D1738773

Articles on American Literature

1900-1950

Articles on American Literature 1900-1950

LEWIS LEARY

Durham, N. C.

DUKE UNIVERSITY PRESS

1954

Cambridge University Press, London, N.W.1, England

Library of Congress Catalogue Number 54-5025

Printed in the United States of America
The Seeman Printery, Inc., Durham, N. C.

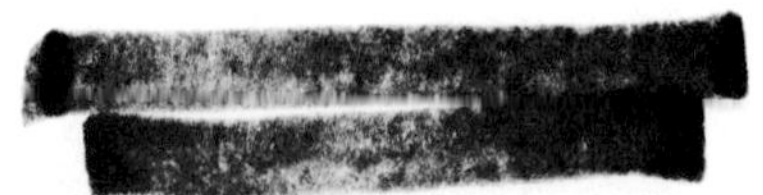

To

JAY B. HUBBELL

Magister

THIS BOOK WAS PUBLISHED WITH THE ASSISTANCE OF THE INCOME FROM THE
P. HUBER HANES FUND

INTRODUCTION

This compilation presents a listing of articles on American literature written in English and appearing in periodicals from 1900 through 1950. It is a revision and extension of the listing published in 1947 as *Articles on American Literature Appearing in Current Periodicals, 1920-1945*. Certain articles in languages other than English have been included, but no systematic search has been made through foreign language periodicals of the period. The term "articles on American literature" has been interpreted broadly in order to include significant reviews and review articles. The purpose of this compilation is to provide as useful and therefore as complete a listing as possible, but the compiler has exercised some selection in omitting articles which have seemed only peripherally concerned with literature in America.

Every person who uses this compilation owes large debts to many people. First among them is Jay B. Hubbell, who in 1929 began the quarterly publication in *American Literature* of "Articles on American Literature Appearing in Current Periodicals" and whose encouragement and advice has been given freely to each of the compilers who succeeded him. Second are members of the Committee on Bibliography of the American Literature Group of the Modern Language Association of America, who for more than twenty years have submitted to the Group Bibliographer their quarterly findings. The library staffs of the University of Pennsylvania and of Duke University have been generous in helping assemble and file materials for this and the previous edition. The Research Council of Duke University has made funds available over a period of years for the employment of assistants who searched file after file of old periodicals, and funds also for the not inconsiderable task of preparing copy for the printers. Scores of fellow students in American literature have supplied the compiler with corrections and additions to the listings as previously published: to name them all would be impracticable, to name a few would be unfair. Jane Cook, who spent six months editing copy, must, however, be remembered, and particualrly Florence Blakely, of the reference staff of the Duke University Library, who has worked with the compiler for four years in correcting, expanding, and editing the listing. Finally, debts are owed to Ashbel Brice of the Duke University Press for effectively solving some complicated problems of composition.

As a revision and extension of the cumulative compilation of 1947, the present volume contains articles as listed in the quarterly check list of "Articles on American Literature Appearing in Current Periodicals" in *American Literature* from 1929 and articles listed in the annual "American Bibliography" in the *Publications of the Modern Language Association of*

America from 1922. It has been checked against, and in some instances has corrected the bibliographical listings in, the *Cambridge History of American Literature* (1917-21), the *Literary History of the United States* (1948), the *Literature of the American People* (1951), Walter Fuller Taylor's *History of American Letters* (1936), Perry Miller and T. H. Johnson's *The Puritans* (1938), Fred B. Millett's *Contemporary American Authors* (1944), Frederick J. Hoffman, Charles Allen, and Carolyn F. Ulrich's *The Little Magazines* (1946), George Arms's *Poetry Explication* (1950), Morton Dauwen Zabel's *Literary Opinion in America* (1951), and the various volumes of the American Writers Series. Separate bibliographies, published and unpublished, of individual authors have been consulted as available.

From 1929 through 1950 it pretends to have examined, with the cooperation of the Committee on Bibliography of the American Literature Group, all pertinent periodicals. From 1900 to 1929 the following periodicals have been searched:

American Historical Review
Anglia
Arena
Atlantic Monthly
Bibliographer
Book Buyer
Bookman (London)
Bookman (New York)
Bulletin of the New York Public Library
Century
Chautauquan
Collections of the Massachusetts Historical Society
Critic
Dial
Egoist
Forum
Harper's Magazine
Harper's Weekly
Independent
Journal of English and Germanic Philology
Lamp
Little Review
Living Age
Maryland Historical Magazine
Masses
Midland
Mississippi Valley Historical Review
Modern Language Notes
Modern Language Quarterly
Modern Language Review
Modern Philology
Nation
New England Magazine
New Republic
North American Review
Notes & Queries

Outlook
Overland Monthly
Pennsylvania Magazine of History and Biography
Poetry
Proceedings of the American Antiquarian Society
Proceedings of the American Philosophical Society
Proceedings of the Massachusetts Historical Society
Proceedings of the Colonial Society of Massachusetts
Publications of the Modern Language Association of America
Publications of the Southern Historical Association
Putnam's Magazine
Quarterly Review
Reader
Scribner's
Seven Arts
Sewanee Review
Smart Set
South Atlantic Quarterly
Studies in Philology
Unpopular Review
Virginia Magazine of History and Biography
Westminster Magazine
William and Mary Quarterly
Yale Review

ABBREVIATIONS

In listing the location of each article an attempt has been made to be as concise and at the same time as clear as possible. The title of the periodical in which an article appears is often abbreviated (see below) and is italicized. It is followed by the volume number in arabic numerals or, if no volume is indicated, by the number (no.) or section (sec.) of the issue in which the article appears. Next follows the date of publication in parentheses; then the pages on which the article is to be found. Dates are listed in the following order: day, month, year; or month (or issue) and year; or, in some instances, simply by year. When preceded by indication of month or issue, the year is abbreviated (01 for 1901). Months are abbreviated: Ja, F, Mr, Ap, My, Je, Jl, Ag, S, O, N, D. For quarterly publications which are dated seasonally, the abbreviations Sp (Spring), Su (Summer), Fl (Fall), Au (Autumn), and Wi (Winter) are used. The titles or portions of titles of certain periodicals are abbreviated as follows:

AAUP	*American Association of University Professors*
Acad	*academic*
Aesth	*aesthetic, aesthetics*
AGR	*American-German Review*
AHR	*American Historical Review*
AL	*American Literature*
Ala	*Alabama*
Am	*America, American*
AN&Q	*American Notes and Queries*
AR	*Antioch Review*
Arch	*archeology, archeological*
Ariz	*Arizona*
Ark	*Arkansas*
AS	*American Speech*
ASR	*American Scandinavian Review*
Assn	*association*
Atl	*Atlantic Monthly, atlantic*
Bibl	*bibliography, bibliographical*
Biog	*biography, biographical*
Biol	*biology, biological*
Bkm	*Bookman*
BNYPL	*Bulletin New York Public Library*
BPLQ	*Boston Public Library Quarterly*
Bul	*bulletin*
Calif	*California*
Cath	*catholic*
CE	*College English*
CEA	*College English Association*
Chri	*Christian*
Chron	*chronicle*
CL	*Comparative Literature*

Col	*college*
Coll	*collection, collections*
Colo	*Colorado*
Contemp	*contemporary*
Crit	*criticism*
Cur	*current*
Dig	*digest*
Ec	*economic, economics*
Ed	*education, educational*
EIHC	*Essex Institute Historical Collections*
EJ	*English Journal*
ELH	*Journal of English Literary History*
Eng	*English*
Expl	*Explicator*
Del	*Delaware*
FAR	*French-American Review*
Fla	*Florida*
FR	*French Review*
Ga	*Georgia*
Gaz	*gazette*
Gen	*general*
Ger	*German*
GQ	*German Quarterly*
GR	*German Review*
Grad	*graduate, graduates*
Harper's	*Harper's Magazine, Harper's Monthly Magazine*
Harper's W	*Harper's Weekly*
H&H	*Hound and Horn*
Hisp	*Hispanic*
Hist	*history, historical, historians*
HLB	*Harvard Library Bulletin*
HLQ	*Huntington Library Quarterly*
Ill	*Illinois*
Ind	*Indiana*
Indep	*independent*
Inst	*institute, institution*
Int	*international*
Ital	*Italica*
J	*journal*
JAF	*Journal of American Folklore*
JEGP	*Journal of English and Germanic Philology*
JHI	*Journal of the History of Ideas*
JQ	*Journalism Quarterly*
JRUL	*Journal of the Rutgers University Library*
KR	*Kenyon Review*
La	*Louisiana*
Lang	*language*
Lib	*library*
Lit	*literary, literature*
Mag	*magazine*
Mass	*Massachusetts*
Med	*medicine*
Merc	*mercury*
Mich	*Michigan*
Minn	*Minnesota*
Miss	*Mississippi*

MLF	*Modern Language Forum*
MLJ	*Modern Language Journal*
MLN	*Modern Language Notes*
MLQ	*Modern Language Quarterly*
MLR	*Modern Language Review*
Mo	*monthly, Missouri*
Mod	*modern*
MP	*Modern Philology*
Munsey's	*Munsey's Magazine*
Mus	*music, musical*
NAR	*North American Review*
Nat	*national*
N E	*New England*
Neb	*Nebraska*
NEQ	*New England Quarterly*
Nev	*Nevada*
NMQR	*New Mexico Quarterly Review*
N&Q	*Notes and Queries*
NRp	*New Republic*
NYFQ	*New York Folklore Quarterly*
Nw	*northwest, northwestern*
NYr	*New Yorker*
Okla	*Oklahoma*
Op	*opinion*
Ore	*Oregon*
ns	*new series*
PAAS	*Proceedings of the American Antiquarian Society*
Pac	*Pacific*
Pam	*pamphlet*
PAPS	*Proceedings of the American Philosophical Society*
PBSA	*Papers of the Bibliographical Society of America*
PBSUV	*Papers of the Bibliographical Society of the University of Virginia*
PCSM	*Publications of the Colonial Society of Massachusetts*
Phil	*philology, philological*
Philos	*philosophy, philosophical*
PMHB	*Pennsylvania Magazine of History and Biography*
PMHS	*Proceedings of the Massachusetts Historical Society*
PMLA	*Publications of the Modern Language Association of America*
Pol	*political, politics*
PQ	*Philological Quarterly*
PR	*Partisan Review*
Proc	*proceedings*
PS	*Pacific Spectator*
Psych	*psychology, psychological*
Pub	*publication, publications*
Pub W	*Publisher's Weekly*
PULC	*Princeton University Library Chronicle*
Q	*quarterly (substantive)*
QJS	*Quarterly Journal of Speech*
QQ	*Queen's Quarterly*
Quar	*quarterly (adjective)*
R	*review*
Rel	*religion, religious*
Res	*research*
RES	*Review of English Studies*

Rev of Rev	*Review of Reviews*
RR	*Romanic Review*
SAQ	*South Atlantic Quarterly*
Sat	*Saturday*
SB	*Studies in Bibliography*
Sci	*science, scientific*
Schol	*scholar, scholastic*
ser	*series*
SFQ	*Southern Folklore Quarterly*
SLM	*Southern Literary Messenger*
So	*southern, south*
SP	*Studies in Philology*
SR	*Sewanee Review*
SRL	*Saturday Review of Literature*
SS	*Scandinavian Studies*
Stud	*studies*
Sw	*southwest, southwestern*
Soc	*society*
Sociol	*sociological, sociology*
Spect	*spectator*
Theol	*theology, theological*
TLS	*London Times Literary Supplement*
TSB	*Thoreau Society Bulletin*
Trans	*transactions*
UKCR	*University of Kansas City Review*
Un	*university*
UTQ	*University of Toronto Quarterly*
VMHB	*Virginia Magazine of History and Biography*
VQR	*Virginia Quarterly Review*
W	*weekly*
WF	*Western Folklore*
WHR	*Western Humanities Review*
WMQ	*William and Mary Quarterly*
WR	*Western Review*
YR	*Yale Review*

Contents

Articles on American Literature
1900-1950

ABBOTT, JACOB (1803-79). Lawrence, W. W. "Rollo and His Uncle George." *NEQ* 18 (S 45) 291-302.
Osgood, Fletcher. "Jacob Abbott: A Neglected New England Author." *N E Mag* ns 30 (Je 04) 471-9.

ABBOTT, LYMAN (1835-1922). Brown, I. V. "Lyman Abbott: Christian Evolutionist." *NEQ* 23 (Je 50) 218-31.

ADAMIC, LOUIS (1899-1951). Mann, Klaus. "Profile of the Month: Louis Adamic." *Decision* 2 (O 41) 76-9.
Remenyi, Joseph. "Louis Adamic, a Portrait." *CE* 5 (N 43) 62-70.

ADAMS, ABIGAIL (1744-1818). Adams, Abigail. "Letter from Abigail Adams to Elbridge Gerry." *PMHS* 57 (My 24) 499-500.
——— "Two Letters from Abigail Adams." *PMHS* 66 (N 28) 24-5.
Forbes, A. B. "Abigail Adams, Commentator." *PMHS* 66 (1942) 126-53.
Hamilton, J. G. de R. "Abigail Adams: A Joy Forever." *Scribner's* 87 (Ja 30) 64-74.

ADAMS, ANDY (1859-1935). Berland, Hal. "The Magnetic West." *N Y Times Book R* (15 Ag 43) 6, 18.
Dobie, Frank. "Andy Adams, Cowboy Chronicler." *SWR* 11 (Ja 26) 92-101.

ADAMS, BROOKS (1848-1927). Aaron, Daniel. "The Unusable Man: An Essay on the Mind of Brooks Adams." *NEQ* 21 (Mr 48) 1-33.
Barnes, H. E. "Brooks Adams on World Utopia." *Cur Hist* 6 (Ja 44) 1-6.
Beard, C. A. "Historians at Work, Brooks and Henry Adams." *Atl* 171 (Ap 43) 87-93.
Blackmur, R. P. "Henry and Brooks Adams: Parallels in Two Generations." *So R* (Au 39) 308-34.
Ford, W. C. "Memoir of Brooks Adams." *PMHS* 60 (My 27) 345-58.

ADAMS, FRANKLIN PIERCE (1881-). Anon. "F. P. A. of the New York *Tribune*." *Everybody's* 34 (My 16) 598-9.
"Elspeth." "Shall We Accost F. P. A.?" *Pub W* 119 (17 Ja 31) 289-91.
Fadiman, Clifton. "The Education of Franklin P. Adams." *NYr* 13 (9 N 35) 81-2.
Phelps, W. L. "Advance of English Poetry." *Bkm* 47 (My 18) 268-9.
Taylor, B. L. "F. P. A." *Am Mag* 77 (Ap 14) 66-8.
Van Doren, Carl. "Day In and Day Out: Adams, Morley, Marquis, and Broun, Manhattan Wits." *Century* 107 (D 23) 309-15.

ADAMS, HENRY (1838-1918). Anon. "At Mr. Adams." *NRp* 15 (25 My 18) 106-8.
——— "Autobiography of a Failure." *Nation* 17 (12 O 18) 403.
——— "The Education of Henry Adams." *Atl* 122 (N 18) 484-91.
——— "Great Failure." *Time* 32 (12 S 38) 69.
——— "Henry Adams." *Unpopular R* 10 (O-D 18) 255-72.
——— "Henry Adams: A British Estimate." *Living Age* 300 (29 Mr 19) 791-4.
——— "Henry Adams and Garibaldi, 1860." *AHR* 25 (Ja 20) 241-55.
——— "A Study in Irony." *Spectator* 122 (22 F 19) 231-3.
——— "A Victim of Twentieth Century Multiplicity." *Cur Op* 66 (F 19) 108-10.

Adams, J. T. "Henry Adams and the New Physics." *YR* 19 (D 29) 283-302.
Aiken, Conrad. "The Lucifer Brothers in Starlight." *Athenaeum* 1 (20 F 20) 243-4.
Alden, J. E. "Henry Adams as Editor: A Group of Unpublished Letters Written to David A. Wells." *NEQ* 11 (Mr 38) 146-52.
Baldensperger, Fernand. "Les Scruples d'un américain attardé." *Correspondant* (Paris) 245 (25 D 20) 1040-62.
Basso, Hamilton. "Mind in the Making." *NYr* 23 (29 Mr 47) 103-6.
Baym, M. I. "The 1858 Catalogue of Henry Adams's Library." *Colophon* ns 3 (Au 38) 483-9.
——— "Henry Adams and the Critics." *Am Schol* 15 (Wi 46) 79-89.
——— "Henry Adams and Henry Vignaud." *NEQ* 17 (S 44) 442-9.
——— "William James and Henry Adams." *NEQ* 10 (D 37) 717-42.
Beard, C. A. "Historians at Work, Brooks and Henry Adams." *Atl* 171 (Ap 43) 87-93.
Becker, Carl. "The Education of Henry Adams." *AHR* 24 (Ap 19) 422-34.
——— "Henry Adams Once More." *SRL* 9 (8 Ap 33) 521, 524.
Bennett, C. A. A. "Of Last Things, Modern Style." *YR* 9 (Jl 20) 890-6.
Bixler, P. H. "Letters of Henry Adams." *YR* 24 (S 34) 112-7.
——— "A Note on Henry Adams." *Colophon* 5 (Je 34) Pt 17.
Blackmur, R. P. "The Expense of Greatness: Three Emphases on Henry Adams." *VQR* 12 (Jl 36) 396-415.
——— "Henry Adams: Three Late Moments." *KR* 2 (Wi 40) 7-29.
——— "Henry and Brooks Adams: Parallels in Two Generations." *So R* 5 (Au 39) 308-34.
——— "The Letters of Marian Adams, 1865-1883." *VQR* 13 (Ap 37) 289-95.
——— "The Novels of Henry Adams." *SR* 51 (Ap 43) 281-304.
Blanchard, Paul. "The Education of Henry Adams." *Mental Hygiene* 4 (Ja 20) 232-42.
Blunt, H. F. "The Mal-Education of Henry Adams." *Cath World* 145 (Ap 37) 46-52.
Bradford, Gamaliel. "Henry Adams." *Atl* 125 (Je 20) 623-34.
Cargill, Oscar. "Letter . . ." *AL* 16 (N 44) 226.
Cater, H. D. "Henry Adams Reports on a German Gymnasium." *AHR* 53 (O 47) 59-74.
Clark, J. A. "Henry Adams Sees His Shadow." *Commonweal* 29 (31 Mr 39) 627-9.
Clement, A. W. "Henry Adams and the Repudiation of Science." *Sci Mo* 64 (My 47) 451.
Coleman, H. T. J. "Henry Adams: A Study in Multiplicity." *QQ* 28 (Jl-S 20) 1-14.
Commager, H. S. "Henry Adams." *SAQ* 26 (Jl 27) 252-65.
——— "Henry Adams, Prophet of Our Disjointed World." *N. Y. Times Mag* (20 F 38) 11, 22.
Cook, A. S. "Six Letters of Henry Adams." *YR* 10 (O 20) 131-40.
——— "Three Letters from Henry Adams to Albert S. Cook." *PR* 2 (S 21) 273-5.
Cournos, John. "Two Famous Failures." *Bkm* 67 (Ag 28) 690-1.
Creek, H. L. "The Medievalism of Henry Adams." *SAQ* 24 (Ja 25) 86-97.
Crothers, S. M. "Education in Pursuit of Henry Adams." *YR* ns 8 (Ap 19) 580-95.
Davis, E. H. "Letters and Comments." *YR* ns 11 (O 21) 218-21.
Delany, S. P. "A Man of Mystery." *NAR* 216 (N 22) 695-704.
Dennett, Thomas. "Five of Hearts." *Scholastic* 38 (4 Mr 36) 6-7.
Dickason, D. H. "Henry Adams and Clarence King: The Record of a Friendship." *NEQ* 17 (Je 44) 229-54.
Dunning, W. A. "Henry Adams on Things in General." *Pol Sci Q* 34 (Je 19) 305-11.
Edwards, H. J. "Henry Adams: Politician and Statesman." *NEQ* 22 (Mr 49) 49-60. 60.
Edwards, Herbert. "The Prophetic Mind of Henry Adams." *CE* 3 (My 42) 708-21.

Elsey, G. M. "The First Education of Henry Adams." *NEQ* 14 (D 41) 679-84.
Ford, W. C. "The Adams Family." *Quar R* 237 (Ap 22) 298-312.
——— "Henry Adams, Historian." *Nation* 106 (8 Je 18) 674-5.
Frewen, M. "The Autobiography of Henry Adams." *Nineteenth Century* 85 (My 19) 980-9.
Glicksberg, C. I. "Henry Adams and the Civil War." *Americana* 33 (O 39) 443-62.
——— "Henry Adams the Journalist." *NEQ* 21 (Je 48) 232-6.
——— "Henry Adams and the Modern Spirit." *Dalhousie R* 27 (O 47) 229-309.
——— "Henry Adams Reports on a Trade Union Meeting." *NEQ* 15 (D 42) 724-8.
Hackett, Francis. "Henry Adams." *NRp* 17 (7 D 18) 169-71.
Holt, W. S. "Henry Adams and the Johns Hopkins University." *NEQ* 11 (S 38) 632-8.
Howe, M. A. De W. "The Elusive Henry Adams." *SRL* 7 (18 O 30) 237-9.
Hume, R. A. "Henry Adams's Quest for Certainty." *Stanford Un Stud Lang & Lit* (1941).
——— "Homage to Henry Adams." *PS* 2 (Su 48) 299-307.
——— "The Style and Literary Background of Henry Adams." *AL* 16 (Ja 45) 296-315.
Irish, M. D. "Henry Adams: The Modern American Scholar." *Am Schol* 2 (Mr 32) 223-9.
Jameson, J. F. "Obituary." *Am Hist Assn Reports* 1 (1918) 71-2.
Jordy, W. H. "Henry Adams and Walt Whitman." *SAQ* 40 (Ap 41) 132-45.
Kronenberger, Louis. "The Education of Henry Adams." *NRp* 98 (15 Mr 39) 155-8.
——— "The Epicurean Stoic." *NRp* 96 (12 O 38) 276-8.
La Farge, Mabel. "Henry Adams." *Commonweal* 18 (19 My 33) 74-5.
——— "Henry Adams: A Niece's Memories." *YR* 9 (Ja 20) 271-85.
Lake, Kirsopp. "Artist and Historian. *Atl* 133 (Ap 24) 528-34.
Laoki, H. J. "Henry Adams: An Unpublished Letter." *Nation* 151 (3 Ag 40) 94-5.
Laughlin, J. L. "Some Recollections of Henry Adams." *Scribner's* 69 (My 21) 576-85.
Leslie, Shane. "The Education of Henry Adams." *Dublin R* 164 (Je 19) 218-32.
——— "Letters of Henry Adams." *YR* 24 (S 34) 112-7.
Lovett, R. M. "The Betrayal of Henry Adams." *Dial* 65 (30 N 18) 468-72.
——— "Henry Adams' Letters." *NRp* 64 (22 O 30) 268-70.
Luquiens, F. B. "Seventeen Letters of Henry Adams." *YR* 10 (O 20) 111-40.
Lydenberg, John. "Henry Adams and Lincoln Steffens." *SAQ* 48 (Ja 49) 42-64.
Miller, R. F. "Henry Adams and the Influence of Woman." *AL* 18 (Ja 47) 291-8.
Mitchell, Stewart. "Henry Adams and Some of His Students." *PMHS* 66 (1942) 294-312.
——— "Letters of Henry Adams, 1858-1891." *NEQ* 4 (Jl 31) 563-8.
More, P. E. "The Education of Henry Adams." *Unpopular R* 10 (O 18) 255-72.
Muller, Gustav. "Henry Adams: Ein Amerikanischer Geschichtsphilosoph." *Hochland* 28 (1930-1) 348-56.
Neufield, Maurice. "The Crisis in Prospect." *Am Schol* 4 (Aut 35) 397-408.
Nichols, R. F. "The Dynamic Interpretation of History." *NEQ* 8 (Je 35) 163-78.
Page, E. "'The Man Around the Corner': An Episode in the Career of Henry Adams." *NEQ* 23 (S 50) 401-3.
Perry, Bliss. "The Adamses." *YR* 20 (Wi 31) 382-3.
Powell, J. W. "Henry Adams and Democratic Education." *Standard* 18 (F 32) 172-8.
Pritchett, V. S. "Books in General." *New Statesman & Nation* 28 (4 N 44) 305.
Quinlivan, Frances. "Irregularities of the Mental Mirror." *Cath World* 163 (Ap 46) 58-65.
Randall, D. A., & Winterich, J. T. "One Hundred Good Novels. Henry Adams: *Democracy*." *Pub W* 136 (15 Jl 39) 180-2.

Rhodes, J. F., & Lodge, N. C. "Henry Adams, '58." *Harvard Grad Mag* 26 (Je 18) 40-6.

Roelofs, G. H. "Henry Adams: Pessimism and the Intelligent Use of Doom." *ELH* 17 (S 50) 214-39.

Rourke, C. M. "The Adams Mind." *Freeman* 3 (23 Mr 21) 43-4.

Sabine, G. H. "Henry Adams, and the Writings of History." *Un Calif Chron* 26 (Ja 24) 31-46.

Shafer, Robert. "Henry Adams." *Int J Ethics* 30 (O 19) 43-57.

Sheldon, W. D. "Why Education Failed to Educate Henry Adams." *SR* 18 (Ja 20) 54-65.

Shepard, Odell. "The Ghost of Henry Adams." *Nation* 147 (22 O 38) 419.

Sherman, S. P. "Evolution in the Adams Family." *Nation* 110 (10 Ap 20) 473-7.

Shoemaker, R. L. "The France of Henry Adams." *FR* 21 (F 48) 292-9.

Shumate, R. V. "The Political Philosophy of Henry Adams." *Am Pol Sci R* 28 (Ag 34) 599-610.

Silver, A. W. "Henry Adams' 'Diary of a Visit to Manchester.'" *AHR* 51 (O 45) 74-89.

Simonds, Katherine. "Living in a Dead World." *SRL* 18 (10 S 38) 5.

——— "The Tragedy of Mrs. Henry Adams." *NEQ* 9 (D 36) 564-82.

Smith, Garnet. "Henry Adams." *Contemp R* 141 (My 32) 617-24.

Spiller, R. E. "Henry Adams: Man of Letters." *SRL* 30 (22 F 47) 11-2, 33-4.

Stone, James. "Henry Adams's Philosophy of History." *NEQ* 14 (S 41) 538-48.

Sullivan, J. W. N. "The Power of Words." *Athenaeum* 1 (21 My 20) 665.

Swift, Lindsay. "A Course of History at Harvard College in the Seventies." *PMHS* 52 (D 18) 69-77.

Taylor, H. O. "'The Education of Henry Adams.'" *Atl* 122 (O 18) 484-91.

Taylor, W. R. "Historical Bifocals on the Year 1800." *NEQ* 23 (Je 50) 172-86.

Thomason, J. W. "The Man Who Knew Everything." *Am Merc* 46 (Ja 39) 99-104.

Thorpe, F. N. "The Political Ideas of John Adams." *PMHB* 44 (Ja 20) 1-46.

Wecter, Dixon. "Harvard Exiles." *VQR* 10 (Ja 34) 244-57.

Weiss, T. "The Nonsense of Winters' Anatomy." *Quar R Lit* 1 (Sp 44) 212-34.

Whipple, T. K. "Henry Adams: First of the Moderns." *Nation* 112 (14 Ap 26) 408-9.

White, William. "The Date of *The Education of Henry Adams.*" *Eng Stud* (Amsterdam) 20 (O 38) 204-5.

Williams, H. H. "The Education of Henry Adams." *Monist* 31 (Ja 21) 149-59.

Williams, Orlo. "Roosevelt and Henry Adams: Doer and Doubler." *National R* 96 (F 31) 279-87.

Winters, Yvor. "Replies . . ." *AL* 16 (N 44) 221-2, 223-5.

Wright, Nathalia. "Henry Adams's Theory of History: A Puritan Defense." *NEQ* 18 (Je 45) 204-10.

Zukofsky, Louis. "Henry Adams: A Criticism in Autobiography." *H&H* 3 (Ap-Je, Jl-S 30) 333-57, 518-30; 4 (O-D 30, Ja-Mr 31) 46-72, 261-4.

ADAMS, JOHN (1704-1740). Carlson, C. L. "John Adams, Matthew Adams, Mather Byles, and the *New England Weekly Journal.*" *AL* 12 (N 40) 347-8.

ADAMS, JOHN (1735-1826). Bowen, C. D. "John Adams and His Bowl." *Atl* 177 (My 46) 120-4.

——— "Young John Adams." *Atl* 14 (S, O, N, D 49) 24-30, 46-52, 70-6, 68-73; 185 (Ja 50) 75-80.

Butterfield, L. H. "The Jefferson-Adams Correspondence in the Adams Manuscript Trust." *Libr Cong Quar J* 5 (F 48) 3-6.

Cary, E. L. "John Adams and Mary Wollstonecraft." *Lamp* 26 (F 03) 35-40.

Coleman, Mrs. G. P. "Randolph and Tucker Letters." *VMHB* 42 (Ap 34) 129-31.

Dorfman, Joseph. "The Regal Republic of John Adams." *Pol Sci Q* 59 (Je 44) 227-47.
Grey, Lennox. "John Adams and John Trumbull in the 'Boston Cycle.'" *NEQ* 4 (Jl 31) 509-14.
Gummere, R. M. "John Adams, *Togatus*." *PQ* 13 (Ap 34) 203-10.
Hamilton, J. G. de Roulhac. "Jefferson and Adams at Ease." *SAQ* 26 (O 27) 359-72.
Haraszti, Zoltán. "John Adams and Rousseau." *Atl* 181 (F 48) 95-100.
——— "John Adams and Turgot." *BPLQ* 1 (Jl 49) 1-22.
——— "John Adams on Condorcet." *More Books* 5 (D 30) 473-99.
——— "John Adams on Dr. Priestly." *More Books* 10 (O 35) 301-18.
——— "John Adams on Frederick the Great." *More Books* 9 (Ap, My 34) 117-33, 161-73.
——— "John Adams on Napoleon and the French." *More Books* 9 (Je 34) 201-31.
——— "John Adams on Religion." *More Books* 9 (D 34) 373-98.
Hedges, J. B. "John Adams Speaks His Mind." *AHR* 47 (Jl 42) 806-9.
Pound, Ezra. "The Jefferson-Adams Correspondence." *NAR* 244 (Wi 37-8) 314-24.
Robathan, D. M. "John Adams and the Classics." *NEQ* 19 (Mr 46) 91-8.
Swift, Lindsay. "Literary Work of John Adams." *Book Buyer* 20 (My 00) 287-8.
Thorpe, F. N. "Adams and Jefferson: 1826-1926." *NAR* 223 (Je-Ag 26) 234-47.
——— "The Political Ideas of John Adams." *PMHB* 44 (Ja 20) 1-46.
Van Lennep, William. "John Adams to a Young Playwright: An Unpublished Letter to Samuel Judah." *HLB* 1 (Wi 47) 117-8.
Von Abele, Rudolph. "The World of John Adams." *Am Merc* 67 (Jl 48) 66-73.

ADAMS, JOHN QUINCY (1767-1848). Bradner, Leicester. "A Verse Translation by John Quincy Adams." *NEQ* 6 (Je 33) 361-3.
Goodfellow, D. M. "The First Boylston Professor of Rhetoric and Oratory." *NEQ* 19 (S 46) 372-89.
——— "'Old Man Eloquent' Visits Pittsburgh." *West Penn Hist Mag* 28 (S-D 45) 99-100
——— "'Your Old Friend, J. Q. Adams.'" *NEQ* 21 (Je 48) 217-31.
Kirby, T. A. "J. Q. Adams and Chaucer." *MLN* 61 (Mr 46) 185-6.
Rahskopf. H. G. "John Quincy Adams: Speaker and Rhetorician." *QJS* 32 (D 46) 435-41.
Von Abele, Rudolph. "John Quincy Adams: Scientific Statesman." *Am Merc* 70 (Ap 50) 449-56.

ADAMS, LÉONIE FULLER (1899-). Sapir, Edward. "Leonie Adams." *Poetry* 27 (F 26) 275-9.
Untermeyer, Louis. "Three Younger Poets." *EJ* 21 (D 32) 787-9.
Zabel, M. D. "A Harrier of Heaven." *Poetry* 35 (Mr 30) 332-6.

ADE, GEORGE (1866-1944). Anon. "How George Ade Did It." *Book Buyer* 25 (N 02) 316-7.
Clark, J. A. "Ade's Fables in Slang: An Appreciation." *SAQ* 46 (O 47) 537-44.
Evans, Bergen. "George Ade, Rustic Humorist." *Am Merc* 70 (Mr 50) 321-9.
Howells, W. D. "Work of George Ade." *NAR* 176 (My 03) 739-43.

AIKEN, CONRAD (1889-). Anon. "Virtues of Abundance: Current Feeling and Tradition." *TLS* (4 S 37) 629-30.
Aiken, Conrad. "The Mechanism of Poetic Inspiration." *NAR* 206 (D 17) 917-24.
Albrecht, W. P. "Aiken's *Mr. Arcularis*." *Expl* 6 (Ap 48).
Blackmur, R. P. "Scapegoat." *H&H* 1 (D 27) 160-3.
Bodenheim, Maxwell. "American Literary Critics." *Double Dealer* 3 (Ap 22) 206-10.
Brown, C. S. "Music and Conrad Aiken." *Ga R* 2 (Sp 48) 40-51.
Carlson, E. W. "The Range of Symbolism in Poetry." *SAQ* 48 (Jl 49) 442-51.

Colum, Padraic. "The Poetry of Mr. Conrad Aiken." *Freeman* 3 (13 Ap 21) 117-8.
Edison, George. "Thematic Symbols in the Poetry of Aiken and MacLeish." *UTQ* 10 (O 40) 12-26.
Fletcher, J. G. "Conrad Aiken—Metaphysical Poet." *Dial* 66 (31 My 19) 558-9.
——— "Poetry of Conrad Aiken." *Dial* 64 (28 Mr 18) 291-2.
Hamalian, Leo. "Aiken's *Silent Snow, Secret Snow.*" *Expl* 7 (N 48) 17.
Hoagland, Clayton. "Explorer of the Ego." *SLM* 2 (Ap 40) 259-63.
Hoffman, D. G. "Poetic Symbols from the Public Domain." *SFQ* 12 (D 48) 293-8.
Kunitz, S. J. "The Poetry of Conrad Aiken." *Nation* 133 (14 O 31) 393-4.
Mencken, H. L. "Conrad Aiken." *Nation* 119 (20 Ag 24) 179.
Moore, Marianne. "If a Man Die." *H&H* 5 (Ja-Mr 32) 313-20.

AKERS, ELIZABETH (1832-1911). Winterich, J. T. "Elizabeth Akers and the Unsubstantial Character of Fame." *Colophon* 4 (O 33) Pt 15.

ALCOTT, BRONSON (1799-1888). Anthony, Katharine. "An Early American Educator." *NAR* 244 (Au 37) 172-83.
Carpenter, F. I. "Bronson Alcott: Genteel Transcendentalist—an Essay in Definition." *NEQ* 13 (Mr 40) 34-8.
Clark, A. M. L. "The Alcotts in Harvard." *N E Mag* ns 22 (Ap 00) 173-80.
Collie, G. L., & Richardson, R. K. "A 'Conversation' of A. Bronson Alcott." *Wisc Mag Hist* 32 (S 48) 85-8.
Edgell, D. P. "Bronson Alcott's 'Autobiographical Index.'" *NEQ* 14 (D 41) 704-15.
——— "Bronson Alcott's 'Gentility.'" *NEQ* 13 (D 40) 699-705.
Gohdes, Clarence. "Alcott's 'Conversation' on the Transcendental Club and *The Dial.*" *AL* 3 (Mr 31) 14-27.
Grose, H. B., Jr. "Notes on *Pedlar's Progress.*" *AL* 10 (My 38) 216-22.
Henry, F. "Henry David Thoreau and Bronson Alcott: A Study of Relationships." *Teachers Col J* 14 (Jl 43) 126-8.
Hoeltje, H. H. "Alcott Came to Concord in Autumn." *Chri Sci Mon* 36 (21 S 44) 6.
——— "Amos Bronson Alcott in Iowa." *Iowa J Hist & Pol* 29 (Jl 31) 375-401.
Marble, A. R. "Alcott as a Pioneer Educator." *Education* 24 (N 03) 153-66.
Mead, David. "Some Ohio Conversations of Amos Bronson Alcott." *NEQ* 22 (S 49) 358-72.
Shepard, Odell. "Sunken Treasure." *SRL* 16 (27 Mr 37) 15-6.
Trowbridge, J. T. "Recollections of Bronson Alcott." *Atl* 91 (Ap 03) 464-7.
Warren, Austin. "The Orphic Sage: Bronson Alcott." *AL* 3 (Mr 31) 3-13.

ALCOTT, LOUISA MAY (1832-88). Anon. "Letter from Louisa M. Alcott to Viola Price Franklin." *Overland Mo* ns 91 (Ag 33) 106.
——— "Louisa M. Alcott Centenary Year." *Pub W* 122 (2 Jl 32) 32-5.
Adams, E. L. "Louisa Alcott's Doomed Manuscript." *More Books* 17 (My 42) 221-2.
Adlow, D. "Louisa Alcott's Sister May." *Chri Sci Mon* 26 (29 Ag 34) 10.
Ahlgren, Stig. "Agnes von Krusenstjerna och Louisa M. Alcott." *Bonniers Litterära Magasin* (Stockholm) 9 (Ap 40) 270-4.
Atkinson, Thelma. "Louisa May Alcott." *MS* 5 (My 34) 5.
Bradford, Gamaliel. "Portrait of Louisa May Alcott." *NAR* 209 (Mr 19) 391-403.
Gerould, K. F. "Miss Alcott's New England." *Atl* 108 (Ag 11) 180-6.
Harden, J. W. "Louisa Alcott's Contribution to Democracy." *Negro Hist Bul* 6 (N 42) 28-32.
Pratt, A. A. "About Little Women." *St Nicholas* 30 (My 03) 631.
Roller, Bert. "When Jo Died." *SR* 36 (Ap 28) 164-70.
Rostenberg, Leona. "Some Anonymous and Pseudonymous Thrillers of Louisa M. Alcott." *PBSA* 37 (Ap-Je 43) 131-40.
Sanborn, F. B. "Reminiscences of Louisa May Alcott." *Independent* 72 (7 Mr 12) 496-502.

Sears, W. P., Jr. "Educational Theories of Louisa May Alcott." *Dalhousie R* 27 (O 47) 327-34.
Shepard, Odell. "The Mother of Little Women." *NAR* 245 (Sp 38) 391-8.
Stern, M. B. "The First Appearance of a 'Little Women' Incident." *AN&Q* 3 (O 43) 99-100.
——— "Louisa Alcott, Civil War Nurse." *Americana* 37 (Ap 43) 296-325.
——— "Louisa Alcott, Trouper." *NEQ* 16 (Je 43) 175-97.
——— "Louisa M. Alcott: An Appraisal." *NEQ* 22 (D 49) 475-98.
——— "Louisa May Alcott's Contributions to Periodicals: 1868-88." *More Books* 18 (N 43) 411-20.
——— "Louisa May Alcott's Self-Criticism." *More Books* 20 (O 45) 339-46.
——— "The Witch's Cauldron to the Family Hearth." *More Books* 18 (O 43) 363-80.
Talbot, Marion. "Glimpses of the Real Louisa May Alcott." *NEQ* 11 (D 38) 731-8.
Turner, L. D. "Louisa May Alcott's 'M. L.'" *J Negro Hist* 14 (O 29) 495-522.
Vincent, E. "Subversive Miss Alcott." *NRp* 40 (22 O 24) 204.
Winterich, J. T. "Romantic Stories of Books . . . *Little Women*." *Pub W* 120 (15 Ag 31) 607-11.

ALDEN, HENRY MILLS (1836-1919). Cooper, F. T. "Alden and the New Realism." *Forum* 41 (Mr 09) 284-8.

ALDRICH, THOMAS BAILEY (1836-1907). Alden, H. M. "Thomas Bailey Aldrich, 1836-1907." *Harper's W* 51 (6 Ap 07) 491, 511.
Barry, J. D. "Mr. Aldrich's Dramatic Poem." *Critic* 46 (Ja 05) 70-3.
Bowen, E. W. "Thomas Bailey Aldrich, a Decade After." *Methodist R* 99 (My 17) 379-90.
Boynton, H. W. The Literary Work of Aldrich." *Putnam's* 2 (Je 07) 259-66.
Corrick, A. Van L. "House of the Bad Boy." *Country Life* 36 (Ag 19) 33-7.
Cowie, Alexander. "Indian Summer Novelist." *NEQ* 15 (D 42) 608-21.
Donaldson, Gilbert. "Thomas Bailey Aldrich." *Reader* 9 (My 07) 657-65.
Grattan, C. H. "Thomas Bailey Aldrich." *Am Merc* 5 (My 25) 41-5.
Greenslet, Ferris. "Aldrich in New York." *Scribner's* 43 (My 08) 609-22.
——— "A Group of Aldrich Letters." *Century* 76 (Ag 08) 495-505.
——— "Thomas Bailey Aldrich." *Nation* 84 (21 Mr 07) 261-9.
Harbour, J. L. "The Author of the Story of a Bad Boy." *St. Nicholas* 34 (Je 07) 676-81.
Howe, M. A. DeW. "Thomas Bailey Aldrich and the *Atlantic*." *Chri Sci Mon* 37 (Ja 45) 6.
Mabie, H. W. "An Appreciation." *Outlook* 84 (24 N 06) 735-40.
——— "A Charming Biography." *Outlook* 90 (28 N 08) 718-21.
MacArthur, James. "Thomas Bailey Aldrich." *Forum* 40 (O 08) 500-3.
More, P. E. "Thomas Bailey Aldrich and Vers de Sociéte." *Nation* 87 (8 O 08) 331-3.
North, E. D. "A Bibliography of the Original Editions of the Works of Thomas Bailey Aldrich." *Book Buyer* 23 (My 01) 296-303.
Peck, H. T. "Thomas Bailey Aldrich." *Bkm* 25 (My 07) 236-8.
Perry, Bliss. "Thomas Bailey Aldrich." *Atl* 99 (My 07) 711-9.
Phelps, Albert. "The Value of Aldrich's Verse." *Atl* 100 (Ag 07) 239-45.
Rideing, W. H. "Glimpses of Thomas Bailey Aldrich." *Putnam's* 7 (Ja 10) 398-406.

ALGER, HORATIO (1834-99). Levy, Newman. "They Made Me What I Am Today." *Atl* 182 (N 43) 115-7.
Rugg, W. K. "A Library Exile." *Chri Sci Mon* 26 (19 N 34) 7.

ALLEN, ETHAN (1738-89). Anderson, G. P. "Who Wrote 'Ethan Allen's Bible'?" *NEQ* 10 (D 37) 585-96.

Buckham, J. W. "Robin Hood of Vermont." *N E Mag* ns 25 (S 01) 102-19.
Doten, Dana. "Ethan Allen's 'Original Something.'" *NEQ* 11 (Je 38) 361-6.
Ericson, E. E. "Mr. Woolston of London, 1788." *NEQ* 171 (17 O 36) 278.
Gohdes, Clarence. "Ethan Allen and His Magnum Opus." *Open Court* 43 (Mr 29) 129-51.
Pell, John. "Ethan Allen's Literary Career." *NEQ* 2 (O 29) 585-602.
Rife, C. W. "Ethan Allen, an Interpretation." *NEQ* 2 (O 29) 561-84.
Schantz, B. T. "Ethan Allen's Religious Ideas." *J Rel* 18 (Ap 38) 183-217.

ALLEN, HERVEY (1889-1949). Allen, Hervey. "The Sources of 'Anthony Adverse.'" *SRL* 10 (13 Ja 34) 401, 408-10.
Bamm, Peter. "Hervey Allens 'Oberst Franklin.'" *Die Literatur* 40 (D 37) 147-8.
Clemens, Cyril. "Hervey Allen and Mark Twain." *Hobbies* (Ap 50) 20.
Cobb, Sanford. "Anthony Hits a Million." *Pub W* 128 (24 Ag 35) 500-3.
Cohn, L. H. "American First Editions: William Hervey Allen, 1889- ." *Pub W* 124 (16 S 33) 914-15.
Cox, Sidney. "Israfel." *SR* 35 (Ap-Je 27) 241-3.
Daniels, Jonathan. "Escape from a Legend." *SRL* 22 (5 Mr 38) 3-4, 16, 18.
Hoffman, D. G. "Poetic Symbols from the Public Domain." *SFQ* 12 (D 48) 294-8.
Kinneman, J. A. "Anthony Adverse or Theodore Canot?" *J Negro Hist* 30 (Jl 45) 304-10.
Laing, Alexander. "Noble Tales." *Poetry* 35 (Mr 30) 342-6.
Monroe, Harriet. "Epic Moods." *Poetry* 27 (N 25) 96-8.
Prezzolini, Giuseppe. "Un Dumas Americano." *Pan* (Milan) 3 (S 34) 127-30.
Siebeneck, H. K. "Hervey Allen and Arthur St. Clair." *West Penn Hist Mag* 30 (S-D 47) 73-94.
Wilson, J. S. "Enter a Novelist." *VQR* 9 (Jl 33) 433-5.
——— "Poe and the Biographers." *VQR* 3 (Ap 27) 313-20.

ALLEN, JAMES LANE (1849-1925). Anon. "The Choir Invisible and Increasing Purpose." *Living Age* 226 (1 S 00) 585-8.
——— "An Interview with James Lane Allen." *Lamp* 27 (S 03) 117-21.
——— "James Lane Allen." *Living Age* 261 (12 Je 09) 689-96.
——— "New Poet." *Outlook* 71 (9 Ag 02) 935-8.
Clemens, Cyril. "An Unpublished Letter from James Lane Allen." *AL* 9 (Ja 45) 355-6.
Cook, E. A. "James Lane Allen." *Bellman* 23 (6 O 17) 378-80.
Finley, J. W. "James Lane Allen." *Rev of Rev* 71 (Ap 25) 419-20.
Hancock, A. E. "The Art of James Lane Allen." *Outlook* 74 (22 Ag 03) 953-5.
Knight, G. C. "Allen's Christmas Trilogy and Its Meaning." *Bkm* 68 (D 28) 411-5.
Marcosson, I. F. "The South in Fiction." *Bkm* 32 (D 10) 360-70.
Maurice, A. B. "James Lane Allen's Country." *Bkm* 12 (O 00) 154-62.
Payne, L. W., Jr. "The Stories of James Lane Allen." *SR* 8 (Ja 00) 45-55.
Sherman, E. B. "The Works of James Lane Allen." *Book Buyer* 20 (Je 00) 374-7.

ALLSTON, WASHINGTON (1779-1843). Chase, G. D. "Some Washington Allston Correspondence." *NEQ* 16 (D 43) 628-34.
Meyer, A. N. "A Portrait of Coleridge by Washington Allston." *Critic* 48 (F 06) 138-41.
Soby, J. T. "Washington Allston, Eclectic." *SRL* 30 (23 Ag 47) 28-9.

ALMQUIST, JONAS LUDWIG (1793-1866). Johnson, E. G. "An Excited Swedish Novelist and the Civil War." *J Ill State Hist Soc* 41 (Je 48) 1-13.
——— "Swedish Author's Only American Story." *J Ill State Hist Soc* 41 (S 48) 285-304.

ALSOP, RICHARD (1761-1815). Benson, A. B. "Scandinavian Influences on the Works of William Dunlap and Richard Alsop." *SS* 9 (N 27) 239-57.

Fucilla, J. G. "An Early American Translation of the Count Ugolino Episode." *MLQ* 11 (D 50) 480.
Zunder, T. A. "A Few New Facts Surrounding Richard Alsop's Death." *AN&Q* 2 (O 42) 101.

AMES, NATHANIEL (1708-64). Jorgenson, C. E. "The New Science in the Almanacs of Ames and Franklin." *NEQ* 8 (D 35) 555-61.
Morrison, S. E. "Squire Ames and Doctor Ames." *NEQ* 1 (Ja 28) 5-31.

ANDERSON, MAXWELL (1888-). Anon. "The Critic's Award." *Chri Sci Mon* 29 (31 Mr 37) 14.
——— "Maxwell Anderson." *Cur Biog* 3 (N 42) 1-4.
Boyce, Benjamin. "Anderson's *Winterset*." Expl 2 (F 44) 32.
Calverton, V. F. "The American Theatre: I. Maxwell Anderson." *Mod Mo* 10 (My 37) 3-5.
Carmer, Carl. "Maxwell Anderson: Poet and Champion." *Theatre Arts Mo* 17 (Je 33) 437-46.
Childs, H. E. "Playgoer's Playwright: Maxwell Anderson." *EJ* 27 (Je 38) 475-85.
Collijn, Gustaf. "Maxwell Anderson." *Bonniers Litterära Magasin* (Stockholm) 9 (N 40) 689-93.
Foster, Edward. "Core of Belief: An Interpretation of the Plays of Maxwell Anderson." *SR* 50 (Ja 42) 87-100.
Gregory, Horace. "Poets in the Theatre." *Poetry* 48 (Jl 36) 221-8.
Halline, A. G. "Maxwell Anderson's Dramatic Theory." *AL* 16 (My 44) 63-81.
Harris, Ainslie. "Maxwell Anderson." *Madison Q* 4 (Ja 44) 30-44.
Isaacs, E. J. R. "Maxwell Anderson." *EJ* 25 (D 36) 795-803.
Healey, R. C. "Anderson, Saroyan, Sherwood: New Directions." *Cath World* 152 (N 40) 174-80.
Kliger, Samuel. "Hebraic Lore in Maxwell Anderson's *Winterset*." *AL* 18 (N 46) 219-32.
Meredith, Burgess. "On the Set with Winterset." *Stage* 14 (D 36) 45-7.
Mersand, Joseph. "Speech in the New Plays: The Poetic Dramas of Shakespeare and Maxwell Anderson Dominate the New York Stage." *Correct Eng* 37 (Mr, Ap 37) 117-8.
Monroe, Harriet. "Quiet Music." *Poetry* 27 (Mr 26) 337-8.
Parks, E. W. "Maxwell Anderson." *Revista do Instituto Brasil-Estados Unidos* (Rio de Janeiro) 7 (Ja-Je 49) 18-21.
Rodell, J. S. "Maxwell Anderson: A Criticism." *KR* 5 (Sp 43) 272-7.
Rosenberg, Harold. "Poetry and the Theatre." *Poetry* 57 (Ja 41) 258-63.
Sampley, A. M. "Theory and Practice in Maxwell Anderson's Poetic Tragedies." *CE* 5 (My 44) 412-8.
Sedgwick, R. H. "Maxwell Anderson: Playwright and Poet." *Stage* 14 (O 38) 54-6.
Steiner, Pauline, & Frenz, Horst. "Anderson and Stallings' *What Price Glory?* and Carl Zuckmayer's *Rivalen*." *GQ* 20 (N 47) 239-51.
Wall, Vincent. "Maxwell Anderson: The Last Anarchist." *SR* 49 (Jl-S 41) 339-69.
Watts, H. H. "Maxwell Anderson: The Tragedy of Attrition." *CE* 4 (Ja 43) 220-30
Wilson, Edmund. "Prize-winning Verse." *NRp* 91 (23 Je 37) 193-4.
Woodbridge, H. E. "Maxwell Anderson." *SAQ* 44 (Ja 45) 55-68.

ANDERSON, SHERWOOD (1876-1941). Anon. "Letters of Sherwood Anderson." *Harper's Bazaar* 73 (F 49) 130.
Aaron, Manley. "American First Editions . . . Sherwood Anderson." *Pub W* 102 (27 Ja 23) 251.
Adams, M. "A Small-Town Editor Airs His Mind." *N Y Times Mag* (22 S 29) 6.
Alexander, D. C. "Sherwood Anderson." *Letters* 2 (F 28) 23-9.

Almy, R. F. "Sherwood Anderson: The Non-Conforming Rediscover." *SRL* 28 (6 Ja 45) 17-8.
Anderson, K. J. "My Brother, Sherwood Anderson." *SRL* 31 (4 S 48) 6-7, 26-7.
Anderson, Sherwood. "An Apology for Crudity." *Dial* 63 (8 N 17) 437-8.
——— "Letters of Sherwood Anderson." *Berkeley* 1 (O 47) 1-4.
——— "A Note on Realism." *Lit R* 3 (25 O 24) 1-2.
——— "Notes Out of a Man's Life." *Vanity Fair* 26 (Mr 26) 47, 98.
——— "On Being Published." *Colophon* pt 1 (F 30) 1-4.
——— "Sherwood Anderson to Theodore Dreiser." *Am Spect* 1 (Je 33) 1.
——— "The Story-Teller's Job." *Book Buyer* 2 (D 36) 8.
——— "When I Left Business for Literature." *Century* 108 (Ag 24) 489-96.
——— "A Writer's Conception of Realism." *Writer* 54 (Ja 41) 3-6.
Arvin, Newton. "Mr. Anderson's New Stories." *Freeman* 8 (5 D 23) 307-8.
Barker, R. H. "The Storyteller Role." *CE* 3 (F 42) 433-42.
Bodenheim, Maxwell. "Psychoanalysis and American Fiction." *Nation* 114 (7 Je 22) 683.
Boynton, P. H. "Sherwood Anderson." *NAR* 224 (Mr-Ap-My 27) 140-50.
Buchanan, A. M. "Sherwood Anderson, Country Editor." *World Tomorrow* 12 (F 29) 248-53.
Calverton, V. F. "Sherwood Anderson." *Mod Q* 2 (Fl 24) 82-118.
Carson, S. "In Reply to Sherwood Anderson." *Mod Mo* 7 (Jl 33) 347, 351.
Chase, C. B. "Sherwood Anderson." *SRL* 4 (24 S 27) 129-30.
Crawford, N. A. "Sherwood Anderson and the Wistfully Faithful." *Midland* 7 (N 22) 297-308.
Dell, Floyd. "How Sherwood Anderson Became an Author." *N Y Herald-Tribune Books* 18 (12 Ap 42) 1-2.
Dickinson, L. R. "Smyth County Hems." *Outlook* 113 (11 Ap 28) 580-2.
Fadiman, Clifton. "Sherwood Anderson: The Search for Salvation." *Nation* 135 (9 N 32) 454-6.
Fagin, N. B. "Sherwood Anderson." *SAQ* 43 (Jl 44) 256-62.
——— "Sherwood Anderson, the Liberator of Our Short Story." *EJ* 16 (Ap 27) 271-9.
——— "Sherwood Anderson and Our Anthropological Age." *Double Dealer* 7 (1925) 91-9.
Faulkner, William. "Prophets of the New Age: Sherwood Anderson." Dallas *Morning News* (26 Ap 25) 7.
Faÿ, Bernard. "Portrait de Sherwood Anderson: américain." *Revue de Paris* (15 O 34) 886-902.
Flanagan, J. T. "The Permanence of Sherwood Anderson." *SWR* 35 (Su 50) 170-7.
Frank, Waldo. "Emerging Greatness." *Seven Arts* 1 (N 16) 73-8.
Geismar, Maxwell. "Anderson's Winesburg." *N Y Times Book R* (18 Jl 43) 4.
Gerould, K. F. "Stream of Consciousness." *SRL* 4 (22 O 27) 234.
Gilman, Lawrence. "The Book of the Month: An American Masterwork." *NAR* 215 (Mr 22) 412-6.
Gozzi, R. D. "A Bibliography of Sherwood Anderson's Contributions to Periodicals." *Newberry Lib Bul* 2 (D 48) 71-82.
Gregory, Alyse. "Sherwood Anderson." *Dial* 75 (S 23) 243-6.
Guido, Augusto. "Cavalli da corsa e vomini dell' Ohio." *La Fiera Letteraria* (Italy) no 43 (23 O 49) 5.
Healey, R. C. "Anderson, Saroyan, Sherwood: New Directions." *Cath World* 42 (N 40) 174-80.
Hellesnes, Nils. "Sherwood Anderson, den einsame Amerikanaren." *Syn og Segn* (Oslo) 53 (N 47) 433-9.
Henderson, A. C. "Mid-America Awake." *Poetry* 11 (Je 18) 155-8.
Howe, Irving. "Sherwood Anderson and the American Myth of Power." *Tomorrow* 8 (Ag 49) 52-4.

——— "Sherwood Anderson and D. H. Lawrence." *Furioso* 5 (Fl 50) 21-33.
Huebsch, B. W. "Footnotes to a Publisher's Life." *Colophon* 7 (Su 37) 406-26.
Jessup, Mary. "A Check-List of the Writings of Sherwood Anderson." *Am Col* 5 (1928) 157-8.
Johnson, A. T. "Realism in Contemporary American Literature: Notes on Dreiser, Anderson, Lewis." *Sw Bul* (S 29) 3-16.
Kaufman, W. "Sherwood Anderson's Advice." *SRL* 33 (26 Ag 50) 21.
Lovett, R. M. "The Promise of Sherwood Anderson." *Dial* 72 (Ja 22) 78-83.
——— "Sherwood Anderson." *EJ* 13 (O 24) 531-9.
——— "Sherwood Anderson." *NRp* 89 (25 N 36) 103-5.
——— "Sherwood Anderson, American." *VQR* 17 (Su 41) 379-88.
McCole, C. J. "Sherwood Anderson, Congenital Freudian." *Cath World* 134 (N 29) 129-33.
Morris, L. S. "Sherwood Anderson, Sick of Words." *NRp* 51 (3 Ag 27) 277-9.
Rosenfeld, Paul. "Sherwood Anderson." *Dial* 72 (Ja 22) 29-42.
——— "Sherwood Anderson's Work." *Anglica* 1 (Ap-Je 46) 66-88.
Sillen, Samuel. "Sherwood Anderson." *New Masses* 39 (25 Mr 41) 23-6.
Smith, Rachel. "Sherwood Anderson: Some Entirely Arbitrary Reactions." *SR* 37 (Ap 29) 159-63.
Sutton, W. A. "Sherwood Anderson: The Advertising Years, 1900-1906." *Nw Ohio Q* 22 (Su 50) 120-57.
——— "Sherwood Anderson: The Cleveland Year, 1906-1907." *Nw Ohio Q* 22 (Wi 49-50) 39-44.
——— "Sherwood Anderson: The Clyde Years." *Nw Ohio Q* 19 (Jl 47) 99-114.
——— "Sherwood Anderson: The Spanish-American War Year." *Nw Ohio Q* 20 (Ja 48) 20-36.
Trilling, Lionel. "Sherwood Anderson." *KR* 3 (Su 41) 293-302.
——— "The World of Sherwood Anderson." *N Y Times Book R* 52 (9 N 47) 67-9.
Van Doren, Carl. "Sinclair Lewis and Sherwood Anderson: A Study of Two Moralists." *Century* 110 (Jl 25) 362-9.
Warren, R. P. "Hawthorne, Anderson and Frost." *NRp* 54 (16 My 28) 399-401.
Whipple, T. K. "Sherwood Anderson." *Lit R* 2 (11 Mr 22) 481-2.

ASCH, SHOLEM (1880-). Cargill, Oscar. "Sholem Asch: Still Immigrant and Alien." *CE* 12 (N 50) 67-77; *EJ* 39 (N 50) 483-90.
Cournos, John. "Three Novelists: Asch, Singer and Schneour." *Menorah J* 25 (Wi 37) 81-91.
Gorman, H. S. "Yiddish Literature and the Case of Sholem Asch." *Bkm* 57 (Je 23) 394-400.
Madison, C. A. "Sholem Asch." *Poet Lore* 46 (Wi 40) 303-37.
Slochower, Harry. "Franz Werfel and Sholem Asch: The Yearning for Status." *Accent* 5 (Au 45) 73-82.

ATHERTON, GERTRUDE (1857-1948). Anon. "Gertrude Atherton Writes Her 56th Book." *Life* 21 (11 N 46) 95-8.
Atherton, Gertrude. "Gertrude Atherton's Record." *SRL* 30 (17 My 47) 22.
Clemens, Cyril. "Gertrude Atherton." *Overland Mo* 90 (O 32) 239-59.
Cooper, F. T. "Gertrude Atherton." *Bkm* 30 (D 09) 357-63.
Harris, W. E. "Gertrude Atherton." *Writer* 39 (Mr 29) 62-4.
Johnson, M. D., & Hopkins, F. M. "American First Editions . . . Gertrude (Franklin) Atherton, 1857- ." *Pub W* 103 (25 Ag 23) 612.
Maurice, A. B. "Gertrude Atherton." *Bkm* 72 (S 30) 62-4.
Mowbray, J. P. "That 'Affair' of Mrs. Atherton's." *Critic* 40 (Je 02) 501-5.
Paterson, Isabel. "Gertrude Atherton, a Personality." *Bkm* 59 (F 24) 632-7.
"Pendennis." "My Types: Gertrude Atherton." *Forum* 58 (N 17) 585-94.

Stevenson, Lionel. "Atherton versus Grundy: The Forty Years' War." *Bkm* 69 (Jl 29) 464-72.
Van Vechten, Carl. "A Lady Who Defies Time." *Nation* 126 (14 F 23) 194, 196.

ATKINSON, BROOKS (1894-). Atkinson, Brooks. "Credo of a Critic." *SRL* 32 (6 Ag 49) 136.

ATWATER, CALEB (1778-1867). Anon. "A Country Fit for Princes." *Palimpsest* 12 (Ap 31) 144-59.

AUDEN, W. H. (1907-). Beach, J. W. "The Poems of Auden and the Prose Diathesis." *VQR* 25 (Su 49) 365-83.
Bloomfield, M. W. "W. H. Auden and *Sawles Warde*." *MLN* 63 (D 48) 548-52.
Bradbury, J. M. "Auden and the Tradition." *WR* 12 (Su 48) 221-9.
Brown, W. C. "Auden's *Sir, No Man's Enemy, Forgiving All*." *Expl* 3 (Mr 45) 38.
Cleophas, Sister M. "Auden's Family Ghosts (or *The String's Excitement*)." *Expl* 7 (O 48) 1.
Flint, C. F. "Auden's *Our Hunting Fathers Told the Story*." *Expl* 2 (O 43) 28.
Griffon, Howard. "Conversation on Cornelia Street: Dialogue with W. H. Auden." *Accent* 10 (Ag 49) 51-8.
Le Compte, C. B. "Which Side Am I Supposed to Be On?" *Expl* 8 (D 49) 21.
Long, R. A. "Auden's *Ode to My Pupils*." *Expl* 6 (Ap 48) 39.
——— "Auden's *Schoolchildren*." *Expl* 7 (F 49) 32.
McCoard, W. B. "An Interpretation of the Times: A Report of the Oral Interpretation of W. H. Auden's *Age of Anxiety*." *QJS* 35 (D 49) 489-95.
Philbrick, F. A. "Auden's *Have a Good Time*." *Expl* 4 (D 45) 21.
Robertson, D. A. "Auden's *Sir, No Man's Enemy, Forgiving All*." *Expl* 3 (My 45) 51.
Schwartz, Delmore. "The Two Audens." *KR* 1 (Wi 39) 43-4.
Valette, Jacques. "État actuel de l'oeuvre de W. H. Auden." *Mercure de France* no 1048 (Ja 50) 714-8.

AUDUBON, JOHN JAMES (1785-1851). Anon. "Audubon Bird Pictures and Leaflets." *School & Soc* 30 (31 Ag 29) 290-1.
Blanck, Jacob. "American First Editions; John James Audubon, 1785-1851." *Pub W* 129 (15 F 36) 832.
Colles, G. W. "Defense of Audubon." *Sci Am* 98 (2 My 08) 311.
Delamain, Jacques. "Un Grand Américain, Audubon." *Formes et Couleurs* (Paris) no 6 (1947).
Fox, H. M. "Audubon as Botanist." *House & Garden* (D 48) 146-7.
Geiser, S. W. "Audubon in Texas." *Sw* R 16 (Au 30) 109-36.
Henson, C. E. "A Note on the Early Travels of John James Audubon in Southern Illinois." *J Ill State Hist Soc* 40 (S 47) 336-9.
Hopkins, F. M. "Audubon's *Birds of America*." *Pub W* 128 (26 O 35) 1545-6.
McDermott, J. F. "Audubon's 'Journey up the Mississippi.'" *J Ill State Hist Soc* 35 (Je 42) 148-73.
Merriam, C. H. "John James Audubon: Pioneer of Science." *Popular Sci* 70 (Ap 07) 301-3.
Peattie, D. C. "The Real Audubon." *Am Merc* 9 (O 26) 219-26.
Richards, I. T. "Audubon, Joseph R. Mason, and John Neal." *AL* 6 (Mr 34) 122-40.
Roberts, T. S. "Audubon." *Bellman* 24 (9 F 18) 158.
Savage, H. L. "John James Audubon: A Backwoodsman in the Salon." *Princeton Un Lib Chron* 5 (Je 44) 129-36.
Schmucker, S. C. "Great American Scientist." *Chautauquan* 48 (O 07) 239-48.
Shelley, D. A. "Audubon to Date." *N Y Hist Soc Q* 30 (Jl 46) 168-73.

Watters, R. C. "Audubon and His Baltimore Patrons." *Md Hist Mag* 34 (Je 39) 138-43.
Weeks, Mangum. "On John James Audubon." *SAQ* 41 (Ja 42) 76-87.
Zabriskie, G. A. "The Story of a Priceless Art Treasure: The Original Water Colors of John James Audubon." *N. Y. Hist Soc Q* 30 (Ap 46) 69-76.

AUSTIN, BENJAMIN (1752-1820). Kaplan, Sidney. "'Honestus' and the Annihilation of the Lawyers." *SAQ* 48 (Jl 49) 401-20.

AUSTIN, MARY (1868-1934). Anon. "Mary Austin." *Bkm* 58 (S 23) 47-52.
Du Bois, A. E. "Mary Austin, 1868-1934." *Sw R* 20 (Sp 35) 231-64.
Field, L. M. "Mary Austin, American." *Bkm* 85 (D 32) 819-21.
Major, Mabel. "Mary Austin in Fort Worth." *N Mex Q* 4 (N 34) 307-10.
Maunsell, Louise. "Mary Austin, American." *Bkm* 85 (D 32) 819-21.
Pearce, T. M. "Mary Austin and the Pattern of New Mexico." *Sw R* 22 (Ja 37) 140-8.
Sergeant, E. S. "Mary Austin: A Portrait." *SRL* 11 (8 S 34) 96.
Steffens, Lincoln. "Mary Austin and the Desert." *Am Mag* 72 (Je 11) 178-81.
Van Doren, Carl. "The American Rhythm." *Century* 104 (N 23) 151-6.
Wynn, Dudley. "Mary Austin, Woman Alone." *VQR* 13 (Sp 37) 243-56.
Young, Vernon. "Mary Austin and the Earth Performance." *Sw R* 35 (Su 50) 153-63.

BABBITT, IRVING (1865-1933). Adams, J. L. "Humanism and Creation." *H&H* 6 (O-D 33) 173-96.
Bandler, Bernard. "The Individualism of Irving Babbitt." *H&H* 3 (O-D 29) 57-70.
Blackmur, R. P. "Humanism and Symbolic Imagination. Notes on Re-reading Irving Babbitt." *So R* 7 (Au 41) 309-25.
Boas, R. P. "The Humanism of Irving Babbitt." *Am R* 3 (Jl-Ag 25) 391-9.
Cappon, A. P. "Irving Babbitt and His Fundamental Thinking." *New Humanist* 6 (S-O 33) 9-13.
Clark, A. F. B. "Irving Babbitt." *Canadian Forum* 14 (O 33) 15-7.
Colum, M. M. "Literature, Ethics, and the Knights of Good Sense." *Scribner's* 87 (D 30) 599-608.
——— "Self-Critical America." *Scribner's* 87 (F 30) 197-206.
DeMille, G. E. "On Being Humanist." *SR* 41 (Ap-Je 33) 249-51.
Dubbel, S. E. "He Searched the Past." *SAQ* 35 (Ja 36) 50-61.
Eliot, T. S. "The Humanism of Irving Babbitt." *Forum* 80 (Jl 28) 37-44.
Elliott, G. R. "Babbitt and Religion." *Am R* 6 (F 34) 487-91.
——— "Irving Babbitt as I Knew Him." *Am R* 8 (N 36) 36-60.
——— "The Religious Dissension of Babbitt and More." *Am R* 9 (Su 37) 252-65.
——— "T. S. Eliot and Irving Babbitt." *Am R* 7 (S 36) 442-54.
Fairley, B. "Open Letter to Professor Irving Babbitt." *Canadian Forum* 14 (O 33) 15-7.
Giese, W. F. "Irving Babbitt, Undergraduate." *Am R* 6 (N 35) 65-94.
Greever, Garland. "Romanticism as a Philosophy of Life." *SR* 28 (Ja-Mr 20) 101-5.
Hecht, Hans. "Irving Babbitt, Rousseau and Romanticism." *Englische Studien* 55 (O 21) 447-57.
Hough, Lynn. "Dr. Babbitt and Vital Control." *London Quar R* 147 (Ja 27).
Hughes, M. Y. "Proud Humility." *SRL* 1 (4 O 24) 162.
Jones, H. M. "Professor Babbitt Cross-Examined." *NRp* 54 (21 Mr 28) 158-60.
Lippmann, Walter. "Humanism as Dogma." *SRL* 6 (15 Mr 30) 817-9.
MacCampbell, Donald. "Irving Babbitt." *SR* 43 (Ap 35) 164-74.
Maddox, N. S. "Irving Babbitt and the Emperor Shun." *Am R* 4 (Ja 26) 74-80.
Mather, F. J. "Irving Babbitt." *Harvard Grad Mag* 42 (D 33) 65-84.

Mercier, L. J. A. "The Legacy of Irving Babbitt." *Harvard Grad Mag* 42 (Je 34) 327-47.
More, P. E. "Irving Babbitt." *Am R* 3 (Ap 34) 23-40.
Morrell, Ray. "Wordsworth and Professor Babbitt." *Scrutiny* 1 (Mr 33) 374-83.
Munson, G. B. "The Socratic Virtues of Irving Babbitt." *Critic* 1 (Ja 34) 494-503.
Nickerson, Hoffman. "Irving Babbitt." *Am R* 2 (F 34) 385-404; *Criterion* 13 (Ja 34) 179-95.
Parkes, H. B. "D. H. Lawrence and Irving Babbitt." *Adelphi* 9 (Mr 35) 328-31.
Richard, Christian. "Irving Babbitt, the Man and the Teacher." *Cath World* 148 (O 38) 44-9.
Richards, P. S. "Irving Babbitt." *Nineteenth Century* 103 (Ap-My 28) 644-55.
Russell, F. T. "Romanticism of Irving Babbitt." *SAQ* 32 (O 33) 399-411.
Salpeter, Harry. "Irving Babbitt, Calvinist." *Outlook & Independent* 155 (16 Jl 30) 421-3, 439.
Seillière, Ernest. "La Reaction contre le naturisme aux Etats-Unis." *Journal des Debats* (6 O 33) 580-3.
Sypher, Wylie. "Irving Babbitt: A Reappraisal." *NEQ* 14 (My 41) 64-76.
Thompson, A. R. "Literature and Irresponsibility." *Am R* 7 (My 36) 192-202.
Warren, Austin. "Portrait of Irving Babbitt." *Commonweal* 24 (26 Je 36) 234-6.
Wilbur, R. "A Word about Babbitt, Romanticism, Mysticism, and the Supernatural." *Commonweal* 21 (25 Ja 35) 364-6.
Wilson, Edmund. "Notes on Babbitt and More." *NRp* 64 (19 Mr 30) 115-20.
——— "Sophocles, Babbitt and Freud." *NRp* 65 (3 D 30) 68-70.

BACHELLER, IRVING (1859-1950). Johnson, Merle. "American First Editions: Irving (Addison) Bacheller, 1859–." *Pub W* 120 (19 D 31) 2645.
Watkins, E. W. "The Irving Bacheller Collection." *N Y Hist Soc Quar Bul* 26 (Jl 42) 64.

BACON, DELIA (1811-59). Kimball, L. E. "Miss Bacon Advances Learning." *Colophon* ns 2 (Su 37) 338-54.

BAGBY, GEORGE WILLIAM (1828-83). Bell, W. H. "A Letter from Alexander H. Stephens to Dr. George W. Bagby." *WMQ* 16 (Jl 36) 359-61.

BAILEY, JACOB (ca. 1750-90). Baker, R. P. "The Poetry of Jacob Bailey, Loyalist." *NEQ* 2 (Ja 29) 58-92.

BAKER, RAY STANNARD (1870-1946). Anderson, W. E. "American First Editions: Ray Stannard Baker (David Grayson) 1870- ." *Pub W* 130 (22 Ag 36) 612-3.
Phillips, J. S. "Alias David Grayson," *Bkm* 43 (Je 16) 394-7.

BAKER, WILLIAM MUMFORD (1825-83). Parrott, T. M., & Thomas, M. H. "William Mumford Baker: Forgotten Princetonian." *PULC* 10 (F 49) 61-80.

BALDWIN, JOSEPH GLOVER (1815-64). Braswell, William. "An Unpublished Letter of Joseph Glover Baldwin." *AL* 2 (N 30) 292-4.
Farish, H. D. "An Overlooked Personality in Southern Life." *N C Hist R* 12 (O 35) 341-53.
Mellen, G. F. "Joseph G. Baldwin and the 'Flush Times.'" *SR* 9 (Ap 01) 171-84.
Wetmore, T. B. "Joseph G. Baldwin." *Ala Hist Soc Trans* 2 (1916) 67-73.

BANCROFT, GEORGE (1800-91). Bancroft, George. "Letter from George Bancroft to Charles P. Huntington." *PMHS* 57 (F 24) 270-1.
Bassett, J. S. "Correspondence of George Bancroft and Jared Sparks, 1823-32." *Smith Col Stud Hist* 2 (Ja 17) 67-143.

Dawes, N. H., & Nichols, F. T. "Revaluing George Bancroft." *NEQ* 6 (Je 33) 278-93.
Jantz, H. S. "German Thought and Literature in New England." *JEGP* 41 (Ja 42) 1-46.
Kraus, Michael. "George Bancroft (1834-1934)." *NEQ* 7 (D 34) 662-86.
Nye, R. B. "George Bancroft, Early Critic of German Literature." *MLN* 58 (F 43) 128-30.
——— "George Bancroft's View of Shakespeare." *Shakespeare Assn Bul* 18 (Jl 43) 109-13.
——— "The Religion of George Bancroft." *J Rel* 19 (Jl 39) 216-33.
Pange, Jean de. "Madame de Staël et les États-Unis." *Revue de Paris* 5 (1 S 33) 150-63.
Roe, A. S. "The Homes and Haunts of George Bancroft." *N E Mag* ns 23 (O 00) 161-80.
Stewart, Watt. "George Bancroft, Historian of the American Republic." *Miss Valley Hist R* 19 (Je 32) 77-86.
Sloane, W. M. "George Bancroft." *Atl* 102 (Ag 08) 275-81.

BANCROFT, HUBERT HOWE (1832-1918). Caughey, J. W. "Hubert Howe Bancroft: Historian of Western America." *AHR* 50 (Ap 45) 461-70.
Lewis, Oscar. "The Launching of Bancroft's 'Native Races.'" *Colophon* ns 1 (Wi 36) 323-32.

BANGS, JOHN KENDRICK (1862-1922). Bangs, F. H. "John Kendrick Bangs and the Acta Columbiana." *Columbia Un Q* 28 (Mr 36) 1-17.
——— "John Kendrick Bangs, Humorist of the Nineties." *Yale Un Lib Gaz* 7 (Ja 33) 53-76.
Corbin, John. "John Kendrick Bangs." *Book Buyer* 20 (Ap 00) 208-9.

BANNISTER, NATHANIEL HARRINGTON (1813-47). Marshall, T. F. "The Birth Date of Nathaniel Harrington Bannister." *AL* 8 (N 36) 306-7.

BARLOW, JOEL (1754-1812). Anon. "A Reviewer's Notebook." *Freeman* 8 (27 F 24) 598-9.
Adams, M. R. "Joel Barlow, Political Romanticist." *AL* 9 (My 37) 113-53.
——— "On the 'Newly Discovered Letter' of Joel Barlow." *AL* 10 (My 38) 224-7.
Armstrong, T. P. "Raleigh and 'The Columbiad.'" *N&Q* 162 (2 Ja 32) 15.
Belote, T. T. "Selections from the Gallipolis Papers." *Quar Pub Hist & Phil Soc Ohio* 2 (Ap-Je 07) 41-52.
Benson, A. B. "An American Poet-Enemy of Gustavus III of Sweden." *SS* 10 (N 28) 104-10.
Blau, J. L. "Joel Barlow, Enlightened Religionist." *JHI* 10 (Je 49) 430-44.
Boynton, P. H. "Joel Barlow Advises the Privileged Orders." *NEQ* 12 (S 39) 477-99.
Coolidge, Theresa. "Arms for Virginia: Joel Barlow to Monroe." *More Books* 22 (F 47) 57-8.
dell' Isola, Maria. "Joel Barlow: Précurseur de la Société des Nations." *Revue de Littérature Comparée* 14 (Ap-Je 34) 283-96.
Dorfman, Joseph. "Joel Barlow: Trafficker in Trade and Letters." *Pol Sci Q* 59 (Mr 44) 83-100.
Howard, Leon. "Joel Barlow and Napoleon." *Huntington Lib Q* 2 (O 38) 37-51.
King, W. B. "First American Satirists." *Conn Mag* 10 (O 06) 403-11.
Leary, Lewis. "Joel Barlow and William Hayley: A Correspondence." *AL* 21 (N 49) 325-34.
——— "Thomas Day on American Poetry: 1786." *MLN* 61 (N 46) 464-6.
Maxfield, E. K. "To the Editors of American Literature." *AL* 10 (N 38) 351-2.

——— "A Newly Discovered Letter from Joel Barlow to His Wife, from Algiers." *AL* 9 (Ja 38) 442-9.

——— "The Tom Barlow Manuscript of the *Columbiad.*" *NEQ* 11 (D 38) 834-42.

Squires, V. P. "Joel Barlow: Patriot, Democrat, and Man of Letters." *Quar J Un No Dak* 9 (Jl 19) 299-308.

Swift, Lindsay. "Our Literary Diplomats." *Book Buyer* 20 (Je 00) 269-73.

Wecter, Dixon. "Joel Barlow and the Sugar Beets." *Colo Mag* 18 (S 41) 179-81.

Zunder, T. A. "Joel Barlow and George Washington." *MLN* 44 (Ap 29) 254-6.

——— "Joel Barlow and Seasickness." *Yale J Biol & Med* 1 (Jl 29) 385-90.

——— "A New Barlow Poem." *AL* 11 (My 39) 206-9.

——— "Notes on the Friendship of Joel Barlow and Tom Paine." *Am Book Coll* 6 (Mr 35) 96-9.

——— "Six Letters of Joel Barlow to Oliver Wolcott." *NEQ* 2 (Jl 29) 475-89.

BARR, AMELIA (1831-1919). Adams, Paul. "Amelia Barr in Texas, 1856-1868." *Sw Hist Q* 49 (Ja 46) 361-73.

BARRY, PHILIP (1896-1949). Cajetan, Brother. "The Pendulum Starts Back." *Cath World* 139 (Mr 35) 650-6.

Carmer, Carl. "Philip Barry." *Theatre Arts Mo* 13 (N 29) 819-26.

BARTLETT, ROBERT (1817-43). Forbes, C. S. "Robert Bartlett, a Forgotten Transcendentalist." *N E Mag* ns (O 00) 211-9.

BARTRAM, JOHN (1699-1777). Cardwell, R. H. "American-English Communications of Three American Scholars, 1700-1775." *Tenn Hist Mag* 2: ser 2 (Jl 32) 227-33.

Harper, Francis. "John Bartram, Diary of a Journey through the Carolinas, Georgia and Florida. '1765-66.'" *Trans Am Philos Soc* 33 (1942) 1-120.

Jenkins, C. F. "The Historical Background of Franklin's Tree." *PMHB* 57 (Jl 33) 193-208.

Lovell, J. H. "The Beginnings of American Science: The First Botanist." *N E Mag* ns 30 (Ag 04) 753-67.

Middleton, W. S. "John Bartram, Botanist." *Sci Mo* 21 (Mr 25) 191-216.

Thatcher, Herbert. "Dr. Mitchell, M.D., F.R.S., of Virginia." *VMHB* 41 (Ja 33) 59-70.

BARTRAM, WILLIAM (1739-1823). Coleridge, E. H. "Coleridge, Wordsworth, and the American Botanist William Bartram." *Trans Royal Soc Lit* 27 (1906) 69-92.

Fagin, N. B. "Bartram's Travels." *MLN* 46 (My 31) 288-91.

Scudder, H. H. "Bartram's 'Travels': A Note on the Use of Bartram's 'Travels' by the Author of 'Nick of the Woods.'" *N&Q* 184 (13 Mr 43) 154-5.

BATES, ERNEST SUTHERLAND (1879-1939). Calverton, V. F. "Ernest Sutherland Bates." *Mod Q* 11 (Fl 39) 2-4.

BATES, KATHARINE LEE (1859-1929). Boyd, E. P. "Katharine Lee Bates: Poet-Teacher." *EJ* 20 (Je 31) 455-62.

BATWELL, DANIEL (ca 1750-90). Rede, Kenneth. "A Note on the Author of *The Times.*" *AL* 2 (Mr 30) 79-82.

BAXTER, RICHARD (1615-91). Powicke, F. J. "Some Unpublished Correspondence of the Rev. Richard Baxter and the Rev. John Eliot, 'The Apostle to the American Indians,' 1656-1682." *Per Bul John Rylands Lib* 15 (Ja, Jl 31) 138-76, 442-6.

BEACH, REX (1877-1949). Clemens, Cyril. "My Friend Rex Beach." *Hobbies* (F 50) 138.

BEADLE, ERASTUS (1821-94). Adimari, Ralph. "The House That Beadle Built." *Am Book Coll* 4 (N, D 33) 221-6, 288-91; 5 (Ja, F, Mr, My-Je, Jl 34) 22-6, 60-3, 92-4, 147-9, 215-7.
Lutes, D. T. "The Dime Novel Delights of Mr. Beadle." *Chri Sci Mon* 34 (1 Ag 42) 6, 15.
——— "Erastus F. Beadle, Dime Novel King." *N Y Hist* 22 (Ap 41) 147-57.

BEEBE, WILLIAM (1877-). Anon. "Une Poésie inattendue." *Journal des Débats* 39 (F 32) 198-9.
Barr, Mark. "Roughing It in the Tropics." *Atl* 140 (N 27) 611-20.
Roosevelt, Theodore. "A Naturalist's Tropical Laboratory." *Scribner's* 61 (Ja 17) 46-64.
Wilson, Edmund. "A Conversation in the Galapagos." *Atl* 136 (N 25) 577-87.

BEECHER, HENRY WARD (1813-87). Anon. "Excerpts from two letters, dated March 31, 1855, and April 18, 1869." *Autograph Album* 1 (D 33) 53.
Abbott, Lyman. "Beecher: A Leader of Men." *Outlook* 105 (18 O 13) 362-4.
——— "Henry Ward Beecher." *Atl* 92 (O 03) 539-51.
——— "Henry Ward Beecher as an Orator." *Outlook* 104 (21 Je 13) 377-81.
Crocker, Lionel. "The Rhetorical Influence of Henry Ward Beecher." *QJS* 18 (F 32) 82-7.
Mead, David. "The Humiliation of Henry Ward Beecher." *Ohio State Arch & Hist Q* 58 (Ja 49) 94-100.
Pond, J. B. "Eccentricities of Genius." *Arena* 25 (F 01) 227-32.

BEECHER, LYMAN (1775-1863). Stowe, L. B. "The First of the Beechers." *Atl* 152 (Ag 33) 209-20.

BEER, THOMAS (1889-1940). Clark, Emily. "Thomas Beer." *SRL* 10 (12 My 34) 689.
Lane, J. W. "Thomas Beer." *Bkm* 74 (N 31) 241-6.
Mumford, Lewis. "Thomas Beer." *SRL* 22 (4 My 40) 3-4, 17.

BEHRMAN, S. N. (1893-). Kaplan, Charles. "S. N. Behrman: The Quandary of the Comic Spirit." *CE* 11 (Mr 50) 317-23.
Krutch, J. W. "The Comic Wisdom of S. N. Behrman." *Nation* 137 (19 Jl 33) 74-6.
Mersand, Joseph. "S. N. Behrman and the American Comedy of Manners." *Players' Mag* 17 (Ap 41) 6-8.

BELASCO, DAVID (1859-1931). Belasco, David. "My Life's Story." *Hearst's Mag* 25 (Ap, My, Je, Jl 14) 297-306, 481-9, 641-52, 767-79; 26 (Ag, S, O, N, D 14) 42-54, 187-200, 454-65, 601-15, 784-97; 27 (Ja, F, Mr, Ap, Je, Jl 15) 41-53, 154-68, 286-7, 319-21, 353-4, 393-4, 422-3, 456, 500-1, 545; 28 (Ag, S, O, N, D 15) 22-3, 70-2, 106-7, 156-8, 178-9, 226-7, 248-9, 296-7, 326-7, 370-1, 397-9, 434-5.
Brock, H. I. "Belasco, Magician of the Stage, Is 75." *N Y Times Mag* (21 Jl 29).
Moses, Montrose. "David Belasco: The Astonishing Versatility of a Veteran Producer." *Theatre Guild Mag* 7 (N 29) 27-30, 51.
Peirce, F. L. "Youth, Art, and Mr. Belasco." *Drama* 7 (My 17) 176-91.
Victor, A. "David Belasco." *Reflex* 2 (Je 28) 66-70.
Young, Stark. "Belasco." *NRp* 67 (17 Je 31) 123-4.

BELKNAP, JEREMY (1744-98). Cole, C. W. "Jeremy Belknap; Pioneer Nationalist." *NEQ* 10 (D 37) 743-51.
Eliot, S. A. "Jeremy Belknap." *PMHS* 66 (1942) 96-106.
Mayo, L. S. "Jeremy Belknap and Ebenezer Hazard." *NEQ* 12 (Ap 29) 183-98.
——— "Jeremy Belknap and J. Q. Adams, 1787." *PMHS* 59 (F 26) 203-10.
——— "Jeremy Belknap's Apologue of the Hen at Pennycook." *PCSM* 27 (Ap 27) 31-6.

BELLAMY, EDWARD (1850-98). Filler, Louis. "Edward Bellamy and the Spiritual Unrest." *Am J Econ & Soc* 8 (Ap 49) 239-49.

Forbes, A. B. "The Literary Quest for Utopia, 1880-1900." *Social Forces* 6 (D 27) 179-89.

Franklin, J. H. "Edward Bellamy and the Nationalist Movement." *NEQ* 11 (D 38) 739-72.

Johnson, Merle. "American First Editions: Edward Bellamy." *Pub W* 126 (22 S 34) 1125.

Levi, A. W. "Edward Bellamy: Utopian." *Ethics* 55 (Ja 45) 131-44.

Madison, C. A. "Edward Bellamy, Social Dreamer." *NEQ* 15 (S 42) 444-66.

Morgan, A. E. "Diagram for a World That Might Be." *Chri Sci Mon* 37 (24 Mr 45) 8.

Sadler, Elizabeth. "One Book's Influence: Edward Bellamy's 'Looking Backward.'" *NEQ* 18 (D 44) 530-55.

Shurter, R. L. "The Literary Work of Edward Bellamy." *AL* 5 (N 33) 229-34.

——— "The Writing of *Looking Backward*." *SAQ* 38 (Jl 39) 255-61.

Tarbell, I. M. "New Dealers of the Seventies: Henry George and Edward Bellamy." *Forum* 92 (S 34) 133-9.

BENCHLEY, ROBERT (1889-1945). Benchley, Robert. "Why Does Nobody Collect Me?" *Colophon* 5 (S 34) Pt 18.

BENÉT, STEPHEN VINCENT (1898-1943). Anderson, Pearl. "A Prize Winner." *Poetry* 19 (Mr 22) 340-43.

Bacon, Leonard. "Stephen Vincent Benét." *SRL* 10 (7 Ap 34) 609.

Becker, Carl. "Benét's Sympathetic Understanding." *Mark Twain Q* 6 (Wi-Sp 43-44) 13.

Benét, Stephen V. "Epic on an American Theme." *New Colophon* 2 (Ja 49) 1-12.

——— "The Sixth Man." *Colophon* 4 (O 33) Pt 15.

Benét, W. R. "My Brother Steve: A Poet Who Never Cared Much about an Ivory Tower." *SRL* 26 (27 Mr 43) 5-7.

——— "Round about Parnassus." *SRL* 7 (27 D 30) 491.

Chubb, T. C. "Recollections of Steve Benét." *Mark Twain Q* 6 (Wi-Sp 43-44) 10-12.

Clemens, Cyril. "A Chat with Stephen Benét." *Mark Twain Q* 6 (Wi-Sp 43-44) 7-9.

——— "For Stephen Benét." *America* 68 (Ag 43) 550.

Daniels, S. R. "A Saga of the American Civil War." *Contemp R* 146 (O 34) 466-71.

Johnson, Merle. "American First Editions, Stephen Vincent Benét." *Pub W* 121 (16 Ja 32) 290-1.

La Farge, Christopher. "The Narrative Poetry of Stephen Vincent Benét." *SRL* 27 (Ag 44) 106-8.

Lovett, R. M. "The American Conflict." *NRp* 56 (29 Ag 28) 51-2.

MacLeish, Archibald, *et al.* "As We Remember Him." *SRL* 26 (27 Mr 43) 7-11.

Monroe, Harriet. "A Cinema Epic." *Poetry* 33 (N 28) 91-6.

Nathan, Robert. "Stephen Vincent Benét and His America." *Mark Twain Q* 6 (Wi-Sp 43-44) 4-5.

North, J. N. "A Playful Tiger." *Poetry* 27 (F 26) 279-81.

O'Neill, Eugene, Jr. "S. V. Benét: 'John Brown's Body.'" *SRL* 32 (6 Ag 49) 34-5.

Spitz, Leon. "Stephen Vincent Benét." *Am Hebrew* 157 (13 F 48) 8, 13.

Wells, H. W. "Stephen Vincent Benét." *CE* 5 (O 43) 8-13.

Wiley, P. L. "The Phaeton Symbol in *John Brown's Body*." *AL* 17 (N 45) 231-42.

Winwar, Frances. "Two Poets, Stephen Vincent and William Rose Benét." *CE* 2 (F 41) 415-27.

Zabel, M. D. "The American Grain." *Poetry* 48 (Jl 36) 276-82.

BENÉT, WILLIAM ROSE (1886-1950). Anon. "Poetry of Benét." *Dial* 56 (16 Ja 14) 67-8.
——— "William Rose Benét." *Bkm* 58 (O 23) 135-9.
Humphries, Rolfe. "Journeyman of Letters." *Poetry* 44 (My 34) 108-11.
Monroe, Harriet. "Benét and the Zodiac." *Poetry* 15 (O 19) 48-51.
North, J. N. "Mr. Benét's Selected Poems." *Poetry* 9 (Mr 17) 322-4.
Wilkinson, Marguerite. "Mirrors of the Renaissance." *Bkm* 52 (Ap 21) 168-70.
Winwar, Frances. "Two Poets, Stephen Vincent and William Rose Benét." *CE* 2 (F 41) 415-27.

BENEZET, ANTHONY (1713-84). Merrill, L. T. "Anthony Benezet: Antislavery Crusader and Apostle of Humanitarianism." *Negro Hist Bul* 9 (F 46) 99-100, 104-6, 108, 111-6.

BENJAMIN, PARK (1809-64). Williams, M. L. "Park Benjamin on Melville's 'Mardi.'" *AN&Q* 8 (D 49) 132-4.

BENNETT, EMERSON (1822-1905). Mills, R. V. "Emerson Bennett's Two Oregon Novels." *Ore Hist Q* 41 (D 40) 367-81.

BENNETT, JAMES GORDON (1795-1872). Croffut, W. A. "Bennett and His Time." *Atl* 47 (F 31) 196-206.

BENSON, STELLA (1892-1933). Gettman, R. A. "Benson's 'The Man Who Missed the Bus.'" *Expl* 3 (D 44).

BERRYMAN, JOHN (1914-   ). Fitzgerald, Robert. "Poetry and Perfection." *SR* 55 (Ag 48) 690-1.

BEVERLY, ROBERT (1673-1722). Wright, L. B. "Beverly's History . . . of Virginia (1705), A Neglected Classic." *WMQ* 1 (Ja 44) 49-64.

BIDDLE, NICHOLAS (1786-1844). Govan, T. P. "An Unfinished Novel by Nicholas Biddle." *Princeton Un Lib Chron* 10 (Ap 49) 124-36.

BIERCE, AMBROSE (1842-1914?). Anon. "A Collection of Bierce Letters." *Un Calif Chron* 34 (Ja 32) 30-48.
——— "English Tribute to the Genius of Ambrose Bierce." *Cur Op* 58 (Je 15) 427.
——— "A Reviewer's Note-Book." *Freeman* 1 (21 Ap 20) 143.
——— "Uno dei dispersi." *Letteratura* (Ja-F 46) 26.
Bierce, Helen. "Ambrose Bierce at Home." *Am Merc* 30 (D 33) 453-8.
Bower-Shore, Clifford. "Ambrose Bierce." *Bkm* (London) 78 (Ag 30) 283-4.
Braddy, Haldeen. "Ambrose Bierce and Guy de Maupassant." *AN&Q* 1 (Ag 41) 67-8.
——— "Trailing Ambrose Bierce." *AN&Q* 1 (Ap, My 41) 5-6, 20.
Cooper, F. T. "Ambrose Bierce: An Appraisal." *Bkm* 33 (Jl 11) 471-80.
Dalziel, Gilbert. "Ambrose Bierce." *TLS* 24 (21 My 25) 352.
deCastro, Adolphe. "Ambrose Bierce as He Really Was." *Am Parade* 1 (O 26) 28-44.
East, H. M., Jr. "Bierce—The Warrior Writer." *Overland Mo* ns 65 (Je 15) 105-7.
Fadiman, Clifton. "Portrait of a Misanthrope." *SRL* 29 (12 O 46) 11-3, 61-2.
Follett, Wilson. "Ambrose Bierce, an Analysis of the Perverse Wit that Shaped His Work." *Bkm* 68 (N 28) 284-9.
——— "Ambrose, Son of Marcus Aurelius." *Atl* 160 (Jl 37) 32-42.
——— "America's Neglected Satirist." *Dial* 65 (18 Jl 18) 49-52.
——— "Bierce in His Brilliant Obscurity." *N Y. Times Book R* (11 O 36) 232.
Goldstein, J. S. "Edwin Markham, Ambrose Bierce, and 'The Man with the Hoe.'" *MLN* 69 (Mr 43) 165-75.
Grattan, C. N. "Ambrose Bierce." *Reviewer* 5 (O 25) 103-4.

Harding, R. G. "Mr. Boythorn-Bierce." *Bkm* 61 (Ag 25) 636-46.
McWilliams, Carey. "Ambrose Bierce." *Am Merc* 16 (F 29) 215-22.
——— "Ambrose Bierce and His First Love." *Bkm* 75 (Je-Jl 32) 254-9.
——— "The Mystery of Ambrose Bierce." *Am Merc* 22 (My 45) 330-7.
Millard, Bailey. "Personal Memories of Ambrose Bierce." *Bkm* 40 (F 15) 653-8.
Miller, A. C. "The Influence of Edgar Allan Poe on Ambrose Bierce." *AL* 4 (My 32) 130-50.
Monaghan, Frank. "Ambrose Bierce and the Authorship of *The Monk and the Hangman's Daughter.*" *AL* 2 (Ja 31) 337-49.
Nathan, G. J. "Ambrose Light." *Am Spect* 2 (F 34) 2.
Nations, L. J. "Ambrose Bierce: The Gray Wolf of American Letters." *SAQ* 25 (Jl 26) 253-68.
Partridge, Eric. "Ambrose Bierce." *London Merc* 16 (O 27) 625-38.
Scheffauer, H. G. "The Satirist in Vacuo." *Freeman* 1 (11 Ag 20) 514-6.
Snell, George. "Poe Redivivus." *Ariz Q* 1 (Su 45) 49-57.
Sterling, George. "The Shadow Maker." *Am Merc* 6 (S 25) 10-9.
——— "A Wine of Wizardry." *Cosmopolitan* 43 (S 07) 551-6.
Thompson, F. Y. "Light on the Bierce Mystery." *John O'London's W* 57 (29 O 48) 513.
Williams, S. T. "Ambrose Bierce and Bret Harte." *AL* 17 (My 45) 179-80.
Wilt, Napier. "Ambrose Bierce and the Civil War." *AL* 1 (N 29) 260-85.

BINYON LAURENCE (1869-1943). Southworth, J. G. "Laurence Binyon." *SR* 43 (Jl-S 35) 343-6.

BIRD, ROBERT MONTGOMERY (1806-54). Quinn, A. H. "Dramatic Works of Robert Montgomery Bird." *Nation* 101 (3 Ag 16) 136-7.
Scudder, H. H. "Bartram's 'Travels': A Note on the Use of Bartram's 'Travels' by the Author of 'Nick of the Woods.'" *N&Q* 184 (13 Mr 43) 154-5.
Thompson, C. S. "Life of Robert Montgomery Bird: Written by His Wife, Mary Mayer Bird . . . with Selections from Bird's Correspondence." *Un Penn Lib Chron* 12 (1944) 71-120; 13 (1945) 1-94.
Williams, C. B. "R. M. Bird's Plans for Novels of the Frontier." *AL* 21 (N 49) 321-4.

BISHOP, JOHN PEALE (1892-1944). Anon. "John Peale Bishop '17: 1892-1944." *Princeton Un Lib Chron* 7 (F 46) 55-6.
Arrowsmith, William. "An Artist's Estate." *Hudson R* 2 (Sp 49) 118-27.
Frank, Joseph. "Force and Form: A Study of John Peale Bishop." *SR* 55 (Ja-Mr 47) 71-107.
Hyman, S. E. "Notes on the Organic Unity of John Peale Bishop." *Accent* 9 (Wi 49) 102-13.
Patrick, J. M., & Stallman, R. W. "John Peale Bishop: A Checklist." *PULC* 7 (F 46) 62-79.
Radford, Manson. "Act of Darkness." *So R* 1 (Jl 35) 205-8.
Stallman, R. W. "Bishop's *Behavior of the Sun.*" *Expl* 5 (O 46) 6.
——— "Bishop's *Perspectives Are Precipices.*" *Expl* 5 (N 46) 8.
——— "Bishop's *Southern Pines.*" *Expl* 4 (Ap 46) 46.
——— "The Poetry of John Peale Bishop." *WR* 11 (Au 46) 5-19.
Tate, Allen. "John Peale Bishop: A Personal Memoir." *WR* 12 (Wi 48) 67-71.
——— "A Note on Bishop's Poetry." *So R* 1 (Au 35) 357-64.
Warren, R. P. "Working Toward Freedom." *Poetry* 43 (Mr 34) 342-6.

BLACKMUR, R. P. (1904-). Baker, Carlos. "R. P. Blackmur: A Checklist." *PULC* 3 (Ap 42) 99-106.
Hyman, S. E. "R. P. Blackmur and the Expense of Criticism." *Poetry* 71 (F 48) 259-70.

Schwartz, Delmore. "The Critical Method of R. P. Blackmur." *Poetry* 53 (O 38) 28-39.
West, R. B., Jr. "An Examination of Modern Critics: R. P. Blackmur." *Rocky Mt R* 8 (Su 45) 139-45.

BLAIR, FRANCIS (1791-1876). Smith, W. E. "Francis P. Blair, Pen-Executive of Andrew Jackson." *Miss Valley Hist R* 17 (Mr 31) 543-56.

BLAND, H. M. (1863-1931). Peterson, M. S. "The Poet Bland and Sixteen Specimen Poems." *Un Neb Stud* (1943) no 3.

BODENHEIM, MAXWELL (1892-1954). Cowley, Malcolm. "Euphues." *Dial* 73 (O 22) 446-8.
Monroe, Harriet. "Maxwell Bodenheim." *Poetry* 25 (Mr 25) 320-7.

BOGAN, LOUISE (1897-). Ford, M. M. "The Flame in Stone." *Poetry* 50 (Je 37) 158-61.
Hubbell, Lindley. "Portrait of Louise Bogan." *Book Buyer* 3 (O 37) 20-1.
Winters, Yvor. "The Poetry of Louise Bogan." *NRp* 60 (16 O 29) 247.
Wolfe, R. L. "Impassioned Austerity." *Poetry* 23 (Mr 24) 335-8.
Zabel, M. D. "The Flower of the Mind." *Poetry* 35 (D 29) 158-62.

BOKER, GEORGE HENRY (1823-90). Beatty, R. C. "Bayard Taylor and George H. Boker." *AL* 6 (N 34) 316-27.
Bradley, Sculley. "George Henry Boker and Angie Hicks." *AL* 8 (N 36) 258-65.
——— "'Hans Breitmann' in England and America." *Colophon* ns 2 (Aut 36) 65-81.
——— "A Newly Discovered American Sonnet Sequence." *PMLA* 40 (D 25) 910-20.
——— "Poe on the New York Stage in 1855." *AL* 9 (N 37) 353-4.
Hubbell, J. B. "Five Letters from George Henry Boker to William Gilmore Simms." *PMHB* 63 (Ja 39) 66-71.
——— "George Henry Boker, Paul Hamilton Hayne, and Charles Warren Stoddard: Some Unpublished Letters." *AL* 5 (My 33) 146-65.
Krutch, J. W. "George Henry Boker, A Little Known American Dramatist." *SR* 25 (O 17) 457-68.
Metcalf, J. C. "An Old Romantic Triangle." *SR* 29 (Ja 21) 45-58.
Quinn, A. H. "The Dramas of George Henry Boker." *PMLA* 32 (1917) 233-66.
——— "George Henry Boker—Playwright and Patriot." *Scribner's* 173 (Je 23) 701-15.
Taylor, G. H. "Check-List to Writings by and about George H. Boker (1823-1890)." *Am Book Coll* 5 (D 34) 372-4.
Urban, Gertrude. "Paolo and Francesca in History and Literature." *Critic* 40 (1902) 425-38.

BOLTON, NATHANIEL (1749-1820). Bolton, C. K. "Nathaniel Bolton, a Forgotten New England Poet." *PAAS* 41 (O 31) 405-20.

BOUCHER, JONATHAN (1738-1804). Anon. "Letters of Rev. Jonathan Boucher." *Md Hist Mag* 7 (Mr, Je, S, D 12) 1-26, 150-65, 286-303, 337-56; 8 (Mr, Je, S, D 13) 34-50, 168-86, 235-56, 338-52; 9 (Mr, S, D 14) 54-67, 232-40, 327-35.
Chorley, E. C. "Correspondence between the Right Reverend John Skinner, Jr., and the Reverend Jonathan Boucher, 1786." *Hist Mag Prot Episc Church* 10 (Je 41) 163-75.
Pate, J. E. "Jonathan Boucher, an American Loyalist." *Md Hist Mag* 25 (S 30) 305-18.
Pennington, E. L. "Some Letters of Bishop William Skinner of Aberdeen, 1822-1827." *Hist Mag Prot Episc Church* 16 (D 47) 373-413.

Read, A. W. "Boucher's Linguistic Pastoral of Colonial Maryland." *Dialect Notes* 6 (D 33) 353-60.
Thompson, M. W. "Jonathan Boucher (1738-1804) by Himself." *Blackwood's* 231 (Mr 32) 315-34.
Walker, R. G. "Jonathan Boucher: Champion of the Minority." *WMQ* 2: ser 3 (Ja 45) 3-14.

BOUCICAULT, DION (1820-90). Kaplan, Sidney. "'Omoo': Melville's and Boucicault's." *AN&Q* 8 (Ja 50) 150-1.
Morris, Clara. "A Memory of Dion Boucicault." *Cosmopolitan* 38 (Ja 05) 273-8.
Peffer, Susan. "Dion Boucicault." *Letters* 2 (Ag 29) 7-18.
Rahill, Frank. "Dion Boucicault." *Theatre Arts* 23 (N 39) 807-13.

BOURNE, RANDOLPH (1886-1918). Anon. "Randolph Bourne [letters]." *Twice a Year* 2 (1939) 79-102; 5-6 (1940-41) 79-98; 7 (1941) 76-90.
Dell, Floyd. "Randolph Bourne." *NRp* 17 (4 Ja 19) 276.
Laski, H. J. "The Liberalism of Randolph Bourne." *Freeman* 1 (19 My 20) 237-8.
Lerner, Max. "Randolph Bourne and Two Conversations." *Twice a Year* 5-6 (1940-41) 54-78.
Madison, C. A. "The Man in the Black Cape. Randolph Bourne: A Literary Radical." *Am Schol* 15 (Su 46) 338-47.
Monroe, Harriet. "Mr. Bourne on Traps." *Poetry* 12 (My 18) 90-4.
Mumford, Lewis. "The Image of Randolph Bourne." *NRp* 64 (24 S 30) 151-2.
Rosenfeld, Paul. "Randolph Bourne." *Dial* 75 (D 23) 545-60.
Teall, Dorothy. "Bourne into Myth." *Bkm* 75 (O 32) 590-9.

BOYD JAMES (1888-1944). Anon. "James Boyd." *Wilson Bul* 5 (N 30) 174-5.
Boyd, James. "Answer Sky." *PULC* 6 (F 45) 61.
——— "Away! Away!" *PULC* 6 (F 45) 62-76.
Burt, Struthers. "James Boyd." *PULC* 6 (F 45) 56-60.
DeVoto, Bernard. "A Novel Hammered Out of Experience." *SRL* 11 (27 Ap 25) 645.
McLaury, Helen, & Young, Malcolm. "James Boyd: A Check-List." *PULC* 6 (F 45) 77-81.
Meade, J. R. "James Boyd." *SRL* 12 (29 Je 35) 10-1.
Stone, Frank. "American First Editions: James Boyd, 1888- ." *Pub W* 135 (15 Ap 39) 1461.
Wilson, J. S. "The South Goes Democratic." *SRL* 3 (28 My 27) 860.

BOYESEN, HJALMAR HJORTH (1848-95). White, G. L. Jr. "H. H. Boyesen: A Note on Immigration." *AL* 13 (Ja 42) 363-71.

BOYLE, KAY (1903-). Anon. "Kay Boyle." *Cur Biog* 3 (Je 42) 13-5.
Harter, Evelyn. "Kay Boyle, Experimenter." *Bkm* 75 (Je 32) 249-53.
Hawkins, A. D. "Death of a Man." *Critic* 27 (Ap 37) 498-501.

BRACKENRIDGE, HENRY MARIE (1786-1871). McDermott, J. F. "Henry Marie Brackenridge and His Writings." *W Penn Hist Mag* 20 (S 37) 181-96.

BRACKENRIDGE, HUGH HENRY (1748-1816). Andrews, J. C. "*The Pittsburgh Gazette*—a Pioneer Newspaper." *W Penn Hist Mag* 15 (N 32) 293-307.
Conner, Martha. "Hugh Henry Brackenridge at Princeton University." *W Penn Hist Mag* 10 (Jl 27) 146-62.
Eakin, Myrl. "Hugh Henry Brackenridge, Lawyer." *W Penn Hist Mag* 10 (Jl 27) 163-75.
Field, A. G. "The Press in Western Pennsylvania to 1812." *W Penn Hist Mag* 20 (D 37) 231-64.

Haviland, T. P. "Hugh Henry Brackenridge and Milton's 'Piedmontese' Sonnet." *N&Q* 176 (8 Ap 39) 243-4.

——— "The Miltonic Quality of Brackenridge's Poem on Divine Revelation." *PMLA* 56 (Je 41) 588-92.

Marsh, Philip. "Hugh Henry Brackenridge: The 'Direct Primary' of 1792." *W Penn Hist Mag* 32 (S-D 49) 115-6.

——— "Hugh Henry Brackenridge: More Essays in the *National Gazette*." *W Penn Hist Mag* 29 (S-D 47) 147-52.

Newlin, C. M. "Hugh Henry Brackenridge, Writer." *W Penn Hist Mag* 10 (1928) 224-56.

Williams, Mildred. "Hugh Henry Brackenridge as a Judge of the Supreme Court of Pennsylvania." *W Penn Hist Mag* 10 (1928) 210-23.

BRADBURY, JOHN (*fl.* 1809). True, R. H. "A Sketch of the Life of John Bradbury, Including His Unpublished Correspondence with Thomas Jefferson." *PAPS* 68 (1929) 133-50.

BRADFORD, ANDREW (1686-1742). DeArmond, A. J. "Andrew Bradford." *PMHB* 62 (O 38) 463-87.

BRADFORD, GAMALIEL (1863-1932). Anon. "Personal Letters of Gamaliel Bradford." *Atl* 153 (Ap 34) 431-40.

Arvin, Newton. "Society and Solitude." *NRp* 76 (18 O 33) 284.

Bolton, C. K. "Gamaliel Bradford, a Memoir." *PMHS* 65 (F 33) 81-91.

Bradford, Gamaliel. "The Journal of a Man of Letters." *Harper's* 166 (Mr, Ap 33) 419-29, 609-19.

Chew, S. W. "O Heart Rise Not Against Me." *YR* 24 (Wi 34) 392-7.

Ezban, Selim. "Gamaliel Bradford et Leopardi." *Ital* 22 (D 45) 205-11.

Fadiman, Clifton. "Other People's Lives." *N Yr* 20 (9 S 33) 77-8.

Forsythe, R. S. "The Journal of Gamaliel Bradford, 1883-1932." *NEQ* 5 (D 33) 830-3.

Greever, Garland. "Saul among the Poets." *SR* 29 (Ap 21) 222-9.

Harris, J. C. "An American Sainte-Beuve: Gamaliel Bradford." *Emory Un Q* 4 (Mr 48) 16-20.

Hicks, Granville. "An Insulated Littérateur." *Nation* 137 (27 S 33) 358-9.

Knickerbocker, W. S. "Gamaliel Bradford Looks at His Art." *SR* 42 (Ja-Mr 34) 91-9.

Lincoln, V. C. "Gamaliel Bradford." *Writer* 38 (My 28) 155-8.

Richards, G. R. B. "The Life and 'Lives' of Gamaliel Bradford." *N Y Herald Tribune Books* 8 (24 Ap 32) 4.

Wagenknecht, Edward. "Psychography, the First Forty Years." *VQR* 3 (Ap 27) 285-91.

Ware, Leonard. "Gamaliel Badford, A Challenge." *Writer* 43 (Je 32) 155-8.

Warren, Dale. "Gamaliel Bradford." *Mod Thinker* 1 (Ag 32) 364-6.

——— "Gamaliel Bradford: A Personal Sketch." *SAQ* 32 (Ja 33) 9-18.

Woodruff, M. D. "Gamaliel Bradford: A Searcher of Souls." *SAQ* 28 (O 29) 419-29.

BRADFORD, JOHN (1749-1830). Clift, G. G. "John Bradford: 'The Caxton of Kentucky': A Bibliography." *AN&Q* 8 (Je 48) 35-41.

BRADFORD, WILLIAM (1590-1657). Bradford, E. F. "Conscious Art in Bradford's 'History of Plymouth Plantation.'" *NEQ* 1 (Ap 28) 133-57.

Gee, C. S. "The Bradford Manuscript." *Church Hist* 6 (Je 37) 136-44.

BRADSTREET, ANNE (1612-72). Crowder, Richard. "'Phoenix Spencers': A Note on Anne Bradstreet." *NEQ* 18 (Je 44) 310.

Starrett, Vincent. "The First American Poet." *Freeman* 5 (17 My 22) 224-5.

Svenson, J. K. "Anne Bradstreet in England: A Bibliographical Note." *AL* 13 (Mr 41) 63-5.

Vancurá, Z. "Baroque Prose in America." *Stud Eng Charles Un* (Prague) 4 (1933) 39-58.

Wegelin, Oscar. "A List of Editions of the Poems of Anne Bradstreet, with Some Additional Books Relating to Her." *Am Book Coll* 4 (Jl 33) 15-6.

Wheelock, M. "Mistress Anne Bradstreet." *Vassar J Undergrad Stud* 5 (My 31) 26-9.

BRAITHWAITE, WILLIAM STANLEY (1878-). Teresa, Sister Francis. "Poet's Discoverer." *Phylon* 5 (O-D 44) 375-8.

BRANN, W. C. (1855-98). Meyer, A. E. "Advocatus Diaboli." *Am Merc* 12 (S 27) 68-74.

BRAY, THOMAS (1685-1730). Lydekker, J. W. "Thomas Bray (1685-1730), Founder of Missionary Enterprise." *Hist Mag Prot Episc Church* 12 (S 43) 187-214.

Oswald, T. C. "Thomas Bray: The Founder of American Libraries." *Am Book Coll* 5 (Mr 34) 80-2.

Wheeler, J. T. "Thomas Bray and the Maryland Parochial Libraries." *Md Hist Mag* 34 (S 39) 246-65.

Wroth, L. C. "Dr. Bray's 'Proposals for the Encouragement of Religion and Learning in the Foreign Plantations'—a Bibliographical Note." *PMHS* 65 (F 36) 518-34.

BREINTNALL, JOSEPH (d. 1746). Bloore, Stephen. "Joseph Breintnall, First Secretary of the Library Company." *PMHB* 59 (Ja 35) 42-56.

Tolles, F. B. "A Note on Joseph Breintnall." *PQ* 21 (Ap 42) 247-9.

BRINNIN, JOHN MALCOLM (1916-). Theobald, John. "The World in a Cross Word." *Poetry* 71 (N 47) 82-90.

BRISBANE, ARTHUR (1864-1936). Anon. "Arthur Brisbane." *Chri Sci Mon* 29 (29 D 36) 14.

BROMFIELD, LOUIS (1896-). Anon. "Louis Bromfield." *Cur Biog* 5 (Jl 44) 8-11.

Bainbridge, John. "Farmer Bromfield: Famous Novelist Preaches the New Agriculture on His Malabar Farm." *Life* 25 (11 O 48) 111-4, 116, 119-20, 122.

Bordeaux, Henry. "Un nouveau romancier Américain: Louis Bromfield." *Revue Hebdomadaire* (16 My 31) 267-75.

Bromfield, Louis. "A Case of Literary Sickness." *SRL* 30 (13 S 47) 7-8, 30.

——— "How I Wrote My Novels." *MS* 2 (Ja 31) 1, 9.

Bromfield, Mary. "The Writer I Live With." *Atl* 186 (Ag 50) 77-9.

Caillé, Pierre-François. "Bromfield et la France." *Les Nouvelles Littéraires* (21 Mr 46) 1, 6.

Derrenbacher, Merle. "Louise Bromfield: A Bibliography." *Bul Bibl* 17 (S-D 41, Ja-Ap 42) 112, 141-5.

Fuller, H. B. "The Bromfield Sage." *Bkm* 65 (Ap 27) 200-3.

Gillet, Louis. "Terre d'Amérique." *Revue des Deux Mondes* 18 (1 N 33) 201-12.

Inescort, Frieda. "Louis Bromfield of Mansfield." *SRL* 10 (14 Ap 34) 629.

LeFèvre, Frédéric. "Une Heure avec Louis Bromfield." *Les Nouvelles Littéraires* 12 (3 N 34) 6.

BROOKHOUSER, FRANK (1900-). Beck, Warren. "After Sherwood Anderson: The Stories of Frank Brookhouser." *UKCR* 14 (Su 48) 297-302.

BROOKS, CLEANTH (1906-). Crane, R. S. "Cleanth Brooks; or, The Bankruptcy of Critical Monism." *MP* 45 (My 48) 226-45.
Hecht, Roger. "Paradox and Cleanth Brooks." *Bard* R 2 (Sp 47) 47-51.
Ransom, J. C. "Poetry: I. The Formal Analysis." *KR* 9 (Su 47) 436-56.
Stallman, R. W. "Cleanth Brooks: A Checklist of His Critical Writings." *UKCR* 14 (Su 48) 317-24.
Strauss, A. B. "The Poetic Theory of Cleanth Brooks." *Centenary R* 1 (Fl 49) 10-22.

BROOKS, MARIA GOWEN (1794-1845). Mabbott, T. O. "Maria del Occidente." *Am Col* 2 (Ag 26) 415-24.

BROOKS, NOAH (1830-1903). Dickinson, H. C. "Noah Brooks & His Castine." *Lamp* 28 (Mr 04) 117-20.
Evans, Frederick. "Noah Brooks." *Lamp* 27 (S 03) 129-32.

BROOKS, PHILLIPS (1835-93). Anon. "The Great Preacher." *Atl* 88 (F 01) 262-9.
Abbott, Lyman. "Phillips Brooks." *Outlook* 67 (30 Mr 01) 717-20.
Brady, C. T. "Phillips Brooks." *Book Buyer* 22 (Mr 01) 121-4.
Deland, Margaret. "Phillips Brooks." *Atl* 166 (Jl 40) 29-37.
Gladden, Washington. "Phillips Brooks: An Estimation." *NAR* 176 (F 03) 257-81.
Hochmuth, Marie. "Phillips Brooks." *QJS* 27 (Ap 41) 227-36.
Newton, R. H. "Phillips Brooks: The Preacher and the Man." *Critic* 38 (Mr 01) 245-51.
Peabody, F. G. "Phillips Brooks and German Preaching." *NAR* 197 (F 13) 246-55.

BROOKS, VAN WYCK (1886-). Anon. "Emerson's New England: A Lost Leadership." *TLS* (22 D 36) 1021-2.
Anderson, Sherwood. "Letters to Van Wyck Brooks." *Story* 19 (S-O 41) 19-62.
Cargill, Oscar. "The Ordeal of Van Wyck Brooks." *CE* 8 (N 46) 55-61.
Collins, Seward. "Criticism in America: The Origins of a Myth." *Bkm* 71 (Je 30) 241-56, 353-64.
Colum, M. M. "An American Critic: Van Wyck Brooks." *Dial* 76 (Ja 24) 33-41.
Dupee, F. W. "The Americanism of Van Wyck Brooks." *PR* 6 (Su 39) 69-85.
Flint, F. C. "A Cycle of New England." *VQR* 13 (Ja 37) 33-41.
Foerster, Norman. "The Literary Prophets." *Bkm* 72 (S 30) 35-44.
Glicksberg, C. I. "Van Wyck Brooks." *SR* 43 (Ap-Je 35) 175-86.
Guerard, Albert, Jr. "The Last Opinions of Van Wyck Brooks." *Rocky Mt R* 6 (Wi 42) 1-3.
Hyman, S. E. "Van Wyck Brooks and Biographical Criticism." *Accent* 7 (Sp 47) 131-49.
Jones, H. H. "The Pilgrimage of Van Wyck Brooks." *VQR* 8 (Jl 32) 439-42.
Kenton, Edna. "Henry James and Mr. Van Wyck Brooks." *Bkm* 62 (O 25) 152-7.
Kohler, Dayton. "Van Wyck Brooks: Traditionally American." *CE* 2 (Ap 41) 629-39.
Maynard, Theodore. "Van Wyck Brooks." *Cath World* (Ja 35) 412-21.
Munson, G. B. "Van Wyck Brooks: His Sphere and His Encroachments." *Dial* 78 (Ja 25) 28-42.
Smith, Bernard. "Van Wyck Brooks." *CE* 4 (N 42) 93-9.
——— "Van Wyck Brooks." *NRp* 88 (26 Ag 36) 69-72.
Wade, J. D. "The Flowering of New England." *So R* 2 (1937) 807-14.
Wellek, René. "Van Wyck Brooks and a National Literature." *Am Prefaces* 7 (Su 42) 292-306.
Wilson, Edmund. "Imaginary Conversations: Mr. Van Wyck Brooks and Mr. Scott Fitzgerald." *NRp* 38 (30 Ap 24) 249-54.
——— "Mr. Brooks' Second Phase." *NRp* 103 (30 S 40) 452-4.

BROUN, HEYWOOD (1888-1939). Anon. "Heywood Broun." *Bkm* 58 (N 23) 275-9.

Adams, F. P. "Comrade Broun." *Nation* 131 (1 O 30) 341-2.

A. R. "The Rabbit that Bit the Bulldog." *N Yr* 3 (1 O 27) 18-22.

Cerf, Bennett. "Heywood Broun." *SRL* 25 (19 D 42) 14-6.

Marshall, Margaret. "Columnists on Parade." *Nation* 146 (21 My 38) 580-3.

Ross, V. P. "Emotional Prodder." *Outlook* 119 (30 O 29) 308-15.

Van Doren, Carl. "Day In and Day Out: Adams, Morley, Marquis and Broun: Manhattan Wits." *Century* 107 (D 23) 309-15.

Woollcott, Alexander. "Heywood Broun." *Bkm* 53 (Jl 21) 443.

BROWN, ALICE (1857-1948). Thompson, C. M. "The Short Stories of Alice Brown." *Atl* 98 (Jl 06) 55-65.

BROWN, CHARLES BROCKDEN (1771-1810). Anon. "The American Pioneer of the New Psychic Romance." *Cur Op* 64 (Ap 18) 278.

——— "American Pioneer Prose Masters: Charles Brocken Brown." *Mentor* 4 (1 My 16) 16-34.

——— "Charles Brockden Brown." *Chautauquan* 64 (S 11) 99-102.

——— "Charles Brockden Brown—First American Novelist." *Bkm* 25 (Mr 07) 3-5.

——— "Supplement to the Guide to the Manuscript Collections in the Historical Society of Pennsylvania." *PMHB* 68 (Ja 44) 98-111.

Blake, W. B. "Brockden Brown and the Novel." *SR* 18 (O 10) 431-43.

Clark, D. L. "Brockden Brown and the Rights of Women." *Un Texas Bul Comp Lit Ser* (22 Mr 22) no 2.

——— "Brockden Brown's First Attempt at Journalism." *Un Texas Stud Eng* 17 (1927) 156-74.

——— "Unpublished Letters of Charles Brockden Brown and W. W. Wilkins." *Un Texas Stud Eng* 17 (Je 48) 76-89.

Cole, C. C., Jr. "Brockden Brown and the Jefferson Administration." *PMHB* 72 (Jl 48) 253-63.

Frank, J. G. "The Wieland Family in Charles Brockden Brown." *Monatshefte* 42 (N 50) 347-53.

Haviland, T. P. "Préciosité Crosses the Atlantic." *PMLA* 59 (Mr 44) 131-41.

Hendrickson, J. C. "A Note on Wieland." *AL* 8 (N 36) 305-6.

Kerlin, R. T. "*Wieland* and *The Raven.*" *MLN* 31 (D 16) 503-5.

Kimball, L. E. "An Account of Hocquet Caritat, XVIII Century New York Circulating Librarian, Bookseller, and Publisher of the First Two Novels of Charles Brockden Brown, 'America's First Professional Man of Letters.'" *Colophon* 5 (S 34) Pt 18.

McDowell, Tremaine. "Scott on Cooper and Brockden Brown." *MLN* 45 (Ja 30) 18-20

Marble, A. R. "The Centenary of America's First Novelist." *Dial* 48 (16 F 10) 109-10.

Marchand, Ernest. "The Literary Opinions of Charles Brockden Brown." *SP* 31 (O 34) 541-66.

Morris, Mabel. "Charles Brockden Brown and the American Indian." *AL* 18 (N 46) 244-7.

Oberholtzer, E. P. "The First American Novelist." *J Am Hist* 1 (1907) 236-40.

Peden, William. "Thomas Jefferson and Charles Brockden Brown." *Md Q* no 2 (1944) 65-8.

Prescott, F. C. "*Wieland* and *Frankenstein.*" *AL* 2 (My 30) 172-3.

Sickels, Eleanor. "Shelley and Charles Brockden Brown." *PMLA* 45 (D 30) 1116-28.

Snell, George. "Charles Brockden Brown: Apocalypticalist." *UKCR* 4 (Wi 44) 131-8.

Stearns, B. M. "A Speculation Concerning Charles Brockden Brown." *PMHB* 59 (Ap 35) 99-105.
Van Doren, Carl. "Early American Realism." *Nation* 99 (12 N 14) 577-8.
——— "Minor Tales of Charles Brockden Brown." *Nation* 100 (14 Ja 15) 46-7.
Warfel, H. R. "Brockden Brown's First Published Poem." *AN&Q* 1 (My 41) 19-20.
——— "Charles Brockden Brown's German Sources." *MLQ* 1 (S 40) 357-65.

BROWN, HARRIET CONNOR (1872-). Petersen, W. J. "Harriet Connor Brown." *Palimpsest* 30 (Ap 49) 135-6.

BROWN, MARGARET WISE (1910-). Bliven, Bruce, Jr. "Child's Best Seller: Margaret Wise Brown, Who Uses Three Pseudonyms, Has Written 53 Books, and Bound One of Them in Bunny Fur." *Life* 21 (2 D 46) 59-62.

BROWN, WILLIAM GARROTT (1868-1913). Stephenson, W. H. "Willam Garrott Brown: Literary Historian and Essayist." *J So Hist* 12 (Ag 46) 313-44.

BROWN, WILLIAM HILL (1765-93). Ellis, Milton. "The Author of the First American Novel." *AL* 4 (Ja 33) 359-68.
——— "Two Notes on the Early American Sonnet." *AL* 5 (N 33) 268-9.
McDowell, Tremaine. "The First American Novel." *Am R* 2 (N 33) 73-81.
——— "Last Words of a Sentimental Heroine." *AL* 4 (My 32) 174-7.

BROWNE, CHARLES FARRAR (1834-67). Anon. "Artemus Ward." *TLS* (26 Ap 34) 289.
——— "Neglected Worthies." *Nation* 107 (17 Ag 18) 165.
Belknap, P. H. "Our Unique Humorist: Artemus Ward." *Dial* 67 (15 N 19) 433-4.
Blodgett, Harold. "Artemus Ward in London." *Mark Twain Q* 2 (Fl 38) 3-5.
Clemens, Cyril. "A Convert Humorist." *America* 67 (26 S 42) 689-90.
Nock, A. J. "Artemus Ward." *SRL* 1 (4 O 24) 157-8.
——— "Artemus Ward's America." *Atl* 154 (S 34) 273-81.
Seitz, D. C. "Artemus Ward Letters." *Am Col* 3 (F 27) 195-8.

BROWNE, JOHN ROSS (1821-75). Johansen, D. O. "J. Ross Browne." *Pac Nw Q* 32 (O 41) 385-401.

BROWNE, WILLIAM HAND (1828-1912). Anon. "The Tabbalbum and a Literary Friendship." *Ex Libris* 3 (Mr 43) 2.

BROWNELL, WILLIAM CRARY (1851-1928). Bandler, Bernard. "The Humanism of W. C. Brownell." *H&H* 2 (1929) 205-22.
Furst, Clyde. "American Prose Masters." *SR* 18 (O 10) 483-9.
Harper, G. M. "W. C. Brownell." *Atl* 105 (Ap 10) 481-90.
Lovett, R. M. "William Crary Brownell." *NRp* 56 (19 O 28) 204-6.
Mabie, H. W. "William Crary Brownell." *Outlook* 78 (3 D 04) 855-7.
Mercier, L. J. A. "W. C. Brownell and Our Neo-Barbarism." *Forum* 81 (Je 29) 376-81.
Sherman, S. P. "Mr. Brownell and Mr. Mencken." *Bkm* 60 (Ja 25) 632-4.
Sturgis, Russell. "William Crary Brownell as Critic on Fine Art." *Int Mo* 5 (Ap 02) 448-67.
Wharton, Edith. "William C. Brownell." *Scribner's* 84 (N 28) 596-602.

BROWNSON, ORESTES (1803-76). Caponigri, A. R. "Brownson and Emerson: Nature and History." *NEQ* 18 (S 45) 368-90.
Conroy, P. R. "The Role of the American Constitution in the Political Philosophy of Orestes A. Brownson." *Cath Hist R* 25 (O 39) 271-86.
Cook, T. I., & Leavelle, A. B. "Orestes A. Brownson's *The American Republic.*" *R Pol* 4 (Ja 42) 77-90.

Ladu, A. I. "The Political Ideas of Orestes A. Brownson, Transcendentalist." *PQ* 12 (Jl 33) 280-9.
LeBreton, D. R. "Orestes Brownson's Visit to New Orleans in 1855." *AL* 16 (My 44) 110-4.
Maynard, Theodore. "Orestes Brownson, Journalist, A Fighter for Truth." *Commonweal* 37 (5 F 43) 390-3.
Mims, H. S. "Early American Democratic Theory and Orestes Brownson." *Sci & Soc* 3 (Sp 39) 166-88.
Parsons, Wilfred. "Brownson, Hecker and Hewitt." *Cath World* 153 (Jl 41) 396-408.
Rowland, J. P. "Brownson and the American Republic Today." *Cath World* 152 (F 41) 537-41.
Ryan, T. R. "Brownson and the Papacy." *Am Eccles R* 114 (F 46) 114-22.
——— "Brownson on Salvation and the Church." *Am Eccles R* 117 (Ag 47) 117-24.
——— "Brownson Speaks of England." *Cath World* 154 (Ja 42) 426-9.
——— "Brownson's Love of Truth." *Cath World* 166 (Mr 48) 537-44.
——— "Brownson's Technique in Apologetics." *Am Eccles R* 118 (Ja 48) 12-22.
Schlesinger, A. M., Jr. "Orestes Brownson, An American Marxist before Marx." *SR* 47 (Jl 39) 317-23.
Wellek, René. "The Minor Transcendentalists and German Philosophy." *NEQ* 15 (D 42) 652-80.

BRUCE, DAVID (d. 1830). Warfel, H. R. "David Bruce, Federalist Poet of Western Pennsylvania." *West Penn Hist Mag* 8 (1925) 175-89, 215-34.

BRYAN, DANIEL (1795-1866). Binns, Elizabeth. "Daniel Bryan, Poe's Poet of 'the Good Old Goldsmith School.'" *WMQ* 23 (O 43) 465-73.

BRYANT, WILLIAM CULLEN (1794-1878). Anon. "Bryant's 'Index Expurgatorius.'" *Scribner's* 165 (Mr 19) 377-79.
——— "Excerpts from two letters, dated April 26, 1875, and Dec. 25, 1876." *Autograph Album* 1 (D 33) 36-7.
Arms, George. "William Cullen Bryant: A Respectable Station on Parnassus." *UKCR* 15 (Sp 49) 215-23.
Bernard, E. G. "Northern Bryant and Southern Hayne." *Colophon* ns 1 (Sp 36) 536-40.
Bestor, A. E., Jr. "Concord Summons the Poets." *NEQ* 6 (S 33) 602-13.
Bohman, G. V. "A Poet's Mother: Sarah Snell Bryant in Illinois." *J Ill State Hist Soc* 33 (Je 40) 166-89.
Bryant, W. C. "Dictionary of the New York Dialect of the English Tongue." *AS* 16 (Ap 41) 157-8.
——— "The Genesis of 'Thanatopsis.'" *NEQ* 21 (Je 48) 163-84.
Chapin, C. C. "Bryant and Some of His Latin American Friends." *Bul Pan Am Union* (N 44) 609-13.
Drew, H. L. "Unpublished Letters of William Cullen Bryant." *NEQ* 10 (Jl 37) 236-355.
Dykes, E. B. "William Cullen Bryant; Apostle of Freedom." *Negro Hist Bul* 6 (N 42) 29-32.
Foerster, Norman. "Nature in Bryant's Poetry." *SAQ* 17 (Ja 18) 10-7.
Friedland, L. S. "Bryant's Schooling in the Liberties of Oratory." *AN&Q* 7 (My 47) 27.
Giovannini, G., & Gurasch, Walter. "Bryant's *Inscription for the Entrance to a Wood.*" *Expl* 4 (Ap 46) 40.
Glicksberg, C. I. "Bryant and the Sedgwick Family." *Americana* 31 (O 37) 626-38.
——— "Bryant and *The United States Review.*" *NEQ* 7 (D 34) 687-701.
——— "Bryant and Whittier." *EIHC* 72 (Ap 36) 111-6.

——— "Bryant on Emerson the Lecturer." *NEQ* 12 (S 39) 530-4.
——— "Bryant, The Poet of Humor." *Americana* 29 (Jl 35) 364-74.
——— "Cooper & Bryant: A Literary Friendship." *Colophon* 5 (Mr 35) Pt 20.
——— "From the 'Pathetic' to the 'Classical': Bryant's Schooling in the Liberties of Oratory." *AN&Q* 6 (Mr 47) 179-82.
——— "Letters by William Cullen Bryant, 1826-1827." *Americana* 33 (Ja 39) 23-41.
——— "Letters of William Cullen Bryant from Florida." *Fla Hist Soc Q* 14 (Ap 36) 255-74.
——— "Longfellow and Bryant." *N&Q* 166 (3 F 34) 77-8.
——— "New Contributions in Prose by William Cullen Bryant." *Americana* 30 (O 36) 573-92.
——— "An Uncollected Poem by William Cullen Bryant." *Am Book Coll* 6 (Ap 35) 131-4.
——— "Whitman and Bryant." *Fantasy* 5 (1935) no 2.
——— "William Cullen Bryant and the American Press." *JQ* 16 (D 39) 356-65.
——— "William Cullen Bryant: Champion of Simple English." *JQ* 26 (S 49) 299-303.
——— "William Cullen Bryant and Communism." *Mod Mo* 8 (Jl 34) 353-9.
——— "William Cullen Bryant and Fanny Wright." *AL* 6 (Ja 35) 427-32.
——— "William Cullen Bryant: A Reinterpretation." *Revue Anglo-Américaine* 11 (Ag 34) 495-503.
Griffin, M. L. "Bryant and the South." *Tulane Stud Eng* 1 (1949) 53-80.
Grubbs, H. A. "Mallarmé and Bryant." *MLN* 62 (Je 47) 410-2.
Herrick, A. H. "Bryant's Beziehungen zur Deutschen Dichtung." *MLN* 32 (Je 17) 344-51.
——— "Chronology of a Group of Poems by W. C. Bryant." *MLN* 31 (Mr 17) 180-2.
Herrick, M. T. "Rhetoric and Poetry in Bryant." *AL* 7 (My 35) 188-94.
Hervey, J. L. "Bryant and 'The New Poetry.'" *Dial* 59 (15 Ag, 28 O, 9 D 15) 92-3, 361-3, 555-7.
——— "A Few Facts About Bryant." *Dial* 59 (14 O 15) 361-3.
——— "Some Further Remarks About Bryant." *Dial* 59 (9 D 15) 555-7.
Hoyt, W. D., Jr. "Some Unpublished Bryant Correspondence." *N Y Hist* 21 (Ja, Ap 40) 63-70, 193-204.
Hubbell, J. B. "A New Letter by William Cullen Bryant." *Ga Hist Q* 26 (S-D 42) 288-90.
Hudson, W. P. "Archibald Alison and William Cullen Bryant." *AL* 12 (Mr 40) 59-68.
Huntress, Keith, & Lorch, F. W. "Bryant and Illinois." *NEQ* 16 (D 43) 634-47.
Jack, A. E. "William Cullen Bryant." *Reader* 5 (D 04) 124-7.
Johnson, W. F. "Thanatopsis, Old and New." *NAR* 224 (N 27) 566-72.
Ladu, A. I. "A Note on Childe Harold and 'Thanatopsis.'" *AL* 11 (Mr 39) 80-1.
Leisy, E. C. "Bryant and Illinois." *SRL* 3 (4 D 26) 407.
Long, H. P. "The Alden Lineage of William Cullen Bryant." *N E Hist & Gen Reg* 102 (Ap 48) 82-6.
Lorch, F. W. "Bryant and Illinois: Further Letters of the Poet's Family." *NEQ* 16 (D 43) 634-47.
Mabbott, T. O. "Bryant and James Grahame." *N&Q* 169 (14 D 35) 420-1.
McDowell, Tremaine. "The Ancestry of William Cullen Bryant." *Americana* 22 (1928) 408-20.
——— "Bryant and the *North American Review*." *AL* 1 (Mr 29) 14-26.
——— "Bryant's Practice in Composition and Revision." *PMLA* 52 (Je 37) 474-502.
——— "Cullen Bryant at Williams College." *NEQ* 1 (O 28) 443-66.
——— "Cullen Bryant Prepares for College." *SAQ* 30 (Ap 31) 125-33.
——— "Edgar Allan Poe and William Cullen Bryant." *PQ* 16 (Ja 37) 83-4.

——— "The Juvenile Verse of William Cullen Bryant." *SP* 26 (Ja 29) 96-116.
——— "An Uncollected Poem by Bryant." *Americana* 28 (Jl 34) 299-301.
——— "William Cullen Bryant and Yale." *NEQ* 3 (O 30) 706-16.
Mathews, Amanda. "The Diary of a Poet's Mother." *Mag Hist* 2 (S 05) 206-9.
Mathews, J. C. "Bryant's Knowledge of Dante." *Ital* 16 (D 39) 115-9.
Miller, R. N. "Nationalism in Bryant's 'The Prairies.'" *AL* 21 (My 49) 227-32.
Monroe, Harriet. "Aere Perennius." *Poetry* 6 (Jl 15) 197-200; *Dial* 59 (14 O 15) 314-5.
——— "Bryant and the New Poetry." *Dial* 59 (14 O 15) 314-5.
——— "William Cullen Bryant Again." *Dial* 59 (25 N 15) 479-80.
Moore, C. L. "Our Pioneer American Poet." *Dial* 38 (1 Ap 05) 223-6.
Mott, F. L. "Youth and Death, 1817-1917." *SR* 26 (Jl 18) 313-8.
Nichols, C. W. "A Passage in 'Thanatopsis.'" *AL* 11 (My 39) 217-8.
Phelps, W. L. "Thanatopsis in the *North American Review.*" *NAR* 201 (F 15) 224-7.
——— "William Cullen Bryant, Father of American Poetry." *Ladies Home J* 40 (Je 23) 14 ff.
Russell, J. A. "The Romantic Indian in Bryant's Poetry." *Educ* 48 (Je 28) 642-9.
Schell, S. "William Cullen Bryant." *Werner's Mag* (S 00).
Schick, J. S. "William Cullen Bryant and Théophile Gautier." *MLJ* 17 (Ja 33) 260-7.
Scholl, J. W. "On the Two Place-Names in 'Thanatopsis.'" *MLN* 28 (D 13) 247-9.
Semple, E. A. "William Cullen Bryant, Poet and Journalist." *Craftsman* 20 (Jl 11) 372-8.
Smith, Frank. "Schoolcraft, Bryant, and Poetic Fame." *AL* 5 (My 33) 170-2.
Spivey, H. E. "William Cullen Bryant Changes His Mind: An Unpublished Letter about Thomas Jefferson." *NEQ* 22 (D 49) 528-9.
Van Doren, Carl. "The Growth of 'Thanatopsis.'" *Nation* 101 (7 O 15) 432-3.
Winterich, J. T. "Early American Books and Printing, Chapter IX (Concluded): Enter the Professional Author." *Pub W* 125 (19 My 34) 1863-6.
Wolfe, T. F. "In the Footprints of Bryant." *Lippincott's* 66 (N 00) 765-72.

BUCK, PEARL (1892-). Benét, S. V. & Rosemary. "Two-World Success Story: Pearl Buck." *N Y Herald-Tribune Books* 8 (18 Ja 42) 21.
Bentley, Phyllis. "The Art of Pearl S. Buck." *EJ* 24 (D 35) 791-800.
Buck, P. S. "Advice to Unborn Novelists." *SRL* 11 (2 Mr 35) 513-4, 520-1.
——— "A Debt to Dickens." *SRL* 13 (4 Ap 36) 11, 20, 25.
——— "The Writing of *East Wind: West Wind.*" *Colophon* 3 (D 32) Pt 12.
Canby, H. S. "The Good Earth, Pearl Buck and the Nobel Prize." *SRL* 21 (19 N 38) 8.
Cowley, Malcolm. "Wang Lung's Children." *NRp* 99 (10 My 39) 24-5.
Johnson, Merle. "American First Editions: Pearl S. Buck 1892- ." *Pub W* 125 (20 Ja 34) 272.
Las Vergnas, Raymond. "Vent de Chine." *Hommes et Mondes* 37 (Ag 49) 678-82.
Shuler, Max. "Pearl Buck (Mrs. Richard Walsh)." *Chri Sci Mon* 28 (29 Ja 36) 5.
——— "We Dream Too Much." *Chri Sci Mon* 28 (29 Ja 36) 54.

BULFINCH, THOMAS (1796-1867). Seybolt, P. S. "American First Editions: Thomas Bulfinch (1796-1867)." *Pub W* 130 (19 D 36) 2424.

BUNNER, HENRY CUYLER (1855-96). Hutton, L. "Henry Cuyler Bunner." *Bkm* 32 (O 10) 196-8.
Jensen, G. E. "Bunner's Letters to Gilder." *AL* 17 (My 45) 161-9.
Leeb, Gabriel. "The United States Twist: Some Plot Revisions by Henry Cuyler Bunner." *AL* 9 (Ja 38) 431-41.
Paine, H. G. "H. C. Bunner and His Circle." *Bkm* 35 (Je 12) 397-406.

BURGESS, GELETT (1866-1951). Begg, Edleen. "Larks, Purple Cows, and Whitmania." *Un Texas Libr Chron* 2 (Sp 47) 190-2.

BURKE, KENNETH (1897-). Bewley, Marius. "Kenneth Burke as Literary Critic." *Scrutiny* 15 (D 48) 254-77.
Du Boise, A. E. "Accepting and Rejecting Kenneth Burke." *SR* 45 (Jl-S 37) 343-56.
Duffey, B. I. "Reality as Language: Kenneth Burke's Theory of Poetry." *WR* 12 (Sp 48) 132-45.
Glicksberg, C. I. "Kenneth Burke: The Critic's Critic." *SAQ* 36 (Ja 37) 74-84.
Parkes, H. B. "Attitudes toward History." *So R* 3 (Sp 38) 693-706.
Rasom, J. C. "An Address to Kenneth Burke." *KR* 4 (Sp 42) 219-37.
Tate, Allen. "A Note on Autotelism." *KR* 11 (Wi 49) 13-6.
Warren, Austin. "Kenneth Burke: His Mind and Art." *SR* 41 (Jl-S 33) 344-63.
Williams, W. C. "Kenneth Burke." *Dial* 76 (Ja 29) 6-8.

BURNETT, FRANCES HODGSON (1849-1924). Maurice, A. B. "Frances Hodgson Burnett's 'Little Lord Fauntleroy.'" *Bkm* 34 (S 11) 35-45.
Roberts, M. F. "Mrs. Burnett's Rose Garden in Kent." *Craftsman* 12 (Ag 07) 537-47.

BURRITT, ELIHU (1810-79). Allen, Devere. "To Pereshore: A Yankee Pilgrimage." *Adelphi* 23 (Jl-S 47) 201-6.
Curti, M. E. "Henry Wadsworth Longfellow and Elihu Burritt." *AL* 7 (N 35) 315-28.

BURROUGHS, JOHN (1837-1921). Anon. "Appreciation." *Nation* 112 (13 Ap 21) 531.
——— "Evolution of John Burroughs." *Cur Op* 70 (My 21) 644-7.
——— "John Burroughs." *Lit Dig* 69 (16 Ap 21) 23-4.
——— "John Burroughs." *Playground* 15 (Jl 21) 259.
——— "John Burroughs and the Balance of Nature." *Cur Op* 70 (My 21) 677-8.
——— "John the Bird Man." *Mentor* 9 (Ag 21) 35.
——— "New England Nature Studies: Thoreau, Burroughs, Whitman." *Edinburgh R* 208 (O 08) 343-66.
——— "Strength and Weakness of John Burroughs." *Cur Op* 71 (Jl 21) 74-5.
——— "Woodchuck Lodge Exercises Mark Burroughs' Centennial." *Chri Sci Mon* 29 (5 Ap 37) 4.
Barrus, Clara. "Whitman and Burroughs as Comrades." *YR* ns 15 (O 25) 59-81.
——— "With John o'Birds and John o'Mountains in the Southwest." *Century* 80 (Ag 10) 521-8.
Burroughs, John. "The Faith of a Naturalist." *NAR* 210 (N 19) 678-88.
Burroughs, Julian. "Boyhood Days of John Burroughs." *Craftsman* 22 (Je, Jl, Ag, S 12) 240-52, 257-67, 525-31, 635-9.
Canby, H. S. "John Burroughs." *SRL* 5 (24 N 28) 393-4.
Chapman, F. M. "John Burroughs, 1837-1921." *Bird Lore* 23 (My 21) 119-23.
Devoe, Alan. "John Burroughs, Inspired Farmer." *Am Merc* 53 (Jl 41) 111-4.
Fisher, G. C. "Reminiscences of John Burroughs." *Natural Hist* 21 (Mr-Ap 21) 113-25.
Foerster, Norman. "Burroughs as Bergsonist." *NAR* 212 (N 20) 670-7.
——— "Burroughs as Ornithologist." *NAR* 214 (Ag 21) 177-82.
——— "The 'Detective Eye' of John Burroughs." *NRp* 26 (13 Ap 21) 186-7.
Fuertes, L. A. "Appreciation." *WR* 4 (13 Ap 21) 338.
Garland, Hamlin. "My Friend John Burroughs," *Century* 102 (S 21) 731-42.
Hartmann, Sadakichi. "Visit to John Burroughs." *Century* 101 (Mr 21) 619-21.
Hier, F. P., Jr. "The End of a Literary Mystery." *Am Merc* 1 (Ap 24) 471-8.
Hudson, W. H. "Truth Plain and Colored." *Living Age* 248 (20 Ja 06) 188-90.
Ingersoll, E. "American Naturalists." *Mentor* 7 (15 Je 19) 7-8.
Lodge, W. M. "John Burroughs." *Overland* ns 77 (Ap 21) 50-2.

Long, W. J. "The Modern School of Nature Study and Its Critics." *NAR* 176 (My 03) 688-98.
Lummis, C. F. "Facing the Mystery." *Ladies Home J* 38 (Ag 21) 132.
Murphy, M. A. "John O'Birds." *St Nicholas* 48 (Jl 21) 780-2.
Parkman, M. R. "John Burroughs—the Seer of Woodchuck Lodge." *St Nicholas* 44 (Ap 17) 486-91.
Perry, Bliss. "John Burroughs as a Man of Letters." *Harvard Grad Mag* 30 (Mr 22) 328-33.
Sharp, Dallas. "Fifty Years of John Burroughs." *Atl* 106 (N 10) 631-41.
——— "Laird of Woodchuck Lodge." *Good Housekeeping* 73 (N 21) 13-4.
Stanley, H. M. "Burroughs as a Prose Writer." *Dial* 32 (1 Ja 02) 7-8.
Tyrrell, Henry. "A John Burroughs Art Exhibition at the Ehrich Galleries." *Art & Archaeology* 11 (Je 21) 259.
Van Dyke, Henry. "John Burroughs." *Rev of Rev* 63 (My 21) 517-9.
West, H. L. "John Burroughs." *Bkm* 49 (My 19) 389-98.

BURT, MAXWELL STRUTHERS (1882-). William, B. C. "Maxwell Struthers Burt." *Bkm* 52 (My 21) 53-8.

BUSHNELL, HORACE (1802-76). Paul, Sherman. "Horace Bushnell Reconsidered." *Etc* 6 (Su 49) 255-9.

BUTLER, WILLIAM ALLEN (1825-1902). Kouwenhoven, J. A. "Some Ado About Nothing." *Colophon* ns 2 (Au 36) 101-13.

BUTTERWORTH, HEZEKIAH (1839-1905). Davol, Ralph. "Hezekiah Butterworth: A Sketch of His Personality." *N E Mag* ns 33 (Ja 06) 507.

BYLES, MATHER (1707-88). Carlson, C. L. "John Adams, Matthew Adams, Mather Byles, and the *New England Weekly Journal*." *AL* 12 (N 40) 347-8.

BYNNER, WITTER (1881-). Blackmur, R. P. "Versions of Solitude." *Poetry* 39 (Ja 32) 217-21.
Deutsch, Babette. "Two Solitudes." *Dial* 67 (4 O 19) 301-2.
Flanner, Hildegarde. "Witter Bynner's Poetry." *Un R* 6 (Je 40) 269-74.
Head, Cloyd. "A Poet Strayed." *Poetry* 22 (Je 23) 158-60.
Henderson, A. C. "Poetic Dramas." *Poetry* 3 (F 14) 184-7.
Long, Haniel. "Mr. Bynner in the South-West." *Poetry* 27 (Mr 26) 331-4.
Monroe, Harriet. "Mr. Bynner in the South-West." *Poetry* 36 (Ag 30) 276-8.
Seiffert, M. A. "A Light-Stepping Caravan." *Poetry* 27 (Mr 26) 331-4.
Wilson, T. C. "Society Portraits." *Poetry* 47 (N 35) 101-3.

BYRD, WILLIAM (1674-1744). Anon. "Letters of the Byrd Family." *VMHB* 35 (Jl, O 27) 221-45, 371-89; 36 (Ja, Ap, Jl, O 28) 36-44, 113-23, 209-22, 353-62; 37 (Ja, Ap, Jl, O 29) 28-33, 101-18, 242-52, 301-15; 38 (Ja, Ap, O 30) 51-63, 145-56, 347-60; 39 (Ap, Jl 31) 139-45, 221-9.
Anon. "Letters of William Byrd, 2d, of Westover, Va." *VMHB* 6 (1901-2) 113-30, 225-51.
Cannon, C. L. "William Byrd II, of Westover." *Colophon* ns 3 (Sp 38) 291-302.
Davis, Margaret. "'Great Dismal' Pictures." *SAQ* 33 (Ap 34) 171-84.
Earle, E. A. "A Virginia Gentleman of Two Centuries Ago." *Dial* 32 (My 02) 308-10.
Houlette, W. D. "The Byrd Library." *Tyler's Quar Hist & Gen Mag* 16 (O 34) 100-9.
——— "William Byrd and Some of His American Descendants." *Tyler's Quar Hist & Gen Mag* 16 (O 34) 93-100.
Johnston, Rebecca. "William Byrd Title Book." *VMHB* 48 (Ja, Ap, Jl, O 40) 31-56, 107-29, 222-37, 328-40; 49 (Ja, Ap, Jl-O 41) 37-50, 174-80, 269-78, 354-63; 50 (Ap, Jl 42) 169-79, 238-63.

Leary, Lewis. "A William Byrd Poem." *WMQ* 4: 3 ser (Jl 47) 356.
Lyle, G. R. "William Byrd, Book Collector." *Am Book Coll* 5 (My-Je, Jl 34) 163-5, 208-9.
Masterson, J. R. "William Byrd in Lubberland." *AL* 9 (My 37) 153-70.
Monahan, K. "William Byrd of Westover, Explorer of Early America." *Scholastic* 31 (18 D 37) 21-3.
Murdock, K. B. "William Byrd and the Virginian Author of *The Wanderer*." *Harvard Stud Phil & Lit* 17 (1935) 129-36.
Riback, W. H. "Some Words in Byrd's Histories." *AS* 15 (O 40) 331-2.
Ryan, E. L. "Letters of the Byrd Family." *VMHB* 39 (Ap, Jl 31) 139-45, 221-9.
Sioussat, St. George. "The *Philosophical Transactions* of the Royal Society in the Libraries of William Byrd of Westover, Benjamin Franklin, and the American Philosophical Society." *PAPS* 93 (My 49) 99-113.
Tyler, Dorothy. "Modern Education and William Byrd of Westover." *SAQ* 43 (Ap 44) 174-80.
Weathers, W. T. "William Byrd: Satirist." *WMQ* 4 (Ja 47) 27-41.
Woodfin, M. H. "The Missing Pages of William Byrd's 'Secret History of the Line.'" *WMQ* 2 (Ja 45) 63-70.
——— "Thomas Jefferson and William Byrd's Histories of the Dividing Line." *WMQ* 1 (O 44) 363-73.
——— "William Byrd and the Royal Society." *VMHB* 40 (Ja, Ap 32) 23-34, 111-23.
Wright, L. B. "The Classical Tradition in Colonial Virginia." *PBSA* 33 (1939) 85-97.
——— "A Shorthand Diary of William Byrd of Westover." *HLQ* 2 (Jl 39) 489-96.
——— "William Byrd I and the Slave Trade." *HLQ* 8 (Ag 45) 379-87.
——— "William Byrd's Defense of Sir Edmund Andros." *WMQ* 2 (Ja 45) 47-62.
——— "William Byrd's Opposition to Governor Francis Nicholson." *J So Hist* 11 (F 45) 68-79.
——— & Tinling, Marion. "William Byrd of Westover, an American Pepys." *SAQ* 39 (Jl 40) 259-74.

CABELL, JAMES BRANCH (1879-). Anon. "James Branch Cabell." *Bkm* 57 (F 23) 741-5.
Allen, G. W. "Jurgen and Faust." *SR* 39 (O-D 31) 485-92.
Barlow, S. L. "The Censor of Art." *NAR* 213 (Mr 21) 346-50.
Beach, J. W. "The Holy Bottle." *VQR* 2 (Ap 26) 175-86.
——— "Pedantic Study of Two Critics." *AS* 1 (Mr 26) 299-306.
Björkman, Edwin. "Concerning James Branch Cabell's Human Comedy." *Lit Dig Int Book R* 2 (D 22) 40, 42, 44.
Boynton, Percy. "Mr. Cabell Expounds Himself." *EJ* 12 (Ap 23) 258-65.
Brewster, P. G. "*Jurgen* and *Figures of Earth* and the Russian Skazki." *AL* 13 (Ja 42) 305-19.
Bulluck, R. D., Jr. "The Cream of the Jest." *N&Q* 169 (17 Ag 35) 115.
Cabell, J. B. "The Genteel Tradition in Sex." *Am Spect* 1 (N 32) 3.
——— "Recipes for Writers." *Colophon* pt 7 (1931) 1-8.
Clark, Emily. "The Case of Mr. Cabell vs. the Author of the Biography." *VQR* 5 (Jl 29) 336-45.
Crowley, Aleister. "Another Note on Cabell." *Reviewer* 3 (Jl 23) 907-14.
Fadiman, Clifton. "James Branch Cabell." *Nation* 136 (12 Ap 33) 409-10.
Fishwick, M. W. "James Branch Cabell, Virginia Novelist." *Commonwealth* 17 (My 50) 35-6.
Follett, Wilson. "A Gossip on James Branch Cabell." *Dial* 64 (25 Ap 18) 392-6.
——— "Ten Times One Makes One." *Dial* 66 (8 Mr 19) 225-8.
Glasgow, Ellen. "The Biography of Manuel." *SRL* 6 (7 Je 30) 1108-10.
Gunther, J. J. "James Branch Cabell: An Introduction." *Bkm* 52 (N 20) 200-6.

Hackett, Francis. "Pardon Me!" *NRp* 90 (24 Mr 37) 207-8.
Hatcher, H. H. "On Not Having Read James Branch Cabell." *Bkm* 72 (F 31) 597-9.
Hergesheimer, Joseph. "James Branch Cabell." *Am Merc* 13 (Ja 28) 38-47.
Himelick, Raymond. "Cabell, Shelley, and the 'Incorrigible Flesh.'" *SAQ* 47 (Ja 48) 88-95.
Hooker, E. N. "Something about Cabell." *SR* 37 (Ap 29) 192-203.
Howard, J. M. "The Fate of Mr. Cabell." *Reading & Collecting* 2 (Ja 38) 5-7.
Howard, Leon. "Figures of Allegory." *SR* 42 (Ja-Mr 34) 54-66.
Jack, P. M. "James Branch Cabell Period." *NRp* 89 (13 Ja 37) 323-6.
Kronenberger, Louis. "Mr. Cabell Suffers No Sea-Change." *N Y Times Book R* 37 (7 F 32) 2.
Le Breton, Maurice. "James Branch Cabell, romancier." *Revue Anglo-Américaine* 11 (D 33, Ja 34) 112-28, 223-6; 12 (F 34) 223-38.
Le Gallienne, Richard. "Master of the Pastiche." *N Y Times Book R* (13 F 21) 3, 22.
Lovett, R. M. "Mr. James Branch Cabell." *NRp* 26 (13 Ap 21) 187-9.
McCole, C. J. "Something About Cabell." *Cath World* 134 (Jl 29) 45-65.
McIntyre, C. F. "Mr. Cabell's Cosmos." *SR* 38 (Jl 30) 278-85.
Palmer, J. H. "James Branch Cabell, Dualist." *Letters* 2 (F 28) 6-14.
Parker, E. R. "A Key to Cabell." *EJ* 21 (Je 32) 431-40.
Parrington, V. L. "The Incomparable Mr. Cabell." *Pac R* 2 (D 21) 359.
Phillips, H. A. "A Novelist's Uphill Road." *World Today* 52 (Jl 28) 152-3.
Rascoe, Burton. "Papé's Illustrations for Cabell's 'Jurgen.'" *Int Studio* 74 (Ja 22) 203-8.
Richardson, E. R. "Richmond and Its Writers." *Bkm* 68 (D 28) 449-53.
Sehrt, E. T. "Die Weltanschauung James Branch Cabells (im Anschluss an seinen Roman *Figures of Earth*)." *Englische Studien* 72 (Ag 38) 355-99.
Untermeyer, Louis. "A Key to Cabell." *Double Dealer* 4 (Jl 22) 29-31.
Van Doren, Carl. "Getting the Groundplan of Mr. Cabell's Work." *Lit Dig Int Book R* 2 (D 24) 12-4.
——— "Irony in Velvet." *Century* 108 (Ag 24) 561-6.
——— "Jurgen in Limbo." *Nation* 115 (6 D 22) 613-4.
——— "Two Heroes of Poictesme." *Century* 109 (N 24) 129-34.
Wagenknecht, Edward. "Cabell: A Reconsideration." *CE* 9 (F 48) 238-46.
Walpole, Hugh. "The Art of James Branch Cabell." *YR* 9 (Jl 20) 684-98.

CABLE, GEORGE WASHINGTON (1844-1925). Anon. "The Author of Old Creole Days." *Outlook* 130 (11 F 25) 213-4.
Basso, Hamilton. "Letters in the South." *NRp* 83 (19 Je 35) 161-3.
Bishop, D. H. "A Commencement in the Eighties: George W. Cable's First Public Address." *Sw R* 18 (Ja 33) 108-14.
Bloom, Margaret. "G. W. Cable: A New Englander in the South." *Bkm* 73 (Je 31) 401-3.
Bourne, Randolph. "From an Older Time." *Dial* 65 (2 N 18) 363.
Bowen, E. W. "George W. Cable: An Appreciation." *SAQ* 18 (Ap 19) 145-55.
Butcher, Philip. "George W. Cable and Booker T. Washington." *J Negro Educ* 17 (Fl 48) 462-8.
——— "George W. Cable and Negro Education." *J Negro Hist* 34 (Ap 49) 119-34.
——— "George W. Cable: History and Politics." *Phylon* 9 (Ap-Je 48) 137-45.
Dart, H. P. "George W. Cable." *La Hist Q* 8 (O 25) 647-53.
Eidson, J. O. "George W. Cable's Philosophy of Progress." *Sw R* 21 (Ja 36) 211-6.
Ekström, Kjell. "The Cable-Howells Correspondence." *Studia Neophilologica* 22 (1950) 48-61.
——— "Cable's Grandissimes and the Creoles." *Studia Neophilologica* 21 (1949) 190-4.

Hale, Walter. "The New Orleans of Cable." *Bkm* 13 (Ap 01) 136-47.
Harwood, W. S. "New Orleans in Fiction." *Critic* 47 (N 05) 426-35.
Johnson, R. U. "Commemorative Tribute to Cable." *Arts & Letters* 57 (1927) 1-6.
Neilson, W. A. "In Memoriam: George W. Cable." Northampton *Hampshire Gazette* (9 F 25).
Nevins, Allen. "A Charming Personality." *SRL* 5 (2 F 29) 1-2.
Orcutt, C. D. "From My Library Walls." *Chri Sci Mon* 37 (17 N 44) 7.
Peabody, E. F. "Mark Twain's Ghost Story." *Minn Hist* 18 (My 37) 28-35.
Powell, L. P. "The Home-Culture Clubs." *Bkm* 11 (Mr 05) 381-9.
Roseboro, Viola. "George W. Cable: The Man and the Novelist." *Book News Mo* 27 (Ap 09) 566-8.
Sancton, Thomas. "A Note on Cable and His Times." *Survey Graphic* 36 (Ja 47) 28.
Street, Appleton. "This Haunted House Has Only Happy Ghosts." *Am Mag* 104 (S 27) 16-7.
Tinker, E. L. "Cable and the Creoles." *AL* 5 (Ja 34) 313-26.
Turner, Arlin. "George W. Cable, Novelist and Reformer." *SAQ* 48 (O 49) 539-45.
——— "George Washington Cable's Literary Apprenticeship." *La Hist Q* 24 (Ja 41) 168-86.
——— "Whittier Calls on George W. Cable." *NEQ* 22 (Mr 49) 92-6.
Warfel, H. R. "George W. Cable Amends a Mark Twain Plot." *AL* 6 (N 34) 328-31.
Wilson, Edmund. "A Citizen of the Union." *NRp* 57 (13 F 29) 352-3.
Wykoff, G. S. "The Cable Family in Indiana." *AL* 1 (My 29) 183-95.

CAHAN, ABRAHAM (1860-1951). Wexelstein, Leon. "Abraham Cahan." *Am Merc* 9 (S 26) 88-94.

CAIN, JAMES MALLAHAN (1892-). Frohock, W. M. "The Tabloid Tragedy of James M. Cain." *Sw R* 34 (Aut 49) 380-6.

CALDWELL, ERSKINE (1903-). Anon. "America's Most Censored Author—An Interview with Erskine Caldwell." *Pub W* 155 (14 My 49) 1960-1; see also (19, 26 Mr; 2, 30 Ap; 7 My 49) 1312, 1438, 1512-5, 1519, 1805-6, 1876.
——— "Denver Police Ban Penguin Edition of 'God's Little Acre.'" *Pub W* 151 (15 F 47) 1135.
Burke, Kenneth. "Caldwell, Maker of Grotesques." *NRP* 82 (10 Ap 35) 232-5.
Carmichael, P. A. "Jeeter Lester." *SR* 48 (Ja 40) 21-9.
Coindreau, M. E. "Erskine Caldwell." *Nouvelle Revue Française* 47 (1 N 36) 908-12.
Couch, W. T. "Landlord and Tenant." *VQR* 14 (Sp 38) 309-12.
Cowley, Malcolm. "The Two Erskine Caldwells." *NRp* 111 (6 N 44) 599-600.
Davidson, Donald. "Erskine Caldwell's Picture Book." *So R* 4 (Jl 38) 15-25.
Ferguson, Otis. "Story-teller's Workshop." *Accent* 1 (Sp 41) 170-3.
Fiore, Ilario. "Caldwell è triste." *Fiera Letteraria* (29 My 49) no 22.
Frohock, W. M. "Erskine Caldwell: Sentimental Gentleman from Georgia." *Sw R* 31 (Aut 46) 351-9.
Grenaud, Pierre. "Mystique Amérigue; 'Les Voies du Seigneur.'" *Revue de la Mediterranée* 9 (N-D 50) 739-40.
Krutch, J. W. "The Case of Erskine Caldwell." *Nation* 146 (20 Ag 38) 190.
Kubie, L. W. "'God's Little Acre': An Analysis." *SRL* 11 (24 N 34) 305-6, 312.
Maclachlan, J. M. "Fold and Culture in the Novels of Erskine Caldwell." *SFQ* 9 (Ja 45) 93-101.
Marion, J. H. "Star-Dust above 'Tobacco Road.'" *Christian Century* 55 (16 F 38) 204-6.
Raymond, Louis-Marcel. "Erskine Caldwell." *La Nouvelle Relève* (Montreal) 5 (Ja 47) 497-505.

Rosati, S. "Erskine Caldwell." *La Nuova Europa* 2 (1945) 42.
Söderberg, Sten. "Nazismen och den moderna realismen: Litterär nazism." *Samtid och Framtid* (Stockholm) 2 (Je-Ag 45) 376-9.
Squire, Marian. "American First Editions: Erskine (Preston) Caldwell 1903- ." *Pub W* 129 (21 Mr 36) 1276.
Wade, J. D. "Sweet Are the Uses of Degeneracy." *So R* 1 (Wi 36) 449-66.

CALVERT, GEORGE HENRY (1803-89). Hagge, C. W. "G. H. Calvert's Translations from the German." *MLN* 57 (Ap 42) 283-4.
Stewart, Randall. "Hawthorne's Contributions to *The Salem Advertiser*." *AL* 5 (Ja 34) 327-41.

CALVERTON, VICTOR FRANCIS (1900-40). Glicksberg, C. I. "V. F. Calverton: Marxism without Dogma." *SR* 46 (Jl-S 38) 338-51.

CAMPBELL, BARTLEY (1843-88). Frenz, Horst. "Bartley Campbell's 'My Partner' in Berlin." *GQ* 17 (Ja 44) 32-5.

CAMPBELL, KILLIS (1872-1937). Law, R. A. "Killis Campbell, 1872-1937." *Un Texas Stud Eng* 17 (1937) 7-14.
Stovall, Floyd, & McDowell, Tremaine. "In Memoriam Killis Campbell, 1872-1937." *AL* 10 (Mr 38) 76.

CANBY, HENRY SEIDEL (1878-). Anon. "Henry Seidel Canby." *Bkm* 60 (S 24) 66-7.
——— "Henry Seidel Canby." *Cur Biog* 3 (S 42) 3-8.
Canby, H. S. "Henry Seidel Canby." *Nation* 119 (8 O 24) 375-6.
Foerster, Norman. "The Literary Historians." *Bkm* 71 (Jl 30) 365-74.
Glicksberg, C. I. "Henry Seidel Canby." *SR* 44 (O-D 36) 420-33.
Schinz, Albert. "Un Examen de conscience par un Américain." *Revue Bleue* 17 (2 S 23) 584-7.

CAREY, MATHEW (1760-1839). Anon. "150 Years of Publishing; Lea and Febiger, Medical Book Publishers of Philadelphia, Celebrate Their Sesquicentennial This Year." *Pub W* 127 (16 F 35) 781-3.
——— "Priestly Letters in this Library." *More Books* 10 (O 35) 319-20.
Bullen, H. L. "Mathew Carey." *Americana Collector* 1 (D 25) 86-92.
Hallenbeck, C. T. "Book-Trade Publicity Before 1800." *PBSA* 32 (1938) 47-56.
Kenney, L. J. "Mathew Carey." *Hist Bul* 21 (Mr 43) 61, 64.
McCadden, H. M. "The Father of The American Book Fair." *Cath World* 144 (F 37) 547-51.

CARITAT, HOCQUET (*fl.* 1797-1807). Kimball, L. E. "An Account of Hocquet Caritat, XVIII Century New York Circulating Librarian, Bookseller, and Publisher of the First Two Novels of Charles Brockden Brown, 'America's First Professional Man of Letters.'" *Colophon* 5 (S 34) Pt 18.

CARLETON, WILL (1845-1912). Corning, A. E. "Memories of Will Carleton." *Bkm* 43 (Ag 16) 606-11.
Finney, B. A. "Will Carleton: Michigan's Poet." *Mich Hist Col* 39 (1915) 191-203.

CARMAN, BLISS (1861-1929). Anon. "Bliss Carman." *Lit Dig* 102 (6 Je 29) 21.
Hathaway, R. H. "Bliss Carman: An Appreciation." *Canadian Mag* 56 (Ap 21) 521-36.
——— "The Poetry of Bliss Carman." *SR* 33 (O 25) 469-83.
Mowbray, J. P. "A New Pagan Lilt." *Critic* 41 (O 02) 308-13.
Roberts, C. G. D. "Bliss Carman." *Dalhousie R* 9 (Ja 30) 409-17.
——— "More Reminiscences of Bliss Carman." *Dalhousie R* 10 (Ap 30) 2-9.

CARMER, CARL (1893-). Van Gelder, Robert. "An Interview with Mr. Carl Carmer." *N Y Times Book R* (11 Ja 42) 2, 4.

CARUTHERS, WILLIAM ALEXANDER (1802-1846). Allen, E. P. "Notes on William Alexander Caruthers." *WMQ* 9 (O 29) 294-7.
Davis, C. C. "Chronicler of the Cavaliers—Some Letters from and to William Alexander Caruthers, M.D. (1802-1846)." *VMHB* 55 (Jl 47) 213-32.
——— "Chronicler of the Cavaliers: Three More Letters from and to William Alexander Caruthers, M.D. (1802-1846)." *VMHB* 57 (Ja 49) 55-66.
——— "An Early Historical Novelist Goes to the Library: William A. Caruthers and His Reading, 1823-29." *BNYPL* 52 (Ap 48) 159-70.
——— "First Climber of Natural Bridge." Richmond *Times-Dispatch* (8 F 48) sec 4: 6D.
——— "The First Climber of the Natural Bridge: A Minor American Epic." *J So Hist* 16 (Ag 50) 277-90.
——— "The Virginia 'Knights' and Their Golden Horseshoes: Dr. William A. Caruthers and an American Tradition." *MLQ* 10 (D 49) 490-507.
——— "A Virginia Romancer and His Reading: Literary Allusions in the Work of William A. Caruthers." *Tyler's Quar Hist & Gen Mag* 30 (Jl 48) 21-33.

CATHER, WILLA (1876-1947). Adams, F. B. Jr. "Willa Cather. Early Years: Trial and Error." *Colophon* n graph s 1 (S 39).
——— "Willa Cather. Middle Years: The Right Road Taken." *Colophon* n graph s 1 (1939) 103-8.
Arms, G. W. "Cather's *My Antonia*." *Expl* 5 (Mr 47) 35.
Baum, Bernard. "Willa Cather's Waste Land." *SAQ* 48 (O 49) 589-601.
Benét, S. V. & Rosemary. "Willa Cather: Civilized and Very American." *N Y Herald-Tribune Books* 17 (15 D 40) 6.
Bloom, E. A. & L. D. "Willa Cather's Novels of the Frontier: A Study in Thematic Symbolism." *AL* 21 (Mr 49) 71-93.
——— "Willa Cather's Novels of the Frontier: The Symbolic Function of 'Machine-Made Materialism.'" *UTQ* 20 (O 50) 45-60.
Bogan, Louise. "American Classic." *NYr* 7 (8 Ag 31) 19-22.
Boynton, P. H. "Willa Cather." *EJ* 13 (Je 24) 373-80.
Brown, E. K. "Homage to Willa Cather." *YR* 36 (S 46) 77-92.
——— "Willa Cather: The Benjamin D. Hitz Collection." *Newberry Lib Bul* 2 (D 50) 158-60.
——— "Willa Cather and the West." *Un Toronto R* 5 (Jl 36) 444-66.
Bullock, Flora. "Willa Cather, Essayist and Dramatic Critic, 1891-1895." *Prairie Schooner* 23 (Wi 49) 393-401.
Burnet, M. R. "Catherton." *Prairie Schooner* 23 (Fl 49) 279-88.
Canby, H. S. "Willa Cather (1876-1947)." *SRL* 30 (10 My 47) 22-4.
Carroll, Latrobe. "Willa Sibert Cather." *Bkm* 53 (My 21) 212-6.
Cather, Willa. "A Letter from Willa Cather." *Commonweal* 7 (23 N 27) 713-4.
——— "My First Novels (There Were Two)." *Colophon* 2 (Je 31) Pt 6.
——— "Nebraska: The End of the First Cycle." *Nation* 117 (5 S 23) 237-8.
——— "The Novel Démeublé." *NRp* 30 (12 Ap 22) supp.
——— "The Personal Side of William Jennings Bryan." *Prairie Schooner* 23 (Wi 49) 331-7.
——— "Shadows on the Rock: A Letter." *SRL* 8 (17 O 31) 216.
——— "When I Knew Stephen Crane." *Prairie Schooner* 23 (Fl 49) 231-7.
Chamaillard, Pierre. "Le Cas de Marian Forrester." *Revue Anglo-Américaine* 8 (Je 31) 419-28.
Cottman, G. S. "The Western Association of Writers." *Ind Mag Hist* 29 (S 33) 187-97.
Cox, Sidney. "My Favorite Forgotten Book." *Tomorrow* 7 (Je 48) 63.

Fadiman, Clifton. "Willa Cather: The Past Recaptured." *Nation* 135 (7 D 32) 563-5.
Fay, E. G. "Borrowing from Anatole France by Willa Cather and Robert Nathan." *MLN* 56 (My 41) 377.
Fisher, D. C. "Daughter of the Frontier." *N Y Times Mag* (28 My 33) 7.
Footman, R. H. "The Genius of Willa Cather." *AL* 10 (My 38) 123-41.
Gierasch, Walter. "Thoreau and Willa Cather." *TSB* 20 (Jl 47) 4.
Hale, E. E. "Willa Cather." *Faculty Papers of Union Col* 26 (Ja 33) 5-17.
Hicks, Granville. "The Case against Willa Cather." *EJ* 22 (N 33) 703-10.
Hinz, J. P. "The Real Alexander's Bridge." *AL* 21 (Ja 50) 473-6.
——— "Willa Cather in Pittsburgh." *New Colophon* (1950) 198-207.
——— "Willa Cather-Prairie Spring." *Prairie Schooner* 23 (Sp 49) 82-9.
——— "Willa Cather, Undergraduate—Two Poems." *AL* 21 (Mr 49) 111-6.
Jessup, M. E. "A Bibliography of the Writings of Willa Cather." *Am Col* 6 (My-Je 28) 67.
Jones, H. M. "The Novels of Willa Cather." *SRL* 17 (6 Ag 38) 3-4.
——— "Willa Cather Returns to the Middle West." *SRL* 12 (3 Ag 35) 7.
Kazin, Alfred. "A State before There Were People in It." *Chri Sci Mon* 35 (30 Ja 43) 6.
Kohler, Dayton. "Willa Cather: 1876-1947." *CE* 9 (O 47) 8-18.
Kronenberger, Louis. "Willa Cather." *Bkm* 74 (Ja 31) 134-40.
McNamara, Robert. "Phases of American Religion in Thornton Wilder and Willa Cather." *Cath World* 135 (S 32) 641-9.
Morris, Lloyd. "Willa Cather." *NAR* 219 (My 24) 641-52.
Mosher, J. C. "Willa Cather." *Writer* 38 (N 26) 528-30.
Moss, David. "American First Editions . . . Willa Sibert Cather, 1875- ." *Pub W* 101 (3 F 22) 321.
Myers, W. L. "The Novel Dedicate." *VQR* 8 (Jl 32) 410-8.
Porterfield, Alexander. "Willa Cather." *London Merc* 13 (Mr 26) 516-24.
Rapin, René. "Willa Cather (1875-1947)." *Etudes de Lettres* (Switzerland) 23 (S-O 50) 39-50.
Reilly, J. J. "A Singing Novelist." *Commonweal* 13 (25 F 31) 464-6.
Schloss, George. "A Writer's Art." *Hudson R* 3 (Sp 50) 151-6.
Scott, W. S. "Cather's *My Antonia.*" *Expl* 5 (Je 47) 58.
Seibel, George. "Willa Cather from Nebraska." *New Colophon* 2 (S 49) 195-208.
Sergeant, E. S. "Willa Cather." *NRp* 43 (17 Je 25) 91-4.
Shively, J. R. "Willa Cather Juvenilia." *Prairie Schooner* 22 (Sp 48) 97-111.
Stalnaker, J. M., & Eggan, F. "American Authors Ranked." *EJ* 18 (Ap 29) 295-307.
Tietjens, Eunice. "Poetry by a Novelist." *Poetry* 23 (Jl 23) 221-3.
Tittle, Walter. "Glimpses of Interesting Americans." *Century* 110 (Jl 25) 309-13.
Trilling, Lionel. "Willa Cather." *NRp* 80 (10 F 37) 10-3.
Wagenknecht, Edward. "Willa Cather." *SR* 37 (Ap 29) 221-39.
Weber, C. J. "Willa Cather's Call on Housman." *Colby Lib Q* ser 2 (N 47) 61-4.
Whipple, T. K. "Willa Cather." *Lit R* 4 (1923) 331-32.
White, G. L., Jr. "Willa Cather." *SR* 50 (Ja-Mr 42) 18-25.
Wilson, J. S. "Shadows on the Rock." *VQR* 7 (O 31) 585-90.
Winsten, Archer. "In Defense of Willa Cather." *Bkm* 74 (Mr 32) 634-40.
Zabel, M. D. "Willa Cather." *Nation* 164 (14 Jl 47) 713-6.

CATHERWOOD, MARY HARTWELL (1847-1902). Anon. "The Illinois Bookshelf: *Spanish Peggy. A Story of Young Illinois,* by Mary Hartwell Catherwood." *J Ill State Hist Soc* 40 (Mr 47) 82-4.
Price, Robert. "Mary Hartwell Catherwood. A Bibliography." *J Ill State Hist Soc* 33 (Mr 40) 68-77.
——— "Mary Hartwell Catherwood's Literary Record of the Great Lakes and French America." *Mich Hist* 30 (O-D 46) 756-63.

——— "Mrs. Catherwood's Early Experiments with Critical Realism." *AL* 17 (My 45) 140-51.
Simonds, W. E. "Mary Hartwell Catherwood." *Critic* 42 (F 03) 169-71.

CAWEIN, MADISON (1865-1914). Howells, W. D. "The Poetry of Madison Cawein." *NAR* 187 (Ja 08) 124-8.
Knight, G. C. "A Note on Madison Cawein." *Letters* 4 (Ag 31) 27-9.
McGill, A. B. "The Other Madison Cawein." *SR* 23 (O 15) 418-28.
——— "The Poetry of Madison Cawein." *SAQ* 5 (O 06) 376-86.
Peckham, H. H. "Madison Cawein." *SAQ* 14 (Jl 15) 279-84.
Rittenhouse, J. B. "Memories of Madison Cawein." *Bkm* 61 (N 22) 305-12.
Royster, J. F. "In Illustration of Madison Cawein's Poetry." *Texas R* 1 (Je 15) 15-20.

CHAMBERS, ROBERT WILLIAM (1865-1933). Anon. "Young Man in a Hurry." *Harper's* 45 (Ag 03) 377-83.
Cooper, F. T. "Robert W. Chambers." *Bkm* 30 (F 10) 613-9.
Hornberger, Theodore. "American First Editions at TxU: V. Robert William Chambers (1865-1933)." *Un Texas Lib Chron* 2 (Sp 47) 193-5.

CHANDLER, ELIZABETH MARGARET (1807-34). Burklund, C. E. "An Early Michigan Poet: Elizabeth Margaret Chandler." *Mich Hist* 30 (Ap 46) 277-88.

CHANNING, WILLIAM ELLERY (1780-1842). Doubleday, N. F. "Channing on the Nature of Man." *J Rel* 23 (O 43) 245-57.
Downs, L. H. "Emerson and Dr. Channing." *NEQ* 20 (D 47) 516-34.
Edgell, D. P. "A Note on Channing's Transcendentalism." *NEQ* 22 (S 49) 394-7.
Hicks, Granville. "Dr. Channing and the Creole Case." *AHR* 37 (Ap 32) 516-25.
——— "A Glance at Channing's Friendships." *Chri Reg* 108 (5, 12 S 29) 723-4, 741-2.
Higginson, T. W. "Two New England Heretics: Channing and Parker." *Independent* 54 (22 My 02) 1234-6.
Hochmuth, Marie. "William Ellery Channing, New England Conversationalist." *QJS* 30 (D 44) 429-39.
Holt, Anne. "William Ellery Channing, 1780-1842." *Hibbert J* 41 (O 42) 42-9.
Ladu, A. I. "Channing and Transcendentalism." *AL* 11 (My 39) 129-37.
Mood, Fulmer, & Hicks, Granville. "Letters to Dr. Channing on Slavery and the Annexation of Texas, 1837." *NEQ* 5 (Jl 32) 587-601.
Patterson, R. L. "The Theology of Channing and the Via Affirmativa." *Anglican Theol R* 26 (O 44) 229-35.
Peabody, F. G. "The Humanism of William Ellery Channing." *Chri Reg* 109 (15 My 30) 407-9.
Schneider, H. W. "The Intellectual Background of William Ellery Channing." *Church Hist* 7 (Mr 38) 3-23.
Schuster, E. M. "Native American Anarchism." *Smith Col Stud Hist* 17 (O 31-Jl 32) 5-202.
Spiller, R. E. "A Case for W. E. Channing." *NEQ* 3 (Ja 30) 55-81.
Virtanen, Reino. "Tocqueville and William Ellery Channing." *AL* 22 (Mr 50) 21-8.

CHANNING, WILLIAM ELLERY (1817-1901). Anon. "A Link with the *Past*." *Dial* 32 (1 Ja 02) 5-6.
Emerson, R. W. "Fresh Leaves from Emerson's Diary: Walks with Ellery Channing." *Atl* 90 (Jl 02) 27-34.
Higginson, T. W. "Walks with Ellery Channing." *Atl* 90 (Jl 02) 27-34.
Marble, A. R. "The Late William Ellery Channing." *Critic* 40 (F 02) 27-34.
Randel, W. P. "Hawthorne, Channing, and Margaret Fuller." *AL* 10 (Ja 39) 472-6.
Sanborn, F. B. "Channing's Verse." *Nation* 76 (1 Ja 03) 10.

——— "Ellery Channing and His Table Talk." *Critic* 47 (Jl, Ag S 05) 76-81, 121-8, 267-72.
——— "Ellery Channing in New Hampshire." *Granite Mo* 32 (Mr 02) 157-64.
——— "Emerson, Thoreau, Channing." *Springfield Republican* (2 Jl 02) 14.
——— "The Maintenance of a Poet." *Atl* 86 (D 00) 819-25.
——— "Thoreau and Ellery Channing." *Critic* 47 (N 05) 444-51.
Silver, R. G. "Ellery Channing's Collaboration with Emerson." *AL* 7 (Mr 35) 84-6.

CHAPMAN, JOHN JAY (1862-1933). Barzun, Jacques. "Against the Grain: John Jay Chapman." *Atl* 179 (F 47) 120-4.
Howe, M. A. DeW. "John Jay Chapman to William James." *Harper's* 174 (D 36) 46-54.
——— "Letters from John Jay Chapman." *Harper's* 175 (S 37) 363-70.
——— "More Letters of John Jay Chapman." *Harper's* 175 (O 37) 530-8.
Stocking, David. "John Jay Chapman and Political Reform." *Am Q* 2 (Sp 50) 62-70.
Wilson, Edmund. "John Jay Chapman." *Atl* 160 (N 37) 581-95.
Wister, Owen. "John Jay Chapman." *Atl* 153 (My 34) 524-39.

CHASE, MARY ELLEN (1887-). Anon. "Mary (Coyle) Chase." *Cur Biog* 6 (O 45) 12-4.
Boynton, P. H. "Two New England Regionalists." *CE* 1 (Ja 40) 291-9.

CHEEVER, GEORGE BARRELL (1807-90). Denny, Margaret. "Cheever's Anthology and American Romanticism." *AL* 20 (Mr 43) 1-9.
Rockwood, R. I. "George Barrell Cheever, Protagonist of Abolition." *PAAS* ns 46 (Ap 36) 82-113.

CHESNUTT, CHARLES WADDELL (1858-1932). Burris, A. M. "American First Editions: Charles Waddell Chesnutt, 1858-1932." *Pub W* 121 (15 My 37) 2033.
Chamberlain, John. "The Negro as Writer." *Bkm* 70 (F 30) 603-11.
Chesnutt, C. W. "Post-Bellum—Pre-Harlem." *Colophon* 2 (F 31) Pt 5.

CHILD, FRANCIS JAMES (1825-96). Gummere, F. B. "A Day with Professor Child." *Atl* 103 (Mr 09) 421-5.
Howe, M. A. DeW. "Il Pesceballo: The Fishball Operetta of Francis James Child." *NEQ* 23 (Je 50) 187-99.

CHILD, LYDIA MARIA (1802-80). Barnes, J. A. "Letters of a Massachusetts Woman Reformer to an Indiana Radical." *Ind Mag Hist* 26 (Mr 30) 46-60.
McDonald, G. D. "A Portrait from Letters of Lydia Maria Child, 1802-1880." *BNYPL* 36 (S 32) 617-22.
Mayo, L. S. "The History of the Legend of Chocorua." *NEQ* 19 (S 46) 302-14.
Streeter, R. E. "Mrs. Child's 'Philothea': A Transcendentalist Novel?" *NEQ* 16 (D 43) 648-54.
Zimmerman, L. M. "An Unpublished Letter of Lydia Maria Child." *Yale Un Lib Gaz* 5 (Jl 30) 15-6.

CHIVERS, THOMAS HOLLEY (1809-58). Chase, Lewis. "Searching for a Lost Poet." *Atlanta J* mag sec (1 O 33) 10, 21.
Mabbott, T. O. "Collation of a Book by T. H. Chivers." *N&Q* 159 (11 O 30) 257.
——— "Numismatic References of Three American Writers." *Numismatist* 46 (N 33) 688.
Newcomer, A. G. "The Poe-Chivers Tradition Re-examined." *SR* 12 (Ja 04) 20-35.
Pitfield, R. L. "Thomas Holley Chivers, M.D." *Gen Mag & Hist Chron* 41 (O 38) 57-75.

——— "Thomas Holley Chivers, 'The Wild Mazeppa of Letters.'" *Gen Mag & Hist Chron* 37 (1934) 73-92.
Scott, W. S. "The Astonishing Chivers: Poet for Plagiarists." *PULC* 5 (Je 44) 150-3.
Woodberry, G. E. "The Poe-Chivers Papers." *Century* 65 (Ja-F 03) 435-47, 545-58.

CHOPIN, KATE (1851-1904). Anon. "Missouri Miniatures: Kate Chopin." *Mo Hist R* 38 (1944) 207-8.

CHURCH, BENJAMIN (1734-76). Vosburgh, M. B. "The Disloyalty of Benjamin Church." *Cambridge Hist Soc Pub* 30 (1945) 47-71.

CHURCHILL, WINSTON (1871-1947). Anon. "Two Etymologies." *Word Study* 9 (N 33) 5-7.
Cooper, F. T. "Winston Churchill." *Bkm* 31 (My 10) 246-53.
Dixon, J. M. "Some Real Persons and Places in 'The Crisis.'" *Bkm* 14 (S 01) 17-20.
Griffin, L. W. "Winston Churchill: American Novelist." *More Books* 23 (N 48) 331-8.
Henderson, Brooks. "Winston Churchill's Country." *Bkm* 41 (Ag 15) 607-19.
Hofstadter, Richard & Beatrice. "Winston Churchill: A Study in the Popular Novel." *Am Q* 2 (Sp 50) 12-28.
Johnson, Merle. "American First Editions: Winston Churchill." *Pub W* 119 (17 Ja 31) 327.
Remick, J. W. "Winston Churchill and His Campaign." *Outlook* 84 (1 S 06) 17-22.
Van Doren, Carl. "Winston Churchill." *Nation* 112 (27 Ap 21) 619-21.
Whitelock, W. W. "Mr. Winston Churchill." *Critic* 40 (F 02) 135-41.

CIARDI, JOHN (1916-). Scott, W. T. "Three Books by John Ciardi." *UKCR* 16 (Wi 49) 119-25.

CLARK, WILLIS GAYLORD (1808-41). Clark, W. G. "Willis Gaylord Clark on American Literature in 1830." *BNYPL* 10 (1906) 181-3.
Dunlap, L. W. "The Letters of Willis Gaylord Clark and Lewis Gaylord Clark." *BNYPL* 42 (Je, Jl, Ag, O, N, D 38) 455-76, 523-48, 613-36, 753-79, 857-81, 933-58.

CLARKE, JAMES FREEMAN (1810-88). Thomas, J. W. "The Fifth Gospel." *MNL* 62 (N 47) 445-9.
——— "James Freeman Clarke as a Translator." *AGR* 10 (D 43) 31-3.

CLEMENS, SAMUEL LANGHORNE (1835-1910). Anon. "Business versus Genius." *Freeman* 1 (14 Jl 20) 412-3.
——— "Copyright in the Days of Mark Twain." *Pub W* 121 (27 F 32) 949.
——— "Dan Beard Tells All about Those 'Yankee' Pictures." *Twainian* 3 (O 43) 4-5.
——— "Ever This Twain Is Met." *Lit Dig* 120 (30 N 35) 19.
——— "Excerpt from a letter dated March 1, 1899." *Autograph Album* 1 (D 33) 44.
——— "Letters to James Redpath from Samuel L. Clemens." *Mark Twain Q* 5 (Wi-Sp 42) 19-21.
——— "Mark Twain." *TLS* (30 N 35) 779-80.
——— "Mark Twain Anticipates Roosevelt." *Word Study* 9 (Ap 34) 4.
——— "Mark Twain and Christian Science." *Harper's Weekly* 46 (27 D 02) 2022; 47 (24 Ja 03) 145.
——— "Mark Twain as Publisher." *Bkm* 36 (Ja 13) 489-94.
——— "Mark Twain Centennial to Be Celebrated." *Pub W* 127 (9 F 35) 697.
——— "The Mark Twain Commemoration." *Columbia Un Q* 28 (1935) 357-78.
——— "Mark Twain: In Memoriam." *Harper's W* 54 (17 D 10) 8-9.
——— "Mark Twain Number." *Bkm* 31 (Je 10).
——— "Mark Twain Number." *Overland Mo* 87 (Ap 29).

——— "Mark Twain's Childhood Sweetheart Recalls Their Romance." *Lit Dig* 56 (23 Mr 18) 70-5.
——— "Mark Twain's First Lecture Tour." *Mark Twain Q* 3 (Su-Fl 39) 3-6, 24.
——— "Mark Twain's New Deal." *SRL* 10 (16 D 33) 352.
——— "Mark Twain's Philosophy." *Monist* 23 (Ap 13) 181-223.
——— "Mark Twain's Private Girls' Club." *Ladies Home J* 29 (F 12) 23, 54.
——— "Not So Good Is Mark's Effort to Show He Can Pen a Poem Like the 'Raven' by Poe." *Twainian* 6 (Jl-Ag 47) 3.
——— "The Originals of Some of Mark Twain's Characters." *Rev of Rev* 42 (Ag 10) 228-30.
——— "A Scotch Tilt against Mark Twain." *Lit Dig* 68 (8 Ja 21) 35.
——— "Taming Mark Twain." *Lit Dig* 67 (13 N 20) 34-5.
——— "Tributes to Mark Twain." *NAR* 191 (Je 10) 827-35.
——— "Twain Trustees Bring Halt to Publication of Story." *Pub W* 153 (17 Ja 48) 233.
——— "Two Etymologies." *Word Study* 9 (N 33) 5-7.
——— "Two Literary Shrines Menaced." *Lit Dig* 65 (29 My 20) 36-7.
——— "Unpublished Letters to Dan Beard." *Mark Twain Q* 7 (Wi-Sp 45-6) 22.
——— "Unpublished Twain Letter." *Mark Twain Q* 8 (Sp-Su 47) 19.
——— "Unpublished Twain Letter." *Mark Twain Q* 8 (Su-Fl 48) 13.
——— "When Mark Twain Petrified the 'Brahmins.'" *Lit Dig* 62 (12 Jl 19) 28-9.
——— "'Youths' Companion' Reveals Twain Tales and Advertisement of 'Huck Finn.'" *Twainian* 5 (Mr-Ap 46) 1-3.
Abbott, Keene. "Tom Sawyer's Town." *Harper's W* 57 (9 Ag 13) 16-7.
Adams, John. "Mark Twain As Psychologist." *Bkm* (London) 39 (Mr 11) 270-2.
——— "Mark Twain, Psychologist." *Dalhousie R* 13 (Ja 34) 417-26.
Ade, George. "Mark Twain and the Old Time Subscription." *Rev of Rev* 41 (Je 10) 703-4.
——— "Mark Twain as Our Emissary." *Century* 81 (D 10) 204-6.
Alden, H. M. "Mark Twain—An Appreciation." *Bkm* 31 (Je 10) 366-9.
Altick, R. D. "Mark Twain's Despair: An Explanation in Terms of His Humanity." *SAQ* 34 (O 35) 359-67.
Altrocchi, J. C. "Along the Mother Lode." *YR* 24 (S 34) 131-45.
Angert, E. H. "Is Mark Twain Dead?" *NAR* 190 (S 09) 318-29.
Archer, William. "The Man That Corrupted Hadleyburg—A New Parable." *Critic* 37 (N 00) 413-5.
Armstrong, C. J. "John Robards—Boyhood Friend of Mark Twain." *Mo Hist R* 25 (1931) 493-8.
——— "Mark Twain's Early Writings Discovered." *Mo Hist R* 24 (Jl 30) 485-501.
——— "Sam Clemens Considered Becoming a Preacher." *Twainian* 4 (My 45) 1.
Arvin, Newton. "Mark Twain: 1835-1935." *NRp* 83 (12 Je 35) 125-7.
Bailey, Millard. "Mark Twain In San Francisco." *Bkm* 31 (Je 10) 369-73.
Balicer, H. C. "Szczepanik's 'Portrait' of Mark Twain." *Pub W* 131 (20 F 37) 968-9.
Beard, D. C. "Mark Twain as a Neighbor." *Rev of Rev* 41 (Je 10) 705-9.
Beck, W. "Huckleberry Finn versus the Cash Boy." *Education* 49 (S 28) 1-13.
Belden, H. M. "Scyld Scefing and Huck Finn." *MLN* 33 (My 18) 315.
Bellamy, G. C. "Mark Twain's Indebtedness to John Phoenix." *AL* 13 (Mr 41) 29-43.
Benson, A. B. "Mark Twain's Contacts with Scandinavia." *SS* 14 (Ag 37) 159-67.
Bergler, Edmund. "Exceptional Reaction to a Joke of Mark Twain." *Mark Twain Q* 8 (Wi 47) 11-2.
Bicknell, Percy. "Mark Twain." *Dial* 53 (16 O 12) 290-2.
Bidewell, G. I. "Mark Twain's Florida Years." *Mo Hist R* 40 (Ja 46) 159-73.
Bigelow, Poultney. "God Speed Mark Twain." *Independent* 52 (25 O 00) 2548-50.
Blair, Walter. "Mark Twain, New York Correspondent." *AL* 11 (N 39) 247-59.

——— "Mark Twain's Way with Words." *Un R* 5 (Au 38) 60-2.
——— "On the Structure of *Tom Sawyer*." *MP* 37 (Ag 39) 75-88.
Blaise, Bunker. "The Mark Twain Society." *SRL* 20 (15 Jl 39) 11-2.
Blanck, Jacob. "*The Gilded Age: A Collation*." *Pub W* 138 (20 Jl 40) 186-88.
——— "Mark Twain's 'Sketches Old and New.'" *Pub W* 132 (30 O 37) 1740-1.
Bland, H. M. "Mark Twain." *Overland Mo* ns 49 (Ja 07) 22-7.
Blearsides, Oliver. "Mark Twain's Characters Come from Real People." *Mark Twain Q* 4 (Su-Fl 41) 16-9.
Blodgett, Harold. "A Note on Mark Twain's Library of Humor." *AL* 10 (Mr 38) 78-80.
Booth, Bradford. "Mark Twain's Comments on Holmes's *Autocrat*." *AL* 21 (Ja 50) 456-63.
——— "Mark Twain's Friendship with Emeline Beach." *AL* 19 (N 47) 219-30.
——— "Mark Twain's Friendship with Emma Beach." *Mark Twain Q* 8 (Wi 47) 4-10.
Bowen, E. W. "Mark Twain." *SAQ* 15 (Jl 16) 250-68.
Bradford, Gamaliel. "Mark Twain." *Atl* 125 (Ap 20) 462-73.
Branch, E. M. "A Chronological Bibliography of the Writings of Samuel Clemens to June 8, 1867." *AL* 18 (My 46) 109-59.
——— "The Two Providences: Thematic Form in 'Huckleberry Finn.'" *CE* 11 (Ja 50) 188-95.
Brashear, M. M. "An Early Mark Twain Letter." *MLN* 44 (Ap 29) 256-9.
——— "Mark Twain Juvenilia." *AL* 2 (Mr 30) 25-53.
"Britannicus." "England and Mark Twain." *NAR* 191 (Je 10) 822-6.
Brooks, Sydney. "England's Ovation to Mark Twain." *Harper's W* 51 (27 Jl 07) 1086-9.
——— "Mark Twain in England." *Harper's W* 51 (20 Jl 07) 1053-4.
Brooks, Van Wyck. "The Genesis of Huck Finn." *Freeman* 1 (31 Mr 20) 59-63.
——— "Lost Prophet." *Freeman* 1 (24 Mr 20) 46-7.
——— "Mark Twain's Humor." *Dial* 68 (Mr 20) 275-91.
——— "Mark Twain's Satire." *Dial* 68 (Ap 20) 424-43.
Brownell, G. H. "About that Heliotype Portrait of Mark Twain in 'Huck Finn.'" *Twainian* 6 (Ja-F 47) 1-2.
——— "About the Program of that 'Babies' Banquet." *Twainian* 4 (N 44) 4-6.
——— "About Twain in Periodicals." *Twainian* 1: no 7 (1939) 4-5.
——— "The After-Dinner Speaker's Best Friend: Mark Twain's Patent Adjustable Speech." *Twainian* 5 (Ja-F 46) 1-3.
——— "Did Twain Write 'The Wrong Ashes'?" *Twainian* 4 (Ap 45) 2-3.
——— "Everybody's Friend." *Twainian* 3 (F 44) 1-4.
——— "The First of Series II, American Travel Letters, in *Alta Californian*." *Twainian* 6 (My-Je 47) 1-3.
——— "From 'Hospital Days.'" *Twainian* 2 (Mr, Ap 43) 1-5, 4-6.
——— "The Home of the Prodigal Son." *Twainian* 2 (Ap 43) 1-3.
——— "'An Important Question' Settled." *Twainian* 2 (F 43) 1-5.
——— "Kipling's Meeting with Mark Twain." *Am Book Coll* 4 (S-O 33) 191-2.
——— "Mark Orates on Death of Democratic Party in 1880 (?)." *Twainian* 6 (Ja-F 47) 2-3.
——— "Mark Twain and the *Hannibal Journal*." *Am Book Coll* 2 (Ag-S, O 32) 173-6, 202-4.
——— "Mark Twain Launches the Chicago Press Club." *Twainian* 4 (Mr 45) 1-2.
——— "Mark Twain Tells of the Daring Deed of Professor Jenkins and His Velocipede." *Twainian* 4 (F 45) 1-4.
——— "Mark Twainiana." *Am Book Coll* 5 (Ap 34) 124-6.
——— "Mark Twain's Eulogy on the 'Reliable Contraband.'" *Twainian* 2 (Je 43) 1-3.
——— "Mark Twain's First Published Effort." *Am Book Coll* 3 (F 33) 92-5.

——— "Mark Twain's Inventions." *Twainian* 3 (Ja 44) 1-5.
——— "Mark Twain's Memory Builder." *Twainian* 3 (D 43) 1-4.
——— "Mark Twain's Tribute to Francis Lightfoot Lee." *Twainian* 3 (N 43) 1-3.
——— "More Twain Found in *New York Weekly.*" *Twainian* 3 (Mr 44) 1-4.
——— "Mr. DeVoto Explains as to Use of the Name 'Mark Twain.'" *Twainian* 4 (Je 45) 2.
——— "New First Issue Point in *Life on the Mississippi.*" *Twainian* 4 (N 44) 1-3.
——— "No Mystery about 'A Mystery Cleared Up.'" *Twainian* 4 (My 45) 1-2.
——— "A Question as to the Origin of the Name, 'Mark Twain.'" *Twainian* 1 (F 42) 4-7.
——— "Second Letter of 'American Travel Letters, Series II.'" *Twainian* 6 (Jl-Ag 47) 4-6.
——— "Seven New Twain Tales Discovered by Chance." *Twainian* 3 (N 43) 3-6.
——— "Some Figures on the 1st Edition of 'Tom Sawyer.'" *Twainian* 7 (Mr-Ap 47) 2.
——— "A Tale of Twain's Shipboard Poem 'Goodbye' or 'The Parting of the Ships.'" *Twainian* 4 (Je 45) 1-2.
——— "That Picture of 'St. Louis Hotel' in 'Life on the Mississippi.'" *Twainian* 6 (S-O 47) 1-3.
——— "Third Letter of 'American Travel Letters,' Series II." *Twainian* 6 (S-O 47) 3-4.
——— "This German Biography Did Not Contain Enough 'Frozen Truth' to Satisfy Twain." *Twainian* 6 (Mr-Ap 47) 1.
——— "Twain 'Ciphers' Loss from Postal Decree." *Twainian* 6 (Mr-Ap 47) 3-4.
——— "Twain Letter Tells of 'Francis Lightfoot Lee.'" *Twainian* 3 (F 44) 4-5.
——— "Twain's Version of Hamlet." *Twainian* 2 (Je 43) 4-6.
——— "Two Hitherto Unknown Twain Tales Found in New York *Tribune.*" *Twainian* 5 (N-D 46) 1-2.
——— "Whence Came 'Well Done, Good and Faithful Servant.'" *Twainian* 5 (Ja-F 46) 3-4.
——— "Where and When Were These Twain Tales First Printed?" *Twainian* 4 (D 44) 1-5.
——— "Who Was Frank Findlay?" *Twainian* 4 (O 44) 1-6.
——— "Why Mark Twain Registered His Name as a 'Trade Mark.'" *Twainian* 4 (Ap 45) 3-4.
——— "The Winner of the Medal." *Twainian* 2 (My 43) 1-4.
Brynes, Asher. "Boy-Men and Man-Boys." *YR* 38 (Wi 49) 223-33.
Burke, Richard. "Mark Twain: An Exhibition." *BNYPL* 40 (Je 36) 499-501.
Burton, W. J. "Mark Twain in Hartford Days." *Mark Twain Q* 1 (Su 37) 5.
Buxbaum, Katherine. "Mark Twain and American Dialect." *AS* 2 (F 27) 233-6.
Campbell, Killis. "From Aesop to Mark Twain." *SR* 19 (Ja 11) 43-9.
Canby, H. S. "Mark Twain." *Lit R* 4 (1923) 201-2.
Carnegie, Andrew, *et al.* "Tributes to Mark Twain." *NAR* 191 (Je 10) 827-35.
Carpenter, C. E. "Mark Twain, 1898." *Mark Twain Q* 1 (Fl 36) 4-5.
Carter, Paul. "Mark Twain and War." *Twainian* 1 (Mr 42) 1-3, 7.
Carus, P. "Mark Twain's Philosophy." *Monist* 6 (Ap 13).
Chapman, J. W. "The Germ of a Book: A Footnote on Mark Twain." *Atl* 150 (D 32) 720-1.
Charpentier, John. "Humour anglais et humour américain. A propos du centenaire de Mark Twain." *Mercure de France* 264 (15 D 35) 475-500.
Childs, M. W. "The Home of Mark Twain." *Am Merc* 9 (S 26) 101-5.
Chubb, Percival. "Mark Twain at Sundown." *Mark Twain Q* 5 (Sp 43) 15-6, 18.
Clemens, Clara. "Recollections of Mark Twain." *NAR* 230 (N-D 30) 522-9, 652-9; 231 (Ja, O 31) 50-7, 433-40.
Clemens, Cyril. "'The Birth of a Legend' Again." *AL* 15 (Mr 43) 64-5.
——— "Contract for *Roughing It.*" *Mark Twain Q* 6 (Su-Fl 44) 5.

——— "F. D. Roosevelt and Mark Twain." *Dalhousie R* 25 (O 45) 339-41.
——— "Harry S. Truman: Mark Twain Enthusiast." *Dalhousie R* 29 (Jl 49) 198-200.
——— "Hervey Allen and Mark Twain." *Hobbies* (Ap 50) 20.
——— "An Incident in Mark Twain's Life." *Slant* 2 (F 45) 7.
——— "Jeremiah Clemens, Novelist and Southern Supporter of Lincoln." *Mark Twain Q* 8 (Wi 50) 13-6.
——— "Margaret Mitchell and Mark Twain." *Hobbies* (O 49) 140.
——— "Mark Twain and Jane Austen." *Overland Mo* 91 (Ja 33) 21.
——— "Mark Twain in St. Louis." *Slant* 1 (O 44) 6, 16.
——— "Mark Twain's Ancestry." *Mark Twain Q* 7 (Wi-Sp 45-46) 8, 24.
——— "Mark Twain's Favorite Book." *Overland Mo* 88 (My 30) 157-8.
——— "Mark Twain's Joan of Arc." *Commonweal* 22 (26 Jl 35) 323-4.
——— "Mark Twain's Reading." *Commonweal* 24 (7 Ag 36) 363-4.
——— "Mark Twain's Religion." *Commonweal* 21 (28 D 34) 254-5.
——— "Mark Twain's Story on the Siamese Twins." *Hobbies* 53 (O 48) 139.
——— "Mark Twain's Washington in 1868." *Mark Twain Q* 5 (Su 42) 1-16.
——— "Scattered Letters of Mark Twain, together with Eulogistic Contributions for His Centennial." *Mo Hist Soc Glimpses of the Past* 2 (N 35) 123-32.
——— "The True Character of Mark Twain's Wife." *Mo Hist R* 24 (O 29) 40-9.
——— "Twainiana." *Hobbies* 48 (O 43) 96.
——— "Twain's Southern Relative, Jeremiah Clemens." *Mark Twain Q* 8 (Sp-Su, Wi 47) 13-4, 15-7.
——— "Unique Origin of Mark Twain's Books." *Mo School J* 60 (Ja 44) 16, 18-9.
——— "Unpublished Recollections of the Original Becky Thatcher." *Mark Twain Q* 4 (Su-Fl 41) 20-3.
——— "A Visit to Paul Elmer More, with Some Letters." *Mark Twain Q* 3 (Su-Fl 39) 18-20, 24.
——— "Winston Churchill and Mark Twain." *Dalhousie R* 24 (Ja 45) 402-5.
Clemens, M. L. "Trailing Mark Twain through Hawaii." *Sunset* 38 (My 17) 7-9.
Clemens, S. L. "Chapters from My Autobiography." *NAR* 183 (7, 21 S, 5, 19 O, 2, 16 N, 7, 21 D 06) 320-30, 449-60, 577-89, 705-16, 833-44, 961-70, 1089-95, 1217-24; 184 (4, 18 Ja, 1, 15 F, 1, 15 Mr, 5, 9 Ap) 1-14, 113-9, 225-32, 337-46, 448-63, 561-71, 673-82, 784-93; 185 (3, 17 My, 7 Je, 5 Jl, 2 Ag) 1-12, 113-22, 241-51, 465-74, 689-98; 186 (S, O, N, D 07) 8-21, 161-73, 327-36, 480-94.
——— "I Shall Probably See Stormfield but Seldom Hereafter." *Twainian* 2 (My 43) 4-6.
——— "Letter Addressed to 'The Hon. Secretary of the Treasury': dated October 13, 1902." *Book News* (Am Book Co, Au 35).
——— "My Methods of Writing." *Mark Twain Q* 8 (Wi-Sp 49) 1.
——— "Private Theatricals." *Twainian* 3 (D 43) 4-5.
——— "Unpublished Chapters From the Autobiography of Mark Twain." *Harper's* 145 (Ag 22) 310-5; 144 (Mr 22) 455-60.
Coad, O. S. "Mrs. Clemens Apologizes for Her Husband." *JRUL* 10 (D 47) 29.
Colby, F. M. "Mark Twain's Illuminating Blunder." *Bkm* 32 (D 10) 354-8.
Coleman, R. A. "Trowbridge and Clemens." *MLQ* 9 (Je 48) 216-23.
Compton, C. H. "Who Reads Mark Twain?" *Am Merc* 31 (Ap 34) 465-71.
Cooper, Lane. "Mark Twain's Lilacs and Laburnums." *MLN* 47 (F 32) 85-7.
Corey, W. A. "Memories of Mark Twain." *Overland Mo* 66 (S 15) 17-24.
Coryell, I. "Josh, of the 'Territorial Enterprise.'" *NAR* 243 (Su 37) 287-95.
Cowie, Alexander. "Mark Twain Controls Himself." *AL* 10 (Ja 39) 488-91.
Davidson, W. E. "Mark Twain and Conscience." *Twainian* 1 (Ap 42) 1-3.
De Lautrec, Gabriel. "Mark Twain." *Mercure de France* 264 (15 N 35) 69-82.
DeVoto, Bernard. "Letters From the Recording Angel." *Harper's* 192 (F 46) 106-9.
——— "Mark Twain about the Jews." *Jewish Frontier* 6 (My 39) 7-9.
——— "The Mark Twain Papers." *SRL* 19 (10 D 38) 14-5.

——— "The Matrix of Mark Twain's Humor." *Bkm* 74 (O 31) 172-8.

——— "The Real Frontier: A Preface to Mark Twain." *Harper's* 163 (Je 31) 60-71.

——— "Those Two Immortal Boys." *Woman's Day* (N 47) 38-9, 131-4.

——— "Tom, Huck and America." *SRL* 9 (13 Ag 32) 37-9.

Dickinson, L. T. "Marketing a Best-Seller: Mark Twain's *Innocents Abroad.*" *PBSA* 41 (Ap-Je 47) 107-22.

——— "Mark Twain's Revisions in Writing *The Innocents Abroad.*" *AL* 19 (My 47) 139-57.

——— "The Sources of *The Prince and the Pauper.*" *MLN* 64 (F 49) 103-6.

Donner, S. T. "Mark Twain as a Reader." *QJS* 33 (O 47) 308-11.

Douglas, Gilbert. "Behind That Door." *N Y World-Telegram* (15 Ag 34) 21.

Dreiser, Theodore. "Mark the Double Twain." *EJ* 24 (O 35) 615-27.

Duffy, Charles. "Mark Twain Writes to Howells." *Mark Twain Q* 8 (Su-Fl 48) 4.

Dugas, Gaile. "Mark Twain's Hannibal." *Holiday* 2 (Ap 47) 102-7.

Eastman, Max. "Mark Twain's Elmira." *Harper's* 175 (My 38) 620-32.

Edwards, P. G. "The Political Economy of Mark Twain's 'Connecticut Yankee.'" *Mark Twain Q* 8 (Wi 50) 2, 18.

Eidson, J. O. "Innocents Abroad, Then and Now." *Ga R* 2 (Su 48) 186-92.

Emberson, F. G. "Mark Twain's Vocabulary: A General Survey." *Un Mo Stud* 10 (Jl 35) 1-53.

Eskew, G. L. "Mark Twain, Steamboat Pilot." *Coronet* 8 (My 40) 100-6.

Farrell, J. T. "Twain's 'Huckleberry Finn' and the Era He Lived In." *N Y Times Book R* (12 D 43) 6, 37.

Fatout, Paul. "Mark Twain Lectures in Indiana." *Ind Mag Hist* 46 (D 50) 363-7.

Feinstein, G. W. "Mark Twain on the Immanence of Authors in Their Writing." *Mark Twain Q* 8 (Wi 47) 13-4.

——— "Mark Twain's Idea of Story Structure." *AL* 18 (My 46) 160-3.

——— "Mark Twain's Regionalism in Fiction." *Mark Twain Q* 7 (Wi-Sp 45-46) 7, 24.

——— "Twain as Forerunner of Tooth-and-Claw Criticism." *MLN* 63 (Ja 48) 49-50.

Ferguson, DeLancey. "The Case for Mark Twain's Wife." *UTQ* 9 (O 39) 9-21.

——— "Huck Finn Aborning." *Colophon* ns 3 (Sp 38) 171-80.

——— "A Letter to the Editors of *American Literature.*" *AL* 11 (My 39) 218-9.

——— "Mark Twain and the Cleveland *Herald.*" *AL* 8 (N 36) 304-5.

——— "Mark Twain's Comstock Duel: The Birth of a Legend." *AL* 14 (Mr 42) 66-70.

——— "Mark Twain's Lost Curtain Speeches." *SAQ* 42 (Jl 43) 262-9.

——— "The Petrified Truth." *Colophon* ns 2 (Wi 37) 189-96.

——— "The Uncollected Portions of Mark Twain's *Autobiography.*" *AL* 8 (Mr 36) 37-46.

Fiedler, Leslie. "Come Back to the Raft Ag'in, Huck Honey!" *PR* 15 (Je 48) 664-71.

Fields, Mrs. J. T. "Bret Harte and Mark Twain in the Seventies. Passages from the Diaries of Mrs. James T. Fields: Edited by M. A. De Wolfe Howe." *Atl* 130 (Jl-D 22) 341-48.

Fischer, Walter. "Mark Twain: Zu seinem 100 Geburtstage . . ." *Neuren Sprachen* 43 (1935) 471-80.

Flack, F. M. "About the Play 'Roughing It' as Produced by Augustin Daly." *Twainian* 5 (Jl-Ag 46) 1-3.

——— "Mark Twain and Music." *Twainian* 2 (O 42) 1-3.

Flanagan, J. T. "Mark Twain on the Upper Mississippi." *Minn Hist* 17 (D 36) 369-84.

Flowers, F. C. "Mark Twain's Theories of Morality." *Mark Twain Q* 8 (Su-Fl 48) 10-1.

France, C. J. "Mark Twain as Educator." *Educ* 21 (Ja 01) 265-74.
Francis, R. L. "Mark Twain and H. L. Mencken." *Prairie Schooner* 24 (Sp 50) 31-40.
Fremersdorff, E. H. "Mark Twain in Australia." *Mark Twain Q* 8 (Sp-Su 47) 20.
Gaither, Rice. "New Steamboating Days on Our Rivers." *N Y Times Mag* (10 N 29) 4-5, 20.
Gary, L. M. "Mark Twain—Boy and Philosopher." *Overland Mo* 91: ser 2 (N 33) 154-55.
Gates, W. B. "Mark Twain to His English Publishers." *AL* 11 (Mr 39) 78-81.
Gay, R. M. "The Two Mark Twains." *Atl* 166 (D 40) 724-6.
Gibson, C. H. "My Last Impression of Mark Twain." *Mark Twain Q* 7 (Wi-Sp 45-46) 5-6.
Gibson, W. M. "Twain and Howells: Anti-Imperialists." *NEQ* 20 (D 47) 435-70.
Gilder, R. W. "A Glance at Twain's Spoken and Written Art." *Outlook* 78 (3 D 04) 842-4.
——— "Mark Twain Detested the Theatre." *Theatre Arts* 28 (F 44) 109-16.
——— "Rodman Gilder Writes That One of These Two Twain Tales Is a Forgery." *Twainian* 4 (Ja 45) 4.
Goodpasture, A. V. "Mark Twain, Southerner." *Tenn Hist Mag* 1 (Jl 31) 253-60.
Granger, Eugenie. "Mark Twain versus Publicity." *Mark Twain Q* 7 (Wi-Sp 45-46) 10.
Grimes, Absalom. "Campaigning With Mark Twain." *Mo Hist R* 21 (Ja 27) 188-201.
Guest, Boyd. "Twain's Concept of Woman's Sphere." *Mark Twain Q* 7 (Wi-Sp 45-46) 1-4.
Hall, D. E. "A Mark Twain Sales Tip." *Mark Twain Q* 7 (Wi-Sp 45-46) 9.
Hamada, Masajiro. "Mark Twain's Conception of Social Justice." *Stud Eng Lit* (Japan) 16 (O 36) 593-616.
Harrison, J. G. "A Note on the Duke in 'Huck Finn': The Journeyman Printer as a Picaro." *Mark Twain Q* 8 (Wi 47) 1-2.
Hawthorne, Hildegarde. "Mark Twain and the Immortal Tom." *St Nicholas* 42 (D 14) 164-6.
Hemminghaus, E. H. "Mark Twain's German Provenience." *MLQ* 6 (D 45) 459-78.
Henderson, Archibald. "The International Fame of Mark Twain." *NAR* 192 (D 10) 804-15.
——— "Laughing Philosopher." *Bkm* 46 (Ja 18) 583-4.
——— "Mark Twain." *Harper's* 118 (My 09) 948-55
——— "Mark Twain." *SAQ* 15 (Jl 15) 250-68.
——— "Mark Twain als Philosoph, Moralist und Soziologe." *Deutsche Revue* 36 (1911) 198-205.
——— "Mark Twain Seen in Three Aspects." *NCR* 2 (5 Mr 11) 6-7, 10.
——— "Mark Twain—Wie er ist." *Deutsche Revue* 34 (1909) 195-205.
Herrick, Robert. "Mark Twain and the American Tradition." *Mark Twain Q* 2 (Wi 37) 8-11.
Hewlett, Maurice. "Mark on Sir Walter." *SR* 29 (Ap 21) 130-3.
Hoben, J. B. "Mark Twain's *Connecticut Yankee:* A Genetic Study." *AL* 18 (N 46) 197-218.
Hollenbach, J. W. "Mark Twain, Story-Teller, at Work." *CE* 7 (Mr 46) 303-12.
Holloway, T. E. "Mark Twain's Turning Point." *Mark Twain Q* 8 (Su-Fl 48) 1-3.
Holmes, Ralph. "Mark Twain and Music." *Century* 104 (O 22) 844-50.
Howe, M. A. DeW. "Bret Hart and Mark Twain in the Seventies." *Atl* 130 (S 22) 341-8.
Howells, W. D. "Editor's Easy Chair." *Harper's* 126 (Ja 13) 310-2; 136 (Mr 18) 602-5.
——— "Mark Twain: An Inquiry." *NAR* 171 (F 01) 306-21; 191 (Je 10) 836-50.

——— "My Memories of Mark Twain." *Harper's* 121 (Je 10) 165-78 (Ag 10) 340-8 (S 10) 512-29.
——— "In Memory of Mark Twain." *Am Acad Proc* 1 (1 N 11) 5-6.
——— "The Surprise Party to Mark Twain." *Harper's W* 44 (15 D 00) 1205.
Hughes, R. M. "A Deserter's Tale." *VMHB* 39 (Ja 31) 21-8.
Hustvedt, S. B. "The Preacher and the Gray Mare." *Calif Folklore Q* 5 (Ja 46) 109-10.
Hutcherson, D. R. "Mark Twain as a Pilot." *AL* 12 (N 40) 353-5.
Hutton, Graham. "Hawkeye, Huck Finn and an English Boy." *Chicago Sun Book Week* 4 (4 My 47) 2.
Hyslop, J. H. "Mark Twain Returns." *Unpartizan R* 12 (O-D 19) 397-409.
Jacobs, W. W. "An Englishman's Opinion of Mark Twain." *Mark Twain Q* 2 (Fl 38) 1-2.
James, G. W. "Mark Twain and the Pacific Coast." *Pac Mo* 24 (Ag 10) 115-32.
James, O. C. "The Everlasting Author." *Overland Mo* 87 (Ap 29) 106.
Jerrold, Walter. "Mark Twain, the Man and the Jester." *Bkm* (London) 38 (Je 10) 111-6.
Johnson, Alvin. "The Tragedy of Mark Twain." *NRp* 22 (14 Jl 20) 201-4.
Johnson, Burgess. "When Mark Twain Cursed Me." *Mark Twain Q* 2 (Fl 37) 8-9.
Jones, Joseph. "The 'Duke's' Tooth-Powder Racket: A Note on *Huckleberry Finn.*" *MLN* 61 (N 46) 468-9.
——— "Utopia as Dirge." *Am Q* 2 (Fl 50) 214-26.
Jordan, Elizabeth. "A Silent Celebrity." *Chri Sci Mon* (30) (4 N 38) 9.
Kemble, E. W. "Illustrating Huckleberry Finn." *Colophon* (F 30) Pt 1.
Kimball, E. A. "Mark Twain, Mrs. Eddy, and Christian Science." *Cosmopolitan* 43 (My 07) 35-41.
King, F. A. "The Story of Mark Twain's Debts." *Bkm* 31 (Je 10) 394-6.
Kitzhaber, A. R. "Götterdämmerung in Topeka: The Downfall of Senator Pomeroy." *Kansas Hist Q* 18 (Ag 50) 243-78.
Klett, A. M. "Meisterschaft, or The True State of Mark Twain's German." *AGR* 7 (D 40) 10-1.
Kyne, P. B. "Great Mono Miracle: An Echo of Mark Twain." *Sunset* 29 (Jl 12) 37-49.
La Cossitt, Henry. "Hail to Hannibal, Honoring Mark Twain." *N Y Times Mag* (1 D 35) 11, 16.
Laverty, C. D. "The Genesis of The Mysterious Stranger." *Mark Twain Q* 8 (Sp-Su 47) 15-9.
Leacock, Stephen. "Mark Twain and Canada." *QQ* 42 (Sp 35) 68-81.
——— "Two Humorists: Charles Dickens and Mark Twain." *YR* 24 (S 34) 118-29.
LeBreton, Maurice. "Un Centenaire: Mark Twain." *Revue Anglo-Américaine* 13 (Je 35) 401-19.
Lederer, Max. "Mark Twain in Vienna." *Mark Twain Q* 7 (Su-Fl 45) 1-12.
Leisy, E. E. "Mark Twain and Isaiah Sellers." *AL* 13 (Ja 42) 398-405.
——— "Mark Twain's Part in *The Gilded Age.*" *AL* 8 (Ja 37) 445-8.
——— "The Quintus Curtius Snodgrass Letters in the New Orleans *Daily Crescent.*" *Twainian* 5 (S-O 46) 1-2.
Lemmonier, Léon. "Les Débuts d'un humoriste." *La Grande Revue* 149 (N 35) 76-88.
——— "L'Enfance de Mark Twain." *Revue de France* 15 (1 N 35) 130-58.
Leupp, F. E. "Mark Twain as Inventor." *Harper's W* 45 (7 S 01) 903.
Liljegren, S. B. "The Revolt against Romanticism in American Literature as Evidenced in the Works of S. L. Clemens." *Studia Neophilologica* 17 (1945) 207-58.
Lillard, R. G. "Contemporary Reaction to 'The Empire City Massacre.'" *AL* 16 (N 44) 198-203.
——— "Evolution or the 'Washoe Zephyr.'" *AS* 18 (D 43) 257-60.

Long, E. H. "Sut Lovingood and Mark Twain's *Joan of Arc.*" *MLN* 64 (Ja 49) 37-9.
Loomis, C. G. "Dan De Quille's Mark Twain." *Pac Hist R* 15 (S 46) 336-47.
Lorch, F. W. "Adrift for Hersey." *Palimpsest* 10 (1929) 372-80.
——— "Albert Bigelow Paine's Visit to Keokuk in 1910." *Iowa J Hist & Pol* 42 (Ap 44) 192-8.
——— "'Doesticks' and *Innocents Abroad.*" *AL* 20 (Ja 49) 446-9.
——— "Lecture Trips and Visits of Mark Twain in Iowa." *Iowa J Hist & Pol* 27 (O 29) 408-56.
——— "Mark Twain and the 'Campaign That Failed.'" *AL* 12 (Ja 41) 454-70.
——— "Mark Twain in Iowa." *Iowa J Hist & Pol* 27 (Jl 29) 409-56.
——— "A Mark Twain Letter." *Iowa J Hist & Pol* 28 (Ap 30) 268-76.
——— "Mark Twain's Early Nevada Letters." *AL* 10 (Ja 39) 486-8.
——— "Mark Twain's Early Views on Western Indians." *Twainian* 4 (Ap 45) 1-2.
——— "Mark Twain's Lecture from *Roughing It.*" *AL* 22 (N 50) 290-307.
——— "Mark Twain's Orphanage Lecture." *AL* 7 (Ja 36) 453-5.
——— "Mark Twain's Philadelphia Letters in the Muscatine *Journal.*" *AL* 17 (Ja 46) 348-51.
——— "Mark Twain's Sandwich Islands Lecture at St. Louis." *AL* 18 (Ja 47) 299-307.
——— "Mark Twain's Trip to Humboldt in 1861." *AL* 10 (N 38) 343-9.
——— "A Note on Tom Blankenship (Huckleberry Finn)." *AL* 12 (N 40) 351-3.
——— "Orion Clemens." *Palimpsest* 10 (O 29) 353-86.
——— "A Source for Mark Twain's 'The Dandy Frightening the Squatter.'" *AL* 3 (N 31) 309-13.
Lowell, C. J. "The Background of Mark Twain's Vocabulary." *AS* (Ap 47) 88-9.
Mabbott, T. O. "Mark Twain's Artillery: A Mark Twain Legend." *Mo Hist R* 25 (O 30) 23-9.
Mabie, H. W. "Mark Twain. The Humorist." *Outlook* 87 (23 N 07) 648-53.
McKay, Donald. "On the Vanishing Trail of Tom Sawyer." *N Y Times Mag* (27 O 29) 8-9.
McKeithan, D. M. "A Letter from Mark Twain to Francis Henry Skrine in London." *MLN* 63 (F 48) 134-5.
——— "Mark Twain's *Tom Sawyer Abroad* and *Jules Verne's Five Weeks in a Balloon.*" *Un Texas Stud Eng* 28 (1949) 257-70.
——— "More about Mark Twain's War with English Critics of America." *MLN* 63 (Ap 48) 221-8.
——— "The Occasion of Mark Twain's Speech *On Foreign Critics.*" PQ 27 (Jl 48) 276-9.
Marcosson, I. F. "Mark Twain as Collaborator." *Mark Twain Q* 2 (Wi 37) 7, 24.
Mason, L. D. "Real People in Mark Twain Stories." *Overland Mo* 89 (Ja 31) 12-4.
Masters, E. L. "Mark Twain: Son of the Frontier." *Am Merc* 36 (S 35) 67-74.
Matthews, Brander. "Mark Twain and the Art of Writing." *Harper's* 141 (O 20) 635-43.
——— "Mark Twain as Speech Maker and Story Teller." *Mentor* 12 (My 24) 24-8.
——— "Memories of Mark Twain." *Sat Eve Post* 192 (6 Mr 20) 14-5.
Maurice, A. B. "Mark Twain's 'The Innocents Abroad.'" *Bkm* 31 (Je 10) 374-9.
Mendelson, M. "Mark Twain Accuses." *Soviet Lit* (My 48) 151-61.
Merrill, W. H. "When Mark Twain Lectured." *Harper's W* 50 (10 F 06) 199.
Meyer, Harold. "Mark Twain on the Comstock." *Sw R* 12 (Ap 27) 197-207.
Michel, Robert. "The Popularity of Mark Twain in Austria." *Mark Twain Q* 8 (Wi 50) 5-6, 19.
Milbank, E. P. "In Mark-Twain Land." *St Nicholas* 46 (Ag 19) 934.
Millard, Bailey. "Mark Twain in San Francisco." *Bkm* 31 (Je 10) 369-73.
——— "When They Were Twenty-One." *Bkm* 37 (My 13) 296-304.

Moffet, S. E. "Mark Twain, Doctor of Letters." *Rev of Rev* 36 (Ag 07) 167-8.
Moffett, W. B. "Mark Twain's Lansing Lecture on *Roughing It*." *Mich Hist* 34 (Je 50) 144-70.
Moore, J. B. "Mark Twain and Copyright." *Mark Twain Q* 3 (Wi 38) 3.
Moore, O. H. "Mark Twain and Don Quixote." *PMLA* 37 (Je 22) 324-46.
Mott, H. S., Jr. "The Origin of Aunt Polly." *Pub W* 134 (11 N 38) 1821-3.
Nye, R. B. "Mark Twain in Oberlin." *Ohio St Arch & Hist Q* 48 (Ja 38) 69-73.
O'Day, E. C. "Stories from the Files." *Overland* ns 75 (Ap-Je 20) 326-8, 407-9, 517-9, 551.
Older, F. "Mark Twain and Jackass Hill." *Overland Mo* 92: ser 2 (Jl 34) 118.
Olson, J. C. "Mark Twain and the Department of Agriculture." *AL* 13 (Ja 42) 408-10.
Orcutt, W. D. "From My Library Walls." *Chri Sci Mon* 37 (17 N 44) 7.
Orians, G. H. "Walter Scott, Mark Twain, and the Civil War." *SAQ* 40 (O 41) 342-59.
Pain, Barry. "The Humour of Mark Twain." *Bkm* (London) 38 (Je 10) 107-11.
Paine, A. B. "A Boy's Life of Mark Twain." *St. Nicholas* (N 15-D 16) 6, 20-1.
——— "Mark Twain." *Harper's* 123 (N 11) 813-28; 124 (D 11, Ja, F, Mr, Ap, My 12) 42-53, 215-28, 419-33, 583-97, 737-51, 934-47; 125 (Je, Jl, Ag, S, O, N 12) 104-19, 249-63, 405-17, 593-605, 767-80, 923-35.
——— "Mark Twain: A Biographical Summary." *Harper's W* 54 (30 Ap 10) 6-10.
——— "Mark Twain at Stormfield." *Harper's* 118 (My 09) 955-8.
——— "Some Mark Twain Letters." *Harper's* 134 (My 17) 781-94; 135 (Jl, Ag, S, O, N 17) 177-86, 378-88, 569-77, 638-47, 812-9.
——— "Unpublished Chapters from the Autobiography of Mark Twain." *Harper's* 144 (F, Mr 22) 273-8, 455-60; 145 (Ag 22) 310-5.
——— "Unpublished Diaries of Mark Twain." *Hearst's Int* 99 (Ag 35) 24-7, 134-6.
Parsons, C. O. "The Devil and Samuel Clemens." *VQR* 23 (Aut 47) 582-606.
Partridge, H. M. "Did Mark Twain Perpetrate Literary Hoaxes." *Am Book Coll* 5 (D 34) 351-7; 6 (Ja, F 35) 20-3, 50-3.
Pattee, F. L. "On the Rating of Mark Twain." *Am Merc* 14 (Je 28) 183-91.
Paullin, C. O. "Mark Twain's Virginia Kin." *WMQ* 15 (Jl 35) 294-8.
Peabody, E. F. "Mark Twain's Ghost Story." *Minn Hist* 18 (Mr 37) 28-35.
Peck, H. T. "Mark Twain a Century Hence." *Bkm* 31 (Je 10) 282-93.
Peckham, H. H. "The Literary Status of Mark Twain, 1877-90." *SAQ* 19 (O 20) 332-40.
Petersen, Svend. "Splendid Days and Fearsome Nights." *Mark Twain Q* 8 (Wi-Sp 49) 3-8, 15.
Phelps, W. L. "Mark Twain." *NAR* 185 (5 Jl 07) 540-8.
——— "Mark Twain." *YR* 25 (Wi 36) 291-310.
——— "Mark Twain, Artist." *Rev of Rev* 41 (Je 10) 702-3.
——— "My Father—Mark Twain." *Scribner's* 91 (Ja 32) 54-5.
——— "Notes on Mark Twain." *Independent* 68 (5 My 10) 956-60.
Phillips, M. J. "Mark Twain's Partner." *Sat Eve Post* 193 (11 S 20) 22-3.
Phillips, R. E. "Mark Twain: More Than Humorist." *Book Buyer* 22 (Ap 01) 196-201.
Pilkington, Walter, & Alsterlund, B. "Mark Twain's Introductory Remarks at the Time of Churchill's First American Lecture." *AN&Q* 5 (Ja 46) 147-8.
Powell, L. C. "An Unpublished Mark Twain Letter." *AL* 13 (Ja 42) 405-7.
Pritchett, V. S. "Books in General." *New Statesman and Nation* 22 (2 Ag 41) 113.
Putnam, Samuel. "The Americanism of Mark Twain." *Mark Twain Q* 2 (Fl 38) 13, 24.
Quaife, M.M. "George in Historyland." *Twainian* 3 (Ja 44) 5-6.
——— "Mark Twain's Military Career." *Twainian* 3 (Je 44) 4-7.
Quick, Dorothy, "A Little Girl's Mark Twain." *NAR* 240 (S 35) 342-8.
——— "My Author's League with Mark Twain." *NAR* 245 (Su 38) 315-29.

R., V. "Walter Scott and the Southern States of America." *N&Q* 169 (9 N 35) 328-30.
Ramsay, R. L., & Emberson, F. G. "A Mark Twain Lexicon." *Un Mo Stud* 13: i-cxix (Ja 38) 1-278.
Rideing, W. H. "Mark Twain in Clubland." *Bkm* 31 (Je 10) 279-82.
——— "Mark Twain's 'The Innocents Abroad.'" *Bkm* 31 (Je 10) 374-82.
Roades, Sister M. T. "Don Quixote and *A Connecticut Yankee in King Arthur's Court.*" *Mark Twain Q* 2 (Fl 38) 8-9.
Robbins, L. H. "Mark Twain's Fame Goes Marching On: His Century Which Closes This Year, Finds Him Still the Best-Loved and Most Widely Read of American Authors." *N Y Times Mag* (21 Ap 35) 4, 16.
Roberts, Harold. "Sam Clemens: Florida Days." *Twainian* 1 (Mr 42) 4-6.
Roberts, R. E. "Mark Twain." *Fortnightly R* ns 827 (N 35) 583-92.
Robertson, Stuart. "Mark Twain in Germany." *Mark Twain Q* 2 (Fl 37) 10-2.
Robinson, M. J. "Mark Twain Lecturer." *Mark Twain Q* 8 (Sp-Su 47) 1-12.
Rodgers, Cleveland. "The Many-Sided Mark Twain." *Mentor* 12 (My 24) 30-1.
Roerich, Nicholas. "Mark Twain in Russia." *Mark Twain Q* 3 (Sp 39) 7.
Rowe, Ida. "Mark Twain's Interest in Nature." *Mark Twain Q* 1 (Su 37) 7, 9-10, 14.
Russell, L. L. "Americanism as Typified by Mark Twain." *Mark Twain Q* 8 (Su-Fl 48) 14-5.
Salls, H. H. "Joan of Arc in English and American Literature." *SAQ* 25 (Ap 36) 167-84.
Schoenemann, F. "Mark Twain and Adolf Wilbrandt." *MLN* 34 (Je 19) 372-4.
——— "Neue Mark-Twain-Studien." *Neueren Sprachen* 44 (1936) 260-72.
Schultz, J. R. "New Letters of Mark Twain." *AL* 8 (Mr 36) 47-51.
Schuster, G. N. "The Tragedy of Mark Twain." *Cath World* 104 (Mr 17) 731-7.
Sherman, S. P. "Mark Twain." *Nation* 90 (12 My 10) 477-80.
Shirley, Philip. "Those 'Poems' by Twain in 'The Wasp' of San Francisco." *Twainian* 5 (Jl-Ag 46) 3-4.
Sillen, Samuel. "Dooley, Twain and Imperialism." *Masses & Mainstream* 1 (D 48) 6-14.
Simboli, Raffaele. "Mark Twain from an Italian Point of View." *Critic* 44 (Je 04) 518-24.
Slade, W. G. "Mark Twain's Educational Views." *Mark Twain Q* 4 (Su-Fl 41) 5-10.
Slater, Joseph. "Music at Col. Grangerford's: A Footnote to *Huckleberry Finn.*" *AL* 21 (Mr 49) 108-11.
Sosey, F. H. "Palmyra and Its Historical Environment." *Mo Hist R* 23 (Ap 29) 361-79.
Squires, J. R. "Mark Twain." *Accent* 9 (Aut 48) 32-3.
Stewart, G. R. "Bret Harte upon Mark Twain in 1866." *AL* 13 (N 41) 263-4.
Stewart, H. L. "Mark Twain on the Jewish Problem." *Dalhousie R* 14 (Ja 35) 455-8.
Stoddart, A. M. "Twainiana." *Independent* 68 (5 My 10) 960-3.
Stong, Phil. "Mark Twain Cruise: Aboard a Modern River Boat, with Sam Clemens' Shade at the Wheel." *Holiday* 5 (Ap 48) 56-62, 86-7, 90, 92, 93, 95, 97.
Street, J. "In Mizzoura." *Colliers* 53 (29 Ag 14) 18-9.
Swain, L. H. "Mark Twain as a Music Critic: A Case Study in Esthetic Growth." *Furman Bul* 19 (Ap 37) 48-53.
Tarkington, Booth. "Mark Twain and Boys." *Mark Twain Q* 1 (Fl 36) 6-7.
Taylor, W. F. "Mark Twain and the Machine Age." *SAQ* 37 (O 38) 384-96.
Templin, E. H. "On Re-reading Mark Twain." *Hispania* 24 (O 41) 269-76.
Ticknor, Caroline. "'Mark Twain's' Missing Chapter." *Bkm* 39 (My 14) 298-309.
Tidwell, J. N. "Mark Twain's Representation of Negro Speech." *AS* 17 (O 42) 174-6.

Trommer, Marie. "Tom Sawyer and the Missing Cat Chapter." *Mark Twain Q* 8 (Wi 50) 3-4.
Troxell, G. M. "Samuel Langhorne Clemens, 1835-1910." *Yale Un Lib Gaz* 18 (Jl 43) 1-5.
Twichell, J. H. "Mark Twain Number." *Mentor* 12 (My 24) 3-58.
Underhill, I. S. "Diamonds in the Rough: Being the Story of Another Book That Mark Twain Never Wrote." *Colophon* 4 (Mr 33) Pt 13.
——— "The Haunted Book: A Further Exploration concerning *Huckleberry Finn.*" *Colophon* ns 1 (Au 35) 281-91.
——— "An Inquiry into *Huckleberry Finn.*" *Colophon* 2 (Je 31) Pt 6.
Vale, Charles. "Mark Twain as an Orator." *Forum* 44 (Jl 10) 1-13.
Van Doren, Carl. "Mark Twain and Bernard Shaw." *Century* 109 (Mr 25) 705-10.
Van Doren, Mark. "A Century of Mark Twain." *Nation* 141 (23 O 35) 472-4.
Verdaguer, Mario. "Humorismo inglés e ironía yanqui." *La Razón* (Panama) 5 (3 Jl 37) 2.
Vogelback, A. L. "Mark Twain: Newspaper Contributor." *AL* 20 (My 48) 111-28.
——— "*The Prince and the Pauper:* A Study in Critical Standards." *AL* 14 (Mr 42) 48-54.
——— "The Publication and Reception of *Huckleberry Finn* in America." *AL* 11 (N 39) 260-72.
Von Hibler, Leo. "Mark Twain und die deutsche Sprache." *Anglia* 65 (N 40) 206-13.
Waggoner, H. H. "Science in the Thought of Mark Twain." *AL* 8 (Ja 37) 357-70.
Walker, Franklin. "An Influence from San Francisco on Mark Twain's *The Gilded Age.*" *AL* 8 (Mr 36) 63-6.
Walsh, E. P. "A Connecticut Yankee of Our Lady's Court." *Cath World* 169 (My 49) 91-7.
Warfel, H. R. "George W. Cable Amends a Mark Twain Plot." *AL* 6 (N 34) 328-31.
Watterson, Henry. "Mark Twain—An Intimate Memory." *Am Mag* 70 (Jl 10) 372-5.
Weatherly, E. A. "Beau Tibbs and Colonel Sellers." *MLN* 59 (My 44) 310-3.
Webster, D. & S. W. "Whitewashing Jane Clemens." *Bkm* 61 (Jl 25) 531-5.
Webster, S. C. "Ghost Life on the Mississippi." *PS* 2 (Aut 48) 485-90.
——— "Mark Twain, Business Man: Letters and Memoirs." *Atl* 173 (Je 44) 37-46; 174 (Jl, Ag, S, O, N 44) 72-80, 71-7, 90-6, 74-80, 100-6.
Wecter, Dixon. "Frank Findlay; or, 'The Thameside Tenderfoot in the Wooly West.'" *Twainian* 6 (Jl-Ag 47) 1-4.
——— "The Love Letters of Mark Twain." *Atl* 180 (N, D 47) 33-9, 66-72.
——— "Mark Twain and the West." *HLQ* 8 (Ag 45) 359-77.
——— "Mark Twain as Translator from the German." *AL* 13 (N 41) 257-64.
——— "Mark Twain's River." *Atl* 182 (O 48) 45-7.
Weisinger, Mort. "Listen! Mark Twain Speaking." *Sat Eve Post* 221 (3 Jl 48) 12.
West, R. B., Jr. "Mark Twain's Idyl of Frontier America." *UKCR* 15 (Wi 48) 92-104.
West, V. R. "Folklore in the Works of Mark Twain." *Un Neb Stud* 10 (1930) 1-87.
Wharton, H. M. "The Boyhood Home of Mark Twain." *Century* 64 (S 02) 675-7.
White, Edgar. "Mark Twain's Printer Days." *Overland Mo* ns 70 (D 17) 573-6.
White, F. M. "Mark Twain as a Newspaper Reporter." *Outlook* 96 (24 D 10) 961-7.
Whiting, B. J. "Guyuscutus, Royal Nonsuch and Other Hoaxes." *SFQ* 8 (D 44) 251-75.
Williams, H. J. E. "Mark Twain." *Bkm* (London) 18 (S 00) 169-74.
Williams, M. L. "Mark Twain's John of Arc." *Mich Alumnus Quar R* 54 (8 My 48) 243-50.

Willson, F. C. "Mark Twain on the Old-Fashioned Spelling Bee." *Twainian* 4 (Mr 45) 2-4.

——— "That 'Gilded Age' Again: An Attempt to Unmuddle the Mystery of the Fifty-Seven Variants." *PBSA* 37 (Ap-Je 43) 141-56.

——— "Twain Spanks a Government Employee for Unofficial Impertinence." *Twainian* 4 (Ja 45) 2, 5.

——— "Twain Tells Us How to Remove Warts and Tatoo Marks." *Twainian* 4 (Je 45) 3-4.

——— "Twain's Tale, 'The Facts Concerning the Recent Important Resignation.'" *Twainian* 5 (My-Je 46) 1-3.

Wilson, R. H. "Malory in the Connecticut Yankee." *Un Texas Stud Eng* 27 (Je 48) 185-205.

Wimberly, L. C. "Mark Twain and the Tichener Bonanza." *Atl* 172 (N 43) 117-9.

Winterich, J. T. "The Life and Works of Bloodgood Haviland Cutter." *Colophon* 1 (My 30) Pt 2.

Wister, Owen. "In Homage to Mark Twain." *Harper's* 171 (O 35) 547-56.

Woodbridge, H. E. "Mark Twain and the 'Gesta Romanorum.'" *Nation* 108 (22 Mr 19) 424-5.

——— "Mark Twain's Fatalism." *Nation* 105 (11 O 17) 399.

Woolf, S. J. "Painting the Portrait of Mark Twain." *Collier's* 45 (14 My 10) 42-4.

Workman, M. T. "The Whitman-Twain Enigma." *Mark Twain Q* 8 (Su-Fl 48) 12-3.

Wyatt, Edith. "An Inspired Critic." *NAR* 205 (Ap 17) 603-15.

Wyman, M. A. "A Note on Mark Twain." *CE* 7 (My 46) 438-42.

Yarmolinsky, Avraham. "The Russian View of American Literature." *Bkm* 44 (S 16) 44-8.

COBB, FRANK IRVING (1869-1923). Pringle, H. F. "The Newspaper Man as an Artist: Frank I. Cobb." *Scribner's* 97 (F 35) 101-10.

Schermerhorn, James. "Frank I. Cobb." *Am Mag* 75 (Ja 13) 29-30.

COBB, IRVIN S. (1876-1944). Anon. "Attempt to Place Irvin S. Cobb among the Immortals." *Cur Op* 54 (Ja 13) 56-7.

——— "Concerning Irving Cobb." *Bkm* 37 (Mr 13) 14-5.

Cobb, I. S. "The Trail of the Lonesome Laugh." *Everybody's* 24 (Ap 11) 467-75.

Davis, R. H. "Irvin S. Cobb, a Paducah Gentleman." *Am Mag* 83 (My 17) 14.

Maurice, A. B. "Irvin S. Cobb." *Bkm* 69 (Jl 29) 511-4.

COBB, JOSEPH B. (1819-58). Buckley, G. T. "Joseph B. Cobb: Mississippi Essayist and Critic." *AL* 10 (My 38) 166-78.

COBBETT, WILLIAM (1763-1835). Adkins, N. F. "Another American Reference to Cobbett." *N&Q* 163 (8 O 32) 258.

——— "William Cobbett." *N&Q* 163 (13 Ag 32) 116.

Reitzel, William. "William Cobbett and Philadelphia Journalism: 1794-1800." *PMHB* 59 (Jl 35) 223-4.

COFFIN, ROBERT P. TRISTRAM (1892-). Benét, W. R. "Man from Maine." *EJ* 25 (S 36) 523-33.

Holden, Raymond. "Holy Strangeness." *Poetry* 47 (Ja 36) 229-31.

Knowlton, E. C. "Descriptive Verse." *SAQ* 34 (Jl 35) 339-40.

Schacht, Marshall. "Two Regions." *Poetry* 53 (N 38) 92-6.

Warren, R. P. "Americanism." *Poetry* 34 (S 29) 334-7.

Zabel, M. D. "An Art of Living Things." *Poetry* 34 (S 29) 356-8.

COLBY, FRANK MOORE (1865-1925). Clark, J. A. "A Touchstone for Intellectuals: Frank Moore Colby." *SR* 47 (Ap-Je 39) 221-34.

COLMAN, BENJAMIN (1673-1747). Davenport, G. H. "An Early Coronation Sermon." *N E Mag* ns 26 (Je 02) 476-80.

Hornberger, Theodore. "Benjamin Colman and the Enlightenment." *NEQ* 12 (Je 39) 227-40.

Paltsits, V. H. "Note on a Benjamin Colman Manuscript." *PMHS* 65 (D 33) 232-3.

CONKLING, HILDA (1910-). Fairchild, H. N. "Belated Appreciation." *Poet Lore* 42 (Wi 35) 267-75.

CONNELLY, MARC (1890-). Carmer, Carl. "The Green Pastures." *NRp* 62 (19 Mr 30) 128-9.

Withington, Robert. "Notes on the Corpus Christi Plays and 'The Green Pastures.'" *Shakespeare Assn Bul* 9 (O 34) 193-7.

Woollcott, Alexander. "Two-Eyed Connelly." *NYr* 6 (12 Ap 30) 29-31.

Young, Starke. "The Green Pastures." *NRp* 62 (19 Mr 30) 128-9.

CONWAY, MONCURE DANIEL (1832-1907). Bassett, J. S. "An Exile from the South." *SAQ* 4 (Ja 05) 82-90.

COOKE, EBENEZER (*fl.* 1708-32). Anon. "An Unpublished Poem by the Author of the Sot Weed Factor." *Md Hist Mag* 14 (Je 19) 172-3.

Pole, J. T. "Ebenezer Cooke and *The Maryland Muse.*" *AL* 3 (N 31) 296-302.

Wroth, L. C. "The Maryland Muse of Ebenezer Cooke." *PAAS* 44 (O 34) 267-355.

COOKE, JOHN ESTEN (1830-86). Collins, Carvel. "John Esten Cooke and Local Color." *SLM* 6 (Ja-F 44) 82-4.

Cooke, J. E. "John Esten Cooke on the Harper Fire of 1853." *BNYPL* 17 (S 13) 780.

Holliday, Carl. "John Esten Cooke as a Novelist." *SR* 13 (Ap 05) 216-22.

Hubbell, J. B. "The War Diary of John Esten Cooke." *J So Hist* 7 (N 41) 526-40.

Wegelin, Oscar. "A Bibliography of the Separate Writings of John Esten Cooke." *Am Col* 1 (D 25) 96-9.

COOKE, PHILIP PENDLETON (1816-50). Hogan, W. J. "An Unpublished Poem of Philip Pendleton Cooke." *Educ Forum* 1 (N 36) 81-6.

COOKE, ROSE TERRY (1827-92). Rugg, W. K. "A Lady Author Comes to Town." *Chri Sci Mon* 29 (13 My 37) 11.

COOLBRITH, INA (1842-1928). Bland, H. M. "The Poets of the Overland." *Overland Mo* 85 (Jl 27) 199-200, 218.

Everett, L. B. "Ina Coolbrith and Jim Beckwith." *Overland Mo* ns 91 (Ag 33) 109.

Kendall, Carlton. "California Pioneer Poetess." *Overland Mo* 87: ser 2 (Ag 29) 229-30.

McCrackin, J. C. "Ina Coolbrith." *Overland Mo* ns 66 (N 15) 448-50.

Stevenson, Lionel. "The Mind of Ina Coolbrith." *Overland Mo* 88: ser 2 (My 30) 150.

Sultzer, K. D. "California's Poet Laureate." *MS.* 4 (Ag 32) 5, 9.

Taylor, Marian. "Ina Coolbrith, California Poet." *Overland Mo* ns 64 (O 14) 326-39.

——— "Poet-Laureate Hostess." *Sunset* 34 (Ja 15) 135-8.

COOPER, JAMES FENIMORE (1789-1851). Anon. "Cooper To-day." *Outlook* 69 (21 D 01) 1037-9.

——— "Letters to Cooper." *Bkm* 43 (Ag 16) 570-5.

——— "She Remembers Cooper." *Lit Dig* 114 (12 N 32) 14-5.

Adkins, N. F. "A Glimpse of Fenimore Cooper in His Last Years." *N&Q* 167 (11 Ag 34) 96-7.

——— "James Fenimore Cooper and the Bread and Cheese Club." *MLN* 47 (F 32) 71-9.
——— "James Fenimore Cooper in France, 1830-1832." *N&Q* 173 (25 S 37) 222-4.
Arndt, K. J. R. "The Cooper-Sealsfield Exchange of Criticism." *AL* 15 (Mr 43) 16-24.
——— "John Christopher Hartwick." *NY Hist* 18 (Jl 37) 293-303.
——— "New Letters from James Fenimore Cooper." *MLN* 41 (F 37) 117-20.
Ballinger, R. H. "Origins of James Fenimore Cooper's *The Two Admirals*." *AL* 20 (Mr 48) 20-3.
Bandy, W. T. "Two Uncollected Letters of James Fenimore Cooper." *AL* 20 (Ja 49) 441-2.
Barba, P. A. "Cooper in Germany." *Ger-Am Annals* ns 12 (1914) 1-46; *Ind Un Stud* (1914) 21.
Birss, J. H. "A Letter of Herman Melville." *N&Q* 162 (16 Ja 32) 39.
Blanck, Jacob. "The Bibliography of American Literature: James Fenimore Cooper." *Pub W* 151 (1 F 47) B83-4.
——— "News from the Rare Book Shop." *Pub W* 133 (23 Ap 38) 1696.
Bolander, L. H. "The Naval Career of James Fenimore Cooper." *U S Naval Inst Proc* 66 (Ap 40) 541-50.
Bonner, W. H. "Cooper and Captain Kidd." *MLN* 61 (Ja 46) 21-7.
Brenner, C. D. "The Influence of Cooper's *The Spy* on Hauff's *Lichtenstein*." *MLN* 30 (N 15) 207-10.
Brownell, W. C. "Cooper." *Scribner's* 39 (Ap 06) 455-68.
Butterfield, L. H. "Judge William Cooper (1754-1809): A Sketch of His Character and Accomplishment." *N Y Hist* 30 (O 49) 385-408.
Byington, S. T. "Mr. Byington's Brief Case (IV)." *AS* 21 (F 46) 37-44.
Canby, H. S. "James Fenimore Cooper." *SRL* 3 (23 Ap 27) 747-9.
Clavel, M. "Du nouveau sur Fenimore Cooper." *Revue Anglo-Américaine* 5 (Ap 28) 342-54; 6 (Ag 29) 532-7; 8 (Ag 31) 538-42; 12 (D 34) 167-70.
Clemens, S. L. "Fenimore Cooper's Further Literary Offenses." *NEQ* 19 (S 46) 291-301.
Cooper, J. F. "Letter from James Fenimore Cooper to George H. Preble." *PMHS* 60 (N 26) 34-5.
——— "Unpublished Letters of James Fenimore Cooper." *YR* 5 (Jl 16) 810-31; 11 (Ja 22) 242-68.
Dargan, E. P. "Balzac and Cooper: *Les Chouans*." *MP* 13 (Ag 15) 193-213.
Davidson, L. J. "Letters from Authors." *Colo Mag* 19 (Jl 42) 122-6.
Davis, E. E. "James Fenimore Cooper Lived Here." *Long Island Forum* 3 (D 40) 253-4.
Dondore, Dorothy. "The Debt of Two Dyed-in-the-Wool Americans to Mrs. Grant's *Memoirs;* Cooper's *Satanstoe,* and Paulding's *The Dutchman's Fireside*." *AL* 12 (Mr 40) 52-8.
Drescher, Rudolph. "My Cooper Collection." *Freeman's J* (Cooperstown, 13 F 29).
Flanagan, J. T. "The Authenticity of Cooper's *The Prairie*." *MLQ* 2 (Mr 41) 98-104.
Foerster, Norman. "The Letters of Fenimore Cooper." *The Freeman* 7 (16 My 23) 235.
Fox, D. R. "James Fenimore Cooper, Aristocrat." *N Y Hist* 22 (Ja 41) 18-24.
Gates, W. B. "Cooper's 'The Sea Lions' and Wilkes' 'Narrative.'" *PMLA* 65 (D 50) 1069-75.
Gibb, M. M. "Leon Gozlan et Fenimore Cooper." *Revue de Littérature Comparée* 10 (Jl-S 30) 485.
Glicksberg, C. I. "Cooper & Bryant: A Literary Friendship." *Colophon* 5 (Mr 35) Pt 20.
Goggio, Emilio. "Cooper's *Bravo* in Italy." *RR* 20 (Jl -S 29) 222-30.
——— "The Italy of James Fenimore Cooper." *MLJ* 29 (Ja 45) 66-71.

Goodfellow, D. M. "The Sources of *Mercedes of Castile.*" *AL* 12 (N 40) 318-28.
Gordan, J. D. "*The Red Rover* Takes the Boards." *AL* 10 (Mr 38) 66-75.
Griggs, E. L. "James Fenimore Cooper on Coleridge." *AL* 4 (Ja 33) 389-91.
Hale, E. E., Jr. "American Scenery in Cooper's Novels." *SR* 18 (Jl 10) 317-32.
Hastings, G. E. "How Cooper Became a Novelist." *AL* 12 (Mr 40) 20-51.
Hicks, Granville. "Landlord Cooper and the Anti-Renters." *AR* 5 (Sp 45) 95-109.
Jones, V. L. "Gustave Aimard." *Sw R* 15 (Su 30) 452-68.
Kirk, Russell. "Cooper and the European Puzzle." *CE* 7 (Ja 46) 198-207.
Kouwenhoven, J. A. "Cooper and the American Copyright Club: An Unpublished Letter." *AL* 13 (N 41) 265.
——— "Cooper's 'Upside Down' Turns Up." *Colophon* ns 3 (Aut 38) 524-30.
Lawrence, D. H. "Studies in Classic American Literature (iv): Fenimore Cooper's Anglo-American Novels." *Eng R* 28 (F 19) 88-99.
——— "Studies in Classic American Literature (v): Fenimore Cooper's Leather-stocking Novels." *Eng R* 28 (Mr 19) 204-19.
Lüdeke. H. "James Fenimore Cooper and the Democracy of Switzerland." *Eng Stud* 27 (1946) 33-4.
Lyman, S. E. "I Could Write You a Better Book than That Myself." *N Y Hist Soc Quar Bul* 29 (O 45) 213-41.
McDowell, Tremaine. "The Identity of Harvey Birch." *AL* 2 (My 30) 111-20.
——— "James Fenimore Cooper as Self-Critic." *SP* 27 (Jl 30) 508-16.
——— "Scott on Cooper and Brockden Brown." *MLN* 45 (Ja 30) 18-20.
Marckwardt, A. H. "The Chronology and Personnel of the Bread and Cheese Club." *AL* 6 (Ja 35) 389-99.
Matthews, Brander. "Fenimore Cooper." *Atl* 100 (S 07) 329-41; *Rev of Rev* 36 (O 07) 503-4 (condensed).
Messac, Régis. "Fenimore Cooper et son influence en France." *PMLA* 43 (D 28) 1199-1201.
Muret, M. "Fenimore Cooper, Américain d'hier." *Journal des Debats* (23 O 31) 670-2.
Muszynska-Wallace, E S. "The Sources of *The Prairie.*" *AL* 21 (My 49) 191-200.
Nelson, Andrew. "James Cooper and George Groghan." *PQ* 20 (Ja 41) 69-73.
Oakley, K. R. "James Fenimore Cooper and *Oak Openings.*" *Mich Hist Mag* 16 (Su 32) 309-20.
Paine, G. L. "Cooper and *The North American Review.*" *SP* 28 (O 31) 799-809.
——— "The Indians of the Leather-Stocking Tales." *SP* 23 (Ja 26) 16-39.
Palfrey, T. R. "Cooper and Balzac: *The Headsman.*" *MP* 29 (F 32) 335-41.
Partridge, Eric. "Fenimore Cooper's Influence on the French Romantics." *MLR* 20 (Ap 25) 174-8.
Pattee, F. L. "Cooper the Critic." *SRL* 5 (15 Je 29) 1107-8.
——— "Cooper's Last of the Mohicans." *Chautauquan* 31 (Je 00) 287-92.
——— "James Fenimore Cooper." *Am Merc* 4 (Mr 25) 289-97.
Pearce, R. H. "The Leatherstocking Tales Re-examined." *SAQ* 46 (O 47) 524-36.
Phelps, W. L. "Fenimore Cooper and His Writings." *N Y Hist* 22 (Ja 41) 27-35.
Pound, Louise. "The Dialect of Cooper's Leather-Stocking." *AS* 2 (S 27) 479.
Routh, James. "The Model of the Leatherstocking Tales." *MLN* 28 (Mr 13) 77-9.
Russell, J. A. "Cooper: Interpreter of the Real and the Historical Indian." *J Am Hist* 23 (1929) 41-71.
Sawyer, E. A. "A Year of Cooper's Youth." *N E Mag* ns 37 (D 07) 498-504.
Scudder, H. H. "Cooper and the Barbary Coast." *PMLA* 62 (S 47) 184-92.
——— "Cooper's *The Crater.*" *AL* 19 (My 47) 109-26.
——— "What Mr. Cooper Read to His Wife." *SR* 36 (Ap 28) 177-94.
Simmonds, W. E. "James Fenimore Cooper." *Reader* 5 (D 04) 127-9.
Snell, George. "The Shaper of American Romance." *YR* 34 (Sp 45) 482-94.
Spiller, R. E. "Cooper's Notes on Language." *AS* 4 (Ap 29) 294-300.

——— "Fenimore Cooper and Lafayette: Friends of Polish Freedom, 1830-1832." *AL* 7 (Mr 35) 56-75.
——— "Fenimore Cooper and Lafayette: The Finance Controversy of 1831-1832." *AL* 3 (Mr 31) 28-44.
——— "Fenimore Cooper: Critic of His Times: New Letters from Rome and Paris, 1830-1831." *AL* 1 (My 29) 131-48.
——— "Fenimore Cooper's Defense of Slave-Owning America." *AHR* 35 (Ap 30) 575-82.
——— "War with the Book Pirates." *Pub W* 132 (30 O 37) 1736-8.
Stedman, E. C. "Poe, Cooper and the Hall of Fame." *NAR* 185 (Ag 07) 801-12.
Stokes, A. P. "James Fenimore Cooper: A Memorial Sermon." *N Y Hist* 22 (Ja 41) 36-45.
Strout, A. L. "Some Unpublished Letters of John Gibson Lockhart to John Wilson Croker." *N&Q* 185 (9 O 43) 217-23.
Sueffer, Carl. "War Lederstumpf ein Deutscher?" *Westermann's Monatsheft* 156 (My 34) 245-9.
Sutton, Walter. "Cooper as Found—1949." *UKCR* 16 (Aut 49) 3-10.
Vandiver, E. P. "James Fenimore Cooper and Shakspere." *Shakespeare Assn Bul* 15 (Ap 40) 110-7.
Waples, Dorothy. "A Letter of James Fenimore Cooper." *NEQ* 3 (Ja 30) 123-32.
Williams, M. L. "Cooper, Lyon, and the Moore-Hascall Harvesting Machine." *Mich Hist* 31 (Mr 47) 26-34.
——— "They Wrote Home about It." *Mich Alumnus Quar R* (Su 45) 337-51.
Wilson, J. G. "Cooper Memorials." *Independent* 53 (31 Ja 01) 251-3.
Winterich, J. T. "Romantic Stories of Books, Second Series, XXII, *The Spy*." *Pub W* 119 (20 Je 31) 2882-6.
Wood, R. K. "Leatherstocking Trail." *Bkm* 41 (Jl 15) 513-21.

COOPER, SUSAN FENIMORE (1813-94). Cunningham, A. K. "Susan Fenimore Cooper: Child of Genius." *N Y Hist* 25 (Jl 44) 339-50.

COTTER, JOSEPH S. (1861-). Kerlin, R. T. "A Poet from Bardstown." *SAQ* 20 (Jl 21) 213-21.

COTTON, JOHN (1854-1652). Anon. "Cromwell to Cotton, After the Battle of Worcester." *BNYPL* 4 (Ja 00) 13-4.
Calder, I. M. "The Authorship of a Discourse About Civil Government . . ." *AHR* 37 (Ja 32) 267-9.
——— "John Cotton and the New Haven Colony." *NEQ* 3 (Ja 30) 82-94.
——— "John Cotton's 'Moses His Judicials.'" *PCSM* 28 (Ap 31) 86-94.
Ford, W. C. "John Cotton's 'Moses His Judicials.'" *PMHS* 16: ser 2 (1903) 274-84.
Greenough, C. N. "On the Authorship of *Singing of Psalms a Gospel Ordinance*, 1647." *PCSM* 20 (Ap 18) 239-47.
Hirsch, E. F. "John Cotton and Roger Williams." *Church Hist* 10 (Mr 41) 38-51.
Hornberger, Theodore. "Puritanism and Science: The Relationship Revealed in the Writings of John Cotton." *NEQ* 10 (S 37) 503-15.
Hosmer, J. K. "Was John Cotton the Preceptor of Henry Vane?" *Nation* 89 (8 Jl 09) 32-3.
King, H. C. "John Cotton and Sir Henry Vane." *Nation* 88 (8 Ap 09) 357-8.
——— "Was John Cotton the Preceptor of Sir Henry Vane?" *Nation* 88 (10 Je 09) 577-8.
Mead, E. M. "John Cotton's Influence on Vane." *Nation* 88 (13 My 09) 484.
Merrill, D. K. "The First American Biography." *NEQ* 11 (Mr 38) 152-4.
Parkes, H. B. "John Cotton and Roger Williams Debate Toleration, 1644-1652." *NEQ* 4 (O 31) 735-56.

COTTON, JOHN, of Acquia Creek (*fl.* 1676). Basler, R. P. "*Bacon's Epitaph,* Made by His Man." *Expl* 2 (D 43) 12.

Hubbell, J. B. "John and Ann Cotton, of 'Queen's Creek,' Virginia." *AL* 10 (My 38) 179-201.

Schorer, C. E. "'One Cotton, of Acquia Creek, Husband of Ann Cotton." *AL* 22 (N 50) 342-5.

COX, WILLIAM (1805?-1847). Taft, K. B. "William Cox: Author of *Crayon Sketches.*" *AL* 16 (Mr 44) 10-8.

COZZENS, JAMES GOULD (1903-). Hicks, Granville. "The Reputation of James Gould Cozzens." *CE* 11 (Ja 50) 177-83; *EJ* 39 (Ja 50) 1-6.

CRAIGIE, PEARL R. (1867-1906). Howells, W. D. "The Fiction of John Oliver Hobbs." *NAR* 183 (21 D 06) 1251-61.

CRANCH, CHRISTOPHER PEARSE (1813-92). Levenson, J. C. "Christopher Pearse Cranch: The Case History of a Minor Artist in America." *AL* 21 (Ja 50) 415-26.

Lind, S. E. "Christopher Pearse Cranch's 'Gnosis': An Error in Title." *MLN* 57 (N 47) 486-8.

CRANE, HART (1899-1932). Anon. "Lettere inedite epoesie scelte." *Inventario* (Au, Wi 46-47) 3, 4.

Beach, J. W. "The Cancelling Out—A Note in Recent Poetry." *Accent* 7 (Su 47) 245-6.

Birss, J. H. "American First Editions: (Harold) Hart Crane (1892-1932)." *Pub W* 125 (16 Je 34) 2223.

Blake, Howard. "Thoughts on Modern Poetry." *SR* 43 (Ap-Je 35) 187-96.

Cowley, Malcolm. "Remembering Hart Crane." *NRp* 104 (14 Ap 41) 504-6.

——— "The Roaring Boy." *NRp* 91 (9 Je 37) 134.

Crane, Hart. "A Discussion with Hart Crane." *Poetry* 25 (O 26) 34-41.

——— "Lettere inedite a poesie scelte." *Inventario* 1 (Au-Wi 46-47) 89-97.

——— "Letters." *H&H* 7 (Jl-S 34) 677-82.

Frank, Joseph. "Hart Crane: American Poet." *SR* 57 (Wi 49) 156-8.

Frank, Waldo. "An Introduction to Hart Crane." *NRp* 74 (15 F 33) 11-6.

Ghiselin, Brewster. "Bridge into the Sea." *PR* 16 (Jl 49) 679-86.

Herman, Barbara. "The Language of Hart Crane." *SR* 58 (Wi 50) 52-67.

Hoffman, F. J. "The Technological Fallacy in Contemporary Poetry: Hart Crane and MacKnight Black." *AL* 21 (Mr 49) 94-107.

Horton, Philip. "The Greenberg Manuscript and Hart Crane's Poetry." *So R* 2 (Su 36) 148-59.

Larrabee, A. "Three Studies in Modern Poetry." *Accent* 3 (Wi 43) 115-21.

Leavis, F. R. "Hart Crane from This Side." *Scrutiny* 7 (Mr 39) 443-6.

Loveman, Samuel. "Hart Crane." *Bodley Book Shop Cat* 92 (1947) 63-4.

Lundkvist, Artur. "Hart Crane." *Ord och Bild* (Stockholm) 51 (1942) 411-4.

Monroe, Harriet. "A Discussion with Hart Crane." *Poetry* 29 (O 26) 34-41.

Moss, Howard. "Disorder as a Myth: Hart Crane's *The Bridge.*" *Poetry* 62 (Ap 43) 32-45.

Ramsey, Warren. "Crane and Laforgue." *SR* 18 (J-S 50) 439-49.

——— "Poesia e platonismo in Hart Crane." *Inventario* 1 (Au-Wi 46-47) 30-69.

Rice, P. B. "The Collected Poems of Hart Crane." *Symposium* 4 (O 33) 483-91.

Savage, D. S. "The Americanism of Hart Crane." *Horizon* 5 (My 42) 302-11.

Shockley, M. S. "Hart Crane's 'Lachrymae Christi.'" *UKCR* 16 (Au 49) 31-6.

Swallow, Alan. "Hart Crane." *UKCR* 16 (Wi 49) 103-18.

Tate, Allen. "Hart Crane and the American Mind." *Poetry* 40 (Jl 32) 210-6.

——— "In Memoriam: Hart Crane." *H&H* 5 (Jl-S 32) 612-9.

——— "A Poet and His Life." *Poetry* 50 (Jl 37) 219-24.
Taylor, Frajam. "Keats and Crane: An Airy Citadel." *Accent* 8 (Au 47) 34-40.
Waggoner, H. H. "Hart Crane and the Broken Parabola." *UKCR* 8 (Su 45) 173-7.
——— "Hart Crane's Bridge to Cathay." *AL* 16 (My 44) 115-30.
Walcutt, C. C. "Crane's *Voyages.*" *Expl* 4 (My 46) 53.
Walton, E. L. "Hart Crane." *Nation* 136 (3 My 33) 508-9.
West, R. B. "Portrait of the Artist as American." *WR* 12 (Su 48) 247-51.
Winters, Yvor. "Hart Crane's Poems." *Poetry* 30 (Ap 27) 47-51.
——— "The Progress of Hart Crane." *Poetry* 36 (Je 30) 153-65.
Zabel, M. D. "The Book of Hart Crane." *Poetry* 42 (Ap 33) 33-9.

CRANE, STEPHEN (1871-1900). Anon. "The All Star Literary Vaudeville." *NRp* 47 (30 Je 26) 162.
——— "English Views of Stephen Crane." *Lit Dig* 21 (17 Jl 00) 13.
——— "How Stephen Crane 'Drew Off' His Poems." *Cur Op* 56 (Je 14) 460.
——— "The Last of Stephen Crane." *Lit Dig* 21 (1 D 00) 647.
——— "The New Art of Description in Fiction." *Lit Dig* 20 (10 F 00) 183.
——— "Redeeming the Red Badge of Courage." *Bkm* 35 (My 04) 235-6.
——— "Revival of Interest in Stephen Crane." *Cur Op* 76 (Ja 24) 39.
——— "Stephen Crane: 'A Wonderful Boy.'" *Lit Dig* 20 (23 Je 00) 750.
——— "Stephen Crane as the American Pioneer of the Free Verse Army." *Cur Op* 62 (Mr 17) 202-3.
——— "A Stephen Crane Letter. . . ." *Colophon* 4 (1930) 1-4.
——— "The Work of Stephen Crane." *Book Buyer* 20 (Jl 00) 433-4.
Angoff, Charles. "A Fiction Without Women." *Am Merc* 33 (N 34) 375-6.
"Applejoy, Petronius." "Stephen Crane Is News." *Cath World* 151 (Ag 40) 586-94.
Barney, E. C. "Stephen Crane." *Overland Mo* ns 90 (D 32) 309.
Barry, J. D. "A Note on Stephen Crane." *Bkm* 13 (Ap 01) 148.
Bates, H. E. "Stephen Crane: A Neglected Genius." *Bkm* 81 (O 31) 10-1.
Beer, Thomas. "Fire Feathers." *SRL* 2 (19 D 25) 425-7.
——— "Henry and the Hat." *Vanity Fair* 18 (Ag 22) 63, 88.
——— "Mrs. Stephen Crane." *Am Merc* 31 (Mr 34) 289-95.
Birss, J. H. "The Death of Stephen Crane." *SRL* 10 (25 N 33) 288.
——— "A Letter of Stephen Crane." *N&Q* 166 (7 Ap 34) 240-1.
——— "Stephen Crane: Letter and Bibliographical Note." *N&Q* 165 (7 O 33) 243.
Bohnenberger, Carl. "Stephen Crane and Robert Barr." *SRL* 10 (16 D 33) 352.
———, & Hill, N. M. "The Letters of Joseph Conrad to Stephen and Cora Crane." *Bkm* 69 (My, Je 29) 225-35, 367-74.
Bragdon, Claude. "The Purple Cow Period." *Bkm* 69 (Jl 29) 475-8.
Brooks, Van Wyck. "Reviewer's Note Book." *Freeman* 4 (18 Ja 22) 455.
Cather, Willa. "When I Knew Stephen Crane." *Library* 1 (23 Je 00) 17-8.
——— "When I Knew Stephen Crane." *Prairie Schooner* 23 (Fl 49) 231-7.
Coblentz, S. A. "Stephen Crane: A Literary Meteor." *N Y Times Book R* (30 D 23) 8.
Collamore, H. B. "The Collector's World." *Lit Observer* 1 (Je-Jl 34).
——— "Some Notes on Modern First Editions." *Colophon* ns 3 (Su 38) 358.
Conrad, Jessie. "Recollections of Stephen Crane." *Bkm* 63 (Ap 26) 134-7.
Conrad, Joseph. "Stephen Crane: A Note without Dates." *Bkm* 50 (F 20) 529-31.
Crane, H. R. "My Uncle, Stephen Crane." *Am Merc* 31 (Ja 34) 24-9.
Craven, Thomas. "Stephen Crane." *Freeman* 8 (22 Ja 24) 475-7.
Daskam, J. D. "The Distinction of Our Poetry." *Atl* 87 (My 01) 696-705.
Dell, Floyd. "Stephen Crane and the Genius Myth." *Nation* 119 (10 D 24) 637-8.
Dickason, D. H. "Stephen Crane and the *Philistine.*" *AL* 15 (N 43) 279-87.
Drake, J. F. "A Stephen Crane Letter." *Colophon* (D 30) Pt 4.
Dreiser, Theodore. "The Great American Novel." *Am Spect* 1 (D 32) 1.
Elconin, V. A. "Stephen Crane at Asbury Park." *AL* 20 (N 48) 275-89.

Fabian, R. C. "Stephen Crane Collection: Report for 1948." *Syracuse Un Alumni News* 30 (D 48) 11, (Ja 49) 11.
Feldman, Abraham. "Crane's Title from Shakespeare." *AN&Q* 8 (Mr 50) 185-6.
Follett, Wilson. "The Second Twenty-Eight Years: A Note on Stephen Crane, 1871-1900." *Bkm* 68 (Ja 29) 532-7.
Ford, F. M. "Stephen Crane." *Am Merc* 37 (Ja 36) 36-45.
——— "Stevie." *N Y Evening Post Lit R* (12 Jl 24) 881-2.
——— "Techniques." *So R* 1 (Jl 35) 20-35.
——— "Three Americans and a Pole." *Scribner's* 90 (O 31) 379-86.
French, Mansfield. "Stephen Crane, Ball Player." *Syracuse Un Alumni News* 15 (4 Ja 34) 1, 4.
Galsworthy, John. "Reminiscences of Conrad." *Scribner's* 77 (O 31) 3-10.
Garland, Hamlin. "Roadside Meetings." *Bkm* 70 (Ja 30) 523-8.
——— "Stephen Crane: Soldier of Fortune." *Sat Eve Post* 173 (28 Jl 00) 16-7.
——— "Stephen Crane as I Knew Him." *YR* ns 3 (Ap 14) 494-506.
Garnett, Edward. "A Gossip on Criticism." *Atl* 117 (F 16) 174-85.
——— "Some Remarks on English and American Fiction." *Atl* 114 (D 14) 747-56.
Gilder, J. B. "Stephen Crane." *Harper's W* 44 (16 Je 00) 560.
Gordon, Caroline. "Stephen Crane." *Accent* 9 (Sp 49) 153-7.
Gregory, Horace. "Stephen Crane's Poems." *NRp* 63 (25 Je 30) 159-60.
Griffith, O. L. "Stephen Crane." *Pub W* 102 (16 S 22) 813.
Hackett, Francis. "Another War: Stephen Crane's *Red Badge of Courage*." *NRp* 11 (30 Je 17) 250-1.
Harriman, K. E. "Last Days of Stephen Crane." *New Hope* 2 (O 34) 12-4.
——— "A Romantic Idealist." *Lit R* 4 (Ap 00) 85-7.
Hertzberg, M. J. "New and Old Data on Stephen Crane." *Torch* 4 (Ap 31) 36-8.
——— "Stephen Crane: A Pioneer Novelist." *World R* 1 (19 O 25) 74.
Hopkins, Claude. "Stephen Crane at Syracuse." *AL* 7 (Mr 35) 82-4.
Howells, W. D. "Editor's Easy Chair." *Harper's* 130 (Ap 15) 797.
Hubbard, Elbert. "Heart to Heart Talks." *Philistine* 11 (S 00) 123-8.
Johnson, Merle. "My Adventures with Stephen Crane." *Bookseller* (8 D 27) 12.
Johnson, W. F. "The Launching of Stephen Crane." *Lit Dig Int Book R* 4 (Ap 26) 288-90.
Jones, C. E. "Stephen Crane: A Bibliography of His Short Stories and Essays." *Bul Bibl* 15 (S-D 35) 149-50, (Ja-Ap 36) 170.
——— "Stephen Crane at Syracuse." *AL* 7 (Mr 35) 82-4.
Keet, A. E. "Stephen Crane, a New York Poet." *Bruno's W* 3 (2 S 16) 951-3.
Linson, C. K. "Stephen Crane." *Sat Eve Post* 177 (11 Ap 03) 19-20.
Littell, Robert. "Notes on Stephen Crane." *NRp* 54 (16 My 28) 391-2.
Lucky, R. E. "Appreciación del poeta Stephen Crane." *Revista Ibero-americana* 5 (O 42) 317-43.
Lüdeke, Henry. "Stephen Cranes Gedichte." *Anglia* 62 (My 38) 410-22.
Lynskey, Winifred. "Crane's *The Red Badge of Courage*." *Expl* 8 (D 49) 18.
McCormick, Lawlor. "If Stephen Crane Had Returned to Texas." *Bunker's Mo* 1 (F 28) 312-8.
Mangione, J. G. "Stephen Crane's Unpublished Letters." Syracuse Un *Chap Book* 2 (My 30) 8-10.
Mankiewicz, H. J. "The Literary Craft of Stephen Crane." *N Y Times Book R* (10 Ja 26) 7.
Martin, T. E. "Stephen Crane: Athlete and Author." Syracuse Un *Argot* 3 (Mr 35) 1-2.
Maurice, A. B. "Old Bookman Days." *Bkm* 66 (S 27) 20-6.
Molyneaux, Peter. "Had Stephen Crane Returned." *Bunker's Mo* 1 (F 28) 312-6.
Monroe, Harriet. "Stephen Crane." *Poetry* 14 (Je 19) 148-52.
Morris, L. R. "The Discourse of the Elders." *Outlook* 129 (14 S 21) 67-8.
Noxon, F. W. "The Real Stephen Crane." *Step Ladder* 14 (Ja 28) 4-9.

Nye, R. B. "Stephen Crane as a Social Critic." *Mod Q* 11 (Su 40) 48-54.
Oliver, Arthur. "Hersey Memories." *N J Hist Soc Proc* 16 (O 31) 454-63.
Overton, Grant. "Do You Remember 'The Red Badge of Courage'?" *Mentor* 17 (O 29) 62.
Paine, R. D. "The Life and Art of Stephen Crane." *Bkm* 58 (23 D 23) 470-1.
Pratt, L. U. "An Addition to the Canon of Stephen Crane." *Res Stud State Col Wash* 7 (1939) 55-8.
——— "The Formal Education of Stephen Crane." *AL* 10 (Ja 39) 460-71.
——— "A Possible Source for *The Red Badge of Courage.*" *AL* 11 (Mr 39) 1-10.
Pritchett, V. S. "Books in General." *New Statesman & Nation* 24 (8 Ag 42) 95.
Pugh, E. "Stephen Crane." *Bkm* (London) 67 (D 74) 162-4.
Randall, D. A., & Winterich, J. T. "One Hundred Good Novels: Crane, Stephen, 'The Red Badge of Courage.'" *Pub W* 136 (21 O 39) 1625-6.
Seitz, D. C. "Stephen Crane: War Correspondent." *Bkm* 76 (F 33) 137-40.
Sewall, R. B. "Crane's *The Red Badge of Courage.*" *Expl* 3 (My 45) 55.
Shroeder, J. W. "Stephen Crane Embattled." *UKCR* 17 (Wi 50) 119-29.
Sidbury, E. C. "My Uncle, Stephen Crane." *Lit Dig Int Book R* 4 (Mr 26) 248-50.
Smith, E. G. "Stephen Crane." *Lafayette Alumnus* 4 (F 32) 16.
Starrett, Vincent. "Stephen Crane." *Colophon* 2 (S 31) Pt 7.
——— "Stephen Crane: An Estimate." *SR* 28 (Jl 20) 405-13.
Stolper, B. J. R. "Unpublished Crane Material." *SRL* 10 (30 D 33) 380.
Van Doren, Carl. "Books and Affairs." *Century* 107 (Ja 24) 476.
——— "Stephen Crane." *Am Merc* 1 (Ja 24) 11-4.
Vosburgh, R. G. "The Darkest Hour in the Life of Stephen Crane." *Criterion* ns 1 (F 01) 26-7.
Walton, E. L. "Stephen Crane: A Poet in Parables." *N Y Times Book R* (14 S 30) 2.
Webster, H. T. "Wilbur F. Hinman's *Corporal Si Klegg* and Stephen Crane's *The Red Badge of Courage.*" *AL* 11 (N 39) 285-93.
Wells, H. G. "Stephen Crane from an English Standpoint." *NAR* 171 (Ag 00) 233-42.
Werner, W. L. "Stephen Crane and 'The Red Badge of Courage.'" *N Y Times Book R* (30 S 45) 4.
Wickham, Harry. "Stephen Crane at College." *Am Merc* 7 (Mr 26) 291-7.
Williams, A. W. "A Stephen Crane Collection." *Antiq Bkm* 1 (My 48) 717-8.
——— "Stephen Crane, War Correspondent." *New Colophon* 1 (Ap 48) 113-24.
Wilson, Edmund. "A Vortex of the Nineties." *NRp* 37 (2 Ja 24) 153-4.
Winterich, J. F. "Made in Japan." *SRL* 9 (28 Ja 33) 406.
——— "The Red Badge of Courage." *Pub W* 118 (20 S 33) 1303-7.
Woolcott, Alexander. "Stephen Crane's *Whilomville Stories.*" *SRL* 16 (23 O 37) 14.
Wyatt, Edith. "Stephen Crane." *NRp* 4 (11 S 15) 148-50.

CRAPSEY, ADELAIDE (1878-1914). Jones, Llewellyn. "Adelaide Crapsey: Poet and Critic." *NAR* 217 (Ap 23) 535-43.
Osborn, M. E. "Three Grey Women." *MLN* 45 (Je 30) 362-3.
——— "The Vocabulary in Adelaide Crapsey's Verse." *AS* 3 (Ag 38) 457-9.

CRAWFORD, FRANCIS MARION (1854-1909). Anon. "Marion Crawford." *Outlook* 91 (17 Ap 09) 856-7.
——— "Marion Crawford Memories." *Bkm* 36 (D 12) 366-9.
——— "Marion Crawford's Workshop." *Bkm* 38 (N 13) 232-3.
——— "The Novels of Mr. Marion Crawford." *Edinburgh R* 204 (Jl 06) 61-80.
Beerbohm, Max. "Crawford versus Dante." *Sat R* 122 (21 Je 02) 6-9.
Benson, A. B. "Marion Crawford's Dr. Claudius." *SS* 12 (F 33) 77-85.

Brett, G. P. "F. Marion Crawford: Novelist and Historian." *Outlook* 91 (24 Ap 09) 915-7.
Chapman, Grace. "Francis Marion Crawford: Some Observations on His Novels." *London Merc* 30 (Jl 34) 244-53.
Cooper, F. T. "Francis Marion Crawford—an Estimate." *Bkm* 29 (My 09) 283-92.
——— "Marion Crawford." *Forum* 41 (My 09) 488-91.
——— "Some Representative American Story Tellers: Francis Marion Crawford." *Bkm* 26 (O 07) 126-36.
Fraser, M. C. "Notes on a Romantic Life." *Collier's* 45 (23 Ap 10) 22-4.
Garrett, C. H. "A Talk with Marion Crawford." *Lamp* 27 (O 03) 216-8.
Hale, L. C. "Crawford's Rome." *Bkm* 15 (Je 02) 350-63.
Walpole, Hugh. "The Stories of Francis Marion Crawford." *YR* 12 (Jl 23) 673-91.
Wharton, Edith. "The Three Francescas." *NAR* 175 (Jl 02) 17-30.

CRÈVECOEUR, J. HECTOR ST. JOHN (1735-1813). Adams, P. G. "Crèvecoeur and Franklin." *Penn Hist* 14 (O 47) 273-9.
——— "Notes on Crèvecoeur." *AL* 20 (N 48) 327-33.
Blake, W. B. "Eighteenth-Century Travellers in America." *Dial* 52 (1 Ja 12) 5-9.
Bourdin, H. L., & Williams, S. T. "The American Farmer Returns." *NAR* 222 (S-N 25) 135-40.
——— "Crèvecoeur on the Susquehanna." *YR* 14 (Ap 25) 552-84.
——— "Crèvecoeur, the Loyalist; The Grotto: An Unpublished Letter." *Nation* 121 (23 S 25) 328-30.
——— "Hospitals [During the Revolution]: An Unpublished Essay by J. Hector St. John Crèvecoeur." *PQ* 5 (Ap 26) 157-65.
——— "Sketch of a Contrast between the Spanish and English Colonies." *Un Calif Chron* 28 (Ap 26) 152-63.
——— "The Unpublished Manuscripts of Crèvecoeur." *SP* 22 (Jl 25) 425-32.
Boynton, P. H. "A Colonial Farmer's Letters." *NRp* 3 (19 Je 15) 168-70.
Crèvecoeur, H. St. J. "Letter From St. Jean de Crèvecoeur to Monsieur Le Duc de la Rochefoucauld." *PMHS* 55 (N 21) 42-6.
Lawrence, D. H. "Studies in Classic American Literature (iii): Henry St. John de Crèvecoeur." *Eng R* 28 (Ja 19) 5-19.
Masterson, J. R. "The Tale of the Living Fang." *AL* 11 (Mr 39) 63-73.
Moore, J. B. "Crèvecoeur and Thoreau." *Papers Mich Acad Sci, Arts, and Letters* 5 (1926) 309-33.
——— "The Rehabilitation of Crèvecoeur." *SR* 35 (Ap 27) 216-30.
Rice, H. C. "The American Farmer's Letters." *Colophon* 5 (S 34) Pt 18.
Sanborn, F. B. "The American Farmer; St. John de Crèvecoeur and His Famous 'Letters.'" *PMHB* 30 (1906) 257-87.
Shelley, P. A. "Crèvecoeur's Contribution to Herder's 'Neger-Idyllen.'" *JEGP* 27 (Ja 38) 48-69.

CROCKETT, DAVID (1786-1836). Anon. "Letters of Davy Crockett." *Am Hist Mag* 5 (Ja 00) 41-7.
Bezanson, W. E. "Go Ahead, Davy Crockett!" *JRUL* 12 (Je 49) 33-7.
Blair, Walter. "Six Davy Crocketts." *Sw R* 25 (Jl 40) 443-62.
Brady, C. T. "David Crockett." *McClure's* 18 (Ja 02) 252-61.
Crowell, C. T. "Davy Crockett." *Am Merc* 4 (Ja 25) 109-15.
Dorson, R. M. "Davy Crockett and the Heroic Age." *SFQ* 6 (Je 42) 95-102.
Foster, A. P. "David Crockett." *Tenn Hist Mag* 9 (25) 166-77.
Loomis, C. G. "Davy Crockett Visits Boston." *NEQ* 20 (S 47) 396-400.
Porter, K. W. "Davy Crockett and John Horse: A Possible Origin of the Coonskin Story." *AL* 15 (Mr 43) 10-5.
Rourke, Constance. "Davy Crockett: Forgotten Facts and Legends." *Sw R* 19 (Ja 34) 149-61.

Shapiro, Irwin. "The All-American Hero." *SRL* 27 (1 Ap 44) 10-1.
Wade, J. D. "The Authorship of David Crockett's Autobiography." *Ga Hist R* 6 (S 22) 265-8.

CROTHERS, RACHEL (1878-). Anon. "Rachel Crothers—Peacemaker for American Social Comedy." *Theatre Arts* 16 (D 32) 971-2.

CROTHERS, SAMUEL McCHORD (1857-1927). Talbot, E. A. "Samuel McChord Crothers." *Mass Mag* 10 (Ja 17) 25-7.

CULLEN, COUNTEE (1903-). Bontemps, Arna. "The Harlem Renaissance." *SRL* 30 (22 Mr 47) 12-3, 44.
Dodson, Owen. "Countee Cullen (1903-1946)." *Phylon* 7 (Ja-Mr 46) 19-20.

CUMMINGS, EDWARD ESTLIN (1894-). Anon. Cummings Number. *Harvard Wake* 5 (Sp 46) 1-77.
——— "The Great 'I Am.'" *SRL* 9 (15 Ap 33) 533, 536.
Adams, R. M. "grasshopper's waltz: the poetry of e. e. cummings." *Cronos* 1 (Fl 47) 1-7.
Arthos, John. "The Poetry of E. E. Cummings." *AL* 14 (Ja 43) 372-83.
Axelrod, Joseph. "Cummings and Phonetics." *Poetry* 65 (N 44) 88-94.
Barrow, H. C., & Steinhoff, W. R. "Cummings' *Anyone Lived in a Pretty How Town*." *Expl* 9 (O 50) 1.
Bishop, J. P. "Incorrect English." *Vanity Fair* 18 (Jl 22) 20.
——— "The Poems and Prose of E. E. Cummings." *So R* 4 (Jl 38) 173-86.
Blackmur, R. P. "Notes on E. E. Cummings' Language." *H&H* 4 (Ja-Mr 31) 163-92.
——— "Twelve Poets." *So R* 7 (Su 41) 187-213.
Blum, W. C. "The Perfumed Paraphrase of Death." *Dial* 76 (Ja 24) 49-52.
Breit, Harvey. "The Case for the Modern Poet." *N Y Times Mag* (3 N 46) 58-61.
Brooker, Bertram. "The Poetry of E. E. Cummings." *Canadian Forum* 10 (Jl 30) 370-1.
Carver, George. "The Enormous Room." *Midland* 7 (N 22) 97-102.
Coblentz, S. A. "What Are They—Poems or Puzzles?" *N Y Times Mag* (13 O 46) 24, 50-3.
DeVries, Peter. "To Be." *Poetry* 64 (Je 44) 158-64.
Dos Passos, John. "Off the Shoals." *Dial* 73 (Jl 22) 97-102.
Finch, John. "New England Prodigal." *NEQ* 12 (D 39) 643-53.
Frankenberg, Lloyd. "An Obligation to Be Gay." *N Y Times Book R* (2 Ap 50) 5, 36.
Gregory, Horace. "The Collected Cummings." *NRp* 84 (27 Ap 38) 368-70.
Hayakawa, S. I. "Is Indeed 5." *Poetry* 52 (Ag 38) 284-92.
Horton, Philip, & Mangan, Sherry. "Two Views of Cummings." *PR* 4 (My 38) 58-63.
Jones, H. M. "The Imagination Does But Seem." *VQR* 8 (Ja 32) 143-50.
Kees, Weldon. "A Supplement from Cummings." *Poetry* 59 (D 41) 162-4.
Kohn, W. F. "The Romance of Actuality." *NRp* 45 (2 D 25) 60-1.
Lesemann, Maurice. "The Poetry of E. E. Cummings." *Poetry* 29 (D 26) 164-9.
Monroe, Harriet. "Flare and Blare." *Poetry* 23 (Ja 24) 211-5.
Moore, Marianne. "A Penguin in Moscow." *Poetry* 42 (Ag 33) 332-7.
——— "People Stare Carefully." *Dial* 80 (Ja 26) 49-52.
Moseley, E. M. "Cummings' *These Children Singing in a Stone A* (*50 Poems, 37*)." *Expl* 9 (O 50) 2.
Munson, G. B. "Syrinx." *Secession* 5 (Jl 23) 2-11.
North, J. N. "Visual Poetry." *Poetry* 31 (Mr 28) 334-8.
Rice, P. B. "Viva." *Symposium* 3 (Ap 32) 270-4.
Rosenfeld, Paul. "The Brilliance of E. E. Cummings." *Nation* 146 (26 Mr 38) 360-3.

——— "The Enormous Cummings." *Twice a Year* 3-4 (Fl-Wi 39, Sp-Su 40) 271-80.
Sage, Robert. "Roughneck Verse." *Transition* 3 (Je 27) 169-72.
Shapiro, Karl. "Prosody as Meaning." *Poetry* 73 (Mr 49) 336-51.
Spencer, Theodore. "50 Poems." *Furioso* 1 (Su 41) 55-6.
——— "Technique as Joy." *Harvard Wake* 5 (Sp 46) 25-7.
Steinberg, Jack. "Cummings *I x I*." *Expl* 8 (D 49) 17.
Tate, Allen. "Personal Convention." *Poetry* 39 (Mr 32) 332-7.
Troy, William. "Cummings' Non-land of Un-" *Nation* 136 (12 Ap 33) 413.
Van Doren, Mark. "First Glance." *Nation* 121 (8 Jl 25) 72.
Vowles, R. B. "Cummings' *Space Being . . . Curved*." *Expl* 9 (O 50) 3.
Wesenberg, A. B. "In Defense of Mr. Cummings." *NRp* 45 (30 D 25) 166.
Whiteley, M. N. S. "Savagely a Maker." *Poetry* 70 (Jl 47) 211-7.

CURTIS, GEORGE WILLIAM (1824-92). Adams, E. L. "George William Curtis and His Friends." *More Books* 14 (S, O 39) 291-303, 353-66.
Norton, Sara, & Howe, M. A. DeW. "War-time Letters of Charles Eliot Norton to George William Curtis." *Atl* 110 (N 12) 597-614.
Seybolt, P. S. "American First Editions: George William Curtis, 1824-1892." *Pub W* 128 (20 Jl 35) 173-4.
Ticknor, Caroline. "Some Early Letters of George William Curtis." *Atl* 114 (S 14) 363-76.

CUSHMAN, CHARLOTTE (1816-76). Smither, Nelle. "Charlotte Cushman's Apprenticeship in New Orleans." *La Hist Q* 31 (O 49) 973-80.

DABNEY, RICHARD (1787-1825). Bradsher, E. L. "Richard Dabney," *SR* 23 (Jl 15) 326-36.

DALY, AUGUSTIN (1839-99). Shipman, C. "Treasures of the Daly Library." *Critic* 36 (Mr 00) 213-9.

DANA, RICHARD HENRY (1787-1879). Anon. "Letters and Comment." *YR* ns 12 (Jl 23) 893-6.
Hoyt, W. D., Jr. "R. H. Dana, Sr. and the Lecture System, 1841." *NEQ* 18 (Mr 45) 93-6.

DANA, RICHARD HENRY, JR. (1815-82). Allen, Walter. "Books in General." *New Statesman & Nation* 31 (18 My 46) 361.
Gallery, D. V. "Too Far before the Mast." *Colophon* ns 2 (Au 36) 60-4.
Hart, J. D. "The Education of Richard Henry Dana, Jr." *NEQ* 9 (Mr 36) 3-25.
——— "An Eyewitness of Eight Months before the Mast." *New Colophon* 3 (1950) 128-31.
——— "Melville and Dana." *AL* 9 (Mr 37) 49-55.
——— "A Note on Sherman Kent's 'Russian Christmas before the Mast.'" *AL* 14 (N 42) 294-8.
——— "The Other Writings of Richard Henry Dana, Jr." *Colophon* 5 (D 34) Pt 19.
Humphry, James, III. "A Letter from Richard Henry Dana." *Colby Lib Q* ser 3: no 10 (My 49) 171-2.
Johnson, Merle. "American First Editions: Richard Henry Dana, Jr., 1815-1882." *Pub W* 119 (20 Je 31) 2891-2.
Kent, Sherman. "Russian Christmas before the Mast." *AL* 13 (Ja 42) 395-8.
London, Jack. "Classic of the Sea." *Independent* 71 (14 D 11) 1297-9.
Weidman, Jerome. "Two Years before the Mast: Richard Henry Dana, Jr." *Holiday* 2 (Ap 47) 123-7, 129, 131-2, 134.
Winterich, J. T. "Once More Westward Ho!" *Pub W* 125 (20 Ja, 17 F 34) 263-5, 791-3.
——— "Two Years before the Mast." *Pub W* 117 (15 Mr 30) 1581-5.

DARGAN, OLIVE TILFORD (*fl.* 1904-47). Knickerbocker, F. W. "American Writers." *TLS* (21 Mr 36) 244.

DAVIDSON, DONALD (1893-). Cater, Catherine "Four Voices Out of the South." *Mich Alumnus Q* (Wi 44) 166-73.
Millspaugh, C. A. "The Long Perspective." *Poetry* 54 (My 39) 108-11.
Monroe, Harriet. "Tennesseans." *Poetry* 31 (Ja 28) 222-4.
Warren, R. P. "A Note on Three Southern Poets." *Poetry* 40 (My 32) 103-13.

DAVIS, JAMES (*ca.* 1750). Perry, F. M. "James Davis, First North Carolina Printer." *Furman Bul* 20 (Ja 38) 21-8.

DAVIS, JOHN (1775-1854). Law, R. A. "The Bard of the Coosawhatchie." *Texas R* 7 (Ja 22) 133-56.

DAVIS, OWEN (1874-). Davis, Owen. "Why I Quit Writing Melodrama." *Am Mag* 78 (S 14) 28-31.

DAVIS, RICHARD HARDING (1864-1916). Anon. "Campaigner under Many Skies." *Outing* 46 (My 05) 183-7.
——— "Richard Harding Davis as Revealed by His Letters." *NRp* 14 (2 Mr 18) 149-50.
Archibald, J. F. J. "Richard Harding Davis: His Home At Marion—His Methods of Work." *Book Buyer* 25 (O 02) 216-20.
Gibson, C. D. "The First Glimpse of Davis." *Scribner's* 60 (Jl 16) 90.
McCutcheon, J. T. "With Davis in Vera Cruz, Brussels, and Salonika." *Scribner's* 60 (Jl 16) 91-7.
Maurice, A. B. "Richard Harding Davis—An Estimate." *Bkm* (My 16) 328-37.
——— "Some Representative American Story Tellers: Richard Harding Davis." *Bkm* 23 (Ap 06) 137-45.
Palmer, Frederick. "Richard Harding Davis." *Scribner's* 80 (N 26) 472-7.
Porter, W. H. "Mr. Davis and the Real Olancho." *Bkm* 15 (Ag 02) 557-61.
Roosevelt, Theodore. "Davis and the Rough Riders." *Scribner's* 60 (Jl 16) 89.
Wood, Leonard. "Richard Harding Davis." *Collier's* 57 (5 Ag 16) 19.

DAVIS, WILLIAM STEARNS (1877-1930). McKendrick, W. S. "William Stearns Davis." *Harvard Grad Mag* 38 (Je 30) 457-62.

DAWSON, WILLIAM (1704-52). Dean, H. L. "An Identification of the 'Gentleman of Virginia.'" *PBSA* 31 (1937) 10-20.

DAY, MAHLON (*ca.* 1750). Weiss, H. B. "Mahlon Day, Early New York Printer, Bookseller and Publisher of Children's Books." *BNYPL* 45 (D 41) 1007-21.

DE BOW, JAMES DUNWOODY BROWNSON (1820-67). Nixon, H. C. "J. D. B. De Bow, Publicist." *Sw R* 20 (Ja 35) 217-9.
Skipper, O. C. "J. D. B. DeBow, the Man." *J So Hist* 10 (N 44) 404-23.

DE CASSERES BENJAMIN (1873-1945). De Casseres, Benjamin, "Why I Am a Romantic." *Thinker* 4 (D 31) 66-9.

DEFOREST, JOHN WILLIAM (1826-1906). McIntyre, C. F. "J. W. DeForest, Pioneer Realist." *Un Wyo Pub* 9 (31 Ag 42) 1-3.

DELAND, MARGARET[TA] (1857-1945). Alden, H. M. "The Author of 'The Iron Woman.'" *Outlook* 99 (11 N 11) 628-32.
Ford, M. K. "Margaret Deland." *Bkm* 25 (Jl 07) 511-9.
Gould, M. D. "Of Margaret Deland and 'Old Chester.'" *Colby Lib Q* ser 2: no 10 (My 49) 167-71.

Howe, M. A. DeW. "Margaret Deland: A Study In Influences." *Outlook* 84 (24 N 06) 731-4.
Humphry, James. "The Works of Margaret Deland." *Colby Lib Q* ser 2: no 8 (N 48) 134-40.
Johnson, Merle. "American First Editions: Margaret Deland, 1857- ." *Pub W* 120 (21 N 31) 2328-9.
McDonald, Donald. "Childhood of Margaret Deland." *Outlook* 64 (17 F 00) 407-10.
Norris, Kathleen. "A Visit to Margaret Deland." *Woman's Home Companion* 42 (N 15) 5.

DELL, FLOYD (1887-). Anon. "Floyd Dell." *Bkm* 57 (Mr 23) 65-71.
Dell, Floyd. "A Literary Self-Analysis." *Mod Q* 4 (Je-S 27) 147-9.
Lewis, Sinclair. "Floyd Dell." *Bkm* 52 (My 21) 245.
Redman, B. R. "Moon-Calf Grows Up." *SRL* 10 (30 S 33) 141, 145.
Sutcliffe, Denham. "New Light on the Chicago Writers." *Newberry Lib Bul* ser 2: no 5 (D 50) 146-57.

DENNIE, JOSEPH (1768-1812). Leary, Lewis. "Joseph Dennie on Benjamin Franklin: A Note on Early American Literary Criticism." *PMHB* 72 (Jl 48) 240-6.
——— "Leigh Hunt in Philadelphia: An American Literary Incident of 1803." *PMBH* 70 (Jl 46) 270-80.
Randall, R. C. "Authors of the Portfolio Revealed by the Hall Files." *AL* 11 (Ja 40) 379-416.

DERBY, GEORGE HORATIO (1823-61). Bellamy, G. C. "Mark Twain's Indebtedness to John Phoenix." *AL* 13 (Mr 41) 29-43.
Farquhar, F. B. "The Topographical Reports of Lieutenant George H. Derby." *Calif Hist Soc Q* 11 (Je 32) 99-123.
Johnston, Charles. "First Jester of California." *Harper's W* 57 (17 My 13) 20.

DeVOTO, BERNARD (1897-). Lewis, Sinclair. "Fools, Liars, and Mr. DeVoto." *SRL* 17 (15 Ap 44) 9, 12.
Thourston, Jarvis. "Bernard DeVoto and Criticism." *Rocky Mt R* 7 (Sp-Su 43) 1, 9, 14-5.
Wilson, Edmund. "Complaints: II. Bernard DeVoto." *NRp* 89 (3 F 37) 405-8.

DICKINS, ASBURY (1780-1861). Nuermberger, R. K. "Asbury Dickins (1780-1861): A Career in Government Service." *N C Hist R* 24 (Je 47) 281-314.

DICKINSON, EMILY (1830-86). Anon. "An Emily Dickinson Letter." *Mt Holyoke Alumnae Q* 9 (Ja 26) 153-5.
——— "Excerpts from a letter dated Jan. 13, 1854, to Edward Everett Hale." *Autograph Album* 1 (D 33) 50.
——— "Two Unpublished Autograph Letters of Emily Dickinson." *Yale Un Lib Gaz* 6 (O 31) 42-3.
——— "The Wounded Poet." *TLS* (6 D 47) 628.
Abbott, L. R. "Emily Dickinson." *Outlook* 140 (10 Je 25) 211-3.
Aiken, Conrad. "Emily Dickinson." *Dial* 76 (Ap 24) 301-8; *Bkm* (London) 67 (O 24) 8-12.
Arms, George. "Dickinson's *I Love to See It Lap the Miles.*" *Expl* 2 (My 44) Q31.
——— "Dickinson's *These Are the Days When Birds Come Back.*" *Expl* 2 (F 44) 29.
———, *et al.*. "*Dickinson's A Bird Came Down the Walk.*" *Expl* 2 (Je 44).
Arnold, H. H. "'From the Garden We Have Not Seen': New Letters of Emily Dickinson." *NEQ* 16 (S 43) 363-75.
Baldi, S. "Appunti per uno studio selle poesia della Dickinson." *Letteratura* 6 (1942) 76-88.
Barbot, M. E. "Emily Dickinson Parallels." *NEQ* 14 (D 41) 689-96.

Barney, H. M. "Fragments from Emily Dickinson." *Atl* 139 (Je 27) 799-801.
———, & Carpenter, F. I. "Unpublished Poems of Emily Dickinson." *NEQ* 5 (Ap 32) 217-20.
Bass, Althea. "A Classmate of Emily Dickinson." *Colophon* 5 (D 34) Pt 19.
Bennett, M. A. "A Note on Josephine Pollitt's *Emily Dickinson: The Human Background of Her Poetry.*" *AL* 2 (N 30) 283-96.
Bianchi, M. D. "Emily Dickinson." *SRL* 1 (2 Ag 24) 1-2.
——— "Selections from the Unpublished Letters of Emily Dickinson to Her Brother's Family." *Atl* 115 (Ja 15) 35-42.
Bingham, M. T. "Emily Dickinson's Handwriting—A Master Key." *NEQ* 22 (Je 49) 229-34.
——— "Poems of Emily Dickinson: Hitherto Published Only in Part." *NEQ* 20 (Mr 47) 3-50.
Birss, J. H. "Emily Dickinson: A Bibliographical Note." *N&Q* 164 (17 Je 33) 421; 165 (15 Jl 33) 29.
——— "A Letter of Emily Dickinson." *N&Q* 163 (17 D 32) 441.
Blackmur, R. P. "Emily Dickinson: Notes on Prejudice and Fact." *So R* 3 (Aut 37) 325-47.
Bloom, Margaret. "Emily Dickinson and Dr. Holland." *Un Calif Chron* 35 (Ja 33) 96-103.
Blunden, Edmund. "Emily Dickinson." *Nation and Athenaeum* 46 (22 Mr 30) 863.
Boynton, P. H. "A New England Nun." *NRp* 39 (25 Je 24) 130-1.
Bradford, Gamaliel. "Emily Dickinson." *Atl* 125 (F 20) 216-26.
Brégy, K. "Emily Dickinson: A New England Anchoress." *Cath World* 120 (D 24) 344-54.
Brown, R. W. "A Sublimated Puritan." *SRL* 5 (6 O 28) 186-7.
Burroughs, F. W. "The Single Hound." *N E Mag* ns 52(D 14) 165-6.
Campbell, H. M. "Dickinson's *The Last Night That She Lived.*" *Expl* 8 (My 50) 54.
Carpenter, F. I. "Dickinson's *Farther in Summer than the Birds.*" *Expl* 8 (Mr 50) 33.
Catel, Jean, "Emily Dickinson: Essai d'Analyse Psychologique." *Revue Anglo-Am* 2 (1925) 394-405.
——— Emily Dickinson, L'Oeuvre." *Revue Anglo-Am* 2 (1925) 105-20.
——— "Sur Emily Dickinson. À Propos de deux livres." *Revue Anglo-Am* 13 (D 35) 140-4.
Chadwick, H. C. "Emily Dickinson: A Study." *Personalist* 10 (O 29) 256-69.
Childs, H. E. "Emily Dickinson, Spinster." *WHR* 3 (O 49) 303-9.
Comings, L. L. "Emily Dickinson." *Mt Holyoke Alumnae Q* 8 (O 24) 133-9.
Connors, D. F. "The Significance of Emily Dickinson." *CE* 3 (Ap 42) 624-33.
Davidson, Frank. "A Note on Emily Dickinson's Use of Shakespeare." *NEQ* 18 (S 45) 407-8.
——— "Some Emily Dickinson Letters." *Ind Q for Bookmen* 1 (O 45) 113-5.
Deutsch, Babette. "Miracle and Mystery." *Poetry* 66 (Ag 45) 274-80.
——— "A Sojourn in Infinity." *Bkm* 69 (My 29) 303-6.
Erskine, John. "The Dickinson Saga." *YR* 35 (S 45) 74-83.
Fletcher, J. G. "Woman and Poet." *SRL* 1 (30 Ag 24) 77-8.
Frank, Josef. "Emily Dickinson (1830-1881)." *Prisma* 6 (Ap 47) 21-3.
French, Yvonne. "Chronicles: Poetry." *London Merc* 29 (D 33) 161-3.
Frump, Timothy. "Emily Dickinson: A Song." *N&Q* 165 (2 D 33) 386.
Glenn, Eunice. "Emily Dickinson's Poetry: A Revaluation." *SR* 51 (O-D 43) 574-88.
Graves, L. B. "The Likeness of Emily Dickinson." *HLB* 1 (Sp 47) 248-51.
Green, C. B. "A Reminiscence." *Bkm* 60 (N 24) 291-3.
Hartley, Marsden. "Emily Dickinson." *Dial* 65 (15 Ag 18) 95-7.
Hillyer, Robert. "Emily Dickinson." *Freeman* 6 (18 O 22) 129-31.

Hindus, Milton. "Emily's Prose: A Note." *KR* 2 (Wi 40) 88-91.
Humiliata, Sister Mary. "Emily Dickinson—Mystic Poet?" *CE* 12 (D 50) 144-9.
Humphries, Rolfe. "A Retouched Portrait." *Measure* (My 24) 16.
James, Sister Mary. "Emily's Neighborhood." *Cath World* 158 (N 43) 143-9.
Kelcher, Julia. "The Enigma of Emily Dickinson." *NMQ* 2 (N 32) 326-32.
Keys, F. W. "A Poet in Time and Space." *NAR* 219 (Je 24) 905-12.
Kirby, J. P. "Dickinson's *A Bird Came Down the Walk*." *Expl* 2 (Je 44) 61.
Klett, A. M. "Doom and Fortitude: A Study of Poetic Metaphor in Annette von Droste-Hülshoff (1797-1848) and Emily Dickinson (1830-1886)." *Monatshefte für Deutschen Unterricht* 37 (Ja 45) 37-54.
Kurth, P. "Emily Dickinson in Her Letters." *Thought* 4 (D 29) 430-9.
Larrabee, A. "Three Studies in Modern Poetry." *Accent* 3 (Wi 43) 115-21.
Lindqvist, Ebba. "Emily Dickinson efter många år." *Ord Och Bild* (Stockholm) 55 (1946) 581-5.
Linscott, R. N. "Emily Dickinson." *Bkm* 71 (Ap-My 30) 228.
MacLean, Kenneth. "Mail from *Tunis*." *UTQ* 20 (O 50) 27-32.
McLean, S. R. "Emily Dickinson at Mount Holyoke." *NEQ* 7 (Mr 34) 25-42.
McNaughton, R. F. "Emily Dickinson on Death." *Prairie Schooner* 23 (Su 49) 203-15.
——— "The Imagery of Emily Dickinson." *Un Neb Stud* 4 (Ja 49) 16-22.
Marcellino, Ralph. "Emily Dickinson." *CE* 7 (N 45) 102-3.
——— "Simonides and Emily Dickinson." *Class J* 42 (D 46) 140.
Matthiessen, F. O. "The Problem of the Private Poet." *KR* 7 (Aut 45) 584-97.
Maynard, Theodore. "The Mystery of Emily Dickinson." *Cath World* 134 (O 31) 70-81.
Miles, Susan. "The Irregularities of Emily Dickinson." *London Merc* 13 (D 25) 145-58.
Monroe, Harriet. "The Single Hound." *Poetry* 5 (D 14) 138-40.
Moore, Marianne. "Emily Dickinson." *Poetry* 41 (Ja 33) 219-26.
Moran, Helen. "Queens Now." *London Merc* 26 (Je 32) 138-46.
Morse, S. F. "Emily Dickinson." *NRp* 86 (15 Ap 36) 282.
Moseley, Edwin. "The Gambit of Emily Dickinson." *UKCR* 16 (Au 49) 11-9.
Parton, Ethel. "Emily Dickinson." *Outlook* 136 (23 Ap 24) 701-2.
Pattee, F. L. "Gentian, Not Rose: The Real Emily Dickinson." *SR* 45 (Ap-Je 37) 180-97.
Pearson, E. L. "Two Poets." *Outlook* 137 (23 Jl 24) 479.
Phelps, W. L. "As I Like It." *Scribner's* 95 (Ap 34) 290.
Pohl, F. J. "The Emily Dickinson Controversy." *SR* 41 (O-D 33) 467-82.
——— "The Poetry of Emily Dickinson." *Amherst Mo* 25 (My 10) 47-50.
Pommer, H. F. "Dickinson's *The Soul Selects Her Own Society*." *Expl* 3 (F 45).
Powell, Desmond. "Emily Dickinson." *Colo Col Pub* Gen ser 200 (My 34) 1-12.
Prescott, F. C. "Emily Dickinson's *Further Poems*." *AL* 1 (N 29) 306-7.
Price, W. J. "Three Forgotten Poetesses." *Forum* 47 (Mr 12) 361-6.
Root, E. M. "Clothes vs. Girl." *Measure* (My 24) 15-18.
R. "Letters from Amherst." *Chri Sci Mon* 29 (30 Je 37) 7.
Sapir, Edward. "Emily Dickinson, A Primitive." *Poetry* 26 (My 25) 97-105.
Schappes, M. U. "Errors in Mrs. Bianchi's Edition of Emily Dickinson's Letters." *AL* 4 (Ja 33) 369-84.
Scott, A. G. "Emily Dickinson's 'Three Gems.'" *NEQ* 16 (D 43) 627-8.
Scott, Wilbur. "Dickinson's *I'll Tell You How the Sun Rose*." *Expl* 7 (N 48) 14.
Sergeant, E. S. "An Early Imagist." *NRp* 4 (14 Ag 15) 52-4.
Sewall, R. B. "Dickinson's *To Undertake Is to Achieve*." *Expl* 6 (Je 48) 51.
Shackford, M. H. "The Poetry of Emily Dickinson." *Atl* 111 (Ja 13) 93-7.
Sherrer, G. B. "A Study of Unusual Verb Construction in the Poems of Emily Dickinson." *AL* 7 (Mr 35) 37-46.
Smith, Grover. "Dickinson's *A Route of Evanescence*." *Expl* 7 (My 49) 54.

Smith, R. St. C. "Dickinson's *I Dreaded That First Robin So*." *Expl* 5 (F 47) 31.
——— "Emily Dickinson: A Bibliographical Note." *N&Q* 193 (1 My 48) 188-9.
Starke, A. H. "Emily Dickinson as a Great Unknown." *Am Book Coll* 5 (Ag-S 34) 245-6.
Strachan, Pearl. "Poets Have Something to Say." *Chri Sci Mon* 40 (14 F 48) 5.
Taggard, Genevieve. "Emily Dickinson." *Nation* 119 (8024) 8-9.
——— "A Little 'Scholar' of 1848." *J Adult Ed* 2 (Ja 30) 75-6.
Tate, Allen. "Emily Dickinson." *Outlook* 149 (15 Ag 28) 621-3.
——— "New England Culture and Emily Dickinson." *Symposium* 3 (Ap 32) 206-26.
Todd, M. L. "Emily Dickinson's Literary Debut." *Harper's* 160 (Mr 30) 471.
Trueblood, C. K. "Emily Dickinson." *Dial* 80 (Ap 26) 301-11.
Untermeyer, Louis. "Emily Dickinson." *SRL* 6 (5 Jl 30) 1169-71.
——— "Thoughts after a Centenary." *SRL* 7 (20 Je 31) 905-6.
Van der Vat, R. "Emily Dickinson (1830-1886)." *Eng Stud* 21 (D 36) 241-60.
Weber, C. J. "Two Notes from Emily Dickinson." *Colby Col Q* 15 (Je 46) 239-40.
Wells, A. M. "Early Criticism of Emily Dickinson." *AL* 1 (N 29) 243-59.
Wells, Carolyn. "Lavinia Dickinson." *Colophon* (S 30) Pt 3.
West, R. B. "Emily's Forest." *Rocky Mt R* 5 (Sp-Su 41) 1.
Whicher, G. F. "A Chronological Grouping of Some of Emily Dickinson's Poems." *Colophon* 4 (Mr 34) Pt 16.
——— "The Deliverance of Emily Dickinson." *N Y Herald Tribune Book R* (13 Ag 50) 2, 12.
——— "Emily's Lover." *N Y Herald Tribune Books* 6 (2 Mr 30) 2.
——— "In Emily Dickinson's Garden." *Atl* 177 (F 46) 64-70.
——— "Some Uncollected Poems by Emily Dickinson." *AL* 20 (Ja 49) 436-40.
———, & Bingham, M. T. "Emily Dickinson's Earliest Friend." *AL* 6 (Mr 34) 3-17, 191-3.
White, William. "Two Unlisted Emily Dickinson Poems." *Colby Lib Q* 3 (F 48) 69-70.
Whiteside, M. B. "Poe and Dickinson." *Personalist* 15 (Aut 34) 315-26.
Wyck, W. V. "Emily Dickinson's Songs Out of Sorrow." *Personalist* 18 (Ap 37) 183-9.
Zabel, M. D. "Christina Rossetti and Emily Dickinson." *Poetry* 37 (Ja 31) 213-6.

DICKINSON, JOHN (1732-1808). Brunhouse, R. L. "The Effect of the Townshend Acts in Pennsylvania." *PMHB* 54 (O 30) 355-73.
Hooker, R. J. "John Dickinson on Church and State." *AL* 16 (My 44) 82-98.
Powell, J. H. "John Dickinson and the Constitution." *PMHB* 60 (Ja 36) 1-14.
——— "John Dickinson, President of the Delaware State, 1781-1782." *Del Hist* (Ja, Jl 46) 1-54, 111-34.
Tolles, F. B. "Light on John Dickinson." *Friends Intelligencer* 104 (1 F 47) 56.

DICKINSON, JONATHAN (1688-1747). Andrews, C. M. "God's Protecting Providence: A Journal of Jonathan Dickinson." *Fla Hist Q* 21 (O 42) 107-26.

DIGGES, THOMAS ATWOOD (1741?-1821?). Elias, R. H. "The First American Novel." *AL* 12 (Ja 41) 419-34.

DILLON, GEORGE (1906-). Freer, A. L. "Baudelaire in English." *Poetry* 48 (Je 36) 158-62.
Lovett, R. M. "George Dillon's Second Volume." *Poetry* 39 (Mr 32) 328-32.
Luhrs, Marie. "Spring Snow." *Poetry* 31 (Mr 28) 343-5.
Untermeyer, Louis. "Three Younger Poets." *EJ* 21 (D 32) 787-99.

DOOLITTLE, HILDA (1886-). Anon. "Hilda Doolittle (H. D.)." *Wilson Bul* 5 (F 31) 356.
Blackmur, R. P. "The Lesser Satisfactions." *Poetry* 41 (N 32) 94-100.

Bryher, W. "Spear-Shaft and Cyclamen-Flower." *Poetry* 19 (Mr 22) 333-7.
Doggett, F. A. "H. D.: A Study in Sensitivity." *SR* 37 (Ja 29) 1-9.
Fletcher, J. G. "From 75 B.C. to 1925 A.D." *SRL* 3 (1 Ja 27) 482.
——— "H. D.'s Vision." *SR* 37 (Ja-Mr 29) 1-9.
Flint, T. S. "The Poetry of H. D." *Egoist* 2 (1 My 15) 72-3.
Macklin, Thomas. "Analysis of Experience in Lyric Poetry." *CE* 9 (Mr 48) 320.
Monroe, Harriet. "H. D." *Poetry* 26 (Ag 25) 268-75.
Seiffert, M. A. "Glacial Bloom." *Poetry* 25 (D 24) 160-4.
Sinclair, May. "The Poems of 'H.D.'" *Fortnightly R* ns 121 (1 Mr 27) 329-45.
Untermeyer, Louis. "The Perfect Imagist." *SRL* 1 (8 N 24) 260.
Watts, H. H. "H. D. and the Age of Myth." *SR* 56 (Sp 48) 287-303.
Williams, W. C. "Something for a Biography." *Gen Mag & Hist Chron* 50 (Su 48) 211-3.

DOS PASSOS, JOHN (1896-). Anon. "Soviet Literature and John Dos Passos." *International Lit* 5 (1933-4) 103-12.
Adams, J. D. "Speaking of Books." *N Y Times Book R* (13 F 48) 2.
Beach, J. W. "Dos Passos: 1947." *SR* 55 (Su 47) 406-18.
Blanck, Jacob. "Exploding the 'Three Soldiers' Myth." *Pub W* 135 (18 Je 38) 2377-8.
Blum, W. C. "A Moralist in the Army." *Dial* 71 (21 N 21) 606-8.
Bower-Shore, C. "John Dos Passos." *Bkm* (London) 85 (D 33) 198-9.
Bradford, C. B. "John Dos Passos—A Defense." *Un R* 8 (Su 42) 267-72.
Calmer, Alan. "John Dos Passos." *SR* 40 (Jl-S 32) 341-9.
Chamberlain, John. "John Dos Passos." *SRL* 20 (3 Je 39) 3-4, 14-5.
Colum, Padriac. "Airways, Inc." *Dial* 86 (My 29) 442.
Cowley, Malcolm. "Afterthoughts on John Dos Passos." *NRp* 88 (9 S 36) 134.
——— "Dos Passos and His Critics." *NRp* 120 (28 F 49) 21-3.
——— "The Poet and the World." *NRp* 70 (27 Ap 32) 303-5.
——— "Reviewers on Parade." *NRp* 93 (2 F 38) 371-2; 94 (9 F 38) 23-4.
Dawson, Coningsby. "Insulting the Army." *N Y Times Book R* (2 O 21) 1, 16-7.
DeVoto, Bernard. "John Dos Passos: Anatomist of Our Times." *SRL* 14 (8 Ag 36) 3-4, 12-3.
Dos Passos, John. "The Business of a Novelist." *NRp* 78 (4 Ap 34) 220.
——— "A Communication." *NRp* 63 (13 Ag 30) 371-2.
Farrell, J. T. "Dos Passos and the Critics." *Am Merc* 47 (Ag 39) 489-94.
Footman, R. H. "John Dos Passos." *SR* 47 (Jl 39) 365-82.
Frohock, W. M. "John Dos Passos: Of Time and Frustration." *Sw R* 33 (Wi, Sp 48) 71-80, 170-9.
Geismar, Maxwell. "Young Sinclair Lewis and Old Dos Passos." *Am Merc* 56 (Mr 43) 624-8.
Gibson, William. "A Dos Passos Checklist." *Book Coll J* 1 (Ap, My 36) 6, 9.
Gold, Michael. "Change the World." *Daily Worker* (26 F 38) 7.
——— "The Education of John Dos Passos." *EJ* 22 (F 33) 87-97.
Hackett, Francis. "Doughboys." *NRP* 28 (5 O 21) 162-3.
Hicks, Granville. "Dos Passos and His Critics." *Am Merc* 68 (My 49) 623-30.
——— "Dos Passos's Gifts." *NRp* 68 (24 Je 31) 157-8.
——— "John Dos Passos." *Bkm* 75 (Ap 32) 32-42.
——— "Politics and John Dos Passos." *AR* 10 (Sp 50) 85-98.
Howe, Irving. "John Dos Passos: The Loss of Passion." *Tomorrow* 7 (Mr 49) 54-7.
Johnson, Merle. "American First Editions: John Dos Passos." *Pub W* 120 (18 Jl 31) 259.
Kallich, Martin. "Bibliography of John Dos Passos." *Bul Bibl* 19 (My-Ag 49) 231-5.
——— "John Dos Passos: Liberty and the Father Image." *AR* 10 (Sp 50) 99-106.

——— "A Textual Note on John Dos Passos' *Journeys between Wars.*" *PBSA* 43 (Jl-S 49) 346-8.
Latorre, Mariano. "John Dos Passos y su última novela." *Atenea* 15 (F 38) 216-22.
Leavis, F. R. "A Serious Artist." *Scrutiny* 1 (S 32) 173-9.
Lerner, Max. "America of John Dos Passos." *Nation* 143 (15 Ag 36) 187-8.
Lewis, Sinclair. "Manhattan at Last!" *SRL* 2 (5 D 25) 361.
McHugh, Vincent. "Dos Passos Trilogy Revalued." *N Y Times Book R* (5 S 43) 8.
Marshall, Margaret. "John Dos Passos." *Nation* 150 (6 Ja 40) 15-8.
Pierhal, Armand. "Le Grand romancier Dos Passos est à Paris." *Nouvelles Littéraires* (5 Je 37) 9.
Posani, Riccardo. "Recensione di 'The Grand Design.'" *Il Ponte* (Italy) (D 49) 1529.
Reid, J. T. "Spain as Seen By Some Contemporary Writers." *Hispania* 20 (My 37) 139-50.
Rosati, Salvatore. "John Dos Passos." *Nuova Antologia* 387 (16 Ap 35) 633-5.
Rugoff, Milton. "Dos Passos, Novelist of Our Time." *SR* 49 (O-D 41) 453-68.
Sartre, Jean-Paul. "A propos de John Dos Passos." *Situation* (Paris) 1 (1947) 14-25.
Schramm, W. L. "Careers at Crossroads." *VQR* 15 (Au 39) 629-30.
Schwartz, Delmore. "John Dos Passos and the Whole Truth." *So R* 4 (O 38) 351-67.
Sillen, Samuel. "Misadventures of John Dos Passos." *New Masses* 32 (4 Jl 39) 21-2.
Solow, Herbert. "Substitution at Left Tackle: Hemingway for Dos Passos." *PR* 4 (Ap 38) 62-4.
Soupault, Philippe. "John Dos Passos." *Europe* 34 (F 34) 282-6.
Trilling, Lionel. "The America of John Dos Passos." *PR* 4 (Ap 38) 26-32.
Wade, Mason. "Novelist of America: John Dos Passos." *NAR* 244 (Wi 37-8) 349-67.
Wilson, Edmund. "Dos Passos and the Social Revolution." *NRp* 58 (17 Ap 29) 256-7.
Whipple, T. K. "Dos Passos and the U. S. A." *Nation* 146 (19 F 38) 210-2.
Zelinski, C., & Pavlenko, P. "Russia to John Dos Passos." *Living Age* 343 (O 32) 178-9.

DOUGLAS, LLOYD (1877-1951). Anon. "The Robe: Novel of Early Christianity Has Become a Popular Classic." *Life* 23 (8 D 47) 90-4.
Bode, Carl. "Lloyd Douglas and America's Largest Parish." *Religion in Life* 19 (Su 50) 440-7.
——— "Lloyd Douglas: Loud Voice in the Wilderness." *Am Q* 2 (Wi 50) 340-52.

DRAKE, JOSEPH RODMAN (1795-1820). Birss, J. H. "American First Editions: Joseph Rodman Drake, 1795-1820." *Pub W* 127 (18 My 35) 1926.
Corning, A. E. "Joseph Rodman Drake." *Bkm* 41 (Jl 15) 574-6.
Wheelock, P. D. "Henry Eckford (1775-1832), an American Shipbuilder." *Am Neptune* 8 (Jl 47) 177-95.
White, F. M. "Honoring an American Poet." *Harper's W* 54 (2 Jl 10) 13-4.
Wilson, J. G. "The Author of 'The American Flag.'" *Century* 80 (Jl 10) 439-44.

DREISER, THEODORE (1871-1945). Anon. "An Arriving Giant in American Fiction." *Cur Lit* 53 (D 12) 696-7.
——— "Dreiser the Great." *Newsweek* 27 (25 Mr 46) 102.
——— "The Liberation of American Literature." *TLS* (15 Je 33).
Anderson, Sherwood. "Dreiser." *Little R* 3 (Ap 16) 5.
——— "Sherwood Anderson to Theodore Dreiser." *Am Spect* 1 (Je 33) 1.
Arnavan, Cyrille. "Theodore Dreiser and Painting." *AL* 17 (My 45) 113-26.
Auerbach, J. S. "Authorship and Liberty." *NAR* 207 (Je 18) 902-17.
Avary, M. L. "Success—and Dreiser." *Colophon* ns 3 (Au 38) 598-604.

Bercovici, Konrad. "Romantic Realist." *Mentor* 16 (My 30) 38-41.
Birss, J. H. "Record of Theodore Dreiser: A Bibliographical Note." *N&Q* 165 (30 S 33) 226.
Bizzari, E. "Dreiser postumo." *Fiera Letteraria* 6 (16 My 49) 6.
Bourne, R. S. "The Art of Theodore Dreiser." *Dial* 62 (14 Je 17) 507-9.
——— "Theodore Dreiser." *NRp* 2 (17 Ap 15) 7-8.
Boynton, Percy. "Theodore Dreiser." *EJ* 12 (Mr 23) 180-8.
Brooks, Van Wyck. "Theodore Dreiser." *UKCR* 16 (Sp 50) 187-97.
Broun, Heywood. "Tragedy in No Man's Land." *Stage* 13 (Ap 36) 35.
Brown, C. T. "Dreiser's *Bulwark* and Philadelphia Quakerism." *Bul Friends Hist Assn* 35 (Au 46) 52-61.
Burgum, E. B. "The America of Theodore Dreiser." *Book Find News* 2 (Mr 46) 10-1, 21.
Chamberlain, John. "Theodore Dreiser." *NRp* 89 (23 D 36) 236-8.
Chesterton, G. K. "Skeptic as Critic." *Forum* 81 (F 29) 65-9.
"Constant Reader." "Words, Words, Words." *NYr* 7 (30 My 31) 69-72.
Cowley, Malcolm. "Sister Carrie's Brother." *NRp* 116 (26 My 47) 23-5.
——— "The Slow Triumph of Sister Carrie." *NRp* 116 (23 Je 47) 24-7.
Dell, Floyd. "Mr. Dreiser and the Dodo." *Masses* 5 (F 14) 17.
——— "Talks with Live Authors: Theodore Dreiser." *Masses* 8 (Ag 16) 36.
Dreiser, Edward. "My Brother, Theodore." *Book Find News* 2 (Mr 46) 14-5.
Dreiser, Theodore. "The Early Adventures of *Sister Carrie*." *Colophon* 2 (F 31) Pt 5.
Duffus, R. L. "Dreiser." *Am Merc* 7 (Ja 26) 71-6.
Elias, R. H. "The Library's Dreiser Collection." *Un Penn Lib Chron* 17 (1950) 78-80.
——— "Theodore Dreiser: or, The World Well Lost." *Book Find News* 2 (Mr 46) 12-3, 22.
Fadiman, Clifton. "Dreiser and the American Dream." *Nation* 125 (19 O 32) 364-5.
Farrell, J. T. "'An American Tragedy.'" *N Y Times Book R* (6 Mr 45) 6, 16.
——— "James T. Farrell Revalues Dreiser's 'Sister Carrie.'" *N Y Times Book R* (4 Jl 43) 3.
——— "Some Aspects of Dreiser's Fiction." *N Y Times Book R* (29 Ap 45) 7, 28.
——— "Theodore Dreiser: In Memoriam." *SRL* 29 (12 Ja 46) 16-7, 27-8.
Fast, Howard. "Dreiser's Short Stories." *New Masses* 60 (3 S 46) 11-2.
Flanagan, J. T. "Theodore Dreiser in Retrospect." *Sw R* 31 (Au 46) 408-11.
Ford, F. M. "Theodore Dreiser." *Am Merc* 40 (Ap 37) 488-96.
Franz, E. W. "The Tragedy of the 'North Woods.'" *NYFQ* 4 (Su 48) 85-97.
Freeman, John. "An American Tragedy." *London Merc* 16 (O 27) 607-14.
Gilkes, Martin. "Discovering Dreiser." *New Adelphi* 2 (D 27, F 28) 178-81.
Gilman, Lawrence. "The Biography of an Amorist." *NAR* 203 (F 16) 290-3.
Gregory, Horace. "In the Large Stream of American Tradition." *N Y Herald-Tribune Books* (24 Mr 46) 1-2.
Hedges, M. H. "Mr. Dreiser." *Dial* 62 (19 Ap 17) 343.
Hellesnes, Nils. "Theodore Dreiser." *Syn og Segn* (Oslo) 53 (Mr 47) 116-20.
Hicks, Granville. "Theodore Dreiser." *Am Merc* 62 (Je 46) 751-6.
Huth, J. F., Jr. "Dreiser and Success: An Additional Note." *Colophon* ns 3 (Su 38) 406-10.
——— "Theodore Dreiser, Success Monger." *Colophon* ns 3 (Wi 38) 120-33.
——— "Theodore Dreiser: 'The Prophet.'" *AL* 9 (My 37) 208-17.
Jackson, Charles. "Theodore Dreiser and Style." *Book Find News* 2 (Mr 46) 16-7.
Johnson, A. T. "Realism in Contemporary American Literature: Notes on Dreiser, Anderson, Lewis." *Sw Bul* (S 29) 3-16.
Johnson, Merle, & Hopkins, F. M. "American First Editions . . . Theodore Dreiser, 1871- ." *Pub W* 107 (22 D 23) 1925.

Jones, H. M. "Theodore Dreiser—A Pioneer Whose Fame Is Secure." *N Y Times Book R* (13 Ja 46) 5.
Lawson, J. L. "Tribute to Theodore Dreiser." *Book Find News* 2 (Mr 46) 19.
Le Verrier, Charles. "Un Grand romancier américain: Theodore Dreiser." *Revue Hebdomadaire* (21 Ja 33) 280-95.
Ludlow, Francis. "Plodding Crusader." *CE* 8 (O 46) 1-7.
McCole, C. J. "The Tragedy of Theodore Dreiser." *Cath World* 132 (O 30) 1-7.
McDonald, E. D. "Dreiser before 'Sister Carrie.'" *Bkm* 67 (Je 28) 369-74.
Marx, Caroline. "Book Marks." *N Y World-Telegram* (25 S 36).
Mayberry, George. "Dreiser: 1871-1945." *NRp* 114 (14 Ja 46) 56.
Mencken, H. L. "The Dreiser Bugaboo." *Seven Arts* 2 (Ag 17) 507-17.
——— "The Life of an Artist." *NYr* 24 (17 Ap 48) 43-57.
Monroe, Harriet. "Dorothy Dudley's Frontiers." *Poetry* 43 (Ja 34) 208-15.
Powys, J. C. "An American Tragedy." *Dial* 75 (Ap 26) 7-13.
——— "Theodore Dreiser." *Little R* 2 (N 15) 7-13.
Radin, Edward. "The Original American Tragedy." *N Y Sunday Mirror Mag Sec* (26 Ja 47) 12-3.
Rolf, Edwin. "Theodore Dreiser." *Poetry* 77 (Je 46) 134.
Ross, W. O. "Concerning Dreiser's Mind." *AL* 18 (N 46) 233-43.
"Scavenger." "The Dionysian Dreiser." *Little R* 2 (O 15) 10-3.
Schneider, Isidor. "Dreiser . . . A Man of Integrity." *Book Find News* 2 (Mr 46) 18, 22.
——— "Theodore Dreiser." *SRL* 10 (10 Mr 34) 533, 534-5.
"Search-light." "Profiles: The Colossus of Children." *NYr* 1 (15 Ag 25) 6-7.
Sebestyén, Karl. "Theodore Dreiser at Home." *Living Age* 339 (D 30) 375-8.
Sherman, S. P. "The Naturalism of Mr. Dreiser." *Nation* 101 (2 D 15) 648-51.
Sillen, Samuel. "Dreiser's *J'Accuse*." *New Masses* 38 (28 Ja 41) 24-6.
Smith, E. H. "Dreiser, after Twenty Years." *Bkm* 53 (Mr 21) 27-39.
Taylor, G. R. S. "The United States as Seen by an American Writer." *Nineteenth Century* 100 (D 26) 803-15.
Tittle, Walter. "Glimpses of Interesting Americans." *Century* 110 (Ag 25) 441-7.
Tjader, Marguerite. "Dreiser's Last Year . . . 'The Bulwark' in the Making." *Book Find News* 2 (Mr 46) 6-7, 20.
Trilling, Lionel. "Dreiser and the Liberal Mind." *Nation* 162 (20 Ap 46) 466, 468-72.
Van Doren, Carl. "Jurgen in Limbo." *Nation* 115 (6 D 22) 613-4.
——— "Theodore Dreiser." *Nation* 112 (16 Mr 21) 400-1.
Vivas, Eliseo. "Dreiser, an Inconsistent Mechanist." *Ethics* 48 (Jl 38) 498-508.
Walcutt, C. C. "Naturalism in 1946; Dreiser and Farrell." *Accent* 6 (Su 46) 263-7.
——— "The Three Stages of Theodore Dreiser's Naturalism." *PMLA* 55 (Mr 40) 266-89.
Waldman, Milton. "A German-American Insurgent." *Living Age* 331 (1 O 26) 43-50.
——— "Theodore Dreiser." *London Merc* 14 (Jl 26) 283-91.
Walker, C. R. "How Big Is Dreiser?" *Bkm* 63 (Ap 26) 146-9.
Wallace, Margaret. "Books—A History Takes Shape." *Indep Woman* 25 (Jl 46) 209.

DU BOIS, WILLIAM EDWARD BURGHARDT (1868-). Redding, J. S. "Portrait: W. E. Burghardt Du Bois." *Am Schol* 18 (Wi 48-49) 93-6.

DUCHÉ, JACOB (1737-98). Hastings, G. E. "Jacob Duché, First Chaplain of Congress." *SAQ* 21 (O 32) 386-400.
Pennington, E. L. "The Work of the Bray Associates in Pennsylvania." *PMHB* 58 (Ja 34) 1-25.

DUNBAR, PAUL LAURENCE (1872-1906). Anon. "Dunbar—Negro Poet." *Chri Sci Mon* 29 (26 Jl 37) 141.

Achille, L. T. "Paul Laurence Dunbar: Poète nègre." *Revue Anglo-Américaine* 12 (Ag 34) 504-20.
Arnold, E. F. "Some Personal Reminiscences of Paul Laurence Dunbar." *J Negro Hist* 17 (O 32) 400-8.
Burch, C. E. "Dunbar's Poetry in Literary English." *Southern Workman* 50 (O 21) 469-73.
——— "The Plantation Negro in Dunbar's Poetry." *Southern Workman* 50 (My 21) 227-9.
Burnham, I. H. "Paul Lawrence Dunbar's Story as Told by His Mother." *MS* 4 (F 33) 3, 9.
Burris, A. M. "Bibliography of Works by Paul Laurence Dunbar . . ." *Am Coll* 5 (N 27) 69-73.
Chamberlain, John. "The Negro as Writer." *Bkm* 70 (F 30) 603-11.
Daniel, T. W. "Paul Laurence Dunbar and the Democratic Ideal." *Negro Hist Bul* 6 (Je 43) 206-8.
Howells, W. D. "Paul Laurence Dunbar." *NAR* 23 (Ap 06) 185-6.

DUNLAP, WILLIAM (1766-1839). Benson, A. B. "Scandinavian Influences on the Works of William Dunlap and Richard Alsop." *SS* 9 (N 27) 239-57.
——— "The Sources of William Dunlap's *Ella, a Norwegian Tale.*" *SS* 19 (N 46) 136-43.
Bowman, M. R. "Dunlap and the 'Theatrical Register' of the *New-York Magazine.*" *SP* 24 (Jl 27) 413-25.
Coad, O. S. "The Dunlap Diaries at Yale." *SP* 24 (Jl 27) 403-12.
——— "The Gothic Element in American Literature before 1835." *JEGP* 24 (1925) 72-93.
Woolsey, T. S. "The American Vasari." *YR* 3 (Jl 14) 778-89.

DUNNE, FINLEY PETER (1867-1936). Adams, F. P. "Mr. Dooley." *NRp* 84 (4 My 38) 390-1.
Canby, H. S. "Mr. Dooley and Mr. Hennessy." *SRL* 14 (9 My 36) 3-4.
Daly, T. A. "I See by th' Pa-apers." *SRL* 14 (9 My 36) 4, 16.
Hackett, Francis. "Mr. Dooley." *NRp* 20 (24 S 19) 235-6.
Kelleher, J. V. "Mr. Dooley and the Same Old World." *Atl* 177 (Je 46) 119-25.
McClure, H. H. "'Mr. Dooley,' Ph. D." *Am Mag* 65 (D 07) 173-4.
Werner, M. R. "Mr. Dooley Alias Peter Finley Dunne." *Bkm* 51 (Ag 20) 674-7.

DURANT, CHARLES S. (*fl.* 1837). Howe, Elizabeth. "A Forgotten Naturalist." *Lamp* 28 (Jl 04) 485-7.

DUYCKINCK, GEORGE (1823-63). Schubert, L. "A Boy's Journal of a Trip into New England in 1838." *EIHC* 86 (Ap 50) 97-105.

DWIGHT, JOHN SULLIVAN (1813-93). McCusker, Honor. "Fifty Years of Music in Boston." *More Books* 12 (O 37) 341-57.
Thomas, J. W. "John Sullivan Dwight: A Translator of American Romanticism." *AL* 21 (Ja 50) 427-41.

DWIGHT, TIMOTHY (1752-1817). Aldridge, A. O. "Timothy Dwight's Posthumous Gift to British Theology." *AL* 21 (Ja 50) 479-81.
Boynton, P. H. "Timothy Dwight and His Connecticut." *MP* 38 (N 40) 193-203.
Buchanan, L. E. "The Ethical Ideas of Timothy Dwight." *Res Stud State Col Wash* 13 (S 45) 185-99.
Ford, W. C. "Some Papers of Aaron Burr." *PAAS* ns 29 (Ap 19) 55-6.
Griswold, A. W. "Three Puritans on Prosperity." *NEQ* 7 (S 34) 475-93.
Hayward, Laurence. "An Early Writer of New England Travels." *N E Mag* ns 23 (N 00) 256-62.
Leary, Lewis. "The Author of *The Triumph of Infidelity.*" *NEQ* 20 (S 47) 377-85.

——— "Thomas Day on American Poetry: 1786." *MLN* 61 (N 46) 464-6.
Zunder, T. A. "Noah Webster and *The Conquest of Canäan.*" *AL* 1 (My 29) 200-2.

EAMES, WILBERFORCE (1855-1937). Lydenberg, H. M. "Wilberforce Eames, 1855-1937." *Am Lib Assn Bul* 22 (Ja 38) 25-7.
Wegelin, Oscar. "Wilberforce Eames, Bookseller." *Am Book Coll* 4 (N 33) 243-4.
Winship, G. P. "Wilberforce Eames: Bookman." *BNYPL* 42 (Ja 38) 3-9.

EARLE, ALICE MORSE (1853-1911). Averill, E. C. "Alice Morse Earle: Writer Who Popularized New England." *Old Time New England* 37 (Ja 47) 73-8.

EASTMAN, MAX (1883-). Eastman, Max. "Bunk about Bohemia." *Mod Mo* 8 (My, Je 34) 200-8, 240-300.
——— "John Reed and the Old Masses." *Mod Mo* 10 (O 36) 19-22.
Glicksberg, C. I. "Max Eastman: Literary Insurgent." *SR* 44 (Jl-S 36) 323-37.
Henderson, A. C. "Child of the Amazons." *Poetry* 3 (O 13) 31-3.
——— "Lazy Criticism." *Poetry* 9 (D 16) 144-9.
Kunitz, S. J. "A Note on Max Eastman." *New Masses* 15 (8 My 34) 24-5.
Mangan, Shirley. "Mush." *Poetry* 39 (O 31) 51-4.
Monroe, Harriet. "Poetry, a Zest for Life." *Poetry* 2 (Jl 13) 140-2.
——— "A Radical-Conservative." *Poetry* 15 (Mr 19) 322-6.
Mussey, H. R. "How to Change Things." *Nation* 127 (15 Ag 28) 159-60.
Scudder, V. D. "The Muse and the Causes." *Survey* 30 (5 Jl 13) 489-90.

EBERHART, RICHARD (1904-). Eberhart, Richard. "Eberhart's *Grave Piece.*" *Expl* 6 (F 48) 23.
——— "Eberhart's The Young Hunter." *Expl* 6 (F 48) 24.

EDMONDS, WALTER DUMAUX (1903-). Anon. "Walter D(umaux) Edmonds." *Cur Biog* 3 (S 42) 10-13.
Edmonds, W. D. "A Novelist Takes Stock." *Atl* 172 (Jl 43) 73-7.
Gay, R. M. "The Historical Novel: Walter D. Edmonds." *Atl* 165 (My 40) 656-8.
Kohler, Dayton. "Walter D. Edmonds: Regional Historian." *EJ* (Coll ed) 27 (Ja 38) 1-11.

EDWARDS, JONATHAN (1703-58). Anon. "A Contemporaneous Account of Jonathan Edwards." *J Presbyterian Hist Soc* 2 (D 03) 125-35.
Aldridge, A. O. "Benjamin Franklin and Jonathan Edwards on Lightning and Earthquakes." *Isis* 41 (Fl 50) 162-4.
——— "Jonathan Edwards and William Godwin on Virtue." *AL* 18 (Ja 47) 308-18.
Billings, T. H. "The Great Awakening." *EIHC* 65 (Ja 29) 89-104.
Burt, Struthers. "Jonathan Edwards and the Gunman." *NAR* 227 (Je 29) 712-8.
C., J. M. "Jonathan Edwards on Multidimensional Space and the Mechanistic Conception of Life." *Science* ns 52 (29 O 20) 409-10.
Cady, E. H. "The Artistry of Jonathan Edwards." *NEQ* 22 (Mr 49) 61-72.
Carpenter, F. I. "The Radicalism of Jonathan Edwards." *NEQ* 4 (O 31) 629-44.
Caskey, E. "If They Were Alive Today. Jonathan Edwards: The First American Philosopher." *Thinker* 4 (O 31) 34-5.
Darrow, Clarence. "The Edwardses and the Jukeses." *Am Merc* 6 (O 25) 147-57.
Davidson, Frank. "Three Patterns of Living." *AAUP Bul* 34 (Su 48) 364-74.
De Normandie, James. "Jonathan Edwards at Portsmouth, New Hampshire." *PMHS* 35 (Mr 01) 16-25.
De Wett, John. "Jonathan Edwards: A Study." *Princeton Theo R* 3 (Ja 04) 21-7.
Dexter, F. B. "On the Manuscripts of Jonathan Edwards." *PMHS* 15: ser 2 (1902) 2-16.
Faust, C. H. "Jonathan Edwards as a Scientist." *AL* 1 (Ja 30) 393-404.
Fisher, G. P. "The Value of Edwards for Today." *Congregationalist and Christian World* 88 (3 O 03) 469-72.

Gardiner, H. N. "The Early Idealism of Jonathan Edwards." *Philos R* 9 (N 00) 573-96.

Gohdes, Clarence. "Aspects of Idealism in Early New England." *Philos R* 39 (N 30) 537-55.

Haroutunian, J. G. "Jonathan Edwards: A Study in Godliness." *J Rel* 11 (Jl 31) 400-19.

——— "Jonathan Edwards: Theologian of the Great Commandment." *Theology Today* 1 (O 44) 361-77.

Harper, W. H. "Edwards: Devotee, Theologian, Preacher." *Interior* 34 (1 O 03) 1272-4.

Hayes, S. P. "An Historical Study of the Edwardean Revivals." *Am J. Psych* 13 (O 02) 550-74.

Hornberger, Theodore. "The Effect of the New Science upon the Thought of Jonathan Edwards." *AL* 9 (My 37) 196-207.

Johnson, T. H. "Jonathan Edwards and the 'Young Folks' 'Bible.'" *NEQ* 5 (Ja 32) 37-54.

——— "Jonathan Edwards as a Man of Letters." *Harvard Sum of Theses* (1934) 332-7.

——— "Jonathan Edwards' Background of Reading." *PCSM* 28 (1935) 193-222.

King, H. C. "Jonathan Edwards as Philosopher and Theologian." *Hartford Seminary R* 14 (N 03) 23-57.

MacCracken, J. H. "The Sources of Jonathan Edwards's Idealism." *Philos R* 11 (Ja 02) 26-42.

Miller, E. W. "The Great Awakening." *Princeton Theo R* 2 (O 04) 545-62.

Miller, Perry. "The Half-Way Covenant." *NEQ* 6 (D 33) 676-715.

——— "Jonathan Edwards on the Sense of the Heart." *Harvard Theo R* 41 (Ap 48) 123-45.

——— "Jonathan Edwards' Sociology of the Great Awakening." *NEQ* 21 (Mr 48) 50-77.

——— "Jonathan Edwards to Emerson." *NEQ* 13 (D 40) 589-618.

Orr, James. "Jonathan Edwards: His Influence in Scotland." *Congregationalist* 88 (3 O 03) 467-9.

Otto, M. C. "A Lesson for Jonathan Edwards." *Humanist* 1 (Jl 41) 38.

Phelps, W. L. "Edwards and Franklin, the Man of God and the Man of the World." *Ladies Home J* 39 (N 22) 16-7.

Rawley, W. E. "The Puritan's Tragic Vision." *NEQ* 17 (S 44) 394-417.

Riley, I. W. "The Real Jonathan Edwards." *Open Court* 22 (D 08) 705-15.

Schneider, H. W. "Jonathan Edwards." *Nation* 131 (26 N 30) 584-5.

Seitz, D. C. "Jonathan Edwards, Consistent Theologian." *Outlook* 143 (Je 26) 315-6.

Seldes, Gilbert. "Jonathan Edwards." *Dial* 84 (Ja 28) 37-46.

Slosson, E. E. "Jonathan Edwards as a Freudian." *Science* ns 52 (24 D 20) 609.

Squires, J. R. "Jonathan Edwards." *Accent* 9 (Au 48) 31-2.

Sullivan, Frank. "Jonathan Edwards, the Contemplative Life, and a Spiritual Stutter." *Los Angeles Tidings* (11 Mr 49) 27.

Suter, Rufus. "An American Pascal: Jonathan Edwards." *Sci Mo* 68 (My 49) 338-42.

——— "The Concept of Morality in the Philosophy of Jonathan Edwards." *J Rel* 14 (Jl 34) 265-72.

——— "The Philosophy of Jonathan Edwards." *Harvard Sum of Theses* (1932) 351-3.

Townsend, H. G. "Jonathan Edwards' Later Observations of Nature." *NEQ* 13 (S 40) 510-8.

——— "The Will and the Understanding in the Philosophy of Jonathan Edwards." *Church Hist* 16 (D 47) 210-20.

Upham, W. P. "Short-Hand Notes of Jonathan Edwards." *PMHS* 35 (F 02) 514-23.
Williams, S. T. "Six Letters of Jonathan Edwards to Joseph Bellamy." *NEQ* 1 (1928) 226-42.
Winship, E. A. "The Human Legacy of Jonathan Edwards." *World's Work* 6 (O 03) 3981-4.
Woodbridge, F. J. E. "Jonathan Edwards." *Philos R* 13 (Jl 04) 393-408.
Wright, Conrad. "Edwards and the Arminians on the Freedom of the Will." *Harvard Theo R* 35 (O 42) 241-61.
Zenos, A. C. "The Permanent and Passing in the Thought of Edwards." *Interior* 34 (1 O 03) 1274-5.

EGGLESTON, EDWARD (1837-1902). Bloom, Margaret. "Eggleston's Notes on Hoosier Dialect." *AS* 9 (D 34) 319-20.
Cary, Edward. "Dr. Edward Eggleston." *Book Buyer* 25 (O 02) 221-3.
Eggleston, G. C. "First of the Hoosiers." *Outlook* 78 (8 O 04) 382-3.
Flanagan, J. T. "The Hoosier Schoolmaster in Minnesota." *Minn Hist* 18 (D 37) 347-70.
——— "The Novels of Edward Eggleston." *CE* 5 (F 44) 250-4.
Haller, J. M. "Edward Eggleston, Linguist." *PQ* 24 (Ap 45) 175-86.
Nicholson, Meredith. "Edward Eggleston." *Atl* 90 (D 02) 804-9.
Randel, William. "Edward Eggleston's Library at Traverse de Sioux." *Minn Hist* 26 (S 45) 242-7.
——— "Zoroaster Higgins: Edward Eggleston as a Political Satirist in Verse." *AL* 17 (N 45) 255-60.
Rawley, J. A. "Edward Eggleston: Historian." *Ind Mag Hist* 40 (D 44) 341-52.
——— "Some New Light on Edward Eggleston." *AL* 11 (Ja 40) 453-8.
Spencer, B. T. "The New Realism and a National Literature." *PMLA* 56 (D 41) 1116-32.
Stone, Edward. "Edward Eggleston's Religious Transit." *Un Texas Stud Eng* 19 (1939) 210-8.
Tooker, L. F. "As I Saw It from an Editor's Desk: The Fiction of the Magazine." *Century* 108 (Je 24) 260-71.
Vest, E. B. "Where *The Hoosier School-Master* Was Written." *J Ill State Hist Soc* 41 (D 48) 475-6.

ELIOT, JOHN (1604-90). Eames, Wilberforce. "Discovery of a Lost Cambridge Imprint: John Eliot's *Genesis,* 1655." *PCSM* 34 (1943) 11-2.
——— "Three Letters of John Eliot." *Bul John Rylands Lib* 5 (Ag 18) 102-10.
Haraszti, Zoltán. "Eliot's Indian Bible." *More Books* 4 (Je 29) 217-22.
Orcutt, W. D. "John Eliot and His Indian Bible." *Chri Sci Mon* 27 (29 O 35) 283.
Powicke, F. J. "Some Unpublished Correspondence of the Rev. Richard Baxter and the Rev. John Eliot." *Bul John Rylands Lib* 15 (Ja, Jl 31) 138-76, 442-6.
Winship, G. P. "Cost of Printing the Eliot Indian Tracts, 1660." *PCSM* 26 (1927) 85-7.
——— "Letters to John Eliot, the Apostle." *PMHS* 53 (Je 20) 189-92.

ELIOT, THOMAS STEARNS (1888-). Anon. "Milton Lost and Regained." *TLS* (29 Mr 47) 140.
——— "Play for a Cathedral." *Chri Sci Mon* 28 (3 D 35) 30.
——— "Reflections." *Time* 55 (6 Mr 50) 22-6.
——— "Thomas Stearns Eliot." *St Louis R* 2 (14 Ja 33) 12-3.
——— "T. S. Eliot Goes Home." *Living Age* 343 (My 32) 234-6.
——— "T. S. Eliot Receives British Order of Merit." *Pub W* 153 (31 Ja 48) 632.
——— "You Must Meet Mr. Eliot." *Scholastic* 50 (10 F 47) 19.
Adair, P. M. "Mr. Eliot's *Murder in the Cathedral.*" *Cambridge J* 4 (N 50) 83-95.

Aiken, Conrad. "After Ash-Wednesday." *Poetry* 45 (D 34) 161-5.
——— "The Scientific Critic." *Freeman* 2 (2 Mr 21) 593-4.
Anceschi, Luciano. "Eliot e la poesia." *La Fiera Letteraria* (Italy) (14 N 48) 34.
——— "T. S. Eliot o delle difficoltà del mondo!" *La Rassegna d'Italia* 3 (Mr 49).
Anér, Kerstin. "Anglarna vid cocktailbricken." *Bonniers Litterära Magasin* 8 (O 50) 593-602.
Arms, G. W., *et al.* "Eliot's *Burbank with a Baedeker: Bleistein with a Cigar.*" *Expl* 3 (My 45).
Arrowsmith, William. "English Verse Drama II: The Cocktail Party." *Hudson R* 3 (Au 50) 411-31.
Astre, Georges-Albert. "T. S. Eliot et la nostalgie de la 'culture.'" *Critique* 5 (S 49) 774-811.
——— "T. S. Eliot, poète spirituel." *Critique* 4 (Ap, My 48) 307-14, 408-21.
Bain, Donald. "T. S. Eliot's *The Cocktail Party.*" *Nine* 2 (Ja 50) 16-22.
Baldini, G. "T. S. Eliot ha parlato a Roma." *Fiera Letteraria* 51 (18 D 47).
Barber, C. L. "T. S. Eliot after Strange Gods." *So R* 6 (Au 40) 387-416.
Barrett, William. "Dry Land, Dry Martini." *PR* 17 (Ap 50) 354-9.
Basler, R. P., & Kirschbaum, Leo. "Eliot's *Sweeney among the Nightingales.*" *Expl* 2 (D 43).
Bates, E. S. "T. S. Eliot: Middle Class Laureate." *Mod Mo* 7 (F 33) 17-24.
Battenhouse, R. W. "Eliot's 'The Family Reunion' as Christian Prophecy." *Christendom* 10 (Su 45) 307-21.
Benét, W. R. "T. S. Eliot and Original Sin." *SRL* 10 (5 My 34) 673, 678.
Bernadette, J. A. "Eliot's Water Imagery: An Adventure in Symbolism." *Adam* 18 (My-Je 50) 25-9.
Berti, L. "Intorno alle note aliotane sulla cultura." *Inventario* (Sp 46).
Blackmur, R. P. "T. S. Eliot." *H&H* 1 (Mr 28) 187-213.
——— "T. S. Eliot in Prose." *Poetry* 42 (Ap 33) 44-9.
——— *et al.* "Mr. Eliot and Notions of Culture: A Discussion." *PR* 11 (Su 44) 302-12.
Blissett, William. "The Argument of T. S. Eliot's *Four Quartets.*" *UTQ* 15 (Ja 46) 115-26.
——— "T. S. Eliot." *Canadian Forum* 28 (Jl 48) 86-7.
Boschere, Jean de. "T. S. Eliot." *L'Age Nouveau* (Paris) 33 (Ja 49) 18-23.
Bradford, Curtis. "Footnotes to *East Coker:* A Reading." *SR* 52 (Ja-Mr 44) 169-75.
——— "Journeys to Byzantium." *VQR* 25 (Sp 49) 205-25.
Breit, Harvey. "An Interview with T. S. Eliot—and Excerpts from His Birthday Book." *N Y Times Book R* (21 N 48) 3.
Brooks, Cleanth. "Three Revolutions in Poetry. III. Metaphysical Poetry and the Ivory Tower." *So R* 1 (Wi 36) 568-83.
——— "*The Waste Land:* An Analysis." *So R* 3 (Su 37) 106-36.
Brotman, D. B. "T. S. Eliot: 'The Music of Ideas.'" *UTQ* 17 (O 48) 20-9.
Brown, C. S. "T. S. Eliot and Die Droste." *SR* 46 (O-D 38) 492-500.
Brown, E. K. "Mr. Eliot and Some Enemies." *UTQ* 8 (O 38) 69-84.
Brown, W. C. "Mr. Eliot without the Nightingales." *UKCR* 14 (Au 47) 31-8.
——— "T. S. Eliot and the Demon of the Ego." *New Humanist* 8 (Je-Jl-Ag 35) 81-5.
Buck Gerhard. "Über die Anspielungen in T. S. Eliots *Waste Land.*" *Anglia* 65 (N 40) 214-25.
Burke, Kenneth. "Acceptance and Rejection." *So R* 2 (Wi 37) 600-32.
Caldwell, J. R. "An Explorer in Poetic Fields." *SRL* 8 (9 Ja 32) 437-9.
Calverton, V. F. "T. S. Eliot: An Inverted Marxian." *Mod Mo* 8 (Jl 34) 372-3.
Campbell, H. M. "An Examination of Modern Critics: T. S. Eliot." *Rocky Mt R* 8 (Su 44) 128-38.
Carter, B. B. "Modern English Poetry." *Cath World* 143 (1936) 292-300.

Catlin, George. "T. S. Eliot and the Moral Issue." *SRL* 32 (2 Jl 49) 7-8, 36-8.
Chapin, K. G. "T. S. Eliot at the National Gallery." *Poetry* 70 (S 47) 328-9.
Chase, Richard. "The Sense of the Present." *KR* 7 (Sp 45) 225-31.
——— "T. S. Eliot in Concord." *Am Schol* 16 (Au 47) 438-43.
Church, R. W. "Eliot on Bradley's Metaphysic." *Harvard Advocate* 125 (D 38) 24-6.
Clark, J. A. "On First Looking into Benson's *Fitzgerald*." *SAQ* 48 (Ap 49) 258-69.
Cleophas, Sister M. "Eliot's *Whispers of Immortality*." *Expl* 8 (D 49) 22.
Collin, W. E. "T. S. Eliot." *SR* 39 (Ja-Mr 31) 13-24.
——— "T. S. Eliot, the Critic." *SR* (O-D 31) 419-24.
Cook, Albert. "Eliot's Waste Land, III (Fire Sermon, 262-265)." *Expl* 6 (O 47) 7.
Coomaraswamy, A. K. "Primordial Images." *PMLA* 61 (Je 46) 601-2.
Cormican, L. A. "Mr. Eliot and Social Biology." *Scrutiny* 17 (Sp 50) 2-13.
Cotten, L. A. "Eliot's *The Waste Land*, I, 43-46." *Expl* 9 (O 50) 7.
Cowley, Malcolm. "T. S. Eliot's Ardent Critics." *N Y Herald Tribune Books* 25 (13 Mr 49) 1-2.
——— "The Religion of Art." *NRp* 77 (3 Ja 34) 216-8.
cummings, e. e. "T. S. Eliot." *Dial* 68 (Je 20) 781-4.
Curtius, E. R. "T. S. Eliot: Das Wueste Land." *Die Neue Rundschau* 3 (1950) 327-45.
D., A. "Some Notes on 'The Waste Land.'" *N&Q* 195 (19 Ag 50) 365-9.
Daiches, David. "Some Aspects of T. S. Eliot." *CE* 9 (D 47) 115-22.
——— "T. S. Eliot." *YR* 38 (Sp 49) 460-70.
Daniells, J. R. "T. S. Eliot and His Relation to T. E. Hulme." *UTQ* 2 (Ap 33) 380-96.
Dawson, N. P. "Enjoying Poor Literature." *Forum* 69 (Mr 23) 1371-7.
Deutsch, Babette. "T. S. Eliot and the Laodiceans." *Am Schol* 9 (Wi 40) 19-30.
Dobson, C. A. "Three of T. S. Eliot's Poems." *New R* (Calcutta) 12 (1940) 361-72.
Dunkel, W. D. "T. S. Eliot's Quest for Certitude." *Theology Today* 7 (Jl 50) 228-36.
Dwyer, D. H. "Eliot's *Ash-Wednesday*, IV, 1-4." *Expl* 9 (O 50) 5.
Edman, Irwin. "Incantations by Eliot." *SRL* 33 (24 Je 50) 56-7.
Eliot, T. S. "A Letter from T. S. Eliot." *Poetry* 76 (My 50) 88.
——— "Die Aufgaben des Versdramas." *Die Neue Rundschau* 2 (1950) 190-203.
——— "From Poe to Valéry." *Hudson R* 2 (Aut 49) 327-43.
——— "Gedichte." *Die Neue Rundschau* 13 (Wi 49) 75-84.
——— "Sagt av Eliot." *Prisma* (Stockholm) 1 (1948) 18-24.
——— "Ueber Kultur and Politik." *Die Wandlung* 4 (Ap 49) 306-16.
Elliott, G. R. "T. S. Eliot and Irving Babbitt." *Am R* 7 (S 36) 442-54.
Enebjelm, Helen. "T. S. Eliots ökenkänsla—En anglo-sachsisk företeelse." *Litteratur, Kunst, Teater* (Stockholm) 2 (1945) 11-5.
Eshelman, W. R. "Eliot's *Gerontion*." *Expl* 4 (Ap 46) 44.
Ferguson, Frances. "Action as Passion: *Tristan* and *Murder in the Cathedral*." *KR* 9 (Sp 47) 201-21.
Fish, C. J. "Eliot's *The Love Song of J. Alfred Prufrock*." *Expl* 8 (Je 50) 62.
Flint, R. W. "The Four Quartets Reconsidered." *SR* 61 (Wi 48) 69-81.
Fluchère, Henri. "L'Attitude critique de T. S. Eliot." *Cahiers du Sud* (Marseilles) 35 (Second Half 48) 499-511.
——— "Un Européen." *Adam* (London) 16 (My 48) 5-6.
Foster, G. W. "The Archetypal Imagery of T. S. Eliot." *PMLA* 60 (Je 45) 567-85.
Fowlie, Wallace. "Eliot and Tchelitchew." *Accent* 5 (Sp 45) 166-70.
——— "Le Mythe de l'enfance—T. S. Eliot et Tchelitchew." *Arts et Lettres* (Paris) 1 (Mr 46) 53-9.
Franciosa, M. "Significato di un premio." *La Fiera Letteraria* (Italy) (14 N 48) 34.

Frank, Waldo. "The 'Universe' of T. S. Eliot." *Adelphi* 5 (F 33) 321-5.
Franzen, Erich. "T. S. Eliot und die Masken Ezra Pounds." *Die Wandlung* 4 (Ag 49) 593-604.
Fraser, G. S. "Mr. Eliot and the Great Cats." *Adam* (London) 16 (My 48) 10-4.
Freimarck, Vincent. "Eliot's *Ash-Wednesday,* II-IV." *Expl* 9 (O 50) 6.
Fry, Edith. "The Poetic Work of T. S. Eliot." *British Annual of Lit* 5 (1948) 8-14.
Fry, Varian. "A Bibliography of the Writings of Thomas Stearns Eliot." *H&H* 1 (Mr, Je 28) 214-8, 320-4.
Fussell, Paul, Jr. "A Note on 'The Hollow Men.'" *MLN* 65 (Ap 50) 254-5.
Gassner, John. "Perspectives." *New Theater* 2 (1936) 10-2, 36-7.
George, R. E. G. "The Return of the Native." *Bkm* 75 (S 32) 423-31.
Gilbert, Katharine. "A Spatial Configuration in Five Recent Poets." *SAQ* 44 (O 45) 422-31.
Gillet, Louis. "M. T. S. Eliot et les faux dieux." *Revue des Deux Mondes* 22 (1 Jl 34) 199-211.
Glazier, Lyle. "Eliot's *The Waste Land,* I, 24-30." *Expl* 8 (F 50) 26.
Glicksberg, C. I. "T. S. Eliot as Critic." *Ariz Q* 4 (Au 48) 225-36.
Greene, E. J. H. "Jules Laforgue et T. S. Eliot." *Revue de Littérature Comparée* (Paris) 22 (Jl-S 48) 363-97.
Gregory, Horace. "The Man of Feeling." *NRp* 79 (16 My 34) 23-4.
Guidacci, Margherita. "I Quartetti di Eliot." *Letteratura* (Italy) 9 (Mr-Ap 47) 110-2.
Guido, A. "Omaggio a Eliot." *La Fiera Letteraria* (Italy) (14 N 49).
Hall, Vernon, Jr. "Eliot's *La Figlia che Piange.*" *Expl* 5 (N 46) 15.
Hamalian, Leo. "Mr. Eliot's *Saturday Evening Service.*" *Accent* 10 (Au 50) 195-206.
Hamilton, K. M. "Wasteland To-Day: Recent Tendencies in the Arts in England." *Dalhousie R* 27 (Ap 47) 33-43.
Harvey-Jellie, W. "T. S. Eliot among the Prophets?" *Dalhousie R* 23 (Ap 38) 83-90.
Häusermann, H. W. "'East Coker' and 'The Family Reunion.'" *Life & Letters Today* 47 (O 45) 32-8.
——— "T. S. Eliots religiöse Entwicklung." *Englische Studien* 69 (Ja 35) 373-91.
Hayward, John. "Den okände T. S. Eliot." *Bonniers Litterära Magasin* (Stockholm) 17 (D 49) 736-41.
Hazlitt, Henry. "The Mind of T. S. Eliot." *Nation* 135 (5 O 32) 312-3.
Hernigman, Bernard. "Two Worlds and Epiphany." *Bard R* 2 (My 48) 156-9.
Heywood, Robert. "Everybody's Cocktail Party." *Renascence* 3 (1950) 28-30.
Hildebrand, K. G. "Eliot." Svensk Tidskrift (Stockholm) 26 (1949) 59-66.
Hillyer, Robert. "The Crisis in American Poetry." *Am Merc* 70 (Ja 50) 65-71.
——— "Poetry's New Priesthood." *SRL* 32 (18 Je 49) 7-9, 38.
Hilton, Charles. "The Poetry of T. S. Eliot." *EJ* 20 (N 31) 749-61.
Hobson, Harold. "The Paradoxical Public." *Chri Sci Mon* (Mag Sec) 42 (25 F 50) 10.
Hodin, J. P. "Bertrand Russell og T. S. Eliot om menneskehetens fremtid." *Samtiden* (Oslo) 56 (1947) 78-89.
——— "The Condition of Man Today: An Interview with T. S. Eliot." *Horizon* 12 (Ag 45) 83-8.
Hogan, J. P. "Eliot's Later Verse." *Adelphi* 28 (Ja-Mr 42) 54-8.
Hook, Sidney. "The Dilemma of T. S. Eliot." *Nation* 160 (20 Ja 45) 69-71.
House, H. "Mr. Eliot as a Critic." *New Oxford Outlook* 1 (My 33) 95-105.
Hubner, Walter. "T. S. Eliot und das neue Drama." *Neuphilologische Zeitschrift* 5 (1950) 337-52.
Jack, P. M. "A Review of Reviews: T. S. Eliot's Four Quartets." *Am Bkm* 1 (Wi 44) 91-9.

Jameson, R. D. "Poetry and Plain Sense: A Note on the Poetic Method of T. S. Eliot." *Tsing Hua R* (Peiping) (N 31).
Johnson, Maurice. "The Ghost of Swift in 'Four Quartets.'" *MLN* 64 (Ap 49) 273.
Kemp, Lysander. "Eliot's *Waste Land,* I, 49-50." *Expl* 7 (Je 49) 60.
——— "Eliot's *The Waste Land,* I, 43-59." *Expl* 8 (F 50) 27.
Kenner, Hugh. "Elliot's Moral Dialectic." *Hudson R* 2 (Au 49) 421-48.
Kinsman, R. S. "Eliot's *The Hollow Men.*" *Expl* 8 (Ap 50) 48.
Kirschbaum, Leo. "Eliot's *Sweeney Among the Nightingales.*" *Expl* 2 (D 43).
Knickerbocker, W. S. "Bellwether." *SR* 41 (Ja-Mr 33) 64-78.
Koch, Vivienne. "Programme Notes on *The Cocktail Party.*" *Poetry Q* 2 (Wi 49) 248-51.
Kramer, Hilton. "T. S. Eliot in New York (Notes on the End of Something)." *WR* 14 (Su 50) 303-5.
Kronenberger, Louis. "T. S. Eliot as Critic." *Nation* 140 (17 Ap 35) 452-3.
Krutch, J. W. "A Poem Is a Poem." *Nation* 137 (13 D 33) 679-80.
Laboulle, M. J. J. "T. S. Eliot and Some French Poets." *Revue de Littérature Comparée* (Ap-Je 36) 389-99.
Lalou, René. "T. S. Eliot: Prix Nobel." *Les Nouvelles Littèraires* (Paris) 1006 (11 N 48) 1.
Larrabee, A. "Three Studies in Modern Poetry." *Accent* 3 (Wi 43) 115-21.
Lea, Richard. "T. S. Eliot's Four Quartets." *Adelphi* ns 21 (Jl-S 45) 186-7.
Leavis, F. R. "Eliot's Later Poetry." *Scrutiny* 11 (Su 42) 65-7.
Lewis, A. O., Jr. "Eliot's Burnt Norton." *Expl* 8 (N 49) 9.
Leyris, Pierre. "Rencontres avec T. S. Eliot." *Figaro Littéraire* (Paris) 3 (13 N 48) 1.
Lindberger, Örgan. "Modern anglosaxisk litteraturkritik." *Bonniers Litterära Magasin* (Stockholm) 18 (D 49) 784-94.
Lindsay, Jack. "Déchéance de T. S. Eliot." *Les Lettres Françaises* (Paris) 8 (11 N 48) 1.
Locke, L. G. "Eliot's *Burbank with Baedeker.*" *Expl* 3 (My 45) 53.
Loring, M. L. S. "T. S. Eliot on Matthew Arnold." *SR* 43 (O-D 35) 479-88.
MacCarthy, Desmond. "T. S. Eliot." *New Statesman* 16 (8 Ja 21) 418-20.
Mackworth, Cecily. "Visite à T. S. Eliot." *Paru* 44 (Jl 48) 11-3.
McLaughlin, J. J. "A Daring Metaphysic: The Cocktail Party." *Renascence* 3 (1950) 15-28.
McLuhan, H. M. "Eliot's *The Hippopotamus.*" *Expl* 2 (My 44) 50.
——— "Mr. Eliot's Historical Decorum." *Renascence* 2 (1950) 9-15.
Malmberg, Bertil. "Hallucinationrealism." *Bonniers Litterära Magasin* (Stockholm) 18 (Ja 49) 45-8.
Martz, L. L. "The Wheel and the Point: Aspects of Imagery and Theme in Eliot's Later Poetry." *SR* 55 (Ja-Mr 47) 126-47.
Matthiessen, F. O. "Eliot's Quartets." *KR* 5 (Sp 43) 161-78.
——— "For an Unwritten Chapter." *Harvard Advocate* 125 (D 38) 22.
Melchiori, G. "Tecnica e poetica nel teatro di Eliot." *La Fiera Letteraria* (Italy) (14 N 48).
Messiaen, Pierre. "Le Sens de l'oeuvre poétique de T. S. Eliot." *Etudes* (Paris) (D 48) 383-5.
Meyer, Christine. "Eliot's *The Hippopotamus.*" *Expl* 8 (O 49) 6.
Meyerhoff, Hans. "Mr. Eliot's Evening Service." *PR* 15 (Ja 48) 131-8.
Mirsky, D. S. "T. S. Eliot et la fin de la poésie bourgeoise." *Échanges* 5 (D 31).
Mononey, M. F. "Mr Eliot and Critical Tradition." *Thought* 21 (S 46) 455-74.
Montgomerie, William. "Harry, Meet Mr. Prufrock (T. S. Eliot's Dilemma)." *Life & Letters Today* 31 (N 41) 115-28.
Moore, Marianne. "It Is Not Forbidden to Think." *Nation* 142 (27 My 35) 680-1.
More, P. E. "The Cleft Eliot." *SRL* 9 (12 N 32) 233, 235.

Morgan, Roberta, and Wohlstetter, Albert. "Observations on 'Prufrock.'" *Harvard Advocate* 125 (D 38) 27-30.
Morris, R. L. "Eliot's 'Game of Chess' and Conrad's 'The Return.'" *MLN* 65 (Je 50) 422-3.
Morrison, Theodore. "*Ash Wednesday:* A Religious History." *NEQ* 11 (Je 38) 266-86.
Muir, Edwin. "T. S. Eliot." *Nation* 121 (5 Ag 25) 162-4.
Nathan, Monique. "James Joyce et T. S. Eliot—Conjonctions et Divergences." *Cahiers du Monde Nouveau* (Paris) 6 (1950) 94-102.
Nicholls, Norah. "A Preliminary Check-List of T. S. Eliot." *Am Book Coll* 3 (F 33) 105-6.
Nicoll, Allardyce. "T. S. Eliot and the Revival of Classicism." *EJ* 23 (Ap 34) 269-78.
Nitze, W. A. "The Waste Land: A Celtic Arthurian Theme." *MP* 43 (Ag 45) 58-62.
O'Connor, W. V. "Gerontion & The Dream of Gerontius." *Furioso* 3 (Wi 47) 53-6.
Oliphant, E. H. C. "Tourneur and Mr. T. S. Eliot." *SP* 32 (O 35) 546-52.
Orsini, N. "Nota in margine ad una poesia di T. S. Eliot." *Letteratura* 33 (Mr-Ap 47) 110-2.
Österling, Anders. "Anförande vid Nobelfesten 1948." *Prisma* (Stockholm) 1 (1948) 18-24.
Otake, Masaru. "T. S. Eliot: The Lyric Prophet of Chaos." *Stud Eng Lit* 16 (O 36) 542-54.
Palmer, H. E. "The Hoax and Earnest in *The Waste Land.*" *Dublin Mag* ns 8 (Ap-Je 33) 11-9.
Pellegrini, Allessandro. "Una conversazione Londonese con T. S. Eliot e i 'Four Quartets.'" *Belfagor* (Florence) 3 (31 Jl 48) 445-52.
Peschmann, Hermann. "The Later Poetry of T. S. Eliot." *Eng* 5 (Au 45) 180-5.
——— "The Significance of T. S. Eliot." *Wind & the Rain* (London) 6 (Au 49) 108-23.
Peter, John. "The Family Reunion." *Scrutiny* 16 (S 49) 219-30.
——— "Sin and Soda—The Cocktail Party." *Scrutiny* 17 (Sp 50) 61-6.
Pick, John. "A Note on the Cocktail Party." *Renascence* 3 (1950) 30-2.
Pocock, D. F. "Symposium on Mr. Eliot's 'Notes.'" *Scrutiny* 17 (Au 50) 273-6.
Pope, J. C. "Prufrock and Raskolnikov." *AL* 17 (N 45) 213-30.
——— "Prufrock and Raskolnikov Again: A Letter from Eliot." *AL* 18 (Ja 47) 319-21.
Pope, M. P. "Eliot's *Gerontion.*" *Expl* 11 (My 48) [Q 16].
Pottle, F. A. "Eliot's *Gerontion.*" *Expl* 4 (Je 48) 55.
Pound, Ezra. "Sagt om Eliot." *Prisma* (Stockholm) 1 (1948) 25.
Praz, Mario. "Eliot e Montale." *La Fiera Letteraria* (Italy) (14 N 48).
——— "La Scuola di Eliot." *La Fiera Letteraria* (Italy) (28 N 48).
——— "T. S. Eliot and Dante." *So R* 2 (Wi 37) 525-48.
Qvamme, B. "T. S. Eliot." *Edda* (Oslo) 43 (Ja-Mr 43) 23-33.
Ransom, J. C. "Eliot and the Metaphysicals." *Accent* 1 (Sp 41) 148-56.
——— "The Inorganic Muses." *KR* 5 (Sp 43) 298-300.
——— "T. S. Eliot as Dramatist." *Poetry* 54 (Ag 39) 264-71.
——— "T. S. Eliot on Criticism." *SRL* 10 (24 Mr 34) 574.
Rees, Garnet. "A French Influence on T. S. Eliot: Rémy de Gourmont." *Revue de Littérature Comparée* 16 (O 36) 760-7.
Reinsberg, Mark. "A Footnote to *Four Quartets.*" *AL* 21 (N 49) 343-4.
Rice, P. B. "Out of the Wasteland." *Symposium* 3 (O 32) 422-42.
Richards, I. A. "The Poetry of T. S. Eliot." *Living Age* 329 (10 Ap 26) 112-5.
Robbins, R. H. "The T. S. Eliot Myth." *Science & Society* 14 (Wi 49-50) 1-28.
Roberts, Michael. "The Poetry of T. S. Eliot." *London Merc* 34 (My 36) 38-44.

Rosario, S. "Postilla al pensiero critico de Eliot." *La Fiera Letteraria* (Italy) (14 N 48).
Rosseaux, André. "Poésie et poétique de T. S. Eliot." *Figaro Littéraire* (Paris) 5 (20 My 50) 2.
Rowland, John. "The Spiritual Background of T. S. Eliot." *New-Church Mag* 61 (Ja-Mr 42) 52-62.
Russell, Peter. "A Note on Eliot's New Play." *Nine* 1 (O 49) 28-9.
Schaar, Claes. "Främmande gudar." *Bonniers Litterära Magasin* (Stockholm) 17 (Mr 50) 205-8.
Schappes, M. U. "The Irrational Malady." *Symposium* 1 (O 30) 518-30.
——— "T. S. Eliot Moves Right." *Mod Mo* 7 (Ag 33) 405-8.
Schoeck, R. J. "T. S. Eliot, Mary Queen of Scots, and Guillaume de Machaut." *MLN* 63 (Mr 48) 187-8.
Schwartz, Delmore. "T. S. Eliot as the International Hero." *PR* 12 (Sp 45) 199-206.
Scott, E. "There Is Humor in T. S. Eliot." *Chri Sci Mon* 36 (11 Ja 44) 6.
Seldes, Gilbert. "T. S. Eliot." *Nation* 115 (6 D 22) 614-6.
Shand, John. "Around 'Little Gidding.'" *Nineteenth Century and After* 136 (S 44) 120-32.
Shapiro, Karl. "The Persistence of Poetry." *Poetry* 76 (My 50) 89-91.
Shapiro, Leo. "The Medievalism of T. S. Eliot." *Poetry* 56 (Jl 40) 202-13.
Shuster, G. N. "Mr. Eliot Returns." *Commonweal* 16 (19 O 32) 581-3.
Sickells, E. M. "Eliot's *The Waste Land,* I, 24-30, and *Ash-Wednesday,* IV-VI." *Expl* 9 (O 50) 4.
——— "Eliot's *The Waste Land* II." *Expl* 7 (D 48) 20.
Smidt, Kristian. "Lyrikeren T. S. Eliot." *Spektrum* (Oslo) no 4 (1947) 181-97.
Smith, F. J. "A Reading of *East Coker.*" *Thought* 21 (Je 46) 272-86.
Smith, Grover. "Charles-Louis Philippe and T. S. Eliot." *AL* 22 (N 50) 254-9.
——— "Eliot's *Gerontion.*" *Expl* 7 (F 49) 26.
——— "Observations on Eliot's 'Death by Water.'" *Accent* 6 (Su 46) 257-63.
——— "Tourneur and *Little Gidding;* Corbière and *East Coker.*" *MLN* 65 (Je 50) 418-21.
——— "T. S. Eliot and Sherlock Holmes." *N&Q* 193 (2 O 48) 431-2.
——— "T. S. Eliot's Lady of the Rocks." *N&Q* 194 (19 Mr 49) 123-5.
Smith, Ray. "Eliot's *The Waste Land,* I, 74-75." *Expl* 9 (O 50) 8.
Spencer, Theodore. "The Poetry of T. S. Eliot." *Atl* 151 (Ja 33) 60-8.
——— "Three Notes on *Murder in the Cathedral.*" *Harvard Advocate* 125 (D 38) 20-1.
Spender, Stephen. "The Artistic Future of Poetry." *NRp* 79 (18 Ap 34) 268-70.
——— "How Pleasant to Know Mr. Eliot." *John O'London's W* 57 (29 O 48) 515.
Stamm, Rudolf. "The Orestes Theme in Three Plays by Eugene O'Neill, T. S. Eliot, and Jean-Paul Sartre." *Eng Stud* 30 (1949) 244-55.
Stolpe, Sven. "T. S. Eliot." *Ord och Bild* (Stockholm) 58 (1949) 89-96.
Stonier, G. W. "Eliot and The Plain Reader." *Fortnightly R* 138 (N 32) 620-9.
Strong, R. "The Critical Attitude of T. S. Eliot." *London Q & Holborn R* 158 (O 33) 513-9.
Stuart, D. A. "Modernistic Critics and Translators." *PULC* 11 (Su 50) 177-98.
Sweeney, J. J. "East Coker: A Reading." *So R* 6 (Sp 41) 771-9.
——— "Little Gidding: Introductory to a Reading." *Poetry* 62 (Jl 43) 216-23.
Tate, Allen. "Irony and Humility." *H&H* 4 (Ja-Mr 31) 290-7.
Taupin, René. "The Classicism of T. S. Eliot." *Symposium* 3 (Ja 32) 64-82.
Tentori, F. "Lorca, Hopkins, Eliot: misure difficili della poesia moderna." *La Fiera Letteraria* 11 (12 Mr 50).
Thompson, T. H. "The Bloody Wood." *London Merc* 29 (Ja 34) 233-9.
Trilling, Lionel. "Elements That Are Wanting." *PR* 7 (S-O 40) 367-79.
Trompeo, P. P. "Cicerone di Eliot." *La Fiera Litteraria* (Italy) (14 N 48).

Turnell, G. M. "Tradition and T. S. Eliot." *Collosseum* 1 (Je 34) 44-54.
Tyndall, W. Y. "The Recantation of T. S. Eliot." *Am Schol* 16 (Au 47) 431-7.
Unger, Leonard. "Notes on *Ash Wednesday.*" *So R* 4 (Sp 39) 745-70.
——— "T. S. Eliot's Rose Garden: A Persistent Theme." *So R* 7 (Sp 42) 667-89.
Untermeyer, Louis. "Disillusion as Dogma." *Freeman* 6 (17 Ja 22) 453.
——— "Irony De Luxe." *Freeman* 1 (30 Je 20) 381-2.
Utley, F. L. "Eliot's *The Hippopotamus.*" *Expl* 3 (N 44).
Valette, Jacques. "T. S. Eliot, Melton et la poésie anglaise." *Mercure de France* (Ag 48) 747-9.
——— "Une Vue conservatrice de la culture." *Mercure de France* 1029 (1 My 49) 162-74.
Valverde, J. M. "T. S. Eliot, desde la Poesiá Americana." *Insula* (Madrid) 4 (15 Ag 50) 1-2.
Vander Vat, D. G. "The Poetry of T. S. Eliot." *Eng Stud* (Amsterdam) 20 (1938) 107-18.
Vincent, C. J. "A Modern Pilgrim's Progress." *QQ* 57 (1950) 346-52.
Vinograd, Sherna. "The Accidental: A Clue to Structure in Eliot's Poetry." *Accent* 9 (Su 49) 231-8.
Vivas, Eliseo. "The Objective Correlative of T. S. Eliot." *Am Bkm* 1 (Wi 44) 7-18.
Waggoner, H. H. "T. S. Eliot and *The Hollow Men.*" *AL* 15 (My 43) 101-26.
Walcutt, C. C. "Eliot's *Sweeney among the Nightingales.*" *Expl* 2 (Ap 44) 48.
——— "Eliot's *Whispers of Immortality.*" *Expl* 7 (N 48) 11.
Ward, Anne. "Speculations on Eliot's Time-World: An Analysis of *The Family Reunion* in Relation to Hulme and Bergson." *AL* 21 (Mr 49) 18-34.
Wecter, Dixon. "The Harvard Exiles." *VQR* 10 (Ap 34) 244-57.
Weiss, T. "T. S. Eliot and the Courtyard Revolution." *SR* 54 (Sp 46) 289-307.
Wheelwright, Philip. "The Burnt Norton Trilogy." *Chimera* 1 (Au 42) 7-18.
Williams, W. C. "The Fatal Blunder." *Quar R Lit* 2 (Wi 44) 125-6.
Williamson, George. "The Structure of *The Waste Land.*" *MP* 47 (F 50) 191-206.
——— "The Talent of T. S. Eliot." *SR* 35 (Jl 27) 284-95.
Wilson, Edmund. "The Poetry of Drouth." *Dial* 73 (D 22) 611-6.
Winters, Yvor. "T. S. Eliot: The Illusion of Reaction." *KR* 3 (Wi, Sp 41) 7-30, 221-39.
Wool, Sandra. "Weston Revisited." *Accent* 10 (Au 50) 207-12.
Wormhoudt, Arthur. "A Psychoanalytic Interpretation of 'The Love Song of J. Alfred Prufrock.'" *Perspective* 2 (Wi 49) 109-17.
Worthington, Jane. "The Epigraphs to the Poetry of T. S. Eliot." *AL* 21 (Mr 49) 1-17.
Wyatt, E. V. "St. Thomas á Becket." *Cath World* 143 (My 36) 207-11.
Zabel, M. D. "The Still Point." *Poetry* 41 (D 32) 152-8.
——— "T. S. Eliot in Mid-Career." *Poetry* 36 (S 30) 330-7.
——— "The Use of the Poet." *Poetry* 44 (Ap 34) 32-7.

EMBURY, EMMA CATHERINE (1806-63). Robbins, J. A. "Mrs. Emma C. Embury's Account Book, A Study of Some of Her Periodical Contributions." *BNYPL* 51 (Ag 47) 479-85.

EMERSON, RALPH WALDO (1803-82). Anon. "L'Amitie de Emerson et Carlyle." *Journal des Economistes* 108 (N 38) 587-95.
——— "Belaboring the 'Brahmans' Again." *Lit Dig* 63 (4 O 19) 31.
——— "Emerson." *Living Age* 292 (17 Mr 17) 674-9.
——— "Emerson and Humanism." *TLS* no 1679 (5 Ap 34) 233-4.
——— "Emerson and Scholars." *Harvard Grad Mag* 14 (Mr 06) 383-91.
——— "Emerson at Lehigh." *Lehigh Alumni Bul* 29 (Ap 42) 15-6.
——— "Emerson in French." *Living Age* 314 (16 S 22) 739-40.

——— "Emerson Published His First Book Anonymously." *Lit Dig* 84 (21 Mr 25) 52.
——— "Emerson, the Citizen." *Nation* 76 (28 My 03) 428.
——— "Emerson's Correspondence with Herman Grimm." *Atl* 91 (Ap 03) 467-79.
——— "French Estimate of Emerson in 1846." *NEQ* 10 (S 37) 447-63.
——— "The Friendship of Emerson and Carlyle." *Hibbert J* 38 (O 39) 102-14.
——— "The Milk of Emerson." *SRL* 3 (4 D 26) 355-64.
——— "Ralph Waldo Emerson." *Blackwood's* 173 (My 03) 714-9.
——— "Ralph Waldo Emerson." *Macmillan's* 88 (My 03) 37-45.
——— "When Mark Twain Petrified the 'Brahmans.'" *Lit Dig* 62 (12 Jl 19) 28-9.
Abbott, L. F. "A Transcendental Humorist." *Outlook* 136 (20 F 24) 299-300.
——— "Two Literary Sportsmen." *Outlook* 147 (12 O 27) 177.
Abel, Darrel. "Strangers in Nature—Arnold and Emerson." *UKCR* 15 (Sp 49) 205-15.
Adams, J. T. "Emerson Re-read." *Atl* 146 (O 30) 484-92.
Adams, Raymond. "Emerson's Brother and the Mousetrap." *MLN* 62 (N 47) 483-6.
Adkins, N. F. "Emerson and the Bardic Tradition." *PMLA* 63 (Je 48) 662-77.
——— "Emerson's 'Days' and Edward Young." *MLN* 63 (Ap 48) 269-71.
Albee, John. "Tribute to Emerson." *Independent* 55 (My 21) 1178-82.
Amacher, R. E. "Emerson's *The Bohemian Hymn.*" *Expl* 5 (Je 47) 55.
——— "Emerson's *Divinity School Address.*" *Expl* 7 (Je 49) 59.
Arms, G. W. "Emerson's *Concord Hymn.*" *Expl* 1 (D 42) 33.
——— "Emerson's *Days.*" *Expl* 4 (N 45) 8.
Baker, Carlos. "Emerson and Jones Very." *NEQ* 7 (Mr 34) 90-9.
——— "The Road to Concord. Another Milestone in the Whitman-Emerson Friendship." *PULC* 9 (Ap 46) 100-17.
Baugh, Hansell. "Emerson and the Elder Henry James." *Bkm* 68 (N 28) 320-22.
Baym, M. I. "Emma Lazarus and Emerson." *Pub Am Jewish Hist Soc* 38 (Je 49) 261-87.
Beach, J. W. "Emerson and Evolution." *UTQ* 3 (Jl 34) 474-97.
Beers, H. A. "Emerson and His Journals." *YR* ns 5 (Ap 16) 568-83.
Benton, Joel. "Emerson's Optimism." *Outlook* 69 (15 Je 01) 407-10.
Bestor, A. E., Jr. "Emerson's Adaptation of a Line from Spenser." *MLN* 49 (Ap 34) 265-7.
Birrell, Augustine. "Prophets on the Wane." *Nation & Athenaeum* (London) 40 (12 Mr 27) 793-4.
Birss, J. H. "Emerson and Poe: A Similitude." *N&Q* 166 (21 Ap 34) 279.
Bixby, J. T. "Emerson as Writer and Man." *Arena* 39 (My 08) 538-43.
——— "Emerson's Message." *Arena* 39 (Je 08) 665-73.
Blair, Walter, & Faust, Clarence. "Emerson's Literary Method." *MP* 42 (N 44) 79-95.
Blake, W. B. "Emerson: A Mystic Who Lives Again in His Journals." *Forum* 52 (O 14) 612-20.
Booth, R. A., & Stromberg, Roland. "A Bibliography of Ralph Waldo Emerson, 1908-20." *Bul Bibl* 19 (D 48) 180-3.
Boynton, H. W. "Emerson." *Reader* 5 (Ja 05) 250-3.
Boynton, P. H. "Democracy in Emerson's Journals." *NRp* 1 (28 N 14) 25-6.
——— "Emerson, A Rediscovered Modern." *Independent* 119 (24 S 27) 294-6.
——— "Emerson in His Period." *Int J Ethics* 39 (Ja 29) 177-89.
——— "Emerson's Feeling Toward Reform." *NRp* 1 (30 Ja 15) 16-8.
——— "Emerson's Solitude." *NRp* 3 (22 My 15) 68-70.
Bradley, Sculley. "Lowell, Emerson, and the *Pioneer.*" *AL* 19 (N (47) 231-44.
Braswell, William. "Melville as a Critic of Emerson." *AL* 9 (N 37) 317-34.
Braun, F. A. "Goethe as Viewed by Emerson." *JEGP* 15 (1916) 23-34.
Brittin, N. A. "Emerson and the Metaphysical Poets." *AL* 8 (Mr 36) 1-21.
Brooks, Van Wyck. "Emerson and the Reformers." *Harper's* 154 (D 26) 114-9.

——— "Emerson in His Time." *NRp* 100 (23 Ag 39) 78-80.
Brown, E. B. "The Modern Emerson." *Critic* 42 (My 03) 440-4.
Brown, S. G. "Emerson." *UKCR* 15 (Au 48) 27-37.
——— "Emerson's Platonism." *NEQ* 18 (S 45) 325-45.
Brownell, W. C. "Emerson." *Scribner's* 46 (N 09) 608-24.
Burke, Kenneth. "Acceptance and Rejection." *So R* 2 (Wi 37) 600-32.
Burroughs, John. "A Glance into Emerson's Journals." *Art World* 3 (N 17) 105-8.
Cameron, K. W. "An Early Prose Work of Emerson." *AL* 22 (N 50) 332-8.
Caponigri, A. R. "Brownson and Emerson: Nature and History." *NEQ* 18 (S 45) 368-90.
Carey, E. L. "Hawthorne and Emerson." *Critic* 45 (Jl 04) 25-7.
——— "Ralph Waldo Emerson." *Dial* 37 (1 D 04) 366-7.
Carpenter, F. I. "Immortality from India." *AL* 1 (N 29) 233-42.
——— "La Pédagogie d'Emerson." *Annales de L'Université de Paris* 4 (Jl-Ag 29) 302-18.
——— "Points of Comparison between Emerson and William James." *NEQ* 2 (Jl 29) 458-74.
——— "Le Romantisme d'Emerson." *Revue Anglo-Américaine* 7 (O-D 29) 1-18, 113-31.
——— "Thoreau et Emerson." *Revue Anglo-Américaine* 7 (F 30) 215-30.
——— "William James and Emerson." *AL* 11 (Mr 39) 39-57.
Carpenter, H. C. "Emerson at West Point." *Educ* 71 (S 50) 57-61.
Cestre, Charles. "Emerson Poete." *Etudes Anglaises* 4 (Ja-Mr 40) 1-14.
Chawner, M. G. "Nature in Emerson's Essays." *NE Mag* ns 32 (Ap 05) 215-9.
Chazin, Maurice. "Emerson's Disciple in Belgium: Marie Mali (1855-1927)." *RR* 24 (O-D 33) 346-9.
——— "Extracts from Emerson in Quinet's Cahiers." *Revue de Littérature Comparée* 15 (Ja-Mr, Ap-Je 35) 136-49, 310-26.
——— "Extracts from Emerson by Edgar Quinet (1844-1845)." *Revue de Littérature Comparée* 15 (Ja-Mr 35) 136-49.
——— "Quinet, an Early Discoverer of Emerson." *PMLA* 48 (Mr 33) 147-63.
Choate, J. H. "Emerson." *Critic* 43 (S 03) 212-6.
Christy, A. E. "Emerson's Debt to the Orient." *Monist* 38 (Ja 28) 38-64.
Clark, H. H. "Emerson and Science." *PQ* 10 (Jl 31) 225-60.
Clark, T. H. "An Emerson Reminiscence." *SAQ* 4 (Jl 05) 284-6.
Coad, O. S. "An Unpublished Lecture by Emerson." *AL* 14 (Ja 43) 421-6.
Cohen, B. B. "'Threnody': Emerson's Struggle with Grief." *Ind Un Folio* 14 (O 48) 13-5.
Coleman, R. A. "Two Meetings with Emerson." *MLN* 65 (N 50) 482-4.
Commager, H. S. "Tempest in a Boston Tea Cup." *NEQ* 6 (D 33) 651-75.
Connor, M. H. "Emerson's Interest in Contemporary Practical Affairs." *EJ* 38 (O 49) 428-32.
Conway, M. D. "Emerson: The Teacher and the Man." *Critic* 42 (My 03) 404-11.
——— "The Ministry of Emerson." *Open Court* 17 (1903) 257-64.
Cooke, G. W. "Emerson and Transcendentalism." *N E Mag* ns 27 (My 03) 264-80.
——— "The Emerson Centennial." *N E Mag* ns 27 (My 03) 255-64.
Cosman, Max. "Emerson's English Traits and the English." *Mark Twain Q* 8 (Su-Fl 48) 7-9.
Crozier, J. B. "Emerson as a Thinker and Man of Letters." *Fortnightly R* 116 (Ag 21) 229-42.
——— "Emerson, Cicero, the Stoics, and Myself." *Contemp R* 112 (S 17) 293-9.
——— "Key to Emerson." *Fortnightly R* 116 (Ag-S 21) 229-42, 383-95.
Cutler, D. B. "An Unpublished Letter of Emerson." *Yale Un Lib Gaz* 4 (Jl 29) 15-7.
Davis, A. E. "Emerson's Thought on Education." *Educ* 45 (F 25) 253-72.

Davis, M. R. "Emerson's 'Reason' and the Scottish Philosophers." *NEQ* 17 (Je 44) 209-28.
Davis, N. C. "Emerson and Ohio: A New Emerson Letter." *Ohio State Arch & Hist Q* 58 (Ja 49) 101-2.
DeCasseres, Benjamin. "Emerson the Individualist." *Bkm* 17 (My 03) 300-2.
——— "Emerson: Sceptic and Pessimist." *Critic* 42 (My 03) 437-40.
Dedmond, F. B. "A New Note on Ralph Waldo Emerson." *N&Q* 195 (24 Je 50) 278-9.
Dewey, John. "The Philosopher of Democracy." *Int J Ethics* 13 (Jl 03) 405-13.
Dillaway, Newton. "Emerson's Remarkable Face." *Chri Sci Mon* 38 (3 Ja 46) 8.
Dow, B. H. "A New Emphasis in American Thought." *Cath World* 145 (O 37) 65-71.
Downs, L. H. "Emerson and Dr. Channing: Two Men from Boston." *NEQ* 20 (D 47) 516-34.
Dykema, K. W. "Why Did Lydia Jackson Become Lidian Emerson?" *AS* 17 (D 42) 285-6.
Edmunds, A. J. "Emerson's Misquotation from Boehme." *N&Q* 175 (23 Jl 38) 63.
Eidson, J. O. "Two Unpublished Letters of Emerson." *AL* 21 (N 49) 335-8.
Eliot, C. W. "Emerson as Seer." *Atl* 91 (Je 03) 844-55.
Elliott, G. R. "Emerson as Diarist (A Middle-Aged View)." *UTQ* 6 (Ap 37) 299-308.
——— "On Emerson's 'Grace' and 'Self-Reliance.'" *NEQ* 2 (Ja 29) 93-104.
Emerson, E. W. "Emerson and Scholars." *Harvard Grad Mag* 14 (Mr 06) 383-91.
——— "Ralph Waldo Emerson." *Bkm* 24 (Je 03) 92-6.
Emerson, R. W. "Three Letters from Ralph Waldo Emerson." *PMHS* 60 (D 26) 83-5.
Erskine, John. "The American Scholar." *Am Schol* 1 (Wi 32) 5-15.
Evans, T. C. "Early English Criticism of Emerson." *Lamp* 26 (Jl 03) 470-3.
Falk, R. P. "Emerson and Shakespeare." *PMLA* 56 (Je 41) 523-43.
Faust, Clarence. "The Background of the Unitarian Opposition to Transcendentalism." *MP* 35 (F 38) 297-324.
Firkins, O. W. "Has Emerson a Future?" *MLN* 45 (D 30) 491-500.
Flanagan, J. T. "Emerson and Communism." *NEQ* 10 (Je 37) 243-61.
——— "Emerson as a Critic of Fiction." *PQ* 15 (Ja 36) 30-45.
Fletcher, E. G. "Emerson's *Days*." *Expl* 5 (Ap 47) 41.
Flewelling, R. T. "Emerson and Adolescent America." *Personalist* 20 (O 39) 343-52.
——— "Emerson and the Middle Border." *Personalist* 16 (S 35) 295-309.
Flower, B. O. "The Poet as a Philosopher." *Arena* 39 (Mr 08) 323-31.
Flugel, F. "Pages from an Autograph Collection." *Un Calif Chron* 28 (O 26) 351-3.
Foerster, Norman. "Emerson as Poet of Nature." *PMLA* 37 (S 22) 599-614.
——— "Emerson on the Organic Principle in Art." *PMLA* 41 (Mr 26) 193-208.
Ford, G. S. "The American Scholar Today." *School & Soc* 40 (17 N 34) 641-51.
Ford, W. C. "Mr. Emerson Was Present." *PMHS* 62 (1930) 130-8.
Forsythe, R. S. "Emerson and 'Moby Dick.'" *N&Q* 177 (23 D 39) 457-8.
Foster, C. H. "Emerson as American Scripture." *NEQ* 16 (Mr 43) 91-105.
Foster, G. R. "The Natural History of the Will." *Am Schol* 15 (Su 46) 277-87.
Francke, Kuno. "Emerson and German Personality." *Int Q* 8 (S 03) 93-107.
Friedrich, Gerhard. "Emersons Inschrift in einem Goethe-Band. Aus dem Englischen übersetzt von Gerhard Friedrich." *Books Abroad* 23 (Wi 49) 29.
Garnett, Richard. "The Secret of Emerson." *Living Age* 231 (16 N 01) 455-8.
Garrod, H. W. "Emerson." *NEQ* 3 (Ja 30) 3-24.
Gass, S. B. "Emerson and the Forgotten Man." *Outlook* 150 (5 S 28) 729-31.
Gerber, J. C. "Emerson and the Political Economists." *NEQ* 22 (S 49) 336-57.
Gilman, Margaret. "Baudelaire and Emerson." *RR* 24 (O 43) 211-22.
Gilmore, A. F. "Was Emerson a Poet?" *Chri Sci Mon* (26 My 37) 6.

Glicksberg, C. I. "Bryant on Emerson the Lecturer." *NEQ* 12 (S 39) 530-4.
Goggio, Emilio. "Emerson's Interest in Italy." *Ital* 17 (S 40) 97-103.
Gohdes, Clarence. "Emerson's English Audience." *Chri Sci Mon* 37 (6 N 44) 7.
——— "A Gossip on Emerson's Treatment of Beauty." *Open Court* 45 (My 31) 315-20.
——— "Some Remarks on Emerson's *Divinity School Address*." *AL* 1 (Mr 29) 27-31.
——— "Whitman and Emerson." *SR* 37 (Ja 29) 79-93.
Gordon, G. A. "Emerson as a Religious Influence." *Atl* 91 (My 03) 577-87.
Gorely, Jean. "Emerson Takes the Road." *Chri Sci Mon* 36 (22 Ag 44) 6.
——— "Emerson's Theory of Poetry." *Poetry R* 22 (Jl-Ag 31) 263-73.
Grover, E. O. "Why Not Professors of Books? A Selling Tip from Ralph Waldo Emerson." *Pub W* 116 (30 N 29) 2591-3.
H, O. N. "Queries from Emerson." *N&Q* 168 (12 Ja 35) 26.
Hagboldt, Peter. "Emerson's Goethe." *Open Court* 46 (Ap 32) 234-44.
Hale, E. E. "Some Emerson Memories." *Outlook* 66 (29 D 00) 1045-6.
Hall, Bolton. "Emerson the Anarchist." *Arena* 37 (Ap 07) 400-4.
Hartwig, G. H. "Emerson on Historical Christianity." *Hibbert J* 37 (Ap 39) 405-12.
——— "An Immortal Friendship (Carlyle and Emerson)." *Hibbert J* 38 (O 39) 102-14.
Hastings, Louise. "Emerson in Cincinnati." *NEQ* 11 (S 38) 443-69.
Henry, Myrtle. "Independence and Freedom as Expressed and Interpreted by Ralph Waldo Emerson." *Negro Hist Bul* 6 (My 43) 173-4.
Hicks, Granville. "A Conversation in Boston." *SR* 39 (Ap-Je 31) 129-41.
——— "Letters to William Francis Channing." *AL* 2 (N 30) 294-8.
Higginson, T. W. "The Personality of Emerson." *Outlook* 74 (23 My 03) 221-7.
Hoeltje, H. H. "Emerson, Citizen of Concord." *AL* 11 (Ja 40) 367-78.
——— "Emerson in Minnesota." *Minn Hist* 2 (Je 30) 145-59.
——— "Emerson in Virginia." *NEQ* 5 (O 32) 753-68.
——— "Emerson's Venture in Western Land." *AL* 2 (Ja 31) 438-40.
——— "Ralph Waldo Emerson in Iowa." *Iowa J Hist and Pol* 25 (Ap 27) 236-76.
Hofmiller, Josef. "R. W. Emerson." *Die Zukunft* 43 (23 My 03) 306-15.
Hogan, Marjorie. "The Philosophy of Ralph Waldo Emerson." *Scholastic* 1 (19 My 47) 50-1.
Holls, F. W. "Correspondence Between Ralph Waldo Emerson and Herman Grimm." *Atl* 91 (Ap 03) 467-79.
Hopkins, V. C. "The Influence of Goethe on Emerson's Aesthetic Theory." *PQ* 27 (O 48) 325-44.
Hotson, C. P. "A Background for Emerson's Poem 'Grace.'" *NEQ* 1 (Ap 28) 124-32; *New-Church Mag* 47 (O-D 28) 219-25.
——— "The Christian Critics and Mr. Emerson." *NEQ* 11 (Mr 38) 29-47.
——— "Corrections as to Emerson's Sources for 'Swedenborg.'" *New Philos* 34 (Ja 31) 309.
——— "Emerson and Swedenborg." *New-Church Mess* 160 (S 30) 274-7.
——— "Emerson and the Doctrine of Correspondence." *New Church R* 46 (Ja, Ap, Jl, O 29) 47-59, 173-86, 304-16, 435-48.
——— "Emerson and the 'New Church Quarterly Review.'" *New-Church Mag* 53 (Jl-S, O-D 29) 169-83, 239-53.
——— "Emerson and the Swedenborgians." *SP* 27 (Jl 30) 517-45.
——— "Emerson, Swedenborg, and B. F. Barret." *New-Church Mag* 50 (O-D 31) 244-52; 51 (Ja-Mr 32) 33-43.
——— "Emerson's Biographical Sources for 'Swedenborg.'" *SP* 26 (Ja 29) 23-36.
——— "Emerson's Boston Lecture on Swedenborg." *New-Church Mag* 51 (Ap-Je 32) 91-101.
——— "Emerson's Manchester Lecture on Swedenborg." *New-Church Mag* 52 (Ja-Mr 33) 48-58.

——— "Emerson's Philosophical Sources for 'Swedenborg.'" *New Philos* 21 (1928) 482-516.

——— "Emerson's Sources for 'Swedenborg.'" *New-Church Mess* 142 (3 F 32) 89-94.

——— "Emerson's Title for 'Swedenborg.'" *New-Church Life* 44 (Jl 29) 390-8.

——— "George Bush and Emerson's 'Swedenborg.'" *New-Church Mag* 50 (Ja-Mr, Ap-Je 31) 22-34, 98-108.

——— "George Bush: Teacher and Critic of Emerson." *PQ* 10 (O 31) 369-83.

——— "Prof. Bush's Reply to Emerson on Swedenborg." *New-Church Mag* 51 (Jl-S, O-D 32) 175-84, 213-23.

——— "A Salford Reply to Emerson's Manchester Lecture on Swedenborg." *New-Church Mag* 52 (Jl-S, O-D 33) 174-85, 232-43.

——— "Sampson Reed, a Teacher of Emerson." *NEQ* 2 (Ap 29) 249-77.

Howard, B. D. "The First French Estimate of Emerson." *NEQ* 10 (S 37) 447-63.

Howe, J. W. "Emerson as I Knew Him." *Critic* 42 (My 03) 411-3.

Howe, M. A. DeW. "Did Anything Happen to Emerson's Memory?" *SRL* 31 (2 Ja 42) 5-6.

Howells, W. D. "Impressions of Emerson." *Harper's W* 47 (16 My 03) 784.

Hubach, R. R. "Emerson's Lectures in Springfield, Illinois, in January, 1853." *AN&Q* 6 (F 47) 164-7.

Hudson, J. W. "The Religion of Emerson." *SR* 28 (Ap 20) 203-12.

Huggard, W. A. "Emerson and the Problem of War and Peace." *Un Iowa Humanistic Stud* 5: no 5 (15 Ap 38) 1-76.

——— "Emerson's Philosophy of War and Peace." *PQ* 22 (O 43) 370-5.

Hummel, Hermann. "Emerson and Nietzsche." *NEQ* 19 (Mr 46) 63-84.

Hyder, C. K. "Emerson on Swinburne: A Sensational Interview." *MLN* 48 (Mr 33) 180-2.

Jackson, S. L. "A Soviet View of Emerson." *NEQ* 19 (Je 46) 236-43.

James, Henry, Sr. "Emerson." *Atl* 94 (D 04) 740-5.

Jones, Joseph. "Emerson and Bergson on the Comic." *CL* 1 (Wi 49) 63-72.

——— "Emerson's *Days*." *Expl* 4 (Ap 46) 47.

Jordan, C. B. "At Emerson's Grave." *Outlook* 74 (2 My 03) 30.

Jorgenson, E. E. "Emerson's Paradise under the Shadow of Swords." *PQ* 11 (Jl 32) 274-92.

Kent, C. W. "Emerson's Last Lecture." *Book Lover* (My-Je 03) 103-4.

Kern, A. C. "Emerson and Economics." *NEQ* 13 (D 40) 678-96.

Kernahan, Coulson. "Is Emerson a Poet?" *National R* 36 (D 00) 523-36.

Kimball, L. E. "Miss [Delia] Bacon Advances Learning." *Colophon* ns 2 (Su 37) 338-54.

Kingsley, M. E. "Outline Study of Emerson's Essays." *Educ* 41 (O 20) 95-109.

Kronman, Jeanne. "Three Unpublished Lectures of Ralph Waldo Emerson." *NEQ* 19 (Mr 46) 98-110.

Kuhn, Helmut. "Carlyle, Ally and Critic of Emerson." *Emory Un Q* 4 (O 48) 171-80.

Ladu, A. I. "Emerson: Whig or Democrat." *NEQ* 13 (S 40) 419-41.

Lee, G. S. "Emerson as a Poet." *Critic* 42 (My 03) 416-29.

Lewin, Walter. "Emerson." *Bkm* 24 (Je 03) 89-92.

Lewis, Albert. "Emerson and War." *School & Soc* 60 (12 Ag 44) 97-9.

——— "Words, Action, and Emerson." *CE* 7 (O 45) 20-5.

Lindeman, E. C. "Emerson: Radical Democrat." *Common Ground* 2: no 2 (1942) 3-6.

——— "Emerson's Pragmatic Mood." *Am Schol* 16 (Wi 46-47) 57-64.

Lloyd, C. F. "Emerson As a Stimulant." *Canadian Bkm* 18 (Jl 36) 1-3.

Mabbott, T. O. "Numismatic References of Three American Writers." *Numismatist* 46 (N 33) 688.

Mabie, H. W. "Concord And Emerson." *Outlook* 74 (2 My 03) 18-29.

——— "Emerson's Journals." *Outlook* 106 (21 F 14) 418-20.
——— "Ralph Waldo Emerson in 1903." *Harper's* 106 (My 03) 903-8.
McDowell, Tremaine. "A Freshman Poem by Emerson." *PMLA* 45 (Mr 30) 326-9.
McEuen, K. A. "Emerson's Rhymes." *AL* 20 (Mr 48) 31-42.
McNulty, J. B. "Emerson's Friends and the Essay on Friendship." *NEQ* 19 (S 46) 390-4.
MacRae, David. "Emerson, a Personal Reminiscence." *Spectator* 90 (20 Je 03) 972.
MacRae, Donald. "Emerson and the Arts." *Art Bul* 20 (Mr 38) 79-95.
Magnus, Philip. "Emerson's Thoughts on Education." *Nineteenth Century* 80 (D 16) 1198-211.
Maitra, Herambachandra. "Emerson from an Indian Point of View." *Harvard Theo R* 4 (1911) 403-17.
Malloy, Charles. "Emerson's 'Bacchus.'" *Arena* 32 (N 04) 504-12.
——— "The Poems of Emerson: 'Days.'" *Arena* 31 (Je 04) 592-602.
——— "The Poems of Emerson: 'Hermione.'" *Arena* 33 (Ja, F, Mr 05) 65-70, 182-7, 289-95.
——— "The Poems of Emerson: 'The Problem.'" *Arena* 32 (Jl, Ag 04) 39-47, 145-50.
——— "The Poems of Emerson: 'The Sphinx.'" *Arena* 31 (F, Mr, Ap, My 04) 138-52, 272-83, 370-80, 494-507.
——— "The Poems of Emerson: 'Uriel.'" *Arena* 32 (S 04) 278-83.
——— "What Bearing upon Emerson's Poems Have Their Titles?" *Poet Lore* 14 (O 03) 65-79.
Marble, A. R. "Emerson as a Public Speaker." *Dial* 34 (16 My 03) 327-9.
——— "First Editions of Emerson." *Critic* 42 (My 03) 430-6.
Marchand, Ernest. "Emerson and the Frontier." *AL* 3 (My 31) 149-75.
Mason, A. H. "Emerson's *Terminus*." *Expl* 4 (Mr 46) 37.
Masson, T. L. "Emerson the Radical." *Bkm* 57 (Je 23) 401-3.
Mathews, J. C. "Emerson's Knowledge of Dante." *Un Texas Stud in Eng* 22 (1942) 171-98.
Meeks, L. H. "The Lyceum in the Early West." *Ind Mag Hist* 29 (Je 33) 87-95.
Melz, C. F. "Goethe and America." *CE* 10 (My 49) 425-31.
Meyer, A. N. "Do We Need Emerson Today?" *Vital Speeches* 5 (15 F 39) 261-4.
Michaud, Régis. "Emerson et Nietzsche." *Revue Germanique* 6 (Jl-Ag 10) 414-21.
——— "Emerson's Transcendentalism." *Am J Psychol* 30 (Ja 19) 73-82.
Mieher, D. "New Appeal of Emerson to Youth." *Scholastic* 32 (28 My 38) 21.
Miller, Perry. "Jonathan Edwards to Emerson." *NEQ* 13 (D 40) 589-618.
Monroe, Harriet. "Emerson in a Loggia." *Poetry* 10 (S 17) 311-5.
Moody, M. M. "The Evolution of Emerson as an Abolitionist." *AL* 17 (Mr 45) 1-21.
Moore, C. L. "Master of Maxims." *Dial* 34 (1 My 03) 293-5.
Moore, J. B. "Emerson on Wordsworth." *PMLA* 41 (Mr 26) 179-92.
——— "The Master of Whitman." *SP* 23 (Ja 26) 77-89.
——— "Thoreau Rejects Emerson." *AL* (N 32) 241-56.
Moravsky, Maria. "Idol of Compensation." *Nation* 108 (28 Je 19) 1004-5.
More, P. E. "The Influence of Emerson." *Independent* 55 (21 My 03) 1183-8.
Mosley, J. R. "The Charm of Emerson." *Arena* 34 (Je 05) 31-8.
Mowat, R. B. "The England Emerson Saw from Americans in England." *Chri Sci Mon* 34 (2 My 42) 8.
Münsterberg, Hugo. "Emerson as Philosopher." *Harvard Psychol Stud* 2 (1906) 16-31.
Murdock, C. A. "Emerson in California." *Pac Unitarian* 11 (My 03) 263-8.
Neilson, W. A. "The American Scholar Today." *Am Schol* 5 (Sp 36) 149-63.
Newton, R. H. "Emerson, the Man." *Arena* 30 (O 03) 359-76.
Nicoll, R. W. "Ralph Waldo Emerson." *NAR* 176 (My 03) 675-87.

Nye, R. B. "Emerson in Michigan and the Northwest." *Mich Hist Mag* 26 (Sp 42) 159-72.
Oliver, E. S. "Emerson's *Days*." *NEQ* 19 (D 46) 518-24.
——— "Melville's Picture of Emerson and Thoreau in *The Confidence Man*." *CE* 8 (N 46) 61-72.
Overstreet, M. M. "Emerson on English Traits." *SRL* 20 (26 Ag 39) 9.
Parkes, H. B. "Emerson." *H&H* 5 (Jl-S 33) 581-601.
Pattee, F. L. "Emerson's 'Self-Reliance.'" *Chautauquan* 30 (Mr 00) 628-33.
Payne, Leonidas. "Poe and Emerson." *Texas R* 7 (O 21) 54-69.
Peck, H. W. "Emerson's 'Brahma': The Poet-Philosopher in the Presence of Diety." *Arena* 33 (Ap 05) 375-6.
Peck, W. E. "A Lost Poem of Emerson?" *Sw R* 12 (Jl 27) 304-5.
Perry, Bliss. "Emerson's Saving Bank." *Nation* 99 (24 S 14) 371-3.
Perry, T. A. "Emerson, the Historical Frame, and Shakespeare." *MLQ* 9 (D 48) 440-7.
Pettegrove, James. "Emerson und der Transzendentalismus in Neu England." *Die Litterarische Welt* 2 (1946) 183-90.
Pettigrew, R. C. "Emerson and Milton." *AL* 3 (Mr 31) 45-59.
Phelps, W. L. "American Philosopher." *Ladies Home J* 40 (Ap 23) 23.
Pochmann, H. A. "Emerson and the St. Louis Hegelians." *AGR* 10 (F 44) 14-7.
——— "The Emerson Canon." *UTQ* 12 (Jl 43) 476-84.
Pollitt, J. D. "Ralph Waldo Emerson's Debt to John Milton." *Marshall R* 3 (D 39) 13-21.
Potter, C. F. "The Hindu Invasion of America." *Mod Thinker* 1 (Mr 32) 16-23.
Pound, Louise. "Emerson as a Romanticist." *Mid-West Q* 2 (Ja 15) 184-95.
Quinn, P. F. "Emerson and Mysticism." *AL* 21 (Ja 50) 397-414.
Randel, W. P. "A Late Emerson Letter." *AL* 12 (Ja 41) 496-7.
Richardson, L. N. "What Rutherford B. Hayes Liked in Emerson." *AL* 17 (Mr 45) 22-32.
Richmond, Mrs. H. L. "Ralph Waldo Emerson in Florida." *Fla Hist Q* (O 39) 75-93.
Roberts, A. J., & Weber, C. J. "Emerson's Visits to Waterville College." *Colby Merc* 5 (1 Ap 34) 41-5.
Roberts, J. R. "Emerson's Debt to the Seventeenth Century." *AL* 21 (N 49) 298-310.
Roz, Firmin. "L'Idéalisme américain: Ralph Waldo Emerson." *Revue des Deux Mondes* 70 (1 F 02) 651-75.
Sadler, M. E. "Emerson's Influence on Education." *Educ R* 26 (D 03) 457-63.
St. Clair, F. Y. "Emerson among the Siphars." *AL* 19 (Mr 47) 73-7.
——— "Emerson's 'Chiser, the Fountain of Life.'" *PQ* 26 (Ja 47) 81-4.
Sanborn, F. B. "A Concord Notebook." *Critic* 47 (O, N 05) 349-56, 444-51.
——— "Emerson and Contemporary Poets." *Critic* 42 (My 03) 413-6.
——— "Emerson, Thoreau, Channing." *Springfield Republican* (2 Jl 02) 14.
——— "Theodore Parker and R. W. Emerson." *Critic* (S 06) 273-81.
Schappes, Morris. "The Letters of Emma Lazarus, 1868-1885." *BNYPL* 53 (Jl, Ag, S 49) 315-34, 367-86, 419-46.
Schottlaender, Rudolf. "Two Dionysians: Emerson and Nietzsche." *SAQ* 39 (Jl 40) 330-43.
Scott, E. B. "Emerson Wins the Nine Hundred Dollars." *AL* 17 (Mr 45) 78-85.
Scudder, Townsend, III. "A Chronological List of Emerson's Lectures on His British Lecture Tour of 1847-1848." *PMLA* 51 (Mr 36) 243-8.
——— "Emerson in Dundee." *Am Schol* 4 (Su 35) 331-44.
——— "Emerson in London and the London Lectures." *AL* 8 (Mr 36) 22-36.
——— "Emerson's British Lecture Tour, 1847-1848, Part I." *AL* 7 (Mr 35) 15-36.
——— "Emerson's British Lecture Tour, 1847-1848, Part II." *AL* 7 (My 35) 166-80.
——— "The Human Emerson." *SRL* 20 (10 Je 39) 3-4, 15.

——— "Incredible Recoil: A Study in Aspiration." *Am Schol* 5 (Wi 36) 35-48.
Shaffer, R. B. "Emerson and His Circle: Advocates of Functionalism." *J Soc Arch Hist* 8 (Jl-D 48) 17-20.
Shaw, C. G. "Emerson the Nihilist." *Int J Ethics* 25 (O 14) 68-86.
Shephard, G. F. "Emerson and Natural Science." *Educ* 59 (Je 39) 590-4.
——— "Emerson's Attitude toward the Classics." *Educ* 54 (Je 34) 626-8.
——— "Emerson's Attitude towards Fine Arts." *Educ* 55 (D 34) 223-5.
Shuster, G. N. "Ancient Vision and the Newer Needs: Philosophy of Emerson." *Cath World* 106 (Mr 18) 733-41.
Sillen, Samuel. "Emerson at War." *New Masses* 47 (25 My 43) 22-4.
Silver, Mildred. "Emerson and the Idea of Progress." *AL* 12 (Mr 40) 1-19.
Silver, R. G. "Ellery Channing's Collaboration with Emerson." *AL* 7 (Mr 35) 84-6.
——— "Emerson as Abolitionist." *NEQ* 6 (Mr 33) 154-8.
——— "Mr. Emerson Appeals to Boston." *Am Book Coll* 6 (My-Je 35) 209-19.
Simison, B. D. "The Letters of Ralph Waldo Emerson: Addenda." *MLN* 55 (Je 40) 425-7.
Sloan, J. M. "Carlyle and Emerson." *Living Age* 309 (21 My 21) 486-9.
Smith, G. J. "Emerson and Whitman." *Conservator* 14 (Je 03) 53-5.
Smith, H. N. "Emerson's Problem of Vocation : A Note on 'The American Scholar.'" *NEQ* 12 (Mr 39) 52-67.
Smith, L. W. "Ibsen, Emerson, and Nietzche: The Individualists." *Popular Sci Mo* 78 (F 11) 147-57.
Stearns, A. W. "Four Emerson Letters to Dr. Daniel Parker." *Tuftonian* 1 (N 40) 6-9.
Steeves, H. R. "Bibliographical Notes on Emerson." *MLN* 32 (N 17) 431-4.
——— "An Ungarnered Emerson Item." *Nation* 100 (20 My 15) 563-4.
Stephen, Leslie. "Emerson." *National R* 36 (F 01) 882-98.
Stevenson, Burton. "More About the Mouse-Trap." *Colophon* ns 1 (Su 35) 71-86.
——— "The Mouse Trap." *Colophon* 5 (D 34) Pt 19.
Stewart, Randall. "The Concord Group." *SR* 44 (O-D 36) 434-46.
Stovall, Floyd. "The Value of Emerson Today." *CE* 3 (F 42) 442-54.
Strauch, C. F. "The Background for Emerson's 'Boston Hymn.'" *AL* 14 (Mr 42) 36-47.
——— "The Date of Emerson's Terminus." *PMLA* 65 (Je 50) 360-70.
——— "Emerson at Lehigh." *Lehigh Alumni Bul* 29 (Ap 42) 15-6.
——— "Emerson's Phi Beta Kappa Poem." *NEQ* 23 (Mr 50) 65-90.
——— "Gérando: A Source for Emerson." *MLN* 58 (Ja 43) 64-7.
——— "The Manuscript Relationships of Emerson's 'Days.'" *PQ* 29 (Ap 50) 199-208.
Sutcliffe, E. G. "Emerson's Theories of Literary Expression." *Un Ill Stud Lang & Lit* 8 (F 23) 9-143.
——— "Whitman, Emerson and the New Poetry." *NRp* 19 (24 My 19) 114-6.
Thompson, F. T. "Emerson and Carlyle." *SP* 24 (Jl 27) 438-53.
——— "Emerson's Indebtedness to Coleridge." *Sp* 23 (Ja 26) 55-76.
——— "Emerson's Theory and Practice of Poetry." *PMLA* 43 (D 28) 1170-84.
Thompson, Ralph. "Emerson and *The Offering for 1829*." *AL* 6 (My 34) 151-7.
Thorp, Willard. "Emerson on Tour." *QJS* 16 (F 30) 19-34.
Thwing, C. F. "The American Scholar: Emerson's Phi Beta Kappa Address (1837)." *Hibbert J* 36 (O 37) 119-31.
——— "Education According to Emerson." *School & Soc* 2 (16 O 15) 551-3.
Tolles, F. B. "Emerson and Quakerism." *AL* 10 (My 38) 142-65.
Torbert, J. K. "Emerson and Swedenborg." *Texas R* 2 (Ap 17) 313-26.
Trent, W. P. "Ralph Waldo Emerson," *Bkm* 17 (Je 03) 421-5.
Trueblood, D. E. "The Influence of Emerson's 'Divinity School Address.'" *Harvard Theo R* 32 (Ja 39) 41-56.

Turpie, M. C. "A Quaker Source for Emerson's Sermon on the Lord's Supper." *NEQ* 17 (Mr 44) 95-101.
Ustick, W. L. "Emerson's Debt to Montaigne." *Wash Un Stud* 9 (1922) 245-62.
W., R. "Shelley, Emerson, and Sir William Osler." *N&Q* 190 (23 Mr 46) 120-1.
Wahr, F. B. "Emerson and the Germans." *Monatsheft für Deutschen Unterricht* 33 (F 41) 49-63.
Warfel, H. R. "Margaret Fuller and Ralph Waldo Emerson." *PMLA* 50 (Je 35) 576-94.
Warren, Austin. "The Concord School of Philosophy." *NEQ* 2 (Ap 29) 199-233.
Wasung, C. J. "Emerson Comes to Detroit." *Mich Hist Mag* 29 (Ja 45) 59-72.
Wellek, René. "Emerson and German Philosophy." *NEQ* 16 (Mr 43) 41-62.
Whiting, B. J. "Emerson, Chaucer, and Thomas Warton." *AL* 17 (Mr 45) 75-8.
Wilkinson, L. A. "Emerson: Militant Pollyanna." *Thinker* 3 (Ap 31) 4, 33-44.
Williams, M. L. "They Wrote Home About It." *Mich Alumnus Quar R* (Su 45) 337-51.
——— "'Why Nature Loves the Number Five.' Emerson Toys with the Occult." *Papers Mich Acad Sci, Arts and Letters* 30 (1944) 639-49.
Williams, S. T. "Unpublished Letters of Emerson." *JEGP* 26 (O-D 27) 475-84.
Williamson, George. "Emerson the Oriental." *Un Calif Chron* 30 (Jl 28) 271-88.
Winterich, J. T. "Romantic Stories of Books, Second Series: Emerson's Essays." *Pub W* 118 (19 Jl 30) 271-5.
Yohannan, J. D. "Emerson's Translations of Persian Poetry from German Sources." *AL* 14 (Ja 43) 407-20.
——— "The Influence of Persian Poetry on Emerson's Work." *AL* 15 (Mr 43) 25-41.
Zeleny, L. D. "The Educational Philosophy of Emerson." *Educ* 45 (D 24) 232-9.
Zink, Harriet. "Emerson's Use of the Bible." *Un Neb Stud Lang, Lit & Crit* 14 (1935) 5-75.

EMMETT, DANIEL D. (1815-1904). Anon. "The Composer of 'Dixie.'" *Critic* 36 (Je 00) 511-2.

ENGLE, PAUL H. (1908-). Anon. "Paul (Hamilton) Engle." *Cur Biog* 3 (Je 42) 20-3.
Engle, Paul. "Five Years of Pulitzer Poets." *EJ* 38 (F 49) 59-65.
Fletcher, J. G. "The American Dream." *Poetry* 45 (F 35) 285-8.
Monroe, Harriet. "Paul Engle's First Book." *Poetry* 42 (Jl 33) 220-2.
Van Gelder, Robert. "An Interview with Iowa's Paul Engle." *N Y Times Book R* (22 Mr 42) 2.
Zabel, M. D. "Because I Love You So." *Poetry* 48 (Jl 36) 228-31.

ENGLISH, THOMAS DUNN (1819-1902). Hunt, W. S. "The Story of a Song." *Proc N J Hist Soc* 51 (Ja 33) 24-33.

ERSKINE, JOHN (1879-1951). Crawford, N. A. "The Professor as Critic." *Poetry* 19 (O 21) 54-7.
Knickerbocker, W. S. "John Erskine." *SR* 35 (Ap-Je 27) 154-74.
Maurice, A. B. "John Erskine." *Bkm* 71 (Ap-My 30) 165-6.
Robinson, H. M. "John Erskine, a Modern Actaeon." *Bkm* 67 (Ag 27) 613-8.
Smith, H. H. "Professor's Progress." *NYr* 3 (10 D 27) 27-9.

EVANS, AUGUSTA (1835-1909). Brewton, W. W. "St. Elmo and St. Twelvemo." *SRL* 5 (22 Je 29) 1123-4.
Calkins, E. E. "St. Elmo: or, Named for a Best Seller." *SRL* 21 (16 D 39) 3-4, 14, 16-7.
Maurice, A. B. "Augusta Jane Evan's 'St Elmo.'" *Bkm* 31 (Mr 10) 35-42.

EVANS, CHARLES N. B. (1850-1932). Hubbell, J. B. "Charles Napoleon Bonaparte Evans: Creator of Jesse Holmes the Fool-Killer." *SAQ* 36 (O 37) 431-46.

EVANS, DONALD (1884-192?). Rosenfeld, Paul. "An American Sonneteer." *Dial* 80 (Mr 26) 197-201.

EVANS NATHANIEL (1742-67). Milligan, B. A. "An Early American Imitator of Milton." *AL* (My 29) 200-6.

Pennington, E. L. "Nathaniel Evans—Some Notes on His Ministry." *PAAS* 50 (Ap 40) 91-7.

EVERETT, EDWARD (1794-1865). Everett, Edward. "Letters from Edward Everett to Charles P. Huntington." *PMHS* 57 (F 24) 269-70, 272-6.

Read, A. W. "Edward Everett's Attitude towards American English." *NEQ* 12 (Mr 39) 112-29.

Streeter, R. E. "Hawthorne's Misfit Politician and Edward Everett." *AL* 16 (Mr 44) 26-8.

FARRELL, JAMES T. (1904-). Anon. "James T. Farrell." *Our Biog* 3 (S 42) 13-6.

——— "Philadelphia Booksellers Arrested; Farrell Hearing Set for May 17." *Pub W* 153 (15 My 48) 2096.

——— "Suit against James T. Farrell Thrown Out of Court." *Pub W* 151 (5 Ap 47) 1923.

Birney, Earle. "The Fiction of James T. Farrell." *Canadian Forum* 19 (Ap 39) 21-4.

Farrell, J. T. "An Introduction to Two Novels." *UKCR* 13 (Sp 47) 217-24.

——— "Lonigan, Lonergan, and New York's Finest." *Nation* 158 (18 Mr 44) 338.

——— "A Novelist Begins." *Atl* 142 (S 38) 330-4.

——— "The Social Obligations of the Novelist: 1. Is the Obligation to 'State' or 'Society?'" *Humanist* 7 (Au 47) 57-62.

——— "The Sovereign Pen." *SRL* 30 (30 D 47) 21, 28.

Frohock, W. M. "James Farrell, the Precise Content." *Sw R* 35 (Wi 50) 39-48.

Glicksberg, C. I. "Contemporary Criticism." *SAQ* 35 (O 36) 445-57.

——— "The Criticism of James T. Farrell." *Sw R* 35 (Su 50) 189-96.

Haas, Irvin, & Gordon, Robert. "American First Editions . . . James T[homas] Farrell (1904-)." *Pub W* 131 (20 Mr 37) 1353.

Hatfield, Ruth. "The Intellectual Honesty of James T. Farrell." *CE* 3 (Ja 42) 337-46.

Howe, Irving. "James T. Farrell: The Critic Calcified." *PR* 14 (S 47) 545-6, 548, 550, 552.

Linebarger, P. M. A. "Stasm: Psychological Warfare and Literary Criticism." *SAQ* 46 (Jl 47) 344-8.

Lovett, R. M. "James T. Farrell." *EJ* 26 (My 37) 347-54.

Stock, Irvin. "Farrell and His Critics." *Ariz Q* 6 (Wi 50) 328-38.

Walcutt, C. C. "Naturalism in 1946; Dreiser and Farrell." *Accent* 6 (Su 46) 263-7.

Willingham, Calder. "Note on James T. Farrell." *Quar R Lit* 2 (Wi 44) 120-4.

FAST, HOWARD (1914-). Anon. "Authors League Protests Ban on 'Citizen Tom Paine.'" *Pub W* 151 (22 F 47) 1252.

——— "Ban on 'Citizen Tom Paine' Raises Storm in New York City." *Pub W* 151 (15 F 47) 1134-5.

Boyer, R. O. "Making an American." *New Masses* 60 (20 Ag 46) 3-6.

Hicks, Granville. "Howard Fast's One-Man Reformation." *EJ* 34 (S 45) 357-62; *CE* 7 (O 45) 1-6.

Morgan, Claude. "Walt Whitman et Howard Fast." *Parallèle 50* no 108 (15 O 48) 5.

Urnov, M. "Howard Fast and America." *Soviet Lit* (Moscow) 11 (1948) 185-91.

FAULKNER, WILLIAM (1897-). Aiken, Conrad. "William Faulkner: The Novel as Form." *Atl* 164 (N 39) 650-4.

Arthos, John. "Ritual and Humor in the Writing of William Faulkner." *Accent* 9 (Au 48) 17-30.

Beck, Warren. "Faulkner and the South." *AR* 1 (Sp 41) 82-94.

——— "Faulkner's Point of View." *CE* 2 (My 41) 736-49.

——— "A Note on Faulkner's Style." *Rocky Mt R* 6 (Sp-Su 42) 5-14.

——— "William Faulkner's Style." *Am Prefaces* 4 (Sp 41) 195-211.

Benét, W. R. "Faulkner as Poet." *SRL* 9 (29 Ap 33) 565.

Bergel, Lienhard. "Faulkner's *Sanctuary*." *Expl* 6 (D 47) 20.

Birney, Earle. "Two William Faulkners." *Canadian Forum* 18 (Je 38) 84-5.

Bowling, Laurence. "Faulkner: Technique of *The Sound and the Fury*." *KR* 10 (Au 48) 552-66.

Boyle, Kay. "Tattered Banners." *NRp* 94 (9 Mr 38) 136-7.

Bradford, Roark. "The Private World of William Faulkner." *'48* 2 (My 48) 83-94.

Brumm, Ursula. "William Faulkner im alten Süden." *Weltstimmen* 19 (May 50) 374-80.

Bunker, Robert. "Faulkner: A Case for Regionalism." *NMQR* 19 (Sp 49) 108-15.

Buttitta, Anthony. "William Faulkner: That Writin' Man of Oxford." *SRL* 18 (21 My 38) 6-8.

Calverton, V. F. "Pathology in Contemporary Literature." *Thinker* 4 (D 31) 7-16.

——— "William Faulkner: Southerner at Large." *Mod Mo* 10 (Mr 38) 11-2.

Calvo, L. N. "El Demonio de Faulkner." *Revista de Occidente* 39 (Ja 33) 98-103.

Campbell, H. M. "Experiment and Achievement." *SR* 51 (Sp 43) 305-20.

——— "Faulkner's *Absalom, Absalom!*" *Expl* 7 (D 48) 24.

——— "Faulkner's *Sanctuary*." *Expl* 4 (Je 46) 61.

——— "Structural Devices in the Works of Faulkner." *Perspective* 3 (Au 50) 209-26.

Canby, H. S. "The School of Cruelty." *SRL* 7 (21 Mr 31) 673-4; 9 (26 Ap 33) 565.

Caraceni, A. "William Faulkner." *Aretusa* 2 (1945) 23-8.

Cecchi, Emilio. "William Faulkner." *Pan* (Milan) 6 (My 34) 64-70.

Chase, Richard. "The Stone and the Crucifixion: Faulkner's Light in August." *KR* 10 (Au 48) 539-51.

Cochran, Louis. "William Faulkner, Literary Tyro of Mississippi." Memphis *Commercial Appeal* (6 N 32) 4.

Coindreau, M. E. "Panorama de la actual literatura joven norteamericana." *Sur* 7 (Mr 37) 49-65.

——— "Le Puritanisme de William Faulkner." *Cahiers du Sud* 12 (Ap 35) 259-67.

——— "William Faulkner." *La Nouvelle Revue Française* 36 (1 Je 31) 926-30.

Colum, Mary. "Faulkner's Struggle with Technique." *Forum* 97 (Ja 37) 25-6.

Cowley, Malcolm. "Poe in Mississippi." *NRp* 89 (4 N 36) 22.

——— "William Faulkner." *Die Amerikanische Rundschau* 3 (Jl 47) 31-40.

——— "William Faulkner Revisited." *SRL* 28 (14 Ap 45) 13-6.

——— "William Faulkner's Human Comedy." *N Y Times Book Rev* (29 O 44) 4.

——— "William Faulkner's Legend of the South." *SR* 53 (Su 45) 13-6.

DeVoto, Bernard. "Witchcraft in Mississippi." *SRL* 15 (31 O 36) 3-4, 14.

Dickmann, Max. "William Faulkner, escritor diabólico." *Revista de las Indias* 13 (Mr 42) 107-16.

Evans. Medford. "Oxford, Mississippi." *Sw R* 15 (Au 29) 46-63.

Evans, Walter. "Faulkner's Mississippi." *Vogue* (1 O 48) 144-9.

Fadiman, Clifton. "Mississippi Frankenstein." *NYr* 14 (21 Ja 39) 60-2.

——— "William Faulkner: Extra-Special, Double-Distilled." *NYr* 12 (31 O 36) 62-4.

——— "The World of William Faulkner." *Nation* 132 (15 Ap 31) 422-3.

Fauchery, Pierre. "La Mythologie faulknérienne dans Pylon." *Espace* (Paris) 3 (Je 45) 106-12.

Faÿ, Bernard. "L'École de l'infortune." *Revue de Paris* 44 (Ag 37) 644-65.
Fielder, L. A. "William Faulkner: An American Dickens." *Commentary* 10 (O 50) 384-7.
Foster, R. E. "Dream as Symbolic Act in Faulkner." *Perspective* 2 (Su 49) 179-94.
Franc, M. "Prokosch non ama Faulkner." *La Fiera Letteraria* (Italy) 3 (15 Ja 50) 16.
Frohock, W. M. "William Faulkner: The Private versus the Public Vision." *Sw R* 34 (Su 49) 281-94.
Geismar, Maxwell. "Ex-Aristocrat's Emotional Education." *SRL* 31 (25 S 48) 8.
Giles, Barbara. "The South of William Faulkner." *Masses and Mainstream* 3 (F 50) 26-40.
Glicksberg, C. I. "William Faulkner and the Negro Problem." *Phylon* 10 (2 Q 49) 153-60.
——— "The World of William Faulkner." *Ariz Q* 5 (Sp 49) 46-58.
Gordon, Caroline. "Notes on Faulkner and Flaubert." *Hudson R* 1 (Su 48) 222-32.
Green, A. W. "William Faulkner at Home." *SR* 40 (Jl-S 32) 294-306.
Greene, Graham. "The Furies of Mississippi." *London Merc* 35 (Mr 37) 517-8.
Harnarck-Fish, Mildred. "William Faulkner." *Die Literatur* (N 35) 64-7.
Harwick, Elizabeth. "Faulkner and the South Today." *PR* 15 (O 48) 1130-4.
Hicks, Granville. "The Past and Future of William Faulkner." *Bkm* 74 (S 31) 17-23.
Hirshliefer, Phyllis. "As Whirlwinds in the South." *Perspective* 2 (Su 49) 225-38.
Hopper, V. F. "Faulkner's Paradise Lost." *VQR* 23 (Su 47) 405-20.
Howe, Irving. "The South and Current Literature." *Am Merc* 47 (O 48) 494-503.
——— "William Faulkner and the Quest for Freedom." *Tomorrow* 9 (D 49) 54-6.
Hudson, Tommy. "William Faulkner: Mystic and Traditionalist." *Perspective* 3 (Au 50) 227-35.
Jackson, J. T. "Delta Cycle: A Study of William Faulkner." *Chimera* 5 (Au 46) 3-14.
Janson, Åke. "William Faulkner." *Bonniers Litterära Magasin* (Stockholm) 10 (D 50) 734-9.
Johnson, C. W. M. "Faulkner's *A Rose for Emily*." *Expl* 6 (My 48) 45.
Kazin, Alfred. "Faulkner: The Rhetoric and the Agony." *VQR* 18 (Su 42) 389-402.
Kohler, Dayton. "William Faulkner and the Social Conscience." *CE* 11 (D 49) 119-27; *EJ* 38 (D 49) 545-52.
Kronenberger, Louis. "Faulkner's Dismal Swamp." *Nation* 146 (19 F 38) 212-4.
Kubie, L. S. "William Faulkner's *Sanctuary:* An Analysis." *SRL* 11 (20 O 34) 218, 224-6.
LaBudde, Kenneth. "Cultural Primitivism in William Faulkner's 'The Bear.'" *Am Q* 2 (Wi 50) 322-8.
Lawson, Strang. "Faulkner's 'The Hamlet.'" *CEA Critic* 10 (D 48) 3.
Leavis, F. R. "Dostoevsky or Dickens." *Scrutiny* 2 (Je 33) 91-3.
LeBreton, Maurice. "Technique et psychologie chez William Faulkner." *Études Anglaises* 1 (S 37) 418-38.
——— "William Faulkner: *Pylon*." *Revue Anglo-Américaine* 12 (O 35) 81-2.
Leibowitz, René. "L'Art tragique de William Faulkner." *Cahiers du Sud* 17 (N 40) 502-8.
Lewis, Wyndham. "A Moralist with a Corn Cob." *Life & Letters* 16 (Je 34) 312-8.
Linn, Robert. "Robinson Jeffers and William Faulkner." *Am Spect* 2 (1933) 1.
Longley, J. L., & Daniel, Robert. "Faulkner's Critics: A Selective Bibliography." *Perspective* 3 (Au 50) 202-8.
Lovati, Georgio. "Faulkner, Soldati and America." *Living Age* 351 (S 36) 71-2.
Lundkvist, Artur. "Amerikansk Prosa." *Bonniers Litterära Magasin* 6 (Mr 37) 197-204.
Lytle, Andrew. "Regeneration for the Man." *SR* 57 (Wi 49) 120-7.

Machlachlan, J. M. "William Faulkner and the Southern Folk." *SFQ* 9 (S 45) 153-67.
McCole, C. J. "The Nightmare Literature of William Faulkner." *Cath World* 141 (Ag 35) 576-83.
Malraux, André. "Préface à 'Sanctuaire' de W. Faulkner." *Nouvelle Revue Française* 41 (N 33) 744-7.
Morra, Umberto. "William Faulkner." *Letteratura* (Italy) 3) (Jl 39) 173-4.
O'Donnell, G. M. "Faulkner's Mythology." *KR* 1 (Su 39) 285-99.
Oliver, M. R. "La Novela norteamericana moderna." *Sur* 9 (Ag 39) 33-47.
Perdeck, A. "William Faulkner." *Critisch Bull* (1934) 209-13.
Peyre, Henri. "American Literature through French Eyes." *VQR* 23 (Su 47) 421-37.
Pick, Robert. "Old-World Views on New-World Writing." *SRL* 32 (20 Ag 49) 7-9, 35-8.
Pilkington, J. P. "Faulkner's *Sanctuary*." *Expl* 4 (Je 46) 61.
Piviano, Fernanda. "Vita di Faulkner." *La Rassegna d'Italia* no 6 (Je 49).
Poirier, William. "Strange Gods in Jefferson, Mississippi." *SR* 53 (Su 45) 44-56.
Pouillon, Jean. "William Faulkner, un Témoin." *Les Temps Modernes* 2 (11 O 46) 172-8.
Powell, S. O. "William Faulkner Celebrates Easter, 1928." *Perspective* 2 (Su 49) 196.
Rascoe, Burton. "Faulkner's New York Critics." *Am Merc* 50 (Je 40) 243-7.
Redman, B. R. "Faulkner's Double Novel." *SRL* 19 (21 Ja 39) 5.
——— "Flights of Fancy." *SRL* 11 (30 Mr 35) 577, 581.
Ricard, J. F. "Les Romans: Faulkner en France." *Confluences* ns 1 (Ja-F 45) 82-5.
Rice, P. B. "The Art of William Faulkner." *Nation* 138 (25 Ap 34) 478.
Rosati, Salvatore. "Letteratura Americana; William Faulkner." *Nuova Antologia* 12 (16 Ja 38) 323-8.
Roth, Russell. "The Brennam Papers: Faulkner in Manuscript." *Perspective* 2 (Su 49) 219-24.
——— "William Faulkner: The Pattern of Pilgrimage." *Perspective* 2 (Su 49) 246-51.
Sartre, J. P. "American Novelists in French Eyes." *Atl* 158 (Ag 46) 114-8.
——— "A Propos de *Le Bruit et la Fureur:* La Temporalité chez Faulkner." *Nouvelle Revue Française* 52 (Je 34) 1057-61.
——— "Sartoris." *Situation* (Paris) 1 (1947) 7-13.
——— "Sartoris, par W. Faulkner." *Nouvelle Revue Française* 26 (F 38) 323-8.
——— "La Temporalité chez Faulkner." *Situation* (Paris) 1 (1947) 70-81.
Schappes, M. U. "Faulkner as Poet." *Poetry* 43 (O 33) 48-52.
Schwartz, Delmore. "The Fiction of William Faulkner." *So R* 7 (Su 41) 145-60.
Signaux, Gilbert. "Sur Faulkner." *La Nef* (Paris) 6 (F 49) 117-20.
Smith, Bradley. "The Faulkner Country." *'48* 2 (My 48) 85-94.
Smith, M. J. "Faulkner of Mississippi." *Bkm* 74 (D 31) 411-7.
Snell, George. "The Fury of William Faulkner." *WR* 11 (Au 46) 29-40.
Söderberg, Sten. "Nazismen och den moderna realismen: Letterär nazism." *Samtid och Framtid* (Stockholm) 2 (Je-Ag 45) 376-9.
Spencer, B. T. "Wherefore Southern Fiction?" *SR* 47 (1939) 500-13.
Spinella, Maria. "Sartoris nelle vita degli U. S. A." *La Fiera Letteraria* (Italy) 3 (31 Jl 47) 31.
Starke, Aubrey. "An American Comedy: An Introduction to a Bibliography of William Faulkner." *Colophon* 5 (D 34) 19.
Stone, Phil. "William Faulkner and His Neighbors." *SRL* 25 (19 S 42) 12.
——— "William Faulkner: The Man and His Work." *Oxford* (Miss) *Mag* 1 (1934) 13-14.
Thompson, A. R. "The Cult of Cruelty." *Bkm* 74 (Ja, F 32) 477-87.
Trilling, Lionel. "The McCaslins of Mississippi." *Nation* 154 (30 My 42) 632-3.

——— "Mr. Faulkner's World." *Nation* 133 (4 N 31) 491-2.
Troy, William. "And Tomorrow." *Nation* 140 (3 Ap 35) 393.
——— "The Poetry of Doom." *Nation* 143 (31 O 36) 524-5.
Vernon, Grenville. "Fallen Angel?" *Commonweal* 15 (20 Ja 32) 332-3.
Vickery, O. W. *"As I Lay Dying." Perspective* 3 (Au 50) 179-91.
Waldman, Milton. "Tendencies of the Modern Novel: America." *Fortnightly R* 140 (D 33) 709-25.
Warren, R. P. "Cowley's Faulkner." *NRp* 65 (12, 26 Ag 46) 176-80, 234-7.
——— "The Snopes World." *KR* 3 (Sp 41) 253-7.
West, R. B. "Atmosphere and Theme in Faulkner's 'A Rose for Emily.'" *Perspective* 2 (Su 49) 239-45.
——— "Faulkner's *A Rose for Emily.*" *Expl* 7 (O 48) 8.
Whan, Edgar. "*Absalom, Absolom!* as Gothic Myth." *Perspective* 3 (Au 50) 192-201.
Whittemore, Reed. "Notes on Mr. Faulkner." *Furioso* 2 (Su 47) 18-25.
Wilson, Edmund. "William Faulkner's Reply to the Civil Rights Program." *NY* 24 (23 O 48) 106, 109-12.
Young, Stark. "New Year's Craw." *NRp* 93 (12 Ja 38) 283-4.

FEARING, KENNETH (1902-). Abbott, C. D. "The Politics of Mr. Fearing." *Un Colo Stud* ser B 2 (O 45) 382-7.
Rosenthal, Macha. "The Meaning of Kenneth Fearing's Poetry." *Poetry* 64 (Jl 44) 208-23.

FERBER, EDNA (1887-). Anon. "Edna Ferber." *Bkm* 54 (Ja 22) 434-9.
——— "Imitative School." *Bkm* 33 (My 12) 225-7.
——— "Our Beautiful Young Idiots." *Lit Dig* 3 (3 O 31) 18-9.
——— "The Way of a Novelist." *Lit Dig* 3 (5 D 31) 14.
Allen, M. P. "'The Odd Women' and 'The Girls.'" *NAR* 216 (N 22) 691-4.
Banning, M. C. "Edna Ferber's America." *SRL* 19 (4 F 39) 5-6.
Bromfield, Louis. "Edna Ferber." *SRL* 12 (15 Je 35) 10-2.
Ferber, Edna. "Pardon My Pointing." *Stage* 15 (Ap 38) 31-5.
Flagg, J. M. "Frills and Ednaferberlows." *Am Mag* 77 (My 14) 102-12.
Forestier, Marie. "L'Amérique se penche sur son passé." *La Revue Nouvelle* 8 (Jl-Ag 48) 92-5.
Johnson, Merle. "American First Editions . . . Edna Ferber." *Pub W* 119 (21 Mr 31) 1611-2.
Overton, Grant. "The Social Critic in Edna Ferber." *Bkm* 64 (O 26) 138-43.
Patrick, Arnold. "Getting into Six Figures." *Bkm* 61 (Ap 25) 164-8.
White, W. A. "Edna Ferber." *World's Work* 59 (Je 30) 36-8.
——— "Edna Ferber in the Forefront of the Reporters of Her Age." *World Today* 59 (Ag 30) 221-5.
——— "A Friend's Story of Edna Ferber." *EJ* 19 (F 30) 101-6.

FERRIL, THOMAS HORNSBY (1896-). Firebaugh, J. J. "Pioneer in the Parlor Car: Thomas Hornsby Ferril." *Prairie Schooner* 21 (Sp 47) 69-85.
Richards, R. F. "Science, Ferril, and Poetry." *Prairie Schooner* 21 (Fl 47) 312-8.
Swallow, Allan. "Two Rocky Mountain Poets." *Rocky Mt R* 3 (Fl 38) 1-3.

FESSENDEN, THOMAS GREEN (1771-1837). Gudde, E. G. "An American Version of Munchausen." *AL* 13 (Ja 42) 372-90.
White, P. G. "Early Poets of Vermont." *Proc Vt Hist Soc* 2 (1917-18) 120-5.

FICKE, ARTHUR DAVISON (1883-). Brown, Gladys. "Arthur Davison Ficke and His Friends." *Yale Un Lib Gaz* 23 (Ja 49) 140-4.
Johnson, Merle. "American First Editions: Arthur Davison Ficke, 1883- ." *Pub W* 124 (19 Ag 33) 513.

FIELD, EUGENE (1850-95). Anon. "Birthplace of Eugene Field." *Chri Sci Mon* 29 (18 D 36) 5.
——— "Excerpts from two letters dated Sept. 3, 1895, and April 23, 1877." *Autograph Album* 1 (D 33) 54.
Burke, H. R. "Eugene Field's Newspaper Days in St. Louis." *Mo Hist R* 41 (Ja 47) 137-46.
Davidson, L. J. "Eugene Field Items." *AN&Q* 1 (Je 41) 37-8.
Field, Roswell. "Eugene Field, A Memory." *Mo Hist R* 44 (Ja 50) 147-67.
Flanagan, J. T. "Eugene Field after Sixty Years." *UKCR* 13 (Sp 45) 167-73.
Goodrich, Mary. "The Vogue in Revival." *Overland Mo* 87 (S 29) 271-2.
Kelsoe, W. A. "Eugene Field's St. Louis Newspaper Work." *Mo Hist R* 27 (O 32) 78-9.
Larned, W. T. "The Mantle of Eugene Field." *Bkm* 41 (Mr 15) 44-57.
Monroe, Harriet. "An Unpublished Letter from Eugene Field." *Poetry* 28 (Ag 26) 268-74.
Ralph, Julian. "Eugene Field, The Many-Sided." *Book Buyer* 24 (F 02) 26-31.
Sparks, G. R. "The Eugene Field of the Saints and Sinners Corner." *Pub W* 120 (7 N 31) 2111-4.
Thompson, Slason. "Eugene Field." *Independent* 54 (20 F 02) 461-2.
Ticknor, Caroline. "Edmond Clarence Stedman and Eugene Field." *Bkm* 27 (Ap 08) 147-51.
——— "Eugene Field and His First Publisher." *Bkm* 39 (Jl 14) 514-26.
Weil, E. E. "Eugene Field." *McBride's* 96 (O 15) 109-16.
Wilson, Francis. "Eugene Field, The Humorist." *Century* 64 (Jl 02) 446-52.

FIELD, ROSWELL MARTIN (1851-1919). Woollcott, Alexander. "In Memoriam: Rose Field." *Atl* 163 (My 39) 643-8.

FIELDS, JAMES THOMAS (1817-81). Charvat, William. "James T. Fields and the Beginnings of Book Promotion, 1840-1855." *HLQ* 8 (N 44) 75-94.
James, Henry. "Mr. and Mrs. James T. Fields." *Atl* 116 (Jl 15) 21-31.

FINDLATER, JANE (1866-). Smith, N. A. "Jane and Mary Findlater, Sister Novelists." *NE Mag* ns 27 (O 02) 186-91.

FINDLATER, MARY (1865-). Smith, N. A. "Jane and Mary Findlater, Sister Novelists." *NE Mag* ns 27 (O 02) 186-91.

FIRKINS, OSCAR W. (1864-1932). Allin, J. B. "Oscar W. Firkins." *Am R* 1 (Je 33) 313-43.

FISHER, DOROTHY CANFIELD (1879-). Boynton, P. H. "Two New England Regionalists." *CE* 1 (Ja 40) 291-9.
Humphrey, Zaphine. "Dorothy Canfield." *Woman Citizen* 10 (Ja 26) 13-4, 36.
Mann, D. L. "Dorothy Canfield: The Little Vermonter." *Bkm* 65 (Ag 27) 695-701.
Phelps, W. L. "Dorothy Canfield Fisher." *EJ* 22 (Ja 33) 1-8.
——— "Dorothy Canfield, Novelist." *SRL* 7 (11 O 30) 199.
Post, Edward. "The Neo-Puritanism of Dorothy Canfield." *Chri Register* (17 Ag 33).
Wyckoff, E. C. "Dorothy Canfield: A Neglected Best Seller." *Bkm* 74 (S 31) 40-4.

FISHER, HENRY LEE (1822-1909). Allen, George. "Two Pennsylvania-Dutch Poets." *AGR* 8 (Ag 42) 10-2, 34.
——— "Two Pennsylvania-Dutch Poets (Part II): Henry Lee Fisher." *AGR* 9 (O 42) 10-3.

FISHER, VARDIS (1895-). Bishop, J. P. "The Strange Case of Vardis Fisher." *So R* 3 (Au 37) 348-59.

FISKE, JOHN (1842-1901). Anon. "John Fiske." *Atl* 88 (Ag 01) 282-4.
——— "John Fiske." *Unpopular R* 10 (Jl-S 18) 160-89.
Abbott, Lyman. "John Fiske's Histories." *Outlook* 69 (16 N 01) 708-11.
Commager, H. S. "John Fiske: An Interpretation." *PMHS* 66 (1942) 332-45.
Davis, A. M. "John Fiske." *Proc Am Acad Arts & Sci* 37 (1902).
Frank, Waldo. "John Fiske." *Educ* 22 (F 02) 331-9.
Green, S. S. "Reminiscences of John Fiske." *PAAS* ns 16 (1902) 421-8.
Guthrie, W. N. "Fiske's 'Through Nature to God.'" *SR* 8 (Ja 00) 12-25.
Hart, A. B. "The Historical Service of John Fiske." *Conn Mag* 7 (1902-3) 611-7.
Holt, Henry. "John Fiske." *Unpopular* R 10 (Jl-S 18) 160-89.
Mason, R. O. "John Fiske and the New Thought." *Arena* 25 (Ap 01) 365-72.
Nye, Russell. "John Fiske and His Cosmic Philosophy." *Papers Mich Acad Sci, Arts & Letters* 28 (1942) 685-98.
Osborn, F. W. "John Fiske as a Schoolboy." *Educ* 22 (D 01) 206-8.
Perry, T. S. "John Fiske: an Appreciation." *Atl* 89 (My 02) 627-37.
Powell, L. C. "John Fiske—Bookman." *PBSA* 35 (O-D 41) 221-54.
Royce, Josiah. "John Fiske." *Unpopular R* 10 (Jl-S 18) 160-89.
——— "John Fiske as Thinker." *Harvard Grad Mag* 10 (S 01) 23-33.
Sanders, J. B. "John Fiske." *Miss Valley Hist R* 17 (S 30) 264-77.
Thayer, W. R. "Memoir of John Fiske." *PMHS* 46 (1913) 167-74.
Van Rensselaer, M. G. "Mr. Fiske and the History of New York." *NAR* 173 (Ag 01) 171-89.

FITCH, CLYDE (1865-1909). Birnbaum, Martin. "Clyde Fitch." *Independent* 67 (15 Jl 09) 123-31.
Eaton, W. P. "The Dramatist As A Man of Letters: The Case of Clyde Fitch." *Scribner's* 47 (Ap 10) 490-7.
Hale, E. E., Jr. "The Obstinacy of Clyde Fitch." *Bkm* 23 (Mr 06) 63-5.
Hamilton, Clayton. "Clyde Fitch." *Bkm* 30 (O 09) 135-8.
Henderson, Archibald. "A Real American Dramatist." *Dial* 61 (7 S 16) 136-8.
Lewis, Addison. "Clyde Fitch and the Printed Play." *Bellman* 22 (3 F 17) 128-30.
Merington, Marguerite. "Clyde Fitch, An Intimate Portrait." *Drama* 14 (D 23) 95-6, 114.

FITZGERALD, F. SCOTT (1896-1940). Anon. "F. Scott Fitzgerald." *Bkm* 57 (My 22) 20-5.
——— "Power without Glory." *TLS* no 2503 (20 Ja 50) 40.
Adams, J. D. "F. Scott Fitzgerald." *Am Merc* 61 (S 45) 373-7.
Adams, T. S. "A Noble Issue." *Gifthorse (Ohio State) 1949* 35-43.
Benét, W. R. "An Admirable Novel." *SRL* 1 (9 My 25) 739-40.
Berryman, John. "F. Scott Fitzgerald." *KR* 8 (Wi 46) 103-12.
Bishop, J. P. "The Missing All." *VQR* 13 (Wi 37) 106-21.
Dos Passos, John. "Fitzgerald and the Press." *NRp* 104 (14 F 41) 213.
Embler, Weller. "F. Scott Fitzgerald and the Future." *Chimera* 4 (Au 45) 48-55.
Fitzgerald, Frances. "Princeton and F. Scott Fitzgerald." *Nassau Lit Mag* 100 (Wi 42) 45-8.
Grattan, C. H. "Tender Is the Night." *Mod Mo* 8 (Jl 34) 375-6.
Gray, James. "Minnesota Muse." *SRL* 16 (12 Je 37) 4-5.
Gurko, Leo & Miriam. "The Essence of F. Scott Fitzgerald." *CE* 5 (Ap 44) 372-6.
Hindus, Maurice. "F. Scott Fitzgerald and Literary Anti-Semitism." *Commentary* 3 (Je 47) 508-16; 4 (Ag 47) 188-9.
Kallich, Martin. "F. Scott Fitzgerald: Money or Morals." *UKCR* 15 (Su 49) 271-80.
Kazin, Alfred. "Fitzgerald: An American Confession." *Quar R Lit* 2 (4Q 46) 341-6.
Leighton, Lawrence. "An Autopsy and a Prescription." *H&H* 5 (Su 32) 519-40.

MacKendrick, P. L. "The Great Gatsby and Trimalchio." *Classical J* 45 (Ap 50) 307-14.
Manning, Andrews. "Fitzgerald and His Brethren." *PR* 12 (Au 45) 545-51.
Marquand, J. P. "Fitzgerald: 'This Side of Paradise.'" *SRL* 32 (6 Ag 49) 30-1.
Marshall, Margaret. "Notes by the Way." *Nation* 152 (8 F 41) 159-60.
Mizener, Arthur. "Fitzgerald in the Twenties." *PR* 17 (Ja 50) 7-38.
——— "The Portable Fitzgerald." *KR* 8 (Sp 46) 343-4.
——— "Scott Fitzgerald and the Imaginative Possession of American Life." *SR* 54 (Ja-Mr 46) 66-86.
——— "Scott Fitzgerald: Moralist of the Jazz Age." *Harper's Bazaar* no 2853 (S 49) 174-8.
——— "The Novel of Manners in America." *KR* 12 (Wi 50) 1-20.
Mosher, J. C. "That Sad Young Man." *NYr* 2 (17 Ap 26) 20-1.
O'Hara, John. "F. Scott Fitzgerald—Odds and Ends." *N Y Times Book R* (8 Je 45) 3-4.
———, & Schulberg, Budd. "In Memory of Scott Fitzgerald." *NRp* 104 (3 Mr 41) 311-2.
Piper, H. D. "The Lost Decade." *Interim* 2 (Sp 45) 39-44.
Powers, J. F. "Dealer in Diamonds and Rhinestones." *Commonweal* 42 (10 Ag 45) 408-10.
Quennell, Peter. "Plutocrat in Fiction." *New Statesman & Nation* 21 (1 F 41) 1123.
R.V.A.S. "The Collected Works of F. Scott Fitzgerald." *NRp* 22 (12 My 20) 362.
Schneider, Isidor. "A Pattern of Failure." *New Masses* 57 (4 D 45) 23-4.
Schorer, Mark. "Fitzgerald's Tragic Sense." *YR* 35 (Au 45) 187-8.
Soupault, Philippe. "Présentation de Scott Fitzgerald." *Renaissances* no 18 (F 46) 93-5.
Troy, William. "Scott Fitzgerald: The Authority of Failure." *Accent* 6 (Au 45) 56-60.
Weir, Charles, Jr. "An Invite with Gilded Edges." *VQR* 20 (Ap 44) 100-13.
Wilson, Edmund. "Imaginary Conversation: Mr. Van Wyck Brooks and Mr. Scott Fitzgerald." *NRp* 38 (30 Ap 24) 249-54.

FLEMING, WALTER L. (1874-1932). Bonham, M. L., Jr. "Walter Lynwood Fleming: Southern Scholar." *SAQ* 38 (Ja 39) 23-30.

FLETCHER, JOHN GOULD (1886-1950). Aiken, Conrad. "Colourism in Poetry." *Freeman* 3 (6 Jl 21) 405-6.
——— "Possessor and Possessed." *Dial* 66 (22 F 19) 189-91.
Blackmur, R. P. "Versions of Fletcher." *Poetry* 47 (Mr 36) 344-7.
Cappon, Alexander. "An Alien among the Imagists: John Gould Fletcher." *Un R* 4 (Sp 38) 165-72.
Crawford, N. A. "Philosophy in Verse." *Poetry* 31 (Ja 28) 216-8.
Davidson, Donald. "In Memory of John Gould Fletcher." *Poetry* 77 (D 50) 154-60.
Deutsch, Babette. "A Lost Address." *Poetry* 52 (S 38) 347-51.
Dudley, Dorothy. "Poet and Theorist." *Poetry* 9 (O 16) 43-7.
Fletcher, J. G. "A Poet's Declaration of Rights." *Poetry* 7 (N 15) 88-9.
Fulkerson, Baucum. "John Gould Fletcher." *SR* 46 (Jl-S 38) 278-88.
Greenslet, Ferris. "The Poetry of John Gould Fletcher." *Egoist* 2 (1 My 15) 73.
Grudin, Louis. "A Naive Mystic." *Poetry* 21 (F 23) 270-5.
Henderson, A. C. "Two Books by Fletcher." *Poetry* 13 (Mr 19) 340-1 [See also 7 (O 15) 44-7].
Loving, Pierre. "Towards Walt Whitman." *Double Dealer* 4 (S 22) 139-42.
Lowell, Amy. "Mr. Fletcher's Verse." *NRp* 3 (15 My 15) 48-9.
Monroe, Harriet. "John Gould Fletcher." *Poetry* 27 (Ja 26) 206-10.
Pender, R. H. "John Gould Fletcher." *Egoist* 3 (N 16) 173-4.

Pound, Ezra. "Peals of Iron." *Poetry* 3 (D 13) 111-3.
Sherry, Laura. "Fletcherian Colors." *Poetry* 19 (D 21) 155-7.
Van Doren, Mark. "Poetic Space and Time." *Nation* 112 (13 Ap 21) 252.
W., E. "Faery-lands Forlorn." *NRp* 9 (18 N 16) 11.
Warren, R. P. "A Note on Three Southern Poets." *Poetry* 40 (My 32) 103-13.
Yarnell, D. A. "John Gould Fletcher." *Un R* 4 (Wi 36) 110-3.
Zabel, M. D. "Dust Discrowned." *Poetry* 33 (Ja 29) 222-4.

FLINT, TIMOTHY (1780-1840). Hamilton, J. A. "Timothy Flint's 'Lost Novel.'" *AL* 22 (Mr 50) 54-6.
Morris, R. L. "Three Arkansas Travellers." *Ark Hist R* 4 (Au 45) 215-30.
Turner, Arlin. "James Kirke Paulding and Timothy Flint." *Miss Valley Hist R* 34 (Je 47) 105-11.
Walker, L. M. "Picturesque New Mexico Revealed in Novel as Early as 1826." *N Mex Hist R* 13 (Jl 38) 325-8.

FLOWER, BENJAMIN ORANGE (1858-1918). Dickason, D. H. "Benjamin Orange Flower, Patron of the Realists." *AL* 14 (My 42) 148-56.
Fairfield, R. P. "Benjamin Orange Flower: Father of the Muckrakers." *AL* 22 (N 50) 272-82.

FLYNT, HENRY (1675-1760). Wilson, D. M. "Tutor Flynt, New England's First Humorist." *N E Mag* ns 23 (N 00) 284-93.

FOOTE, MARY HALLOCK (1847-1938). Davidson, L. J. "Letters from Authors." *Colo Mag* 19 (Jl 42) 122-6.

FORD, PAUL LEICESTER (1865-1902). Maurice, A. B. "Paul Leicester Ford." *Bkm* 10 (F 00) 563-6.

FOSS, SAM WALTER (1858-1911). Flower, B. O. "A New England Poet of the Common Life." *Arena* 26 (O 01) 391-410.

FOSTER, HANNAH WEBSTER (1759-1840). Shurter, R. L. "Mrs. Hannah Webster Foster and the Early American Novel." *AL* 4 (N 32) 306-8.

FOSTER, STEPHEN COLLINS (1826-64). Adkins, N. F. "A Note on the Bibliography of Stephen C. Foster." *N&Q* 163 (5 N 32) 331-2.
Bowman, J. G. "A Singer to Pioneers." *Atl* 156 (Jl 35) 83-8.
Burnett, J. G. "National Elements in Stephen Foster's Art." *SAQ* 21 (O 22) 322-6.
Crosby, A. F. "The Man Who Wrote 'Old Folks at Home.'" *Bkm* 38 (F 14) 615-7.
DeVoto, Bernard. "Stephen Foster's Songs." *Harper's* 183 (Je 41) 109-12.
Fletcher, E. G. "Stephen Collins Foster, Dramatic Collaborator." *Colophon* ns 1 (Su 35) 33-9.
Hodges, Fletcher. "Foster and the South." *SLM* 2 (F 40) 89-96.
——— "A Pittsburgh Composer and His Memorial." *West Penn Hist Mag* 21 (Je 38) 77-106.
Holliday, Carl. "Stephen Collins Foster." *Overland Mo* 88 (Jl 30) 199.
Howard, J. T. "History Bunked." *West Penn Hist Mag* 20 (Mr 37) 57-61.
——— "Stephen Foster and His Publishers." *Mus Q* 20 (Ja 34) 77-95.
——— "Stephen Foster's Contribution to Our American Life." *Pitt* 7 (Sp 41) 37-9.
Jillson, W. R. "State and National Collections of Fosteriana." *Ky State Hist Soc Reg* 32 (Jl 34) 270-3.
Lilly, J. K. "Fosteriana at Foster Hall." *Colophon* 4 (O 33) Pt 15.
Oberndorfer, A. S. F. "Life and Songs of Stephen C. Foster." *Am Col* 2 (Jl 20) 391-3.
Whitmer, T. C. "Stephen Foster, an American." *Musician* 18 (D 13) 801-2.
Young, Stark. "Massa's in Cold, Cold Ground." *NRp* 91 (19 My 37) 46-7.

FOX, JOHN (1863-1919). Page, T. N. "John Fox, Jr." *Scribner's* 66 (D 19) 674-83.

FRANK, WALDO (1889-). Colum, M. M. "Rahab." *Freeman* 5 (26 Ap 22) 162-4.
Davidson, Donald. "Waldo Frank." *Am R* 4 (D 34) 233-8.
Douglas, A. D. "Waldo Frank—Poet." *SRL* 1 (1 N 24) 244.
Gilman, Lawrence. "Franko-American." *NAR* 211 (Ja 20) 133-7.
Glicksberg, C. I. "Waldo Frank: Critic of America." *SAQ* 35 (Ja 36) 13-26.
Harrison, C. Y. "An Open Letter to Waldo Frank." *Mod Mo* 10 (Ja 37) 6-8.
Hughes, M. Y. "The Rediscovery of America." *SR* 37 (Jl-S 29) 379-81.
Jocelyn, John. "Getting at Waldo Frank." *SR* 40 (O-D 32) 405-13.
Josephson, Matthew. "Instant Note on Waldo Frank." *Broom* 2 (D 22) 57-60.
Littell, Robert. "Waldo Frank." *NRp* 36 (26 S 23) 12-4.
Rees, Richard. "Waldo Frank's Masterpiece." *Adelphi* 10 (Je 35) 147-53.
Rosenfeld, Paul. "The Novels of Waldo Frank." *Dial* 70 (Ja 21) 95-105.
Salaberry, R. C. "Waldo Frank et le nouvel idéal américain." *Mercure de France* 219 (15 Ap 30) 353-62.
Valle, R. H. "Diálogo con Waldo Frank." *Universidad* 3 (Ja 37) 36-44.

FRANKLIN, BENJAMIN (1706-90). Anon. "Acquisition of Benjamin Franklin Collection of Yale University." *School & Soc* 44 (29 Ag 36) 267-8.
——— "Benjamin Franklin and Freedom." *J Negro Hist* 4 (Ja 19) 41-50.
——— "Franklin's Earliest Manuscript." *Gen Mag* 37 (Jl 35) 447-50.
——— "Letter of Benjamin Franklin to Philip Mazzei." *WMQ* 9 (O 29) 323.
——— "List of Works in the New York Public Library by or Relating to Benjamin Franklin." *BNYPL* 10 (Ja 06) 29-83.
——— "Poem on the Death of Franklin." *Proc N J Hist Soc* 15 (Ja 30) 109.
——— "Selections from the Correspondence of Hugh Roberts and Benjamin Franklin." *PMHB* 38 (1914) 287-311.
——— "Some Letters of Franklin's Correspondents." *PMHB* 27 (1903) 151-75.
——— "Some New Franklin Papers." *Un Penn Alumni Bul* (Jl 03) 500.
——— "Tips from the Publishers." *Pub W* 151 (1 F 47) 567.
Abernethy, T. P. "The Origin of the Franklin-Lee Imbroglio." *N C Hist R* 15 (Ja 38) 41-52.
Adams, P. G. "Crèvecoeur and Franklin." *Penn Hist* 14 (O 47) 273-9.
Adams, R. G. "And Sold by Messrs. Franklin and Hall." *PMHB* 55 (Ja 31) 24-31.
——— "Notes and Queries." *Colophon* ns 2 (Au 37) 602-10.
——— "A Passy Passport." *JRUL* 5 (D 41) 5-8.
Aldridge, A. O. "Benjamin Franklin and Jonathan Edwards on Lightning and Earthquakes." *Isis* 41 (Fl 50) 162-4.
——— "Benjamin Franklin and The Maryland Gazette." *Md Hist Mag* 44 (S 49) 177-89.
——— "The Debut of American Letters in France." *FAR* 3 (Ja-Mr 50) 1-23.
——— "Franklin and the Ghostly Drummer of Tedworth." *WMQ* 3 ser 7 (O 50) 559-67.
——— "Franklin and Jackson on the French War." *PAPS* 94 (1950) 396-7.
——— "Franklin as Demographer." *J Ec Hist* 9 (My 49) 25-44.
——— "Franklin's Deistical Indians." *PAPS* 94 (1950) 398-410.
——— "Franklin's Letters on Indians and Germans." *PAPS* 94 (1950) 391-5.
——— "Franklin's 'Shaftesburian' Dialogues Not Franklin's: A Revision of the Franklin Canon." *AL* 21 (My 49) 151-9.
Ames, H. V. "The Public Career of Benjamin Franklin. A Life of Service." *PMHB* 55 (Jl 31) 193-207.
Babler, O. F. "Benjamin Franklin and Adam Mickiewicz." *N&Q* 192 (15 N 47) 498.

Bache, Franklin. "Where Is Franklin's First Chart of the Gulf Stream?" *PAPS* 76 (1936) 731-42.

Bache, R. M. "Smoky Torches in Franklin's Honor." *Critic* 48 (Je 06) 561-6.

Baldwin, A. H. "His Mother's Kindred." *Americana* 35 (Ja, Ap-Je 41) 7-32, 276-318.

Barbeu-Dubourg, Jacques. "Letters of Barbeu-Dubourg to Franklin, 1768-1775." *PMHS* 56 (N 22) 127-56.

Bennett, J. H. "Benjamin Franklin and John Selden." *AL* 15 (Mr 43) 63-5.

Biddison, Philip. "The Magazine Franklin Failed to Remember." *AL* 4 (My 32) 177-80.

Bloore, Stephen. "Samuel Keimer: A Footnote to the Life of Franklin." *PMHB* 54 (Jl 30) 255-87.

Boyd, J. P. "Dr. Franklin: Friend of the Indians." *J Franklin Inst* 234 (O 42) 311-30.

Bridgewater, D. W. "Notable Additions to the Franklin Collection." *Yale Un Lib Gaz* 20 (O 45) 21-8.

Brigham, C. S. "Franklin's German Newspaper, 1751-52." *PMHS* 56 (My 23) 301-5.

Browne, C. A. "Joseph Priestley [1733-1804] and the American 'Fathers.'" *Am Schol* 4 (Sp 35) 133-47.

Bullen, H. L. "Benjamin Franklin, and What Printing Did for Him." *Am Col* 2 (My 26) 284-91.

Cadman, P. F. "Souvenir of Franklin in Paris." *Gen Mag and Hist Chron* 46 (Sp 44) 138-51.

Cardwell, R. H. "American-English Correspondence of Three American Scholars, 1700-1775." *Tenn Hist Mag* 2: ser 2 (Jl 32) 227-33.

Cestre, Charles. "Franklin, homme représentative." *Revue Anglo-Américaine* 5 (Je, Ag 28) 409-23, 505-22.

Chinard, Gilbert. "Abbé Lefebvre de la Roche's Recollections of Benjamin Franklin." *Am Phil Soc Lib Bul* 94 (Je 50) 214-21.

——— "Conseils de Franklin pour l'utilisation du Maïs." *FAR* 1 (Ja-Mr 48) 17-20.

——— "Dr. Franklin Negotiates, December, 1777." *PAPS* 92 (5 My 48) 101-4.

——— "Les Amites américains de Mme. D'Houdetot." *Bibliothèque de la Revue Comparée* 7 (1924) 5-10.

——— "Looking Westward." *J Franklin Inst* 234 (Jl 42) 1-16.

Choate, J. H. "Benjamin Franklin." *Critic* 48 (Ja 06) 51-67.

Clapp, Margaret. "An Editor for Franklin's Autobiography." *Chri Sci Mon* 40 (11 D 47) 8.

Cohen, I. B. "Benjamin Franklin and Aeronautics." *J Franklin Inst* 232 (Ag 41) 101-28.

——— "Benjamin Franklin and the Mysterious 'Dr. Spence.'" *J Franklin Inst* 235 (Ja 43) 1-25.

——— "Benjamin Franklin as Scientist and Citizen." *Am Schol* 12 (Au 43) 474-81.

——— "Franklin's Experiments on Heat Absorption as a Function of Color." *Isis* 34 (Su 43) 404-7.

——— "How Practical Was Benjamin Franklin's Science?" *PMHB* 69 (O 45) 284-93.

Conway, Eleanor. "Dr. Abeloff's Franklin Collection." *N Y Hist Soc Quar Bul* 26 (Jl 42) 65-6.

Coulson, Thomas. "Benjamin Franklin and the Post Office." *J Franklin Inst* 210 (S 50) 191-212.

Covell, Elizabeth. "The Visits of Benjamin Franklin to Newport." *Newport Hist Soc Bul* 103 (Ja 45) 1-16.

Crane, V. W. "Benjamin Franklin and the Stamp Act." *PCSM* 32 (1937) 56-77.

——— "Benjamin Franklin on Slavery and American Liberties." *PMHB* 62 (Ja 38) 1-11.

——— "Certain Writings of Benjamin Franklin on the British Empire and the American Colonies." *PBSA* 28 (1934) 1-27.

——— "Franklin's Political Journalism in England." *J Franklin Inst* 233 (Mr 42) 205-24.

——— "Three Fables by Benjamin Franklin." *NEQ* 9 (S 36) 499-504.

Crawford, M. C. "An Important Franklin Discovery." *Outlook* 82 (20 Ja 06) 117-21.

——— "Franklin and the French Intriguers." *Appleton's* 7 (F 06) 220-31.

Davidson, Frank. "Three Patterns of Living." *AAUP Bul* 34 (Su 48) 364-74.

Dean, E. J. "Benjamin Franklin." *Negro Hist Bul* 6 (Ja 43) 78, 87.

Dickinson, A. D. "Another Old Yellow Book." *Gen Mag and Hist Chron* 30 (O 27) 3-7.

Distler, T. A. "Franklin's Two Colleges." *Gen Mag & Hist Chron* 48 (Wi 46) 117-24.

Dos Passos, John. "Two Eighteenth-Century Careers: I. Benjamin Franklin. II. Daniel Defoe." *NRp* 103 (11, 18 N 40) 654-7.

Dreppard, C. W. "The Franklin Stove." *Am Heritage* ns 1 (Wi 50) 52-3.

Duane, Russell. "Benjamin Franklin." *PAPS* 66 (1927) 729-35.

Dvoichenko-Markoff, Eufrosina. "Benjamin Franklin, the American Philosophical Society, and the Russian Academy." *PAPS* 151 (29 Ag 47) 250-7.

Eames, Wilberforce. "The Antigua Press and Benjamin Mecom, 1748-1765." *PAAS* ns 38 (O 28) 303-48.

Eddy, G. S. "Account Book of Benjamin Franklin Kept by Him during His First Mission to England as Provincial Agent, 1757-1762." *PMHB* 55 (Ap 31) 97-133.

——— "Comments on the State of Franklin Scholarship, with Directions for Possible Research." *Colophon* ns 2: no 4 (Au 37) 602-16.

——— "Correspondence between Dr. Benjamin Franklin and John Walter, Regarding the Logographic Process of Printing." *PAAS* ns 38 (O 28) 349-63.

——— "Dr. Benjamin Franklin's Library." *PAAS* ns 34 (O 24) 206-26.

——— "Ramble Through the Mason-Franklin Collection." *Yale Un Lib Gaz* 10 (Ap 36) 65-90.

——— "A Work Book of the Printing House of Benjamin Franklin and David Hall, 1759-1766." *BNYPL* 34 (Ag 30) 575-89.

Eliot, C. W. "Benjamin Franklin." *Science* ns 23 (1 Je 06) 833-9.

Eliot, T. D. "The Relations between Adam Smith and Benjamin Franklin before 1776." *Pol Sci Q* 39 (Mr 24) 67-96.

Falls, W. F. "Buffon, Franklin, et deux académies américaines." *RR* 29 (F 38) 37-47.

Farrand, Max. "Benjamin Franklin Memoirs." *Huntington Lib Bul* no 10 (O 36) 49-78.

——— "Self-Portraiture: The Autobiography." *J Franklin Inst* 233 (Ja 42) 1-16.

Fay, Bernard. "Franklin et Mirabeau." *Revue de la Littérature Comparée* 8 (Ja-Mr 28) 5-28.

——— "Les Débuts de Franklin en France." *Revue de Paris* (1 F 31) 577-605.

——— "His Excellency Mr. Franklin." *Forum* 79 (Mr 28) 319-34.

——— "Learned Societies in Europe and America in the Eighteenth Century." *AHR* 37 (Ja 32) 255-66.

——— "Le Triomphe de Franklin en France." *Revue de Paris* (15 F 31) 872-96.

Ford, W. C. "Franklin's Accounts against Massachusetts." *PMHS* 56 (N 22) 94-102.

——— "Franklin's *New England Courant*." *PMHS* 57 (Ap 24) 336-53.

——— "The French Manuscript of Franklin's Autobiography." *Nation* 86 (21 My 08) 462-3.

——— "One of Franklin's Friendships." *Harper's* 113 (S 06) 626-33.

Foster, J. W. "Franklin as a Diplomat." *Independent* 60 (11 Ja 06) 84-9.

Franklin, Benjamin. "Letters from Franklin to William Hodgson." *PMHS* 56 (N 22) 156-60.

——— "Letters of Benjamin Franklin." *PMHB* 40 (Ja 16) 480-4.

Gallacher, S. A. "Franklin's *Way to Wealth:* A Florilegium of Proverbs and Wise Sayings." *JEGP* 48 (Ap 49) 229-51.

Garrison, F. W. "Franklin and the Physiocrats." *Freeman* 8 (24 O 23) 154-6.

Gerig, J. L. "A Washington Letter to Franklin." *RR* 22 (Ap-Je 31) 173-4.

Griswold, A. W. "Three Puritans on Prosperity." *NEQ* 7 (S 34) 475-93.

Gummere, R. M. "Socrates at the Printing Press: Benjamin Franklin and the Classics." *Classical W* 26 (5 D 32) 57-9.

Hart, A. B. "Benjamin Franklin." *Mentor* 6 (15 My 18) 1-11.

Harvey, E. N. "Benjamin Franklin's View of the Phosphorescence of the Sea." *PAPS* 83 (Ag 40) 341-8.

Haviland, T. P. "Franklin's General Magazine, 1741." *Gen Mag & Hist Chron* 48 (Wi 46) 125-38.

——— "Of Franklin, Whitefield, and the Orphans." *Ga Hist R* 29 (D 45) 211-6.

Hedges, J. B. "John Adams Speaks His Mind." *AHR* 47 (Jl 42) 806-9.

Hoffman, R. V. "New Jersey in the Revolutionary Scene." *Americana* 36 (1942) 22-66.

Horner, G. F. "Franklin's *Do-Good Papers* Re-examined." *SP* 37 (Jl 40) 501-23.

Huckel, Oliver. "Benjamin Franklin and George Whitefield—Founding Fathers." *Gen Mag & Hist Chron* 40 (Jl 38) 372-82.

Hughes, M. M. "Benjamin Franklin, Lover." *Cornhill* 149 (Ja 34) 101-6.

Jenkins, C. F. "Franklin Returns from France—1785." *PAPS* 92 (27 D 48) 417-32.

Jernegan, M. W. "Benjamin Franklin's Electrical Kite and Lightning Rod." *NEQ* 1 (1928) 180-96.

Jorgenson, C. E. "Benjamin Franklin and Rabelais." *Classical J* 29 (Ap 34) 538-40.

——— "The New Science in the Almanacs of Ames and Franklin." *NEQ* 8 (D 35) 555-61.

——— "Sidelights on Benjamin Franklin's Principles of Rhetoric." *Revue Anglo-Américaine* 11 (F 34) 209-23.

——— "The Source of Benjamin Franklin's Dialogues between Philocles and Horatio (1730)." *AL* 6 (N 34) 337-9.

Kirkland, F. R. "Jefferson and Franklin." *PMHB* 71 (Jl 47) 218-22.

——— "Three Franklin Letters." *PMHB* 72 (Ja 48) 70-6.

——— "Three Mecom-Franklin Letters." *PMHB* 72 (Jl 48) 264-72.

——— "An Unknown Franklin Cartoon." *PMHB* 73 (Ja 49) 76-9.

Kite, E. S. "Benjamin Franklin—Diplomat." *Cath World* 142 (O 35) 28-37.

Knollenberg, Bernhard. "Benjamin Franklin—'Philosophical Revolutionist.'" *J Franklin Inst* 233 (Je 42) 517-23.

Lane, W. C. "Harvard College and Franklin." *PCSM* 10 (Ja 06) 229-39.

Lawrence, D. H. "Studies in Classic American Literature: II. Franklin." *Eng R* 27 (D 18) 397-408.

Leary, Lewis. "Joseph Dennie on Benjamin Franklin: A Note on Early American Literary Criticism." *PMHB* 72 (Jl 48) 240-6.

Less, Frank. "The Parisian Suburb of Passy in the Days of Franklin." *Arch Rec* 12 (D 02) 669-83.

Lingelbach, W. E. "B. Franklin, Printer—New Source Materials." *PAPS* 92 (5 My 48) 79-100.

Lodge, H. C. "Franklin and His Times." *Independent* 60 (11 Ja 06) 72-9.

McAdie, A. "The Date of Franklin's Kite Experiment." *PAAS* ns 34 (O 24) 188-205.

——— "Franklin and Lightning." *Atl* 136 (Jl 25) 67-73.

MacDonald, William. "The Fame of Franklin." *Atl* 96 (O 05) 450-62.

McKenzie, R. T. "A New View of Benjamin Franklin." *Century* 88 (Jl 14) 416-7.

McKillop, A. D. "Some Newtonian Verses in *Poor Richard.*" *NEQ* 21 (S 48) 383-5.
McMurtrie, D. C. "The Correspondence of Peter Timothy, Printer of Charleston [S. C.] with Benjamin Franklin." *S C Hist & Gen Mag* 35 (O 34) 123-9.
McPharlin, Paul. "Franklin's 'Cato Major,' 1774." *Pub W* 144 (4 D 43) 2111-8.
Madelin, L. "Franklin a Passy." *Bul de la Soc Hist d'Auteuil et de Passy* 12 (1933-4) 75-85.
Malone, Kemp. "Benjamin Franklin on Spelling Reform." *AS* 1 (N 25) 96-100.
Marsh, Philip. "The Manuscript Franklin Gave to Jefferson." *Lib Bul Am Philos Soc* (1946) 45-8.
Mason, W. S. "Franklin and Galloway, Some Unpublished Letters." *PAAS* ns 34 (O 24) 227-58.
Masterson, J. R. "A Foolish *Oneida* Tale." *AL* 10 (Mr 38) 53-65.
Mathews, L. K. "Benjamin Franklin's Plan for a Colonial Union, 1750-1775." *Am Pol Sci R* 8 (Ag 14) 393-412.
Miller, C. R. D. "Franklin and Carli's *Lettere Americane.*" *MP* 28 (F 30) 359-60.
Millikan, R. A. "Benjamin Franklin and His Electrical Experiments." *J Franklin Inst* 248 (Ag 49) 162-7.
——— "Benjamin Franklin as a Scientist." *J Franklin Inst* 232 (N 41) 407-23.
More, P. E. "Franklin in Literature." *Independent* 60 (11 Ja 06) 98-104.
Moses, E. C. "The Religion of Benjamin Franklin." *Arena* 40 (N 08) 434-7.
Mugridge, D. H. "Scientific Manuscripts of Benjamin Franklin." *Lib Congress J of Current Acquisitions* 4 (Ag 47) 12-21.
Mulder, Arnold. "Benjamin Franklin: Teacher of Composition." *CE* 3 (F 42) 480-6.
Mustard, W. P. "Poor Richard's Poetry." *Nation* 82 (22 Mr, 5 Ap 06) 239, 279.
Oberholtzer, E. P. "Franklin's Philosophical Society." *Popular Sci* 60 (Mr 02) 430-7.
Oswald, J. C. "The Portraits of Franklin." *Am Printer* 76 (1923) 49-54.
Owen, E. D. "Where Did Benjamin Franklin Get the Idea for His Academy?" *PMHB* 58 (Ja 34) 86-94.
Pace, Antonio. "Franklin and Machiavelli." *Symposium* 1 (My 47) 36-42.
Pange, C. J. de. "Madame de Staël et les Etats-Unis." *Revue de Paris* 5 (1 S 33) 150-63.
Pepper, G. W. "Molding the Constitution." *J Franklin Inst* 233 (My 42) 413-34.
Pepper, William. "Benjamin Franklin, Founder of the University." *Gen Mag & Hist Chron* 40 (Ap 38) 318-24.
Pettengil, G. E. "Franklin, Priestley and the Samuel Vaughan, Jr. Manuscripts, 1775-1782." *J Franklin Inst* 247 (Mr 49) 195-204.
Phelps, W. L. "Edwards and Franklin, The Man of God and the Man of the World." *Ladies' Home J* 39 (N 22) 16-7.
Phillips, W. L. "Franklin's Version of the 'Lord's Prayer': A Restoration of the Text." *AL* 22 (N 50) 338-41.
Pitt, A. S. "Franklin and the Quaker Movement against Slavery." *Bul Friends' Hist Assn* 32 (Sp 43) 13-31.
——— "Franklin and William Penn's *No Cross, No Crown.*" *MLN* 54 (Je 39) 466-7.
——— "The Sources, Significance, and Date of Franklin's 'An Arabian Tale.'" *PMLA* 57 (Mr 42) 155-68.
Quinlan, M. J. "Dr. Franklin Meets Dr. Johnson." *PMHB* 73 (Ja 49) 34-44.
Read, Conyers. "Benjamin Franklin, It Seems, Was No Idealist." *Chri Sci Mon* 37 (27 F 45) 6.
——— "Dr. Franklin as the English Saw Him." *J Franklin Inst* 233 (F 42) 105-33.
——— "The English Elements in Benjamin Franklin." *PMHB* 64 (Jl 40) 314-30.
Riddell, W. R. R. "Benjamin Franklin and Colonial Money." *PMHB* 54 (Ja 30) 52-64.

Roelker, W. G. "The Franklin-Greene Correspondence." *PAPS* 92 (19 Jl 48) 186-93.
Rogers, J. F. "The Physical Franklin." *SAQ* 15 (Ja 16) 18-24.
Rosengarten, J. G. "Franklin's Bagatelles." *PAPS* 40 (30 Jl 01) 87-134.
Ross, E. D. "Benjamin Franklin as an Eighteenth-Century Agricultural Leader." *J Pol Econ* 37 (F 29) 52-72.
Ross, J. F. "The Character of Poor Richard: Its Source and Alteration." *PMLA* 55 (S 40) 785-94.
Rotch, A. L. "Benjamin Franklin and the First Balloons." *PAAS* 18 (Ap 07) 259-74.
——— "Benjamin Franklin's Original Letters about Balloons." *PAAS* 19 (Ap 08) 100-6.
——— "Did Benjamin Franklin Fly His Electrical Kite before He Invented the Lightning Rod?" *PAAS* 18 (O 06) 18-23.
Ruggles, L. B. "A Few Things Recalled by the Franklin Bicentenary." *Critic* 48 (Ja 06) 40-50.
Sachse, J. F. "The Masonic Chronology of Benjamin Franklin." *PMHB* 30 (1906) 238-41.
Scott, J. B. "Franklin—Political Philosopher." *PAPS* 71 (1932) 217-24.
Seeber, E. D. "Franklin's 'Drinkers Dictionary' Again." *AS* 15 (F 40) 103-5.
Shelling, R. I. "Benjamin Franklin and the Dr. Bray Associates." *PMHB* 63 (Jl 39) 282-93.
Sioussat, St. G. L. "*The Philosophical Transactions* of the Royal Society in the Libraries of William Byrd of Westover, Benjamin Franklin, and the American Philosophical Society." *PAPS* 93 (My 49) 99-113.
Smyth, A. H. "Franklin as a Printer." *Independent* 60 (11 Ja 06) 84-9.
——— "Franklin's Social Life in France." *Putnam's* 1 (O, N, D 06, Ja 07) 30-41, 167-73, 310-6, 431-8.
Sonneck, O. G. "Franklin's Relation to Music." *Music* 19 (N 00) 1-14.
Spiller, R. E. "Benjamin Franklin: Student of Life." *J Franklin Inst* 233 (Ap 42) 309-29.
Steell, Willis. "Franklin and Voltaire." *Forum* 77 (Je 27) 900-2.
Stone, R. C. "Cato and Franklin on Buying." *Classical J* 42 (Ja 47) 242.
Strowbridge, S. S. "Franklin, the Homespun." *Chri Sci Mon* 35 (21 O 43) 6.
Thaler, Alwin. "Franklin and Fulke Greville." *PMLA* 56 (D 41) 1059-64.
Thatcher, Herbert. "Dr. Mitchell, M.D., F.R.S., of Virginia." *VMHB* 41 (Ja 33) 59-70.
Townsend, A. H. "The Franklin Fable." *EJ* 25 (Mr 36) 215-23.
Trent, W. P. "New Editions of Franklin." *Forum* 37 (Ja 06) 398-410.
Van Doren, Carl. "The Beginnings of the American Philosophical Society." *PAPS* 87 (1943) 277-89.
——— "Concluding Paper" [in "Meet Dr. Franklin" series]. *J Franklin Inst* 234 (N 42) 415-29.
——— "The First American Man of Letters." *Mich Alumnus Quar R* 45 (Su 39) 283-98.
——— "Franklin's Neglected Maxims." *SRL* 18 (20 Ag 38) 15-7.
——— "Meet Dr. Franklin." *J Franklin Inst* 232 (D 41) 509-18.
———, & Cohen, I. B. "Reviews of *Benjamin Franklin: A Biographical Sketch,* by Carl L. Becker." *WMQ* 4: ser 3 (Ap 47) 229-32.
Walcutt, C. C. "Franklin and Goldsmith on Sheep's Tales." *N&Q* 178 (16 D 39) 23.
Warren, Joseph. "Trusts for Accumulation of Income: The Wills of Benjamin Franklin and Peter Thellusson." *PMHS* 66 (1942) 346-56.
Wecter, Dixon. "Benjamin Franklin and an Irish 'Enthusiast.'" *HLQ* 4 (Ja 41) 205-34.
——— "Burke, Franklin, and Samuel Petrie." *HLQ* 3 (Ap 40) 315-38.

—— "Francis Hopkinson and Benjamin Franklin." *AL* 12 (My 40) 200-17.

—— "Thomas Paine and the Franklins." *AL* 12 (N 40) 306-17.

Williams, David. "More Light on Franklin's Religious Ideas." *AHR* 43 (Jl 38) 803-13.

Winterich, J. T. "Early American Books and Printing: Benjamin Franklin." *Pub W* 131 (1932) 2212-6.

Wolfe, Mrs. I. R. "Letter from William C. Rives in Regard to the Portrait of Franklin." *VMHB* 40 (Ja 32) 77-8.

Woodruff, L. L. "Erasmus Darwin and Benjamin Franklin." *Science* ns 46 (21 S 17) 291-2.

Woodward, C. R. "Benjamin Franklin: Adventure in Agriculture." *J Franklin Inst* 234 (S 42) 207-88.

Wright, L. B. "Franklin's Legacy to the Gilded Age." *VQR* 22 (Mr 46) 268-79.

Wroth, L. C. "Benjamin Franklin: The Printer at Work." *J Franklin Inst* 234 (Ag 42) 105-32.

Wykoff, G. S. "Problems concerning Franklin's 'A Dialogue between Britain, France, Spain, Holland, Saxony, and America.'" *AL* 11 (Ja 40) 439-48.

FRANKLIN, WILLIAM (1730?-1813). Knollenberg, Bernhard. "Three Letters of William Franklin." *Yale Un Lib Gaz* 21 (O 46) 18-27.

FREDERIC, HAROLD (1856-98). Johnson, Merle. "American First Editions: Harold Frederic (1856-1898)." *Pub W* 126 (15 D 34) 2164.

McWilliams, Carey. "Harold Frederic: 'A Country Boy of Genius.'" *Un Calif Chron* 25 (1933) 21-34.

Walcutt, C. C. "Harold Frederic and American Naturalism." *AL* 11 (Mr 39) 11-22.

FREEMAN, MARY WILKINS (1852-1930). Levy, B. M. "Mutations in New England Local Color." *NEQ* 19 (S 46) 338-58.

FRENCH, ALICE (1850-1934). Sewell, Rebecca. "Clover Bend Plantation." *Sw R* 21 (Ap 36) 312-8.

FRENEAU, PETER (1760-1816). Davis, R. B., & Seigler, M. B. "Peter Freneau, Carolina Republican." *J So Hist* 13 (Ag 47) 395-405.

FRENEAU, PHILIP (1752-1832). Anon. "The Father of American Poetry." *Dial* 34 (16 Je 03) 405-6.

—— "Philip Freneau, the Poet of the Revolution." *Nation* 75 (24 Jl 02) 78.

Ainsworth, E. G. "An American Translator of Ariosto: Philip Freneau." *AL* 4 (Ja 33) 393-5.

Arms, G. W. "Freneau's *The Indian Burying Ground.*" *Expl* 2 (My 44) 55.

Beatty, J. M. "Churchill and Freneau." *AL* 2 (My 30) 121-30.

Benson, A. B. "The Misconception in Philip Freneau's 'Scandinavian War Song.'" *JEGP* 28 (Ja 29) 111-6.

Bowen, E. W. "Philip Freneau, The Poet of The American Revolution." *SR* 11 (Ap 03) 213-20.

Brown, R. W. "Classical Echoes in the Poetry of Philip Freneau." *Classical J* 45 (O 49) 29-34.

Burnett, V. S. "Freneau Revises." *JRUL* 10 (Je 47) 63-4.

Calverton, V. F. "Philip Freneau: An Apostle of Freedom." *Mod Mo* 7 (O 33) 533-46.

Clark, H. H. "The Literary Influences of Philip Freneau." *SP* 22 (Ja 25) 1-33.

—— "What Made Freneau the Father of American Poetry?" *SP* 26 (Ja 29) 1-22.

—— "What Made Freneau the Father of American Prose?" *Trans Wisc Acad Sci, Arts & Letters* 25 (1930) 39-50.

Dondore, Dorothy. "Freneau's *The British Prison-Ship* and Historical Accuracy." *EJ* (Col ed) 28 (Mr 39) 228-30.

Forman, S. E. "The Political Activities of Philip Freneau." *Johns Hopkins Un Stud Hist & Pol Sci* 20 (S-O 02) 1-105.
Gibbens, V. E. "A Note on Three Lyrics of Philip Freneau." *MLN* 59 (My 44) 313-5.
Grundy, J. O. "Philip Freneau, Jersey Patriot and Poet of the Revolution." *Proc N J Hist Soc* ns 14 (O 29) 481-8.
Gummere, R. M. "Apollo on Locust Street." *PMHB* 56 (Ja 32) 68-96.
Hallenbeck, C. T. "A Note for Future Editors of Freneau's Poems." *AL* 4 (Ja 33) 391-3.
Haviland, T. P. "A Measure for the Early Freneau's Debt to Milton." *PMLA* 55 (D 40) 1033-40.
Holbert, G. K. "Barney, Forgotten Hero." *Hist Soc Reg* 41 (Ap 43) 138-46.
Hopkins, P. T. "On a Popular Poet." *Poet Lore* 32 (D 21) 581-5.
Hustvedt, S. B. "Philippic Freneau." *AS* 4 (O 28) 1-18.
Johnson, Merle. "American First Editions. Philip Freneau (1752-1832)." *Pub W* 122 (16 Jl 32) 213-4.
Kirk, Rudolf. "Freneau's 'View' of Princeton." *JRUL* 3 (D 39) 20-5.
——— "Two Poems by Philip Freneau." *JRUL* 1 (D 37) 31-2.
Leary, Lewis. "Account of the Island of Bermuda." *Bermuda Hist Q* 5 (My 48) 54, 98-100.
——— "Father Bombo's Pilgrimage." *PMHB* 66 (O 42) 459-78.
——— "The First Biography of Philip Freneau." *Proc N J Hist Soc* 65 (Jl 47) 117-25.
——— "The Log of the Brig Rebecca, October 15—November 7, 1779." *JRUL* 5 (Je 42) 65-70.
——— "The Manuscript of Philip Freneau's 'The British Prison-Ship.'" *JRUL* 6 (D 42) 1-28.
——— "Phaeton in Philadelphia: Jean Pierre Blanchard and the First Balloon Ascension in America, 1793." *PMHB* 67 (Ja 43) 49-60.
——— "Philip Freneau and Monmouth County." *Monmouth County Hist Assn Bul* 1 (Jl 48) 59-82.
——— "Philip Freneau at Seventy." *JRUL* 1 (Je 38) 1-13.
——— "Philip Freneau in Charleston." *S C Hist & Gen Mag* 42 (Jl 41) 89-98.
——— "Philip Freneau on the Cession of Florida." *Fla Hist Q* 21 (Jl 42) 40-3.
——— "Philip Freneau's Captain Hanson." *AN&Q* 2 (Jl 42) 51-2.
——— "Philip Freneau's Father." *JRUL* 2 (Je 39) 46-52.
——— "Philip Freneau's Records of Sea Voyages." *JRUL* 11 (Je 48) 94-6.
——— "*The Time-Piece:* Philip Freneau's Last Venture in Newspaper Editing." *PULC* 2 (F 41) 65-74.
——— "An Uncollected Item in the Bibliography of Philip Freneau." *AL* 6 (N 34) 331-4.
Mabbott, T. O. "Freneau's *On a Honey Bee Drinking*." *Expl* 5 (Je 47) 57.
Malone, Ted. "Freneau, America's First Poet." *Vermonter* 51 (Ja 46) 19-25.
Marble, A. R. "Philip Freneau, America's First Poet." *N E Mag* ns 29 (D 03) 421-35.
Marsh, P. M. "Freneau and Jefferson: The Poet-Editor Speaks for Himself about the *National Gazette* Episode." *AL* 8 (My 36) 180-9.
——— "Freneau and the Bones of Columbus." *MLN* 60 (F 45) 121-4.
——— "A Freneau Fragment." *JRUL* 10 (Je 47) 60-2.
——— "Freneau's 'Hezekiah Salem.'" *NEQ* 18 (Je 45) 256-9.
——— "Freneau's Last Home." *Proc N J Hist Soc* 57 (Ap 39) 108-13.
——— "From 'Ezekiah Salem' to 'Robert Slender,' the Pseudonymic Creations of Peter Zenger and Philip Freneau." *MLN* 61 (N 46) 447-51.
——— "The Griswold Story of Freneau and Jefferson." *AHR* 51 (O 45) 68-73.
——— "Jefferson and Freneau." *Am Schol* 16 (Sp 47) 201-10.
——— "A Lost Fragment of Freneau's 'The Spy.'" *JRUL* 13 (Je 50) 61-3.

——— "Madison's Defense of Freneau." *WMQ* 3: ser 3 (Ap 46) 269-80.
——— "Monroe's Draft of the Defense of Freneau." *PMHB* 71 (Ja 47) 73-6.
——— "Philip Freneau and Francis Hopkinson." *Proc N J Hist Soc* 63 (Jl 45) 141-9.
——— "Philip Freneau and His Circle." *PMHB* 63 (Ja 39) 37-59.
——— "Philip Freneau and James Madison, 1791-1793." *Proc N J Hist Soc* 65 (O 47) 189-94.
——— "Philip Freneau and the Theatre." *Proc N J Hist Soc* 66 (Ap 48) 96-105.
——— "Philip Freneau, Our Sailor Poet." *Am Neptune* 6 (Ap 46) 115-20.
——— "Philip Freneau to Peter Freneau." *JRUL* 10 (D 46) 28-30.
——— "Philip Freneau's Manuscript of 'The Spy.'" *JRUL* 9 (D 45) 23-7.
——— "Philip Freneau's Personal File of the *Freeman's Journal*." *Proc N J Hist Soc* 57 (Jl 39) 163-70.
——— "A Reply to Lewis Leary." *AL* 21 (N 49) 344-6.
——— "Was Freneau a Fighter?" *Proc N J Hist Soc* 56 (Jl 38) 211-8.
———, & Ellis, Milton. "A Broadside of Freneau's *The British Prison Ship*." *AL* 10 (Ja 39) 476-80.
Masters, E. C. "Philip Freneau." *Un R* 2 (Su 36) 227-35.
More, P. E. "Philip Freneau." *Nation* 85 (10 O 03) 320-3.
Northrup, C. S. "The Laureate of the Revolution." *Dial* 33 (1 Ag 02) 55-8.
Pattee, F. L. "Bibliography of Freneau." *Bibliographer* 1 (Ja 02) 96-106.
——— "Philip Freneau." *Chautauquan* 31 (Ag 00) 467-75.
——— "Philip Freneau as Postal Clerk." *AL* 4 (Mr 32) 61-2.
Rockefeller, G. C. "New Jersey Printing before 1800." *Proc N J Hist Soc* 55 (O 37) 295-7.
Smith, Frank. "Philip Freneau and *The Time-Piece and Literary Companion*." *AL* 4 (N 32) 270-87.

FROST, ROBERT (1875-). Anon. "Frost and Masters." *Poetry* 9 (Ja 17) 202-7.
——— Part of a letter, dated December 14, 1932, in which Frost refers to Amy Lowell, Ezra Pound, and others. *Autograph Album* 1 (D 33) 56.
——— "Pawky Poet." *Time* 56 (9 O 50) 76-82.
——— "The 'Poet of Frost.'" *Lit Dig* 66 (17 Jl 20) 32-3.
——— "Robert Frost." *Bkm* 57 (My 23) 304-8.
——— "Robert Frost, a Check-list Bibliography." *Reading & Collecting* (S 37) 15.
——— "Robert (Lee) Frost." *Cur Biog* 3 (S 42) 18-22.
Abbot, Waldo. "Robert Frost: Professor of English." *Mich Alumnus* 32 (12 D 25) 208-9.
Abercrombie, Lascelles. "A New Voice." *Nation* 15 (13 Je 14) 423-4.
Anthony, Joseph. "Robert Frost, the Farmer-Poet." *Farm & Fireside* 45 (Je 21) 4.
Aykroyed, G. O. "The Classical in Robert Frost." *Poet Lore* 40 (Wi 29) 610-4.
Bartlett, Donald. "A Friend's View of Robert Frost." *N H Troubadour* 16 (N 46) 22-5.
Baxter, Sylvester. "New England's New Poet." *Rev of Rev* 51 (Ap 15) 432-4.
Benjamin, P. L. "Robert Frost—Poet of Neighborliness." *Survey* 45 (27 N 20) 318-9.
Berkelman, R. G. "Robert Frost and the Middle Way." *CE* 3 (Ja 42) 347-53.
Blackmur, R. P. "The Instincts of a Bard." *Nation* 142 (24 Je 36) 819.
Boutell, H. S. "A Bibliography of Robert Frost." *Colophon* 1 (My 30) Pt 2.
Bowles, E. S. "Robert Frost: A Belated Appreciation." *Granite Mo* 57 (Jl 25) 267-70.
Bowra, C. M. "Robert Frost." *Adelphi* 27 (N 50) 46-64.
Boynton, P. H. "Robert Frost." *EJ* 11 (O 22) 455-62.
Bradley, W. A. "Four American Poets." *Dial* 61 (14 D 16) 528-30.
Breit, Harvey. "Talk with Robert Frost." *N Y Times Book R* (27 N 49) 20.
Browne, G. H. "Robert Frost, a Poet of Speech." *Independent* 86 (22 My 16) 283-4.

Campbell, H. M. "Frost's *Sitting by a Bush in Broad Sunlight.*" *Expl* 5 (D 46) 18.
Carroll, G. H. "New England Sees It Through." *SRL* 13 (9 N 35) 3-4, 14, 17.
Cestre, Charles. "Amy Lowell, Robert Frost, and Edwin Arlington Robinson." *John Hopkins Alumni Mag* 14 (Mr 26) 363-88.
Clark, Sylvia. "Robert Frost: The Derry Years." *N H Troubadour* 16 (N 46) 13-6.
Clausen, B. C. "A Portrait for Peacemakers." *Friends' Intelligencer* 101 (29 Ja 44) 71-2.
Clymer, Shubnick. "Robert Frost the Realist." *Yankee* 1 (O 35) 22-5.
Colum, Padriac. "Poetry of Robert Frost." *NRp* 9 (23 D 16) 219.
Conrad, L. H. "Robert Frost." *Landmark* 12 (O 30) 643-6.
Cook, R. L. "Frost as a Parablist." *Accent* 10 (Au 49) 33-41.
——— "Frost Country." *Vt Life* 3 (Su 49) 15-7.
——— "Poet in the Mountains." *WR* 11 (Sp 47) 175-81.
——— "Robert Frost: A Time to Listen." *CE* 7 (N 45) 66-71.
——— "Robert Frost as Teacher." *CE* 8 (F 47) 251-5.
——— "Robert Frost's Asides on His Poetry." *AL* 19 (Ja 48) 351-9.
Corbin, H. H., Jr., & Hendricks, C. H. "Frost's *Neither Out Far Nor in Deep.*" *Expl* 1 (My 43) 58.
Cowley, Malcolm. "Frost: A Dissenting Opinion." *NRp* 111 (11, 18 S 44) 312-3, 345-7.
Cox, S. H. "New England and Robert Frost." *NMQR* 4 (My 34) 89-94.
——— "Robert Frost and Poetic Fashion." *Am Schol* 18 (Wi 48-49) 78-86.
——— "Robert Frost at Plymouth." *N H Troubadour* 16 (N 46) 18-22.
——— "The Sincerity of Robert Frost." *NRp* 12 (25 Ag 17) 109-11.
Croff, Grace. "A Side-Light on Robert Frost." *Christmas Books* (Hunter Col) (D 37) 29-30.
Dabbs, J. M. "Robert Frost and the Dark Woods." *YR* 23 (Mr 34) 514-20.
——— "Robert Frost, Poet of Action." *EJ* 25 (Je 36) 443-51.
DeVoto, Bernard. "The Critics and Robert Frost." *SRL* 17 (1 Ja 38) 3-4, 14-5.
Dudley, Dorothy. "The Acid Test." *Poetry* 23 (Mr 24) 328-35.
Dupee, F. W. "Frost and Tate." *Nation* 160 (21 Ap 45) 464.
Dyer, W. A. "Overlooking the Common." *Amherst Record* 93 (20 Mr 35) 2, 6.
Eckert, R. P., Jr. "Robert Frost in England." *Mark Twain Q* 3 (Sp 40) 14-6.
Elliott, G. R. "The Neighborliness of Robert Frost." *Nation* 109 (6 D 19) 713-5.
——— "An Undiscovered America in Frost's Poetry." *VQR* 1 (Jl 25) 205-15.
Emerson, Dorothy. "Robert Frost." *Schol* 29 (19 S 36) 6-7.
Engle, Paul. "About Robert Frost." *Am Prefaces* 3 (Ap 39) 100.
Fair, J. F. "Robert Frost Visits the Demonstration Class." *EJ* 20 (F 31) 124-8.
Farrar, John. "Robert Frost and Other Green Mountain Writers." *EJ* 16 (O 27) 581-7.
Feuillerat, Albert. "Poètes américains d'aujourd'hui: M. Robert Frost." *Revue des Deux Mondes* 17 (S 23) 185-210.
Fisher, D. C. "Robert Frost's Hilltop." *Bkm* 64 (D 26) 403-5.
Fletcher, J. G. "Robert Frost the Outlander." *Mark Twain Q* 3 (Sp 40) 5-8.
Greeme, M. T. "Robert Frost at Home." *Chri Sci Mon* 15 (15 Ag 49) 14.
McCord, David. "Robert Frost." *Harvard Alumni Bul* 26 (29 My 24) 985-7.
McGiffert, John. "Something in Robert Frost." *EJ* 34 (N 45) 469-71.
McMillen, L. "A Modern Allegory." *Hudson R* 1 (Sp 48) 105-8.
Mardenborough, Aimee. "Robert Frost: The Old and the New." *Cath World* 168 (D 48) 232-6.
Melcher, F. G. "American First Editions . . . Robert (Lee) Frost, 1875- ." *Pub W* 102 (6 Ja 23) 24.
——— "Robert Frost and His Books." *Colophon* 1: pt 2 (My 30) 1-7.
Mitchell, Stewart. "Notes on Nightingales." *NEQ* 4 (Ap 32) 404-7.
Monroe, Harriet. "Frost and Masters." *Poetry* 9 (Ja 17) 202-7.
——— "A Frugal Master." *Poetry* 35 (Mr 29) 333-6.

——— "Robert Frost." *Poetry* 25 (D 24) 146-51.
Moore, Merrill. "Poetic Agrarianism, Old Style." *SR* 45 (O-D 37) 507-9.
Moore, Virginia. "Robert Frost of New Hampshire." *YR* 20 (Mr 31) 627-9.
Morse, Stearns. "Robert Frost and New Hampshire." *N H Troubadour* 16 (N 46) 6-8.
——— "The Wholeness of Robert Frost." *VQR* 19 (S 43) 412-6.
Morton, David. "The Poet of the New Hampshire Hills." *Outlook* 135 (19 D 23) 688-9.
Munson, G. B. "Robert Frost." *SRL* 1 (28 Mr 25) 625-6.
——— "Robert Frost and the Humanistic Temper." *Bkm* 81 (Jl 30) 419-22.
Nash, Ray. "The Poet and the Pirate." *New Colophon* 2 (F 50) 311-21.
Newdick, R. S. "Bibliographies and Exhibits of the Work of Robert Frost." *Amherst Grad Q* 26 (N 36) 79-80.
——— "Children in the Poems of Robert Frost." *Ohio Schools* 15 (S 37) 286-7, 313.
Foster, C. H. "Robert Frost and the New England Tradition." *Un Colo Stud* 2: ser B (O 45) 370-81.
Freeman, John. "Robert Frost." *London Mercury* 13 (D 25) 176-87.
Frost, Robert. "The Constant Symbol." *Atl* 178 (O 46) 50-2.
——— "Speaking of Loyalty." *Amherst Graduates' Q* 37 (Ag 48) 271-6.
Garnett, Edward. "A New American Poet." *Atl* 116 (Ag 15) 214-21.
Gregory, Horace. "Robert Frost." *New Freeman* 3 (1 Ap 31) 60-2.
Hedges, M. H. "Creative Teaching: Robert Frost's Assumption of a Professorship of Literature in Amherst College." *School & Soc* 7 (26 Ja 18) 117-8.
Hicks, Granville. "The World of Robert Frost." *NRp* 65 (3 D 30) 77-8.
Hillyer, Robert. "A Letter to Robert Frost." *Atl* 158 (Ag 36) 158-63.
——— "Robert Frost 'Lacks Power.'" *NEQ* 4 (Ap 32) 402-4.
Hoffman, D. G. "Frost's *For Once, Then Something.*" *Expl* 9 (N 50) 17.
Holden, Raymond. "North of Boston." *NYr* 7 (6 Je 31) 24-7.
Holmes, John. "Close-up of an American Poet at 75." *N Y Times Mag* (26 Mr 50) 12, 72, 73, 75-7.
Hopper, V. F. "Robinson and Frost." *SRL* 13 (2 N 35) 9.
Horton, R. W., & Thompson, Lawrance. "Frost." *CEA Critic* 11 (F 49) 4-5.
Janney, F. L. "Robert Frost." *Hollins Alumnae Q* 9 (1935) 10-5.
Jarrell, Randall. "The Other Robert Frost." *Nation* 165 (29 N 47) 590-601.
Jones, Llewellyn. "Robert Frost." *Am R* 2 (Mr 24) 165-71.
Lambuth, David. "The Unforgettable Robert Frost." *N H Troubadour* 16 (N 46) 25-9.
Lindley, F. V. "Robert Frost." *Groton School Q* 7 (O 33) 583-95.
Long, W. S. "Frost." *CEA Critic* 10 (N 48) 4.
——— "Design in the Books of Robert Frost." *Reading & Coll* 1 (S 37) 5-6, 15.
——— "The Early Verse of Robert Frost and Some of His Revisions." *AL* 7 (My 35) 181-7.
——— "Foreign Responses to Robert Frost." *Colophon* ns 2 (Wi 37) 289-90.
——— "Robert Frost and the American College." *J Higher Educ* 7 (My 36) 237-43.
——— "Robert Frost and the Classics." *Classical J* 35 (Ap 40) 403-16.
——— "Robert Frost and the Dramatic." *NEQ* 10 (Je 37) 262-9.
——— "Robert Frost and the Sound of Sense." *AL* 9 (N 37) 289-300.
——— "Robert Frost as Teacher." *EJ* 25 (O 36) 632-7.
——— "Robert Frost: Impressions and Observations." *Ohio Stater* 2 (My 36) 18-9.
——— "Robert Frost Looks at War." *SAQ* 38 (Ja 39) 52-9.
——— "Robert Frost Speaks Out." *SR* 45 (Ap-Je 37) 239-41.
——— "Robert Frost, Teacher and Educator: An Annotated Bibliography." *J Higher Educ* 7 (Je 36) 342-4.
——— "Robert Frost's Other Harmony." *SR* 48 (Jl 40) 409-18.
——— "Some Notes on Robert Frost and Shakespeare." *Shakespeare Assn Bul* 12 (Jl 37) 187-9.

——— "Three Poems by Robert Frost." *AL* 7 (N 35) 329.
——— "Uncollected Poems of Robert Frost." *Book Coll J* 2 (F 37) 1-2.
O'Donnell, W. G. "Parable in Poetry." *VQR* 25 (Sp 49) 269-82.
——— "Robert Frost and New England: A Revaluation." *YR* 37 (Su 48) 698-712.
Ortiz-Vargas, Alfredo. "Perfiles anglo-americanas." *Revista Ibero Americana* 4 (F 42) 163-76.
——— "Robert Frost." *N Mex Q* 14 (Wi 44) 403-8.
Parks, E. W. "Robert Frost." *Boletin do Instituto Brasil-Estados Unidos* (Rio de Janeiro) 8 (Mr 50) 2.
Paz, Octavio. "Visita al poeta Robert Frost." *Sur* 14 (N 45) 33-9.
Perrine, Laurence. "Frost's *Neither Out Far Nor In Deep.*" *Expl* 7 (Ap 49) 46.
Polle, Ernest. "Robert Frost Was Here." *N H Troubadour* 16 (N 46) 10-2.
Pound, Ezra. "A Boy's Will." *Poetry* 2 (My 13) 72-4.
——— "Modern Georgics." *Poetry* 5 (D 14) 127-30.
Prévost, Jean. "Robert Frost." *Nouvelle Revue Française* (1 My 39) 818-40.
Richards, E. A. "A Note on Robert Frost." *MS* 2 (F 31) 4.
Root, E. T. "New England Honors Her Leading Poet." *Christian Century* 53 (15 Ap 36) 581.
Ryan, A. S. "Frost's *A Witness Tree.*" *Expl* 7 (Mr 49) 39.
Saul, G. B. "Brief Observations on Frost and Stephens." *News Letter Col Eng Assn* 4 (O 42) 6.
Schwartz, Karl. "Robert Frost—Ein Dichter New Englands." *Hochschule und Ausland* 13 (Mr 35) 46-50.
Sergeant, E. S. "Robert Frost, A Good Greek Out of New England." *NRp* 84 (30 S 35) 144-8.
Smith, Fred. "The Sound of a Yankee Voice." *Commonweal* 15 (13 Ja 32) 297-8.
Spitz, Leon. "Robert Frost's Job Drama." *Am Hebrew* 157 (12 S 47) 13, 89.
Thomas, C. W. "Double Wisdom." *Wisc State J* (21 Je 36) 4.
Thompson, Lawrance. "An Early Frost Broadside." *New Colophon* 1 (Ja 48) 5-12.
Tilley, M. P. "Notes from Conversations with Robert Frost." *Inlander* 20 (F 18) 3-8.
Untermeyer, Louis. "Play in Poetry." *SRL* 17 (26 F 38) 3-4, 14, 16.
——— "Robert Frost: Revisionist." *Am Merc* 39 (S 36) 123-5.
Van Doren, Carl. "The Soil of the Puritans, Robert Frost: Quintessence and Subsoil." *Century* 105 (F 23) 629-36.
Van Doren, Mark. "The Permanence of Robert Frost." *Am Schol* 5 (Sp 36) 190-8.
——— "Robert Frost." *Nation* 117 (19 D 23) 715-6.
Viereck, Peter. "Parnassus Divided." *Atl* 184 (O 49) 67-70.
Waggoner, H. H. "Frost's *A Masque of Reason.*" *Expl* 4 (Mr 46) 32.
——— "The Humanistic Idealism of Robert Frost." *AL* 13 (N 41) 207-23.
Walcutt, C. C. "Frost's *Death of the Hired Man.*" *Expl* 3 (O 44).
Warren, C. H. "An Original, Ordinary Man." *Bkm* (London) 65 (Ja 31) 262-4.
Warren, R. P. "Hawthorne, Anderson, and Frost." *NRp* 54 (16 My 28) 399-401.
Webster, H. T. "Frost's *West Running Brook.*" *Expl* 8 (F 50) 32.
Whicher, G. F. "Frost at Seventy." *Am Schol* 14 (Au 45) 412-4.
——— "Out for Stars: A Meditation on Robert Frost." *Atl* 171 (My 43) 64-7.
Whipple, T. H. "Robert Frost." *Lit R* 4 (22 Mr 24) 605-6.
White, N. I. "Robert Frost's First Collected Edition." *SAQ* 30 (O 31) 439-40.
Wilkinson, Marguerite. "Poets of the People." *Touchstone* 3 (Ap 18) 7-74.
Wilson, J. S. "Robert Frost: American Poet." *VQR* 7 (Ap 31) 316-20.
Winterich, J. T. "Robert Frost: A Chronological Survey." *SRL* 14 (8 Ag 36) 21.
Winters, Yvor. "Robert Frost: Or, the Spiritual Drifter as Poet." *SR* 56 (Au 48) 564-96.

FULLER, HENRY BLAKE (1857-1929). Lovett, R. M. "Fuller of Chicago." *NRp* 60 (21 Ag 29) 16-8.

Mabbott, T. O. "Henry B. Fuller: His Pseudonym." *N&Q* 163 (31 D 32) 477.
Schultz, Victor. "Henry Blake Fuller: Civilized Chicagoan." *Bkm* 70 (S 29) 34-8.
Van Vechten, Carl. "Henry Blake Fuller." *Double Dealer* 3 (Je 22) 289-99.

FULLER, MARGARET (1810-50). Barbour, F. M. "Margaret Fuller and the British Reviewers." *NEQ* 9 (D 36) 618-25.
Bradford, Gamaliel. "Portrait of Margaret Fuller." *NAR* 210 (Jl 19) 109-21.
Braun, F. A. "Margaret Fuller's Translation and Criticism of Goethe's *Tasso*." *JEGP* 13 (1914) 202-13.
Burton, R. C. "Margaret Fuller's Criticism of the Fine Arts." *CE* 6 (O 44) 18-23.
Cairns, W. B. "The 'Dryad Song.'" *AL* 1 (N 29) 305.
Carpenter, R. V. "Margaret Fuller in Northern Illinois." *J Ill State Hist Soc* 2 (Ja 10) 7-22.
Fuller, Margaret. "Margaret Fuller on Literary London in 1846." *BNYPL* 5 (D 01) 455-6.
Hess, M. W. "Margaret Fuller and Browning's Childe Roland." *Personalist* 28 (Au 47) 376-83.
Hicks, Granville. "A Conversation in Boston." *SR* 39 (Ap-Je 31) 129-43.
——— "Margaret Fuller to Sarah Helen Whitman: An Unpublished Letter." *AL* 1 (Ja 30) 419-21.
Jones, L. C. "A Margaret Fuller Letter to Elizabeth Barrett Browning." *AL* 9 (Mr 37) 70-1.
McMaster, H. N. "Margaret Fuller as a Literary Critic." *Un Buffalo Stud* 7 (1928) 35-100.
McNeal, T. H. "Poe's *Zenobia:* An Early Satire on Margaret Fuller." *MLQ* 11 (Je 50) 215-6.
Madison, C. A. "Margaret Fuller: Transcendental Rebel." *AR* 2 (Fl 42) 422-38.
Marble, A. R. "Margaret Fuller as Teacher." *Critic* 43 (O 03) 334-45.
Martin, W. E., Jr. "A Last Letter of Margaret Fuller Ossoli." *AL* 5 (Mr 33) 66-9.
Meyer, A. N. "The Real Margaret Fuller." *Bkm* 17 (Ag 03) 596-600.
Minot, J. C. "True Daughter of Genius." *N E Mag* ns 42 (My 10) 294-5.
Munsterberg, Margaret. "Margaret Fuller Centenary." *BPLQ* 2 (Jl 50) 245-66.
Nicholas, Edward. "It Is I, Margaret Fuller." *Harper's* 199 (Jl 49) 66-76.
Orr, E. W. "Two Margaret Fuller Manuscripts." *NEQ* 11 (D 38) 794-802.
Randel, W. P. "Hawthorne, Channing, and Margaret Fuller." *AL* 10 (Ja 39) 472-6.
Rostenberg, Leona. "Diary of Timothy Fuller in Congress, January 12-March 15, 1818." *NEQ* 12 (S 39) 521-9.
——— "Margaret Fuller and Elizabeth Barrett Browning." *AN&Q* 2 (F 43) 163-5.
——— "Margaret Fuller's Roman Diary." *J Mod Hist* 12 (Je 40) 209-20.
——— "Mazzini to Margaret Fuller, 1847-1849." *AHR* 47 (O 41) 73-80.
Sanborn, F. B. "Women of Concord." *Critic* 48 (Mr 06) 251-7.
Schultz, A. R. "Margaret Fuller—Transcendentalist Interpreter of American Literature." *Monatshefte für Deutschen Unterricht* 34 (1942) 169-82.
Slochower, Harry. "Margaret Fuller and Goethe." *Germanic R* 7 (Ap 32) 130-44.
Stern, M. B. "The House of Expanding Doors; Ann Lynch's Soirées, 1846." *N Y Hist* 23 (Ja 42) 42-51.
——— "Margaret Fuller and *The Dial*." *SAQ* 40 (Ja 41) 11-21.
——— "Margaret Fuller's Schooldays in Cambridge." *NEQ* 13 (Je 40) 207-22.
——— "Margaret Fuller's Stay in Providence, 1837-1838." *Americana* 34 (Jl 40) 353-69.
——— "Margaret Fuller's Summer in the West (1843)." *Mich Hist Mag* 30 (Au 41) 300-30.
Thomas, J. W. "A Hitherto Unpublished Poem by Margaret Fuller." *AL* 15 (Ja 44) 411-5.
——— "A Hitherto Unpublished Textual Criticism by James Freeman Clarke of Margaret Fuller's Translation of *Tasso*." *Monatshefte* 41 (F 49) 89-92.

Wallace, Margaret. "Margaret Fuller, Critic." *Bkm* 69 (Mr 29) 60-7.
Warfel, H. R. "Margaret Fuller and Ralph Waldo Emerson." *PMLA* 50 (Je 35) 576-94.
Warren, Austin. "Hawthorne, Margaret Fuller, and 'Nemesis.'" *PMLA* 54 (Je 39) 613-5.
West, Kenyon. "Margaret Fuller." *Outlook* 95 (4 Je 10) 271.

GALE, ZONA (1874-1938). Anon. "Zona Gale." *Bkm* 57 (Ap 23) 168-72.
Gale, Zona. "The Novel and the Spirit." *YR* 12 (O 22) 41-55.
——— "Period Realism." *YR* 23 (S 33) 111-24.
Hurst, Fannie. "Zona Gale." *Bkm* 52 (Ap 21) 123.
Smith, B. W. "Zona Gale." *Writer* 37 (Mr 27) 95-6.

GALES, WINIFRED AND JOSEPH (1786-1860). Eaton, Clement. "Winifred and Joseph Gales, Liberals in the Old South." *J So Hist* 10 (N 44) 461-74.

GARLAND, HAMLIN (1860-1940). Anon. "Garland in Ghostland: A Book-Study." *Arena* 34 (Ag 05) 206-16.
——— "A Reviewer's Notebook." *Freeman* 3 (13 Ap 21) 118-9.
Bacheller, Irving. "A Little Story of Friendship." *Mark Twain Q* 4 (Su 40) 14.
Bowen, E. W. "Hamlin Garland, The Middle-West Short Story Writer." *SR* 17 (O 19) 411-22.
Chamberlain, J. E. "Hamlin Garland in Boston." *Mark Twain Q* 4 (Su 40) 13.
Clemens, Cyril. "A Lunch with Hamlin Garland." *Mark Twain Q* 4 (Su 40) 5-8.
Flannagan, J. T. "Hamlin Garland, Occasional Minnesotan." *Minn Hist* 22 (Je 41) 157-8.
Gale, Zona. "National Epics of the Border." *YR* 11 (Jl 22) 852-6.
Garland, Hamlin. "Books of My Childhood." *SRL* 7 (15 N 30) 347.
——— "Limitations of Authorship in America." *Bkm* 59 (My 24) 257-62.
——— "My Aim in Cavanagh." *World's Work* 20 (1910) 13569.
——— "Roadside Meetings of a Literary Nomad." *Bkm* 70 (O-D 29, Ja, F 30) 138-52, 246-57, 392-406, 514-28, 625-38; 71 (Mr, Ap, My, Je-Jl 30) 44-57, 196-208, 302-13, 423-34.
——— "Some of My Youthful Enthusiasms." *EJ* 20 (Je 31) 355-62.
Goldstein, J. B. "Two Literary Radicals." *AL* 17 (My 45) 152-60.
Hill, E. B. "American First Editions . . . Hamlin Garland." *Pub W* 102 (21 Ap 23) 1270.
Hornberger, Theodore. "American First Editions at TxU: Hamlin Garland." *Lib Chron Un Texas* 1 (Su 44) 27-9.
Howells, W. D. "Mr. Garland's Books." *NAR* 196 (O 12) 523-8.
Mott, F. L. "Exponents of the Pioneers." *Palimpsest* 11 (F 30) 61-6.
Nevins, Allan. "Garland and the Prairies." *Lit R* 2 (11 Ag 22) 881-2.
Raw, R. M. "Hamlin Garland, the Romanticist." *SR* 36 (Ap 28) 202-10.
Sibley, Carroll. "Hamlin Garland: Delightful Host." *Mark Twain Q* 4 (Su 40) 3-4.
Simpson, Claude. "Hamlin Garland's Decline." *Sw R* 26 (Ja 41) 223-34.
Sparks, G. R. "The Eugene Field of the Saints and Sinners Corner." *Pub W* 120 (7 N 31) 2111-4.
Van Doren, Carl. "Contemporary American Novelists." *Nation* 113 (23 N 21) 596-7.

GARRISON, WILLIAM LLOYD (1805-79). Garrison, W. L. "Letter from William Lloyd Garrison to Samuel E. Sewall." *PMHS* 57 (D 23) 209-11.
——— "Letters of William Lloyd Garrison to John B. Vashon." *J Negro Hist* 12 (Ja 27) 33-40.
Hicks, Granville. "Letters to William Francis Channing." *AL* 2 (N 30) 294-8.
Higginson, T. W. "Garrison and Whittier." *Independent* 59 (7 D 05) 1310-6.
Tolstoi, Leo. "Garrison and Non-Resistance." *Independent* 56 (21 Ap 04) 881-3.

Villard, O. G. "Gandhi's New England Background." *Common Sense* 11 (O 42) 323-33.

GAYARRÉ, CHARLES ÉTIENNE ARTHUR (1805-95) . "Four Letters from Charles Gayarré." *La Hist Q* 12 (Ja 29) 28-32.
Kendall, J. S. "The Last Days of Charles Gayarré." *La Hist Q* 15 (Jl 32) 359-75.
Nelson, J. H. "Charles Gayarré, Historian and Romancer." *SR* 33 (O 25) 427-38.
Richardson, F. D. "A Last Evening with Judge Gayarré." *La Hist Q* (Ja 31) 81-5.
Tinker, E. L. "Charles Gayarré, 1805-95." *PBSA* 27 (1933) 24-64.

GEORGE, HENRY (1839-97). Anon. "The Henry George Controversy." *Independent* 56 (26 My 04) 1169-74.
——— "Henry George Exhibition." *BNYPL* 31 (N 27) 899-903.
Geiger, G. R. "The Forgotten Man: Henry George." *AR* 1 (Fl 41) 291-307.
Johnson, E. H. "The Economics of Henry George's 'Progress and Poverty.'" *J Pol Econ* 18 (N 10) 714-35.
Madison, C. A. "Henry George, Prophet of Human Rights." *SAQ* 43 (O 44) 349-60.
Miller, M. M. "Henry George: Philosopher of the Natural Order." *Letters* 4 (My 31) 23-31.
Nock, A. J. "Henry George: Unorthodox American." *Scribner's* 94 (N 33) 274-9, 315-20.
Sawyer, R. A. "Henry George and the Single Tax." *BNYPL* 30 (Jl, Ag S 26) 481-503, 571-98, 685-716.
Tarbell, I. M. "New Dealers of the Seventies." *Forum* 92 (S 34) 133-9.

GEROULD, KATHERINE FULLERTON (1879-1944). Bennett, C. A. "Life through Fiction, the Knight's Move." *Bkm* 63 (My 26) 308-12.
Brooks, Cleanth, & Warren, R. P. "Dixie Looks at Mrs. Gerould." *AR* 6 (Mr 36) 585-95.
Gerould, K. F. "Newest Woman." *Atl* 109 (My 12) 606-11.
Gilman, Lawrence. "The Strange Case of Mrs. Gerould." *NAR* 211 (Ap 20) 564-8.

GHISELIN, BREWSTER (1910-). Swallow, Alan. "Brewster Ghiselin." *Intermountain R* 2 (Wi 38) 4, 8.

GILDER, RICHARD WATSON (1844-1909). Anon. "Mr. Gilder's Political Activities." *Century* 79 (F 10) 625-37.
Lansdale, M. H. "Life-Work and Homes of Richard Watson Gilder." *Century* 81 (Mr 11) 716-33.
Mabie, H. W. "Mr. Gilder's Poetry." *Bkm* 30 (Ja 10) 489-91.
——— "Richard Watson Gilder: An Appreciation." *Bkm* 30 (Ja 10) 488-9.
Matthews, Brander. "Richard Watson Gilder." *NAR* 191 (Ja 10) 39-48.
Stark, L. M. "Gilder Poetry Collection." *BNYPL* 52 (Jl 48) 341-54.
Viereck, G. S. "Reminiscences of Richard Watson Gilder." *Forum* 43 (Ja 10) 73-8.
Warfel, H. R. "George W. Cable Amends a Mark Twain Plot." *AL* 6 (N 34) 328-31.
Woodberry, G. E., *et al.* "Mr. Gilder's Public Activities." *Century* 79 (F 10) 625-37.

GILDERSLEEVE, BASIL LANNEAU (1831-1924). Smith, C. F. "Basil Lanneau Gildersleeve: An Intimate View." *SR* 32 (Ap 24) 162-75.

GILLETTE, WILLIAM (1855-1937). Brock, H. I. "Sherlock Holmes Returns to the Stage." *N Y Times Mag* (10 N 29) 14, 20.
Frenz, Horst, & Campbell, L. W. "William Gillette on the London Stage." *QQ* 52 (Wi 45-6) 443-57.

GILMAN, MRS. SAMUEL (1794-1888). "Letters of a Confederate Mother." *Atl* 137 (Ap 26) 503-15.

GILMER, FRANCIS (179?-1826). Davis, R. B. "Forgotten Scientists in Georgia and South Carolina." *Ga Hist Q* 27 (S 43) 271-84.
——— "Forgotten Scientists in Old Virginia." *VMHB* 46 (Ap 38) 97-111.

GLASGOW, ELLEN (1874-1945). Anon. "Miss Glasgow's Novels and Poems." *World's Work* 5 (N 02) 2790-2.
Adams, J. D. "Speaking of Books." *N Y Times Book R* sec 2 (2 D 45) 2.
Brickell, Herschel. "Miss Glasgow and Mr. Marquand." *VQR* 17 (Su 41) 405-17.
Canby, H. S. "Ellen Glasgow: Ironic Tragedian." *SRL* 18 (10 S 38) 3-4, 14.
——— "Ellen Glasgow: A Personal Memory." *SRL* 28 (22 D 45) 13.
Chamberlayne, L. P. "Virginia." *SR* 21 (O-D 13) 500-3.
Clark, Emily. "Ellen Glasgow." *VQR* 5 (Ap 29) 182-91.
Collins, Joseph. "Gentlemen, the Ladies." *N Y Times Book R* 3 (23 D 23) 10, 23.
Cooper, F. T. "Ellen Glasgow." *Bkm* 29 (Ag 09) 613-8.
Egly, W. H. "Bibliography of Ellen Anderson Gholson Glasgow." *Bul Bibl* 17 (S 40) 47-50.
Field, L. M. "Miss Glasgow at Home." *N Y Times Book R* 3 (30 Jl 22) 21.
Forestier, Marie. "L'Amérique se penche sur son passé." *La Revue Nouvelle* 8 (Jl-Ag 48) 92-5.
Freeman, D. S. "Ellen Glasgow: Idealist." *SRL* 12 (31 Ag 35) 11-2.
Glasgow, Ellen. "One Way to Write Novels." *SRL* 11 (8 D 34) 335, 344, 350.
Haardt, Sara. "Ellen Glasgow and the South.' *Bkm* 79 (Ap 29) 133-9.
Henderson, Archibald. "Recent Novels of Note." *SR* 12 (O 04) 456-64.
——— "Soil and Soul." *SRL* 1 (18 Jl 25) 907.
Jones, H. M. "Product of the Tragic Muse." *SRL* 23 (5 Mr 41) 5.
Mann, Dorothea. "Ellen Glasgow, Citizen of the World." *Bkm* 64 (N 26) 265-71.
Marcosson, I. F. "The Personal Ellen Glasgow." *Bkm* 29 (Ag 09) 619.
Meade, J. R. "Ellen Glasgow, A True Genius." *Writer* 41 (O 30) 239-41.
Mencken, H. L. "A Southern Sceptic." *Am Merc* 24 (Ag 33) 504.
Mims, Edwin. "The Social Philosophy of Ellen Glasgow." *J Social Forces* 4 (Mr 26) 495-503.
Ormond, J. R. "Some Recent Products of the New School of Southern Fiction." *SAQ* 3 (Jl 04) 285-9.
Overton, Grant. "Ellen Glasgow's Arrow." *Bkm* 61 (My 25) 291-6.
Parker, W. R. "Ellen Glasgow: A Gentle Rebel." *EJ* (Col ed) 20 (Mr 31) 187-94.
Rawlings, M. K. "Regional Literature of the South." *CE* 1 (F 40) 381-9.
Reid, J. D. "The Ellen Glasgow Collection of Ceramic Dogs." *Commonwealth* 16 (F 49) 13, 30-1.
Richardson, E. R. "Richmond and Its Writers." *Bkm* 68 (D 28) 449-53.
Rogers, Cameron. "Realism and the Romantic South." *World's Work* 50 (My 25) 99.
Rouse, H. B. "Ellen Glasgow in Retrospect." *Emory Un Q* 6 (Mr 50) 30-40.
Snelling, Paula. "Ellen Glasgow and Her South." *N Ga R* 6 (Wi 41) 26-7.
Stone, Grace. "Ellen Glasgow's Novels." *SR* 50 (Jl-S 42) 289-300.
Tyler, A. M. "Ellen Glasgow." *Book News Mo* 30 (Ag 12) 843-8.
Villard, Léonie. "L'Oeuvre d'Ellen Glasgow, romancière américaine." *Revue Anglo-Américaine* 11 (D 33) 97-111.
Wilson, J. S. "Ellen Glasgow." *VQR* 9 (O 33) 595.
——— "Ellen Glasgow, Ironic Idealist." *VQR* 15 (Wi 39) 121-6.
——— "Two American Novels." *VQR* 11 (O 35) 620-5.
Young, Stark. "Deep South Notes, VI: At Sheltered Valley." *NRp* 72 (7 S 32) 100-2.
——— "Prefaces to Distinction." *NRp* 75 (7 Je 33) 101.

GLASPELL, SUSAN (1882-1948). Crawford, B. J. "Susan Glaspell." *Palimpsest* 11 (D 30) 517-21.

Lewisohn, Ludwig. "Susan Glaspell." *Nation* 111 (3 N 20) 509-10.
——— "The Verge." *Nation* 113 (14 D 21) 708-9.

GODFREY, THOMAS (1736-63). Carlson, C. L. "A Further Note on Thomas Godfrey in England." *AL* 9 (Mr 37) 73-6.
——— "Thomas Godfrey in England." *AL* 7 (N 35) 302-9.
Gegenheimer, A. F. "Thomas Godfrey: Protege of William Smith." *Penn Hist* 9 (O 42) 233-51; 10 (Ja 43) 26-43.
George, Dorothy. "More Evidence on an Early Theatrical Withdrawal." *AN&Q* 2 (O 42) 100-1.
Henderson, Archibald. "Thomas Godfrey, American Dramatist: Carolina Days." *Everywoman's Mag* 1 (Ag 17) 19-24.
——— "Thomas Godfrey: The First American Playwright and Our First Carolina Playmaker." *Carolina Play-Book* 1 (Mr 28) 9-10.
Pollock, T. C. "Rowe's *Tamerlane and The Prince of Parthia*." *AL* 6 (My 34) 158-62.
Quinn, A. H. "The Prince of Parthia, A Tragedy. By Thomas Godfrey." *SAQ* 16 (O 17) 369-72.
Woolf, H. B. "Thomas Godfrey: Eighteenth-Century Chaucerian." *AL* 12 (Ja 41) 486-90.

GODKIN, EDWIN LAWRENCE (1831-1902). Anon. "The Late Edwin Lawrence Godkin." *Critic* 40 (Jl 02) 82-4.
Bishop, J. B. "Personal Recollections of E. L. Godkin." *Century* 64 (Ag 02) 694-700.
Bryce, J. B. "Two Editors." *Nation* 101 (8 Jl 15) 41.
Howells, W. D. "A Great New York Journalist." *NAR* 185 (3 My 07) 44-53.
Nevins, Allan. "E. L. Godkin: Victorian Liberal." *Nation* 171 (22 Jl 50) 76-9.
Ogden, Rollo. "Letters of E. L. Godkin." *Scribner's* 4 (Mr 07) 292-303.
Rhodes, J. F. "Edwin Lawrence Godkin." *Atl* 102 (S 08) 320-34.
Stoke, H. W. "Edwin Lawrence Godkin, Defender of Democracy." *SAQ* 30 (O 31) 339-49.
Stone, I. F. "Free Inquiry and Free Endeavor." *Nation* 150 (10 F 40) 150, 158-61.
Villard, O. G. "Edwin Lawrence Godkin: A Great American Editor." *SAQ* 5 (Jl 07) 288-99.
——— "Godkin's 'Nation.'" *Nation* 150 (10 F 40) 152-4.
Wrage, E. J. "E. L. Godkin and the *Nation*." *So Speech J* 15 (D 49) 100-11.

GOODRICH, SAMUEL GRISWOLD (1793-1860). Bates, A. C. "The Knights of the Round Table." *Bul Conn Hist Soc* 7 (O 40) 2-4.

GOOKIN, DANIEL (1612-87). Brigham, C. S. "Elegy on Urian Oakes, 1681, by Daniel Gookin, Jr." *PCSM* 20 (Ap 18) 247-52.

GORDON, CAROLINE (1895-). Lytle, Andrew. "Caroline Gordon and the Historic Image." *SR* 57 (Au 49) 560-86.
Ragan, David. "Portrait of a Lady Novelist." *Mark Twain Q* 8 (Wi 47) 18-20.

GRADY, HENRY WOODFIN (1850-89). Wade, J. D. "Henry W. Grady." *So R* 3 (Ja 38) 479-509.

GRAYSON, WILLIAM J. (1788-1863). Parks, E. W. "Legaré and Grayson: Types of Classical Influence on Criticism in the Old South." *Sw R* 22 (Jl 37) 354-65.
Stoney, S. G. "The Autobiography of William John Grayson." *S C Hist and Gen Mag* 48 (Jl, O 47) 125-33, 189-97; 49 (Ja, Ap, Jl 48) 23-40, 88-103, 163-70.

GREELEY, HORACE (1811-72). Anon. "Horace Greeley on B. F. Wade as President." *Tyler's Quar Hist & Gen Mag* 14 (Ja 33) 153.

Adcock, A. St. J. "A Great American Journalist: A Note on the Centenary of Horace Greeley." *Bkm* (London) 39 (Mr 11) 273-5.
Bradford, Gamaliel. "Horace Greeley." *Am Merc* 1 (Ap 24) 385-93.
Brophy, L. P. "Horace Greeley Socialist." *N Y Hist* 29 (Jl 48) 309-17.
Commons, J. R. "Horace Greeley and the Working Class Origins of the Republican Party." *Pol Sci Q* 24 (S 09) 468-88.
Croffut, W. A. "Horace Greeley Knows His Business." *Atl* 145 (F 30) 228-39.
Cushman, R. S. "Horace Greeley's Early New England Home." *N E Mag* ns 21 (Ja 00) 556-65.
Holmes, Mrs. P. B. "Horace Greeley's New Hampshire Diary." *Hist N H* 2 (Ap 45) 7-11.
Lillard, R. G. "Hank Monk and Horace Greeley." *AL* 14 (My 42) 126-34.
Mabbott, T. O. "Greeley's Estimate of Poe." *Autograph Album* 1 (D 33) 14-6, 61.
Ross, E. D. "Horace Greeley and the South, 1865-1872." *SAQ* 16 (O 17) 324-38.
——— "Horace Greeley and the West." *Miss Valley Hist R* 20 (Je 33) 63-74.
Williams, M. L. "Horace Greeley and Michigan Cooper." *Mich Hist* 34 (N 50) 120-32.

GREEN, ANNA KATHARINE (1846-1935). Rohlfs, Charles. "American First Editions: (Mrs.) Anna Katharine Green (Rohlfs), (1846-1935)." *Pub W* 127 (20 Ap 35) 1617-8.
Woodward, Kathleen. "Anna Katharine Green." *Bkm* 70 (O 29) 168-70.

GREEN, DUFF (1791-1875). Green, F. M. "Duff Green, Militant Journalist of the Old School." *AHR* 52 (Ja 47) 247-64.

GREEN, JULIEN (1900-). Bespalov, Rachel. "Notes sur Julien Green." *Nouvelle Revue Française* 46 (1 Mr 36) 416-28.
Brace, Marjorie. "The Case of Julien Green." *Accent* 2 (Au 41) 42-4.
Brock, I. W. "Julien Green: A French Novelist with a Southern Background." *Emory Un Q* 1 (Mr 45) 31-43.
——— "Julien Green: The Mood and Style of His Novels." *Emory Un Q* 1 (D 45) 259-64.
Chevalley, A. "The Case of Julien Green." *SRL* 4 (Mr 28) 565-6.
Darbelnet, J. "Un Écrivan américain d'expression française." *Bul des Etudes Françaises* 25 (My-Je 45) 31-5.
Green, Julien. "How a Novelist Begins." *Atl* 168 (D 41) 743-52.
Jaloux, E. "Julien Green." *Bkm* 67 (Mr 28) 34-5.
Kohler, Dayton. "Julien Green: Modern Gothic." *SR* 40 (Ap-Je 32) 139-48.
Lehner, Frederick. "Julien Green." *FR* 15 (Mr 42) 385-94.
Marshall, R. H. "Characterization in the Novels of Julien Green." *Bard R* 1 (Fl 46) 36-50.
Steell, W. "Anne and Julien Green." *Bkm* 75 (Ag 32) 349-53.

GREEN, PAUL (1894-). Anon. "Justice to the South in a Play." *Lit Dig* 3 (24 O 31) 17.
Carmer, Carl. "Paul Green—the Making of an American Dramatist." *Theatre Arts* 16 (D 32) 995-1006.
Clark, B. H. "Notes on Paul Green." *Drama* 15 (Ja 26) 137, 155.
——— "Paul Green." *Theatre Arts* 12 (O 28) 730-6.
Isaacs, E. J. R. "Paul Green—a Case in Point." *Theatre Arts* 25 (Jl 41) 489-98.
Jones, H. M. "Paul Green." *Sw R* 14 (O 28) 1-8.
Malone, A. E. "An American Folk-Dramatist: Paul Green." *Dublin Mag* ns 6 (Ap-Je 29) 31-42.
Meade, J. R. "Paul Green." *Bkm* 74 (Ja-F 32) 503-7.
Young, Stark. "The Shadow of Wings." *NRp* 68 (14 O 31) 234-6.

GREENHOW, ROBERT (1800-54). Barbee, D. R. "Robert Greenhow." *WMQ* 13 (Jl 33) 182-3.

GREGORY, HORACE (1898-). Blackmur, R. P. "The Ribbon of Craft." *Poetry* 42 (Jl 33) 217-22.
Burke, Kenneth. "The Hope in Tragedy." *Poetry* 46 (Jl 35) 227-30.
Humphries, Rolfe. "Catullus Resartus." *Poetry* 39 (N 31) 93-6.
Kunitz, S. J. "Horace Gregory's First Book." *Poetry* 38 (Ap 31) 41-5.
Rosenthal, M. L. "Horace Gregory: The Catullus Translations." *Accent* 10 (Sp 50) 175-84.

GRIDLEY, JEREMY (1700-65). Reeves, J. K. "Jeremy Gridley, Editor." *NEQ* 17 (Je 44) 265-81

GRIFFITH, MARY (*fl.* 1830). Adkins, N. F. "An Early American Story of Utopia." *Colophon* ns 1 (Su 35) 123-32.

GRIGGS, SUTTON E. (1872-). Gloster, Hugam. "Sutton E. Griggs, Novelist of the New Negro." *Phylon* 4 (O-D 43) 335-45.

GRISWOLD, RUFUS WILMOT (1815-57). Horaszti, Zoltán. "The Correspondence of R. W. Griswold." *BPLQ* 1 (Jl, O 49) 61-74, 156-65; 2 (Wi, Ap, Jl, O 50) 77-84, 172-9, 269-75, 354-68.
McCusker, Honor. "The Correspondence of R. W. Griswold." *More Books* 16 (Mr, Ap, My, Je 41) 105-16, 152-6, 190-6, 286-9; 18 (F, S 43) 67-8, 322-33.
Neu, J. L. "Rufus Wilmot Griswold." *Un Texas Stud in Eng* no 5 (1925) 101-65.

GUEST, EDGAR A. (1881-). Cline, Leonard. "Eddie Guest: Just Glad." *Am Merc* 6 (N 25) 322-7.

GUINEY, LOUISE IMOGEN (1861-1920). Brown, Alice. "An American Poet: Louise Imogen Guiney." *NAR* 213 (Ap 21) 502-17.
Donelin, M. C. "Louise Imogen Guiney." *J Am Irish Hist Soc* 28 (1930) 107-11.
Earl, Michael. "Letters of Louise Imogen Guiney." *Bkm* 55 (Ap, Ag 22) 163-9, 591-6; 56 (F 23) 705-9.
——— "Three Poets in a Golden Clime." *Cath World* 142 (F 36) 551-61.
Putnam, Herbert. *Report Lib Cong* (1934) 19.
Ryan, Corlctta. "Louise Guiney's Own 'Patrius' to a Younger Friend." *N Y Times Book R* (3 Je 23).
Tenison, E. M. "A Bibliography of Louise Imogen Guiney, 1861-1920." *Bkm J & Print Coll* ns 7 (D 22, Ja, Mr 23) 86-7, 123-4, 181-2.

GUNTHER, JOHN (1901-). Bradley, D. F. "Gunther to Haddon to Harper." *Pub W* 152 (5 Jl 47) 43-4.
Rovere, R. H. "Inside." *NYr* 23 (23 Ag 47) 30-9.

GUTHRIE, ALFRED BERTRAM, JR. (1901-). Breit, Harvey. "Talk with A. B. Guthrie, Jr." *N Y Times Book R* (23 O 49) 39.

GUTHRIE, WILLIAM NORMAN (1868-1944). Henneman, J. B. "Two Younger Poets." *SR* 10 (Ja 02) 68-79.

HALDEMAN-JULIUS, EMANUEL (1889-1951). Mordell, Albert. "Haldeman-Julius as a Writer on Freethought." *Critic & Guide* 4 (D 50) 1-24.
Yarros, V. S. "Haldeman-Julius Bookshelf." *Critic & Guide* 4 (D 50) 25-32.

HALE, EDWARD EVERETT (1822-1909). Bowen, E. W. "Edward Everett Hale." *SAQ* 17 (Jl 18) 231-42.
Frothingham, P. R. "Memoir of Edward Everett Hale." *PMHS* 55 (Ap 22) 307-18.
Garver, A. S. "Edward Everett Hale." *PAAS* 20 (O 09) 60-9.

Hale, E. E. "Memories of a Hundred Years." *Outlook* 72 (4 O 02) 301-14.
Hale, E. E., Jr. "Edward Everett Hale." *Outlook* 85 (6 Ap 07) 801-5.
Higginson, T. W. "Edward Everett Hale." *Outlook* 92 (19 Je 09) 403-6.
Mead, E. D. "Edward Everett Hale." *N E Mag* ns (Jl 09) 521-9.
Merriam, G. S. "Reminiscences of Edward Everett Hale." *Outlook* 96 (12 N 10) 581-91.
Whicher, G. F., & Bingham, M. T. "Emily Dickinson's Earliest Friend." *AL* 6 (My 34) 191-3.

HALE, SARA JOSEPHA (1788-1879). Strong, Ola. "The Woman to Thank for Thanksgiving." *Holland's Mag* 69 (N 50) 15.

HALL, HAZEL (1886-1924). Munroe, Harriet. "Hazel Hall." *Poetry* 24 (Jl 24) 210-3.
Powell, L. C. "A Note on Hazel Hall and Her Poetry." *Gen Mag & Hist Chron* 37 (1933) 14-25.

HALL, JAMES (1793-1868). Donald, David. "The Autobiography of James Hall, Western Literary Pioneer." *Ohio State Arch & Hist Q* 56 (Jl 47) 295-305.
Eckert, R. P., Jr. "The Path of the Pioneer." *Colophon* ns 3 (Wi 36) 404-21.
Flanagan, J. T. "An Early Collection of American Tales." *HLQ* 3 (O 39) 103-5.
——— "James Hall and the Antiquarian and Historical Society of Illinois." *J Ill State Hist Soc* 34 (D 41) 439-52.
James, D. L. "Judge James Hall: A Literary Pioneer in the Middle West." *Ohio Arch & Hist Soc Pub* 18 (1909) 468-83.
Shultz, Esther. "James Hall in Shawnee Town." *J Ill State Hist Soc* 22 (Ap 29, Ja 30) 388-400.
——— "James Hall in Vandalia." *Ill State Hist Soc J* 23 (Ap 30) 92-112.
Welch, M. D. "James Norman Hall: Poet and Philosopher." *SAQ* 39 (Ap 40) 140-50.

HALLECK, FITZ-GREENE (1790-1867). Adkins, N. F. "Two Unpublished Letters of Fitz-Greene Halleck." *Am Book Coll* 5 (O, N 34) 301-4, 323-4.
Birss, J. H. "American First Editions: Fitz-Greene Halleck. 1790-1867." *Pub W* 127 (15 Je 35) 2306.
Taft, K. B. "The First Printing of Halleck's 'The Winds of March Are Humming.'" *N Y Hist Soc Quar Bul* 27 (Ap 43) 35-6.
Ward, S. M. "A Romantic Episode in the Life of the Poet, Fitz-Greene Halleck." *Bkm* 47 (Jl 18) 499-502.

HALLIBURTON, THOMAS CHANDLER (1796-1865). Anon. "Testi Americana: II. T. C. Halliburton (1855)." *Anglica* 1 (Ap-Je 46) 20-3.
Harvey, D. C. "The Centenary of Sam Slick." *Dalhousie R* 16 (Ja 37) 429-40.
Wood, R. K. "The Creator of the First Yankee of Literature." *Bkm* 41 (Ap 15) 152-60.

HAMILTON, ALEXANDER (1757-1804). Davisson, Ora. "The Early Pamphlets of Alexander Hamilton." *QJS* 30 (Ap 44) 168-73.
Marsh, Philip. "Hamilton and Monroe." *Miss Valley Hist R* 34 (D 47) 459-68.
Vandenberg, A. H. "Alexander Hamilton: The Greatest Horatio Alger Story in the History of America." *Life* 23 (7 Jl 47) 65-9.

HAMMETT, DASHIEL (1894-). Sanderson, E. "Ex-Detective Hammett." *Bkm* 74 (Ja, F 32) 477-87, 516-8.

HARBAUGH, HENRY (1817-67). Allen, George. "Two Pennsylvania Dutch Poets." *AGR* 8 (Ag 34) 10-2, 34.

HARBEN, WILLIAM NATHANIEL (1858-1919). Howells, W. D. "Mr. Harben's Georgia Fiction." *NAR* 191 (Mr 10) 356-63.

HARDING, REBECCA (1831-1910). Downey, Fairfax. "Portrait of a Pioneer." *Colophon* 3 (D 32) Pt 12.

HARLAND, HENRY (1861-1905). Henderson, Archibald. "Recent Novels of Note." *SR* 12 (O 04) 456-64.

O'Brien, Justin. "Henry Harland, an American Forerunner of Proust." *MLN* 54 (Je 39) 420-8.

HARRIS, BENJAMIN (*fl.* 1673-1716). Ford, W. C. "Benjamin Harris, Printer and Bookseller." *PMHS* 57 (O 23) 34-68.

——— "Harris's 'Protestant Tutor.'" *PMHS* 60 (Je 27) 374-80.

Monaghan, Frank. "Benjamin Harris." *Colophon* 3 (D 32) Pt 12.

Muddiman, J. G. "Benjamin Harris, the First American Journalist, Sarrah and Vasavour Harris, Booksellers." *N&Q* 163 (20 Ag, 27 Ag, 3 S, 24 S, 15 O 32) 129-33, 147-50, 166-70, 223, 273-4.

HARRIS, CORRA (1869-1935). Dickey, C. H. "Something about the Circuit Rider by the Circuit Rider's Wife." *Richmond Times-Dispatch* (24 F 35) 3, 12.

HARRIS, GEORGE WASHINGTON (1814-69). Blair, Walter. "Sut Lovingood." *SRL* 15 (7 N 36) 3-4, 16.

Day, Donald. "The Humorous Works of George W. Harris." *AL* 14 (Ja 43) 391-406.

——— "The Life of George Washington Harris." *Tenn Hist Q* 6 (Mr 47) 3-38.

——— "The Political Satires of George W. Harris." *Tenn Hist Q* 4 (D 45) 320-38.

HARRIS, JOEL CHANDLER (1848-1908). Anon. "Joel Chandler Harris Writes Interestingly of the Warm Springs of Meriwether County, Georgia." *Emory Un Q* 3 (Mr 47) 54-7.

Baker, R. S. "Joel Chandler Harris." *Outlook* 78 (5 N 04) 595-603.

Bowen, E. W. "Joel Chandler Harris." *Reformed Church R* 4 (Jl 19) 357-69.

Brown, Wenzell. "Anansi and Brer Rabbit." *Am Merc* 69 (O 49) 438-43.

Cousins, P. "The Debt of Joel Chandler Harris to Joseph Addison Turner." *Chimes* 42 (Mr 30) 3-10.

Dauner, Louise. "Myth and Humor in the Uncle Remus Fables." *AL* 20 (My 48) 129-43.

English, T. H. "In Memory of Uncle Remus." *SLM* 2 (F 40) 77-83.

——— "Joel Chandler Harris's Earliest Literary Project." *Emory Un Q* 2 (O 46) 176-85.

——— "Memorializing Pride in an Adopted Son: Emory Library Holds Famous Uncle Remus Manuscripts." *Emory Alumnus* 5 (Mr 29) 7-8.

——— "The Twice-Told Tale and Uncle Remus." *Ga R* 2 (Wi 48) 447-60.

Ferguson, T. E. "Joel Chandler Harris." *Texas R* 6 (Ap 21) 214-21.

Flanders, B. H. "Two Forgotten Youthful Works of Joel Chandler Harris." *SAQ* 38 (Jl 39) 278-83.

Gavigan, W. V. "Two Gentlemen of Georgia." *Cath World* 145 (Ag 37) 584-9.

Gayle, Margot. "Georgia's Aesop." *Holland's Mag* 67 (D 48) 8-9.

Harman, H. E. "Joel Chandler Harris." *Bkm* 61 (Je 25) 433-6.

——— "Joel Chandler Harris: The Prose Poet of the South." *SAQ* 17 (Jl 18) 243-8.

Harris, Julia C. "Joel Chandler Harris—Fearless Editor." *Emory Alumnus* 5 (Mr 29) 9-10.

——— "Joel Chandler Harris: The Poetic Mind." *Emory Un Q* 3 (Mr 47) 21-9.

——— "Sage of Br'er Rabbit." *Bkm* (S 18) 50-6.

——— "Uncle Remus at Home and Abroad." *SLM* 2 (F 40) 84-6.

Harris, L. M. "The Passing of Uncle Remus." *Independent* 65 (23 Jl 08) 190-2.
Hess, M. W. "The Man Who Knew Uncle Remus." *Cath World* 166 (D 47) 254-8.
Hubbell, J. B. "Two Letters of Uncle Remus." *Sw R* 23 (Ja 38) 216-23.
Lee, J. W. "Joel Chandler Harris." *Century* 77 (Ap 09) 891-7.
Mabbott, T. O. "Joel Chandler Harris: A Debt to Poe." *N&Q* 166 (3 Mr 34) 151.
Miller, H. P. "Bibliography of Joel Chandler Harris." *Emory Alumnus* 5 (Mr 29) 13-4, 22.
Parsons, E. C. "Joel Chandler Harris and Negro Folklore." *Dial* 66 (17 My 19) 491-3.
Pickett, L. C. "Uncle Remus." *Lippincott's* 89 (Ap 12) 572-8.
Stafford, John. "Patterns of Meaning in *Nights with Uncle Remus*." *AL* 18 (My 46) 89-108.
Ticknor, Caroline. "Some Glimpses of the Author of 'Uncle Remus.'" *Bkm* 27 (Ag 08) 551-7.
Wade, J. D. "Joel Chandler Harris." *VQR* 8 (Ja 32) 123-7.
——— "Profits and Losses in the Life of Joel Chandler Harris." *Am R* 1 (Ap 33) 17-35.
Winterich, J. T. "Romantic Stories of Books . . . *Uncle Remus*." *Pub W* 118 (5 N 30) 2279-83.
Wooten, K. H. "Tribute to Uncle Remus." *St Nicholas* 45 (D 17) 130-1.

HARRIS, WILLIAM TORREY (1835-1909). Berle, A. A., Sr. "W. T. Harris—Pragmatic Hegelian." *J Phil* 45 (26 F 48) 121-33.

HART, ALBAN J. X. (1798-1879). Walser, Richard. "'Old Field Teacher' Literary Puzzle Solved by Research After 107 Years." *Durham* [N. C.] *Morning Herald* (21 Ap 46) sec 4, 1.

HART, JOEL TANNER (1810-77). Mitchell, S. D. "A Sketch of Josiah Hart and Poems by Joel T. Hart." *Ky State Hist Soc Reg* 42 (Ja 44) 19-25.

HART, MOSS (1904-). Gilder, Rosamund. "The Fabulous Hart." *Theatre Arts* 28 (F 44) 89-98.

HARTE, BRET (1836-1902). Anon. "Bret Harte." *Dial* 32 (16 My 02) 337-8.
——— "Bret Harte and the Pioneers of '49." *Blackwood's* 191 (Ap 12) 581-4.
——— "Bret Harte Revived." *Overland Mo* 89 (D 31) 19.
——— "Excerpts from Eight Letters." *Autograph Album* 1 (D 33) 65-6.
——— "A Reviewer's Note-Book." *Freeman* 1 (25 Ag 20) 574-5.
Brete Harte Number. *Overland Mo* 40 (S 02) 201-45.
Altrocchi, J. C. "Along the Mother Lode." *YR* 24 (S 34) 131-45.
Batten, G. R. "Bret Harte and Early California. *Overland Mo* 71 (Ap 18) 295-300.
Blanck, Jacob. "The Question of Bret Harte's *Mliss*." *Pub W* 130 (28 N 36) 2102-5.
Bland, H. M. "Bret Harte's First School." *Overland Mo* 86 (Jl 28) 239.
Booth, B. A. "Unpublished Letters of Bret Harte." *AL* 16 (My 44) 131-42.
Booth, Bradford. "Bret Harte Goes East: Some Unpublished Letters." *AL* 19 (Ja 48) 318-35.
Bowen, E. W. "Francis Bret Harte." *SR* 24 (Jl 16) 287-302.
Boyd, M. S. "Some Letters of Bret Harte." *Harper's* 105 (O 02) 773-6.
Bradsher, E. L. "The Place of Bret Harte in English Prose." *Texas R* 4 (Jl 19) 339-49.
Brooks, Noah. "Bret Harte: A Study and an Appreciation." *Book Buyer* 22 (Je 02) 358-62.
Byers, S. H. M. "Bret Harte in Switzerland." *Overland Mo* 42 (O, N 02) 291-7, 426-32.

Canby, H. S. "Bret Harte's Tragedy." *SRL* 8 (30 Ja 32) 485-8.
Chesterton, G. K. "American Humor and Bret Harte." *Critic* 41 (Ag 02) 170-4.
Clemens, W. M. "Bret Harte's Country." *Bkm* 13 (My 01) 223-37.
Davis, H. I. "Bret Harte and His Jewish Ancestor, Bernard Hart." *Pub Am Jewish Hist Soc* 32 (1932) 99-111.
Doub, R. A. "A Trip through the Bret Harte Country." *Overland Mo* ns 60 (S 12) 234-6.
Douglas, James. "Bret Harte." *Bkm* 15 (Jl 02) 466-7.
Duffus, R. L. "Eyes Scan the Country of Bret Harte." *N Y Times Mag* (23 Ag 36) 9, 17.
Elliott, S. R. "Glimpses of Bret Harte." *Reader* 10 (Jl 07) 122-7.
Fields, Mrs. J. T. "Bret Harte and Mark Twain in the Seventies." *Atl* 130 (Jl-D 22) 341-8.
Fulton, R. L. "Bret Harte and Truthful James." *Overland Mo* 66 (Ag 15) 89-98.
——— "Glimpses of the Mother Lode." *Bkm* 39 (Mr 14) 49-57.
Gohdes, Clarence. "A Check-List of Bret Harte's Works in Book Form Published in the British Isles." *Bul Bibl* 18 (My-Ag, S-D 43) 19, 36-9.
Harte, R. B. "Grandpa: A Reminiscence of Bret Harte by His Grandson." *Overland Mo* ns 68 (D 16) 528-9.
Hazard, L. L. "Eden to Eldorado." *Un Calif Chron* 25 (1933) 107-21.
Horwill, H. W. "News and Views of Literary London." *N Y Times Book R* (6 S 36) 8.
Howe, M. A. DeW. "Bret Harte and Mark Twain in the Seventies." *Atl* 130 (S 22) 341-8.
Howells, W. D. "Editor's Easy Chair." *Harper's* 108 (D 03) 153-9.
——— "Reminiscences of Bret Harte." *Overland Mo* 40 (S 02) 226-7.
James, G. W. "Bret Harte." *Overland* ns 78 (D 21) 10-8.
——— "The Founding of the *Overland Monthly*." *Overland Mo* ns 52 (Jl 08) 3-12; 86 (Jl 28) 199-200.
Kyne, P. B. "Trailing Bret Harte." *Sunset* 31 (Jl 13) 97-107.
Mackall, L. L. "Bret Harte Exhibition." *N Y Herald-Tribune Books* 12 (30 Ag 36) 21.
May, E. R. "Bret Harte and the *Overland Monthly*." *AL* 22 (N 50) 260-71.
Merwin, H. C. "Bret Harte." *Atl* 90 (Ag 02) 260-8.
——— "Bret Harte's Heroines." *Atl* 102 (S 08) 297-307.
Mitchell, L. A. "Bret Harte's Literary Tribute to the West." *Overland Mo* 86 (Jl 28) 215.
Murdock, C. A. "Bret Harte in Humboldt." *Overland Mo* 40 (S 02) 201-7.
Nock, A. J. "Bret Harte as a Parodist." *Bkm* 69 (My 29) 246-50.
Peixotto, E. C. "Through Bret Harte's Country." *Scribner's* 34 (N 03) 533-40.
Randall, D. A., & Winterich, J. T. "One Hundred Good Novels. Harte, Bret: *The Luck of Roaring Camp*." *Pub W* 136 (25 N 39) 1985-1986.
Root, S. W. "Three Lost Years of Bret Harte's Life." *Overland Mo* 90 (O 32) 229-30, 246, 249, 253.
Stewart, G. R., Jr. "A Bibliography of the Writings of Bret Harte in the Magazines and Newspapers of California, 1857-1871." *Un Calif Pub Eng* 3: no 3 (1933) 119-70.
——— "The Bret Harte Legend." *Un Calif Chron* 30 (Jl 28) 338-50.
——— "Bret Harte on the Frontier." *Sw R* 11 (Ap 26) 265-73.
——— "Bret Harte upon Mark Twain in 1866." *AL* 13 (N 41) 263-4.
——— "Some Bret Harte Satires." *Frontier* 13 (Ja 33) 93-101.
——— "The Year of Bret Harte's Birth." *AL* 1 (Mr 29) 78.
Stokes, F. M. "Fred Stocking and His Service to California Literature." *Overland Mo* ns 59 (F 12) 111-4.
Stocking, F. M. "The Passing of 'Tennessee.'" *Overland Mo* 42 (D 03) 539-43.
——— "The Real Tennessee's Partner." *Overland Mo* 40 (S 02) 240-5.

Strachey, Lionel. "Bret Harte." *Critic* 40 (Je 02) 557-8.
Tamony, Peter. "Writers Supported by Government Sinecures." *AN&Q* 8 (D 49) 138-9.
Vázquez-Arjona, G. "Spanish and Spanish-American Influences on Bret Harte." *Revue Hispanique* 76 (Ag 29) 573-621.
Weber, C. J. "Harte and Hardy." *Colby Lib Q* 1 (O 43) 57-8.
Williams, S. T. "Ambrose Bierce and Bret Harte." *AL* 17 (My 45) 179-80.
Winterich, J. T. "Romantic Stories of Books . . . *The Luck of Roaring Camp.*" *Pub W* 117 (24 My 30) 2639-43.

HASTINGS, SARAH (1773-1812). Hastings, G. E. "Sally Hastings (1773-1812), Poet and Pioneer." *Americana* 36 (Jl 42) 301-415.
Howard, Leon. "Literature and the Frontier: The Case of Sally Hastings." *ELH* 7 (Mr 40) 68-82.

HAWTHORNE, JULIAN (1846-1934). Stevenson, Lionel. "The Dean of American Letters." *Bkm* 73 (Ap 31) 164-72.
Weber, C. J. "More about Lowell's 'Dead Rat.'" *NEQ* 9 (D 36) 686-8.

HAWTHORNE, NATHANIEL (1804-64). Anon. "Hawthorne." New York *Times* (13 S 48) 16.
——— "Books Read by Nathaniel Hawthorne, 1822-50." *EIHC* 68 (Ja 32) 65-87.
——— "Catalogue of Portraits in the Essex Institute." *EIHC* 71 (Ap 35) 150-1.
——— "Hawthorne and Thoreau." *T. P.'s Weekly* 6 (22 S 05) 369.
——— "The Hawthorne Statue." *Atl* 94 (Jl 04) 140-1.
——— "Hawthorne's 'Pot-8-O'Club' at Bowdoin College." *EIHC* 67 (Jl 31) 225-32.
——— "Puritan Romancer." *TLS* 2495 (25 N 49) 770.
Adkins, N. F. "The Early Projected Works of Nathaniel Hawthorne." *PBSA* 39 (1945) 119-55.
Arvin, Newton. "The Relevance of Hawthorne." *New Student* 7 (1928) 3-5.
Astrov, Vladimir. "Hawthorne and Dostoievski as Explorers of the Human Conscience." *NEQ* 15 (Je 42) 296-319.
Bader, A. L. "Those Mesmeric Victorians." *Colophon* ns 3 (Su 38) 335-53.
Baldensperger, Fernand. "A propos de 'Nathaniel Hawthorne en France.'" *MLN* 56 (My 41) 343-5.
Beers, H. A. "Fifty Years of Hawthorne." *YR* 4 (Ja 15) 300-15.
Blodgett, Harold. "Hawthorne as Poetry Critic; Six Unpublished Letters to Lewis Mansfield." *AL* 12 (My 40) 173-84.
Bode, Carl. "Hawthorne's *Fanshawe:* The Promising of Greatness." *NEQ* 23 (Je 50) 235-42.
Brooks, V. W. "Retreat from Utopia." *SRL* 13 (22 F 36) 3-4, 14, 16, 18.
Brown, E. K. "Hawthorne, Melville, and 'Ethan Brand.'" *AL* 3 (Mr 31) 72-5.
Brownell, W. C. "Hawthorne." *Scribner's* 43 (Ja 08) 69-84.
Buckingham, L. H. "Hawthorne and the British Income Tax." *AL* 11 (Ja 40) 451-3.
Burnham, P. E. "Hawthorne's *Fanshawe* and Bowdoin College." *EIHC* 80 (Ap 44) 131-8.
Burton, K. "Rose of All Hawthorne's." *Cath World* 142 (F 36) 562-6.
Cable, L. L. "Old Salem and the Scarlet Letter." *Bkm* 26 (D 07) 398-403.
Cantwell, Robert. "Hawthorne and Delia Bacon." *Am Q* 1 (Wi 49) 343-60.
Cargill, Oscar. "Nemesis and Nathaniel Hawthorne." *PMLA* 52 (S 37) 848-62.
Carlisle, Kathryn. "Wit and Humor in Nathaniel Hawthorne." *Bard R* 3 (Ap 49) 86-93.
Carlton, W. N. C. "Hawthorne's First Book—*Fanshawe: A Tale.*" *Am Col* 4 (Je 27) 82-6
Carpenter, F. I. "Puritans Preferred Blondes: The Heroines of Melville and Hawthorne." *NEQ* 9 (Je 36) 253-72.
——— "Scarlet A Minus." *CE* 5 (Ja 44) 173-80.
Cary, E. L. "Hawthorne and Emerson." *Critic* 45 (Jl 04) 25-7.
Chandler, E. L. "Hawthorne's *Spectator.*" *NEQ* 4 (Ap 31) 289-330.

——— "A Study of the Sources of the Tales and Romances Written by Nathaniel Hawthorne Before 1853." *Smith Col Stud Mod Lang* 7: no 4 (Jl 26) 1-64.
Chase, Richard. "The Progressive Hawthorne." *PR* 16 (Ja 49) 96-100.
Cherry, F. N. "A Note on the Source of Hawthorne's 'Lady Eleanore's Mantle.'" *AL* 6 (Ja 35) 437-9.
——— "The Sources of Hawthorne's 'Young Goodman Brown.'" *AL* 5 (Ja 34) 342-8.
Cohen, B. B. "The Composition of Hawthorne's 'The Duston Family.'" *NEQ* 21 (Je 48) 236-41.
——— "'The Gray Champion.'" *Ind Un Folio* 13 (F 48) 11-2.
——— "Hawthorne and Legends." *Hoosier Folklore* 7 (S 48) 94-5.
——— "A New Critical Approach to the Works of Hawthorne." *Wayne Eng Remembrancer* 4 (Je 50) 43-7.
Coleridge, M. E. "Questionable Shapes of Nathaniel Hawthorne." *Littell's Living Age* 242 (6 Ag 04) 348-53.
Commager, H. S. "Hawthorne as Editor." *AHR* 47 (Ja 42) 358-9.
Conway, M. D. "My Hawthorne Experience." *Critic* 45 (Jl 04) 21-5.
——— "The Secret of Hawthorne." *Nation* 88 (30 Je 04) 509-10.
Cook, E. C. "Nathaniel Hawthorne's Growth as an Artist." *MS* 2 (My 30) 4.
Cooke, A. L. "The Shadow of Martinus Scriblerus in Hawthorne's 'The Prophetic Pictures.'" *NEQ* 17 (D 44) 597-604.
——— "Some Evidences of Hawthorne's Indebtedness to Swift." *Un Texas Stud Eng* 18 (8 Jl 38) 140-62.
Copeland, C. T. "Hawthorne's Use of His Materials." *Critic* 45 (Jl 04) 56-60.
Cowley, Malcolm. "Hawthorne in the Looking Glass." *SR* 56 (Au 48) 545-63.
——— "Hawthorne in Solitude." *NRp* 119 (2 Ag 48) 19-23.
——— "100 Years Ago: Hawthorne Set a Great New Pattern." *N Y Herald Tribune Book R* (6 Ag 50) 1, 13.
Dana, H. W., & Hawthorne, Manning. "'The Maiden Aunt of the Whole Human Race': Frederika Bremer's Friendship with Longfellow and Hawthorne." *ASR* 37 (S 49) 217-29.
Dauner, Louise. "The Case of Tobias Pearson." *AL* 21 (Ja 50) 464-72.
Davidson, Frank. "Hawthorne's Hive of Honey." *MLN* 61 (Ja 46) 14-21.
——— "Hawthorne's Use of Pattern from *The Rambler*." *MLN* 63 (D 48) 545-8.
——— "Thoreau's Contribution to Hawthorne's *Mosses*." *NEQ* 20 (D 47) 535-42.
De Casseres, Benjamin. "Emperor of Shadows." *Critic* 45 (Jl 04) 37-45.
Desmond, M. E. "Associations of Hawthorne." *Cath World* 74 (Ja 02) 455-65.
Dony, Françoise. "Romantisme et Puritanisme chez Hawthorne, à propos de la 'Lettre Pourpre.'" *Etudes Anglaises* 4 (Ja-Mr 40) 15-30.
Doubleday, N. F. "Hawthorne and Literary Nationalism." *AL* 12 (Ja 41) 447-53.
——— "Hawthorne's Criticism of New England Life." *CE* 2 (Ap 41) 639-53.
——— "Hawthorne's Hester and Feminism." *PMLA* 54 (S 39) 825-8.
——— "Hawthorne's Inferno." *CE* 1 (My 40) 658-70.
——— "Hawthorne's Satirical Allegory." *CE* 3 (Ja 42) 325-37.
——— "Hawthorne's Use of Three Gothic Patterns." *CE* 7 (F 46) 250-62.
——— "The Theme of Hawthorne's 'Fancy's Show Box.'" *AL* 10 (N 38) 341-3.
Durston, J. H. "14 Unknown Hawthorne Works Reported Found by Collector." N Y *Herald Tribune* (12 S 48) 15.
Everett, L. B. "How the Great Ones Did It." *Overland* ns 88 (Mr 30) 88.
Ferguson, J. D. "Earliest Translation of Hawthorne." *Nation* 100 (7 Ja 15) 14-5.
Flanagan, J. T. "The Durable Hawthorne." *JEGP* 49 (Je 50) 88-96.
Fogle, R. H. "Ambiguity and Clarity in Hawthorne's 'Young Goodman Brown.'" *NEQ* 18 (D 45) 448-65.
——— "An Ambiguity of Sin or Sorrow." *NEQ* 21 (S 48) 342-9.
——— "The Problem of Allegory in Hawthorne's *Ethan Brand*." *UTQ* 17 (Ja 48) 190-203.

——— "The World and the Artist: A Study of Hawthorne's 'The Artist of the Beautiful.'" *Tulane Stud Eng* 1 (1949) 31-52.
Foster, C. H. "Hawthorne's Literary Theory." *PMLA* 57 (Mr 42) 241-54.
Gallup, D. C. "On Hawthorne's Authorship of 'The Battle Omen.'" *NEQ* 9 (D 36) 690-9.
Gavigan, W. V. "Hawthorne and Rome." *Cath World* 103 (Ag 32) 555-9.
Gerber, J. C. "Form and Content in *The Scarlet Letter.*" *NEQ* 17 (Mr 44) 25-55.
Gerould, K. F. "Call It Holy Ground." *Atl* 163 (Ja 39) 74-82.
Gibbens, V. E. "Hawthorne's Note to 'Dr. Heidegger's Experiment.'" *MLN* 60 (Je 45) 408-9.
Goldstein, J. S. "The Literary Source of Hawthorne's *Fanshawe.*" *MLN* 60 (Ja 45) 1-8.
Goodspeed, C. E. "Nathaniel Hawthorne and the Museum of the East India Marine Society." *Am Neptune* 5 (O 45) 266-72.
Gray, Maxwell. "Hawthorne the Mystic." *Nineteenth Century & After* 87 (Ja 20) 118-25.
Gribble, Francis. "Hawthorne from an English Point of View." *Critic* 45 (Jl 04) 20-3.
——— "Two Centenaries: Nathaniel Hawthorne and George Sand." *Fortnightly R* 82 (Ag 04) 260-78.
Griffiths, T. M. "'Montpelier' and 'Seven Gables': Knox's Estate and Hawthorne's Novel." *NEQ* 16 (S 43) 432-43.
Griswold, M. J. "American Quaker History in the Works of Whittier, Hawthorne, and Longfellow." *Americana* 34 (Ap 40) 220-63.
H., R. "Hawthorne in More Cheerful Mood." *Chri Sci Mon* 27 (1 Jl 35) 7.
Hall, L. S. "Hawthorne: Critic of Society. The Making of an American Philosophy." *SRL* 26 (22 My 43) 28, 30, 32.
Hannigan, D. F. "Hawthorne's Place in Literature." *Living Age* 231 (14 D 01) 720-4.
Hart, J. E. "*The Scarlet Letter:* One Hundred Years After." *NEQ* 23 (S 50) 381-95.
Haselmayer, L. A. "Hawthorne and the Cenci." *Neophilologus* 27 (1941) 59-64.
Haskell, R. I. "The Great Carbuncle." *NEQ* 10 (S 37) 533-5.
——— "Sensings and Realizations on Reading 'The Great Stone Face.'" *Educ* 43 (My 23) 544-50.
Hastings, Louise. "An Origin for 'Dr. Heidegger's Experiment.'" *AL* 9 (Ja 38) 403-10.
Hawthorne, Hildegarde. "Hawthorne and Melville." *Lit R* 2 (4 F 22) 406.
Hawthorne, Julian. "Books of Memory." *Bkm* 61 (Jl 25) 567-71.
——— "A Daughter of Hawthorne." *Atl* 142 (S 28) 372-7.
——— "A Group of Hawthorne Letters." *Harper's* 108 (Mr 04) 602-7.
——— "Hawthorne and His Circle." *Nation* 77 (19 N 03) 410-1.
——— "Hawthorne, Man of Action." *SRL* 3 (21 Ap 27) 727-8.
——— "Hawthorne's Last Years." *Critic* 45 (Jl 04) 67-71.
——— "The Making of *The Scarlet Letter.*" *Bkm* 74 (D 31) 401-11.
——— "Nathaniel Hawthorne's Blue Cloak." *Bkm* 75 (S 32) 501-6.
——— "Such Is Paradise." *Century* 105 (D 27) 157-69.
Hawthorne, Manning. "Aunt Ebe: Some Letters of Elizabeth M. Hawthorne." *NEQ* 20 (Je 47) 209-31.
——— "The Friendship between Hawthorne and Longfellow." *EJ* 28 (Mr 39) 221-3; *Eng Leaflet* 39 (F 40) 25-30.
——— "A Glimpse of Hawthorne's Boyhood." *EIHC* 83 (Ap 47) 178-84.
——— "Hawthorne and 'The Man of God.'" *Colophon* 2 (Wi 37) 262-82.
——— "Hawthorne and Utopian Socialism." *NEQ* 12 (D 39) 726-30.
——— "Hawthorne's Early Years." *EIHC* 74 (Ja 38) 1-21.
——— "Maria Louisa Hawthorne." *EIHC* 75 (Ap 39) 103-34.

——— "Nathaniel and Elizabeth Hawthorne, Editors." *Colophon* ns 1 (S 39).
——— "Nathaniel Hawthorne at Bowdoin." *NEQ* 13 (Je 40) 246-79.
——— "Nathaniel Hawthorne Prepares for College." *NEQ* 11 (Mr 38) 66-8.
——— "Parental and Family Influences on Hawthorne." *EIHC* 76 (Ja 40) 1-13.
Hayford, Harrison. "Hawthorne, Melville, and the Sea." *NEQ* 19 (D 46) 435-52.
Heilman, R. B. "Hawthorne's 'The Birthmark': Science as Religion." *SAG* 48 (O 49) 575-83.
Hicks, Granville. "A Conversation in Boston." *SR* 39 (Ap-Je 31) 129-42.
Hillman, M. V. "Hawthorne and Transcendentalism." *Cath World* 93 (My 11) 199-212.
Hoeltje, H. H. "Hawthorne's Review of *Evangeline.*" *NEQ* 23 (Je 50) 232-5.
Horwill, H. W. "Hawthorne's America." *Critic* 45 (Jl 04) 71-3.
Howe, Irving. "Hawthorne and American Fiction." *Am Merc* 68 (Mr 49) 367-74.
Howe, M. A. DeW. "The Tale of Tanglewood." *YR* 32 (D 42) 323-36.
——— "With Hawthorne at Tanglewood." *Chri Sci Mon* 38 (15 Jl 46) 6.
Howells, W. D. "The Personality of Hawthorne." *NAR* 177 (D 03) 872-82.
Hungerford, E. B. "Hawthorne Gossips about Salem." *NEQ* 6 (S 33) 445-69.
Ibershoff, C. H. "Hawthorne's Philosophy of Life." *Outlook* 126 (15 S 20) 124.
Jepson, G. E. "Hawthorne in the Boston Custom House." *Bkm* 19 (Ag 04) 573-80.
Johnston, Helen. "American Boy and Nathaniel Hawthorne—Now." *Educ R* 54 (N 17) 413-4.
Jones, Llewellyn. "Mr. Hawthorne's Scarlet Letter." *Bkm* 57 (Ja 24) 622-5.
Kane, R. J. "Hawthorne's 'The Prophetic Pictures' and James's 'The Lion.'" *MLN* 65 (Ap 50) 257-8.
Kern, A. A. "Hawthorne's *Feathertop* and 'R. L. R.'" *PMLA* 52 (Je 37) 503-10.
——— "The Sources of Hawthorne's 'Feathertop.'" *AS* 46 (D 31) 1253-9.
Kesselring, M. L. "Hawthorne's Reading, 1828-1850." *BNYPL* 53 (F, Mr, Ap 49) 55-71, 121-38, 173-94.
Kiling, Carlos. "Hawthorne's View of Sin." *Personalist* 13 (Ap 32) 119-30.
Kimball, L. E. "Miss [Delia] Bacon Advances Learning." *Colophon* ns 2 (Su 37) 338-54.
Kingery, R. E. "Disastrous Friendship." *Hobbies* 45 (Ja 41) 98.
Kouwenhoven, J. A. "Hawthorne's Notebooks and *Doctor Grimshawe's Secret.*" *AL* 5 (Ja 34) 349-58.
Lang, Andrew. "Hawthorne's Tales of Old Greece." *Independent* 62 (4 Ap 07) 792-4.
Langemann, J. K. "'Husband to the Month of May.'" *Chri Sci Mon* 38 (13 Jl 46) 4-5.
Latimer, G. P. "The Tales of Poe and Hawthorne." *NE Mag* ns 30 (Ag 04) 693-703.
Lawrence, D. H. "Studies in Classic American Literature (vii): Nathaniel Hawthorne." *Eng R* 28 (My 19) 404-17.
Leaf, Munro. "*House of Seven Gables,* by Nathaniel Hawthorne, Who Had Ghosts in His Own Garrett." *Am Mag* 131 (Mr 41) 62.
Lewin, Walter. "Nathaniel Hawthorne." *Bkm* (London) 26 (Jl 04) 121-8.
Lueders, E. G. "The Melville-Hawthorne Relationship in *Pierre* and *The Blithedale Romance.*" *WHR* 4 (Au 50) 323-34.
Lundblad, Jane. "Nathaniel Hawthorne and the Tradition of Gothic Romance." *Studia Neophilologica* 19 (1946) 1-92.
Mabie, H. W. "Nathaniel Hawthorne." *NAR* 179 (Jl 04) 12-23.
McDowell, Tremaine. "Nathaniel Hawthorne and the Witches of Colonial Salem." *N&Q* 166 (3 Mr 34) 152.
Manning, C. A. "Hawthorne and Dostoyevsky." *Slavonic R* 14 (Ja 36) 417-24.
Marble, A. R. "Gloom and Cheer in Hawthorne." *Critic* 45 (Jl 04) 28-36.
Marsh, Philip. "Hawthorne and Griswold." *MLN* 63 (F 48) 132-3.
Matherly, E. P. "Poe and Hawthorne as Writers of the Short Story." *Educ* 40 (Ja 20) 294-306.

Matthews, J. C. "Hawthorne's Knowledge of Dante." *Un Texas Stud Eng* 20 (1940) 157-65.
Merrill, L. J. "The Puritan Policeman." *Am Soc R* 10 (D 45) 766-76.
Metzdorf, R. F. "Hawthorne's Suit against Ripley and Dana." *AL* 12 (My 40) 235-41.
Miller, H. P. "Hawthorne Surveys His Contemporaries." *AL* 12 (My 40) 228-35.
Mills, Barriss. "Hawthorne and Puritanism." *NEQ* 21 (Mr 48) 78-102.
More, P. E. "Hawthorne: Looking Before and After." *Independent* 56 (30 Je 04) 1489-94.
——— "The Origins of Hawthorne and Poe." *Independent* 54 (16 O 02) 2453-60.
——— "The Solitude of Nathaniel Hawthorne." *Atl* 88 (N 01) 588-99.
Morison, S. E. "Melville's 'Agatha' Letter to Hawthorne." *NEQ* 2 (Ap 29) 296-307.
Mulder, Arnold. "An Immoral Moral." *Freeman* 5 (9 Ag 22) 517-8.
Mumford, Lewis. "Influence of Hawthorne on Melville." *Am Merc* 15 (D 28) 428-90.
Munger, T. T. "The Centenary of Hawthorne." *Century* 68 (Jl 04) 482-3.
——— "Notes on the Scarlet Letter." *Atl* 93 (Ap 04) 521-35.
Myers, Gustave. "Hawthorne and the Myths about Puritans." *Am Spect* 2 (Ap 34) 1.
Nevins, W. S. "Nathaniel Hawthorne's Removal from the Salem Custom House." *EIHC* 53 (Ap 17) 97-132.
Orians, G. H. "The Angel of Hadley in Fiction: A Study of the Sources of Hawthorne's 'The Grey Champion.'" *AL* 4 (N 32) 257-69.
——— "Hawthorne and 'The Maypole of Merry-mount.'" *MLN* 53 (Mr 38) 159-67.
——— "New England Witchcraft in Fiction." *AL* 2 (Mr 30) 54-71.
——— "Scott and Hawthorne's *Fanshawe*." *NEQ* 11 (Je 38) 388-94.
——— "The Source of Hawthorne's 'Roger Malvin's Burial.'" *AL* 10 (N 38) 313-8.
——— "The Sources and Themes of Hawthorne's 'The Gentle Boy." *NEQ* 14 (D 41) 664-78.
Osborne, J. B. "Nathaniel Hawthorne as American Consul." *Bkm* 16 (Ja 03) 461-4.
Parkes, H. B. "Poe, Hawthorne, Melville: An Essay in Sociological Criticism." *PR* 16 (F 49) 157-65.
Pearce, R. H. "Hawthorne and the Twilight of Romance." *YR* 27 (Sp 48) 487-506.
Pearson, N. H. "Anonymous Editor." *SRL* 24 (26 Jl 41) 18.
——— "A Sketch by Hawthorne." *NEQ* 6 (Mr 33) 136-44.
Perry, Bliss. "The Centenary of Hawthorne." *Atl* 94 (Ag 04) 195-206.
Pfeiffer, K. G. "The Prototype of the Poet in 'The Great Stone Face.'" *Res Stud State Col Wash* 9 (Je 41) 100-8.
Phelps, W. L. "Nathaniel Hawthorne and Puritanism." *Ladies Home J* 40 (Mr 23) 15.
Pickard, S. T. "Is 'Hawthorne's First Diary' a Forgery?" *Dial* 33 (16 S 02) 155.
Pritchard, J. P. "Hawthorne's Debt to Classical Literary Criticism." *Classical W* 29 (2 D 35) 41-5.
Pritchett, V. S. "Books in General." *New Statesman & Nation* 24 (24 O 42) 275.
——— "Hawthorne at Brook Farm." *New Statesman & Nation* 28 (N 44) 323.
Pryce-Jones, Allan. "Hawthorne in England." *Life & Letters* 50 (Ag 46) 71-80.
Rahv, Philip. "The Dark Lady of Salem." *PR* 8 (S-O 41) 362-81.
Randall, D. A., & Winterich, J. T. "One Hundred Good Novels: Hawthorne, Nathaniel, 'The Scarlet Letter.'" *Pub W* 137 (16 Mr 40) 1181-2.
Randel, W. P. "Hawthorne, Channing, and Margaret Fuller." *AL* 10 (Ja 39) 472-6.
Read, Herbert. "Hawthorne." *H&H* 3 (Ja-Mr 30) 213-29.
Reed, A. L. "Self-Portraiture in the Works of Nathaniel Hawthorne." *SP* 23 (Ja 26) 40-54.

Ringe, D. L. "Hawthorne's Psychology of the Head and Heart." *PMLA* 65 (Mr 50) 120-32.

Roberts, J. E. "Sophia Hawthorne, Editor." *SRL* 29 (23 D 39) 9.

Robinson, H. M. "Materials of Romance." *Commonweal* 10 (16 O 29) 622-3.

Roper, Gordon. "The Originality of Hawthorne's *The Scarlet Letter*." *Dalhousie R* 29 (Ap 50) 62-79.

Ross, E. C. "A Note on *The Scarlet Letter*." *MLN* 37 (Ja 22) 58-9.

Russell, A. J. "Hawthorne and the Romantic Indian." *Educ* 48 (F 28) 381-6.

Sampson, M. W. "Nathaniel Hawthorne." *Reader* 5 (Ap 05) 775-8.

Schubert, Leland. "A Boy's Journal of a Trip into New England in 1838." *EIHC* 86 (Ap 50) 97-105.

——— "Hawthorne and George W. Childs and the Death of W. D. Ticknor." *EIHC* 84 (Ap 48) 164-8.

——— "Hawthorne Used the Melodic Rhythm of Repetition." *Chri Sci Mon* 37 (15 Mr 45) 6.

Scudder, H. H. "Hawthorne's Use of *Typee*." *N&Q* 187 (21 O 44) 184-6.

Seitz, D. C. "Fanshawe at the American Top." *Pub W* 119 (16 My 31) 244.

Shroeder, J. W. "'That Inward Sphere': Notes on Hawthorne's Heart Imagery and Symbolism." *PMLA* 65 (Mr 50) 106-19.

Smyth, A. H. "Hawthorne's 'Great Stone Face.'" *Chautauquan* 31 (Ap 00) 75-9.

——— "Hawthorne's Marble Faun." *Chautauquan* 30 (F 00) 522-6.

Spiller, R. E. "Critical Revaluations." *SRL* 10 (13 Ja 34) 406.

——— "The Mind and Art of Nathaniel Hawthorne." *Outlook* 149 (22 Ag 28) 50-2.

Stewart, Randall. "The Concord Group." *SR* 44 (O-D 36) 434-46.

——— "Editing Hawthorne's Notebooks." *More Books* 20 (S 45) 299-315.

——— "Ethan Brand." *SRL* 5 (27 Ap 29) 967.

——— "Hawthorne and Politics; Unpublished Letters to William R. Pike." *NEQ* 5 (Ap 32) 237-63.

——— "Hawthorne and the Civil War." *SP* 34 (Ja 37) 91-106.

——— "Hawthorne and *The Faerie Queene*." *PQ* 12 (Ap 33) 196-206.

——— "Hawthorne in England: The Patriotic Motive in the Notebooks." *NEQ* 8 (Mr 35) 3-13.

——— "The Hawthornes at the Wayside, 1860-1864." *More Books* 19 (S 44) 263-79.

——— "Hawthorne's Contributions to *The Salem Advertiser*." *AL* 5 (Ja 34) 327-41.

——— "Hawthorne's Last Illness and Death." *More Books* 19 (O 44) 303-13.

——— "Hawthorne's Speeches at Civil Banquets." *AL* 7 (Ja 36) 415-23.

——— "Letters to Sophia." *HLQ* 7 (Ag 44) 387-95.

——— "Mrs. Hawthorne's Financial Difficulties. Selections from Her Letters to James T. Fields, 1865-1868." *More Books* 21 (F 46) 43-53.

——— "Mrs. Hawthorne's Quarrel with James T. Fields." *More Books* 21 (S 46) 254-63.

——— "'Pestiferous Gail Hamilton,' James T. Fields, and the Hawthornes." *NEQ* 17 (S 44) 418-23.

——— "Recollections of Hawthorne by His Sister Elizabeth." *AL* 16 (Ja 45) 316-31.

——— "Two Uncollected Reviews by Hawthorne." *NEQ* 9 (S 36) 504-9.

Stoddard, R. H. "Reminiscences of Hawthorne and Poe." *Independent* 54 (20 N 02) 2756-8.

Streeter, R E. "Hawthorne's Misfit Politician and Edward Everett." *AL* 16 (Mr 44) 26-8.

Symons, Arthur. "Hawthorne." *Lamp* 28 (Mr 04) 102-7.

Tapley, H. S. "Hawthorne's 'Pot-8-0 Club' at Bowdoin College." *EIHC* 67 (Jl 31) 225-32.

Thorner, H. E. "Hawthorne, Poe, and a Literary Ghost." *NEQ* 7 (Mr 34) 146-54.

Ticknor, Caroline. "Hawthorne and His Publisher." *Dial* 56 (1 Ja 14) 13-6.

Ticknor, H. M. "Hawthorne as Seen by His Publishers." *Critic* 45 (Jl 04) 23-6.
Trollope, Anthony. "The Genius of Nathaniel Hawthorne." *NAR* 201 (F 15) 313-4.
Turner, Arlin. "Autobiographical Elements in Hawthorne's 'The Blithedale Romance.'" *Un Texas Stud in Eng* 15 (1935) 39-62.
——— "Hawthorne and Reform." *NEQ* 15 (D 42) 700-14.
——— "Hawthorne as Self-Critic." *SAQ* 37 (Ap 38) 132-8.
——— "Hawthorne at Martha's Vineyard." *NEQ* 11 (Je 38) 394-400.
——— "Hawthorne's Literary Borrowings." *PMLA* 51 (Je 36) 543-62.
——— "A Note on Hawthorne's Revisions." *MLN* 51 (N 36) 426-9.
Tuttiett, M. G. "Hawthorne the Mystic." *Nineteenth Century* 87 (Ja 20) 118-25.
Tykessen, Elizabeth. "Från bokhyllan." *Bonniers Litterära Magasin* (Stockholm) 15 (Jl-Ag 47) 497-9.
Van Doren, Carl. "Flower of Puritanism: Hawthorne's *Scarlet Letter.*" *Nation* 111 (8 D 20) 649-50.
Voigt, G. P. "Hawthorne and the Roman Catholic Church." *NEQ* 19 (S 46) 394-7.
——— "Nathaniel Hawthorne, Author for Preachers." *Lutheran Church Q* 21 (Ja 43) 82-6.
Waggoner, H. H. "Hawthorne's Beginning: 'Alice Doane's Appeal.'" *UKCR* 16 (Su 50) 254-60.
——— "Hawthorne's 'Canterbury Pilgrims': Theme and Structure." *NEQ* 22 (S 49) 373-87.
——— "Nathaniel Hawthorne: The Cemetery, the Prison, and the Rose." *UKCR* 14 (Sp 48) 175-90.
Waples, Dorothy. "Suggestions for Interpreting *The Marble Faun.*" *AL* 13 (N 41) 224-39.
Ward, W. S. "Nathaniel Hawthorne and Brook Farm." *Letters* 4 (Ag 31) 6-14.
Warren, Austin. "Hawthorne, Margaret Fuller, and 'Nemesis.'" *PMLA* 54 (Je 39) 613-5.
——— "Hawthorne's Reading." *NEQ* 8 (D 35) 480-97.
Warren, R. P. "Hawthorne, Anderson, and Frost." *NRp* 54 (16 My 28) 399-401.
Weber, C. J. "A Hawthorne Centenary." *Colby Merc* 7 (My 42) 97-102.
Wegelin, Christof. "Europe in Hawthorne's Fiction." *ELH* 14 (S 47) 219-45.
Werner, W. L. "The First Edition of Hawthorne's *The Scarlet Letter.*" *AL* 5 (Ja 34) 359.
Whibley. Charles. "Two Centenaries." *Blackwood's Mag* 176 (Ag 04) 255-62.
Winterich, J. T. "Good Second Hand Condition." *Pub W* 121 (18 Je 32) 2423-4.
Winters, Yvor. "Maule's Curse: Hawthorne and the Problem of Allegory." *Am R* 9 (S 37) 339-61.
Woodberry, G. E. "Hawthorne and Everett." *Nation* 75 (9 O 02) 283.
——— "The Literary Age of Boston." *Harper's* 106 (F 03) 424-30.
Wright, Nathalia. "Hawthorne and the Praslin Murder." *NEQ* 15 (Mr 42) 5-14.
Zangwill, O. L. "A Case of Paramnesia in Nathaniel Hawthorne." *Character & Personality* 13 (Mr-Je 45) 246-60.
Zunder, T. A. "Walt Whitman and Hawthorne." *MLN* 47 (My 32) 314-6.

HAY, JOHN (1838-1905). Adams, Brooks. "John Hay." *McClure's Mag* 19 (Je 02) 173-82.
Bender, C. A. "Another Forgotten Novel." *MLN* 41 (My 26) 319-22.
Bishop, J. B. "A Friendship with John Hay." *Century* 71 (Mr 06) 773-80.
Chapman, A. S. "The Boyhood of John Hay." *Century* 78 (Je 09) 444-54.
Gilder, J. B. "Glimpses of John Hay." *Critic* 47 (Ag, S 05) 112-3, 248-52.
Hicks, Granville. "The Conversion of John Hay." *NRp* 67 (10 Je 31) 100-1.
Howells, W. D. "John Hay in Literature." *NAR* 181 (S 05) 343-51.
Louitt, W. E. "The Love of a Nun." *Colophon* ns 2 (Au 37) 504-10.
Mellen, G. F. "John Hay—Littérateur." *Methodist R* 34: ser 5 (Jl-Ag 18) 547-56.
Moore, J. B. "John Hay: An Estimate." *SRL* 10 (11 N 33) 249-51.

Stanton, Theodore. "John Hay and the Bread Winners." *Nation* 103 (1916) 130-1.
Thayer, W. R. "John Hay's Policy of Anglo-Saxonism." *World's Work* 35 (N 17) 33-41.

HAYNE, PAUL HAMILTON (1830-86). Anon. "Unpublished Letters of Wilkie Collins to Paul H. Hayne." *Bkm* 37 (Mr 13) 66-71.
Anderson, Charles. "Poet of the Pine Barrens." *Ga R* (Fl 47) 280-93.
Bernard, E. G. "Northern Bryant and Southern Hayne." *Colophon* ns 1 (Sp 36) 536-40.
Brown, J. T., Jr. "Paul Hamilton Hayne." *SR* 14 (Ap 06) 236-47.
Coleman, R. A. "Hayne Writes to Trowbridge." *AL* 10 (Ja 39) 483-6.
Davis, R. B. "Paul Hamilton Hayne to Dr. Francis Peyre Porcher." *SP* 44 (Jl 47) 327-9.
——— "An Unpublished Poem by Paul Hamilton Hayne." *AL* 18 (Ja 47) 327-9.
Dedmond, F. B. "Paul Hamilton Hayne and the Poe Westminster Memorial." *Md Hist Mag* 45 (Je 50) 149-51.
Ferguson, J. D. "A New Letter of Paul Hamilton Hayne." *AL* 5 (Ja 34) 368-70.
Griffin, M. L. "Whittier and Hayne: A Record of a Friendship." *AL* 19 (Mr 47) 41-58.
Hayne, P. H. "Five Letters from Paul Hamilton Hayne to Horatio Woodman." *PMHS* 54 (Ja 21) 178-84.
Hench, A. L. "Three Letters to the Haynes from Richard Blackmore." *AL* 4 (My 32) 199-207.
Holliday, Carl. "Paul Hamilton Hayne." *SR* 14 (Ap 06) 236-43.
Hoole, W. S. "Seven Unpublished Letters of Paul Hamilton Hayne." *Ga Hist Q* 22 (S 38) 273-85.
Hubbell, J. B. "George Henry Boker, Paul Hamilton Hayne, and Charles Warren Stoddard: Some Unpublished Letters." *AL* 5 (My 33) 146-65.
——— "Some New Letters of Constance Fenimore Woolson." *NEQ* 14 (D 41) 715-35.
McKeithan, D. M. "Communication to the Editor [Unpublished Letters]." *J So Hist* 10 (N 44) 498-9.
——— "A Correspondence Journal of Paul Hamilton Hayne." *Ga Hist Q* 27 (S-D 42) 249-72.
——— "A Note on Hayne's Ancestry." *Ga Hist Q* 24 (Je 40) 166-7.
——— "Paul Hamilton Hayne and *The Southern Bivouac*." *Un Texas Stud Eng* 17 (1937) 112-23.
——— "Paul Hamilton Hayne Writes to the Granddaughter of Patrick Henry." *Ga Hist Q* 32 (Mr 48) 22-8.
——— "Paul Hamilton Hayne's Reputation in Augusta at the Time of His Death." *Un Texas Stud Eng* 18 (1938) 163-73.
——— "An Unpublished Poem of Paul Hayne." *SLM* 1 (S 39) 591-2.
Routh, James. "Two Fugitive Poems of Paul Hamilton Hayne." *JEGP* 17 (1918) 426-9.
Shaw, H. J. "Paul Hamilton Hayne to Richard Henry Stoddard, July 1, 1866." *AL* 4 (My 32) 195-9.
Starke, Aubrey. "Sidney Lanier and Paul Hamilton Hayne: Three Unpublished Letters." *AL* 1 (Mr 29) 32-9.
Thompson, Maurice. "The Last Literary Cavalier." *Critic* 38 (Ap 01) 352-4.

HEARN, LAFCADIO (1850-1904). Anon. "Letters and the Arts: Lafcadio Hearn." *Living Age* 341 (O 31) 180.
——— "Letters of a Poet to a Musician: Lafcadio Hearn to Henry E. Krehbiel." *Critic* 48 (Ap 06) 309-18.
——— "Rare Manuscripts." *Life* 20 (15 Ap 46) 101-5.
Abbott, H. V. "Lafcadio Hearn." *SAQ* 6 (Ap 07) 189-99.

Amenomori, Nobushige. "Lafcadio Hearn, the Man." *Atl* 96 (O 05) 510-25.
Andromedas, Nicholas. "Ancestry of Lafcadio Hearn's Mother." *Athene* 11 (Ag 50) 28-9, 60.
Ballenberg, Kathleen. "Lafcadio Hearn—A Writer's Writer." *MS* 3 (Jl 31) 3, 9.
Beck, E. C. "Letters of Lafcadio Hearn to His Brother." *AL* 4 (My 32) 167-73.
——— "Letters of Lafcadio Hearn to His Brother." *EJ* (Col ed) 20 (Ap 31) 287-92.
Bedinger, G. R. "Japanese Sources of Lafcadio Hearn." *Independent* 73 (21 N 12) 1166-70.
Binyon, Laurence. "Lafcadio Hearn on Victorian Poets." *Living Age* 303 (6 D 19) 601-3.
Bisland, Elizabeth. "Japanese Letters of Lafcadio Hearn.' *Atl* 104 (D 09) 721-33; 105 (Ja, F 10) 19-31, 200-13.
——— "Some Martinique Letters of Lafcadio Hearn." *Harper's* 142 (Mr 21) 516-25.
Blake, W. B. "The Problem of Lafcadio Hearn." *Dial* 52 (1 Ap 12) 503-8.
Boynton, P. H. "Lafcadio Hearn." *VQR* 3 (Jl 27) 418-34.
Cowley, Malcolm. "Lafcadio Herum-san." *NRp* 120 (18 Ap 49) 22-4.
Davis, F. H. "Lafcadio Hearn." *Forum* 51 (Mr 14) 447-54.
——— "Lafcadio Hearn." *Living Age* 309 (16 Ap 21) 34-40.
Edwards, Osman. "Lafcadio Hearn on the Decadent School." *Craftsman* 13 (O 07) 14-21.
——— "Some Unpublished Letters of Lafcadio Hearn." *Trans & Proc Japan Soc* 16 (1917-8) 16-35.
——— "Things English and Japanese: Unpublished Letters of Lafcadio Hearn." *Craftsman* 13 (N 07) 140-8.
Emerson, Margaret. "Lafcadio Hearn's Funeral." *Critic* 46 (Ja 05) 34-8.
Espey, J. J. "The Two Japans of Lafcadio Hearn." *PS* 4 (Sp 50) 342-51.
Foxwell, E. "Reminiscences of Lafcadio Hearn." *Trans & Proc Japan Soc* 8 (1907-9) 68-94.
Gookin, F. W. "The Self-Revelation of Lafcadio Hearn." *Dial* 41 (16 D 06) 448-50.
Greenslet, Ferris. "Lafcadio Hearn." *Atl* 99 (F 07) 261-72.
Hendrick, Ellwood. "Lafcadio Hearn." *BNYPL* 33 (D 29) 854-61.
Joya, Mock. "Hearn Sen-sei." *Bkm* 39 (Ap 14) 172-8.
Kennard, Mrs. Arthur. "The Real Lafcadio Hearn." *Nineteenth Century* 65 (F 09) 258-71.
Kinnosuké, Adachi. "Mr. Hearn's Japanese Shadowings." *Critic* 38 (Ja 01) 29-30.
Kneeland, H. T. "Lafcadio Hearn's Brother." *Atl* 131 (Ja 23) 20-7.
Koizumi, Setsuko. "The Last Days of Lafcadio Hearn." *Atl* 119 (Mr 17) 349-51.
——— "Reminiscences of Lafcadio Hearn." *Atl* 122 (S 18) 342-51.
Langton, D. H. "Lafcadio Hearn." *Manchester Q* 31 (Ja 12) 1-23.
Lawless, R. M. "A Note on Lafcadio Hearn's Brother." *AL* 10 (Mr 38) 80-3.
Marsh, E. C. "Lafcadio Hearn." *Forum* 40 (Ag 08) 175-80.
Masamuné, H. "New Light on Lafcadio Hearn." *Contemp Japan* 2 (S 33) 270-80.
Mims, Edwin. "The Letters of Lafcadio Hearn." *SAQ* 10 (Ap 11) 149-58.
Monahan, Michael. "The Celtic Strain In Lafcadio Hearn." *Forum* 51 (My 14) 779-81.
——— "Lafcadio Hearn: A French Estimate." *Forum* 49 (Mr 13) 356-66.
More, P. E. "Lafcadio Hearn; The Meeting of Three Ways." *Atl* 91 (F 03) 204-11.
Noguchi, Yone. "A Japanese Appreciation of Lafcadio Hearn." *Atl* 105 (Ap 10) 521-6.
——— "Lafcadio Hearn: A Dreamer." *Cur Lit* 38 (Je 05) 521-3.
Porter, K. A. "A Disinherited Cosmopolitan." *N Y Herald Tribune Books* (16 F 30) 22.
Rhodes, Harrison. "Lafcadio Hearn." *Bkm* 25 (Mr 07) 73-5.

Rosenbaum, S. G. "On the Centenary of Lafcadio Hearn." *N Y Herald Tribune Book R* (31 D 50) 6.
Rudkin, H. E. "Lafcadio Hearn." *N&Q* 177 (9 D 39) 419-22.
Rutland, Lucille. "Lafcadio Hearn and Denny Corcoran." *Double Dealer* 3 (F 22) 96-9.
Sisson, M. H. "A Bibliography of Lafcadio Hearn." *Bul Bibl* 15 (My-Ag, S-D 33, Ja-Ap, My-Ag 34) 6-7, 32-4, 55-6, 73-5.
Snell, George. "Poe Redivivus." *Ariz Q* 1 (Su 45) 49-57.
Stempel, Daniel. "Lafcadio Hearn: Interpreter of Japan." *AL* 20 (Mr 48) 1-19.
Stewart, W. C. "Note on Lafcadio Hearn." *Contemp R* 102 (O 12) 543-51.
Tinker, E. L. "Lafcadio Hearn and the Sense of Smell." *Bkm* 58 (Ja 24) 519-27.
Van Briessen, Fritz. "Lafcadio Hearn: dekadent? aesthet? exotist?" *Englische Studien* 71 (Je 37) 372-83.

HEGGEN, THOMAS O. (1919-1949). Anon. "Thomas O. Heggen." *Pub W* 155 (28 My 49) 2170.
Cohn, Victor. "Mister Heggen." *SRL* 32 (11 Je 49) 19.

HELLMAN, LILLIAN (1905-). Clark, B. H. "Lillian Hellman." *CE* 6 (D 44) 127-33.
Isaacs, E. J. R. "Lillian Hellman: A Playwright on the March." *Theatre Arts* 28 (Ja 44) 19-24.

HELPER, HINTON ROWAN (1829-1909). Barbee, D. R. "Hinton Rowan Helper." *Tyler's Quar Hist & Gen Mag* 15 (Ja 34) 145-72.
Polk, William. "The Hated Helper." *SAQ* 30 (Ap 31) 177-89.
Reuben-Sheeler, J. "Hinton Rowan Helper." *Negro Hist Bul* 9 (Mr 46) 137-41.

HEMINGWAY, ERNEST (1898-). Anon. "Tiger, Tiger." *SRL* 17 (16 O 37) 88.
Adams, J. D. "Ernest Hemingway." *EJ* (Col ed) 28 (F 39) 87-94.
Allen, Hugh. "The Dark Night of Ernest Hemingway." *Cath World* 150 (F 40) 522-9.
Baker, Carlos. "The Hard Trade of Mr. Hemingway." *Delphian Q* 23 (Jl 40) 12-7.
Barea, Arturo. "Not Spain but Hemingway." *Horizon* 3 (My 41) 350-61.
Bessie, Alvah. "Hemingway's 'For Whom the Bell Tolls.'" *New Masses* 37 (5 N 40) 25-9.
Bishop, J. P. "Homage to Hemingway." *NRp* 89 (11 N 36) 39-42.
——— "The Missing All." *VQR* 13 (Wi 37) 107-21.
Bizzari, E. "Croce con prefazione di Hemingway." *Fiera Letteraria* (2 My 46) 4.
Brooks, Cleanth, & Warren, R. P. "The Killers." *Am Prefaces* 7 (Sp 42) 195-209.
Burgum, E. B. "Hemingway's Development." *New Masses* 29 (22 N 38) 21-3.
Bütow, Hans. "Ernest Hemingway, ein Schriftsteller aus U. S. A." *Frankfurter Zeitung* (5 Jl 34) 335-6.
Calverton, V. F. "Ernest Hemingway: Primevalite." *Mod Mo* 10 (D 37) 6-7.
Campbell, Kenneth. "An Appreciation of Hemingway." *Am Merc* 44 (Jl 38) 288-91.
Canby, H. S. "Chronicle and Comment." *Bkm* 70 (F 30) 641-7.
——— "Farewell to the Nineties." *SRL* 10 (28 O 33) 217.
Cecchi, E. "Ernest Hemingway." *Mercurio* 2 (1945) 111-23.
Cohn, L. H. "A Note on Ernest Hemingway." *Colophon* ns 1 (Su 35) 119-22.
Coindreau, M. E. "*To Have and to Have Not,* par Ernest Hemingway." *Nouvelle Revue Française* 26 (Mr 38) 501-4.
Cowley, Malcolm. "A Farewell to Spain." *NRp* 73 (30 N 32) 76-7.
——— "Hemingway and the Hero." *NRp* 101 (4 D 44) 754-8.
——— "Hemingway at Midnight." *NRp* 111 (14 Ag 44) 190-5.
——— "Hemingway in Madrid." *NRp* 96 (2 N 38) 367-8.
——— "Notes for a Hemingway Omnibus." *SRL* 27 (23 S 44) 7-8, 23-4.

——— "A Portrait of Mister Pape." *Life* 25 (10 Ja 49).
Daiches, David. "Ernest Hemingway." *CE* 2 (My 41) 735-6.
Daniel, R. A. "Hemingway and His Heroes." *QQ* 54 (Wi 47-8) 471-85.
Delpech, Jeanine. "Ernest Hemingway romancier de la vie dangereuse." *Nouvelles Littéraires* (3 Ap 37) 9.
Dewing, Arthur. "The Mistake about Hemingway." *NAR* 232 (O 31) 364-71.
Dodd, L. W. "Simple Annals of the Callous." *SRL* 4 (19 N 27) 322-3.
Eastman, Max. "Bull in the Afternoon." *NRp* 75 (7 Je 33) 94-7.
——— "Red Blood and Hemingway." *NRp* 75 (28 Je 33) 184.
Engstrom, A. G. "Dante, Flaubert, and 'The Snows of Kilimanjaro.'" *MLN* 65 (Mr 50) 203-5.
Fadiman, Clifton. "Ernest Hemingway: An American Byron." *Nation* 136 (18 Ja 33) 63-5.
——— "Hemingway." *NYr* 13 (16 O 37) 76-7.
——— "A Letter to Mr. Hemingway." *NYr* 9 (28 O 33) 58-9.
Fallada, Hans. "Ernest Hemingway oder woran liegt es?" *Die Literatur* 33 (S 31) 672-4.
Farrell, J. T. "Ernest Hemingway, Apostle of a 'Lost Generation.'" *N Y Times Book R* (1 Ag 43) 6, 14.
Fenimore, Edward. "English and Spanish in *For Whom the Bell Tolls.*" *ELH* 10 (Mr 43) 73-86.
Fitzgerald, F. S. "How to Waste Material: A Note on My Generation." *Bkm* 63 (My 26) 262-5.
Frankenberg, Lloyd. "Themes and Characters in Hemingway's Latest Period." *So R* 7 (Sp 42) 776-88.
Frohock, W. M. "Ernest Hemingway: Violence and Discipline: I." *Sw R* 32 (Wi 47) 89-97.
——— "Ernest Hemingway: Violence and Discipline: II." *Sw R* 32 (Sp 47) 184-93.
Galantière, L. "The Brushwood Boy at the Front." *H&H* 3 (Ja-Mr 30) 259-62.
Garnett, David. "Books in General." *New Statesman & Nation* 7 (10 F 34) 192.
Geismar, Maxwell. "No Man Alone Now." *VQR* 17 (S 41) 517-34.
Gordon, Caroline. "Notes on Hemingway and Kafka." *SR* 57 (Sp 49) 215-26.
Hackett, Francis. "Hemingway: 'A Farewell to Arms.'" *SRL* 32 (6 Ag 49) 32-3.
Halliday, E. M. "Hemingway's *In Our Time.*" *Expl* 7 (Mr 49) 35.
Hemingway, Ernest. "Monologue to the Maestro." *Esquire* 4 (O 35) 21 ff.
Hemphill, George. "Hemingway and James." *KR* 11 (Wi 49) 50-60.
Herrick, Robert. "What Is Dirt?" *Bkm* 70 (N 29) 258-62.
Jameson, Storm. "The Craft of the Novelist." *Eng R* 58 (Ja 34) 28-43; *Mod Thinker* 4 (Mr 34) 290-302.
John, Edgar. "Farewell the Separate Peace." *SR* 48 (Jl-S 40) 289-300.
Johnson, Merle. "American First Editions: Ernest Hemingway." *Pub W* 121 (20 F 32) 870.
Kazin, Alfred. "The Indignant Flesh." *NYr* 26 (9 S 50) 101-3.
Kirstein, Lincoln. "The Canon of Death." *H&H* 6 (Ja-Mr 33) 336-41.
Leighton, Lawrence. "An Autopsy and a Prescription." *H&H* 5 (Jl-S 32) 519-39.
Lewis, Wyndham. "The Dumb Ox, a Study of Ernest Hemingway." *Am R* 6 (Je 34) 289-312.
Littell, Robert. "Notes on Hemingway." *NRp* 51 (10 Ag 27) 303-6.
Lovett, R. M. "Ernest Hemingway." *EJ* 21 (O 32) 609-17.
Lundkvist, Artur. "Ernest Hemingway." *Bonniers Littërara Magasin* 8 (Mr 39) 198-204.
Mann, Klaus. "Ernest Hemingway." *Neue Schweizer Rundschau* 24 (1931) 272-7.
Matthews, T. S. "Nothing Ever Happens to the Brave." *NRp* 60 (9 O 29) 208-10.
Mecredy, M. B. "A Reported Trend in Novel Writing." *Dalhousie R* 26 (Ja 47) 454-8.

Orton, Vrest. "Some Notes Bibliographical and Otherwise on the Books of Ernest Hemingway." *Pub W* 117 (15 F 30) 884-6.
Parker, Dorothy. "The Artist's Reward." *NYr* (30 N 29) 28-31.
Paul, Elliott. "Hemingway and the Critics." *SRL* 16 (6 N 37) 3-4.
Praz, Mario. "Hemingway in Italy." *PR* 15 (O 48) 1086-1160.
Rahv, Philip. "The Social Muse and the Great Kudu." *PR* 4 (D 37) 16-20.
Rascoe, Burton. "Contemporary Reminiscences." *Arts & Decoration* 24 (N 25) 57, 79.
Redman, B. R. "The Champ and His Critics." *SRL* 33 (28 O 50) 15-6, 38.
Reid, J. T. "Spain as Seen by Some Contemporary Writers." *Hispania* 20 (My 37) 139-50.
Root, E. M. "The Aesthetic Puritans." *Christian Century* 44 (25 Ag 37) 1043-5.
Savage, D. S. "Ernest Hemingway." *Hudson R* 1 (O 48) 380-401.
Schneider, Marcel. "Ernest Hemingway." *Espace* (Paris) (Je 45) 98-105.
Schwartz, Delmore. "Ernest Hemingway's Literary Situation." *So R* 3 (Ap 38) 769-82.
Sickels, E. M. "Farewell to Cynicism." *CE* 3 (O 41) 31-8.
Söderberg, Sten. "Nazismen och den moderna realismen: Litterär nazism." *Samtid och Framtid* (Stockholm) 2 (Je-Ag 45) 376-9.
Solow, Herbert. "Substitution at Left Tackle: Hemingway for Dos Passos." *PR* 4 (Ap 38) 62-4.
Stein, Gertrude. "Hemingway: A Portrait." *Ex Libris* (D 23) 192.
——— "Ernest Hemingway and the Post-War Decade." *Atl* 152 (Ag 33) 197-208.
Tavernier, René. "Hemingway—Pages Inédites, traduites et présentées par René Tavernier." *Confluences* ns 2 (Mr 45) 142-72.
Tedlock, E. W., Jr. "Hemingway's 'The Snows of Kilimanjaro.'" *Expl* 8 (O 49) 7.
Walcutt, C. C. "Hemingway's *The Snows of Kilimanjaro*." *Expl* 7 (Ap 49) 43.
Warren, R. P. "Hemingway." *Die Amerikanische Rundschau* 3 (D 47) 89-104.
——— "Hemingway." *KR* 9 (Wi 47) 1-28.
——— "Novelist-Philosophers—X: Hemingway." *Horizon* 15 (Ap 47) 156-79.
West, R. B. "Ernest Hemingway: Death in the Evening." *AR* 4 (D 44) 569-80.
——— "Ernest Hemingway: The Failure of Sensibility." *SR* 53 (Wi 45) 120-35.
Wilson, Edmund. "Ernest Hemingway, Bourbon Gauge of Morale." *Atl* 163 (Jl 39) 36-46.
——— "The Sportsman's Tragedy." *NRp* 53 (14 D 27) 102-3.
Young, Philip. "Hemingway's *A Farewell to Arms*." *Expl* 7 (O 48) 7.

HENDERSON, ARCHIBALD (1877-). Polk, W. T. "Archibald Henderson." *SLM* 3 (D 41) 564-7.

HENTZ, CAROLINE L. (1800-56). Ellison, R. C. "Mrs. Hentz and the Green-Eyed Monster." *AL* 22 (N 50) 345-50.

HERBERT, HENRY WILLIAM (1807-58). Henderson, R. W. "The Godolphin Arabian. Is It a Herbert Translation?" *Book Buyer* 3 (D 37) 18.
Randall, D. A. "A 'Frank Forester' Check List." *Pub W* 122 (24 S 32) 1276.

HERGESHEIMER, JOSEPH (1880-1954). Anon. "Hergesheimer, Literary Meteor or Newly Discovered Star?" *Cur Op* 68 (F 20) 229-33.
——— "Joseph Hergesheimer." *Bkm* 54 (My 22) 247-51
Boynton, P. H. "Joseph Hergesheimer." *EJ* 16 (My 27) 335-45.
Cabell, J. B. "About One and Another: A Note as to Joseph Hergesheimer." *N Y Herald Tribune Books* 6: sec 1 (15 Je 30) 6.
——— "In Respect to Joseph Hergesheimer." *Bkm* 50 (N-D 19) 267-73.
Drake, M. E. "American First Editions . . . Joseph Hergesheimer." *Pub W* 102 (30 D 22) 2221.
Fadiman, Clifton. "The Best People's Best Novelist." *Nation* 136 (15 F 33) 175-7.

Fischer, Walther. "Joseph Hergesheimer." *J Pol Econ* 1 (1925) 393-412.
Follett, Wilson. "Factualist versus Impressionist." *Dial* 66 (3 My 19) 449-51.
Gagnot, Berthe. "Un Romancier Americain: Joseph Hergesheimer." *Revue Anglo-Amer* 3 (Ag 26) 505-10.
George, W. L. "Joseph Hergesheimer." *Bkm* (London) 58 (S 20) 193-4.
Glasgow, Ellen. "The Biography of Manuel." *SRL* 6 (7 Je 30) 1108-10.
Gray, J. B. "An Author and His Town: West Chester and Joseph Hergesheimer Get Used to Each Other." *Bkm* 67 (Ap 28) 159-64.
Haardt, Sara. "Joseph Hergesheimer's Methods." *Bkm* 69 (Je 29) 398-403.
Hergesheimer, Joseph. "Art." *Am Merc* 9 (N 26) 257-63.
——— "Biography and Bibliographies." *Colophon* 2 (D 31) Pt 8.
——— "The Profession of Novelist." *NRp* 30 (12 Ap 22) supp.
——— "Scholasticus, in se Scholia Facit. Or, Java Head Revisited." *PULC* 3 (F 42) 52-5.
——— "Some Veracious Paragraphs." *Bkm* 48 (S 18) 8-12.
Kelley, Leon. "America and Mr. Hergesheimer." *SR* 40 (Ap-Je 32) 171-93.
Latham, G. W. "Joseph Hergesheimer." *Canadian Forum* 11 (Ap 31) 260-1.
Phillips, H. A. "A Novelist's Uphill Road." *World Today* 52 (Jl 28) 151-4.
Priestly, J. B. "Joseph Hergesheimer, an English View." *Bkm* 63 (My 26) 272-80.
Rascoe, Burton. "Contemporary Reminiscences." *Arts & Decoration* 21 (Ag 24) 36, 66-7.
Shaw, Vivian. "Blood and Irony." *Dial* 73 (Mr 22) 310-3.
Van Vechten, Carl. "How I Remember Joseph Hergesheimer." *Yale Un Lib Gaz* 22 (Ja 48) 87-92.
West, Geoffrey. "Joseph Hergesheimer: An Appreciation." *Eng R* 53 (O 31) 556-64; *VQR* 8 (Ja 32) 95-108.

HERNE, JAMES A.. (1839-1901). Bucks, D. S., & Nethercot, A. H. "Ibsen and Herne's *Margaret Fleming:* A Study of the Early Ibsen Movement in America." *AL* 17 (Ja 46) 311-33.
Garland, Hamlin, Enneking, J. J., & Flower, B. O. "James A. Herne: Actor, Dramatist, and Man." *Arena* 26 (S 01) 282-91.
Morton, Frederick. "James A. Herne." *Theatre Arts* 24 (D 40) 899-902.
Quinn, A. H. "Ibsen and Herne—Theory and Facts." *AL* 19 (My 47) 171-7.
Waggoner, H. H. "The Growth of a Realist: James A. Herne." *NEQ* 15 (Mr 42) 62-73.

HERRICK, ROBERT (1868-1938). Anon. "Robert Herrick." *NRp* 97 (18 Ja 39) 302.
——— "Robert Herrick on the American Novel." *Rev of Rev* 49 (My 14) 621-2.
Aldrich, T. B. "Robert Herrick." *Century* 59 (Mr 00) 678-88.
Arvin, Newton. "Homage to Robert Herrick." *NRp* 82 (6 Mr 35) 93-5.
Björkman, Edwin. "The Americanism of Robert Herrick." *Rev of Rev* 43 (Mr 11) 380-1.
Cooper, F. T. "Robert Herrick." *Bkm* 28 (D 08) 350-7.
Dell, Floyd. "Chicago in Fiction." *Bkm* 38 (N 13) 274-5.
Hicks, Granville. "Robert Herrick, Liberal." *NRp* 67 (17 Je 31) 129-30.
Hale, Swinburne. "Mr. Robert Herrick and His Realism." *Harvard Mo* 36 (My 03) 105-11.
Holland, J. A. "Together: A Nietzschean Novel." *SR* 16 (O 08) 812-20.
Howells, W. D. "The Novels of Robert Herrick." *NAR* 189 (Je 09) 812-20.
Kazin, Alfred. "Three Pioneer Realists." *SRL* 20 (8 Jl 39) 3-4.
Krutch, J. W. "The Longest Journey." *Nation* 121 (7 O 25) 388-9.
Lüdeke, Henry. "Robert Herrick: Novelist of American Democracy." *Eng Stud* 18 (Ap 36) 49-57.
Neilsen, Harald. "Robert Herrick." *Poet-Lore* 19 (S 08) 337-63.

Nevius, Blake. "The Idealistic Novels of Robert Herrick." *AL* 21 (Mr 49) 56-70.
Seldes, G. V. "The American Novel." *Harvard Mo* 56 (Mr 13) 1-11.
Stead, W. T. "Modern Wives." *Rev of Rev* 38 (O 08) 378-82.
Van Doren, Carl. "Robert Herrick." *Nation* 113 (31 Ag 21) 230-1.

HERSEY, JOHN (1914-). Guilfoil, Kelsey. "John Hersey: Fact and Fiction." *EJ* 39 (S 50) 355-60.
Hersey, John. " Soviet Writers Discuss *A Bell for Adano*." *Am R on the Soviet Union* 7 (F 46) 20-5.
Rugoff, Milton. "John Hersey—From Documentary Journalism to the Novelist's Art." *N Y Herald Tribune Book R* 27 (20 Ag 50) 3, 13.

HEWITT, JOHN HILL (1801-90). Harwell, R. B. "John Hill Hewitt Collection." *So Atl Bul* 13 (Mr 48) 305.
——— "A Reputation by Reflection: John Hill Hewitt and Edgar Allan Poe." *Emory Un Q* 3 (Je 47) 104-14.
Hewitt, J. H. "'Atlanta to the Sea.'" *Emory Un Q* 3 (D 47) 248-51.

HEYWARD, DUBOSE (1885-1940). Anon. "Charleston (and Gershwin) Provide Folk Opera." *Lit Dig* 120 (26 O 35) 18.
Clark, Emily. "Dubose Heyward." *VQR* 6 (O 30) 546-56.
Cohen, Hennan. "American First Editions: DuBose Heyward." *Pub W* 129 (18 Ap 36) 163.
de Saint Jean, Robert. "DuBose Heyward dans sa cabane." *Nouvelles Littéraires* 12 (24 Mr 34) 8.
Heyward, DuBose. "Porgy and Bess Return on Wings of Song." *Stage* 13 (O 35) 25-8.
Monroe, Harriet. "The Old South." *Poetry* 22 (My 23) 89-92.
——— "A Poet of the Carolinas." *Poetry* 25 (D 24) 164-7.
Watkins, Wren. "DuBose Heyward." *SLM* 2 (Jl 40) 422-5.
White, N. I. "Skylines and Horizons." *SAQ* 22 (O 24) 377-8.
Wilson, J. S. "The Perennial Rooster." *VQR* 2 (Ja 26) 15-55.

HICKS, ELIAS (1748-1830). Burgess, Janna. "Walt Whitman and Elias Hicks." *Friends' Intelligencer* 101 (Ja 44) 54-5.
Forbush, Bliss. "Elias Hicks—Prophet of an Era." *Bul Friends Hist Assn* 38 (Sp 49) 11-9.
——— "The Newly Discovered Manuscript Journal of Elias Hicks: A Study of the Writing and Editing of a Quaker Journal." *Bul Friends Hist Assn* 39 (Sp 50) 16-26.

HICKS, GRANVILLE (1901-). Anon. "Granville Hicks." *Cur Biog* 3 (My 42) 43-6.
Farrell, J. T. "Mr. Hicks: Critical Vulgarian." *Am Spect* 4 (Ap 36) 21-6.
Glicksberg, C. I. "Granville Hicks and Marxist Criticism." *SR* 45 (Ap 37) 129-40.
Gregory, Horace. "Two Poets in Search of an Absolute." *Nation* 138 (14 F 34) 189-91.
Matthiessen, F. O. "The Great Tradition: A Counter Statement." *NEQ* 7 (Je 34) 223-4.

HIGGINSON, THOMAS WENTWORTH (1823-1911). Bowen, E. W. "Thomas Wentworth Higginson." *SR* 23 (O 15) 429-42.
Frost, R. H. "Thoreau's Worcester Friends: III. Thomas Wentworth Higginson. His Worcester Years." *Nature Outlook* 5 (My 47) 4-7, 33.
Jackson, A. W. "Col. Thomas Wentworth Higginson." *N E Mag* ns 25 (D 01) 446-63.
Mead, E. D. "Thomas Wentworth Higginson." *N E Mag* ns 44 (My 11) 397-412.

Munsterberg, Margaret. "Letters by Thomas Wentworth Higginson." *More Books* 22 (F 47) 52-6.
White, F. E. "Thomas Wentworth Higginson's Idea of Democracy." *Negro Hist Bul* 6 (D 42) 55, 71.

HILLYER, ROBERT (1895-). Anon. "News Notes." *Poetry* 74 (Ag 49) 308.
Blackmur, R. P. "In Search of a Soul." *Poetry* 39 (Mr 32) 340-2.
Gregory, Horace. "At the Cross-Roads." *Poetry* 31 (Je 28) 165-7.
Haraszti, Zoltán. "Robert Hillyer's *Riverhead*." *NEQ* 9 (Je 36) 273-80.
Hicks, Granville. "A Letter to Robert Hillyer." *NRp* 92 (20 O 37) 308.
Hillyer, Robert. "Robert Hillyer." *Lyric* 27 (Su 47) 59, 77-80.
Holden, Raymond. "The Pence of Persistence." *Poetry* 45 (N 34) 99-103.
Knister, Raymond. "Carmus and Others." *Poetry* 25 (F 25) 281-3.
Luhrs, Marie. "Delicate and Pure." *Poetry* 29 (F 27) 284-6.
Millspaugh, C. A. "Harvard Has It." *Poetry* 51 (F 38) 267-70.
Speyer, Leonora, & Hillyer, Robert. "Two Poets on the Teachings of Poetry." *SRL* 29 (23 Mr 46) 13-4, 52-4.

HOFFMAN, CHARLES FENNO (1806-84). Taylor, Anthony. "American First Editions: Charles Fenno Hoffman, 1806-1884." *Pub W* 132 (18 D 37) 2312.

HOLLAND, JOSIAH GILBERT (1819-81). Bloom, Margaret. "Emily Dickinson and Dr. Holland." *Un Calif Chron* 35 (Ja 33) 96-103.

HOLLEY, MARIETTA (1836-1926). Butler, E. P. "Marietta Holley." *Mark Twain Q* 2 (Fl 37) 13.

HOLMES, ABIEL (1763-1837). Howe, M. A. DeW. "'Yaratildia,' a Note on Abiel Holmes." *PMHS* 62 (My 29) 155-8.

HOLMES, GEORGE FREDERICK (1820-97). Wish, Harvey. "George Frederick Holmes and the Southern Periodical Literature of the Mid-Nineteenth Century." *J So Hist* 7 (Ag 41) 343-56.

HOLMES, OLIVER WENDELL (1809-94). Anon. "Excerpt from a letter dated May 29, 1880." *Autograph Album* 1 (D 33) 69.
——— "Oliver Wendell Holmes on 'Pseudo-Critics' in 1850." *BNYPL* 4 (N 00) 356-7.
Adkins, N. F. "'The Chambered Nautilus'; Its Scientific and Poetic Backgrounds." *AL* 9 (Ja 38) 458-65.
Anderson, C. R. "Two Letters from Lanier to Holmes." *AL* 18 (Ja 47) 321-6.
Andrews, M. L. "Oliver Wendell Holmes—Doctor and Gentleman." *Nation* 89 (11 N 09) 456-7.
Arms, George. "Holmes' *The Chambered Nautilus*." *Expl* 4 (My 46) 51.
——— "Holmes' *The Living Temple*." *Expl* 2 (N 43) 15.
——— "'To Fix the Image All Unveiled and Warm.'" *NEQ* 19 (D 46) 534-7.
Ballantine, W. G. "Oliver Wendell Holmes." *NAR* 190 (Ag 09) 178-93.
Bicks, E. M. "A Note on the Medical Works of Oliver Wendell Holmes." *Annals Medical Hist* 4 (S 32) 487-90.
Bowen, C. D. "Flag at the Peak: A Holmes Letter." *Atl* 175 (Ap 45) 101.
Brooks, Van Wyck. "Dr. Holmes; Forerunner of the Moderns." *SRL* 14 (27 Je 36) 3-4, 13-5.
Burton, Richard. "Oliver Wendell Holmes." *Reader* 5 (Ap 05) 778-82.
Canby, H. S. "Breakfast with Dr. Holmes." *SRL* 5 (26 Ja 29) 1-2.
Christy, B. H. "The Ship of Pearl." *AL* 9 (My 37) 245-7.
Clark, H. H. "Dr. Holmes: A Re-interpretation." *NEQ* 12 (Mr 39) 19-34.
Coolidge, R. D. "Holmes and the Trees." *N E Mag* ns 40 (Ag 09) 701-6.
Crothers, S. M. "The Autocrat and His Fellow-Boarders." *Atl* 104 (Ag 09) 237-44.

Currier, T. F. "The Autocrat of the Breakfast Table: A Bibliographical Study." *PBSA* 38 (1934) 284-311.
——— "Oliver Wendell Holmes, Poet Laureate of Harvard." *PMHS* 67 (1945) 436-51.
Doubleday, N. F. "Dr. Holmes and the Faith in the Future." *CE* 4 (F 43) 281-8.
Eliot, C. W. "Oliver Wendell Holmes." *Harvard Grad Mag* 31 (Je 23) 457-565.
Ferguson, J. D. "Allusions in Oliver Wendell Holmes." *N&Q* 166 (28 Ap 34) 297.
——— "The Unfamiliar Autocrat." *Colophon* ns 1 (Wi 36) 388-96.
Fitz, Reginald. "President Eliot and Dr. Holmes Leap Forward." *HLB* 1 (Sp 47) 212-20.
Flanagan, J. T. "Dr. Holmes Advises Young Ignatius Donnelly." *AL* 13 (Mr 41) 59-61.
Garland, Alice. "Easing a Poet's Conscience." *Chri Sci Mon* 36 (30 N 44) 9.
Grattan, C. H. "Oliver Wendell Holmes." *Am Merc* 4 (Ja 25) 37-41.
Hayakawa, S. I. "The Boston Poet-Laureate: Oliver Wendell Holmes." *Stud Eng Lit* (Japan) 16 (O 36) 572-92.
——— "Holmes's Lowell Institute Lectures." *AL* 8 (N 36) 281-90.
Holmes, O. W. "My Hunt after 'The Captain.' (Dec. 1862)." *Atl* 150 (N 32) 638-49.
Howe, M. A. DeW. "Dr. Holmes, the Friend and Neighbor." *YR* 7 (Ap 18) 562-78.
Jerrold, Walter. "Oliver Wendell Holmes." *Bkm* (London) 36 (Ag 09) 209-13.
Kent, R. G. "An Unpublished Letter of Oliver Wendell Holmes." *AL* 20 (N 48) 333-6.
Kern, A. C. "Dr. Oliver Wendell Holmes Today." *UKCR* 16 (Sp 48) 191-9.
Knickerbocker, W. S. "His Own Boswell: A Note on the Poetry of Oliver Wendell Holmes." *SR* 41 (O-D 33) 454-66.
Lewis, Stewart. "The True Story of Oliver Wendell Holmes." *Independent* 67 (9 D 09) 1313.
Linn, Irving. "Dean Swift, Pope Innocent, and Oliver Wendell Holmes." *PQ* 16 (Jl 37) 317-20.
Linn, J. W. "Holmes as a Humorist." *Un Chicago Mag* 2 (N 09) 16-23.
Lokensgard, H. O. "Holmes Quizzes the Professor." *AL* 13 (My 41) 157-62.
——— "Oliver Wendell Holmes's Phrenological Character." *NEQ* 13 (D 40) 711-8.
Mabbott, T. O. "Abraham Lincoln on a Poem by Oliver Wendell Holmes." *N&Q* 163 (24 D 32) 458.
Orcutt, W. D. "From My Library Walls." *Chri Sci Mon* 36 (26 Ja 44) 6.
Reid, Sydney. "Oliver Wendell Holmes." *Independent* 54 (29 Ag 02) 2057-8.
Rideing, W. H. "Some Boston Memories." *N E Mag* ns 42 (Je 10) 417-26.
Roditi, Edouard. "Oliver Wendell Holmes as Novelist." *Accent* 1 (Wi 45) 23-33; *Ariz Q* 1 (Wi 45) 22-33.
Russell, J. A. "Oliver Wendell Holmes—Dartmouth Professor." *Dartmouth Alumni Mag* 33 (D 41) 20, 88.
Schurz, Carl. "Reminiscences of a Long Life." *McClure's* 28 (Ja 07) 259-60.
Scudder, H. H. "The 'Contentment' of Dr. Holmes." *AL* 20 (Ja 49) 443-6.
Seebie, R. H. "Oliver Wendell Holmes." *Manchester Q* 20 (1901) 232-58.
Sellers, C. C. "Four Letters of Dr. Holmes." *YR* ns 14 (Ja 25) 410-3.
Small, M. R. "First and Last Surviving Poems of Dr. Oliver Wendell Holmes." *AL* 15 (Ja 44) 416-20.
——— "Oliver Wendell Holmes Still the Poet Laureate at Eighty-Four." *Am Schol* 13 (Sp 44) 244-6.
Townsend, F. S. "The Religion of Oliver Wendell Holmes." *Methodist R* 91 (Jl 09) 605-11.
Trowbridge, J. T. "Recollections of Oliver Wendell Holmes." *Atl* 91 (My 03) 600-5.
Turner, E. S. "The Autocrat's Theology." *Putnam's* 6 (S 09) 662-7.

Viets, H. R. "Oliver Wendell Holmes, Physician." *Am Schol* 3 (Wi 34) 5-11.
Wilson, J. G. "Dr. Holmes and Old Ironsides." *Bkm* 19 (My 04) 315.
Winterich, J. T. "Autocrat of the Breakfast Table." *Pub W* 119 (17 Ja 31) 317-21.
Withington, Robert. "A Note on *The Autocrat,* III and IV." *MLN* 46 (My 31) 293.
——— "The Patriotism of the Autocrat." *Harvard Grad Mag* (Je 28) 523-32.
——— "Religio Duorum Medicorum." *Int J Ethics* 43 (Je 39) 413-28.
Worth, Wallace. "The Autocrat in Profile." *Colophon* ns 1 (Je 39) 2.

HOOKER, THOMAS (1586-1647). Mead, E. D. "Thomas Hooker's Farewell Sermon in England." *PMHS* 46 (1913) 253-74.
Miller, Perry. "Thomas Hooker and the Democracy of Early Connecticut." *NEQ* 4 (O 31) 663-712.

HOPKINS, LEMUEL (1750-1801). Steiner, W. R. "Dr. Lemuel Hopkins, One of the Celebrated Hartford Wits, and a Forgotten, Distinguished American Student of Tuberculosis." *Johns Hopkins Hosp J* 21 (Ja 10) 16-27.

HOPKINS, SAMUEL (1721-1803). Elsbree, O. W. "Samuel Hopkins and His Doctrine of Benevolence." *NEQ* 8 (D 35) 534-50.

HOPKINSON, FRANCIS (1737-91). Anon. "Letter of George Washington to Francis Hopkinson, 1789." *PMHB* 38 (1914) 461-3.
Arrowood, C. F. "Educational Themes in the Writings of Francis Hopkinson." *Peabody J Educ* 6 (N 28) 145-60.
Gegenheimer, A. F. "The Pirating of Francis Hopkinson's *Science*." *AL* 17 (My 45) 170-3.
——— "A Satire on Early Commencements." *Gen Mag & Hist Chron* 46 (Wi 44) 84-91.
——— "An Unpublished Letter of Francis Hopkinson to George Washington." *AL* 14 (N 42) 308-10.
Hastings, G. E. "The Bible: An Unpublished Poem of Francis Hopkinson." *Living Church* 86 (1926) 83-4.
——— "Francis Hopkinson and the American Flag." *Americana* 33 (Jl 39) 1-23; *Gen Mag & Hist Chron* 42 (O 39) 46-63.
——— "Francis Hopkinson and the Anti-Federalists." *AL* 1 (Ja 30) 405-18.
——— "John Bull and His American Descendants." *AL* 1 (Mr 29) 40-68.
——— "Two Uncollected Essays by Francis Hopkinson." *Gen Mag & Hist Chron* 41 (Jl 39) 416-22.
Leary, Lewis. "Francis Hopkinson, Jonathan Odell, and 'The Temple of Cloacina.'" *AL* 15 (My 43) 183-91.
MacPike, E. E. "The Battle of the Kegs." *N&Q* 175 (12 N 38) 354-5.
Marble, A. R. "Francis Hopkinson: Man of Affairs and Letters." *N E Mag* ns 27 (N 02) 289-302.
Pennington, E. L. "The Work of the Bray Associates in Pennsylvania." *PMHB* 58 (Ja 34) 1-25.
Wecter, Dixon. "Francis Hopkinson and Benjamin Franklin." *AL* 12 (My 40) 200-17.

HOPKINSON, JOSEPH (1770-1842). Hart, C. H. "'Hail Columbia.' and Its First Publication. A Critical Inquiry." *PMHB* 34 (1910) 162-6.
Sonneck, O. G. "The First Edition of 'Hail Columbia.'" *PMHB* 40 (1916) 426-58.

HORGAN, PAUL (1903-). Carter, Alfred. "On the Fiction of Paul Horgan." *N Mex Q* 7 (Ag 37) 207-16.

HOUGH, EMERSON (1857-1923). Grahame, Pauline. "A Novelist of the Unsung." *Palimpsest* 11 (F 30) 67-77.

HOVEY, RICHARD (1864-1900). Laing, Alexander. "A Forgotten Arthurian." *Dartmouth Alumni Mag* 22 (F 30) 258-62.
Marchand, Ernest. "Hovey's First Flight." *Dartmouth Alumni Mag* 31 (Je 39) 15-6.
Page, C. H. "Richard Hovey's 'Taliesin'—A Poet's Poem." *Bkm* 11 (Ap 00) 125-31.
Russell, J. A. "The Hoveys." *Dartmouth Alumni Mag* 20 (1928) 236-9.
Von Ende, Amelie. "The Ethical Message of Richard Hovey's Poem in Drama." *Poet Lore* 20 (Ja-F 09) 69-76.
Ward, L. "Richard Hovey." *Harvard Mo* 31 (D 00) 111-7.

HOWARD, BRONSON (1842-1908). Halline, A. G. "Bronson Howard's *The Amateur Benefit.*" *AL* 14 (Mr 42) 74-6.
Hamilton, Clayton. "Bronson Howard." *Bkm* 28 (S 08) 55-6.
Marshall, T. F. "Performances of Bronson Howard's *The Amateur Benefit.*" *AL* 14 (N 42) 311-2.
Matthews, Brander. "Bronson Howard." *NAR* 188 (O 08) 504-13.

HOWARD, SIDNEY (1891-1939). Clark, B. H. "His Voice Was American." *Theatre Arts* 33 (Ap 49) 27-30.
——— "Letters from Sidney Howard." *Theatre Arts* 25 (Ap 41) 276-86.
Krutch, J. W. "The Dramatic Variety of Sidney Howard." *Nation* 137 (13 S 33) 294-5.

HOWARTH, E. C. (1827-99). Wegelin, Oscar. "New Jersey's Best Woman Poet." *Am Book Coll* 6 (Ap 35) 134-6.

HOWE, EDGAR WATSON (1853-1937). Crawford, N. A. "Kansas Honors a Genius." *Midwest* 1 (O 34) 1, 2.
Dick, Everett. "Ed Howe, a Notable Figure on the Sod-House Frontier." *Neb Hist Mag* 18 (Ap-Je 37) 138-42.
Van Doren, Carl. "Prudence Militant. E. W. Howe: Village Sage." *Century* 106 (My 23) 151-6.
Williams, W. F. "The Founder of the Don't Worry Club." *World To-day* 21 (S 11) 1084-5.

HOWE, JOSEPH (1804-73). Chisholm, J. A. "Hitherto Unpublished Letters of Joseph Howe." *Dalhousie R* 12 (O 32) 309-14.
——— "More Letters of Joseph Howe." *Dalhousie R* 12 (Ja 33) 481-96.
Munroe, David. "Joseph Howe as Man of Letters." *Dalhousie R* 20 (Ja 41) 451-7.

HOWE, JULIA WARD (1819-1910). Anon. "How I Wrote the Battle Hymn of the Republic." *Ladies Home J* 26 (My 19) 43.
Cooke, G. W. "Mrs. Howe as Poet, Lecturer and Club-Woman." *N E Mag* ns 26 (Mr 02) 3-21.
Higginson, T. W. "Julia Ward Howe." *Outlook* 85 (26 Ja 07) 167-78.
Mahon, A. W. "Queen of Hearts." *Canadian Mag* 56 (F 21) 349.
Maud, C. E. "Mrs. Julia Ward Howe." *Fortnightly* 93 (F 10) 268-73.
Orcutt, W. D. "From My Library Walls." *Chri Sci Mon* 35 (3 Ag 43) 6.
Painter, Florence. "Julia Ward Howe." *Putnam's* 6 (My 09) 148-55.
Parkman, M. R. "Julia Ward Howe: The Singer of a Nation's Song." *St Nicholas* 44 (Jl 17) 790-5.
Richards, L. E., & Elliott, Maud. "Julia Ward Howe." *Delineator* 87 (O, N, D 15) 5-6, 10, 20-1; 88(Ja, F, Mr 16) 12-3, 17-8, 19.
Robert, Jeanne. "Julia Ward Howe." *Rev of Rev* 43 (F 11) 252-3.

HOWE, MARK ANTONY DE WOLFE (1864-1950). Cather, Willa. "The House on Charles Street." *Lit R* 3 (1922) 173-4.
Pier, A. S. "Mark Howe of Boston." *Atl* 185 (Ap 50) 75-8.

HOWE, SAMUEL GRIDLEY (1801-76). Bennett, Whitman. "No Stuffed Shirts." *Pub W* 151 (14 Je 47) B513-5.
Straker, R. L. "Samuel G. Howe to Horace Mann." *NEQ* 16 (S 43) 476-96.

HOWELLS, WILLIAM DEAN (1837-1920). Anon. "Celebrating the Eightieth Birthday of William Dean Howells." *Cur Op* 62 (Ap 17) 278.
——— "Genial Wisdom at Eighty." *Nation* 104 (8 Mr 17) 261-2.
——— "His Friends Greet William Dean Howells at Eighty." New York *Sun* 5 (25 F 17) 10.
——— "Howells' *A Hazard of New Fortunes*." *Expl* 1 (N 42) 14.
——— Howells' at Eighty, Receives Notable Tributes as the Dean of American Letters." *Cur Op* 62 (My 17) 357.
——— "Howells Number." *Book News Mo* 26 (Je 08).
——— "Looking Backward: The Lady of the Aroostook?" *Lit R* 3 (25 N 22) 243.
——— "Mr. Howells." *Lit Dig* 65 (29 My 20) 34-5.
——— "Mr Howells in England." *Lit Dig* 65 (19 Je 20) 37.
——— "Mr. Howells' World." *Freeman* 1 (26 My 20) 248.
——— "Public meeting held at the Stuart Gallery, New York Public Library, New York, March 1st, 1921, in memory of William D. Howells." *Am Acad Proc* 2 (1 Jl 21) 1-21.
——— "The Safe and Sane Genius of William Dean Howells." *Cur Op* 69 (Jl 20) 93-6.
——— "Sketch." *Cur Hist Mag* (New York *Times*) 12 (Je 20) 398-9.
——— "Smiling Aspects of Life." *TLS* (9 O 48) 568.
——— "A Tribute to William Dean Howells." *Harper's W* 56 (9 Mr 12) 27-34.
——— "William Dean Howells." *Nation* 110 (22 My 20) 673.
——— "William Dean Howells." *Rev of Rev* 61 (Je 20) 644.
——— "William Dean Howells." *SRL* 15 (13 Mr 37) 8.
——— "William Dean Howells: March 1, 1837—May 11, 1920." *NAR* 212 (Jl 20) 1-16.
——— "William Dean Howells, Printer, Journalist, Poet, Novelist." *Lit Dig* 65 (12 Je 20) 53, 54, 57.
Alden, H. M. "Editor's Study." *Harper's* 134 (My 17) 903-4.
——— "William Dean Howells." *Bkm* 49 (Jl 19) 549-54.
Arms, George. "'Ever Devotedly Yours': The Whitlock-Howells Correspondence." *JRUL* 10 (D 46) 1-19.
——— "Further Inquiry into Howells' Socialism." *Sci & Soc* 3 (Sp 39) 245-8.
——— "Howells's *A Hazard of New Fortunes*." *Expl* 1 (N 42) 14.
——— "Howells' New York Novel: Comedy and Belief." *NEQ* 21 (S 48) 313-25.
——— "Howells' Unpublished Prefaces." *NEQ* 17 (D 44) 580-91.
——— "The Literary Background of Howells's Social Criticism." *AL* 14 (N 42) 260-76.
——— "A Novel and Two Letters." *JRUL* 8 (D 44) 9-13.
——— "'Silas Lapham,' 'Daisy Miller' and the Jews." *NEQ* 16 (Mr 43) 118-22.
———, & Gibson, W. M. "A Bibliography of William Dean Howells." *BNYPL* 50 (S, N 46) 675-98, 857-68.
——— "Five Interviews with William Dean Howells." *Americana* 37 (Ap 43) 257-95.
Arvin, Newton. "The Usableness of Howells." *NRp* 91 (30 Je 37) 227-8.
Atherton, Gertrude. "Why Is American Literature Bourgeois?" *NAR* 278 (My 04) 771-81.
Ayscough, John. "Of Some Americans." *Cath World* 116 (O 22) 41-55.
Bass, A. L. "The Social Consciousness of William Dean Howells." *NRp* 26 (13 Ap 21) 192-4.
Belcher, H. G. "Howells's Opinions on the Religious Conflicts of His Age as Exhibited in Magazine Articles." *AL* 15 (N 43) 262-78.

Blodgett, Harold. "A Note on *Mark Twain's Library of American Humor.*" *AL* 10 (Mr 38) 78-80.
Boyd, Ernest. "Readers and Writers." *Independent* 114 (20 Ja 25) 20.
Boynton, P. H. "William Dean Howells." *Lit R* 1 (23 Ap 21) 22.
——— "William Dean Howells." *NRp* 33 (31 Ja 23) 256-7.
Brooks, Van Wyck. "Mr. Howells at Work at Seventy-two." *World's Work* 18 (My 09) 11547-9.
Budd, L. J. "William Dean Howells' Debt to Tolstoi." *Am Slavic & East Eur R* 9 (D 50) 292-301.
Cady, E. H. "Armanda Palacio Valdés Writes to William Dean Howells." *Symposium* 2 (My 48) 19-37.
——— "Howells in 1948." *UKCR* 15 (Wi 48) 83-91.
——— "The Neuroticism of William Dean Howells." *PMLA* 61 (Mr 46) 229-38.
——— "A Note on Howells and 'The Smiling Aspects of Life.'" *AL* 17 (My 45) 175-8.
——— "William Dean Howells and the *Ashtabula Sentinel.*" *Ohio State Arch & Hist Q* 53 (Ja-Mr 44) 39-51.
Carter, E. S. "The Palpitating Divan." *CE* 11 (My 50) 423-8; *EJ* 39 (My 50) 237-42.
——— "William Dean Howells' Theory of Critical Realism." *ELH* 16 (Je 49) 151-66.
Cary, E. L. "William Dean Howells: A Point of View." *Lamp* 29 (Ja 05) 597-604.
Clarkson, H. W. "Our Debt to Mr. Howells." *Harper's W* 56 (9 Mr 12) 6.
Clemens, S. L. "William Dean Howells." *Harper's* 113 (Jl 06) 221-5.
Cobley, W. D. "William Dean Howells: 1837-1920." *Manchester Q* 51 (1925) 93-120.
Colby, F. M. "The Casual Reader: Curiosities of Literary Controversy." *Bkm* 28 (O 08) 124-6.
Commager, H. S. "The Return to Howells." *Spectator* 158 (28 My 48) 642-3.
Cooke, D. G. "The Humanity of William Dean Howells." *Texas R* 6 (O 20) 6-25.
DeMille, G. E. "The Infallible Dean." *SR* 36 (Ap 28) 148-56.
Drake, F. C. "William Dean Howells Helped This Young Man Write a Play." *Lit Dig* 65 (19 Je 20) 56-8.
Dreiser, Theodore. "The Real Howells." *Ainslee's* 5 (Mr 00) 137-42.
Duffy, Charles. "Mark Twain Writes to Howells." *Mark Twain Q* 8 (Su-Fl 48) 4.
Edwards, Herbert. "Howells and the Controversy over Realism in American Fiction." *AL* 3 (N 31) 237-48.
Ekstrom, Kjell. "The Cable-Howells Correspondence." *Studia Neophilologica* 22 (1950) 48-61.
Erskine, John. "William Dean Howells." *Bkm* 51 (Je 20) 385-9.
Ferguson, J. D. "New Letter of Paul Hamilton Hayne." *AL* 5 (Ja 34) 368-70.
Firkins, O. W. "Howells Always Found the Right Word." *Chri Sci Mon* 37 (22 Ja 45) 6.
——— "Last of the Mountaineers." *SRL* 5 (16 Mr 29) 774-5.
——— "William Dean Howells." *SR* 29 (Ap 21) 171-6.
Follett, H. T., & Wilson. "Contemporary Novelists: William Dean Howells." *Atl* 119 (Mr 17) 362-72.
Fréchette, A. H. "William Dean Howells." *Canadian Bkm* 2 (Jl 20) 9-12.
Freman, M. W. "A Woman's Tribute to Mr. Howells." *Lit Dig* 44 (9 Mr 12) 485.
Garland, Hamlin. "A Great American." *Lit R* 1 (5 Mr 21) 1-2.
——— "Meetings with Howells." *Bkm* 45 (Mr 17) 1-7.
——— "Roadside Meetings of a Literary Nomad. II, William Dean Howells and Other Memories of Boston." *Bkm* 70 (N 29) 246-50.
——— "Sanity in Fiction." *NAR* 176 (N 03) 336-48.
——— "William Dean Howells, Master Craftsman." *Art World* 1 (Mr 17) 411-2.
Gettman, R. A. "Turgenev in England and America." *Un Ill Stud* 27 (1941) 51-63.

Getzels, J. W. "William Dean Howells and Socialism." *Sci & Soc* 2 (Su 38) 376-86.
Gibson, W. M. "Mark Twain and Howells, Anti-imperialists." *NEQ* 20 (D 47) 435-70.
——— "Materials and Form in Howells's First Novels." *AL* 19 (My 47) 158-66.
———, & Arms, George. "A Bibliography of William Dean Howells." *BNYPL* 51 (Ja, F, My, Je, Jl, Ag 47) 49-56, 91-105, 341-5, 384-8, 431-57, 486-512.
Gilder, G. L. "Howells and Some of His Friends." *Critic* 38 (F 01) 165-8.
Gilman, Lawrence. "Dean of American Letters." N Y *Times* sec 5 (16 My 20) 254-5.
Gosse, E. W. "The Passing of William Dean Howells." *Living Age* 306 (10 Jl 20) 98-100.
——— "The World of Books, W. D. Howells." *Sunday Times* (London) (8 Mr 25) 8.
Grattan, C. H. "Howells: Ten Years After." *Am Merc* 20 (My 30) 42-50.
Grey, R. "William Dean Howells: The Last." *Fortnightly R* 115 (Ja 21) 154-63.
Hackett, Francis. "William Dean Howells." *NRp* 10 (21 Ap 17) 3-5.
Hale, E. E. "The Dean of American Letters." *Dial* 33 (16 N 02) 323-4.
Harlow, Virginia. "William Dean Howells and Thomas Sergeant Perry." *BPLQ* 1 (O 49) 134-50.
Hazard, L. L. "Howells a Hundred Years Later." *Mills Q* 20 (F 38) 167-72.
Hellman, G. S. "The Letters of Howells to Higginson." *Annual Report Bibl Soc* 27 (1929) 20-52.
——— "The Reminiscences of Mr. Howells." *Bkm* 13 (Mr 01) 67-71.
Howells, W. D. "Howells' Unpublished Prefaces." *NEQ* 17 (D 44) 580-91.
——— "Literary Recollections." *NAR* 195 (Ap 12) 550-8.
——— "Part of Which I Was." *NAR* 201 (Ja 15) 135-41.
——— "Recollections of an Atlantic Editorship." *Atl* 100 (N 07) 594-606.
James, Henry. "Literary Recollections." *NAR* 195 (Ap 12) 558-62.
Jones, H. M. "A Study of Howells." *Freeman* 7 (25 Ap 23) 163.
Kazin, Alfred. "Howells: A Late Portrait." *AR* 1 (Je 41) 216-33.
Kirk, Rudolf & C. M. "'The Howells Family' by Richard J. Hinton." *JRUL* 14 (D 50) 14-23.
——— "'Poems of Two Friends.'" *JRUL* 4 (Je 41) 33-44.
Lappin, H. A. "The Passing of W. D. Howells." *Cath World* 111 (Jl 20) 445-53.
Lawrence, C. E. "An Appreciation of William Dean Howells." *Bkm* (London) 52 (Je 17) 88-91.
——— "William Dean Howells as a Novelist." *Living Age* 294 (21 Jl 17) 173-7.
Lessing, O. E. "William Dean Howells." *Das literarische Echo* 15 (1 N 12) 155-61.
Liveright, Horace. "The Case of W. D. Howells." N Y *Times* sec 3 (7 Ap 24) 26.
Mabie, H. W. "William Dean Howells." *Outlook* 111 (1 D 15) 786-7; *Am Acad Proc* 2 (N 16) 51-2.
Malone, Clifton. "The Realism of William Dean Howells." *Quar Bul Okla Baptist Un* 34 (F 49) 3-22.
Marston, F. C., Jr. "An Early Howells Letter." *AL* 18 (My 46) 163-5.
Martin, E. S. "W. D. Howells." *Harper's* 141 (Jl 20) 265-6.
Matthews, Brander. "Mr. Howells as a Critic." *Forum* 32 (Ja 02) 629-38.
Medrano, H. J. "William Dean Howells." *Cuba Contemporánea* 23 (Jl 20) 252-6.
Morby, E. S. "William Dean Howells and Spain." *Hisp R* 14 (Jl 46) 187-212.
Mordell, Albert. "William Dean Howells and the Classics." *Stratford Mo* ns 2 (S 24) 199-205.
Morris, Lloyd. "Conscience in the Parlor: William Dean Howells." *Am Schol* 18 (Au 49) 407-16.
Mowbray, J. P. "Mr. Howells's Réchauffé." *Critic* 42 (Ja 03) 21-6.
Muirhead, J. F. "Howells and Trollope." *Living Age* 308 (Ja 21) 304-9.

——— "W. D. Howells, the American Trollope." *Landmark* 2-3 (D 20, Ja 21) 53-6, 812-6.
Pennell, Joseph. "Adventures of an Illustrator, with Howells in Italy." *Century* 104 (My 22) 135-41.
Phelps, W. L. "An Appreciation." *NAR* 212 (Jl 20) 17-20.
——— "William Dean Howells." *YR* 10 (O 20) 99-109.
Preston, H. W. "The Latest Novels of Howells and James." *Atl* 91 (Ja 03) 77-82.
Quinn, A. H. "The Art of William Dean Howells." *Century* 100 (S 20) 675-81.
Rankin, D. S. "William Dean Howells: 1837-1920." *Commonweal* 26 (22 O 37) 597-8.
Ratcliffe, S. K. "William Dean Howells." *New Statesman* 15 (22 My 20) 195-6.
Reardon, M. S. R., III. "My Visit to William Dean Howells." *Mark Twain Q* 8 (Su-Fl 48) 5, 11.
Reeves, J. K. "The Way of a Realist: A Study of Howells' Use of the Saratoga Scene." *PMLA* 65 (D 50) 1035-52.
Reid, Forrest. "W. D. Howells." *Irish Statesman* 1 (4 O 19) 333-4, 359-60.
Rein, D. M. "Howells and the *Cosmopolitan*." *AL* 21 (Mr 49) 49-55.
Richardson, L. N. "Men of Letters and the Hayes Administration." *NEQ* 15 (Mr 42) 117-27.
Rood, Henry. "W. D. Howells at 75." N Y *Times* (25 F 12) 4.
——— "William Dean Howells, Some Notes of a Literary Acquaintance." *Ladies Home J* 37 (S 20) 42, 154-7.
Sanborn, F. B. "Literary Recollections." *NAR* 195 (Ap 12) 562-6.
Schwartz, H. B. "The Americanism of William Dean Howells." *Methodist R* 101 (Mr 18) 226-32.
Sinclair, R. B. "Howells in the Ohio Valley." *SRL* 38 (6 Ja 45) 22-3.
Smith, Bernard. "Howells: The Genteel Radical." *SRL* 11 (11 Ag 34) 41-2.
Snell, George. "Howells' Grasshopper." *CE* 7 (My 46) 444-52.
Starke, A. H. "William Dean Howells and Sidney Lanier." *AL* 3 (Mr 31) 79-82.
——— "William Dean Howells Refuses an Interview." *AL* 10 (Ja 39) 492-4.
Strunsky, Simeon. "About Books, More or Less." N Y *Times* sec 3 (24 F 24) 4.
Tarkington, Booth. "Mr. Howells." *Harper's* 141 (Ag 20) 346-50.
Taylor, W. F. "On the Origin of Howells's Interest in Economic Reform." *AL* 2 (Mr 30) 3-14.
——— "William Dean Howells and the Economic Novel." *AL* 4 (My 32) 103-13.
——— "William Dean Howells, Artist and American." *SR* 46 (Jl-S 38) 288-303.
Thomas, B. P. "A Unique Biography of Lincoln." *Bul Lincoln Assn* 35 (Je 34) 3-8.
Thomas, E. M. "Mr. Howell's Way of Saying Things." *Putnam's* 4 (Jl 08) 443-7.
Tomlinson, May. "Fiction and Mr. Howells." *SAQ* 20 (O 21) 360-7.
Tooker, L. F. "As I Saw It from an Editor's Desk: The Fiction of the Magazine." *Century* 108 (Je 24) 260-71.
Towne, C. H. "The Kindly Howells." *Touchstone* 7 (Jl 20) 280-2.
Trites, W. B. "William Dean Howells." *Forum* 49 (F 13) 217-40.
Van Westrum, A. S. "Mr. Howells and American Aristocracies." *Bkm* 25 (Mr 07) 67-73.
——— "Mr. Howells on Love and Literature." *Lamp* 28 (F 04) 27-31.
Walsh, W. S. "William Dean Howells Believes in the Future." N Y *Herald* (30 D 00) 13.
Whiteley, M. N. S. "A Visit to W. D. Howells." *Mark Twain Q* 2 (Fl 37) 7, 24.
Wilkins-Freeman, M. E. "A Woman's Tribute to Mr. Howells." *Lit Dig* 44 (9 Mr 12) 485.
Wilson, C. D., & Fitzgerald, D. B. "A Day in Howells's 'Boy's Town.'" *N E Mag* ns 36 (My 07) 289-97.
Wister, Owen. "William Dean Howells." *Atl* 160 (D 37) 704-13.
Wright, Conrad. "The Sources of Mr. Howells's Socialism." *Sci & Soc* 2 (Fl 38) 514-7.

Wyatt, Edith. "National Contribution." *NAR* 196 (S 12) 339-52.

HOYT, CHARLES HALE (1860-1900). Hunt, D. L. "Charles H. Hoyt: Playwright-Manager." *Theatre Annual* (1932) 42-50.

HUBBARD, ELBERT (1856-1915). Allen, F. L. "Elbert Hubbard." *Scribner's* 104 (S 38) 12-4, 49-51.
Hunter, David. "Elbert Hubbard and 'A Message to Garcia.'" *New Colophon* 1 (Ja 48) 27-35.
Maynard, Laurens. "Walt Whitman and Elbert Hubbard." *Contemp R* 28 (D 17) 151-2.
Vail, R. W. G. "'A Message to Garcia': A Bibliographical Puzzle." *BNYPL* 34 (F 30) 71-8.

HUBBARD, FRANK McKINNEY (1868-1930). Chamberlin, J. H. "Abe Martin: Hoosier Sage." *SRL* 27 (24 Je 44) 19-21.

HUBBARD, WILLIAM (*c.* 1621-1704). Anon. "Hubbard's Narrative, 1677." *Colophon* ns 1 (Wi 36) 456-7.
Adams, R. G. "William Hubbard's 'Narrative,' 1677: A Bibliographical Study." *PBSA* 33 (1939) 25-39.
Brigham, C. B. "John Hubbard's Poem on the Death of Jonathan Law." *Am Col* 3 (N 26) 88-9.
Murdock, K. B. "William Hubbard and the Provincial Interpretation of History." *PAAS* 52 (Ap 42) 15-37.

HUGHES, HATCHER (1883-). Leake, Grace. "Southern Personalities: Hatcher Hughes, Dramatist." *Holland's* 56 (F 37) 12, 67.

HUGHES, LANGSTON (1902-). Birss, J. H. "Langston Hughes." *Pub W* 130 (28 N 36) 21-35.
Bontemps, Arna. "The Harlem Renaissance." *SRL* 30 (22 Mr 47) 12-3, 44.
Chamberlain, John. "The Negro as Writer." *Bkm* 70 (Ja 30) 603-11.
Hughes, Langston. "Simple and Me." *Phylon* 6 (O-D 45) 349-52.
Parker, J. W. "'Tomorrow' in the Writings of Langston Hughes." *CE* 10 (My 49) 438-40.
Peterkin, Julia. "Negro Blue and Gold." *Poetry* 31 (O 27) 44-7.
Schoell, F. L. "Un Poète Nègre." *Revue Politique et Littéraire (Revue Bleue)* 67 (20 Jl 29) 436-8.

HUMPHREYS, DAVID (1752-1818). Marble, A. R. "David Humphreys: His Services to American Freedom and Industry." *N E Mag* ns 29 (F 04) 690-704.

HUNEKER, JAMES GIBBONS (1860-1921). Colby, F. M. "James Huneker's Pathos of Distance." *Harper's Weekly* 57 (10 My 13) 17.
Fay, E. C. "Huneker's Criticism of French Literature." *FR* 14 (D 40) 130-7.
Mencken, H. L. "James Huneker." *Century* 102 (Je 21) 191-7.
Pritchard, J. P., & Raines, J. M. "James Gibbons Huneker, Critic of the Seven Arts." *Am Q* 2 (Sp 50) 53-61.
Smith, Bernard. "Huneker, Man of the Tribe." *SRL* 10 (19 Ag 33) 49-50.
Van Roosbroeck, G. L. "Review of *Essays,* by James Huneker, 1929." *RR* 22 (Ja-Mr 31) 62-4.

HURST, FANNIE (1889-). Anon. "Fannie Hurst." *Bkm* 58 (Ja 24) 552-6.
Hurst, Fannie. "Fannie Hurst, by Herself." *Mentor* 14 (Ap 28) 50-1.
Hurston, Z. N. "Fannie Hurst." *SRL* 16 (9 O 37) 15-6.
Maurice, A. B. "Fannie Hurst." *Bkm* 69 (My 29) 258-60.
Roberts, M. F. "Fannie Hurst, Art Collector." *Arts & Decoration* 43 (N 35) 9-11, 51.

Salpeter, Harry. "Fannie Hurst, Sob-sister of American Fiction." *Bkm* 73 (Ag 31) 612-3.
Van Gelder, Robert. "An Interview with Miss Fannie Hurst." *NY Times Book R* (25 Ja 42) 2, 18.

HURSTON, ZORA NEALE (1903-). Gloster, H. M. "Zora Neale Hurston, Novelist and Folklorist." *Phylon* 4 (Ap-Je 43) 153-9.

HUTCHINSON, THOMAS (1711-80). Mayo, C. B. "Additions to Hutchinson's *History of Massachusetts Bay*." *PMHS* 59 (1949) 11-74.

IDELL, ALBERT EDWARD (1901-). Anon. "Albert E(dward) Idell." *Cur Biog* 4 (O 43) 26-8.

IMLAY, GILBERT (*c.* 1754-1828?). Emerson, O. F. "Notes on Gilbert Imlay, Early American Writer." *PMLA* 39 (Je 24) 406-39.
Krumplemann, J. T. "Du Pratz's History of Louisiana (1763), a Source of Americanisms, Especially of Those Attributed to Imlay." *AS* 20 (F 45) 45-50.
Rusk, R. L. "The Adventures of Gilbert Imlay." *Ind Un Stud* 10 (Mr 23) 3-26.
Wyatt, E. F. "The First American Novel." *Atl* 144 (O 29) 466-75.

INGALLS, JOHN (*fl.* 1849). Vail, R. W. G. "California Letters of the Gold Rush Period: The Correspondence of John Ingalls, 1849-1851." *PAAS* 47 (Ap 37) 145-82.

INGERSOLL, ROBERT (1833-99). Sunderland, J. T. "Ingersoll after Nine Years." *Arena* 4 (Mr 09) 295-301.

INGRAHAM, JOSEPH HOLT (1809-66). French, W. G. "A 'Lost' American Novel." *AL* 21 (Ja 50) 477-8.
Seitz, D. C. "A Prince of Best Sellers." *Pub W* 119 (21 F 31) 940.

IRVING, PETER (1771-1838). Beach, L. B., *et al.* "Peter Irving's Journals." *BNYPL* 44 (Ag, S, N, D, 40, Ja 41) 589-608, 649-70, 745-72, 814-42, 888-914.
Smith, F. P. "Peter Irving, Translator of *Jean Sbogar*." *Franco-Am R* 1 (Sp 37) 341-6.

IRVING, WASHINGTON (1783-1859). Anon. "Catalogue of the Seligman Collection of Irvingiana." *BNYPL* 30 (F 26) 83-109.
——— "Excerpts from two letters, dated Dec. 16, 1845, and Dec. 20, 1829." *Autograph Album* 1 (D 33) 71-2.
——— "Letter from Washington Irving to George A. Ward, 1842." *EIHC* 83 (Ja 47) 85.
——— "Manuscript Division Accessions during 1942." *BNYPL* 47 (F 43) 91-8.
——— "A Master of the Obsolete: Washington Irving in the Shadows." *TLS* (21 Mr 36) 229-30.
——— "Our Christmas Visitor. An American at Bracebridge Hall." *TLS* (21 N 42) 565-6.
——— "Rare Manuscripts." *Life* 20 (15 Ap 46) 101-5.
——— "Washington Irving Exhibition." *BNYPL* 18 (N 14) 1255.
Adkins, N. F. "Irving's 'Wolfert's Roost': A Bibliographical Note." *N&Q* 164 (21 Ja 33) 42.
——— "An Uncollected Tale by Washington Irving." *AL* 5 (Ja 34) 364-7.
Axson, Stockton. "Washington Irving and the Knickerbocker Group." *Rice Inst Pamphlet* 20 (Ap 33) 178-95.
Beach, L. B. "Washington Irving." *UKCR* 14 (Su 48) 259-66.
Beers, H. A. "The Singer of the Old Swimmin' Hole." *YR* 9 (Ja 20) 395-402.
Bennett, S. S. "The Cheves Family of South Carolina." *S C Hist & Gen Mag* 35 (O 34) 130-52.

Benson, A. B. "Scandinavians in the Works of Washington Irving." *SS* 9 (Ag 27) 207-23.

Birss, J. H. "New Verses by Washington Irving." *AL* 4 (N 32) 296.

Blackburn, P. C. "Irving's Biography of James Lawrence." *BNYPL* 36 (N 32) 742-3.

Blanck, Jacob. "The Authorship of 'Salmagundi.'" *Pub W* 130 (28 N 36) 2101.

——— "*Salmagundi* and Its Publisher." *PBSA* 41 (1st Quar 47) 1-32.

Boll, Ernest. "Charles Dickens and Washington Irving." *MLQ* 5 (D 44) 453-67.

Bowen, E. W. "Washington Irving's Place in American Literature." *SR* 14 (Ap 06) 171-83.

Campbell, Killis. "The Kennedy Papers: A Sheaf of Unpublished Letters from Washington Irving." *SR* 25 (Ja 17) 1-19.

Canby, H. S. "Irving the Federalist." *SRL* 3 (25 D 26) 461-3.

Commins, Saxe. "America's First Man of Letters." *SRL* 28 (1 S 45) 5-7.

Davis, R. B. "James Ogilvie and Washington Irving." *Americana* 35 (Jl 41) 435-58.

De Wolfe, Elsie. "The Old Washington Irving House in New York as It Is Today." *Delineator* 78 (O 11) 214-5.

Eaton, V. L. "The Leonard Kebler Gift of Washington Irving First Editions." *Lib Cong Quar J* 5 (F 48) 9-13.

Folsom, Merrill. "Irving's Restored Home Open to Public at Tarrytown." N Y *Times* (2 O 47) 29C.

Foreman, Grant. "An Unpublished Report by Captain Bonneville." *Chron Okla* 10 (S 32) 326-30.

Furst, Clyde. "A Century of Washington Irving." *SR* 21 (O 13) 402-20.

Gardner, J. H. "One Hundred Years Ago in the Region of Tulsa." *Chron Okla* 11 (Je 33) 765-85.

Gates, W. B. "Washington Irving in Mississippi." *MLN* 58 (F 43) 130-1.

Goggio, Emilio. "Washington Irving and Italy." *RR* 21 (Ja-Mr 30) 26-33.

——— "Washington Irving's Works in Italy." *RR* 22 (O-D 31) 301-3.

Greenlaw, Edward. "Washington Irving's Comedy of Politics." *Texas R* 1 (Ap 16) 291-306.

Hale, E. E. "Washington Irving." *Reader* 5 (D 04) 122-4.

Hastings. G. E. "John Bull and His American Descendants." *AL* 1 (Mr 29) 40-68.

Hellman, G. S. "Irving's Washington: and an Episode in Courtesy." *Colophon* (Mr 30) Pt 1.

——— "The Washington Irving Collection Formed by Isaac N Seligman." *BNYPL* 24 (My 20) 275-9.

Hespelt, E. H. "Irving's Version of Byron's *The Isles of Greece.*" *MLN* 42 (F 27) 111.

——— "Washington Irving's Notes on Fernán Caballero's Stories." *PMLA* 49 (D 34) 1129-39.

———, & Williams, S. T. "Two Unpublished Anecdotes by Fernán Caballero Preserved by Washington Irving." *MLN* 49 (Ja 34) 25-31.

Hoffman, L. M. "Irving's Use of Spanish Sources in *The Conquest of Granada.*" *Hispania* 28 (N 45) 483-98.

Kirby, T. A. "Carlyle and Irving." *ELH* 13 (Mr 46) 59-63.

——— "Irving and Moore: A Note on Anglo-American Literary Relations." *MLN* 62 (Ap 47) 251-5.

Kirk, Rudolf & Clara. "Letters of Washington Irving." *JRUL* 10 (D 46) 20-7.

——— "Letters of Washington Irving. Part Two—From Italy to Paris and London." *JRUL* 9 (Je 46) 36-58.

——— "Seven Letters of Washington Irving." *JRUL* 9 (D 45) 1-22.

Laird, C. G. "Tragedy and Irony in *Knickerbocker's History.*" *AL* 12 (My 40) 157-72.

Langfield, W. R. "The Poems of Washington Irving." *BNYPL* 34 (N 30) 763-99.

——— "Washington Irving—A Bibliography." *BNYPL* 36 (Je, Jl, Ag, S, O, N, D 32) 415-22, 487-94, 561-72, 627-36, 683-9, 755-78, 829-41.
Laughlin, Clara. "Two Famous Bachelors." *Book Buyer* 25 (O 02) 241-7.
Le Fevre, Louis. "Paul Bunyan and Rip Van Winkle." *YR* 36 (S 46) 66-76.
Leisy, E. E. "Irving and the Genteel Tradition." *Sw R* 21 (Ja 36) 223-7.
Lloyd, F. V., Jr. "Irving's *Rip Van Winkle.*" *Expl* 4 (F 46) 26.
Luquer, T. T. P. "Correspondence of Washington Irving and John Howard Payne." *Scribner's* 48 (O, N 10) 461-82, 597-616.
Mabbott, T. O. "An Unwritten Drama." *Am Col* 1 (N 25) 64-6.
Mabie, H. W. "A Diplomatist of Old New York." *Outlook* 111 (15 D 15) 921-3.
——— "The Washington Irving Country." *Outlook* 72 (6 D 02) 821-9.
McCarter, P. K. "The Authorship and Date of The Haunted Ship." *AL* 11 (N 39) 294-5.
McDermott, J. F. "Washington Irving Had Come Home." *Chri Sci Mon* 37 (8 Ja 45) 6.
McDowell, G. T. "General James Wilkinson in The Knickerbocker *History of New York.*" *MLN* 41 (Je 26) 353-9.
Mapes, E. S. "Where Irving Worked and Wandered." *Critic* 41 (O 02) 329-32.
Mathews, J. C. "Washington Irving's Knowledge of Dante." *AL* 10 (Ja 39) 480-3.
Miller, H. E. "In the Sleepy Hollow Country." *N E Mag* ns 23 (D 00) 449-67.
Morris, G. D. "Washington Irving's Fiction in the Light of French Criticism." *Ind Un Stud* 30 (My 16) 3-24.
Olive, W. J. "Davenant and Davenport." *N&Q* 144 (23 Jl 49) 320.
Pacey, W. C. D. "Washington Irving and Charles Dickens." *AL* 16 (Ja 45) 332-9.
Paltsits, V. H. "Washington Irving and Frederick Saunders." *BNYPL* 36 (Ap 32) 218-9.
Parsons, C. O. "Washington Irving Writes from Granada." *AL* 6 (Ja 35) 439-43.
Pemberton, T. E. "Washington Irving in England." *Munsey's* 30 (Ja 04) 552-8.
Pochmann, H. A. "Irving's German Sources in *The Sketch Book.*" *SP* 27 (Jl 30) 477-507.
——— "Irving's German Tour and Its Influence on His Tales." *PMLA* 45 (D 30) 1150-87.
Price, G. R. "Washington Irving's Librettos." *Music & Letters* (London) 24 (O 48) 348-55.
Putnam, G. P. "Washington Irving." *Forum* 75 (Mr 26) 397-409.
Reichart, W. A. "Baron Von Gumppenberg, Emily Foster, and Washington Irving." *MLN* 60 (My 45) 333-5.
——— "Washington Irving as a Source for Borel and Dumas." *MLN* 51 (Je 36) 388-9.
——— "Washington Irving, the Fosters, and the Forsters." *MLN* 50 (Ja 35) 35-9.
——— "Washington Irving's Friend and Collaborator: Barham John Livius, Esq." *PMLA* 56 (Je 41) 513-41.
Richards, I. T. "John Neal's Gleanings in Irvingiana." *AL* 8 (My 36) 170-9.
Russell, A. J. "Irving: Recorder of Indian Life." *J Am Hist* 45 (Mr 31) 185-95.
Sanford, O. M. "An Irving Centennial Fifty Years Ago." *Americana* 27 (O 33) 456-61.
Seigler, M. B. "Washington Irving to William C. Preston: An Unpublished Letter." *AL* 19 (N 47) 256-9.
Sheridan, P. H. D. "Sunnyside on the Hudson." *Buick Mag* 9 (Ap 48) 12.
Simison, B. D. "Washington Irving's Notebook of 1810." *Yale Un Lib Gaz* 29 (Jl 49) 1-16.
Small, M. R. "A Possible Ancestor of Diedrich Knickerbocker." *AL* 2 (Mr 30) 21-4.
Smith, F. P. "Washington Irving, the Fosters, and Some Poetry." *AL* 9 (My 37) 228-32.
Snell, George. "Washington Irving: A Revaluation." *MLQ* 7 (S 46) 303-10.

Spaulding, K. A. "A Note on *Astoria:* Irving's Use of the Robert Stuart Manuscript." *AL* 22 (My 50) 150-7.
Spiller, R. E. "War with the Book Pirates." *Pub W* 132 (30 O 37) 1736-8.
Starke, Aubrey. "Irving's 'Haunted Ship'—A Correction." *AL* 6 (Ja 35) 444-5.
Streeter, F. B. "Knickerbocker on the Prairie." *Aerend* 3 (Fl 32) 229-30.
Taylor, J. F. "Washington Irving's Mexico: A Lost Fragment." *Bkm* 41 (Ag 15) 665-9.
Thoburn, J. B. "Centennial of the Tour on the Prairies by Washington Irving (1832-1932)." *Chron Okla* 10 (S 32) 426-33.
Thompson, Ralph. "Irving's 'Haunted Ship.'" *AL* 6 (Ja 35) 443-4.
Van Wart, R. B. "Washington Irving and Scotland." *Blackwood's Mag* 266 (S 49) 257-63.
Webster, C. M. "Irving's Expurgation of the 1809 *History of New York.*" *AL* 4 (N 32) 293-5.
——— "Washington Irving as Imitator of Swift." *N&Q* 166 (28 Ap 34) 295.
Wegelin, Christof. "Dickens and Irving: The Problem of Influence." *MLQ* 7 (Mr 46) 83-91.
Williams, Laurence. "The Ghost in Irving Place." *Bkm* 30 (S 09) 53-5.
Williams, S. T. "The First Version of the Writings of Washington Irving in Spanish." *MP* 28 (N 30) 185-201.
——— "Letters of Washington Irving: Spanish Fêtes and Ceremonies." *YR* 17 (O 27) 99-117.
——— "Sunnyside: The Home of Our First Man of Letters." *House & Garden* (Jl 48) 51-5, 106.
——— "Unpublished Letters of Washington Irving." *YR* 16 (Ap 27) 459-84.
——— "Washington Irving and Andrew Jackson." *Yale Un Lib Gaz* 19 (Ap 45) 67-9.
——— "Washington Irving and Fernán Caballero." *JEGP* 29 (Jl 30) 352-66.
——— "Washington Irving and Matilda Hoffman." *AS* 1 (Je 26) 463-9.
——— "Washington Irving, Matilda Hoffman, and Emily Foster." *MLN* 48 (Mr 33) 182-6.
——— "Washington Irving's First Stay in Paris." *AL* 2 (Mr 30) 15-20.
——— "Washington Irving's Religion." *YR* 15 (Ja 26) 414-6.
———, & Beach, L. B. "Washington Irving's Letters to Mary Kennedy." *AL* 6 (Mr 34) 44-65.
———, & Leisy, E. E. "Polly Holman's Wedding Notes by Washington Irving." *Sw R* 19 (Jl 34) 449-54.
Wilson, J. L. "Washington Irving's 'Celebrated English Poet.'" *AL* 18 (N 46) 247-9.
Winterich, J. T. "Early American Books and Printing: Enter the Professional Author." *Pub W* 125 (17 Mr, 21 Ap 34) 1148-50, 1547-50.
Winters, Yvor. "Maule's Curse: Hawthorne and the Problem of Allegory." *Am R* 9 (S 37) 339-61.
Woodberry, G. E. "Knickerbocker Era of American Letters." *Harper's* 105 (O 02) 677-83.
Yarborough, M. C. "Rambles with Washington Irving: Quotations from an Unpublished Autobiography of William C. Preston." *SAQ* 29 (O 30) 423-39.
Zabriskie, G. A. "A Little About Washington Irving." *N Y Hist Soc Quar Bul* 29 (Ja 44) 5-15.
Zeydel, E. H. "Washington Irving and Ludwig Tieck." *PMLA* 46 (S 31) 946-7.
Zinsser, W. K. "Ghosts No Longer Haunt the Hudson Valley." N Y *Herald-Tribune* (5 O 41) 14C.
Zirkle, Mary. "Meeting the West." *Chri Sci Mon* 29 (20 Mr 37) 4.

JACKSON, HELEN HUNT (1831-85). Anon. "How Ramona Was Written." *Atl* 86 (N 00) 712-4.

——— "*Ramona* and Helen Hunt Jackson's Centenary." *Pub W* 120 (10 O 31) 1701-2.
Davidson, L. J. "Letters from Authors." *Colo Mag* 19 (Jl 42) 122-6.
Kelly, E. A. "Grandma Varner and Tommy." *Overland Mo* ns 50 (S 07) 255-9.
Nevins, Allan. "Helen Hunt Jackson, Sentimentalist vs. Realist." *Am Schol* 10 (Su 41) 269-85.
Pound, Louise. "Biographical Accuracy and 'H. H.'" *AL* 2 (Ja 31) 418-21.
Stellmann, L. J. "The Man Who Inspired *Ramona*." *Overland Mo* ns 50 (S 07) 252-5.

JAMES, HENRY (1843-1916). Anon. "Cher Maître and Mon Bon." *TLS* (25 S 48) 540.
——— "The Death of Henry James." *TLS* (17 Ap 43) 187.
——— "Gulf of Henry James." *Nation* 111 (20 O 20) 441.
——— "The Heiress: Play Based on James's Novel Joins Broadway's String of Sober Hits." *Life* 23 (3 N 47) 149-50, 153.
——— "Henry James: A Last Glimpse." *Living Age* 301 (31 My 19) 541-3.
——— "Henry James and the English Association." *Scrutiny* 14 (D 46) 131-3.
——— "A Henry James Centenary Exhibition." *Colby Lib Q* 1 (1943) 34-44.
——— "Henry James' Failure as a Dramatist Exposed by a London Critic." *Cur Op* 63 (O 17) 247.
——— Henry James Number of the *Little Review*. *Lit R* 5 (Ag 18).
——— "Henry James Reprints." *TLS* (5 F 49) 96.
——— "James the Dramatist." *TLS* no 2501 (6 Ja 50) 8.
——— "Letters and Comment." *YR* 13 (O 23) 206-8.
——— "Mr. James' Variant." *Atl* 94 (S 04) 426-7.
——— "Notes." *Nation* 86 (2 Ja, 5 Mr 08) 11, 215.
——— "Novels of Henry James." *Living Age* 310 (30 Jl 21) 267-71.
——— "A Reviewer's Notebook." *Freeman* 3 (24 Ag 21) 574-5; 4 (8 F 22) 526-7.
——— "Secret of Henry James' Style as Revealed by His Typist." *Cur Op* 63 (Ag 17) 118.
——— "Two Unpublished Letters." *H&H* 7 (Ap-Je 34) 414-6.
——— "The World of Henry James." *Living Age* 289 (22 Ap 16) 229-32.
Adams, J. R. "At Isella: Some Horrible Printing Corrected." *Mark Twain Q* 5 (Sp 43) 10, 23.
——— "Henry James: Citizen of Two Countries." *TLS* (17 Ap 43) 188, 190.
Anderson, Quentin. "Henry James and the New Jerusalem." *KR* 8 (Au 46) 515-66.
——— "Henry James, His Symbolism and His Critics." *Scrutiny* 15 (D 47) 12-8.
——— "The Two Henry Jameses." *Scrutiny* 14 (S 47) 242-51.
Arvin, Newton. "Henry James and the Almighty Dollar." *H&H* 7 (Ap-Je 34) 434-43.
Auden, W. H. "At the Grave of Henry James." *PR* 8 (Jl-Ag 41) 266-70.
——— "Henry James and the Artist in America." *Harper's* 197 (Jl 48) 36-40.
——— "Henry James's 'The American Scene.'" *Horizon* 15 (F 47) 77-90.
Ayscough, John. "Of Some Americans." *Cath World* 116 (O 22) 41-55.
Barrett, Lawrence. "Young Henry James, Critic." *AL* 20 (Ja 49) 385-400.
Barzun, Jacques. "James the Melodramatist." *KR* 5 (Au 43) 508-21.
Beach, J. W. "The Novel from James to Joyce." *Nation* 132 (10 Je 31) 634-6.
——— "The Sacred and Solitary Refuge." *Furioso* 3 (Wi 47) 23-7.
Beer, Thomas. "The Princess Far Away." *SRL* 1 (25 Ap 25) 701-2, 707.
Benson, A. C. "Henry James." *Cornhill Mag* ns 40 (N 16) 511-9.
Berland, Alwyn. "Henry James." *UKCR* 18 (Wi 50) 94-108.
Berti, Luigo. "Saggio su Henry James." *Inventario* 1 (Au-Wi 46-7) 78-88.
Bethurum, Dorothy. "Morality and Henry James." *SR* 31 (Jl 23) 324-30.

Bewley, Marius. "Appearance and Reality in Henry James." *Scrutiny* 17 (Su 50) 90-114.
——— "James's Debt to Hawthorne." *Scrutiny* 16 (Wi 49) 178-95, 301-17; 17 (Sp 50) 14-37.
——— "Maisie, Miles and Flora, the Jamesian Innocents." *Scrutiny* 17 (Au 50) 255-63.
Beyer, William. "The State of the Theatre." *School & Soc* 71 (8 Ap 50) 213-7.
Bixler, J. S. "Letters from Henry James to Theodule A. Ribot." *Colby Lib Q* 1 (1945) 153-61.
Blackmur, R. P. "The Critical Prefaces." *H&H* 7 (Ap-Je 34) 444-77.
——— "In the Country of the Blue." *KR* 5 (Au 43) 595-617.
——— "The Sacred Fount." *KR* 4 (Au 42) 328-52.
——— "The Sphinx and the Housecat." *Accent* 6 (Au 45) 60-3.
Bogan, Louise. "James on a Revolutionary Theme." *Nation* 146 (23 Ap 38) 471-4.
——— "The Portrait of New England." *Nation* 161 (1 D '48) 582-3.
Boit, Louise. "Henry James as Landlord." *Atl* 178 (Ag 46) 118-21.
Bosanquet, Theodora. "Henry James." *Fortnightly R* 101 (Je 17) 995-1009; *Living Age* 294 (11 Ag 17) 346-7.
——— "Henry James as a Literary Artist." *Bkm* 45 (Ag 17) 571-81.
——— "The Record of Henry James." *YR* 10 (O 20) 143-56.
Boughton, Alice. "A Note by His Photographer." *H&H* 7 (Ap-Je 34) 478-9.
Bowen, E. W. "Henry James, the Realist: An Appreciation." *Methodist R* 101 (My 18) 410-9.
Boyd, E. A. "Henry James Self-Revealed." *Freeman* 1 (25 Ag 20) 563-4.
Bradford, Gamaliel. "Portrait of Henry James." *NAR* 213 (F 21) 211-24.
Bragdon, Claude. "The Figure in Mr. James's Carpet." *Critic* 44 (F 04) 146-50.
——— "The Letters of Henry James." *Freeman* 1 (8 S 20) 619.
Brooks, Sydney. "Henry James at Home." *Harper's W* 48 (8 O 04) 1548-9.
Brooks, Van Wyck. "Henry James: The American Scene." *Dial* 75 (Jl 23) 29-42.
——— "Henry James: The First Phase." *Dial* 74 (My 23) 433-50.
——— "Henry James: An International Episode." *Dial* 75 (S 23) 225-38.
——— "Henry James of Boston." *SRL* 22 (13 Jl 40) 3-4.
——— "Our Illustrious Expatriate." *Freeman* 1 (28 Ap 20) 164-5.
Brown, E. K. "James and Conrad." *YR* 35 (D 45) 265-85.
——— "Two Formulas for Fiction." *CE* 8 (O 46) 7-17.
Brownell, W. C. "Henry James." *Atl* 95 (Ap 05) 496-519.
Burrell, J. A. "Henry James: A Rhapsody of Youth." *Dial* 63 (27 S 17) 260-2.
Bynner, Witter. "On Henry James' Centennial: Lasting Impressions of a Great American Writer." *SRL* 26 (22 My 43) 23, 26, 28.
——— "A Word or Two with Henry James." *Critic* 46 (F 05) 146-8.
Cairns, W. B. "Character-Portrayal in the Work of Henry James." *Un Wisc Stud* 2 (S 18) 314-22.
——— "Meditations of a Jacobite." *Dial* 60 (30 Mr 16) 313-6.
Canby, H. S. "Henry James." *Harper's W* 291 (25 My 16) 291.
——— "The Return of Henry James." *SRL* 31 (24 Ja 48) 9-10, 34-5.
Cantwell, Robert. "A Little Reality." *H&H* 7 (Ap-Je 34) 494-505.
——— "The Return of Henry James." *NRp* 81 (12 D 34) 119-21.
Carter, E. S. "The Palpitating Divan." *EJ* 39 (My 50) 237-42.
Cary, E. L. "Henry James." *Scribner's* 36 (O 04) 394-400.
Cestre, Charles. "La France dans l'oeuvre de Henry James." *Revue Anglo-Américaine* 10 (O 32) 1-13, 112-22.
Clark, A. F. B. "Henry James." *McGill Un Mag* 18 (F 19) 45-68.
Clark, Edwin. "Henry James and the Actors." *PS* 3 (Wi 49) 84-99.
Clemens, Cyril. "Henry James, 1843-1916." *Mark Twain Q* 5 (Sp 43) 1.
——— "A Visit to Henry James' Old Home." *Mark Twain Q* 5 (Sp 43) 9.

Clemens, Katherine. "Alice James, Neglected Sister." *Mark Twain Q* 6 (Su-Fl 44) 6-7.
Colby, F. M. "In Darkest James." *Bkm* 16 (N 02) 259-60.
——— "The Queerness of Henry James." *Bkm* 15 (Je 02) 396-7.
Conrad, Joseph. "Henry James: An Appreciation." *NAR* 180 (Ja 05) 102-8; 203 (Ap 16) 585-91.
Cooper, F. T. "The American Scene." *NAR* 185 (17 My 07) 214-8.
Cooper, Harold. "Trollope and Henry James." *MLN* 57 (N 43) 558.
Cornelius, R. D. "The Clearness of Henry James." *SR* 17 (Ja 19) 1-8.
Coward, T. R. "The Letters of Henry James." *Freeman* 1 (8 S 20) 618-9.
Cowley, Malcolm. "The Two Henry Jameses." *NRp* 112 (5 F 45) 177-80.
Croly, Herbert. "Henry James and His Countrymen." *Lamp* 28 (F 04) 47-53.
Daiches, David. "Sensibility and Technique: Preface to a Critique." *KR* 5 (Au 43) 569-79.
Dargan, E. P. "Henry James the Builder." *NRp* 7 (17 Je 16) 171-4.
Davray, H. D. "Un Deraciné Anglo-Américain: Henry James d'après sa correspondence." *Mercure de France* 146 (15 F 21) 68-84.
de la Mare, Walter. "Henry James." *Living Age* 289 (8 Ap 16) 122-4.
de la Roche, Mazo. "Reading Henry James Aloud." *Mark Twain Q* 5 (Sp 43) 8.
Delétang, Yanette. "Henry James." *Vie Art Cité* 14 (1950) 50-1.
Draper, Muriel. "I Meet Henry James." *Harper's* 156 (Mr 28) 416-21.
Dunbar, O. H. "Henry James as a Lecturer." *Critic* 47 (Jl 05) 24-5.
Dunbar, V. R. "Addenda to 'Biographical and Critical Studies of Henry James, 1941-1948.'" *AL* 22 (Mr 50) 56-61.
——— "A Note on the Genesis of *Daisy Miller*." *PQ* 27 (Ap 48) 184-6.
——— "The Revision of *Daisy Miller*." *MLN* 65 (My 50) 311-7.
——— "A Source for *Roderick Hudson*." *MLN* 63 (My 48) 303-10.
Dupee, F. W. "Henry James and the Play." *Nation* 171 (8 Jl 50) 40-2.
Durham, F. H. "Henry James' Dramatization of His Novels." *Bul Citadel* 6 (1942) 51-64.
Dwight, H. G. "Henry James—in His Own Country." *Putnam's* 2 (My, Jl 07) 164-70, 433-42.
Edel, Léon. "The Exile of Henry James." *UTQ* 2 (Jl 33) 530-32.
——— "Henry James and *The Outcry*." *UTQ* 18 (Jl 49) 340-6.
——— "Henry James and the Poets." *Poetry* 62 (S 43) 328-34.
——— "Henry James Discoveries." *TLS* (29 Jl 39) 460.
——— "Henry James: The War Chapter, 1914-1916." *UTQ* 10 (Ja 41) 125-38.
——— "The James Revival." *Atl* 182 (S 48) 96-8.
——— "A Note on the Translations of H. James in France." *Revue Anglo-Américaine* 7 (Ag 30) 539-40.
——— "The Text of Henry James's Unpublished Plays." *HLB* 3 (Au 49) 395-406.
Edgar, Pelham. "The Art of Henry James." *Nat R* 83 (Jl 24) 730-9.
——— "Henry James and His Method." *Proc Royal Soc Canada* 12: ser 3 (1919) 225-40.
——— "Henry James the Essential Novelist." *QQ* 39 (My 32) 181-92.
——— "The Letters of Henry James." *QQ* 28 (Ja 21) 283-7.
——— "Three Novels of Henry James." *Dalhousie R* 4 (Ja 25) 467-75.
Egan, M. F. "The Revelation of an Artist in Literature." *Cath World* 111 (Je 20) 289-300.
Eliot, T. S. "The Hawthorne Aspect." *Little R* 5 (Ag 18) 44-53.
Elton, Oliver. "The Novels of Mr. Henry James." *Quar R* 198 (O 03) 358-79.
Evans, Oliver. "James's Air of Evil: 'The Turn of the Screw.'" *PR* 16 (F 49) 175-87.
Fadiman, Clifton. "En kommentar till 'Europa.'" *Bonniers Litterära Magasin* (Stockholm) 17 (F 48) 99-100.

——— "The Revival of Interest in Henry James." *N Y Herald-Tribune Books* 21 (14 Ja 45) 1-2.
Fagin, N. B. "Another Reading of *The Turn of the Screw.*" *MLN* 56 (Mr 41) 196-202.
Fenton, Edna. "The Plays of Henry James." *Theatre Arts* 12 (My 28) 347-52.
Ferguson, A. R. "Some Bibliographical Notes on the Short Stories of Henry James." *AL* 21 (N 49) 292-7.
Fergusson, Francis. "The Drama in *The Golden Bowl.*" *H&H* 7 (Ap-Je 34) 407-13.
——— "James's Idea of Dramatic Form." *KR* 5 (Au 43) 495-507.
Fielding, H. M. "Henry James, the Lion." *Reader* 5 (F 05) 364-7.
Fleet, Simon. "The Nice American Gentleman." *Vogue* (19 O 49) 136, 138.
Follett, Wilson. "Henry James and the Untold Story." *Dial* 63 (6 D 17) 579-81.
——— "Henry James's Portrait of Henry James." *N Y Times Book R* (23 Ag 36) 2, 16.
——— "The Simplicity of Henry James." *Am R* 1 (My-Je 23) 315-25.
——— & H. T. "Henry James." *Atl* 117 (Je 16) 801-11.
Forbes, E. L. "Dramatic Lustrum: A Study of the Effect of Henry James's Theatrical Experience on His Later Novels." *NEQ* 11 (Mr 38) 108-20.
Ford, F. M. "Henry James." *Am Merc* 36 (N 35) 315-27.
——— "Techniques." *So R* 1 (1935) 20-35.
——— "Three Americans and a Pole." *Scribner's* 90 (O 31) 378-86.
France, W. C. "Henry James as a Lecturer." *Bkm* 21 (Mr 05) 71-2.
Fullerton, Morton. "The Art of Henry James." *Quar R* 212 (Ap 10) 393-408; *Living Age* 265 (11 Je 10) 643-52.
Garland, Hamlin. "Roadside Meetings of a Literary Nomad." *Bkm* 71 (Jl 30) 427-32.
Gettman, R. A. "Henry James's Revision of *The American.*" *AL* 16 (Ja 45) 279-95.
Gide, André. "Henry James." *YR* 19 (Mr 30) 641-3.
Gill, W. A. "Henry James and His Double." *Atl* 100 (1907) 458-66; *Fortnightly R* 92 (1 O 09) 689-700.
Gilman, Lawrence. "The Book of the Month." *NAR* 201 (My 15) 757-60.
——— "Henry James in Reverie." *NAR* 203 (Ja 17) 123-9.
——— "The Letters of Henry James." *NAR* 211 (My 20) 682-90.
Gosse, Edmund. "Henry James." *London Merc* 1 (Ap 20) 673-84; 2 (My 20) 29-41; *Scribner's* 67 (Ap, My 20) 422-30, 548-57.
Grattan, C. H. "The Calm within the Cyclone." *Nation* 134 (17 F 32) 201-3.
Greene, Graham. "Books in General." *New Statesman & Nation* 39 (28 Ja 50) 101-2.
——— "Henry James." *La Table Ronde* (Paris) no 29 (My 50) 9-22.
Gretton, M. S. "Mr. Henry James and His Prefaces." *Contemp R* 101 (Ja 12) 69-78; *Living Age* 272 (3 F 12) 287-95.
Guedalla, Philip. "The Crowner's Quest." *New Statesman* 12 (15 F 19) 421-2.
Hackett, Francis. "Stylist on Tour." *NRp* 2 (1 My 15) 320-1.
Hale, E. E. "Henry James." *Dial* 60 (16 Mr 16) 259-62.
——— "The Impressionism of Henry James." *Union Col Faculty Papers* 2 (Ja 31) 3-17.
——— "The Rejuvenation of Henry James." *Dial* 44 (16 Mr 08) 174-6.
Hamilton, Clayton. "Disengaged." *Forum* 61 (Ap 09) 342-3.
Hamilton, E. C. "Biographical and Critical Studies of Henry James." *AL* 20 (Ja 49) 424-35.
Harlow, Virginia. "Thomas Sergeant Perry and Henry James." *BPLQ* 1 (Jl 49) 43-60.
Harvitt, Hélène. "How Henry James Revised *Roderick Hudson.*" *PMLA* 39 (Mr 24) 203-27.
Havens, R. D. "Henry James' 'The Impressions of a Cousin.'" *MLN* 65 (My 50) 317-9.

——— "A Misprint in 'The Awkward Age.'" *MLN* 60 (N 45) 497.
——— "The Revisions of *Roderick Hudson*." *PMLA* 40 (Je 25) 433-4.
Hays, H. R. "Henry James, the Satirist." *H&H* 7 (Ap-Je 34) 514-22.
Heilman, R. B. "The Freudian Reading of *The Turn of the Screw*." *MLN* 62 (N 47) 433-45.
——— "'The Turn of the Screw' as Poem." *UKCR* 14 (Su 48) 277-89.
Hellman, G. S. "Stevenson and Henry James: The Rare Friendship between Two Stylists." *Century* 111 (Ja 26) 336-45.
Hemphill, George. "Hemingway and James." *KR* 11 (Wi 49) 50-60.
Herrick, Robert. "Tolstoi and Henry James." *YR* 12 (O 22) 181-6.
——— "A Visit to Henry James." *YR* 12 (Jl 23) 724-41; 13 (O 23) 206-8.
Hoare, D. M. "A Note on Henry James." *New Adelphi* 2 (Mr-My 29) 247-8.
Honig, Edwin. "The Merciful Fraud." *Tiger's Eye* 1 (15 O 49) np.
Hoskins, Katherine. "Henry James and the Future of the Novel." *SR* 54 (Wi 46) 87-101.
Hough, Graham. "Books in General." *New Statesman & Nation* 37 (16 Ap 49) 382.
Houser, Z. L. "Early Years of Henry James." *Mark Twain Q* 8 (Wi-Sp 49) 9-10.
Howe, M. DeW. "The Letters of Henry James to Mr. Justice Holmes." *YR* 38 (Sp 49) 410-33.
Howells, W. D. "Editor's Easy Chair." *Harper's* 102 (Ja 00) 318-20.
——— "Mr. Henry James's Later Work." *NAR* 176 (Ja 03) 125-37; 203 (Ap 16) 572-84.
——— "Mr. James's Masterpiece." *Harper's Bazaar* 36 (Ja 02) 9-14.
Hoxie, E. F. "Mrs. Grundy Adopts Daisy Miller." *NEQ* 19 (D 46) 474-84.
Hueffer, F. M. "Thus to Revisit . . . ." *Dial* 69 (Jl, Ag, S 20) 52-60, 132-41, 239-46; 70 (Ja 21) 14-23.
——— "Two Americans." *Lit R* 1 (9, 26 Mr 21) 1-2, 1-2.
Huneker, J. G. "The Lesson of the Master." *Bkm* 51 (My 20) 364-8.
I, B. de C. "Henry James at Work." *Manchester Guardian W* 59 (23 S 48) 12.
James, Henry. "The Ambassadors—Project of a Novel." *H&H* 7 (Ap-Je 34) 541-62.
——— "Two Unpublished Letters." *H&H* 7 (Ap-Je 34) 414-6.
Johnson, Arthur. "A Comparison [with Melville] of Manners." *NRp* 20 (27 Ag 19) 113-5.
Jones, D. M. "Henry James." *London Quar R* 126 (Jl 16) 117-20.
Jones-Evans, Mervyn. "Henry James's Year in France." *Horizon* 14 (Jl 46) 52-60.
Jordan, Elizabeth. "Henry James at Dinner." *Mark Twain Q* 5 (Sp 43) 7.
K., Q. "Before the Play." *NRp* 16 (7 S 18) 172.
——— "Henry James's Workshop." *NRp* 13 (1 D 17) 119-21.
Kane, R. J. "Hawthorne's 'The Prophetic Pictures' and James's 'The Lion.'" *MLN* 65 (Ap 50) 257-8.
——— "Virgin Soil and *The Princess Casamassima*." *Gifthorse* (Ohio State) 1949 25-9.
Kayser, Rudolf. "Henry James: Ein europäischer Amerikaner." *Neue Schweizer Rundschau* 13 (D 50) 480-4.
Kazin, Alfred. "Our Passion in Our Task." *NRp* 108 (15 F 43) 215-8.
Kelly, C. P. "The Early Development of Henry James." *Un Ill Stud* 15 (Jl 16).
Kenton, Edna. "The Ambassadors: Project of Novel." *H&H* 7 (Ap-Je 34) 541-62.
——— "Henry James and Mr. Van Wyck Brooks." *Bkm* 62 (O 25) 152-7.
——— "Henry James in the World." *H&H* 7 (Ap-Je 34) 506-13.
——— "Henry James to the Ruminant Reader." *Arts* 6 (N 24) 245-55.
——— "The 'Plays' of Henry James." *Theatre Arts* 12 (My 28) 347-52.
——— "Some Bibliographical Notes on Henry James." *H&H* 7 (Ap-Je 34) 535-40.
Kerner, David. "A Note on *The Beast in the Jungle*." *UKCR* 17 (Wi 50) 109-18.
Kirk, Rudolf. "Five Letters of Henry James." *JRUL* 12 (Je 49) 54-8.
Knights, L. C. "Henry James and the Trapped Spectator." *So R* 4 (Ja 39) 600-15.

L., P. "Henry James's Quality." *NRp* 6 (11 Mr 16) 152-4.
LaFarge, John. "Henry James's Letters to the LaFarges." *NEQ* 22 (Je 49) 173-92.
Larrabee, H. A. "The Jameses—Financier, Heretic, Philosopher." *Am Schol* 1 (O 32) 401-13.
Leach, Anna. "Henry James: An Appreciation." *Forum* 55 (Ap 16) 551-64.
Leavis, F. R. "The Appreciation of Henry James." *Scrutiny* 14 (Sp 47) 229-37.
——— "George Eliot (IV): 'Daniel Deronda' and 'The Portrait of a Lady.'" *Scrutiny* 14 (D 46) 102-31.
——— "Henry James." *Scrutiny* 5 (Mr 37) 398-417.
——— "Henry James and the Function of Criticism." *Scrutiny* 15 (Sp 48) 98-104.
——— "Henry James's First Novel." *Scrutiny* 14 (S 47) 295-301.
——— "James's 'What Maisie Knew': A Disagreement." *Scrutiny* 17 (Su 50) 115-27.
——— "'The Portrait of a Lady' Reprinted." *Scrutiny* 15 (Su 48) 235-41.
Leavis, Q. D. "Henry James: The Stories." *Scrutiny* 14 (Sp 47) 223-9.
——— "The Institution of Henry James." *Scrutiny* 15 (D 47) 68-74.
Le Clair, R. C. "Henry James and Minny Temple." *AL* 21 (Mr 49) 35-48.
Lee, Vernon. "The Handling of Words: Meredith, Henry James." *Eng R* 5 (Je 10) 427-34.
Leighton, Lawrence. "Armor against Time." *H&H* 7 (Ap-Je 34) 373-84.
Lerner, Daniel. "The Influence of Turgenev on Henry James." *Slavonic Yearbook* 20 (1941) 28-54.
Levy, B. M. "'The High Bid' and the Forbes-Robertsons." *CE* 8 (Mr 47) 284-92.
Lewis, J. H. "The Difficulties of Henry James." *Poet Lore* 39 (Sp 28) 117-9.
Lind, S. E. "Henry James." *TLS* (27 N 48) 667.
Littell, Phillip. "Henry James as Critic." *NRp* 1 (21 N 14) 26-8.
——— "Henry James's Quality." *NRp* 6 (11 Mr 16) 152-4.
——— "Henry James's Way of Writing English." *NRp* 13 (29 D 17) 254.
——— "James's Sacred Fount." *NRp* 3 (3 Jl 15) 234.
——— "Landscape by Henry James." *NRp* 6 (18 Mr 16) 191.
Livesay, J. F. B. "Henry James and His Critics." *Dalhousie R* 7 (Ap 27) 80-8.
Loomis, C. B. "An Attempt to Translate Henry James." *Bkm* 21 (Jl 05) 464-6.
Lowndes, M. B. "Henry James in War Time." *Mark Twain Q* 5 (Sp 43) 8.
Lubbock, Percy. "Henry James." *Quar R* 226 (Jl 16) 60-74; *Living Age* 190 (16 S 16) 733-41.
MacCarthy, Desmond. "Mr. Henry James and His Public." *Independent R* 6 (My 05) 105-10.
——— "Money, Birth and Henry James." *New Statesman* 9 (21 Jl 17) 375-6.
——— "The World of Henry James." *Life & Letters* 5 (N 30) 352-65; *Living Age* 339 (Ja 31) 491-8; *SRL* 8 (29 Ag 31) 81-3.
MacDonell, Annie. "Henry James as a Critic." *Bkm* 43 (Ap 16) 219-22.
McElderry, B. R., Jr. "Henry James and 'The Whole Family.'" *PS* 4 (Su 50) 352-60.
——— "The Uncollected Stories of Henry James." *AL* 21 (N 49) 279-91.
McFarlane, I. D. "A Literary Friendship—Henry James and Paul Bourget." *Cambridge J* 4 (D 50) 144-61.
McGill, V. J. "Henry James: Master Detective." *Bkm* 72 (N 30) 251-6.
McIntyre, Clara. "The Later Manner of Henry James." *PMLA* 27 (1912) 354-71.
MacKenzie, Compton. "Henry James." *Life & Letters* 39 (D 43) 147-55.
——— "My Meetings with Henry James." *Mark Twain Q* 6 (Su-Fl 44) 6-7.
McLane, James. "A Henry James Letter." *YR* 14 (O 24) 205-8.
Marsh, E. C. "Henry James: Auto-Critic." *Bkm* 30 (O 09) 138-43.
Matthews, Brander. "Henry James and The Theatre." *Bkm* 51 (Je 20) 389-95.
Matthiessen, F. O. "Henry James's Portrait of the Artist." *PR* 11 (Wi 44) 71-87.
——— "James and the Plastic Arts." *KR* 5 (Au 43) 533-50.
——— "The Painter's Sponge and Varnish Bottle: Henry James's Revision of *The*

Portrait of a Lady." *Am Bkm* 1 (Wi 44) 49-68.
Maurois, André. "Ecrivains américains." *Revue de Paris* 54 (Ap 47) 9-24.
Michaud, Régis. "William et Henry James d'après leur correspondence." *Revue de France* (22 S 22) 145-59.
Miller, Warren. "Henry James in Hollywood." *Masses & Mainstream* 2 (D 49) 81-3.
Moore, Marianne. "Henry James as a Characteristic American." *H&H* 7 (Ap-Je 34) 363-72.
Morgan, Louise. "The Weakness of Henry James." *Outlook* (London) 57 (6 F 26) 89.
Mortimer, Raymond. "Henry James." *Horizon* 7 (My 43) 314-29.
Moses, Montrose. "Henry James as a Letter Writer." *Outlook* 125 (20 My 20) 167-8.
Moult, Thomas. "Dedicated to Art." *Eng R* 31 (Ag 20) 183-6.
Mowbray, J. P. "The Apotheosis of Henry James." *Critic* 41 (N 02) 409-14.
Munson, Gorham. "The Real Thing: A Parable for Writers of Fiction." *UKCR* 16 (Su 50) 261-4.
Nadal, E. S. "Personal Recollections of Henry James." *Scribner's* 68 (Jl 20) 89-97.
Neff, J. C. "Henry James the Reporter." *N Mex Q* 8 (F 38) 9-14.
Nowell-Smith, Simon. "Mr. H——." *TLS* (28 D 46) 643.
Oliver, Clinton. "Henry James as a Social Critic." *AR* 7 (Su 47) 243-58.
Orcutt, W. D. "Celebrities off Parade: Henry James." *Chri Sci Mon* 26 (24 Ag 34) 12.
——— "From My Library Walls." *Chri Sci Mon* 35 (17 Ag 43) 7.
Pacey, W. C. D. "Henry James and His French Contemporaries." *AL* 13 (N 41) 240-56.
Pallache, J. C. "The Critical Faculty of Henry James." *Un Calif Chron* 26 (O 24) 399-410.
Pennell, Joseph. "In London with Henry James." *Century* 103 (F 22) 543-8.
Perry, R. B. "Henry James in Italy." *Harvard Grad Mag* 41 (Je 33) 189-200.
——— "The James Collection." *Harvard Un Lib Notes* 4 (Mr 42) 74-9.
Phelps, W. L. "Henry James." *YR* 5 (Jl 16) 783-97.
——— "Henry James: America's Analytical Novelist." *Ladies' Home J* 40 (N 23) 174-5.
——— "Henry James, Reviewer." *Lit R* 1 (4 Je 21) 4.
Popkin, Henry. "Pretender to the Drama." *Theatre Arts* 33 (D 49) 32-5, 91.
Porter, K. A. "The Days Before." *KR* 5 (Au 43) 481-94.
Pound, Ezra. "The Middle Years." *Little Rev* 5 (Ag 18) 5-41.
Preston, H. W. "The Latest Novels of Howells and James." *Atl* 91 (Ja 03) 77-82.
Putt, S. G. "A Henry James Jubilee, II." *Cornhill Mag* 160 (Sp 47) 284-97.
Qvamme, B. "Henry James." *Edda* (Oslo) 44 (Ja-Je 44) 73-85.
Raeth, C. J. "Henry James's Rejection of 'The Sacred Fount.'" *ELH* 16 (D 49) 308-24.
Rahv, Phillip. "Attitudes to Henry James." *NRp* 108 (15 F 43) 220-24.
——— "The Heiress of All the Ages." *PR* 10 (My-Je 43) 227-47.
Randell, W. L. "The Art of Mr. Henry James." *Fortnightly R* 105 (1 Ap 16) 620-32; *Living Age* 290 (29 Jl 16) 281-9.
——— "Henry James as Humanist." *Fortnightly R* ns 110 (S 21) 459-69.
Reed, Glenn. "Another Turn on James's 'The Turn of the Screw.'" *AL* 20 (Ja 49) 413-23.
Roberts, Morley. "Meetings with Some Men of Letters." *QQ* 39 (F 32) 65-70.
Roberts, Morris. "Henry James and the Art of Foreshortening." *RES* 22 (Jl 46) 207-14.
——— "Henry James's Final Period." *YR* 37 (Au 47) 60-7.
Roditi, Edouard. "Oscar Wilde and Henry James." *UKCR* 15 (Au 48) 52-6.

Roellinger, F. X., Jr. "Psychical Research and 'The Turn of the Screw.'" *AL* 20 (Ja 49) 401-12.
Roscoe, E. S. "Henry James at the Reform Club." *Bkm* 60 (Ja 25) 584-5.
Rosenfeld, Paul. "The Henry James Revival." *Commonweal* 43 (11 Ja 46) 329-32.
Rosenzweig, Saul. "The Ghost of Henry James." *PR* 11 Fl (44) 436-55; *Character and Personality* 12 (D 43) 79-100.
Rouse, H. B. "Charles Dickens and Henry James: Two Approaches to the Art of Fiction." *Nineteenth-Century Fiction* 5 (S 50) 151-7.
Russell, John. "Books in General." *New Statesman & Nation* 29 (26 My 45) 339.
——— "Henry James and the Leaning Tower." *New Statesman & Nation* 25 (17 Ap 43) 254-5.
Sampson, George. "Letters in Criticism." *Bkm* (London) 18 (My 20) 76-7.
Schneider, Isidor. "The Rediscovery of Henry James." *New Masses* 55 (28 My 45) 23-4.
Schuyler, Montgomery. "Henry James." *N Y Times Book R* 13 (11, 18 Ja 08) 5, 30.
——— "Henry James's Short Stories." *Lamp* 26 (Ap 03) 231-5.
Scott, Dixon. "Henry James." *Bkm* (London) 43 (Mr 13) 299-306.
——— "In Defence of Henry James." *Bkm* (London) 45 (Mr 14) 302-7.
Seldes, G. V. "Henry James: An Appreciation." *Harvard Mo* 53 (D 11) 92-100.
Seznec, Jean. "Lettres de Tourgueneff à Henry James." *CL* 1 (Su 49) 193-209.
Sherman, S. P. "Aesthetic Idealism of Henry James." *Nation* 104 (5 Ap 17) 393-9.
Short, R. W. "The Sentence Structure of Henry James." *AL* 17 (My 46) 71-88.
——— "Some Critical Terms for Henry James." *PMLA* 65 (S 50) 667-80.
Sigaux, Gilbert. "Les Ambassadeurs." *La Nef* no 71-2 (D 50, Ja 51) 197-9.
Smith, J. A. "Henry James and R. L. Stevenson." *London Merc* 34 (S 36) 412-20.
Smith, L. P. "Notes on Henry James." *Atl* 172 (Ag 43) 75-7.
——— "Slices of Cake." *New Statesman & Nation* 25 (15 Je 43) 367-8.
Specker, Heidi. "The Change of Emphasis in the Criticism of Henry James." *Eng Stud* 29 (Ap 48) 33-47.
Spender, Stephen. "A Modern Writer in Search of a Moral Subject." *London Merc* 31 (D 34) 128-33.
——— "The School of Experience in the Early Novels." *H&H* 7 (Ap-Je 34) 417-33.
——— "A World Where the Victor Belonged to the Spoils." *N Y Times Book R* (12 Mr 44) 3.
Squire, J. C. "Three Unpublished Letters and a Monologue by Henry James." *London Merc* 6 (S 22) 492-501.
Steegmuller, Francis. "Flaubert's Sundays, Maupassant and Henry James." *Cornhill Mag* no 974 (Sp 48) 124-30.
Stevens, George. "The Return of Henry James." *SRL* 28 (3 Mr 45) 7-8, 30, 32-3.
Stewart, Randall. "The Moral Aspects of Henry James's 'International Situation.'" *Un R* 9 (Wi 43) 109-13.
Stone, Edward. "A Further Note on *Daisy Miller* and Cherbuliez." *PQ* 29 (Ap 50) 213-6.
——— "Henry James's First Novel." *BPLQ* 2 (Ap 50) 167-71.
——— "Henry James's Last Novel." *BPLQ* 2 (O 50) 348-53.
Sweeney, J. L. "The Demuth Pictures." *KR* 5 (Au 43) 522-32.
Swinnerton, Frank. "A Superb Performance." *Mark Twain Q* 5 (Sp 43) 2.
———, *et al.* "Henry James Number." *Mark Twain Q* 5 (Sp 43) 1-10.
"Thersites." "Talk on Parnassus." *N Y Times Book R* (24 My 49) 7, 27.
Tintner, A. R. "The Spoils of Henry James." *PMLA* 61 (Mr 46) 239-51.
Tooker, L. F. "The Fiction of the Magazine." *Century* 108 (Je 24) 260-71.
Trilling, Lionel. "The Princess Casamassima." *Horizon* 17 (Ap 48) 267-95.
Troy, William. "The Altar of Henry James." *NRp* 108 (15 F 31) 228-30.
——— "Henry James and Young Writers." *Bkm* 73 (Je 31) 351-8.

Vivas, Eliseo. "Henry and William James: Two Notes." *KR* 5 (Au 43) 580-94.
Wade, Allen. "Henry James as Dramatic Critic." *Theatre Arts* 27 (D 43) 735-40.
Wagenknecht, Edward. "Our Contemporary Henry James." *CE* 10 (D 48) 123-32.
Walbrook, H. M. "Henry James and the English Theatre." *Nineteenth Century* 80 (Jl 16) 141-5; *Living Age* 190 (19 Ag 16) 505-8.
——— "Henry James and the Theatre." *London Merc* 20 (O 29) 612-6.
——— "The Novels of Henry James." *Fortnightly R* 127 (My 30) 680-91.
Waldock, A. J. A. "Mr. Edmund Wilson and *The Turn of the Screw*." *MLN* 62 (My 47) 331-4.
Walkley, A. B. "Henry James and His Letters." *Fortnightly R* ns 107 (Je 20) 864-73.
Walpole, Hugh. "Henry James, A Reminiscence." *Horizon* 1 (F 40) 74-80.
Warren, Austin. "James and His Secret." *SRL* 8 (28 My 32) 759.
——— "Myth and Dialectic in the Later Novels." *KR* 5 (Au 43) 551-68.
Warren, R. P., ed. "The Henry James Number." *KR* 5 (Au 43) 481-617.
Waterlow, S. P. "Memories of Henry James." *New Statesman & Nation* 26 (6 F 32) 514-5.
——— "The Work of Mr. Henry James." *Independent R* 4 (N 04) 236-43.
Weber, C. J. "Henry James and Thomas Hardy." *Mark Twain Q* 5 (Sp 43) 3-4.
——— "A Unique Henry James Item." *Colby Libr Q* 2 (Ap 48) 123.
Wells, H. G. "Wells and Henry James." *New Statesman & Nation* 25 (12 Je 43) 385.
West, Rebecca. "Reading Henry James in War Time." *NRp* 2 (27 F 15) 98-100.
Westcott, Glenway. "A Sentimental Contribution." *H&H* 7 (Ap-Je 34) 523-34.
Wharton, Edith. "A Backward Glance." *Ladies' Home J* 51 (F 34) 19, 73, 78, 80.
——— "Henry James in His Letters." *Quar R* 234 (Jl 20) 188-202.
Wheelwright, John. "Henry James and Stanford White." *H&H* 7 (Ap-Je 34) 480-93.
White, J. W. "Professor White's Interpretation of Henry James's Action." *Spectator* 115 (14 Ag 15) 204-5.
Whitford, R. C. "The Letters of Henry James." *SAQ* 19 (O 20) 371-3.
Williams, Blanche. "The Depth of Henry James." *Mark Twain Q* 5 (Sp 43) 5-6.
Williams, Orlo. "The Ambassadors." *Criterion* 8 (S 28) 47-64.
Wilson, Edmund. "The Ambiguity of Henry James." *H&H* 7 (Ap-Je 34) 385-406.
——— "The Exploration of Henry James." *NRp* 50 (16 Mr 27) 112-3.
——— "The Novels of Henry James." *NRp* 44 (14 O 25) 203.
Winters, Yvor. "Henry James and the Relation of Morals to Manners." *Am R* 9 (O 37) 482-503.
Wolff, R. L. "The Genesis of 'The Turn of the Screw.'" *AL* 13 (Mr 41) 1-8.
Wyatt, Edith. "Henry James: An Impression." *NAR* 203 (Ap 16) 592-9.
Young, Filson. "A Bunch of Violets." *Eng R* 22 (Ap 16) 317-20; *Living Age* 289 (27 My 16) 568-9.
Young, R. E. "An Error in *The Ambassadors*." *AL* 22 (N 50) 245-53.
Young, Vernon. "The Question of James." *Ariz Q* 1 (Wi 45) 57-62.
Zabel, M. D. "Henry James' Place." *Nation* 156 (24 Ap 43) 597-9.
——— "The Poetics of Henry James." *Poetry* 45 (F 35) 270-6.

JAMES, WILLIAM (1842-1910). Anon. "William James: A Belated Acknowledgment." *Atl* 123 (Ap 19) 568-70.
Ament, W. S. "William James as a Man of Letters." *Personalist* 23 (Sp 42) 199-206.
Barzun, Jacques. "William James as Artist." *NRp* 108 (15 F 43) 218-20.
Baum, Maurice. "The Attitude of William James toward Science." *Monist* 42 (O 32) 585-604.
——— "The Development of James's Pragmatism Prior to 1879." *J Philos* 30 (5 Ja 33) 43-51.

Baym, M. I. "William James and Henry Adams." *NEQ* 10 (D 37) 717-42.
Bixler, J. S. "Two Questions Raised by William James's Essay on 'The Moral Equivalent of War.'" *Harvard Theol R* 25 (Ap 42) 117-29.
——— "William James and Our Changing World." *Am Schol* 1 (1932) 392-400.
Björkman, Edwin. "William James." *Rev of Rev* 37 (Ja 08) 45-8.
——— "William James: Builder of American Ideals." *Rev of Rev* 42 (O 10) 463-7.
Bruce, H. A. "William James." *Outlook* 96 (10 S 10) 68-70.
Buchler, Justus. "The Philosopher, the Common Man and William James." *Am Schol* 11 (Au 42) 416-26.
Carpenter, F. I. "Points of Comparison between Emerson and William James." *NEQ* 2 (Jl 29) 458-74.
Compton, C. H. "Who Reads William James?" *SAQ* 25 (O 26) 403-9.
Delattre, Floris. "William James: Bergsonien." *Revue Anglo-Américain* (1923) 1-24, 135-44.
Dewey, John. "A Philosopher Who Believed in Life." *Independent* 69 (8 S 10) 533-6.
Edman, Irwin. "For a New World." *NRp* 108 (15 F 43) 224-8.
——— "William James: 1842-1942." *Nation* 154 (17 Ja 42) 67-8.
Evans, E. G. "William James and His Wife." *Atl* 144 (S 29) 374-87.
Foerster, Norman. "Open Minds: A Text from William James." *Dial* 54 (1 My 13) 364-7.
Fries, Horace. "William James—January 11, 1842. Philosopher of the Practical." *Humanist* 2 (Sp 42) 20-3.
Gilman, Lawrence. "The Book of the Month: The Letters of William James." *NAR* 213 (Mr 21) 411-6.
Goldmark, Josephine. "An Adirondack Friendship: Letters from William James." *Atl* 154 (S 34) 265-72.
Hackett, Francis. "William James as Highbrow." *NRp* 8 (23 S 16) 184-6.
Hedges, M. H. "Physician as Hero—William James." *Forum* 52 (D 14) 880-1.
——— "Seeking the Shade of William James." *Forum* 53 (Ap 15) 441-8.
Hodges, George. "William James." *Outlook* 85 (23 F 07) 448-51.
Howe, M. A. DeW., ed. "John Jay Chapman to William James." *Harper's* 174 (D 36) 46-54.
Jacks, L. P. "William James and His Letters." *Atl* 128 (Jl-D 21) 197-203.
James, Henry. "Familiar Letters of William James." *Atl* 126 (Jl-D 20) 1-15, 163-75, 305-17.
Jastrow, Joseph. "American Academician." *Educ R* 41 (Ja 11) 27-33.
——— "The Legacy of William James." *Dial* 52 (1 Ja 12) 12-4.
Kallen, H. M. "William James." *Dial* 63 (30 Ag 17) 141-3.
——— "William James." *Nation* 91 (8 S 10) 210-1.
Levinson, R. B. "Sigwart's *Logik* and William James." *JHI* 8 (O 47) 475-83.
Lippmann, Walter. "Open Mind: William James." *Everybody's* 23 (D 10) 800-1.
Lovejoy, A. O. "William James as Philosopher." *Int J Ethics* 21 (Ja 11) 125-53.
Lyman, E. W. "The William James Centenary." *Humanist* 2 (Wi 42) 137-9.
——— "William James: Philosopher of Faith." *J Rel* 22 (Je 42) 233-50.
McCreary, J. K. "William James and Modern Value Problems." *Personalist* 31 (Sp 50) 126-34.
MacDonald, M. I. "The Common Sense of William James." *Craftsman* 19 (N 10) 135-9.
Macy, John. "Ex Libris." *Freeman* 2 (23 F, 2 Mr 21) 574-5, 598-9.
——— "William James as a Man of Letters." *Bkm* 32 (Ap 11) 205-9.
Mayhall, Jane. "William James and the Modern Mood." *AR* 8 (S 48) 291-365.
Michaud, Régis. "William et Henry James d'après leur correspondence." *Revue de France* (S 22) 145-59.
Moore, T. V. "The Pragmatism of Henry James." *Cath World* 90 (D 09) 341-50.

Otto, M. C. "On a Certain Blindness in William James." *Ethics* 53 (Ap 43) 184-91.
Parkes. H. B. "William James." *H&H* 7 (O-D 33) 6-28.
Patrick, G. T. W. "Mind Emergent." *VQR* 1 (O 25) 364-79.
Perry, R. B. "William James et M. Henri Bergson. Lettres (1902-1910)." *Revue des Deux Mondes* (15 O 33) 783-824.
Pratt, C. A. "Teachers, Students, and Professor James." *Critic* 36 (F 00) 119-21.
Putnam, J. J. "William James." *Atl* 106 (D 10) 835-48.
Raymond, M. E. "Memories of William James." *NEQ* 10 (S 37) 419-29.
Royce, Josiah. "James as a Philosopher." *Sci* ns 34 (14 Jl 11) 33-45.
Russell, Bertrand. "The Philosophy of William James." *Living Age* 267 (1 O 10) 52-5.
Slattery, C. L. "The Debt of the Church to William James." *Outlook* 98 (22 Jl 11) 643-6.
Stein, Leo. "Exercises in Criticism . . . William James." *Am Schol* 17 (Sp 48) 161-5.
——— "William James." *Am Merc* 9 (S 26) 68-70.
Trueblood, C. K. "The Education of William James." *Dial* 83 (O 27) 301-14.
Vivas, Eliseo. "Henry and William James: Two Notes." *KR* 5 (Au 43) 580-94.

JANVIER, THOMAS ALLIBONE (1849-1913). Seybolt, P. S. "American First Editions: Thomas A. Janvier, 1849-1913: Check List." *Pub W* 128 (23 N 35) 1924.

JARRELL, RANDALL (1914-). Spender, Stephen. "Randall Jarrell's Landscape." *Nation* 166 (1 My 48) 476.

JEFFERS, ROBINSON (1887-). Anon. "Rats, Lice, and Poetry." *SRL* 17 (23 O 37) 8.
——— "Robinson Jeffers: Bard." *Mag of Sigma Chi* 50 (My-Je 31) 292-6.
Adamic, Louis. "Robinson and Una Jeffers: A Portrait of a Great American Poet and His Wife." *San Franciscan* 3 (Mr 29) 16, 29.
Arms, George. "Jeffers' *Fire on the Hills.*" *Expl* 1 (My 43) 59.
Arvin, Newton. "The Paradox of Jeffers." *New Freeman* 1 (17 My 30) 230-2.
Bassett, W. K. "Wherein One Poet Talks Not and Another Shoots Squirrels." *Carmel Cymbal* 1 (15 Je 26) 3, 11.
Benét, W. R. "Round about Parnassus." *SRL* 8 (16 Ja 32) 461.
Brown, E. K. "The Coast Opposite Humanity." *Canadian Forum* 18 (Ja 39) 309-10.
Brown, M. W. "Robinson Jeffers: A Poet Who Studied Medicine." *Med J & Record* 130 (5 N 29) 535-9.
Busch, Niven. "Duel on a Headland." *SRL* 11 (9 Mr 35) 533.
Calverton, V. F. "Pathology in Contemporary Literature." *Thinker* 4 (D 31) 7-16.
Canby, H. S. "North of Hollywood." *SRL* 10 (7 O 33) 162.
Carpenter, F. I. "Death Comes for Robinson Jeffers." *Un R* 7 (D 40) 97-105.
——— "The Values of Robinson Jeffers." *AL* 11 (Ja 40) 353-66.
Cestre, Charles. "Robinson Jeffers." *Revue Anglo-Américain* 4 (1927) 489-502.
Church, S. H. "A Pittsburgh Poet Discovered." *Carnegie Mag* 2 (N 28) 180-2.
Cunningham, C. C. "The Rhythm of Robinson Jeffers' Poetry as Revealed by Oral Reading." *QJS* 32 (O 46) 351-7.
Daly, James. "Roots Under the Rocks." *Poetry* 26 (Ag 25) 278-85.
Davis, H. L. "Jeffers Denies Us Twice." *Poetry* 31 (F 28) 274-9.
De Casseres, Benjamin. "Robinson Jeffers." Un N C *Daily Tar Heel* 40 (24 Ja 32) 1.
——— "Robinson Jeffers: Tragic Terror." *Bkm* 66 (N 27) 262-6.
Dell, Floyd. "Shell-Shock and the Poetry of Robinson Jeffers." *Mod Q* 3 (S-D 26) 268-73.
Ficke, A. D. "A Note on the Poetry of Robinson Jeffers." *Carmelite* 1 (19 D 28) 17.

Flanner, Hildegarde. "Two Poets: Jeffers and Millay." *NRp* 89 (27 Ja 37) 379-82.
Fletcher, J. G. "The Dilemma of Robinson Jeffers." *Poetry* 43 (Mr 34) 338-42.
Flewelling, R. T. "Tragic Drama—Modern Style." *Personalist* 20 (Jl 39) 229-41.
Gates, G. G. "The Bread That Every Man Must Eat Alone." *CE* 4 (D 42) 170-4.
Gibson, W. H., & Horton, Philip. "Robinson Jeffers: Pro . . . [and] Con." Princeton Un *Nassau Lit* 91 (N 32) 11-23.
Gierasch, Walter. "Robinson Jeffers." *EJ* (Col ed) 28 (Ap 39) 284-95.
Glicksberg, C. I. "The Poetry of Doom and Despair." *Humanist* 7 (Au 47) 69-76.
Gorman, H. "Jeffers, Metaphysician." *SRL* 4 (17 S 27) 115.
Hackman, Martha. "Whitman, Jeffers, and Freedom." *Prairie Schooner* 20 (Fl 46) 182-4.
Hagemeyer, Dora. "How Jeffers and Laurence 'Do' the Atmosphere." *Carmel Cymbal* 1 (18 My 26) 6, 11.
Hale, W. H. "Robinson Jeffers: A Lone Titan." *Yale Lit Mag* 95 (D 29) 31-5.
Hatcher, Harlan. "The Torches of Violence." *EJ* 23 (F 34) 91-9.
Hayden, A. E. "Robinson Jeffers: Poet-Philosopher." *Un R* 5 (Su 39) 235-8.
Humphries, Rolfe. "More About Robinson Jeffers." *NRp* 62 (9 Ap 30) 222.
——— "Poet or Prophet?" *NRp* 61 (15 Ja 30) 228-9.
——— "Robinson Jeffers." *Mod Mo* 8 (Ja, F 35) 680-9, 748-53.
——— "Two Books by Jeffers." *Poetry* 40 (Je 32) 154-8.
Jeffers, Robinson. "A Few Memories." *Overland Mo* 85 (N 27) 329, 351.
——— "First Book." *Colophon* 10 (My 32) Pt 10.
Jeffers, Una. "A Correction." Princeton Un *Nassau Lit* 91 (Ja 33) 41.
Johnson, Merle. "(John) Robinson Jeffers, 1887—." *Pub W* 117 (19 Ap 30) 2143.
Johnson, W. S. "The 'Savior' in the Poetry of Robinson Jeffers." *AL* 15 (My 43) 159-68.
Karo, L. M. "Robinson Jeffers." *Present Day Am Lit* 4 (Mr 31) 154-65.
Lehman, B. H. "The Most Significant Tendency in Modern Poetry." *Scripps Col Papers* no 2 (Mr-Ap 29) 1-12.
——— "Robinson Jeffers." *SRL* 8 (5 S 31) 91-9.
Lind, L. R. "The Crisis in Literature Today." *SR* 47 (Ja-Mr 30) 47-50.
Macdonald, Dwight. "Robinson Jeffers." *Miscellany* 1 (Jl, S 30) 1-10, 1-24.
McWilliams, Carey. "Robinson Jeffers: An Antitoxin." *Los Angeles Saturday Night* 9 (3 Ag 29) 5.
Marchand, L. A. "Robinson Jeffers—Poet Extraordinary." *MS* 3 (O 31) 3, 9.
——— "A Viewpoint on Jeffers." *Carmelite* 4 (19 N 31) 11.
Mayfield, J. S. "Robinson Jeffers Receives a Convert." *Overland Mo* 86 (Ag 28) 279-80.
Miller, Benjamin. "Toward a Religious Philosophy of the Theatre." *Personalist* 20 (O 34) 361-76.
Monroe, Harriet. "Power and Pomp." *Poetry* 28 (Ja 26) 160-4.
Morris, L. S. "Robinson Jeffers: The Tragedy of a Modern Mystic." *NRp* 54 (16 My 28) 386-90.
Pinckney, Josephine. "Jeffers and MacLeish." *VQR* 8 (Jl 32) 443-7.
Powell, L. C. "Leaves of Grass and Granite Boulders." *Carmelite* 4 (22 O 31) 8-9.
Rice, P. B. "Jeffers and the Tragic Sense." *Nation* 141 (23 O 35) 480-2.
Robinson, A. C. "Jeffer's Mother." *Time* 19 (25 Ap 32) 8.
Roddy, Joseph. "View from a Granite Tower." *Theatre Arts* 33 (Je 49) 32-6.
Schwartz, Delmore, & Taylor, Frajam. "The Enigma of Robinson Jeffers." *Poetry* 55 (O 34) 30-8.
Short, R. W. "The Tower Beyond Tragedy." *So R* 7 (Su 41) 132-4.
Sterling, George. "Rhymes and Reactions." *Overland Mo* 84 (N 25) 411.
——— "A Tower by the Sea." *San Francisco R* 1 (F-Mr 26) 248-9.
Swallow, Alan. "The Poetry of Robinson Jeffers." *Intermountain R* 2 (Fl 37) 8-9.
Van Doren, Mark. "Judas, Savior of Jesus." *Nation* 130 (1 Ja 30) 20-1.
Vivas, Elisea. "Robinson Jeffers." *New Student* 8 (Ap 29) 13-5.

Waggoner, H. H. "Science and the Poetry of Robinson Jeffers." *AL* 10 (N 38) 275-88.
Walton, E. L. "Beauty of Storm Disproportionately." *Poetry* 51 (Ja 38) 209-13.
Wann, Lewis. "Robinson Jeffers—Counterpart of Walt Whitman." *Personalist* 19 (Jl 38) 297-308.
Watts, H. H. "Multivalence in Robinson Jeffers." *CE* 3 (N 41) 109-20.
——— "Robinson Jeffers and Eating the Serpent." *SR* 49 (Ja 41) 39-55.
Wells, H. W. "A Philosophy of War: The Outlook of Robinson Jeffers." *CE* 6 (N 44) 81-8.
White, William. "Some Unnoticed Jeffers Poems." *PBSA* 34 (D 40) 362-3.
——— "Uncollected Poems of Robinson Jeffers." *AN&Q* 1 (Ja 42) 149-51.
Winters, Yvor. "Robinson Jeffers." *Poetry* 35 (F 30) 279-86.
Wronecki, Jeanne. "Un Poète américain d'aujourd'hui: Robinson Jeffers." *Revue de France* 2 (15 Mr 39) 283-6.
Zabel, M. D. "The Problem of Tragedy." *Poetry* 33 (Mr 29) 336-40.

JEFFERSON, THOMAS (1743-1826). Anon. "Excerpts from two letters." *Autograph Album* 1 (D 33) 74-5.
——— "Jefferson Issue." *Ethics* 53 (Jl 43) 237-310.
——— "Jefferson Letter: Indians Present Old Script to Princeton Library." *Life* 21 (2 D 46) 44.
——— "Letters of Thomas Jefferson to William Short." *WMQ Hist Mag* 12 (O 33) 287-304.
Adams, Elizabeth. "Unpublished Letters by Thomas Jefferson." *More Books* 18 (Ap 43) 155-62.
Adams, J. T. "Jefferson and Hamilton Today: The Dichotomy in American Thought." *Atl* 141 (Ap 28) 443-50.
Adams, R. G. "Notes and Queries." *Colophon* ns 3 (Wi 38) 134-6.
Beard, C. A. "Jefferson in America Now." *YR* 25 (Wi 36) 241-57.
———, *et al.*. "Jefferson Number." *Miss Valley Hist R* 30 (S 43) 159-214.
Becker, Carl. "What Is Still Living in the Philosophy of Thomas Jefferson?" *AHR* 48 (Jl 43) 691-706; *PAPS* 87 (1943) 200-10.
Berman, E. D., & McClintock, E. C., Jr. "Thomas Jefferson and Rhetoric." *QJS* 33 (F 47) 1-8.
Bernstein, Samuel. "Jefferson and the French Revolution." *Sci & Soc* 7 (Sp 43) 115-40.
Bevan, E. R. "Thomas Jefferson in Annapolis." *Md Hist Mag* 41 (Je 46) 115-24.
Blanck, Jacob. "Antiquarian Book Notes." *Antiquarian Bkm* 1 (21 F 48) 299-300.
Bourgin, F. P., & Merriam, C. E. "Jefferson as a Planner of National Resources." *Ethics* 53 (Jl 43) 284-92.
Bowers, C. G. "Jefferson and the Freedom of the Human Spirit." *Ethics* 53 (Jl 43) 237-45.
——— "Jefferson, Master Politician." *VQR* 2 (Jl 26) 321-33.
Bryan, M. R. "Thomas Jefferson through the Eyes of His Contemporaries." *Princeton Un Lib Chron* 9 (Je 48) 219-24.
Bullock, H. D. "Mr. Jefferson, Musician." *Etude* 61 (O 43) 633-4.
——— "The Papers of Thomas Jefferson." *Am Archivist* 4 (O 41) 238-49.
Butterfield, L. H. "The Jefferson-Adams Correspondence in the Adams Manuscript Trust." *Lib Cong Quar J* 5 (F 48) 3-6.
——— "The Papers of Thomas Jefferson." *Am Archivist* 12 (Ap 49) 131-47.
Carrière, J. M. "The Manuscript of Jefferson's Unpublished Errata List for Abbé Morellet's Translation of the *Notes on Virginia*." *Papers Bibl Soc Un Va* 1 (1948-9) 3-24.
——— "Mr. Jefferson Sponsors a New French Method." *FR* 19 (My 46) 394-405.
Chamberlayne, C. G. "Three Old Letters." *VMHB* 43 (Ja 35) 63-5.

Chandler, J. A. C. "Jefferson and William and Mary College." *WMQ Hist Mag* 14 (O 34) 304-7.
Chinard, Gilbert. "Jefferson among the Philosophers." *Ethics* 53 (Jl 43) 255-68.
——— "Jefferson and Ossian." *MLN* 38 (Ap 23) 201-5.
——— "Jefferson and the American Philosophical Society." *PAPS* 87 (1943) 263-78.
——— "Jefferson and the Physiocrats." *Un Calif Chron* 33 (Ja 31) 18-31.
Coleman, Mrs. G. P. "Randolph and Tucker Letters." *VMHB* 42 (O 34) 317-24.
Commager, H. S. "Thomas Jefferson Still Survives." *Pub W* 143 (10 Ap 43) 1504-6.
Corbin, John. "From Jefferson to Wilson." *NAR* 210 (Ag 19) 172-85.
Curtis, T. E. "The True Thomas Jefferson." *Outlook* 70 (25 Ja 02) 239-41.
Diamond, Sigmund. "Some Jefferson Letters." *Miss Valley Hist R* 28 (S 43) 235-42.
Dickinson, John. "The Old Political Philosophy and the New." *PAPS* 87 (1943) 246-62.
Dodd, W. E. "Napoleon Breaks Thomas Jefferson." *Am Merc* 5 (Jl 25) 303-13.
Dumbauld, Edward. "Les Demeures Parisiennes de Thomas Jefferson." *FAR* 1 (Ja-Mr 48) 68-75.
Fucilla, J. G. "An American Diplomat in Settecento Italy." *Ital* 26 (Mr 49) 78-101.
Gabriel, R. H. "Thomas Jefferson and Twentieth-Century Rationalism." *VQR* 26 (Su 50) 321-35.
Garrison, F. W. "Jefferson and the Physiocrats." *Freeman* 8 (31 O 23) 180-2.
Gould, W. D. "The Religious Opinions of Thomas Jefferson." *Miss Valley Hist R* 20 (S 33) 191-208.
Griswold, A. W. "The Agrarian Democracy of Thomas Jefferson." *Am Pol Sci R* 40 (Ag 46) 657-81.
Hamilton, J. G. deR. "Jefferson and Adams at Ease." *SAQ* 26 (O 27) 359-72.
Haworth, P. L. "Thomas Jefferson—Poet." *Bkm* 31 (Ag 10) 647-50.
Hench, A. L. "Jefferson and Ossian." *MLN* 43 (D 28) 537.
Henline, Ruth. "A Study of *Notes on Virginia* as an Evidence of Jefferson's Reaction against the Theories of the French Naturalists." *VMHB* 55 (Ap 47) 233-46.
Herzberg, M. J. "Thomas Jefferson as a Man of Letters." *SAQ* 13 (O 14) 310-27.
Hirsch, Rudolf. "Notes and Queries." *Colophon* ns 3 (Wi 38) 134-9.
Kallen, H. M. "The Arts and Thomas Jefferson." *Ethics* 53 (Jl 43) 269-83.
Kimball, Fiske. "Form and Function in the Architecture of Jefferson." *Mag of Art* 40 (Ap 47) 150-3.
——— "In Search of Jefferson's Birthplace." *VMHB* 51 (O 43) 313-25.
Kimball, Marie. "Jefferson and the Arts." *PAPS* 87 (1943) 238-45.
——— "Jefferson in Paris." *NAR* 248 (Au 39) 73-86.
——— "Jefferson's Farewell to Romance." *VQR* 4 (Jl 28) 402-19; 7 (Ja 31) 81-95.
——— "A Playmate of Thomas Jefferson." *NAR* 213 (F 21) 145-56.
——— "Thomas Jefferson's Rhine Journey." *AGR* 13 (O, D 46, F 47) 4-9, 11-5, 4-8.
——— "Unpublished Correspondence of Mme de Staël with Thomas Jefferson." *NAR* 208 (Jl 18) 63-71.
Kirk, R. A. "Jefferson and the Faithless." *SAQ* 40 (Jl 41) 220-7.
Kirkland, F. R. "Jefferson and Franklin." *PMHB* 71 (Jl 47) 218-22.
Koch, Adrienne. "Philosopher-Statesmen of the Republic." *SR* 55 (Su 47) 384-405.
Krock, Arthur. "Jefferson's Stepchildren." *Am Merc* 7 (F 26) 129-35.
Lingelbach, A. L. "Jefferson Today." *Cur Hist* 5 (N 43) 225-8.
Lucs, F. A. "Thomas Jefferson: Palaeontologist." *Natural Hist* 26 (My-Je 26) 328-30.
Lucke, J. R. "Some Correspondence with Thomas Jefferson concerning the Public Printers." *PBS Un Va* 1 (1948-9) 25-38.
McAdie, A. "Thomas Jefferson at Home." *PAAS* ns 40 (Ap 30) 27-46.

Malone, Dumas. "Polly Jefferson and Her Father." *VQR* 7 (Ja 31) 81-95.
Marraro, H. W. "Four Versions of Jefferson's Letter to Mazzei." *WMQ* 22 (Ja 42) 18-29.
——— "Jefferson Letters Concerning the Settlement of Mazzei's Virginia Estate." *Miss Valley Hist R* 30 (S 43) 235-42.
Marsh, P. M. "Freneau and Jefferson: The Poet-Editor Speaks for Himself about the National Gazette Episode." *AL* 8 (My 36) 180-9.
——— "Jefferson and Freneau." *Am Schol* 16 (Sp 47) 201-10.
——— "Jefferson and Journalism." *HLQ* 9 (F 46) 209-12.
——— "Jefferson's 'Conduct' of the *National Gazette*." *Proc N J Hist Soc* 63 (Ap 45) 69-73.
——— "Jefferson's Retirement as Secretary of State." *PMHB* 69 (Jl 45) 220-4.
——— "The Manuscript Franklin Gave to Jefferson." *Lib Bul Am Philos Soc* (1946) 45-8.
——— "The Vindication of Mr. Jefferson." *SAQ* 45 (Ja 46) 61-7.
Martin, E. T. "Thomas Jefferson's Interest in Science and the Useful Arts." *Emory Un Q* 2 (Je 46) 65-73.
Mellen, G. F. "Thomas Jefferson and Higher Education." *N E Mag* ns 26 (Jl 02) 607-16.
Merriam, C. E. "The Political Theory of Jefferson." *Pol Sci Q* 17 (Mr 02) 24-45.
Montgomery, H. C. "Thomas Jefferson as a Philologist." *Am J Phil* 65 (O 44) 367-71.
Morris, Mabel. "Jefferson and the Language of the American Indian." *MLQ* 6 (Mr 45) 31-4.
Morris, R. S. "Jefferson as a Lawyer." *PAPS* 87 (1943) 211-5.
Osborn, H. F. "Thomas Jefferson the Pioneer of American Paleontology." *Sci* 69 (19 Ap 29) 410-3.
Padover, S. K. "Jefferson's Prose Poem: The Declaration of Independence." *Am Merc* 54 (F 42) 165-71.
Peden, William. "A Book Peddler Invades Monticello." *WMQ* 3 ser 6 (O 49) 631-6.
——— "Some Notes Containing Thomas Jefferson's Library." *WMQ* 1 (Jl 44) 265-72.
——— "Thomas Jefferson and Charles Brockden Brown." *Md Q* no 2 (1944) 65-8.
Pound, Ezra. "The Jefferson-Adams Correspondence." *NAR* 244 (Wi 37-8) 314-24.
Prescott, F. C. "Jefferson and Bishop Burnet." *AL* 7 (Mr 35) 87.
Quinn, P. F. "Agrarianism and the Jeffersonian Philosophy." *R Pol* 2 (Ja 40) 87-104.
Roberts, J. G. "An Exchange of Letters between Jefferson and Quesnay de Beaurepaire." *VMHB* 50 (Ap 42) 134-42.
Sand, Norbert. "The Classics in Jefferson's Theory of Education." *Classical J* 40 (N 44) 92-8.
Schachner, Nathan. "Jefferson: The Man and the Myth." *Am Merc* 65 (Jl 47) 46-52.
Schick, J. S. "Poe and Jefferson." *VMHB* 54 (O 46) 316-20.
Schneider, H. W. "The Enlightenment of Thomas Jefferson." *Ethics* 53 (Jl 43) 246-54.
Sellers, H. W. "Letters of Thomas Jefferson to Charles Willson Peale, 1796-1825." *PMHB* 28 (1904) 136-54, 295-319, 403-20.
Shaffer, K. R. "Copy to Mr. Jefferson about the Sale of His Library to Congress." *Ind Q for Bkm* 1 (Jl 45) 55-9.
Shapley, Harlow. "Notes on Thomas Jefferson as a Natural Philosopher." *PAPS* 87 (1943) 234-7.
Smith, Dorothy, & Ruese, Nina. "He Wrote the Declaration." *Chri Sci Mon* 37 (30 Je 45) 3.

Smith, T. V. "Thomas Jefferson and the Perfectibility of Man." *Ethics* 53 (Jl 43) 293-310.
Thomas, C. M. "Date Inaccuracies in Thomas Jefferson's Writings." *Miss Valley Hist R* 19 (Je 32) 87-90.
Thorpe, F. N. "Adams and Jefferson: 1826-1926." *NAR* 223 (Je-Jl-Ag 26) 234-47.
True, R. H. "A Sketch of the Life of John Bradbury, Including His Unpublished Correspondence with Thomas Jefferson." *PAPS* 68 (1929) 133-50.
——— "Thomas Jefferson's Gardening Book." *PAPS* 76 (1936) 939-46.
Vandiver, E. P. "Thomas Jefferson's Religion." *Lutheran Church Q* 17 (Jl 45) 300-5.
Warren, Charles. "Why Jefferson Abandoned the Presidential Speech to Congress." *PMHS* 57 (N 23) 123-72.
Washburn, C. G. "Who Was the Author of the Declaration of Independence?" *PAAS* ns 38 (Ap 28) 51-62.
Wilson, M. L. "Thomas Jefferson—Farmer." *PAPS* 87 (1943) 216-22.
Wilstach, Paul. "Jefferson Out of Harness." *Am Merc* 4 (Ja 25) 63-8.
Wiltse, C. M. "Jeffersonian Democracy: A Dual Tradition." *Am Pol Sci R* 28 (O 34) 838-51.
——— "Thomas Jefferson on the Law of Nations." *Am J Int Law* 29 (Ja 35) 66-81.
Woodfin, M. H. "Thomas Jefferson and William Byrd's Manuscript Histories of the Dividing Line." *WMQ* 1 (O 44) 363-73.
Wright, L. B. "The Classical Tradition in Colonial Virginia." *PBSA* 33 (1939) 85-97.
——— "Thomas Jefferson and the Classics." *PAPS* 87 (1943) 223-33.
Wyman, W. I. "Thomas Jefferson and the Patent System." *J Patent Office Soc* 1 (S 18).

JEMISON, MARY (1743-1833). Strecker, Frederick. "My First Year as a Jemisonian." *Colophon* 2 (S 31) Pt 7.

JEWETT, SARAH ORNE (1849-1909). Anon. "A Letter by Sarah Orne Jewett." *Colby Merc* 7 (Ap 42) 82-3.
——— "The New England Spirit." *TLS* (22 N 47) 602.
Boleman, B. A. "Deephaven and the Woodburys." *Colophon* ns 3 (S 39).
Chapman, E. M. "The New England of Sarah Orne Jewett." *YR* 3 (O 13) 157-72.
Floyd, O. B. "Sara Orne Jewett's Advice to a Young Writer." *YR* 26 (Wi 37) 430-2.
Grattan, C. H. "Sarah Orne Jewett." *Bkm* 69 (My 26) 296.
Marble, A. R. "A True Daughter of New England." *Dial* 51 (1 N 11) 337-9.
Shackford, M. H. "Sarah Orne Jewett." *SR* 30 (Ja 22) 20-6.
Thompson, C. M. "The Art of Miss Jewett." *Atl* 94 (O 04) 485-97.
Weber, C. J. "More Letters from Sarah Orne Jewett." *Colby Lib Q* ser 2 (N 49) 201-6.
——— "New England through French Eyes Fifty Years Ago." *NEQ* 20 (S 47) 385-96.
——— "Three More Jewett Letters." *Colby Lib Q* 2 (F 50) 216-8.
——— "Whittier and Sarah Orne Jewett." *NEQ* 18 (S 45) 401-7.

JOHNSON, JAMES WELDON (1871-1938). Aery, W. A. "James Weldon Johnson: American Negro of Distinction." *School & Soc* 48 (3 S 38) 291-4.
Gale, Zona. "Autobiography of Distinction." *World Tomorrow* 17 (4 Ja 34) 20-1.
Johnson, C. S. "American Background of the American Negro." *Am Federationist* 35 (Ja 28) 49-53.
Monroe, Harriet. "Negro Sermons." *Poetry* 30 (Ag 27) 291-3.
Rosenberg, Harold. "Truth and the Academic Style." *Poetry* 49 (O 36) 49-51.
Villard, O. G. "Issues and Men." *Nation* 149 (9 Jl 38) 44.
Wohlforth, Robert. "Dark Leader." *NYr* 9 (30 S 33) 22-6.

JOHNSON, OWEN (1878-). Hooker, Brian. "Johnson's Stories at Yale." *Bkm* 35 (My 12) 309-12.
Maurice, A. B. "Owen Johnson." *Bkm* 39 (Je 14) 416-20; 70 (D 29) 414-6.

JOHNSON, SAMUEL (1696-1772). Hornberger, Theodore. "Samuel Johnson of Yale, and King's College." *NEQ* 8 (S 35) 378-97.
Schneider, H. W. "A Note on the Samuel Johnson Papers." *AHR* 31 (Jl 26) 724-6.

JOHNSON, SAMUEL (1709-84). Burkett, Eva. "The American Samuel Johnson and His Dictionaries." *PQ* 19 (Jl 40) 295-305.
Gibson, M. J. "America's First Lexicographer, Samuel Johnson, Jr." *AS* 11 (D 36) 283-92; 12 (F 37) 19-30.
——— "Identifying Samuel Johnson, Jr." *NEQ* 9 (D 36) 688-9.

JOHNSON, WALTER ROGERS (1794-1852). Pettengill, G. E. "Walter Rogers Johnson." *J. Franklin Inst* 250 (Ag 50) 93-113.

JOHNSTON, MARY (1870-1936). Dixon, Thomas. "Mary Johnston's Virginia." *Bkm* 12 (N 00) 237-8.
Johnson, Merle. "American First Editions: Mary Johnston, 1870- ." *Pub W* 118 (19 Jl 30) 276-7.
Sherman, C. D. "The Rediscovery of Mary Johnston." *SLM* 4 (S 42) 431-2.
Wagenknecht, Edward. "The World and Mary Johnston." *SR* 44 (Ap-Je 36) 188-206.

JOHNSTON, RICHARD MALCOLM (1822-98). Gavigan, M. V. "Two Gentlemen of Georgia." *Cath World* 145 (Ag 37) 584-9.
Long, F. T. "The Life of Richard Malcolm Johnston in Maryland, 1867-1898." *Md Hist Mag* 34 (D 39) 305-24; 35 (S 40) 270-86; 36 (Mr 41) 54-69.
Parks, E. W. "Professor Richard Malcolm Johnston." *Ga Hist Q* 25 (Mr 41) 1-15.

JONES, CHARLES COLCOCK (1831-93). Bonner, J. C. "Charles Colcock Jones: The Macaulay of the South." *Ga Hist Q* 27 (D 43) 324-8.

JONES, ROBERT EDMOND (1887-). Young, Stark. "Robert Edmond Jones." *NRp* 212 (23 Ap 45) 556.

JONES, WILLIAM A. (1817-1900). Stafford, John. "William A. Jones, Democratic Literary Critic." *HLQ* 12 (My 49) 289-302.

JORDAN, DAVID STARR (1851-1931). Dickason, D. H. "David Starr Jordan as a Literary Man." *Ind Mag Hist* 37 (D 41) 345-58.

JOSSELYN, JOHN (*fl.* 1638-75). Mood, Fulmer. "Notes on John Josselyn, Gent." *PCSM* 28 (1935) 24-36.

JUDAH, SAMUEL (*fl.* 1820). Van Lennep, William. "John Adams to a Young Playwright: An Unpublished Letter to Samuel Judah." *Harvard Lib Bul* 1 (Wi 47) 117-8.

JUDD, SYLVESTER (1813-53). Brockway, P. J. "Sylvester Judd, Novelist of Transcendentalism." *NEQ* 13 (D 40) 654-77.

JUDSON, EDWARD ZANE CARROL (1823-86). Holbrook, S. H. "Life and Times of Ned Buntline." *Am Merc* 64 (My 47) 599-605.

KANTOR, MACKINLAY (1904-). Kantor, Mackinlay. "First Blood." *Colophon* ns 2 (Su 37) 317-22.
——— "My Memoirs of the Civil War." *Colophon* ns 1 (Sp 36) 541-8.

KAUFMAN, GEORGE S. (1889-). Carmer, Carl. "George Kaufman—Playmaker to Broadway." *Theatre Arts* 16 (O 32) 807-15.
Chapman, John. "The Gloomy Dean." *Sat Eve Post* 210 (1 Ja 38) 16, 33-4.
Corbin, John. "George Kaufman." *SRL* 9 (21 Ja 33) 385-6.
Krutch, J. W. "The Random Satire of George S. Kaufman." *Nation* 137 (9 Ag 33) 156-8.
Lembke, R. W. "The George S. Kaufman Plays as Social History." *QJS* 33 (O 47) 341-7.
Moses, M. J. "George S. Kaufman." *NAR* 237 (Ja 34) 76-83.
Woolcott, Alexander. "The Deep Tangled Kaufman." *NYr* 5 (18 My 29) 26-9.

KAZIN, ALFRED (1915-). Hicks, Granville. "The Ground Alfred Kazin Stands On." *AR* 3 (Sp 43) 21-31.

KEENAN, HENRY FRANCIS (1850-?). Bender, C. A. "Another Forgotten Novel." *MLN* 41 (My 26) 319-22.

KEIMER, SAMUEL (1688-1739). Bloore, S. "Samuel Keimer: A Footnote to the Life of Franklin." *PMHB* 54 (Jl 30) 255-87.
Carlson, C. L. "Samuel Keimer: A Study in the Transit of English Culture to Colonial Pennsylvania." *PMHB* 61 (O 37) 357-86.

KELLOGG, ELIJAH (1813-1901). Ray, I. T. "Rev. Elijah Kellogg—Author and Preacher." *N E Mag* ns 26 (Je 02) 434-48.

KELLY, GEORGE (1887-). Carmer, Carl. "George Kelly." *Theatre Arts Mo* 15 (Ap 31) 322-30.
Crowder, Florence. "Up from Vaudeville." *Letters* 5 (F 32) 29-33.
Krutch, J. W. "The Austerity of George Kelly." *Nation* 137 (30 Ag 33) 240-2.
McCarthy, Mary. "Something about the Weather." *PR* 14 (Mr-Ap 47) 174-8.
Maisel, Edward. "The Theatre of George Kelly." *Theatre Arts* 31 (F 47) 33-42.
Van Druten, John. "Small Souls and Great Plays." *Theatre Arts* 11 (Jl 27) 493-8.
White, Kenneth. "George Kelly and Dramatic Device." *H&H* 4 (Ap-Je 31) 384-400.

KENNEDY, JOHN PENDLETON (1795-1870). Campbell, Killis. "The Kennedy Papers." *SR* 25 (Ja, Ap, Jl 17) 1-19, 193-208, 348-60.
Forman, H. C. "The Rose Croft in Old St. Mary's." *Md Hist Mag* 35 (Mr 40) 26-31.
Gallagher, F. X. "The Gentleman from Maryland." *Evergreen Q* 5 (Fl 48) 48-55.
Johnson, Merle. "American First Editions: John Pendleton Kennedy (1795-1870)." *Pub W* 122 (20 Ag 32) 589.
Moore, J. R. "Kennedy's *Horse-Shoe Robinson:* Fact or Fiction?" *AL* 4 (My 32) 160-6.
Uhler, J. E. "Kennedy's Novels and His Posthumous Works." *AL* 3 (Ja 32) 469-77.

KETTELL, SAMUEL (1800-55). Johnston, Charles. "Jester of Old Massachusetts." *Harper's Weekly* 16 (26 O 12) 24.

KEY, FRANCIS SCOTT (1779-1843). Anon. "Excerpt from a letter, dated July 16, 1823." *Autograph Album* 1 (D 33) 76.
——— "Francis Scott Key Home." *State and Local News Hist News* 3 (Jl 46) 1.
Howard, McHenry. "Date of Francis Scott Key's Birth." *Md Hist Mag* 2 (Je 07) 137-40.
Johnson, Christopher. "Key Family." *Md Hist Mag* 5 (Je 10) 194-200.
Key, F. S. "Letters of Francis Scott Key to Roger Brooke Taney." *Md Hist Mag* 5 (Mr 10) 23-37.

Lippencott, M. E. "O'er the Land of the Free." *N Y Hist Soc Quar Bul* 25 (Ja 41) 28-36.
Pickett, L. C. "Poet of the Flag." *Lippincott's* 90 (Jl 12) 45-52.
Wroth, L. C. "Francis Scott Key as Churchman." *Md Hist Mag* 4 (Je 09) 154-70.

KEYES, FRANCES PARKINSON (1885-). Bourgeois, M. K. "Lady of Letters." *Holland's Mag* 45 (D 46) 24-5.

KILMER, JOYCE (1886-1918). Brégy, Katherine. "Joyce Kilmer, Poet and Patriot." *Outlook* 122 (23 Jl 19) 467-9.
Faherty, W. B. "Wisconsin's Kilmer Memorial." *Wisc Mag Hist* 26 (S 42) 61-71.
Le Gallienne, Richard. "Joyce Kilmer." *Bkm* 48 (O 18) 133-9.
Williams, Constance, *et al.* "American Verse Quotation." *N&Q* 173 (7 Ag 37) 104.

KING, GRACE ELIZABETH (1851-1932). Beer, William. "List of Writings of Grace King." *La Hist Q* 6 (Jl 23) 378-9.
Cocks, R. S. "The Fiction of Grace King." *La Hist Q* 6 (Jl 23) 353-9.
Faust, M. E. "In Memoriam: Grace King." *Bkm* 75 (Ag 32) 360-1.
Gilmer, E. M. "Dorothy Dix Talks on Miss King." *La Hist Q* 6 (Jl 23) 359-62.
Guyol, L. H. "A Southern Author in Her New New Orleans Home." *La Hist Q* 6 (Jl 23) 365-74.
Kendall, J. S. "A New Orleans Lady of Letters." *La Hist Q* 19 (Ap 36) 436-65.
Nott, G. W. "Grace King, Southern Novelist and Historian of Louisiana." *SLM* (N 23) 13-4.
Vaughan, Bess. "A Bio-Bibliography of Grace Elizabeth King." *La Hist Q* 17 (O 34) 752-70.

KIRKLAND, JACK (1901-). Day, Dorothy. "Tobacco Road." *Commonweal* 39 (N 43) 140-1.

KIRKLAND, JOSEPH (1830-94). Flanagan, J. T. "Joseph Kirkland, Pioneer Realist." *AL* 11 (N 39) 273-84.
——— "A Note on Joseph Kirkland." *AL* 12 (Mr 40) 107-8.
La Budde, K. J. "A Note on the Text of Joseph Kirkland's *Zury*." *AL* 20 (Ja 49) 452-5.

KNIGHT, SARAH KEMBLE (1666-1727). Titus, Anson. "Madam Sarah Knight, Her Diary and Her Times." *Bostonian Soc Pub* 9 (1912) 99-126.

KNORTZ, KARL (1841-1918). Frenz, Horst. "Karl Knortz, Interpreter of American Literature and Culture." *AGR* 13 (D 46) 27-30.

KNOWLES, FREDERIC LAWRENCE (1869-1905). French, J. L. "The Younger Poets of New England." *N E Mag* ns 33 (D 05) 424-8.

KREYMBORG, ALFRED (1883-). Carmer, Carl. "American Poets." *Theatre Arts* 14 (F 30) 177-8.
Crawford, N. A. "For Assimilators of Culture." *Poetry* 36 (My 30) 110-2.
——— "A Poet's Progress." *Poetry* 44 (Ag 34) 269-74.
Johns, Orrick. "Plays for Poet-Mimes." *Drama* 7 (Ag 18) 414-6.
Mansfield, M. S. "Whimsical Wisdom." *Poetry* 29 (Ja 27) 226-8.
Michelson, Max. "The Radicals." *Poetry* 8 (Je 16) 151-5.
Monroe, Harriet. "A Staccato Poet." *Poetry* 9 (O 16) 51-4.
Seiffert, M. A. "Kreymborg's Plays for Poet-mimes." *Poetry* 13 (Ja 19) 224-7.
Sherry, Laura. "Little Theatre Rhythms." *Poetry* 18 (Jl 21) 218-21.
Zabel, M. D. "Souvenirs." *Poetry* 35 (D 29) 168-9.

KRUTCH, JOSEPH WOOD (1893-). Baugh, Hansell. "Mutations of the Novel." *SR* 29 (O-D 31) 507-10.

Beach, J. W. "Mr. Krutch and Ideal Values in Literature." *International J Ethics* 48 (Jl 38) 487-97.
Glicksberg, C. I. "Joseph Wood Krutch: Critic of Despair." *SR* 44 (Ja-Mr 36) 77-93.
Grattan, C. H. "Open Letters to Lewisohn, Krutch, and Mumford." *Mod Mo* 7 (Ap 33) 175-81.
Hill, Helen. "Pause before Resurrection." *VQR* 9 (Ap 33) 313-5.
Hoffman, R. J. S. "Mr. Krutch and Europe." *Am R* 4 (N 34) 56-66.
Perry, R. B. "The Modern Distemper." *SRL* 5 (1 Je 29) 1063-4.

KYNE, PETER B. (1880-). Bode, Carl. "Cappy Ricks and the Monk in the Garden." *PMLA* 64 (Mr 49) 59-69.

LADD, JOSEPH BROWN (1764-86). Leary, Lewis. "A Forgotten Charleston Poet: Joseph Brown Ladd, 1764-1786." *Americana* 36 (O 42) 571-88.
——— "Joseph Brown Ladd of Charleston, 1764-1786." *So Atl Bul* 8 (D 42) 304.
——— "Ossian in America: A Note." *AL* 14 (N 42) 305-6.
——— "The Writings of Joseph Brown Ladd." *Bul Bibl* 18 (Ja-Ap 45) 131-3.

LA FARGE, OLIVER (1901-). Allen, Charles. "The Fiction of Oliver La Farge." *Ariz Q* 1 (Wi 45) 74-81.
Binsse, H. L. "Heaven in a Rage." *Commonweal* 44 (13 S 46) 527-8.
Bird, John. "The Future of Oliver La Farge." *Bkm* 72 (S 30) 11-4.
Bunker, Robert. "Oliver La Farge: In Search of Self." *N Mex Q* 20 (Su 50) 211-24.

LAMAR, MIRABEAU (1798-1859). Graham, Philip. "An Unsigned Poem by Mirabeau Lamar." *Un Texas Stud Eng* 13 (1933) 113-5.

LAMB, HAROLD (1892-). Hoffman, A. S. "Harold Lamb and Historical Romance." *Bkm* 71 (Mr 30) 40-3.

LANIER, SIDNEY (1842-81). Anon. "Lanier and Music." *Reader* 8 (Jl 06) 218-20.
——— "Sidney Lanier." *Johns Hopkins Alumni Mag* 5 (N 16) 1-2.
——— "Sidney Lanier." *Johns Hopkins News Letter* (12 F 29) 3-4.
Adams, R. G. "Notes and Queries: Correction by Lanier." *Colophon* ns 2 (Au 36) 153.
Allen, G. W. "Sidney Lanier as a Literary Critic." *PQ* 17 (Ap 38) 121-38.
Anderson, Charles. "Poet of the Pine Barrens." *Ga R* 1 (Fl 47) 280-93.
——— "Preparation for the Publication of the Centennial Edition of Sidney Lanier." *Year Book of Am Philos Soc* (1943) 234-8.
——— "Two Letters from Lanier to Holmes." *AL* 18 (Ja 47) 321-6.
Avery, M. L. "Lanier Urged for Hall of Fame." *Atlanta J* (30 Ap 33).
Baskervill, W. M. "Southern Literature." *PMLA* 7 (1892) 89-100.
Bassett, J. S. "The Struggles of Sidney Lanier." *Methodist R* 49 (Ja 00) 3-27.
Billing, B. M. "On Wings of Song." *SLM* 2 (Ja 40) 13-8.
Birss, J. H. "A Humorous Quatrain by Lanier." *AL* 5 (N 33) 270.
Bocock, Macklin. "Life of Sidney Lanier in Music and Poetry." *Va Gaz* (12 F 37) 6.
Bopes, C. F. "A Lost Occasional Poem by Sidney Lanier." *AL* 5 (N 33) 269.
Bourgeois, Y. R. "Sidney Lanier et le Goffic." *Revue Anglo-Amer* 8 (Je 31) 431-2.
Bradford, Gamaliel. "Portrait of Sidney Lanier." *NAR* 211 (Je 20) 805-17.
Cady, F. W. "Writings of Sidney Lanier." *SAQ* 13 (Ap 14) 156-73.
Christy, Arthur. "The Orientalism of Sidney Lanier." *Aryan Path* 5 (O 34) 638-41.
Clarke, G. H. "Some Early Letters and Reminiscences of Sidney Lanier." *Independent* 61 (8 N 06) 1092-8.
Cottman, G. S. "James F. D. Lanier." *Ind Mag Hist* 22 (Je 26) 194-202.

Daniel, R. N. "Sidney Lanier." *Furman Stud* 31 (Wi 48) 35-45.
Dobbin, I. L. "Lanier at the Peabody." *Peabody Bul* (Ap-My 11) 4-5.
Doyle, T. A. "The Indomitable Courage of Sidney Lanier." *Cath World* 156 (D 42) 293-301.
Ellerbe, J. E. "Sidney Lanier." *Confederate Veteran* 31 (Je 23) 210-1.
Fagin, N. B. "Sidney Lanier: Poet of the South." *Johns Hopkins Alumni Mag* 20 (Mr 32) 232-41.
Few, W. P. "Sidney Lanier as a Student of English Literature." *SAQ* 2 (Ap 03) 157-68.
Fletcher, J. G. "Sidney Lanier." *UKCR* 16 (Wi 49) 97-102.
Foerster, Norman. "Lanier as a Poet of Nature." *Nation* 108 (21 Je 19) 981-3.
French, J. C. "First Drafts of Lanier's Verse." *MLN* 48 (Ja 33) 27-31.
——— "New Lanier Letters." *Ex Libris* 4 (My 35) 3-4.
Furst, Clyde. "Concerning Sidney Lanier." *MLN* 14 (N 99) 197-205.
Garland, Hamlin. "Roadside Meetings of a Literary Nomad." *Bkm* 70 (D 29) 403-6.
Gibson, Count D. "The Wonderful Marshes of Glynn." *Emory Un Q* 3 (Je 47) 116-21.
Gilman, D. C. "The Launching of a University." *Scribner's* 31 (Mr 02) 327-36.
——— "Pleasant Incidents of an Academic Life." *Scribner's* 31 (My 02) 614-24.
——— "Reminiscences of Sidney Lanier." *Pathfinder* 1 (S 06) 205.
——— "Sidney Lanier: Reminiscences and Letters." *SAQ* 4 (Ap 05) 115-22.
Goodnow, F. J. "Lanier and the University." *John Hopkins Alumni Mag* 14 (Je 26) 503-5.
Graham, Philip. "Lanier and Science." *AL* 4 (N 32) 288-92.
——— "Lanier's Reading." *Un Texas Stud Eng* 11 (1931) 63-89.
——— "A Note on Lanier's Music." *Un Texas Stud Eng* 17 (1937) 107-11.
Greenlaw, Edwin. "A Sidney Lanier Professorship at Johns Hopkins." *Johns Hopkins Alumni Mag* 18 (Ja 29) 136-41.
Guest, Boyd. "Sidney Lanier's Feminine Ideal." *Ga Hist Q* 32 (S 48) 175-8.
Hankins, J. DeW. "Unpublished Letters of Sidney Lanier." *SLM* 2 (Ja 40) 5-11.
Harman, H. E. "Sidney Lanier—A Study." *SAQ* 14 (O 15) 301-6.
——— "A Study of Sidney Lanier's 'The Symphony.'" *SAQ* 17 (Ja 18) 32-9.
Henneman, J. B. "The Biography of Sidney Lanier." *SR* 14 (Jl 06) 352-7.
——— "The National Element in Southern Literature." *SR* 11 (Jl 03) 345-66.
Hollar, R. H. "Lanier, Agrarian Poet-Prophet." *SLM* 3 (F 41) 71-3.
Hubbell, J. B. "A Commencement Address by Sidney Lanier." *AL* 2 (Ja 31) 385-404.
——— "A Lanier Manuscript." *Lib Notes* (Duke Un) 2 (N 37) 2-3.
Huckel, Oliver. "The Genius of the Modern in Lanier." *Johns Hopkins Alumni Mag* 14 (Je 26) 484-503.
Jackson, L. E. "Sidney Lanier in Florida." *Fla Hist Soc Q* 15 (O 36) 118-24.
———, & Starke, Aubrey. "New Light on the Ancestry of Sidney Lanier." *VMHB* 43 (Ap 35) 160-8.
Kaufman, M. F. "Sidney Lanier, Poet Laureate of the South." *Methodist R* 82 (Ja 00) 94-107.
Kelly, Frederick. "Lanier's House on Denmead Street." *Md Hist Mag* 36 (Je 41) 231-2.
——— "Sidney Lanier at the Peabody Institute." *Peabody Bul* (D 39).
Kent, C. W. "A Study of Lanier's Poems." *PMLA* 7 (Ap 92) 33-63.
Klemm, G. "Sidney Lanier: Poet, Man and Musician." *Etude* 59 (My 41) 299-300.
Kuhl, E. P. "Sidney Lanier and Edward Spencer." *SP* 27 (Jl 30) 462-76.
Lamar, Mrs. W. D., *et al.* "Sidney Lanier Committee." *United Daughters of Confederacy Mag* 11 (F 48) 8-9.
Lanier, C. A. "Sidney Lanier." *Gulf States Hist Mag* 2 (Jl 03) 9-17.
Lanier, H. W. "In a Poet's Workshop: Poems Outlines by Sidney Lanier." *Century* 76 (O 08) 847-50.

Leary, Lewis. "The Forlorn Hope of Sidney Lanier." *SAQ* 46 (Ap 47) 263-71.
Le Gallienne, Richard. "The Poetry of Lanier." *Living Age* 224 (31 Mr 00) 840-3.
Mabie, H. W. "Sidney Lanier." *Outlook* 71 (24 My 02) 236-9.
McCowan, H. S. "Sidney Lanier, Bard of the South." *Self-Culture* 10 (Ja 00) 398-400.
McNaspy, A. T. "Sidney Lanier, Bard of the South.' *Signet* 12 (O 31) 16-20.
Magruder, M. L. "The Laniers." *SLM* 2 (Ja 40) 26-7.
Malone, Kemp. "Sidney Lanier." *Johns Hopkins Alumni Mag* 21 (Mr 33) 224-49.
Mayfield, J. S. "Lanier in Lastekas." *Sw R* 17 (O 31) 20-38.
——— "Lanier's Trail in Texas." *Texas Mo* 3 (Mr 29) 329-37.
——— "Sidney Lanier in Texas." *Texas Mo* 2 (D 28) 650-67.
——— "Sidney Lanier's Friendship with Charlotte Cushman." *Atlanta J* (21 Jl 35).
——— "Sidney Lanier's Immoral Bird." *Am Book Coll* 6 (My-Je 35) 200-3.
——— "Sidney Lanier's War Experiences." *Macon Telegraph* (31 Jl 37).
Miles, J. T. "Lanier." *SLM* 1 (S 39) 599.
Moore, E. H. "Sidney Lanier." *Ala Hist Q* 5 (Sp 43) 35-46.
Northrup, M. N. "Sidney Lanier: Recollections and Letters." *Lippincott's* 75 (Mr 05) 302-15.
Oehser, P. H. "The Poet Who Sang a Song." *Light &Life Evangel* 38 (4 F 34) 1.
——— "Sidney Lanier, Nature Poet." *Nature Mag* 35 (N 42) 468, 500.
Oliphant, Jean. "Wesleyan College Presents Sidney Lanier, Flutist." *Wesleyan Alumnae* 1 (Ja 25) 4-9.
Olney, Clark. "Archaisms in the Poetry of Sidney Lanier." *N&Q* 166 (28 Ap 34) 292-4.
Orr, Oliver. "Sidney Lanier's Fame and Memorials." *SLM* 2 (Ja 40) 28-32.
Oxnam, G. B. "Sidney Lanier, a Prophet of the Social Awakening." *Methodist R* 99 (Ja 17) 86-90.
Payne, L. W., Jr. "Sydney Lanier's Lectures." *SR* 11 (O 03) 452-62.
Pickett, L. C. "The Sunrise Poet." *Lippincott's* 88 (D 11) 851-8.
Pollard, E. B. "The Spiritual Message of Sidney Lanier." *Homiletic R* 74 (Ag 17) 91-5.
Ransom, J. C. "Hearts and Heads." *Am R* 2 (Mr 34) 554-71.
Rede, Kenneth. "Lanier's 'Owl against Robin.'" *Am Col* 3 (O 26) 27-30.
——— "The Sidney Lanier Memorial Alcove." *Am Book Coll* 3 (My-Je 33) 300-4.
Reese, L. W. "The Spirituality of Lanier." *Johns Hopkins Alumni Mag* 14 (Je 26) 482-4.
Roberts, F. S. "The Lanier Brothers of Georgia." *Confederate Veteran* 27 (O 19) 376.
Roquie, M. B. "Sidney Lanier, Poet-Musician." *Etude* 55 (S 37) 576, 617.
Roseberg, M. T. "Sidney Lanier, Poet of Democracy." *SLM* 6 (Mr-Ap 44) 195-9.
Sapir, Edward. "The Musical Foundations of Verse." *JEGP* 20 (2nd Quar 21) 213-28.
Shackford, J. A. "Sidney Lanier as Southerner." *SR* 48 (Ap, Jl, O 40) 153-73, 348-55, 480-93.
Shepherd, H. E. "Sidney Lanier." *Cur Lit* 32 (Ja 02) 108-11.
Short, J. S. "Sidney Lanier at Johns Hopkins." *Johns Hopkins Alumni Mag* 5 (N 16) 7-24.
——— "Sidney Lanier, 'Familiar Citizen of the Town.'" *Md Hist Mag* 35 (Je 40) 121-46.
Sillard, P. A. "Sidney Lanier and His Poetry." *Am Cath Quar R* 44 (Ja 19) 33-9.
Smith, C. F. "Sidney Lanier as Poet." *Methodist R* 51 (Mr-Ap 02) 196-210.
Snoddy, J. S. "Color and Motion in Sidney Lanier." *Poet-Lore* 4 (O-D 00) 558-70.
Spiller, R. E. "Sidney Lanier: Ancestor of Anti-Realism." *SRL* 21 (10 Ja 48) 6-7 24.
Starke, Aubrey. "The Agrarians Deny a Leader." *Am R* 2 (Mr 34) 534-53.
——— "Annulet Andrews: Poet." *SAQ* 35 (Ap 36) 194-200.

——— "Lanier, the Unknown Man." *Atlanta J* (20 Ag 33) 6, 18.
——— "Lanier's Appreciation of Whitman." *Am Schol* 2 (O 33) 398-408.
——— "More about Lanier." *NRp* 76 (1 N 33) 337-8.
——— "An Omnibus of Poets." *Colophon* 4 (Mr 34) Pt 16.
——— "Sidney Lanier and Paul Hamilton Hayne: Three Unpublished Letters." *AL* 1 (Mr 29) 32-9.
——— "Sidney Lanier as a Musician." *Musical Q* 20 (O 34) 384-400.
——— "Sidney Lanier, Man of Science in the Field of Letters." *Am Schol* 2 (O 33) 389-97.
——— "An Uncollected Sonnet by Sidney Lanier." *AL* 7 (Ja 36) 460-3.
——— "William Dean Howells and Sidney Lanier." *Am R* 3 (Mr 31) 79-82.
———, & Harrison, J. M. "Maternal Ancestors of Sidney Lanier." *VMHB* 44 (Ja, Ap 36) 73-80, 160-74.
Swiggett, G. L. "Sidney Lanier." *Conservative R* 5 (S 01) 187-92.
Tate, Allen. "More about Lanier." *NRp* 76 (1 N 33) 338.
——— "A Southern Romantic." *NRp* 76 (30 Ag 33) 67-70.
Thorpe, H. C. "Sidney Lanier: Poet for Musicians." *Musical Q* 11 (Jl 25) 373-82.
Voigt, G. P. "Sidney Lanier." *SRL* 13 (4 Ap 36).
Warren, R. P. "The Blind Poet: Sidney Lanier." *Am R* 2 (N 33) 27-45.
Watkins, M. A. "Sidney Lanier, Musician, Poet of the Confederacy." *Confederate Veteran* 40 (D 32) 426-7.
Whicher, G. F. "Lanier: Inheritor of Unfulfilled Fame." *N Y Herald-Tribune Books* 23 (25 Ag 46) 1-2.
——— "Sidney Lanier's Letters." *Forum* 104 (O 46) 354-8.
White, E. L. "Reminiscences of Sidney Lanier." *Johns Hopkins Alumni Mag* 17 (Je 29) 329-31.
Whiteside, M. B. "Lanier and the Path to Fame." *Westminster Mag* 16 (S 31) 57-61.
Wood, Clement. "The Influence of Poe and Lanier on Modern Literature." *SLM* 1 (Ap 39) 237-40.
——— "Lanier's Religion Was Unorthodox." *SLM* 1 (S 39) 641.
Woolen, Mrs. L. L. "Sidney Lanier." *United Daughters of Confederacy Mag* 11 (F 48) 10-1.
Woolf, W. P. "The Poetry of Sydney Lanier." *SR* 10 (Jl 02) 325-40.
——— "Sydney Lanier as Revealed in His Letters." *SR* 8 (Jl 00) 346-64.
Wright, Nathalia. "The East Tennessee Background of Sidney Lanier's *Tiger-Lilies*." *AL* 19 (My 47) 127-38.

LARDNER, RING (1885-1933). Anon. "Ring Lardner, Interpretor of Life." *Lit Dig* 118 (14 O 33) 19.
Anderson, Sherwood. "Four American Impressions." *NRp* 32 (11 O 22) 171-3.
——— "Meeting Ring Lardner." *NYr* 9 (25 N 33) 36, 38.
Bibesco, Elizabeth. "Lament for Lardner." *Living Age* 345 (D 33) 366-8.
Douglas, Donald. "Ring Lardner as Satirist." *Nation* 122 (26 My 26) 584-5.
Fadiman, Clifton. "Ring Lardner and the Triangle of Hate." *Nation* 136 (22 Mr 33) 315-7.
Farrell, J. T. "Ring Lardner's Success-Mad World." *N Y Times Book R* (18 Je 44) 8, 18.
Fitzgerald, F. S. "Ring." *NRp* 76 (11 O 33) 254-5.
Kasten, M. C. "The Satire of Ring Lardner." *EJ* 36 (Ap 47) 192-5.
Matthews, T. S. "Lardner, Shakespeare and Chekhov." *NRp* 59 (22 My 29) 35-6.
Mencken, H. L. "A Humorist Shows His Teeth." *Am Merc* 8 (Je 26) 254.
Nevins, Allan. "The American Moron." *SRL* 5 (8 Je 29) 89-90.
Overton, Grant. "Ring W. Lardner's Bell-Lettres." *Bkm* 62 (S 25) 44-9.
R., D. "The Reigning Jester." *Independent* 114 (23 My 25) 590.
Tittle, Walter. "Glimpses of Interesting Americans." *Century* 110 (Jl 25) 313-7.

Van Doren, Carl. "Beyond Grammar: Ring Lardner, Philologist among the Low-brows." *Century* 106 (Jl 23) 471-5.
Wheeler, J. M. "Ring Lardner." *Collier's* 81 (17 Mr 28) 16, 44.
Wilson, Edmund. "Mr. Lardner's American Characters." *Dial* 77 (Jl 24) 69-72.

LAWRENCE, JOSEPHINE (*ca.* 1900-). Guilfoil, Kelsey. "Josephine Lawrence: The Voice of the People." *EJ* 38 (S 49) 365-70.

LAZARUS, EMMA (1849-87). Baym, M. I. "Emma Lazarus and Emerson." *Pub Am Jewish Hist Soc* 38 (Je 49) 261-87.
——— "Emma Lazarus's Approach to Renan." *Pub Am Jewish Hist Soc* 36 (Ja 47) 17-29.
——— "A Neglected Translator of Italian Poetry: Emma Lazarus." *Ital* 21 (D 44) 175-85.
Burton, Katherine. "A Princess in Israel." *Cath World* 157 (My 43) 190-5.
Mordell, Albert. "Some Final Words on Emma Lazarus." *Pub Am Jewish Hist Soc* 39 (Mr 50) 321-7.
——— "Some Neglected Phases of Emma Lazarus's Genius." *Jewish Forum* 32 (O 49) 181-2, 187.
Price, W. J. "Three Forgotten Poetesses." *Forum* 47 (Mr 12) 361-76.
Schappes, M. U. "The Letters of Emma Lazarus, 1868-1885." *BNYPL* 53 (Jl, Ag, S 49) 315-34, 367-86, 419-46.

LEA, HENRY CHARLES (1825-1909). Anon. "150 Years of Publishing: Lea and Febiger, Medical Book Publishers of Philadelphia, Celebrate Their Sesquicentennial This Year." *Pub W* 127 (16 F 35) 781-3.

LEE, ARTHUR (1740-92). Smith, G. C. "Dr. Arthur Lee: Political Pamphleteer of Pre-Revolutionary Virginia." *Madison Q* 3 (My 43) 130-7.

LEE, RICHARD (1732-94). Lee, Richard. "Narrative of Richard Lee." *Proc Vt Hist Soc* 11 (Je 43) 77-94.

LEE, RICHARD II (1647-1714). Ellis, Milton. "Richard Lee II, Elizabethan Humanist or Middle-Class Planter?" *WMQ* 21 (Ja 41) 29-32.
Wright, L. B. "Richard Lee II, a Belated Elizabethan in Virginia." *HLQ* 2 (1938) 1-35.

LEE, SAMUEL (1625-91). Hornberger, Theodore. "Samuel Lee (1625-1691), A Clerical Channel for the Flow of New Ideas to Seventeenth Century New England." *Osiris* 1 (Ja 36) 341-55.

LEGARÉ, HUGH (1797-1843). Davis, R. B. "The Early American Lawyer and the Profession of Letters." *HLQ* 12 (F 49) 191-205.
Ramage, B. J. "Hugh Swinton Legaré." *SR* 10 (Ja, Ap 02) 43-55, 167-80.

LEGARÉ, JAMES M. (1823-59). Davis, C. C. "A Letter from the Muses: Publication and Critical Reception of James M. Legaré's *Orta-Undis, and Other Poems* (1848)." *N C Hist R* 26 (O 49) 417-38.
——— "Poet, Painter and Inventor: Some Letters by James Mathewes Legaré, 1823-1859." *N C Hist R* 21 (Jl 44) 215-31.
Parks, E. W. "Legaré and Grayson: Types of Classical Influence on Criticism in the Old South." *Sw R* 22 (Jl 37) 354-65.

LEGGETT, WILLIAM (1801-39). Glicksberg, C. I. "William Leggett, Neglected Figure of American Literary History." *J Q* 25 (Mr 48) 52-8.
Hofstadter, Richard. "William Leggett, Spokesman of Jacksonian Democracy." *Pol Sci Q* 58 (D 43) 581-94.

Proctor, P. S., Jr. "William Leggett (1801-1839) ; Journalist and Liberator." *PBSA* 46 (3 Q 50) 239-53.

LELAND, CHARLES GODFREY (1824-1903). Bradley, Sculley. "'Hans Breitmann' in England and America." *Colophon* ns 2 (Au 36) 65-81.
Glicksberg, C. I. "Charles Godfrey Leland and *Vanity Fair*." *PMHB* 62 (Jl 38) 309-23.
——— "A Friend of Walt Whitman." *Am Book Coll* 6 (Mr 35) 91-4.
Masefield, John. "Hans Breitmann." *Academy* (4 Ap 03).
Pennell, E. R. "A Bundle of Old Letters." *Atl* 95 (Mr 05) 309-28.
Thalmann, Marianne. "Hans Breitmann." *PMLA* 54 (Je 39) 578-88.

LEONARD, WILLIAM ELLERY (1876-1944). Boehme, Traugott. "Mr. Leonard's Fables." *Open Court* 23 (N 19) 709-12.
Cason, C. E. "William Ellery Leonard." *VQR* 4 (Jl 28) 359-66.
Clough, W. O. "William Ellery Leonard, Teacher." *Prairie Schooner* 20 (Sp 46) 23-7.
Duffy, Charles. "A Letter from Leonard to Charles Bulger." *Akron Alumnus* (Jl 48) np.
——— "W. E. Leonard's Annotations in a Copy of 'Poems, 1916-1917.'" *MLN* 63 (Mr 48) 185-7.
Fairclough, H. R. "The Classics and Our Twentieth Century Poets." *Stanford Un Pub* 2 (1927) 1-50.
Griswold, Louise. "The Poetical Work of William Ellery Leonard." *Quar J Un No Dak* 2 (Ja 26) 149-63.
Jones, H. M. "William Ellery Leonard." *Double Dealer* 8 (My 26) 332-8.
Jorgenson, C. E. "William Ellery Leonard." *Am Prefaces* 1 (Ja 36) 51-4.
Leiser, Clara. "A Little about William Ellery Leonard." *Un R* 2 (Wi 35) 103-10.
——— "William Ellery Leonard: Some Memories and New Poems." *Tomorrow* 8 (My 49) 37-41.
Leonard, W. E. "The Poetic Process from the Inside." *Bkm* 75 (Ag 32) 327-33.
Lewisohn, Ludwig. "Poet and Scholar." *Nation* 116 (6 Je 23) 660-1.
——— "The Problem of Modern Poetry." *Bkm* 48 (Ja 19) 550-7.
Meyer, E. L. "William Ellery Leonard." *Am Merc* 32 (Jl 34) 334-40.
Minton, A. "William Ellery Leonard." *Plain Talk* 7 (Jl 30) 110-6.
Monroe, Harriet. "A Modern Agonist." *Poetry* 27 (F 26) 272-5.
Scott, W. T. "Professor as Poet." *Poetry* 67 (F 46) 260-5.
Taylor, W. S., & Culler, E. K. "The Problem of the Locomotive-God." *J Abnormal Psychol* 23 (O 29) 342-99; 25 (O 31) 340-1.

LERNER, ALAN JAY (1918-). Krumpelmann, J. T. "Gerstaecker's 'Germelshausen' and Lerner's 'Brigadoon.'" *Monatshefte* 40 (N 48) 396-400.

LESLIE, ELIZA (1787-1858). Smith, O. D. "Charles and Eliza Leslie." *PMHB* 74 (O 50) 512-27.

LE VERT, MRS. OCTAVIA (1810-77). Anon. "Madame Le Vert's Diary." *Ala Hist Q* 3 (Sp 41) 31-54.
Keis, P. P. "Mrs. Le Vert Visits the Brownings." *Res Stud State Col Wash* 17 (Je 49) 67-72.

LEWIS, JAMES FRANKLIN (1903-). Fletcher, J. G. "On the Poetry of James Franklin Lewis." *UKCR* 13 (Wi 46) 151-3.
Raymund, Bernard. "The Spiral Stair: On Some of the Later Poems of James Franklin Lewis." *UKCR* 13 (Wi 46) 153-4.
Waggoner, H. H. "Poet and Scientist." *UKCR* 13 (Wi 46) 148-51.

LEWIS, RICHARD (1699?-1733?). Carlson, C. L. "Richard Lewis and the Reception of His Work in England." *AL* 9 (N 37) 301-16.

Norris, W. B. "Some Recently-found Poems of the Calverts." *Md Hist Mag* 32 (Je 37) 112-36.

LEWIS, SINCLAIR (1885-1951). Anon. "Lewis Travels Far." *Lit Dig* 115 (4 Mr 33) 18-9.

——— "Newspaper Comments on the Dreiser-Lewis Quarrel." *Lit Dig* 109 (Ap 31) 15-6.

——— "A Reviewer's Notebook." *Freeman* 6 (18 O 22) 142-3.

——— "Sinclair Lewis." *Bkm* 55 (S 22) 54-9.

——— "Sinclair Lewis." *SRL* 7 (22 N 30) 357.

——— "W.P.A. to Present Sinclair Lewis Play." *Chri Sci Mon* 28 (22 Ag 36) 2.

Abbott, L. F. "Honoré de Balzac and Sinclair Lewis." *Outlook* 146 (6 Jl 27) 307-9.

Ames, Russell. "Sinclair Lewis Again." *CE* 10 (N 48) 77-80.

Anderson, Sherwood. 'Four American Impressions." *NRp* 32 (11 O 22) 171-3.

Baker, J. E. "Sinclair Lewis, Plato, and the Regional Escape." *EJ* (Col ed) 28 (Je 39) 460-72.

Baldensperger, Fernand. "Un romancier Américain d'aujourd'hui, M. Sinclair Lewis." *Correspondant* 301 (25 D 25) 835-54.

Beck, Warren. "How Good Is Sinclair Lewis?" *CE* 9 (Ja 48) 173-80.

Bellesort, André. "Sinclair Lewis." *Correspondant* 324 (10 Je 31) 119-28.

Benét, W. R. "The Earlier Lewis." *SRL* 10 (20 Ja 34) 421-2.

Binsse, H. L., & Trounstine, J. J. "Europe Looks at Sinclair Lewis." *Bkm* 72 (Ja 31) 453-7.

Bogardus, E. S. "Social Distance in Fiction: Analyses of Main Street." *Sociology & Social Res* 14 (N-D 29) 174-80.

Boynton, P. H. "Sinclair Lewis." *EJ* 16 (Ap 27) 251-60.

Cabell, J. B. "A Note as to Sinclair Lewis." *Am Merc* 20 (Ag 30) 394-7.

Calverton, V. F. "The Prodigal Lewis." *Mod Mo* 10 (F 38) 11-3, 16.

——— "Sinclair Lewis, the Last of the Literary Liberals." *Mod Mo* 8 (Mr 34) 77-86.

Canby, H. S. "Fighting Success." *SRL* 1 (7 Mr 25) 575.

——— "Schmaltz, Babbitt & Co." *SRL* 4 (24 Mr 28) 697-8.

——— "Sinclair Lewis." *ASR* 19 (F 31) 73-6.

——— "Sinclair Lewis's Art of Work." *SRL* 10 (10 F 34) 465-73.

Cantwell, Robert. "Sinclair Lewis." *NRp* 88 (21 O 36) 298-301.

Chesterton, G. K. "Chesterton Sums Us Up—Paradoxically." *N Y Times Mag* 80 (12 Jl 31) 405.

Compton, C. H. "The Librarian and the Novelist." *SAQ* 26 (O 27) 392-403.

Cowley, Malcolm. "Nobel Prize Oration." *NRp* 88 (19 Ag 36) 36-8.

Crocker, Lionel. "Sinclair Lewis on Public Speaking." *QJS* 21 (Ap 35) 232-7.

Davis, Elmer. "Sinclair Lewis's Hick of Genius." *SRL* 10 (27 Ja 34) 433, 437.

DeCasseres, Bernard. "Portraits en Brochette." *Bkm* 73 (Jl 31) 487-8.

Deming, Charlotte. "Sinclair Lewis." *Der Gral* (Ap 31) 637-43.

DeVilleneuve, R. "Le Nationalisme de Sinclair Lewis." *Mercure de France* 280 (1 D 37) 286-307.

DeVoto, Bernard. "Sinclair Lewis." *SRL* 9 (22 Ja 33) 397-8.

Durtain, Luc. "Un Témoin des États-Unis: Le Romancier Sinclair Lewis." *Revue Hebdomadaire* (30 N 29) 554-64.

Elgström, Anna Lenah. "Sinclair Lewis gör come back." *Samtid och Framtid* 2 (S 45) 428-35.

Fadiman, Clifton. "Nobel Prizewinner." *NYr* 11 (13 Jl 35) 56-8.

Faÿ, Bernard. "Portrait de Sinclair Lewis: l'Américain à rebroussepoil." *Revue de Paris* (15 My 34) 401-16.

Fischer, Walther. "Samuel Dodsworth bereist Europa." *Nachrichten der Giessener Hochschulgesellschaft* 9 (Je 33) 31-42.

Fisk, E. E. "The Chesterton-Drinkwater-Lewis Affair." *Bkm* 58 (Ja 24) 538-40.

Flanagan, J. T. "A Long Way to Gopher Prairie: Sinclair Lewis's Apprenticeship." *Sw R* 32 (Au 47) 403-13.
Forsythe, Robert. "Sinclair Lewis's Good Intentions." *New Masses* 25 (30 N 37) 12.
Gale, Zona. "The American Village Defended." *N Y Times Mag* 80 (19 Jl 31) 1-2, 21.
Gannett, Lewis. "Sinclair Lewis: 'Main Street.'" *SRL* 32 (6 Ag 49) 31-2.
Gauss, C. S. "Sinclair Lewis *vs* His Education." *Sat Eve Post* 204 (26 D 31) 20-1, 54-6.
Geismar, Maxwell. "Diarist of the Middle-Class Mind." *SRL* 30 (1 N 47) 9-10, 42-5.
——— "Young Sinclair Lewis and Old Dos Passas." *Am Merc* 56 (My 43) 624-8.
Grunwald, Henry Anatole. "Main Street 1947." *Life* 22 (23 Je 47) 100-2, 104, 107-8, 110, 113-4.
Gurko, Leo & Miriam. "The Two Main Streets of Sinclair Lewis." *CE* 4 (F 43) 288-92.
Hansen, Harry. "Fashions in Fiction." *Forum* 89 (Mr 33) 152-5.
Hibler, Leo von. "Sinclair Lewis und die Amerikanische Wirtschaft." *Anglia* 59 (Jl 35) 448-60.
Hicks, Granville. "Sinclair Lewis and the Good Life." *EJ* 25 (Ap 36) 265-73.
——— "Sinclair Lewis's Stink Bomb." *New Masses* 26 (25 Ja 38) 19-20.
Hoyt, B. T. "Sinclair Lewis as Seen by an Average Reader." *MS* 5 (D 33) 5.
Horton, T. D. "Sinclair Lewis: The Symbol of an Era." *NAR* 248 (Wi 39-40) 374-93.
Hülsenbeck, Richard. "Sinclair Lewis." *Living Age* 339 (Ja 31) 479-82.
Johnson, A. T. "Realism in Contemporary American Literature: Notes on Dreiser, Anderson, Lewis." *SW Bul* (S 29) 3-16.
Jones, H. M. "Mr. Lewis's America." *VQR* 7 (Jl 31) 427-32.
Karlfeldt, E. A. "Sinclair Lewis and the Nobel Prize." *SRL* 7 (10 Ja 31) 524-5.
Krutch, J. W. "Dodsworth." *Nation* 138 (14 Mr 34) 311-2.
LeVerrier, Charles. "La Femme affranchie d'après M. Sinclair Lewis: Ann Vickers." *Revue Hebdomadaire* (13 My 33) 228-38.
Lewis, Sinclair. "And That Was Me." *NYr* 12 (2 Ja 37) 20-1.
——— "Breaking into Print." *Colophon* ns 2 (Wi 37) 217-21.
——— "Enemies of the Book." *Pub W* 129 (23 My 36) 2011-4.
——— "I'm an Old Newspaperman Myself." *Cosmopolitan* no 730 (Ap 47) 27.
——— "Main Street's Been Paved." *Nation* 119 (10 S 24) 260.
——— "Mr. Lorimer and Me." *Nation* 127 (25 Jl 28) 81-2.
——— "Self-Conscious America." *Am Merc* 6 (O 25) 135.
Loiseau, Jean. "La Croisade de Sinclair Lewis." *Etudes Anglaises* 2 (Ap-Je 38) 120-33.
McCole, C. J. "The Future Significance of Sinclair Lewis." *Cath World* 132 (D 30) 314-22.
McNally, W. J. "Mr. Babbitt Meet Mr. Lewis." *Nation* 125 (21 S 27) 278-81.
Mainsard, Joseph. "Les Américains d'après S. Lewis." *Etudes* 211 (14 Ap 30) 23-47.
Marshall, Archibald. "Gopher Prairie." *NAR* 215 (Mr 22) 394-402.
Maurice, A. B. "Sinclair Lewis." *Bkm* 69 (Mr 29) 52-3.
Morris, Lloyd. "Sinclair Lewis—His Critics and the Public." *NAR* 245 (Su 38) 381-90.
Mumford, Lewis. "The America of Sinclair Lewis." *Cur Hist* 33 (Ja 31) 529-33.
Murry, J. M. "The Hell It Can't." *Adelphi* 11 (Mr 36) 321-7.
Muzzey, D. S. "Sinclair Lewis's Attack on the Clergy." *Standard* 17 (Jl 27) 7-10.
Neumann, Henry. "Arrowsmith, a Study in Vocational Ethics." *Am R* 4 (Mr 26) 184-92.
O'Dell, G. E. "The American Mind and Main Street." *Standard* 8 (Jl 22) 17-20.

Overton, Grant. "The Salvation of Sinclair Lewis." *Bkm* 61 (Ap 25) 179-85.
Phelps, W. L. "As I Like It." *Scribner's* 89 (Mr 31) 325-8; 93 (Ap 33) 256.
——— "Mr. Lewis's Fourteenth Novel." *Scribner's* 99 (Ja 36) 59-60.
Russell, F. T. "The Growing Up of Sinclair Lewis." *Un Calif Chron* 32 (Jl 30) 319-24.
——— "The Young Mr. Lewis." *Un Calif Chron* 30 (O 28) 417-27.
Seligmann, H. J. "The Tragi-Comedy of Main Street." *Freeman* 2 (17 N 20) 237.
Sherwood, R. E. "Is the Nobel Prize an Insult?" *Scribner's* 89 (Ja 31) 11-2.
Shillito, Edward. "'Elmer Gantry' and the Church in America." *Nineteenth Century* 101 (My 27) 739-48.
Soule, G. H., Jr. "A Novelist with a Future." *Book News Mo* 34 (Ja 16) 208-10.
Spitz, Leon. "Sinclair Lewis' Prof. Gottlieb." *Am Hebrew* 158 (3 D 48) 2, 10.
Stolbert, Benjamin. "Sinclair Lewis." *Am Merc* 53 (O 41) 450-60.
Van Doren, Carl. "The Real Sinclair Lewis." *N Y Herald-Tribune Mag* (17 F 35) 5, 22.
——— "Sinclair Lewis and Sherwood Anderson." *Century* 110 (Jl 25) 362-9.
Velte, F. M. "Sinclair Lewis." *Mod Librarian* 3 (Ap 33) 129-34, 136.
Waldeman, Milton. "Sinclair Lewis." *London Merc* 13 (Ja 26) 273-81.
Williams, Michael. "Babbittry into Vickery." *Commonweal* 17 (22 Mr 33) 567-9.
——— "The Sinclair Lewis Industry." *Commonweal* 5 (30 Mr 27) 577-9.
Woodward, W. E. "Sinclair Lewis Gets the Job." *SRL* 30 (1 N 47) 10-1.
——— "The World and Sauk Centre." *NYr* 10 (27 Ja, 3 F 34) 24-7, 24-7.
Zweig, Arnold. "Improvisation über Sinclair Lewis." *Die Literatur* 33 (Ja 31) 185-6.

LEWISOHN, LUDWIG (1882-). Adeney, Marcus. "A Voice from Israel." *Canadian Bkm* 12 (S 30) 179-82.
Austin, Mary. "Up Stream." *Dial* 72 (22 Je 22) 634-9.
Bates, E. S. "Lewisohn into Crump." *Am Merc* 31 (Ap 34) 441-50.
Brande, Dorothea. "Mr. Lewisohn Interprets America." *Am R* 2 (D 33) 189-98.
Bridges, H. J. "Mr. Lewisohn versus America." *Standard* 8 (Jl 23) 14-23.
Goldberg, Isaac. "Ludwig Backstream Lewisohn." *Am Spect* 2 (O 36) 13-4.
Grattan, C. H. "Open Letters to Lewisohn, Krutch, and Mumford." *Mod Mo* 7 (Ap 33) 175-81.
Lewisohn, Ludwig. "Ludwig Lewisohn." *Nation* 117 (21 N 23) 583-4.
Lowell, Amy. "The Case of Modern Poetry versus Professor Lewisohn." *Bkm* 48 (D 19) 558-66.
Moody, M. H. "Impressions of Expression." *SR* 40 (O-D 32) 506-8.
Snider, C. L. "Tolerance." *VQR* 2 (O 26) 623-30.
Wharton, Don. "Dorothy Thompson." *Scribner's* 101 (My 37) 9-14.

LEYPOLDT, FREDERICK (1835-84). Osborne, M. A. "Some Memories of My Father and Mother." *Pub W* 151 (18 Ja 47) 284-5.
Rider, Fremont. "The Origin and Early History of the Weekly." *Pub W* 151 (18 Ja 47) 272-8.
Scherer, George. "Frederick Leypoldt and the Dragon." *AGR* 10 (D 43) 6-9.

LIBBEY, LAURA JEAN (1862-1924). Gold, Louis. "Laura Jean Libbey." *Am Merc* 24 (S 31) 47-52.

LIDDELL, MARK H. (1866-1936). More, P. E. "Rhythm and the Science of Poetry." *SR* 10 (O 02) 406-17.

LIEBER, FRANCIS (1800-72). Freidel, Frank. "Francis Lieber, Charles Sumner, and Slavery." *J So Hist* 9 (F 43) 75-93.
——— "Lieber's Contribution to the International Copyright Movement." *HLQ* 8 (F 45) 200-6.

LINCOLN, ABRAHAM (1809-65). Anon. "The Gettysburg Address." *TLS* no 2, 466 (6 My 49) 304.
——— "Lincoln as His Friends and Admirers Knew Him during His Life Time." *Touchstone* 2 (N 17) 94-7.
——— "Lincoln's Pocket." *Friends' Intelligencer* 102 (10 F 45) 86-7.
——— "Poetical Cult of Lincoln." *Nation* 108 (17 My 19) 777.
Angle, P. M. "Four Lincoln Firsts." *PBSA* 36 (1Q 42) 1-17.
——— "The Minor Collection: A Criticism." *Atl* 143 (Ap 29) 516-25.
Ayres, P. W. "Lincoln as a Neighbor." *Rev of Rev* 57 (F 18) 183-5.
Barton, W. E. "A Noble Fragment: Beveridge's Life of Lincoln." *Miss Valley Hist R* 15 (Mr 29) 497-510.
Basler, R. P. "Abraham Lincoln—Artist." *NAR* 245 (Sp 38) 144-53.
——— "Abraham Lincoln's Rhetoric." *AL* 11 (My 39) 167-82.
——— "The Authorship of the 'Rebecca' Letters." *Abraham Lincoln Q* 2 (Je 42) 80-90.
——— "Who Wrote the 'Letter to Mrs. Bixby'?" *Lincoln Herald* 45 (F 43) 9-14.
Bayne, J. T. "Tad Lincoln's Father." *Atl* 133 (My 24) 660-5.
Benzanson, W. E. "Lincoln and Douglas and the Naughty Nursery Rhyme." *JRUL* 14 (D 50) 9-13.
Berry, M. F. "Lincoln—the Speaker." *QJS* 17 (F, Ap 31) 25-40, 177-90.
Blanck, Jacob. "Antiquarian Book Notes." *Antiq Bkm* 1 (7 F 48) 219-20.
Bready, J. W. "Shaftesbury and Lincoln." *Dalhousie R* 8 (Ap 28) 67-72.
Burt, S. W. "Lincoln on His Own Story Telling." *Century* 73 (F 07) 499-502.
Chapman, J. J. "Lincoln and Hamlet." *NAR* 209 (Mr 19) 371-9.
Charnwood, Lord. "Concerning Abraham Lincoln." *Living Age* 308 (19 F 21) 481-4.
——— "More About Lincoln." *Living Age* 306 (10 Jl 20) 100-8.
——— "Some Further Notes on Abraham Lincoln." *Living Age* 305 (15 My 20) 404-13.
Cooper, C. H. "The Writings of Abraham Lincoln." *Dial* 41 (16 Ag 06) 84-5.
Cushman, E. C. "Broadside Poems of Lincoln." *Am Col* 6 (Ap 28) 34-7.
Dahlberg, W. A. "Lincoln the Wit." *QJS* 31 (D 45) 424-7.
Fesler, J. W. "Lincoln's Gettysburg Address." *Ind Mag Hist* 40 (S 44) 209-26.
Fortenbaugh, Robert. "Lincoln as Gettysburg Saw Him." *Penn Hist* 14 (Ja 47) 1-12.
Griffith, A. H. "Lincoln Literature, Lincoln Collections, and Lincoln Collectors." *Wisc Mag Hist* 15 (D 31) 148-67.
Hamilton, J. G. deR. "The Many-Sided Lincoln." *Am Merc* 5 (Je 25) 129-35.
Herrick, Cheesman. "The Americanism of Lincoln." *NAR* 215 (F 22) 179-87.
Holliday, Carl. "Lincoln's God." *SAQ* 18 (Ja 19) 15-23.
Hubbell, J. B. "Lincoln's First Inaugural." *AHR* 36 (Ja 31) 550-2.
Jordan, P. D. "Some Lincoln and Civil War Songs." *Abraham Lincoln Q* 2 (1942) 127-42.
Lambert, W. H. "Unpublished Letters of Abraham Lincoln." *PMHB* 37 (1903) 60-2.
Landon, F. "Canadian Opinion of Abraham Lincoln." *Dalhousie R* 2 (O 22) 329-34.
Lincoln, Abraham. "The Bear Hunt: An Original Ballad Never Before Printed." *Atl* 135 (F 25) 277-9.
Lindstrom, R. C. "Lincoln the Religionist." *Chri Sci Mon* 36 (5 F 44) 3.
Lorant, Stefan. "Where Are the Lincoln Papers?" *Life* 23 (25 Ag 47) 45-6, 48, 51.
Mabbott, T. O. "Abraham Lincoln on a Poem by Oliver Wendell Holmes." *N&Q* 163 (24 D 32) 458.
MacKay, W. K. "Philadelphia during the Civil War, 1861-1865." *PMHB* 70 (Ja 46) 3-51.
Minor, W. F. "Lincoln the Lover." *Atl* 142 (D 28) 838-56; 143 (Ja, F 29) 1-14, 215-25.

Monaghan, Jay. "An Analysis of Lincoln's Funeral Sermons." *Ind Mag Hist* 41 (Mr 45) 31-44.
Morgan, A. E. "New Light on Lincoln's Boyhood." *Atl* 125 (F 20) 208-18.
Nadal, E. S. "Some Impressions of Lincoln." *Scribner's* 39 (Mr 06) 368-77.
Nicolay, Helen. "The Writing of *Abraham Lincoln: A History*." *J Ill State Hist Soc* 42 (S 49) 259-71.
O'Connor, T. P. "Lincoln's Personality: An English Study." *Living Age* 306 (4 S 20) 594-606.
Park, J. H. "Lincoln and Contemporary English Periodicals." *Dalhousie R* 6 (O 26) 297-311.
Pennypacker, I. R. "The Lincoln Legend." *Am Merc* 1 (Ja 24) 1-7.
——— "Washington and Lincoln: The Father and the Savior of the Country." *PMHB* 56 (Ap 32) 97-109.
Perry, J. R. "The Poetry of Lincoln." *NAR* 193 (F 11) 213-20.
Phillips, C. "Poets' Lincoln." *Cath World* 107 (My 18) 145-60.
Randall, J. G. "Lincoln in the Role of Dictator." *SAQ* 28 (Jl 29) 236-52.
Reed, L. B. "Outline of Lincoln Literature." *Dial* 34 (16 Mr 03) 189-91.
Richter, Werner. "Portraet Abraham Lincolns." *Neue Rundschau* (Fruehjahr 49) 218-36.
Roberts, Octavia. "A. Lincoln Gives a Ball." *Chri Sci Mon* 38 (12 F 46) 8.
Roosevelt, Theodore. "Roosevelt's Tribute to Lincoln." *Rev of Rev* 59 (F 19) 161-2.
Rutledge, Archibald. "Lincoln and the Theory of Secession." *SAQ* 41 (O 42) 370-83.
Sandburg, Carl. "Abraham Lincoln." *Atl* 179 (F 47) 62-5.
Sollars, E. S. "Campaign Verse of Abraham Lincoln." *Cath World* 144 (F 33) 536-541.
Stanton, R. B. "Abraham Lincoln: Personal Memories of the Man." *Scribner's* 68 (Jl 20) 32-41.
Stoddard, W. O. "Face to Face with Lincoln." *Atl* 135 (Mr 25) 332-9.
Swisher, J. A. "Lincoln in Iowa." *Iowa J Hist & Pol* 43 (Ja 45) 69-84.
Townsend, W. H. "Lincoln and Liquor." *Atl* 153 (F 34) 129-42.
Villard, Henry. "Recollections of Lincoln." *Atl* 93 (F 04) 165-74.
Warren, L. A. "Herndon's Contribution to Lincoln Mythology." *Ind Mag Hist* 41 (S 45) 221-44.
——— "Lincoln's Pioneer Father." *N E Hist & Gen Reg* 84 (O 30) 389-400.
Wessen, E. J. "Lincoln Bibliography—Its Present Status and Needs." *PBSA* 34 (4Q 40) 327-48.
Whipple, W. "Abraham Lincoln, the Greatest American Humorist." *Hampton* 28 (F 12) 28-30.
Whitcomb, P. S. "Lincoln's 'Gettysburg Address.'" *Tyler's Quar Hist & Gen Mag* 12 (Ap 31) 221-35.
White, C. T. "Lincoln and Three Methodists." *Methodist R* 47 (Ja-F 31) 38-45.
Williams, Talcott. "Lincoln the Reader." *Rev of Rev* 61 (F 20) 193-6.
Wilson, J. G. "Lincoln's Gettysburg Address." *Independent* 74 (24 Ap 13) 910-2.

LINDERMAN, FRANK BIRD (1869-1938). Van de Water, F. F. "The Work of Frank B. Linderman." *Frontier & Midland* 19 (Sp 39) 148-52.

LINDSAY, HOWARD (1889-). Beiswanger, George. "Lindsay and Crouse." *Theatre Arts* 28 (F 44) 79-88.

LINDSAY, VACHEL (1879-1931). Anon. "An Evangelist in Rhyme." *Nation* 103 (16 D 31) 658.
——— "Mr. Vachel Lindsay Explains America." *Living Age* 307 (11 D 20) 671-3.
——— "Poems of Lindsay." *Rev of Rev* 49 (F 14) 245.
——— "Poet of Promise." *Independent* 77 (12 Ja 14) 72-3.
——— "Poetry of Vachel Lindsay." *Dial* 57 (16 O 14) 281-3.

——— "Vachel Lindsay." *SRL* 8 (9 Ja 32) 437.
——— "Vachel Lindsay in London." *Lit Dig* 65 (15 My 20) 43.
——— "Vachel Lindsay Sees a New Heaven Descending upon the Earth." *Cur Op* 69 (S 20) 371-3.
——— "Why Vachel Lindsay Swears by the Log Cabin." *Lit Dig* 88 (20 F 26) 50.
Aiken, Conrad. "A Letter from Vachel Lindsay." *Bkm* 74 (Mr 32) 598-601.
Amacher, R. E. "Lindsay's *The Sante-Fé Trail.*" *Expl* 5 (Mr 47) 33.
——— "Off 'The Sante-Fé Trail.'" *AL* 20 (N 48) 337.
Anderson, Sherwood. "Lindsay and Masters." *NRp* 85 (25 D 35) 194-5.
Armstrong, A. J. "Letters of Vachel Lindsay to A. Joseph Armstrong." *Baylor Bul* 43 (S 40) i-xiv, 1-121.
——— "Vachel Lindsay as I Knew Him." *Mark Twain Q* 5 (Fl-Wi 42-3) 6-11.
Avery, E. L. "Vachel Lindsay in Spokane." *PS* 3 (Su 49) 338-52.
Bader, A. L. "Lindsay Explains 'The Congo.'" *PQ* 27 (Ap 48) 190-2.
——— "Vachel Lindsay on 'The Sante Fé Trail.'" *AL* 19 (Ja 48) 360.
Bartlett, A. H. "Voices from the Great Inland States (Sandburg and Lindsay)." *Poetry R* 15 (Mr-Ap 24) 101-10.
Benjamin, P. L. "Vachel Lindsay—A Folk Poet." *Survey* 47 (15 O 21) 73-4.
Canby, H. S. "Vachel Lindsay." *SRL* 8 (9 Ja 32) 437.
Davies, Charles, & Lucas, Llewellyn. "Two Aspects of Vachel Lindsay." *Poetry & the Play* 11 (S-N 27) 294-303.
Davison, Edward. "Nicholas Vachel Lindsay." *London Merc* 17 (Ap 28) 652-5.
DeCasseres, B. "Five Portraits on Galvanized Iron." *Am Merc* 9 (D 26) 396-7.
Drinkwater, John. "Two American Lives." *Quar R* (London) 266 (Ja 36) 122-35.
DuBois, A. E. "Lindsay, and Especially Masters." *SR* 44 (Jl-S 36) 377-82.
Edwards, Davis. "The Real Source of Vachel Lindsay's Poetic Technique." *QJS* 33 (Ap 47) 182-95.
Fiske, A. L. "Walking with Lindsay." *Commonweal* 15 (10 F 32) 409-11.
Frank, Glenn. "The Rodin of American Poetry." *Century* 102 (Ag 21) 638-40.
Gorman, H. S. "Vachel Lindsay: Evangelist of Poetry." *NAR* 219 (Ja 24) 123-8.
Graham, Stephen. "Vachel Lindsay." *Spectator* 5 (23 Ja 32) 104.
Hackett, Francis. "In the American Language." *NRp* 21 (11 F 20) 321-2.
——— "Vachel Lindsay." *NRp* 9 (18 N 16) 6-7.
Henderson, A. C. "The Congo and Other Poems." *Poetry* 5 (Mr 15) 296-9.
Jones, Llewellyn. "Vachel Lindsay: American Poet." *Chri Century* 48 (23 D 31) 1619-20.
Lee, C. P. "Adulation and the Artist." *SRL* 22 (10 Ag 40) 7, 18-9.
Lesemann, Maurice. "Two Trampers, and a Poem." *Poetry* 22 (Jl 23) 212-5.
Lindsay, Vachel. "Adventures of a Literary Tramp." *Outlook* 91 (2, 9 Ja, 6, 13 F 09) 36-9, 86-90, 312-6, 357-9.
——— "Adventures While Preaching the Gospel of Beauty." *Forum* 50 (S, O, N, D 13) 296-307, 500-10, 671-84, 827-38; 51 (Ja, F 14) 57-67, 232-41.
MacFarlane, P. C. "Vagabond Poet." *Collier's* 51 (6 S 13) 7-8.
Masters, E. L. "The Tragedy of Vachel Lindsay." *Am Merc* 29 (Jl 33) 357-69.
——— "Vachel Lindsay." *Bkm* 64 (O 26) 156-60.
——— "Vachel Lindsay and America." *SRL* 12 (10 Ag 35) 3-4, 16.
Monroe, Harriet. "Celestial Jazz." *Poetry* 16 (My 20) 101-4.
——— "Lindsay." *Poetry* 39 (Ja 32) 206-12.
——— "The Lindsay Biography." *Poetry* 47 (Mr 36) 337-44.
——— "Lindsay's Poems." *Poetry* 3 (F 14) 182-3.
——— "Notes and Queries from Mr. Lindsay." *Poetry* 17 (F 21) 262-6.
——— "Still Alive." *Poetry* 11 (Ja 18) 214-7.
——— "Vachel Lindsay." *Poetry* 24 (My 24) 90-5.
Moore, Marianne. "An Eagle in the Ring." *Dial* 75 (N 23) 498-505.
Moses, W. R. "Vachel Lindsay: Ferment of the Poet's Mind." *So R* 1 (Sp 36) 828-36.

O'Connor, N. J. "Vachel Lindsay: Poet-Prophet of the Middle West." *Landmark* 2 (D 20) 805-8.
Rittenhouse, J. B. "Contemporary Poetry." *Bkm* 46 (Ja 18) 575-7.
——— "Vachel Lindsay." *SAQ* 32 (Jl 33) 266-82.
Roberts, Octavia. "Nicholas Vachel Lindsay." *Am Mag* 74 (Ag 12) 422-4.
Robinson, H. M. "The Ordeal of Vachel Lindsay." *Bkm* 75 (Ap 32) 6-9.
Spencer, Hazelton. "The Life and Death of Vachel Lindsay." *Am Merc* 25 (Ap 32) 455-62.
Starke, Aubrey, *et al.* "They Knew Vachel Lindsay: A Symposium of Personal Reminiscences." *Latin Q* 1 (Au 34) 128-40.
Tietjens, Eunice. "Bids for Premature Judgment." *Poetry* 22 (S 23) 330-3.
Trombly, A. E. "Vachel Lindsay's Prose." *Sw R* 13 (Jl 28) 459-68.
Untermeyer, Louis. "Vachel Lindsay." *SRL* 2 (25 O 25) 236.
——— "Vachel Lindsay: 1879-1931." *SRL* 8 (12 D 31) 368.
Van Doren, Carl. "Salvation with Jazz: Vachel Lindsay, Evangelist in Verse." *Century* 103 (Ap 23) 951-6.
Warren, Austin. "The Case of Vachel Lindsay." *Accent* 6 (Su 46) 230-9.
Wilkinson, Marguerite. "Poets of the People." *Touchstone* 2 (F 18) 510-2.
Wimberly, L. C. "Vachel Lindsay." *Frontier & Midland* 14 (Mr 34) 212-6.

LINN, JOHN BLAIR (1777-1804). Leary, Lewis. "John Blair Linn." *WMQ* 3 ser 4 (Ap 47) 148-76.
——— "The Writings of John Blair Linn (1777-1804)." *Bul Bibl* 19 (S-D 46) 18-9.

LIPPARD, GEORGE (1822-54). Cowie, Alexander. "Monk Hall, Shame of Philadelphia." *N Y Times Book R* (22 O 44).
Jackson, Joseph. "A Bibliography of the Works of George Lippard." *PMHB* 54 (Ap 30) 131-54.
——— "George Lippard: Misunderstood Man of Letters." *PMHB* 59 (O 35) 376-91.

LOCKE, DAVID ROSS (1838-88). Ransome, J. C. "David Ross Locke: Civil War Propagandist." *Nw Ohio Q* 20 (Ja 48) 5-19.
——— "David Ross Locke: The Post-war Years." *Nw Ohio Q* 20 (Su 48) 144-58.

LODGE, HENRY CABOT (1850-1924). Lord, A., & Morse, J. T., Jr. "Henry Cabot Lodge." *PMHS* 58 (N 24) 97-110.
Washburn, C. G. "Memoir of Henry Cabot Lodge." *PMHS* 58 (Ap 25) 324-76.

LODOWICK, CHRISTIAN (1660-1728). Jantz, H. S. "Christian Lodowick (1660-1728) of Newport and Leipzig." *R I Hist* 3 (O 44) 111-7; 4 (Ja 45) 13-26.

LOMAX, JOHN (1872-1948). Day, Donald. "John Lomax and His Ten Thousand Songs." *SRL* 28 (22 S 45) 5-7.

LONDON, JACK (1876-1916). Anon. "Excerpts from two letters, dated August 7, 1901, and July 27, 1906." *Autograph Album* 1 (D 33) 83-4.
——— "Jack London as a Farmer." *Touchstone* 6 (Mr 20) 416-21.
——— "Jack London as His Wife Charmion Knew Him." *Cur Op* 71 (N 21) 645-8.
——— "Jack London Number." *Overland Mo* 90 (My 32).
Baggs, M. L. "The Real Jack London in Hawaii." *Overland Mo* ns 69 (My 17) 405-10.
Bailey, Millard. "Jack London, Farmer." *Bkm* 44 (O 16) 151-6.
——— "Valley of the Moon Ranch." *Overland Mo* ns 69 (My 17) 411-5.
Barry, J. D. "Personal Qualities of Jack London." *Overland Mo* ns 69 (My 17) 431-2.
Bland, H. M. "Jack London: Traveler, Novelist and Social Reformer." *Craftsman* 9 (F 06) 607-19.
——— "John Barleycorn at the Plow." *Sunset* 33 (Ag 14) 347-9.

——— "The Work of Jack London." *Overland Mo* ns 56 (My 04) 410-6.
Bosworth, Hobart. "My Jack London." *Mark Twain Q* 5 (Fl-Wi 42-3) 2-5, 24.
Bosworth, L. A. M. "Is Jack London a Plagiarist?" *Independent* 62 (14 F 07) 247-50.
Bowen, E. W. "Jack London's Place in American Literature." *Reformed Church R* 4 ser 24 (Jl 20) 306-15.
Briggs, J. E. "Tramping with Kelly through Iowa: A Jack London Diary." *Palimpsest* 7 (My 26) 129-64.
Brody, A. "Jack London via Moscow." *Nation* 125 (28 D 27) 740.
Burroughs, John. "Real and Sham Natural History." *Atl* 91 (Mr 03) 60-3.
Colbron, G. I. "The Eternal Masculine." *Bkm* 35 (O 10) 16.
——— "Jack London: What He Was and What He Accomplished." *Bkm* 44 (Ja 17) 441-51.
Connell, S. "Jack London Wooed Fame through the *Overland Monthly*." *Overland Mo* ns 76 (O 20) 65-71.
Crossman, R. H. S. "The Prophecies of Jack London." *New Statesman and Nation* 17 (8 Je 40) 14.
Dargan, E. P. "Jack London in Chancery." *NRp* 10 (21 Ap 17) 7-8.
Dickason, D. H. "A Note on Jack London and David Starr Jordan." *Ind Mag Hist* 38 (D 42) 407-10.
Eames, Ninetta. "Haunts of Jack London." *Cosmopolitan* 40 (D 05) 227-30.
——— "Jack London." *Overland Mo* ns 52 (My 00) 321-4.
Flowers, B. O. "Jack London at Harvard." *Arena* 35 (F 06) 18-9.
Friedland, L. S. "Jack London as Titan." *Dial* 62 (25 Ja 17) 49-51.
Graham, Stephen. "Jack London." *Eng R* 38 (My 24) 732-7.
Grattan, C. H. "Jack London." *Bkm* 68 (F 29) 667-71.
Groos, K. "Die Verwendung der Eidetik als Kunstmittel in J. Londons Roman Martin Eden." *Zeitschrift für angewandte Psychologie* 33 (1929) 417-38.
Hawkes, E. G. "Jack London: A Brief Sketch of His Life." *Overland Mo* 90 (My 32) 109-10.
Houck, C. B. "Jack London's Philosophy of Life." *Overland Mo* 84 (Ap, My 26) 103-4, 120, 136-7, 141, 147, 149.
Howard, Eric. "Men around London." *Esquire* 13 (Je 40) 62, 183-6.
Hueffer, O. M. "Jack London." *Living Age* 292 (13 Ja 17) 124-6.
James, G. W. "A Study of Jack London in His Prime." *Overland Mo* 69 (My 17) 361-99.
Kellogg, B. W. "Treasures from the Snark's Cruise." *Overland Mo* 90 (My 32) 113-4.
Kronenberger, Louis. "Jack London as Legend." *Nation* 127 (22 O 38) 680-1.
Lane, R. W. "Life and Jack London." *Sunset* 39 (O, N, D 17) 17-20, 29-32, 21-3; 40 (Ja, F, Mr, Ap, My 18) 34-7, 30-4, 27-30, 21-5, 28-32.
Langdon, B. "Mrs. Jack London's Log of the Snark." *Overland Mo* ns 69 (My 17) 447-50.
Larkin, E. L. "Recollections of Jack London." *Overland Mo* ns 69 (My 17) 433-4.
Lay, Wilfrid. "John Barleycorn under Psychoanalysis." *Bkm* 45 (Mr 17) 47-54.
London, C. R. "My Husband—An Old Contributor." *Overland Mo* 90 (My 32) 101-7, 120.
London, Jack. "Rods and Gunnels." *Bkm* 44 (O 16) 177-80.
——— "What Life Means to Me." *Cosmopolitan* 40 (Mr 06) 526-30.
McDevitt, William. "Jack London's Father's Autobiography." *Hobbies* 50 (F 46) 121, 128-9.
Marshall, L. R. "Mrs. Jack London's New Viewpoint." *Overland Mo* ns 69 (My 17) 400-4.
Mumford, Lewis. "Jack London." *NRp* 30 (29 Mr 22) 145-7.
Murphy, C. G. "Library Collected by Jack London." *Overland Mo* 90 (My 32) 111-2.

Pease, Frank. "Impressions of Jack London." *Seven Arts* 1 (Mr 17) 522-30.
Romm, Charles. "Jack London, a Bibliographical Checklist, 1876-1916." *Pub W* 103 (4 F 23) 1021.
Russack, Martin. "Jack London, America's First Proletarian Writer." *New Masses* 22 (4 Ja 29) 12-4.
Silver, G. V. "Jack London's Women." *Overland Mo* ns 74 (Jl 19) 24-8.
Sinclair, Upton. "About Jack London." *Masses* 9 (N, D 17).
——— "Is This Jack London?" *Occult R* 52 (1930) 394-400; 53 (1931) 10-4.
Stellman, L. J. "Jack London—The Man." *Overland Mo* ns 70 (O 17) 385-7.
——— "Jack London, Super-boy." *Sunset* 38 (F 17) 42.
Viereck, G. S. "The Ghost of Jack London." *Liberty* 8 (10 O 31) 15-8.
Walcutt, C. C. "Naturalism and the Superman in the Novels of Jack London." *Papers Mich Acad Sci, Arts & Letters* 24 (1938) 89-107.
Walling, A. S. "Memoirs of Jack London." *Masses* 9 (Jl 17) 13-7.
Whipple, T. K. "Jack London—Wonder Boy." *SRL* 17 (24 S 38) 3-4, 16-7.
Williams, P. S. "Jack London, Lecturer." *Overland Mo* ns 48 (O 06) 247-50.

LONGFELLOW, HENRY WADSWORTH (1807-82). Anon. "Belaboring the 'Brahmans' Again." *Lit Dig* 63 (4 O 19) 31.
——— "Diminishing Poet." *Lit Dig* 71 (22 O 21) 25-6.
——— "Dramatization of Evangeline." *Bkm* 38 (N 13) 221-3.
——— "Evangeline Again." *Chri Sci Mon* 29 (25 O 37) 14.
——— "Longfellow in Latin America." *Bul Pan Am Union* 46 (Mr 18) 345-52.
——— "A Longfellow Letter." *Letters* 3 (N 29) 31-4.
——— "Longfellow's 'Wreck of the Hesperus': 'The Reef of Norman's Woe.'" *N&Q* 167 (28 Jl 34) 59.
——— "When Mark Twain Petrified the 'Brahmans.'" *Lit Dig* 62 (12 Jl 19) 28-9.
Adkins, N. F. "Longfellow and the Italian Risorgimento." *PMLA* 48 (Mr 33) 311.
Aldrich, T. B. "The Centenary of Longfellow." *Atl* 99 (Mr 07) 379-88.
Amacher, R. E. "Longfellow's *Jugurtha.*" *Expl* 6 (F 48) 29.
———, & Falk, R. P. "Words by Longfellow." *JRUL* 10 (D 47) 29-32.
Appel, J. J. "'A Simile' Said to Have Been Written by Henry Wadsworth Longfellow for *The Israelite.*" *Pub Am-Jewish Hist Soc* 40 (D 50) 182-3.
Appelmann, A. H. "Longfellow's *Poems on Slavery* in Their Relation to Freiligrath." *MLN* 30 (Ap 15) 101-2.
——— "The Relation of Longfellow's Evangeline to Tegnér's Frithiofs Saga." *Pub Soc for the Advancement of Scand Stud* 4 (Jl 15).
Arms, George. "Longfellow's *Divina Commedia. Sonnet 1.*" *Expl* 2 (O 43) 7.
——— "Longfellow's Hymn to the Night." *Expl* 1 (O 42) 7.
——— "'Moby-Dick' and 'The Village Blacksmith.'" *N&Q* 192 (3 My 47) 187-8.
——— "The Revision of 'My Lost Youth.'" *MLN* 61 (Je 46) 389-92.
Arndt, K. J., & Groen, H. J. "Sealsfield, the Greatest American Author." *AGR* 7 (Je 41) 12-5.
Averill, E. C. "Longfellow Undiscovered." *MLN* 49 (Je 34) 423.
——— "An Undiscovered Bit of Verse by Longfellow." *MLN* 49 (My 34) 311-2.
Axon, W. E. A. "On the Sources of Longfellow's Tales of a Wayside Inn." *Royal Soc Lit Trans* 30 (1911) 159-72.
Baldensperger, Fernand. "An Unpublished Letter by Longfellow." *MLN* 21 (F 06) 64.
Bangs, E. M. "An Historic Mansion." *N E Mag* ns 27 (F 03) 695-713.
Bestor, A. E., Jr. "Concord Summons the Poets." *NEQ* 6 (S 33) 602-13.
Bowen, Edwin. "Longfellow Twenty Years After." *SR* 13 (Ap 05) 164-76.
Bradford, Gamaliel. "Portraits of American Authors." *Bkm* 42 (N 15) 248-61.
Brebner, J. B. "The Brown MSS and Longfellow." *Canadian Hist R* 17 (Je 36) 172-8.
Cadbury, H. J. "Evangeline." *Friends Intelligencer* 104 (15 N 47) 618.

Cammett, Stephen. "Early Homes of Longfellow." *Century* 73 (Mr 07) 647-57.
Campbell, Killis. "Marginalia on Longfellow, Lowell, and Poe." *MLN* 42 (D 27) 516-21.
Campbell, T. M. "Longfellow and the Hexameter." *MLN* 23 (Mr 08) 96.
Carman, Bliss. "Longfellow." *Reader* 6 (Je 05) 110-5.
Chamberlain, W. A. "Longfellow's Attitude toward Goethe." *MP* 16 (Je 18) 57.
Charvat, William. "Let Us Then Be Up and Doing." *EJ* (Col ed) 18 (My 39) 374-83.
——— "Longfellow's Income from His Writings, 1840-1852." *PBSA* 38 (1Q 44) 9-21.
Clausen, Julius. "Longfellow and Scandinavia . . . with Some Unpublished Letters." *ASR* 16 (D 28) 732-40.
Coad, O. S. "The Bride of the Sea." *AL* 9 (Mr 37) 71-3.
Colton, Arthur. "Longfellow: An Essay in Reputations." *Bkm* 76 (F 33) 128-33.
Courson, Della. "The Art of Evangeline." *Educ* 20 (F 00) 362-4.
Crawford, M. C. "Longfellow: Poet of Places." *Putnam's* 1 (F 07) 522-34.
Curti, M. E. "Henry Wadsworth Longfellow and Elihu Burritt." *AL* 7 (N 35) 315-28.
Dana, H. W. L. "Longfellow on Spain." *New Masses* 27 (12 Ap 38) 92-5.
——— "'Sail On, O Ship of State!': How Longfellow Came to Write These Lines 100 Years Ago." *Colby Lib Q* 2 (F 50) 210-4.
———, & Hawthorne, Manning. "'The Maiden Aunt of the Whole Human Race': Frederika Bremer's Friendship with Longfellow and Hawthorne." *ASR* 37 (S 49) 217-29.
DiGiovanni, Margaret. "The Italian Friends of Longfellow." *Ital* 17 (D 40) 144-7.
Dole, N. H. "Longfellow and Mendelssohn." *Dial* 60 (17 F 16) 112-4.
Doyle, H. G. "Longfellow as Professor at Harvard." *Hispania* 27 (O 44) 320-9.
Dunn, E. C. "Longfellow the Teacher." *NAR* 211 (F 20) 259-65.
Durand, H. M. "Longfellow's Conquest of England." *Outlook* 85 (16 F 07) 355-9.
Eckstorm, F. H. "Pigwacket and Parson Symmes." *NEQ* 9 (S 36) 378-402.
Edgren, Hjalmar. "Antecedents of Longfellow's 'King Robert of Sicily.'" *Poet Lore* 14 (Ja-Mr 03) 127-31.
Eliot, C. W. "Address." *Cambridge Hist Soc Pub* 2 (F 07) 57-9.
Elliott, G. R. "Gentle Shades of Longfellow." *Sw R* 10 (Ap 25) 34-53.
Englekirk, J. E. "Notes on Longfellow in Spanish America." *Hispania* 25 (O 42) 295-308.
Estève, Edmond. "Longfellow et la France." *Bowdoin Col Bul* no 146 (O 25) 3-25.
Fiske, C. F. "Mercerized Folklore in Hiawatha." *Poet Lore* 31 (D 20) 538-75.
Flanders, B. H. "An Uncollected Longfellow Translation." *AL* 7 (My 35) 205-7.
Freneau, Peter. "When Longfellow Was a Portland Lad." *Delineator* 66 (Jl 05) 73-5.
Gavigan, W. V. "Longfellow and Catholicism." *Cath World* 138 (O 33) 42-50.
Gilbert, Creighton. "On Longfellow's Translation of a Michael Angelo Sonnet." *PQ* 27 (Ja 48) 57-62.
Glicksberg, C. I. "Longfellow and Bryant." *N&Q* 166 (3 F 34) 77-8.
Goggio, Emilio. "Italian Influences on Longfellow's Works." *RR* 16 (Jl-S 25) 208-22.
——— "The Sources of Longfellow's *Michael Angelo*." *RR* 25 (O-D 34) 314-24.
Gohdes, Clarence. "A Check List of Volumes by Longfellow Published in the British Isles during the Nineteenth Century." *Bul Bibl* 17 (S-D 40) 46; (Ja-Ap, My-Ag 41) 67-9, 93-6.
——— "Longfellow and His Authorized English Publishers." *PMLA* 55 (D 40) 1165-79.
Gorman, H. S. "Longfellow's Golden Years." *Bkm* 64 (N 26) 320-3.
Gribble, Francis. "Henry Wadsworth Longfellow." *Fortnightly R* ns 81 (1 F 07) 241-50; *Putnam's* 1 (F 07) 515-21.

Griswold, M. J. "American Quaker History in the Works of Whittier, Hawthorne, and Longfellow." *Americana* 34 (Ap 40) 220-63.
Haight, G. S. "Longfellow and Mrs. Sigourney." *NEQ* 3 (Jl 30) 532-7.
Hale, Henry. "Hiawatha Played by Real Indians." *Critic* 47 (Jl 05) 41-9.
Hall, H. M. "Longfellow's Letters to Samuel Ward." *Putnam's* 3 (O, N, D 07) 38-43, 165-71, 301-8.
Hart, J. M. "Hoffmann and Longfellow." *Nation* 84 (9 Ja 07) 26-7.
Hastings, William. "Longfellow's Influence on Musical Composition." *Étude* 55 (Jl 37) 433-4.
Hatfield, J. T. "Longfellow and Germany." *AGR* 5 (S 38) 8-10.
——— "The Longfellow-Freiligrath Correspondence." *PMLA* 48 (D 33) 1223-93.
——— "Longfellow's 'Lapland Song.'" *PMLA* 45 (D 30) 1188-92.
——— "Professor Hatfield Replies to Mr. Thompson." *AL* 6 (My 34) 193-5.
——— "An Unknown Prose Tale by Longfellow." *AL* 3 (My 31) 136-49.
Hawthorne, Manning. "The Friendship between Hawthorne and Longfellow." *Eng Leaflet* 39 (F 40) 25-30.
——— "Hawthorne and 'The Man of God.'" *Colophon* ns 2 (Wi 37) 262-82.
———, & Dana, H. W. L. "The Origin of Longfellow's *Evangeline*." *PBSA* 41 (3Q 47) 165-203.
Hecht, David. "Lavrov and Longfellow." *Russian R* 5 (Sp 46) 90-6.
——— "Longfellow in Russia." *NEQ* 19 (D 46) 531-4.
Hervey, J. L. "The Distinction of Longfellow." *Dial* 60 (20 Ja 16) 49-51.
Heywood, C. B. M. "Hiawatha at Cambridge." *London Merc* 27 (N 32) 6-30.
Higginson, M. T. "New Longfellow Letters." *Harper's* 106 (Ap 03) 779-86.
——— "The Youth of Longfellow." *Independent* 62 (21 F 07) 416-9.
Hilen, Andrew. "The Longfellows and the Stokoes: A Forgotten Friendship." *Studia Neophilologica* 33 (1950) 17-36.
Hill, M. G. "Some of Longfellow's Sources for the Second Part of *Evangeline*." *PMLA* 31 (2 N 16) 161-80.
Howells, W. D. "The Art of Longfellow." *NAR* 184 (1 Mr 07) 472-85; *Cambridge Hist Soc Pub* 2 (F 07) 60-72.
——— "Editor's Easy Chair." *Harper's* 104 (Ap 02) 833-6.
Huebener, Theodore. "Longfellow's Estimate of Heine." *GQ* 21 (Mr 48) 117-9.
——— "Longfellow's French Grammar." *FR* 22 (My 49) 448-51.
Jackson, D. K. "Some Unpublished Letters of John R. Thompson and Augustin L. Taveau." *WMQ* 16 (Ap 36) 206-21.
Johnson, A. "The Relation of Longfellow to Scandinavian Literature." *ASR* 16 (Ja 15) 40-6.
——— "Some Unpublished Longfellow Letters." *Ger-Am Annals* 5 (My-Je 07).
Johnson, C. L. "Longfellow's Beginnings in Foreign Languages." *NEQ* 20 (S 47) 317-28.
——— "Three Notes on Longfellow." *Harvard Stud & Notes in Phil & Lit* 14 (1932) 249-71.
Johnson, V. "Homes of Two Neighbors, Poet and Blacksmith." *St Nicholas* 44 (O 17) 1129-32.
Jones, H. M. "The Longfellow Nobody Knows." *Outlook* 149 (8 Ag 28) 577-9, 586.
Kip, H. Z. "The Origin of Longfellow's 'The Arrow and the Song.'" *PQ* 9 (Ja 30) 76-8.
Kirk, Rudolf. "A Longfellow Letter." *JRUL* 6 (Je 43) 62-3.
Kramer, Sidney. "There was a Little Girl: Its First Printing, Its Author, Its Variants." *PBSA* 40 (4Q 46) 287-310.
Krumpelmann, J. T. "Longfellow's *Golden Legend* and the *Armer Heinrich* Theme in Modern German Literature." *JEGP* 25 (2Q 26) 173-92.
LeGallienne, Richard. "On Re-reading Longfellow." *Harper's W* 62 (29 Ja 16) 112-4.

Legler, H. E. "Longfellow's Hiawatha: Bibliographical Notes concerning Its Origin, Its Translations, and Its Contemporary Parodies." *Lit Coll* 9 (Ja 04) 12-4.

Leighly, John. "Inaccuracies in Longfellow's Translations of Tegnér's 'Nattvardsbaren.'" *SS* 21 (N 49) 171-80.

Long, O. W. "Goethe and Longfellow." *GR* 7 (Ap 32) 145-75.

Longfellow, H. W. "Letter from H. W. Longfellow to Peleg Sprague." *PMHS* 56 (N 22) 160-1.

Longfellow, Samuel. "The Five of Clubs." *Chri Sci Mon* 30 (22 O 38) 9.

——— "The Old Portland Academy: Longfellow's 'Fitting School.'" *NEQ* 18 (Je 45) 247-51.

Mabbott, T. O. "A Longfellow Parody: From Thomas Moore." *AN&Q* 4 (My 44) 22-3.

Mabie, H. W. "Longfellow the Poet." *Outlook* 92 (26 Je 09) 512-4.

——— "Sonnets from the Divine Comedy." *Outlook* 91 (23 Ja 09) 175-8.

McCourt, E. A. "The Canadian Historical Novel." *Dalhousie R* 26 (Ap 46) 30-6.

MacMechan, Archibald. "Evangeline and the Real Acadians." *Atl* 99 (F 07) 202-13.

Matenko, Percy. "Fragments from Longfellow's Workshop: Novalis." *GR* 22 (F 47) 32-41.

Mathews, J. C. "Echoes of Dante in Longfellow's Poetry." *Ital* 26 (D 49) 242-59.

Mayer, M. J. "The Land of Evangeline." *Critic* 41 (Ag 02) 108-12.

Millard, Clifford. "The Acadians in Virginia." *VMHB* 40 (Jl 32) 241-58.

Miller, R. B. "Baron of Saint Castine—American Pioneer." *Americana* 28 (Ja 34) 92-7.

Murdock, K. B. "Andrews Norton's Estimate of Longfellow." *AL* 1 (Mr 29) 77.

Norton, C. E. "Longfellow and His Hexameters." *MLN* 23 (N 08) 231.

Nyland, Waino. "*Kalevela* as a Reputed Source of Longfellow's *Song of Hiawatha.*" *AL* 22 (Mr 50) 1-20.

Pattee, F. L. "Evangeline: An Epic." *Chautauquan* 30 (Ja 00) 415-20.

Pearson, N. H. "Both Longfellows." *UKCR* 16 (Su 50) 245-53.

Perry, Bliss. "The Centenary of Longfellow." *Atl* 99 (Mr 07) 379-88.

——— "Longfellow as a Citizen." *Outlook* 92 (26 Je 09) 511-2.

Pritchard, J. P. "The Horatian Influence upon Longfellow." *AL* 4 (Mr 32) 22-39.

Rea, J. D. "Longfellow's Nature." *MP* 18 (My 20) 48.

Richards, I. T. "Longfellow in England." *PMLA* 51 (D 36) 1123-40.

Russell, J. A. "Longfellow: The Interpreter of the Historical and Romantic Indian." *J Am Hist* 22 (1928) 327-47.

——— "Longfellow's Dartmouth Influence." *Dartmouth Alumni Mag* 29 (Mr 37) 13-4.

Saylor, H. L. "The Real Evangeline." *Bkm* 18 (S 03) 17-25.

Scholl, J. W. "Longfellow and Schiller's 'Lied von der Glocke.'" *MLN* 28 (F 13) 49-50.

Schramm, W. L. "Hiawatha and Its Predecessors." *PQ* 11 (O 32) 321-43.

Schurz, Carl. "Reminiscences of a Long Life." *McClure's* 28 (Ja 07) 259-60.

Shelley, P. A. "An Exchange of Letters with Longfellow." *PMLA* 60 (Je 45) 611-6.

Smith, C. P. "Longfellow's Castle on the Oxbow." *Chri Sci Mon* 38 (10 Jl 46) 8.

Steele, R. B. "The Meter of 'Evangeline.'" *MLN* 9 (N 94) 413-8.

——— "The Poetry of Longfellow." *SR* 13 (Ap 05) 177-97.

Stewart, Randall. "Hawthorne's Contributions to *The Salem Advertiser.*" *AL* 5 (Ja 34) 327-41.

Strachan, Pearl. "Poets Have Something to Say." *Chri Sci Mon* 40 (14 F 48) 5.

Swan, M. W. S. "Professor Longfellow: Scandinavian Book Buyer." *HLB* 4 (Au 50) 259-73.

Thayer, W. R. "The Longfellow Celebration at Cambridge." *Nation* 84 (7 Mr 07) 219-20.

———, *et al.* "Longfellow." *PMHS* 40 (F 07) 564-87.

Thompson, Lawrance. "An Inquiry into the Importance of 'Boston Prize Poems.'" *Colophon* ns 1 (1940) 55-62.
——— "Longfellow Sells *The Spanish Student*." *AL* 6 (My 34) 141-50.
——— "Longfellow's Original Sin of Imitation." *Colophon* ns 1 (Su 35) 97-106.
——— "Longfellow's Projected *Sketch Book of New England*." *Colophon* 4 (O 33) Pt 15.
Thompson, Ralph. "Additions to Longfellow Bibliography, Including a New Prose Tale." *AL* 3 (N 31) 303-98.
Thompson, Stith. "The Indian Legend of Hiawatha." *PMLA* 37 (Mr 22) 128-40.
Thornton, H. H. "An Early American Textbook." *Ital* 8 (D 31) 110-1.
Thorstenberg, Edward. "The *Skeleton in Armour* and *The Frithiof Saga*." *MLN* 25 (Je 10) 189-92.
Trent, W. P. "Recent Tributes to Longfellow." *Forum* 38 (Ap-Je 07) 554-8.
Ullmann, S. "Composite Metaphors in Longfellow's Poetry." *RES* 18 (Ap 42) 219-28.
Untermeyer, Louis. "With New England Roots." *Chri Sci Mon* 39 (28 Ja 47) 7.
Warnack, H. C. "An Unpublished Letter from Longfellow on Evangeline." *Poet Lore* 14 (O 02) 108-10.
Weber, C. J. "Rebekah Owen Corrects a Sonnet of Longfellow's." *NEQ* 14 (Mr 41) 141-4.
White, G. L., Jr. "Longfellow's Interest in Scandinavia during the Years 1835-1845." *SS* 17 (My 42) 70-82.
Winslow, Erving. "Historical Inaccuracies in Longfellow's Evangeline." *Dial* 60 (3 F 16) 105-7.
Worden, J. P. "Longfellow's Tales and Their Origin." *Anglia* 23 (1901) 316-22.
Yeigh, Frank. "The Drama of Hiawatha, a Mana-bozho." *Canadian Mag* 17 (Jl 01) 207-17.

LONGSTREET, AUGUSTUS BALDWIN (1790-1870). Gilbert, Creighton. "Emory Portraits II: Four Figures of the College Campus." *Emory Un Q* 4 (Mr 48) 40-54.
Longstreet, A. B. "An Unreprinted *Georgia Scene*." *Emory Un Q* 2 (Je 46) 100-1.
Weber, C. J. "A Connecticut Yankee in King Alfred's Country." *Colophon* ns 1 (Sp 36) 525-35.

LORD, WILLIAM WILBERFORCE (1819-1907). Randall, D. A. "Footnote on a Minor Poet." *Colophon* ns 3 (Au 38) 587-97.

LOVEJOY, ELIJAH PARISH (1802-37). Palmer, N. D. "The Conversion of Elijah Parish Lovejoy and Its Results." *Colby Lib Q* ser 2 (N 47) 53-8.

LOW, JOHN (*ca.* 1750-1830). Moss, S. A. "The Low Family of New York City, Publishers, 1795-1829." *BNYPL* 47 (F 43) 87-90.

LOWELL, AMY (1874-1925). Anon. "Amy Lowell." *Bkm* 58 (D 23) 418-24.
Aiken, Conrad. "Miss Lowell Abides Our Question." *Dial* 67 (19 O 19) 331-3.
——— "The Technique of Polyphonic Prose." *Dial* 65 (2 N 18) 346-8.
Allen, Hervey. "Amy Lowell as Poet." *SRL* 3 (5 F 27) 557-8.
——— "The Passing of Amy Lowell." *Bkm* 61 (Jl 25) 519-23.
Ayscough, Florence. "Amy Lowell and the Far East." *Bkm* 63 (Mr 26) 11-8.
Benét, W. R. "Amy Lowell and Other Poets." *YR* 11 (O 21) 175-80.
Boynton, P. H. "Amy Lowell." *EJ* 11 (N 22) 527-35.
Bradley, W. A. "Four American Poets." *Dial* 61 (14 D 16) 528-30.
Campbell, Killis. "Lowell's Uncollected Poems." *PMLA* 38 (D 23) 933-7.
Carlson, E. W. "The Range of Symbolism in Poetry." *SAQ* 48 (Jl 49) 442-51.
Catel, Jean. "Mort d'Amy Lowell." *Mercure de France* 181 (1 Ag 25) 826-31.

Cestre, Charles. "Amy Lowell, Robert Frost, and Edwin Arlington Robinson." *Johns Hopkins Alumni Mag* 14 (Mr 26) 363-88.

——— "L'Oeuvre Poétique d'Amy Lowell." *Revue Anglo-Américaine* 2 (Ag 25) 481-500.

Chew, S. C. "Miss Lowell's Biography of Keats." *NAR* 221 (Mr 25) 545-55.

Colum, Padraic. "A World in High Visibility." *Freeman* 4 (14 S 21) 18-9.

Damon, S. F. "East Wind, West Wind." *YR* 16 (Ap 27) 587-91.

Dole, N. H. "The Bellman's Notebook." *Bellman* 20 (19 F 16) 210-1.

Erskine, John. "John Keats and Amy Lowell." *VQR* 1 (Jl 25) 271-5.

Fletcher, J. G. "Herald of Imagism." *So R* 1 (Sp 36) 813-27.

——— "Living History." *Poetry* 10 (Je 17) 149-53.

——— "Miss Lowell's Discovery: Polyphonic Prose." *Poetry* 6 (Ap 15) 32-6.

Frost, Robert. "Letter, dated December 14, 1932." *Autograph Album* 1 (D 33) 56.

Hammond, Josephine. "Amy Lowell and the Pretorian Cohorts." *Personalist* 1 (O 20) 14-36.

Isoré, Pierre. "L'Originalité d'Amy Lowell." *Revue Anglo-Américaine* 6 (Ap 29) 317-26.

Kemp, Frances. "Bibliography of Amy Lowell." *Bul Bibl* 15 (My-Ag, S-D 33, Ja-Ap 34) 8-9, 25-6, 50-3.

Kizer, H. B. "Amy Lowell: A Personality." *NAR* 207 (My 18) 736-47.

Lippmann, Walter. "Miss Lowell and Things." *NRp* 6 (18 Mr 16) 178-9.

Lomax, J. A. "Amy Lowell at Baylor." *Sw R* 32 (Sp 47) 133-4.

Lovett, R. M. "Amy Lowell." *NRp* 43 (27 My 25) 17.

Loving, Pierre. "Towards Walt Whitman." *Double Dealer* 4 (S 22) 139-42.

Lowes, J. L. "The Poetry of Amy Lowell." *SRL* 2 (3 O 25) 169-70, 174-5.

MacLeish, Archibald. "Amy Lowell and the Art of Poetry." *NAR* 221 (Mr 25) 508-21.

Monroe, Harriet. "Amy Lowell." *Poetry* 25 (Mr 25) 32-8.

——— "Amy Lowell on Keats." *Poetry* 26 (Jl 25) 220-6.

——— "The Amy Lowell Scholarships." *Poetry* 26 (Ag 25) 276-7.

——— "In Bardic Robes." *Poetry* 29 (Mr 27) 336-42.

——— "A Daughter of the Caesars." *Poetry* 47 (Ja 36) 212-9.

——— "A Decorative Colorist." *Poetry* 9 (Ja 17) 207-9.

——— "Her Books and Herself." *Poetry* 31 (Mr 28) 338-43.

——— "A Keen East Wind." *Poetry* 29 (D 26) 160-3.

——— "The Limnal Lindsay." *Poetry* 29 (Ja 27) 217-21.

——— "Memories of Amy Lowell." *Poetry* 26 (Jl 25) 208-14.

——— "Miss Lowell and Polyphonic Prose." *Poetry* 13 (N 18) 97-102.

——— "Miss Lowell on Tendencies." *Poetry* 11 (D 17) 151-6.

——— "That Bookshelf." *Poetry* 15 (O 19) 39-42.

Patterson, W. M. "New Verse and New Prose." *NAR* 207 (F 18) 257-67.

Perkins, E. W. "Amy Lowell of New England." *Scribner's* 82 (Sp 27) 329-35.

Pratt, J. W. "*Can Grande's Castle*. By Amy Lowell." *SAQ* 18 (Jl 19) 264-7.

Schwartz, W. L. "A Study of Amy Lowell's Far Eastern Verse." *MLN* 43 (Mr 28) 145-52.

Scott, W. T. "Amy Lowell after Ten Years." *NEQ* 8 (Ag 39) 320-30.

Sergeant, E. S. "Amy Lowell Memory Sketch." *NRp* 44 (18 N 25) 322-6.

Smith, M. C. "American First Editions . . . Amy Lowell." *Pub W* 102 (19 My 23) 1515.

Snyder, E. D. "Poe and Amy Lowell." *MLN* 43 (Mr 28) 152-3.

Tittle, Walter. "Glimpses of Interesting Americans." *Century* 110 (Je 25) 177-80.

Tupper, James. "The Poetry of Amy Lowell." *SR* 28 (Ja 20) 37-53.

Untermeyer, Louis. "Amy Lowell—Storm-center." *Independent* 87 (28 Ag 16) 306.

——— "Storm Center in Brookline; Amy Lowell as I Remember Her." *Harper's* 179 (Ag 39) 265-75.

Wilkinson, Marguerite. "Amy Lowell." *Touchstone* 7 (Je 20) 219-20.

——— "Poets of the People; Amy Lowell." *Touchstone* 2 (Ja 18) 416-9.
Yeaman, Virginia. "Amy Lowell at Sevenels." *Forum* 74 (Jl 25) 76-9.

LOWELL, JAMES RUSSELL (1819-91). Anon. "Excerpts from two letters, dated January 25, 1853, and August 21, 1848." *Autograph Album* 1 (D 33) 85.
——— "International Significance of the Lowell Centenary." *Cur Op* 66 (Ap 19) 251-2.
——— "Letters of James Russell Lowell. 1843-54." *BNYPL* 4 (O 00) 339-45.
——— "Lowell at His Best." *Freeman* 1 (23 Je 20) 357-8.
——— "Lowell's English Accents." *Lit Dig* 61 (5 Ap 19) 32-3.
——— "Testi Americana: I. J. R. Lowell (1846)." *Anglica* 1 (F 46) 27-32.
——— "Visit of Lowell to Chicago in 1887." *Dial* 55 (16 Ag 13) 101.
Adkins, N. F. "A Borrowing of Lowell from George Chapman." *AL* 5 (My 33) 172-5.
Altick, R. D. "Was Lowell an Historical Critic?" *AL* 14 (N 42) 250-9.
Armitage, W. H. G. "Some New Letters of James Russell Lowell." *N&Q* 195 (13 My 50) 359-73.
Bail, H. V. "Harvard's Commemoration Day: July 21, 1865." *NEQ* 15 (Je 42) 259-79.
——— "James Russell Lowell's Ode Recited at the Commemoration of the Living and Dead Soldiers of Harvard University, July 21, 1865." *PBSA* 37 (Jl-S 43) 169-202.
Beatty, R. C. "Lowell's Commonplace Books." *NEQ* 18 (S 45) 391-401.
Bernard, E. G. "New Light on Lowell as an Editor." *NEQ* 10 (Je 37) 337-41.
Bester, A. E., Jr. "Concord Summons the Poets." *NEQ* 6 (S 33) 602-13.
Boynton, P. H. "Lowell in His Times." *NRp* 18 (22 F 19) 112-4.
Bradley, Sculley. "Lowell, Emerson, and the *Pioneer*." *AL* 19 (N 47) 231-44.
Brownell, W. C. "Lowell." *Scribner's* 41 (F 07) 220-35.
Cairns, W. B. "James Russell Lowell: A Centenary View." *Nation* 108 (22 F 19) 274-7.
Campbell, Killis. "Bibliographical Notes on Lowell." *Un Texas Stud Eng* 4 (1924) 115-9.
——— "Lowell's Uncollected Poems." *PMLA* 38 (D 23) 933-7.
——— "Marginalia on Longfellow, Lowell and Poe." *MLN* 42 (D 27) 516-21.
——— "Three Notes on Lowell." *MLN* 38 (F 23) 121-2.
Chapman, E. M. "The Bigelow Papers Fifty Years After." *YR* ns 6 (O 16) 120-34.
Chrisman, L. H. "Lowell and His Interpretation of Life." *Methodist R* 102 (My 19) 366-78.
Clark, H. H. "Lowell—Humanitarian, Nationalist, or Humanist?" *SP* 27 (Jl 30) 411-41.
——— "Lowell's Criticism of Romantic Literature." *PMLA* 41 (Mr 26) 209-28.
Crowe, M. D. "James Russell Lowell—Author, Teacher, Public Servant." *Negro Hist Bul* 6 (F 43) 102-3, 119.
Davis, R. B. "A Variant of Lowell's 'I Go to the Ridge in the Forest.'" *MLN* 61 (Je 46) 392-5.
DeMille, G. E. "The Critic from Cambridge." *SR* 32 (O 24) 446-63.
DeRiano, E. G. "Mr. Lowell and His Spanish Friends." *Century* 60 (Je 00) 292-3.
Doyle, H. G. "An Interesting Letter of James Russell Lowell." *Hisp R* 31 (N 48) 398-400.
Duncan, E. H. "Lowell's 'Battle of the Kettle and Pot.'" *AL* 15 (My 43) 127-38.
Edes, H. H. "Letters from James Russell Lowell to W. H. Furners." *PCSM* 8 (Ap 03) 134-7.
Eliot, C. W. "James Russell Lowell as a Professor." *Harvard Grad Mag* 27 (Je 19) 482-7.

Flower, B. O. "James Russell Lowell as a Poet of Freedom and Human Rights." *Arena* 41 (Mr 09) 309-17.
Foerster, Norman. "The Creed of Lowell as Literary Critic." *SP* 14 (Jl 27) 454-73.
——— "Lowell as a Poet of Nature." *SR* 25 (O 17) 422-42.
Fuess, C. M. "Some Forgotten Political Essays of Lowell." *PMHS* 62 (1930) 3-13.
Galsworthy, John. "The Community of Language." *NAR* 209 (Ap 19) 523-7.
Gibbs, Lincoln. "A Brahmin's Version of Democracy." *AR* 1 (Sp 41) 50-62.
Glicksman, Harry. "Lowell on Milton's *Areopagitica*." *MLN* 35 (Mr 20) 185-6.
Golann, Ethel. "A Lowell Autobiography." *NEQ* 7 (Je 34) 356-64.
Goodspeed. G. T. "A Unique Lowell Item." *Am Col* 3 (Mr 27) 241-3.
Grandgent, C. H. "From Franklin to Lowell: A Century of New England Pronunciation." *PMLA* 14 (1899) 207-39.
Grattan, C. H. "Lowell." *Am Merc* 2 (My 24) 63-9.
Griffin, M. L. "Lowell and the South." *Tulane Stud Eng* 2 (1950) 75-102.
Grubb, Edward. "The Socialism of James Russell Lowell." *NE Mag* ns 6 (Jl 92) 676-8.
Hale, E. E., Jr. "James Russell Lowell." *Reader* 6 (Jl 05) 233-6.
Hart, J. M. "James Russell Lowell." *PMLA* 7 (1892) 25-31.
Harte, Bret. "A Few Words about Mr. Lowell." *New R* 5 (S 91) 193-201.
Heil, J. A. "Die Volkssprache im Nordosten der Vereinigten Staaten von Amerika, dargestellt auf Grund der Biglow Papers von James Russell Lowell." *Giessener Beiträge zur Erforschung der Sprache und Kultur Englands Nordamerikas* 3 (1927) 205-311.
Henry, H. T. "James Russell Lowell's Moral Intuitions." *Cath Ed R* 22 (Ja 24) 6-17.
——— "Music in Lowell's Prose and Verse." *Musical Q* 24 (O 24) 546-72.
——— "Religious Intimations in the Writings of James Russell Lowell." *Cath Ed R* 21 (S 23) 398-408.
Horwill, H. W. "Lowell's Influence in England." *N E Mag* ns 27 (N 02) 321-5.
Howe, M. A. DeW. "Elwood and Charles Street. Letters of Lowell and Diaries of Mrs. Fields." *Atl* 130 (Jl-D 22) 464-9.
——— "*Il Pesceballo:* The Fishball Operetta of Francis James Child." *NEQ* 23 (Je 50) 187-99.
——— "Victorian Poets: A Side Light." *Atl* 152 (Ag 33) 224-7.
Howells, W. D. "A Personal Retrospect of James Russell Lowell." *Scribner's* 28 (S 00) 363-78.
Jackson, W. A. "J. R. Lowell and John Locke." *NEQ* 19 (Mr 46) 113-4.
Jameson, J. F. "Lowell and Public Affairs." *Rev of Rev* 4 (O 91) 287-91.
Jenkins, W. G. "Lowell's Criteria of Political Values." *NEQ* 7 (Mr 34) 115-41.
Johnson, W. H. "James Russell Lowell." *Critic* 40 (F 02) 121-5.
Joyce, H. E. "A Bibliographical Note on James Russell Lowell." *MLN* 35 (Ap 20) 249-50.
Kies, P. P. "Lowell and the Two Doras." *Res Stud State Col Wash* 16 (1948) 179-84.
Killheffer, Marie. "A Comparison of the Dialect of 'The Biglow Papers' with the Dialect of Four Yankee Plays." *AS* 3 (F 28) 222-36.
Lange, A. F. "James Russell Lowell as a Critic." *Calif Un Chron* 8 (1906) 352-64.
Lockwood, Ferris. "Mr. Lowell on Art-Principles." *Scribner's* 15 (F 94) 186-9.
Low, Sidney. "Lowell and His Poetry." *Fortnightly R* 56 (1 S 91) 310-24.
Mabbott, T. O. "A Review of Lowell's Magazine." *N&Q* 178 (29 Je 40) 457-8.
——— "A Supposedly New Poem by James Russell Lowell." *N&Q* 188 (27 Ja 45) 34.
McEuen, K. A. "Lowell's Puns." *AS* 22 (F 47) 24-33.
Mead, E. D. "Lowell's *Pioneer*." *N E Mag* ns 5 (O 91) 235-58.
Miller, F. DeW. "An Artist Sits for Lowell." *BPLQ* 2 (O 50) 378-9.
Mims, Edwin. "Lowell as a Citizen." *SAQ* 1 (Ja 02) 27-40.

Moore, C. L. "Arnold and Lowell." *Dial* 45 (16 S 08) 157-9.
Mulhauser, Ruth. "Sainte Beuve, Lowell, and the *Atlantic Monthly.*" *Harvard Lib Bul* 2 (Wi 48) 126-7.
Nadal, E. S. "London Recollections of Lowell." *Harper's* 132 (F 16) 366-72.
Nichols, E. J. "Identification of Characters in Lowell's *A Fable for Critics.*" *AL* 4 (My 32) 191-4.
Norton, C. E. "James Russell Lowell." *Harper's* 86 (My 93) 846-57.
Norton, Sara, & Howe, M. A. DeW. "Letters of Charles Eliot Norton to James Russell Lowell." *Atl* 110 (D 12) 759-75.
Nye, R. B. "Lowell and American Speech." *PQ* 18 (Jl 39) 249-56.
Parsons, E. S. "Lowell's Conception of Poetry." *Colo Coll Pub* (language series) 2 (S 08) 67-84.
Perry, Bliss. "James Russell Lowell." *Harvard Grad Mag* 27 (Je 19) 482-91.
Pettigrew, R. C. "Lowell's Criticism of Milton." *AL* 3 (Ja 32) 457-62.
Pound, Louise. "Lowell's 'Breton Legend.'" *AL* 12 (N 40) 348-50.
Pritchard, J. P. "A Glance at Lowell's Classical Reading." *AL* 21 (Ja 50) 442-55.
——— "Lowell's Debt to Horace's *Ars Poetica.*" *AL* 3 (N 31) 259-76.
Rice, Wallace. "Lowell on Human Liberty." *Dial* 34 (1 Ja 03) 14-6.
Roberts, R. E. "James Russell Lowell (1819-1891.)" *Bkm* (London) 55 (Mr 19) 185-9.
——— "James Russell Lowell: A British Estimate." *Living Age* 301 (26 Ap 19) 231-5.
Robertson, J. M. "Criticism and Science." *NAR* 209 (My 19) 690-6.
——— "Lowell as Critic." *NAR* 209 (F 19) 246-62.
Ruud, M. B. "James Russell Lowell, an American University Man." *Un No Dak J* 9 (Jl 19) 351-9.
Scoggin, G. C. "James Russell Lowell and 'Il Pesceballo.'" *Nation* 105 (18 O 17) 437-8.
Sedgwick, Ellery. "Lowells, Inc." *SRL* 29 (21 S 46) 5-6, 37-8.
Seigler, M. B. "Lowell's *The Courtin'.*" *Expl* 8 (N 49) 14.
Smith, F. D. "Mr. Wilbur's Posthumous Macaronics." *Quar J Un No Dak* 10 (1920) 436-43.
Smith, J. H. "The Biglow Papers as an Argument against the Mexican War." *PMHS* 45 (My 12) 602-11.
Spencer, Herman. "A Possible Lowell Origin." *MLN* 23 (Ja 08) 29-30.
Swift, Lindsay. "Our Literary Diplomats: Part IV." *Book Buyer* ns 21 (S 00) 90-8.
Thayer, W. R. "James Russell Lowell as a Teacher: Recollections of His Last Pupil." *Scribner's* 68 (O 20) 473-80.
Voss, Arthur. "Backgrounds of Lowell's Satire in 'The Biglow Papers.'" *NEQ* 23 (Mr 50) 47-64.
——— "*The Biglow Papers* in England." *AL* 21 (N 49) 340-2.
——— "The Evolution of Lowell's 'The Courtin'.'" *AL* 15 (Mr 43) 42-50.
——— "James Russell Lowell." *UKCR* 15 (Sp 49) 224-33.
——— "Lowell, Hood and the Pun." *MLN* 63 (My 48) 346-7.
——— "Lowell's 'A Legend of Brittany.'" *MLN* 61 (My 46) 343-5.
Warren, Austin. "Lowell on Thoreau." *SP* 27 (Jl 30) 442-62.
Weber, C. J. "Lowell: Poet and Friendly Critic." *Colby Lib Q* 1 (Mr 43) 19-23.
——— "Lowell's 'Dead Rat in the Wall.'" *NEQ* 9 (S 36) 468-72.
——— "Lowell's Visit to Waterville." *Colby Merc* 6 (N 35) 54-6.
——— "More about Lowell's 'Dead Rat.'" *NEQ* 9 (D 36) 686-8.
White, William. "Two Versions of Lowell's 'Function of the Poet.'" *PQ* 20 (O 41) 587-96.
Will, T. E. "A Poet of Freedom." *Arena* 31 (Mr 04) 262-71.
Winterich, J. T. "Romantic Stories of Books, Second Series: *The Biglow Papers.*" *Pub W* 119 (21 Mr 31) 1605-10.

Wurfl, G. "Lowell's Debt to Goethe." *Penn State Col Stud* 1 (1936) 1-89.

LOWELL, ROBERT (1917-). Anon. "Prize Poet: Robert Lowell Wins the Pulitzer Award." *Life* 20 (19 My 47) 91-2, 94.
Elton, William. "A Note on Robert Lowell." *Poetry* 71 (D 47) 138-9.
Engle, Paul. "Five Years of Pulitzer Poets." *EJ* 38 (F 49) 62-3.
Jarrell, Randall. "From the Kingdom of Necessity." *Nation* 164 (18 Ja 47) 74-5.

LOWELL, ROBERT TRAILL SPENCE (1816-91). Blodgett, Harold. "Robert Traill Spence Lowell." *NEQ* 16 (D 43) 578-91.

LOWRY, ROBERT (1826-99). Cantini, Roberto. "Robert Lowry, piccolo uomo." *Fiera Letteraria* no 10 (6 Mr 49).

LUMMIS, CHARLES FLETCHER (1859-1928). DuBois, C. G. "Charles F. Lummis, Author and Man." *Critic* 40 (Ap 02) 326-30.
Field, Ben. "Charles Fletcher Lumnis." *Overland Mo* 87 (Jl 29) 197-203.
Newmark, Marco. "Charles Fletcher Lummis." *Hist Soc So Calif Q* 32 (Mr 50) 45-60.

MABIE, HAMILTON WRIGHT (1845-1916). Anon. "Hamilton Wright Mabie, Critic and Essayist." *Rev of Rev* 55 (F 17) 204-5.
——— "Mr. Mabie's Life and Work." *Outlook* 115 (10 Ja 17) 51-2.
Abbott, Lyman. "Hamilton Wright Mabie." *Outlook* 115 (10 Ja 17) 49-51.

McCLELLAND, MARY GREENWAY (1853-95). Holman, H. R. "Mary Greenway McClelland, 1853-1895." *VMHB* 56 (Jl 48) 294-8.

McCULLERS, CARSON (1917-). Blanzat, Jean. "Frankie Adams de Carson McCullers." *Figaro Littéraire* no 190 (10 D 49) 7.

McFEE, WILLIAM (1881-). Elder, A. J. "William McFee, Engineer and Author." *Bkm* 44 (S 16) 57-62.
McFee, William. "Getting into Print." *Colophon* (F 30) Pt 1.
North, Jessica. "The Wrong-Headed Poets." *Poetry* 34 (Je 29) 156-60.
Shay, Frank. "American First Editions . . . William McFee." *Pub W* 102 (9 D 22) 2054.

McHENRY, JAMES (1785-1845). Coad, O. S. "James McHenry: A Minor American Poet." *JRUL* 8 (Je 45) 33-64.

McJILTON, JOHN NELSON (1805-75). Terwilliger, W. B. "John Nelson McJilton: Humorist, Divine Educator." *Md Hist Mag* 32 (D 37) 301-31.

McKAY, CLAUDE (1890-). Burris, A. M. "American First Editions: Claude McKay, 1889- ." *Pub W* 132 (30 O 37) 1767-8.

MACKAYE, PERCY (1875-). Abbott, E. H. "Masque of Masques." *Outlook* 113 (7 Je 16) 308-10.
Baker, G. P. "The Pageant and Masque of St. Louis." *World's Work* 28 (Ag 14) 389-99.
Botkin, B. A. "Folk Speech in the Kentucky Mountain Cycle of Percy Mackaye." *AS* 6 (Ap 31) 267-76.
Colby, F. M. "Percy MacKaye's Mater." *Bkm* 28 (N 08) 222-4.
Collier, John. "Caliban by the Yellow Sands." *Survey* 36 (1 Jl 16) 343-50.
Crowley, Allister. "Percy MacKaye." *International* 11 (1917) 47.
Dickinson, T. H. "The Epic of the World Finder." *VQR* 4 (Ap 28) 275-8.
Farwell, Arthur. "The Pageant and Masque of St. Louis." *Rev of Rev* 50 (Ag 14) 187-93.

Firkins, O. W. "Percy MacKaye." *Nation* 103 (14 D 16) 562-4.
Knaufft, Ernst. "Two Great Pageants." *Rev of Rev* 53 (My 16) 593-7.
Roberts, M. F. "The Dramatic Engineer and the Civic Theatre." *Craftsman* 26 (My 14) 139-47.
——— "Rehearsing a Community Masque." *Craftsman* 28 (Ag 16) 483-8.
Sherry, Laura. "Pageantry and Rhetoric." *Poetry* 19 (O 21) 51-3.
Wells, H. W. "Percy Mackaye's Plays on *Hamlet*." *Shakespeare Assn Bul* 24 (Ap 49) 85-90.
Zabel, M. D. "A Mountain Folk Play." *Poetry* 32 (S 28) 352-4.

MACKAYE, STEELE (1842-94). Eaton, W. P. "Steele MacKaye, or the Dreamer Delivered." *Theatre Arts* 11 (N 27) 827-37.
MacKaye, Percy. "Steele MacKaye, Dynamic Artist of the American Theatre." *Drama* 4 (D 11) 138-61.
S., C. G. "Artists, Idealists and Steele MacKaye." *Mask* 14 (Ja-Mr 28) 22-3.

MACLEISH, ARCHIBALD (1892-). Anon. "The First American Ballet." *Living Age* 348 (Mr 35) 87-8.
Aiken, W. E. "Poetic Form in *Conquistador*." *MLN* 51 (F 36) 107-9.
Amacher, R. E. "MacLeish's 'L'An Trentiesme de Mon Eage.'" *Expl* 6 (Ap 48) 42.
Blackmur, R. P. "A Modern Poet in Eden." *Poetry* 28 (S 26) 339-42.
Blake, Howard. "Thoughts on Modern Poetry." *SR* 43 (Ap-Je 35) 187-96.
Chamberlain, John. "Archibald MacLeish." *SRL* 20 (24 Je 39) 10-1.
Dangerfield, George. "Archibald MacLeish: An Appreciation." *Bkm* 72 (Ja 31) 493-6.
Denison, Merrill. "Radio and the Writer." *Theatre Arts* 22 (My 38) 365-70.
Deutsch, Babette. "Certain Good." *VQR* 10 (Ap 34) 298-302.
Donnald, Elizabeth. "An Ideal of Confidence Reflected by Some Contemporary American Poets." *Furman Bul* 22 (Ap 40) 3-17.
Eaten, W. P. "MacLeish, Lecturer." *Commonweal* 27 (25 Mr 38) 602-3.
Edison, George. "Thematic Symbols in the Poetry of Aiken and MacLeish." *UTQ* 10 (O 40) 12-6.
Fitts, Dudley. "To Karthage Then I Came." *H&H* 4 (Jl-S 31) 637-41.
Gillmor, Frances. "The Curve of the Continent." *NMQR* 4 (My 34) 114-22.
Gregory, Horace. "Poets in the Theatre." *Poetry* 48 (Jl 36) 221-8.
Honig, Edwin. "History, Document, and Archibald MacLeish." *SR* 48 (Jl 40) 385-96.
Humphries, Rolfe. "Archibald MacLeish." *Mod Mo* 8 (Je 34) 264-70, 274.
Isaacs, H. R. "The Fall of Another City." *Theatre Arts* 23 (F 39) 147-9.
Jones, Llewellyn. "Archibald MacLeish: A Modern Metaphysical." *EJ* 24 (Je 35) 441-51.
Kirstein, Lincoln. "Arms and Men." *H&H* 5 (Ap-Je 32) 484-92.
Kohler, Dayton. "MacLeish and the Modern Temper." *SAQ* 38 (O 39) 416-26.
Kreymborg, Arthur. "'The Moon Is Dead.'" *SRL* 10 (27 Ja 34) 435.
Lash, Kenneth. "Myth and the Conquest of Mexico." *NMQR* 17 (Sp 47) 38-44.
Lind, L. R. "The Crisis in Literature Today." *SR* 47 (Ja-Mr 39) 50-4.
Lundkvist, Artur. "En Amerikansk poet." *Bonniers Litterära Magasin* (Stockholm) 10 (S 41) 555-62.
MacLeish, Archibald. "Modern Instances: Notebooks, 1924-1938." *Poetry* 73 (O, N 48) 33-42, 88-96.
——— "The Writer and Revolution." *SRL* 11 (26 Ja 35) 441-2.
MacMullan, H. M. "Poems, 1924-33." *Sw R* 20 (Wi 34) 2, 4-6.
Magil, A. B. "Mr. MacLeish Hesitates." *New Masses* 31 (30 My 39) 21-2.
Melcher, F. G. "Check List of Archibald MacLeish." *Pub W* 124 (15 Jl 33) 180.
Mizener, Arthur. "The Poetry of Archibald MacLeish." *SR* 44 (O 38) 501-19.
Monroe, Harriet. "Archibald MacLeish." *Poetry* 38 (Je 31) 150-5.

Myhr, I. L. "MacLeish's . . . *& Forty-Second Street.*" *Expl* 3 (Ap 45).
Pinckney, Josephine. "Jeffers and MacLeish." *VQR* 8 (Jl 32) 443-7.
Powell, Charles. "The Poetry of 1933." *Manchester Guardian Weekly Supplement* 29 (8 D 33) 9.
Rice, P. B. "Poets and the Wars." *Nation* 140 (13 F 35) 189-92.
Rosenberg, Harold. "The God in the Car." *Poetry* 52 (S 38) 334-42.
Sanders, Gerald. "MacLeish's *Pony Rock.*" *Expl* 2 (O 43) 8.
Schappes, M. U. "The Direction of A. MacLeish." *Symposium* 3 (O 32) 476-94.
Sickels, E. M. "Archibald MacLeish and American Democracy." *AL* 15 (N 43) 223-37.
Sillen, Samuel. "Archibald MacLeish, the Irresponsible." *New Masses* 35 (11 Je 40) 24-6.
Thurber, Gerrish. "MacLeish Published Books." *Lib J* 64 (N 39) 864-6.
Van Ghent, Dorothy. "The Poetry of Archibald MacLeish." *Sci & Soc* 5 (Fl 38) 500-11.
Wade, Mason. "The Anabasis of A. MacLeish." *NAR* 243 (Su 37) 330-43.
Waggoner, H. H. "Archibald MacLeish and the Aspect of Eternity." *CE* 4 (Ap 43) 402-12.
Wilson, Edmund. "Archibald MacLeish and 'The Word.'" *NRp* 103 (1 Jl 40) 30-2.
——— "The Omelet of A. MacLeish." *NYr* 14 (14 Ja 39) 23-4.
Zabel, M. D. "Cinema of Hamlet." *Poetry* 44 (Je 34) 150-9.
——— "The Compromise of A. MacLeish." *Poetry* 36 (Ag 30) 270-5.
——— "The Poet on Capitol Hill." *PR* 8 (Ja-Mr 41) 2-19, 128-45.

McMASTER, JOHN BACH (1852-1932). Hutchinson, W. T. "John Bach McMaster, Historian of the American People." *Miss Valley Hist R* 16 (Je 29) 23-49.

MacNEICE, LOUIS (1907-). Brown, S. G. "Some Poems of Louis MacNeice." *SR* 51 (Wi 43) 64-72.
Dupee, F. W. "Cecil Day Lewis and Louis MacNeice." *Nation* 161 (13 O 45) 380.

MADISON, JAMES (1751-1836). Adair, Douglass. "The Authorship of the Disputed Federalist Papers." *WMQ* 1 (Ap, Jl 44) 97-122, 235-64.
——— "James Madison's Autobiography." *WMQ* 2 (Ap 45) 191-209.
Alderman, E. A. "A Madison Letter and Some Digressions." *NAR* 217 (Je 23) 785-96.
Koch, Adrienne. "Philosopher-Statesmen of the Republic." *SR* 55 (Su 47) 384-405.
Marsh, Philip. "Madison's Defense of Freneau." *WMQ* 3 (Ap 46) 269-80.
——— "Philip Freneau and James Madison, 1791-1793." *Proc N J Hist Soc* 65 (O 47) 189-94.
Moore, W. C. "James Madison, the Speaker." *QJS* 31 (Ap 45) 155-62.
Schaedler, L. C. "James Madison, Literary Craftsman." *WMQ* 3 (O 46) 515-33.

MAILER, NORMAN (1923-). Maurois, André. "La Guerre, jugée par un romancier américain." *Nouvelles Littéraires* (Paris) 29 (27 Ag 50) 5.

MAJOR, CHARLES (1856-1913). Hepburn, W. M. "The Charles Major Manuscripts in the Purdue University Libraries." *Ind Quar for Bkm* 2 (Jl 46) 71-81.

MANN, HORACE (1796-1859). Roberts, Josephine. "Horace Mann and the Peabody Sisters." *NEQ* 18 (Je 45) 164-80.

MARCH, WILLIAM (1893-). Crowder, Richard. "The Novels of William March." *UKCR* 15 (Wi 48) 111-29.

MARKHAM, EDWIN (1852-1940). Anon. "A Conversation with Edwin Markham on the Poet as a Teacher." *Arena* 28 (D 02) 634-7.
——— "Edwin Markham." *Chri Sci Mon* 29 (16 F 37) 14.

Bland, H. M. "Edwin Markham and His Art." *Overland Mo* ns 50 (O 07) 333-7.
——— "Edwin Markham: The Boy, the Man, His Art." *Overland Mo* 66 (O 15) 333-40.
Bromer, E. S. "Edwin Markham, the Poet of Democracy." *Reformed Church R* 15: ser 4 (Ap 11) 165-86.
Clemens, Cyril. "The Poetical Education of Edwin Markham." *Overland Mo* 90 (Ap 32) 86-7.
———, *et al.* "Edwin Markham Number." *Mark Twain Q* 4 (Sp 41) 1-20.
Field, B. F. "California's Literary Wealth." *Overland Mo* 89 (N 31) 19-20.
——— "Edwin Markham and His Eightieth Birthday Celebration." *Overland Mo* 90 (Jl 32) 143-4.
——— "Edwin Markham, Dean of American Poets." *Overland Mo* 91 (N 33) 147-8.
Flower, B. O. "Edwin Markham, A Prophet-Poet of the Fraternal State." *Arena* 27 (Ap 02) 391-411.
——— "Edwin Markham: The Poet-Prophet of Democracy." *Arena* 35 (F 06) 139-46.
Goldstein, J. S. "Edwin Markham, Ambrose Bierce, and 'The Man with the Hoe.'" *MLN* 58 (Mr 43) 165-75.
——— "Escapade of a Poet." *Pacific Hist R* 13 (S 44) 303-13.
——— "Two Literary Radicals." *AL* 17 (My 45) 152-60.
Grose, G. R. "Edwin Markham: Poet of the Social Conscience." *Personalist* 17 (Ap 36) 149-56.
Harris, L. H. "Markham's 'The Man with the Hoe.'" *Expl* 3 (Mr 45).
Johnson, Merle. "American First Editions: Edwin Markham (1852-)." *Pub W* 126 (21 Jl 34) 220.
Markham, Edwin. "Letter from Edwin Markham to *The Overland Monthly.*" *Overland Mo* 89 (N 31) 14.
——— "What Life Means to Me." *Cosmopolitan* 41 (Je 06) 185-8.
Millard, Bailey. "The Launching of a Famous Poem." *Bkm* 27 (My 08) 267-72.
Monahan, Michael. "Edwin Markham's Poetry." *Stratford J* 5 (S 19) 140-3.
Towne, C. H. "Edwin Markham, 1852-1940." *Poetry* 56 (Ap 40) 30-1.

MARQUAND, JOHN PHILLIPS (1893-). Benét, Stephen & Rosemary. "J. P. Marquand, a Really Remarkable Writer." *N Y Herald-Tribune Books* 17 (16 Mr 41) 5.
Bisbee, T. D. "J. P. Marquand's Tales of Two Cities." *SRL* 24 (5 Jl 41) 11, 14.
Boynton, P. H. "The Novel of Puritan Decay: From Mrs. Stowe to John Marquand." *NEQ* 13 (D 40) 626-37.
Brickell, Herschel. "Miss Glasgow and Mr. Marquand." *VQR* 17 (Su 41) 405-17.
Butterfield, Roger. "John P. Marquand: America's Famous Novelist of Manners." *Life* 17 (31 Jl 44) 64-73.
Fiske, C. M. "John P. Marquand: Something of an Apley Himself." *SRL* 19 (10 D 38) 10-1.
Hatcher, Harlan. "John Phillips Marquand." *CE* 1 (N 39) 107-18; *EJ* 28 (S 39) 507-18.
Hellman, G. T. "How to Take the World in Your Stride after Being Tipped Off by J. P. Marquand." *NYr* 19 (23 O 43) 20-1, 23.
Hicks, Granville. "Marquand of Newburyport." *Harper's* 200 (Ap 50) 105-8.
Van Gelder, Robert. "An Interview with a Best-Selling Author: John P. Marquand." *Cosmopolitan* 122 (Mr 47) 18, 150-2.
——— "Marquand Unburdens Himself." *N Y Times Book R* (7 Ap 40) 20-1.
White, William. "John P. Marquand: A Preliminary Checklist." *Bul Bibl* 19 (S-D 49) 268-71.
——— "Marquandiana." *Bul Bibl* 20 (Ja-Ap 50) 8-12.
——— "Mr. Marquand's 'Mr. Moto.'" *AS* 23 (Ap 48) 157-8.

MARQUIS, DONALD ROBERT PERRY (1878-1937). Anon. "Don Marquis, American Minstrel." *Cur Op* 73 (N 22) 662-4.
——— "Don Marquis and His Place in the Sun." *Cur Op* 67 (Ap 19) 119.
——— "Don Marquis of the *Evening Sun.*" *Everybody's* 34 (Je 16) 720-1.
Crowell, C. T. "The Fun of Don Marquis." *Atl* 178 (N 46) 129-31.
DeVoto, Bernard. "The Easy Chair: Almost Toujours Gai." *Harper's* 200 (Mr 50) 49-52.
Gilder, Rodman. "American First Editions: Don (Robert Perry) Marquis, 1878- ." *Pub W* 132 (17 Jl 37) 209-10.
Kirby, Rollin. "Don Marquis: Delayed Elizabethan." *Am Merc* 64 (Mr 47) 337-40.
Marquis, Don. "Don Marquis." *Everybody's* 42 (Ja 20) 29, 85.
Morley, Christopher. "Don Marquis: An Appreciation." *Tomorrow* 9 (My 50) 52-3.
——— "O Rare Don Marquis." *SRL* 17 (8 Ja 38) 13-4.
Tittle, Walter. "Glimpses of Interesting Americans." *Century* 110 (Ag 25) 437-41.
Van Doren, Carl. "Day In and Day Out. Adams, Morley, Marquis and Broun: Manhattan Wits." *Century* 107 (D 23) 309-15.

MARSH, GEORGE PERKINS (1801-82). Kliger, Samuel. "George Marsh and and the Gothic Tradition in America." *NEQ* 19 (D 46) 524-31.

MARSH, JAMES (1794-1842). Dewey, John. "James Marsh and American Philosophy." *JHI* 2 (Ap 40) 131-50.
Nicolson, Marjorie. "James Marsh and the Vermont Transcendentalists." *Philos R* 34 (Ja 25) 28-50.

MARSHALL, HUMPHREY (1756-1841). Jackson, Joseph. "The Aliens: A Patriotic Poem by Humphrey Marshall." *Am Col* 1 (N 25) 45-50.

MASON, JOHN (*c.* 1600-72). Hutt. F. W. "Puritan John Mason." *Americana* 26 (Ja 32) 7-11.

MASTERS, EDGAR LEE (1869-1950). Anon. "Another Walt Whitman." *Lit Dig* 52 (4 Mr 16) 564-5.
——— "Edgar Lee Masters." *Bkm* 55 (Ag 22) 572-6.
——— "Frost and Masters." *Poetry* 9 (Ja 17) 202-7.
Altrocchi, Rudolph. "Edgar Lee Masters and Joinville." *MLN* 45 (Je 30) 360-2.
Amacher, R. E. "Masters' *The Lost Orchard.*" *Expl* 7 (Mr 49) 38.
Anderson, Sherwood. "Lindsay and Masters." *NRp* 85 (25 D 35) 194-5.
Baldensperger, Fernand. "Une Confession poetique de l'ouest americain." *Correspondant* 297 (25 D 24) 833-47.
Boynton, P. H. "The Voice of Chicago: Edgar Lee Masters and Carl Sandburg." *EJ* 11 (D 22) 610-20.
Bradley, W. A. "Four American Poets." *Dial* 61 (14 D 16) 528-30.
Braithwaite, W. S. "Spoon River Anthology." *Forum* 55 (Ja 16) 114-7.
Chandler, J. C. "Mr. Masters' 'Spoon River.'" *Un R* 2 (Wi 35) 92-5.
——— "The Spoon River Country." *J Ill State Hist Soc* 14: nos 3-4 (1921-22) 252-329.
Childs, H. E. "Agrarianism and Sex." *SR* 41 (Jl-S 33) 331-42.
Coffin, R. P. T. "Poets of the People." *VQR* 13 (Ja 37) 126-31.
Deaton, M. B. "Masters' 'The Lost Orchard.'" *Expl* 8 (N 49) 16.
DuBois, A. E. "Lindsay, and Especially Masters." *SR* 44 (Jl-S 36) 377-82.
——— "Shelley, Browning and Masters." *Personalist* 18 (O 37) 405-16.
Dudley, Dorothy. "Large Measures." *Poetry* 12 (Je 18) 150-4.
E., R. F. "Portrait in Line Introducing Edgar Lee Masters." *Book Buyer* 2 (F 37) 18.
Fletcher, J. G. "Masters and Men." *Poetry* 49 (Mr 37) 343-7.
Francoisa, M. "Dedica per Lee Masters." *La Fiera Letteraria* no 11 (12 Mr 50).

Freer, A. L. "Spoon River to the Open Sea." *Poetry* 21 (D 22) 154-8.
Gilman, Lawrence. "Moving Picture Poetry." *NAR* 202 (Ag 15) 271-6.
Henderson, A. C. "Spoon River Anthology." *Poetry* 6 (Je 15) 145-9.
Irwin, O. C. "More about Spoon River." *Dial* 60 (25 My 16) 498-9.
Jones, Llewellyn. "Edgar Lee Masters, Critic of Life." *Am R* 2 (S 24) 517-23.
Kilmer, Joyce. "Edgar Lee Masters: The Spoon River Anthologist." *Bkm* 44 (N 16) 264-5.
Loomis, R. S. "In Praise of Spoon River." *Dial* 60 (27 Ap 16) 415-6.
——— "Spoon River Once More." *Dial* 61 (22 Je 16) 14-5.
Masters, E. L. "The Genesis of Spoon River." *Am Merc* 28 (Ja 33) 38-55.
——— "Introduction to Chicago." *Am Merc* 31 (Ja 34) 49-59.
——— "Literary Boss of the Middle West." *Am Merc* 34 (Ap 35) 450-5.
——— "William Marion Reedy." *AS* 9 (Ap 34) 96-8.
Monroe, Harriet. "Edgar Lee Masters." *Poetry* 24 (Jl 24) 204-10.
——— "Frost and Masters." *Poetry* 9 (Ja 17) 202-7.
——— "Spoon River Again." *Poetry* 25 (F 25) 273-8.
Phelps, W. L. "The Advance of English Poetry in the Twentieth Century." *Bkm* 47 (My 18) 262-6.
Powys, J. C. "Edgar Lee Masters." *Bkm* 69 (Ag 29) 650-5.
——— "Edgar Lee Masters' Recent Poetry." *Un R* 4 (Wi 37) 88-94.
Pratt, J. W. "Whitman and Masters: A Contrast." *SAQ* 16 (Ap 17) 155-8.
Puranen, Erkki. "Edgar Lee Masters ja 'Spoon River Anthology.'" *Kirjallisyydentutkijain Seuran* (Helsingfors) 9 (1947) 88-116.
Savelli, G. "Ristampa di Lee." *La Fiera Letteraria* (16 Ja 48).
Scott, Evelyn. "The Test of Maturity." *Poetry* 50 (Jl 37) 215-9.
Seiffert, M. A. "Starved Rock." *Poetry* 16 (Je 20) 151-6.
Sloan, M. B. "Edgar Lee Masters—A Portrait." *Un R* 1 (Su 35) 4-6.
Untermeyer, Louis. "Spoon River Critics." *Masses* 8 (Ap 16) 20.
Van Gelder, Robert. "An Interview with Mr. Edgar Lee Masters." *N Y Times Book R* (15 F 42) 2, 28.
Van Wyck, William. "Edgar Lee Masters and Twentieth Century Prosody." *Personalist* 17 (Ja 37) 75-80.
Wilkinson, Marguerite. "Poets of the People." *Touchstone* 3 (My 18) 172-7.
Wisewell, C. E. "Marivaux and E. L. Masters." *Revue de Littérature Comparée* 10 (Ap-Je 30) 298-303.
Wright, W. H. "Mr. Masters' 'Spoon River Anthology': A Criticism." *Forum* 55 (Ja 16) 109-13.

MATHER, COTTON (1663-1728). Barbee, D. R. "Did James F. Shunk Forge the Cotton Mather Letter? The Answer Is: Definitely No." *Tyler's Quar Hist & Gen Mag* 27 (Ja 46) 179-205.
Chrisman, L. H. "Cotton Mather." *Methodist R* 5 ser 44 (Jl 28) 529-40.
Davies, David. "Coleridge's Marginalia in Mather's *Magnalia.*" *HLQ* 2 (Ja 39) 233-40.
Francke, Kuno. "The Beginning of Cotton Mather's Correspondence with August Hermann Francke." *PQ* 5 (Jl 26) 193-5.
Friedman, L. M. "Cotton Mather and the Jews." *Pub Am Jewish Hist Soc* no 26 (1918) 201-10.
Greenough, C. N. "A Letter Relating to the Publication of Cotton Mather's Magnalia." *PCSM* 26 (1927) 296-312.
Griswold, A. W. "Three Puritans on Prosperity." *NEQ* 7 (S 34) 475-93.
Haraszti, Zoltán. "Cotton Mather and the Witchcraft Trials." *More Books* 15 (My 40) 170-84.
Holmes, T. J. "Cotton Mather and His Writings on Witchcraft." *PBSA* 18 (1924) 31-59.
——— "The Mather Bibliography." *PBSA* 31 (1937) 57-76.

——— "The Mather Collection at Cleveland." *Colophon* 4 (Je 33) Pt 14.
Hopkins, F. M. "The Mather Library Sold: Passes from William Gwinn Mather of Cleveland Who Collected It to Tracy W. MacGregor of Washington." *Pub W* 128 (21 D 35) 2243-4.
Hornberger, Theodore. "Cotton Mather's Annotations on the First Chapter of Genesis." *Un Texas Stud Eng* 18 (1938) 112-22.
——— "The Date, the Source, and the Significance of Cotton Mather's Interest in Science." *AL* 6 (Ja 35) 413-20.
Jones, M. B. "Some Bibliographical Notes on Cotton Mather's 'The Accomplished Singer.'" *PCSM* 28 (1935) 186-93.
Kittredge, G. L. "Cotton Mather's Election into the Royal Society." *PCSM* 14 (D 11) 81-114.
——— "Cotton Mather's Scientific Communications to the Royal Society." *PAAS* 26 (Ap 16) 18-57.
——— "Further Notes on Cotton Mather and the Royal Society." *PCSM* 14 (Ap 12) 281-92.
——— "Notes on Witchcraft." *PAAS* 18 (1907) 148-212.
——— "Some Lost Works of Cotton Mather." *PMHS* 45 (F 12) 418-79.
Murdock, K. B. "Cotton Mather and the Rectorship of Yale College." *PCSM* 26 (1927) 388-401.
——— "Notes on Cotton and Increase Mather." *Proc Unitarian Hist Assn* 1 (1926) 22-4.
Nordell, P. G. "Cotton Mather in Love." *Harper's* 153 (O 26) 566-72.
Porter, K. A. "Affectation of Praehiminincies." *Accent* 2 (Sp, Su 42) 131-8, 226-32.
——— "A Bright Particular Faith." *H&H* 7 (Ja-Mr 34) 46-52.
Quincy, J. P. "Cotton Mather and the Supernormal in New England History." *PMHS* 40 (N 06) 439-53.
Rice, H. C. "Cotton Mather Speaks to France: American Propaganda in the Age of Louis XIV." *NEQ* 16 (Je 43) 198-233.
Thayer, W. S. "Cotton Mather's Rules of Health." *Johns Hopkins Hospital Bul* 16 (S 05) 293-300.
Thompson, Lawrance. "Notes on Some Collectors in Colonial Massachusetts." *Colophon* ns 2 (Au 36) 82-100.
Turtle, J. H. "The Libraries of the Mathers." *PAAS* ns 20 (1910) 269-356.
——— "William Whiston and Cotton Mather." *PCSM* 13 (1912) 197-204.
Watters, R. E. "Biographical Technique in Cotton Mather's *Magnalia*." *WMQ* 2 (Ap 45) 154-63.
Widder, Milton. "Mather Books for Posterity." *Cleveland Press* sec 2 (9 O 35) 1.
Zirkle, Conway. "More Records of Plant Hybridization before Koelreuter." *J Heredity* 25 (Ja 34) 3-18.
——— "Some Forgotten Records of Hybridization and Sex in Plants." *J Heredity* 23 (N 32) 433-48.
——— "The Theory of Concentric Spheres: Edmund Halley, Cotton Mather, and John Cleves Symmes." *Isis* 37 (Jl 47) 155-7.

MATHER, INCREASE (1639-1723). Cadbury, H. J. "Harvard College Library and the Libraries of the Mathers." *PAAS* 50 (Ap 40) 20-48.
Green, S. A. "Notebook of Increase Mather." *PMHS* 33 (Ja 00) 397-412.
Holmes, T. J. "The Mather Collection at Cleveland." *Colophon* 4 (Je 33) Pt 14.
Jantz, H. S. "Henning Witte and Increase Mather." *NEQ* 18 (S 45) 408.
Loomis, C. G. "An Unnoted German Reference to Increase Mather." *NEQ* 14 (Je 41) 374-6.
McCutcheon, R. P. "*The Observator* and Increase Mather." *PCSM* 24 (D 21) 313-7.
Murdock, K. B. "Increase Mather's Experiences as Colonial Agent." *PCSM* 27 (1932) 200-4.

——— "Notes on Increase and Cotton Mather." *Proc Unitarian Hist Assn* 1 (1926) 22-4.
Walz, J. A. "Increase Mather and Dr. Faust, an American 'Faustsplitter.'" *GR* 15 (F 40) 20-31.

MATHER, NATHANAEL (1631-97). Cone, K. M. "A Colonial Boyhood." Atl 88 (N 01) 651-60.

MATHER, RICHARD (1596-1699). Anon. "The Preface to *The Bay Psalm Book*." *More Books* 4 (Je 29) 223-9.
Holmes, T. J. "Notes on Richard Mather's 'Church Government.'" *PAAS* ns 33 (1923) 291-6.

MATHER, SAMUEL (1706-85). Holmes, T. J. "Samuel Mather of Witney, 1674-1733." *PCSM* 26 (1927) 312-22.
Matthews, Albert. "Samuel Mather." *PCSM* 18 (1917) 206-28.

MATTHEWS, BRANDER (1852-1929). Hamilton, Clayton. "Brander." *Scribner's* 86 (Jl 29) 82-7.
Trent, W. P. "Brander Matthews as a Dramatic Critic." *International Q* 4 (Ag 01) 289-93.
Williams, B. C. "Brander Matthews—A Reminiscence." *MS* 1 (Jl 29) 1, 9.

MATTHIESSEN, FRANCIS OTTO (1902-50). Hart, H. N. "Francis Otto Matthiessen." *Cath World* 171 (S 50) 448-51.
Howe, Irving. "The Sentimental Fellow-Traveling of F. O. Matthiessen." *PR* 15 (O 48) 1125-9.
Poggioli, Renato. "In memoria di 'Matty.'" *Inventaria* 3 (Sp 50).

MAURY, MATTHEW F. (1806-73). Byrd, Admiral Richard. "Maury—A Great Citizen." *SLM* 3 (O-N 41) 477-8.
Ellsberg, Commander Edward. "Maury beneath the Seas." *SLM* 3 (O-N 41) 481.
Gainos, F. P. "Maury—The Educator." *SLM* 3 (O-N 41) 479-80.
Jackson, D. K. "Matthew Fontaine Maury—Editor of the 'Messenger.'" *SLM* 3 (O-N 41) 484-8.
Lewis, C. L. "Maury and the 'Messenger.'" *SLM* 1 (Mr 39) 165-71.
——— "Maury—First Meteorologist." *SLM* 3 (O-N 41) 482-3.
Werth, J. R. "Maury—First American International Leader." *SLM* 3 (O-N 41) 473-6.

MAXWELL, WILLIAM (fl. 1796). Byrd, C. K. "Some Notes on W. Maxwell and the *Maxwell Code*." *Ind Quar for Bkm* 2 (Ap 46) 54-60.
Coindreau, M. E. "William Maxwell." *Revue de Paris* 55(F 48) 120-6.

MAYLEM, JOHN (1739-?). Wroth, L. C. "John Maylem: Poet and Warrior." *PCSM* 32 (1937) 87-120.

MEEK, ALEXANDER BEAUFORT (1814-65). Figh, M. G. "Alexander Beaufort Meek, Pioneer Man of Letters." *Ala Hist R* 2 (Su 40) 127-51.
Canby, H. S. "Mr. Meek on America." *SRL* 7 (Ap 16 32) 661, 664.

MELVILLE, HERMAN (1819-91). Anon. "Another Significant American Centenary." *Cur Op* 67 (S 19) 184-5.
——— "Herman Melville's 'Pierre.'" *TLS* no 1500 (30 O 30) 884.
——— "Herman Melville's Silence." *TLS* no 1173 (10 Jl 24) 433.
——— "Journal of Melville's Voyage in a Clipper Ship." *NEQ* 2 (Ja 29) 120-39.
——— "Manuscript Division Accessions during 1942." *BNYPL* 47 (F 43) 91-8.
——— "Melville and His Public." *AN&Q* 2 (Ag 42) 67-71.
——— "Melville's 'Agatha' Letter to Hawthorne." *NEQ* 2 (Ap 29) 296-307.

——— "Melville's Journey: The Conflict of Heart and Mind." *TLS* (12 Ja 46) 18.
——— "Mystery of Herman Melville." *Cur Op* 71 (O 21) 502-3.
——— "Neglected American Classic." *Lit Dig* 70 (16 Jl 21) 26.
——— "A Reviewer's Notebook." *Freeman* 4 (26 O, 21 D 21) 166-7, 358-9; 6 (14 F 23) 550-1; 7 (9 My, 16 My, 30 My 23) 214-5, 238-9, 286-7.
——— "Some Melville Letters." *Nation and Athenaeum* 29 (13 Ag 21) 712-3.
A., S. P. "Toward the Whole Evidence on Melville as a Lecturer." *AN&Q* 2 (O 42) 111-2.
Aaron, Darill. "An English Enemy of Melville." *NEQ* 8 (D 35) 561-7.
——— "Melville and the Missionaries." *NEQ* 8 (S 35) 404-8.
Adams, F. B., Jr. "The Crow's Nest." *Colophon* ns 2: No 1 (Au 36) 148-54.
Adkins, N. F. "A Note on Herman Melville's 'Typee.'" *NEQ* 5 (Ap 32) 348-51.
Almy, R. R. "J. N. Reynolds: A Brief Biography with Particular Reference to Poe and Symmes." *Colophon* ns 2 (Wi 37) 227-45.
Ament, W. S. "Bowdler and the Whale." *AL* 4 (Mr 32) 39-47.
——— "Some Americanisms in Moby Dick." *AS* 7 (Je 32) 365-7.
Anderson, C. R. "Contemporary American Opinions of *Typee* and *Omoo*." *AL* 9 (Mr 37) 1-25.
——— "The Genesis of *Billy Budd*." *AL* 12 (N 40) 329-46.
——— "Melville's English Debut." *AL* 11 (Mr 39) 23-38.
——— "A Reply to Herman Melville's *White-Jacket* by Rear-Admiral Thomas O. Selfridge, Sr." *AL* 7 (My 35) 123-44.
——— "The Romance of Scholarship: Tracking Melville in the South Seas." *Colophon* ns 3 (Sp 38) 259-79.
Arms, George. "'Moby-Dick' and 'The Village Blacksmith.'" *N&Q* 192 (3 My 47) 187-8.
Arvin, Newton. "Melville and the Gothic Novel." *NEQ* 22 (Mr 49) 33-48.
——— "Melville's *Mardi*." *Am Q* 2 (Sp 50) 71-81.
——— "Melville's Shorter Poems." *PR* 16 (O 49) 1034-46.
Ashley, C. W. "A Possible Verse Parody of *Moby-Dick*." *AN&Q* 2 (Jl 42) 62-3.
Auden, W. H. "The Christian Tragic Hero." *N Y Times Book R* 50 (16 D 45) 1, 21.
Baker, Carlos. "Of Art and Artifacts." *N Y Times Book R* 52 (10 Ag 47) 2.
Belgion, Montgomery. "Heterodoxy on *Moby Dick?*" *SR* 55 (Ja-Mr 47) 108-25.
Berkelman, R. G. "*Moby Dick*: Curiosity or Classic?" *EJ* (col ed) 27 (N 38) 742-55.
Beverley, Gordon. "Herman Melville's Confidence." *TLS* no 2493 (11 N 49) 733.
Birrell, Augustine. "The Great White Whale." *Athenaeum* no 4735 (28 Ja 21) 99-100; *Living Age* 308 (12 Mr 21) 659-61.
Birss, J. H. "Another, but Later, Redburn." *AN&Q* 6 (Ja 47) 150.
——— "A Book Review of Herman Melville." *NEQ* 5 (Ap 32) 346-8.
——— "Herman Melville and Blake." *N&Q* 166 5 (My 34) 311.
——— "Herman Melville and the *Atlantic Monthly*." *N&Q* 167 (29 S 34) 223-4.
——— "Herman Melville Lectures in Yonkers." *Am Book Coll* 5 (F 34) 50-2.
——— "International Copyright: A New Letter of Herman Melville." *N&Q* 173 (4 D 37) 402.
——— "A Letter of Herman Melville." *N&Q* 162 (16 Ja 32) 39.
——— "Melville and James Thompson ('B. V.')" *N&Q* 174 (5 Mr 38) 171-2.
——— "'A Mere Sale to Effect' with Letters of Herman Melville." *New Colophon* 1 (Jl 48) 239-55.
——— "*Moby Dick* under Another Name." *N&Q* 164 (25 Mr 33) 206.
——— "A Note on Melville's *Mardi*." *N&Q* 162 (4 Je 32) 404.
——— "An Obscure Melville Letter." *N&Q* 167 (15 O 32) 275.
——— "A Satire on Melville in Verse." *N&Q* 165 (9 D 33) 402.
——— *"The Story of Toby, a Sequel to Typee."* *Harvard Lib Bul* 1 (Wi 47) 118-9.

——— "Toward the Whole Evidence on Melville as a Lecturer." *AN&Q* 3 (Ap 43) 11-2.
——— "'Travelling,' a New Lecture by Herman Melville." *NEQ* 7 (D 34) 725-8.
——— "Whitman and Herman Melville." *N&Q* 164 (22 Ap 33) 280.
Blackmur, R. P. "The Craft of Herman Melville." *VQR* 14 (Sp 38) 266-82.
Blanck, Jacob. "News from the Rare Book Sellers." *Pub W* 152 (23 Ag 47) B122.
Braswell, William. "The Early Love Scenes of Melville's *Pierre*." *AL* 22 (N 50) 283-9.
——— "Melville as a Critic of Emerson." *AL* 9 (N 37) 317-34.
——— "Melville's Use of Seneca." *AL* 12 (Mr 40) 98-104.
——— "A Note on 'The Anatomy of Melville's Fame.'" *AL* 5 (Ja 34) 360-4.
——— "The Satirical Temper of Melville's *Pierre*." *AL* 7 (Ja 36) 424-38.
Brooks, Van Wyck. "Melville in the Berkshires." *Tiger's Eye* 1 (O 47) 47-52.
Brown, E. K. "Hawthorne, Melville, and 'Ethan Brand.'" *AL* 3 (Mr 31) 72-5.
Cahoon, Herbert. "Herman Melville and W. H. Hudson." *AN&Q* 8 (D 49) 131-2.
Canby, H. S. "Conrad and Melville." *Lit R* 2 (1922) 383-94.
Carpenter, F. I. "Puritans Preferred Blondes: The Heroines of Melville and Hawthorne." *NEQ* 9 (Je 36) 253-72.
Charvat, William. "Melville's Income." *AL* 15 (N 43) 251-61.
Chase, Richard. "An Approach to Melville." *PR* 16 (My-Je 47) 285-95.
——— "Dissent on *Billy Budd*." *PR* 15 (N 48) 1212-8.
——— "Melville's *Confidence Man*." *KR* 11 (Wi 49) 122-40.
Colcord, Lincoln. "Notes on 'Moby Dick.'" *Freeman* 5 (23 Ag 30) 559-62, 585-7.
Collins, Carvel. "Melville's *Moby Dick*." *Expl* 4 (F 46) 27.
Colum, Padriac. "*Moby Dick* as an Epic: A Note." *Measure* 13 (Mr 22) 16-8.
Connor, C. H. "Moby Dick" *CEA Critic* 10 (O 48) 3.
Cook, R. L. "Big Medicine in 'Moby Dick.'" *Accent* 8 (Wi 48) 102-9.
Cournot, Michael. "Essai sur Melville." *L'Arche* 3 (Ag-S 46) 42-52.
Damon, S. F. "Pierre the Ambiguous." *H&H* 2 (Ja-Mr 29) 107-18.
——— "Why Ishmael Went to Sea." *AL* 2 (N 30) 281-3.
Davis, M. R. "The Flower Symbolism in 'Mardi.'" *MLQ* 2 (D 41) 625-38.
——— "Melville's Midwestern Lecture Tour, 1859." *PQ* 20 (Ja 41) 46-57.
DeVoto, Bernard. "Editions of 'Typee.'" *SRL* 5 (24 N 28) 406.
Dix, W. S. "Herman Melville and the Problem of Evil." *Rice Inst Pam* 35 (Jl 48) 81-107.
Duffield, Brainerd. "Moby Dick: A Modern Adaptation." *Line* 1 (Ap-My 48) 32-40.
Duffy, Charles. "A Source for the Conclusion of Melville's 'Moby Dick.'" *N&Q* 181 (15 N 41) 278-9.
——— "Toward the Whole Evidence on Melville as a Lecturer." *AN&Q* 2 (Jl 42) 58.
Eby, E. H. "Herman Melville's 'Tartarus of Maids.'" *MLQ* 1 (Mr 40) 95-100.
Eliot, Alexander. "Melville and Bartleby." *Furioso* 3 (Fl 47) 11-21.
Erskine, John. "A Whale of a Story." *Delineator* (O 29) 15 ff.
Fadiman, Clifton. "Herman Melville." *Atl* 172 (O 43) 88-91.
Fagin, N. B. "Herman Melville and the Interior Monologue." *AL* 6 (Ja 35) 433-4.
Feltenstein, Rosalie. "Melville's 'Benito Cereno.'" *AL* 19 (N 47) 245-55.
Ferris, M. L. D. "Herman Melville." *Bul Soc Am Authors* 6 (S 01) 289-93.
Fiedler, L. A. "Out of the Whale." *Nation* 169 (19 N 49) 494-6.
Forsythe, R. S. "Emerson and 'Moby Dick.'" *N&Q* 177 (23 D 39) 457-8.
——— "Herman Melville in Honolulu." *NEQ* 8 (Mr 35) 99-105.
——— "Herman Melville in Tahiti." *PQ* 16 (O 37) 344-57.
——— "Herman Melville in the Marquesas." *PQ* 15 (Ja 36) 1-15.
——— "Herman Melville's Father Murphy." *N&Q* 172 (10, 17 Ap 37) 254-8, 272-6.
——— "Herman Melville's 'The Town-Ho's Story.'" *N&Q* 168 (4 My 35) 314.
——— "More upon Herman Melville in Tahiti." *PQ* 17 (Ja 38) 1-17.

——— "Mr. Lewis Mumford and Melville's *Pierre*." *AL* 2 (N 30) 286-9.
——— "An Oversight by Herman Melville." *N&Q* 172 (24 Ap 37) 296.
Foster, Elizabeth. "Melville and Geology." *AL* 17 (Mr 45) 50-65.
Freeman, F. B. "The Enigma of Melville's 'Daniel Orme.'" *AL* 16 (N 44) 208-11.
Galland, René. "Herman Melville et 'Moby-Dick.'" *Revue Anglo-Américaine* 5 (O 27) 1-9.
Garnett, R. S. "Moby-Dick and Mocha Dick: A Literary Find." *Blackwood's* 226 (D 29) 841-58.
Gary, L. M. "Rich Colors and Ominous Shadows." *SAQ* 37 (Ja 38) 41-5.
Gilman, W. H. "Melville's Liverpool Trip." *MLN* 60 (D 46) 543-7.
——— "A Note on Herman Melville in Honolulu." *AL* 19 (My 47) 169.
Giona, Jean. "Pour saluer Melville." *Nouvelle Revue Française* 26 (1 Ap 40) 433-58.
Giovanni, G. "Melville and Dante." *PMLA* 65 (Mr 50) 329.
——— "Melville's *Moby Dick*." *Expl* 5 (O 46) 7.
——— "Melville's *Pierre* and Dante's *Inferno*." *PMLA* 64 (Mr 49) 70-8.
Gleim, W. S. "A Theory of *Moby Dick*." *NEQ* 2 (Jl 29) 402-19.
Gohdes, Clarence. "Gossip about Melville in the South Seas." *NEQ* 10 (S 37) 526-31.
——— "Melville's Friend 'Toby.'" *MLN* 59 (Ja 44) 52-5.
Hall, J. B. "Moby Dick: Parable of a Dying System." *WR* 14 (Sp 50) 223-6.
Hamalian, Leo. "Melville's Art." *Expl* 8 (Mr 50) 40.
Haraszti, Zoltán. " Melville Defends *Typee*." *More Books* 22 (Je 47) 203-8.
Hart, J. D. "Melville and Dana." *AL* 9 (Mr 37) 49-55.
——— "A Note on Sherman Kent's 'Russian Christmas before the Mast.'" *AL* 14 (N 42) 294-8.
Hawthorne, Hildegarde. "Hawthorne and Melville." *Lit R* 2 (4 F 22) 406.
Hayford, Harrison. "Hawthorne, Melville, and the Sea." *NEQ* 19 (D 46) 435-52.
——— "The Significance of Melville's 'Agatha' Letters." *ELH* 13 (D 46) 299-310.
——— "Two New Letters of Herman Melville." *ELH* 11 (Mr 44) 76-83.
———, & Davis, Merrell. "Herman Melville as Office-Seeker." *MLQ* 10 (Je, S 49) 168-73, 377-88.
Heflin, W. L. "Melville's Third Whaler." *MLN* 64 (Ap 49) 241-5.
——— "The Source of Ahab's Lordship over the Level Loadstone." *AL* 20 (N 48) 323-7.
Hillway, Tyrus. "Melville and the Spirit of Science." *SAQ* 48 (Ja 49) 77-88.
——— "Melville as Critic of Science." *MLN* 65 (Je 50) 411-4.
——— "Melville's Art: One Aspect." *MLN* 62 (N 47) 477-80.
——— "Melville's *Billy Budd*." *Expl* 4 (N 45).
——— "Melville's Geological Knowledge." *AL* 21 (My 49) 232-7.
——— "Melville's Use of Two Pseudo-Sciences." *MLN* 64 (Mr 49) 145-50.
——— "A Note on Melville's Lecture in New Haven." *MLN* 60 (Ja 45) 55-7.
——— "Pierre, the Fool of Virtue." *AL* 21 (My 49) 201-11.
——— "Some Recent Articles Relating to Melville (January 1947 to September 1948)." *Melville Soc News Letter* 4 (1 N 48).
——— "Taji's Abdication in Herman Melville's *Mardi*." *AL* 16 (N 44) 204-7.
——— "Taji's Quest for Certainty." *AL* 18 (Mr 46) 27-34.
——— "The Unknowns in Whale Lore." *AN&Q* 8 (Ag 48) 68-9.
Hoffman, D. G. "Melville in the American Grain." *SFQ* 14 (S 50) 185-91.
——— "Melville's 'Story of China Aster.'" *AL* 22 (My 50) 137-49.
Hollis, Sophie. "Moby Dick: A Religious Interpretation." *Cath World* 163 (My 46) 158-62.
Homas, G. C. "The Dark Angel: The Tragedy of Herman Melville." *NEQ* 5 (O 32) 699-730.
Howard, Leon. "Melville and Spenser—A Note on Criticism." *MLN* 46 (My 31) 291-2.
——— "Melville's Struggle with the Angel." *MLQ* 1 (Je 40) 195-206.

——— "A Predecessor of *Moby Dick.*" *MLN* 49 (My 34) 310-1.
Howarth, R. G. "Melville and Australia." *N&Q* 193 (1 My 48) 188.
Hudson, H. H. "The Mystery of Herman Melville." *Freeman* 3 (27 Ap 21) 156-7.
Hughes, R. G. "Melville and Shakespeare." *Shakespeare Assn Bul* 7 (Jl 32) 103-12.
Hull, William. "Moby Dick: An Interpretation." *Etc* 5 (Au 47) 8-21.
Hunt, Livingston. "Herman Melville as a Naval Historian." *Harvard Grad Mag* 39 (S 30) 22-30.
Huntress, Keith. "Melville's Use of a Source for *White Jacket.*" *AL* 17 (Mr 45) 66-74.
——— "A Note on Melville's *Redburn.*" *NEQ* 18 (Je 45) 259-60.
Jaffé, David. "Some Sources of Melville's Mardi." *AL* 9 (Mr 37) 56-61.
Johnson, Arthur. "A Comparison [with Henry James] of Manners." *NRp* 20 (27 Ag 19) 113-5.
Jones, Joseph. "Ahab's 'Blood Quench': Theater or Metallurgy?" *AL* 18 (Mr 46) 35-7.
——— "Melville: A 'Humorist' in 1890." *AN&Q* 8 (Ag 48) 68.
Josephson, Matthew. "The Transfiguration of Herman Melville." *Outlook* 150 (19 S 28) 809-11, 832, 836.
Kaplan, Sidney. "'Omoo': Melville's and Boucicault's." *AN&Q* 8 (Ja 50) 150-1.
Kazin, Alfred. "The Inmost Leaf." *NRp* 111 (18 D 44) 218-20.
——— "On Melville as Scripture." *PR* 17 (Ja 50) 67-75.
Kimpel, B. D. "Two Notes on Herman Melville." *AL* 16 (Mr 44) 29-32.
Kummer, George. "Herman Melville and the Ohio Press." *Ohio State Arch & Hist Q* 41 (Ja 36) 34-5.
Larrabee, S. A. "Herman Melville's Early Years in Albany." *N Y Hist* 15 (Ap 34) 144-59.
——— "Melville against the World." *SAQ* 34 (O 35) 410-8.
Lease, Benjamin. "Melville's Gally, Gallow." *AS* 25 (O 50) 186.
Levin, Harry. "Don Quijote y Moby-Dick." *Realidad* 2 (1947) 254-67.
Lewis, R. W. B. "Melville on Homer." *AL* 22 (My 50) 166-77.
Leyda, Jay. "An Albany Journal of Gansevoort Melville." *BPLQ* 2 (O 50) 327-47.
——— "Ishmael Melvill: Remarks on Board of Ship *Amazon.*" *BPLQ* 1 (O 49) 199-34.
——— "White Elephant vs. White Whale." *Town & Country* 101 (Ag 47) 68 ff.
Lloyd, F. V., Jr. "Melville's First Lectures." *AL* 13 (Ja 42) 391-5.
Lucas, F. L. "Herman Melville." *New Statesman* 18 (1 Ap 22) 730-1.
Lueders, E. G. "The Melville-Hawthorne Relationship in *Pierre* and *The Blithedale Romance.*" *WHR* 4 (Au 50) 323-34.
Lundkvist, Artur. "Herman Melville." *Bonniers Litterära Magasin* (Stockholm) 11 (D 42) 773-86.
Lutwack, L. I. "Herman Melville and the *Atlantic Monthly Critics.*" *HLQ* 13 (S 50) 414-6.
Mabbott, T. O. "Herman Melville." *N&Q* 162 (27 F 32) 151-2.
——— "A Letter of Herman Melville." *N&Q* 176 (28 Ja 39) 60.
——— "Melville's *Moby Dick.*" *Expl* 8 (N 49) 15.
——— "Poem by Herman Melville." *N&Q* 162 (27 F 32) 151-2.
——— "A Source for the Conclusion of Melville's 'Moby Dick.'" *N&Q* 181 (26 Jl 41) 47-8.
McCloskey, J. C. "*Moby-Dick* and the Reviewers." *PQ* 25 (Ja 46) 20-31.
McCutcheon, R. P. "The Technique of Melville's Israel Potter." *SAQ* 27 (Ap 28) 161-74.
MacMehan, A. McK. "The Best Sea Story Ever Written." *Humane R* 7 (O 01) 242-52.
Mansfield, L. S. "Glimpses of Herman Melville's Life in Pittsfield, 1850-1851." *AL* 9 (Mr 37) 26-48.
——— "Melville's Comic Articles on Zachary Taylor." *AL* 9 (Ja 38) 411-8.

Maquet, Jean. "Sur Melville." *Critique* 1 (Ag- S 46) 229-30.
Marshall, H. P. "Herman Melville." *London Merc* 11 (N 24) 56-70.
Mather, F. J., Jr. "Herman Melville." *SRL* 5 (27 Ap 29) 945-6.
——— "Herman Melville." *Weekly R* 1 (9, 16 Ag 19) 276-8, 298-301.
Maugham, W. S. "Moby Dick." *Atl* 181 (Je 48) 98-104.
Metcalf, E. M. "A Pilgrim by Land and Sea." *Horn Book* 3 (F 27) 3-11.
Meynell, Viola. "Herman Melville." *Dublin R* 166 (Ja-Mr 20) 96-105; *Living Age* 304 (20 Mr 20) 715-20.
Mills, G. H. "The Castaway in *Moby-Dick*." *Un Texas Stud Eng* 39 (1950) 231-48.
——— "The Significance of 'Arcturus' in *Mardi*." *AL* 14 (My 42) 158-61.
Mordell, Albert. "Melville and 'White Jacket.'" *SRL* 7 (4 Jl 31) 946.
Morison, S. E. "Melville's 'Agatha' Letter to Hawthorne." *NEQ* 2 (Ap 29) 296-307.
Morpurgo, J. E. "Herman Melville and England." *Month* (London) 4 (S 50) 180-6.
Morris, L. R. "Melville: Promethean." *Open Court* 45 (S, O 31) 513-26, 621-35.
Mumford, Lewis. "Influence of Hawthorne on Melville." *Am Merc* 15 (D 28) 428-90.
——— "The Significance of Herman Melville." *NRp* 56 (10 O 28) 212-4.
——— "The Writing of 'Moby Dick.'" *Am Merc* 15 (D 28) 482-90.
——— "The Young Olympian." *SRL* 5 (15 D 28) 514-5.
Myers, H. A. "Captain Ahab's Discovery: The Tragic Meaning of *Moby Dick*." *NEQ* 15 (Mr 42) 15-34.
Nash, J. V. "Herman Melville, 'Ishmael' of American Literature." *Open Court* 40 (D 26) 734-42.
Nichol, J. W. "Melville's 'Soiled' Fish of the Sea." *AL* 21 (N 49) 338-9.
Oliver, E. S. "'Cock-A-Doodle-Do!' and Transcendental Hocus-Pocus." *NEQ* 21 (Je 48) 204-16.
——— "Melville's Goneril and Fanny Kemble." *NEQ* 18 (D 45) 489-500.
——— "Melville's Picture of Emerson and Thoreau in *The Confidence Man*." *CE* 8 (N 46) 61-72.
——— "A Second Look at 'Bartleby.'" *CE* 6 (My 45) 431-9.
Olson, Charles. "Lear and Moby Dick." *Twice a Year* 1 (1938) 165-89.
Opitz, E. A. "Herman Melville: An American Seer." *Contemp R* no 972 (D 46) 348-53.
Owlett, F. C. "Herman Melville (1819-1891): A Centenary Tribute." *Bkm* (London) 56 (Ag 19) 164-7.
P., B. A. "Ageless and Edible." *AN&Q* 7 (D 47) 141.
Paltsits, V. G. "Family Correspondence of Herman Melville." *BNYPL* 33 (Jl, Ag 29) 507-25, 575-625.
Parkes, H. B. "Poe, Hawthorne, Melville: An Essay in Sociological Criticism." *PR* 16 (F 49) 157-65.
Parks, A. W. "Leviathan: An Essay in Interpretation." *SR* 47 (Ja-Mr 39) 130-2.
Pattee, F. L. "Herman Melville." *Am Merc* 10 (Ja 27) 33-43.
Paul, Sherman. "Melville's 'The Town-Ho's Story.'" *AL* 21 (My 49) 212-21.
——— "Morgan Neville, Melville, and the Folk Hero." *N&Q* 194 (Je 49) 278.
Pavese, Cesare. "Herman Melville." *La Cultura* 11 (Ja-Mr 32) 83-93.
Pirano, F. "'Moby Dick' di Herman Melville." *Convivium* 15 (1943) 209-43.
Pommer, H. F. "Herman Melville and the Wake of the *Essex*." *AL* 20 (N 48) 290-304.
——— "Melville as Critic of Christianity." *Friends' Intelligencer* 102 (24 F 45) 121-3.
——— "Melville's 'The Gesture' and the Schoolbook Verses." *AN&Q* 6 (Ja 47) 150-1.
Potter, David. "The Brodhead Diaries, 1846-1849." *JRUL* 11 (D 47) 21-7.
——— "Reviews of *Moby Dick*." *JRUL* 3 (Je 40) 62-5.
Proctor, P. S. "A Source for the Flogging Incident in *White-Jacket*." *AL* 22 (My 50) 176-82.

Purcell, J. M. "Melville's Contribution to English." *PMLA* 56 (S 41) 797-808.
Quennell, Peter. "The Author of *Moby Dick.*" *New Statesman* 33 (24 Ag 29) 604.
Quinn, A. H. "The Creator of Moby Dick." *YR* ns 12 (O 22) 205-9.
Rahv, Phillip. "Melville and His Critics." *PR* 17 (S-O 50) 732-5.
Randall, D. A., & Winterich, J. T. "One Hundred Good Novels, Melville, Herman: 'Moby Dick.'" *Pub W* 137 (24 Ja 40) 255-7.
Riegel, O. W. "The Anatomy of Melville's Fame." *AL* 3 (My 31) 195-204.
Ritchie, M. C. "Herman Melville." *QQ* 37 (Wi 30) 36-61.
Roberts, Morley. "The Sea in Fiction." *QQ* 37 (Wi 30) 18-35.
Rousseaux, Andre. "Mardi." *Figaro Litteraire* 5 (9 D 50) 2.
Sackman, Douglas. "The Original of Melville's 'Apple Tree Table.'" *AL* 11 (Ja 40) 448-51.
Schiffman, Joseph. "Critical Problems in Melville's 'Benito Cereno.'" *MLQ* 11 (S 50) 317-24.
——— "Melville's Final Stage, Irony: A Re-examination of *Billy Budd* Criticism." *AL* 22 (My 50) 128-36.
Scott, W. D. "Some Implications of the Typhoon Scenes in *Moby Dick.*" *AL* 12 (Mr 40) 91-8.
Scudder, H. H. "Melville's *Benito Cereno* and Captain Delano's Voyages." *PMLA* 43 (Je 28) 502-32.
Sealts, M. M., Jr. "Did Melville Write 'October Mountain'?" *AL* 22 (My 50) 178-82.
——— "Herman Melville's 'I and My Chimney.'" *AL* 13 (My 41) 142-54.
——— "Melville and the Shakers." *PBSUV* 2 (1949-50) 105-14.
——— "Melville's Friend Atahalpa." *N&Q* 194 (22 Ja 49) 37-8.
——— "Melville's Reading: A Check-List of Books Owned and Borrowed." *HLB* 2 (Sp, Au 48) 141-63, 378-92; 3 (Wi, Sp, Au 49) 119-30, 268-77, 407-21; 4 (Wi 50) 98-109.
——— "The Publication of Melville's *Piazza Tales.*" *MLN* 59 (Ja 44) 56-9.
Short, R. W. "Melville as Symbolist." *UKCR* 15 (Au 49) 38-49.
Simon, Jean. "Recherches australiennes sur Herman Melville." *Revue Anglo-Américaine* 13 (D 35) 114-30.
Slochower, Harry. *"Moby Dick."* *Am Q* 2 (Fl 50) 259-69.
Spangler, E. R. "Harvest in a Barren Field: A Counterpoint." *WR* 14 (Su 50) 305-7.
Starke, A. H. "A Note on Lewis Mumford's Life of Herman Melville." *AL* 1 (N 29) 304-5.
Stevens, H. R. "Melville's Music." *Musicology* 2 (Jl 49) 405-21.
Stewart, Randall. "Ethan Brand." *SRL* 5 (27 Ap 29) 967.
——— "Hawthorne's Contributions to *The Salem Advertiser.*" *AL* 5 (Ja 34) 327-41.
Stonier, G. W. "Books in General." *New Statesman & Nation* 27 (5 F 44) 95.
Strachey, J. St. L. "Herman Melville: Mariner and Mystic." *Spectator* 128 (6 My 22) 559-60.
Sullivan, J. W. N. "Herman Melville." *TLS* no 1123 (26 Jl 23) 493-4.
"Thersites." "Talk on Parnassus." *N Y Times Book R* (24 My 49) 7, 27.
Thomas, Russell. "Melville's Use of Some Sources in *The Encantadas.*" *AL* 3 (Ja 32) 432-56.
——— "Yarn for Melville's *Typee.*" *PQ* 15 (Ja 36) 16-29.
Thorp, Willard. "Did Melville Review *The Scarlet Letter?*" *AL* 14 (N 42) 302-5.
——— "'Grace Greenwood' Parodies *Typee.*" *AL* 9 (Ja 38) 455-7.
——— "Herman Melville's Silent Years." *Un R* 3 (Su 37) 254-62.
——— "Redburn's Prosy Old Guidebook." *PMLA* 53 (D 38) 1145-56.
Tomlinson, H. M. "A Clue to 'Moby Dick.'" *Lit R* 2 (5 N 21) 141-2.
——— "Two Americans and a Whale." *Harper's* 152 (Ap 26) 618-21.
Van Doren, Carl. "The Later Work of Herman Melville." *Double Dealer* 3 (Ja 22) 9-20.

——— "Lucifer from Nantucket." *Century* 110 (Ag 25) 494-501.
——— "Melville before the Mast." *Century* 108 (Je 24) 272-7.
——— "A Note of Confession." *Nation* 127 (5 D 28) 622.
Victor, A. O. "Five Inches of Books." *Yale Un Lib Gaz* 22 (Ap 48) 127-8.
Vincent, H. P. "'White Jacket': An Essay in Interpretation." *NEQ* 22 (S 49) 304-15.
von Abele, Rudolph. "Melville and the Problem of Evil." *Am Merc* 65 (N 47) 592-8.
Wagenknecht, Edward. "Our Contemporary, Herman Melville." *EJ* 39 (Mr 50) 121-8.
Waggoner, H. H. "A Possible Verse Parody of *Moby-Dick* in 1865." *AN&Q* 2 (Ap 42) 3-6.
Wainger, B. M. "Herman Melville: A Study in Disillusion." *Union Col Bul* 25 (Ja 32) 35-62.
Walcutt, C. C. "The Fire Symbolism in *Moby Dick*." *MLN* 59 (My 44) 304-10.
Warren, R. P. "Melville the Poet." *KR* 8 (Sp 46) 208-23.
Watson, E. L. G. "Melville's *Pierre*." *NEQ* 3 (Ap 30) 195-234.
——— "Melville's Testament of Acceptance." *NEQ* 6 (Je 33) 318-27.
——— "'Moby Dick.'" *London Merc* 3 (D 20) 180-6.
Watters, R. E. "Boston's Salt-Water Preacher." *SAQ* 45 (Jl 46) 350-61.
——— "Melville's 'Isolatoes.'" *PMLA* 60 (D 45) 1138-48.
——— "Melville's Metaphysics of Evil." *UTQ* 9 (Ja 40) 170-82.
——— "Melville's 'Sociality.'" *AL* 17 (Mr 45) 33-49.
Weaks, Mabel. "Long Ago and 'Faraway': Traces of Melville in the Marquesas in the Journals of A. G. Jones, 1854-1855." *BNYPL* 52 (Jl 48) 362-9.
Weaver, R. M. "The Centennial of Herman Melville." *Nation* 109 (2 Ag 29) 145-6.
——— "Herman Melville." *Bkm* 54 (D 21) 318-26.
——— "Journal of Melville's Voyage in a Clipper Ship." *NEQ* 2 (Ap 29) 120-5.
Weber, Walter. "Some Characteristic Symbols in Herman Melville's Novels." *Eng Stud* 30 (O 49) 217-24.
Weeks, Donald. "Two Uses of *Moby Dick*." *Am Q* 2 (Su 50) 165-76.
Wegelin, Oscar. "Herman Melville as I Recall Him." *Colophon* ns 1 (Su 35) 21-4.
Weir, Charles, Jr. "Malice Reconciled: A Note on Billy Budd." *UTQ* 13 (Ap 44) 276-85.
Wells, H. W. "Herman Melville's *Clarel*." *CE* 4 (My 43) 478-83.
——— "*Moby Dick* and Rabelais." *MLN* 38 (F 23) 123.
——— "An Unobstrusive Democrat: Herman Melville." *SAQ* 43 (Ja 44) 46-51.
White, William. "Herman Melville, a New Source." *N&Q* 180 (7 Je 41) 403.
Williams, M. L. "Horace Greeley Reviews *Omoo*." *PQ* 27 (Ja 48) 94-6.
——— "Park Benjamin on Melville's 'Mardi.'" *AN&Q* 8 (D 49) 132-4.
——— "Some Notices and Reviews of Melville's Novels in American Religious Periodicals, 1846-1849." *AL* 22 (My 50) 121-7.
——— "Two Hawaiian-Americans Visit Herman Melville." *NEQ* 23 (Mr 50) 97-9.
Williams, S. T. "'Follow Your Leader': Melville's 'Benito Cereno.'" *VQR* 23 (Wi 47) 61-76.
Winterich, J. T. "Romantic Stories of Books, Second Series, IV: 'Moby Dick.'" *Pub W* 1166 (16 N 29) 2391-4.
Woolf, Leonard. "Herman Melville." *Nation & Athenaeum* 33 (1 S 23) 688.
Wright, Nathalia. "Biblical Allusion in Melville's Prose." *AL* 12 (My 40) 185-99.
——— "A Source for Melville's *Clarel*: Dean Stanley's *Sinai and Palestine*." *MLN* 62 (F 47) 110-6.

MENCKEN, HENRY LOUIS (1880-). Anon. "H. L. Mencken." *Bkm* 54 (F 22) 551-4.
——— "Mr. Mencken and the Prophets." *Freeman* 2 (13 O 20) 103-4.
Angoff, Charles. "Mencken Twilight." *NAR* 246 (Wi 38-9) 216-32.

Armstrong, Everhardt. "Mencken and America." *Nineteenth Century* 101 (Ja 27) 117-25.
Arvin, Newton. "The Role of Mr. Mencken." *Freeman* 6 (27 D 22) 381-2.
Babbitt, Irving. "The Critic and American Life." *Forum* 79 (F 28) 161-76.
Barzun, Jacques. "Mencken's America Speaking." *Atl* 177 (Ja 46) 62-5.
Beach, J. W. "Pedantic Study of Two Critics." *AS* 1 (Mr 26) 299-306.
Boyd, E. A. "Mencken, or Virtue Rewarded." *Freeman* 2 (2 F 21) 491-2.
Boynton, P. H. "American Literature and the Tart Set." *Freeman* 1 (7 Ap 20) 88-9.
Bridges, H. J. "Presenting Mr. H. L. Mencken." *Standard* 16 (Ap 27) 237-48.
Buckner, R. H. A. "H. L. Mencken." *Landmark* 11 (Ja 29) 29-32.
Butterfield, Roger. "Mr Mencken Sounds Off." *Life* 21 (5 Ag 46) 4-46, 48, 51-2.
Calverton, V. F. "H. L. Mencken: A Devaluation." *Mod Mo* 10 (N 36) 7-11.
Chesterton, G. K. "The Sceptic as Critic." *Forum* 81 (F 29) 65-9.
Clark, J. A. "H. L. Mencken: An Obituary." *Am Spect* (D 36-Ja 37) 11-2.
Collins, S. B. "Criticism in America." *Bkm* 71 (Je, Jl 30) 241-56, 353-64, 400-15.
Ely, C. B. "The Sorrows of Mencken." *NAR* 225 (Ja 28) 23-6.
Espey, W. R. "The Baltimore 'Sun' Goes Down." *Nation* 148 (4 F 39) 153-6.
Fitzgerald, F. S. "Baltimore Anti-Christ." *Bkm* 52 (Mr 21) 79-81.
Francis, R. L. "Mark Twain and H. L. Mencken." *Prairie Schooner* 24 (Sp 50) 31-40.
Gillis, J. M. "Mencken, Moralist!" *Cath World* 139 (Je 34) 257-66.
Gilman, Lawrence. "The American Language." *NAR* 209 (My 19) 697-703.
Harrold, C. F. "Two Critics of Democracy." *SAQ* 27 (Ap 28) 130-41.
Johnson, G. W. "The Congo, Mr. Mencken." *Reviewer* (Jl 23) 887-93.
Kelley, W. A. "At the Sign of the Basilisk." *Methodist R* 108 (Jl 25) 518-27.
Kronenberger, Louis. "H. L. Mencken." *NRp* 88 (7 O 36) 243-5.
——— "An Ill-Will Tour of the American Mind." *SRL* 32 (6 Ag 49) 38, 40, 42.
Lippmann, Walter. "H. L. Mencken." *SRL* 3 (11 D 26) 413-4.
——— "Near Machiavelli." *NRp* 30 (31 My 22) 12-4.
McFee, William. "Mencken and Mencken, or the Gift of Tongues." *Bkm* 53 (D 21) 361-3.
Manchester, William. "Mencken and the Mercury." *Harper's* 201 (Ag 50) 65-73.
——— "Mencken and the Twenties." *Harper's* 201 (Jl 50) 62-72.
Manning, Jack. "Interesting People: H. L. Mencken." *Am Mag* 144 (S 47) 101.
Maynard, Theodore. "Mencken Leaves 'The American Mercury.'" *Cath World* 139 (Ap 34) 10-20.
Melamed, S. M. "H. L. Mencken's Encyclopedia of Platitudes." *Reflex* 6 (My 30) 3-17.
Mencken, H. L. "H. L. Mencken." *Nation* 117 (5 D 23) 647-8.
——— "On Breaking into Type." *Colophon* (F 30) Pt 1.
——— "Postscripts to *The American Language:* The Life and Time of *O. K.*" *NYr* 25 (1 O 49) 56-60.
——— "Testament." *Rev of Rev* 76 (O 27) 413-6.
Michaud, Régis. "Henry Mencken ou le collectionneur de préjugés." *Nouvelles Littéraires* 7 (9 Je 28) 8.
Monroe, Harriet. "Mephistopheles and the Poet." *Poetry* 28 (Jl 26) 210-5.
Moss, David. "American First Editions . . . H. L. (Henry Louis) Mencken." *Pub W* 102 (28 Ap 23) 1327-8.
Parshley, H. M. "H. L. Mencken: An Appreciation." *Am R* 3 (Ja-F 25) 72-84.
Phelps, W. L. "As I Like It." *Scribner's* 88 (Ag 30) 205-8.
Rascoe, Burton. "Those Who Can, Criticize." *Bkm* 66 (F 28) 670-6.
Ratcliffe, S. K. "Mencken, An English Plaint." *NRp* 26 (13 Ap 21) 191-2.
Salisbury, William. "Mencken, The Foe of Beauty." *Am Parade* 1 (Jl 26) 34-49.
Saroyan, William. "The American Clowns of Criticism." *Overland Mo* ns 87 (Mr 29) 77-8.

Schneider, Isodor. "Mencken, A Portrait in Shadows." *New Masses* 33 (29 S 39) 17-8.
Semper, I. J. "H. L. Mencken and Catholicism." *Cath World* 136 (S 30) 641-50.
——— "H. L. Mencken, Doctor Rhetoricus." *Cath World* 134 (O 29) 30-41.
Sergeant, E. S. "H. L. Mencken." *Nation* 124 (16 F 27) 174-6.
Shaw, Albert. "Mencken and His Aims." *Rev of Rev* 76 (O 27) 412.
Sherman, S. P. "Mr. Brownell and Mr. Mencken." *Bkm* 60 (Ja 25) 632-4.
Simrell, E. V. "H. L. Mencken, the Rhetorician." *QJS* 13 (N 27) 399-412.
Sinclair, Upton. "Mr. Mencken Calls on Me." *Bkm* 66 (N 27) 254-6.
Swinnerton, Frank. "The Great Mencken Fight." *Bkm* 64 (D 26) 463-7.
Tacke, C. A. "H. L. Mencken." *New World Mo* 1 (F 30) 124-32.
Van Doren, Carl. "Smartness and Light." *Century* 105 (Mr 23) 791-6.
Williams, Michael. "Mr. Mencken's Bible for Boobs." *Commonweal* 11 (2 Ap 30) 607-10.
Wilson, Edmund. "H. L. Mencken." *NRp* 27 (1 Je 21) 10-3.

MERRILL, STUART (1863-1915). Chinard, Gilbert. "Letters of Stuart Merrill to Rudmose Brown." *PULC* 8 (Je 47) 168-71.

MERTON, THOMAS (1915-). Anon. "L'Amérique parle 'contemplation.'" *Etudes* (Paris) (F 50) 261-2.
Lissner, Will. "Toast of the Avant-Garde: A Trappist Poet." *Cath World* 166 (F 48) 424-32.
Thielen, J. A. "Thomas Merton: Poet of the Contemplative Life." *Cath World* 169 (My 49) 86-90.

MIDDLETON, GEORGE (1880-). Middleton, George. "Autumnal Appraisal." *N Y Times Book R* 52 (14 D 47) 20.

MILES, GEORGE HENRY (1824-71). Hurley, Doran. "Our First Dramatist." *America* 65 (29 N 41) 213-4.

MILLAY, EDNA ST. VINCENT (1892-1950). Anon. "Edna St. Vincent Millay." *Bkm* 55 (N 22) 272-8.
Barry, Griffin. "Vincent." *NYr* 3 (12 F 27) 25-7.
Beatty, Jerome. "'Best Sellers' in Verse: The Story of Edna St. Vincent Millay." *Am Mag* 43 (Ja 32) 37, 102-6.
Benét, W. R. "Round About Parnassus." *SRL* 11 (10 N 34) 279.
Bishop, J. P. "A Diversity of Opinions." *Poetry* 51 (N 37) 99-104.
Bogan, Louise. "Conversion into Self." *Poetry* 45 (F 35) 277-9.
Booth, B. A. "Millay's *Euclid Alone Has Looked on Beauty Bare.*" *Expl* 6 (O 47) 5.
Breuer, E. "Edna St. Vincent Millay." *Pictorial R* 33 (N 31) 50-7.
Burton, Katherine. "Edna St. Vincent Millay." *Commonweal* 2 (11 Mr 38) 544-5.
Bynner, Witter. "Edna St. Vincent Millay." *NRp* 41 (10 D 24) 14-5.
Chubb, T. C. "Shelley Grown Old." *NAR* 245 (Sp 38) 170-80.
Ciardi, John. "Edna St. Vincent Millay: A Figure of Passionate Living." *SRL* 33 (11 N 50) 8-9, 77.
Clemens, Cyril. "The Passing of Edna Vincent Millay." *Hobbies* (D 50) 140-1.
Colum, Padraic. "Miss Millay's Poems." *Freeman* 4 (2 N 21) 189-90.
Conrad, L. H. "Edna St. Vincent Millay." *Landmark* 15 (Je 33) 297-300.
Dabbs, J. M. "Edna St. Vincent Millay: Not Resigned." *SAQ* 37 (Ja 38) 54-66.
Davison, Edward. "Edna St. Vincent Millay." *EJ* 16 (N 27) 671-82.
Dickson, Arthur. "Millay's *Euclid Alone Has Looked on Beauty Bare.*" *Expl* 6 (My 48) 49.
DuBois, A. E. "Edna St. Vincent Millay." *SR* 43 (Ja-Mr 35) 80-104.
Elton, William. "Millay's *What's This of Death.*" *Expl* 7 (Mr 49) 37.

Fisher, E. K. "Edna St. Vincent Millay's Youth." *St Nicholas* 63 (S, O 36) 48-52.
Flanner, Hildegarde. "Two Poets: Jeffers and Millay." *NRp* 89 (27 Ja 37) 379-82.
Freer, A. L. "Baudelaire in English." *Poetry* 48 (Je 36) 158-62.
Gierasch, Walter. "Millay's *Memorial to D. C.: Elegy.*" *Expl* 2 (My 44).
Hennecke, Hans. "Edna St. Vincent Millay." *Neue Rundschau* 49 (Jl 38) 627-8.
Humphries, Rolfe. "Miss Millay as Artist." *Nation* 153 (30 D 41) 644-5.
Kies, P. P. "Notes on Millay's *The King's Henchman.*" *Res Stud State Col Wash* 14 (1946) 435-6.
Kohn, J. S. "Some Undergraduate Printings of Edna St. Vincent Millay." *Pub W* 138 (30 N 40) 2026-9.
MacDougall, A. R. "Husband of a Genius." *Delineator* 125 (O 34) 21, 40-1.
McInnis, E. "New Writers." *Canadian Forum* 11 (Ag 31) 424-5.
Monroe, Harriet. "Advance or Retreat?" *Poetry* 38 (Jl 31) 216-21.
——— "Edna St. Vincent Millay." *Poetry* 24 (Ag 24) 260-6.
——— "First Books in Verse." *Poetry* 13 (D 18) 167-8.
——— "Miss Millay in Opera." *Poetry* 30 (Ap 27) 42-6.
——— "Miss Millay's New Book." *Poetry* 33 (Ja 29) 210-4.
Nelson, June. "Miss Millay's 'The Fatal Interview.'" *Standard* 19 (Ja 32) 145-8.
Niemeyer, C. A., & Gay, R. M. "Millay's *Euclid Alone Has Looked on Beauty Bare.*" *Expl* 1 (N 42) 16.
Parks, E. W. "Edna St. Vincent Millay." *SR* 38 (Ja-Mr 30) 42-9.
Preston, J. H. "Edna St. Vincent Millay." *VQR* 3 (Jl 27) 342-55.
Ransom, J. C. "The Poet as Woman." *So R* 2 (1937) 783-806.
Rice, P. B. "Edna Millay's Maturity." *Nation* 139 (14 N 34) 568, 570.
Smole, A. K. "Rolfius and Miss Millay." *NRp* 67 (15 Jl 31) 237.
Strobel, Marion. "A Flourish of Trumpets." *Poetry* 19 (D 21) 151-4.
Tate, Allen. "Miss Millay's *Sonnets.*" *NRp* 66 (6 My 31) 335-6.
Van Doren, Carl. "Youth and Wings." *Century* 107 (Je 23) 310-6.

MILLER, ARTHUR (1915-). Kennedy, Sighle. "Who Killed the Salesman?" *Cath World* 171 (My 50) 110-6.
Schneider, D. E. "Play of Dreams." *Theatre Arts* 33 (O 49) 18-21.
Shea, A. A. "Death of a Salesman." *Canadian Forum* 29 (Jl 49) 86-7.

MILLER, HENRY (1891-). Bataille, Georges. "La Morale de Miller." *Critique* 1 (Je 46) 3-17.
Brady, M. E. "The New Cult of Sex and Anarchy." *Harper's* 194 (Ap 47) 312-22.
Chiaromonte, Nicola. "The Return of Henry Miller." *NRp* 111 (4 D 44) 751-2.
Chonez, Claudine. "Henry Miller: Du Pansexualisme à l'Angélisme." *Empédocle* (Paris) 2 (Jl-Ag 50) 74-80.
Durrell, Lawrence. "Studies in Genius: VIII—Henry Miller." *Horizon* 20 (Jl 49) 45-61.
Fowlie, Wallace. "Henry Miller, Prophète Americain." *Arts et Lettres* no 5 (Ière Année) 115-22.
——— "Shadow of Doom: An Essay on Henry Miller." *Accent* 5 (Au 44) 49-53.
Glicksberg, C. I. "Henry Miller: Individualist in Extremis." *Sw R* 33 (Su 48) 289-95.
Greer, Scott, *et al.* "To Be or Not: 4 Opinions on Henry Miller's *The Smile at the Foot of the Ladder.*" *Tiger's Eye* no 5 (20 O 48) 68-72.
Muller, H. J. "The Worlds of Henry Miller." *KR* 2 (Su 40) 312-8.
Neiman, Gilbert. "No Rubbish, No Albatrosses." *Rocky Mt R* 9 (Wi 45) 69-76.
Perles, Alfred. "Henry Miller in Villa Seurat." *Life & Letters Today* 41 (Je 44) 148-56.
Pierhal, Armand. "Éclaircissement sur Henry Miller." *La Neff* 4 (My 47) 23-9.
Quéval, Jean. "Henry Miller." *Poésie 47* no 37 (1947) 110-4.
Smith, Harrison. "The New Coast of Bohemia." *SRL* 30 (16 Ag 47) 18.

Vouga, Daniel. "Sur Henry Miller." *Suisse Contemporaine* (Lausanne) no 1 (Ja 47) 34-8.
Weiss, T. "Kenneth Patchen and Chaos as Vision." *Briarcliff Q* 3 (Jl 46) 127-34.

MILLER, JOAQUIN (1841?-1913). "Joaquin Miller's Memorial Number." *Overland Mo* ns 75 (F 20) 93-148.
Anon. "A Reviewer's Notebook." *Freeman* 3 (6 Ap 21) 94-5.
——— "Work of Joaquin Miller." *Dial* 54 (1 Mr 13) 165-7.
Akin, M. E. "Joaquin Miller's After-dinner Speech." *Overland Mo* ns 52 (S 08) 278-9.
Beebe, B. B. "Letters of Joaquin Miller." *Frontier* 12 (N 31-My 32) 121-4, 223-8, 344-7.
Bland, H. M. "Joaquin Miller: His Life and His Art." *Craftsman* 20 (Ag 11) 496-504.
Boynton, P. H. "Joaquin Miller." *NRp* 10 (24 F 17) 99-101.
Dunbar, J. R. "Joaquin Miller: Sedition and Civil War." *Pac Hist Q* 19 (F 50) 31-6.
——— "Some Letters of Joaquin Miller to Frederick Locker." *MLQ* 11 (D 50) 438-44.
Flower, B. O. "Joaquin Miller: A Nature-Loving Poet of Progress." *Arena* 22 (D 04) 603-15.
Garland, Hamlin. "The Poet of the Sierras." *Sunset* 30 (Je 13) 765-70.
Gettman, R. A. "A Note on Columbia College." *AL* 3 (Ja 32) 480-2.
Gohdes, Clarence. "Some Letters of Joaquin Miller to Lord Houghton." *MLQ* 3 (Je 42) 297-306.
Heywood, B. E. "Tally-ho, the Mountain Play." *Overland Mo* ns 73 (Je 19) 467-71.
Hubbard, Elbert. "Poet of the Sierras." *Hearst's* 23 (Ap 13) 662-3.
Lorch, F. W. "A Note on Joaquin Miller." *AL* 3 (Mr 31) 75-8.
Millard, Bailey. "Wild Joaquin." *Bkm* 28 (D 08) 342-9.
Miller, Joaquin. "The Indiana Boyhood of the Poet of the Sierras." *Ind Mag Hist* 30 (Je 34) 153-60.
——— "The Poet of the Sierras on His Problem Poem Dealing with Love after Marriage." *Arena* 37 (Mr 07) 271-3.
Peterson, M. S. "The Border Days of Joaquin Miller." *Frontier* 11 (My 31) 362-75, 410.
——— "Joaquim Miller: An Introductory Sketch." *Revue Anglo-Américaine* 9 (D 30) 114-22.
Ramsay, L. P. "The Birthplace of Joaquin Miller." *AL* 8 (My 36) 204-5.
Richards, J. S. "Joaquin Miller's California Diary." *Frontier & Midland* 16 (Au 35) 35-40.
Sherburne, E. B. "Joaquin Miller's Cabin." *Overland Mo* ns 61 (Mr 13) 226-7.
Shipley, M. "California's Great Poet." *Overland Mo* ns 75 (Je 20) 476, 537.
Sterling, George. "Joaquin Miller." *Am Merc* 7 (F 26) 220-9.
Taylor, Marian. "Joaquin Miller, Poet." *Overland Mo* ns 63 (F 14) 109-19.
Thompson, H. C. "Reminiscences of Joaquin Miller and Canyon City." *Ore Hist Q* 45 (D 44) 326-36.
Tsushima, S. "Joaquin Miller and Japan." *Nation* 96 (29 My 13) 5445.
Turner, Arlin. "Joaquin Miller in New Orleans." *La Hist Q* 22 (Ja 39) 216-25.
Veach, G. E. "The Indiana Boyhood of the Poet of the Sierras." *Ind Mag Hist* 30 (Je 34) 153-60.
Waterhouse, A. J. "Poet of the Sierras." *Sunset* 30 (Ap 13) 393-6.

MILLER, SAMUEL (1769-1850). Jantz, H. S. "The Samuel Miller Papers at Princeton." *PULC* 4 (F-Ap 43) 68-75.
——— "Samuel Miller's Survey of German Literature, 1803." *GR* 16 (D 41) 267-77.

MITCHELL, DONALD GRANT (1822-1908). Dunn, W. H. "James Whitcomb Riley and Donald G. Mitchell." *PMLA* 41 (S 26) 767-9.
Grattan, C. H. "Ik Marvel." *Am Merc* 7 (Ja 26) 83-6.
Kimball, A. R. "Master of Edgewood." *Scribner's* 27 (F 00) 184-93.
Marble, A. R. "The Charm of Ik Marvel." *Atl* 97 (F 06) 213-9.
More, P. E. "Donald G. Mitchell." *Nation* 86 (13 F 08) 144-5.
Seyholt, P. S. "American First Editions: Donald G. Mitchell (Ik Marvel) (1822-1908)." *Pub W* 7 (Ja 39) 83-6.
W., D. G. "Donald Grant Mitchell." *Yale Un Lib Gaz* 20 (Ap 46) 66-7.
Wilson, A. F. "Ik Marvel and Edgewood Farm: A Revery Come True." *Outlook* 90 (24 O 08) 391-6.

MITCHELL, MARGARET (1905-49). Anon. "Margaret Mitchell." *Pub W* 154 (20 Ag 49) 746.
Clark, G. R. "G. W. T. W." *Harper's* 198 (F 49) 97-8.
Clemens, Cyril. "Margaret Mitchell and Mark Twain." *Hobbies* (O 49) 140.
Rosenbaum, B. "Why Do They Read It?" *Scribner's* 102 (Ag 37) 23-4, 69-70.

MITCHELL, S. WEIR (1829-1914). Anon. "S. Weir Mitchell Number." *Book News Mo* 26 (O 07) 83-94.
Earnest, Ernest. "Weir Mitchell as Novelist." *Am Schol* 17 (Su 48) 314-22.
Farrand, Max. "Hugh Wynne: A Historical Novel." *Wash Hist Q* 1 (Ap 07) 101-8.
Hinsdale, Guy. "Recollections of Weir Mitchell." *Gen Mag & Hist Chron* 50 (Su 48) 248-54.
——— "S. Weir Mitchell, Poet, Novelist, Friend, Physician." *Gen Mag & Hist Chron* 38 (Ap 36) 303-13.
Mitchell, S. W. "Boyhood in the Red City, a Fragment of Autobiography." *Gen Mag & Hist Chron* 51 (Su 49) 151-6.
——— "Pennsylvania Student Life a Century Ago." *Gen Mag & Hist Chron* 52 (Wi 50) 65-75.
Oberholtzer, E. P. "Personal Memories of Weir Mitchell." *Bkm* 39 (Ap 14) 132-8.
Quinn, A. H. "Weir Mitchell: Artist, Pioneer and Patrician." *Century* 120 (Wi 30) 139-48.
Richardson, L. N. "S. Weir Mitchell at Work." *AL* 11 (Mr 39) 58-65.
Schauffler, R. H. "Versatility and Dr. S. Weir Mitchell." *Century* 87 (D 14) 267-9.
Schelling, F. E. "S. Weir Mitchell, Poet and Novelist." *Gen Mag & Hist Chron* 32 (Ap 30) 323-37.
Taylor, J. M. "Personal Glimpses of S. Weir Mitchell." *Annals Med Hist* ns 1 (S 29) 583-98.

MONK, MARIA (*c.* 1817-50). Thompson, Ralph. "The Maria Monk Affair." *Colophon* 5 (Je 34) Pt 17.

MONROE, HARRIET (1860-1936). Anon. "Poetry and Miss Monroe." *SRL* 9 (30 Jl 32) 13, 17.
Boie, Mildred. "A Wider Audience for Poetry." *NAR* 245 (Su 38) 408-14.
Gregory, Horace. "The 'Unheard of Adventure,' Harriet Monroe and *Poetry*." *Am Schol* 6 (Sp 37) 195-200.
Hayakawa, S. I. "Harriet Monroe as Critic." *Stud Eng* (Tokyo) 14 (1934) 1-7.
Monroe, Harriet. "Editorial Amenities." *Poetry* 14 (Ag 19) 262-6.
——— "The Enemies We Have Made." *Poetry* 4 (My 14) 61-4.
——— "Looking Backward." *Poetry* 33 (O 28) 32-8.
——— "These Five Years." *Poetry* 11 (O 17) 33-41.
——— "Twenty-One." *Poetry* 43 (O 33) 32-7.
Zabel, M. D. "Harriet Monroe." *Poetry* 49 (N 36) 85-93.
——— "Poetry's Quarter Century." *Poetry* 51 (O 37) 28-34.

MOODY, WILLIAM VAUGHN (1869-1910). Adkins, N. F. "The Poetic Philosophy of William Vaughn Moody." *Texas R* 9 (Ja 24) 97-112.
Barr, N. O., & Caffin, C. H. "William Vaughn Moody." *Drama* 2 (Ja 24) 177-211.
Blackmur, R. P. "Moody in Retrospect." *Poetry* 38 (S 31) 334-5.
Buchham, J. W. "The Doubt and Faith of William Vaughn Moody." *Homiletic R* 75 (My 18) 349-53.
Chislett, William. "Sources of William Vaughn Moody's Thammuz." *Dial* 60 (13 Ap 16) 370.
——— "William Vaughn Moody and William Blake." *Dial* 59 (2 S 15) 142.
Gilder, J. B. "William V. Moody." *Critic* 39 (S 01) 224-6.
Glasheen, F. J. & Adaline. "Moody's 'Ode in Time of Hesitation.'" *CE* 5 (D 43) 121-9.
Hegedorn, Herman. "William Vaughn Moody." *Independent* 74 (6 F 13) 314-6.
Harrington, F. H. "Literary Aspects of American Anti-Imperialism, 1898-1902." *NEQ* 10 (D 37) 650-67.
Jones, H. M. "William Vaughn Moody: An American Milton." *Double Dealer* 4 (1922) 79-86.
Lewis, C. M. "William Vaughn Moody." *YR* 2 (Jl 13) 688-703.
Lovett, R. M. "Memories of William Vaughn Moody." *Atl* 147 (Mr 31) 385-93.
McKeithan, D. M. "A Note on William Vaughn Moody's 'An Ode in Time of Hesitation.'" *AL* 9 (N 37) 349-51.
Mason, D. G. "Letters of William Vaughn Moody." *Atl* 112 (Ag, S 13) 167-76, 404-13.
Munson, G. B. "The Limbo of American Literature." *Broom* 2 (Je 22) 259-60.
Payne, W. M. "The Poetry of Mr. Moody." *Dial* 30 (1 Je 01) 365-9.
——— "William Vaughn Moody." *Dial* 53 (16 D 12) 484-6.
Rose, G. B. "Two Poets." *SR* 9 (Jl 01) 329-36.
Shackford, M. H. "Moody's *The Fire Bringer* for Today." *SR* 26 (O 18) 407-16.
Shorey, Paul. "The Poetry of William Vaughn Moody." *Un Rec* 13 (1927) 172-200.
Sinclair, May. "Three Poets of Today." *Atl* 98 (S 06) 325-35; *Fortnightly R* 86 (1 S 06) 429-34.
Soule, George. "A Great Pilgrim-Pagan." *Little R* 1 (Ja 14) 2-9.
Walker, C. R. "The Poetry of William Vaughn Moody." *Texas R* 1 (S 15) 144-53.

MOORE, CHARLES LEONARD (1854-?). Guthrie, W. N. "An American Poetic Drama." *SR* 9 (Ap 01) 215-9.

MOORE, CLEMENT CLARKE (1779-1863). West, H. L. "Who Wrote 'Twas the Night before Christmas'?" *Bkm* 52 (D 20) 300-5.

MOORE, JOHN TROTWOOD (1858-1929). Hervey, John. "Sweet Singer of Tennessee." *Hoof Beats* 15 (My 47) 6-7, 36, 37.

MOORE, MARIANNE (1887-). Anon. "News Notes." *Poetry* 74 (Ag 49) 308.
Brooks, Cleanth. "Miss Marianne Moore's Zoo." *Quar R Lit* 4 (1948) 179-83.
Burke, Kenneth. "Motives and Motifs in the Poetry of Marianne Moore." *Accent* 2 (Sp 42) 157-69.
Fowlie, Wallace. "Under the Equanimity of Language." *Quar R Lit* 4 (1948) 175-7.
Frankenberg, Lloyd. "The Imaginary Garden." *Quar R Lit* 4 (1948) 210-22.
Koch, Vivienne. "The Peaceable Kingdom of Marianne Moore." *Quar R Lit* 4 (1948) 157-67.
Lewis, May. "Marianne Moore: An Appreciation." *Forum* 96 (23 S 36) 48-9.
Monroe, Harriet. "Symposium on Marianne Moore." *Poetry* 19 (Ja 22) 208-16.
Moore, Marianne. "Selections from a Poet's Reading Diary." *Tiger's Eye* 1 (O 47) 22-8.
Ransom, J. C. "On Being Modern with Distinction." *Quar R Lit* 4 (1948) 140-1.

Stevens, Wallace. "About One of Marianne Moore's Poems." *Quar R Lit* 4 (1948) 143-7.
Sylvester, W. A. "Moore's *The Fish.*" *Expl* 7 (F 49) 30.
Untermeyer, Louis. "Poetry or Wit?" *Freeman* 6 (7 F 23) 524.
Westcott, Glenway. "Concerning Miss Moore's Observations." *Dial* 77 (Ja 25) 1-4.
Williams, W. C. "Marianne Moore." *Dial* 78 (My 25) 393-401.
———, *et al.* "Marianne Moore Issue." *Quar R Lit* 4 (1948) 125-223.
Winters, Yvor. "Holiday and Day of Wrath." *Poetry* 26 (Ap 25) 39-44.
Zabel, M. D. "A Literalist of the Imagination." *Poetry* 47 (Mr 36) 326-36.

MOORE, MERRILL (1903-). Fitts, Dudley. "The Sonnets of Merrill Moore." *SR* 47 (Ap-Je 39) 268-93.
Holden, Raymond. "Activities of an Amateur." *Poetry* 47 (O 35) 49-52.
McCord, David. "M-m-m-m-m." *SRL* 19 (7 Ja 39) 10.
Untermeyer, Louis. "Merrill Moore." *SR* 43 (Ja-Mr 35) 58-61.
Wells, F. L. "The Mental Measure of Merrill Moore." *Life & Letters Today* 21 (Mr 39) 27-35.
Winters, Yvor. "Merrill Moore's Poems." *Poetry* 36 (My 30) 104-6.

MORE, PAUL ELMER (1864-1937). Arvin, Newton. "The Everlasting No." *Freeman* 3 (1 Je 21) 283-4.
Bart, P. J. "The Christianity of Paul Elmer More." *Cath World* 135 (Ag 32) 542-7.
Bourne, Randolph. "Paul Elmer More." *NRp* 7 (1 Ap 16) 245-7.
Brett, G. S. "Paul Elmer More: A Study." *UTQ* 4 (Ap 35) 279-95.
Brewster, Dorothy. "When Right Meets Left." *Nation* 113 (27 Jl 21) 101-2.
Brown, S. G. "Toward an American Tradition." *SR* 47 (O 39) 476-97.
Cory, H. E. "An Aristocratic Voice in the Wilderness." *Dial* 61 (22 Je 16) 16-20.
Eliot, T. S. "A Commentary." *Criterion* 16 (Jl 37) 666-70.
Elliott, G. R. "More's Chistology." *Am R* 9 (Ap 37) 35-46.
——— "Mr. More and the Gentle Reader." *Bkm* 69 (Ap 29) 143-7.
——— "The Religious Dissension of Babbitt and More." *Am R* 9 (Su 37) 252-65.
Grattan, C. H. "The So-Called Humanism of Paul Elmer More." *New Humanist* 8 (N-D 35) 219-23.
Gregory, Horace. "On Paul Elmer More and His Shelbourne Essays." *Accent* 4 (Sp 44) 140-9.
Hackett, Francis. "Mr. More Moralizes." *NRp* 26 (6 Ap 21) 163-4.
Harper, G. M. "More's Shelburne Essays." *Atl* 98 (O 06) 561-70.
Krans, H. S. "Three Distinguished Critics." *Putnam's* 1 (Mr 07) 752-4.
Leander, Folke. "More—'Puritan *à rebours.*'" *Am Schol* 7 (Au 38) 438-53.
Leo, Brother. "Paul Elmer More." *Cath World* 116 (N 22) 198-211.
Mather, F. J., Jr. "Paul Elmer More, 1864-1937." *Proc Am Acad Arts & Sci* (My 38) 368-72.
Mercier, L. J. A. "The Challenge of Paul Elmer More." *Harvard Grad Mag* 34 (Je 26) 556-69.
Moore, C. A. "Berkeley's Influence on Popular Literature." *SAQ* 14 (Jl 15) 263-78.
More, L. T. "The Priest and the Boy." *SR* 50 (Ja 42) 49-56.
——— "Shelburne Revisited: An Intimate Glimpse of Paul Elmer More." *SR* 48 (O 40) 457-60.
Morrow, Felix. "The Serpent's Enemy." *Symposium* 1 (Ap 30) 168-93.
Murry, J. M. "Puritan or Platonist?" *Dial* 71 (Ag 21) 236-41.
Parkes, H. B. "Paul Elmer More: Manichean." *H&H* 5 (Ap-Je 32) 477-83.
Peck, H. W. "Some Aspects of the Criticism of Paul Elmer More." *SR* 26 (Ja 18) 63-84.
Pittenger, W. N. "Paul Elmer More As Theologian." *Am Church Mo* 41 (Je 37) 353-61.
Richards, P. S. "An American Platonist." *Nineteenth Century* 105 (Ap 29) 479-89.

——— "The Religious Philosophy of Paul Elmer More." *Criterion* 16 (Ja 37) 205-19.
Rinaker, Clarissa. "The Dualism of Mr. P. E. More." *Philos R* 26 (Jl 17) 409-20.
Seillière, Ernest. "La Réaction contre le Naturisme aux États-Unis." *J des Debats* (13 O 33) 580-2.
Shafer, Robert. "Paul Elmer More: A Note on His Verse and Prose Written in Youth, with Two Unpublished Poems." *AL* 20 (Mr 48) 43-51.
Sherman, S. P. "Mr. P. E. More and the Wits." *Weekly R* 2 (17 Ja 20) 54-6.
Spaeth, J. D. "Conversations with Paul Elmer More." *SR* 51 (O-D 43) 532-45.
Stamm, Rudolf. "Paul Elmer Mores Suche nach einer lebendigen Tradition." *Englische Studien* 72 (O 37) 58-72.
Tait, M. D. C. "The Humanism of Paul Elmer More." *UTQ* 16 (Ja 47) 109-22.
Tate, Allen. "The Fallacy of Humanism." *H&H* 3 (Ja-Mr 30) 234-58.
Warren, Austin. "Mr. More Discovers Christianity." *SR* 36 (Ap-Je 28) 246-50.
Wilson, Edmund. "Mr. More and the Mithraic Bull." *NRp* 91 (26 My 37) 64-8.
——— "Notes on Babbitt and More." *NRp* 62 (19 Mr 30) 115-20.
Young, Stark. "Art and Decision." *NRp* 91 (21 Jl 37) 307-8.
——— "Dear Mr. Wilson." *NRp* 91 (9 Je 37) 130-1.
Zabel, M. D. "An American Critic." *Poetry* 50 (S 37) 330-6.
Zeitlin, Jacob. "Stuart P. Sherman and Paul Elmer More: Correspondence." *Bkm* 70 (S 29) 43-53.

MORLEY, CHRISTOPHER (1890-). Altick, R. D. "Average Citizen in Grub Street: Christopher Morley after Twenty-five Years." *SAQ* 41 (Ja 42) 18-31.
Canby, H. S. "Christopher Morley." *EJ* 19 (Ja 30) 9-11.
Gordon, M. M. "*Kitty Foyle* and the Concept of Class as Culture." *Am J Soc* 53 (N 47) 210-7.
Kammer, A. S. "Wallace Stevens & Christopher Morley." *Furioso* 3 (Wi 48) 50-8.
McCord, David. "Christopher Morley." *EJ* 19 (Ja 30) 1-9.
Matthews, T. S. "Christopher Morley." *NRp* 54 (21 Mr 28) 167-9.
Mendoza, Aaron. "American First Editions . . . Christopher Morley." *Pub W* 102 (2 Je 23) 1705-6.
Morley, Christopher. "The Eighth Sin." *Colophon* pt 3 (1930) 1-8.
O'Sullivan, Vincent. "America and the English Literary Tradition." *Living Age* 303 (18 O 19) 170-6.
Stone, W. M. "My Christopher Morley's." *Am Book Coll* 3 (Ja 23) 33-7.
Van Doren, Carl. "Day In and Day Out. Adams, Morley, Marquis and Broun: Manhattan Wits." *Century* 107 (D 23) 309-15.

MORSE, JEDEDIAH (1761-1826). Johnson, Clifton. "The First American Geography." *N E Mag* ns 27 (Jl 03) 516-24.
Morse, Jedediah. "Letter from Jedediah Morse to John Stockdale." *PMHS* 57 (O 23) 70-1.
Turnem, Leonard. "Letters of a Young Geographer." *NEQ* 14 (D 41) 696-704.

MORTON, NATHANIEL (1613-86). Lord, Arthur. "Editions of Morton's New England's Memorial." *PCSM* 26 (1927) 158-62.

MORTON, SARAH WENTWORTH (1759-1846). MacDowell, Tremaine. "The First American Novel." *Am R* 2 (N 33) 73-81.
——— "Last Words of a Sentimental Heroine." *AL* 4 (My 32) 174-7.

MORTON, THOMAS (1590?-1647). Banks, C. E. "Thomas Morton of Merry Mount." *PMHS* 58 (D 24) 147-92; 59 (N 25) 92-5.
Connors, D. F. "Thomas Morton of Merry Mount: His First Arrival in New England." *AL* 11 (My 39) 160-6.

MOTLEY, JOHN LOTHROP (1814-77). Motley, J. L. "Motley Writes Ticknor a Letter of Appreciation." *Chri Sci Mon* 37 (7 Mr 45) 9.

Schantz, B. T. "Motley's 'The Chevalier de Sataniski.'" *AL* 13 (My 41) 155-7.

MOTLEY, WILLARD (1912-). Jarrett, T. D. "Sociology and Imagery in a Great American Novel." *EJ* 38 (N 49) 518-20.

MOULTON, LOUISE CHANDLER (1835-1908). Anon. "Checklist of the Writings of Louise Chandler Moulton." *PAAS* ns 43 (O 33) 234-6.

Rittenhouse, J. B. "Louise Chandler Moulton and Her London Friendships." *Bkm* 28 (F 09) 601-7.

MUIR, JOHN (1838-1914). Baker, R. S. "John Muir." *Outlook* 74 (6 Je 03) 365-77.

Barrus, Clara. "With John o'Birds and John o'Mountains in the Southwest." *Century* 80 (Ag 10) 521-8.

Bland, H. M. "John Muir." *Overland Mo* ns 47 (Jl 06) 517-25.

Clarken, G. G. "At Home with John Muir." *Overland Mo* ns 52 (Ag 08) 125-8.

Johnson, R. U. "Personal Impressions of John Muir." *Outlook* 80 (3 Je 05) 303-6.

Millard, Bailey. "A Skyland Philosopher." *Bkm* 26 (F 08) 593-9.

Pearson, L. E. "John Muir, Poet-Naturalist." *Poet-Lore* 36 (Ja 25) 45-62.

Roosevelt, Theodore. "John Muir: An Appreciation." *Outlook* 109 (6 Ja 15) 27-8.

Schunk, Fred. "Sierra Hymns." *NAR* 246 (Au 38) 185-91.

Strother, French. "John Muir." *World's Work* 13 (Mr 05) 637-54.

Van Hise, C. R. "John Muir." *Sci* ns 45 (2 F 17) 103-9.

Wolfe, L. M. "An Unpublished Journal of John Muir." *NAR* 245 (Sp 38) 24-51.

Wyatt, Edith. "John Muir." *NRp* 2 (20 F 15) 69-71.

Young, S. H. "John Muir in His Laboratory—Alaska." *World Outlook* 4 (My 18) 6-7.

MUMFORD, LEWIS (1895-). Ayres, C. E. "Talking of Cities." *So R* 4 (Au 38) 227-34.

Buchanan, Scott. "Mumford Tilts at Windmills." *VQR* 10 (Jl 34) 447-51.

Duff, Edward. "Lewis Mumford: The Post-Christian in an Anti-Christian World." *Commonweal* 37 (30 O 42) 38-42.

Farrell, J. T. "Faith of Lewis Mumford." *So R* 6 (Wi 41) 417-38.

Foerster, Norman. "The Literary Prophets." *Bkm* 72 (S 30) 39-44.

Forsythe, R. S. "Mr. Lewis Mumford and Melville's *Pierre*." *AL* 2 (N 30) 286-9.

Glicksberg, C. I. "Lewis Mumford and the Organic Synthesis." *SR* 45 (Ja-Mr 37) 55-73.

Grattan, C. H. "Open Letters to Lewisohn, Krutch, and Mumford." *Mod Mo* 7 (Ap 33) 175-81.

Jones, H. M. "Metropolis and Utopia." *NAR* 246 (Au 38) 170-8.

Rourke, Constance. "In Time of Hesitation." *Nation* 148 (18 F 39) 206-7.

MUNFORD, ROBERT (d. 1784). Canby, Courtlandt. "Robert Munford's *The Patriots*." *WMQ* 6 (Jl 49) 437-502.

Hubbell, J. B., & Adair, Douglass. "Robert Munford's *The Candidates*." *WMQ* 5 (Ap 48) 217-57.

MUNFORD, WILLIAM (1775-1825). Davis, R. B. "Homer in Homespun." *SLM* 1 (O 39) 647-51.

MUNSEY, FRANK ANDREW (1854-1925). Duffus, R. L. "Mr. Munsey." *Am Merc* 2 (Jl 24) 297-304.

MURFREE, MARY NOAILLES (1850-1922). Johnson, Merle. "American First Editions: Mary Noailles Murfree (Charles Egbert Craddock, 1850-1922)." *Pub W* 126 (18 Ag 34) 510.

Parks, E. W. "Craddock's First Pseudonym." *E Tenn Hist Soc Pub* 6 (1934) 67-80.
Waldo, Frank. "The Southern Appalachians." *N E Mag* ns 24 (My 01) 231-47.
Wright, Nathalia. "A Note on the Setting of Mary Noailles Murfree's 'The "Harnt" That Walks Chilhowee.'" *MLN* 62 (Ap 47) 272.

MURRAY, JUDITH SARGENT (1751-1820). Jorgenson, C. E. "Gleanings from Judith Sargent Murray." *AL* 12 (Mr 40) 73-8.

NATHAN, GEORGE JEAN (1882-). Anon. "George Jean Nathan." *Bkm* 59 (Ag 24) 695-700.
——— "George Jean Nathan." *Cur Biog* 6 (Ap 45) 32-6.
——— "Slapstick Satirist." *Cur Op* 63 (Ag 17) 95.
Boyd, Ernest. "George Jean Nathan." *Theatre Arts* 11 (Ja 27) 58-64.
Hazlitt, Henry. "George Jean Nathan." *Nation* 132 (18 F 31) 186-7.
Isaacs, E. J. R. "The Critical Arena: I. The Theatre of George Jean Nathan." *Theatre Arts* 26 (F 42) 104-12.
Johnson, M. D., & Hopkins, F. M. "American First Editions . . . George Jean Nathan." *Pub W* 103 (28 Jl 23) 380.
Kronenberger, Louis. "An Ill-Will Tour of the American Mind." *SRL* 32 (6 Ag 49) 38, 40, 42.
Saroyan, William. "The American Clowns of Criticism." *Overland Mo* ns 87 (Mr 29) 77-8, 92-3.
Shaw, C. G. "Through the Magnifying Glass." *NYr* 3 (15 O 27) 30-1.
Van Gelder, Robert. "An Interview with George Jean Nathan." *N Y Times Book R* (1 F 42) 2, 20.

NATHAN, ROBERT (1894-). Benét, S. V. & Rosemary. "Robert Nathan: A World of His Own." *N Y Herald Tribune Book R* (4 My 41) 6.
Dorian, E. M. "Robert Nathan: Novelist of Simplicity." *SR* 41 (Ap-Je 33) 129-43.
Fay, E. G. "Borrowing from Anatole France by Willa Cather and Robert Nathan." *MLN* 56 (My 41) 377.
Redman, B. R. "Expert in Depression: A Portrait of Robert Nathan." *SRL* 11 (13 O 34) 206.
Smith, Rex. "A Master of Fantasy." *Overland Mo* 87 (F 29) 41-2.
Spitz, Leon. "Robert Nathan's Jewish Types." *Am Hebrew* 158 (12 N 48) 10, 14, 15.
Tapley, Robert. "Robert Nathan: Poet and Ironist." *Bkm* 76 (N 32) 607-14.

NEAL, JOHN (1793-1876). Guest, Boyd. "John Neal and 'Women's Rights and Women's Wrongs.'" *NEQ* 18 (D 45) 508-15.
Lease, Benjamin. "John Neal: Yankee Extraordinary." *Ill Tech Engineer* 13 (D 47) 11-3, 38, 40.
Pollard, J. A. "John Neal, Doctor of American Literature." *Bul Friends' Hist Assn* 32 (Sp 43) 5-12.
Richards, I. T. "Audubon, Joseph R. Mason, and John Neal." *AL* 6 (My 34) 122-40.
——— "John Neal's Gleaning in Irvingiana." *AL* 8 (My 36) 170-9.
——— "Mary Gove Nichols and John Neal." *NEQ* 7 (Je 34) 335-55.
Rubin, J. J. "John Neal's Poetics as an Influence on Whitman and Poe." *NEQ* 14 (Je 41) 359-62.
Yorke, Dean. "Yankee Neal." *Am Merc* 19 (Mr 30) 361-8.

NEIHARDT, JOHN G. (1881-). Adkins, N. F. "A Study of John G. Neihardt's 'Song of Three Friends.'" *AS* 3 (Ap 28) 276-90.
Beach, J. W. "Fourth Dimensional." *Poetry* 28 (S 26) 350-2.
Cuff, R. P. "Neihardt's Epic of the West." *CE* 9 (N 47) 69-72.

Lee, G. S. "Deciding about a New Author." *Putnam's* 4 (Jl 08) 473-4.
Monroe, Harriet. "A Laurelled Poem." *Poetry* 17 (N 20) 94-8.
——— "The Nebraska Laureate." *Poetry* 18 (Jl 21) 212-3.
——— "What of Mr. Neihardt?" *Poetry* 30 (My 27) 99-104.
Van Slyke, Berenice. "Neihardt's Epic." *Poetry* 27 (Mr 26) 328-31.

NEVILLE, MORGAN (1783-1840). Flanagan, J. T. "Morgan Neville: Early Western Chronicler." *West Penn Hist Mag* 21 (D 38) 255-66.

NEWELL, ROBERT HENRY (1836-1901). Meredith, Mamie. "Local Discolor." *AS* 6 (Ap 31) 260-3.

NEWTON, EDWARD (1863-1940). Birss, J. H. "American First Editions: Alfred Edward Newton (1863-): Checklist." *Pub W* 126 (3 N 34) 1664-5.
Tinker, C. B. "The Caliph of Books: A. E. N." *Atl* 172 (D 43) 102-6.

NICHOLSON, SIR FRANCIS (1655-1728). Boas, F. S. "A Herod Play from America." *Contemp R* 144 (N 33) 575-80.
Downey, Fairfax. "The Governor Goes A-Wooing." *VMHB* 55 (Ja 47) 6-19.

NILES, HEZEKIAH (1777-1839). Luxon, N. N. "H. Niles, the Man and the Editor." *Miss Valley Hist R* 28 (Je 41) 27-40.

NIMS, JOHN FREDERICK (1913-). Ciardi, John. "John Frederick Nims and the Modern Idiom." *UKCR* 14 (Wi 47) 105-10.

NOBLE, LOUIS LEGRAND (1813-82). Burklund, C. E. "An Early Michigan Poet: Louis Legrand Noble." *Mich Hist* 31 (Je 47) 192-9.

NORRIS, FRANK (1870-1902). Anon. "Frank Norris's Werewolf." *Cur Op* 56 (Je 14) 455-6.
——— "Last Work of Frank Norris." *Harper's W* 47 (14 Mr 03) 433.
Armes, W. D. "Concerning the Work of the Late Frank Norris." *Sunset* 10 (D 02) 165-75.
Bixler, P. H. "Frank Norris's Literary Reputation." *AL* 6 (My 34) 109-21.
Britten, F. H. "'Prissy' Frank Norris." *N Y Herald Tribune Books* (23 Ag 31) 13.
Burgess, Gelett. "One More Tribute to Frank Norris." *Sunset* 10 (Ja 03) 246.
Cassady, E. E. "Muckraking in the Gilded Age." *AL* 13 (1941) 134-41.
Chamberlain, John. "The 'Prentice Days of Frank Norris." *N Y Times Book R* (3 My 31) 2, 10.
Clift, D. H. "The Artist in Frank Norris." *Pac Mo* 17 (Mr 07) 313-22.
Cooper, F. T. "Frank Norris." *Bkm* 16 (D 02) 334-5.
——— "Frank Norris's 'The Octopus.'" *Bkm* 13 (My 01) 245-7.
Cowley, Malcolm. "Naturalism's Terrible McTeague." *NRp* 116 (5 My 47) 31-3.
Dobie, C. C. "Frank Norris, or Up from Culture." *Am Merc* 13 (Ap 28) 412-24.
Duffus, R. L. "Norris in Retrospect." *N Y Times Book R* 52 (8 Je 47) 5.
Edgett, E. F. "Norris's Posthumous Novel." *Boston Eve Transcript* sec 2 (22 Ap 14) 8.
Edwards, Herbert. "Zola and the American Critics." *AL* 4 (1932) 114-29.
Flower, B. O. "The Trust in Fiction: A Remarkable Social Novel." *Arena* 27 (My 02) 547-54.
Garland, Hamlin. "The Work of Frank Norris." *Critic* 42 (Mr 03) 216-8.
Goodrich, Arthur. "Frank Norris." *Cur Lit* 33 (D 02) 764.
Grattan, C. H. "Frank Norris." *Bkm* 69 (Jl 29) 506-10.
——— "Frank Norris." *Nation* 135 (30 N 32) 535-6.
Hellman, Geoffrey. "Trail-blazer of Realism." *N Y Herald Tribune Books* (4 D 32) 25.
Howells, W. D. "Frank Norris." *NAR* 175 (D 02) 769-78.

——— "The Last Work of Frank Norris." *Harper's W* 47 (14 Mr 03) 433.
Kazin, Alfred. "Three Pioneer Realists." *SRL* 20 (8 Jl 39) 3-4, 14-5.
Levick, M. B. "Frank Norris." *Overland Mo* 45 (Je 05) 504-8.
McKee, Irving. "Notable Memorials to Mussel Slough." *Pac Hist R* 17 (Ja 48) 19-27.
Martin, W. E., Jr. "The Establishment of the Order of Printings in Books Printed from Plates: Illustrated in Frank Norris's *The Octopus,* with Full Collations." *AL* 5 (Mr 33) 17-28.
——— "Frank Norris's Reading at Harvard College." *AL* 7 (My 35) 203-4.
——— "Two Uncollected Essays by Frank Norris." *AL* 8 (My 36) 190-8.
Meyer, G. W. "A New Interpretation of *The Octopus.*" *CE* 4 (Mr 43) 351-9.
Millard, Bailey. "A Significant Literary Life." *Out West* 18 (Ja 03) 49-55.
Peixotto, Ernest. "Romanticist under the Skin." *SRL* 9 (27 My 33) 613-5.
Preston, H. W. "The Novels of Mr. Norris." *Atl* 91 (My 03) 691-2.
Reninger, H. W. "Norris Explains *The Octopus:* A Correlation of His Theory and Practice." *AL* 12 (My 40) 218-27.
Stephens, H. M. "The Work of Frank Norris: An Appreciation." *Un Calif Chron* 16 (Ja 13).
Wagenknecht, Edward. "Frank Norris in Retrospect." *VQR* 6 (Ap 30) 313-20.
Walcutt, C. C. "Frank Norris and the Search for Form." *UKCR* 14 (Wi 47) 126-36.
——— "Frank Norris on Realism and Naturalism." *AL* 13 (Mr 41) 61-3.
Walker, Franklin. "Frank Norris at the University of Califfornia." *Un Calif Chron* 33 (Jl 31) 320-49.
Wister, Owen. "'The Pit—A Story of Chicago': The Last and Best Novel of the Late Frank Norris." *World's Work* 5 (F 03) 3133-4.
Wright, H. M. "In Memoriam—Frank Norris." *Un Calif Chron* 5 (O 02) 240-5.

NORTON, ANDREWS (1786-1853). Heindel, R. H. "Transatlantic Cross Currents." *Harvard Alumni Bul* (4 N 38).

NORTON, CHARLES ELIOT (1827-1908). Anon. Charles Eliot Norton number. *Harvard Grad Mag* 16 (1907).
Higginson, T. W. "Charles Eliot Norton." *Outlook* 90 (31 O 08) 491-4.
Howells, W. D. "Charles Eliot Norton: A Reminiscence." *NAR* 198 (D 13) 836-48.
Littlefield, Walter. "Charles Eliot Norton." *Century* 87 (Mr 14) 780-1.
Norton, C. E. "Three Letters from Charles Eliot Norton to Beadle and Company." *PMHS* 50 (F 17) 196-9.
Shaffer, R. B. "Ruskin, Norton and Memorial Hall." *HLB* 3 (Sp 49) 213-31.
Sioussat, St. G. L. "The Letters of Charles Eliot Norton." *SR* 24 (Ap 16) 229-34.
Snyder, H. N. "Ruskin's Letters to Charles Eliot Norton." *SAQ* 4 (Ap 05) 115-22.
Sumner, Charles. "Letters from Charles Sumner to Charles Eliot Norton." *PMHS* 58 (N 24) 135-6.
Thayer, W. R. "Charles Eliot Norton." *Nation* 87 (29 O 08) 403-6.
Warren, Austin. "Mr. Norton of Shady Hill." *Am R* 8 (N 36) 86-114.
Wendell, Barrett. "Charles Eliot Norton." *Atl* 103 (Ja 09) 82-8.

NYE, EDGAR WATSON (1850-96). Anon. "Letters of Riley and Bill Nye." *Harper's* 138 (Mr 19) 473-84.
Blair, Walter. "The Popularity of Nineteenth-Century American Humorists." *AL* 3 (My 31) 175-94.
Davidson, L. J. "Bill Nye and *The Denver Tribune.*" *Colo Mag* 4 (1928) 13-8.
Nye, E. W. "'Bill Nye' on the Art of Lecturing." *Century* 58 (Je 10) 316-9.
Watson, Edgar. "Bill Nye's Experience." *Annals of Wyo* 16 (Ja 44) 65-70.

O'BRIEN, FITZ-JAMES (*c.* 1828-62). Fatout, Paul. "An Enchanted Titan." *SAQ* 30 (Ja 31) 51-9.

Reilly, J. J. "A Keltic Poe." *Cath World* 110 (Mr 20) 751-62.
Wolle, Francis. "Fitz-James O'Brien in Ireland and England, 1828-1851." *AL* 14 (N 42) 234-49.
——— "'Violina' by Fitz-James O'Brien." *Un Colo Stud* 2: ser B (O 45) 328-36.

ODELL, JONATHAN (1737-1818). Leary, Lewis. "Francis Hopkinson, Jonathan Odell, and 'The Temple of Cloacina.'" *AL* 15 (My 43) 183-91.
Rede, Kenneth. "A Note on the Author of *The Times.*" *AL* 2 (Mr 30) 79-82.

ODETS, CLIFFORD (1906-). Gassner, John. "The Long Journey of Talent." *Theatre Arts* 33 (Jl 49) 25-30.
Isaacs, E. J. R. "Clifford Odets." *Theatre Arts* 23 (Ap 39) 257-64.
McCarten, John. "Revolution's Number One Boy." *NYr* (22 Ja 38) 21-7.
Vernon, Grenville. "Clifford Odets." *Commonweal* 29 (16 D 38) 215.
Warshow, R. S. "Poet of the Jewish Middle Class." *Commentary* 1 (My 46) 17-22.

ODIORNE, THOMAS (1769-1851). Howard, Leon. "Thomas Odiorne: An American Predecessor of Wordsworth." *AL* 10 (Ja 39) 417-36.

OGILVIE, JAMES (1760-1820). Davis, R. B. "James Ogilvie, an Early American Teacher of Rhetoric." *QJS* 28 (O 42) 289-97.

OGLETHORPE, JAMES EDWARD (1696-1785). Kirk, Rudolph. "A Latin Poem by James Edward Oglethorpe." *Ga Hist Q* 32 (Mr 48) 29-31.

O'HARA, JOHN (1905-). Anon. "John O'Hara." *N Y Herald Tribune Books* 26 (28 Ag 49) 2.

O'HARA, THEODORE (1820-67). Herbert, M. S. "Colonel Theodore O'Hara, Author of 'The Bivouac of the Dead.'—Soldier, Orator, Poet and Journalist." *Ky State Hist Soc Reg* 39 (Jl 41) 230-6.

O'NEILL, EUGENE (1888-). Anon. "Counsels of Despair." *TLS* no 2410 (10 Ap 48) 197-9.
——— "*Emperor Jones* in a Raucous Triumph." *Lit Dig* 115 (21 Ja 33) 15.
——— "Eugene O'Neill." *Writer* 38 (D 26) 585-7.
——— "Movie of the Week: Mourning Becomes Electra." *Life* 23 (8 D 47) 63-6.
——— "Mr. Eugene O'Neill. An Iconoclast in the Theatre." *TLS* (8 My 37) 353-4.
——— "O'Neill before the Cross." *Living Age* 347 (F 35) 554-56.
——— "The Ordeal of Eugene O'Neill." *Time* 48 (21 O 46) 71-2, 74-6, 78.
Anderson, John. "Eugene O'Neill." *Theatre Arts* 15 (N 31) 938-42.
Arestad, Sverre. "The Iceman Cometh and The Wild Duck." *SS* 20 (F 48) 1-11.
Baker, G. P. "O'Neill's First Decade." *YR* ns 15 (Jl 26) 789-92.
Baldensperger, Fernand. "Eugene O'Neill, Prix Nobel de Littérature." *Revue Bleue* (6 F 37) 73-8.
Barbetti, E. "O'Neill sulla scena italiana." *Anglica* (D 46) 6.
Barron, Samuel. "The Dying Theater." *Harper's* 172 (D 35) 108-17.
Basso, Hamilton. "The Tragic Sense." *NYr* 24 (28 F, 6 Mr, 13 Mr 48) 34-8, 40, 42-3; 34-8, 40, 43-4; 37-40, 42, 44, 47.
Battenhouse, R. W. "'Mourning Becomes Electra.'" *Christendom* 7 (Su 42) 332-45.
——— "'Strange Interlude' Restudied." *Religion in Life* 15 (Sp 46) 202-13.
Baughan, E. A. "Plays of Eugene O'Neill." *Fortnightly R* 119 (My 23) 852-60.
Baury, Louis. "Mr. O'Neill's New Plays." *Freeman* 5 (3 My 22) 184-5.
Bentley, Eric. "The Return of Eugene O'Neill." *Atl* 178 (N 46) 64-6.
Bird, C. "Eugene O'Neill—The Inner Man." *Theatre Mag* 39 (Je 24) 9, 60.
Blackburn, Clara. "Continental Influences on Eugene O'Neill's Expressionistic Dramas." *AL* 13 (My 41) 103-33.
Boyd, Ernest. "Eugene O'Neill and Others." *Bkm* 69 (Ap 29) 179-81.

——— "A Great American Dramatist." *Freeman* 3 (6 Jl 21) 404-5.

Breese, J. M. "Home on the Dunes." *Country Life* 45 (N 23) 72-6.

Brie, Friedrich. "Eugene O'Neill als Nachfolger der Griechen." *Germanisch-Romanische Monatsschrift* 21 (Ja-F 33) 46-59.

Brown, J. M. "All O'Neilling." *SRL* 29 (19 O 46) 26-30.

——— "Canned Drama." *SRL* (13 D 47) 22-4.

Canby, H. S. "Scarlet Becomes Crimson." *SRL* 8 (7 N 31) 257-8.

Carpenter, F. I. "The Romantic Tragedy of Eugene O'Neill." *CE* 6 (F 45) 250-8.

Catel, Jean. "Eugene O'Neill." *Mercure de France* 274 (1 Mr 37) 422-6.

Cestre, Charles. "Eugene O'Neill." *Etudes Anglaises* 1 (Ja 37) 93-4.

——— "Eugene O'Neill et les surgissements du trefond." *Revue Anglo-Amér* 6 (1928) 131-44.

Chiesura, Giogio. "Intoro a una commedia di O'Neill." *Letteratura* (Italy) 9 (My-Je 47) 16-30.

Clark, B. H. "Aeschylus and O'Neill." *EJ* 21 (N 32) 699-710.

——— "Eugene O'Neill: A Chapter in Biography." *Theatre Arts* 10 (My 26) 325-30, 333-6.

——— "The Eugene O'Neill Collection." *Yale Un Lib Gaz* 18 (Jl 43) 5-8.

——— "The Hairy Ape." *Freeman* 5 (26 Ap 22) 160-1.

——— "O'Neill—New Risen Attic Stream?" *Am Schol* 6 (Su 37) 304-12.

Conrad, L. H. "Eugene O'Neill." *Landmark* 11 (Jl 29) 413-6.

Corbin, John. "O'Neill and Aeschylus." *SRL* 8 (30 Ap 32) 693-5.

Crawford, Jack. "A Broadway Philosopher." *Drama* 12 (1922) 117-8, 142.

Davidson, L. J. "Lazarus in Modern Literature." *EJ* (Col Ed) 18 (Je 29) 16-23.

DeCasseres, Benjamin. "Eugene O'Neill: From Cardiff to Xanadu." *Theatre Mag* 46 (Ag 27) 10, 58.

DeVoto, Bernard. "Minority Report." *SRL* 15 (21 N 36) 3-4, 16.

Dirvana, Nesterin. "Théatre Pur et Rythme Biologique." *Dialogues* (Istanbul) 1: no 1 (Je 49) 87-105.

Dobrée, Bonamy. "Mr. O'Neill's Latest Play." *SR* 56 (Wi 48) 118-26.

——— "The Plays of Eugene O'Neill." *So R* 2 (Wi 37) 435-46.

Dony, Francoise. "La tragédie d'Eugène O'Neill et l'idée de fatalité." *Revue de l'Univérsitaire de Bruxelles* (D 35) 170-88.

——— "Vices et vertus du personnage O'Neillien." *Renaissance* 1 (O-D 45) 589-98.

Dukes, Ashley. "The English Scene: O'Neill Succeeds." *Theatre Arts* 22 (F 38) 101-7.

Eastman, F. "Eugene O'Neill and Religion." *Christian Century* 50 (26 Jl 33) 955-7.

Eaton, W. P. "American Drama Flowers: Eugene O'Neill as a Great Playwright." *World's Work* 55 (N 26) 105-8.

——— "Eugene O'Neill as a Dramatist." *Theatre Arts* 4 (O 20) 286-9.

Edel, Leon. "Eugene O'Neill: The Face and the Mask." *UTQ* 7 (O 37) 18-34.

Fagin, N. B. "Eugene O'Neill Contemplates Mortality." *Open Court* 45 (Ap 31) 208-19.

Fergusson, Francis. "Eugene O'Neill." *H&H* 3 (Ja-Mr 30) 145-60.

——— "Mr. O'Neill's New Play." *Am R* 2 (F 34) 491-5.

Frenz, Horst. "Eugene O'Neill in France." *Books Abroad* 19 (Sp 44) 140-1.

——— "Eugene O'Neill in Russia." *Poet Lore* 49 (Au 43) 241-7.

——— "Eugene O'Neill on the London Stage." *QQ* 54 (Su 47) 223-30.

——— "List of Foreign Editions and Translations of Eugene O'Neill's Dramas." *Bul Bibl* 18 (S-D 43) 33-4.

——— 'O'Neill Collections I Have Seen." *Ind Quar for Bkm* 2 (Ja 45) 27-34.

Fulchignoni, Enrico. "Il Drammaturgo." *Fiera Letteraria* no 24 (12 Je 47).

Garland, Robert. "Eugene O'Neill and This Big Business of Broadway." *Theatre Arts* 9 (Ja 25) 3-6, 9-12, 15-6.

Geddes, Virgil. "Eugene O'Neill." *Theatre Arts* 15 (N 31) 943-6.

Geier, Woodrow. "O'Neill's Miracle Play." *Religion in Life* 16 (Au 47) 515-26.
——— "O'Neill's 'Dynamo' and the Village Experiments." *Drama* 8 (Ap 29) 199-201, 222-3.
Gillet, Louis. "La Clef des songes." *Revue des Deux Mondes* 49 (15 Ja 29) 453-64.
Griffin, W. J. "The Cariocas Discover O'Neill." *Theatre Arts* 31 (Ag 47) 44-6.
Halman, D. F. 'O'Neill and the Untrained Playwright." *Writer* 38 (Jl 28) 215-7.
Haucher, Dorothy. "Modern Dramatic Structure: Eugene O'Neill." *Un Mo Stud* 3 (O 28) 125-58.
Hayward, I. N. "Strindberg's Influence on Eugene O'Neill." *Poet Lore* 39 (Ja-D 28) 596-604.
Helburn, Theresa. "O'Neill: An Impression." *SRL* 15 (21 N 36) 10.
Hilton, James. "The Short Plays of Eugene O'Neill." *Bkm* (London) 84 (S 33) 288-9.
Hofmannsthal, Hugo. "Eugene O'Neill." *Freeman* 7 (21 Mr 23) 39-41.
Hopkins, V. C. "'The Iceman' Seen through 'The Lower Depths.'" *CE* 11 (N 49) 81-7.
Isaacs, E. J. R. "Meet Eugene O'Neill." *Theatre Arts* 30 (O 46) 567-87.
Janney, J. "Perfect Ending." *Am Mag* 117 (Ap 34) 39, 110, 112.
Jones, Carless. "A Sailor's O'Neill." *Revue Anglo-Amér* 12 (F 35) 226-9.
Katzin, Winifred. "The Great God O'Neill." *Bkm* 68 (S 28) 61-6.
Kemelman, H. G. "O'Neill and Highbrow Melodrama." *Bkm* 75 (S 32) 482-91.
Kemp, Harry. "Out of Provincetown: A Memoir of Eugene O'Neill." *Theatre Mag* 51 (Ap 30) 22-3, 66.
Kirchner, Gustav. "Eugene O'Neill: The Iceman Cometh." *Neuphilologische Zeitschrift* 1 (1950) 28-37.
Knickerbocker, F. W. "A New England House of Atreus." *SR* 40 (Ap-Je 32) 249-54.
Krutch, J. W. "The God of Stumps." *Nation* 119 (26 N 24) 578-80.
——— "O'Neill Again." *Nation* 134 (17 F 32) 210-1.
——— "O'Neill's Tragic Sense." *Am Schol* 16 (Su 47) 283-90.
Kühnemund, Richard. "Das Drama Eugene O'Neills." *Anglia* 52 (S 28) 242-87.
Lamm, Martin. "Problemet Eugene O'Neill." *Bonniers Litterära Magasin* 16 (O 47) 633-9.
Lanoire, Maurice. "Eugene O'Neill." *Revue de Paris* (1 F 37) 595-612.
Lewisohn, Ludwig. "The Development of Eugene O'Neill." *Nation* 114 (22 Mr 22) 349-50.
Loving, P. "Eugene O'Neill." *Bkm* 53 (Ag 21) 511-20.
Lowell, J., Jr. "Eugene O'Neill's Darker Brother." *Theatre Arts* 32 (F 48) 45-8.
Lundkvist, Artur. "Eugene O'Neill." *Bonniers Litterära Magasin* 5 (D 36) 784-6.
McAneny, M. L. "Eleven Manuscripts of Eugene O'Neill." *PULC* 4 (Ap 43) 86-9.
Macgowan, Kenneth. "Broadway at the Spring: Broadway Sees Its First Impressionistic Play." *Theatre Arts* 6 (Jl 22) 179-82, 187-90.
——— "The O'Neill Soliloquy." *Theatre Guild* Mag 6 (F 29) 23-5.
McQuire, K. "Beyond 'Strange Interlude.'" *Drama* 19 (Mr 29) 172, 189-90.
Mackall, L. L. "Notes for Bibliophiles: Eugene O'Neill's Bibliography." *N Y Herald Tribune Books* 91 (9 Ag 31) 15.
Mainsard, Joseph. "Le Théâtre d'Eugène O'Neill." *Étude* 212 (5 O 30) 57-8.
Malone, A. E. "The Plays of Eugene O'Neill." *Contemp R* 129 (Mr 26) 363-72.
Malone, Kemp. "The Diction of Strange Interlude." *AS* 6 (O 30) 19-28.
Martínez-Hague, Carlos. "Eugene O'Neill, Premio Nobel." *Letras* (Lima) 2 (1936) 427-32.
Montgomery, Guy. "Strange Interlude." *Un Calif Chron* 30 (Jl 28) 364-8.
Moses, M. J. "The 'New' Eugene O'Neill." *NAR* 236 (D 33) 543-9.
Mullett, M. B. "The Extraordinary Story of Eugene O'Neill." *Am Mag* 94 (N 22) 34, 112, 114, 116, 118, 120.

Naranjo Martinez, Enrique. "Perfiles Angloamericanos. I. Eugene O'Neill." *Revista Iberoamericana* 8 (My 44) 61-102.
Nathan, Adele. "Eugene G. O'Neill: 1916." *N Y Times Mag* (6 O 46) 34-5.
Nathan, G. J. "The American Dramatist." *Am Merc* 17 (Ag 29) 500.
——— "The Case of O'Neill." *Am Merc* 13 (Ap 28) 500-2.
——— "Eugene O'Neill nach Zwölf Jahren." *Prisma* 8 (My 47) 45-6.
——— "O'Neill: A Critical Summation." *Am Merc* 63 (D 46) 713-9.
——— "O'Neill's Finest Play." *Am Merc* 11 (Ag 27) 499-506.
——— "O'Neill's Latest." *Am Merc* 8 (F 26) 247-9.
——— "O'Neill's New Play." *Am Merc* 9 (Ag 26) 499-505.
Nicholls, Norah. "Checklist of Eugene O'Neill." *Bkm* (London) 84 (S 33) 300.
Norwood, Gilbert. "The Art of Eugene O'Neill." *Dalhousie R* 21 (Jl 41) 143-57.
O'Neill, Eugene. "Memoranda on Masks." *Am Spect* 1 (N 32) 3.
——— "Second Thoughts." *Am Spect* 1 (D 32) 2.
Ortiz-Vargas, Alfredo. "Perfiles anglo-americanos: Eugene O'Neill." *Revista Iberoamericana* 8 (My 44) 61-102.
Parks, E. W. "Eugene O'Neill." *Revista de Instituto Brasil-Estados Unidos* 8 (Ja-Je 50) 52-5.
——— "Eugene O'Neill's Symbolism." *SR* 43 (O-D 35) 436-50.
Perry, William. "Does the Buskin Fit O'Neill?" *UKCR* 15 (Su 49) 281-7.
Prideaux, Tom. "Eugene O'Neill." *Life* 21 (14 O 46) 102-4, 106, 108, 110, 113-4, 116.
Quinn, A. H. "Eugene O'Neill. Poet and Mystic." *Scribner's* ns 80 (O 26) 368-72.
Roland, Betty. "O'Neill in Sidney." *Theatre Arts* 30 (O 46) 527-30.
Rosenfeld, Paul. "O'Neill into Opera." *NRp* 52 (22 F 33) 47-8.
Sayler, O. M. "Delving into the Subconscious." *Freeman* 2 (24 N 20) 256-7.
——— "Eugene O'Neill, Master of Naturalism." *Drama* 11 (Mr 21) 189-90.
——— "The Real Eugene O'Neill." *Century* 103 (Ja 22) 351-9.
Sergeant, E. S. "O'Neill, the Man with a Mask." *NRp* 50 (16 Mr 27) 91-5.
Shay, Frank. "American First Editions . . . Eugene (Gladstone) O'Neill." *Pub W* 106 (14 Ap 25) 1216.
Skinner, R. D. "O'Neill, and the Poet's Quest." *NAR* 240 (Je 35) 54-67.
Slochower, Harry. "Eugene O'Neill's Lost Moderns." *Un R* 9 (Au 43) 32-7.
Smith, John. "If I Had Written 'Mourning Becomes Electra.'" *Mod Thinker* 1 (Ag 32) 359-63.
Soupolt, Philippe. "Le Théatre aux États-Unis." *Revue de Paris* 3 (Je 33) 936-44.
Stamm, Rudolf. "The Dramatic Experiments of Eugene O'Neill." *Eng Stud* 28 (F 47) 1-15.
——— "A New Play by Eugene O'Neill." *Eng Stud* 29 (O 48) 138-45.
——— "The Orestes Theme in Three Plays by Eugene O'Neill, T. S. Eliot, and Jean-Paul Sartre." *Eng Stud* Luedeke Anniv No (1949) 244-55.
Steinhauer, H. "Eros and Psyche: A Nietzschean Motif in Anglo-American Literature." *MLN* 64 (Ap 49) 217-28.
Stevens, T. W. "How Good Is Eugene O'Neill?" *EJ* 26 (Mr 37) 179-86.
Sullivan, Frank. "Life Is A Bowl of Eugene O'Neills." *NYr* 7 (21 N 31) 17-8.
Sutton, Graham. "Eugene O'Neill." *Bkm* (London) 64 (My 23) 126-8.
Tapper, Bonno. "Eugene O'Neill's World View." *Personalist* 18 (Ja 37) 40-8.
Tetauer, F. "Eugene O'Neill." *Apollon* 2 (1924-5) 10-3, 30-1, 40-1.
Trilling, Lionel. "Eugene O'Neill." *NRp* 88 (23 S 36) 176-8.
Vernon, G. "Our Native Dramatist Comes into His Own." *Theatre Mag* 41 (My 25) 20, 80.
von Hofmannsthal, Hugo. "Eugene O'Neill." *Freeman* 6 (21 Mr 23) 39-41.
von Wiegand, Charmion. "The Quest of Eugene O'Neill." *New Theatre* 2 (S 35) 12-7, 30-2.
Whipple, T. K. "The Tragedy of Eugene O'Neill." *NRp* 41 (21 Ja 25) 222-5.
White, A. F. "The Plays of Eugene O'Neill." *West Res Un Bul* 25 (1923) 20-36.

Woodbridge, H. E. "Eugene O'Neill." *SAQ* 37 (Ja 38) 22-35.
Woolf, S. J. "Eugene O'Neill Returns after Fifty Years." *N Y Times Mag* (15 S 45) 61-2.
——— "O'Neill Plots a Course for the Drama." *N Y Times Mag* 81 (4 O 31) 6.
Young, Stark. "Eugene O'Neill." *NRp* 32 (15 N 22) 307-8.
——— "Eugene O'Neill's New Play." *NRp* 68 (11 N 31) 352-5.

O'REILLY, JOHN BOYLE (1844-90). Bledsoe, Thomas. "John Boyle O'Reilly; Poet-Prophet of Democracy." *Crisis* 52 (Ja 45) 18-9, 28.
Clemens, Cyril. "John Boyle O'Reilly: Neglected New England Poet." *Poet Lore* no 4 (Wi 48) 361-72.
Finn, B. A. "John Boyle O'Reilly, 1884-1944." *Cath World* 159 (Ag 44) 410-6.
Stockley, W. F. P. "Reminiscences of John Boyle O'Reilly." *Cath World* 140 (Mr 35) 664-72; 141 (Ap 35) 73-81.

OSTENSO, MARTHA (1900-). Anon. "Writer of Novels Wants to Do Play." *Chri Sci Mon* 29 (17 Ag 37) 12.

O'SULLIVAN, VINCENT (1872-). McWilliams, Carey. "Vincent O'Sullivan." *SAQ* 30 (O 31) 394-404.

OTIS, JAMES (1725-83). Gates, F. P. "James Otis and Jonathan Swift: Comments upon Their Literary Relationship." *NEQ* 5 (Ap 32) 344-6.
M., M. "Polemics of James Otis." *More Books* 17 (Mr 42) 115.
Mullett, C. F. "Some Political Writings of James Otis, Collected with an Introduction by C. F. Mullett." *Un Mo Stud* 4 (Jl, O 29) 259-432.

OWEN, ROBERT DALE (1801-77). Himes, N. E. "Robert Dale Owen, the Pioneer of American Neo-Malthusianism." *Am J Soc* 35 (Ja 30) 529-47.

PAGE, THOMAS NELSON (1853-1922). Anon. "Idealist in Prose." *Outlook* 87 (30 N 07) 742-3.
——— "Thomas Nelson Page." *Outlook* 132 (15 N 22) 468-9.
Fuller, H. B. "Thomas Nelson Page." *Freeman* 7 (18 Jl 23) 450-2.
Gordon, A. C. "Thomas Nelson Page: An Appreciation." *Scribner's* 73 (Ja 23) 75-80.
Harrington, F. H. "Literary Aspects of American Antiquarianism." *NEQ* 10 (D 37) 650-67.
Holman, Harriet. "A Letter from Henry W. Grady Regarding Southern Authors and the Piedmont Chautauqua." *Ga Hist Q* 30 (D 46) 308-11.
Jacobs, C. F. "Thomas Nelson Page." *J Nat Educ Assn* 12 (F 23) 59.
Kent, C. W. "Thomas Nelson Page." *SAQ* 6 (Ap 07) 263-71.
Mims, Edwin. "Thomas Nelson Page." *Atl* 100 (Jl 07) 109-15.
Orcutt, W. D. "Celebrities Off Parade." *Chri Sci Mon* 27 (22 Mr 35) 12.
Quinn, A. H. "Passing of a Literary Era." *SRL* 1 (21 Mr 25) 609-10.
Tree, Ronald. "Thomas Nelson Page." *Forum* 69 (Ja 23) 1137-42.

PAGE, WALTER HINES (1855-1918). Connor, R. D. W. "Walter Hines Page: A Southern Nationalist." *J Soc Forces* 2 (Ja 24) 164-8.
Gibson, J. M. "Walter Hines Page Has Been 'Forgiven.'" *SAQ* 32 (Jl 33) 283-83.
Grattan, C. H. "The Walter Hines Page Legend." *Am Merc* 6 (S 25) 39-51.
Mims, Edwin. "Walter Hines Page: Friend of the South." *SAQ* 18 (Ap 19) 97-115.

PAINE, ROBERT TREAT (1773-1811). Hale, Philip. "A Boston Dramatic Critic of a Century Ago." *PMHS* 59 (My 26) 312-24.

PAINE, THOMAS (1737-1809). Anon. "The English Voltaire, Tom Paine: Citizen of the World." *TLS* no 1826 (30 Ja 37) 65-6.

——— "Part of a Letter of James Monroe, dated Jan. 7, 1796." *Autograph Album* 1 (D 33) 89.

Abel, Darrel. "The Significance of the Letter to the Abbé Raynal in the Progress of Thomas Paine's Thought." *PMHB* 66 (Ap 42) 191-204.

Aldridge, A. O. "Why Did Thomas Paine Write on the Bank?" *PAPS* 93 (S 49) 309-15.

Bizardel, Yvon. "Paine le Ressuscité." *Les Lettres Françaises* (20 S 46) 3.

Calverton, V. F. "Thomas Paine: God-Intoxicated Revolutionary." *Scribner's* 95 (Ja 34) 15-22.

Clark, H. H. "An Historical Interpretation of Thomas Paine's Religion." *Un Calif Chron* 25 (Ja 33) 56-87.

——— "Thomas Paine's Relation to Voltaire and Rousseau." *Revue Anglo-Américaine* 9 (Ap, Je 32) 305-18, 393-405.

——— "Thomas Paine's Theories of Rhetoric." *Trans Wisc Acad Sci, Arts & Letters* 28 (1933) 307-39.

——— "Toward a Reinterpretation of Thomas Paine." *AL* 5 (My 33) 133-45.

Colby, Elbridge. "Letters from Thomas Hardy to Thomas Paine." *Nation* 106 (18 My 18) 589-91.

Connell, J. M. "Thomas Paine—The Man As He Was." *Hibbert J* 35 (Ja 37) 213-26.

Cordasco, Francesco. "Tom Paine Silenced." *AN&Q* 8 (Ja 50) 150.

Dickson, H. E. "The Jarvis Portrait of Thomas Paine." *N Y Hist Soc Q* 34 (Ja 50) 5-11.

Dodd, W. E. "Tom Paine." *Am Merc* 21 (D 30) 477-83.

Dorfman, Joseph. "The Economic Philosophy of Thomas Paine." *Pol Sci Q* 53 (S 38) 372-86.

Enson, R. C. K. "Tom Paine's Bicentenary." *London Spect* 5 (29 Ja 37) 163-4.

Falk, R. P. "Thomas Paine and the Attitude of the Quakers to the American Revolution." *PMHB* 63 (Jl 39) 302-10.

——— "Thomas Paine: Deist or Quaker?" *PMHB* 62 (Ja 38) 52-63.

Fast, Howard. "Who Was Tom Paine?" *New Masses* 54 (27 F 45) 23-4.

Flynn, E. G. "Tom Paine Was an Alien, Too." *New Masses* 38 (18 F 41) 41.

Garrison, F. W. "Paine and the Physiocrats." *Freeman* 8 (7 N 23) 205-6.

Gibbens, V. E. "Tom Paine and the Idea of Progress." *PMHB* 66 (Ap 42) 191-204.

Hogue, Caroline. "The Authorship and Date of 'The American Patriot's Prayer.'" *AL* 2 (My 30) 168-72.

Kellog, L. P. "Letter of Thomas Paine, 1793." *AHR* 29 (Ap 24) 501-5.

Kramer, Sidney. "'My Much Loved America . . .'" *Lib Cong Quar J* 1 (Jl-S 43) 17-22.

Landin, H. W. "Some Letters of Thomas Paine and William Short on the Nootka Sound Crisis." *J Mod Hist* 13 (S 41) 357-474.

Laske, H. J. "A Valiant Pamphleteer." *Manchester Guardian W* 36 (5 F 37) 116.

McCloy, S. T. "Rationalists and Religion in the Eighteenth Century." *SAQ* 46 (O 47) 467-82.

Matthews, Albert. "Thomas Paine and the Declaration of Independence." *PMHS* 43 (1910) 245-6.

Meng, J. J. "Thomas Paine, French Propagandist in the United States." *Rec Am Cath Hist Soc Phila* 57 (Mr 46) 1-21.

Miller, Perry. "Thomas Paine, Rationalist." *Nation* 162 (23 F 46) 228-32.

Muzzey, D. S. "Thomas Paine and American Independence." *Am R* 4 (My-Je 26) 278-88.

Nicholson, Marjorie. "Thomas Paine, Edward Nares, and Mrs. Piozzi's Marginalia." *Huntington Lib Bul* no 10 (O 36) 103-33.

Palmer, R. R. "Tom Paine: Victim of the Rights of Men." *PMHB* 66 (Ap 42) 161-75.

Paradyne, Henry. "Misunderstood Patriot." *Harper's W* 53 (5 Je 09) 15.
Penniman, Howard. "Thomas Paine—Democrat." *Am Pol Sci R* 37 (Ap 43) 244-62.
Persinger, C. E. "The Political Philosophy of Thomas Paine." *Un Neb Grad Bul* 3: ser 6 (Jl 01) 54-74.
Seitz, D. C. "Thomas Paine, Bridge Builder." *VQR* 3 (O 27) 571-84.
Smith, Frank. "The Authorship of 'An Occasional Letter on the Female Sex.'" *AL* 2 (N 30) 277-80.
——— "The Date of Thomas Paine's First Arrival in America." *AL* 3 (N 31) 317-8.
——— "New Light on Thomas Paine's First Year in America, 1775." *AL* 1 (Ja 30) 347-71.
Ward, E. F. "Thomas Paine." *Negro Hist Bul* 6 (Ja 43) 80-93.
Wecter, Dixon. "Hero in Reverse." *VQR* 18 (Ap 42) 243-59.
——— "Thomas Paine and the Franklins." *AL* 12 (N 40) 306-17.
Woodress, J. L., Jr. "The 'Cold War' of 1790-1791: Documented by a Collection of Eighteenth-Century Pamphlets in the Duke University Library." Duke Un *Lib Notes* no 20 (Jl 48) 7-18.
Woodward, W. E. "Tom Paine." *Am Merc* 61 (Jl 45) 72-9.
Zunder, T. A. "Notes on the Friendship of Joel Barlow and Tom Paine." *Am Book Coll* 6 (Mr 35) 96-9.

PARKER, CARLETON H. (1879-1918). Parker, C. S. "An American Idyll: Episodes in the Life of Carleton H. Parker." *Atl* 123 (Ja-Je 19) 299-310, 497-512.

PARKER, DOROTHY (1893-). Johnson, Merle. "American First Editions: Dorothy Parker (Rothschild) (1893-)." *Pub W* 125 (17 Mr 34) 1154.
Luhrs, Marie. "Fashionable Poetry." *Poetry* 30 (Ap 27) 52-4.
Maurois, André. "Écrivains américains." *Revue de Paris* 54 (Ap 47) 9-24.
North, Sterling. "More Than Enough Rope." *Poetry* 33 (D 28) 156-8.
Rosenberg, Harold. "Nor Rosemary, nor Rue." *Poetry* 39 (D 31) 159-61.
Van Doren, Mark. "Dorothy Parker." *EJ* 23 (S 34) 535-43.

PARKER, THEODORE (1810-60). Angoff, Charles. "Theodore Parker." *Am Merc* 10 (Ja 27) 81-8.
Christie, F. A. "Theodore Parker and Modern Theology." *Meadville J* 25 (O 30) 3-17.
Commager, H. S. "The Dilemma of Theodore Parker." *NEQ* 6 (Je 33) 257-77.
——— "Tempest in a Boston Tea Cup." *NEQ* 6 (D 33) 651-75.
——— "Theodore Parker, Intellectual Gourmand." *Am Schol* 3 (Su 34) 106-23.
Hicks, Granville. "Letters to William Francis Channing." *AL* 2 (N 30) 294-8.
Higginson, T. W. "Two New England Heretics: Channing and Parker." *Independent* 54 (22 My 02) 1234-6.
Ladu, A. I. "The Political Ideals of Theodore Parker." *SP* 38 (Ja 41) 106-23.
Mead, Theodore. "Theodore Parker in Ohio." *Nw Ohio Q* 21 (Wi 48-9) 18-23.
Newbrough, G. F. "Reason and Understanding in the Works of Theodore Parker." *SAQ* 47 (Ja 48) 64-75.
Sanborn, F. B. "Theodore Parker and John Brown." *Outlook* 93 (4 D 09) 791-2.
——— "Theodore Parker and R. W. Emerson." *Critic* 49 (S 06) 273-81.
Smith, H. S. "Was Theodore Parker a Transcendentalist?" *NEQ* 23 (S 50) 351-64.
West, Kenyon. "The Two Memorials to Theodore Parker in Florence, Italy." *N E Mag* ns 43 (D 10) 332-5.

PARKMAN, FRANCIS (1823-93). Alvord, C. W. "Francis Parkman." *Nation* 117 (10 O 23) 394-6.
Bassett, J. S. "Francis Parkman, the Man." *SR* 10 (Jl 02) 285-301.

——— "Letters of Francis Parkman to Pierre Margry." *Smith Col Stud Hist* 8 (Ap-Jl 23) 123-308.
DeVoto, Bernard. "The Easy Chair." *Harper's* 198 (Ap 49) 52-5.
Doughty, H. "Parkman's Dark Years: Letters to Mary Dwight Parkman." *Harvard Lib Bul* 4 (Wi 50) 53-85.
Fanteux, Aegidius. "Francis Parkman." *Bul des Recherches Historique* 31 (Je 25) 177-83.
Gregory, J. T. "The Parkman Club." *Wisc Mag Hist* 11 (Mr 28) 309-19.
Johnson, Merle. "American First Editions: Francis Parkman, 1823-1893." *Pub W* 127 (19 Ja 35) 263-4.
Kellen, W. V. "The Parkman Centenary in Canada." *PMHS* 57 (D 23) 190-2.
Lodge, H. C. "Francis Parkman." *PMHS* 56 (Je 23) 319-35.
MacDonald, William. "Francis Parkman." *Lit R* 4 (1923) 37-8.
McGloin, J. B. "Francis Parkman on the Jesuits." *Hist Bul* 25 (Mr 47) 57-9.
Peckham, H. H. "The Sources and Revisions of Parkman's 'Pontiac.'" *PBSA* 17 (O-D 43) 293-307.
Perry, Bliss. "Some Personal Qualities of Francis Parkman." *YR* 13 (Ap 24) 443-8.
Robinson, Doane. "Parkman Not in Dakota." *So Dak Hist Coll* 12 (1924) 103-7.
Russell, J. A. "Parkman and the Real Indian." *J Am Hist* 22 (1926) 121-9.
——— "What We Owe to Francis Parkman." *Dalhousie R* 3 (O 23) 330-41.
Schafer, Joseph. "Francis Parkman, 1823-1923." *Miss Valley Hist R* 10 (Mr 24) 351-64.
Schramm, W. L. "A New Englander on the Road to Oregon." *NEQ* 13 (Mr 40) 49-64.
——— "Parkman's Novel." *AL* 9 (My 37) 218-27.
Sullivan, James. "Sectionalism in Writing History." *J N Y State Hist Assn* 2 (Ap 21) 73-88.
Walsh, J. E. "*The California and Oregon Trail:* A Bibliographical Study." *New Colophon* 3 (1950) 279-85.
Wrong, G. M. "Francis Parkman." *Canadian Hist R* 4 (D 23) 289-303.
Wyatt, E. F. "Francis Parkman: 1823-1893." *NAR* 218 (O 23) 484-96.

PARRINGTON, VERNON LOUIS (1871-1929). Cappon, A. P. "Parrington: A Liberal of the Northwest." *New Humanist* 5 (Ja-F 32) 1-9.
Hicks, Granville. "The Critical Principles of V. L. Parrington." *Sci & Soc* 3 (Fl 39) 142-64.
Hofstader, Richard. "Parrington and the Jeffersonian Tradition." *JHI* 2 (O 41) 391-400.
Trilling, Lionel. "Parrington, Mr. Smith and Reality." *PR* 5 (Ja 40) 24-40.

PARRISH, ANNE (1888-). Scott, W. T. "Anne Parrish's Novels." *UKCR* 17 (Ag 50) 52-9.

PARSONS, THOMAS WILLIAM (1819-92). Haraszti, Zoltán. "Letters by T. W. Parsons." *More Books* 13 (O, N, D 38) 243-67, 408-28, 472-93; 14 (Ja 39) 11-20.
Warren, Austin. "T. W. Parsons, Poet and Translator of Dante." *More Books* 13 (S 38) 287-303.

PARTON, MRS. SARA PAYSON (WILLIS) (1811-72). Eckert, R. P. "Friendly Fragrant Fanny Ferns." *Colophon* 5 (S 34) Pt 18.

PASTORIUS, FRANCIS DANIEL (1651-*c.*1720). Jenkins, C. F. "Francis Daniel Pastorius." *AGR* 1 (D 34) 22-5.
Turner, B. P. "William Penn and Pastorius." *PMHB* 57 (Ja 33) 66-90.

PATCHEN, KENNETH (1911-). Fletcher, Ian. "Stopping the Rot." *Nine* 2 (Ja 50) 50-1.

Untermeyer, J. S. "The Problem of Patchen." *SRL* 30 (22 Mr 47) 15-6.
Weiss, T. "Kenneth Patchen and Chaos as Vision." *Briarcliff Q* 3 (Jl 46) 127-34.
Wilder, A. N. "A Poet and the Class Struggle: Two Stages." *Poetry* 56 (Ap 40) 32-9.

PATTEE, FRED LEWIS (1863-1950). Werner, W. L. "Fred Lewis Pattee: Author, Scholar, Teacher." *Headlight on Books at Penn State* 17 (Je 48) 1-16.

PAUL, ELLIOT (1891-). Anon. "Elliot Paul." *N Y Herald Tribune Books* 26 (11 S 49) 2.
Van Gelder, Robert. "An Interview with Mr. Elliot Paul." *N Y Times Book R* (1 Mr 42) 2, 23.

PAULDING, JAMES KIRKE (1778-1860). Anon. "Correspondence Addressed to John C. Calhoun." *Annual Report Am Hist Assn* (1929).
Adkins, N. F. "James K. Paulding's *Lion of the West*." *AL* 3 (N 31) 249-58.
——— "A Study of James K. Paulding's *Westward Ho!*" *Am Col* 3 (Mr 27) 221-9.
Conklin, W. T. "Paulding's Prose Treatment of Types and Frontier Life before Cooper." *Un Texas Stud Eng* 19 (1939) 163-71.
Davidson, Frank. "Paulding's Treatment of the Angel of Hadley." *AL* 7 (N 35) 330-2.
Dondore, Dorothy. "The Debt of Two Dyed-in-theWool Americans to Mrs. Grant's *Memoirs:* Cooper's *Satanstoe* and Pauling's *The Dutchman's Fireside*." *AL* 12 (Mr 40) 52-8.
Robbins, J. A. "Some Unrecorded Poems of James Kirk Paulding: An Annotated Check-List." *SB* 3 (1950) 229-40.
Turner, Arlin. "James Kirke Paulding and Timothy Flint." *Miss Valley Hist R* 34 (Je 47) 105-11.
Watkins, F. C. "The Political Career of James Kirk Paulding." *Emory Un Q* 4 (1948) 225-35.
Wegelin, Oscar. "A Bibliography of the Separate Publications of James Kirke Paulding, Poet, Novelist, Humorist, Statesman, 1779-1860." *PBSA* 12 (Ja-Ap 18) 34-40
Williams, M. L. "Paulding Satirizes Owenism." *Ind Mag Hist* 44 (D 48) 355-65.
——— "Paulding's Contributions to the *Columbia Magazine*." *AL* 21 (My 49) 222-7.
——— "A Tour of Illinois in 1842." *J Illinois State Hist Soc* 42 (S 49) 292-312.
Winterich, J. T. "Early American Books and Printing, Chapter I, 'Westward Ho!' " *Pub W* 120 (19 S 31) 1267-71.

PAYNE, JOHN HOWARD (1791-1852). Bass, A. "From the Notebook of John Howard Payne." *Frontier & Midland* 14 (Ja 34) 139-46.
Coburn, F. W. " 'Sweet Home' Again—Revived Reminiscences of John Howard Payne." *Musician* 21 (D 16) 727.
Foreman, Grant. "John Howard Payne and the Cherokee Indians." *AHR* 37 (Jl 32) 723-50.
Heartman, C. F., & Weiss, H. B. "John Howard Payne: A Bibliography." *Am Book Coll* 3 (Ja, Mr, Ap, My-Je 33) 55-7, 181-4, 224-8, 305-7; 4 (Jl, Ag 33) 27-9, 78-82.
Howard, A. H. "The Romance of Home Sweet Home." *Holland's Mag* (O 29) 18-9, 37.
Leary, Lewis. "John Howard Payne's Southern Adventure: 1835." Duke Un *Lib Notes* no 19 (F 48) 2-11.
———, & Turner, Arlin. "John Howard Payne in New Orleans." *La Hist Q* 31 (Ja 48) 110-22.

Luquer, T. T. P. "Correspondence of Washington Irving and John Howard Payne." *Scribner's* 48 (O, N 10) 461-82, 597-616.

——— "When Payne Wrote 'Home Sweet Home!': Letters from Paris, 1822-1823." *Scribner's* 58 (D 15) 742-54.

——— "Writing a Play in a Debtor's Prison." *Scribner's* 69 (Ja-F 21) 66-81, 237-46.

MacDougall, A. R. "John Howard Payne (1791-1852)." *Americana* 33 (O 39) 463-75.

Morris, Muriel. "Mary Shelley and John Howard Payne." *London Merc* 22 (S 30) 443-50.

Payne, J. H. "The Green Corn Dance." *Chron Okla* 10 (Je 32) 170-95.

Stearns, M. B. "John Howard Payne as an Editor." *AL* 5 (N 33) 215-20.

PEABODY, ELIZABETH PALMER (1804-94). Roberts, J. E. "Elizabeth Peabody and the Temple School." *NEQ* 15 (S 42) 497-508.

——— "Horace Mann and the Peabody Sisters." *NEQ* 18 (Je 45) 164-80.

Tapley, H. S. "Elizabeth Peabody's Letters to Maria Chase of Salem, relating to Lafayette's Visit in 1824." *EIHC* 85 (O 49) 360-8.

Wilson, J. B. "Grimm's Law and the Brahmin's." *NEQ* 16 (Mr 43) 106-9.

PEABODY, JOSEPHINE PRESTON (1874-1922). French, J. L. "The Younger Poets of New England." *N E Mag* ns 33 (D 05) 424-8.

Stimpson, M. S. "Josephine Preston Peabody: America's Dramatic Poet." *N E Mag* ns 42 (My 10) 271-7.

Winter, William. "Drift toward Fairyland." *Harper's W* 55 (18 F 11) 18.

PEATTIE, DONALD CULROSS (1898-). Van Doren, Mark. "A New Naturalist." *NAR* 244 (Au 37) 162-71.

Weeks, Mangum. "Artist and Backwoodsman." *VQR* 13 (Ja 37) 140-3.

PECK, BRADFORD (*fl.* 1900). Davies, W. E. "A Collectivist Experiment Down East: Bradford Peck and the Coöperative Association of America." *NEQ* 20 (D 47) 471-91.

PEIRCE, CHARLES SANDERS (1839-1914). Carpenter, F. I. "Charles Sanders Peirce: Pragmatic Transcendentalist." *NEQ* 14 (Mr 41) 34-48.

Feibleman, James. "A Systematic Presentation of Peirce's Ethics." *Ethics* 53 (Ja 43) 98-109.

Goudge, T. A. "Charles Peirce: Pioneer in American Thought." *UTQ* 12 (Jl 43) 403-14.

Hartshorne, Charles. "Charles Sanders Peirce's Metaphysics of Evolution." *NEQ* 14 (Mr 41) 49-63.

Weiss, Paul. "Charles Sanders Peirce." *SR* 50 (Ap-Je 42) 184-92.

Wiener, P. P. "Peirce's Metaphysical Club and the Genesis of Pragmatism." *JHI* 7 (Ap 46) 218-33.

PENHALLOW, SAMUEL (1665-1726). Adams, E. L. "The Wars of New England." *More Books* 15 (Mr 40) 87-101.

PENN, WILLIAM (1644-1718). Cadbury, H. J. "Intercepted Correspondence of William Penn, 1670." *PMHB* 70 (O 46) 349-72.

——— "Penn, Collison, and the Royal Society." *Bul Friends Hist Assn* 36 (Sp 47) 19-24.

——— "William Penn's Journal: Kent and Sussex, 1672." *PMHB* 68 (O 44) 419-29.

Comfort, William. "William Penn's Religious Background." *PMHB* 68 (O 44) 341-58.

Drake, T. E. "William Penn's Experiments in Race Relations." *PMHB* 68 (O 44) 372-87.
Gray, E. J. "Penn and the Poets." *Friend* 118 (26 O 44) 133-5.
Pitt, A. S. "Franklin and William Penn's *No Cross, No Crown.*" MLN 54 (Je 39) 466-7.
Powell, J. H. "William Penn's Writings: An Anniversary Essay." *Penn Hist* 11 (O 44) 233-59.
Turner, B. P. "William Penn and Pastorius." *PMHB* 57 (Ja 33) 66-90.
White, T. R. "Influence of William Penn on International Relations." *PMHB* 68 (O 44) 388-97.
Wright, L. M. "William Penn and the Royal Society." *Bul Friends Hist Assn* 30 (Sp 41) 8-70.

PERCIVAL, JAMES GATES (1795-1856). Benson, A. B. "James Gates Percival, Student of German Culture." *NEQ* 2 (O 29) 603-24.
——— "James Gates Percival's Relation to Scandinavian Culture." *SS* 10 (1929) 136-46.
Coleman, A. P. "James Gates Percival and the Slavonic Culture." *Slavia* 16 (Je 41) 65-75.
Eckert, R. P., Jr. "A Poet and His Library." *Colophon* 4 (O 33) Pt 15.

PERRY, NORA (1841-96). Ticknor, Caroline. "A New England Singer." *Lamp* 26 (Je 03) 363-74.

PERRY, THOMAS SERGEANT (1845-1928). Harlow, Virginia. "Thomas Sergeant Perry and Henry James." *BPLQ* 1 (Jl 49) 43-60.
——— "William Dean Howells and Thomas Sergeant Perry." *BPLQ* 1 (O 49) 135-50.

PETERKIN, JULIA (1880-). Bennett, Isadora. "Lang Syne's Miss." *Bkm* 69 (Je 29) 357-66.
Law, R. A. "Mrs. Peterkin's Negroes." *Sw R* 14 (Jl 29) 455-61.
Peterkin, Julia. "What I Believe." *Forum* 84 (Jl 30) 48-52.
Taggard, E. K. "Julia Peterkin of 'Lang Syne.'" *Scholastic* 27 (14 D 35) 6.
Yates, Irene. "Conjures and Cures in the Novels of Julia Peterkin." *SFQ* 10 (Je 46) 137-49.

PETERS, SAMUEL ANDREW (1735-1826). Middlebrook, Samuel. "Samuel Peters: A Yankee Munchausen." *NEQ* 20 (Mr 47) 75-87.

PETRY, ANN (1911-). Greene, Marjorie. "Ann Petry Planned to Write." *Opportunity* 24 (Ap-Je 46) 78-9.
Ivy, James. "Ann Petry Talks about First Novel." *Crisis* 53 (F 46) 48-9.

PHELPS, ELIZABETH STUART (1815-52). Hotson, C. P. "'The Gates Ajar.'" *New-Church Mag* 56 (Jl-S 37) 168-78.
Stewart, J. A. "At the Home of Mrs. Elizabeth Stuart Phelps." *N E Mag* ns 31 (S 04) 141-3.

PHELPS, WILLIAM LYON (1865-1943). Bakeless, John. "William Lyon Phelps, Book Booster." *Am Merc* 36 (N 35) 265-72.
Brownell, G. H. "Billy Phelps Joins the Innumerable Caravan." *Twainian* 3 (O 43) 1-4.

PHILLIPS, DAVID GRAHAM (1867-1911). Anon. "Phillips, a Novelist with a Vision." *Cur Lit* 50 (Mr 11) 326-9.
——— "Phillips' Methods." *Bkm* 33 (Mr 11) 6-13.
——— "Phillips' Posthumous Work." *Bkm* 39 (Mr 14) 19-20.

Feldman, Abraham. "David Graham Phillips: His Works and His Critics." *Bul Bible* 19 (My-Ag, S-D 48) 144-6, 177-9.
Filler, Louis. "An American Odyssey: The Story of Susan Lenox." *Accent* 1 (Au 40) 22-9.
——— "Murder in Gramercy Park." *AR* 6 (Wi 46-7) 495-508.
Flower, B. O. "David Graham Phillips: A Novelist with Democratic Ideals." *Arena* 31 (Mr 04) 236-43.
——— "David Graham Phillips: A Twentieth-Century Novelist of Democracy." *Arena* 35 (My 06) 252-7.
Flower, B. O. "Light-Fingered Gentry: A Book Study." *Arena* 38 (D 07) 702.
Hicks, Granville. "David Graham Phillips, Journalist." *Bkm* 73 (My 31) 257.
Marcosson, I. F. "The Significance of Susan Lennox." *Bkm* 45 (Mr 17) 25.
Nathan, G. J. "Literary Tarzan No. 2." *Am Spect* 2 (Ag 34) 2.
Winter, Calvin. "David Graham Phillips." *Bkm* 32 (F 11) 611-9.

PHILLIPS, WENDELL (1811-84). Anon. "Excerpts from two letters dated March 21, 1855, and April 18, 1869." *Autograph Album* 1 (D 33) 53.
Barnard, R. H. "The Speeches of Wendell Phillips." *QJS* 18 (N 32) 571-84.
Dole, N. H. "A Bundle of Cheerful Letters." *N E Mag* ns 39 (F 09) 649-55; 40 (Mr, Ap 09) 38-45, 180-4.
Hagan, H. H. "Wendell Phillips." *SR* 21 (Jl 13) 324-40.
Hincke, C. L. "Wendell Phillips." *N E Mag* 48 (D 12) 488-91.
Wyman, L. C. B. "Reminiscences of Wendell Phillips." *N E Mag* ns 27 (F 03) 725-40.

PIATT, JOHN JAMES (1835-1917). Dowler, Clare. "John James Piatt, Representative Figure of a Momentous Period." *Ohio State Arch & Hist Q* 45 (Ja 36) 1-26.
Howells, W. D. "Editor's Easy Chair." *Harper's* 135 (Jl 17) 291-3.

PIERPONT, JOHN (1785-1866). DeLong, H. C. "John Pierpont." *Medford Hist Register* 4 (O 03) 75-89.
Manchester, I. A. "John Pierpont, Poet and Preacher." *Hall of Memory* 1 (Ja 32) 3-5, 28-30.
Winterich, J. T. "Savonarola of Hollis Street: 1785-1866." *Colophon* 5 (Mr 35) Pt 20.

PIKE, ALBERT (1809-91). Donoghue, David. "Explorations of Albert Pike in Texas." *Sw Hist Q* 39 (O 35) 135-8.

PINCKNEY, SUSANNA SHULRICK HAYNE (1843-?). Sonnichsen, C. L. "Miss Sue Pinckney and Her Private World." *Sw R* 29 (Au 43) 80-92.

PINKERTON, ALLAN (1819-84). Willson, Frank. "American First Editions: Allan Pinkerton, 1819-1884." *Pub W* 130 (28 N 36) 2135-6.

PINKNEY, EDWARD COOTE (1802-28). Melton, W. F. "Edward Coote Pinkney." *SAQ* 11 (O 12) 328-36.
——— "The Influence of Petrarch upon Edward Coote Pinckney." *MLN* 28 (Je 13) 199-200.
Ross, C. H. "Edward Coote Pinckney." SR 4 (M 96) 287-98.
Simmons, J. P. "Edward Coote Pinckney—American Cavalier Poet." *SAQ* 28 (O 29) 406-18.

PLUMMER, JONATHAN (1761-1819). Higgin, R. W. "The Memoirs of Jonathan Plummer, Jr. (1761-1819)." *NEQ* 8 (Mr 35) 84-98.
Vail, R. W. G. "Writings of Jonathan Plummer." *PAAS* ns 43 (O 33) 248-53.

POE, EDGAR ALLAN (1809-49). Anon. "Account of a Rare Dumas Manuscript Describing Poe's Visit to Paris in 1832." *N Y Times* (15 D 29) 19.
——— "Concerning the Portrait of 'Edgar.'" *SLM* 2 (D 40) 652.
——— "Edgar Allan Poe." *Wiley Bul* 33 (Wi 50) 4-5.
——— "From Edgar A. Poe to Mr. John Allan." *SLM* 3 (Ja 41) 22-8.
——— "Important Unpublished Poe Material." *Bodley Book Shop Cat* no 1 (1935) 38.
——— "Israfel in the Laboratory." *TLS* no 2488 (7 O 49) 648.
——— "Lady Editor Who Paid Poe Fifty Cents Per Page." *Cur Op* 62 (Mr 17) 204.
——— "Letter by Poe Is Discovered." *Richmond News-Leader* (16 Mr 36).
——— "Letters of Edgar Allan Poe, 1845-49." *BNYPL* 6 (Ja 02) 7-11.
——— "Local Authority Says New Poe Discovery Rings True." *Richmond News-Leader* (15 Ap 35) 13.
——— "Long Letter by Poe to Irving Revealed." *N Y Times* (12 Ja 30) 1, 19.
——— "The Manuscript of Poe's 'Eulalie.'" *BNYPL* 18 (D 14) 1461-3.
——— "New Light on Poe's Tragic Love Affair with Sarah Helen Whitman." *Cur Op* 61 (D 16) 416.
——— "New Poe Letter Is to Be Sold." *Richmond News-Leader* (5 O 35) 4.
——— "A Note on David Poe as Actor." *Pub W* 117 (21 Je 30) 3041-2.
——— "Poe a Bricklayer in 1834?" *AN&Q* 3 (Je 43) 36.
——— "Poe Centenary." *BPLQ* 1 (O 49) 151-5.
——— "Poe Letters and Manuscripts Found in a Pillow-Case." *Cur Op* 70 (Je 21) 823-4.
——— "Poe the Pathfinder—a German Poet's Worshipful Tribute." *Cur Op* 62 (F 17) 121-2.
——— "Poe's New Reputation." *UKCR* 14 (O 43) 17-9.
——— "Poe's Student Days at the University of Virginia." *Bkm* 44 (Ja 17) 517-25.
——— "Religion of Edgar Allan Poe." *Cur Op* 69 (S 20) 408-10.
——— "A Reviewer's Notebook." *Freeman* 5 (19 Ap 22) 142-3.
——— "Satanic Streak in Poe's Genius." *Cur Lit* 48 (Ja 10) 93-6.
——— "Some Poe Questions." *Bkm* 36 (D 12) 354-5.
——— "An Unpublished Letter from Edgar Allan Poe." *Quarto* (O 49) extra no to accompany no 19.
Abel, Darrel. "Edgar Poe: A Centennial Estimate." *UKCR* 16 (Wi 49) 77-96.
——— "A Key to the House of Usher." *Un Toronto R* 18 (Ja 49) 176-85.
Adams, P. G. "Poe, Critic of Voltaire." *MLN* 57 (Ap 42) 273-5.
Adkins, N. F. "'Chapter on American Cribbage': Poe and Plagiarism." *PBSA* 42 (3Q 48) 169-210.
——— "Poe's Borrowings." *N&Q* 167 (28 Jl 34) 67-8.
——— "Poe's 'Ulalume.'" *N&Q* 164 (14 Ja 33) 30-1.
Albee, John. "Poe and Aristotle." *Dial* 34 (16 Mr 03) 192.
Alderman, E. A. "Edgar Allan Poe and the University of Virginia." *VQR* 1 (Ap 25) 78-84.
Allan, Carlisle. "Cadet Allan Poe, U.S.A." *Am Merc* 39 (Ag 33) 446-55.
Allen, M. S. "Poe's Debt to Voltaire." *Un Texas Stud Eng* 15 (1935) 63-75.
Almy, R. F. "J. N. Reynolds: A Brief Biography with Particular Reference to Poe and Symmes." *Colophon* ns 2 (Wi 37) 227-45.
Alterton, Margaret. "An Additional Source for Poe's 'The Pit and the Pendulum.'" *MLN* 47 (Je 33) 349-56.
——— "An Additional Source of Poe's Critical Theory." *Un Iowa Stud* 2 (1926).
Archibald, R. C. "Music and Edgar Allan Poe." *N&Q* 189 (7 S 40) 170-1.
Arnavon, Cyrille. "Poe cent ans après." *Langues Modernes* no 5 (S-O 49) 28-39.
Arndt, K. J. "Poe's 'Politian' and Goethe's 'Mignon.'" *MLN* 49 (F 34) 101-4.
Astrov, Vladimir. "Dostoievsky on Edgar Allan Poe." *AL* 14 (Mr 42) 70-4.
B., F. "Placing Poe." *Chri Sci Mon* 26 (19 N 34) 12.

Babler, O. F. "Czech Translations of Poe's 'Raven.'" *N&Q* 192 (31 My 47) 235.
——— "German Translations of Poe's 'Raven.'" *N&Q* 174 (1 Ja 38) 9-10.
Bailey, J. O. "The Geography of Poe's 'Dream-Land' and 'Ulalume.'" *SP* 45 (Jl 48) 512-23.
——— "Poe's 'Palaestine.'" *AL* 13 (Mr 41) 44-58.
——— "Poe's 'Stonehenge.'" *SP* 38 (O 41) 645-51.
——— "Sources of Poe's *Arthur Gordon Pym,* 'Hans Pfaal,' and Other Pieces." *PMLA* 57 (Je 42) 513-35.
Bailey, M. E. "Dove and Raven." *Atl* 132 (N 23) 647-56.
Baker, H. T. "Coleridge's Influence on Poe's Poetry." *MLN* 25 (Mr 10) 94-5.
——— "Poe and Hazlitt." *Nation* 87 (8 O 08) 335.
——— "Source of the Raven." *Nation* 91 (22 D 10) 601-2.
Baldini, Garbieli. "Un Poeta della nostra epoca." *La Fiera Letteraria* no 41 (9 O 49) 1.
Baldwin, Summerfield. "The Aesthetic Theory of Edgar Poe." *SR* 26 (Ap 18) 210-21.
Bandy, W. T. "A Source of Poe's 'The Premature Burial.'" *AL* 19 (My 47) 167-8.
Basler, R. P. "Byronism in Poe's 'To One in Paradise.'" *AL* 9 (My 37) 232-6.
——— "The Interpretation of 'Ligeia.'" *CE* 5 (Ap 44) 363-72.
——— "Poe's *The City in the Sea.*" *Expl* 5 (F 46) 30.
——— "Poe's *The Valley of Unrest.*" *Expl* 5 (D 46) 25.
——— "Poe's *Ulalume.*" *Expl* 2 (My 44).
Basore, J. W. "Poe as an Epicurean." *MLN* 25 (Mr 10) 86-7.
Baum, P. F. "Poe's 'To Helen.'" *MLN* 64 (My 49) 289-97.
Bayless, Joy. "Another Rufus W. Griswold as a Critic of Poe." *AL* 6 (Mr 34) 69-72.
Béguin, Albert. "Grandeur d' Edgar Poe." *Les Nouvelles Littéraires* no 1156 (27 O 49) 5.
——— "Il Cenario di Edgar Allan Poe." *Il Ponte* (Italy) (D 49) 1497-1500.
Belden, H. M. "Poe's Criticism of Hawthorne." *Anglia* 23 (1901) 376-404.
——— "Poe's 'The City in the Sea' and Dante's City of Dis." *AL* 7 (N 35) 332-4.
Benson, A. B. "Scandinavian References in the Works of Poe." *JEGP* 40 (Ja 41) 73-90.
——— "Sources of Poe's 'A Descent into the Maelstrom.'" *JEGP* 46 (Jl 47) 298-301.
Berti, Luigi. "Il Poe critico." *Inventorio* (Italy) 2 (Su 49) 1-11.
Birss, J. H. "Emerson and Poe: A Similitude." *N&Q* 166 (21 Ap 34) 279.
——— "Poe in Fordham: A Reminiscence." *N&Q* 173 (18 D 37) 440.
Blair, Walter. "Poe's Conception of Incident and Tone in the Tale." *MP* 41 (My 44) 228-40.
Blake, W. B. "Edgar Allan Poe: A Centenary Outlook." *Dial* 46 (16 F 09) 103-5.
Bledsoe, T. F. "On Poe's 'Valley of Unrest.'" *MLN* 61 (F 46) 91-2.
Block, L. J. "Edgar Allan Poe." *SR* 18 (O 10) 385-403.
Boll, Ernest. "The Manuscript of 'The Murders of the Rue Morgue,' and Poe's Revisions." *MP* 40 (My 43) 302-15.
Bolton, R. P. "The Poe Cottage at Fordham." *Trans Bronx Soc Arts, Sci & Hist* (1922).
Bond, F. D. "Poe as an Evolutionist." *Popular Sci Mo* 71 (S 07) 267-74.
Booth, B. A. "The Identity of Annabel Lee." *CE* 7 (O 45) 17-9.
Bowen, E. W. "Poe Fifty Years After." *Forum* 31 (Je 01) 501-10.
Boynton, P. H. "Poe and Journalism." *EJ* 21 (My 32) 345-51.
Bradley, Sculley. "Poe and the New York Stage in 1855." *AL* 9 (N 37) 353-4.
Brigham, C. S. "Edgar Allan Poe's Contributions to *Alexander's Weekly Messenger.*" *PAAS* ns 52 (Ap 42) 45-125.
Brown, W. C. "The English Professor's Dilemma." *CE* 5 (Ap 44) 380-5.
Brownell, W. C. "Poe." *Scribner's* 45 (Ja 09) 69-84.

Bruce, P. A. "Background of Poe's University Life." *SAQ* 10 (Jl 11) 212-26.
——— "Certain Literary Aspects of Poe." *SR* 22 (Ja 14) 38-49.
——— "Edgar Allan Poe and Mrs. Whitman." *SAQ* 12 (Ap 13) 129-40.
——— "Was Poe a Drunkard?" *SAQ* 11 (Ja 12) 37-9.
Bruno, Guido. "Poe and O. Henry." *Bruno's W* 3 (29 Jl 16) 874-5.
Cain, L. J. "Edgar Poe et Valéry." *Mercure de France* no 1041 (My 50) 81-94.
Cairns, W. B. "Poe's Use of the Horrible." *Dial* 50 (1 Ap 11) 251-2.
——— "Some Notes on Poe's 'Al Aaraaf.'" *MP* 13 (My 15) 35-44.
Campbell, Killis. "Bibliographical Notes on Poe." *Nation* 89 (23, 30 D 09) 623-4, 657-8.
——— "A Bit of Chiversian Mystification." *Un Texas Stud Eng* 10 (1930) 152-4.
——— "Contemporary Opinion of Poe." *PMLA* 36 (Je 21) 142-66.
——— "Gleanings in the Bibliography of Poe." *MLN* 32 (My 17) 267-72.
——— "Items That Have Escaped Poe Bibliographers." *Nation* 93 (19 O 11) 362-3.
——— "Marginalia on Longfellow, Lowell, and Poe." *MLN* 42 (D 27) 516-21.
——— "Miscellaneous Notes on Poe." *MLN* 28 (Mr 13) 65-9.
——— "New Notes on Poe's Early Years." *Dial* 60 (17 F 16) 143-6.
——— "Poe and the *Southern Literary Messenger* in 1837." *Nation* 89 (1 Jl 09) 9-10.
——— "The Poe Canon." *PMLA* 27 (1912) 325-53.
——— "Poe Documents in the Library of Congress." *MLN* 25 (Ap 10) 127-8.
——— "The Poe-Griswold Controversy." *PMLA* 34 (1919) 436-64.
——— "Poe, Stevenson, and Béranger." *Dial* 47 (16 N 09) 374-5.
——— "Poe's Indebtedness to Byron." *Nation* 88 (11 Mr 09) 248-9.
——— "Poe's Knowledge of the Bible." *SP* 27 (Jl 30) 546-51.
——— "Poe's Reading." *Un Texas Stud Eng* 5 (1925) 166-96.
——— "Poe's Reading: *Addenda and Corrigenda.*" *Un Texas Stud Eng* 7 (1927) 175-80.
——— "Poe's Treatment of the Negro and Negro Dialect." *Un Texas Stud Eng* 16 (1936) 107-14.
——— "Recent Books about Poe." *SP* 24 (Jl 27) 474-9.
——— "The Relation of Poe to His Times." *SP* 20 (Jl 23) 293-301.
——— "Some Unpublished Documents Relating to Poe's Early Years." *SR* 20 (Ap 12) 201-12.
——— "The Source of Poe's 'Some Words with a Mummy.'" *Nation* 90 (23 Je 10) 625-6.
——— "Three Notes on Poe." *AL* 4 (Ja 33) 385-8.
——— "Who Was 'Outis'?" *Un Texas Stud Eng* 8 (1928) 107-9.
Cardoso, Lucio. "Edgar Poe." *Revista de Instituto Brasil Estados Unidos* 2 (S 44) 68-76.
Cargill, Oscar. "A New Source for 'The Raven.'" *AL* 8 (N 36) 291-4.
Carlton, W. N. C. "The Authorship of English Notes by Quarles Quickens Reviewed." *Am Col* 1 (F 26) 186-90.
Carter, H. H. "Some Aspects of Poe's Poetry." *Arena* 37 (Mr 07) 281-5.
Carter, J. F. "Edgar Poe's Last Night in Richmond." *Lippincott's* 70 (N 02) 562-6.
Cauthen, I. B. "Music and Edgar Allan Poe." *N&Q* 194 (5 Mr 49) 103.
——— "Poe's *Alone:* Its Background, Source, and Manuscript." *SB* 3 (1950) 284-91.
Cestre, Charles. "Poe et Baudelaire." *Revue Anglo-Américaine* 21 (Ap 34) 322-30.
Charvat, William. "A Note on [the publication of] Poe's 'Tales of the Grotesque and Arabesque.'" *Pub W* 150 (23 N 46) 2957-8.
Chase, Lewis. "John Bransby, Poe's Schoolmaster." *Athenaeum* no 4605 (My 16) 221-2.
——— "More Notes on Poe's First School in London." *Dial* 60 (25 My 16) 499.
——— "A New Poe Letter." *AL* 6 (Mr 34) 66-9.
——— "Poe's First London School." *Dial* 60 (11 My 16) 458-9.

——— "Poe's Playmates in Kilmarnock." *Athenaeum* no 4611 (N 16) 554.

——— "Poe's School at Stoke Newington." *Athenaeum* no 4606 (Je 16) 294.

——— "Why Was 'The Raven' First Published Anonymously?" *Nation* 102 (10 F 16) 15-6.

Cherry, F. N. "The Source of Poe's 'Three Sundays in a Week.'" *AL* 2 (N 30) 232-5.

Clark, D. L. "The Sources of Poe's 'The Pit and the Pendulum.'" *MLN* 24 (Je 29) 349-56.

Clough, W. O. "The Use of Color Words by Edgar Allan Poe." *PMLA* 45 (Je 30) 598-613.

Coad, O. S. "The Meaning of Poe's 'Eldorado.'" *MLN* 59 (Ja 44) 59-61.

Cobb, Palmer. "Edgar Allan Poe and Friedrich Spielhagen. Their Theory of the Short Story." *MLN* 25 (Mr 10) 67-72.

——— "The Influence of E. T. A. Hoffmann on the Tales of Edgar Allan Poe." *SP* 3 (1908) 1-104.

——— "Poe and Hoffmann." *SAQ* 8 (Ja 09) 68-81.

Coburn, F. W. "Poe as Seen by the Brother of 'Annie.'" *NEQ* 16 (S 43) 468-76.

Cody, Sherwin. "Poe as a Critic." *Putnam's* 5 (Ja 09) 438-40.

——— "Poe's Contribution to American Literary History." *Dial* 35 (16 S 03) 161-2.

Colton, C. B. "George Hooker Colton and the Publication of 'The Raven.'" *AL* 10 (N 38) 319-30.

Cooke, A. L. "The Popular Conception of Edgar Allan Poe from 1850 to 1890." *Un Texas Stud Eng* 22 (1942) 22-46.

Cooper, C. B. "Tintinnabulation." *MLN* 41 (My 26) 318.

Courson, Della. "Poe and The Raven." *Educ* 20 (My 00) 566-70.

Cowley, Malcolm. "Aidgarpo." *NRp* 113 (5 N 45) 607-10.

Cox, J. L. "Poe as Critic." *EJ* 21 (N 32) 757-63.

Crawford, P. P. "Lewis and Clark's Expedition as a Source of Poe's 'Journal of Julius Rodman.'" *Un Texas Stud Eng* 12 (1932) 158-70.

Culver, F. B. "Lineage of Edgar Allan Poe and the Complex Pattern of the Family Genealogy." *Md Hist Mag* 37 (D 42) 420-2.

Darnall, F. M. "The Americanism of Edgar Allan Poe." *EJ* 16 (Mr 27) 185-92.

Daughrity, K. L. "Notes: Poe and *Blackwood's*." *AL* 2 (N 30) 289-92.

——— "Poe's 'Quiz on Willis.'" *AL* 5 (Mr 33) 55-62.

——— "Source for a Line of Poe's 'Ulalume.'" *N&Q* 161 (11 Jl 31) 27.

Davidson, Frank. "A Note on Poe's 'Berenice.'" *AL* 11 (My 39) 212-3.

Dávila, Carlos. "Poe y el centenario de la novela policíaca." *America* 33 (Ap-Je 47) 21-3.

Davis, H. C. "Poe's Stormy Voyage in 1827 Is Described." *News & Courier* (Charleston, S. C.) (5 Ja 41).

Davis, R. B. "Poe and William Wirt." *AL* 16 (N 44) 212-20.

Dedmond, F. B. "Paul Hamilton Hayne and the Poe Westminster Memorial." *Md Hist Mag* 45 (Je 50) 149-51.

DeMille, G. E. "Poe as Critic." *Am Merc* 4 (Ap 25) 433-40.

DeTernant, Andrew. "Edgar Allan Poe and Alexander Dumas." *N&Q* 157 (28 D 29) 456.

Didier, E. L. "Edgar Allan Poe in Society." *Bkm* 28 (Ja 09) 455-60.

——— "The Poe Cult." *Bkm* 16 (D 02) 336-40.

Dietz, F. M. "Poe's First and Final Love." *SLM* 5 (Mr 43) 38-47.

Doherty, Edward. "The Spectacles: The Lost Short Story by Edgar Allan Poe." *Liberty* 15 (24 S 38) 12-4.

Douglas, Norman. "Edgar Allan Poe from an English Point of View." *Putnam's* 5 (Ja 09) 433-8.

Dredd, Firmin. "Poe And Secret Writing." *Bkm* 28 (Ja 09) 450-1.

Dubedout, E. J. "Edgar Poe et Alfred de Musset." *MLN* 22 (Mr 07) 71-6.

DuBois, A. E. "The Jazz Bells of Poe." *CE* 2 (D 40) 230-44.

Du Bos, Charles. "Poe and the French Mind." *Athenaeum* (7, 14 Ja 21) 26-7, 54-5.
Dudley, F. A. "*Tintinnabulation:* And a Source of Poe's 'The Bells.'" *AL* 4 (N 32) 296-300.
Duffy, Charles. "Poe's Mother-in-Law; Two Letters to Bayard Taylor." *AN&Q* 2 (Ja 43) 148.
Dunlop, G. B. "A Poe Story." *TLS* (12 Ja 44) 36.
Durham, F. M. "A Possible Relationship between Poe's 'To Helen' and Milton's *Paradise Lost,* Book IV." *AL* 16 (Ja 45) 340-3.
Eastman, Max. "Poe, Whitman et la poésie des temps nouveaux." *Europe* 15 (1927) 443-62.
Echagüe, J. P. "El Amor en la literatura." *Boletin de la Academia Argentina de Letras* 9 (Jl-S 41) 373-499.
Edmunds, A. J. "German Translations of Poe's 'Raven.'" *N&Q* 174 (5 F 38) 106.
Eliot, T. S. "Edgar Poe et la France." *La Table Ronde* (D 48) 1973-92.
——— "From Poe to Valéry." *Hudson R* 2 (Au 49) 327-43.
——— "Note sur Mallarmé et Poe." *Nouvelle Revue Française* 14 (N 26) 524-6.
Elwell, T. E. "A Poe Story." *TLS* (23 O 43) 516.
Engel, Claire-Elaine. "L'Etat des travaux de Poe en France." *MP* 29 (My 32) 482-8.
Englekirk, J. E., Jr. "A Critical Study of Two Tales by Amado Nervo." *NMQR* 2 (F 32) 53-65.
——— "'My Nightmare.'—The Last Tale by Poe." *PMLA* 52 (Je 37) 511-27.
——— "'The Raven' in Spanish America." *Spanish R* 1 (N 34) 52-6.
——— "The Song of Hollands, an Inedited Tale Ascribed to Poe." *NMQR* 1 (Ag 31) 247-70.
Evans, M. G. "Poe in Amity Street." *Md Hist Mag* 36 (D 41) 363-80.
Fagin, N. B. "Poe-Drama Critic." *Theatre Annual* (1946) 23-8.
Faures, André. "Edgar Poe." *Nouvelles Littéraires* (7 Ap 34) 22.
Ferguson, J. D. "Charles Hine and His Portrait of Poe." *AL* 3 (Ja 32) 463-8.
Foerster, Norman. "Quantity and Quality in Poe's Aesthetic." *SP* 20 (Jl 23) 310-35.
Fontainas, A. "Ce qu' ont pensé d'Edgar Allan Poe ses contemporains." *Mercure de France* 225 (15 Ja 31) 312-24.
——— "Un Témoignage sur Edgar Poe." *Figaro* (21 Je 30).
Forsythe, R. S. "Poe's 'Nevermore': A Note." *AL* 7 (Ja 36) 439-52.
Françon, Marcel. "Poe et Baudelaire." *PMLA* 60 (S 45) 841-59.
French, J. C. "The Day of Poe's Burial." Baltimore *Sun* (3 Je 49) 14.
——— "Poe and the *Baltimore Saturday Visiter.*" *MLN* 33 (My 18) 257-67.
——— "Poe's Literary Baltimore." *Md Hist Mag* 32 (Je 37) 101-12.
Friedman, W. F. "Edgar Allan Poe, Cryptographer." *AL* 8 (N 36) 266-80; *Signal Corps Bul* 97 (Jl-S 37) 41-53, 98 (O-D 37) 54-75.
Garnett, R. S. "The Mystery of Edgar Allan Poe." *Blackwood's* 227 (F 30) 235-98.
Gates, W. B. "Poe's *Politian* Again." *MLN* 49 (D 34) 561.
Ghiselin, Brewster. "Reading Sprung Rhythms." *Poetry* 70 (My 47) 86-93.
Gilder, J. L. "Biography and Letters." *Critic* 42 (Je 03) 499-502.
Goodwin, K. C. "Old Documents and Their Marketing." *Daughters Am Revolution Mag* 67 (S 33) 539-46.
Gordan, J. D. "Edgar Allan Poe. An Exhibition on the Centenary of His Death October 7, 1849. A Catalogue of the First Editions, Manuscripts, Autograph Letters from the Berg Collection." *BNYPL* 53 (O 49) 471-91.
Gosse, W. E. "The Centenary of Poe." *Contemp R* 95 (F 09) 1-8.
Gravely, W. H., Jr. "An Incipient Libel Suit Involving Poe." *MLN* 60 (My 45) 308-11.
——— "Thomas Dunne English's *Walter Woofe*—A Reply to 'A Minor Poe Mystery.'" *PULC* 5 (1944) 108-14.
Graves, C. M. "Landmarks of Poe in Richmond." *Century* 67 (Ap 04) 909-20.

Greenlaw, Edward. "Poe in the Light of Literary History." *Johns Hopkins Alumni Mag* 18 (Je 30) 273-90.
Gregory, Horace. "Within the Private View." *PR* 10 (My-Je 43) 263-74.
Griggs, E. L. "Five Sources of Edgar Allan Poe's 'Pinakidia.'" *AL* 1 (My 29) 196-9.
Grubb, Gerald. "The Personal and Literary Relationships of Dickens and Poe." *Nineteenth-Century Fiction* 5 (Je, S, D 50) 1-22, 101-20, 209-21.
Gruener, G. "Notes on the Influence of E. T. A. Hoffman upon Edgar Allan Poe." *PMLA* 19 (Mr 04) 1-25.
——— "Poe's Knowledge of German." *MP* 2 (Je 04) 125-40.
Hale, E. E., Jr. "Edgar Allan Poe." *Reader* 5 (Mr 05) 487-90.
Hamilton, Robert. "Poe and the Imagination." *Quar R* 227 (O 50) 514-25.
Harrison, J. A. "New Glimpses of Poe." *Independent* 52 (6 S 00) 2158-61.
——— "A Poe Miscellany." *Independent* 61 (1 N 06) 1044-51.
———, & Dailey, C. F. "Poe and Mrs. Whitman: New Light on a Romantic Episode." *Century* 77 (Ja 09) 439-52.
Harwell, R. B. "A Reputation by Reflection: John Hill Hewitt and Edgar Allan Poe." *Emory Un Q* 3 (Je 47) 104-14.
Heartman, C. F. "The Curse of Edgar Allan Poe." *Am Book Coll* 4 (Jl 33) 45-9.
——— "A Remarkable Addition to the Poe Census." *Am Book Coll* 3 (Ap 33) 246.
Hoagland, Clayton. "The Universe of Eureka: A Comparison of the Theories of Eddington and Poe." *SLM* 1 (My 39) 307-13.
Holsapple, C. K. *"The Masque of the Red Death* and *I Promessi Sposi."* *Un Texas Stud Eng* 18 (1938) 137-9.
——— "Poe and Conradus." *AL* 4 (Mr 32) 62-6.
Hoole, W. S. "Poe in Charleston, S. C." *AL* 6 (Mr 34) 78-80.
Howard, W. L. "Poe and His Misunderstood Personality." *Arena* 31 (Ja 04) 78-83.
Howells, W. D. "Edgar Allan Poe." *Harper's W* 53 (16 Ja 09) 12-3.
Hubbell, J. B. "'O Tempora! O, Mores,' A Juvenile Poem by Edgar Allan Poe." *Un Colo Stud* 2: ser B (O 45) 314-21.
——— "Poe's Mother, with a Note on John Allan." *WMQ* 21 (Jl 41) 250-4.
Hudson, R. L. "Poe and Disraeli." *AL* 8 (Ja 37) 492-16.
Hughes, David. "The Influence of Poe." *Fortnightly R* ns no 964 (N 49) 342-3.
Hungerford, Edward. "Poe and Phrenology." *AL* 2 (N 30) 209-31.
Hunter, W. B., Jr. "Poe's 'The Sleeper' and *Macbeth.*" *AL* 20 (Mr 48) 55-7.
Huntress, Keith. "Another Source for Poe's 'The Narrative of Arthur Gordon Pym.'" *AL* 16 (Mr 44) 19-25.
Hurley, L. B. "A New Note in the War of the Literati." *AL* 7 (Ja 36) 376-94.
Hutcherson, D. R. "The *Philadelphia Saturday Museum* Text of Poe's Poems." *AL* 5 (Mr 33) 36-48.
——— "Poe's Reputation in England and America, 1850-1909." *AL* 14 (N 42) 211-33.
Ingraham, J. H. "Edgar Allan Poe's Lost Poem 'The Beautiful Physician.'" *Bkm* 28 (Ja 09) 452-4.
——— "Edgar Poe and Some of His Friends." *Bkm* (London) 35 (Ja 09) 167-73.
Jackowska, S. I. O. "The Raven." *Chri Sci Mon* 27 (8 Ag 35) 12.
——— "Le Rehabilitation d'Edgar Poe." *Nouvelle Revue* 124 (Mr 33) 103-15.
Jackson, D. K. "An Estimate of the Influence of 'The Southern Literary Messenger.'" *SLM* 1 (1939) 508-14.
——— "Four of Poe's Critiques in the Baltimore Newspapers." *MLN* 10 (Ap 35) 251-6.
——— "Poe and the 'Messenger.'" *SLM* 1 (Ja 39) 5-11.
——— "Poe Notes: 'Pinakidia' and 'Some Ancient Greek Authors.'" *AL* 5 (N 33) 258-67.
——— "Poe's Knowledge of Law during the *Messenger* Period." *AL* 10 (N 38) 331-9.

——— "'Some Ancient Greek Authors': A Work of Edgar A. Poe." *N&Q* 166 (26 My 34) 368.
——— "Some Unpublished Letters of T. W. White to Lucian Minor." *Tyler's Quar Hist & Gen Mag* 17 (Ap 36) 224-43.
Jackson, Joseph. "George Lippard: Misunderstood Man of Letters." *PMHB* 59 (O 35) 376-91.
——— "Poe's Signature to 'The Raven.'" *SR* 26 (Jl 18) 272-5.
Jaloux, Edmond. "Rencontres avec Edgar Poe." *1935* (27 Mr 35) 9.
January, J. P. "Edgar Allan Poe's 'Child Wife': With An Unpublished Acrostic by Her to Her Husband." *Century* 78 (O 09) 894-6.
Jillson, Willard. "The Beauchamp-Sharp Tragedy in American Literature." *Register Ky State Hist Soc* 36 (1938) 54-60.
Johnston, M. C. "Rubén Darío's Acquaintance with Poe." *Hispania* 17 (O 34) 271-8.
Jones, J. J. "Poe's 'Nicéan Barks.'" *AL* 2 (Ja 31) 433-8.
Jones, L. C. "A Margaret Fuller Letter to Elizabeth Barrett Browning." *AL* 9 (Mr 37) 70-1.
Jones, P. M. "Poe and Baudelaire: The 'Affinity.'" *MLR* 40 (O 45) 279-83.
——— "Poe, Baudelaire and Mallarmé: A Problem of Literary Judgment." *MLR* 39 (Jl 44) 236-46.
Jones, R. S. "The Influence of Edgar Allan Poe on Paul Valéry, prior to 1900." *CL Stud* 21-2 (1946) 10-5.
Julien-Cain, L. "Edgar Poe et Valery." *Mercure de France* 309 (1 My 50) 81-94.
Kane, Margaret. "Edgar Allan Poe and Architecture." *SR* 41 (Ja-Mr 32) 149-60.
Kent, C. W. "Poe's Student Days at the University of Virginia." *Bkm* 13 (Jl 01) 430-40.
Kerlin, R. T. "*Wieland* and *The Raven.*" *MLN* 31 (D 16) 503-5.
Kern, A. A. "Poe's Theory of Poetry." *Bul Randolph-Macon Woman's Col* 19 (1932) 10-3.
——— "Was Poe Accurate?" *Nation* 97 (23 O 13) 381-2.
King, Lucille. "Notes on Poe's Sources." *Un Texas Stud Eng* 10 (1930) 128-34.
Kirby, J. P. "Poe's *Ulalume.*" *Expl* 1 (O 42) 8.
Kogan, Bernard. "Poe, the 'Penn,' and the 'Stylus.'" *SLM* 2 (Ag 40) 442-5.
Krappe, E. S. "A Possible Source for Poe's 'The Tell-Tale Heart' and 'The Black Cat.'" *AL* 12 (Mr 40) 84-8.
Krutch, J. W. "The Strange Case of Poe." *Am Merc* 6 (N 25) 349-56.
Kummer, George. "Another Poe-Coleridge Parallel?" *AL* 8 (Mr 36) 72.
Lafleur, L. J. "Edgar Allan Poe, as Philosopher." *Personalist* 22 (O 41) 401-5.
Lalou, René. "Edgar Poe et la France." *L'Education Nationale* (Paris) no 4 (26 Ja 50) 7-8.
Laser, Marvin. "The Growth and Structure of Poe's Concept of Beauty." *ELH* 15 (Mr 48) 69-84.
Latimer, G. D. "The Tales of Poe and Hawthorne." *N E Mag* 30 (Ag 04) 692-703.
Lauvrière, Émile. "Edgar Poe et le Freudisme." *La Grande Revue* 142 (O 33) 565-87.
Laverty, Carroll. "The Death's-Head on the Gold-Bug." *AL* 12 (Mr 40) 88-91.
——— "A Note on Poe in 1838." *MLN* 64 (Mr 49) 174-6.
——— "Poe in 1847." *AL* 20 (My 48) 163-8.
Law, R. A. "A Source for Annabel Lee." *JEGP* 21 (2Q 22) 341-6.
Lawrence, D. H. "Studies in Classic American Literature (vi): Edgar Allan Poe." *Eng R* 28 (Ap 19) 278-91.
Leary, Lewis. "Poe's *Ulalume.*" *Expl* 6 (F 48) 25.
LeBreton, Maurice. "Edgar Poe et Macaulay." *Revue Anglo-Américaine* 21 (O 35) 38-42.
Lemonnier, Léon. "Baudelaire et Mallarmé, traducteurs d'Edgar Poe." *Les Langues Modernes* 43 (Ja-F 49) 47-57.

——— "Edgar Poe et la roman scientifique française." *La Grande Revue* 133 (Ag 30) 214-23.
——— "Edgar Poe et le théâtre de mystère et de terreur." *La Grande Revue* 130 (My 29) 379-96.
——— "Edgar Poe et les parnassiens françaises." *La Revue de Littérature Comparée* 9 (O-D 29) 728-36.
——— "L'Influence d'Edgar Poe sur les conteurs françaises symbolistes et décadents." *Revue de Littérature Comparée* 13 (Ja-Mr 33) 102-34.
——— "L'Influence d'Edgar Poe sur quelque conteurs réalistes." *Revue de Littérature Comparée* 11 (Jl-S 31) 451-65.
——— "L'Influence d'Edgar Poe sur Villiers de l'Isle-Adam." *Mercure de France* 246 (15 S 33) 604-19.
Lewis, C. L. "Edgar Allan Poe and the Sea." *SLM* 3 (Ja 41) 5-10.
Lind, S. E. "Poe and Mesmerism." *PMLA* 62 (D 47) 1077-94.
Lloyd, J. A. T. "Who Wrote 'English Notes?'" *Colophon* ns 1 (Su 35) 107-18.
Lograsso, A. H. "Poe's Piero Maroncelli." *PMLA* 58 (S 43) 780-9.
Lot, Fernand. "Edgar Poe mis a nu?" *Revue Bleue* 23 (D 34) 901-5.
Lyne, Mrs. William. "Reminiscences of Mrs. William Lyne of Orange." *WMQ* 13 (Jl 33) 184-5.
Mabbott, T. O. "Additions to 'A List of Poe's Tales.'" *N&Q* 183 (12 S 42) 163-4.
——— "Allusions to a Spanish Joke in Poe's 'A Valentine.'" *N&Q* 169 (14 S 35) 189.
——— "Antediluvian Antiquities: A Curiosity of American Literature and a Source of Poe's." *Am Col* 4 (Jl 27) 124-6.
——— "The Astrological Symbolism of Poe's 'Ulalume.'" *N&Q* 161 (11 Jl 31) 27.
——— "Dumas on Poe's Visit to Paris." *N Y Times* (22 D 29) 5.
——— "An Early Discussion of Poe." *N&Q* 191 (7 S 46) 102.
——— "Echoes of Poe in Rossetti's 'Beryl Song.'" *N&Q* 168 (2 F 35) 77.
——— "Edgar Allan Poe: A Find." *N&Q* 150 (3 Ap 26) 241.
——— "English Publications of Poe's 'Valdemar Case.'" *N&Q* 183 (21 N 42) 311-2.
——— "Evidence that Poe Knew Greek." *N&Q* 185 (17 Jl 43) 39-40.
——— "A Few Notes on Poe." *MLN* 35 (Je 20) 372-4.
——— "The First Publication of Poe's 'Raven.'" *BNYPL* 47 (Ag 43) 581-4.
——— "George H. Derby: A Debt to Poe." *N&Q* 166 (10 Mr 34) 171.
——— "German Translations of Poe's 'Raven.'" *N&Q* 174 (29 Ja 38) 88.
——— "Greeley's Estimate of Poe." *Autograph Album* 1 (D 33) 14-6, 61.
——— "Joel Chandler Harris: A Debt to Poe." *N&Q* 166 (3 Mr 34) 151.
——— "A Letter of Poe's Sister." *N&Q* 169 (28 D 35) 457.
——— "Letters from George W. Eveleth to Edgar Allan Poe." *BNYPL* 26 (Mr 22) 171-95.
——— "Letters from Mary E. Hewitt to Poe." *Christmas Books* (Hunter Col) (D 37) 116-21.
——— "A Lost Jingle by Poe." *N&Q* 179 (23 N 40) 371.
——— "Newly-Identified Reviews by Edgar Poe." *N&Q* 163 (17 D 32) 441.
——— "Newly-Identified Verses by Poe." *N&Q* 177 (29 Jl 39) 77-8.
——— "Numismatic References of Three American Writers." *Numismatist* 46 (N 33) 688.
——— "On Poe's 'Tales of the Folio Club.'" *SR* 36 (Ap 28) 171-6.
——— "Palindromes (and Edgar Poe)." *N&Q* 191 (30 N 47) 238-9.
——— "Poe and Ash Upson." *N&Q* 172 (8 My 37) 330-1.
——— "Poe and Dr. Lardner." *AN&Q* 3 (N 43) 115-7.
——— "Poe and the Artist John P. Frankenstein." *N&Q* 182 (17 Ja 42) 31-2.
——— "Poe and the Philadelphia Irish Citizen." *J Am Irish Hist Soc* 29 (1930-1) 121-31.
——— "A Poe Manuscript." *BNYPL* 28 (F 24) 103-5.

——— "Poe on Intemperance." *N&Q* 183 (18 Jl 42) 34-5.
——— "Poe's Balloon Hoax." *N Y Sun* (23 Ja 43) 6.
——— "Poe's *City in the Sea*." *Expl* 4 (O 45) 31.
——— "Poe's *Israfel*." *Expl* 2 (Je 44).
——— "Poe's Obscure Contemporaries." *AN&Q* 1 (F 42) 166-7.
——— "Poe's Original Conundrums." *N&Q* 184 (5 Je 43) 328-9.
——— "Poe's 'Raven': First Inclusion in a Book." *N&Q* 185 (9 O 43) 225.
——— "Poe's Tale, 'The Lighthouse.'" *N&Q* 182 (25 Ap 42) 226-7.
——— "Poe's 'The Sleeper' Again." *AL* 21 (N 49) 339-40.
——— "Poe's *To Helen*." *Expl* 1 (Je 43) 16.
——— "Poe's *To the River*." *Expl* 3 (Je 45) 22.
——— "Poe's *Ulalume*." *Expl* 1 (F 43) 6.
——— "Poe's *Ulalume*." *Expl* 6 (Je 48) 57.
——— "Poe's Ulalume." *N&Q* 164 (25 F 33) 143.
——— "Poe's Word 'Porphyrogene.'" *N&Q* 177 (2 D 39) 403.
——— "Poe's Word 'Tintinnabulation.'" *N&Q* 175 (26 N 38) 387.
——— "Puckle and Poe." *N&Q* 164 (25 Mr 33) 205-6.
——— "A Review of Lowell's Magazine." *N&Q* 178 (Je 40) 457-8.
——— "Another Source of Poe's Play, 'Politian.'" *N&Q* 194 (25 Je 49) 279.
——— "The Source of the Title of Poe's 'Morella.'" *N&Q* 172 (9 Ja 37) 26-7.
——— "The Sources of Poe's 'Eldorado.'" *MLN* 60 (My 45) 312-4.
——— "The Text of Poe's Play 'Politian.'" *N&Q* 189 (14 Jl 45) 14.
——— "Ullahanna—A Literary Ghost." *AN&Q* 1 (S 41) 83.
——— "An Unfavorable Reaction to Poe, in 1842." *N&Q* 194 (19 Mr 49) 122-3.
——— "An Unpublished Letter to Poe." *N&Q* 174 (28 My 38) 385.
——— "Unrecorded Texts of Two Poe Poems." *AN&Q* 8 (Ag 48) 67-8.
——— "The Writing of Poe's 'The Bells.'" *AN&Q* 2 (O 42) 110.
Mabie, H. W. "To Helen and Israfel." *Outlook* 91 (24 Ap 09) 955-7.
McCabe, L. R. "A Pilgrimage to Poe's Cottage." *Book Buyer* 25 (Ja 03) 592-8.
McCasker, Honor. "The Correspondence of R. W. Griswold." *More Books* 16 (Mr-Je 41) 105-16, 152-6, 190-6, 286-9.
McDowell, Tremaine. "Edgar Allan Poe and William Cullen Bryant." *PQ* 16 (Ja 37) 83-4.
McElderry, B. R., Jr. "The Edgar Allan Poe Collection." Un So Calif *Lib Bul* no 4 (Ja 48) 4-6.
McKeithan, D. M. "Two Sources of Poe's *Narrative of Arthur Gordon Pym*." *Un Texas Stud Eng* 13 (1933) 116-37.
McLean, S. R. "Poeana. I. A Valentine." *Colophon* ns 1 (Au 35) 183-7.
———, & Whitty, J. H. "Poeana." *Colophon* ns 1 (Au 35) 188-91.
McNeal, T. H. "Poe's *Zenobia*: An Early Satire on Margaret Fuller." *MLQ* 11 (Je 50) 215-6.
Macy, John. "Ex Libris." *Freeman* 2 (9 Mr 21) 622-3.
——— "The Fame of Poe." *Atl* 102 (D 08) 835-43.
Marble, A. R. "Willis and Poe: A Retrospect." *Critic* 48 (Ja 06) 24-6.
Marchand, Ernest. "Poe as Social Critic." *AL* 6 (Mr 34) 28-43.
Marion, Denis. "La Méthod intellectuelle de Poe." *Mesures* 6 (Ap 40) 89-127.
Markham, Edwin. "The Poetry of Poe." *Arena* 32 (Ag 04) 170-5.
Mason, Leo. "Poe-Script." *Dickensian* 42 (Sp 46) 79-81.
Matherly, E. P. "Poe and Hawthorne as Writers of the Short Story." *Educ* 40 (Ja 20) 294-306.
Matthews, Brander. "Poe and the Detective Story." *Scribner's* 42 (S 07) 287-93.
——— "Poe's Cosmopolitan Fame." *Century* 81 (D 10) 271-5.
Matthews, J. C. "Did Poe Read Dante?" *Un Texas Stud Eng* 18 (1938) 123-36.
Matthiessen, F. O. "Poe." *SR* 54 (Sp 46) 175-205.
Melton, W. F. "Poe's Mechanical Poem." *Texas R* 3 (Ja 18) 133-8.
——— "Some Autobiographical Notes in Poe's Poetry." *SAQ* 11 (Ap 12) 175-9.

Melville, Lewis. "The Centenary of Edgar Allan Poe." *Nineteenth Century* 65 (Ja 09) 140-52.
"Menander." "The Aesthetic of Poe." *TLS* (17 Je 44) 291.
Meyer, E. "Consulation d'Edgar Poe sur un crime. Edgar Poe à M. le Directeur de 'La Grande Revue' du pays de la soif eternelle." *La Grande Revue* 144 (Mr 34) 114-8.
Michaud, Régis. "Baudelaire et Edgar A. Poe." *Revue de Littérature Comparée* 19 O-D 38) 666-84.
Mierow, H. E. "A Classical Allusion in Poe." *MLN* 31 (Mr 16) 184-5.
——— "Stephen Phillips and Edgar Allan Poe." *MLN* 32 (D 17) 499-501.
Miller, A. C. "The Influence of Edgar A. Poe on Ambrose Bierce." *AL* 4 (My 32) 130-50.
Miller, F. DeW. "The Basis for Poe's 'The Island of the Fay.'" *AL* 14 (My 42) 135-40.
Mitchell, McBurney. "Poe and Spielhagen; Novelle and Short-Story." *MLN* 29 (F 14) 36-41.
Mohr, F. K. "The Influence of Eichendorff's 'Ahnung und Gegenwart' on Poe's 'Masque of the Red Death.'" *MLQ* 10 (Mr 49) 3-15.
Monroe, Harriet. "Poe and Longfellow." *Poetry* 29 (F 27) 266-74.
Moore, C. L. "The Case of Poe and His Critics." *Dial* 47 (16 N 09) 367-70.
——— "Poe's Place as a Critic." *Dial* 34 (16 F 03) 111-2.
Moore, J. R. "Poe, Scott, and 'The Murders in the Rue Morgue.'" *AL* 8 (Mr 36) 52-8.
More, P. E. "A Note on Poe's Method." *SP* 20 (Jl 23) 302-9.
——— "The Origins of Hawthorne and Poe." *Independent* 54 (16 O 02) 2453-60.
Morley, Christopher. "The Allergy of Roderick Usher." *TLS* no 2, 462 (9 Ap 49) 233.
Morris, G. D. "French Criticism of Poe." *SAQ* 14 (O 15) 324-9.
Morrison, Robert. "Poe's *The Lake: To —.*" *Expl* 7 (D 48) 22.
Neale, W. G., Jr. "The Source of Poe's 'Morella.'" *AL* 9 (My 37) 237-9.
Newcomer, A. G. "The Poe-Chivers Tradition Re-Examined." *SR* 12 (Ja 04) 20-35.
Nordstedt, George. "Poe and Einstein." *Open Court* 44 (Mr 30) 173-80.
——— "Prototype of 'The Raven.'" *NAR* 224 (D 27) 692-701.
Norman, E. K. "Poe's Knowledge of Latin." *AL* 6 (Mr 34) 72-7.
Norris, W. B. "Poe's Balloon Hoax." *Nation* 91 (27 O 10) 389-90.
Noulet, E. "L'Influence d'edgar Poe sur la poésie Française." *Études Littéraires* (Mexico) (1945) 79-126.
Olivero, Frederico. "Symbolism in Poe's Poetry." *Westminster R* 180 (Ag 13) 201-7.
O'Neill, E. H. "The Poe-Griswold-Harrison Texts of the 'Marginalia.'" *AL* 15 (N 43) 238-50.
Oras, Ants. "'The Bells' of Edgar Allan Poe and 'A Prophecy' by John Keats." *Apophoreta Tartuensia* (Stockholm) 2 (1949) 88-94.
Ostrom, J. W. "Another Griswold Forgery in a Poe Letter." *MLN* 58 (My 43) 394-6.
——— "A Poe Correspondence Re-Edited." *Americana* 34 (Jl 40) 409-46.
——— "Two 'Lost' Poe Letters." *AN&Q* 1 (Ag 41) 68-9.
——— "Two Unpublished Poe Letters." *Americana* 36 (Ja 42) 67-71.
Page, C. H. "Poe In France." *Nation* 88 (14 Ja 09) 32-4.
Parkes, H. B. "Poe, Hawthorne, Melville: An Essay in Sociological Criticism." *PR* 16 (F 49) 157-65.
Parks, E. W. "Edgar Allan Poe como Critico." *Diario de São Paulo* (Brazil) (9 O 49) 3.
Pasolini, Desideria. "Traduzione e Scelta dai Marginalia di E. A. Poe." *L'Immagine* no 12 (Mr-Ap 49).
Pattee, F. L. "Poe's Ulalume." *Chautauquan* 35 (Ag 00) 552-3.

Payne, L. W. "Poe and Emerson." *Texas R* 7 (O 21) 54-69.
Pettigrew, R. C. "Poe's Rime." *AL* 4 (My 32) 151-9.
———, & M. M. "A Reply to Floyd Stovall's Interpretation of 'Al Aaraaf.'" *AL* 8 (Ja 37) 439-45.
Philips, Edith. "The French of Edgar Allan Poe." *AS* 2 (Mr 27) 270-4.
Pickett, L. C. "Poet of the Night." *Lippincott's* 90 (S 12) 326-33.
Pittman, Diana. "Key to the Mystery of Edgar Allan Poe." *SLM* 3 (Ag, S 41) 367-77, 418-24; (F, Ap 42) 81-5, 143-68.
——— "Key to the Mystery of 'Ulalume.'" *SLM* 3 (Ag 41) 371-7.
Poe, E. E. "Poe, the Weird Genius." *Cosmopolitan* 46 (F 09) 243-52.
Pollock, A. "A Play about Poe." *Chri Sci Mon* 28 (17 N 36) 8.
Pope-Hennessy, Una. "A Letter to the Editors." *AL* 7 (N 35) 334.
Posey, M. N. "Notes on Poe's *Hans Pfaal.*" *MLN* 45 (D 30) 501-7.
Pound, Louise. "On Poe's 'The City in the Sea.'" *AL* 6 (Mr 34) 22-7.
——— "Poe's 'The City in the Sea' Again." *AL* 8 (Mr 36) 70-1.
Prescott, F. C. "Poe's Definition of Poetry." *Nation* 88 (4 F 09) 110.
Quarles, Diana. "Poe and International Copyright." *SLM* 3 (Ja 41) 4.
Quinn, A. H. "The Marriage of Poe's Parents." *AL* 11 (My 39) 209-12.
Randall, David. "Robertson's Poe Bibliography." *Pub W* 125 (21 Ap 34) 1540-3.
Rasor, C. L. "Possible Sources of 'The Cask of Amontillado.'" *Furman Stud* 31 (Wi 49) 46-50.
Rede, Kenneth. "New Poe Manuscript." *Am Col* 3 (D 26) 100-2.
——— "Poe Notes: From an Investigator's Notebook." *AL* 5 (Mr 33) 49-54.
——— "Poe's Annie: Leaves from Lonesome Years." *Am Col* 4 (Ap 27) 21-8.
———, & Heartman, C. F. "A Census of First Editions and Source Materials by or Relating to Edgar Allan Poe in American Public and Private Collections." *Am Book Coll* 1 (Ja, F, Mr, Ap, My, Je 32) 45-9, 80-4, 143-7, 207-11, 274-7, 339-43; 2 (Jl, Ag-S, O, N, D 32) 28-32, 141-53, 232-4, 290-2, 338-42.
Redman, Catherine. "Edgar Allan Poe—Soldier." *Quartermaster R* 16 (Ja, F 37) 18-21, 73-4.
Rendall, V. "Dumas and Poe." *TLS* (28 N 29) 1001.
Rhea, R. L. "Some Observations on Poe's Origins." *Un Texas Stud Eng* 10 (1930) 135-46.
Rhodes, S. A. "The Influence of Poe on Baudelaire." *RR* 18 (O-D 27) 329-33.
Richards, I. T. "A New Poe Poem." *MLN* 42 (Mr 27) 158-62.
Richardson, C. F. "Edgar Allan Poe, World-Author." *Critic* 41 (Ag 02) 138-47.
——— "Poe's Doctrine of Effect." *Un Calif Pub Mod Phil* 11 (1928) 179-86.
Roberts, W. "A Dumas Manuscript: Did Edgar Allan Poe Visit Paris?" *TLS* (21 N 29) 978.
Routh, James. "Notes on the Sources of Poe's Poetry: Coleridge, Keats, Shelley." *MLN* 29 (Mr 14) 72-5.
Rubin, J. J. "John Neal's Poetics as an Influence on Whitman and Poe." *NEQ* 14 (Je 41) 359-62.
Ryan, Sylvester. "A Poe Oversight." *CE* 11 (Ap 50) 408.
Saintsbury, George. "Edgar Allan Poe." *Dial* 83 (D 27) 451-63.
Sartain, William. "Edgar Allan Poe—Some Facts Recalled." *Art World* 2 (Jl 17) 320-3.
Scheffauer, H. G. "The Baiting of Poe." *Overland Mo* ns 53 (Je 09) 591-4.
Schick, J. S. "The Origin of 'The Cask of Amontillado.'" *AL* 6 (Mr 34) 18-21.
——— "Poe and Jefferson." *VMHB* 54 (O 46) 316-20.
Schreiber, C. F. "A Close-up of Poe." *SRL* 3 (9 O 26) 165-7.
——— "Mr. Poe at His Conjurations Again." *Colophon* 1 (Mr. My 30) Pt 2.
Schubert, Leland. "James William Carling: Expressionist Illustrator of 'The Raven.'" *SLM* 4 (Ap 42) 173-81.
Schwartz, W. L. "The Influence of E. A. Poe on Judith Gautier." *MLN* 42 (Mr 27) 171-3.

Scudder, H. H. "Poe's 'Balloon Hoax.'" *AL* 21 (My 49) 179-90.
Shepherd, L. M. "A New Portrait of Edgar Allan Poe." *Century* 91 (Ap 16) 906-7.
Shockley, M. S. "*Timour, the Tartar,* and Poe's *Tamerlane.*" *PMLA* 54 (D 41) 1103-6.
Shulte, A. P., & Wilson, J. S. "Facts About Poe: Portraits and Daguerreotypes of Edgar Allan Poe, with a Sketch of the Life of Poe." *Un Va Rec* 10 no 8.
Silver, R. G. "A Note about Whitman's Essay on Poe." *AL* 6 (Ja 35) 435-6.
Smart, C. A. "On the Road to Page One." *YR* 37 (Wi 48) 242-56.
Smith, C. A. "Poe and the Bible." *Davidson Col Mag* 36 (1920) 1-4.
Smith, G. P. "Poe's 'Metzengerstein.'" *MLN* 48 (Je 33) 356-9.
Smith, H. E. "Poe's Extension of His Theory of the Tale." *MP* 16 (Ag 18) 195-203.
Smith, J. M. "A New Light on Poe." *SLM* 1 (S 39) 575-81.
Snell, George. "First of the New Critics." *Quar R Lit* 2 (Su 45) 333-40.
Snyder, E. D. "Poe and Amy Lowell." *MLN* 43 (Mr 28) 152-3.
Somerville, J. A. "The 'Ifs' in Poe's Life." *SLM* 1 (D 39) 860.
Sparks, Archibald. "Edgar Allan Poe: Bibliography." *N&Q* 159 (27 D 30) 465.
Spivey, H. E. "Poe and Lewis Gaylord Clark." *PMLA* 54 (D 39) 1124-32.
Stanard, M. M. "Was Poe Never Ethical?" *Nation* 92 (25 My 11) 527.
Starke, Aubrey. "Poe's Friend Reynolds." *AL* 11 (My 39) 152-9.
Starrett, Vincent. "One Who Knew Poe." *Bkm* 64 (O 27) 196-201.
——— "A Poe Mystery Uncovered: *The Lost Minerva Review of Al Aaraaf.*" *SRL* 26 (1 My 43) 4-5, 25.
Stedman, E. C. "Poe, Cooper, and the Hall of Fame." *NAR* 185 (Ag 07) 801-12.
——— "Poe's Cottage at Fordham." *Century* 73 (Mr 07) 770-3.
Stern, M. B. "The House of the Expanding Doors: Ann Lynch's Soirees, 1846." *N Y Hist* 23 (Ja 42) 42-51.
Stoddard, R. H. "Reminiscences of Hawthorne and Poe." *Independent* 54 (20 N 02) 2756-8.
Stonier, G. W. "Books in General." *New Statesman & Nation* 24 (29 Ag 42) 143.
Stovall, Floyd. "An Interpretation of Poe's 'Al Aaraaf.'" *Un Texas Stud Eng* 9 (1929) 106-33.
——— "Poe as a Poet of Ideas." *Un Texas Stud Eng* 11 (1931) 56-62.
——— "Poe's Debt to Coleridge." *Un Texas Stud Eng* 10 (Jl 30) 70-127.
——— "The Women in Poe's Poems and Tales." *Un Texas Stud Eng* 5 (1925) 197-209.
Suarés, André. "Edgar Poe." *Nouvelles Littéraires* 12 (7 Ap 34) 1-2.
Tannenbaum, Libby. "The Raven Abroad: Some European Illustrations of the Work of Edgar Allan Poe." *Mag of Art* 37 (1944) 123-7.
Tate, Allen. "Our Cousin, Mr. Poe." *PR* 16 (D 49) 1207-19.
——— "Three Commentaries: Poe, James, and Joyce." *SR* 58 (Wi 50) 1-15.
Taylor, Archer. "Poe's Dr. Lardner, and 'Three Sundays in a Week.'" *AN&Q* 3 (Ja 44) 153-5.
Taylor, Bayard. "Poe's Last Manuscript." *Am Clipper* 1 (N 34) 64.
Taylor, W. F. "Israfel in Motley." *SR* 42 (Jl-S 34) 330-9.
Tello de la Piña, Raquel. "La Necrofilia en Allan Poe." *Humanidades* 1 (D 43) 101-13.
Thorner, H. E. "Hawthorne, Poe, and a Literary Ghost." *NEQ* 7 (Mr 34) 146-54.
Thorp, Willard. "Two Poe Letters at Princeton." *PULC* 10 (F 49) 91-4.
Ticknor, Caroline. "Ingram—Discourager of Poe Biographies." *Bkm* 44 (S 16) 8-14.
Tinker, C. B. "Poetry and the Secret Impulse." *YR* 16 (Ja 27) 275-86.
Townsend-Warner, Sylvia. "Cross Out Louisa." *New Statesman & Nation* 8 (17 N 34) 730.
Traylor, M. G. "'To Keep It in Beauty': The Poe Shrine." *SLM* 1 (Ap 39) 263-8.
Triplett, E. B. "A Note on Poe's 'The Raven.'" *AL* 10 (N 38) 339-41.
Trompio, P. P. "Poe a Roma." *La Nuova Europa* 2 (1945).

Turnbull, Mrs. L. "New Statue of Edgar Allan Poe by Sir Moses Ezekiel." *Art & Arch* 5 (My 17) 306-8.
Turner, Arlin. "Another Source of Poe's 'Julius Rodman.'" *AL* 8 (Mr 36) 69-70.
——— "A Note on Poe's 'Julius Rodman.'" *Un Texas Stud Eng* 10 (1930) 147-57.
——— "Sources of Poe's 'A Descent into the Maelstrom.'" *JEGP* 46 (Jl 47) 298-301.
——— "Writing of Poe's 'The Bells.'" *AN&Q* 2 (Ag 42) 73.
———, & Mabbott, T. O. "Two Poe Hoaxes by the Same Hand." *AN&Q* 2 (Ja 43) 147-8.
Valette, Jacques. "Chronique sur Edgar Poe." *Mercure de France* no 1037 (1 Ja 50) 161-3.
Van Doorn, Willem. "Edgar Poe en Ulalume." *Levende Talen* (Groningen) no 151 (1949).
Varner, Cornelia. "Notes on Poe's Use of Contemporary Materials in Certain of His Stories." *JEGP* 32 (Ja 33) 77-80.
Varner, J. G. "Note on a Poem Attributed to Poe." *AL* 8 (Mr 36) 66-8.
——— "Poe and Miss Barrett." *TLS* (11 Ap 35) 224.
——— "Poe and Miss Barrett of Wimpole Street." *Four Arts* 2 (Ja-F 35) 4-5, 14-5, 17.
——— "Poe's *Tale of Jerusalem* and *The Talmud*." *Am Book Coll* 6 (F 35) 56-7.
Vincent, H. P. "A Sarah Helen Whitman Letter about Edgar Allan Poe." *AL* 13 (My 41) 162-7.
Walcutt, C. C. "The Logic of Poe." *CE* 2 (F 41) 438-44.
Wallace, A. R. "Leonainie Problem." *Fortnightly R* 81 (Ap 04) 706-11.
Warfel, H. R. "Poe's Dr. Percival: A Note on *The Fall of the House of Usher*." *MLN* 54 (F 39) 129-31.
Wegelin, Oscar. "Poe's First Printer." *Am Col* 3 (O 26) 31.
——— "The Printer of Poe's Tamerlane." *N Y Hist Soc Quar Bul* 24 (Ja 40) 23-5.
Weiss, S. A. "Reminiscences of Edgar Allan Poe." *Independent* 56 (5 My 04) 1010-4; 57 (25 Ag 04) 443-8.
Wells, Gabriel. "Poe as a Mystic." *Am Book Coll* 5 (F 34) 54-5.
Wells, Ross. "College 'Lit' First to Recognize Poe." *Richmond Times Dispatch* (6 O 35) 6.
Werner, W. L. "Poe's *Israfel*." *Expl* 2 (Ap 44) 44.
——— "Poe's Theories and Practice in Poetic Technique." *AL* 2 (My 30) 157-65.
Whiteside, M. B. "Poe and Dickinson." *Personalist* 15 (Au 34) 315-26.
Whiting, M. B. "The Life-Story of Edgar Allan Poe." *Bkm* (London) 35 (Ja 09) 173-81.
Whitt, Celia. "Poe and the *Mysteries of Udolpho*." *Un Texas Stud Eng* 17 (1937) 124-31.
Whitty, J. H. "Discoveries in the Uncollected Poems of Edgar Allan Poe." *Nation* 102 (27 Ja 16) 105-6.
——— "Edgar Allan Poe." *Lit R* 3 (1923) 918.
——— "Edgar Allan Poe in England and Scotland." *Bkm* 44 (S 16) 14-21.
——— "First and Last Publication of Poe's *Raven*." *Pub W* 130 (17 O 36) 1635.
——— "Letters Touching the Early Life of Edgar Allan Poe." *Nation* 95 (18 Jl 12) 55.
——— "A New Poe Letter: Hitherto Unpublished Note Deals with Strange Cryptogram." *Richmond Times Dispatch* (21 Jl 35) 15.
——— "The Passing of Poe's English Biographer." *Dial* 61 (22 Je 16) 15.
——— "Poe Portrait." *Century* 92 (Ag 16) 635.
——— "Poeana. II. A Parrot." *Colophon* ns 1 (Au 35) 188-90.
——— "Poem to Mark Tomb of Mother." *Richmond Times Dispatch* (6 O 35) 3.
——— "Poe's Writing Influenced by Richmond Gardens." *Richmond News Leader* (24 Ap 37).
——— "Three Poems by Edgar Allan Poe." *Nation* 107 (7 D 18) 699-700.

Wiener, P. P. "Poe's Logic and Metaphysic." *Personalist* 14 (O 33) 268-74.
Williams, S. T. "New Letters about Poe." *YR* 14 (Jl 25) 755-73.
Williams, Valentine, & Crawford, Alice. "The Detective in Fiction." *Fortnightly R* 128 (S 30) 380-92.
Wilson, Edmund. "Poe as a Literary Critic." *Nation* 155 (31 O 42) 452-3.
Wilson, J. G. "Memorials of Edgar Allan Poe." *Independent* 53 (25 Ap 01) 940-2.
Wilson, J. S. "The Devil Was in It." *Am Merc* 24 (O 31) 215-20.
——— "The Letters of Edgar A. Poe to George W. Eveleth." *Un Va Alumni Bul* 17 (Ja 24) 34-59.
——— "Poe's Philosophy of Composition." *NAR* 223 (D-Ja-F 27) 675-84.
——— "Unpublished Letters of Edgar Allan Poe." *Century* 107 (Mr 24) 652-6.
——— "The Young Man Poe." *VQR* 2 (Ap 26) 238-53.
Wilt, Napier. "Poe's Attitude toward His Tales: A New Document." *MP* 25 (Ag 27) 101-5.
Wimsatt, W. K., Jr. "Mary Rogers, John Anderson, and Others." *AL* 21 (Ja 50) 482-4.
——— "Poe and the Chess Automaton." *AL* 11 (My 39) 138-51.
——— "Poe and the Mystery of Mary Rogers." *PMLA* 55 (Mr 41) 230-48.
——— "What Poe Knew about Cryptography." *PMLA* 58 (S 43) 754-79.
Winters, Yvor. "Edgar Allan Poe: A Crisis in the History of American Obscurantism." *AL* 8 (Ja 37) 379-401.
Wood, Clement. "The Influence of Poe and Lanier on Modern Literature." *SLM* 1 (Ap 39) 237-42.
Woodberry, G. E. "The Poe-Chivers Papers." *Century* 65 (Ja F 03) 435-47, 545-58.
Worthen, S. C. "Poe and the Beautiful Cigar Girl." *AL* 20 (N 48) 305-12.
——— "A Strange Aftermath of the Mystery of 'Marie Roget' (Mary Rogers)." *Proc N J Hist Soc* 60 (Ap 42) 116-23.
Wylie, C. P., Jr. "Mathematical Allusions in Poe." *Sci Mo* 63 (S 46) 227-35.
Yarmolinsky, Avrahm. "The Russian View of American Literature." *Bkm* 44 (S 16) 44-8.
Yewdale, M. S. "Edgar Allan Poe, Pathologically." *NAR* 212 (N 20) 686-96.

POLLARD, PERCIVAL (1869-1911). Munson, G. B. "A Forgotten American Critic." *Freeman* 2 (20 O 20) 135-6.

POOLE, ERNEST (1880-). Anon. "Ernest Poole." *Bkm* 41 (Ap 17) 115-8.
——— "Ernest Poole." *Book News Mo* 30 (Ag 15) 565-6.
——— "Ernest Poole." *Wilson Bul* 6 (S 31) 24.
Holt, Hamilton. "The Problem of Poverty, by an Aristotelian." *Unpopular R* 6 (O 16) 245-63.
More, P. E. "The Problem of Poverty, by a Platonist." *Unpopular R* 6 (O 16) 231-45.

PORTER, ELEANOR HODGMAN (1868-1920). Colbron, G. I. "The Popularity of Pollyanna.'" *Bkm* 41 (My 15) 297-8.

PORTER, KATHARINE ANNE (1894-). Birss, J. H. "American First Editions . . . Katherine Anne Porter." *Pub W* 133 (18 Ja 38) 2382.
Hartley, Lodwick. "Katherine Anne Porter." *SR* 48 (Ap 40) 201-16.
Sylvester, W. A. "Selected and Critical Bibliography of the Uncollected Works of Katherine Anne Porter." *Bul Bibl* 19 (Ja-Ap 47) 36.
Warren, R. P. "Katherine Anne Porter (Irony with a Center)." *KR* 4 (Wi 42) 29-42.
West, R. B., Jr. "Katherine Anne Porter: Symbol and Theme in 'Flowering Judas.'" *Accent* 7 (Sp 47) 182-8.
Young, V. A. "The Art of Katherine Anne Porter." *NMQR* 15 (Au 45) 326-41.

PORTER, WILLIAM SYDNEY (1862-1910). Anon. "Chronicle and Comment." *Bkm* 34 (O 11) 115-8.

Anon. "The Finding of Unknown O. Henry Stories." *Redbook* 68 (Ja 37) 7.

——— "How O. Henry's Greatest Story Came to Be Written." *Cur Op* 64 (Je 18) 421.

——— "O. Henry Our Literary De Valera." *Lit Dig* 65 (15 My 20) 43-4.

——— "O. Henry's Biographer." *Bkm* 37 (Mr 13) 2-3.

——— "O. Henry's Short Stories." *NAR* 187 (My 08) 781-3.

——— "Old O. Henrys." *Lit Dig* 123 (10 Ap 37) 25.

——— "The Personal O. Henry." *Bkm* 29 (Je 09) 345-6.

Adams, Paul. "O Henry and Texas." *Bellman* 23 (22 S 17) 319-23.

Adcock, A. St. J. "O. Henry." *Bkm* (London) 50 (S 16) 153-7; *Littell's Living Age* 291 (25 N 16) 482-8.

Beaty, John. "O Henry's Life and Position." *SR* 25 (Ap 17) 237-43.

Boissard, G. A. "O. Henry's Pen Name." *SRL* 15 (9 Ja 37) 13-4.

Boyd, David. "O. Henry's Road of Destiny." *Americana* 31 (O 37) 579-608.

Bruno, Guido. "Poe and O. Henry." *Bruno's W* 3 (29 Jl 16) 874-5.

Burton, R. A. "Debauch of O. Henry." *Bellman* 24 (26 (Ja 18) 93.

Clarkson, P. S. "A Decomposition of *Cabbage and Kings.*" *AL* 7 (My 35) 195-202.

——— "Whence 'O. Henry'?" *SRL* 10 (13 Ja 34) 404.

Cobley, W. D. "O. Henry." *Manchester Q* 37 (1918) 316-39.

Courtney, L. W. "O. Henry's Case Reconsidered." *AL* 14 (Ja 43) 361-71.

Davis, R. H. "I Go in Search of O. Henry." *Golden Book* 11 (Ap 30) 44.

Denison, Lindsay. "Sydney Porter—O. Henry." *Am. Mag* 70 (S 10) 605.

Echols, E. C. "O. Henry and the Classics—II." *Classical J* 44 (D 48) 209-11.

——— "O. Henry's 'Shaker of the Attic Salt.'" *Classical J* 43 (My 48) 488-9.

Firkins, O. W. "O. Henry." *Weekly R* 1 (13 S 19) 384-6.

Forman, H. J. "O. Henry's Short Stories." *NAR* 187 (My 08) 781-3.

Gates, W. B. "O. Henry and Shakespere." *Shakespeare Assn Bul* 19 (Ja 44) 20-5.

Goerch, Carl. "O. Henry's Brother Lives in Ayden." *State* (N. C.) 2 (24 N 34) 1, 26.

Gohdes, Clarence. "Some Letters by O. Henry." *SAQ* 38 (Ja 39) 31-9.

Hall, Gilman. "Tarkington and O. Henry." *Everybody's* 17 (O 07) 567.

Henderson, Archibald. "O. Henry: After a Decade." *So R* 1 (Ap 20) 15-8.

——— "O. Henry and North Carolina." *Nation* 100 (14 Ja 15) 49-50.

——— "O. Henry, Artist and Fun-Maker." *Un N C Mag* 51 (N 20) 18-20.

——— "O. Henry—A Contemporary Classic." *SAQ* 22 (Jl 23) 270-8.

——— "O. Henry: His Life and Art." *Alumni News* (N C State Normal Col) 4 (1916) 1-2.

Henderson, I. B. "The Courtship of O. Henry." *State* (N. C.) 2 (9 F 35) 8.

——— "How O. Henry Began His Writing Career." *State* (N. C.) 2 (2 F 35) 5.

——— "Sara Coleman Porter." *State* (N. C.) 2 (26 Ja 35) 3.

Hollis, D. W. "The Persecution of O. Henry." *Austin Am-Statesman Sunday Mag* (16, 23, 30 Ag; 6, 13, 20, 27 S; 4 O 25) 1-11; 10, 14; 10, 14; 6-7; 6-7; 6-7; 6-7.

Hubbell, J. B. "Charles Napoleon Evans, Creator of Jesse Holmes the Fool-Killer." *SAQ* 36 (O 37) 431-46.

Irwin, Will. "O. Henry, Man and Writer." *Cosmopolitan* 49 (S 10) 447-9.

Jones, Joseph. "Don Pomposo: Mr. W. S. Porter." *MLN* 57 (F 43) 131.

Jung, Margetta. "O. Henry in Manhattan." *Sw* R 26 (Jl 39) 411-5.

Kercheville, F. M. "O. Henry and Don Alfonso." *NMQR* 1 (N 31) 367-88.

Larned, W. T. "Prof. Leacock and the Other Professors." *NRp* 9 (13 Ja 17) 299.

Leacock, Stephen. "O. Henry and His Critics." *NRp* 9 (2 D 16) 120-2.

Lomax, J. A. "Henry Steger and O. Henry." *Sw R* 24 (Ap 39) 299-316.

Long, E. H. "O. Henry's Christmas Stories." *SLM* 1 (D 39) 795-7.

Mabbott, T. O. "Queries from O. Henry's 'The Pendulum.'" *N&Q* 169 (5 O 35) 249.

McAdam, George. "Crossways of 'Roads of Destiny.'" *N Y Times Book R* (3 Je 23).
McCormick, Lawlor. "O. Henry in Texas." *Bunker's Mo* 1 (F 28) 319.
Maurice, A. B. "About New York with O. Henry." *Bkm* 38 (S 13) 49-57.
Mims, Edwin. "Professor Smith's O. Henry Biography." *SAQ* 16 (Ap 17) 167-9.
Mohler, E. F. "The City of Too Many Caliphs." *Cath World* 111 (S 20) 756-61.
Morley, Christopher. "I Visit the Prison . . ." *SRL* 10 (9 D 33) 325.
Narsy, Raoul. "O. Henry through French Eyes." *Living Age* 303 (11 O 19) 86-8.
Nathan, G. J. "O. Henry in His Own Bagdad." *Bkm* 31 (Jl 10) 477-9.
Newbolt, Frank. "Letter to a Dead Author." *Nineteenth Century* 82 (O 17) 825-34.
O'Quinn, Trueman. "O. Henry in Austin." *Sw Hist Q* 43 (O 39) 143-57.
Page, A. W. "Little Pictures of O. Henry: III." *Bkm* 37 (Je, Jl, Ag 13) 381-7, 498-508, 607-16; 38 (O 13) 169-77.
Pattee, F. L. "The Journalization of American Literature." *Unpopular R* 7 (Ap-Je 17) 374-94.
Patterson, E. L. "O. Henry and Me." *Everybody's* 30 (F 14) 205-10.
Paxton, Matthew. "An O. Henry Story That Was Not Written." *Bkm* (London) 76 (Jl 29) 204.
Payne, L. W., Jr. "The Humor of O. Henry." *Texas R* 4 (O 18) 18-37.
Peck, H. T. "The American Story Teller." *Bkm* 31 (Ap 10) 131-7.
Porter, W. S. "Part of a letter, dated November 27, 1903." *Autograph Album* 1 (D 33) 12, 94.
Ratchford, Fanny. "The Rolling Stone: The Life History of an O. Henry Rarity." *Colophon* 5 (Je 34) Pt 17.
Richardson, C. F. "O. Henry and New Orleans." *Bkm* 39 (My 14) 281-7.
Robinson, Duncan, *et al.* "O. Henry's Austin." *Sw R* 24 (Jl 39) 388-410.
Rollins, H. E. "O. Henry." *SR* 22 (Ap 14) 213-32.
——— "An O. Henry Cocktail." *HLB* 1 (Wi 47) 119-20.
——— "O. Henry's Texas." *Texas R* 4 (Jl 19) 295-307.
——— "O. Henry's Texas Days." *Bkm* 40 (O 14) 154-65.
——— "The Rolling Stone." *Nation* 99 (2 Jl 14) 11-2.
Seibel, George. "O. Henry and the Silver Dollar." *Bkm* 73 (Ag 31) 593-7.
Sillard, P. A. "Appreciation of O. Henry." *Cath World* 115 (S 22) 785-9.
Smith, C. A. "O. Henry." *Nation* 106 (11 My 18) 567.
——— "The Strange Case of Sydney Porter and O. Henry." *World's Work* 33 (D 16) 412-4.
Stanton, Theodore. "O. Henry in France." *Dial* 60 (11 My 16) 450-3.
Steger, H. P. "O. Henry: New Facts about the Great Author." *Cosmopolitan* 53 (O 12) 655-63.
——— "O. Henry—Who He Is and How He Works." *World's Work* 18 (Je 09) 11724-6.
——— "On O. Henry's Trail." *Cosmopolitan* 53 (O 12) 655-7.
——— "Some O. Henry Letters and the Plunkville Patroit." *Independent* 73 (5 S 12) 543-7.
Stratton, Florence, & Burke, Vincent. "O. Henry's Own Short Story." *Bunker's Mo* 2 (Jl 28) 30-9.
Tinker, E. L. "Why O. Henry?" *Bkm* 61 (Je 25) 436-7.
Travis, Edmunds. "O. Henry Enters the Shadows." *Bunker's Mo* 1 (My 28) 669-84.
——— "O. Henry's Austin Years." *Bunker's Mo* 1 (Ap 28) 495-508.
——— "The Triumph of O. Henry." *Bunker's Mo* 1 (Je 28) 839-52.
Van Doren, Carl. "O. Henry." *Texas R* 2 (Ja 17) 248-59.
Williams, W. W. "The Quiet Lodger of Irving Place." *Am Book Coll* 5 (Mr, Ap, My-Je 34) 72-6, 118-22, 136-9.
Woollcott, Alexander. "O. Henry, Playwright." *Bkm* 56 (O 22) 152-7; *Golden Book* 19 (My 34) 570-6.

PORTER, WILLIAM T. (1809-58). Eberstadt, Lindley. "The Passing of a Noble 'Spirit.'" *PBSA* 44 (4Q 50) 272-3.

POST, CHARLES CYREL (1846-1906). "A Significant Memorial to Mussel Slough." *Pac Hist R* 18 (N 49) 501-4.

POUND, EZRA (1885-). Anon. "Bollingen Prize in Poetry." *Annual Report, Libr Cong* (30 Je 49) 88-94.
——— "The Case against the *Saturday Review of Literature.*" *Poetry* (special issue, first printing O 49).
——— "Congressmen Seek Inquiry into Bollingen Award." *Pub W* 156 (20 Ag 49) 742.
——— "Ezra (Loomis) Pound." *Cur Biog* 3 (N 42) 62-5.
——— "Ezra Pound Issue." *Quar R Lit* 5 no 2 (1949) 103-200.
——— "News Notes." *Poetry* 74 (Ap 49) 56, 59.
——— "Pound Sterling." *Life and Letters* 15 (Ag 34) 632-6.
——— "A Reviewer's Note-Book." *Freeman* 1 (16 Je 20) 334-5.
——— "To Define True Madness." *Canadian Forum* 29 (S 49) 125.
——— "Understanding the News." *Scholastic* 54 (2 Mr 49) 15.
Adams, R. M. "A Hawk and a Handsaw for Ezra Pound." *Accent* 8 (Su 48) 205-14.
Aiken, Conrad. "Personae." *Poetry* 44 (Ag 34) 276-9.
Aldington, Richard. "A Book for Literary Philosophers." *Poetry* 16 (Jl 20) 213-6.
——— "The Poetry of Ezra Pound." *Egoist* 2 (1 My 15) 71-2.
Barrett, William. "A Prize for Ezra Pound." *PR* 16 (Ap 49) 344-7.
Barry, Iris. "The Ezra Pound Period." *Bkm* 74 (O 31) 159-71.
Beck, Warren. "Boundaries of Poetry." *CE* 4 (Mr 43) 346-7.
Benét, W. R. "Poets in Collected Editions." *YR* 17 (Ja 28) 366-74.
Berryman, John. "The Poetry of Ezra Pound." *PR* 16 (Ap 49) 377-94.
Berti, L. "Poesia e minetismo con Ezra Pound." *Letteratura* 4 (1940) 140-5; 5 (1941) 123-34.
Blackmur, R. P. "Masks of Ezra Pound." *H&H* 7 (Ja-Mr 34) 177-212.
Bodenheim, Maxwell. "Isolation of Carved Metal." *Dial* 72 (Ja 22) 87-91.
Bottrall, Ronald. "XXX Cantos of Ezra Pound." *Scrutiny* 2 (S 33) 112-22.
Bronner, Milton. "A Panel of Poets." *Bkm* 38 (S 13) 154-61.
Brown, J. I. "A Troubadour at Hamilton." *Hamilton Lit Mag* 62 (1932) 53-63.
Canby, H. S. "Ezra Pound." *SRL* 28 (15 D 45) 10.
Carnevali, Emanuel. "Irritation." *Poetry* 15 (Ja 20) 211-21.
Cerf, Bennett. "The Case of Ezra Pound." *SRL* 29 (23 Mr 46) 32-6, 49-53.
Cowley, Malcolm. "The Battle over Ezra Pound." *NRp* 121 (3 O 49) 17-20.
Delmer, S. "Ezra Pound." *Zeitschrift für Französischen und Englischen Unterricht* 29 (1930) 92-110.
Dillon, George. "A Note on the Obvious." *Poetry* 68 (S 46) 322-5.
Drummond, John. "Il Caso di Ezra Pound." *Fiera Lettaria* no 16 (17 Ap 49).
Dudek, Louis. "Correspondence." *Canadian Forum* 29 (N 49) 185-6.
Eberhart, Richard. "Pound's New Cantos." *Quar R Lit* 5 (1949) 174-91.
Eliot, T. S. "Ezra Pound." *Poetry* 68 (S 39) 326-39.
——— "Isolated Superiority." *Dial* 84 (Ja 28) 4-7.
Enriques Agnoletti, E. "Il Caso Ezra Pound." *Il Ponte* (Italy) (O 49) 1327.
Fitts, Dudley. "Music Fit for the Odes." *H&H* 4 (Ja-Mr 31) 278-89.
Fitzgerald, Robert. "Mr. Pound's Good Governors." *Accent* 1 (Wi 41) 121-2.
Forsell, Lars. "Ezra Pound." *Bonniers Litterära Magasin* (Stockholm) 18 (O 49) 608-18.
Geddes, Virgil. "Ezra Pound Today." *Poetry* 21 (N 22) 95-100.
Gilkes, Martin. "Discovery of Ezra Pound." *English* 2 no 8 (1938) 74-83.
Glicksberg, C. I. "Ezra Pound and the Fascist Complex." *SAQ* 46 (Jl 47) 349-58.
Gorman, H. S. "Bolingbroke of Bards." *NAR* 219 (Je 24) 855-65.
Gregory, Horace. "The A.B.C. of Ezra Pound." *Poetry* 46 (Ag 35) 279-85.

——— "The Search for a Frontier." *NRp* 75 (26 Jl 33) 292-4.
Grigson, Geoffrey. "Aspects of Modern Poetry." *New Statesman & Nation* 8 (15 D 34) 899.
Hale, W. G. "Pegasus Impounded." *Poetry* 14 (Ap 19) 52-5.
Hauserman, H. W. "W. B. Yeats's Criticism of Ezra Pound." *Eng Stud* 29 (Ag 48) 97-109.
Healy, J. V. "An Adjunct to the Muses' Diadem: A Note on E. P." *Poetry* 68 (S 46) 339-40.
Hillyer, Robert. "Treason's Strange Fruit: The Case of Ezra Pound and the Bollingen Award." *SRL* 32 (11 Je 49) 9-11, 28.
Hume, Robert. "The Contribution of Ezra Pound." *English* 8 (Su 50) 60-5.
Kenner, Hugh. "In the Caged Panther's Eyes." *Hudson R* 1 (Wi 49) 580-6.
——— "The Rose in the Steel Dust." *Hudson* R 3 (Sp 50) 66-124.
Laughlin, James. "Ezra Pound's Propertius." *SR* 44 (O-D 38) 480-91.
Leesemann, Maurice. "Mr. Pound and the Younger Generation." *Poetry* 30 (Jl 27) 216-22.
Lewis, Wyndham. "Ezra: The Portrait of a Personality." *Quar R Lit* 5 no 2 (1949) 136-44.
Loving, Pierre. "Towards Walt Whitman." *Double Dealer* 4 (S 22) 139-42.
McClure, John. "New Poems of Ezra Pound." *Double Dealer* 2 (My 22) 269-71.
Mangan, Sherry. "Poetry for Scholars, Scholarship for Poets." *Poetry* 41 (Mr 33) 336-9.
Michelson, Max. "A Glass-blower of Time." *Poetry* 11 (Mr 18) 330-3.
Monroe, Harriet. "Ezra Pound." *Poetry* 26 (My 25) 90-7.
Moore, Marianne. "The Cantos." *Poetry* 39 (O 31) 37-50.
——— "A Draft of Cantos." *Criterion* 13 (Ap 34) 482-5.
Paige, D. D. "Letters of Ezra Pound." *Hudson R* 3 (Sp 50) 53-66.
Patchen, Kenneth. "Ezra Pound's Guilt." *Renascence* 2 (F 46) 3-4.
Peel, Robert. "The Poet as Artist and Citizen." *Chri Sci Mon* (9 D 50) 7.
Pound, Ezra. "D'Artagnan Twenty Years After." *Criterion* 16 (Jl 37) 606-17.
——— "A Few Don'ts by an Imagiste." *Poetry* 1 (Mr 13) 200-6.
——— "Indiscretions, or Une Revue de Deux Mondes." *Quar R Lit* 5 no 2 (1949) 105-35.
——— "Letters to a Young Poet from Ezra Pound." *Poetry* 76 (S 50) 342-51.
——— "The Wisdom of Poetry." *Forum* 47 (Ap 12) 497-501.
Prestin, J. H. "Three American Poets." *VQR* 3 (Jl 27) 450-62.
Ransom, J. C. "Mr. Pound and the Broken Tradition." *SRL* 11 (19 Ja 35) 434.
Rice, Wallace. "Ezra Pound and Poetry." *Dial* 54 (1 My 13) 370-1.
Richardson, Lawrence. "Ezra Pound's Homage to Propertius." *Yale Poetry R* no 6 (1947) 21-9.
Sandburg, Carl. "The Work of Ezra Pound." *Poetry* 7 (O 16) 249-57.
Schlauch, Margaret. "The Anti-Humanism of Ezra Pound." *Sci & Soc* 13 (Su 49) 258-69.
Schwartz, Delmore. "Ezra Pound's Very Useful Labors." *Poetry* 51 (Mr 38) 324-39.
Sillen, Samuel. "A Prize for Ezra Pound." *Masses & Mainstream* 2 (Ap 49) 3-6.
Sinclair, May. "The Reputation of Ezra Pound." *Eng R* 30 (Ap 20) 326-35; *NAR* 211 (My 20) 658-68.
Speirs, John. "Mr. Pound's Propertius." *Scrutiny* 3 (S 34) 409-18.
Stuart, D. R. "Modernistic Critics and Translators." *PULC* 11 (Su 50) 177-98.
Tate, Allen. "Ezra Pound's Golden Ass." *Nation* 132 (10 Je 31) 632-4.
——— "Laundry Bills." *Poetry* 41 (N 32) 107-12.
——— "Poetry and Politics." *NRp* 75 (2 Ag 33) 308-11.
Taupin, René. "La Poésie d'Ezra Pound." *Revue Anglo-Américaine* 8 (F 31) 221-36.
Tichenor, G. H. "This Man Is a Traitor." *PM* (15 Ag 43) 3-5.
Untermeyer, Louis. "Ezra Pound, Proseur." *NRp* 16 (17 Ag 18) 83-4.

Valette, Jacques. "Ezra Pound." *Mercure de France* no 1025 (Ja 49) 160-3.
Watts, H. H. "The Devices of Pound's Cantos." *Quar R Lit* 5 no 2 (1949) 147-75.
——— "Philosopher at Bay." *Cronos* 2 (Mr 48) 1-16.
——— "Pound's Cantos: Means to an End." *Yale Poetry R* no 6 (1947) 9-20.
West, R. B. "Excerpts from a Journal: 1949." *WR* 14 (Wi 50) 82, 151-9.
——— "Ezra Pound and Contemporary Criticism." *Quar R Lit* 5 (1949) 192-200.
Williams, D. P. "The Background of *The Pisan Stanzas.*" *Poetry* 73 (Ja 49) 216-21.
Williams, W. C. "Ezra Pound: Lord Ga-Ga!" *Decision* 2 (S 41) 16-24.
——— "Something for a Biography." *Gen Mag & Hist Chron* 50 (Su 48) 211-13.
Zukovsky, Louis. "The Cantos of Ezra Pound." *Criterion* 10 (Ap 31) 424-40.

POYDRAS, JULIEN (*c.* 1740-1824). Tinker, E. L. "Louisiana's Earliest Poet: Julien Poydras and the Paeans to Galvez." *BNYPL* 37 (O 33) 839-47.

PRESCOTT, WILLIAM HICKLING (1796-1859). Angus-Butterworth, L. M. "William Hickling Prescott." *SAQ* 44 (Ap 45) 217-26.
Charvat, William. "Prescott's Political and Social Attitudes." *AL* 13 (Ja 42) 320-30.
Clark, H. H. "Literary Criticism in the *North American Review,* 1815-1835." *Trans Wisc Acad Sci, Arts, & Letters* 32 (1940) 299-350.
Means, P. A. "A Re-examination of Prescott's Account of Early Peru." *NEQ* 4 (O 31) 645-62.
Mood, Fulmer, & Hicks, Granville. "Letters to Dr. Channing on Slavery and the Annexation of Texas, 1837." *NEQ* 5 (Jl 32) 587-601.
Ogden, Rollo. "Prescott the Man." *Atl* 93 (Mr 04) 320-37.

PRINCE, THOMAS (1687-1758). Forbes, A. B. "Thomas Prince Scientist and Historian." *PCSM* 28 (1935) 100-4.
Hornberger, Theodore. "The Science of Thomas Prince." *NEQ* 9 (Mr 36) 26-42.
Thompson, Lawrance. "Notes on Some Collectors in Colonial Massachusetts." *Colophon* ns 2 (Au 36) 82-100.
Tilton, E. M. "Lightning-Rods and the Earthquake of 1755." *NEQ* 13 (Mr 40) 85-97.

PROKOSCH, FREDERIC (1909-). Bataille, Georges. "Un Nouveau romancier américain." *Critique* 2 (My 47) 387-9.
Bishop, J. P. "Final Dreading." *Poetry* 49 (Mr 37) 337-9.
Brest, René. "Un Américain juge les Américains." *Les Nouvelles Littéraires* 29 (9 F 50) 1.
Metzel, Boris. "Entretien avec Frédéric Prokosch." *Paru* (France) no 61 (Je 50) 18-21.
Morse, S. F. "Spectre over Europe." *Poetry* 53 (N 38) 89-92.
Nimier, Roger. "L'Amérique." *La Table Ronde* (Paris) no 26 (F 50) 138-40.
Rubin, J. J. "Young Man of Letters." *SR* 46 (Ja-Mr 38) 122-4.
Tian, Enzo. "Prokosch o del viaggio." *Fiera Letteraria* no 4 (23 Ja 49).

PROUD, ROBERT (1728-1813). Powell, J. H. "Robert Proud, Pennsylvania's First Historian." *Penn Hist* 13 (Ap 46) 85-112.

PULITZER, JOSEPH (1847-1911). St. Johns, G. S. "Joseph Pulitzer." *Mo Hist R* 25 (Ja, Ap, Jl 31) 201-18, 404-20, 563-75; 26 (O 31, Ja, Ap 32) 54-67, 163-78, 267-80.
——— "Joseph Pulitzer, Early Life in St. Louis and His Founding of the *Post-Dispatch* up to 1883." *Mo Hist R* 6 (Ja, Ap 32) 163-78, 267-80.
Seitz, D. C. "The Portrait of an Editor." *Atl* 134 (Ag 24) 289-300.

PUTNAM, PHELPS (1894-1948). Matthiessen, F. O. "Phelps Putnam (1894-1948)." *KR* 11 (Wi 49) 61-82.
Rosenfeld, Paul. "An Affirmative Romantic." *Bkm* 74 (Mr 32) 607-13.

Zabel, M. D. "Phelps Putnam and America." *Poetry* 40 (S 32) 335-44.

QUIMBY, PHINEAS PARKHURST (1802-66). Holmes, S. W. "Phineas Parkhurst Quimby: Scientist of Transcendentalism." *NEQ* 17 (S 44) 356-80.

QUINCY, ELIZA SUSAN (1773-1850). Howe, M. A. DeW. "The New England Scene, 1814-1821: Passages from the Journal of Eliza Susan Quincy." *Atl* 178 (Ag 46) 94-100.

RALPH, JAMES (*c.* 1695-1762). Kenny, R. W. "James Ralph: An Eighteenth-Century Philadelphian in Grub Street." *PMHB* 64 (Ap 40) 218-42.

RAMSAY, DAVID (1749-1815). Brunhouse, R. L. "David Ramsay's Publication Problems, 1784-1808." *PBSA* 39 (1Q 45) 51-67.

RANDALL, JAMES RYDER (1839-1908). Uhler, J. E. "James Ryder Randall in Louisiana." *La Hist Q* 21 (Ap 38) 3-17.

RANDOLPH, JOHN (1773-1833). Coleman, Mrs. G. P. "Randolph and Tucker Letters." *VMHB* 42 (Ja 34) 47-52.
Coleman, Mary H. "Whittier on John Randolph of Roanoke." *NEQ* 8 (D 35) 551-5.

RANSOM, JOHN CROWE (1888-). Baker, J. E. "Philosopher and New Critic." *SR* 50 (Ap-Je 42) 167-70.
Beatty, R. C. "John Crowe Ransom as Poet." *SR* 52 (Su 44) 347-66.
Blum, Morgan. "The Fugitive Particular: John Crowe Ransom." *WR* 14 (Wi 50) 85-102.
Brooks, Cleanth. "The Doric Delicacy." *SR* 56 (Su 48) 406-14.
Burgum, E. B. "An Examination of Modern Critics: John Crowe Ransom." *Rocky Mt R* 8 (Sp 44) 87-93.
Campbell, H. M. "John Crowe Ransom." *Sw R* 24 (Jl 39) 476-89.
Carne-Ross, D. C. "Ransom's 'Judith of Bethulia.'" *Nine* 2 (My 50) 91-5.
Cater, Catherine. "Four Voices Out of the South." *Mich Alumnus Q* (Wi 44) 166-73.
Ford, N. F. "Empson's and Ransom's Mutations of Texts." *PQ* 29 (My 50) 81-4.
Henderson, A. C. "An American Georgian." *Poetry* 36 (Ap 30) 51-2.
Jarrell, Randall. "John Ransom's Poetry." *SR* 56 (Su 48) 378-90.
Knickerbocker, W. S. "Mr. Ransom and the Old South." *SR* 39 (Ap-Je 31) 222-38.
——— "The Theological Home Brew." *SR* 39 (Ja-Mr 31) 103-11.
Luhrs, Marie. "A Conjurer." *Poetry* 30 (Je 27) 162-5.
Lynskey, Winifred. "A Critic in Action: Mr. Ransom." *CE* 5 (F 44) 239-49.
Matthiessen, F. O. "Primarily Language." *SR* 56 (Su 44) 394-400.
Nemerov, Howard. "Summer's Flare and Winter's Flaw." *SR* 56 (Su 48) 418-22.
Schwartz, Delmore. "Instructed of Much Mortality." *SR* 54 (Su 46) 443-6.
Stauffer, D. A. "Portrait of the Critic Poet as Equilibrist." *SR* 56 (Su 48) 430.
Stocking, F. H., & Mason, Ellsworth. "Ransom's *Here Lies a Lady.*" *Expl* 8 (O 49) 1.
Warren, R. P. "John Crowe Ransom: A Study in Irony." *VQR* 11 (Ja 35) 93-112.
——— "A Note on Three Southern Poets." *Poetry* 40 (My 32) 103-13.
——— "Pure and Impure Poetry." *KR* 5 (Sp 43) 237-40.

RAWLINGS, MARJORIE KINNAN (1896-1953). Anon. "Majorie Kinnan Rawlings." *Cur Biog* 3 (Jl 42) 65-8.
Morris, Lloyd. "A New Classicist." *NAR* 246 (Au 38) 179-84.
Reid, Mary. "*The Yearling* on the Screen." *Holland's Mag* 66 (Ap 46) 11, 18.

READ, OPIE (1852-1939). Morris, R. L. "Opie Read, Arkansas Journalist." *Ark Hist Q* 2 (S 43) 246-54.

READ, THOMAS BUCHANAN (1822-72). Ford, H. S. "Thomas Buchanan Read and the Civil War: The Story of 'Sheridan's Ride.'" *Ohio State Arch & Hist Q* 56 (Jl 47) 215-27.
Moore, C. L. "A Neglected American Poet." *Dial* 56 (1 Ja 14) 7-9.

REALF, RICHARD (1834-78). Stimson, J. W. "An Overlooked American Shelley." *Arena* 30 (Jl 03) 15-26.

REED, JOHN (1887-1920). Eastman, Max. "John Reed and the Old Masses." *Mod Mo* 10 (O 36) 19-22, 31.
Hicks, Granville. "The Legend of John Reed." *New Masses* 25 (19 O 37) 9-11.
Madison, C. A. "John Reed: Rebel into Revolutionary." *UKCR* 13 (Wi 46) 97-109.
Steffens, Lincoln. "John Reed." *Freeman* 2 (3 N 20) 181.

REEDY, WILLIAM MARION (1862-1920). Winkler, Jean. "William Marion Reedy." *St Louis R* 2 (28 Ja, 11 F 33) 5-7, 7-10.

REESE, LIZETTE WOODWORTH (1856-1935). Adams, Leonie. "Winter Bloom." *Poetry* 42 (Ap 34) 40-2.
Dowling, A. W. "Lizette Woodworth Reese: An Appreciation." *SLM* 2 (F 40) 98-104.
Harriss, R. P. "April Weather: The Poetry of Lizette Woodworth Reese." *SAQ* 29 (Ap 30) 200-7.
Luhrs, Marie. "A Child Comes and Goes." *Poetry* 31 (F 28) 283-4.
Monroe, Harriet. "Faint Perfume." *Poetry* 23 (Mr 24) 341-2.
——— "Honor to Lizette Reese." *Poetry* 47 (F 36) 277-8.
Rhode, R. D. "Lizette W. Reese: 'Fair Gospeler.'" *Personalist* 31 (Au 50) 390-8.

REID, CHRISTIAN (1846-1920). Henderson, Archibald. "Christian Reid." *SR* 18 (Ap 10) 223-32.

REMINGTON, FREDERICK (1861-1909). Allen, E. D. "Frederick Remington—Author and Illustrator." *BNYPL* 51 (D 45) 895-912.

REPPLIER, AGNES (1858-1950). Adams, Mildred. "Our Miss Repplier." *Bkm* 65 (Je 27) 410-2.
Browne, E. H. "The Abiding Art of Agnes Repplier." *Thought* 5 (D 30) 396-410.
Chase, M. E. "The Dean of American Essayists." *Commonweal* 18 (18 Ag 33) 384-6.
Flanagan, J. T. "A Distinguished American Essayist." *SAQ* 44 (Ap 45) 162-9.
Reilly, Joseph. "A Daughter of Addison." *Cath World* 148 (N 38) 158-66.
Repplier, Agnes. "The Happiness of Writing an Autobiography." *Atl* 133 (F 24) 200-7.
——— "Miss Repplier's Reply." *Nation* 100 (8 Ap 15) 385.
Stratton, G. M. "Crooked Thinking in Regard to War." *Nation* 100 (8 Ap 15) 384-5.
Wade, Mason. "Agnes Repplier at Eighty." *NRp* 93 (8 D 37) 140.

REYNOLDS, JEREMIAH N. (1799?-1858). Almy, R. F. "J. N. Reynolds: A Brief Biography with Particular Reference to Poe and Symmes." *Colophon* ns 2 (Wi 37) 227-45.

RHODES, EUGENE MANLOVE (1869-1934). Dobie, J. F. "Gene Rhodes; Cowboy Novelist." *Atl* 183 (Je 49) 75-7.

RICE, CALE YOUNG (1872-1943). Farquhar, E. F. "The Poetry of Cale Young Rice." *Letters* 4 (N 30, F 31) 30-42, 24-40.

RICE, ELMER (1892-). Collins, R. L. "The Playwright and the Press: Elmer Rice and His Critics." *Theatre Annual* 7 (1948-9) 35-58.
Jennings, Richard. [*Street Scene.*] *Spectator* 145 (27 S 30) 407.

Levin, Meyer. "Elmer Rice." *Theatre Arts* 16 (Ja 32) 54-62.
Rice, Elmer. "Things I Have Never Done." *NYr* 7 (15 Ag 31) 24, 26.

RICHARDSON, ABBY SAGE (1837-1900). Stern, M. B. "Trials by Gotham, 1870: The Career of Abby Sage Richardson." *N Y Hist* 28 (Jl 47) 271-87.

RICHTER, CONRAD (1890-). Carpenter, F. I. "Conrad Richter's Pioneers: Reality and Myth." *CE* 12 (N 50) 77-82.
Kohler, Dayton. "Conrad Richter: Early American." *CE* 8 (F 47) 221-7.
Sutherland, Bruce. "Conrad Richter's America." *NMQR* 15 (Wi 45) 413-22.

RIDGE, LOLA (1871-1941). Aiken, Conrad. "The Literary Abbozzo." *Dial* 66 (25 Ja 19) 83-4.
Carnevali, Emmanuel. "Crucible." *Poetry* 17 (Mr 21) 332-4.
Flanner, Hildegarde. "Miss Ridge's Quest." *Poetry* 47 (O 35) 40-2.
Hackett, Francis. "Lola Ridge's Poetry." *NRp* 17 (16 N 18) 76-7.
Kreymborg, Alfred. "A Poet in Arms." *Poetry* 13 (Mr 19) 335-40.
Monroe, Harriet. "A Banner in the Wind." *Poetry* 30 (Je 27) 154-9.
——— "A Symphony of the Cross." *Poetry* 36 (Ap 30) 36-40.

RIDING, LAURA (1901-). Hays, H. R. "The Expatriate Consciousness." *Poetry* 54 (My 39) 101-4.
Wheelright, John. "Multiplied Bewilderment." *Poetry* 40 (Ag 32) 288-90.

RIGGS, LYNN (1899-). Campbell, W. S. "Lynn Riggs: Poet and Dramatist." *Sw R* 15 (Au 29) 64-70.
Glover, J. W. "Plays from Oklahoma." *Theatre Arts* 13 (F 29) 154-5.
Lowe, R. L. "The Lyrics of Lynn Riggs." *Poetry* 37 (Mr 31) 347-9.
Mitchell, Lee. "A Designer at Work." *Theatre Arts* 18 (N 34) 874-7.
Vestal, Stanley. "Lynn Riggs, Poet and Dramatist." *Sw R* 15 (Ag 29) 64-71.

RILEY, JAMES WHITCOMB (1849-1916). Anon. "Portrait." *Mentor* 9 (Je 21) 33.
——— "The Riley Home at Greenfield." *Ind Hist Bul* 14 (Ap 37) 151-2.
Beers, H. A. "The Singer of the Old Swimmin' Hole." *YR* ns 9 (Ja 20) 395-402.
Chomel, M. C. "An Interview with James Whitcomb Riley." *Lamp* 26 (My 03) 289-95.
Cottman, G. S. "Some Reminiscences of James Whitcomb Riley." *Ind Mag Hist* 14 (Je 18) 99-107.
——— "The Western Association of Writers." *Ind Mag Hist* 29 (S 33) 187-97.
Dunn, W. H. "James Whitcomb Riley and Donald G. Mitchell." *PMLA* 41 (S 26) 767-9.
Eitel, E. H. "The Letters of James Whitcomb Riley." *Harper's* 136 (F, My 18) 313-26, 840-51.
——— "Letters of Riley and Bill Nye." *Harper's* 138 (Mr 19) 473-84.
——— "A Poet and His Child Friends: James Whitcomb Riley's Letters to Children." *Harper's* 136 (D 17) 1-14.
——— "The Real Orphant Annie." *Ladies' Home* J 32 (N 15) 54.
——— "Riley and the Kids." *Collier's* 56 (9 O 15) 23-4.
Harvey, George. "In Memoriam: James Whitcomb Riley." *NAR* 204 (S 16) 421-5.
Hitt, G. C. "James Whitcomb Riley." *Ind Mag Hist* 32 (S 36) 189-206.
Howland, H. H. "How Riley Came Into His Own." *Bkm* 33 (Mr 11) 67-75.
Hughes, E. H. "James Whitcomb Riley." *Methodist R* 98 (N 16) 837-49.
Hyman, H. R. "James Whitcomb Riley's Complete Works." *Bkm* 38 (O 13) 163-8.
Laughlin, C. E. "James Whitcomb Riley's Antipathies and Whimsies." *Cur Op* 61 (N 16) 2-4.

Masters, E. L. "James Whitcomb Riley: A Sketch of His Life and an Appraisal of His Work." *Century* 114 (O 27) 704-15.
Mitchell, J. F. "James Whitcomb Riley's Home Folks." *Ladies' Home J* 19 (Ja 02) 7.
Monroe, Harriet. "James Whitcomb Riley." *Poetry* 8 (S 16) 305-7.
Nicholson, Meredith. "James Whitcomb Riley." *Atl* 118 (O 16) 503-14.
Peattie, D. C. "Riley as a Nature Poet." *SRL* 16 (3 Jl 37) 10.
Price, Robert. "James Whitcomb Riley in 1876." *Ind Mag Hist* 35 (Je 39) 129-40.
Richards, L. P. "James Whitcomb Riley on a Country Newspaper." *Bkm* 20 (S 04) 18-24; 44 (S 16) 79-87.
Tevis, C. V. "'Jim' Riley." *Bkm* 35 (Ag 12) 637-45.
——— "Memories and the Last Meeting." *Bkm* 44 (S 16) 22-7.
White, W. A. "Poet Come Out of Tailholt." *Collier's* 56 (25 D 15) 3-4.
Wyatt, Edith. "Inventor of Language." *NRp* 8 (19 Ag 16) 71-2.

RINEHART, MARY ROBERTS (1876-). Hellman, G. T. "Mary Roberts Rinehart." *Life* 20 (25 F 46) 55-6, 58, 61-2.

RIPLEY, GEORGE (1802-80). Gohdes, Clarence. "Getting Ready for Brook Farm." *MLN* 49 (Ja 34) 36-9.
Schulz, A. R., & Pochmann, H. A. "George Ripley: Unitarian, Transcendentalist, or Infidel?" *AL* 14 (Mr 42) 1-19.
Simmons, Edward. "A Boy Grew Up in the Old Manse." *Chri Sci Mon* 39 (21 Mr 47) 7.

ROBERTS, ELIZABETH MADOX (1886-1941). Anon. "Elizabeth Madox Roberts." *Wilson Bul* 4 (My 30) 418.
Adams, J. D. "Elizabeth Madox Roberts." *VQR* 12 (Ja 36) 80-90.
Buchan, A. M. "Elizabeth Madox Roberts." *Sw R* 25 (Jl 40) 463-81.
Janney, F. L. "Elizabeth Madox Roberts." *SR* 45 (O-D 37) 388-410.
Tate, Allen. "The Elizabeth Madox Roberts Papers." *Lib Cong Quar J Cur Acquisitions* 1 (O-D 43) 29-31.
Teasdale, Sara. "A Child Sings." *Poetry* 38 (Jl 31) 227-9.
Van Doren, Mark. "Elizabeth Madox Roberts." *EJ* 21 (S 32) 521-8.
Westcott, Glenway. "Elizabeth Madox Roberts: A Personal Note." *Bkm* 71 (Mr 30) 12-5.
Winters, Yvor. "Under the Tree." *Poetry* 22 (Ap 23) 45-8.

ROBERTS, KENNETH (1885-). Albert, George. "Bibliography of Kenneth Lewis Roberts." *Bul Bibl* 17 (S-D 42, Ja-Ap 43) 191-2, 218-9; 18 (My-Ag, S-D 43) 13-5, 34-46.
Baker, Carlos. "The Novel and History: Kenneth Roberts." *Delphian Q* 24 (Ja 41) 15-20.
Stone, Frank. "American First Editions: Kenneth (Lewis) Roberts (1885-)." *Pub W* 132 (16 O 37) 1595-6.
Williams, B. A. "Kenneth Roberts." *SRL* 18 (25 Je 38) 8-10.

ROBINSON, EDWIN ARLINGTON (1869-1935). Anon. "An American Bard and the British Reviewers." *Living Age* 315 (28 O 22) 244.
——— "Appreciation of the Poetry of Edwin Arlington Robinson." *Scribner's* 66 (D 19) 763-4.
——— "E. A. Robinson." *News-Week* 6 (16 N 35) 47.
——— "Edwin Arlington Robinson." *Bkm* 57 (Ja, Mr 23) 565-9, 107-8.
——— "Edwin Arlington Robinson." *Lib J* 61 (15 F 36) 138.
——— "Edwin Arlington Robinson." *Our World W* 2 (4 My 25) 205.
——— "Edwin Arlington Robinson." *Outlook* 105 (6 D 14) 736.
——— "Edwin A. Robinson." *Wilson Bul* 3 (N 28) 326.
——— "Edwin Arlington Robinson's Sombre Muse." *Cur Op* 74 (My 23) 549-50.

——— "News Notes." *Poetry* 74 (My 49) 122.
——— "A Poet's Birthday." *Lit Dig* 64 (10 Ja 20) 32-3.
——— "A Poet's Birthday." *Outlook* 123 (24 D 19) 535.
——— "Robinson as a Poet Born Ahead of His Time." *Cur Op* 72 (Ap 22) 525-7.
——— "Two Friends of Robinson." *Colby Lib Q* no 9: ser 2 (F 49) 147-52.
Adams, Léonie. "The Ledoux Collection of Edwin Arlington Robinson." *Lib Cong Quar J Cur Acquisitions* 7 (N 49) 9-13.
Aiken, Conrad. "A Letter from America." *London Merc* 5 (Je 22) 196-8.
——— "The Poetry of Mr. E. A. Robinson." *Freeman* 4 (F 20) 43-6.
Allen, Hervey. "The Poetry of Edwin Arlington Robinson." *Reviewer* 4 (O 23) 56-8.
App, A. J. "Edwin Arlington Robinson's Arthurian Poems." *Thought* 10 (D 35) 468-79.
Arns, Karl. "Amerikas Grösster Lebender Dichter im Urteil Seiner Zeitgenossen." *Zeitschrift für Französischen und Englischen Unterricht* (Berlin) 26 (1928) 500-13.
——— "Edwin Arlington Robinson." *Germanisch-romanische Monatsschrift* (Heidelberg 12 (Jl-Ag 24) 224-33.
Bates, R. C. "Edwin Arlington Robinson's *Three Poems.*" *Yale Un Lib Gaz* 8 (O 33) 81-2.
——— "The Robinson Gift." *Yale Un Lib Gaz* 17 (O 42) 33-5.
Beatty, Frederika. "Edwin Arlington Robinson as I Knew Him." *SAQ* 43 (O 44) 375-81.
Beebe, L. M. "Dignified Faun: A Portrait of E. A. R." *Outlook & Independent* 155 (27 Ag 30) 647-50, 677.
Benét, W. R. "E. A." *Forum* 93 (Je 35) 381.
Berryman, John. "Note on E. A. Robinson." *Nation* 141 (10 Jl 35) 38.
Blackmur, R. P. "'Verse That Is to Easie.'" *Poetry* 43 (Ja 34) 221-5.
Blanck, Jacob. "News from the Rare Book Sellers." *Pub W* 152 (22 N 47) B354.
Bogan, Louise. "Tilbury Town and Beyond." *Poetry* 37 (Ja 31) 216-21.
Bois, Jules. "Le Poète américain de la conscience—Edwin Arlington Robinson." *Revue Politique et Littéraire* 66 (16 Je 28) 369-74.
Boynton, P. H. "Edwin Arlington Robinson." *EJ* 11 (S 22) 383-91.
Brown, David. "E. A. Robinson's Later Poems." *NEQ* 10 (S 37) 487-502.
——— "A Note on *Avon's Harvest.*" *AL* 9 (N 37) 343-9.
——— "Some Rejected Poems of Edwin Arlington Robinson." *AL* 7 (Ja 36) 395-414.
Brown, R. W. "Mrs. MacDowell and Her Colony." *Atl* 184 (Jl 49) 42-6.
Burns, Winifred. "Edwin Arlington Robinson in the Hands of the Reviewers." *Poet Lore* 48 (Su 42) 164-75.
Burton, Richard. "Robinson as I Saw Him." *Mark Twain Q* 2 (Sp 38) 8.
Carlson, C. L. "Robinsoniana." *Colby Merc* 6 (D 39) 281-4.
Carpenter, F. I. "Tristram the Transcendent." *NEQ* 11 (S 38) 501-23.
Cestre, Charles. "Amy Lowell, Robert Frost, and Edwin Arlington Robinson." *Johns Hopkins Alumni Mag* 14 (Mr 26) 363-88.
——— "Avec Edwin Arlington Robinson dans l'inferno de l'art." *Revue Anglo-Américaine* 12 (Ap 35) 323-8.
——— "Le Dernier poème d'Edwin Arlington Robinson: *Cavender's House.*" *Revue Anglo-Américaine* (Ag 29) 489-507.
——— "Edwin Arlington Robinson, artiste dans les jeux de l'humour et de la fantaisie." *Revue Anglo-Américaine* 11 (F 34) 246-51.
——— "Edwin Arlington Robinson—Maker of Myths." *Mark Twain Q* 2 (Sp 38) 3-8, 24.
——— "L'Oeuvre poètique d'Edwin Arlington Robinson." *Revue Anglo-Américaine* 1 (Ap 24) 279-94.
——— "Récit, drame et symbole chez Edwin Arlington Robinson." *Revue Anglo-Américaine* 9 (Je 32) 405-13.

——— "Le Tristan d'Edwin Arlington Robinson." *Revue Anglo-Américaine* 5 (1927-8) 97-110, 219-28.
Collamore, H. B. "Robinson and the War." *Colby Lib Q* 1 (Mr 43) 30-1.
Colton, A. W. "Edwin Arlington Robinson." *Lit R* 3 (23 Je 23) 781-2.
Conrad, L. H. "The Critic's Poet." *Landmark* 15 (Ja 33) 23-6.
Corning, H. McK. "Edwin Arlington Robinson." *Voices* no 64 (Ap 32) 255-7.
Cowley, Malcolm. "Edwin Arlington Robinson: Defeat and Triumph." *NRp* 119 (6 D 48) 26-30.
——— Untitled article in section called "This Week." *NRp* 82 (17 Ap 35) 268-9.
Crowder, Richard. "E. A. Robinson's Camelot." *CE* 9 (N 47) 72-9.
——— "E. A. Robinson's Craftsmanship: Opinions of Contemporary Poets." *MLN* 61 (Ja 46) 1-14.
——— "E. A. Robinson's Symphony: *The Man Who Died Twice.*" *CE* 11 (D 49) 141-4.
——— "The Emergence of E. A. Robinson." *SAQ* 45 (Ja 46) 89-98.
——— " 'Here Are the Men . . .'; E. A. Robinson's Male Character Types." *NEQ* 18 (S 45) 346-67.
——— "Robinson's *For a Dead Lady.*" *Expl* 5 (D 46) 60.
——— "Robinson's *The Field of Glory.*" *Expl* 8 (F 50) 31.
——— "Robinson's *Luke Havergal.*" *Expl* 7 (N 48) 15.
——— "Robinson's *An Old Story.*" *Expl* 4 (D 45) 22.
——— "Robinson's *The Sheaves.*" *Expl* 4 (Mr 46) 38.
Daly, James. "The Inextinguishable God." *Poetry* 27 (O 25) 40-4.
Daniels, Mable. "Robinson's Interest in Music." *Mark Twain Q* 2 (Sp 38) 15, 24.
Dauner, Louise. "Avon and Cavender: Two Children of the Night." *AL* 14 (Mr 42) 55-65.
——— "The Pernicious Rib: E. A. Robinson's Concept of the Feminine Character." *AL* 15 (My 43) 139-58.
——— "Vox Clamantis: Edwin Arlington Robinson as a Critic of American Democracy." *NEQ* 15 (S 42) 401-26.
Davidson, L. J. "Lazarus in Modern Literature." *EJ* (coll ed) 18 (Je 29) 16-23.
Deutsch, Babette. "A New Light on Lancelot." *Poetry* 16 (Jl 20) 217-9.
——— "A Sophisticated Mystic." *Reedy's Mirror* 26 (22 Mr 18) 166-7.
Doyle, J. R. "The Shorter Novels of E. A. Robinson." *Bul Citadel* 6 (1942) 3-18.
Drinkwater, John. "Edwin Arlington Robinson." *YR* 11 (Ap 22) 467-76; *Fortnightly R* 111 (1 Ap 22) 649-60.
DuBois, A. E. "The Cosmic Humorist." *Mark Twain Q* 2 (Sp 38) 11-3.
Dudley, Dorothy. "Wires and Cross-wires." *Poetry* 24 (My 24) 96-103.
Emerson, Dorothy. "Edwin Arlington Robinson: Looking Back on Our First Contemporary Poet." *Scholastic* 26 (12 O 35) 9-10.
Evans, Nancy. "Edwin Arlington Robinson." *Bkm* 75 (N 32) 675-81.
Farrar, John. "The Literary Spotlight." *Bkm* 56 (Ja 23) 565-9.
Figueira, Gastón. "Poetas y prosistas americanos: I. Edwin Arlington Robinson. II. Thomas Wolfe." *Revista Iberoamericana* 11 (O 46) 329-32.
Fletcher, J. G. "Edwin Arlington Robinson." *Spectator* (London) 130 (10 F 23) 216.
——— "Mr. Edwin Arlington Robinson Abroad." *Living Age* 311 (17 D 21) 744.
——— "Mr. Robinson's Poems." *Nation & Athenaeum* 30 (19 N 21) 307-8.
——— "Portrait of Edwin Arlington Robinson." *NAR* 244 (Au 37) 24-6.
Flint, F. C. *"Matthias at the Door."* *Symposium* 3 (Ap 32) 237-48.
French, J. L. "The Younger Poets of New England." *N E Mag* ns 33 (D 05) 424-8.
Gierasch, Walter. "Robinson's *Luke Havergal.*" *Expl* 3 (O 44) 8.
Gorman, H. S. "Edwin Arlington Robinson." *NRp* 29 (8 F 22) 311-3.
Gregory, Horace. "The Weapon of Irony." *Poetry* 45 (D 34) 158-61.
———, & Zaturenska, Marya. "The Vein of Comedy in E. A. Robinson's Poetry." *Am Bkm* 1 (Fl 44) 43-64.

Hammond, Josephine. "The Man against the Sky—Edwin Arlington Robinson." *Personalist* 10 (Jl 29) 178-84.
Hardon, R. V. "The President's Poetical Protégé." Boston *Evening Transcript* (31 O 05) 12.
Henderson, L. J. "Edwin Arlington Robinson." *Proc Am Acad Arts & Sci* 70 (Mr 36) 570-3.
Hicks, Granville. "The Talents of Mr. Robinson." *Nation* 131 (8 O 30) 382.
Hillyer, Robert. "E. A. Robinson and His 'Tristram.'" *New Adelphi* 2 (S 28) 90-4.
——— "Edwin Arlington Robinson." *Harvard Alumni Bul* 37 (24 My 35) 992-4.
Hogan, C. B. "Edwin Arlington Robinson; New Bibliographical Notes." *PBSA* 35 (2Q 41) 115-44
——— "A Poet at the Phonic Shrine." *Colophon* ns 3 (Su 38) 359-63.
Hopper, V. F. "Robinson and Frost." *SRL* 13 (2 N 35) 18.
Hudson, H. H. "Edwin Arlington Robinson." *Lit Dig* 107 (25 O 30) 24.
——— "Robinson and Praed." *Poetry* 61 (F 43) 612-20.
Hughes, Merritt. "Un Poeta Americano: Edwin Arlington Robinson." *Il Giornal di Politica e di Letteratura* (Rome) 14 (S 30) 809-27.
Hutchinson, Percy. "The Poetry of E. A. Robinson." *N Y Times Book R* (21 Ap 35) 2, 11.
Isaacs, E. J. R. "Edwin Arlington Robinson: A Descriptive List of the Lewis M. Isaacs Collection of Robinsoniana." *BNYPL* 52 (My 48) 211-33.
Isaacs, L. M. "E. A. Robinson Speaks of Music." *NEQ* 22 (D 49) 499-510.
Jacobs, W. D. "E. A. Robinson's 'Mr. Flood's Party.'" *CE* 12 (N 50) 110.
Jane, M. C. "Journey to Head Tide." *Chri Sci Mon* (Mag sec) 42 (25 F 50) 10.
Johnson, Edgar. "Edwin Robinson Sonnets." *Lit R* (1 D 28) 8.
Jones, Llewellyn. "Edwin Arlington Robinson." *Am R* 1 (Mr-Ap 23) 180-9.
Kilmer, Joyce. "A Classic Poet." *N Y Times Book R* (8 S 12) 487.
——— "E. A. Robinson Defines Poetry." *N Y Times Book R* (2 Ap 16) 12.
Latham, G. W. "Robinson at Harvard." *Mark Twain Q* 2 (Sp 38) 19-20.
Latham, H. S. "Edwin Arlington Robinson." *Pub W* 103 (17 Mr 23) 945.
Ledoux, L. V. "In Memoriam: Edwin Arlington Robinson." *SRL* 11 (13 Ap 35) 621.
——— "Psychologist of New England." *SRL* 12 (19 O 35) 3-4, 16, 18.
Le Gallienne, Richard. "Three American Poets." *Forum* 45 (Ja 11) 80-90.
Lowell, Amy. "A Bird's Eye View of E. A. Robinson." *Dial* 72 (F 22) 130-42.
MacKaye, Percy. "'E. A.'—A Milestone for America." *NAR* 211 (Ja 20) 121-7.
MacVeagh, Lincoln. "Edwin Arlington Robinson." *NRp* 2 (10 Ap 15) 267-8.
Markham, Edwin. "Robinson, My Hand to You." *N Y American* (13 F 09) 13.
Mason, D. G. "Early Letters of Edwin Arlington Robinson." *VQR* 13 (Wi 37) 52-69.
——— "Edwin Arlington Robinson: A Group of Letters." *YR* 25 (Je 36) 860-4.
——— "Letters of Edwin Arlington Robinson to Daniel Gregory Mason." *VQR* 13 (Sp 37) 223-40.
Mather, F. J., Jr. "E. A. Robinson: Poet." *SRL* 6 (11 Ja 30) 629-30.
Maynard, Theodore. "Edwin Arlington Robinson." *Cath World* 141 (Je 35) 266-75.
Monroe, Harriet. "Edwin Arlington Robinson." *Poetry* 25 (Ja 25) 206-17.
——— "On Foreign Ground." *Poetry* 31 (D 27) 160-7.
——— "Mr. Robinson in Camelot." *Poetry* 10 (Jl 17) 211-3.
——— "Mr. Robinson's Jubilee." *Poetry* 15 (F 20) 265-7.
——— "A Pioneer." *Poetry* 8 (Ap 16) 46-8.
——— "Robinson as Man and Poet." *Poetry* 46 (Je 35) 150-7.
Morris, Lloyd. "The Rare Genius of Edwin Arlington Robinson." *World* R 5 (12 D 27) 182-3.
Morrison, Theodore. "Two Harvard Poets." *Harvard Alumni Bul* 26 (29 My 24) 983-5.
Munson, G. B. "Edwin Arlington Robinson." *SRL* 3 (21 My 27) 839-40.

North, Jessica. "A Classic of Indirection." *Poetry* 34 (Jl 29) 233-6.
Notopoulos, J. A. "Sophocles and Captain Craig." *NEQ* 17 (Mr 44) 109.
Ownbey, E. S. "Robinson's *Mr. Flood's Party,* 17-24." *Expl* 8 (Ap 50) 47.
Parlett, M. M. "Robinson's *Luke Havergal.*" *Expl* 3 (Je 45).
Payne, L. W., Jr. "The First Edition of E. A. Robinson's *The Peterborough Idea.*" *Un Texas Stud Eng* 19 (1939) 219-31.
Peltier, Florence. "Edwin Arlington Robinson, Himself." *Mark Twain Q* 1 (Su 37) 6, 11-4.
Perrine, Laurence. "Robinson's *Eros Turannos.*" *Expl* 8 (D 49) 20.
——— "Robinson's *Tristram.* *Expl* 6 (My 48) 44; 7 (Mr 49) 33.
——— "Robinson's *Veteran Sirens.*" *Expl* 6 (N 47) 13.
Perry, Bliss. "Poets Celebrate E. A. Robinson's Birthday." *N Y Times Book R* (21 D 19) 765-6.
Pettit, Henry. "Robinson's *The Whip.*" *Expl* 1 (Ap 43).
Phelps, W. L. "As I Like It." *Scribner's* 89 (Ja 31) 95.
Pipkin, E. E. "The Arthur of Edwin Arlington Robinson." *EJ* 19 (Mr 30) 183-95.
Raven, A. A. "Robinson's *Luke Havergal.*" *Expl* 3 (D 44).
Richards, L. E. "Edwin Arlington Robinson." *Horn Book Mag* 12 (Ja-F 36) 52-3.
——— "Recollections of 'E. A.' as a Boy in Gardiner." *N Y Herald Tribune Books* (12 My 35) 10.
Robbins, H. C. "The Classicism of Edwin Arlington Robinson." *Congregational Q* 14 (Ap 36) 166-71.
Robinson, E. A. "The First Seven Years." *Colophon* (D 30) Pt 3.
——— "The Peterborough Idea." *NAR* 204 (S 16) 448-54.
Roming, E. D. "Tilbury Town and Camelot." *Un Colo Stud* 19 (Je 32) 303-26.
Roosevelt, Kermit. "An Appreciation of the Poetry of Edwin Arlington Robinson." *Scribner's* 66 (D 19) 763-4.
Roosevelt, Theodore. "The Children of the Night." *Outlook* 80 (12 Ag 05) 913-4.
Rosenberg, Harold. "Judgment and Passion." *Poetry* 41 (D 32) 158-61.
Roth, Samuel. "A Bookshop Night's Adventure." *Bkm* 58 (O 23) 140-6.
——— "Edwin Arlington Robinson." *Bkm* 50 (Ja 20) 507-11.
——— "Robinson—Bridges—Noyes, 1920: The Three Taverns." *Bkm* 52 (D 20) 361.
Saben, Mowry. "Memories of Edwin Arlington Robinson." *Colby Merc* 7 (Ja 41) 13-4.
St. Clair, George. "E. A. Robinson and Tilbury Town." *NMQR* 4 (My 34) 95-107.
——— "Edwin Arlington Robinson on Time." *NMQR* 9 (Ag 39) 150-6.
Sapir, Edward. "Poems of Experience." *Freeman* 5 (19 Ap 22) 141-2.
Schmitt, H. G. "Some Robinson Letters in My Collection." *Colby Lib Q* 1 (Ja 43) 8-12.
Schönemann, Friedrich. "E. A. Robinson." *Literatur* 35 (My 33) 446-8.
Scott, W. T. "Edwin Arlington Robinson." *Brown Lit Q* 2 (N 29) 13-8.
——— "'Great and Austere Poet.'" *Poetry* 70 (My 47) 94-8.
——— "Robinson to Robinson." *Poetry* 54 (My 39) 92-100.
——— "The Unaccredited Profession." *Poetry* 50 (Je 37) 150-4.
Sinclair, May. "Three American Poets of Today." *Fortnightly R* 86 (1 S 06) 429-34; *Atl* 98 (S 06) 330-3.
Smith, C. P., *et al.* "Some Personal Tributes to Edwin Arlington Robinson." *SRL* 11 (20 Ap 35) 632.
Squire, J. C. "Edwin Arlington Robinson." *London Merc* 13 (F 26) 401-12.
Stovall, Floyd. "The Optimism behind Robinson's Tragedies." *AL* 10 (Mr 38) 1-23.
Super, R. H. "Robinson's *For a Dead Lady.* *Expl* 3 (Je 45); 5 (Je 47) 60.
Sutcliffe, Denham. "Edwin Arlington Robinson, a Product of Seventeenth Century Puritanism." Bates Col *Garnet* (My 35) 29-32.
——— "The Original of Robinson's Captain Craig." *NEQ* 16 (S 43) 407-31.
Tate, Allen. "Again, O Ye Laurels." *NRp* 76 (25 O 33) 312-3.

Theis, O. F. "Edwin Arlington Robinson." *Forum* 51 (F 14) 305-12.
Todrin, Boris. "Edwin Arlington Robinson." *Book Coll J* 1 (Jl 36) 1, 4.
Torrence, O. H. D. "The Poet at the Dinner Table." *Colophon* ns 3 (Wi 38) 92-9.
Ulrich, Dorothy. "Edwin Arlington Robinson." *Avocations* 2 (Je 38) 248-53.
Van Doorn, Willem. "How It Strikes a Contemporary." *Eng S* 7 (O 26) 129-42.
Van Doren, Mark. "Edwin Arlington Robinson." *Nation* 140 (17 Ap 35) 434.
Van Norman, C. E. "Captain Craig." *CE* 2 (F 41) 462-75.
Waggoner, H. H. "E. A. Robinson and the Cosmic Chill." *NEQ* 13 (Mr 40) 65-84.
Waldo, Fullerton. "The Earlier E. A. R.: Some Memories of a Poet in the Making." *Outlook* 129 (30 N 21) 531-2, 534.
Walsh, W. T. "Some Recollections of E. A. Robinson." *Cath World* 155 (Ag 42) 522-31.
Wearing, Thomas. "Edwin Arlington Robinson—New England Poet—Philosopher." *Colgate-Rochester Divinity School Bul* 14 (F 42) 162-74.
Weaver, R. M. "Some Currents and Backwaters of Contemporary Poetry: Lancelot." *Bkm* 51 (Je 20) 457-8.
Weber, C. J. "Additions to Our Robinson Collection." *Colby Merc* 7 (My 42) 94-6.
——— "The Cottage Lights of Wessex." *Colby Merc* 6 (F 36) 64-7.
——— "E. A. Robinson and Hardy." *SRL* 11 (27 Ap 35) 648; *Nation* 140 (1 My 35) 140.
——— "E. A. Robinson's Translation of Sophocles." *NEQ* 17 (D 44) 604-5.
——— "The Jubilee of Robinson's *Torrent*." *Colby Lib Q* 2 (F 47) 1-12.
——— "A New Poem by Edwin Arlington Robinson." *Colby Lib Q* 2 (F 47) 12-3.
——— "Poet and President." *NEQ* 16 (D 43) 615-26.
——— "A Robinson Wild-Goose Chase." *Colby Merc* 7 (My 42) 96.
——— "Robinson's Prose: A Retraction." *Colby Lib Q* 1 (Mr 43) 31-2.
——— "Three Newly Discovered Articles by Edwin Arlington Robinson." *Colby Merc* 7 (D 41) 69-72.
——— "To More 'Torrents.'" *Colby Lib Q* (Ag 48) 122-3.
——— "With Admiration and Love." *Colby Lib Q* 2 (My 48) 85-108.
White, N. I. "Collected Poems." *SAQ* 21 (Jl-S 22) 365-9.
White, William. "E. A. Robinson and A. E. Housman." *Colby Lib Q* 2 (Ag 47) 42-3.
Wilkinson, Marguerite. "A Biographer of Souls." *Woman's Press* 21 (My 27) 329-31.
Williams, A. M. "Edwin Arlington Robinson, Journalist." *NEQ* 15 (D 42) 715-24.
Wilson, Edmund. "Mr. Robinson's Moonlight." *Dial* 74 (My 23) 515-7.
Winters, Yvor. "A Cool Master." *Poetry* 19 (F 22) 278-88.
——— "Religious and Social Ideas in the Didactic Work of E. A. Robinson." *Ariz Q* 1 (Sp 45) 70-85.
Wisehart, M. K. "'By Jove!' Said Roosevelt, 'It Reads Like the Real Thing!'" *Am Mag* 105 (Ap 28) 34-5.
Zabel, M. D. "Edwin Arlington Robinson." *Commonweal* 17 (15 F 33) 436-8.
——— "Robinson in America." *Poetry* 46 (Je 35) 157-62.

ROBINSON, MARIUS RACINE (1867-). Nye, R. B. "Marius Robinson, a Forgotten Abolitionist Leader." *Ohio State Arch & Hist Q* 55 (Ap-Je 46) 138-54.

ROBINSON, ROWLAND EVANS (1833-1900). Bailey, H. L. "The Chronicler of 'Danvis Folks.'" *N E Mag* ns (D 00) 430-7.
Dorr, J. C. R. "Rowland Robinson." *Atl* 44 (Ja 01) 116-9.

ROE, E. P. (1838-88). Maurice, A. B. "E. R. Roe's 'Barriers Burned Away.'" *Bkm* 33 (My 11) 247-53.

ROGERS, NATHANIEL PEABODY (1794-1846). Adams, Robert. "Nathaniel Peabody Rogers: 1794-1846." *NEQ* 20 (S 47) 365-76.

ROGERS, ROBERT (1731-95). Paltsits, V. H. "Journal of Robert Rogers . . . [1760-1]." *BNYPL* 37 (Ap 33) 261-76.

ROGERS, WILL (1879-1935). Martin, G. "The Wit of Will Rogers." *Am Mag* 88 (N 19) 34, 106-18.

Pringle, H. F. "King Babbitt's Court Jester." *Outlook & Independent* 157 (8 Ap 31) 496-8.

RÖLVAAG, O. E. (1876-1931). Anon. "Ole Edvart Rölvaag." *ASR* 19 (Ja 32) 7-9.

Baker, J. E. "Western Man Against Nature: *Giants in the Earth.*" CE 4 (O 42) 1926.

Bjork, Kenneth. "The Unknown Rölvaag: Secretary in the Norwegian-American Historical Association." *Norwegian-Am Stud & Records* 11 (1940) 114-49.

Boynton, P. H. "O. E. Rölvaag and the Conquest of the Pioneer." *EJ* (col ed) 18 (S 29) 535-42.

Colcord, Lincoln. "Rölvaag the Fisherman Shook His Fist at Fate." *Am Mag* 105 (7 Mr 28) 36-7, 188-92.

Haugen, E. I. "Rölvaag." *Norwegian-Am Stud & Records* 7 (1933) 53-73.

Jorgenson, Theodore. "The Main Factors in Rölvaag's Authorship." *Norwegian-Am Stud & Records* 10 (1938) 135-51.

Olson, J. E. "Rölvaag's Novels of Norwegian Pioneer Life in the Dakotas." *SS* 9 (Ag 26) 45-55.

Rölvaag, O. E. "When a Novelist Is in a Hurry." *SS* 9 (Ag 26) 61-8.

Solum, N. O. "The Sources of the Rölvaag Biography." *Norwegian-Am Stud & Records* 11 (1940) 150-9.

ROMBERG, JOHANNES CHRISTLIEB NATHANIEL (1808-91). Metzanthin-Raunick, Selma. "Johannes Christlieb Nathaniel Romberg, German Poet of Texas." *AGR* 12 (F 46) 32-5.

ROOSEVELT, FRANKLIN DELANO (1882-1945). Adams, F. B., Jr. "The President as Author." *Colophon* ns 1 (Sp 36) 487-97.

Schiffman, Joseph. "Observations on Roosevelt's Literary Style." *QJS* 25 (Ap 49) 222-6.

ROOSEVELT, THEODORE (1858-1919). Beers, H. A. "Roosevelt as Man of Letters." *YR* ns 8 (Jl 19) 694-709.

Bradford, Gamaliel. "The Fury of Living: Theodore Roosevelt." *Harper's* 162 (F 31) 353-64.

Bridges, Robert. "Roosevelt As a Writer for Young Men." *Lamp* 28 (My 04) 311-4.

Cordingly, N. E. "Extreme Rarities in the Published Works of Theodore Roosevelt." *PBSA* 39 (1Q 45) 20-50.

Egan, M. F. "Theodore Roosevelt in Retrospect." *Atl* 123 (Je 19) 676-85.

Gilder, J. B. "A Man of Letters in the White House." *Critic* 39 (N 01) 401-9.

Utley, G. B. "Theodore Roosevelt's 'Winning of the West': Some Unpublished Letters." *Miss Valley Hist R* 30 (Mr 44) 495-507.

ROSENFELD, PAUL (1890-1946). Mumford, Lewis. "The Wisdom of Paul Rosenfeld." *Ariz Q* 4 (Sp 48) 35-45.

ROSS, HAROLD (1892-1951). Kramer, Dale, & Clark, G. R. "Harold Ross and the New Yorker: a Landscape with Figures." *Harper's* 186 (Ap 43) 510-21.

ROURKE, CONSTANCE (1885-1941). Allen, G. W. "Humor in America." *SR* 40 (Ja-Mr 32) 111-3.

Hyman, S. E. "Constance Rourke and Folk Criticism." *AR* 7 (Fl 47) 418-34.

Kelsey, Vera. "Lotta." *Theatre Arts* 12 (N 28) 844-5.

Marshall, Margaret. "Constance Rourke; Artist and Citizen." *Nation* 157 (21 Je 41) 726-8.

——— "Constance Rourke in the Critics' Den." *Nation* 155 (24 O 42) 418-20.
Weeks, Mangum. "Artist and Backwoodsman." *VQR* 13 (Ja 37) 140-3.

ROWLANDSON, MARY (*c.* 1635-*c.* 78). Nelson, J. "Mary Rowlandson's Narrative." *Americana* 27 (Ja 33) 45-62.

ROWSON, SUSANNA HASWELL (*c.* 1762-1824). Howay, F. W. "A Short Account of Robert Haswell." *Wash Hist Q* 24 (Ap 33) 83-90.
Sargent, M. E. "Susanna Rowson." *Medford Hist R* (Ap 04).
Vail, R. W. "Susanna Haswell Rowson, the Author of *Charlotte Temple:* A Bibliographical Study." *PAAS* 42 (Ap 32) 47-160.

ROYALL, ANNE NEWPORT (1769-1854). Blankenhorn, Heber. "The Grandma of the Muckrakers." *Am Merc* 12 (S 27) 87-93.

ROYCE, JOSIAH (1855-1916). Brown, S. G. "From Provincialism to the Great Community: The Social Philosophy of Josiah Royce." *Ethics* 59 (O 48) 14-34.
Chapman, J. J. "Portrait of Josiah Royce, the Philosopher." *Outlook* 122 (2 Jl 19) 372-7.
Cohen, M. R. "Josiah Royce." *NRp* 8 (14 O 16) 264-6.
Robinson, D. S. "Josiah Royce: California's Gift to Philosophy." *Personalist* 31 (Au 50) 52-68.
Slattery, C. L. "Josiah Royce." *Outlook* 121 (15 Ja 19) 114-5.

RUFFNER, HENRY (1789-1861). Davis, C. C. "*Judith Bensaddi* and the Reverend Doctor Henry Ruffner: The Earliest Appearance in American Fiction of the Jewish Problem?" *Pub Am Jewish Hist Soc* 39 (D 49) 115-42.

RUKEYSER, MURIEL (1913-). Brinnin, J. M. "Muriel Rukeyser: The Social Poet and the Problem of Communication." *Poetry* 61 (Ja 43) 554-75.
Gierasch, Walter. "Reading Modern Poetry." *CE* 2 (O 40) 32-3.
Untermeyer, Louis. "The Language of Muriel Rukeyser." *SRL* 22 (10 Ag 40) 11-3.

RUPPIUS, OTTO (1819-64). Schrader, F. F. "Otto Ruppius, a Career in America." *AGR* 9 (Ja 43) 28-33.

RUSH, BENJAMIN (1745-1813). Butterfield, L. H. "Benjamin Rush as a Promoter of Useful Knowledge." *PAPS* 92 (8 Mr 48) 26-36.
——— "Dr. Benjamin Rush's Journal of a Trip to Carlisle in 1784." *PMHB* 74 (O 50) 443-56.
——— "Dream of Benjamin Rush." *YR* ns 40 (D 50) 297-319.
——— "Love and Valor; or, Benjamin Rush and the Leslies of Edinburgh." *PULC* 9 (N 47) 1-12.
——— "The Reputation of Benjamin Rush." *Penn Hist* 17 (Ja 50) 3-22.
——— "A Survey of the Benjamin Rush Papers." *PMHB* 70 (Ja 46) 78-11.
Osgood, C. G. "An American Boswell." *PULC* 5 (Ap 44) 85-91.

RUSH JAMES (1786-1869). Gray, G. W., & Hale, L. L. "James Rush, Dramatist." *QJS* 29 (F 43) 55-61.

RUSSELL, IRWIN (1853-79). Campbell, E. S. "Three Mississippi Poets of the Nineteenth Century." *J Miss Hist* 5 (1943) 38-40.
Harrell, L. D. S. "A Bibliography of Irwin Russell." *J Miss Hist* 8 (Ja 46) 3-23.
Kendall, J. S. "Irwin Russell in New Orleans." *La Hist Q* 14 (Jl 31) 321-45.
Kern, A. A. "Biographical Notes on Irwin Russell." *Texas R* 2 (O 16) 140-9.
——— "The Unpublished Verse of Irwin Russell." *SAQ* 11 (Jl 12) 244-50.
Nott, G. W. "Irwin Russell, First Dialect Author." *SLM* 1 (D 39) 809-14.

RUSSELL, JOHN (1885-). Flanagan, J. T. "John Russell of Bluffdale." *J Ill State Hist Soc* 42 (S 49) 272-91.

RUTLEDGE, ARCHIBALD (1883-). Rutledge, Archibald. "A Plantation Boyhood." *Atl* 150 (Ag 32) 163-70, 351-7.

RUXTON, GEORGE FREDERICK (1820-48). Sutherland, Bruce. "George Frederick Ruxton in North America." *Sw* R 30 (Au 44) 86-91.

RYAN, ABRAHAM JOSEPH (1836-86). Anon. "Father Ryan, Poet-Priest of the South." *Records Am Cath Hist Soc* 39 (1928) 33-6.
Clemens, Cyril. "Poet Priest of the Confederacy." *Ave Maria* 57 (20 F 43) 238-41.
Hewlett, J. H. "An Unknown Poem by Father Ryan." *MLN* 44 (Ap 29) 259-61.
White, Kate. "Father Ryan—The Poet-Priest of the South." *SAQ* 18 (Ja 19) 69-74.

SALINGER, HERMAN (1905-). Waggoner, H. H. "The Angel of Our Thirst: Herman Salinger's Romantic Sensibility." *UKCR* 13 (Sp 47) 189-92.

SALTUS, EDGAR (1855-1921). Anon. "The Glittering Genius of Edgar Saltus." *Cur Lit* 43 (Jl 07) 46-8.
——— "The Stylist Who Created a Mythology of Manhattan." *Cur Op* 65 (O 18) 254-5.
Colles, Ramsay. "A Publicist: Edgar Saltus." *Westminster R* 162 (O 04) 463-74.
Hartmann, Sadakichi. "The Edgar Saltus I Knew." *Bkm* 58 (S 23) 17-9.
Hubbard, Elbert. "Heart to Heart Talks with Philistines by the Pastor of His Flock." *Philistine* 25 (O 07) 129-43.
Kitchen, P. H. "A Note on the Art of Edgar Saltus." *MS* 2 (D 30) 3.
——— "Sorcerer of Syllables." *Open Road* (Mr-Ap 43) 15-7.
Munson, G. B. "The Limbo of American Literature." *Broom* 2 (Je 22) 250-60.
Overton, Grant. "How about This Fellow Saltus?" *Bkm* 61 (Ag 25) 644-6.
Saltus, Marie. "Reply to Sadakichi Hartmann." *Bkm* 58 (Ja 24) 597-8.
Sonnenschein, Hugo. "Edgar Saltus: Don't Rush Him." *Brentano's Book Chat* (S-O 25) 27-30.
Symons, Arthur. "Edgar Saltus." *Vanity Fair* 16 (Mr 20) 18-9.
Van Vechten, Carl. "Edgar Saltus: A Postscript." *Double Dealer* 2 (O 21) 162-4.

SANBORN, FRANKLIN BENJAMIN (1831-1917). Hellman, G. S. "An Unpublished Concord Journal by Frank Sanborn." *Century* ns 103 (Ap 22) 825-35.
Swift, Lindsay. "Tribute to Franklin Benjamin Sanborn." *PMHS* 50 (Mr 17) 209-13.

SANDBURG, CARL (1878-). Anon. "The Poet of American Industrialism." *Living Age* 308 (22 Ja 21) 231-4.
Allen, Charles. "Cadenced Free Verse." *CE* 9 (Ja 48) 195-9.
Anderson, Sherwood. "Carl Sandburg." *Bkm* 54 (D 21) 360-1.
Arvin, Newton. "Carl Sandburg." *NRp* 88 (9 S 36) 119-21.
Bartlett, A. H. "Voices from the Great Inland States (Sandburg and Lindsay)," *Poetry R* 15 (Mr-Ap 24) 101-10.
Bas, R. R. "Sandburg's *Early Lynching.*" *Expl* 1 (Je 43).
Benét, S. V. & Rosemary. "Sandburg: Son of the Lincoln Countryside." *N Y Herald-Tribune Books* 18 (14 D 41) 8.
Benjamin, P. L. "A Poet of the Common-Place." *Survey* 45 (2 O 20) 12-3.
Boynton, P. H. "The Voice of Chicago: Edgar Lee Masters and Carl Sandburg." *EJ* (D 22) 610-20.
Bradley, W. A. "Four American Poets." *Dial* 61 (14 D 16) 528-30.
Cargill, Oscar. "Carl Sandburg: Crusader and Mystic." *CE* 11 (Ap 50) 365-72; *EJ* 39 (Ap 50) 177-84.
Carnevali, Emanuel. "Our Great Carl Sandburg." *Poetry* 22 (F 21) 266-72.
——— "The Sandburg-Sarett Recital." *Poetry* 15 (F 20) 271-2.
Compton, C. H. "Who Reads Carl Sandburg?" *SAQ* 28 (Ap 29) 190-200.
Crowder, Richard. "Sandburg's *Caboose Thoughts.*" *Expl* 4 (My 46) 52.

Deutsch, Babette. "Poetry for the People." *EJ* 26 (Ap 37) 265-74.
Elgstrom, A. H. "Carl Sandburg." *Ord och Bild* (Stockholm) 53 (1944) 528-39.
Emrich, Duncan. "The Poet and the General: Carl Sandburg Meets General Eisenhower." *SRL* 31 (20 Mr 48) 9-11, 45-7.
Hansen, Henry. "Carl Sandburg—Poet of the Prairie." *Pictorial R* 26 (S 25) 114-8.
Hoffman, D. G. "Sandburg and 'The People': His Literary Populism Appraised." *AR* 10 (Su 50) 265-78.
Holcomb, E. L. "Whitman and Sandburg." *EJ* 17 (S 28) 549-55.
Jenkins, Alan. "Portrait of a Poet at College." *SAQ* 49 (O 50) 478-82.
Jones, H. M. "Backgrounds of Sorrow." *VQR* 3 (Ja 27) 111-23.
Jones, Llewellyn. "Carl Sandburg, Formalist." *Am R* 2 (Jl-Ag 24) 356-62.
Loeber, William. "The Literary Tough." *Double Dealer* 2 (F 22) 105-7.
Lunderbergh, Holger. "Carl Sandburg." *ASR* 24 (Sp 38) 49-51.
Melcher, F. G. "American First Editions . . . Carl Sandburg." *Pub W* 102 (20 Ja 23) 149.
Monroe, Harriet. "Carl Sandburg." *Poetry* 24 (S 24) 320-6.
——— "Chicago Granite." *Poetry* 8 (My 16) 90-3.
Munson, G. B. "The Single Portent of Carl Sandburg." *Double Dealer* 6 (O 24) 17-26.
Nash, J. V. "Carl Sandburg: An American Homer." *Open Court* 44 (O 30) 633-9.
Oldsey, B. S. "Sandburg's *Broken-Faced Gargoyles*." *Expl* (My 49) 50.
Ortiz-Vargas, Alfredo. "Perfiles anglo-americanas." *Revista Ibero-americana* 4 (1940) 163-76.
Paelik, Martin. "Smoke and Steel." *Englische Studien* 62 (Mr 28) 415-20.
Pound, Ezra. "Ezra Pound on Sandburg." *Double Dealer* 3 (My 22) 206-10.
Ramsdell, C. W. "Carl Sandburg's *Lincoln*." *So R* 6 (Wi 41) 439-53.
Rascoe, Burton. "Carl Sandburg." *Lit R* 5 (27 S 24) 1-2.
Rosenfeld, Paul. "Carl Sandburg." *Bkm* 53 (Jl 21) 389-96.
——— "Carl Sandburg and Photography." *NRp* 61 (22 Ja 30) 251-2.
Sandburg, Carl. "Sandburg's Words at New Salem." *J Ill State Hist Soc* 14 (Sp 50) 7-14.
——— "Trying to Write." *Atl* 186 (S 50) 31-3.
Schenk, W. P. "Carl Sandburg—A Bibliography." *Bul Bibl* 16 (D 36) 4-7.
Shoemaker, D. C. "Carl Sandburg at Flat Rock." *So Packet* 4 (Ag 48) 1-4.
Skinner, C. L. "Songs That Give Reason for Singing." *NAR* 223 (D-F 26-7) 695-700.
Sloan, M. B. "Carl Sandburg—A Portrait." *Un R* 2 (Sp 36) 151-4.
Spitz, Leon. "Carl Sandburg's Bible Texts." *Am Hebrew* 158 (8 O 48) 8, 13.
Untermeyer, Louis. "Enter Sandburg." *Masses* 8 (Jl 16) 30.
Van Doren, Carl. "Flame and Slag. Carl Sandburg: Poet with Both Fists." *Century* 106 (S 23) 786-92.
West, Rebecca. "The Voice of Chicago." *SRL* 3 (4 S 26) 81-3.
Yust, Walter. "Carl Sandburg, Human Being." *Bkm* 52 (Ja 21) 285-90.
Zabel, M. D. "Sandburg's Testament." *Poetry* 49 (O 36) 33-45.

SANDYS, GEORGE (1578-1644). Attenborough, J. M. "George Sandys: Traveller and Poet." *Westminster R* 163 (Je 05) 643-55.
Bowers, Fredson, & Davis, R. B. "George Sandys: A Bibliographical Catalogue of Printed Editions in England to 1700." *BNYPL* 14 (Ap, My, Je 50) 159-81, 223-44, 280-6.
Davis, R. B. "Early Editions of George Sandys's 'Ovid': The Circumstances of Production." *PBSA* 35 (4Q 41) 255-76.
——— "George Sandys and Two Uncollected Poems." *HLQ* 12 (N 48) 105-11.
——— "George Sandys, Poet-Adventurer." *Americana* 33 (Ap 39) 180-95.
——— "George Sandys *v.* William Stansby: The 1632 Edition of Ovid's *Metamorphoses*." *Library* (London) 3: ser 5 (D 48) 193-212.

——— "Two New Manuscript Items for a George Sandys Bibliography." *PBSA* 37 (3Q 43) 215-22.

SANTAYANA, GEORGE (1863-1952). Anon. "George Santayana." *Cur Biog* 5 (Ap 44) 39-44.

——— "Reprints and New Editions." *N Y Herald-Tribune Books* 18 (21 Mr 37) 16.

Aaron, Daniel. "A Postscript to *The Last Puritan*." *NEQ* 9 (D 36) 683-6.

Barrett, William. "The Conclusion of Mr. Santayana's Philosophy." *So R* 7 (Sp 42) 904-25.

——— "History of an Unhistorical Mind." *PR* 11 (Su 44) 313-21.

Bowers, R. H. "Santayana and Browning: A Postscript." *N&Q* 194 (1 O 49) 433-4.

Brett, G. S. "The Achievement of Santayana." *UTQ* 9 (O 39) 22-37.

Brown, S. G. "Lucretius and Santayana: A Study in Classical Materialism." *NMQR* 15 (Sp 45) 5-17.

Buchler, Justus. "George Santayana's *The Last Puritan*." *NEQ* 9 (Je 36) 281-5.

Buckham, J. W. "Santayana's *Last Puritan* Again." *Personalist* 18 (Jl 37) 292-300.

Canby, H. S. "The American Santayana." *SRL* 15 (17 Ap 37) 3-4, 14.

Cecchi, E. "L'Autobiografiadi G. Santayana." *Il Mondo* 1 (1945) 12.

Clemens, Cyril. "An American Philosopher in Exile, George Santayana." *Mark Twain Q* 1 (Fl 36) 10-2.

Cohen, M. R. "On American Philosophy: George Santayana." *NRp* 23 (21 Jl 20) 221-3.

Colum, Padriac. "Santayana's 'Discipline' of Mind and Heart." *N Y Herald-Tribune Books* 22 (31 Mr 46) 4.

Cory, Daniel. "The Later Philosophy of Mr. Santayana." *Criterion* 15 (Ap 36) 379-92.

——— "Santayana in Europe." *Atl* 173 (My 44) 53-62.

——— "A Study of Santayana." *J Philos Stud* 2 (Jl 27) 349-64.

Dell, Stanley. "Truth of History—History of Truth: A Comment on George Santayana's *The Idea of Christ in the Gospels*." *Chimera* 5 (Au 46) 41-51.

Duron, Jacques. "Santayana, Espagnol d'Amérique." *Les Nouvelles Littéraires* no 1207 (19 O 50) 7.

Edman, Irwin. "Santayana at Seventy." *SRL* 10 (16 D 33) 349-50.

Falconi, Carlo. "Incontro sul Celio con George Santayana." *La Fiera Letteraria* (Italy) no 43 (23 O 49) 1, 4.

Firuski, Maurice. "American First Editions: George Santayana, 1863- ." *Pub W* 129 (20 Je 36) 2463-4.

Gilbert, Katherine. "Santayana's Doctrine of Aesthetic Expression." *Philos R* 25 (1926) 221-35.

Gray, J. G. "Plato the Greek and Santayana the Cosmopolitan." *Am Schol* 12 (Sp 43) 186-204.

Hazen, B. F. "The Last Puritan." *Cronos* 1 (Su 47) 1-5.

Howgate, G. W. "The Essential Santayana." *Mark Twain Q* 5 (Wi-Sp 42) 7-18.

——— "Santayana and Humanism." *SR* 43 (Ja-Mr 35) 49-57.

Kallen, H. M. "America and the Life of Reason." *J Philos* 18 (29 S, 13 O 29) 533-51, 568-75.

Knickerbocker, W. S. "Figaro among the Philosophers: George Santayana." *SR* 50 (Ap-Je 41) 250-65.

Lamprecht, S. P. "Naturalism and Agnoticism in Santayana." *J Philos* 30 (12 O 33) 561-74.

——— "Santayana Then and Now." *J Philos* 25 (27 S 28) 533-50.

Lane, J. W. "The Dichotomy of George Santayana." *Cath World* 140 (O 34) 20-8.

Larrabee, H. A. "George Santayana." *SR* 39 (Ap-Je 31) 209-21.

——— "Robert Bridges and George Santayana." *Am Schol* 1 (1932) 167-82.

——— "Santayana: Philosopher for America." *SR* 39 (Jl-S 31) 325-38.

——— "Santayana through Austrian Eyes." *Books Abroad* 4 (Ja 30) 19-20.

Leavis, Q. D. "The Critical Writings of George Santayana." *Scrutiny* 3 (D 35) 278-95.
——— "Tragedy and the Medium: A Note on Mr. Santayana's Tragic Philosophy." *Scrutiny* 12 (Au 44) 249-60.
MacCampbell, Donald. "Santayana's Debt to New England." *NEQ* 8 (Je 35) 203-14.
McDowall, Arthur. "Three Philosopher-Poets." *Living Age* 310 (23 Jl 21) 200-8.
MacLeish, Archibald. "Santayana, the Poet." *Bkm* 62 (O 25) 187-9.
Miller, D. S. "Mr. Santayana and William James." *Harvard Grad Mag* (Mr 21) 348-64.
Mumford, Lewis. "Mr. Santayana's Philosophy." *Freeman* 7 (23 My 23) 258-60.
Münsterberg, Margaret. "Santayana and His Pilgrim's Progress." *Am Merc* 12 (My 36) 115-20.
——— "Santayana at Cambridge." *Am Merc* 1 (Ja 24) 69-74.
O'Neill, George. "Poetry, Religion and Professor Santayana." *Stud* 10 (S 21) 451-63.
Papajewski, Helmut. "Santayana's 'The Last Puritan' und seine Kulturkritik des Amerikanismus." *Germanisch-Romanische Monatschrift* 30 (Ja-Mr 42) 21-39.
Pellizzi, C. "Santayana e i puritani." *Fiera Letteraria* no 25 (19 Je 47).
Randall, J. H., Jr. "The Latent Idealism of a Materialist." *J Philos* 28 (19 N 31) 645-60.
Ransom, J. C. "Art and Mr. Santayana." *VQR* 13 (Su 37) 420-36.
Ratner, Joseph. "George Santayana: a Philosophy of Piety." *Monist* 34 (Ap 24) 236-59.
——— "George Santayana's Theory of Religion." *J Religion* 3 (S 23) 458-75.
Rice, P. B. "George Santayana." *KR* 2 (Au 40) 469-71.
——— "George Santayana: The Philosopher as Poet." *KR* 2 (Au 40) 460-75.
Rosenfeld, Paul. "Carl Sandburg." *Bkm* 53 (Jl 21) 389-96.
Saglio, H. T. "Implications of *The Life of Reason*." *J Philos* 28 (24 S 31) 533-44.
Santayana, George. "Brief History of Myself." *SRL* 13 (F 36) 13.
——— "A Change of Heart." *Atl* 182 (D 48) 52-6.
Smith, D. F. "George Santayana and the Last Puritan." *NMQR* 7 (F 37) 39-45.
Smith, Herbert. "George Santayana." *Am R* 1 (Mr-Ap 23) 190-204.
Ten, M. H. "George Santayana's Theory of Knowledge." *J Philos* 20 (12 Ap 23) 197-211.
Terzian, Shohig. "Santayana at Harvard, 1882-1912." *Mark Twain Q* 5 (Wi-Sp 42) 3-6.
Trueblood, C. K. "A Rhetoric of Intuition." *Dial* 84 (My 28) 401-4.
Watkin, E. I. "The Philosophy of George Santayana." *Dublin R* 182 (Ja 28) 32-45.
Wilson, Edmund. "Santayana at the Convent of the Blue Nuns." *NYr* 22 (6 Ap 46) 55-62.
Zardoya, Concha. "Poesía y Estilo de George Santayana." *Cuadernos Americanos* (Mexico) 49 (Ja-F 50) 130-56.

SARETT, LEW (1888-). Frink, Maurice. "Out a'Fishing with Lew Sarett." *Nature* 16 (Ag 30) 113-6.
Henderson, A. C. "Tall Timber and a Loon." *Poetry* 17 (D 20) 158-61.
McCole, C. J. "Lew Sarett." *Writer* 39 (My 29) 120-3.
Monroe, Harriet. "Beasts and Humans." *Poetry* 39 (D 31) 155-7.
——— "Lew Sarett and Our Aboriginal Inheritance." *Poetry* 27 (N 25) 88-95.

SAROYAN, WILLIAM (1908-). Burgum, E. B. "The Lonesome Young Man on the Flying Trapeze." *VQR* 20 (Su 44) 392-403.
Carpenter, F. I. "The Time of William Saroyan's Life." *PS* 1 (Wi 47) 88-98.
Castello, G. C. "I Giorni della vita." *Il Ponte* (F 46) 2.
E. D. C. "Il Mio nome è Aram." *Fiera Letteraria* no 24 (12 Je 47).
Fadiman, Clifton. "71 Varieties." *NYr* 12 (22 F 36) 67-9.
Hatcher, Harlan. "William Saroyan." *EJ* 28 (Mr 39) 169-77.

Healey, R. C. "Anderson, Saroyan, Sherwood: New Directions." *Cath World* 152 (N 40) 174-80.
Lévy, Raoul. "A propos de Saroyan." *Les Temps Modernes* no 6 (1 Mr 46) 1122-6
Mersand, Joseph. "William Saroyan and the American Imagination." *Players Mag* 17 (Ja 41) 9.
Nathan, G. J. "First Nights & Passing Judgments." *Esquire* 13 (F 40) 78, 117.
——— "Saroyan: Whirling Dervish of Fresno." *Am Merc* 51 (N 40) 303-8.
Rahv, Philip. "William Saroyan: A Minority Report." *Am Merc* 57 (S 43) 371-7.
Remenyi, Joseph. "William Saroyan: A Portrait." *CE* 6 (N 44) 92-100.
Wilson, Edmund. "The Boys in the Back Room: William Saroyan." *NRp* 103 (18 N 40) 697-8.

SAXON, LYLE (1891-1946). Leisure, H. L. "Presenting Lyle Saxon." *SLM* 2 (S 40) 509-10.

SCHINDLER, SOLOMON (1842-1915). Mann, A. "Solomon Schindler: Boston Radical." *NEQ* 23 (D 50) 453-76.

SCHOOLCRAFT, HENRY ROWE (1793-1864). Hallowell, A. I. "Concordance of Ojibwa Narratives in the Published Works of Henry R. Schoolcraft." *AS* 59 (Ap-Je 46) 136-53.
Orians, G. H. "The Souvenir of the Lakes." *Quar Bul Hist Soc Nw Ohio* 11 (Ap-Jl 39) 1-24.
Rust, J. D. "Henry Rowe Schoolcraft and George Eliot." *Mich Hist* 24 (Mr 50) 29-34.
Streeter, F. B. "Henry Rowe Schoolcraft." *Am Col* 5 (O 27) 2-8.

SCHUTZE, MARTIN (1866-1950). Guthrie, W. N. "A New Star." *SR* 12 (Jl 04) 354-60.

SCOTT, EVELYN (1893-). Anon. "Evelyn Scott." *Wilson Bul* 4 (D 29) 150.
——— "Portrait in Line Introducing Evelyn Scott." *Book Buyer* 3 (My 37) 15.
Fitts, Dudley. "The Verse of Evelyn Scott." *Poetry* 36 (S 30) 338-43.
Gregory, Horace. "The Narrow House of Victorian England." *SRL* 10 (26 My 34) 709, 713.
Lovett, R. M. "The Evolution of Evelyn Scott." *Bkm* 70 (O 29) 153-6.
Radford, Manson. "Bread and a Sword." *So R* 3 (Sp 38) 824-8.
Ridge, Lola. "Evelyn Scott." *Poetry* 17 (Mr 21) 334-7.
Salpeter, Harry. "Portrait of a Disciplined Artist." *Bkm* 74 (N 31) 281-6.

SCOTT, WINFIELD (1786-1866). Ciardi, John. "Winfield Townley Scott." *UKCR* 13 (Wi 46) 119-20.

SCUDDER, HORACE ELISHA (1838-1902). Allen, A. V. G. "Horace E. Scudder: An Appreciation." *Atl* 91 (Ap 03) 549-60.
Hersholt, Jean. "The Two Never Met." *SRL* 29 (21 D 46) 18-9.

SEABURY, SAMUEL (1729-96). Pennington, E. L. "Some Letters of Bishop William Skinner of Aberdeen, 1822-1827." *Hist Mag Prot Episc Church* 16 (D 47) 373-413.

SEALSFIELD, CHARLES (1793-1864). Arndt, K. J. "The Cooper-Sealsfield Exchange of Criticism." *AL* 15 (Mr 43) 16-24.
——— "Sealsfield's Early Reception in England and America." *GR* 18 (O 43) 176-95.
———, & Groen, H. J. "Sealsfield—'The Greatest American Author.'" *AGR* 7 (Je 41) 12-5.

Heller, Otto. "Charles Sealsfield, a Forgotten Discoverer of the Valley of the Mississippi." *Mo Hist R* 31 (Jl 37) 382-405.
——— "Plagiarism on Charles Sealsfield." *JEGP* 7 (D 08) 130-3.
——— "Some Sources of Charles Sealsfield." *MP* 7 (Ap 10) 587-92.
Krumpelmann, J. T. "Charles Sealsfield's Americanisms." *AS* 19 (O 44) 196-9.
McMillan, J. B. "Lexical Evidence from Charles Sealsfield." *AS* 18 (Ap 43) 117-27.
Preston, A. B. "Sealsfield Sources." *Ger-Am Annals* ns 9 (1911) 31-9.
Schroeder, A. E. "New Sources of Charles Sealsfield." *JEGP* 46 (Je 47) 70-4.

SEDGWICK, ANNE DOUGLAS (1873-1935). Forbes, Ester. "Anne Douglas Sedgwick and Her Novels." *Bkm* 69 (Ag 29) 568-74.
Overton, Grant. "The Security of Anne Douglas Sedgwick and Her Novels." *Bkm* 65 (Ap 27) 125-32.
Phelps, W. L. "Anne Sedgwick, American Novelist." *Forum* 72 (O 24) 515-9.
Selincourt, Basil de (ed). "Anne Douglas Sedgwick's Letters: A Portrait." *Forum* 96 (S 36) 111-5.

SEDGWICK, CATHARINE MARIA (1789-1867). Fess, G. M. "Catharine Sedgwick and Crèvecoeur." AL 15 (Ja 44) 420-1.
Glicksberg, C. I. "Bryant and the Sedgwick Family." *Americana* 31 (O 37) 626-38.
Schantz, B. T. "Sir Christopher Gardiner in Nineteenth Century American Fiction." *NEQ* 11 (D 38) 807-17.
Sedgwick, H. D. "The Sedgwicks of Berkshire." *Col Berkshire Hist & Sci Soc* 3 (1900) 90-106.
Stearns, B. M. "Miss Sedgwick Observes Harriet Martineau." *NEQ* 7 (S 34) 533-41.

SEEGER, ALAN (1888-1916). Anon. "Unknown, His Grave." *Lit Dig* 108 (31 Ja 31) 16.
Gillet, L. B. "Poets in the War." *NAR* 209 (Je 19) 822-36.
Mott, F. L. "Youth and Death, 1817-1917." *SR* 26 (Jl 18) 313-8.
Reeves, Harrison. "The Tragedy of Alan Seeger." *NRp* 10 (10 Mr 17) 160-2.
Roberts, W. A. "The Alan Seeger I Knew." *Bkm* 47 (Ag 18) 585-90.
Terrin, Charles. "Alan Seeger, poète-légionnaire." *La Légion Étrangère* (France) no 21 (1950) 32-5.

SETON, ERNEST THOMPSON (1860-1946). Anon. "Necrology." *N Mex Hist R* 22 (Ja 47) 107.

SEWALL, SAMUEL (1652-1730). Anon. "The Sins and Mercies of a Harvard Student." *More Books* 11 (S 36) 277-85.
Dykema, K. W. "Samuel Sewall Reads John Dryden." *AL* 14 (My 42) 157-61.
Ford, W. C. "Samuel Sewall and Nicholas Noyes on Wigs." *PCSM* 20 (1920) 109-28.
Harden, J. W. "Judge Sewall and Anti-Slavery Sentiment in Colonial New England." *Negro Hist Bul* 6 (Mr 43) 125, 143.
Harding, Walter. "A Volume from Samuel Sewall's Library." *JRUL* 14 (D 50) 31.
Howard, C. H. C. "Chief Justice Samuel Sewall." *EIHC* 37 (1901) 161-76.
Kittredge, G. L. "Letters of Samuel Lee and Samuel Sewall Relating to New England and the Indians." *PCSM* 14 (1913) 142-55.
Lawrence, H. W. "Samuel Sewall, Revealer of Puritan New England." *SAQ* 33 (Ja 34) 20-37.
Winship, G. P. "Samuel Sewall and the New England Company." *PMHS* 67 (1941-4) 55-110.

SHAPIRO, KARL (1913-). Daiches, David. "The Poetry of Karl Shapiro." *Poetry* 66 (Ag 45) 266-73.
Engle, Paul. "Five Years of Pulitzer Poets." *EJ* 38 (F 49) 62-3.

Glicksberg, C. I. "Karl Shapiro and the Personal Accent." *Prairie Schooner* 22 (Sp 48) 44-52.
Kohler, Dayton. "Karl Shapiro: Poet in Uniform." *CE* 7 (F 46) 243-9; EJ 35 (F 48) 63-8.
O'Connor, W. V. "Karl Shapiro: The Development of a Talent." *CE* 10 (N 48) 71-5.
——— "Shapiro on Rime." *KR* 8 (Wi 46) 116, 119-21.
Scannell, Vernon. "The Poetry of Karl J. Shapiro." *Adelphi* 25 (Ja-Mr 49) 157-8.
Seif, Morton. "Poet's Journey: The Struggle in the Soul of Karl Shapiro." *Menorah J* 37 (Wi 49) 51-8.
Shapiro, Karl. "Prosody as Meaning." *Poetry* 73 (Mr 49) 336-51.
———, & Smith, W. J. "Two Transatlantic Statements." *Poetry* 6 (F 47) 273-7.
Shockley, M. S. "Shapiro's 'World.'" *AL* 21 (Ja 50) 485.

SHAW, HENRY WHEELER (1818-85). Anon. "Neglected Worthies." *Nation* 107 (17 Ag 18) 165.
Clements, Cyril. "Josh Billings: A Neglected Humorist." *Overland Mo* 92 (Ja 34) 12.
Jones, Joseph. "Josh Billings: Some Yankee Notions of Humor." *Un Texas Stud Eng* 23 (1943) 148-61.
——— "Josh Billings Visits a Mark Twain Shrine." *AN&Q* 4 (S 44) 83-4.
Mudge, James. "A Philosophical Humorist." *Methodist R* 101 (Mr 18) 209.

SHEEAN, VINCENT (1899-). Kliger, Samuel. "Theme and Structure in Vincent Sheean's 'Personal History.'" *CE* 9 (Mr 48) 312-6.

SHEPARD, THOMAS (1605-49). Davis, A. M. "A Few Words about the Writings of Thomas Shepard." *Pub Cambridge Hist Soc* 3 (1908) 79-89.
——— "Hints on Contemporary Life in the Writings of Thomas Shepard" *PCSM* 12 (1911) 136-62.
Shepard, Thomas. "The Autobiography of Thomas Shepard." *PCSM* 27 (1932) 343-400.

SHERMAN, FRANCIS (1871-1926). Roberts, C. G. D. "Francis Sherman." *Dalhousie R* 14 (Ja 35) 419-27.

SHERMAN, STUART P. (1881-1926). Anon. "The Life and Times of Stuart Sherman." *Bkm* 70 (N 29) 289-305.
——— "Professor Sherman's Tradition." *Freeman* 2 (27 O 20) 151-3.
——— "A Reviewer's Notebook." *Freeman* 6 (29 N 22) 286-7.
——— "Stuart P. Sherman." *Bkm* 54 (Je 22) 354-8.
Arvin, Newton. "Stuart Sherman." *H&H* 3 (Ap-Je 30) 304-13.
Burgum, E. B. "Stuart Sherman." *EJ* 19 (F 30) 137-50.
Canby, H. S. "Stuart P. Sherman: 'The American Scholar.'" *SRL* 6 (5 O 29) 201-2.
Carson, Gerald. "Mr. Stuart Sherman Discovers Aphrodite Pandemos." *Bkm* 63 (Je 26) 289-96.
Colum, Mary. "Stuart P. Sherman." *SRL* 2 (26 Je 26) 881-2.
DeMille, G. E. "Stuart P. Sherman: The Illinois Arnold." *SR* 35 (Ja 27) 78-93.
Elliott, G. R. "Stuart Sherman and the War Age." *Bkm* 71 (Ap-My 30) 173-81.
Foerster, Norman. "The Literary Historians." *Bkm* 71 (Jl 30) 365-74.
Heaton, Charles. "A Philosophical Litterateur." *Monist* 28 (O 18) 608-12.
Perry, Bliss. "Stuart Sherman." *YR* 19 (D 29) 386-9.
Van Doren, Carl. "The Great and Good Tradition: Stuart P. Sherman, Scourge of Sophomores." *Century* 106 (Ag 23) 631-6.
Warren, Austin. "Humanist into Journalist." *SR* 38 (Jl-S 30) 357-65.
Zeitlin, Jacob. "Correspondence of S. P. Sherman and Paul Elmer More." *Bkm* 70 (S 29) 43-53.

SHERWOOD, ROBERT (1896-). Breit, Harvey. "An Interview with Robert E. Sherwood." *N Y Times Book R* 54 (13 F 49) 23.
Campbell, O. J. "Robert Sherwood and His Times." *CE* 4 (F 43) 275-80.
Gassner, John. "Robert Emmet Sherwood." *Atl* 169 (Ja 42) 26-33.
Healey, R. C. "Anderson, Saroyan, Sherwood: New Directions." *Cath World* 152 (N 40) 174-80.
Isaacs, E. J. R. "Robert Sherwood." *Theatre Arts* 23 (Ja 39) 31-40.
Sherwood, R. E. "Footnote to a Preface." *SRL* 32 (6 Ag 49) 130, 132, 134.

SHILLABER, BENJAMIN PENHALLOW (1814-90). Clemens, Cyril. "Benjamin Shillaber and His 'Carpet Bag.'" *NEQ* 14 (S 41) 519-37.
——— "Shillaber and the Carpet Bag." *Mark Twain Q* 7 (Wi-Sp 45-6) 11-21.
——— "Shillaber's Birth and Childhood." *Mark Twain Q* 6 (Su-Fl 44) 9-11, 24.
Coleman, R. A. "Trowbridge and Shillaber." *NEQ* 20 (Je 47) 232-46.
Masters, E. L. "Benjamin Penhallow Shillaber." *Mark Twain Q* 4 (Fl-Wi 40-1) 22, 24.
Meine, F. J. "Shillaber's Place in American Literature." *Mark Twain Q* 6 (Su-Fl 44) 8.

SHOREY, PAUL (1857-1934) Putnam, E. J. "Paul Shorey." *Atl* 161 (Je 38) 795-804.

SIGOURNEY, LYDIA HUNTLEY (1791-1865). Collin, G. L. "Lydia Huntley Sigourney." *N E Mag* ns 27 (S 02) 15-20.
Haight, G. S. "Longfellow and Mrs. Sigourney." *NEQ* 3 (Jl 30) 532-7.
Jordan, P. D. "The Source of Mrs. Sigourney's 'Indian Girl's Burial.'" *AL* 4 (N 32) 300-5.

SILL, EDWARD ROWLAND (1841-87). Arvin, Newton. "The Failure of E. R. Sill." *Bkm* 72 (F 31) 581-9.
Baker, E. L. "Edward Rowland Sill, Poet-Teacher." *Overland Mo* 83 (Ap 25) 154-5, 175-6.
Dix, W. F. "The Poems of Edward Rowland Sill." *Outlook* 72 (1 N 02) 554-6.
P., W. B. "Sill's Poetry." *Atl* 90 (Ag 02) 271-5.

SIMITIÈRE, PIERRE EUGÈNE DU (d. 1874?). Huth, Hans. "Pierre Eugène du Simitière and the Beginnings of the American Historical Museum." *PMHB* 69 (O 45) 315-25.

SIMMS, WILLIAM GILMORE (1806-70). Anon. "Correspondence Addressed to John C. Calhoun." *Annual Report Am Hist Assn* (1929).
Deen, F. H. "A Comparison of Simms's *Richard Hurdis* with Its Sources." *MLN* 60 (Je 45) 406-8.
——— "The Genesis of *Martin Faber* in *Caleb Williams*." *MLN* 59 (My 44) 315-7.
Higham, J. W. "The Changing Loyalties of William Gilmore Simms." *J So Hist* 9 (My 43) 210-23
Holman, C. H. "Simms and the British Dramatists." *PMLA* 65 (Je 50) 346-59.
——— "William Gilmore Simms' Picture of the Revolution as a Civil Conflict." *J So Hist* 15 (N 49) 441-62.
Hoole, W. S. "A Note on Simms's Visits to the Southwest." *AL* 6 (N 34) 334-6.
——— "Simms' *Michael Bonham*, a 'Forgotten' Drama of the Texas Revolution." *Sw Hist Q* 46 (Ja 42) 255-61.
——— "William Gilmore Simms's Career as Editor." *Ga Hist Q* 19 (Mr 35) 47 ff.
Hubbell, J. B. "Five Letters from George Henry Boker to William Gilmore Simms." *PMHB* 63 (Ja 39) 66-71.
Jackson, D. K. "Some Unpublished Letters of John R. Thompson and Augustin L. Taveau." *WMQ* 16 (Ap 36) 206-21.
Jarrell, H. M. "Falstaff and Simms's Porgy." *AL* 3 (My 31) 204-13.

——— "Simms's Visits to the Southwest." *AL* 5 (Mr 33) 29-35.
Jillson, Willard. "The Beauchamp-Sharp Tragedy in American Literature." *Register Ky State Hist Soc* 36 (1938) 54-60.
McDavid, R. I., Jr. "*Ivanhoe* and Simms' *Vasconselos*." *MLN* 56 (Ap 41) 294-7.
Morris, J. A. "Gullah in the Stories and Novels of William Gilmore Simms." *AS* 22 (F 47) 46-53.
——— "The Stories of William Gilmore Simms." *AL* 14 (Mr 42) 20-35.
Odell, A. T. "Letters . . . to James H. Hammond." *Bul Furman Un* 26 (Ma 43) 3-15.
——— "William Gilmore Simms in the Post-War Years." *Bul Furman Un* 29 (My 46) 5-20.
Russell, J. A. "Southwestern Border Indians in the Writings of William Gilmore Simms." *Educator* 51 (N 30) 144-57.
Salley, A. S., Jr. "A Bibliography of William Gilmore Simms." *Pub So Hist Assn* 11 (S 07) 343-4.
Stewart, Randall. "Hawthorne's Contributions to *The Salem Advertiser*." *AL* 5 (Ja 34) 327-41.
Stone, Edward. "*Caleb Williams* and *Martin Faber:* A Contrast." MLN 62 (N 47) 480-3.
Stoney, S. G. "The Memoirs of Frederick Adolphus Porcher." *S C Hist & Gen Mag* 47 (Ja, Ap 46) 32-52, 83-108.
Wegelin, Oscar. "Simms's First Publication." *N Y Hist Soc Quar Bul* 25 (Ja 41) 26-7.
——— "William Gilmore Simms: A Short Sketch, with a Bibliography of His Separate Writings." *Am Book Coll* 3 (F, Mr, Ap, My-Je 33) 113-6, 149-51, 216-8, 284-6.
Whaley, G. W. "A Note on Simms's Novels." *AL* 2 (My 30) 173-4.
Wilson, J. G. "William Gilmore Simms." *Book News Mo* 30 (Je 12) 711-5.

SINCLAIR, UPTON (1878-). Bantz, Elizabeth. "Upton Sinclair: Book Reviews and Criticisms Published in German and French Periodicals and Newspapers." *Bul Bibl* 18 (1946) 204-6.
Calverton, V. F. "The Upton Sinclair Enigma." *Nation* 132 (4 F 31) 133-4.
Cantwell, Robert. "Upton Sinclair." *NRp* 90 (24 F 37) 69-71.
Dell, Floyd. "The Artist in Revolt." *Bkm* 65 (My 27) 316-22.
——— "Upton Sinclair in America." *New Masses* 29 (N 28) 6-7.
Garlin, Sender. "Upton Sinclair, Reactionary Utopian." *New Masses* 15 (22 My 34) 10-2.
Grattan, C. H. "Upton Sinclair on Current Literature." *Bkm* 75 (Ap 32) 61-4.
Harris, Mrs. L. M. "Upton Sinclair and Helicon Hall." *Independent* 62 (28 Mr 07) 711-3.
Hicks, Granville. "The Survival of Upton Sinclair." *CE* 4 (Ja 43) 213-20.
Hitchcock, C. N. "The Brass Check. . . ." *J Pol Econ* 29 (Ap 21) 336-48.
Jordan-Smith, P. "Upton Sinclair." *World Tomorrow* 8 (D 25) 378.
Kauffman, Kurt. "Upton Sinclair, The Brass Check." *Englische Studien* 56 (Ja 22) 162-5.
Lippmann, Walter. "Upton Sinclair." *SRL* 4 (3 Mr 28) 641-3.
Lovett, R. M. "Upton Sinclair." *EJ* 17 (O 28) 706-14.
Mordell, Albert. "Haldeman-Julius and Upton Sinclair." *Critic & Guide* 4 (F 50) 94-119.
Morris, L. S. "Upton Sinclair." *NRp* 54 (7 Mr 28) 90-3.
Rogers, P. P. "Francisco Rojas González and *The Jungle*." *MLF* 35 (1950) 39-41.
Sinclair, Upton. "Farewell to Lanny Budd." *SRL* 32 (13 Ag 49) 18-9, 38.
——— "New Helicon Hall." *Independent* 67 (9 S 09) 580-3.
——— "Planning the Model State." *Mod Thinker* 5 (O 34) 23-5.
——— "To My Readers." *New Masses* 28 (19 Jl 38) 10-1.

——— "What Life Means to Me." *Cosmopolitan* 41 (O 06) 591-5.
Spitz, Leon. "Upton Sinclair and Nazism." *Am Hebrew* 158 (22 O 48) 2.
——— "Upton Sinclair on Zionism." *Am Hebrew* 158 (31 D 48) 6, 15.
Talbert, E. W. "A Comment on 'The Goose Step.'" *School & Soc* 18 (27 O 23) 491-7.
Van Doren, Carl. "Upton Sinclair." *Nation* 113 (28 S 21) 347-8.
Whyte, J. H. "Upton Sinclair: Puritan and Socialist." *Mod Scot* 3 (1932) 149-55.
Wilson, Edmund. "Lincoln Steffens and Upton Sinclair." *NRp* 72 (28 S 32) 173-5.

SINGMASTER, ELSIE (1879-). Kohler, Dayton. "Elsie Singmaster." *Bkm* 72 (F 31) 621-6.

SMITH, CHARLES HENRY (1826-1903). Anon. "'Bill Arp'—Humorist." *Tyler's Quar Mag* 31 (Jl 49) 25-33.
Figh, M. G. "Folklore in Bill Arp's Works." *SFQ* 12 (S 48) 169-75.
Ginther, J. E. "Charles Henry Smith, Alias 'Bill Arp.'" *Ga R* 4 (Wi 50) 313-21.

SMITH, ELIHU HUBBARD (1771--98). Cronin, J. E. "Elihu Hubbard Smith and the New York Theatre (1793-1798)." *N Y Hist* 31 (Ap 50) 136-48.
Rugg, W. K. "American Poems, Selected and Original." *Chri Sci Mon* 18 (16 Ap 36) 7.

SMITH, FRANCIS HOPKINSON (1838-1915). Anon. "'Hop' Smith." *Bkm* 41 (My 15) 247-9.
Hornberger, Theodore. "The Effect of Painting in the Fiction of F. Hopkinson Smith." *Un Texas Stud Eng* 23 (1943) 162-92.
——— "Painters and Painting in the Writing of F. Hopkinson Smith." *AL* 16 (Mr 44) 1-10.
Mabie, H. W. "Hopkinson Smith and His Work." *Book Buyer* 25 (Ag 02) 17-20.
Page, T. N. "Francis Hopkinson Smith." *Scribner's* 58 (S 15) 305-13.
Van Westrum, A. S. "Francis Hopkinson Smith, Novelist." *Lamp* 28 (Je 04) 383-9.

SMITH, JOHN (1580-1631). Cameron, Alexander. "First Admiral of New England." *N E Mag* ns 30 (Mr 04) 51-67.
Davis, R. B. "The First American Edition of Captain John Smith's *True Travels* and *General Historie*." *VMHB* 48 (Ap 39) 97-108.
Fishwick, M. W. "Virginians on Olympus. I. The Last Great Knight Errant." *VMHB* 58 (Ja 50) 40-57.
Ford, W. C. "Captain John Smith's Map of Virginia." *Ga R* 14 (Jl 24) 433-43.
Glenn, Keith. "Captain John Smith and the Indians." *VMHB* 52 (O 44) 228-48.
Morse, J. M. "John Smith and His Critics: A Chapter in Colonial Historiography." *J So Hist* 1 (My 35) 123-37.
Southall, J. P. C. "Captain John Smith (1580-1631) and Pocahontas (1595?-1617)." *Tyler's Quar Hist & Gen Mag* 28 (Ap 47) 209-25.
Story, I. C. "The Elizabethan Prelude." *Pac Un Stud Lit* 3 (1940) 1-12.

SMITH, LILLIAN (1897-). Anon. "Lillian Smith." *Cur Biog* 5 (My 44) 49-52.
——— "Lillian Smith." *N Y Herald-Tribune Books* 26 (30 O 49) 2.
DeVoto, Bernard. "The Decision in the *Strange Fruit* Case: The Obscenity Statute in Massachusetts." *NEQ* 19 (Je 46) 147-83.
Dumble, W. R. "A Footnote to Negro Literature." *Negro Hist Bul* 9 (Ja 46) 82-4, 94-5.
Smith, Lillian. "Personal History of *Strange Fruit*." *SRL* 28 (17 F 45) 9-10.
——— "Why I Wrote *Killers of the Dream*." *N Y Herald-Tribune Books* 26 (17 Jl 49) 2.
——— "Why I Wrote *Strange Fruit*." *SLM* 3 (N 45) 81-2.

SMITH, LOGAN PEARSALL (1865-1946). Connolly, Cyril. "Logan Pearsall Smith." *New Statesman & Nation* 31 (9 Mr 46) 172; *Atl* 177 (Je 46) 129-32.

SMITH, MARGARET CAMERON (1867-). Hillyer, Robert. "An American Victorian." *Forum* 94 (Ag 35) 109-14.

SMITH, RICHARD PENN (1799-1854). Mabbott, T. O. "Richard Penn Smith's Tragedy of *Caius Marius.*" *AL* 2 (My 30) 141-56.

SMITH, SAMUEL STANHOPE (1750-1819). Bowers, D. F. "The Smith-Blair Correspondence, 1786-1791." *PULC* 4 (Je 43) 123-34.

SMITH, THORNE (1892-1934). Haas, Irvin. "American First Editions: (James) Thorne Smith (Jr.) 1893-1934." *Pub W* 130 (28 N 36) 2134.

SMITH, WILLIAM (1727-1803). Gegenheimer, A. F. "A Satire on Early Commencements." *Gen Mag & Hist Chron* 46 (Wi 44) 84-91.

Hornberger, Theodore. "A Note on the Probable Source of Provost William Smith's Famous Curriculum for the College of Philadelphia." *PMHB* 58 (O 34) 370-7.

SMITH, WILLIAM MOORE (1759-1821). Haviland, T. P. "'Attend! Be Firm! Ye Fathers of the State': An Account of the Commencement, College of Philadelphia, May 17, 1775." *Gen Mag & Hist Chron* 52 (Sp 50) 129-37.

SNELLING, WILLIAM JOSEPH (1804-48). Emch, Lucille. "An Indian Tale by William J. Snelling." *Minn Hist* 26 (S 45) 211-21.

Flanagan, J. T. "William Joseph Snelling, Forgotten Critic." *PQ* 16 (O 37) 376-93.

Woodall, A. E. "William Joseph Snelling and the Early Northwest." *Minn Hist* 10 (D 29) 367-85.

SPAFFORD, HORATIO GATES (1778-1832). Boyd, J. P. "Horatio Gates Spafford: Inventor, Author, Promoter of Democracy." *PAAS* 51 (O 41) 279-350.

SPARKS, JARED (1789-1866). Stearns, Malcolm, Jr. "The Utopian College of Jared Sparks." *NEQ* 15 (S 42) 512-5.

SPENCER, THEODORE (1902-1950). Matthiessen, F. O. "Theodore Spencer." *Contemp Poetry* 10 (O 50) 36-8.

Viereck, Peter. "Tribute to Theodore Spencer." *Epoch* 2 (Wi 49) 156.

SPEYER, LEONORA (1872-). Speyer, Leonora, & Hillyer, Robert. "Two Poets on the Teachings of Poetry." *SRL* 29 (23 Mr 46) 13-4, 52-4.

SPINGARN, J. E. (1875-1939). Boyesen, Bayard. "Creative Criticism." *Dial* 63 (16 Ag 17) 95-8.

SPOONER, LYSANDER (1808-87). Alexander, A. J. "The Ideas of Lysander Spooner." *NEQ* 23 (Je 50) 200-17.

SPRAGUE, ACHSA W. (d. 1862). Sprague, A. W. "Selections from Achsa W. Sprague's Diary and Journal." *Proc Vt Hist Soc* ns 9 (S 41) 131-84.

Twynham, Leonard. "Achsa W. Sprague (1827-1862)." *Proc Vt Hist Soc* ns 9 (D 41) 271-9.

STARNES, EBENEZER (d. *ca.* 1870). Miller, H. P. "The Authorship of *The Slave-holder Abroad.*" *J So Hist* 10 (F 44) 92-4.

STEDMAN, EDMUND CLARENCE (1833-1908). Anon. "Selections from the Literary Correspondence of Edmund Clarence Stedman." *Mag Hist* 25 (S-O 17) 140-51.

Boynton, H. W. "Edmund Clarence Stedman." *Putnam's* 4 (Je 08) 357-61.

DeMille, G. E. "Stedman, Arbiter of the Eighties." *PMLA* 41 (S 26) 756-66.
Hay, John. "Edmund Clarence Stedman." *Putnam's* 1 (O 16) 15-6.
Higginson, T. W. "Edmund Clarence Stedman." *Atl* 101 (Mr 08) 418-23.
Howells, W. D. "Editor's Easy Chair." *Harper's* 122 (F 11) 471-4.
Kirk, Rudolph. "'Kearny at Seven Pines.'" *JRUL* 8 (Je 45) 70-1.
Peck, H. T. "Edmund Clarence Stedman." *Bkm* 27 (Mr 08) 31-4.
Pritchard, J. P. "Stedman and Horatian Criticism." *AL* 5 (My 33) 166-9.
Stedman, Laura. "A Poet in War-Time." *Harper's* 120 (My 10) 938-47.
———, & Gould, G. M. "Some Lighter Verse by Stedman." *Bkm* 34 (F 12) 592-8.
Ticknor, Caroline. "Edmund Clarence Stedman and Eugene Field." *Bkm* 27 (Ap 08) 147-51.
Tinker, C. B. "Pan in Wall Street." *SRL* 10 (23 D 33) 365-6.

STEELE, WILBUR DANIEL (1886-). Elser, F. B. "Oh, Yes . . . Wilbur Daniel Steele." *Bkm* 62 (F 26) 691-4.

STEENDAM, JACOB (*c.* 1616-*c.* 1672). Anon. "New York City's First Poet." *N Y Times Mag* (3 N 29) 16.

STEFFENS, LINCOLN (1866-1936). Lovett, R. M. "Lincoln Steffens, Realist." *NRp* 66 (15 Ap 31) 243-4.
Lydenberg, John. "Henry Adams and Lincoln Steffens." *SAQ* 48 (Ja 49) 42-64.
Madison, C. A. "Muckraker's Progress." *VQR* 22 (Su 46) 405-20.
Nock, A. J. "Lincoln Steffens." *SRL* 7 (9 My 31) 809-10.
Steffens, Lincoln. "The Influence of My Father on My Son." *Atl* 159 (My 37) 525-30.
Wilson, Edmund. "Lincoln Steffens and Upton Sinclair." *NRp* 72 (28 S 32) 173-5.

STEIN, GERTRUDE (1874-1946). Anon. "Speaking of Pictures: Gertrude Stein Left a Hodgepodge Behind Her." *Life* 23 (18 Ag 47) 14-6.
Aiken, Conrad. "We Ask in Bread." *NRp* 78 (4 Ap 34) 219.
Aldington, Richard. "The Disciples of Gertrude Stein." *Poetry* 17 (O 20) 35-40.
Anderson, Sherwood. "Four American Impressions." *NRp* 32 (11 O 22) 171.
——— "Gertrude Stein." *Am Spect* 2 (Ap 34) 3.
——— "The Work of Gertrude Stein." *Little R* 8 (Sp 22) 29-32.
Braque, Georges, *et al.* "Testimony against Gertrude Stein." *transition* 23 (Jl 35) suppl.
Burke, Kenneth. "Engineering with Words." *Dial* 74 (Ap 23) 408.
Burnett, Whit. "Conversations with Gertrude Stein." *Story* (My 35) 2, 98.
Canby, H. S. "Cheating at Solitaire." *SRL* 11 (17 N 34) 290.
——— "Dressmakers for Art." *SRL* 10 (24 Mr 34) 572.
Cerf, Bennett. "Trade Winds." *SRL* 25 (5 S 42) 20.
Chamberlain, Dorothy. "Gertrude Stein, Amiably." *NRp* 104 (7 Ap 41) 477.
Church, Ralph. "A Note on the Writing of Gertrude Stein." *transition* 14 (Fl 28) 14-8.
Cowley, Malcolm. "Gertrude Stein: Writer or Word Scientist." *N Y Herald-Tribune Books* (24 N 46) 1.
Davies, H. S. "Narration by Gertrude Stein." *Criterion* 15 (Jl 36) 61.
Eagleson, Harvey. "Gertrude Stein: Method in Madness." *SR* 44 (Ap-Je 36) 164.
Elias, R. H. "Letters." *Story* 10 (F 37) 55.
Evans, Oliver. "The Americanism of Gertrude Stein." *Prairie Schooner* 22 (Sp 48) 70-4.
——— "Gertrude Stein as Humorist." *Prairie Schooner* 21 (Sp 47) 97-102.
Faÿ, Bernard. "Gertrude Stein, poète de l'Amérique." *Revue de Paris* (15 N 35) 294-313.
Gallup, D. C. "A Book Is a Book." *New Colophon* 1 (Ja 48) 67-80.
——— "Always Gtrde Stein." *Sw R* 34 (Su 49) 254-8.

——— "The Gertrude Stein Collection." *Yale Un Lib Gaz* 22 (O 47) 22-32.
Haines, George, IV. "Gertrude Stein and Composition." *SR* 57 (Su 49) 411-24.
Herbst, Josephine. "Miss Porter and Miss Stein." *PR* 15 (My 48) 568-72.
Janzon, Åke. "Gertrude Stein." *Bonniers Litterära Magasin* 7 (S 50) 528-31.
Lane, J. W. "The Craze for Craziness." *Cath World* 144 (D 36) 306-9.
Levinson, Ronald. "Gertrude Stein, William James, and Grammar." *Am J Psychol* 54 (Ja 41) 124-32.
Pearson, N. H. "The Gertrude Stein Collection." *Yale Un Lib Gaz* 16 (Ja 42) 45-7.
Porter, K. A. "Gertrude Stein: A Self-Portrait." *Harper's* 195 (D 47) 519-28.
Rago, Henry. "Gertrude Stein." *Poetry* 69 (N 46) 93-7.
Riding, Laura. "The New Barbarian and Gertrude Stein." *transition* 1 (Je 27) 153-68.
Ronnebeck, Arnold. "Gertrude Was Always Giggling." *Books Abroad* 19 (Wi 45) 3-7.
Sawyer, Julian. "Gertrude Stein: A Bibliography, 1941-1948." *Bul Bibl* 19 (My-Ag, S-D 48) 152-6, 183-7.
——— "Gertrude Stein (1874-): A Checklist Comprising Critical and Miscellaneous Writings about Her Work, Life and Personality from 1913-1942." *Bul Bibl* 17 (Ja-Ap 43) 211-2; 18 (My-Ag 43) 11-3.
Schmalhausen, S. D. "Gertrude Stein or Light on the Literary Enuresis." *Mod Q* 5 (Fl 29) 3-9.
Skinner, B. F. "Has Gertrude Stein a Secret?" *Atl* 153 (Ja 34) 50-7.
Smith, Harrison. "A Rose for Remembrance." *SRL* 32 (10 Ag 46) 11.
Stein, Gertrude. "Bibliography." *transition* 3 (F 29) 47-55.
——— "The War and Gertrude Stein." *Atl* 152 (Jl 33) 56-69.
——— "Your United States."' *Atl* 160 (O 37) 459-68.
Ulrich, D. L. "Gertrude Stein in Summer." *Avocation* 3 (F 39) 5.
Wilcox, Wendell. "A Note on Stein and Abstraction." *Poetry* 55 (F 40) 254-7.

STEINBECK, JOHN (1902-). Aamot, Per. "John Steinbeck—drommeren of hverdagen." *Samtiden* (Oslo) 51 (1940) 506-13.
Abramson, Ben. "John Steinbeck." *Reading & Collecting* (D 36) 4-5.
Baker, Carlos. "'In Dubious Battle' Revalued." *N Y Times Book R* (25 Jl 43) 4, 16.
——— "Steinbeck of California." *Delphian Q* 23 (Ap 40) 40-5.
Berkelman, R. G. "George Sterling on 'The Black Vulture.'" *AL* 10 (My 38) 223-4.
Besouchet, Lidia. "Amando Fontes y Steinbeck." *Nosotros* 7 (S 42) 322-5.
Bracher, Frederick. "Steinbeck and the Biological View of Man." *PS* 2 (Wi 48) 14-29.
Burgum, E. B. "The Sensibility of John Steinbeck." *Sci & Soc* 10 (Sp 46) 132-47.
Calverton, V. F. "Steinbeck, Hemingway, and Faulkner." *Mod Q* 11 (Fl 39) 36-44.
Carpenter, F. I. "John Steinbeck: American Dreamer." *Sw R* 26 (Jl 41) 454-67.
——— "The Philosophical Joads." *CE* 2 (Ja 41) 315-25.
Champney, Freeman. "John Steinbeck, Californian." *AR* 7 (Fl 47) 345-62.
Cousins, Norman. "Bankrupt Realism." *SRL* 30 (8 Mr 47) 22-3.
Davis, Elmer. "The Steinbeck Country." *SRL* 18 (24 S 38) 11.
Fairley, Barker. "John Steinbeck and the Coming Literature." *SR* 50 (Ap 42) 145-61.
Forestier, Marie. "Steinbeck et son oeuvre." *La Revue Nouvelle* 5 (Mr 47) 253-61.
Frohock, W. M. "John Steinbeck's Men of Wrath." *Sw R* 31 (Sp 46) 144-52.
Gannett, Lewis. "John Steinbeck: Novelist at Work." *Atl* 176 (D 45) 55-61.
Gibbs, L. R. "John Steinbeck, Moralist." *AR* 2 (Su 42) 172-84.
Gierasch, Walter. "Steinbeck's *The Red Pony,* II, 'The Great Mountains.'" *Expl* 4 (Mr 46) 39.
Hyman, S. E. "Some Notes on John Steinbeck." *AR* 2 (Su 42) 185-200.
Jackson, J. H. "John Steinbeck: A Portrait." *SRL* 17 (25 S 37) 11-2.

Jones, C. E. "Proletarian Writing and John Steinbeck." *SR* 48 (O 40) 445-56.
Mjöberg, Jöran. "Den ansvarlösa godheten: Till John Steinbecks etik." *Ord och Bild* (Stockholm) 55 (1946) 509-13.
Nevius, Blake. "Steinbeck: One Aspect." *PS* 3 (Su 49) 302-11.
Powell, L. C. "American First Editions . . . John Steinbeck." *Pub W* 137 (17 Ap 37) 1701.
——— "Toward a Bibliography of John Steinbeck." *Colophon* ns 3 (Au 38) 558-68.
Rascoe, Burton. "John Steinbeck." *EJ* (col ed) 27 (Mr 38) 205-16.
Richards, E. C. "The Challenge of John Steinbeck." *NAR* 243 (Su 37) 406-13.
Rosati, S. "Letteratura inglese: l'ultimo Steinbeck." *La Nuova Europa* 2 (1945) 31.
Ross, W. O. "John Steinbeck: Naturalism's Priest." *CE* 10 (My 49) 432-7.
Shedd, Margaret. "Of Mice and Men." *Theatre Arts* 17 (O 37) 774-80.
Shockley, M. S. "The Reception of *The Grapes of Wrath* in Oklahoma." *AL* 15 (Ja 44) 351-61.
Sillen, Samuel. "Censoring 'The Grapes of Wrath.'" *New Masses* 32 (12 S 39) 23-4.
Steinbeck, John. "Critics, Critics Burning Bright." *SRL* 33 (11 N 50) 20-1.
——— "The Novel Might Benefit by the Discipline and Terseness of the Drama." *Stage* 15 (Ja 38) 50-1.
Tarr, E. W. "Steinbeck on One Plane." *SRL* 30 (20 D 47) 20.
Van Gelder, Robert. "Interview with a Best-Selling Author: John Steinbeck." *Cosmopolitan* no 730 (Ap 47) 18.
Whipple, T. K. "Steinbeck through a Glass, though Brightly." *NRp* 96 (12 O 38) 274-5.

STERLING, GEORGE (1869-1926). Anon. George Sterling Numbers. *Overland Mo* 85 (N, D 27).
Austin, Mary. "George Sterling at Carmel." *Am Merc* 11 (My 27) 65-72.
——— "A Poet in Outland." *Overland Mo* 85 (N 27) 331, 351.
Bassett, W. K. "Wherein One Poet Talks Not and Another Shoots Squirrels." *Carmel Cymbal* 1 (15 Je 26) 3, 11.
Bender, Albert. "George Sterling: The Man." *Overland Mo* 85 (D 27) 362.
Berkelman, R. G. "George Sterling on 'The Black Vulture.'" *AL* 10 (My 38) 223-4.
Bland, H. M. "The Poets of the Overland." *Overland Mo* 85 (Jl 27) 199-200, 218.
——— "Sterling, the Poet of the Seas and Stars." *Overland Mo* ns 64 (D 14) 540-8.
Cooksley, S. B. "George Sterling—An Appreciation." *Overland Mo* 84 (S 25) 333-5.
Dobie, C. C. "The Man Who Short-Changed Himself." *Overland Mo* 85 (N 27) 327.
Douglas, George. "Glimpses of George Sterling." *Overland Mo* 85 (N 27) 333.
Field, Ben. "Literary Magazines in the Western World." *Overland Mo* 86 (O 28) 341-2.
——— "Los Angeles to George Sterling." *Overland Mo* 85 (Mr 27) 71.
——— "Memories of George Sterling." *Overland Mo* 85 (N 27) 334-5.
Gray, Donald. "Sterling in Type." *Overland Mo* 85 (N 27) 328, 350.
Hopper, James. "The Martyr." *Overland Mo* 85 (N 27) 335, 347.
Howard, Eric. "Men Around London." *Esquire* 13 (Je 40) 62, 183-6.
Jeffers, Robinson. "A Few Memories." *Overland Mo* 85 (N 27) 329, 351.
Johnson, Merle. "American First Editions: George Sterling (1869-1926)." *Pub W* 119 (18 Ap 31) 2023-4.
Jones, Idwal. "King of Bohemia." *Overland Mo* 85 (N 27) 332-3.
Lee, B. V. "Justice." *Overland Mo* 85 (Mr 27) 74.
Lewis, Austin. "George Sterling at Play." *Overland Mo* 85 (N 27) 344-5.
London, C. K. "As I Knew Him." *Overland Mo* 85 (D 27) 360-1.
——— "George Sterling as I Knew Him." *Overland Mo* 85 (Mr 27) 69-70, 76, 80, 83, 87, 90.
Mencken, H. L. "Sterling." *Overland Mo* 85 (D 27) 363.

O'Day, E. F. "1809-1926." *Overland Mo* 85 (D 27) 357-8, 383.
——— "George Sterling." *San Francisco Water* 7 (Jl 28) 9-12, 13.
Phelan, J. D. "George Sterling." *Overland Mo* 85 (N 27) 343.
Rorty, James. "Living Inseparables." *Overland Mo* 85 (D 27) 366.
Sinclair, Upton. "My Friend George Sterling." *Bkm* 66 (S 27) 30-2; *Overland Mo* 85 (D 27) 365.
Smith, C. A. "George Sterling—An Appreciation." *Overland Mo* 85 (My 27) 79.
Turner, E. "George Sterling." *San Francisco R* 2 (N-D 26) 97-8.

STERLING, JAMES (*fl.* 1718-55). Wroth, L. C. "James Sterling: Poet, Priest, and Prophet of Empire." *PAAS* ns 41 (Ap 31) 25-76.

STEVENS, WALLACE (1879-). Arms, G. A., *et al.* "Stevens' *The Anecdote of the Jar.*" *Expl* 3 (N 44).
Baker, Howard. "Wallace Stevens and Other Poets." *So R* 1 (Au 35) 373-96.
Benét, W. R. "Three Poets and a Few Opinions." *NAR* 243 (Sp 37) 195-201.
Bewley, Marius. "The Poetry of Wallace Stevens." *PR* 16 (S 49) 895-915.
Blackmur, R. P. "Examples of Wallace Stevens." *H&H* 5 (Ja-Mr 32) 223-55.
Blake, Howard. "Thoughts on Modern Poetry." *SR* 43 (Ap-Je 35) 187-96.
Breit, Harvey. "Sanity That Is Magic." *Poetry* 62 (Ap 43) 48-50.
Brinnin, J. M. "Plato, Phoebus and the Man from Hartford." *Voices* 121 (Sp 45) 30-7.
Cunningham, J. V. "The Poetry of Wallace Stevens." *Poetry* 85 (1949) 149-65.
Ferry, D. R. "Stevens' *Sea Surface Full of Clouds.*" *Expl* 6 (Je 48) 56.
Fitzgerald, Robert. "Thoughts Revolved." *Poetry* 51 (D 37) 153-7.
Ford, C. H. "Verlaine in Hartford." *View* 1 (S 40) 1, 6.
Gay, R. M. "Stevens' *Le Monocle de Mon Oncle.*" *Expl* 6 (F 48) 27.
Gregory, Horace. "An Examination of Wallace Stevens in a Time of War." *Accent* 3 (Au 42) 57-61.
Hays, H. R. "Laforgue and Wallace Stevens." *RR* 25 (Jl-S 34) 242-8.
Heringman, Bernard. "Two Worlds and Epiphany." *Bard R* 2 (My 48) 156-9.
——— "Wallace Stevens: The Use of Poetry." *ELH* 16 (D 49) 325-36.
Herzberg, Max, & Stevens, Wallace. "Stevens' *The Emperor of Ice Cream.*" *Expl* 7 (N 48) 18.
Kammer, A. S. "Wallace Stevens & Christopher Morley." *Furioso* 3 (Wi 48) 50-8.
Kirby, J. B. "Stevens' *Anecdote of the Jar.*" *Expl* 1 (N 44) 16.
Laros, Fred. "Wallace Stevens Today." *Bard R* 2 (Sp 47) 8-15.
Lash, Kenneth, & Thackaberry, Robert. "Stevens' *The Emperor of Ice Cream.*" *Expl* 6 (Ap 48) 36.
Lowell, Robert. "Imagination and Reality." *Nation* 166 (5 Sp 47) 400-2.
Martz, L. L. "Wallace Stevens: The Romance of the Precise." *Yale Poetry R* 2 (Ag 46) 13-20.
Monroe, Harriet. "A Cavalier of Beauty." *Poetry* 23 (Mr 24) 322-7.
——— "He Plays to the Present." *Poetry* 47 (D 35) 153-7.
Moore, Marianne. "Unanimity and Fortitude." *Poetry* 49 (F 37) 268-72.
Munson, G. B. "The Dandyism of Wallace Stevens." *Dial* 79 (N 25) 413-7.
O'Connor, W. V. "The Politics of a Poet." *Perspective* 1 (Su 48) 206-9.
——— "Tension and Structure in Poetry." *SR* 51 (Au 43) 557-60.
——— "Wallace Stevens and Imagined Reality." *WR* 12 (Sp 48) 156-63.
——— "Wallace Stevens on 'The Poems of Our Climate.'" *UKCR* 15 (Wi 48) 105-10.
Pauker, John. "A Discussion of 'Sea Surface Full of Clouds.'" *Furioso* 5 (Fl 50) 34-46.
Powys, Llewellyn. "The Thirteenth Way." *Dial* 77 (Jl 24) 45-50.
Seiffert, M. A. "The Intellectual Tropics." *Poetry* 23 (D 23) 154-60.
Simons, Hi. "The Comedian as the Letter C: Its Sense and Its Significance." *So R* 5 (Wi 40) 453-68.

——— "The Genre of Wallace Stevens." *SR* 53 (Au 45) 566-79.
——— "The Humanism of Wallace Stevens." *Poetry* 61 (N 42) 448-52.
——— "Wallace Stevens and Mallarmé." *MP* 43 (My 46) 235-59.
Stocking, F. H. "Stevens' *Bantams in Pine-Woods*." *Expl* 3 (Ap 45).
——— "Stevens' *The Comedian of the Letter C*." *Expl* 3 (Mr 45) 43.
——— "Stevens' *The Ordinary Woman*." *Expl* 4 (O 45) 4.
——— "Stevens' *Peter Quince at the Clavier*." *Expl* 5 (My 47) 47.
Symons, Julian. "A Short View of Wallace Stevens." *Life & Letters Today* 26 (S 40) 215-24.
Sypher, Wylie. "Connoisseur in Chaos: Wallace Stevens." *PR* 13 (Wi 46) 83-94.
Tate, Allen, *et al.* "The Wallace Stevens Number." *Harvard Advocate* 127 (D 40).
Tejera, V. "Wallace Stevens' *Transport to Summer*." *J Phil* 45 (26 F 48) 137-9.
Vance, Will. "Wallace Stevens: Man Off the Street." *SRL* 29 (23 Mr 46) 8.
Viereck, Peter. "Some Notes on Wallace Stevens." *Contemp Poetry* 7 (Wi 48) 14-5.
Weiss, T. "The Nonsense of Winters' Anatomy." *Quar R Lit* 1 (Sp 44) 212-34.
Zabel, M. D. "The Harmonium of Wallace Stevens." *Poetry* 39 (D 31) 148-54.

STICKNEY, TRUMBULL (1874-1904). Blackmur, R. P. "Stickney's Poetry." *Poetry* 42 (Je 33) 158-63.
Moody, W. V. "The Poems of Trumbull Stickney." *NAR* 183 (16 N 06) 1005-18.

STILES, EZRA (1727-95). Clark, C. H. "The 18th Century Diary of Ezra Stiles." *NAR* 208 (S 18) 410-22.
Parsons, Francis. "Ezra Stiles of Yale." *NEQ* 9 (Je 36) 286-316.

STILL, JAMES (1906-). Cobb, Ann. "A Note on James Still." *Mountain Life & Work* 12 (Ap 36) 28.
Kohler, Dayton. "Jesse Stuart and James Still, Mountain Regionalists." *CE* 3 (Mr 42) 523-33.

STOCKTON, AUNIS BOUDINOT (*fl.* 1750-80). Butterfield, L. H. "Aunis and the General: Mrs. Stockton's Poetic Eulogies of George Washington." *PULC* 7 (N 45) 19-39.
——— "Morven: A Colonial Outpost of Sensibility, with Some Hitherto Unpublished Poems by Aunis Boudinot Stockton." *PULC* 6 (N 44) 1-15.

STOCKTON, FRANK R. (1834-1902). Bowen, E. W. "The Fiction of Frank R. Stockton." *SR* 18 (Jl 20) 452-62.
——— "Frank R. Stockton." *SR* 11 (O 03) 474-8.
Howells, W. D. "Mr. Stockton and All His Works." *Book Buyer* 20 (F 00) 19-21.
——— "Stockton's Novels and Stories." *Atl* 87 (Ja 01) 136-8.
Mabie, H. W. "Frank R. Stockton." *Book Buyer* 22 (Je 02) 355-6.
Pforzheimer, W. L. "The Lady, the Tiger, and the Author." *Colophon* ns 1 (Au 35) 261-70.
Werner, W. L. "The Escapes of Frank Stockton." *Essays in Honor of A. Howry Espenshade* (1937) 21-45.

STODDARD, CHARLES WARREN (1843-1909). Bland, H. M. "Charles Warren Stoddard." *Overland Mo* ns 47 (Ap 06) 374-80.
——— "The Poets of the Overland." *Overland Mo* 85 (Jl 27) 199-200, 218.
Hubbell, J. B. "George Henry Boker, Paul Hamilton Hayne, and Charles Warren Stoddard: Some Unpublished Letters." *AL* 5 (My 33) 146-65.
O'Neill, Francis. "Stoddard, Psalmist of the South Seas." *Cath World* 105 (Jl 17) 651-62.

STODDARD, RICHARD HENRY (1825-1903). Fenn, W. P. "Richard Henry Stoddard's Chinese Poems." *AL* 11 (Ja 40) 417-38.
Gilder, J. B. "Mr. Stoddard at Seventy-Five." *Critic* 37 (S 00) 215.

Hitchcock, Ripley. "Richard Henry Stoddard: Some Personal Notes." *Lamp* 26 (Je 03) 403-9.
Howells, W. D. "Editor's Easy Chair." *Harper's* 108 (Ja 04) 478-81.
Northup, C. S. "Recollections of a Notable Literary Life." *Dial* 35 (1 N 03) 299-301.
Shaw, Harry, Jr. "Paul Hamilton Hayne to Richard Henry Stoddard, July 1, 1866." *AL* 4 (My 32) 195-9.
Shipman, Carolyn. "A Poet's Library." *Critic* 42 (Ap 03) 315-23.

STODDARD, SOLOMON (1643-1729). Miller, Perry. "Solomon Stoddard." *Harvard Theol R* 34 (O 41) 277-320.

STOWE, HARRIET BEECHER (1811-96). Anon. "Last Days for Uncle Tom." *N Y Times Mag* (80) (12 Jl 31) 18.
——— "Part of a Letter, dated March, 1870, to Edward Everett Hale." *Autograph Album* 1 (D 33) 104.
——— "'Uncle Tom' in Russia." *Lit Dig* 114 (2 Jl 32) 16.
——— "'Uncle Tom's' Effect on a Contemporary Reporter." *Ill State Hist J* 41 (S 48) 305.
Ames, E. W. "First Presentation of Uncle Tom's Cabin." *Americana* (N 11).
Beeton, M. M. "Mr. Beeton and 'Uncle Tom.'" *TLS* (4 Jl 42) 331.
Bellows, S. B. "Paging Sam Lawson." *Chri Sci Mon* 35 (11 Ag 43) 8.
Boynton, P. H. "The Novel of Puritan Decay: From Mrs. Stowe to John Marquand." *NEQ* 13 (D 40) 626-37.
Burns, Wayne, & Sutcliffe, E. G. "*Uncle Tom* and Charles Reade." *AL* 18 (Ja 46) 334-47.
Eaton, G. D. "Harriet Beecher Stowe." *Am Merc* 10 (Ap 27) 449-59.
Fleming, B. J. "Harriet Beecher Stowe, Militant Dreamer." *Negro Hist Bul* 6 (Je 43) 195-6.
Foster, C. H. "The Genesis of Harriet Beecher Stowe's *The Minister's Wooing*." *NEQ* 21 (D 48) 493-517.
Garwood, H. P. "Mr. Beeton and 'Uncle Tom.'" *TLS* (16 My 42) 250.
Jerrold, Walter. "The Author of 'Uncle Tom': Some Centenary Notes." *Bkm* (London) 40 (S 11) 241-5.
Johnson, Merle. "American First Editions: Harriet (Elizabeth) Beecher Stowe, 1811-1896." *Pub W* 120 (16 Ap 32) 1738-9.
Howe, J. W. "Harriet Beecher Stowe." *Reader* 5 (Mr 05) 613-7.
Klingberg, F. J. "Harriet Beecher Stowe and Social Reform in England." *AHR* 43 (Ap 38) 542-52.
Lee, Wallace, *et al.* "Is *Uncle Tom's Cabin* Anti-Negro?" *Negro Digest* (Ja 46) 68-72.
McDowell, Tremaine. "The Use of Negro Dialect by Harriet Beecher Stowe." *AS* 6 (Je 31) 322-6.
Mackay, C. D'A. "The Harriet Beecher Stowe Centenary." *N E Mag* ns 44 (Je 11) 345-60.
Maurice, A. B. "Famous Novels and Their Contemporary Critics." *Bkm* 16 (Mr 03) 23-30.
Maxfield, E. K. "'Goody Goody' Literature and Mrs. Stowe." *AS* 4 (F 29) 189-202.
Pierson, Ralph. "A Few Library Highlights of 1850-52." *Am Book Coll* 2 (Ag-S 32) 156-60.
Pilcher, Velona. "The Variorum Stowe." *Theatre Arts* 10 (Ap 26) 226-39.
Pruette, L. "Harriet Beecher Stowe and the Universal Backdrop." *Bkm* 64 (S 26) 18-23.
Purcell, J. M. "Mrs. Stowe's Vocabulary." *AS* 13 (O 38) 230-1.
Randall, D. A., & Winterich, J. T. "One Hundred Good Novels: Stowe, Harriet Beecher: Uncle Tom's Cabin." *Pub W* 137 (18 My 40) 1931-2.

Rogers, J. M. "Uncle Tom's Cabin in Kentucky." *Era* 10 (S 02) 262-8.
Sanborn, F. B. "Mrs. Stowe and Her Uncle Tom." *Bibliotheca Sacra* 68 (O 11) 674-83.
Scheffler, Herbert. "Bücher die Welt bewegten." *Die Literatur* 41 (Ag 39) 663-5.
Seiler, Grace. "Harriet Beecher Stowe." *CE* 11 (D 49) 127-37.
Stowe, C. E. "Harriet Beecher Stowe: Friend of the South." *Outlook* 98 (10 Je 11) 300-3.
Talbot, William. "Uncle Tom's Cabin; First English Editions." *Am Book Coll* 3 (My-Je 33) 292-7.
Ward, Aileen. "In Memory of 'Uncle Tom.'" *Dalhousie R* 20 (O 40) 235-8.
Weed, G. L. "The True Story of Eliza." *Independent* 55 (17 S 03) 2224-6.

STRACHEY, WILLIAM (*fl.* 1606-18). Cawley, R. R. "Shakspere's Use of the Voyagers in *The Tempest.*" *PMLA* 41 (S 26) 688-726.
Sanders, C. R. "William Strachey, the Virginia Colony and Shakespeare." *VMHB* 57 (Ap 49) 115-32.

STRANGE, ROBERT (1796-1854). Walser, Richard. "Senator Strange's Indian Novel." *N C Hist R* 26 (Ja 49) 2-27.

STREET, JAMES (1903-). Leisure, Harold. "James Street: Literary Handyman." *SLM* 4 (Jl 42) 325-6.
Parker, W. C. "The Path of Street." *Holland's Mag* 68 (Mr 49) 7, 13.

STRIBLING, T. S. (1881-). Bates, E. S. "Thomas Sigismund Stribling." *EJ* 24 (F 35) 91-100.
Dickens, Byrom. "T. S. Stribling and the South." *SR* 42 (Jl-S 34) 341-9.
Jarrett, T. D. "Stribling's Novels." *Phylon* 4 (O-D 43) 345-50.
LeBreton, Maurice. "L'Evolution sociale dans les états du sud d'après T. S. Stribling." *Etudes Anglaises* 1 (Ja 37) 36-52.
Stone, Frank. "American First Editions: T(homas) S(igismund) Stribling 1881- ." *Pub W* 132 (21 Ag 37) 592.
Warren, R. P. "T. S. Stribling: A Paragraph in the History of Critical Realism." *Am R* 2 (F 34) 463-86.
Wilson, J. S. "Poor White and Negro." *VQR* 8 (O 32) 621-4.

STUART, JESSE (1905-). Kohler, Dayton. "Jesse Stuart and James Still, Mountain Regionalists." *CE* 3 (Mr 42) 523-33.
Salmon, Charlotte. "Jesse Stuart." *Sw R* 21 (Ja 36) 163-8.
Shelburne, Marguerite. "Jesse Stuart, Young Man of the Mountains." *Holland's Mag* 66 (D 47) 8-9.
Sturgill, V. L. "Genius of W-Hollow." *SLM* 2 (Mr 40) 155-8.

STURGIS, HOWARD OVERING (1855-1920). Jamieson, John. "An Edwardian Satirist." *Chimera* 4 (Wi 46) 49-54.

SUCKOW, RUTH (1892-). Baker, J. E. "Regionalism in the Middle West." *Am R* 4 (Mr 35) 603-14.
Dodd, L. W. "A Test Case." *SRL* 3 (27 N 26) 330-1.
Frederick, J. T. "Ruth Suckow and the Middle Western Literary Movement." *EJ* (col ed) 20 (Ja 31) 1-8.

TABB, JOHN B. (1845-1909). Anon. "John Banister Tabb: Priest and Poet." *TLS* (24 Mr 45) 138.
——— "Poems of John B. Tabb." *Living Age* 204 (9 N 07) 372-5.
——— "Poet and Priest." *Outlook* 93 (11 D 09) 807-8.
——— "The Tabbalbum and a Literary Friendship." *Ex Libris* 3 (Mr 43) 2.
Barry, J. J. "Father Tabb." *Cath Educ R* 42 (Mr 44) 149-55.
——— "Father Tabb (1845-1909)." *Irish Mo* 73 (Ap 45) 141-7.

Bregy, K. "Of Father Tabb." *Cath World* 114 (D 21) 308-18.
Clements, Cyril. "John Banister Tabb." *Cath Dig* 11 (O 47) 99-101; *Servite* 39 (Ag 47) 43-7.
Connor, D. J. "Father Tabb's Poetical References." *Cath World* 115 (My 22) 242-8.
Crane, W. O. "Some Tabb Discoveries." *America* 72 (7 O 44) 12.
Goodwin, E. B. "Poet for the Winter Evening." *Cath World* 73 (My 01) 208-16.
Humiliata, Sister Mary. "Religion and Nature in Father Tabb's Poetry." *Cath World* 165 (Jl 47) 330-6.
Jacobi, J. B. "The Large Philosophy in the Little Poems of Father Tabb." *Am Cath Quar R* 40 (Ja 15) 33-47.
Kelly, J. B. "The Poetry of a Priest." *Cath World* 103 (My 16) 228-33.
Kessler, Emile. "Tabb and Wordsworth." *Cath World* 143 (Ag 36) 572-6.
Kincheloe, H. G. "Father Tabb: A Neglected Southern Poet." *Furman Bul* 20 (Ja 38) 46-52.
Litz, F. E. "Father Tabb: Writer of Prose." *Cath World* 160 (Mr 45) 499-507.
Lovett, H. M. "Father Tabb's Memorial: John B. Tabb Memorial Library for Children, Richmond, Virginia." *Commonweal* 14 (20 My 31) 65-6.
Mabbott, T. O. "A New Poem by Father Tabb." *N&Q* 190 (20 Ap 46) 166.
McDevitt, William. "Father Tabb at St. Charles' College." *Cath World* 156 (Ja 43) 412-9.
Mather, F. J. "The Poetry of Father Tabb." *Nation* 89 (2 D 09) 534-6.
Meynell, Alice. "Father Tabb as a Poet." *Cath World* 90 (F 10) 577-82.
O'Brien, J. L. "A Contemporaneous Poet." *Am Cath Quar R* 35 (Ap 10) 355-63.
Reilly, D. "Father Tabb." *Dominicana* 17 (D 32) 261-4.
Starke, Aubrey. "Father John B. Tabb: A Checklist." *Am Book Coll* 6 (Mr 35) 101-4.
——— "Tabbiana." *Colophon* ns 3 (Su 38) 427-34.
Tabb, J. B. "Some Notes on My Life: Written at St. Charles College 1896." *Borromean* 10 (D 36) 25-7.
Washington, B. R. "Father Tabb's Memorial: Reply." *Commonweal* 14 (24 Je 31) 214-5.

TAGGARD, GENEVIEVE (1894-). Field, S. B. "Chiseled Lines." *Poetry* 28 (Jl 26) 221-4.
Knister, Raymond. "Hawaiian Flights." *Poetry* 26 (My 25) 108-9.
North, Jessica. "The Edge of the Sword." *Poetry* 45 (D 34) 168-70.
Wilson, Edmund. "A Poet of the Pacific." *NRp* 61 (12 D 28) 99-100.
Zabel, M. D. "An Early Retrospect." *Poetry* 33 (D 28) 154-6.
Zaturensky, Marya. "Enameled Poems." *Poetry* 22 (Ap 23) 43-5.

TARKINGTON, BOOTH (1869-1946). Anon. "The Personal Booth Tarkington." *Bkm* 43 (Ja 16) 505-10.
Barrett, C. H. "Booth Tarkington." *Outlook* 72 (6 D 02) 817-9.
Bennett, C. D. "Booth Tarkington, 1869-1946: An Appreciation." *Emory Un Q* 2 (O 46) 161-9.
Boynton, P. H. "Booth Tarkington." *EJ* 12 (F 23) 117-25.
Brownell, G. H. "Booth Tarkington." *Twainian* 5 (My-Je 46) 5.
Clark, B. H. "Booth Tarkington, Dramatist." *Outlook* 132 (4 O 22) 202-4.
Collins, Joseph. "The New Mr. Tarkington." *Bkm* 65 (Mr 27) 12-21.
Corbett, E. F. "Tarkington and the Veiled Lady." *Am R* 3 (S-O 25) 601-5.
Currie, Barton. "Hints to Tarkingtonians." *Colophon* 3 (F 32) Pt 9.
Dennis, A. W. "Getting Booth Tarkington Educated." *World's Work* 59 (Ja 30) 57-60.
Doubleday, Russell. "Booth Tarkington of the Midlands." *Lit Dig Int Book R* 4 (F 24) 224-5.
Eaton, W. P. "Tarkington versus Trotzky." *Freeman* 2 (20 O 20) 137-8.
Garrett, C. H. "Booth Tarkington." *Outlook* 72 (6 D 02) 817-9.

Hall, Gilman. "Tarkington and O. Henry." *Everybody's* 17 (O 07) 567.
Helys, Marc. "Un Romancier régionaliste américain, Booth Tarkington." *Correspondant* 292 (25 Ag 23) 644-62.
Holliday, R. C. "Tarkingtonapolis." *Bkm* 48 (S 18) 84-92.
Kelly, F. C. "When Riley Discovered Tarkington." *Colliers* 71 (10 My 23) 22.
Marshall, Archibald. "The Novelist's Workshop." *YR* ns 11 (Jl 22) 803-24.
Maurice, A. B. "Booth Tarkington." *Bkm* 68 (D 28) 445-8.
——— "Newton Booth Tarkington." *Bkm* 24 (F 07) 605-16.
Roberts, R. E. "Booth Tarkington." *Bkm* 55 (Ja 19) 123-7; *Living Age* 192 (1 Mr 19) 541-5.
Tarkington, Booth. "Young Literary Princeton Fifty Years Ago." *PULC* 7 (N 45) 1-5.
Wyatt, E. F. "Booth Tarkington: The Seven Ages of Man." *NAR* 216 (O 22) 499-512.

TATE, ALLEN (1899-). Anon. "Allen Tate." *Book Buyer* 3 (N 37) 9-10.
Amyx, Clifford. "The Aesthetics of Allen Tate." *WR* 13 (Sp 49) 135-44.
Beatty, R. C. "Allen Tate as Man of Letters." *SAQ* 47 (Ap 48) 226-41.
Brooks, Cleanth, & Van Doren, Mark. "Modern Poetry: A Symposium." *Am R* 8 (F 37) 427-56.
Burke, Kenneth. "Tentative Proposal." *Poetry* 50 (My 37) 96-100.
Cater, Catherine. "Four Voices Out of the South." *Mich Alumnus Q* (Wi 44) 166-73.
Dupee, F. W. "Frost and Tate." *Nation* 160 (21 Ap 45) 464.
Flint, F. C. "Poems, 1928-1931." *Symposium* 3 (Jl 32) 407-14.
Glicksberg, C. I. "Allen Tate and the Mother Earth." *SR* 45 (Jl-S 37) 284-95.
Horrell, Joe. "Some Notes on Conversion in Poetry." *So R* 7 (Su 41) 119-22.
Knickerbocker, W. S. "The Return of a Native." *SR* 38 (O-D 30) 479-83.
Koch, Vivienne. "The Poetry of Allen Tate." *KR* 11 (Su 49) 355-78.
Mason, A. H. "Tate's *Again the Native Hour*." *Expl* 7 (D 48) 23.
Mizener, Arthur. "'The Fathers' and Realistic Fiction." *Accent* 7 (Wi 47) 101-9.
Monk, S. H. "Tate's *Again the Hour*." *Expl* 6 (Je 48) 58.
Morgan, Frederick. "Recent Poetry." *Hudson R* 1 (Su 48) 263-4.
Morse, S. T. "Second Reading." *Poetry* 51 (F 38) 262-6.
Nemerov, Howard. "The Current of the Frozen Stream: An Essay on the Poetry of Allen Tate." *Furioso* 3 (Fl 48) 50-61.
Russell, Peter. "A Note on the Poetry of Allen Tate." *Nine* 2 (My 50) 89-90.
Schwartz, Delmore. "The Poetry of Allen Tate." *So R* 5 (Wi 40) 419-38.
Shafer, Robert. "Humanism and Impudence." *Bkm* 70 (Ja 30) 489-98.
Tate, Allen. "Narcissus as Narcissus." *VQR* 14 (Wi 38) 108-22.
——— "Prefazione inedita e piccola antologia lirica." *Inventario* 1 (Au-Wi 46-7) 69-77.
Thorp, Willard. "Allen Tate: A Checklist." *PULC* 3 (Ap 42) 85-98.
Walcutt, C. C. "Tate's *The Cross*." *Expl* 6 (Ap 48) 41.
Zabel, M. D. "The Creed of Memory." *Poetry* 40 (Ap 32) 34-9.
——— "A Critic's Poetry." *Poetry* 33 (F 29) 281-4.

TAYLOR, BAYARD (1825-78). Armstrong, Ralph. "Bayard Taylor's Romance." *Bkm* 42 (N 15) 270-5.
Beatty, R. C. "Bayard Taylor and George H. Boker." *AL* 6 (N 34) 316-27.
——— "A Mind Divided." *Am R* 3 (Ap 34) 77-95.
——— "Swinburne and Bayard Taylor." *PQ* 13 (Jl 34) 297-9.
Flanagan, J. T. "Bayard Taylor's Minnesota Visit." *Minn Hist* 19 (D 38) 399-418.
Frenz, Horst. "Bayard Taylor and the Reception of Goethe in America." *JEGP* 41 (Ap 42) 125-39.
Glicksberg, C. I. "Walt Whitman and Bayard Taylor." *N&Q* 173 (3 Jl 37) 5-7.
Hubbell, J. B. "A Lanier Manuscript." Duke Un *Lib Notes* 2 (N 37) 2-3.

Krumpelmann, J. T. "The Genesis of Bayard Taylor's Translation of Goethe's *Faust*." *JEGP* 42 (O 43) 551-62.

Lieder, F. W. C. "Bayard Taylor's Adaptation of Schiller's *Don Carlos*." *JEGP* 16 (Ja 17) 27-52.

Mabie, H. W. "Bayard Taylor: Adventurer." *Bkm* 42 (Mr 16) 51-9.

Meeks, L. H. "The Lyceum in the Early West." *Ind Mag Hist* 29 (Je 33) 87-93.

Prahl, A. J. "Bayard Taylor and Goethe." *MLQ* 7 (Je 46) 205-18.

——— "Bayard Taylor in Germany." *GQ* 18 (Ja 45) 16-25.

——— "Bayard Taylor's Letters from Russia." *HLQ* 9 (Ag 46) 411-8.

——— "An Unpublished Letter of Bayard Taylor." *MLN* 61 (Ja 46) 55-7.

Quinby, A. W. "The Spell of a Sylvan Story." *Critic* 41 (Ag 02) 131-7.

Rogers, E. R. "The Poetry of Bayard Taylor—An Appreciation." *SAQ* 3 (O 04) 243-8.

Schultz, J. R. "Features of Colorado Life as Seen by Bayard Taylor." *Colo Mag* 12 (S 35) 161-8.

——— "An Unpublished Poem of Bayard Taylor." *AL* 5 (Ja 34) 367-8.

Stedman, Laura. "Bayard Taylor." *NAR* 201 (Je 15) 904-7.

Taylor, Bayard. "Poe's Last Manuscript." *Am Clipper* 1 (N 34) 64.

Warnock, Robert. "Bayard Taylor's Unpublished Letters to His Sister Annie." *AL* 7 (Mr 35) 47-55.

——— "Unpublished Lectures of Bayard Taylor." *AL* 5 (My 33) 123-32.

TAYLOR, EDWARD (*c.* 1644-1729). Brown, W. C. "Edward Taylor: American 'Metaphysical.'" *AL* 16 (N 44) 186-97.

Giovannini, G. "Taylor's *The Glory of and Grace in the Church Set Out*." *Expl* 6 (F 48) 26.

Johnson, T. H. "The Discovery of Edward Taylor's Poetry." *Colophon* ns 1 (Je 39).

——— "Edward Taylor: A Puritan 'Sacred Poet.'" *NEQ* 10 (Je 37) 290-322.

——— "A Seventeenth-Century Printing of Some Verses of Edward Taylor." *NEQ* 14 (Mr 41) 139-41.

——— "Some Edward Taylor Gleanings." *NEQ* 16 (Je 43) 280-96.

——— "The Topical Verses of Edward Taylor." *PCSM* 34 (1943) 513-54.

Lind, S. E. "Edward Taylor: A Revaluation." *NEQ* 21 (D 48) 518-30.

Macdonald, Allan. "A Sailor Among the Transcendentalists." *NEQ* 8 (S 35) 307-19.

Pearce, R. H. "Edward Taylor: The Poet as Puritan." *NEQ* 23 (Mr 50) 31-46.

Warren, Austin. "Edward Taylor's Poetry: Colonial Baroque." *KR* 3 (Su 41) 355-71.

Weathers, W. T. "Edward Taylor, Hellenistic Puritan." *AL* 18 (Mr 46) 18-26.

Wright, Nathalia. "The Morality Tradition in the Poetry of Edward Taylor." *AL* 18 (Mr 46) 1-17.

TAYLOR, EDWARD ROBESON (1838-1923). Millard Bailey. "The Poet Mayor of San Francisco." *Bkm* 27 (Jl 08) 467-73.

TEASDALE, SARA (1884-1933). Anon. "Sara Teasdale." *NRp* 74 (15 F 33) 6.

——— "Sara Teasdale." *Pub W* 123 (4 F 33) 539.

——— "Sara Teasdale." *Wilson Bul* 5 (S 30) 4.

Aiken, Conrad. "'It Is in Truth a Pretty Toy.'" *Dial* 78 (F 25) 107-14.

Colum, Padriac. "Sara Teasdale's Poems." *NRp* 15 (22 Je 18) 239-41.

Deutsch, Babette. "The Solitary Ironist." *Poetry* 51 (D 37) 148-53.

Fisher, Irene. "Strange Victory: One Woman's Life." *NMQR* 4 (My 34) 123-6.

Monroe, Harriet. "Sara Teasdale." *Poetry* 25 (F 25) 262-8.

——— "Sara Teasdale." *Poetry* 42 (Ap 33) 30-3.

——— "Sara Teasdale's Prize." *Poetry* 12 (Ag 18) 264-9.

Rittenhouse, J. B. "Sara Teasdale." *Bkm* 65 (My 27) 290-4.

Smith, M. C. "American First Editions . . . Sara Teasdale." *Pub W* 102 (5 My 23) 1380.
Untermeyer, Louis. "Sara Teasdale." *SRL* 9 (11 F 33) 426.
Wilkinson, Margaret. "Sara Teasdale's Poems." *Forum* 65 (F 21) 229-35.

THAXTER, CELIA (1835-94). Albee, John. "Memories of Celia Thaxter." *N E Mag* ns 24 (Ap 01) 166-72.
Stubbs, M. W. "Celia Leighton Thaxter 1835-1894." *NEQ* 8 (D 35) 518-33.
Westbrook, P. D. "Celia Thaxter's Controversy with Nature." *NEQ* 20 (D 47) 492-415.

THOMAS, AUGUSTUS (1857-1934). Brooks, Van Wyck. "Augustus Thomas." *World's Work* 18 (5 Ag 09) 11882-5.
Hapgood, Norman. "Augustus Thomas and the Time Spirit." *Harper's W* 58 (22 N 13) 25.
Matthews, Brander. "Augustus Thomas on His Methods." *Art World* 2 (S 17) 510-1.
Nathan, G. J. "In Memoriam." *Am Merc* 8 (My 26) 117-20.

THOMASON, JOHN W. (1893-). Dobie, F. J. "John W. Thomason: An Appreciation." *Sw R* 29 (Su 44) 10.

THOMPSON, DOROTHY (1894-). Dale, Warren. "Off the Record with a Columnist." *SRL* 27 (Je 44) 13-4, 27.

THOMPSON, JOHN R. (1823-73). Graves, C. M. "Thompson the Confederate." *Lamp* 29 (O 04) 181-90.
Jackson, D. K. "Some Unpublished Letters of John R. Thompson and Augustin L. Taveau." *WMQ* 16 (Ap 36) 206-21.

THOMPSON, MAURICE (1844-1901). Kraut, M. K. "Maurice Thompson at Home." *Independent* 53 (21 F 01) 416-8.

THOMPSON, WILLIAM TAPPAN (1812-82). Miller, H. P. "The Background and Significance of *Major Jones's Courtship*." *Ga Hist Q* 30 (D 46) 267-96.

THOMSON, MORTIMER NEAL (1831-75). Kuethe, J. L. "Q. K. Philander Doesticks, P. B., Neologist." *AS* 12 (Ap 37) 111-6.
Lorch, F. W. "'Doesticks' and *Innocents Abroad*." *AL* 20 (Ja 49) 446-9.

THOREAU, HENRY DAVID (1817-62). Anon. "Hawthorne and Thoreau." *T.P.'s Weekly* 6 (22 S 05) 369.
——— "Henry David Thoreau." *Seven Arts* 2 (Jl 17) 383-6.
——— "New England Nature Studies: Thoreau, Burroughs, Whitman." *Edinburgh R* 208 (O 08) 343-66.
——— "Notes and Comment." *NYr* 25 (7 My 49) 23.
——— "Theosophist Unaware." *Theosophy* 32 (My, Je 44) 290-5, 330-4.
——— "Thoreau and Music." *TSB* 18 (Ja 47) 2-3.
——— "Thoreau as a Born Supernaturalist." *Cur Op* 67 (Jl 19) 44.
——— "Thoreau Championed by Emerson's Son." *Cur Op* 63 (S 17) 194-5.
——— "The Thoreau Collection of the Pierpont Morgan Library of New York City." *TSB* 19 (Ap 47) 2.
——— "Thoreau on the Kindley Relations." *Scribner's* 67 (Mr 20) 379.
——— "Thoreau's Cabin Site Marked with Granite at Walden Pond." Boston *Herald* (13 Jl 47).
——— "Thoreau's Early Declaration of Independence for American Literature." *Cur Op* 63 (Jl 17) 47-8.
——— "Thoreau's Plan of a Farm." *TSB* 20 (Jl 47) 2.
——— "Tolstoy's Admiration for Thoreau." N Y *Times* (29 S 28) 6.

——— "Walden Pond—A Century After Thoreau Lived There." *N Y Herald-Tribune* (18 S 48).
——— "Widening Influence of Thoreau." *Cur Lit* 45 (Ag 08) 170-1.
Adams, J. D. "Speaking of Books." *N Y Times Book R* (6 Je 47) 2.
Adams, Raymond. "The Bibliographical History of Thoreau's *A Week on the Concord and Merrimack Rivers.*" *PBSA* 43 (1Q 49) 39-47.
——— "A Bibliographical Note on *Walden.*" *AL* 2 (My 30) 166-8.
——— "'Civil Disobedience' Gets Printed." *TSB* 28 (Jl 49) 1-2.
——— "An Early and Overlooked Defence of Thoreau." *TSB* 32 (Jl 50) 1, 2.
——— "Emerson's House at Walden." *TSB* 24 (Jl 48) 2-6.
——— "An Irishman on Thoreau: A Stillborn View of *Walden.*" *NEQ* 13 (D 40) 697-9.
——— "Thoreau and Immortality." *SP* 26 (Ja 29) 58-66.
——— "Thoreau and the Photographs." *Photo-Era* 46 (My 31) 239-43.
——— "Thoreau at Harvard." *NEQ* 13 (Mr 40) 24-33.
——— "Thoreau at Walden." *Un N C Ext Bul* 34 (N 44) 1-17.
——— "Thoreau Buried Twice." *SRL* 10 (16 S 33) 111.
——— "Thoreau's Burials." *AL* 12 (Mr 40) 105-7.
——— "Thoreau's Diploma." *AL* 17 (My 45) 174-5.
——— "Thoreau's Growth at Walden." *Chri Reg* 124 (Jl 45) 268-70.
——— "Thoreau's Literary Apprenticeship." *SP* 29 (O 32) 617-29.
——— "Thoreau's Science." *Sci Mo* 60 (My 45) 379-82.
——— "Thoreau's Sources for 'Resistance to Civil Government.'" *SP* 42 (Jl 45) 640-53.
Allen, F. H. "English as She Is Edited." *Atl* 113 (Mr 14) 42-5.
——— "Thoreau's Arm: A Correction." *Bul Mass Audubon Soc* 33 (Ja 50) 385.
——— "Thoreau's *Collected Poems.*" *AL* 17 (N 45) 250-67.
——— "Thoreau's Knowledge of Birds." *Nation* 91 (22 S 10) 261.
——— "Thoreau's Translations from Pindar." *TSB* 26 (Ja 49) 3-4.
Allen, M. S., Earle, Osborne, & Egdell, D. P. "Walden and How to Teach It." *CEA News Letter* 9 (D 47) 3-4.
Allison, H. M. "Man and Mountain." *Appalachia* (Je 47) 361-3.
Atkinson, J. B. "Concerning Thoreau's Style." *Freeman* 6 (12 S 22) 8-10.
——— "Thoreau the Radical." *Freeman* 1 (28 Jl 20) 468-9.
Baatz, W. H. "Henry David Thoreau." *Rochester Lib Bul* 5 (Wi 50) 35-9.
Babcock, F. L. "Adventure in Living." *Chri Cent* 62 (28 Mr 45) 395-6.
——— "Thoreau's House." *N Y Herald-Tribune* (4 S 47).
Bailly, A. "Les Grandes figures: Henry David Thoreau (1817-1862)." *L'Unique* (Orleans) 49 (Je-Jl 50); 50 (O 50).
Beardsley, George. "Thoreau as a Humorist." *Dial* 28 (1 Ap 00) 241-3.
Benson, A. B. "Scandinavian Influences in the Writings of Thoreau." *SS* 16 (My, Ag 41) 201-11, 241-56.
Berry, E. G. "Thoreau in Canada." *Dalhousie R* 23 (Ap 43) 68-74.
Birss, J. H. "Thoreau and Thomas Carew." *N&Q* 164 (28 Ja 33) 63.
Bode, Carl. "A New College Manuscript of Thoreau's." *AL* 21 (N 49) 311-20.
——— "Thoreau Finds a House." *SRL* 29 (20 Jl 46) 15.
——— "Thoreau's Last Letter." *NEQ* 19 (Je 46) 244.
Boyd, David. "Thoreau, the Rebel Idealist." *Americana* 30 (Ja, Ap 36) 89-118, 286-323.
Brawner, J. P. "Thoreau as Wit and Humorist." *SAQ* 44 (Ap 45) 170-6.
Brooks, Van Wyck. "Thoreau, Master of Simplicity." *Reader's Dig* 30 (My 37) 25.
Buckell, H. "A Thoreau Pilgrimage." *NAR* 238 (O 34) 376-7.
Buckley, Frank. "Thoreau and the Irish." *NEQ* 13 (S 40) 389-400.
Burnham, P. E., & Collins, Carvel. "Contribution to a Bibliography of Thoreau, 1938-1945." *Bul Bibl* 19 (S-D 46, Ja-Ap 47) 16-8, 37-9.
Burroughs, John. "A Critical Glance into Thoreau." *Atl* 123 (Je 19) 777-86.

Burroughs, Julian. "Burroughs and Thoreau." *TSB* 21 (O 47) 2.
Canby, H. S. "American Challenge: A Study of Walden." *SRL* 20 (2 S 39) 10-2, 16.
——— "Back to Walden." *Cath World* 134 (Ja 32) 478-80.
——— "The Man Who Did What He Wanted." *SRL* 15 (26 D 36) 3-4, 15.
——— "The Modern Thoreau." *Dial* 59 (15 Jl 15) 54-5.
——— "A Self-Appointed Interpreter to Americans." *Chri Sci Mon* 38 (3 D 45) 8.
——— "Thoreau and the Machine Age." *YR* 20 (Mr 31) 517-31.
——— "Thoreau! A New Estimate." *SRL* 22 (3 D 49) 15-6.
——— "Thoreau in History." *SRL* 20 (15 Jl 39) 3-4, 14-5.
——— "Thoreau in Search of a Public." *Am Schol* 8 (Au 39) 431-44.
——— "Thoreau, the Great Eccentric." *SRL* 4 (26 N 27) 337-9.
——— "Two Women." *NAR* 248 (Au 39) 18-32.
Carberg, Warren. "Thoreau Fame Still Expands." Boston *Post* (27 Jl 47).
Carter, G. T. "Thoreau, the Great Transcendentalist." *Lit Coll* 8 (O 04) 169-77; *Hobbies* 54 (Ag 49) 139-42.
Casey, Alfredo. "Tiempo y ambiente de Henry David Thoreau." *La Prensa* (Buenos Aires) (8 Ja 50).
Cestre, Charles. "Thoreau et Emerson." *Revue Anglo-Américaine* 7 (F 30) 215-30.
——— "Thoreau et la dialectique." *Revue Anglo-Américaine* 7 (F 30) 230-3.
Chamberlin, J. E. "Thoreau's Last Pencil." *Mag Hist* 22 (My 16) 173-6.
Christy, Arthur. "A Thoreau Fact-Book." *Colophon* 4 (Mr 34) Pt 16.
Coleman, G. P. "Thoreau and His Critics." *Dial* 40 (1 Je 06) 352-6.
Collins, T. L. "Thoreau's Coming of Age." *SR* 49 (Ja 41) 57-66.
Combellack, C. R. B. "Marx und Thoreau." *Die Amerikanische Rundschau* 28 (D 49) 21-6.
——— "Two Critics of Society." *PS* 3 (Au 49) 440-5.
Cook, R. L. "Thoreau in Perspective." *UKCR* 14 (Wi 47) 117-25.
Cosman, Max. "Apropos of John Thoreau." *AL* 12 (My 40) 241-3.
——— "Thoreau and Nature." *Personalist* 21 (Au 40) 289-93.
——— "Thoreau and Staten Island." *Long Island Hist* 6 (Ja-Mr 43) 1-2, 7-8.
——— "Thoreau Faced War." *Personalist* 25 (Wi 44) 73-6.
——— "A Yankee in Canada." *Canadian Hist R* 20 (Mr 44) 33-7.
Cournas, John. "Gaugin and Thoreau: A Comparison." *Bkm* 67 (Jl 28) 548-51.
——— "Hater of Shams." *Century* 116 (Je 28) 140.
Crosbie, Mary. "The Poet by His Pond." *John O'London's Weekly* 56 (3 O 47) 621.
Crowell, Reid. "Henry Thoreau at Walden Pond." *Classmate* 55 (Ag 48) 3-4.
Dabbs, J. M. "Thoreau—The Adventurer as Economist." *YR* 36 (Su 47) 667-72.
Dale, D. "Natural Mystics." *Am Cath Q* 39 (Ja 14) 167-73.
Davenport, E. B. "Thoreau in Vermont." *Vt Botanical Club Bul* 3 (Ap 08).
Davidson, Frank. "Thoreau's Contribution to Hawthorne's *Mosses*." *NEQ* 20 (D 47) 535-42.
Davies, John. "A Letter from England." *TSB* 21 (O 47) 2-3.
——— "Thoreau and the Ethics of Food." *Vegetarian Messenger* 44 (F 47) 40-1.
DeArmond, Fred. "Thoreau and Schopenhauer: An Imaginary Conversation." *NEQ* 5 (Ja 32) 55-64.
Deevey, E. S. "A Re-Examination of Thoreau's 'Walden.'" *Quar R Biol* 17 (Mr 42) 1-11.
Dewey, John. "John Dewey on Thoreau." *TSB* 30 (Ja 50) 1.
Dunton, E. K. "The Old and New Estimate of Thoreau." *Dial* 33 (16 D 02) 464-6.
Eckstorm, F. H. "The Death of Thoreau's Guide." *Atl* 93 (Je 04) 736-46.
——— "Thoreau's Maine Woods." *Atl* 102 (Jl-Ag 08) 16-18, 242-50.
Emerson, E. W. "Centenary of Henry David Thoreau: 1817-1862." *Bkm* (London) 52 (Je 17) 81-4.

Eulau, Heinz. "Wayside Challenger—Some Remarks on the Politics of Henry David Thoreau." *AR* 9 (Wi 49) 509-22.
Fabulet, Louis. "Henry David Thoreau et l'amitie." *Europe* 6 (1924) 434-9.
Flanagan, J. T. "Thoreau in Minnesota." *Minn Hist* 16 (Mr 35) 35-46.
Fletcher, F. "Henry D. Thoreau, Oriental." *Open Court* 44 (Ag 30) 510-2.
Foerster, Norman. "Humanism of Thoreau." *Nation* 105 (5 Jl 17) 9-12.
——— "The Intellectual Heritage of Thoreau." *Texas R* 2 (Ja 17) 192-212.
——— "Thoreau and 'The Wild.'" *Dial* 63 (28 Je 17) 8-11.
——— "Thoreau as Artist." *SR* 29 (Ja 21) 2-13.
Ford, N. A. "Henry David Thoreau, Abolitionist." *NEQ* 19 (S 46) 359-71.
Francis, R. G. "Thoreau's Mask of Serenity." *Forum* 106 (Ja 47) 72-7.
——— "Two Brothers." *Dalhousie R* 9 (Ap 29) 48-52.
Frost, R. H. "Theo Brown, Friend of Thoreau." *Nature Outlook* 2 (My 44) 15-9.
——— "Thoreau's Worcester Friends." *Nature Outlook* 3 (My 45) 116-8; 4 (N 46) 16-8; 5 (My 47) 4-7, 33.
Gierasch, Walter. "Thoreau and Willa Cather." *TSB* 20 (Jl 47) 4.
Gleason, H. W. "Winter Rambles in Thoreau's Country." *Nat Geo Mag* 37 (F 20) 165-80.
Glick, W. P. "Thoreau and the 'Herald of Freedom.'" *NEQ* 22 (Je 49) 193-204.
Gohdes, Clarence. "Henry Thoreau, Bachelor of Arts." *Classical J* 23 (F 28) 323-36.
Gorley, C. P. "Thoreau and the Land." *Landscape Arch* 24 (Ap 34) 58-9.
Green, M. H. "Raritan Bay Union, Eagleswood, New Jersey." *Proc N J Hist Soc* 68 (Ja 50) 1-20.
Guilford, Kelsey. "The Thoreau Cultists." Chicago *Tribune* (1 D 46).
Guillet, Cephas. "The Thoreau Family." *TSB* 19 (Ap 47) 3.
H., C. C. "Walden Centenary." N Y *Sun* (6 S 47).
Harding, Walter. "Additions to the Thoreau Bibliography." *TSB* 10-33 (45-50) [quarterly].
——— "A Bibliography of Thoreau in Poetry, Fiction, and Drama." *Bul Bibl* 18 (My-Ag 43) 15-8.
——— "A Century of Thoreau." *Audubon Mag* 47 (Mr-Ap 45) 80-4.
——— "A Check List of Thoreau's Lectures." *BNYPL* 70 (F 48) 78-87.
——— "The Correspondence of Sophia Thoreau and Marianne Dunbar." *TSB* 23 (O 50) 1-3.
——— "Gandhi and Thoreau." *TSB* 23 (Ap 48).
——— "In Defense of Thoreau." *Yankee* 11 (Mr 47) 26-7.
——— "The Significance of Thoreau's Walden." *Humanist* 5 (Au 45) 115-21.
——— "Thoreau." *Word* (Glasgow) 8 (O 46) 21.
——— "Thoreau and Horace Greeley." *TSB* 11 (Ap 45).
——— "Thoreau and the Concord Lyceum." *TSB* 30 (Ja 50) 3-4.
——— "Thoreau and the Negro." *Negro Hist Bul* 10 (O 46).
——— "Thoreau: Pioneer of Civil Disobedience." *Fellowship* 12 (Jl 46) 118-9, 131.
——— "Uncle Charlie Comes to Concord." *Nature Outlook* 7 (Fl 48) 7-9.
Harper, G. A. "The Moon and Thoreau." *Nature Study* 18 (N 22) 317-9.
Hausman, L. A. "Thoreau on Monadnock." *TSB* 25 (O 48) 2-3.
Haydon, W. T. "Thoreau: Philosopher, Poet, Naturalist." *Bkm* (London) 52 (Je 17) 84-7; *Living Age* 294 (4 Ag 17) 300-3.
Hayward, Adrian. "The White Pond Tree." *Nature Outlook* 4 (N 45) 29-31.
Henry, F. "Henry David Thoreau and Bronson Alcott: A Study of Relationships." *Teachers Col J* 14 (Jl 43) 126-8.
Hillway, Tyrus. "The Personality of H. D. Thoreau." *CE* 6 (Mr 45) 328-30.
Hinckley, E. B. "Thoreau and Beston: Two Observers of Cape Cod." *NEQ* 4 (Ap 31) 216-29.
Hoeltje, H. H. "Thoreau and the Concord Academy." *NEQ* 21 (Mr 48) 103-9.
——— "Thoreau as Lecturer." *NEQ* 19 (D 46) 485-94.
——— "Thoreau in Concord and Town Records." *NEQ* 12 (Je 39) 349-59.

Hollis, C. C. "Thoreau and the State." *Commonweal* 50 (9 S 49) 530-3.
Holmes, J. H. "Thoreau's Civil Disobedience." *Chri Century* 66 (29 Je 49) 787-9.
Howe, W. D. "Henry David Thoreau." *Reader* 5 (F 05) 372-6.
Hubbell, G. S. "Walden Revisited." *SR* 37 (S 29) 283-94.
Hurd, H. E. "Henry David Thoreau—A Pioneer in the Field of Education." *Educ* 49 (F 29) 372-6.
Hyman, S. T. "Henry Thoreau in Our Time." *Atl* 178 (N 46) 137-46.
Ingersoll, E. "American Naturalists." *Mentor* 7 (15 Je 19) 5-7.
Kalman, David. "A Study of Thoreau." *TSB* 22 (Ja 48) 1-3.
Kaufman, L. R. "Thoreau's Philosophy of Life." *Columbia Lit Mo* 8 (My 00) 241-7.
Keiser, Albert. "New Thoreau Material." *MLN* 44 (Ap 29) 253-4.
——— "Thoreau's Manuscripts on the Indians." *JEGP* 27 (Ap 28) 183-99.
Kennedy, D. E. "Thoreau in Old Dunstable." *Granite State Mag* 4 (D 07) 247-50.
Kilbourne, F. W. "Thoreau and the White Mountains." *Appalachia* 14 (Je 19) 356-67.
Kingsley, M. E. "Outline Study of Thoreau's *Walden*." *Educ* 41 (Mr 21) 452-65.
Krutch, J. W. "A Kind of Pantheism." *SRL* 23 (10 Je 50) 7.
——— "Walden Revisited." *Nation* 136 (3 My 33) 506-7.
Kwiat, J. J. "Thoreau's Philosophical Apprenticeship." *NEQ* 18 (Mr 45) 51-69.
Lafonatine, A. "Henri Thoreau, un Example de la culture Franco-Américaine." *Revue Hebdomadaire* 28 (1 Mr 19) 85-99.
Laughlin, Clara. "Two Famous Bachelors." *Book Buyer* 25 (O 02) 241-7.
Leach, Joseph. "Thoreau's Borrowings in 'Walden.'" *N&Q* 184 (24 Ap 43) 269.
Leighton, Walter. "Henry Thoreau—an Estimate." *Arena* 30 (N 03) 489-98.
Leisy, E. E. "Francis Quarles and Henry D. Thoreau." *MLN* 60 (My 45) 335-6.
——— "Sources of Thoreau's Borrowing in *A Week*." *AL* 18 (Mr 46) 37-44.
——— "Thoreau and Ossian." *NEQ* 18 (Mr 45) 96-8.
——— "Thoreau's Borrowings in 'Walden.'" *AN&Q* 2 (N 42) 121.
Lennon, F. B. "The Voice of the Turtle." *TSB* 15 (Ap 46).
Leviero, H. P. "Walden Pond Preserves Site Thoreau Used as a Sanctuary." *N Y Herald-Tribune* (31 Ag 47).
Lewis, Sinclair. "One Man Revolution." *Newsweek* 10 (20 N 37) 33; *SRL* 17 (11 D 37) 19.
Longstreth, T. M. "An Idyll out of Season." *Chri Sci Mon* 36 (4 Mr 44) 6.
——— "On Thoreau's Coldness." *Chri Sci Mon* 36 (25 Ag 44) 6.
——— "Our Most Famous Hill." *Chri Sci Mon* 35 (5 N 43) 6.
Loomis, Grant. "Thoreau and Zimmermann." *NEQ* 10 (D 37) 789-92.
Lorch, F. W. "Thoreau and the Organic Principle in Poetry." *PMLA* 53 (Mr 38) 286-302.
Ludlow, Robert. "Thoreau and the State." *Commonweal* 50 (23 S 49) 581-2.
Mabie, H. W. "A Theocritus of Cape Cod." *Atl* 110 (Ag 12) 207-15.
——— "Thoreau, a Prophet of Nature." *Outlook* 80 (3 Je 05) 278-82.
McAtee, W. L. "Adaptationist Naivete." *Sci Mo* 48 (Mr 39) 253-5.
McGill, F. T. "Thoreau and College Discipline." *NEQ* 15 (Je 42) 349-53.
Mackaye, Benton. "Thoreau en Ktaadn." *Living Wilderness* 9 (S 44) 3-6.
Madison, C. A. "Henry David Thoreau: Transcendental Individualist." *Ethics* 54 (Ja 44) 110-23.
Mann, Thomas. "Nietzsche in the Light of Modern Experience." *Commentary* 5 (Ja 48) 18.
Manning, Clarence. "Thoreau and Tolstoi." *NEQ* 16 (Je 43) 234-43.
Marble, A. R. "Where Thoreau Worked and Wandered." *Critic* 40 (Je 02) 509-16.
Mathews, J. C. "Thoreau's Reading in Dante." *Italica* 27 (Je 50) 77-81.
Michaud, Regis. "Henry David Thoreau." *Vie des Peuples* 14 (Ag 24) 27-44.
Moore, J. B. "Crèvecoeur and Thoreau." *Papers Mich Acad Sci, Arts & Letters* 5 (1926) 309-33.
——— "Thoreau Rejects Emerson." *AL* 4 (N 32) 241-56.

Mordell, Albert. "Roosevelt and Thoreau." *SRL* 30 (13 S 47) 23.
More, P. E. "A Hermit's Notes on Thoreau." *Atl* 87 (Je 01) 857-64.
——— "Thoreau and German Romanticism." *Nation* 83 (8, 15 N 06) 388-90, 411-2.
Morgan, Charles. "*Walden* and Beyond." London *Times* (8 N 47) 3.
Munson, G. B. "Dionysian in Concord." *Outlook* 149 (29 Ag 28) 690-2.
——— "The Lesson of Thoreau." *Thinker* 3 (Mr 31) 3, 7-20.
Muret, Maurice. "Un poète-naturalist amèricain." *La Revue* 42 (15 Ag, 1 S 02) 428-36, 572-80.
Oliver, E. S. "Melville's Picture of Emerson and Thoreau in *The Confidence Man.*" *CE* 8 (N 46) 61-72.
——— "A Second Look at 'Bartleby.'" *CE* 6 (My 45) 431-9.
Paul, Sherman. "The Wise Silence: Sound as the Agency of Correspondence in Thoreau." *NEQ* 22 (D 49) 511-27.
Peairs, Edith. "The Hound, the Bay Horse, and the Turtle-Dove: A Study of Thoreau and Voltaire." *PMLA* 52 (S 37) 863-9.
Peattie, D. C. "Is Thoreau a Modern?" *NAR* 245 (Sp 38) 159-69.
Perry, J. B. "Was Thoreau a Lover of Nature?" *Critic* 42 (Ag 03) 152.
Powys, Llewellyn. "Thoreau: A Disparagement." *Bkm* 69 (Ap 29) 163-5.
Pritchard, J. P. "Cato in Concord." *Classical W* 36 (5 O 42) 3-4.
Ramsay, C. T. "Pilgrimage to the Haunts of Thoreau." *N E Mag* ns 50 (N, D 13) 371-83, 434-42; 52 (Ap 14) 67-71.
Raysor, T. M. "The Love Story of Thoreau." *SP* 23 (O 26) 457-63.
Russell, E. H. "A Bit of Unpublished Correspondence between Henry Thoreau and Isaac Hecker." *Atl* 90 (S 02) 370-6.
——— "Thoreau's Maternal Grandfather." *PAAS* 19 (1909) 66-76.
Russell, J. A. "Thoreau: The Interpreter of the Real Indian." *QQ* 35 (Ag 27) 37-48.
Salt, H. S. "Gandhi and Thoreau." *Nation & Athenaeum* 46 (1 Mr 30) 728.
——— "Henry David Thoreau and the Humane Study of Natural History." *Humane R* (O 03) 220-9.
——— "Thoreau and Gilbert White." *New Age* (15 N 00).
——— "Thoreau and Jeffries." *Nature Notes* 11 (F 00) 22-3.
Sanborn, F. B. "Thoreau and Confucius." *Nation* 90 (12 My 10) 481.
——— "Thoreau and Ellery Channing." *Critic* 47 (N 05) 444-51.
——— "Thoreau in His Journals." *Dial* 42 (16 F 07) 107-11.
——— "Thoreau in Twenty Volumes." *Dial* 41 (16 O 06) 232-4.
Sanchez, L. B. "Henry David Thoreau." *Revista Iberoamericana* 6 (F 43) 95-102.
Schultz, Howard. "A Fragment of Jacobean Song in Thoreau's *Walden.*" *MLN* 63 (Ap 48) 271-2.
Schuster, E. M. "Native American Anarchism." *Smith Col Stud Hist* 17 (O 31, Jl 32) 5-202.
Shepard, Odell. "Paradox of Thoreau." *Scribner's* 68 (S 20) 335-42.
——— "Thoreau and Columella: A Comment." *NEQ* 11 (S 38) 605-6.
Smith, F. M. "Thoreau." *Critic* 37 (Jl 00) 60-7.
Southworth, J. G. "Thoreau, Moralist of the Picturesque." *PMLA* 49 (S 34) 971-4.
Sterne, M. B. "Approaches to Biography." *SAQ* 45 (Jl 46) 362-71.
Stewart, C. D. "A Word for Thoreau." *Atl* 156 (Jl 35) 110-6.
Stewart, Randall. "The Concord Group." *SR* 44 (O-D 36) 434-46.
——— "The Growth of Thoreau's Reputation." *CE* 7 (Ja 46) 208-14.
Straker, R. L. "Thoreau's Journey to Minnesota." *NEQ* 14 (S 41) 549-55.
Stromberg, R. N. "Thoreau and Marx: A Century After." *Social Stud* 40 (F 49) 53-6.
Swanson, E. B. "The Manuscript-Journal of Thoreau's *Last Journey.*" *Minn Hist* 20 (Je 39) 169-73.
Teale, E. W. "Thoreau's Walden." *Life* 23 (22 S 47) 70-1, 73.

Templeman, W. D. "Thoreau, Moralist of the Picturesque." *PMLA* 47 (S 32) 864-89.
Thomas, W. S. "Marti and Thoreau: Pioneers of Personal Freedom." *Dos Pueblos* (Havana) (Ag 49) 1-3.
——— "Thoreau as His Own Editor." *NEQ* 15 (Mr 42) 101-3.
Tomlinson, H. M. "Two Americans and a Whale." *Harper's* 152 (Ap 26) 618-21.
Torrey, Bradford. "Thoreau as a Diarist." *Atl* 95 (Ja 05) 5-18.
Utley, F. L. "Thoreau and Columella: A Study in Reading Habits." *NEQ* 11 (Mr 38) 171-80.
Vivas, Eliseo. "Thoreau: The Paradox of Youth." *New Student* 7 (1928) 5-8, 15.
Wade, J. S. "A Contribution to a Bibliography from 1909-1936 of Henry David Thoreau." *J N Y Entomological Soc* 47 (Je 39) 163-203.
——— "Friendship of Two Old-Time Naturalists." *Sci Mo* 23 (Ag 26) 152-60.
——— "Henry Thoreau and His Journals." *Nature Mag* 16 (Jl 27) 153-4.
Walcutt, C. C. "Thoreau in the Twentieth Century." *SAQ* 39 (Ap 40) 168-84.
Walker, Roy. "The Natural Life: An Essay on Thoreau." *Vegetarian News* (London) 26 (Sp 48) 3-8.
Wallis, C. L. "Gandhi's Source Book." *Chri Reg* 128 (S 49) 31-2.
Walters, J. C. "Henry David Thoreau." *Manchester Q* 145 (Ja 18) 25-43.
Warren, Austin. "Lowell, on Thoreau." *SP* 27 (Jl 30) 442-62.
Watson, Ella. "Thoreau Visits Plymouth." *TSB* 21 (O 47) 1.
Weiss, John. "Weiss on Thoreau." *TSB* 21 (O 47) 3.
Wells, H. W. "An Evaluation of Thoreau's Poetry." *AL* 16 (My 44) 99-109.
West, H. F. "Values in Thoreau." *TSB* 20 (Jl 47) 1.
Wheeler, J. A. "Duty of Civil Disobedience." *Money* 14 (Je 49) 4.
Wheeler, Mrs. Caleb. "The Thoreau Houses." *TSB* 31 (Ap 50).
Whitcomb, Robert. "The Thoreau 'Country.'" *Bkm* 73 (Jl 31) 458-61.
White, E. B. "One Man's Meat." *Harper's* 179 (Ag 39) 329-32.
White, F. "Thoreau's Observations on Fogs, Clouds and Rain." *Nature Study* 17 (O 21) 296-8.
White, V. C. "Thoreau's Opinion of Whitman." *NEQ* 8 (Je 35) 262-4.
White, William. "A Henry David Thoreau Bibliography, 1908-1937." *Bul Bibl* 16 (Ja-Ap, My-Ag, S-D 38; Ja-Ap, My-Ag, S-D 39) 90-2, 111-3, 131-2, 163, 181-2, 199-202.
Whitford, K. "Thoreau and the Woodlots of Concord." *NEQ* 23 (S 50) 291-306.
Winterich, J. T. "Romantic Stories . . . *Walden*." *Pub W* 116 (21 S 29) 1363-8.
Wood, J. P. "English and American Criticism of Thoreau." *NEQ* 6 (D 33) 733-46.
——— "Mr Thoreau Writes a Book." *New Colophon* 1 (O 48) 367-76.
Wyllie, E. M. "Thoreau Trails." *Holiday* 4 (S 48) 105-14.

THORPE, THOMAS BANGS (1815-78). Blair, Walter. "The Technique of the Big Bear of Arkansas." *SW R* 28 (Su 43) 426-35.

THURBER, JAMES (1894-). Anon. "James Thurber: The Comic Prufrock." *Poetry* 63 (D 43) 150-9.
Downing, Francis. "Thurber." *Commonweal* 41 (9 Mr 45) 518-9.
Follmer, H. D. "Thurberism." *Mark Twain Q* 8 (Wi-Sp 49) 14-5.
Goldwyn, Samuel, & Thurber, James. "Goldwyn vs. Thurber: Producer and Author Dispute Over 'Walter Mitty.'" *Life* 23 (18 Ag 47) 19-20.

TICKNOR, GEORGE (1791-1871). Cuthbertson, Stuart. "George Ticknor's Interest in Spanish-American Literature." *Hispania* 16 (My 33) 117-26.
Doyle, H. G. "George Ticknor." *MLJ* 22 (O 37) 3-37.
Ford, J. D. M. "George Ticknor." *Hispania* 32 (N 49) 423-5.
Guillén, Jorge. "George Ticknor, Lover of Culture." *More Books* 17 (O 42) 359-75.
Hespelt, E. H. "Ticknor's First Book from Argentina." *Hispania* 32 (N 49) 433-5.

Waxman, S. M. "George Ticknor, a Pioneer Teacher of Modern Languages." *Hispania* 32 (N 49) 426-32.
Whittem, A. F. "An Unpublished Letter in French by George Ticknor." *PMLA* 48 (Mr 33) 164-6.
Zeydel, E. H. "George Ticknor and Ludwig Tieck." *PMLA* 44 (S 29) 892-901.

TIETJENS, EUNICE (1884-1944). North, J. N. "Eunice Tietjens: A Memorial." *Poetry* 65 (N 44) 104-8.
Sutcliffe, Denham. "New Light on the Chicago Writers." *Newberry Lib Bul* 5 ser 2 (D 50) 146-57.

TIMROD, HENRY (1828-67). Axson, Stockton. "A Southern Poet: Henry Timrod." *Chautauquan* 30 (Mr 00) 573-6.
Bowen, R A. "Henry Timrod's Poetry." *Book Buyer* 22 (Je 01) 385-7.
Cardwell, G. A., Jr. "The Date of Henry Timrod's Birth." *AL* 7 (My 35) 207-8.
——— "William Henry Timrod, the Charleston Volunteers, and the Defense of St. Augustine." *N C Hist R* 18 (Ja 41) 27-37.
Fidler, William. "Henry Timrod: Poet of the Confederacy." *SLM* 2 (O 40) 527-32.
——— "Seven Unpublished Letters of Henry Timrod." *Ala R* 2 (Ap 49) 139-49.
——— "Unpublished Letters of Henry Timrod." *SLM* 2 (O, N, D 40) 532-5, 605-11, 645-51.
Mabbott, T. O. "Some Letters of Henry Timrod." *Am Col* 3 (F 27) 191-5.
Parks, E. W. "Timrod's College Days." *AL* 8 (N 36) 294-6.
——— "Timrod's Concept of Dreams." *SAQ* 48 (O 49) 584-8.
Patton, Lewis. "An Unpublished Poem by Henry Timrod." *AL* 10 (My 38) 222-3.
Routh, J. E., Jr. "The Poetry of Henry Timrod." *SAQ* 9 (Jl 10) 267-74.
——— "Some Fugitive Poems of Timrod." *SAQ* 2 (Ja 03) 74-7.
——— "An Unpublished Poem of Timrod." *SAQ* 7 (Ap 08) 177-9.
Seigler, M. B. "Henry Timrod and Sophie Sosnowski." *Ga Hist Q* 31 (S 47) 172-80.
Taylor, Rupert. "Henry Timrod's Ancestress, Hannah Caesar." *AL* 9 (Ja 38) 419-30.
Voigt, G. P. "New Light on Timrod's 'Memorial Ode.'" *AL* 4 (Ja 33) 395-6.
——— "Timrod in the Light of Newly Revealed Letters." *SAQ* 37 (Jl 38) 263-9.
——— "Timrod's Essays in Literary Criticism." *AL* 6 (My 34) 163-7.

TIPPMANN, HUGO KARL (1875-). Posselt, Erich. "The Story of an American Poet." *AGR* 17 (O 50) 25-6.

TORRENCE, RIDGELY (1875-). Newdick, R. S. "Ridgely Torrence '97." *Princeton Alumni W* 36 (3 Ap 36) 569-70.
Sinclair, May. "Three American Poets of Today." *Atl* 98 (S 06) 325-35; *Fortnightly R* 86 (1 S 06) 330-3.

TORREY, BRADFORD (1843-1912). Badger, Kingsbury. "Bradford Torrey: New England Nature Writer." *NEQ* 18 (Je 45) 234-46.
Wright, B. "Bradford Torrey." *More Books* 23 (D 48) 363-71.

TOURGÉE, ALBION WINEGAR (1838-1905). Becker, G. J. "Albion W.Tourgée: Pioneer in Social Criticism." *AL* 19 (Mr 47) 59-72.
Nye, R. B. "Judge Tourgée and Reconstruction." *Ohio State Arch & Hist Q* 50 (Ap 41) 101-14.

TRENT, WILLIAM PETERFIELD (1862-1939). Henneman, J. B. "Two Younger Poets." *SR* 10 (Ja 02) 68-79.
Knickerbocker, W. S. "Trent at Sewanee." *SR* 48 (Ap 40) 145-52.

TRILLING, LIONEL (1905-). Lewis, R. W. B. "Lionel Trilling and the New Stoicism." *Hudson R* 3 (Su 50) 313-20.

TRINE, RALPH WALDO (1866-). Anon. "'In Tune with the Infinite,' Famous Best Seller, Now 50 Years Old." *Pub W* 151 (22 F 47) 1251-2.

TROWBRIDGE, J. T. (1827-1916). Coleman, R. A. "Trowbridge and Clemens." *MLQ* 9 (Je 48) 216-23.
——— "Trowbridge and Shillaber." *NEQ* 20 (Je 47) 232-46.
——— "Trowbridge and Whitman." *PMLA* 63 (Mr 48) 262-73.
Howells, W. D. "Editor's Easy Chair." *Harper's* 108 (F 04) 481-2.

TRUMBULL, JOHN (1750-1831). Anon. Part of a letter of John Trumbull, dated April 4, 1820. *Autograph Album* 1 (D 33) 108-9.
Byington, S. T. "Mr. Byington's Brief Case (IV)." *AS* 21 (F 46) 37-44.
Cogan, C. I. "John Trumbull, Satirist." *Colonnade* 14 (1919-22) 83-4.
Conley, K. A. "A Letter of John Trumbull." *NEQ* 11 (Je 38) 372-4.
Cowie, Alexander. "John Trumbull as a Critic of Poetry." *NEQ* 11 (D 38) 773-93.
——— "John Trumbull as Revolutionist." *AL* 3 (N 31) 287-95.
——— "John Trumbull Glances at Fiction." *AL* 12 (Mr 40) 69-75.
Grey, Lennox. "John Adams and John Trumbull in the 'Boston Cycle.'" *NEQ* 4 (Jl 31) 509-14.
Leisy, E. E. "John Trumbull's Indebtedness to Thomas Warton." " *MLN* 36 (My 21) 313-4.
Starr, H. W. "A Note on Gray and Trumbull." *N&Q* 162 (14 Je 47) 254-5.
——— "Trumbull and Gray's 'Bard.'" *MLN* 62 (F 47) 116-9.
Turner, L. D. "John Trumbull's 'The Correspondent,' No. 8." *J Negro Hist* 14 (O 29) 493-5.
Vail, R. W. G. "Report of the Librarian: John Trumbull Checklist." *PAAS* 44 (O 34) 231-3.

TUCKER, BENJAMIN R. (1854-1939). Madison, C. A. "Benjamin R. Tucker: Individualist and Anarchist." *NEQ* 16 (S 43) 444-67.

TUCKER, GEORGE (1775-1861). Helderman, L. C. "A Satirist in Old Virginia." *Am Schol* 6 (Au 37) 481-97.
——— "A Social Scientist of the Old South." *J So Hist* 2 (My 36) 148-74.
Spengler, J. J. "Population Theory in the Ante-Bellum South." *J So Hist* 2 (Ag 36) 360-89.

TUCKER, NATHANIEL (1750-1897). Clark, J. C. "The First English Translator of 'Divine Providence.'" *New Church R* 10 (1903) 237-42.
Leary, Lewis. "Introducing Nathaniel Tucker." *Bermuda Hist Q* 4 (Ag-S 47) 132-5.
——— "The Published Writings of Nathaniel Tucker, 1750-1807." *Bul Bibl* 20 (Ja-Ap 50) 5-6.

TUCKER, NATHANIEL BEVERLEY (1784-1851). Anon. "Beverley Tucker to Wyndham Robertson." *WMQ* 9 (Ap 29) 126.
——— "Virginia Appeals to Connecticut." *Tyler's Quar Hist & Gen Mag* 18 (O 36) 87-8.
McDermott, J. F. "Nathaniel Beverley Tucker in Missouri." *WMQ* 20 (O 40) 504-7.
Woodfin, M. H. "Nathaniel Beverley Tucker." *Richmond College Hist Papers* 2 (1917) 9-42.

TUCKER, ST. GEORGE (1752-1827). Anon. "The Tucker Letters from Williamsburg." *Bermuda Hist Q* 3 (F, My, N 46) 24-37, 73-86, 204-12.
——— "The Tucker Papers." *Bermuda Hist Q* 4 (Ag-S 47) 104-15.
Coleman, Mrs. G. P. "Randolph and Tucker Letters." *VMHB* 42 (Ja, Ap 34) 47-52, 129-31; 43 (Ja 35) 41-6.
Leary, Lewis. "St. George Tucker Attends the Theater." *WMQ* 5 (Jl 48) 396-7.
Riley, E. M. "St. George Tucker's Journal of the Siege of Yorktown, 1781." *WMQ* 5 (Jl 48) 375-95.

TUCKERMAN, FREDERICK GODDARD (1821-73). Eaton, W. P. "A Forgotten American Poet." *Forum* 41 (Ja 09) 62-70.

TULLY, JIM (1891-). Hughes, M. Y. "Jim Tully: Poet or Picaro?" *SR* 37 (O-D 29) 389-98.

TURNER, FREDERICK JACKSON (1861-1932). Craven, Avery. "Frederick Jackson Turner, Historian." *Wisc Mag Hist* 25 (Je 42) 408-24.
Dale, E. E. "Memories of Frederick Jackson Turner." *Miss Valley Hist R* 30 (D 43) 339-58.
Farrand, Max. "Frederick Jackson Turner, a Memoir." *PMHS* 65 (My 35) 432-40.
Mood, Fulmer. "The Development of Frederick Jackson Turner as a Historical Thinker." *PCSM* 34 (1943) 283-352.
——— "Frederick Jackson Turner and the Milwaukee *Sentinel*, 1884." *Wisc Mag Hist* 34 (Au 50) 21-8.
Pierson, G. W. "Recent Studies of Turner and the Frontier Doctrine." *Miss Valley Hist R* (34 (D 47) 453-8.
Shafer, J. "The Author of the 'Frontier Hypothesis.'" *Wisc Mag Hist* 15 (S 31) 86-103.

TURNER, JOSEPH ADDISON (1826-68). "Cincinnatus." "The 'Countryman': A Lone Chapter in Plantation Publishing." *AN&Q* 5 (D 45) 131-5.
——— "Joseph Addison Turner: Publisher, Planter, and Countryman." *AN&Q* 5 (N 45) 115-9.

TYLER, MOSES COIT (1835-1900). Borson, R. M. "Moses Coit Tyler, Historian of the American Genesis." *Sw R* 26 (Jl 41) 416-27.
Burr, G. L. "The Late Professor Moses Coit Tyler." *Critic* 38 (F 01) 136-7.
——— "Moses Coit Tyler." *Am Hist Assn Report* 1 (1901) 187-95.
Trent, W. P. "Moses Coit Tyler." *Forum* 31 (Ag 01) 750-8.

TYLER, ROYALL (1757-1826). Balch, Marston. "Jonathan the First." *MLN* 46 (My 31) 281-8.
Forsythe, R. S. "'The Algerine Captive,' 1802." *N&Q* 172 (29 My 37) 389-90.
Killheffer, Marie. "A Comparison of the Dialect of the 'Biglow Papers' with the Dialect of Four Yankee Plays." *AS* 3 (F 28) 222-36.
Nethercot, A. H. "The Dramatic Background of Royall Tyler's *The Contrast*." *AL* 12 (Ja 41) 435-46.
Tupper, Frederick. "Royall Tyler, Man of Law and Man of Letters." *Proc Vt Hist Soc* 4 (1928) 65-101.

UNDERWOOD, FRANCIS HENRY (1825-94). Perry, Bliss. "The Editor Who Was Never the Editor." *Atl* 100 (N 07) 658-78.

UNTERMEYER, LOUIS (1885-). Deutsch, Babette. "Louis Untermeyer's *Buch der Liebe*." *Bkm* 67 (N 25) 323-6.
Fuller, H. B. "A Parodist." *Poetry* 8 (S 16) 321-2.
Gorman, H. S. "Roast Leviathan." *NRp* 35 (15 Ag 23) 338-9.
Henderson, A. C. "The Old Adam." *Poetry* 17 (Ja 21) 212-6.
Lowell, Amy. "A Poet of the Present." *Poetry* 11 (D 17) 157-64.
Peckham, H. H. "The Poetry of Louis Untermeyer." *SAQ* 17 (Ja 18) 58-64.
Sale, W. M. "Another Exile." *Poetry* 52 (Ap 38) 46-51.
Wilson, Edmund. "The Poet as Politician." *NRp* 45 (2 D 25) 42-3.

UPDIKE, DANIEL BERKELEY (1860-1941). Howe, M. A. DeW. "Updike of Merrymount: the Scholar-Printer." *Atl* 169 (My 42) 588-96.

UPSON, ARTHUR (1877-1908). Beach, J. W. "Beach Tells of Arthur Upson's Life on Minnesota Campus." *Minn Chats* 28 (1 Mr 46) 1.

VAN DOREN, CARL (1885-1951). Glicksberg, C. I. "Carl Van Doren, Scholar and Skeptic." *SR* 46 (Ap-Je 38) 223-34.
Krutch, J. W. "A Generous Presence." *Nation* 171 (12 Ag 51) 150-1.

VAN DOREN, MARK (1894-). Baker, Howard. "A Note on the Poetry of Mark Van Doren." *So R* 1 (Wi 36) 601-8.
Monroe, Harriet. "Slants and Whimsies." *Poetry* 31 (O 27) 47-50.
Moore, Marianne. "Victorious Defeats." *Poetry* 40 (Jl 32) 222-4.
Strobel, Marion. "Mellowness." *Poetry* 25 (F 25) 279-81.
Wood, Katherine. "The Van Doren Brothers in American Letters." *CE* 2 (N 40) 91-102.
Zabel, M. D. "But Still of Earth." *Poetry* 36 (Ap 30) 50-1.

VAN DYKE, HENRY (1852-1933). Anon. "Henry Van Dyke." *Nation* 104 (11 Ja 17) 54-5.
——— Henry Van Dyke Number. *Book News* 24 (My 06) 605-17.
Mabie, H. W. "Henry Van Dyke." *Bkm* 38 (S 13) 20-1.
——— "Henry Van Dyke." *Century* 67 (F 04) 579-81.
Norris, E. M. "Some Writers of the Princeton Faculty." *Critic* 42 (Je 03) 511-2.
Patterson, E. V. "Writers of New Jersey." *Book News* 35 (Jl 17) 406-7.

VAN VECHTEN, CARL (1880-). Beach, J. W. "The Peacock's Tail." *AS* 1 (N 25) 65-73.
Gloster, H. M. "The Van Vechten Vogue." *Phylon* 6 (Au 45) 310-4.
Schuyler, G. S. "Carl Van Vechten." *Phylon* 11 (4Q 50) 362-8.
Van Vechten, Carl. "Notes for an Autobiography." *Colophon* (S 30) Pt 3.

VEBLEN, THORSTEIN (1857-1929). Aaron, Daniel. "Thorstein Veblem: Moralist and Rhetorician." *AR* 7 (Fl 47) 381-90.
Brodersen, Arvid. "Thorstein Veblen." *Syn og Segn* (Oslo) 46 (My-Je 40) 251-60.

VERPLANCK, GULIAN CROMMELIN (1786-1870). Harvey, S. K. "A Bibliography of the Miscellaneous Prose of Gulian Crommelin Verplanck." *AL* 8 (My 36) 199-203.
Marckwardt, A. H. "The American Scholar: Two Views." *Papers Mich Acad Sci, Arts & Letters* 18 (1932) 525-38.

VERY, JONES (1813-80). Baker, Carlos. "Emerson and Jones Very." *NEQ* 7 (Mr 34) 90-9.
Bartlett, W. I. "Early Years of Jones Very—Emerson's 'Brave Saint.'" *EIHC* 73 (Ja 37) 1-23.
——— "Jones Very—The Harvard Years." *EIHC* 74 (Jl 38) 213-38.
Berthoff, W. B. "Jones Very: New England Mystic." *BPLQ* 2 (Ja 50) 63-75.
Burns, P. P. "Jones Very." *Howard Col Bul* 80 (1923) 42-66.
Gohdes, Clarence. "Alcott's 'Conversations' on the Transcendental Club and *The Dial*." *AL* 3 (Mr 31) 14-28.
Hammell, G. M. "Jones Very—A Son of the Spirit." *Methodist R* 83 (Ja 01) 20-30.
Winters, Yvor. "Jones Very: A New England Mystic." *Am R* 7 (My 36) 159-78.

VIERECK, PETER (1916-). Ciardi, John. "Peter Viereck—The Poet and the Form." *UKCR* 15 (Su 49) 297-302.
Viereck, Peter. "My Kind of Poetry." *SRL* 32 (27 Ag 49) 7-8, 35-6.
——— "Parnassus Divided." *Atl* 184 (O 49) 67-70.
——— "Tribute to Theodore Spencer." *Epoch* 2 (Wi 49) 156.

VILLARD, OSWALD GARRISON (1872-1949). Gannett, Lewis. "Villard and His 'Nation.'" *Nation* 171 (22 Jl 50) 79-82.

WALKER, MARGARET (1915-). Anon. "Margaret Walker." *Cur Biog* 4 (N 43) 57-9.

WALLACE, LEWIS (1827-1905). Anon. "The Winner of the Chariot Race." *Nation* 80 (23 F 05) 148-9.
Forbes, J. D. "Lew Wallace, Romantic." *Ind Mag Hist* 44 (D 48) 385-92.
McKee, Irving. "The Early Life of Lew Wallace." *Ind Mag Hist* 37 (S 41) 205-16.
McMillen, W. "A Century of Lew Wallace and a Half Century of 'Ben Hur.'" *Mentor* 15 (My 27) 33-5.
Nicholson, Meredith. "Lew Wallace." *Reader* 5 (Ap 05) 571-5.
Rich, J. W. "General Lew Wallace at Shiloh." *Iowa J Hist & Pol* 18 (Ap 20) 301-8.

WALLIS, SEVERN TEACKLE (1816-94). Scott, F. B. "Letters of Severn Teackle Wallis." *Md Hist Mag* 39 (Je 44) 121-40.

WARD, CHRISTOPHER (1868-). Able, A. H., III. "Christopher Ward: A Literary Appreciation." *Del Notes* 20 (N 47) 77-84.

WARD, NATHANIEL (*c.* 1578-1652). Dibble, R. F. "'The Simple Cobbler of Aggawam.'" *SAQ* 19 (Ap 20) 163-70.
Ericson, E. E. "Ward or the Devil." *AL* 9 (Mr 37) 76-7.
Fussell, E. S. "Ward, Women, and Webster." *AN&Q* 8 (F 50) 166-7.
Holliday, Carl. "The First American Satirist." *SR* 16 (Jl 08) 309-15.
Thompson, J. H. "The First American Humorist, Nathaniel Ward, the Simple Cobbler of Aggawam." *Reading & Collecting* 2 (F-Mr 38) 17-8.
Vancura, Z. "Baroque Prose in America." *Stud Eng Charles Un* (Prague) 4 (1933) 39-58.

WARNER, CHARLES DUDLEY (1829-1900). Mabie, H. W. "Charles D. Warner." *Critic* 37 (D 00) 547-9.
Peck, H. T. "Charles Dudley Warner." *Bkm* 12 (D 00) 268-77.
Twitchell, J. H. "Qualities of Warner's Humor." *Century* 65 (Ja 03) 378-80.

WARREN, MERCY OTIS (1728-1814). Ford, W. C. "Mrs. Warren's 'The Group.'" *PMHS* 62 (O 28) 15-22.
Marble, A. R. "Mistress Mercy Warren: Real Daughter of the American Revolution." *N E Mag* ns 27 (Ap 03) 163-80.

WARREN, ROBERT PENN (1905-). Amacher, R. E. "Warren's *Original Sin: A Short Story*." *Expl* 8 (My 50) 52.
Baker, J. E. "Irony in Fiction: 'All the King's Men.'" *CE* 9 (D 47) 122-30.
Basso, Hamilton. "The Huey Long Legend." *Life* 21 (9 D 46) 106-8, 110, 112, 115-6, 118-21.
Bentley, Eric. "The Meaning of Robert Penn Warren's Novels." *KR* 10 (Su 48) 407-24.
Brooks, Cleanth, & Van Doren, Mark. "Modern Poetry: A Symposium." *Am R* 8 (F 37) 427-56.
Cargill, Oscar. "Anatomist of Monsters." *CE* 9 (O 47) 1-8.
Cater, Catherine. "Four Voices Out of the South." *Mich Alumnus Q* (Wi 44) 166-73.
Girault, N. R. "The Narrator's Mind as Symbol: An Analysis of 'All the King's Men.'" *Accent* 7 (Su 47) 220-34.
Gordon, C. M. "Warren's *Original Sin: A Short Story*." *Expl* 9 (D 50) 21.
Heilman, R. B. "Melpomene as Wallflower; or, the Reading of Tragedy." *SR* 55 (Ja-Mr 47) 154-66.
Hendry, Irene. "Regional Novel: The Example of Robert Penn Warren." *SR* 53 (Ja 45) 84-102.

Humbolt, Charles. "The Lost Cause of Robert Penn Warren." *Masses & Mainstream* 1 (Jl 48) 8-23.
Nemorov, Howard. "The Phoenix in the World." *Furioso* 3 (Sp 48) 36-46.
Runnquist, Ake. "Pärlan i ostronet: Några drag i Robert Penn Warrens romaner." *Bonniers Litterära Magasin* (Stockholm) 16 (N 47) 725-32.
Southard, W. P. "The Religious Poetry of Robert Penn Warren." *KR* 7 (Au 45) 653-76.
Stallman, R. W. "Robert Penn Warren: A Checklist of His Critical Writings." *UKCR* 14 (Au 47) 78-83.
Stuart, J. L. "The Achievement of Robert Penn Warren." *SAQ* 47 (O 48) 570-4.
Zabel, M. D. "Problems of Knowledge." *Poetry* 48 (Ap 36) 37-41.

WASHINGTON, GEORGE (1732-99). Anon. "Washington's Farewell Address." *BNYPL* 39 (F 35) 91-3.
Barck, D. C. "Proposed Memorials to Washington in New York City, 1802-1847." *N Y Hist Soc Quar Bul* 15 (O 31) 79-90.
Beatty, A. R. "Letters of George Washington." *YR* 21 (Sp 32) 466-82.
Benson, N. L. "Washington: Symbol of the United States in Mexico, 1800-1823." *Un Texas Lib Chron* 2 (Sp 47) 175-82.
Bryan, W. A. "George Washington: Symbolic Guardian of the Republic, 1850-1861." *WMQ* 7 (Ja 50) 53-63.
Chesterton, G. K. "George Washington." *Fortnightly R* 137 (1 Mr 32) 303-10.
Clemens, J. R. "George Washington's Pronunciation." *AS* 7 (Ag 32) 438-41.
Frey, G. R. "George Washington in German Fiction." *AGR* 12 (Je 46) 25-6, 37.
Gerig, J. L. "A Washington Letter to Franklin." *RR* 22 (Ap-Je 31) 173-4.
Guedalla, Philip. "General George Washington: In Tradition and in Fact." *Harper's* 150 (D 24) 98-106.
Haraszti, Zoltán. "A Notable Bequest of Washingtoniana." *More Books* 6 (F 31) 49-57.
——— "Washington Bicentennial Exhibit." *More Books* 7 (Ap 32) 79-97.
——— "Washington Letters in This Library." *More Books* 7 (Mr 32) 43-55.
Hart, A. B. "A Study of Washington Biography." *Pub W* 119 (19 F 31) 820-2.
——— "Washington to Order." *PMHS* 60 (D 26) 66-81.
Hay, J., Jr. "George Washington: Literary Man." *Pub W* 121 (27 F 32) 943-4.
Jackson, Joseph. "Washington in Philadelphia." *PMHB* 56 (Ap 32) 110-55.
McGroarty, W. B. "The Death of Washington." *VMHB* 54 (Ap 46) 152-6.
Mead, E. D. "Recent Washington Literature in England." *PMHS* 61 (D 27) 42-55.
Moses, M. J. "His Excellency, George Washington." *Theatre Arts* 16 (F 32) 137-46.
Paltsits, V. L. "Washington's Note-Book [1757]." *BNYPL* 24 (Ag 20) 431-5.
Pennypacker, I. R. "Washington and Lincoln: The Father and the Savior of the Country." *PMHB* 56 (Ap 32) 97-109.
Preston, J. H. "The Rebirth of George Washington." *Forum* 87 (Mr 32) 136-41.
Read, A. W. "British Travellers on George Washington's English." *N&Q* 175 (2 Jl 38) 7.
Smyth, M. W. "Contemporary Songs and Verses about Washington." *NEQ* 5 (Ap 32) 281-92.
Stillwell, M. B. "Checklist of Eulogies and Funeral Orations on the Death of George Washington." *BNYPL* 20 (My 16) 403-50.
van der Kemp, Francis. "Eulogy of George Washington . . . February 22, 1800." *BNYPL* 20 (F 16) 103-13.
Van Dyke, Paul. "Washington." *PAPS* 71 (1932) 191-206.
Zunder, T. A. "Joel Barlow and George Washington." *MLN* 44 (Ap 29) 254-6.

WASSON, GEORGE SAVARY (1855-1932). Eckstorm, F. H. "George Savary Wasson: Artist and Writer 1855-1932." *EIHC* 79 (Ja 43) 47-59.

WATTERSON, HENRY (1840-1921). Beard, W. E. "Henry Watterson—Last of the Oracles." *Tenn Hist Mag* 1 (Jl 31) 233-52.
Peck, H. T. "Henry Watterson." *Bkm* 18 (F 04) 635-8.
Pringle, H. F. "Kentucky Bourbon: Marse Henry Watterson." *Scribner's* 97 (Ja 35) 10-8.

WEBB, JOHN (1824-87). Rice, J. A. "Two Schoolteachers." *Harper's* 184 (Ja 42) 201-9.

WEBSTER, DANIEL (1782-1852). Bradford, J. W. "Could Daniel Webster Teach in New York's Schools?" *Nation* 109 (2 Ag 19) 147.
Clapp, C. B. "The Speeches of Daniel Webster: A Bibliographical Review." *PBSA* 13 (1919) 3-63.
Davis, W. T. "Memories of Daniel Webster in Public and Private Life." *N E Mag* ns 26 (Ap 02) 187-209.
Duniway, C. A. "Daniel Webster and the West." *Minn Hist* 9 (Mr 28) 3-15.
Foster, H.D. "Webster's Seventh of March Speech and the Secession Movement, 1850." *AHR* 27 (Ja 22) 245-70.
Haraszti, Zoltán. "A Webster Exhibit." *More Books* 7 (Ja-F 32) 3-10.
Lower, A.R.M. "An Unpublished Letter of Daniel Webster." *NEQ* 12 (Je 39) 360-4.
McCall, S. W. "Daniel Webster." *Atl* 88 (N 01) 600-14.
Mills, G. E. "Misconceptions concerning Daniel Webster." *QJS* 29 (D 43) 423-8.
Wilson, C. A. "Familiar 'Small College' Quotations: I, Daniel Webster and Dartmouth." *Colophon* ns 3 (Wi 38) 7-23.

WEBSTER, NOAH (1758-1843). Andrews, F. D. "The Centenary of Noah Webster's Dictionary of the English Language." *Vineland Hist Mag* 14 (Ja 29) 102-3.
Benét, W. R. "Noah's Ark: The Origin and Making of Webster's International Dictionary." *SRL* 15 (2 Ja 37) 3-4, 14-6.
Berthold, Arthur. "Launching *The Herald*." *BNYPL* 39 (Jl 35) 519-20.
Laird, Charlton. "Etymology, Anglo-Saxon, and Noah Webster." *AS* 21 (F 46) 3-15.
Malone, Kemp. "A Linguistic Patriot." *AS* 1 (O 25) 26-31.
Mulder, Arnold. "Noah Webster's Prophecy." *CE* 55 (Ja 44) 196-200.
Partch, C. F. "Noah Webster: The Schoolmaster of Our Republic." *JRUL* 2 (Je 39) 39-45.
Read, A. W. "Noah Webster as a Euphemist." *Dial Notes* 6 (1934) 385-91.
——— "Noah Webster's Project in 1801 for a History of American Newspapers." *JQ* 11 (1934) 258-75.
——— "The Philological Society of New York, 1788." *AS* 9 (Ap 34) 131-6.
Shores, Louis. "Noah Webster's Dictionary." *Scholastic* 26 (14 Ap 28) 8, 11.
Smith, G. F. "Noah Webster's Conservatism." *AS* 25 (My 50) 101-4.
Thompson, E. E. "Noah Webster and Amherst College." *Amherst Grad Q* 22 (Ag 33) 289-99.
Wagenknecht, Edward. "The Man behind the Dictionary." *VQR* 5 (Ap 29) 246-58.
Warfel, H. R. "Centenary of Noah Webster's Bible." *NEQ* 7 (S 34) 578-82.
Warthin, A. S. "Noah Webster as Epidemiologist." *J Am Med Assn* 80 (17 Mr 34) 755-64.
Winslow, C. E. A. "The Epidemiology of Noah Webster." *Trans Conn Acad Arts & Sciences* 32 (Ja 34) 21-109.
Zunder, T. A. "Noah Webster and *The Conquest of Canäan*." *AL* 1 (My 29) 200-2.
——— "Noah Webster as a Student Orator." *Yale Un W* 25 (26 Mr 26) 16-8.

WEEMS, MASON LOCKE (1759-1825). Adams, R. G. "The Historical Illustrations in Weems's Washington." *Colophon* (D 32) Pt 8.
——— "It Was Old Parson Weems Who Began It." *N Y Times Mag* 80 (5 Jl 31) 10.

Bayley, M. W. "The Parson and the Cherry Tree." *Chri Sci Mon* 37 (17 F 45) 3.
Bryan, W. A. "The Genesis of Weems' *Life of Washington*." *Americana* 36 (Ap 42) 147-65.
——— "Three Unpublished Letters of Parson Weems." *WMQ* 23 (Jl 43) 272-7
Foster, J. W. "Weems Genealogy." *Md Hist Mag* 28 (S 33) 265-71.
Hart, A. B. "American Historical Liars." *Harper's* 131 (O 15) 732-4.
Ingrahim, C. A. "Mason Locke Weems. A Great American Author and Distributor of Books." *Americana* 25 (O 31) 469-85.
Newton, A. E. "Parson Weems's Washington Once More." *Colophon* ns 1 (Wi 36) 367-70.
Norris, W. B. "The Historian of the Cherry Tree." *National Mag* 16 (F 10) 46-52.
——— "Weems." *Nation* 94 (29 F 12) 207-8.
Skeel, Mrs. Roswell. "Mason Locke Weems: A Postscript." *New Colophon* 3 (1950) 243-9.

WEISSELBERG, MARIE ANNA (1835-1911). Vines, M. J. "A Pioneer Poet of Texas." *AGR* 14 (Je 48) 28-31.

WELLER, GEORGE (1907-). Gwynn, F. L. "The Education of Epes Todd." *Harvard Alumni Bul* 51 (12 F 49) 388-91.

WELTY, EUDORA (1909-). Clark, Eleanor. "Old Glamour, New Gloom." *PR* 16 (Je 49) 631-6.
Warren, R. P. "The Love and Separateness in Miss Welty." *KR* 6 (Sp 44) 246-59.
Welty, Eudora. "The Reading and Writing of Short Stories." *Atl* 183 (F, Mr 49) 46-9, 54-8.

WENDELL, BARRETT (1855-1921). Eaton, W. P. "Barrett Wendell." *Am Merc* 5 (Ag 25) 448-55.
Lowell, A. L. "Memoir of Barrett Wendell." *PMHS* 55 (D 21) 174-84.
Rhodes, J. F., *et al.* "Tribute to Barrett Wendell." *PMHS* 54 (F 21) 195-203.

WESCOTT, GLENWAY (1901-). Kohler, Dayton. "Glenway Wescott: Legend-Maker." *Bkm* 73 (Ap 31) 142-5.
Quinn, P. F. "The Case History of Glenway Wescott." *Frontier & Midland* 19 (Au 39) 11-6.

WEST, NATHANAEL (1904-40). Ross, Alan. "The Dead Centre: An Introduction to Nathanael West." *Horizon* 18 (O 48) 284-96.

WHARTON, EDITH (1862-1937). Anon. "International Novelist." *Chri Sci Mon* 29 (16 Ag 37) 221.
Boynton, P. H. "Edith Wharton." *EJ* 12 (Ja 23) 24-32.
Boynton, W. H. "Mrs. Wharton's Manner." *Nation* 97 (30 O 13) 404-5.
Brown, E. K. "Edith Wharton." *Etudes Anglaises* 2 (Ja-Mr 38) 16-26.
Burdett, Osbert. "Edith Wharton." *London Merc* 13 (N 25) 13, 52-61.
Canby, H. S. "Edith Wharton." *SRL* 16 (21 Ag 37) 6-7.
Chanler, Mrs. Winthrop. "Winters in Paris." *Atl* 158 (O 36) 476-80.
Chapman, H. W. L. "Books in General." *New Statesman & Nation* 29 (20 Ja 45) 43.
Cooper, F. T. "The Bigger Issues in Some Recent Books." *Bkm* 36 (N 11) 312.
Cross, W. L. "Edith Wharton." *Bkm* 63 (Ag 26) 641-6.
——— "Great Novelist of the American Scene." *World R* 8 (My 29) 234.
de Valdiva, O. A. "Edith Wharton." *Andean Q* 5 (Su 44) 8-21, 39-58; 6 (Wi 44) 56-73.
Dwight, H. G. "Edith Wharton." *Putnam's* 3 (F 08) 590-6.
Flanner, Janet. "Dearest Edith." *NYr* 5 (2 Mr 29) 26-7.

Follett, Wilson. "What Edith Wharton Did—and Might Have Done." *N Y Times Book R* (5 S 37) 2, 14.
Gilbertson, Catherine. "Mrs. Wharton." *Century* 119 (Au 29) 112-9.
Gilman, Lawrence. "The Book of the Month: Mrs. Wharton Reverts to Shaw." *NAR* 206 (Ag 17) 304-7.
Hackett, Francis. "Mrs. Wharton's Art." *NRp* 10 (10 F 17) 50-2.
Herrick, Robert. "Mrs. Wharton's World." *NRp* 2 (13 F 15) 40-2.
Hooker, Brian. "Some Springtime Verse." *Bkm* 29 (Je 09) 367-8.
Huneker, James. "Three Disagreeable Girls." *Forum* 52 (N 14) 772-5.
Johnson, M. D., & Hopkins, F. M. "American First Editions . . . Edith Wharton." *Pub W* 102 (10 Mr 23) 796.
Kazin, Alfred. "The Lady and the Tiger: Edith Wharton and Theodore Dreiser." *VQR* 17 (Wi 41) 101-19.
Leavis, Q. D. "Henry James's Heiress: The Importance of Edith Wharton." *Scrutiny* 7 (D 38) 261-76.
Lubbock, Percy. "The Novels of Edith Wharton." *Quar R* 223 (Ja 15) 182-201; *Living Age* 284 (6 Mr 15) 604-16.
McCole, C. J. "Some Notes on Edith Wharton." *Cath World* 146 (Ja 38) 425-31.
Parrington, V. L. "Our Literary Aristocrat." *Pac R* 6 (Je 21) 157-60.
Phelps, W. L. "An Appreciation." *Delineator* 120 (F 32) 7.
Randall, D. A. "A Bibliography of the Writings of Edith Wharton by Lavinia Davis." *Pub W* 123 (17 Je 33) 1975-6.
Ransom, J. C. "Characters and Character: A Note on Fiction." *Am R* 6 (Ja 36) 271-88.
Repplier, Agnes. "Edith Wharton." *Commonweal* 29 (25 N 38) 125-6.
Roberts, R. E. "Edith Wharton." *Bkm* 58 (S 23) 262-4.
Russell, F. T. "Edith Wharton's Use of Imagery." *EJ* 21 (Je 32) 452-60.
——— "Melodramatic Mrs. Wharton." *SR* 45 (O-D 32) 425-37.
Sedgwick, H. D. "The Novels of Mrs. Wharton." *Atl* 98 (Ag 06) 217-28.
Sedgwick, R. D. "Ethan Frome." *Stage* 13 (F 36) 20-3.
Sencourt, Robert. "Edith Wharton." *Cornhill Mag* 157 (Je 38) 721-36.
——— "The Poetry of Edith Wharton." *Bkm* 73 (Jl 31) 478-86.
Sholl, A. M. "The Work of Edith Wharton." *Gunton's* (N 03) 426-32.
Smith, L. P. "Slices of Cake." *New Statesman & Nation* 25 (5 Je 43) 367-8.
Trueblood, C. K. "Edith Wharton." *Dial* 68 (Ja 20) 80-91.
Van Doren, Carl. "Contemporary American Novelists." *Nation* 112 (12 Ja 21) 40-1.
Waldstein, Charles. "Social Ideals." *NAR* 182 (Je 06) 840-52; 183 (Jl 06) 125-6.
Wharton, Edith. "Confessions of a Novelist." *Atl* 151 (Ap 33) 385-92.
——— "The Great American Novel." *YR* 16 (Jl 27) 646-56.
——— "A Little Girl's New York." *Harper's* 186 (Mr 38) 356-64.
——— "The Writing of *Ethan Frome*." *Colophon* 3 (S 32) Pt 11.
Willcox, L. C. "Edith Wharton." *Outlook* 81 (25 N 05) 719-24.
Wilson, Edmund. "Justice to Edith Wharton." *NRp* 95 (29 Je 38) 209-13.
Winter, Calvin. "Edith Wharton." *Bkm* 33 (My 11) 202-9.

WHEATLEY, PHILLIS (1753?-84). Holmes, Wilfred. "Phillis Wheatley." *Negro Hist Bul* 6 (F 43) 117-8.
Matthews, Albert. "The Writings of Phillis Wheatley." *N&Q* 159 (12 Jl 30) 30-1.
Quarles, Benjamin. "A Phillis Wheatley Letter." *J Negro Hist* 34 (O 49) 462-4.

WHEELER, EDWARD L. (1859-1922). Fee, C. A. "Deadwood Dick's Danger Ducks: A 'Novel of Oregon.'" *Ore Hist Q* 45 (Je 44) 177-86.

WHEELOCK, JOHN HALL (1886-). Hubbell, J. B. "The Poetry of John Hall Wheelock." *Sw R* 12 (O 26) 60-7.
Monroe, Harriet. "A Love of Earth." *Poetry* 15 (Mr 20) 343-5.
Scott, Evelyn. "The Tone of Time." *Poetry* 50 (My 37) 100-3.

Wheelock, J. H. "Author Unknown." *Book Buyer* 2 (D 36) 22.
——— "Rhyme in Poetry." *Book Buyer* 3 (D 37) 12-3.
Zabel, M. D. "Poems Stately and Grave." *Poetry* 31 (F 28) 280-2.

WHIPPLE, EDWIN PERCY (1819-86). Sutcliffe, Denham. "'Our Young American Macaulay,' Edwin Percy Whipple, 1819-1886." *NEQ* 19 (Mr 46) 3-18.

WHITE, E. B. (1899-). Beck, Warren. "E. B. White." *EJ* 35 (Ap 46) 175-81; *CE* 7 (Ap 46) 367-73.

WHITE, JOHN (1575-1648). White, John. "The Planter's Plea." *PMHS* 62 (Je 29) 363-425.

WHITE, JOHN BLAKE (1781-1859). Weidner, P. R. "The Journal of John Blake White." *S C Hist & Gen Mag* 42 (Ap-Jl, O 41) 55-71, 169-86; 43 (Ja, Mr, Je 42) 35-46, 103-17, 161-74.

WHITE, RICHARD GRANT (1821-85). Falk, R. P. "Critical Tendencies in Richard Grant White's Shakespeare Commentary." *AL* 20 (My 48) 144-54.

WHITE, STEWART EDWARD (1873-1946). Clark, Ward. "Stewart Edward White." *Bkm* 31 (Jl 10) 486-92.
Denison, Lindsay. "Stewart Edward White." *Bkm* 17 (My 03) 308-11.
Maurice, A. B. "Stewart Edward White." *Bkm* 69 (Ag 29) 588-9.
Wright, Edward. "Stewart Edward White." *Bkm* (London) 46 (Ap 14) 31-3.

WHITE, THOMAS WILLIS (*fl.* 1834-64). Devine, R. B. "Thomas Willis White." *SLM* 1 (Ag 39) 503-7.
Jackson, D. K. "Some Unpublished Letters of T. W. White to Lucian Minor." *Tyler's Quar Hist & Gen Mag* 17 (Ap 36) 224-43; 18 (Jl 36) 32-49.

WHITE, WILLIAM ALLEN (1868-1944). C., E. D. "William Allen White: Lovable American." *Chri Sci Mon* 38 (8 Mr 46) 14.
Canby, H. S. "William Allen White: A Personal Tribute." *SRL* 27 (5 F 44) 16.
Maurois, André. "A Man from Kansas: The Story of William Allen White." *UKCR* 12 (Sp 46) 188-91.
Mencken, H. L. "The Last of the Victorians." *Smart Set* 29 (O 09) 153-5.
Pick, F. W. "A Great American Journalist." *Contemp R* 171 (Ja 47) 27-31.
White, W. A. "Young Kansas Editor." *Atl* 177 (Mr 46) 39-47.

WHITECOTTON, MOSES (1777-1849). Brewster, Paul. "Moses Whitecotton, Hoosier Balladist and Rhymester." *Hoosier Folklore* 8 (Je-S 49) 45-7.

WHITEFIELD, GEORGE (1714-70). King, C. H. "George Whitefield: Dramatic Evangelist." *QJS* 19 (Ap 33) 165-75.

WHITMAN, WALT (1819-92). Anon. "Backward Glances." *TLS* (4 O 47) 507.
——— "A Canadian Interview with Walt Whitman." *AN&Q* 3 (My, Je 43) 19-24, 35-6.
——— "Celebrating Walt Whitman as a Liberator." *Cur Op* 57 (Je 19) 392-3.
——— "De Tocqueville and Whitman." *Nation* 109 (22 N 19) 655.
——— "Edward Carpenter." *Manchester Guardian W* 21 (5 Jl 29) 18.
——— "English Appreciation of Whitman." *Atl* 92 (N 03) 714-6.
——— "In 'The Week.' An incident relative to Walt Whitman's being placed in the Hall of Fame." *NRp* 67 (27 My 31) 30.
——— "A Lonely Whitmanite." *Lit Dig* 57 (15 Je 18) 29-30.
——— "New England Nature Studies: Thoreau, Burroughs, Whitman." *Edinburgh R* 208 (O 08) 343-66.
——— "New Light on Whitman's Contradictory Gospel." *Cur Op* 67 (O 19) 246-7.

——— "A Poet of the Cosmic Consciousness." *Brotherhood* (London) 19 (14 Ap 06) 142-8.
——— "Poets in Politics." *TLS* (10 My 47) 225.
——— "A Precursor of Whitman." *NAR* 185 (21 Je 07) 463-4.
——— "A Reviewer's Notebook." *Freeman* 3 (18 My 21) 238-9.
——— "Walt for Our Day." *Lit Dig* 61 (21 Je 19) 28-9.
——— "Walt Whitman and His Noblest Woman-Friend." *Cur Op* 65 (D 18) 394-5.
——— "Walt Whitman as an Old-Fashioned Conservative." *Cur Op* 70 (Mr 21) 383-5.
——— "Walt Whitman as Musical Prophet." *Musical Am* 16 (15 Ap 17) 12-4.
——— "Walt Whitman's America." *Conservator* 28 (N 17) 134-6.
——— "Walt Whitman's 'Grandee Spain Succumbing.'" *Mo R* (My 03) 151-7.
——— "Walt Whitman's Vogue in Europe." *Cur Op* 64 (My 18) 349-50.
——— "Whitman and Traubel as Prophets Rejected." *Cur Op* 69 (Ag 20) 233-6.
——— "The Whitman Collection: Some New Manuscripts." *Lib Chron Un Penn* 14 (Ap 47) 29-31.
——— "Whitmanie." *Conservator* 29 (My 18) 40-2.
——— "Whitman's Birthplace." *AN&Q* 8 (Ja 50) 160.
——— "Whitman's Home to be Preserved as a Literary Shrine." *Cur Op* 69 (O 20) 527-9.
——— "With Walt Whitman in Camden." *Seven Arts* 2 (S 17) 627-37.
Abbott, L. D. "The Democracy of Whitman and the Democracy of Socialism." *Conservator* 13 (N 02) 136.
——— "Walt Whitman and His Influence in American Poetry." *Poetry R* 1 (O 12) 473-5.
Adams, C. M. "Whitman's Use of 'Grass.'" *AN&Q* 6 (F 47) 167-8.
Adkins, N. F. "Walt Whitman and William Motherwell: 'Goodbye My Fancy.'" *N&Q* 169 (12 O 35) 268-9.
Admari, Ralph. "Leaves of Grass—First Edition." *Am Book Coll* 5 (My-Je 34) 150-2.
Alegria, Fernando. "Walt Whitman en Hispanoamerica." *Revista Iberoamericaine* 8 (1944).
Alexander, C. C. "A Note on Walt Whitman." *AL* 9 (My 37) 242-3.
Allen, G. W. "Biblical Analogies for Walt Whitman's Prosody." *Revue Anglo-Américaine* 12 (Ag 33) 490-507.
——— "Biblical Echoes in Whitman's Works." *AL* 6 (N 34) 302-15.
——— "On the Trochaic Meter of 'Pioneers! O Pioneers!'" *AL* 20 (Ja 49) 449-51.
——— "Walt Whitman and Jules Michelet." *Etudes Anglaises* 1 (My 37) 230-7.
——— "Walt Whitman Bibliography, 1918-1934." *Bul Bibl* 15 (S-D 34) 84-8.
——— "Walt Whitman Bibliography, 1935-1942." *Bul Bibl* 17 (Ja-Ap 43) 209-10.
——— "Walt Whitman in Comparative Literature." *CL News Letter* 2 (D 43) 4-5.
——— "Walt Whitman—Nationalist or Proletarian." *EJ* 26 (Ja 37) 48-52.
——— "Walt Whitman's 'Long Journey' Motif." *JEGP* 38 (Ja 39) 76-95.
——— "Walt Whitman's Reception in Scandinavia." *PBSA* 40 (4Q 46) 259-75.
Amacher, R. E. "Whitman's *Passage to India.*" *Expl* 9 (D 50) 2.
Arms, G. W. "Whitman's *To a Locomotive in Winter.*" *Expl* 5 (N 46) 14.
Arvin, Newton. "Whitman's Individualism." *NRp* 71 (6 Jl 32) 212-3.
Asselineau, Roger. "A propos Walt Whitman." *Les Langues Modernes* (Paris) 42 (Ag-S-O 48) 446-9.
——— "Walt Whitman, Child of Adam? Three Unpublished Letters to Whitman." *MLQ* 10 (Mr 49) 91-5.
Atkinson, J. B. "Walt Whitman's Democracy." *Freeman* 3 (13 Ap 21) 106-8.
Atkinson, W. W. "My Recollections of Whitman." *New Thought Mag* (Ja 10) 6-9.
Baker, Carlos. "The Road to Concord. Another Milestone in the Whitman-Emerson Friendship." *PULC* 9 (Ap 46) 100-17.
Baker, Portia. "Walt Whitman and *The Atlantic Monthly.*" *AL* 6 (N 34) 283-301.

——— "Walt Whitman's Relations with Some New York Magazines." *AL* 7 (N 35) 274-301.
Baldensperger, F. "Walt Whitman and France." *Columbia Un Q* 21 (Jl 19) 298-309.
Barker, Elsa. "What Whitman Learned from the East." *Canada Mo* 10 (O 11) 438-43.
Barrus, Clara. "Whitman and Burroughs as Comrades." *YR* 15 (O 25) 59-81.
Basler, R. P. *"Out of the Cradle Endlessly Rocking."* *Expl* 5 (Je 47) 59.
Beatty, R. C. "Whitman's Political Thought." *SAQ* 46 (Ja 47) 72-83.
Beaver, Joseph. "Walt Whitman, Star-Gazer." *JEGP* 48 (Jl 49) 307-19.
Beck, Maxmilian. "Walt Whitman's Intuition of Reality." *Ethics* 53 (O 42) 14-24.
Begg, Edleen. "Larks, Purple Cows, and Whitmania." *Un Texas Lib Chron* 2 (Sp 47) 190-2.
Benson, A. B. "Walt Whitman's Interest in Swedish Writers." *JEGP* 31 (Jl 32) 332-45.
Bergman, Herbert. "'Chicago': An Uncollected Poem Possibly by Whitman." *MLN* 65 (N 50) 478-81.
——— "A Poet's Western Visit." *Mo Hist R* 8 (Ja 49) 74.
——— "Sir Edwin Arnold and Walt Whitman." *N&Q* 193 (21 Ag 48) 366.
——— "Walt Whitman on New Jersey: An Uncollected Essay." *Proc N J Hist Soc* 66 (O 48) 139-54.
——— "Walt Whitman Parodies." *AN&Q* 8 (Ag 48) 74.
——— "Whitman in June, 1885: Three Uncollected Interviews." *AN&Q* 8 (Jl 48) 51-6.
——— "Whitman on His Poetry and Some Poets: Two Uncollected Interviews." *AN&Q* 8 (F 50) 103-5.
——— "Whitman on Politics, Presidents, and Hopefuls." *AN&Q* 8 (My 48) 19-26.
Bernard, E. G. "Some New Whitman Manuscript Notes." *AL* 8 (Mr 36) 59-63.
Berry, E. G. "Whitman's Canadian Friend." *Dalhousie R* 24 (Ap 44) 77-82.
Bicknell, P. F. "An Aged Poet in His Daily Talk." *Dial* 56 (16 Je 14) 493-4.
——— "The Real and the Ideal Whitman." *Dial* 40 (1 Mr 06) 144-6.
Birss, J. H. "A Note on 'O Captain! My Captain!'" *N&Q* 161 (26 S 31) 233.
——— "Notes on Whitman." *N&Q* 143 (29 O 32) 311-2.
——— "A Satire on Whitman." *N&Q* 164 (7 Ja 33) 6-7.
——— "Whitman and Herman Melville." *N&Q* 164 (22 Ap 33) 280.
——— "Whitman on Arnold: An Uncollected Comment." *MLN* 47 (My 32) 316-7.
Blanck, Jacob. "News from the Rare Book Sellers." *Pub W* 153 (27 S 47) B201-2.
Blodgett, Harold. "Walt Whitman in England." *Am Merc* 17 (Ag 29) 490-6.
——— "Whitman and Buchanan." *AL* 2 (My 30) 131-40.
——— "Whitman and Dowden." *AL* 1 (My 29) 171-82.
Boatwright, M. C. "Whitman and Hegel." *Un Texas Stud Eng* 9 (1929) 134-50.
Boyd, Ernest. "The Father of Them All." *Am Merc* 6 (D 25) 451-8.
Boynton, P. H. "I, Walt Whitman." *NRp* 19 (31 My 19) 141-3.
——— "Soil Preparation and Grass Seed." *NRp* 31 (19 Jl 22) 225-6.
——— "Walt Whitman—a Centenary View." *Nation* 108 (31 My 19) 866-7.
——— "Whitman's Idea of the State." *NRp* 7 (10 Je 16) 139-41.
Bozard, J. F. "Horace Traubel's Socialistic Interpretation of Whitman." *Furman Bul* 20 (Ja 38) 35-45.
Bradford, Gamaliel. "Portraits of American Authors." *Bkm* 42 (Ja 16) 533-48.
Bradley, Sculley. "The Fundamental Metrical Principles in Whitman's Poetry." *AL* 10 (Ja 39) 457-9.
——— "Mr. Walter Whitman." *Bkm* 76 (Mr 33) 227-32.
——— "The Problem of a Variorum Edition of Whitman's *Leaves of Grass*." *Eng Inst Annual* (1941) 129-58.
——— "Walt Whitman and the Postwar World." *SAQ* 42 (Jl 43) 220-4.
——— "Walt Whitman on Timber Creek." *AL* 5 (N 33) 235-46.

——— "Walt Whitman, Poet of the Present War." *Gen Mag & Hist Chron* 45 (O 42) 7-14.
Bradsher, E. L. "Walt Whitman and a Modern Problem." *SR* 22 (Ja 14) 86-95.
Bredvold, L. I. "Walt Whitman." *Dial* 53 (1 N 12) 323-5.
Bromer, E. S. "Is Walt Whitman the Best Representative of America's Independent Spirit in Poetry?" *Reformed Church R* 16 (Jl 12) 346-66.
Brooks, Van Wyck. "A French View of Whitman." *Freeman* 1 (31 Mr 20) 68-9.
——— "A Lost Prophet." *Freeman* 1 (24 Mr 20) 46-7.
Brophy, John. "The Walt Whitman Legend." *John O'London's W* 40 (15 Jl 38) 12.
Brown, C. H. "Young Editor Whitman: An Individualist in Journalism." *JQ* 27 (Sp 50) 141-8.
Brown, H. D. "Whitman and the America of Today." *Conservator* 28 (Ag 17) 86-8.
Bruère, R. W. "Walt Whitman." *Reader* 5 (Mr 05) 490-4.
Burgess, Janna. "Walt Whitman and Elias Hicks." *Friends' Intelligencer* 101 (1944) 54-5.
Burke, Kenneth. "Acceptance and Rejection." *So R* 2 (Wi 37) 600-32.
C., C. C. "Theosophy in Secular Literature—Walt Whitman." *Theosophical Q* 8 (Jl 10) 28-44.
Cairns, W. B. "Swinburne's Opinion of Whitman." *AL* 3 (My 31) 125-36.
——— "Walt Whitman." *YR* ns 8 (Jl 19) 737-54.
Calder, E. M. "Personal Recollections of Walt Whitman." *Atl* 99 (Je 07) 825-34.
——— "William O'Connor and Walt Whitman." *Conservator* 17 (My 06) 42.
Campbell, Killis. "The Evolution of Whitman as Artist." *AL* 6 (N 34) 254-63.
——— "Miscellaneous Notes on Whitman." *Un Texas Stud Eng* 14 (1934) 116-22.
Canby, H. S. "Who Speaks for New World Democracy?" *SRL* 26 (16 Ja 43) 3-4, 16-8.
Carpenter, F. I. "Walt Whitman's 'Eidolon.'" *CE* 3 (Mr 42) 534-45.
Catel, Jean. "L'Atelier de Walt Whitman." *Revue Anglo-Américaine* 6 (Ag 29) 527-30.
——— "Un Inédit de Walt Whitman." *Etudes Anglaises* 3 (1 O 39) 359-60.
——— "Poésie moderne aux Etats-Unis." *Revue des Cours et Conférences* (15, 30 My 33) 210-24, 345-57.
——— "Le Roman d'amour de Walt Whitman." *Revue Anglo-Américaine* 1 (1924) 197-212.
——— "Walt Whitman Pendant la Guerre de Secession d'Après des Documents Inédits." *Revue Anglo-Américaine* (1926) 410-9.
Cestre, Charles. "Un intermède de la renommée de Walt Whitman en France." *Revue Anglo-Américaine* 12 (D 35) 136-40.
——— "Walt Whitman, l'inadapté." *Revue Anglo-Américaine* 7 (Je 30) 385-409.
——— "Walt Whitman, le mystique, le lyrique." *Revue Anglo-Américaine* 6 (Ag 30) 482-505.
——— "Walt Whitman, le poète." *Revue Anglo-Américaine* 7 (O 30) 19-42.
——— "Walt Whitman, Poet of Self." *Un Calif Chron* 25 (Jl 23) 318-43.
Chace, F. M. "A Note on Whitman's Mockingbird." *MLN* 61 (F 46) 93-4.
Clark, G. D. "Walt Whitman in Germany." *Texas R* 6 (Ja 21) 123-37.
Clark, H. A. "The Awakening of the Soul: Whitman and Maeterlinck." *Conservator* 11 (Je 00) 56-8.
Coad, O. S. "Seven Whitman Letters." *JRUL* 8 (D 44) 18-26.
——— "A Walt Whitman Manuscript." *JRUL* 2 (D 38) 6-10.
——— "A Whitman Letter." *JRUL* 6 (D 42) 29.
——— "Whitman as Parent." *JRUL* 7 (D 43) 31-2.
——— "Whitman vs. Parton." *JRUL* 4 (D 40) 1-8.
Coleman, R. A. "Further Reminiscences of Walt Whitman." *MLN* 63 (Ap 48) 266-8.
——— "Trowbridge and Whitman." *PMLA* 63 (Mr 48) 262-73.
Colum, Padraic. "Poetry of Walt Whitman." *NRp* 19 (14 Je 19) 213-5.

Cooke, A. L. "American First Editions at TxU: Walt Whitman." *Un Texas Lib Chron* 2 (Je 36) 95-105.
——— "A Note on Whitman's Symbolism in 'Song of Myself.'" *MLN* 65 (Ap 50) 228-32.
——— "Notes on Whitman's Musical Background." *NEQ* 19 (Je 46) 224-35.
——— "Whitman's Background in the Industrial Movements of His Time." *Un Texas Stud Eng* 15 (1935) 76-91
——— "Whitman's Indebtedness to the Scientific Thought of His Day." *Un Texas Stud Eng* 16 (1936) 115-24.
Cowley, Malcolm. "Walt Whitman: The Miracle." *NRp* 114 (18 Mr 46) 385-8.
——— "Walt Whitman: The Philosopher." *NRp* 117 (29 S 47) 29-31.
——— "Walt Whitman: The Secret." *NRp* 144 (8 Ap 46) 481-4.
——— "Whitman: The Poet." *NRp* 117 (20 O 47) 27-30.
Coy, Rebecca. "A Study of Whitman's Diction." *Un Texas Stud Eng* 16 (Jl 36) 115-24.
Crocker, Lionel. "The Rhetorical Influences of Henry Ward Beecher." *QJS* 18 (F 32) 82-7.
——— "Walt Whitman's Interest in Public Speaking." *QJS* 26 (D 40) 657-67.
Cronyn, G. W. "The Idealism of the Real: Claude Monet and Walt Whitman." *Columbia Mo* (My 08).
Crosby, Ernest. "Walt Whitman's Children of Adam." *Philistine* 23 (Ag 06) 65-8.
Cunningham, Clarence. "A Defense of Walt Whitman's 'Leaves of Grass.'" *Arena* 33 (Ja 05) 55-8.
Curti, Merle. "Walt Whitman, Critic of America." *SR* 36 (Ap 28) 130-8.
Daniel, L. C. "Two Etchings for Walt Whitman's 'Song of the Open Road.'" *Forum* 93 (Ja 35) 32-3.
Dart, W. K. "Walt Whitman in New Orleans." *Pub La Hist Soc* 7 (1915) 97-112.
Davenport, W. E. "Identity of Whitman's Work and Character." *Conservator* 13 (F 03) 181.
DeCasseres, Benjamin. "Enter Walt Whitman." *Philistine* 25 (N 07) 161-72.
Dell, Floyd. "Walt Whitman, Anti-Socialist." *NRp* 3 (15 Je 15) 85.
Diyardin, Edouard. "Les Premiers Poètes du Vers Libre." *Mercure de France* 146 (F-Mr 21) 577-621.
DuBois, A. E. "On Being Born as Whitman Was." *Un R* 9 (Wi 42) 129-38.
Dugdale, Clarence. "Whitman's Knowledge of Astronomy." *Un Texas Stud Eng* 16 (1936) 124-37.
Dyer, L. H. "Walt Whitman." *Wilshire's Mag* (N 02) 76-83.
Dykes, E. B. "Democracy and Walt Whitman." *Negro Hist Bul* 6 (My 43) 175-7.
Dykes, M. M. "'A Nondescript Monster' with 'Terrible Eyes.'" *Nw Mo State Teachers Col Stud* 4 (Je 40) 3-32.
Eastman, Max. "Walt Whitman: Poet of Democracy." *Reader's Dig* 42 (Je 43) 29-33.
Eby, E. H. "Did Whitman Write 'The Good Gray Poet'?" *MLQ* 11 (D 50) 445-9.
Eccles, Caroline. "An Appreciation of Walt Whitman." *Quest* 3 (Ja 12) 349-59.
Eleanor, Sister Mary. "Hedge's 'Prose Writers of Germany' as a Source of Whitman's Knowledge of German Philosophy." *MLN* 61 (Je 46) 381-8.
Elliott, G. R. "Browning's Whitmanism." *SR* 37 (Ap 29) 164-71.
Erskine, John. "Whitman's Prosody." *SP* 20 (Jl 23) 336-44.
Falk, R. P. "Shakespere's Place in Walt Whitman's America." *Shakespeare Assn Bul* 17 (Ap 42) 86-96.
——— "Walt Whitman and German Thought." *JEGP* 40 (Jl 41) 315-30.
Fawcett, Waldo. "One Hundred Critics Gauge Walt Whitman's Fame." *N Y Times Book R* (10 Je 23).
Ferm, E. B. "The Democracy of Walt Whitman." *Mother Earth* 1 (Ja-F 07) 11-2.
Figueira, Gastón. "Poetas y prosistas de América: Walt Whitman." *Revista Iberoamericana* 11 (Je 46) 113-6.

Finkel, W. L. "Sources of Walt Whitman's Manuscript Notes on Physique." *AL* 22 (N 50) 308-31.
——— "Walt Whitman's Manuscript Notes on Oratory." *AL* 22 (Mr 50) 29-52.
——— "Whitman and the Calendar." *Word Study* 25 (F 50) 3-4.
Firkins, O. W. "Walt Whitman." *Weekly R* 1 (31 My 19) 56-8.
Fletcher, E. G. "'Pioneers! O Pioneers!'" *AL* 19 (N 47) 259-61.
——— "Walt Whitman." *NAR* 219 (Mr 24) 355-66.
——— "Walt Whitman's Beginnings." *Freeman* 3 (4 My 21) 188.
Foerster, Norman. "Whitman and the Cult of Confusion." *NAR* 213 (Je 21) 799-812.
——— "Whitman as a Poet of Nature." *PMLA* 31 (D 16) 736-58.
Francis, Sculley. "Walt Whitman." *Andean Q* 2 (Ja 43) 52-61.
Freedman, F. B. "Walt Whitman and Heinrich Zschokke: A Further Note." *AL* 15 (My 43) 181-2.
Frend, G. G. "Walt Whitman as I Remember Him." *Bkm* (L) 22 (Jl 27) 203.
Frenz, Horst. "American Literature and World Literature." *CL News Letter* 2 (F 44) 4-6.
——— "Karl Knortz, Interpreter of American Literature and Culture." *AGR* 13 (D 46) 27-30.
——— "Walt Whitman's Letters to Karl Knortz." *AL* 20 (My 48) 155-63.
Frump, Timothy. "A Whitman Manuscript." *N&Q* 166 (24 Mr 34) 206.
Fulghum, W. B., Jr. "Whitman's Debt to Joseph Gostwick." *AL* 12 (Ja 41) 491-6.
Furness, C. J. "Walt Whitman Looks at Boston." *NEQ* 1 (1928) 353-70.
——— "Walt Whitman's Estimate of Shakespeare." *Harvard Stud & Notes in Phil & Lit* 14 (1932) 1-33.
——— "Walt Whitman's Politics." *Am Merc* 16 (Ap 29) 459-66.
——— "Winwar, *American Giant: Walt Whitman and His Times*." *AL* 13 (Ja 42) 423-32.
Gamberale, Luigi. "Life and Work of Walt Whitman." *Conservator* 15 (S 04) 103-6.
Garrison, C. G. "Walt Whitman, Christian Science and Vedanta." *Conservator* 15 (F 05) 182-5.
Glicksberg, C. I. "A Friend of Walt Whitman." *Am Book Coll* 6 (Mr 35) 91-4.
——— "Walt Whitman and Bayard Taylor." *N&Q* 173 (3 Jl 37) 5-7.
——— "Walt Whitman and Heinrich Zschokke." *N&Q* 166 (2 Je 34) 382-4.
——— "Walt Whitman and 'January Searle.'" *AN&Q* 6 (Jl 46) 51-3.
——— "Walt Whitman in 1862." *AL* 6 (N 34) 264-82.
——— "Walt Whitman in New Jersey: Some Unpublished Manuscripts." *NJ Hist Soc Proc* 55 (Ja 37) 42-6.
——— "Walt Whitman in the Civil War." *Revue Anglo-Américaine* 9 (Ap 32) 327-8.
——— "Walt Whitman Parodies: Provoked by the Third Edition of 'Leaves of Grass.'" *AN&Q* 7 (Mr 48) 163-8.
——— "A Walt Whitman Parody." *AL* 6 (Ja 35) 436-7.
——— "Walt Whitman, the Journalist." *Americana* 30 (Jl 36) 474-90.
——— "Whitman and Bryant." *Fantasy* 5 (1935) 2.
——— "A Whitman Discovery." *Colophon* ns 1 (Au 35) 227-33.
Gohdes, Clarence. "The 1876 English Subscription for Whitman." *MLN* 50 (Ap 35) 257-8
——— "A Note on Whitman's Use of the Bible as a Model." *MLQ* 2 (Mr 41) 105-8.
——— "Whitman and Emerson." *SR* 37 (Ja 29) 79-93.
Goodale, David. "Some of Walt Whitman's Borrowings." *AL* 10 (My 38) 202-13.
Gosse, Edmund. "Whitman Centenary." *Living Age* 302 (5 Jl 19) 41-3.
Hackman, Martha. "Whitman, Jeffers, and Freedom." *Prairie Schooner* 20 (Fl 46) 182-4.
Halkin, Simon. "A Song of Joys." *Bitzaron, the Hebrew Mo of Am* 22 (1950) 92-100.

Hamilton, Clayton. "Walt Whitman as a Religious Seer." *Forum* 42 (Jl 09) 80-5.
Harned, T. B. "Slanderers of Whitman." *Conservator* 18 (D 07) 151-4.
——— "Walt Whitman in the Present Crisis of Our Democracy." *Conservator* 16 (Ja 06) 167-8.
Harris, L. H. "Walt Whitman as Artist and Teacher." *SAQ* 20 (Ap 21) 120-36.
Harrison, R. C. "Walt Whitman and Shakespeare." *PMLA* 44 (D 29) 1201-38.
Hartmann, Sadakichi. "Salut au Monde: A Friend Remembers Whitman." *Sw R* 12 (Jl 27) 262-7.
Hartt, G. M. "Whitman: An Inspiration to Democracy." *Conservator* 19 (Ag 08) 87-8.
Hays, Will. "The Birth of a Bible." *Texas R* 8 (O 23) 21-31.
Hertel, Leo. "Walt Whitmans Kenntnis Deutscher Literatur." *GQ* 21 (Ja 48) 16-24.
Hervey, J. L. "The Growth of the Whitman 'Legend.'" *Dial* 59 (24 Je 15) 12-4.
Hier, F. P., Jr. "The End of a Literary Mystery." *Am Merc* 1 (Ap 24) 471-8.
Holcomb, E. L. "Whitman and Sandburg." *EJ* 17 (S 28) 549-55.
Holloway, Emory. "Childhood Traits in Whitman." *Dial* 72 (F 22) 169-77.
——— "Early Poems of Walt Whitman." *Nation* 102 (10 F 16) 15; 103 (21 D 16) 5-6.
——— "Early Writings of Walt Whitman." *Nation* 102 (10 F 16) 15; 103 (21 D 16) 5-6.
——— "Early Writings of Walt Whitman." *Nation* 101 (14 O 15) 463.
——— "More Light on Whitman." *Am Merc* 2 (F 24) 183-9.
——— "Notes from a Whitman Student's Scrapbook." *Am Schol* 2 (My 33) 269-78.
——— "Some New Whitman Letters." *Am Merc* 16 (F 29) 183-8.
——— "Some Recently Discovered Poems by Walt Whitman." *Dial* 60 (13 Ap 16) 369-70.
——— "The Walt Whitman Exhibition." *BNYPL* 29 (N 25) 763-6.
——— "Walt Whitman in New Orleans." *YR* ns 5 (O 15) 166-83.
——— "Walt Whitman's First Free Verse." *Nation* 105 (27 D 17) 717.
——— "Walt Whitman's History of Brooklyn Just Found." *N Y Times* (17 S 16).
——— "Walt Whitman's Love Affair." *Dial* 69 (N 20) 473-83.
——— "Walt Whitman's Visit to the Shakers." *Colophon* 4 (Mr 33) Pt 13.
——— "Whitman and the War's Finale." *Colophon* (F 30) Pt 1.
——— "Whitman as Critic in America." *SP* 20 (Jl 23) 345-69.
——— "Whitman as Journalist." *SRL* 8 (23 Ap 32) 679-80.
——— "Whitman His Own Press Agent." *Am Merc* 18 (D 29) 482-8.
——— "A Whitman Manuscript." *Am Merc* 3 (D 24) 475-80.
——— "Whitman on the War's Finale." *Colophon* 1 (Mr 30) Pt 1.
——— "Whitman's Embryonic Verse." *Sw R* 10 (Jl 25) 28-40.
——— "Whitman's Message for Today." *Am Merc* 62 (F 46) 202-6.
Howard, Leon. "For a Critique of Whitman's Transcendentalism." *MLN* 47 (F 32) 79-85.
——— "Walt Whitman and the American Language." *AS* 5 (Ag 30) 441-51.
Howe, M. A. DeW. "The Spell of Whitman." *Atl* 98 (D 06) 849-55.
Hubach, R. R. "A Kansas City Newspaper Greets Walt Whitman." *N&Q* 185 (18 D 43) 365-6.
——— "Three Uncollected St. Louis Interviews of Walt Whitman." *AL* 14 (My 42) 141-7.
——— "An Uncollected Whitman Letter." Duke Un *Lib Notes* no 23 (Ja 50) 13.
——— "Walt Whitman and Taliessin." *AL* 18 (Ja 47) 329-31.
——— "Walt Whitman in Kansas." *Kansas Hist Q* 10 (My 41) 150-5.
——— "Walt Whitman Visits St. Louis." *Mo Hist R* 37 (Jl 43) 386-94.
Hubbell, J. B. "De Tocqueville and Whitman." *Nation* 109 (22 N 19) 655.
Hult, G. E. "Whitman Once More." *Un No Dak Quar J* 9 (Jl 19) 309-31.
Hume, R. A. "Walt Whitman and the Peace." *CE* 6 (Mr 45) 313-9.
——— "Wine with Walt." *SAQ* 41 (O 42) 437-40.

Hungerford, Edward. "Walt Whitman and His Chart of Bumps." *AL* 2 (Ja 31) 350-84.
Irwin, F. J. "The Religion of Walt Whitman." *Truth Seeker* (11 Mr 05) 147.
Jacobsen, A. "Walt Whitman in Germany since 1914." *GR* 1 (Ap 26) 132-41.
Jannacconne, P. "Poetry of Walt Whitman." *Conservator* 11 (1900) 21, 38, 53, 120, 135; 12 (1901) 7.
Johnson, C. W. M. "Whitman's *Out of the Cradle Endlessly Rocking.*" *Expl* 5 (My 47) 52.
Johnson, M. O. "Walt Whitman as a Critic of Literature." *Un Neb Stud* 16 (1938) 1-73.
Johnston, A. C. "Personal Memories of Walt Whitman." *Bkm* 46 (D 17) 402-13.
Johnston, Bertha. "Walt Whitman and the American Teacher." *Conservator* 20 (Jl, Ag, S 09) 70, 85, 102.
Johnston, John. "Walt Whitman—The Poet of Nature." *Fortnightly R* 93 (1 Je 10) 1123-36.
Johnston, J. H. "Half Hours with Whitman." *Everywhere* 21 (Ja 08) 212-4.
Jones, P. M. "Influence of Walt Whitman on the Origin of the 'Vers Libre.'" *MLR* 11 (Ap 16) 186-94.
——— "Whitman in France." *MLR* 10 (Ja 15) 1-27.
Jordy, W. H. "Henry Adams and Walt Whitman." *SAQ* 40 (Ap 41) 132-45.
Keller, E. L. "Walt Whitman: The Last Phase." *Putnam's* 6 (Je 09) 331-7.
Kelley, W. V. "The Deification of 'One of the Roughs.'" *Homiletic R* 42 (S 01) 202-8.
Kennedy, W. S. "On the Trail of the Good Gray Poet." *Conservator* 17 (F 07) 82-5.
Kirkland, Winifred. "Americanization and Walt Whitman." *Dial* 66 (31 My 19) 537-9.
Knapp, Adeline. "A Whitman Coincidence." *Critic* 44 (My 04) 467-8.
Lafourcade, Georges. "Swinburne and Walt Whitman." *MLR* 22 (Ja 27) 84-6; *Revue Anglo-Américaine* 8 (O 31) 49-50.
Lang, C. Y. "A Further Note on Swinburne and Whitman." *MLN* 64 (Mr 49) 176-7.
Laporte, P. M. "Cézanne and Whitman." *Mag of Art* 37 (S 44) 223-7.
Law-Robertson, Harry. "Walt Whitman in Deutschland." *Giessener Beiträge zur Deutschen Philologie* 42 (1935).
Leconte, Joseph. "Un Poète américain: Walt Whitman." *La Vie Intellectuelle* 1 (15 F 08).
Lee, G S. "Order for the Next Poet." *Putnam's* 1 (Mr 07) 697-703; 2 (Ap 07) 99-107.
Leighton, Walter. "Whitman's Note of Democracy." *Arena* 28 (Jl 02) 61-5.
Leonard, M. H. "Walt Whitman to His Followers." *SAQ* 16 (Jl 17) 222-6.
Lessing, O. F. "Walt Whitman and His German Critics Prior to 1910." *Am Col* 3 (O 26) 7-15.
Lessing, O. F. "Walt Whitman's Message." *Open Court* 33 (Ag 19) 449-62.
——— "Whitman and German Critics." *JEGP* 9 (Ja 10) 85-98.
Lewis, R. W. B. "The Danger of Innocence: Adam as Hero in American Literature." *YR* 29 (Sp 50) 473-90.
Lindsay, Vachel. "Walt Whitman." *NRp* 37 (5 D 23) 3-5.
Loving, Pierre. "Towards Walt Whitman." *Double Dealer* 4 (S 22) 139-42.
Lowell, Amy. "Walt Whitman and the New Poetry." *YR* 16 (Ap 27) 502-19.
Lucchese, Romeo. "Dopo Whitman la vera poesia americana." *La Fiera Letteraria* (Italy) no 43 (23 O 49) 5.
Mabbott, T. O. "Early Quotations and Allusions of Walt Whitman." *N&Q* 150 (6 Mr 26) 169-70.
——— "Notes on Walt Whitman's 'Franklin Evans.'" *N&Q* 149 (12 D 25) 419-20.
——— "Some Account of Sojourner Truth." *Am Col* 4 (Ap 27) 18-20.

——— "Walt Whitman and the *Aristidean.*" *Am Merc* 2 (Je 24) 205-7.
——— "Walt Whitman and the *Brooklyn Freeman.*" *N&Q* 183 (26 S 42) 186-7.
——— "Walt Whitman and William Motherwell." *N&Q* 168 (4 My 35) 314.
——— "Walt Whitman's ''Tis but Ten Years Since.'" *AL* 15 (Mr 43) 61-2.
——— "Walt Whitman's Use of 'Libertad.'" *N&Q* 174 (21 My 38) 367-8.
——— "Whitman: Notes on Emerson." *N&Q* 185 (26 F 44) 14.
——— "Whitman's Lines on Duluth." *AL* 3 (N 31) 316-7.
——— "Whitman's *Song of Myself,* XXIV, 19." *Expl* (Ap 47) 43.
——— "William Winter's Serious Parody of Walt Whitman." *AL* 5 (Mr 33) 63-6.
———, & Silver, R. G. "Mr. Whitman Reconsiders." *Colophon* 3 (F 32) Pt 9.
Mabie, H. W. "American Life in Whitman's Poetry." *Outlook* 75 (5 S 03) 67-78.
McCain, Rea. "Walt Whitman in Italy." *Ital* 20 (Mr 43) 4-16.
——— "Walt Whitman in Italy: A Bibliography." *Bul Bibl* 17 (Ja-Ap, My-Ag 41) 66-7, 92-3.
McCusker, Honor. "*Leaves of Grass:* First Editions and Manuscripts in the Whitman Collection." *More Books* 13 (My 38) 179-92.
McIlwraith, J. N. "A Dialogue in Hades: Omar Khayyám and Walt Whitman." *Atl* 89 (Je 02) 808-12.
Mackall, L. L. "Whitman and Bucke. Notes for Bibliophiles." *N Y Herald-Tribune Books* 12 (12 Ap 36) 23.
Mann, Klaus. "The Present Greatness of Walt Whitman." *Decision* 1 (Ap 41) 14-30.
Mansell-Jones, P. "Whitman and the Origins of the 'vers-libre.'" *French Stud* (Oxford, England) 2 (Ap 48) 129-39.
Martí, José. "Martí in His Own Words. I. Walt Whitman." *Bul Pan Am Union* 2 (My 45) 270-2.
Mary Eleanor, Sister. "Hedge's *Prose Writers of Germany* as a Source of Whitman's Knowledge of German Philosophy." *MLN* 61 (Je 46) 381-8.
Mathews, J. C. "Walt Whitman's Reading of Dante." *Un Texas Stud Eng* 19 (1939) 177-9.
Maxwell, William. "Some Personalist Elements in the Poetry of Whitman." *Personalist* 12 (Jl 31) 190-9.
Maynard, Laurens. "Walt Whitman and Elbert Hubbard." *Conservator* 28 (D 17) 151-2.
Mead, Leon. "Walt Whitman." *Conservator* 11 (Ag 00) 90-2.
Mendelssohn, M. "Walt Whitman." *New World* (Moscow) 22 (Mr 45) 183-8.
Merrill, Stuart. "Une Lettre . . . à propos de Walt Whitman." *Mercure de France* 102 (Ap 13) 890-2.
——— "La Question Walt Whitman." *Mercure de France* 706 (16 N 13) 329-36.
Meyer, A. N. "Two Portraits of Whitman." *Putnam's* 4 (S 08) 707-10.
Miller, F. H. "Some Unpublished Letters of Walt Whitman's." *Overland Mo* 43 (Ja 04) 61-3.
Mirsky, D. S. "Walt Whitman: Poet of American Democracy." *Dialectics* 1 (1937) 11-29.
Molinoff, Katherine. "Walt Whitman at Smithtown." *Long Island Forum* 4 (Ag 41) 179-80, 182-4.
Möller, Tyge. "Walt Whitman." *Conservator* 20 (Ja 10) 165-8.
Monroe, Harriet. "Walt Whitman." *Poetry* 14 (My 19) 89-94.
Monroe, W. S. "Recent Walt Whitman Literature in America." *Revue Anglo-Américaine* 7 (D 30) 138-41.
——— "Swinburne's Recantation of Walt Whitman." *Revue Anglo Américaine* 8 (Ap 31) 347-52.
Moore, J. B. "The Master of Whitman." *SP* 23 (Ja 26) 77-89.
Moore, J. R. "Walt Whitman: A Study in Brief." *SR* 25 (Ja 17) 80-92.
Morgan, Claude. "Walt Whitman and Howard Fast." *Parallèle* 50: no 108 (15 O 48) 5.
Morgan, J. A. "Early Reminiscences of Walt Whitman." *AL* 13 (Mr 41) 9-17.

——— "A Reply." *AL* 13 (Ja 42) 414-6.
Mouray, Gabriel. "Walt Whitman." *Conservator* 21 (My, Je 10) 37, 53.
Mufson, Thomas. "Walt Whitman, Poet of the New Age." *Twentieth Century* 2 (Jl 10) 325-30.
Muzzey, D. S. "The Ethical Message of Walt Whitman." *Ethical Record* 4 (My 03) 147-51.
Myers, H. A. "Whitman's Conception of the Spiritual Democracy, 1855-1856." *AL* 6 (N 34) 239-53.
——— "Whitman's Consistency." *AL* 8 (N 36) 243-57.
Nathan, Hans. "Walt Whitman and the Marine Band." *More Books* 18 (F 43) 47-56.
Naumburg, Edward, Jr. "A Collector Looks at Walt Whitman." *PULC* 3 (N 41) 1-18.
Neumann, H. "Walt Whitman." *Am Schol* 2 (My 33) 261-8.
Noguchi, Yone. "Whitmanism and Its Failure." *Bkm* 49 (Mr 19) 95-7.
O'Higgins, Harvey. "Alias Walt Whitman." *Harper's* 158 (My 29) 698-707.
O'Leary, R. D. "Swift and Whitman as Exponents of Human Nature." *Int J Ethics* 24 (Ja 14) 183-201.
Osmaston, F. P. "The 'Coarseness' of Whitman." *Quest* 3 (Jl 12) 766-70.
Paine, Gregory. "The Literary Relations of Whitman and Carlyle with Especial Reference to Their Contrasting Views on Democracy." *SP* 36 (Jl 39) 550-63.
Parry, Albert. "Walt Whitman in Russia." *Am Merc* 33 (S 34) 100-7.
Parsons, O. W. "Whitman the Non-Hegelian." *PMLA* 58 (D 43) 1073-93.
Pentecost, H. O. "Walt Whitman's View of Life." *Truth Seeker* (7 Mr 14).
Platt, I. H. "A Poet Who Could Wait." *Book News* 24 (Ap 06) 545-9.
——— "The Silence of Whitman." *Conservator* 13 (Je 02) 56-7.
——— "Whitman's Superman." *Conservator* 16 (F 06) 182-3.
Pollard, Marguerite. "The Universality of Whitman." *Theosophist* 35 (D 13) 373-81.
Pound, Louise. "Doubtful Whitman Lore." *AL* 13 (Ja 42) 411-3.
——— "Note on Walt Whitman and Bird Poetry." *EJ* 19 (Ja 30) 31-6.
——— "Walt Whitman and Italian Music." *Am Merc* 6 (S 25) 58-63.
——— "Walt Whitman and the Classics." *Sw R* 10 (Ja 25) 75-83.
——— "Walt Whitman and the French Language." *AS* 1 (My 26) 421-9.
——— "Walt Whitman's Neologisms." *Am Merc* 4 (F 25) 199-201.
Powell, L. C. "Leaves of Grass and Granite Boulders." *Carmelite* 4 (22 O 31) 8-9.
Pratt, J. W. "Whitman and Masters: A Contrast." *SAQ* 16 (Ap 17) 155-8.
Pritchett, V. S. "Books in General." *New Statesman & Nation* 28 (30 S 44) 223-4.
Rahv, Philip. "Paleface and Redskin." *KR* 1 (Su 39) 251-6.
Randall, H. F. "Whitman and Verhaeren—Priests of Human Brotherhood." *FR* 16 (O 42) 36-43.
Ratcliffe, S. K. "Walt Whitman." *Literature* (16 F 01).
Reed, H. B. "The Heraclitan Obsession of Walt Whitman." *Personalist* 15 (Sp 34) 125-38.
Reeves, Harrison. "À propos de Walt Whitman." *Mercure de France* 103 (16 Je 13) 893-5.
Remenyi, Joseph. "Walt Whitman in Hungarian Literature." *AL* 16 (N 44) 181-5.
Rhodes, S. A. "The Influence of Walt Whitman on André Gide." *RR* 31 (Ap 40) 156-71.
Rhys, Ernest. "Walt Whitman—1819-1892." *Bkm* (London) 56 (My 19) 66-8.
——— "Walt Whitman's *Leaves of Grass.*" *Everyman* 1 (28 F, 7 Mr 13) 623, 656-7.
Ridley, H. "Walt Whitman and Anne Gilchrist." *Dalhousie R* 11 (Ja 32) 521-6.
Robinson, Victor. "Walt Whitman." *Altruria Mag* (My 07) 14-25.
Robinson, W. J. "Walt Whitman and Sex." *Conservator* 24 (Je 13) 53-5.
Rodgers, Cleveland. "Walt Whitman, the Politician." *Lit R* 4 (1923) 57-8.

Romig, E. D. "More Roots for Leaves of Grass." *Un Colo Stud* 2: ser B (O 45) 322-8.
——— "The Paradox of Walt Whitman." *Un Colo Stud* 5 (Je 26) 95-132.
——— "Walt Whitman: 1819-1919." *Outlook* 122 (7 My 19) 34-7.
Roos, Carl. "Walt Whitman's Letters to a Danish Friend." *Orbis Litterarum* 7 (1949) 31-60.
Ross, E. C. "Whitman's Verse." *MLN* 45 (Je 30) 363-4.
Rubin, J. J. "John Neal's Poetics as an Influence on Whitman and Poe." *NEQ* 14 (Je 41) 359-62.
——— "Tupper's Possible Influence on Whitman's Style." *AN&Q* 1 (O 41) 101-2.
——— "Whitman and Carlyle: 1846." *MLN* 53 (My 38) 370.
——— "Whitman and the Boy-Forger." *AL* 10 (My 38) 214-5.
——— "Whitman as a Dramatic Critic." *QJS* 28 (F 42) 45-9.
——— "Whitman in 1840: A Discovery." *AL* 9 (My 37) 239-42.
——— "Whitman on Byron, Scott, and Sentiment." *N&Q* 176 (11 Mr 39) 171.
——— "Whitman's *New York Aurora*." *AL* 11 (My 39) 214-7.
Santayana, George. "Genteel American Poetry." *NRp* 3 (29 My 15) 94-5.
Schinz, Albert. "À propos de Walt Whitman." *Mercure de France* 107 (1 F 14) 669-71.
——— "Walt Whitman, a World Poet?" *Lippincott's* (O 13) 466-74.
Schumann, D. W. "Enumerative Style and Its Significance in Whitman, Rilke, Werfel." *MLQ* 3 (Je 42) 171-204.
Scott, Dixon. "Walt Whitman." *Bkm* (London) 46 (My 14) 81-5.
Scott, F. N. "A Note on Walt Whitman's Prosody." *JEGP* 7 (2Q 08) 134-53.
Scovel, J. M. "Walt Whitman as I Knew Him." *National Mag* 20 (My 04) 165-9.
Sengfelder, Bernhard. "Walt Whitman." *Deutsche Rundschau* (Stuttgart) 70 (N 47) 108-14.
Sheffauer, Herman. "Whitman in Whitman's Land." *Fortnightly R* 91 (Ja 15) 128-37; *NAR* 201 (F 15) 206-16.
Shepard, Esther. "An Error of Omission in Mabbott and Silver's 'Walt Whitman's "'Tis but Ten Years Since."'" *AL* 15 (Ja 44) 421.
Sherrinsky, Harald. "Walt Whitman in modernen deutschen Uebersetzungen." *Neuphilologische Zeitschrift* 3 (1950) 189-91.
Shipley, Maynard. "Democracy as Religion." *Open Court* 33 (Jl 19) 385-93.
——— "Walt Whitman's Message." *Conservator* 17 (S 06) 102-5.
Sholes, C. W. "Walt Whitman: His Poetry and Philosophy." *Pac Mo* 6 (S 01) 141-3.
Sillen, Samuel. "Walt Whitman: The War Years." *New Masses* 42 (31 Mr 42) 22-3.
Silver, R. G. "Concerning Walt Whitman." *N&Q* 167 (11 Ag 34) 96.
——— "For the Bright Particular Star." *Colophon* ns 2 (Wi 37) 197-216.
——— "A Note about Whitman's Essay on Poe." *AL* 6 (Ja 35) 435-6.
——— "Oscar Makes a Call." *Colophon* 5 (Mr 35) Pt 20.
——— "A Parody on Walt Whitman." *N&Q* 167 (1 S 34) 150.
——— "Seven Letters of Walt Whitman." *AL* 7 (Mr 35) 76-81.
——— "Thirty-one Letters of Walt Whitman." *AL* 8 (Ja 37) 417-38.
——— "Walt Whitman: First Appearance of 'Virginia—the West.'" *N&Q* 175 (12 N 38) 348-49.
——— "Walt Whitman's Lecture in Elkton." *N&Q* 170 (14 Mr 36) 190-1.
——— "Whitman." N Y *Times* (3 N 35) sec 4: 9.
——— "Whitman and Dickens." *AL* 5 (Ja 34) 370-1.
——— "Whitman in 1850: Three Uncollected Articles." *AL* 19 (Ja 48) 301-17.
——— "Whitman Interviews Himself." *AL* 10 (Mr 38) 84-7.
Simonds, W. E. "Walt Whitman, Fifty Years After." *Dial* 41 (16 N 06) 317-20.
Sixbey, G. L. "'Chanting the Square Deific'—A Study in Whitman's Religion." *AL* 9 (My 37) 171-95.

Skinner, C. M. "Walt Whitman as Editor." *Atl* 92 (N 03) 679-86.
Smith, F. M. "Whitman's Debt to Carlyle's *Sartor Resartus*." *MLQ* 3 (Mr 42) 51-65.
——— "Whitman's Poet-Prophet and Carlyle's Hero." *PMLA* 55 (D 40) 1146-64.
Smith, G. J. "Emerson and Whitman." *Conservator* 14 (Je 03) 53-5.
——— "Whitman's Reading of Life." *Poet Lore* 17 (Au 06) 79-94.
Snyder, J. E. "Walt Whitman's Woman." *Socialist Woman* (F 09).
Soto Paz, Rafael. "Un gran poeta." *America; Revista de la Associatión de Escritores y Artistas Americanos* 10 (Je 41) 5.
Spiegelman, Julia. "Walt Whitman and Music." *SAQ* 41 (Ap 42) 167-76.
Spitzer, Leo. "'Explication de Texte' Applied to Whitman's 'Out of the Cradle Endlessly Rocking.'" *ELH* 16 (S 49) 229-49.
Springer, Otto. "Walt Whitman and Ferdinand Freiligrath." *AGR* 11 (D 44) 22-6, 38.
Starr, W. T. "Jean Giono and Walt Whitman." *FR* 14 (D 40) 118-29.
Steell, Willis. "Walt Whitman's Early Life on Long Island." *Munsey's* 40 (Ja 09) 497-502.
Stevenson, Philip. "Walt Whitman's Democracy." *New Masses* 27 (14 Je 33) 129-33.
Stewart, G. R. "Whitman and His Own Country." *SR* 33 (Ap 25) 210-8.
Story, I. C. "The Structural Pattern of *Leaves of Grass*." *Pac Un Bul* 38 (Ja 42) 2-12.
Stovall, Floyd. "Main Drifts in Whitman's Poetry." *AL* 4 (Mr 32) 3-22.
——— [On Whitman's "Calamus" poems.] *PULC* 3 (F 42) 68-9.
Strauch, C. F. "The Structure of Walt Whitman's 'Song of Myself.'" *EJ* (col ed) 27 (S 38) 597-607.
Sutcliffe, E. G. "Whitman, Emerson and the New Poetry." *NRp* 19 (24 My 19) 114-6.
Swan, Tom. "Walt Whitman: The Man. His Book. His Message." *Open Road* 1 (Jl, Ag, N 07).
Swayne, Mattie. "Whitman's Catalogue Rhetoric." *Un Texas Stud Eng* 21 (1941) 162-78.
Symons, Arthur. "Note on Walt Whitman." *Bellman* 24 (9 F 18) 154-5.
Thayer, W. R. "Personal Recollections of Walt Whitman." *Scribner's* 65 (Je 19) 674-87.
Thorstenberg, Edward. "The Walt Whitman Cult in Germany." *SR* 19 (Ja 11) 71-86.
Tolles, F. B. "A Quaker Reaction to *Leaves of Grass*." *AL* 19 (My 47) 170-1.
Toruno, A. F. "El Sentido humano de la poesia social de Walt Whitman." *Comizahualt* 4 (Je 44) 1-5, 23-7.
Traubel, Horace. "The Code of a Gentleman." *Conservator* 17 (Ja 07) 168-72.
———. "Estimates of Well-Known Men." *Century* 83 (D 11) 250-6.
——— "Getting Whitman Right and Wrong." *Conservator* 25 (Jl 14) 77.
——— "The Good Gray Poet at Home." *Sat Eve Post* (13 My, 3 Je, 16 Ag 05).
——— "Leaves from Whitman's Later Life." *Critic* 41 (O 02) 319-27.
——— "Talks with Walt Whitman." *Am Mag* 64 (Jl 07) 281-8.
——— "Walt Whitman at Fifty Dollars a Volume and How He Came to It." *Era* 11 (Je 03) 523-9.
——— "Walt Whitman on Himself." *Am Merc* 3 (O 24) 186-92.
——— "Walt Whitman's America." *Conservator* 28 (N 17) 134-6.
——— "Walt Whitman's New Publishers." *Conservator* 18 (Ag 17) 92.
——— "Walt Whitman's Respect for the Body." *Physical Culture* 10 (S 03) 246-50.
——— "Whitman in Old Age." *Century* 74 (S, O 07) 740-55, 911-22.
——— "Whitman on His Contemporaries." *Am Merc* 2 (Jl 24) 328-32.
——— "Whitmania." *Conservator* 29 (My 18) 40-2.

——— "With Walt Whitman in Camden." *Century* 71 (N 05) 82-98; *Forum* 46 (O, N, D 11) 400-14, 589-600, 709-19; 47 (Ja 12) 78-89; 54 (Jl, Ag, S 15) 77-85, 187-99, 318-27; *Seven Arts* 2 (S 17) 627-38.
——— See also *Conservator* 12-30 (Ja 00-Je 19) *passim.*
Trent, J. C. "Walt Whitman—A Case History." *Surgery, Gynecology & Obstetrics* 87 (Jl 48) 113-21.
Trilling, Lionel. "Sermon on a Text from Whitman." *Nation* 160 (24 F 45) 214-20.
Trowbridge, J. T. "Reminiscences of Walt Whitman." *Atl* 89 (F 02) 163-75.
Turina, Pepita. "Walt Whitman, Cotidano y Eterno." *Anales de la Universidad de Chile* 45-6 (1942) 190-205.
Untermeyer, Louis. "Whitman Centenary." *NRp* 18 (22 Mr 19) 245-7.
Van Doren, Mark. "Walt Whitman, Stranger." *Am Merc* 35 (Jl 35) 277-85.
von Ende, Amelia. "Walt Whitman and Arno Holz." *Poet Lore* 16 (Su 05) 61-5.
——— "Walt Whitman and the Germans Today." *Conservator* 18 (Je 07) 55-7.
——— "Walt Whitman in Germany." *Conservator* 14 (Ja, F 04) 167, 183.
——— "Whitman's Following in Germany." *Conservator* 14 (Ap 03) 23-5.
W. "Walt Whitman—a Sketch." *Universal Brotherhood Path* 16 (D 01) 502-11.
Walcutt, C. C. "Whitman's 'Out of the Cradle Endlessly Rocking.'" *CE* 10 (F 49) 277-9.
Wallace, J. W. "Whitman's Personality." *Bkm* (London) 56 (My 19) 68-9.
Ware, Lois. "Poetic Conventions in *Leaves of Grass.*" *SP* 26 (Ja 29) 47-57.
Weathers, W. T. "Whitman's Poetic Translations of His 1855 Preface." *AL* 19 (Mr 47) 21-40.
Wecter, Dixon. "Walt Whitman as Civil Servant." *PMLA* 58 (D 43) 1094-1109.
Wells, Carolyn. "On Collecting Whitman." *Colophon* ns 1 (1939) 47-54.
Wentworth, Franklin. "The Breaker of Seals." *Conservator* 16 (Jl 05) 69-71.
Werner, W. L. "Whitman's 'The Mystic Trumpeter' as Autobiography." *AL* 1 (Ja 36) 455-8.
Whicher, S. E. "Whitman's *Out of the Cradle Endlessly Rocking.*" *Expl* 5 (F 47) 28.
White, C. Y. "A Whitman Ornithology." *Cassinia* 25 (1945) 12-22.
White, Eliot. "Walt Whitman and the Living Present." *Conservator* 24 (O 13) 117.
——— "Walt Whitman's Significance to a Revolutionist.'" *Conservator* 22 (Jl 11) 71-2.
White, V. C. "Thoreau's Opinion of Whitman." *NEQ* 8 (Je 35) 262-4.
White, William. "Walt Whitman and Sir William Osler." *AL* 11 (Mr 39) 73-7.
——— "Walt Whitman on Osler: 'He Is a Great Man.'" *Bul Hist Med* 15 (Ja 40) 79-90.
Whitman, Walt. "An American Primer." *Atl* 93 (Ap 04) 460-70.
Wiley, A. N. "Reiterative Devices in *Leaves of Grass.*" *AL* 1 (My 29) 161-70.
Willcox, L. C. "Walt Whitman." *NAR* 183 (Ag 06) 281-96.
Williams, F. H. "An Appreciation of Walt Whitman." *Columbia Mo* 5 (My 08) 7.
——— "Individuality as Whitman's Primary Motive." *Conservator* 11 (Jl 00) 71-3.
Williams, M. L. "Whitman Today." *UKCR* 14 (Su 48) 267-76.
Williams, S. T. "The Adrian Van Sinderen Collection of Walt Whitman." *Yale Un Lib Gaz* 15 (Ja 41) 49-53.
Winterich, J. T. "Walt Whitman and Leaves of Grass." *Golden Book* (My 29) 79.
Winwar, Frances. "Walt Whitman's 'Dark Lady.'" *Un R* 9 (Sp 43) 191-7.
——— "Whitman's Calamus Poems." *PULC* 3 (F 42) 66-8.
Woodhull, M. G. "Walt Whitman: A Memory Picture." *Lit Era* 8 (Mr 01) 159-60.
Woodward, F. L. "Walt Whitman: A Prophet of the Coming Race." *Theosophical R* 32 (Ag 03) 508-15.
Workman, M. T. "The Whitman-Twain Enigma." *Mark Twain Q* 8 (Su-Fl 48) 12-3.
Wyatt, E. F. "The Answerer: Walt Whitman." *NAR* 209 (My 19) 672-82.
——— "A Peace-Lover's War Epic." *NRp* 11 (30 Je 17) 242-4.

——— "Whitman and Anne Gilchrist." *NAR* 210 (S 19) 388-400.
Yarmolinsky, Avraham. "The Russian View of American Literature." *Bkm* 44 (S 16) 44-8.
Yorke, Dane. "Whitman in Camden." *Am Merc* 8 (Jl 26) 355-62.
Zarek, O. "Walt Whitman and German Poetry." *Living Age* 316 (10 F 23) 334-7.
Zeiger, Arthur. "In Defense of Whitman." *To-morrow* 9 (Je 50) 54-6.
Zueblin, Charles. "Walt Whitman, Prophet and Democrat." *Ford Hall Folks* 2 (28 D 13).
Zunder, T. A. "Walt Whitman and Nathaniel Hawthorne." *MLN* 47 (My 32) 314-6.
——— "Whitman Interviews Barnum." *MLN* 48 (Ja 33) 40.
——— "William B. Marsh: The First Editor of the *Brooklyn Daily Eagle*." *Am Book Coll* 4 (Ag 33) 93-5.

WHITTIER, JOHN GREENLEAF (1807-92). Anon. "Letters from John G. Whittier to Superintendent of Schools in Cincinnati." *EIHC* 67 (O 31) 408.
——— "An Unknown Whittier Poem." *N E Mag* ns 29 (N 03) 273-5.
——— "Unpublished Whittier Poems." *N E Mag* ns 29 (F 04) 783-6.
——— "A Whittier Note." *Bul Friends' Hist Assn* 18 (Au 39) 102.
Abbott, Lyman. "Snap-shots of My Contemporaries. John G. Whittier, Mystic." *Outlook* 127 (19 Ja 21) 96-8.
Adams, E. L. "Whittier's Choice for Congress." *More Books* 18 (N 43) 432-3.
Adkins, N. F. "Sources of Some of Whittier's Lines." *N&Q* 164 (8 Ap 33) 242.
——— "Two Uncollected Sketches of Whittier." *NEQ* 6 (Je 33) 364-71.
——— "Whittier's 'The Barefoot Boy.'" *N&Q* 165 (5 Ag 33) 78-9.
Barrows, M. M. "The Love Story of Whittier's Life: Personal Reminiscences of the Poet's Sweetheart, Evelina Bray." *N E Mag* ns 32(Ap 05) 173-9.
Beckford, W. H. "A Reminiscence of Whittier." *Book News Mo* 33 (S 14) 13-4.
Beffel, J. N. "Dark Day in New England." *Am Merc* 56 (Ap 43) 481-5.
Bennett, R. M. "An Unpublished Whittier Letter." *JRUL* 9 (D 45) 30-2.
Bishop, D. H. "John Greenleaf Whittier." *SAQ* 7 (Ja 08) 61-74.
Boynton, H. W. "John Greenleaf Whittier, an Appreciation." *Putnam's* 3 (D 07) 274-80.
Bray, Evelina. "Letter from Evelina Bray to John Greenleaf Whittier." *EIHC* 69 (Ja 33) 88.
Bruère, R. W. "Walt Whitman." *Reader* 5 (Mr 05) 490-4.
Buckham, J. W. "The Unforgotten Whittier." *N E Mag* ns 29 (S 03) 44-51.
Byington, S. T. "Mr Byington's Brief Case (IV)." *AS* 21 (F 46) 37-41.
Cadbury, H. J. "Whittier's Early Quaker Poems." *NEQ* 18 (Je 45) 251-6.
Carpenter, G. R. "The Range of Whittier's Pen." *Book News Mo* 26 (D 07) 263-4.
Carruth, F. W. "The Real Barbara Frietchie." *Bkm* 13 (Jl 01) 418-21.
Carter, G. F. "A Footnote on Whittier." *N E Mag* ns 34 (Je 06) 432.
——— "The Home and Birthplace of Whittier." *Lit Coll* 8 (Jl 04) 65-72.
——— "Some Little-known Whittierana." *Lit Coll* 7 (Ap 04) 169-72.
Chapin, H. M. "Whittier's 'Palatine' Discovered." *Am Col* 3 (D 26) 118-22.
Christy, Arthur. "Orientalism in New England: Whittier." *AL* 1 (Ja 30) 372-92.
——— "The Orientalism of Whittier." *AL* 5 (N 33) 247-57.
Coad, O. S. "The Bride of the Sea." *AL* 9 (Mr 37) 71-3.
Coleman, M. H. "Whittier on John Randolph of Roanoke." *NEQ* 8 (D 35) 551-5.
Coolidge, Theresa. "Whittier Introduces Elizabeth Lloyd Howell." *More Books* 22 (D 46) 29.
Currier, T. F. "Alexander Pushkin by John Greenleaf Whittier." *Friends' Intelligencer* 94 (Mr 37) 159.
——— "The Epping Oak." *Exeter News-Letter* (19 Je 41) 10.
——— "Whittier and 'Mary.'" *NEQ* 6 (D 33) 801-2.
——— "Whittier and the Amesbury-Salisbury Strike." *NEQ* 8 (Mr 35) 105-12.
——— "Whittier and the *New England Weekly Review*." *NEQ* 6 (S 33) 589-97.

——— "The Whittier Leaflet 'Pericles.'" *Lib Q* 4 (Ap 34) 175-8.
——— "Whittier's 'Lines in an Album.'" *NEQ* 9 (D 36) 699-700.
——— "Whittier's Philadelphia Friends in 1838." *Bul Friends' Hist Assn* 27 (Au 38) 58-72.
——— "Whittier's 'The Demon Lady:'" *NEQ* 10 (D 37) 776-80.
———, & Emerson, D. E. "Whittier's 'To ——— with a Copy of Woolman's Journal.'" *Bul Friends' Hist Assn* 30 (Au 41) 69-74.
Cuyler, T. L. "Recollections of a Long Life." *Cur Lit* 33 (O 02) 121-5.
Delavan, Wayne. "Whittier Promoted Free Kansas." *Aerend* 12 (Sp 41) 81-6.
Desmond, M. E. "Associations of Whittier." *Cath World* 75 (Je 02) 353-68.
——— "The Story of Whittier's 'Captain's Well.'" *Cath World* 71 (Ag 00) 595-604.
——— "The Story of Whittier's 'Countess.'" *Cath World* 72 (Ja 01) 478-88.
Dolbee, Cora. "Kansas and 'The Prairied West' of John G. Whittier." *EIHC* 81 (O 45) 307-47; 82 (Ap 46) 155-73.
Doyle, Joseph. "An Uncollected Poem of Whittier." *NEQ* 22 (Mr 49) 96-7.
Drew, H. L. "The Schoolmaster in *Snow-Bound.*" *AL* 9 (My 37) 243-4.
Emerson, D. E. "Whittier, Woolman's *Journal,* and Caroline Neagus." *Bul Friends' Hist Assn* 30 (Au 41) 74-9.
Ericson, E. E. "'John Hort' and 'Skipper Ireson.'" *NEQ* 10 (S 37) 531-2.
Fabian, R. C. "Some Uncollected Letters of John Greenleaf Whittier to Gerritt Smith." *AL* 22 (My 50) 158-63.
Fleming, B. J. "John Greenleaf Whittier, Abolition Poet." *Negro Hist Bul* 6 (D 42) 54, 64, 66.
Foerster, Norman. "Nature in Whittier." *Nation* 104 (4 Ja 17) 15-7.
——— "Whittier as Lover." *Freeman* 6 (14 F 23) 549-50.
Forsythe, R. S. "An Uncollected Poem by Whittier." *AL* 4 (My 32) 194-5.
Freeman, D. C. "John Greenleaf Whittier and His Birthplace." *EIHC* 86 (O 50) 229-310.
Glicksberg, C. I. "Bryant and Whittier." *EIHC* 72 (Ap 36) 111-6.
Gribble, Francis. "John Greenleaf Whittier." *Fortnightly R* 89 (Ja 09) 137-47; *Living Age* 256 (F 08) 287-95.
Griffin, M. L. "Whittier and Hayne: A Record of a Friendship." *AL* 19 (Mr 47) 41-58.
Griggs, E. L. "John Greenleaf Whittier and Thomas Clarkson." *AL* 7 (Ja 36) 458-60.
Griswold, M. J. "American Quaker History in the Works of Whittier, Hawthorne, and Longfellow." *Americana* 34 (Ap 40) 220-63.
Hale, E. E. "Impression of Whittier." *Outlook* 87 (21 D 07) 860-1.
Harvey-Jellie, W. "A Forgotten Poet." *Dalhousie R* 19 (Ap 39) 91-100.
Hawley, C. A. "Correspondence between John Greenleaf Whittier and Iowa." *Iowa J Hist & Pol* 35 (Ap 37) 115-41.
——— "The Growth of Whittier's Reputation in Iowa." *Bul Friends' Hist Assn* 28 (Au 39) 67-102.
——— "Jennie Shrader." *Palimpsest* 18 (S 37) 285-98.
——— "John Greenleaf Whittier and His Middle Western Correspondents." *Bul Friends' Hist Assn* 28 (Sp 39) 19-29.
——— "Whittier and Iowa." *Iowa J Hist & Pol* 34 (Ap 36) 115-43.
——— "Whittier and Nebraska." *Bul Friends' Hist Assn* 30 (Sp 41) 17-43.
Hicks, Granville. "Letters to William Francis Channing." *AL* 2 (N 30) 294-8.
Higginson, T. W. "Garrison and Whittier." *Independent* 59 (7 D 05) 1310-6.
——— "John Greenleaf Whittier." *Independent* 63 (19 D 07) 1492-7.
——— "The Place of Whittier among Poets." *Reader* 5 (F 05) 368-72.
——— "Whittier as Combatant in the Days of the Abolitionists." *Book News Mo* 26 (D 07) 259-62.
Hoxie, E. F. "Harriet Livermore: 'Vixen and Devotee.'" *NEQ* 18 (Mr 45) 39-50.

Hoyt, M. W. "Rambles in Whittier-land." *Granite State Mag* 6 (Ag, S 11) 217-24, 257-64; 7 (O, N, D 11) 17-24, 69-78.
Hume, Elizabeth. "Neighbor to a Poet." *EIHC* 76 (O 40) 345-54.
——— "Summers with a Poet." *EIHC* 75 (O 39) 313-25.
Hurd, H. E. "Paradoxes in the Life and Poetry of John Greenleaf Whittier." *Poetry R* 17 (Ag 26) 261-7.
Kingsley, M. E. "A Quaker Poet in Puritan New England." *Poet Lore* 21 (O 10) 330-6.
Kirk, Rudolph. "Whittier and Miss Piatt." *JRUL* 7 (Je 44) 63.
Lancaster, H. C. "Henri Bordeaux and *Maud Muller*." *MLN* 27 (Ja 12) 30-1.
Lee, E. D. "John Greenleaf Whittier." *Westminster R* 169 (Ja 08) 78-92.
McEuen, K. A. "Whittier's Rhymes." *AS* 20 (F 45) 51-7.
Marble, A. R. "Elizabeth Whittier and the Amesbury Home." *Outlook* 87 (7 S 07) 29-35.
——— "Some Friendships of Whittier: With Letters Hitherto Unpublished." *Dial* 43 (16 D 07) 409-10.
Maulsby, D. L. "Whittier's New Hampshire." *NE Mag* ns 22 (Ag 00) 631-47.
Mordell, Albert. "Another Note on Whittier." *NEQ* 7 (Je 34) 324-5.
——— "Whittier and Lucy Hooper." *NEQ* 7 (Je 34) 316-25.
Perry, Bliss. "Whittier for Today." *Atl* 100 (D 07) 851-9.
Phelps, W. L. "A Noteworthy Letter of Whittier's." *Century* 64 (My 02) 15-7.
——— "Whittier." *NAR* 186 (D 07) 602-6.
Phillips, S. W. "Further Light on the Question of the Residence of John Greenleaf Whittier." *EIHC* 69 (Ja 33) 89.
Pickard, S. T. "A Merry Woman's Letters to a Quiet Poet." *Ladies' Home J* 17 (D 99, Ja 00) 7-8, 9-10.
——— [Miscellaneous bibliographical and textual notes.] *Independent* 55-72 (00-12) *passim.*
Pollard, J. A. "Whittier on Labor Unions." *NEQ* 12 (Mr 39) 99-102.
——— "Whittier's Esteem in Great Britain." *Bul Friends' Hist Assn* 38 (Sp 49) 33-6.
Powell, Desmond. "Whittier." *AL* 9 (N 37) 335-42.
Quynn, D. M., & W. R. "Barbara Frietschie." *Md Hist Mag* 37 (S, D 42) 227-54, 400-3.
Rantoul, R. S. "Some Personal Recollections of the Poet Whittier." *EIHC* 37 (Ap 00) 129-44.
Russell, J. A. "The Original Element in Whittier's Writings." *Granite Mo* 60 (1928) 217-23.
Sanborn, F. B. "Whittier as Man, Poet, and Reformer." *Bibliotheca Sacra* 65 (Ap 08) 193-213.
Sayles, N. L. "A Note on Whittier's *Snow-Bound*." *AL* 6 (N 34) 336-7.
Schaedler, L. C. "Whittier's Attitude toward Colonial Puritanism." *NEQ* 21 (S 48) 350-67.
Schurz, Carl. "Reminiscences of a Long Life." *McClure's* 28 (Ja 07) 259-60.
Scott, Kenneth. "The Source of Whittier's 'The Dead Ship of Harpswell.'" *Am Neptune* 6 (Jl 46) 223-7.
Scott, W. T. "Poetry in America: A New Consideration of Whittier's Verse." *NEQ* 7 (Je 34) 258-75.
Shackford, M. H. "A Child's Impressions of Whittier." *Lamp* 28 (Jl 04) 470-2.
——— "Whittier and Some Cousins." *NEQ* 15 (S 42) 467-96.
Shepard, G. F. "Letters of Lucy Larcom to the Whittiers." *NEQ* 3 (Jl 30) 501-18.
Smallwood, O. T. "The Historical Significance of Whittier's Anti-Slavery Poems as Reflected by Their Political and Social Background." *J Negro Hist* 35 (Ap 50) 150-73.

Snyder, E. D. "John Greenleaf Whittier to William J. Alinson: Nineteen Unpublished Letters from the Quaker Poet to His Friend in Burlington, N. J." *Bul Friends' Hist Assn* 37 (Sp 48) 17-35.

——— "Notes on Whittier and Haverford College." *Bul Friends' Hist Assn* 25 (Sp 36) 7-10.

——— "Whittier Returns to Philadelphia after a Hundred Years." *PMHB* 62 (Ap 38) 140-57.

——— "Whittier's Letters to Ann Elizabeth Wendell." *Bul Friends' Hist Assn* 29 (Au 40) 69-92.

———, & Hewitt, A. B. "Letters of John Greenleaf Whittier in the Roberts Collection at Haverford College." *Bul Friends' Hist Assn* 25 (Sp 36) 33-43.

Sparhawk, F. C. "Glimpses of Whittier." *Lippincott's* 80 (D 07) 786-93.

Stearns, Bertha-Monica. "John Greenleaf Whittier, Editor." *NEQ* 13 (Je 40) 280-304.

Stedman, E. C. "The Whittier Home Association." *Independent* 54 (22 My 02) 1231-3.

Stewart, Randall. "Two Uncollected Reviews by Hawthorne." *NEQ* 9 (S 36) 504-9.

T., H. S. "John Greenleaf Whittier Manuscripts: The Oak Knoll Collection." *EIHC* 67 (Ap 31) 113-8.

Taylor, C. M. "The 1849 Best Seller." *Bul Friends' Hist Assn* 38 (Sp 49) 26-7.

——— "Some Whittier First Editions Published in the British Isles." *J Friends' Hist Soc* 42 (1950) 41-5.

——— "Whittier vs. Garrison." *EIHC* 82 (Jl 46) 249-78.

Thaler, Alwin. "Tennyson and Whittier." *PQ* 28 (O 49) 518-9.

Thompson, Ralph. "The *Liberty Bell* and Other Anti-Slavery Gift Books." *NEQ* 7 (Mr 34) 154-68.

Thwing, J. W. "Reminiscences of Whittier." *Granite State Mo* 3 (Mr, My 07) 89-98, 185-94.

Tilton, E. M. "Making Whittier Definitive." *NEQ* 12 (Je 39) 281-314.

Turner, Arlin. "Whittier Calls on George W. Cable." *NEQ* 22 (Mr 49) 92-6.

Weber, C. J. "Whittier and Sarah Orne Jewett." *NEQ* 18 (S 45) 401-7.

Wells, H. W. "The New England Quaker." *Chri Sci Mon* 37 (3 N 44) 9.

Whittier, J. G. "Rhymes (for S. Lewis)." *Bul Friends' Hist Assn* 25 (Sp 36) 11.

Wood, R. K. "A New Pilgrim in Whittierland." *Bkm* 38 (Ja 14) 481-9.

Woodman, Mrs. A. J. "Reminiscences of John Greenleaf Whittier's Life at Oak Knoll." *EIHC* 44 (Ap 08) 97-122.

Woodwell, R. H. "The Hussey Ancestry of the Poet Whittier." *EIHC* 70 (Ja 34) 58-68.

WHITTIER, MATTHEW FRANKLIN (1812-83). Griffin, L. W. "Matthew Franklin Whittier, 'Ethan Spike.'" *NEQ* 14 (D 41) 646-63.

WIDENER, HARRY ELKINS (1855-1912). Newton, A. E. "A Remembrance of Harry Elkins Widener." *Atl* 122 (Jl-D 18) 351-6.

WIGGIN, KATE DOUGLAS (1856-1923). Gibson, Ashley. "Kate Douglas Wiggin." *Bkm* (London) 38 (Jl 10) 149-58.

More, N. A. "Kate Douglas Wiggin: An Appreciation." *Overland Mo* 87 (Ja 29) 18, 28.

van Westrum, A. S. "Kate Douglas Wiggin, Litt.D. (Bowdoin)." *Lamp* 29 (Ja 05) 585-90.

Winter, Calvin. "Kate Douglas Wiggin." *Bkm* 32 (N 10) 237-43.

WIGGLESWORTH, MICHAEL (1631-1705). Anon. "Michael Wigglesworth's *Meat out of the Eater*." *Yale Un Libr Gaz* 5 (Ja 31) 45-7.

Jones, M. B. "Notes for a Bibliography of Michael Wigglesworth's *Day of Doom* and *Meat out of the Eater*." *PAAS* 39 (Ap 29) 77-84.

Matthiessen, F. O. "Michael Wigglesworth: A Puritan Artist." *NEQ* 1 (D 28) 491-504.

WILCOX, ELLA WHEELER (1850-1919). De Ford, M. A. "Poetess of Passion." *Am Merc* 32 (Ag 34) 435-9.

WILDE, RICHARD HENRY (1789-1847). Beall, C. B. "Un Tassista americano di cent'anni fa, R. H. Wilde." *Bergomum* 17 (Je 39) 91-9.
Starke, A. H. "The Dedication of Richard Henry Wilde's *Hesperia*." *Am Book Coll* 6 (My-Je 35) 204-9.
——— "Richard Henry Wilde." *Am Book Coll* 4 (N, D 33) 226-32, 285-8; (Ja 34) 7-10.
——— "Richard Henry Wilde in New Orleans and the Establishment of the University of Louisiana." *La Hist Q* 17 (O 34) 605-24.

WILDER, THORNTON (1897-). Anon. "The Economic Interpretation of Thornton Wilder." *NRp* 65 (26 N 30) 31-2.
Adcock, St. John. "Thornton Wilder." *Bkm* (London) 75 (Mr 29) 316-9.
Alder, Henry. "Thornton Wilder's Theatre." *Horizon* 12 (Ag 45) 89-98.
Bergholz, Harry. "Thornton Wilder." *Englische Studien* 65 (F 31) 301-6.
Blackmur, R. P. "Thornton Wilder." *H&H* 3 (Jl-S 30) 586-9.
Blanzat, Jean. "Le Port du Roi Saint-Louis: En Voiture pour le Ciel de Thornton Wilder." *Le Figaro Littéraire* (Paris) 4 (6 Ap 49) 5.
Brown, E. K. "A Christian Humanist: Thornton Wilder." *UTQ* 4 (Ap 35) 356-70.
Brown, J. M. "Wilder: 'Our Town.'" *SRL* 32 (6 Ag 49) 33-4.
Campbell, Joseph, & Robinson, H. M. "The Skin of Whose Teeth? The Strange Case of Mr. Wilder's New Play and 'Finnegan's Wake.'" *SRL* 25 (19 D 42) 3-4, (13 F 43) 16, 18-9.
Casstello, G. C. "Wilder: aperta serenità." *Fiera Letteraria* no 8 (20 F 49).
Chambrun, C. L. "L'Américanisme de Thornton Wilder." *Revue Anglo-Américaine* 8 (Ap 31) 341-4.
Dodd, L. W. "The Ways of Man to Man." *SRL* 4 (3 D 27) 371.
Fadiman, Clifton. "The Quality of Grace." *SRL* 125 (14 D 27) 187.
Farrar, John. "The Editor Recommends—." *Bkm* 63 (Je 20) 478.
Firebaugh, J. J. "The Humanism of Thornton Wilder." *PS* 4 (Au 50) 426-38.
Fischer, Walther. "Thornton Wilder's *The Bridge of San Luis Rey* und Prosper Merimées *Le Carosse du Saint-Sacrement*." *Anglia* 60 (Ja 36) 234-40.
Gardner, Martin. "Thornton Wilder and the Problem of Providence." *Un R* 7 (D 40) 83-91.
Gold, Michael. "Thornton Wilder: Prophet of the Genteel Christ." *NRp* 64 (22 O 30) 266-7.
Isaacs, E. J. R. "Thornton Wilder in Person." *Theatre Arts* 27 (Ja 43) 21-30.
Kohler, Dayton. "Thornton Wilder." *EJ* (coll ed) 28 (Ja 39) 1-11.
Loving, P. "The Bridge of Casuistry." *This Quarter* 2 (Jl-Ag-S 29) 150-61.
McNamara, Robert. "Phases of American Religion in Thornton Wilder and Willa Cather." *Cath World* 135 (S 32) 641-9.
Parmenter, Ross. "Novelist and Playwright." *SRL* 18 (Je 38) 10-1.
Peci, Enzo. "The Ides of March di Wilder." *La Rassegna d'Italia* (F 49).
Phelps, W. L. "As I Like It." *Scribner's* 83 (F 28) 224-5.
——— "Men Now Famous." *Delineator* 117 (S 30) 94-6.
Rebora, Roberto. "Wilder a Milano." *Fiera Letteraria* no 2 (9 Ja 49).
Tritsch, Walther. "Thornton Wilder in Berlin." *Living Age* 341 (Mr-Ag 31) 44-7.
Twitchett, E. G. "Mr. Thornton Wilder." *London Merc* 22 (My 30) 32-9.
Wilder, Thornton. "Ein Brief des Asinius Pollio an Vergil und Horaz." *Die Neue Rundschau* 11 (Su 48) 300-13.
Wilson, Edmund. "The Antrobuses and the Earwickers." *Nation* 156 (30 Ja 43) 167-8.

——— "Thornton Wilder." *NRp* 55 (8 Ag 28) 303-5.

WILLARD, FRANCES E. (1839-98). Bradford, Gamaliel. "Frances Elizabeth Willard." *Atl* 125 (Ja 20) 65-75.

WILLIAMS, BEN AMES (1889-). Roberts, Kenneth. "Ben Ames Williams." *Colby Lib Q* 1 (Ja 43) 5-6.

WILLIAMS, OSCAR (1900-). Eberhart, Richard. "Oscar Williams—Selected Poems." *Contemp Poetry* 8 (Wi 49) 12, 13.

WILLIAMS, ROGER (*c.* 1603-83). Anon. "Illustrations Connected with Roger Williams' Life." *R I Hist Soc Coll* 29 (Ap 36) 33-4.
——— "Important Roger Williams Letter." *R I Hist Soc Coll* 27 (Jl 34) 85-92.
Burrage, H. S. "Why Was Roger Williams Banished?" *Am J Theol* 5 (Ja 01) 1-17.
Carpenter, E. J. "Roger Williams and the Plantations at Providence." *N E Mag* ns 26 (My 02) 353-64.
Easton, Emily. "Mary Barnard." *R I Hist Soc Coll* 29 (Jl 36) 65-80.
Ernst, J. E. "New Light on Roger Williams' Life in England." *R I Hist Soc Coll* 22 (O 29) 97-103.
——— "Roger Williams and the English Revolution." *R I Hist Soc Coll* 24 (Ja 31) 1-58.
Freund, Michael. "Roger Williams, Apostle of Complete Religious Liberty." *R I Hist Soc Coll* 26 (O 33) 101-33.
H., B. C. "Roger Williams' Funeral." *R I Hist Soc Coll* 27 (Ap 34) 54.
Harkness, R. E. "Roger Williams: Prophet of Tomorrow." *J Religion* 15 (O 35) 400-25.
Hirsch, E. F. "John Cotton and Roger Williams: Their Controversy concerning Religious Liberty." *Church Hist* 10 (Mr 41) 38-51.
Ives, J. M. "Roger Williams, Apostle of Religious Bigotry." *Thought* 6 (D 31) 478-92.
King, H. M. "Roger Williams and the Pilgrims." *Nation* 86 (7 My 08) 421-2.
Moreland, Marc. "Roger Williams: Discipline for Today." *Phylon* 6 (2Q 45) 136-40.
Parkes, H. B. "John Cotton and Roger Williams Debate Toleration, 1644-1652." *NEQ* 4 (O 31) 735-56.
Peattie, D. C. "Roger Williams—First Modern American." *Reader's Dig* 49 (D 46) 65-9.
Stead, G. A. "Roger Williams and the Massachusetts-Bay." *NEQ* 7 (Je 34) 235-57.
Swan, B. F. "Roger Williams and the Insane." *R I Hist* 5 (Jl 46) 65-70.
——— "An Unpublished Letter of Roger Williams." *R I Hist* 3 (O 44) 139-40.
Watson, W. L. "A Short History of Jamestown on the Island of Conanicut, Rhode Island." *R I Hist Soc Coll* 26 (Ap 33) 37-59.
Wiener, F. B. "Roger Williams' Contribution to Modern Thought." *R I Hist Soc Coll* 28 (Ja 35) 1-20.
Wroth, L. C. "Variations in Five Copies of Roger Williams's *Key to the Language of America*." *R I Hist Soc Coll* 29 (O 36) 120-1.

WILLIAMS, THOMAS LANIER (1914-). Anon. "E'proprio vero quello che dice Williams?" *L'Ultima* (Italy) (25 Mr 48).
——— "'A Streetcar Named Desire.'" *Life* 23 (15 D 47) 101-2.
Barnett, Lincoln. "Tennessee Williams." *Life* 24 (16 F 48) 113, 114, 116, 118, 121-2, 124, 126-7.
Carroll, Sidney. "A Streetcar Named Tennessee." *Esquire* 29 (My 48) 46.
Gassner, John. "Tennessee Williams: Dramatist of Frustration." *CE* 10 (O 48) 1-7.
Josephson, Lennart. "Tennessee Williams dramatik." *Bonniers Litterära Magasin* (Stockholm) 18 (Mr 49) 207-11.

Lewis, R. C. "A Playwright Named Tennessee." *N Y Times Mag* (7 D 47) 19, 67, 69-70.
Mattia, E. G. "Intervista con Williams." *La Fiera Letteraria* (Italy) (27 F 48).
Moor, Paul. "A Mississippian Named Tennessee." *Harper's* 197 (Jl 48) 63-71.
Taylor, Harry. "The Dilemma of Tennessee Williams." *Masses & Mainstream* 1 (Ap 48) 51-6.

WILLIAMS, WILLIAM (1710-90). Flexner, J. T. "The Amazing William Williams: Painter, Teacher, Musician, Stage Designer, Castaway [and Novelist]." *Mag of Art* 37 (N 44) 243-6, 276-8.

WILLIAMS, WILLIAM CARLOS (1883-). Anon. "News Notes." *Poetry* 72 (Je 48) 171.
Bartlett, H. B. "Koral Grisaille." *Poetry* 17 (Mr 21) 329-32.
Burke, Kenneth. "William Carlos Williams, the Methods of." *Dial* 82 (F 27) 94-8.
Gierasch, Walter. "Williams' *Tract.*" *Expl* 3 (Mr 45) 35.
Lechlitner, Ruth. "The Poetry of William Carlos Williams." *Poetry* 54 (S 39) 326-35.
Moore, Marianne. "A Poet of the Quattrocento." *Dial* 82 (Mr 27) 213-5
Morgan, Frederick. "William Carlos Williams: Imagery, Rhythm, Form." *SR* 55 (Au 47) 670-8.
O'Connor, W. V. "Symbolism and the Study of Poetry." *CE* 6 (Ap 46) 376-9.
Pound, Ezra. "Dr. Williams' Position." *Dial* 75 (N 28) 395-404.
Rakosi, Carol. "William Carlos Williams." *Symposium* 4 (O 33) 439-47.
Rosenfeld, Paul. "Williams the Stylist." *SRL* 19 (11 F 39).
Stearns, M. W. "Syntax, Sense, Sound and Dr. Williams." *Poetry* 66 (Ap 45) 38-9.
Strobel, Marion. "Middle-aged Adolescence." *Poetry* 23 (N 23) 103-5.
Williams, W. C. "Notes toward an Autobiography." *Poetry* 74 (My 49) 94-111.
——— "Some Notes toward an Autobiography: The Childish Background." *Poetry* 72 (Je, Ag 48) 147-55, 264-70.
——— "Something for a Biography." *Gen Mag & Hist Chron* 50 (Su 48) 211-2.

WILLIS, NATHANIEL PARKER (1806-67). Daughrity, K. L. "Poe's 'Quiz on Willis.'" *AL* 10 (Mr 33) 55-62.
Fenn, W. P. "The Source of One of Willis's Sketches." *AL* 6 (Ja 35) 421-6.
Hicks, Granville. "A Literary Swell." *Bkm* 16 (Mr 29) 361-9.
Mabbott, T. O. "N. P. Willis and Lincoln." *AN&Q* 6 (D 46) 133-4.
Marble, A. R. "Willis and Poe: A Retrospect." *Critic* 48 (Ja 06) 24-6.
Paston, G. "The Penciller by the Way: Nathaniel Parker Willis." *Cornhill Mag* ns 11 (S 01) 326-45.
Peck, H. T. "N. P. Willis and His Contemporaries." *Bkm* 24 (S 06) 33-43.
Scudder, H. H. "Thackeray and N. P. Willis." *PMLA* 57 (Je 42) 589-92
Shulman, David. "N. P. Willis and the American Language." *AS* 23 (F 48) 39-47.
Wegelin, Christof. "Social Criticism in the Fiction of N. P. Willis." *AL* 20 (N 48) 313-22.

WILLIS, SARAH PAYSON (1811-72). Eckert, R. P., Jr. "Friendly Fragrant Fanny Fern." *Colophon* 5 (S 34) Pt 18.
Parton, Ethel. "Fanny Fern at the Hartford Female Seminary." *N E Mag* ns 24 (Mr 01) 94-8.

WILLKIE, WENDELL (1892-1944), Bromley, D. D. "The Education of Wendell Willkie." *Harper's* 181 (O 40) 477-85.

WILSON, ALEXANDER (1766-1813). Folsom, J. F. "Alexander Wilson as a Bloomfield Schoolmaster." *Proc N J Hist Soc* 15 (Ap 30) 199-210.

WILSON, AUGUSTA EVANS (1835-1909). Fidler, W. P. "Augusta Evans Wilson as Confederate Propagandist." *Ala R* 2 (Ja 49) 32-44.

WILSON, EDMUND (1895-). Anon. "Doubleday's Appeal Heard in 'Hecate County' Case." *Pub W* 151 (17 My 47) 2499.
——— "Edmund Wilson." *Cur Biog* 6 (Ap 45) 59-62.
——— "'Hecate' Conviction Stands as Supreme Court Splits." *Pub W* 154 (6 N 48) 1974-5.
——— "'Hecate County' Conviction Upheld in New York Appeal." *Pub W* 152 (22 N 47) 2414.
——— "U. S. Supreme Court Will Hear 'Hecate County' Appeal." *Pub W* 153 (27 Mr 48) 1457-8.
——— "Womrath Reports Prize-Winners in 'Hecate County' Contest." *Pub W* 150 (7 D 46) 3106; see also (2, 9 N, 7 D 46) 2608, 2726, 3104.
Boyd, Ernest. "Edmund Wilson's Essays." *SRL* 19 (26 Mr 38) 10.
Brown, E. K. "The Method of Edmund Wilson." *UTQ* 11 (O 41) 105-11.
Clark, J. A. "The Sad Case of Edmund Wilson." *Commonweal* 28 (8 Jl 38) 292-5.
DeVoto, Bernard. "My Dear Edmund Wilson." *SRL* 15 (13 F 37) 8.
Dupee, F. W. "Edmund Wilson's Criticism." *PR* 4 (My 38) 48-51.
Fiess, Edward. "Edmund Wilson: Art and Ideas." *AR* 1 (Fl 41) 356-67.
Flint, F. C. "A Critique of Experimental Poetry." *VQR* 13 (Su 37) 453-7.
Freeman, Joseph. "Edmund Wilson's Globe of Glass." *New Masses* 27 (12 Ap 38) 73-9.
Gauss, Christian. "Edmund Wilson, the Campus and the Nassau 'Lit.'" *PULC* 5 (F 44) 41-50.
Glicksberg, C. I. "Edmund Wilson: Radicalism at the Crossroads." *SAQ* 36 (O 37) 466-77.
Hicks, Granville. "The Intransigence of Edmund Wilson." *AR* 6 (Wi 46-7) 550-62.
Howe, Irving. "Edmund Wilson: A Revaluation." *Nation* 167 (16 O 48) 430-1.
Jerome, V. J. "Edmund Wilson: To the Munich Station." *New Masses* 32 (4 Ap 39) 23-4.
McCarty, Norma. "Edmund Wilson." *NAR* 246 (Au 38) 192-7.
Mizener, Arthur. "Edmund Wilson: A Check List." *PULC* 5 (F 44) 62-78.
Pritchett, V. S. "Books in General." *New Statesman & Nation* 37 (19 F 49) 183.
Schwartz, Delmore. "The Writing of Edmund Wilson." *Accent* 2 (Sp 42) 177-86.
Snell, George. "An Examination of Modern Critics, II: Edmund Wilson. The Historical Critic." *Rocky Mt R* 8 (Wi 44) 36-44.
West, Geoffrey. "Literary Detection." *TLS* (30 My 42) 271.
Wilson, Edmund. "Thoughts on Being Bibliographed." *PULC* 5 (F 44) 51-61.
Wilson, T. C. "The Muse and Edmund Wilson." *Poetry* 52 (Je 38) 144-52.
Zabel, M. D. "Marginalia of a Critic." *Poetry* 35 (Ja 30) 222-6.

WILSON, WOODROW (1856-1924). Athearn, C. R. "Woodrow Wilson's Philosophy." *Methodist R* 5 ser 112 (S-O 29) 683-8.
Barnes, H. E. "Woodrow Wilson." *Am Merc* 1 (Ap 24) 479-90.
Bradford, Gamaliel. "Brains Win and Lose: Woodrow Wilson." *Atl* 147 (F 31) 152-64.
Daniel, M. L. "Woodrow Wilson—Historian." *Miss Valley Hist R* 21 (D 34) 361-74.
Dickinson, T. H. "Bernard Shaw and Woodrow Wilson." *VQR* 7 (Ja 31) 1-17.
Eliot, C. W. "Woodrow Wilson." *Atl* 133 (Je 24) 815-23.
Harper, G. M. "Woodrow Wilson's 'History of the American People.'" *Book Buyer* 25 (Ja 03) 589-92.
Johnson, G. W. "The Ghost of Woodrow Wilson." *Harper's* 183 (Je 41) 1-9.
McKean, D. D. "Notes on Woodrow Wilson's Speeches." *QJS* 16 (Ap 30) 176-84.
MacRae, D. A. "An Appreciation of Woodrow Wilson." *Dalhousie R* 4 (Ap 24) 86-97.
Stephenson, W. H. "The Influence of Woodrow Wilson on Frederick Jackson Turner." *Agr Hist* 19 (O 45) 249-53.

Whyte, Frederic. "President Wilson as a Man of Letters." *Bkm* (London) 55 (O 18) 6-8.

WINSOR, KATHLEEN (1919-). Anon. "Boston Booksellers' Role in 'Forever Amber' Decision." *Pub W* 151 (5 Ap 47) 1905.
——— "'Forever Amber' Clearance Upheld in Massachusetts." *Pub* W 154 (23 O 48) 1813-4.
——— "Kathleen Winsor." *Cur Biog* 7 (D 46) 55-6.

WINTER, WILLIAM (1836-1917). Harting, Hugh. "William Winter." *N&Q* 185 (6 N 43) 288.
McGraw, C. S. "William Winter: Critic of the Brown Decades." *QJS* 31 (Ap 45) 162-7.

WINTERS, YVOR (1900-). Barrett, William. "Temptations of St. Yvor." *KR* 9 (Au 47) 532-51.
Blackmur, R. P. "A Note on Yvor Winters." *Poetry* 57 (N 40) 144-52.
Cunningham, J. V. "Obscurity and Dust." *Poetry* 21 (Je 23) 163-5.
Drummond, D. F. "Yvor Winters: Reason and Judgment." *Ariz Q* 5 (Sp 49) 5-19.
Fitzgerald, Robert. "Against the Grain." *Poetry* 50 (Je 37) 173-7.
Horton, Philip. "The California Classicism." *Poetry* 51 (O 37) 48-52.
Howells, Thomas. "Yvor Winters, Anatomist of Nonsense." *Poetry* 63 (N 43) 86-96.
Humphries, Rolfe. "Foreword, with Poems." *Poetry* 45 (F 35) 288-91.
Ransom, J. C. "Yvor Winters: The Logical Critic." *So R* 6 (Wi 41) 558-83.
Schwartz, Delmore. "A Literary Provincial." *PR* 12 (Wi 45) 138-42.
——— "Primitivism and Decadence." *So R* 3 (Au 38) 288-91.
Swallow, Alan. "The Sage of Palo Alto." *Rocky Mt R* 4 (Sp-Su 40) 1-3.
——— "Yvor Winters." *Rocky Mt R* 9 (Fl 44) 31-7.
Weiss, T. "The Nonsense of Winters' Anatomy." *Quar R Lit* 1 (Sp, Su 44) 212-34, 300-18.
West, R. B. "The Language of Criticism." *Rocky Mt. R* 8 (Fl 43) 12-3, 15.
Zabel, M. D. "A Poetry of Ideas." *Poetry* 37 (Ja 31) 225-30.

WINTHER, SOPHUS (1894-). Powell, Desmond. "Sophus Winther: The Grimsen Trilogy." *ASR* 36 (Su 48) 144-7.
Whicher, G. F. "Dane in America." *Forum* 105 (N 46) 450-4.

WINTHROP, ADAM (1559-1623). Kittredge, G. L. "Verses by Adam Winthrop." *PCSM* 27 (Ap 29) 187-94.

WINTHROP, JOHN (1588-1649). Anon. "The First Year, 1630-1631, of the Journal of John Winthrop." *PMHS* 62 (Je 29) 329-61.
Gray, Stanley. "The Political Thought of John Winthrop." *NEQ* 3 (O 30) 681-705.
Grinnell, F. W. "John Winthrop and the Constitutional Thinking of John Adams." *PMHS* 63 (F 31) 91-119.
Johnson, E. A. J. "Economic Ideas of John Winthrop." *NEQ* 3 (Ap 30) 235-50.

WINTHROP, JOHN (1606-76). Greenberg, Herbert. "The Authenticity of the Library of John Winthrop, the Younger." *AL* 8 (Ja 37) 448-52.
Mood, Fulmer. "John Winthrop, Jr., on Indian Corn." *NEQ* 10 (Mr 37) 121-33.
Steiner, W. R. "Governor John Winthrop, Jr. of Connecticut, as a Physician." *Johns Hopkins Hospital Bul* 14 (1903) 294-302.

WINTHROP, THEODORE (1828-61). Colby, Elbridge. "Bibliographical Notes on Theodore Winthrop." *BNYPL* 21 (Ja 17) 3-13.
——— "The Plates of the Winthrop Books." *BNYPL* 22 (F 18) 87-90.
Gates, W. B. "Theodore Winthrop, Early American Novelist." *Letters* 3 (Ag 30) 14-21.

Hunt, W. S. "An American Dickens." *Proc N J Hist Soc* 15 (O 30) 446.

WIRT, WILLIAM (1772-1834). Davis, R. B. "Poe and William Wirt." *AL* 16 (No 44) 212-20.
Hubbell, J. B. "William Wirt and the Familiar Essay in Virginia." *WMQ* 23 (Ap 43) 136-52.

WISE, JEREMIAH (*d.* 1756). Murdock, K. B. "Jeremiah Wise's Sermon on the Suitableness and Benefit of Prayer in Affliction, 1717." *PCSM* 26 (1927) 235-6.

WISE, JOHN (1652-1725). McElroy, P. S. "John Wise: The Father of American Independence." *EIHC* 81 (Jl 45) 201-26.
Mackaye, J. M. "The Founder of American Democracy." *N E Mag* ns 29 (S 03) 73-83.
Rossiter, C. L. "John Wise: Colonial Democrat." *NEQ* 22 (Mr 49) 3-32.
Story, I. C. "John Wise, Congressional Democrat." *Pac Un Bul* 36 (Mr 39) 3.
Waters, T. F. "John Wise of Chebacco." *Pub Ipswich Hist Soc* no 26 (1927) 1-23.

WISTER, OWEN (1860-1938). Angell, J. R. "The University and Free Speech." *Un Chicago Mag* (Mr 16) 207-8.
Boynton, H. W. "A Word on the Genteel Critic: Owen Wister's Quack Novels and Democracy." *Dial* 59 (14 O 15) 303-6.
Hubbell, J. B. "Owen Wister's Work." *SAQ* 29 (O 30) 440-3.
Marsh, E. C. "Representative American Story Tellers: Owen Wister." *Bkm* 27 (Jl 08) 456-8.
Ritchie, R. W. "Some Scenes of 'The Virginian.'" *Bkm* 44 (Ja 17) 460-3.
Woollcott, Alexander. "Wisteria." *NYr* 6 (30 Ag 30) 30.

WOLFE, THOMAS (1900-38). Anon. "Edward Aswell Succeeds Perkins as Administrator of Wolfe Estate." *Pub W* 152 (9 Ag 47) 531.
——— "Whitmanesque Rhapsody." *TLS* (1 F 47) 61.
Albrecht, W. P. "Time as Unity in Thomas Wolfe." *NMQR* 19 (Au 49) 320-9.
——— "The Title of *Look Homeward, Angel: A Story of the Buried Life*." *MLQ* 11 (Mr 50) 50-7.
Ames, R. S. "Wolfe, Wolfe!" *Am Spect* 3 (Ja 35) 5-6.
Armstrong, A. W. "As I Saw Thomas Wolfe." *Ariz Q* 2 (Sp 46) 5-14.
Askew, Ruth. "The Harp of Death for Thomas Wolfe." *Sw R* 33 (Au 48) 348.
Aswell, E. C., & Terry, J. S. "En Route to a Legend: Two Interpretations of Thomas Wolfe." *SRL* 31 (27 N 48) 1-3, 34-6.
Baker, Carlos. "Thomas Wolfe's Apprenticeship." *Delphian Q* 23 (Ja 40) 20-5.
Barr, Stringfellow. "The Dandridges and the Gants." *VQR* 6 (Ap 30) 310-3.
Basso, Hamilton. "Thomas Wolfe, A Portrait." *NRp* 87 (24 Je 36) 199-202.
Bates, E. S. "Thomas Wolfe.'" *EJ* 26 (S 37) 519-27; *Mod Q* 11 (Fl 38) 86-8.
Bishop, J. P. "The Sorrows of Thomas Wolfe." *KR* 1 (Wi 39) 7-17.
Braswell, William. "Thomas Wolfe Lectures and Takes a Holiday." *CE* 1 (O 39) 11-22.
Bridgers, A. P. "Thomas Wolfe: Legends of a Man's Hunger for His Youth." *SRL* 11 (6 Ap 35) 599, 609.
Brown, E. K. "Thomas Wolfe: Realist and Symbolist." *UTQ* 10 (Ja 41) 153-66.
Burgum, E. B. "Thomas Wolfe's Discovery of America." *VQR* 22 (Su 46) 421-37.
Canaday, Julia. "'Dixieland': Home of Tom Wolfe Always Seemed in Need of Paint." Durham (N C) *Morning Herald* (29 Ag 48) sec 4: 3.
Canby, H. S. "The River of Youth." *SRL* 11 (9 Mr 35) 529-30.
Cargill, Oscar. "Gargantua Fills His Skin." *UKCR* 16 (Au 49) 20-30.
Carpenter, F. I. "Thomas Wolfe: The Autobiography of an Idea." *UKCR* 12 (Su 46) 179-88.
Church, Margaret. "Thomas Wolfe: Dark Time." *PMLA* 64 (S 49) 629-38.

Collins, T. L. "Thomas Wolfe." *SR* 50 (O-D 42) 487-504.
Cowley, Malcolm. "Profiles." *NYr* (8 Ap 44) 30-43.
——— "Wolfe and the Lost People." *NRp* 105 (3 N 41) 592-4.
Daniels, Jonathan. "Thomas Wolfe." *SRL* 18 (24 S 38) 8.
Davis, Ruth. "Look Homeward, Angel." *SRL* 29 (5 Ja 46) 13-4, 31-2.
Delakas, Daniel. "L'Expérience française de Thomas Wolfe." *Revue de Littérature Comparée* 24 (Jl-S 50) 417-36.
Ehrsam, T. G. "I Knew Thomas Wolfe." *Book Coll J* 1 (Je 36) 1, 3.
Fadiman, Clifton. "Thomas Wolfe." *NYr* 11 (9 Mr 35) 68-70.
Falk, Robert. "Thomas Wolfe and the Critics." *CE* 5 (Ja 44) 186-92.
Figueira, Gastón. "Poetasy prosistas americanos: I. Edwin Arlington Robinson. II. Thomas Wolfe." *Revista Iberoamericana* 11 (O 46) 329-32.
Frohock, W. M. "Thomas Wolfe: Of Time and Neurosis." *Sw R* 33 (Au 48) 349-60.
Geismar, Maxwell. "Thomas Wolfe: The Hillman and the Furies." *YR* 35 (Su 46) 649-66.
Glicksberg, C. I. "Thomas Wolfe." *Canadian Forum* 16 (Ja 36) 24-5.
Haugen, Einar. "Thomas Wolfes siste bok." *Samtiden* (Oslo) 55 (1946) 641-5.
Heiderstadt, Dorothy. "Studying under Thomas Wolfe." *Mark Twain Q* 8 (Wi 50) 7-8.
Hutzell, J. K. "As They Recall Thomas Wolfe." *So Packet* 4 (Ap 48) 4, 9-10.
——— "Thomas Wolfe and 'Altamont.'" *So Packet* 4 (Ap 48) 1-4.
Jack, P. M. "Remembering Thomas Wolfe." *N Y Times Book R* (2 O 38) 2, 28.
Jones, H. M. "Thomas Wolfe's Short Stories." *SRL* 13 (30 N 35) 13.
Kauffman, Bernice. "Bibliography of Periodical Articles by Thomas Wolfe." *Bul Bibl* 17 (My-Ag 42) 162-5.
Kennedy, R. S. "Thomas Wolfe at Harvard, 1920-1923." *HLB* 4 (Sp, Au 50) 172-90, 304-19.
Koch, F. H. "Thomas Wolfe, Playmaker." *Carolina Playbook* (S 39) 65-9.
Kohler, Dayton. "All Fury Spent: A Note on Thomas Wolfe." *SLM* 1 (Ag 39) 560-4.
——— "Thomas Wolfe: Prodigal and Lost." *CE* 1 (O 39) 1-10.
Kussy, Bella. "The Vitalist Trend and Thomas Wolfe." *SR* 50 (Jl-S 42) 306-23.
Little, Thomas. "The Thomas Wolfe Collection of William B. Wisdom." *HLB* 1 (Au 47) 280-7.
Macauley, Thurston. "Thomas Wolfe: A Writer's Problems." *Pub W* 134 (24 D 38) 2150-2.
McCole, C. J. "Thomas Wolfe Embraces Life." *Cath World* 143 (Ap 36) 42-8.
McElderry, B. R., Jr. "The Autobiographical Problem in Thomas Wolfe's Earlier Novels." *Ariz Q* 4 (Wi 48) 315-24.
McGovern, Hugh. "A Note on Thomas Wolfe." *NMQR* 17 (Su 47) 198-200.
Maclachlan, J. M. "Folk Concepts in the Novels of Thomas Wolfe." *SFQ* 9 (D 45) 175-86.
Magnus, Peter. "Thomas Wolfe." *Syn og Segn* (Oslo) 53 (Mr 47) 138-44.
Middleton, L. R. "Further Memories of Tom Wolfe." *Am Merc* 64 (Ap 47) 413-20.
——— "Reminiscences of Tom Wolfe." *Am Merc* 63 (N 46) 544-9.
Norwood, Hayden. "Julia Wolfe: Web of Memory." *VQR* 20 (Ap 44) 236-50.
Perkins, M. E. "Thomas Wolfe." *HLB* 1 (Au 47) 269-79.
Powell, Desmond. "Of Thomas Wolfe." *Ariz Q* 1 (Sp 45) 28-36.
Pugh, C. E. "Of Thomas Wolfe." *Mark Twain Q* 7 (Su-Fl 45) 13-4.
Pusey, W. W., III. "The German Vogue of Thomas Wolfe." *GR* 23 (Ap 48) 131-48.
Roberts, J. M., Jr. "Former *Morning Herald* Staff Member Gives Views on Thomas Wolfe's Mother." Durham (N C) *Morning Herald* (26 Ja 47) sec 1: 6.
Shoenberner, Franz. "Wolfe's Genius Seen Afresh." *N Y Times Book R* (4 Ag 46) 1, 25.

Simpson, C. M., Jr. "A Note on Wolfe." *Fantasy* 6 (1939) 17-21.
——— "Thomas Wolfe: A Chapter in His Biography." *Sw R* 25 (Ap 40) 308-21.
Solon, S. L. "The Ordeal of Thomas Wolfe." *Mod Q* 11 (Wi 39) 45-53.
Spitz, Leon. "Was Wolfe an Anti-Semite?" *Am Hebrew* 158 (19 N 48) 5.
Stearns, M. M. "The Metaphysics of Thomas Wolfe." *CE* 6 (Ja 45) 193-9.
Thompson, Lawrance. "Tom Wolfe, Amerikas Skildrare." *Bonniers Litterära Magasin* 8 (S 39) 541-6.
Volkening, H. T. "Tom Wolfe: Penance No More." *VQR* 15 (Sp 39) 196-215.
Wade, J. D. "Prodigal." *So R* 1 (Jl 35) 192-8.
Walser, Richard. "Some Notes on Wolfe's Reputation Abroad." *Carolina Q* 1 (Mr 49) 37-48.
Warren, R. P. "A Note on the Hamlet of Thomas Wolfe." *Am R* 5 (My 35) 191-208.
Wolfe, Thomas. "Portrait of a Player." *Theatre Annual* 6 (1947) 43-54.
——— "Something of My Life." *SRL* 31 (7 F 48) 6-8.
——— "The Story of a Novel." *SRL* 12 (14, 21, 28 D 35) 3-4, 12, 14, 16; 3-4, 15; 3-4, 14-6.
——— "What a Writer Reads." *Book Buyer* 1 (D 35) 13-4.
——— "Writing Is My Life: Letters of Thomas Wolfe." *Atl* 178 (D 46) 60-6.

WOLFF, ALBERT (1835-91). Downs, L. G. "Some Sources for Northwest History: The Writings of Albert Wolff." *Minn Hist* 27 (D 46) 327-9.

WOODBERRY, GEORGE EDWARD (1855-1930). Anon. "A Critic of American Letters." *Current Lit* 34 (N 02) 513-4.
——— "Letters from George Edward Woodberry to Charles Buttell Loomis, Jr." *Bkm* 74 (Ja-F, Mr 32) 542-51, 654-8.
Bradley, W. A. "George Edward Woodberry." *Sheaf* (N 05) 18-20.
Cane, Melville. "George Edward Woodberry: A Student's Memories." *Prairie Schooner* 22 (Fl 48) 292-8.
Cory, H. E. "A Breviary for Critics." *Dial* 59 (15 Ag 15) 98-103.
DeVoto, Bernard. "The Maturity of American Literature." *SRL* 27 (5 Ag 44) 14-8.
Dixon, E. M. "Lectures by Professor Woodberry." *Smith Col Mo* 12 (Mr, Ap 05) 388-91, 450-3.
Dole, N. H. "George E. Woodberry." *J Ed* 86 (13 D 17) 596.
Erskine, John. "George Edward Woodberry." *SRL* 1 (16 My 25) 761.
——— "George Edward Woodberry, 1855-1930: An Appreciation." *BNYPL* 34 (My 30) 279-81.
Hawkins, P. R. "A List of Writings by and about George Edward Woodberry." *BNYPL* 34 (My 30) 282-96.
Hovey, R. B. "George Edward Woodberry: Genteel Exile." *NEQ* 23 (D 50) 504-26.
Jenkins, Oliver. "George Edward Woodberry: An Essay." *Poet and Critic* 1 (S 30) 8-10.
Kellock, Harold. "Woodberry, A Great Teacher." *Nation* 130 (29 Ja 30) 120-2.
Ledoux, Louis. "George Edward Woodberry." *SRL* 6 (11 Ja 30) 638.
——— 'The Poetry of George Edward Woodberry." *Pathfinder* 2 (F 08) 10-6.
Mabie, H. W. "Poet or Critic?" *Outlook* 64 (14 Ap 00) 875-7.
Macy, John. "A Voice from the Past." *Freeman* 3 (6 Jl 21) 402-4.
McGrew, E. L. "Notes on the Poetry of George Edward Woodberry." *Smith Col Bul* 12 (Ap 05) 446-9.
Monroe, Harriet. "A Modern Solitary." *Poetry* 11 (N 17) 103-5.
More, P. E. "The Double Mr. Woodberry." *Weekly R* 4 (23 F 21) 180-1.
Rosenberg, J. N., & Benét, W. R. "George Edward Woodberry: Two Estimates." *N Y Herald Tribune Books* 9 (9 Jl 33) 1-2.
Roskauer, J. M. "The Greatest Teacher I Ever Knew." *SRL* 27 (28 O 44) 12-3.
Sampson, Alden. "The Double Mr. Woodberry." *Weekly R* 4 (23 Mr 21) 97.

Seward, S. S. "George Edward Woodberry." *Stanford Sequoia* 10 (20 My 01) 414-20.
Thwing, C. F. "George Edward Woodberry." *Harvard Grad Mag* 38 (Je 30) 433-43.
Van Doren, Mark. "Aria and Recitative." *Nation* 111 (13 O 20) 414.
——— "George Edward Woodberry." *Nation* 114 (1 Mr 22) 261-2.
West, R. B. "Truth, Beauty, and American Criticism." *UKCR* 14 (Wi 47) 137-48.
Wimberly, L. C. "Oscar Wilde Meets Woodberry." *Prairie Schooner* 2 (Sp 47) 108-16.

WOODWARD, HENRY W. (1832-1921). Maloney, A. B. "Poet of the Oregon Backwoods: Henry W. Woodward." *Ore Hist Q* 50 (Je 49) 122-33.

WOODWORTH, SAMUEL (1785-1842). Coad, O. S. "The Plays of Samuel Woodworth." *SR* 17 (Ap 19) 163-75.
Duffy, Charles. "'Scenes of My Childhood.'" *AL* 13 (My 41) 167.
Taft, K. B. "'Scenes of My Childhood': A Comment." *AL* 13 (Ja 42) 410-1.

WOOLLCOTT, ALEXANDER (1887-1943). Brown, J. M. "A Woollcott in Print." *SRL* 29 (16, 23 Mr 46) 38-42, 40-4.
Gibbs, Wolcott. "Big Nemo." *NYr* 14 (18, 24 Mr, 1 Ap 39) 24-9, 24-9, 22-7.
Isaacs, E. J. R. "The Critical Arena: II. The Theatre of Alexander Woollcott." *Theatre Arts* 26 (Mr 42) 191-200.
Winterich, J. I. "This Is Woollcott." *SRL* 11 (23 F 35) 505.

WOOLMAN, JOHN (1720-72). Darlington, M. E. "A Woolman Document." *JRUL* 5 (D 41) 61-2.
Davidson, Frank. "Three Patterns of Living." *AAUP Bul* 34 (Su 48) 364-74.
deLevie, Dagobert. "John Woolman and the Brute Creation." *Friends Intelligencer* 105 (24 Ap 48) 235-6.
Jones, R. M. "Evidences of the Influence of Quietism on John Woolman." *Friends Intelligencer* 105 (20 Mr 48) 131-2.
Kent, M. "John Woolman, Mystic and Reformer." *Hibbert J* 26 (Ja 28) 302-13.
Lask, J. S. "John Woolman: Crusader for Freedom." *Phylon* 5 (1 Q 44) 30-40.
Rogers, E. W. "John Woolman's Journal." *Nation* 89 (1 Jl 09) 11.
Spiller, R. E. "John Woolman on War." *JRUL* 5 (D 41) 60-91.
Tolles, F. B. "Free Produce, Undyed Clothing, and Beards: The Testimonies of Joshua Evans." *Friends Intelligencer* 100 (Je 43) 378.
——— "John Woolman's List of 'Books Lent.'" *Bul Friends Hist Assn* 31 (Au 42) 72-81.
Wilson, E. C. "John Woolman: A Social Reformer of the Eighteenth Century." *Econ R* 11 (Ap 01) 170-89.

WOOLSON, CONSTANCE FENIMORE (1840-94). Harris, M. "Constance Fenimore Woolson." *SRL* 5 (21 D 29) 590.
Hubbell, J. B. "Some New Letters of Constance Fenimore Woolson." *NEQ* 14 (D 41) 715-35.
Pattee, F. L. "Constance Fenimore Woolson and the South." *SAQ* 38 (Ap 39) 130-41.
Richardson, L. N. "Constance Fenimore Woolson, 'Novelist Laureate' of America." *SAQ* 39 (Ja 40) 18-36.

WRIGHT, CHAUNCEY (1830-75). Blau, J. L. "Chauncey Wright: Radical Empiricist." *NEQ* 19 (D 46) 495-517.
Wiener, P. P. "Chauncey Wright's Defense of Darwin and the Neutrality of Science." *JHI* 6 (Ja 45) 19-45.

WRIGHT, HAROLD BELL (1872-1944). Cooper, F. T. "The Popularity of Harold Bell Wright." *Bkm* 40 (Ja 15) 498-500.

Kenamore, Clair. "A Curiosity in Best-Seller Technique." *Bkm* 47 (Jl 18) 538-44.
Millard, Bailey. "The Personality of Harold Bell Wright." *Bkm* 44 (Ja 17) 463-9.

WRIGHT, RICHARD (1909-). Baldwin, James. "Everybody's Protest Novel." *Zero* (Paris) 1 (Sp 49) 54-8.
Basso, Hamilton. "Thomas Jefferson and the Black Boy." *NYr* 21 (10 Mr 45) 86-9.
Bland, Edward. "Social Forces Shaping the Negro Novel." *Negro Q* 1 (1945) 241-8.
Brewster, Dorothy. "From Phillis Wheatly to Richard Wright." *Negro Q* 1 (1945) 80-3.
Brown, Sterling. "The Negro Author and His Publishers." *Negro Q* 1 (1945) 7-20.
Burgum, E. B. "The Promise of Democracy in the Fiction of Richard Wright." *Sci & Soc* 7 (S 43) 338-53.
Cayton, Horace. "Frightened Children of Frightened Parents." *Twice a Year* 12-3 (Sp-Su, Fl-Wi 45) 262-9.
Cohn, D. L. "The Negro Novel: Richard Wright." *Atl* 165 (My 40) 659-61.
Delpech, Jeanne. "An Interview with Native Son." *Crisis* 17 (N 50) 625-6, 678.
Ellison, Ralph. "Richard Wright's Blues." *AR* 5 (Je 45) 198-211.
Fadiman, Clifton. "A Black American Tragedy." *NYr* 16 (2 Mr 40) 60-1.
Fleurent, Maurice. "Richard Wright à Paris." *Paru* no 25 (D 46) 7-8.
Ford, J. W. "The Case of Richard Wright." *Daily Worker* 21 (5 S 44) 6.
Ford, N. A. "Juvenile Delinquent Becomes Famous Writer." *Afro-American* 2 (22 Ja 49) 5.
Gold, Mike. "Change the World." *Daily Worker* 17 (17, 29 Ap 40) 7.
Rosenthal, Jean. "Native Son—Backstage." *Theatre Arts* 25 (Je 41) 407-8.
Sillen, Samuel. "Bigger Thomas on the Boards." *New Masses* 39 (8 Ap 41) 27-8.
——— "The Meaning of Bigger Thomas." *New Masses* 35 (21 My 40) 26-8.
——— "'Native Son': Pros and Con." *New Masses* 35 (21 My 40) 23-6.
——— "The Response to 'Native Son.'" *New Masses* 35 (23 Ap 40) 25-6.
Webb, Constance. "What Next for Richard Wright." *Phylon* 10 (1949) 161-6.
White, R. K. "Black Boy: A Value Analysis." *J Abnormal Psych* 42 (O 47) 460-1.
Wright, Richard. "Naissance d'un roman nègre." *La Nef* no 44 (Jl 48) 43-64.
———, & Frasconi, Antonio. "Exchange of Letters." *Twice a Year* 12-3 (1945) 255-61.

WRIGHT, WILLARD HUNTINGTON (1888-1939). E., R. F. "Portrait in Line Introducing S. S. Van Dine." *Book Buyer* 2 (Ap 36) 14.
Mencken, H. L. "America Produces a Novelist." *Forum* 55 (Ap 16) 490-6.

WRIGHT, WILLIAM (*fl.* 1876-89). Lillard, R. G. "Dan De Quille, Comstock Reporter and Humorist." *Pac Hist R* 13 (S 44) 251-9.
Loomis, C. G. "The Tall Tales of Dan De Quille." *Calif Folklore Q* 5 (Ja 46) 26-71.

WYETH, JOHN ALLAN (1845-1922). Gailor, T. F. "General Forrest." *SR* 9 (Ja 01) 1-12.

WYLIE, ELINOR (1885-1928). Amacher, R. E. "Wylie's *Castilian*." *Expl* 7 (N 48) 16.
——— "Wylie's *The Tortoise in Eternity*." *Expl* 6 (Mr 48) 33.
Burdett, Osbert. "The Novels of Elinor Wylie." *Eng R* 59 (0 34) 488-90, 492.
Cabell, J. B. "Sanctuary in Porcelain." *VQR* 6 (Jl 30) 335-41.
Cluck, Julia. "Elinor Wylie's Shelley Obsession." *PMLA* 56 (S 41) 841-60.
Deutsch, Babette. "Proud Lady." *VQR* 8 (O 32) 618-20.
Dillon, George. "A Light Never upon Land or Sea." *Poetry* 34 (Jl 29) 230-3.
Gorman, H. S. "Daughter of Donne." *NAR* 219 (My 24) 679-86.
Johnson, Merle. "American First Editions: Elinor Holt Wylie." *Pub W* 116 (21 D 29) 2845-6.

Kohler, Dayton. "Elinor Wylie: Heroic Mask." *SAQ* 36 (Ap 37) 218-28.
Lüdeke, Henry. "Venetian Glass: The Poetry and Prose of Elinor Wylie." *Eng Stud* 20 (D 38) 241-50.
Macklin, Thomas. "Analysis of Experience in Lyric Poetry." *CE* 9 (Mr 48) 316-20.
MacLeish, Archibald. "Black Armour." *NRp* 37 (5 D 23) 16-8.
Monroe, Harriet. "Elinor Wylie." *Poetry* 33 (F 29) 266-72.
Sergeant, E. S. "Elinor Wylie, Intricate and Crystal." *NRp* 49 (1 D 26) 36-9.
Untermeyer, Louis. "Elinor Wylie's Poetry." *SRL* 8 (21 My 32) 741-2.
Van Doren, Carl. "Elinor Wylie: a Portrait from Memory." *Harper's* 173 (S 36) 358-67.
Walbridge, E. E. "Incense and Praise." *Colophon* pt 16 (1934) 1-8.
Walcutt, C. C. "Critic's Taste or Artist's Intention." *UKCR* 12 (Su 46) 479-82.
Wilson, Edmund, & Colum, Mary. "In Memory of Elinor Wylie." *NRp* 57 (6 Ja 29) 316-9.
Wylie, Elinor. "Portrait in Black Paint." *NYr* 3 (19 Mr 27) 24.
Zabel, M. D. "The Pattern of the Atmosphere." *Poetry* 40 (Ag 32) 273-82.

YALE, ELIHU (1649-1721). Bingham, Hiram. "Elihu Yale: Governor, Collector and Benefactor." *PAAS* 47 (Ap 37) 93-144.

YOUNG, STARK (1881-). Bentley, Eric. "An American Theatre Critic!" *KR* 12 (Wi 50) 138-47.
Clark, Emily. "Stark Young's South." *VQR* 11 (O 35) 626-8.
Isaacs, E. J. R. "The Theatre of Stark Young." *Theatre Arts* 26 (Ap 42) 257-65.
Martin, Abbott. "Stark Young and the Ransomists." *SR* 38 (Ja-Mr 30) 114-5.
Payne, L. W. "American First Editions: Stark Young (1881-)." *Pub W* 127 (16 Mr 35) 1164-5.
——— "A New Southern Poet: Stark Young of Mississippi." *SAQ* 8 (O 09) 316-27.

ZENGER, JOHN PETER (1697-1746). McCombs, C. F. "John Peter Zenger, Printer." *BNYPL* 37 (1933) 1031-4.
Winterich, J. T. "Early American Books and Printing (Chap. V: Gentlemen of the Press)." *Pub W* 123 (20 My 33) 1624-5.

ALMANACS, ANNUALS, AND GIFT BOOKS. Anon. "Catalogue of Annuals and Gift Books in the New York Public Library." *BNYPL* 6 (Jl 02) 270-5.
——— "Check List of New York City Almanacs in the New York Public Library." *BNYPL* 5 (My 01) 186-9.
——— "List of Almanacks, Ephemerides, etc., and of Works Relating to the Calendar, in the New York Public Library." *BNYPL* 7 (Jl, Ag 03) 246-67, 281-302.
——— "Literary Annuals and Gift Books in the New York Public Library." *BNYPL* 6 (1902) 271 *ff*.
——— "Passing of an old Almanac." *Educ* 20 (F 00) 382.
Bates, A. C. "Check List of Connecticut Almanacs, 1709-1805." *PAAS* ns 24 (Ap 14) 93-215.
——— "Part of an Almanack." *PAAS* 52 (Ap 42) 38-44.
Booth, B. A. "A Note on an Index to the American Annuals and Gift Books." *AL* 10 (N 38) 349-50.
——— "Taste in Annuals." *AL* 14 (N 42) 299-302.
Brigham, C. S. "An Account of American Almanacs and Their Value in Historical Study." *PAAS* ns 35 (1925) 1-25, 194-209.
——— "Exhibition of American Almanacs, Oct., 1925." *PAAS* ns 35 (1925) 210-8.
Carpenter, F. I. "The Genteel Tradition: A Reinterpretation." *NEQ* 15 (S 43) 427-43.
Chapin, H. M. "Check List of Rhode Island Almanacs, 1643-1850." *PAAS* ns 35 (Ap 15) 19-54.

Cumings, Elizabeth. "A Bundle of Old Almanacs." *N E Mag* ns 27 (S 02) 49-58.
Edes, H. H. "Titan's New Almanack for the Year of Christian Account 1729." *PCSM* 7 (F 01) 198-202.
Greenough, C. N. "New England Almanacs, 1766-1775, and the American Revolution." *PAAS* 45 (O 35) 288-316.
Hunt, W. S. "Gift Books and Annuuals." *Proc N J Hist Soc* 52 (Ja 34) 14-9.
James, A. E. "Literary Annuals and Gift Books." *JRUL* 1 (Je 38) 14-21.
Jorgenson, C. E. "The New Science in the Almanacs of Ames and Franklin." *NEQ* 8 (D 35) 555-61.
Leach, Joseph. "Crockett's Almanacs and the Typical Texan." *Sw R* 35 (Sp 50) 88-95.
Littlefield, G. E. "Notes on the Calendar and the Almanac." *PAAS* ns 34 (1914) 11-64.
Lovely, N. W. "Notes on New England Almanacs." *NEQ* 8 (Je 35) 264-77.
Matthews, Albert. "John Tulley's Almanacs, 1687-1702." *PCSM* 13 (D 10) 207-23.
Nichols, C. L. "Checklist of Maine, New Hampshire and Vermont Almanacs." *PAAS* ns 38 (Ap 28) 63-163.
——— "Notes on the Almanacs of Massachusetts." *PAAS* 22 (Ap 12) 15-134.
Paltsits, V. H. "The Almanacs of Roger Sherman 1750-1761." *PAAS* 18 (Ap 07) 213-58.
Robinson, H. M. "The Almanac." *Bkm* 75 (Je-Jl 32) 251-8.
Shelley, P. A. "Annuals and Gift Books as American Intermediaries of Foreign Literature." *CL News Letter* 3 (My 45) 59-62.
——— "A Token of the Season." *Headlight on Books at Penn State* 14 (D 44) 1-36
Thompson, Ralph. "*The Liberty Bell* and Other Anti-Slavery Gift-Books." *NEQ* 7 (Mr. 34) 159-68.
Wall, A. J. "A List of New York Almanacs, 1694-1850." *BNYPL* 24 (My, Je, Jl, Ag, S, O 20) 287-96, 335-55, 389-413, 443-60, 508-19, 543-57.

AMERICAN LITERATURE, AIMS AND METHODS. Anon. "Americanism in Literature." *Outlook* 72 (6 D 02) 772-4.
——— "Literature in a Democracy." *Outlook* 71 (9 Ag 02) 908-9.
——— "A Series of Essays on American Civilization in the Twentieth Century." *School & Soc* 49 (15 Ja 49) 38-9.
Anderson, Sherwood. "An Apology for Crudity." *Dial* 63 (8 N 17) 437-8.
Angoff, Charles. "Three Notes on American Literature." *NAR* 247 (Sp 39) 38-41.
Arvin, Newton. "Individualism and American Writers." *Nation* 133 (14 O 31) 391-3.
Ashby, N. M. "Aliment for Genius." *AL* 8 (Ja 37) 371-8.
Atherton, Gertrude. "Why Is American Literature Bourgeois?" *NAR* 178 (My 04) 771-81.
Bacon, J. D. "Is American Literature Bourgeois?" *NAR* 179 (Jl 04) 105-18.
Baker, T. J. "American Literature in the Colleges." *NAR* 209 (Je 19) 781-5.
Barzun, Jacques. "The Literature of Ideas." *SRL* 27 (5 Ag 44) 25-8.
Baym, Max. "Apropos a New Record of American Literature." *Occidental* 5 (My 49) 1-5.
Bell, B. I. "The Decay of Intelligence in America." *Criterion* 14 (Ja 35) 193-203.
Berdan, J. M. "American Literature in the High Schools." *Arena* 29 (Ap 03) 337-44.
Blair, Walter. "Roots of American Idealism." *Un R* 6 (Je 40) 275-81.
Björkman, Edwin. "An Open Letter to President Wilson on Behalf of American Literature." *Century* 87 (Ap 14) 887-9.
Bogan, Louise. "Modernism in American Literature." *Am Q* 2 (Su 50) 99-111.
Bolwell, R. W. "Concerning the Study of Nationalism in American Literature." *AL* 10 (Ja 39) 405-16.
Bourne, Randolph. "Traps for the Unwary." *Dial* 64 (28 Mr 18) 277-9.
Boyd, E. A. "American Literature or Colonial?" *Freeman* 1 (17 Mr 20) 13-5.

Boyd, James. "The Prospect for American Literature." *Outlook* 152 (7 Ag 29) 587-600.
Boynton, P. H. "American Neglect of American Literature." *Nation* 102 (4 My 16) 478-80.
Bradsher, E. L. "Americanism in Literature." *SR* 35 (Ja 27) 94-102.
——— "Nationalism in Our Literature." *NAR* 213 (Ja 21) 109-18.
Brooks, Van Wyck. "On Creating a Usable Past." *Dial* 64 (11 Ap 18) 337-41.
——— "War's Heritage to Youth." *Dial* 64 (17 Ja 18) 47-50.
Bryce, James. "Stray Thoughts on American Literature." *NAR* 201 (Mr 15) 357-62.
Bunker, John. "Nationality and the Case of American Literature." *SR* 17 (Ja 19) 82-91.
Burch, E. E. "The Sources of New England Democracy: A Controversial Statement in Parrington's *Main Currents in American Thought.*" *AL* 1 (My 29) 115-30.
Calverton, V. F. "The American Writer Loses Faith." *Cur Hist* 36 (My 32) 161-5.
——— "The Liberation of American Literature." *Scribner's* ns 91 (Mr 32) 143-6.
Canby, H. S. "The American Tradition in Literature." *SRL* 22 (31 Ag 40) 3-4, 15-6.
——— "Current Literature and the Colleges." *Harper's* 131 (Jl 15) 230-6.
——— "Defining American Literature." *SRL* 16 (29 My 37) 8, 17.
——— "The Making of American Literature." *SRL* 31 (24 Jl 48) 6-7, 29-30.
Cardwell, G. A., Jr. "On Scholarship and Southern Literature." *SAQ* 40 (Ja 41) 60-72.
Carpenter, F. I. "Nationalism and the American Scholar." *Delphian Q* 25 (1942) 23-4.
Clark, H. H. "Nationalism in American Literature." *UTQ* 2 (Jl 33) 491-519.
——— "Suggestions Concerning a History of American Literature." *AL* 12 (N 40) 268-96.
Colum, M. M. "The American Mind in Literature." *Forum* 90 (D 33) 330-4.
——— "Literature, Ethics, and the Knights of Good Sense." *Scribner's* ns 87 (Je 30) 599-608.
——— "Self-Critical America." *Scribner's* 87 (F 30) 197-206.
Coulborn, Ruston, *et al.* "The American Culture: Studies in Definition and Prophecy." *KR* 3 (Sp 40) 143-90.
DeVoto, Bernard. "The Maturity of American Literature." *SRL* 27 (5 Ag 44) 13-8.
——— "Time without a Theme." *SRL* 32 (6 Ag 49) 27-9.
Dos Passos, J. R., Jr. "Against American Literature." *NRp* 8 (14 O 16) 269-71.
Effelberger, Hans. "Das nationale Gesicht Amerikas in der Literatur." *Neueren Sprachen* 43 (1935) 451-9.
——— "Neue Entwicklungstendenzen in der amerikanischen Literatur der Gegenwart." *Neueren Sprachen* 44 (1936) 154-61.
Eliot, T. S. "American Literature." *Athenaeum* No 4643 (25 Ap 19) 236-7.
Farrar, John. "The Condition of American Writing." *EJ* 38 (O 49) 421-8; *CE* 11 (O 49) 1-8.
Fast, Howard. "American Literature and the Democratic Tradition." *CE* 8 (Mr 47) 279-84.
Fine, Benjamin. "Education in Review: Need for Greater Study of American Literature Is Stressed in National Survey of Colleges." *N Y Times* (31 O 48) sec 4: 9E.
Fischer, V. W. "Angloamerikanische Kultur—und Literatur-beziehungen in neuerer Zeit." *Archiv für das Studium der Neueren Sprachen* 184 (S 43) 11-31.
Flanagan, J. T. "American Literature in American Colleges." *CE* 1 (Mr 40) 513-9.
Francke, Kuno. "The Study of National Culture." *Atl* 99 (Mr 07) 409-16.
Frenz, Horst. "American Literature and World Literature." *CL News Letter* 2 (F 44) 4-6.
Friederich, W. P., & Gohdes, Clarence. "A Department of American and Comparative Literature." *MLJ* 33 (F 49) 135-7.
Gohdes, Clarence. "On the Study of Southern Literature." *WMQ* 16 (Ja 36) 81-7.

——— "The Study of American Literature in the United States." *Eng Stud* 20 (1938) 61-6.
Goodman, Paul. "The Chance for Popular Culture." *Poetry* 74 (Je 49) 157-65.
Gorer, Geoffrey. "America and the World: A Psychological Study." *Cornhill* no 972 (Au 47) 401-16.
Greever, Garland. "Aspects of Individualism in American Literature." *Personalist* 23 (Au 42) 353-68.
Gregory, Horace, *et al.* " 'Good News' in American Literature: A Symposium." *New Masses* 25 (12 O 37) 17-9.
Guérard, Albert. "Nationality and Literature." *Books Abroad* 7 (Ap 33) 135-7.
——— "The Prospect for American Literature." *Pub W* 129 (1 F 36) 593-8.
Gurko, Leo. "American Literature: the Forces Behind Its Growing Up." *CE* 7 (Mr 46) 319-22.
Hart, J. D. "The Need for the Study of American Literature Today." *Call Number* 3 (6 Ag 42) 2-6.
Holloway, Emory. "The American Tradition and the Future." *CE* 4 (Ap 43) 417-22.
Howells, W. D. "Professor Barrett Wendell's Notions of American Literature." *NAR* 172 (Ap 01) 623-40.
——— "Puritanic Influences on American Literature." *Harper's W* 46 (16 Ag 02) 1110.
Hyman, S. E., & Lewis, R. W. B. "Two Views of the American Writer." *Hudson R* 2 (Wi 50) 600-20.
Jacobs, W. D. "A Modest Proposal." *CE* 10 (Ap 49) 379-88.
Jones, H. M. "American Scholarship and American Literature." *AL* 8 (My 36) 115-24.
——— "The Orphan Child of the Curriculum." *EJ* 25 (My 36) 376-88.
——— "Patriotism—But How?" *Atl* 162 (N 38) 585-92.
——— "Salvaging Our Literature." *Am Schol* 2 (My 33) 347-62.
Kern, A. C. "American Literature in the Teaching of American History." *Miss Valley Hist R* 30 (S 43) 243-5.
Larsen, H. A. "The Cowardice of American Literature." *Forum* 48 (O 12) 443-9.
Lawrence, D. H. "Studies in Classic American Literature: I. The Spirit of Place." *Eng R* 27 (N 18) 320-31.
——— "Studies in Classic American Literature (viii): The Two Principles." *Eng R* 28 (Je 19) 477-89.
Leisy, E. E. "American Literature in Colleges and Universities." *School & Soc* 23 (27 F 26) 307-9.
——— "Folklore in American Literature." *CE* 8 (D 46) 122-9.
——— "Literary Versions of American Folk Materials." *WF* 7 (Ja 48) 43-9.
——— "Materials for Investigations in American Literature, 1926." *SP* 24 (Jl 27) 480-3.
——— "The Significance of Recent Scholarship in American Literature." *CE* 2 (N 40) 115-25.
Lewis, Sinclair. "Self-Conscious America." *Am Merc* 6 (O 25) 129-39.
Mabie, H. W. "Provincialism in American Life." *Harper's* 134 (Mr 17) 579-84.
McDowell, Tremaine. "American Studies and the New Interdepartmentalism." *School & Soc* 68 (25 S 48) 196-200.
McElwain, Dora. "Today and Yesterday in American Literature." *EJ* 25 (F 36) 121-7.
McGlinchee, Claire. "American Literature in American Music." *Mus Q* 31 (Ja 45) 101-19.
Matthews, Brander. "An American Critic on American Literature." *Forum* 43 (Ja 10) 78-86.
——— "A Suggestion for Teachers of American Literature." *Educ R* 21 (Ja 01) 11-6.

——— "What Is American Literature." *Bkm* 44 (N 16) 218-23.
Mencken, H. L. "The American Future." *Am Merc* 40 (F 37) 129-36.
——— "The American Tradition." *Lit R* 4 (1923) 277-8.
——— "The National Literature." *YR* 9 (Jl 20) 804-17.
Moore, C. L. "All-America vs. All-England in Modern Literature." *Dial* 54 (16 Mr 13) 225-6.
——— "American Literary Instinct." *Dial* 38 (16 F 05) 113-6
——— "Interregnum in American Literature." *Dial* 48 (1 My 10) 307-8.
More, P. E. "The Modern Current in American Literature." *Revue de Paris* (15 D 27) 858-79; *Forum* 79 (Ja 28) 127-36.
Munson, G. B. "Impractibility of the American Writer." *SR* 34 (Jl-S 31) 257-61.
——— "The Literary Profession in America." *SR* 39 (O-D 31) 398-425.
Nock, A. J. "The Return of the Patriots." *VQR* 8 (Ap 42) 161-74.
Nuhn, Ferner [Suckow, Ruth]. "Teaching American Literature in American Colleges." *Am Merc* 13 (F 28) 328-31.
Osborn, M. E. "Too Much Incoherencey." *SLM* 4 (Mr 42) 114-8.
Paine, Gregory. "American Literature a Hundred and Fifty Years Ago." *SP* 42 (Jl 45) 385-402.
——— "Trends in American Literary Scholarship." *SP* 29 (O 32) 630-43.
Parker, G. F. "Some American Literary Needs." *SR* 18 (Ja 10) 1-22.
Pattee, F. L. "American Literature in the College Curriculum." *Educ R* 97 (My 24) 266-72.
Pearce, T. M. "American Tradition and Our Histories of Literature." *AL* 14 (N 42) 276-84.
Pearson, N. H. "Surveying American Literature." *CE* 1 (Ap 40) 583-8.
Phillips, William. "Portrait of the Artist as an American." *Horizon* 16 (O 47) 12-9.
Pound, Ezra. "Where Is American Culture?" *Nation* 126 (18 Ap 28) 443-4.
Quinn, A. H. "American Literature and American Politics." *PAAS* 54 (Ap 44) 59-112.
——— "American Literature as a Subject for Graduate Study." *Educ R* 64 (Je 22) 7-15.
——— "The Merry Chase of Fact." *YR* 19 (D 29) 373-85.
——— "New Frontiers of Research." *Scribner's ns* 99(F 31) 95-7.
Rahv, Philip. "Paleface and Redskin." *KR* 1 (Su 39) 251-6.
Rouse, H. B. "Democracy, American Literature, and Mr. Fast." *EJ* 36 (Je 47) 321-3.
Samson, Leon. "Americanism: A Substitute for Socialism." *Mod Mo* 7 (Jl 33) 367-72.
Sandin, E. V. "The Stepchild of the College Curriculum: American Literature." *School & Soc* 63 (9 F 46) 99-100.
Schlesinger, A. M. "Social History in American Literature." *YR* 18 (S 28) 135-47.
Schoonmaker, E. D. "What Our Universities Are Doing for American Literature." *Arena* 35 (My 06) 498-503.
Sedgwick, W. E. "The Materials for American Literature: A Critical Problem of the Early Nineteenth Century." *Harvard Stud & Notes in Phil & Lit* 17 (1935) 145-62.
——— "The Problem of American Literature as Seen by Contemporary Critics." *Harvard Summ Theses* (1935) 333-4.
Shaw, Roger. "American Nationalism: A Study." *Contemp R* 144 (Jl 33) 82-9.
Sherman, S. P. "For the Higher Study of American Literature." *YR* 12 (Ap 23) 469-75.
Shockley, M. S. "American Literature in American Education." *CE* 8 (O 46) 23-30.
Slusser, Herbert. "One Afternoon's Prospective." *Cath World* 145 (My 36) 154-63.
Snyder, F. B. "What Is American 'Literature?'" *SR* 35 (Ap 27) 207-15.
Spencer, B. T. "An American Literature Again." *SR* 57 (Wi 49) 56-72.

——— "The New Realism and a National Literature." *PMLA* 56 (D 41) 1116-32.
Spiller, R. E. "The Verdict of Sidney Smith." *AL* 1 (Mr 29) 3-13.
Stewart, Randall. "Three Views of the Individual as Reflected in American Literature." *CE* 5 (Mr 44) 297-302.
Stovall, Floyd. "The Function of Literature in a Democracy." *CE* 6 (My 45) 440-4.
——— "What Price American Literature?" *SR* 49 (O-D 41) 469-75.
Strout, A. L. "Culture and Cult: American vs. English Literature." *SR* 47 (Ja-Mr 39) 96-105.
Thorp, Willard. "The Training of College Teachers of American Literature." *CE* 8 (Ap 47) 360-5.
Trent, W. P. "American Literature." *Dial* 28 (1 My 00) 335-40.
Trilling, Lionel. "Contemporary American Literature in Its Relation to Ideas." *Am Q* 1 (Fl 49) 195-208.
Van Doren, Carl. "Post-war: The Literary Twenties." *Harper's* 173 (Jl, Ag 36) 148-56, 274-82.
——— "Toward a New Canon." *Nation* 134 (13 Ap 32) 429-30.
Voigt, G. P. "The Spiritual Aspect of Recent American Literature." *Lutheran Church Q* 17 (1944) 3-13.
Webb, Winifred. "The Spirit of American Literature." *Arena* 36 (Ag 06) 121-4.
Winters, Yvor. "On the Possibility of a Co-operative History of American Literature." *AL* 12 (N 40) 298-305.
Wittke, Carl. "National Unity and Cultural Diversity." *AGR* 11 (F 45) 31-2, 36.
Wood, G. A. "American Books and the American Dream." *Fortnightly R* ns no 989 (My 49) 341-5.
Wright, L. B. "Toward a New History of American Literature." *AL* 12 (N 40) 283-7.

BIBLIOGRAPHY, SERIAL. Anon. "Bibliography of Books by and about Negroes." *Mo Summary Race Relations.* Annually in August since 1943 (on first appearance called "Book Notes").
Boggs, R. S. "Folklore Bibliography." *SFQ.* Annually in March.
Bond, D. F. (1939-), McDermott, J. F. (1939-40), and Tucker, J. E. (1941-4). "Bibliography of Anglo-French and Franco-American Studies." *RR.* Annually in October, 1941-9, in April, 1939-41.
Carrière, J. M., *et al.* "Anglo-French and Franco-American Studies." *FAR.* Annually in April-September since 1949.
Forbes, A. B. (1929-48), and Whitehill, W. M. (1948-). "Bibliography of New England." *NEQ.* Annually in April.
Haberman, F. W. "A Bibliography of Rhetoric and Public Address." *QJS.* Annually in April.
Hubbell, J. B. (1929-31), Gohdes, Clarence (1931-8), Paine, G. L. (1938-41), Leary, Lewis (1941-). "Articles on American Literature Appearing in Current Periodicals." *AL.* Irregularly to May, 1930; quarterly since March, 1931.
Chester, Giraud, *et al.* "In the Periodicals [Articles on Speech]." *QJS.* Quarterly.
Johnson, Walter, *et al.* "American Scandinavian Bibliography." *SS.* Annually in May.
Kennedy, A. G. (1928-37), Dobbie, E. V. K. (1936-), Trevino, S. N. (1936-), Hench, A. L. (1937-9), Heflin, W. A. (1939-42), Jones, Joseph (1942-8), Atwood, E. B. (1942-50), Ives, Sumner (1948-). "Bibliography [of American Speech]." *AS* Quarterly since December, 1936; preceded by monthly "Bibliographical" section.
Leisy, E. E. (1929-38), Paine, Gregory (1938-40), Adams, Raymond (1941-5), Leary, Lewis (1945-). "Research in Progress." *AL.* Quarterly, since March, 1929.
Merwin, Fred, *et al.* "Press and Communications: An Annotated Bibliography of Journalism Subjects in American Magazines." *Jour Q.* Quarterly since 1930.
Odum, G. G., and Spivey, Herman. "Bibliography of Southern Literary Culture." *So Atl Bul.* Annually in April since 1942.

Pochman, H. A. (1941-2), Zucher, A. E. (1941-3), Reichmann, Felix (1943-4), Cuntz, Dieter (1942-). "Anglo-German Bibliography." *JEGP*. Annually in April from 1935 to 1941. *AGR*. Annually in April since 1942.

Pollard, Lancaster. "An Bibliography of the Pacific Northwest." *Pacific Nw Q*. Annually in April since 1942.

Spingarn, A. B. "Bibliography of Books by Negro Authors." *Crisis*. Annually in February since 1937.

Thornton, M. L. "North Carolina Bibliography." *N C Hist Q*. Annually in April since 1934.

BIBLIOGRAPHY, SPECIAL. Anon. "Book List to Promote Good Will." *Chri Sci Mon* 27 (18 My 35) 8.

——— "A Check List of Papers Read before the Savannah Historical Research Association That Have Appeared in Print: A Guide to the Unpublished Papers in the Files of the Savannah Historical Research Association." *Ga Hist Quar* 28 (S 44) 213-23.

——— "Check List of Works Relating to the Social History of the City of New York—Its Clubs, Charities, *Hospitals*, etc." *BNYPL* 5 (Je 01) 261-94.

——— "A List of Articles Published in *More Books*, 1906-1935." *More Books* 10 (D 35) 391-5.

——— "Manuscript Collections in the New York Public Library." *BNYPL* 5 (Jl 01) 306-36.

——— "The New Bibliography of American Literature." *Lib J* 69 (5 Je 44) 549-50.

——— "New Mexicana." *New Mexico Quar* 2 (Ag 32) 245-50.

Austin, Mary. "Spanish Manuscripts in the Southwest." *Sw R* 19 (Jl 34) 402-9.

Bach, R. F. "Early American Architecture and the Allied Arts." *Arch Rec* 59 (1926) 265-73, 328-34, 483-8, 525-32; 60 (1926) 65-70; 63 (1928) 577-80; 64 (1928) 70-2, 150-2, 190-2.

Barrett, C. W. "Some Bibliographical Adventuring in America." *PBSA* 44 (1Q 50) 17-28.

Benson, A. B. "Peter Kalm's Writings on America." *SS* 12 (My 33) 89-98.

Benton, E. J. "The Western Reserve Historical Society and Its Library." *Col and Res Lib* 6 (D 44) 23-9.

Billington, R. A. "Tentative Bibliography of Anti-Catholic Propaganda in the United States (1800 to 1860)." *Cath Hist Rec* 18 (Ja 33) 492-513,

Blanck, Jacob. "The Bibliography of American Literature." *Pub W* 138 (17 N 45) 2242-73; 152 (22 N 47) 2409-11.

——— "The Problems of Bibliographical Description of Nineteenth-Century American Books." *PBSA* 36 (2Q 42) 124-36.

Bobbitt, M. R. "A Bibliography of Etiquette Books Published in America before 1900." *BNYPL* 51 (D 47) 687-720.

Booth, B. A. "A Note on an Index to the American Annuals and Gift Books." *AL* 10 (N 38) 349-50.

Bowman, J. R. "A Bibliography of *The First Book of the American Chronicles of the Times*, 1774-1775." *AL* 1 (Mr 29) 69-73.

Brayer, H. O. "Preliminary Guide to Indexed Newspapers in the United States, 1850-1900." *Miss Valley Hist Rev* 33 (S 46) 237-55.

Brigham, C. S. "Bibliography of American Newspapers, 1690-1820." *PAAS* ns 22 (O 13) 247-403; 24 (O 14) 363-449; 25 (Ap, O 15) 128-293, 396-501; 26 (Ap, O 16) 80-184, 413-60; 27 (Ap, O 17) 117-274, 375-513; 28 (Ap, O 18) 63-133, 291-322; 29 (Ap 19) 129-80; 30 (Ap 20) 80-150; 32 (Ap 22) 81-214.

——— "Daniel Hewett's List of Newspapers and Periodicals in the United States in 1828." *PAAS* ns 44 (O 34) 265-96.

Brinton, E. S. "Books by and about the Rogerenes." *BNYPL* 59 (Ap 45) 627-48.

Buck, S. J. "The Bibliography of American Travel: A Project." *PBSA* 22 (1928) 52-9.

——— "The Status of Historical Bibliography in the United States." *PMHB* 63 (O 39) 390-400.
Cadbury, H. J. "Quaker Research in Progress or Unpublished." *Bul Friends' Hist Assn* 33 (1944) 33-4, 90-1.
Campbell, Killis. "Recent Additions to American Literary History." *SP* 33 (Jl 36) 534-43.
Collins, C. E. "Nineteenth-Century Fiction of the Southern Appalachians." *Bul Bibl* 17 (S-D 42,Ja-Ap 43) 186-90, 215-9.
Cope, Jackson, Davis, O. B., Henderson, Samuel, Larson, E. A., and Smeale, Joseph. "Addenda to *Articles on American Literature Appearing in Current Periodicals, 1920-1945*." *AL* 22 (Mr 50) 61-74.
Dougherty, C. T. "Novels of the Middle Border: A Critical Bibliography for Historians." *Hist Bul* 25 (My 47) 77-8, 85-8.
Ducharme, Jacques. "Bibliographie franco-américaine." *Bul de la Société Historique Franco-Américaine* (1942) 97-108.
Dunlap, M. E. "A Selected Annotated List of Books by or about the Negro." *Negro Coll Q* 3 (Mr, Je, S 45) 40-5, 94-6, 153-8.
English, E. D. "Author List of Caroliniana in the University of South Carolina Library." *Bul Un S C* 134 (D 23).
English, T. H. "The Treasure Room of Emory University." *Sw R* 29 (Au 43) 30-6.
Engstfeld, C. P. "Bibliography of Alabama Authors." *Howard Col Bul* 81 (1924) 1-44.
Flanagan J. T. "A Bibliography of Middle Western Farm Novels." *Minn Hist* 23 (Je 42) 113-25.
Ford, W. C. "Broadsides, Ballads, etc., Printed in Massachusetts, 1639-1800." *CMHS* 75 (1922).
Garrison, C. W. "List of Manuscript Collections in the Library of Congress to July, 1931." *Annual Report Am Hist Assn* 1 (1931) 123-233.
Gerald, J. E. "A Selected Bibliography [on Journalism] from British Journals." *JQ* 22 (1945) 72-4, 184-7, 292-6, 380-6.
Gillis, M. R. "Materials for Writers in California State Library." *Overland Mo* 79 (Ag-S 31) 22.
Granniss, R. S. "Series of Books about Books." *Colophon* ns 1 (Sp 36) 549-64.
Grattan, C. H. "An American Bookshelf." *Pub W* 134 (2 S 33) 655-62.
Green, C. H. "North Carolina Books and Authors of the Year: A Review." *N C Hist R* 23 (Ap 46) 228-38.
Griffin, M. L. "A Bibliography of New Orleans Magazines." *La Hist Q* 18 (Jl 35) 493-556.
Halpert, Herbert. "Work in Progress." *JAF* 61 (Ja-Mr 48) 71-81.
Henry, E. A. "Doctoral Dissertations Accepted—Ten Years of History." *Col and Res Lib* 5 (S 44) 309-14.
Heyl, Lawrence. "Sources of Information Covering Research in Progress and University Dissertations." *School and Soc* 29 (Je 29) 808-10.
Hirsch, Rudolf. "A List of Recent Bibliographies." *BNYPL* 42 (F 38) 108-32.
Irvine, D. D. "The Fate of Confederate Archives." *AHR* 44 (Jl 39) 823-41.
Jenks, W. L. "Calendar of Michigan Copyrights." *Mich Hist Mag* 14 (Sp, Wi 30) 150-5, 311-3; 15 (Wi 31) 126-9.
Jilson, W. R. "A Bibliography of Early Western Travel in Kentucky: 1674-1824." *Ky State Hist Soc Reg* 42 (Ap 45) 99-119.
——— "A Bibliography of Lexington, Kentucky." *Ky State Hist Soc Reg* 44 (Jl, O 46) 151-86, 259-90; 45 (Ja 47) 39-70.
——— "Bibliography of Lincoln County, Chronologically Arranged and Annotated." *Ky State Hist Soc Reg* 35 (O 37) 339-59.
——— "A Bibliography of the Lower Blue Licks." *Ky State Hist Reg* 42 (O 44) 297-311; 43 (Ja 45) 24-58.

Johnson, Merle. "Additions and Corrections, Some Contributions from Collectors and Dealers . . . Since *American First Editions* Was Published. Together with Some Discoveries of Our Own." *Pub W* 115 (1929) 2113-4, 2845-6; 116 (1929) 282-3, 1966-7.

——— "Additions to American Firsts." *Pub W* 119 (17 Ja 31) 327-9.

Jones, H. M. "Fifty Guides to American Civilization." *SRL* 29 (12 O 46) 15-6, 47.

Karpinski, L. C. "Manuscript Maps of America in European Archives." *Mich Hist Mag* 14 (Wi 30) 5-14.

Kraus, J. E. "Missouri in Fiction: A Review and a Bibliography." *Mo Hist R* 42 (Ap, Jl 48) 209-25, 310-24.

Kurath, Hans. "A Bibliography of American Pronunciation." *Language* 5 (1929) 155-62.

La Drière, Craig. "Annotated Bibliography of Recent Publications in Literary Theory and Criticism." *Am Bkm* 1 (Fl 44) 74-121.

Landis, B. Y. "Democracy: A Reading List." *Bul Am Lib Assn* 34 (Ja 40).

Landrey, K. B. "A Bibliography of Books Written by Children of the Twentieth Century." *More Books* 12 (Ap 37) 149-57.

Lash, J. S. "The American Negro and American Literature: A Check List of Significant Commentaries." *Bul Bibl* 19 (Ja-Ap 47) 33-6.

Lawson, H. J. "The Negro in American Drama." *Bul Bibl* 17 (Ja, My 40) 7-8, 27-30.

Leary, Lewis. "Doctoral Dissertations in American Literature, 1933-1948." *AL* 20 (My 48) 169-230.

Leavitt, S. E., and Russell, H. K. "Theses in English and Modern Foreign Languages Accepted in the Colleges of North Carolina, South Carolina, Georgia, Florida, and Alabama." *So Atl Bul* 4 (Ap 38) 1-15.

Lehmer, D. N. "The Literary Material in the Colonial Records of North Carolina." *Un Calif Chron* 30 (Ap 28) 125-39.

Leisy, E. E., and Hubbell, J. B. "Doctoral Dissertations in American Literature [to 1933]." *AL* 4 (Ja 33) 419-65.

Lincoln, Waldo. "Bibliography of American Cooking Books, 1742-1860." *PAAS* ns 39 (Je 33) 85-225.

McCormack, H. G. "A Provisional Guide to Manuscripts in the South Carolina Historical Society." *S C Hist and Gen Mag* 46 (Ja, Ap, Jl, O 45) 49-53, 104-9, 171-5, 214-7; 47 (Ja 46) 53-7; 48 (Ja 47) 48-52.

McKay, G. L. "American Book Auction Catalogues, 1913-1934. A Union List." *BNYPL* 39 (1935) 141-66, 388-410, 461-78, 490-521, 561-76, 638-63, 724-44, 815-28, 891-914, 955-80; 40 (1936) 56-78, 139-65, 375-90, 535-57, 671-703, 775-800, 859-77, 955-84, 1065-98.

McMurtrie, D. C. "The Bibliography of American Imprints." *Pub W* 144 (20 N 43) 1939-44.

——— "Locating the Printed Source Materials in United States History; with a Bibliography of Lists of Regional Imprints." *Miss Valley Hist R* 31 (D 44) 369-406.

MacPike, E. F. "American and Canadian Diaries, Journals and Notebooks." *Bul Bibl* 18 (My-Ag, S-D 44, Ja-Ap, My-Ag 45) 91-2, 107-15, 133-5, 156-8.

Marchmann, Watt. "Florida Bibliography, 1941." *Tequesta* I (Ag 42) 65-70.

Monaghan, Frank. "French Travellers in the United States, 1765-1931." *BNYPL* 36 (Mr, Ap, Je, Jl, Ag, S, O 32) 163-89, 250-61, 427-38, 503-20, 587-96, 637-45, 690-702.

Moss, David. "A Bibliography of Little Magazines Published in America since 1900." *Contact* 1 (F-O 32) 91, 109, 111-24, 134-9.

Mugridge, Donald. "Recent Americana." *Lib Congress J* 1 (Jy-S 43) 42-4.

Nichols, C. L. "Checklist of Maine, New Hampshire and Vermont Almanacs." *PAAS* ns 38 (Ap 28) 63-163.

O'Neill, E. H. "Plans for a Bibliography of American Literature." *AL* 11 (Mr 39) 81-3.

Paltsits, V. H. "Proposal of Henry Stevens for a 'Bibliographia Americana' to the Year 1700, to Be Published by the Smithsonian Institution." *PBSA* 36 (4 Q 42) 245-66.

Pollard, Lancaster. "A Check List of Washington Authors." *Pac Nw Q* 21 (Ja 40) 3-96; 35 (Jl 44) 233-66.

Porter, Dorothy. "Early American Negro Writing: A Bibliographical Study." *PBSA* 39 (3Q 45) 192-268.

Procter, D. B. "Early American Negro Writings." *PBSA* 39 (3 Q 45) 192-269.

Quinn, A. H., and O'Neill, E. H. "The Bibliography of American Literature at Philadelphia." *J Documentation* (London) 3 (D 47) 177-87.

Quinn, Kirker. "American Poetry 1930-1940." *Accent* 1 (Su 41) 213-28.

Rawlings, K. W. "Trial List of Kentucky Newspapers and Periodicals before 1866." *Proc N J Hist Soc* 56 (Jl 38) 263-87.

Richardson, L. N. "On Using Johnson's *American First Editions* and Other Sources." *AL* 9 (Ja 38) 449-55.

Roach, G. W. "Guide to Depositories of Manuscript Collections in New York State (Exclusive of New York City)." *N Y Hist* 24 (Ap, Jl, O 43) 265-70, 417-22, 560-4; 25 (Ja Ap 44) 64-8, 226-7.

Rose, L. A. "A Bibliographical Survey of Economic and Political Writings, 1865-1900." *AL* 15 (Ja 44) 381-410.

Rosenburg, R. P. "Bibliographies of Theses in America." *Bul Bibl* 18 (S-D 45) 181-2..

Rugg, H. G. "Modern Authors in New England Libraries." *Col and Res Lib* 6 (D 44) 54-7.

Samuel, Edith. "Index to Deaths Mentioned in *The American Mercury,* 1724-1746." *PMHB* 18 (Ja 34) 37-60.

Saunders, Lyle. "A Guide to the Literature of the Southwest." *N M Quar R* 15 (Au 45) 397-404; 17 (Sp, Su 47) 118-25, 273-9.

Schaper, Joseph. "A Question of 'Firsts' Again." *Wis Hist Mag* 16 (S 32) 102-4.

Shearer, A. H. "French Newspapers in the United States before 1800." *PBSA* 14 (1920) 45-147.

Smith, R. W. "Catalogue of the Chief Novels and Short Stories by American Writers Dealing with the Civil War and Its Effects, 1861-1899." *Bul Bibl* 16 (S 35) 193-4; 17 (S 40, Ja-Ap 41) 10-2, 33-5, 53-5, 72-5.

Stanton, M. B. "A Checklist of Washington Authors, 1943-1950." *Pac Nw R* 41 (Jl 50) 254-72.

Sullivan, H. J. "North Dakota Literary Trails." *Quar J Un N D* 23 (1933) 99-103.

Swindler, W. F. "Graduate Theses in the Field of Journalism, 1936-1945." *JQ* 22 (1945) 231-54.

Tinker, E. D. "Bibliography of the French Newspapers and Periodicals of Louisiana." *PAAS* ns 42 (O 32) 247-370.

Tullis, C. H. "Publications of the Texas State Historical Association, July, 1857, through April, 1937." *Sw Hist R* 14 (Ap 37) 188-95.

Vail, R. W. G. "A Message to Garcia: A Bibliographical Puzzle." *BNYPL* 34 (F 30) 71-8.

——— "Sabin's *Dictionary.*" *PBSA* 31 (1937) 1-9.

Walsh, M. J. "Contemporary Broadside Editions of the Declaration of Independence." *HLB* 3 (Wi 48) 31-43.

Walters, W. O. "American Imprints, 1648-1797, in the Huntington Library, Supplementing Evans' *American Bibliography.*" *Huntington Lib Bul* 3 (Ja 33) 1-95.

Weiss, H. B. "American Chapbooks, 1722-1842." *BNYPL* 49 (Jl, Ag 45) 491-8, 587-96.

——— "American Letter Writers, 1698-1943." *BNYPL* 48 (D 44) 959-81; 49 (Ja 45) 25-61.

——— "A Catalogue of the American, English, and Foreign Chapbooks in the New York Public Library." *BNYPL* 39 (1935) 3-34, 105-26, 181-92, 789-810.

——— "Hannah More's Cheap Repository Tracts in America." *BNYPL* 50 (Jl, Ag 46) 539-49, 634-41.

Wheat, C. I. "The Literature of the Gold Rush." *New Colophon* 2 (Ja 49) 54-67.

Wheeler, E. F. "A Bibliography of Wyoming Writers." *Un Wyo Pub* 6 (15 F 39) 2, 11-37.

Wilkinson, N. B. "Current Writings on Pennsylvania." *Penn Hist* 16 (O 49) 326-30.

Wilson, L. R. "Resources of Research Libraries." *Col and Res Lib* 5 (Je 44) 259-66.

———, & Downs, R. B. "Special Collections for the Study of History and Literature in the Southeast." *PBSA* 28 (1934) 97-131.

Winkler, E. W. "Check List of Texas Imprints, 1846-1876." *Sw Hist Q* 49 (Ap 46) 532-84.

——— "Check List of Texas Imprints, 1861-1876." *Sw Hist Q* 52 (Jl 48) 66-82.

Yarmolinski, Avrahm. "Bibliographical Studies in Early Polish Americana." *BNYPL* 38 (Ap 34) 223-40; 40 (My 36) 427-36.

——— "Studies in Russian Americana." *BNYPL* 47 (Ja 43) 52-4.

BIOGRAPHY. Anon. "A New Departure in Biography." *Atl* 98 (Jl 06) 139-40.

——— "A Reviewer's Note-Book." *Freeman* 2 (13 O 20) 118-9.

Barnes, H. E. "The Fathers at Work and Play." *Am Merc* 8 (My 26) 54-60.

Brecher, Ruth & Edward. "Footprints in the Sands of Time: *The Dictionary of American Biography*." *Am Schol* 14 (D 44) 106-14.

Cantwell, Robert. "The Autobiographers." *NRp* 84 (27 Ap 38) 354-6.

Chamberlain, John. "Walking the Tightrope: An Inquiry into the Art of Political Biography." *Mod Mo* 7 (Mr 33) 105-9.

Commager, H. S. "Memoirs: The Personal Touch." *N Y Times Book R* 52 (3 Ag 47) 1, 20.

Field, L. M. "Biographical New Dealing." *NAR* 238 (D 34) 546-52.

——— "Biography Boom." *NAR* 230 (O 30) 433-40.

Fuess, C. M. "Debunkery and Biography." *Atl* 151 (Mr 33) 347-57.

Hart, A. B. "A Study of Washington Biography." *Pub W* 119 (19 F 31) 820-2.

Hergesheimer, Joseph. "Biography and Bibliographies." *Colophon* 2 (D 31) Pt 8.

Johnson, Allen. "Tendencies of Recent American Biography." *YR* ns 1 (Ap 12) 390-403.

Johnson, Edgar. "American Biography and the Modern World." *NAR* 245 (Su 38) 364-80.

Jones, C. E. "Collected Biographies to 1825." *Bul Bibl* 17 (My-Ag 41) 90-2.

Jones, H. M. "Methods in Contemporary Biography." *EJ* 21 (Ja, F 32) 43-51, 113-22.

Long, J. C. "Biography Now and Tomorrow." *SRL* 29 (18 My 46) 16-7.

Matthews, Brander. "American Autobiography." *Munsey's* 49 (S 13) 988-92.

Merrill, D. K. "The First American Biography." *NEQ* 11 (Mr 38) 152-4.

Mounsell, L. F. "Biographical New Dealing." *NAR* 238 (D 34) 546-52.

O'Neill, E. H. "Modern American Biography." *NAR* 240 (D 35) 488-97.

Schindler, M. C. "Fictitious Biography." *AHR* 42 (Jl 37) 680-90.

Schlesinger, A. M. "Biography of a Nation of Joiners." *AHR* 50 (O 44) 1-25.

Schuyler, Montgomery. "American Biography." *Putnam's* 3 (O 07) 100-5.

Stern, M. B. "Approaches to Biography." *SAQ* 45 (Jl 46) 362-71.

Thayer, W. R. "Recent American Biographies and Letters." *NAR* 213 (My 21) 681-96.

Wolseley, R. E. "The Journalist as Autobiographer." *SAQ* 42 (Ja 43) 38-44.

Wright, L. H. "Traditional Errors in American Biography." *HLQ* 5 (Ja 42) 273-6.

CHILDREN'S LITERATURE. Binsse, H. L. "Children's Books—1946." *Commonweal* 45 (15 N 46) 119-24.
Brigham, C. S. "Exhibition of Children's Books before 1800." *PAAS* 37 (O 27) 210-7.
Commager, H. S. "Super: This Must Go In! Editing the St. Nicholas Anthology." *Pub W* 154 (30 O 48) 1874-7.
Davis, M. G. "Writing about America." *SRL* 29 (10 Ag 46) 30-1.
Edmonds, M. D. "Literature and Children." *NAR* 244 (Au 37) 148-61.
Gruenberg, S. M. "Reading for Children." *Dial* 63 (6 D 17) 575-7.
Hislop, Codman. "The Americanization of Mother Goose." *Colophon* ns 3 (Su 38) 435-40.
Hopkins, F. M. "Early American Juveniles." *Pub W* 116 (16 N 29) 2395-9.
Kiefer, Monica. "Early American Childhood in the Middle Atlantic Area." *PMHB* 68 (Ja 44) 3-37.
Moses, M. J. "Convalescent 'Children's Literature.'" *NAR* 221 (Mr 25) 528-39.
Rosenbach, A. S. W. "Early American Children's Books." *Pub W* 123 (20 My 33) 1620-4.
Royer, Mary. "The Amish and Mennonite Theme in American Literature for Children." *Mennonite Quar R* 19 (O 45) 285-91.
Rugg, W. K. "Books for Children, 1839-1879." *Chri Sci Mon* 27 (5 O 35) 263.
Stearns, M. M. "The Good Die Young." *JRUL* 5 (Je 42) 71-7.
Stone, W. M. "The History of Little Goody Two-Shoes." *PAAS* ns 49 (O 39) 333-70.
Warren, J. C. "Children's Story Books." *PMHS* 55 (Mr 22) 237-8.
Weiss, H. B. "Joseph Yeager, Early American Engraver, Publisher of Children's Books, and Railroad President." *BNYPL* 36 (S 32) 611-6.
Wright, L. M. "Culture through Lectures." *Iowa J Hist & Pol* 39 (Ap 40) 115-63.
Wyat, E. A. "Schools and Libraries in Petersburg, Virginia, Prior to 1861." *Tyler's Quar Hist & Gen Mag* 19 (O 37) 65-86.

DIARIES AND LETTERS. Anon. "Diary of John Early, Bishop of the Methodist Episcopal Church, South." *VMHB* 39 (Ja, Ap 31) 41-5, 146-51.
Adams, Horace. "A Puritan Wife on the Frontier." *Miss Valley Hist R* 27 (Je 40) 67-84.
Barkley, A. H. "Constantine Samuel Rafinesque." *Letters* 2 (Ag 29) 30-6.
Barnes, J. A. "Letters of a Massachusetts Woman Reformer to an Indiana Radical." *Ind Mag Hist* 26 (Mr 30) 46-60.
Beale, H. K. "The Diary of Edward Bates, 1839-1866." *Annual Report Am Hist Assn* 4 (1930) 1-685.
Benson, A. B. "Frederika Bremer's Unpublished Letters to the Downings." *SS* 11 (1931) 1-10, 39-53, 71-8, 109-24, 149-72, 215-28, 264-74.
Bradford, Gamaliel. "A Confederate Pepys." *Am Merc* 6 (D 25) 470-8.
Cadbury, H. J. "John Farmer's First American Journey, 1711-1714." *PAAS* 53 (Ap 43) 79-95.
Coburn, F. W. "Theodore Edson and His Diary." *Hist Mag Protestant Episc Church* 14 (D 45) 307-21.
Fairies, Elizabeth. "The Miami Country, 1750-1815, as Described in Journals and Letters." *Ohio State Arch & Hist Q* 57 (Ja 48) 48-65.
Fessler, W. J. "Captain Nathan Boone's Journal." *Chron Okla* 7 (Mr 29) 58-105.
Fisher, Josephine. "The Journal of Esther Burr." *NEQ* 3 (Ap 30) 297-315.
Galpin, W. F. "Letters Concerning the 'Universal Republic.'" *AHR* 34 (Jl 29) 779-86.
Gohdes, Clarence. "Three Letters by James Kay Dealing with Brook Farm." *PQ* 17 (O 38) 377-88.
Harazti, Zoltán. "Brook Farm Letters." *More Books* 12 (F, Mr 37) 49-68, 93-114.
Harker, M. H. "Journal of a Quaker Maid." *VQR* 11 (Ja 35) 61-81.

Hicks, Granville. "Letters to William Francis Channing." *AL* 2 (N 30) 294-8.

Higginson, Francis. "Higginson's Journal of His Voyage to New England." *PMHS* 62 (Je 29) 281-321.

Jordan, P. D. "Letters of Eliab Parker Mackintire, of Boston, 1845-1863." *BNYPL* 38 (O, N 34) 831-65, 954-77.

Lillard, R. G. "A Literate Woman in the Mines: The Diary of Rachel Haskell." *Miss Valley Hist R* 31 (Je 44) 81-98.

Mabbott, T. O. "Correspondence of John Tomlin." *N&Q* 166 (6 Ja 34) 6-7.

MacPike, E. F. "American and Canadian Diaries, Journals, and Notebooks." *Bul Bibl* 18 (My-Ag, S-D 44; Ja-Ap, My-Ag 45) 91-2, 107-15, 133-5, 156-8.

Pearce, R. H. "Sterne and Sensibility in American Diaries." *MLN* 59 (Je 44) 403-7.

Potter, D. "The Brodhead Diaries, 1846-1849." *JRUL* 10 (D 47) 21-7.

Sedgwick, Henry Dwight. "On Letter Writing." *YR* ns 8 (Ja 19) 372-90.

Shipton, C. K. "The Autobiographical Memoranda of John Brock, 1636-1659." *PAAS* 53 (Ap 43) 96-105.

Webber, M. L. "Josiah Smith's Diary, 1780-1781." *S C Hist & Gen Mag* 33 (Ja, Ap, Jl, 0 32) 1-28, 79-116, 197-207, 281-9; 34 (Ja, Ap, Jl, O 33) 31-9, 67-84, 138-48, 194-210.

Weiss, H. B. "American Letter-Writers, 1698-1943." *BNYPL* 48 (D 44) 959-82; 49 (Ja 45) 36-61.

Wendell, Barrett. "A Gentlewoman of Boston, 1742-1805." *PAAS* ns 29 (O 19) 242-93.

FICTION. Anon. "The Beadle Collection." *BNYPL* 26 (Jl 22) 555-628.

——— "Cardinal Points in American Fiction." *Independent* 54 (20 N 02) 2784-6.

——— "The Case of Fiction." *Harper's* 139 (S 19) 572-8.

——— "Editor's Study." *Harper's* 105 (Jl 02) 313-5.

——— "Fiction in the U. S.: We Need a Novelist to Recreate American Values instead of Wallowing in the Literary Slums." *Life* 25 (16 Ag 48) 24.

——— "The Growth of Science-Fiction and Fantasy Publishing in Book Form." *Pub W* 154 (25 D 48) 2464-9.

——— "The Hour Glass." *Epoch* 1 (Fl 47) 87-91.

——— "The Modern Dime Novel." *N E Mag* 48 (S 12) 305-7.

——— "The Novels of the Second World War." *Pub W* 154 (23 O 48) 1802-8.

——— "Novels of Western Life." *Bkm* 32 (S 10) 20-1.

——— "On Beginning to Write a Novel." *Harper's* 173 (Jl 36) 179-88.

——— "Recent Reflections of a Novel Reader." *Atl* 116 (O 15) 499-511; 117 (My 16) 632-42.

——— "The School of Cruelty." *SRL* 7 (21 F 31) 609.

——— "Shapers of the Modern Novel: A Catalogue of an Exhibition." *PULC* 11 (Sp 50) 134-41.

Able, A. H. III. "Fiction as a Mirror of Delaware Life." *Del Hist* (Mr 48) 37-53.

——— "A Short View of Contemporary Fiction." *Del Notes* ser 21 (1948) 19-35.

Adams, J. D. "Contrasts in British and American Fiction." *EJ* (coll ed) 27 (Ap 38) 287-94.

Adkins, N. F. "An Early American Story of Utopia." *Colophon* ns 1 (Su 35) 123-32.

Admari, Ralph. "Ballou, the Father of the Dime Novel." *Am Book Coll* 4 (S-O 33) 121-9.

——— "Bibliography of Dime Novels." *Am Book Coll* 5 (Jl 34) 215-7.

Agar, Herbert. "Cynicism and Sentimentality in America." *New Statesman & Nation* ns 3 (28 Je 31) 7, 17.

Allen, Hervey. "History and the Novel." *Atl* 173 (F 44) 119-21.

Allen, J. L. "The Gentleman in American Fiction." *Bkm* 32 (N 10) 309.

———, Howells, W. D., Garland, Hamlin, Mabie, H. W., & Bangs, J. K. "Will the Novel Disappear?" *NAR* 175 (S 02) 289-98.

Amunátequi, Francisco. "Jóvenes autores americanos." *Atenea* (Santiago de Chile) 15 (Ag 38) 283-8.
Angoff, Charles. "Three Notes on American Literature." *NAR* 247 (Sp 41) 38-41.
Arvin, Newton. "Fiction Mirrors America." *Cur Hist* 42 (S 35) 610-6.
——— "Jeunes auteurs américains." *Formes et Couleurs* no 6 (1947) np.
Astre, Georges-Albert. "Sur le roman américain." *Critique* 2 (Ap 47) 302-15.
Atherton, Gertrude. "The American Novel in England." *Bkm* 30 (F 10) 632-40.
Austin, Mary. "The Folk Story in America." *SAQ* 33 (Ja 34) 10-19.
——— "Regionalism in American Fiction." *EJ* 21 (F 32) 97-107.
——— "Sex in American Literature." *Bkm* 57 (Je 23) 385-93.
Aydelotte, W. O. "The Detective Story as a Historical Source." *YR* 39 (Au 49) 76-95.
Bacheller, Irving. "American Backgrounds for Fiction: The North Country of New York." *Bkm* 38 (F 14) 624-8.
Bader, Arno. "The Gallant Captain and Brother Jonathan." *Colophon* ns 2 (Au 36) 114-29.
Bailey, J. O. "An Early American Utopian Fiction." *AL* 14 (N 42) 285-93.
Baker, Howard. "The Contemporary Short Story." *So R* 3 (Wi 38) 576-96.
——— "An Essay on Fiction with Examples." *So R* 7 (Au 41) 385-406.
——— "In Praise of the Novel: The Fiction of Huxley, Steinbeck and Others." *So R* 5 (Sp 40) 778-800.
Baldwin, James. "Everybody's Protest Novel." *PR* 16 (Je 49) 578-85.
Bangs, J. K., *et al.* "The Decay of the Novel." *Critic* 42 (F 03) 149-60.
Banning, M. C. "Changing Moral Standards in Fiction." *SRL* 20 (1 Jl 39) 3-4, 14.
Baring-Gould, W. S. "Little Superman, What Now?" *Harper's* 193 (S 46) 283-8.
Barzun, Jacques. "Our Non-Fiction Novelists." *Atl* 178 (Jl 46) 129-32.
Bataille, Georges. "La Soveraineté de la fête et le roman américain." *Critique* 5: no 39 (Ag 49) 675-81.
Beach, J. W. "New Intentions in the Novel." *NAR* 218 (Ag 23) 233-45.
——— "Unripe Fruits." *YR* 16 (O 26) 134-47.
Beary, T. J. "Religion and the Modern Novel." *Cath World* 166 (D 47) 203-11.
Beck, Warren. "Art and Formula in the Short Story." *CE* 5 (N 43) 55-62.
Beffel, J. N. "The Fauntleroy Plague." *Bkm* 65 (Ap 27) 135-7.
Bender, E. H. "Three Amish Novels." *Mennonite Quar R* 19 (O 45) 273-84.
Bennett, Arnold. "The Future of the American Novel." *NAR* 195 (Ja 12) 76-83.
Bentley, Phyllis. "The American Novel To-day." *TLS* (20 My 39) 296, 298.
——— "I Look at American Fiction." *SRL* 20 (13 My 39) 3-4, 14-5.
Bergsveinsson, Sveinn. "Sagaen og den haardkogte Roman." *Edda* (Oslo) 42 (Ja-Mr 42) 56-62.
Berreman, J. V. "An Empirical Test of the Theory of Fugitive Behavior." *Res Stud State Col Wash* 10 (Mr 42) 45-52.
Berti, Luigi. "Critica del romanzo americano." *Fiera Letteraria* no 16 (17 Ap 49).
Billups, E. P. "Some Principles for the Representation of the Negro Dialect in Fiction." *Texas R* 8 (Ja 23) 99-123.
Boatright, M. C. "The Tall Tale in Texas." *SAQ* 30 (Jl 31) 271-9.
Bodenheim, Maxwell. "Psychoanalysis and American Fiction." *Nation* 114 (7 Je 22) 683.
Bowen, E. W. "Is the Novel Decadent?" *SAQ* 2 (Jl 03) 261-6.
Boynton, H. W. "A Glance at Current American Fiction." *Nation* 88 (4 F 09) 106-8.
——— "Literature and Fiction." *Atl* 89 (My 02) 706-11.
——— "Realism and Recent American Fiction." *Nation* 102 (6 Ap 16) 380-2.
——— "A Word on the Genteel Critic." *Dial* 59 (14 O 15) 303-6.
Boynton, P. H. "American Authors Today: The Short Story." *EJ* 12 (My 23) 325-33.
——— "The Novel of Puritan Decay." *NEQ* 13 (D 40) 626-35.

Boys, R. C. "The American College in Fiction." *CE* 7 (Ap 46) 379-87.
Brace, Marjorie. "Thematic Problems of the American Novelist." *Accent* 6 (Au 45) 44-53.
Bradford, Gamaliel. "Fiction as Historical Material." *PMHS* 48 (Mr 15) 326-32.
Bradsher, E. L. "Some Aspects of the Early American Novel." *Texas R* 3 (Ap 18) 241-58.
Brawley, Benjamin. "The Negro in American Fiction." *Dial* 60 (11 My 16) 445-50.
Brickell, Herschel. "Colonial Hero." *NAR* 244 (Wi 37-8) 405-13.
——— "The Contemporary Short Story." *UKCR* 15 (Su 49) 267-70.
——— "The Present State of Fiction." *VQR* 25 (Wi 49) 92-8.
Brody, Alter. "Yiddish in American Fiction." *Am Merc* 7 (F 26) 205-7.
Brooks, Obed. "The Problem of the Social Novel." *Mod Q* 6 (Au 32) 77-82.
Brown, E. B. "Moral Hesitations of the Novelist." *Atl* 90 (O 02) 545-8.
Brown, H. R. "The Great American Novel." *AL* 7 (Mr 35) 1-14.
Brown, M. W. "The Ash Can School." *Am Q* 1 (Su 49) 127-34.
Brudno, E. S. "The American Novel." *Bkm* 19 (Je 04) 414-7.
Buck, P. S. "Fiction and the Front Page." *YR* 25 (Mr 36) 477-87.
Bulloch, J. M. "Tendencies of the American Novel." *Lamp* 26 (Mr 03) 110-2.
Burke, Kenneth. "A Decade of American Fiction." *Bkm* 69 (Ag 29) 561-7.
Burt, Struthers. "What's Left for the Novelist?" *NAR* 232 (Ag 31) 118-25.
Bushnell, R. T. "Banned in Boston." *NAR* 229 (My 30) 518-25.
Cahen, Jacques-Fernand. "Cause et déchéance de la littérature noire." *Le Divan* (Paris) no 268 (O-D 48) 455-69.
——— "Du roman américain." *Le Divan* (Paris) no 267 (Jl-S 48) 393-406.
Cajeton, Brother E. G. "The Pendulum Swings Back." *Cath World* 140 (Mr 35) 650-6.
Canby, H. S. "Fiction Tells All." *Harper's* 171 (Ag 35) 308-15.
——— "Free Fiction." *Atl* 116 (Jl 15) 60-8.
——— "Neither Prurients nor Prudes." *SRL* 20 (20 Ap 39) 8.
——— "An Open Letter to the Realists." *SRL* 30 (3 My 47) 20.
——— "On a Certain Condescension toward Fiction." *Century* 95 (F 18) 549-54.
——— "The Reviewing of Books." *Atl* 180 (Ap 47) 115-8.
——— "Sentimental America." *Atl* 121 (Ap 18) 500-6.
Cantwell, Robert. "A Warning to Pre-War Novelists." *NRp* 91 (23 Je 37) 177-80.
Carruth, F. W. "Boston in Fiction." *Bkm* 14 (N, D 01, Ja, F 02) 236-54, 364-85, 507-21, 590-604.
——— "Washington in Fiction." *Bkm* 15 (Jl 02) 451-63.
Cary, E. L. "Mortality in Modern Fiction." *Book Buyer* 22 (F 01) 18-9.
——— "A New Element in Fiction." *Book Buyer* 23 (Ag 01) 26-8.
Cater, Catherine. "Myth and the Contemporary Southern Novelist: A Note." *Midwest J* 2 (Wi 49) 1-8.
Chamberlain, John. "The Business Man in Fiction." *Fortune* 38 (N 48) 134-6, 138, 139, 142, 144, 148.
Champney, Freeman. "Literature Takes to the Woods." *AR* 4 (Su 44) 246-56.
——— "Protofascism in American Literature." *AR* 4 (Fl 44) 338-48.
——— "Utopia, Ltd." *AR* 8 (Fl 48) 259-80.
Chapman, A. "The New West and the Old Fiction." *Independent* 54 (9 Ja 02) 98-100.
Chapman, Maristan. "Is Our Ink Well?: A Catalog Comment upon Southern Novelists from 1917-1934." *Westminster Mag* 23 (Ja-Mr 35) 259-77.
Chevalier, H. M. "Farewell to Purity." *Mod Mo* 8 (Mr 34) 100-4, 111.
Cline, R. I. "The Tar-Baby Story." *AL* (Mr 30) 72-8.
Coad, O. S. "The Gothic Element in American Literature before 1835." *JEGP* 24 (1Q 25) 72-93.
Cochran, Elizabeth. "Historical Fiction and the Teaching of History." *Social Educ* 14 (F 50) 65-8.

Colbron, G. I. "The American Novel in Germany." *Bkm* 39 (Mr 14) 45-9.
———, *et al.* "The Relation of the Novel to the Present Social Unrest." *Bkm* 40 (N 14) 276-303.
Collins, C. E. "Nineteenth Century Fiction of the Southern Appalachians." *Bul Bibl* 17 (S-D 42; Ja-Ap 43) 186-90, 215-8.
Colum, M. M. "The American Short Story." *Dial* 62 (19 Ap 17) 345-7.
——— "The Psychopathic Novel." *Forum* 91 (Ap 34) 219-23.
Compton, C. H. "The Librarian and the Novelist." *SAQ* 26 (O 27) 392-403.
Cooper, F. T. "Morality in Fiction." *Bkm* 38 (F 14) 666-72.
——— "Pathology in Fiction." *Bkm* 35 (Jl 12) 530-4.
Cory, H. E. "The Senility of the Short-Story." *Dial* 62 (3 My 17) 379-81.
Couch, W. T. "The Agrarian Romance." *SAQ* 36 (O 37) 419-30.
Cowie, Alexander. "My Case against Contemporary American Fiction." *SRL* 28 (29 S 45) 15, 44-6.
——— "The New Heroine's Code for Virtue." *Am Schol* 4 (Sp 35) 190-202.
——— "The Vogue of the Domestic Novel: 1850-1870." *SAQ* 41 (O 42) 416-24.
Cowley, Malcolm. "The Generation That Wasn't Lost." *CE* 5 (F 44) 233-9.
——— "New Tendencies in the Novel: Pure Fiction." *NRp* 121 (28 N 49) 32-5.
——— "'Not Men': A Natural History of American Naturalism." *KR* 9 (Sp 47) 414-35.
——— "Two Wars—and Two Generations. The Novelists' Climate in the Twenties, and His Legacy to the Novelist of Today." *NY Times Book R* (25 Jl 48) 1, 20.
Croly, Herbert. "Some Really Historical Novels." *Lamp* 26 (Jl 03) 509-13.
Cross, Wilbur. "The New Fiction." *YR* ns 11 (Ap 22) 449-66.
——— "Some Novels of 1920." *YR* ns 9 (Ja 21) 396-411.
Crothers, S. M. "The Unfailing Charm of Some Novels." *Atl* 142 (Ag 28) 190-8.
Curti, Merle. "Dime Novels and the American Tradition." *YR* 26 (Je 37) 761-78.
Dane, Clemence. "American Fairy Tales." *Fortnightly R* ns 139 (Ap 36) 464-70; *NAR* 242 (Au 36) 143-52.
Dangerfield, George. "Invisible Censorship." *NAR* 244 (Wi 37-8) 334-48.
Davidson, Donald. "The 43 Best Southern Novels for Readers and Collectors." *Pub W* 127 (27 Ap 35) 1675-6.
Daviess, M. T. "American Backgrounds for Fiction: Tennessee." *Bkm* 38 (D 13) 394-9.
Davis, R. G. "Fiction and Thinking." *Epoch* 1 (Sp 48) 87-96.
Dawson, W. J. "The Modern Short Story." *NAR* 190 (D 09) 799-810.
Dell, Floyd. "Chicago in Fiction." *Bkm* 38 (N, D 13) 270-7, 374-9.
——— "Sex in American Fiction." *Am Merc* 66 (Ja 48) 84-90.
Dempsey, David. "The Novelist and the Soldier." *N Y Times Book R* (9 D 45) 1, 28, 30.
Derleth, August. "America in Today's Fiction." *Pub W* 139 (3 My 41) 1820-5.
——— "The Cult of Incoherence." *Mod Thinker* 2 (D 32) 612-8.
DeVoto, Bernard. "American Novels: 1939." *Atl* 165 (Ja 40) 66-74.
——— "Fiction and the Everlasting *IF*." *Harper's* 177 (Je 38) 42-9.
——— "Fiction Fights the Civil War." *SRL* 17 (18 D 37) 3-4, 15-6.
Dickson, Lovat. "The American Novel in England." *Pub W* 134 (29 O 38) 1586-90.
Dixon, Thomas. "American Backgrounds for Fiction: North Carolina." *Bkm* 38 (Ja 14) 511-21.
Dorson, R. M. "Dialect Stories of the Upper Peninsula: A New Form of American Folklore." *JAF* 61 (Ap-Je 49) 113-50.
Dougherty, C. T. "Novels of the Middle Border: A Critical Bibliography for Historians." *Hist Bul* 25 (My 47) 77-8, 85-8.
Dreiser, Theodore. "The Great American Novel." *Am Spect* 1 (D 32) 1.
DuBois, A. E. "The Art of Fiction." *SAQ* 40 (Ap 41) 112-22.
Earle, M. T. "New York Types in Fiction." *Book Buyer* 20 (Ap 00) 199-202.
——— "Novels That Are Documents." *Lamp* 27 (Ja 04) 603-5.

Eaton, W. P. "Revolt from Realism." *VQR* 10 (O 34) 515-28.
Edmonds, W. D. "How You Begin a Novel." *Atl* 158 (Ag 36) 189-92.
——— "A Novelist Takes Stock." *Atl* 172 (Jl 43) 73-7.
Emch, L. B. "Ohio in Short Stories, 1824-1829." *Ohio Arch & Hist Q* 53 (Jl-S 44) 209-50.
English, Jack. "Can a Catholic Write a Novel?" *Am Merc* 31 (Ja 34) 90-5.
Erskine, John. "American Business in the American Novel." *Bkm* 73 (Jl 31) 449-51.
Evans, Oliver. "Letter from Rome." *Prairie Schooner* 23 (Fl 49) 299-301.
Everett, William. "The Political Novel." *Atl* 101 (Je 08) 850-7.
Fadiman, Clifton. "The American Novel of the Truce." *SRL* 27 (5 Ag 44) 19-21.
Farrar, John. "Novelists and/or Historians." *SRL* 28 (17 F 45) 7-8.
——— "Sex Psychology in Modern Fiction." *Independent* 117 (11 D 26) 668-70.
Farrell, J. T. "The Social Obligations of the Novelist: I. Is the Obligation to 'State' or 'Society?'" *Humanist* 7 (Au 47) 57-62.
——— "Social Themes in American Realism." *EJ* 35 (Je 46) 309-14.
——— "Some Observations on Naturalism, So Called, in American Fiction." *AR* 10 (Su 50) 247-64.
Fast, Howard. "Realism and the Soviet Novel." *New Masses* 57 (11 D 45) 15-6, 25-6.
Fatout, Paul. "The Enchanted Titan." *SAQ* 30 (Ja 31) 51-9.
——— "Yarning in the 1850's." *Am Schol* 3 (Su 34) 281-93.
Faÿ, Bernard. "L'Ecole de l'infortune ou la nouvelle génération littéraire aux États-Unis." *Revue de Paris* (Ag 37) 644-65.
Field, L. M. "American Novelists vs. the Nation." *NAR* 235 (Je 33) 552-60.
——— "Emancipating the Novel." *NAR* 240 (S 35) 318-24.
——— "Heroines Back at the Hearth." *NAR* 236 (Ag 33) 176-83.
——— "The Modest Novelists." *NAR* 235 (Ja 33) 63-9.
——— "Mothers in Fiction." *NAR* 237 (Mr 34) 250-6.
——— "Not for Love." *NAR* 233 (Ap 32) 363-8.
——— "Philo Vance & Co., Benefactors." *NAR* 235 (Mr 33) 254-60.
——— "Sentimentality a la Mode." *NAR* 228 (D 29) 682-5.
——— "War Makes the Hero." *NAR* 235 (Ap 33) 370-5.
——— "What's Wrong with the Men?" *NAR* 231 (Mr 31) 234-40.
——— "What's Wrong with the Women?" *NAR* 232 (S 31) 274-80.
Firkins, O. W. "Undepicted America." *YR* 20 (S 30) 140-50.
Flanagan, J. T. "A Bibliography of Middle Western Farm Novels." *Minn Hist* 23 (Je 42) 156-8.
——— "An Early Tale of the Falls of St. Anthony." *Minn Hist* 25 (Je 44) 165-7.
——— "The Middle Western Farm Novel." *Minn Hist* 23 (Je 42) 113-25.
——— "The Middle Western Historical Novel." *J. Ill State Hist Soc* 37 (Mr 44) 7-47.
——— "Novels of the Midlands." *Chicago Sun Book Week* 4 (4 My 47) 4.
——— "Some Minnesota Novels, 1920-1950." *Minn Hist* 31 (S 50) 145-57.
———, & Grismer, R. L. "Mexico in American Fiction prior to 1850." *Hispania* 23 (D 40) 307-18.
Flower, B. O. "Fashions in Fiction." *Arena* 30 (S 03) 287-94.
Follett, Wilson. "Humanism and Fiction." *Atl* 122 (O 18) 503-12.
——— "Sentimentalist, Satirist, and Realist; Notes on Some Recent Fiction." *Atl* 118 (O 16) 490-502.
——— "The War as Critic." *Atl* 119 (My 17) 660-70.
Ford, J. L. "Chance for an American Dickens." *Munsey's* 23 (My 00) 281-5.
Foster, T. H. "Collecting Iowa Dime Novels." *Palimpsest* 30 (Je 49) 169-72.
Frederick, J. T. "New Techniques in the Novel." *EJ* 24 (My 35) 355-63.
Frey, J. R. "George Washington in American Fiction." *VMHB* 55 (O 47) 342-9.
Fuller, H. B. "Chicago Novels." *Lit R* 2 (18 Mr 22) 501-2.
——— "New Forms of Short Fiction." *Dial* 62 (8 Mr 17) 167-9.

——— "A Plea for Shorter Novels." *Dial* 63 (30 Ag 17) 139-41.

Gaines, F. P. "The Racial Bar Sinister in American Romance." *SAQ* 25 (O 26) 398-402.

Gale, Zona. "Period Realism." *YR* 23 (Au 33) 111-24.

Gallachèr, S. A. "The Ideal Hero of Antiquity and His Counterpart in the Comic Strip of Today." *SFQ* (Je 47) 141-8.

Garcia, O. M. "Quarto novelistas de romantismo Norte-Americano." *Revista de Instituto Brasil Estados Unidos* 2 (S 44) 35-53.

Garland, Hamlin. "Sanity in Fiction." *NAR* 176 (Mr 03) 336-48.

Garnett, Edward. "Some Remarks on American and English Fiction." *Atl* 114 (D 14) 747-56.

Gass, S. B. "Modernism and the Novel." *Forum* 79 (My 28) 757-64.

Gavigan, W. V. "Nuns in Novels." *Cath World* 140 (N 34) 186-95.

Gehman, R. B. "Imagination Run Wild." *NRp* 120 (17 Ja 49) 15-8.

George, W. L. "Do We Despise the Novelist?" *Harper's* 136 (Mr 18) 581-90.

Gerould, Katherine. "The American Short Story." *YR* 13 (Jl 24) 642-63.

Gilder, J. L. "American Historical Novelists." *Independent* 53 (5 S 01) 2096-102.

Gill, W. A. "Some Novelists and the Business Man." *Atl* 112 (S, O 13) 374-85, 506-15.

Gisolfi, A. M. "'The Beach of Heaven': Italy 1943-45 in American Fiction." *Ital* 27 (S 50) 199-207.

Glasgow, Ellen. "The Novel in the South." *Harper's* 143 (D 28) 93-100.

Glicksberg, C. I. "The Furies in Negro Fiction." *WR* 13 (Wi 49) 107-14.

——— "Modern Literature and the Sense of Doom." *Ariz Q* 6 (Au 50) 208-17.

——— "Negro Fiction in America." *SAQ* 45 (O 46) 477-88.

——— "Proletarian Fiction in the United States." *Dalhousie R* 22 (Ap 37) 22-32.

Gould, Gerald. "Novels English and American." *Atl* 142 (Jl 28) 125-34.

Green, Julian. "How a Novelist Begins." *Atl* 168 (D 41) 743-52.

Grunt, O. P. "Ny amerikansk litteratur." *Samtiden* (Oslo) 54 (1945) 312-23; 55 (1946) 387-96.

Guianan, J. W. "The Catholic and the Novel." *Cath Churchman* 5 (Mr-Ap 42) 112-4.

Hackett, A. P. "New Novelists of 1945." *SRL* 29 (16 F 46) 8-10.

Hackett, Francis. "The Novel and Human Personality." *N Y Times Book R* 53 (15 Ag 48) 1, 15.

Hale, E. E. "The Earlier 'Realism.'" *Union Col Bul* 25 (Ja 32) 3-11.

Hansen, Harry. "Literary Fashions." *Forum* 89 (Mr 33) 152-5.

Harben, W. H. "American Backgrounds for Fiction: Georgia." *Bkm* 38 (O 13) 186-92.

Harris, Mrs. L. H. "Fiction North and South." *Critic* 43 (S 03) 273-5.

——— "Neurotic Symptoms in Recent Fiction." *Independent* 55 (19 N 03) 2725-8.

Harrison, H. S. "The Last Days of the Devastators." *YR* 18 (S 28) 88-103.

Harrison, J. G. "Nineteenth-Century American Novels on American Journalism." *JQ* 22 (S, D 46) 215-24, 335-48.

Hart, I. H. "The Most Popular Books of Fiction Year by Year in the Post-War Period." *Pub W* 123 (28 Ja 33) 364-7.

Harvey, C. M. "The Dime Novel in American Life." *Atl* 100 (Jl 07) 37-45.

Harwood, W. S. "New Orleans in Fiction." *Critic* 47 (N 05) 426-35.

Hasley, Louis. "The Stream of Consciousness Method." *Cath World* 144 (N 37) 210-3.

Hatcher, Harlan. "The New Vogue of Historical Fiction." *EJ* 26 (D 37) 775-84.

Haviland, T. P. "Preciosité Crosses the Atlantic." *PMLA* 59 (Mr 44) 131-41.

Hawkins, E. W. "The Stream of Cconsciousness Novels." *Atl* 138 (S 26) 356-60.

Hazard, E. P. "First Novelists of 1947." *SRL* 21 (14 F 48) 8-12.

Henderson, Archibald. "Aspects of Contemporary Fiction." *Arena* 36 (Jl 06) 1-9.

Hergesheimer, Joseph. "The Feminine Nuisance in Literature." *YR* 10 (Jl 21) 716-25.
Herrick, Robert. "The American Novel." *YR* 3 (Ap 14) 419-37.
——— "The Background of the American Novel." *YR* 3 (Ja 14) 213-33.
——— "The Shape of Postwar Literature." *CE* 5 (My 44) 407-12.
——— "What Is Happening to Our Fiction?" *Nation* 129 (4 D 29)673-4.
——— "Writers in the Jungle." *NRp* 80 (17 O 34) 259-61.
Herron, I. H. "The American Small Town in Fiction." *Duke Un Archive* 44 (Ja 32) 8-15.
Hersey, John. "The Novel of Contemporary History." *Atl* 184 (N 49) 80-4.
Heydrick, B. A. "The [American] Novel." *Chautauquan* 64 (S, O 11) 25-40, 165-84.
——— "The [American] Short Story." *Chautauquan* 64 (N 11) 313-34.
Heyward, D. B. "New Theory of Historical Fiction." *Pub W* 122 (13 Ag 32) 511-2.
Hicks, Granville. "American Fiction since the War." *EJ* 37 (Je 48) 271-6.
——— "P-N Fiction." *EJ* 35 (D 46) 525-30; *CE* 8 (D 46) 107-12.
——— "Romancers of the Left." *New Masses* 28 (23 Ag 38) 22-3.
Hitt, Helen. "History in Pacific Northwest Novels." *Ore Hist Q* 51 (S 50) 180-206.
Hock, C. H. "The Mormons in Fiction." *Un Colo Stud* 26 (N 41) 94-6.
Hordahl, A. D. "Norwegian-American Fiction 1880-1928." *N Am Stud & Records* 5 (1930) 61-83.
Howells, W. D. "American Fiction." *Harper's* 105 (O 02) 802-5.
——— "Certain of the Chicago School of Fiction." *NAR* 176 (My 03) 734-46.
——— "The New Historical Romances." *NAR* 171 (D 00) 935-48.
——— "A Novelist on Art." *Lit Dig* 20 (2 Je 00) 662-3.
——— "A Possible Difference in English and American Fiction." *NAR* 173 (Jl 01) 134-44.
——— "Some Anomalies of the Short Story." *NAR* 173 (S 01) 422-32.
Howland, H. H. "An Historical Revival." *Pub W* 125 (9 Je 34) 2135-7.
Hubbell, J. B. "Cavalier and Indentured Servant in Virginia Fiction." *SAQ* 26 (Ja 27) 22-39.
Hudson, A. P. "The Singing South." *SR* 44 (Jl 36) 268-95.
Hull, H. R. "The Literary Drug Traffic." *Dial* 67 (6 S 19) 190-2.
Huston, A. J. "A List of Maine Novels." *Pub W* 128 (6 Jl 35) 12-3.
Hutchinson, W. H. "The 'Western Story' as Literature." *WHR* 3 (Ja 49) 33-7.
J., W. H. "Modern American Fiction: Odd Words." *N&Q* 192 (12 Jl 47) 304.
Johnson, A. T. "Realism in Contemporary Literature." *Sw Bul* (S 29) 3-16
Johnson, R. B. "The Tyranny of Local Color." *Critic* 48 (Mr 06) 266-8.
Jones, A. E., Jr. "Darwinism and Its Relationship to Realism and Naturalism in American Fiction, 1860-1890." *Drew Un Bul* 38 (D 50) 3-21.
Jordan-Smith, Paul. "The Westward Movement in Fiction—1947." *PS* 2 (Wi 48) 107-12.
Josephson, Matthew. "The Young Generation: Its Young Novelists." *VQR* 9 (Ap 33) 243-61.
Kazin, Alfred. "American Naturalism: Reflections from Another Era." *NMQR* 20 (Sp 50) 50-60.
Keller, A. F., Jr. "The Clergyman in Recent Fiction." *Lutheran Church Q* 20 (Ap 47) 193-8.
Kelly, F. F. "American Style in American Fiction." *Bkm* 41 (My 15) 299-302.
Kempton, K. P. "The American Short Story: A Year of the 'Best.'" *N Y Times Book R* (29 F 48) 4.
Kent, Michael. "Realism and Reality: A Plea for Truth in Fiction." *Cath World* 163 (Je 46) 225-9.
Kirkwood, M. M. "Value in the Novel Today." *UTQ* 12 (Ap 43) 282-96.
Koeves, Tibor. "Symbols Wearing Pants." *United Nations World* 2 (D 48) 41-4.

Kohler, Dayton. "Time in the Modern Novel." *EJ* 37 (S 48) 331-40; *CE* 10 (O 48) 15-24.
Koller, Katherine. "The Puritan Preacher's Contribution to Fiction." *HLQ* 11 (Ag 48) 321-40.
Krutch, J. W. "New Morals for Old: Modern Love and Modern Fiction." *Nation* 118 (25 Je 24) 735-6.
LaFarge, Christopher. "Say It with Fiction." *SRL* 27 (23 F 44) 3-7.
LaFarge, Oliver. "Alien Races in Fiction." *NAR* 244 (Au 37) 202-5.
Lawrence, J. C. "A Theory of the Short Story." *NAR* 205 (F 17) 274-86.
Lehmann-Haupt, H. "The Picture Novel Arrives in America." *Pub W* 117 (1 F 30) 609-12.
Leisy, E. E. "The American Historical Novel." *Un Colo Stud* 2 (O 45) ser B.
——— "The Novel in America: Notes for a Survey." *Sw R* 22 (O 36) 88-100.
Lerner, Max. "The Historian, the Novelist, and the Faith." *NRp* 119 (6 D 48) 16.
Levin, Harry. "Definizione del realismo." *Inventario* (Italy) (Au 49) 8-14.
Lewis, C. L. "American Short Stories of the Sea." *U S Naval Inst Proc* 57 (Mr 41) 371-7.
Lewis, Wyndham. "'Detachment' and the Fictionist." *Eng R* 59 (O, N 34) 441-52, 564-73.
Lewisohn, Ludwig. "The Crisis of the Novel." *YR* 22 (Mr 33) 553-4.
Linford, Madeline. "Novels of the Year." *Manchester Guardian W* (8 D 33) 4-5.
Loomis, C. B. "How to Write a Novel for the Masses." *Atl* 87 (Mr 01) 421-4.
Loomis, C. G. "A Tall Tale Miscellany, 1830-1866." *WF* 6 (Ja 47) 28-41.
Lovett, R. M. "The Beginning of the Short Story in America." *Reader* 6 (Ag 05) 347-52.
Ludlow, Francis. "Her Infinite Variety." *CE* 7 (Ja 46) 181-8.
Lundbergh, Holger. "New Swedish Note in American Fiction." *Am Swedish Mo* 12-3 (N 44) 24-5.
Lundkvist, Artur. "Amerikansk Prosa." *Bonniers Litterära Magasin* 6 (Mr 37) 197-204.
——— "Böcker från Amerika." *Bonniers Litterära Magasin* 10 (Ja, F 41) 37-42, 127-34; 16 (My-Je, Jl-Ag 47) 412-7, 489-94.
——— "Bocker från Vaster." *Bonniers Litterära Magasin* 10 (Ja, F 41) 37-42, 127-34; 16 (My-Je, Jl-Ag 47) 412-7, 489-94.
——— "Böcker från Vaster." *Bonniers Litterära Magasin* 9 (Ja 40) 28-36; 11 (Su 42) 448-57; 13 (Ap 44) 332-42; 14 (Ap 47) 304-11.
Mabie, H. W. "American Fiction Old and New." *Outlook* 102 (26 O 12) 417-24.
——— "A Comment on the Short Story." *Outlook* 89 (16 My 08) 118-20.
McAfee, Helen. "The Literature of Disillusion." *Atl* 132 (Ag 23) 225-34.
——— "Rebuttal by the Novelists." *YR* ns 13 (Ap 24) 531-48.
McClure, H. H. "The Newspaper Novel." *Bkm* 31 (Mr 10) 60-1.
McDermott, J. F. "Novels and Other Worthless Books." *Am Book Coll* 5 (Ag-S 34) 259-61.
McDowell, Tremaine. "An American Robinson Crusoe." *AL* 1 (N 29) 307-9.
——— "The Big Three in Yankee Fiction." *SR* 36 (Ap 28) 157-63.
——— "Notes on Negro Dialect in the American Novel to 1821." *AS* 5 (Ap 30) 291-6.
——— "Sensibility in the Eighteenth-Century American Novel." *SP* 24 (Jl 27) 383-402.
Machell, Roger. "The American Best-Seller." *Nineteenth Century & After* 141 (Ja 47) 23-30.
Manning, Clarence. "Socialist Realism and the American Success Novel." *SAQ* 48 (Ap 49) 213-9.
Marble, A. R. "The Novel of American History." *Dial* 32 (1 Je 02) 369-72.
Marcosson, I. F. "The South in Fiction: Kentucky and Tennessee." *Bkm* 32 (D 10) 360-70.

Martin, H. R. "American Backgrounds for Fiction: The Pennsylvania Dutch." *Bkm* 38 (N 13) 244-7.

Matthews, Brander. "American Character in American Fiction." *Munsey's* 49 (Ag 13) 794-8.

——— "The Modern Novel and the Modern Play." *NAR* 180 (N 05) 699-711.

——— "Writing in Haste and Repenting at Leisure." *Bkm* 43 (Ap 16) 135-9.

Maurice, A. B. "Makers of Modern American Fiction." *Mentor* 6 (1 S 18) 1-11.

——— "The Politician as Literary Material." *Bkm* 11 (Ap 00) 120-1.

Menard, Edith. "Jews in Fiction." *Am Hebrew* 55 (29 Mr 46) 5, 12.

Mertner, Edgar. "Zur Theorie der Short Story in England und Amerika." *Anglia* 65 (N 40) 188-205.

Meyer, G. W. "The Original Social Purpose of the Naturalistic Novel." *SR* 1 (O-D 42) 563-79.

Miles, Hamish. "Tendencies of the Modern Novel." *Fortnightly R* 140 (N 33) 576-83.

Millard, Bailey. "San Francisco in Fiction." *Bkm* 31 (Ag 10) 585-97.

Miller, Benjamin. "Mythological Naturalism." *J Rel* 22 (Jl 42) 270-87.

Mino, Edwin. "Time and the Modern Novel." *Atl* 165 (Ap 40) 535-7.

Mirrieless, E. R. "The American Short Story." *Atl* 167 (Je 41) 714-22.

——— "Moral Tales, Past and Present." *Atl* 139 (My 27) 663-71.

Mizener, Arthur. "The Novel of Manners in America." *KR* 12 (Wi 50) 1-19.

Monkhouse, Allan. "Society and the Novel." *Atl* 156 (S 35) 369-71.

Monroe, N. E. "Contemporary Fiction and Society." *SLM* 2 (Je 40) 363-7.

Moore, H. T. "The American Novel Today." *London Merc* 31 (Mr 35) 461-7.

Morgan, A. E. "First American Utopian Story." *AN&Q* 2 (Ap 42) 9-10.

Morgan, Dale. "Mormon Story Tellers." *Rocky Mt R* 7 (Fl 42) 1-7.

——— "The New Psychology in Old Fiction." *SRL* 26 (21 Ag 37) 3-4, 11.

Morley, S. G. "La novelistica del 'Cowboy' y la del Gaucho." *Revista Iberoamericana* 7 (F 44) 255-70.

Morris, Lloyd. "Heritage of a Generation of Novelists." *N Y Herald Tribune Books* 26 (25 S 49) 12-3, 74.

——— "More Historical Novels." *NAR* 243 (Su 37) 395-400.

——— "Some Recent American Fiction." *NAR* 241 (Je 36) 274-88.

Moses, M. J. "The South in Fiction: The Trail of the Lower South." *Bkm* 33 (Ap 11) 161-72.

Mott, Frank. "The Beadles and Their Novels." *Palimpsest* 30 (Je 49) 173-89.

——— "Pioneer Iowa in Beadle Fiction." *Palimpsest* 30 (Je 49) 190-208.

Mowery, W. B. "Convention of Themes in the Magazine Short Story." *Texas R* 8 (Jl 23) 369-83.

Muller, H. J. "Impressionism and Fiction." *Am Schol* 7 (Su 38) 255-367.

Munson, Gorham. "The Recapture of the Storyable." *Un R* 9 (Au 43) 37-44.

Myers, W. L. "The Novel and the Past." *VQR* 14 (Au 38) 567-78.

——— "The Novel and the Simple Soul." *VQR* 13 (Ag 37) 501-12.

——— "The Novel Dedicate." *VQR* 8 (Jl 32) 410-8.

Nathan, G. J. "Business Men's Novels." *Bkm* 30 (O 09) 132-4.

——— "Exit 'Sophistication.'" *Am Merc* 52 (F 41) 227-32.

——— "The Short Story Famine." *Bkm* 32 (Ja 11) 535-8.

Nicholson, Meredith. "The Open Season for American Novelists." *Atl* 116 (O 15) 456-66.

Noll, A. H. "Recent Books about American Bishops." *SR* 16 (Ap 08) 248-53.

Norris, Frank. "The Responsibilities of a Novelist." *Critic* 40 (D 02) 537-40.

O'Brien, E. J. "The American Short Story." *Eng Lit & Ed R* 9 (N 38) 4-8.

O'Connor, W. V. "Mannequin Mythology: The Fashion Journals." *Poetry* 72 (Ag 48) 284-8.

O'Faoláin, Séan. "The Modern Novel." *VQR* 11 (Jl 35) 339-51.

Orians, G. H. "Censure of Fiction in American Romances and Magazines, 1789-1810." *PMLA* 52 (Mr 37) 195-214.
——— "The Indian Hater in Early American Fiction." *J Am Hist* 27 (1933) 34-44.
——— "New England Witchcraft in Fiction." *AL* 2 (Mr 30) 54-71.
Orsini, Napoleone. "American Influence in Italy." *CEA Critic* 10 (O 48) 1, 4.
P., B. "The Short Story." *Atl* 90 (Ag 02) 241-52.
Page, A. W. "Novels That Sell 100,000." *World's Work* 26 (Je 13) 220-7.
Pattee, F. L. "The Present State of the Short Story." *EJ* 12 (S 23) 439-49.
Pearce, R. H. "Sterne and Sensibility." *MLN* 59 (Je 44) 403-7.
Peery, William. "What Do You Read, My Lord?" *Am Schol* 6 (Su 37) 271-81.
Pennell, E. R. "Our Tragic Comics." *NAR* 211 (F 20) 248-58.
Perry, Bliss. "Salmon Not Running." *SRL* 6 (4 N 29) 474-5.
Petroni, Guglielmo. "La Lezione del romanzo americano." *Fiera Letteraria* 18 (I My 49).
Phelps, R. S. "The Lady in Fiction." *NAR* 205 (My 17) 766-74.
Phelps, W. L. "Realism and Reality in Fiction." *Century* 85 (Ap 13) 864-8.
Poore, Charles. "1946: The Fiction Writer's World." *N Y Times Book R* (30 Je 46) 1, 22.
Pratt, C. A. "Epidemic of Idealism in Fiction." *Putnam's* 2 (My 07) 183-7.
Rahv, Philip. "On the Decline of Naturalism." *PR* 9 (N-D 42) 483-93.
——— "Proletarian Literature." *So R* 4 (Ja 39) 616-28.
Raine, W. M. "Anent the Short Story." *Era* 12 (N 03) 480-2.
Randel, William. "Nostalgia for the Ivy." *SRL* 30 (29 N 47) 9-11, 39.
Randolph, Vance. "Recent Fiction and the Ozark Dialect." *AS* 6 (Ag 31) 425-8.
Regan, Patricia. "Realism—Or Is It?" *Cath World* 168 (Je 48) 235-42.
Rice, Wallace. "The Vulgate in American Fiction." *Am Merc* 12 (D 27) 464-6.
Robbins, L. H. "'Deadeye Dick' Has Become a Collector's Item." *N Y Times Mag* (19 S 37) 10-1, 25.
Rogers, W. H. "Form in the Art Novel." *Helicon* 2 (1939) 1-7.
Runes, D. D. "The Twilight of Literature." *Mod Thinker* 1 (Ag 32) 323-4.
Runnquist, Åke. "Den ensamme spårhunden. Några drag hos den hårdkotta romanen och dress hjälter." *Bonniers Litterära Magasin* 18 (Ap 49) 291-7.
Sale, W. M., Jr. "The Content of Fiction." *Epoch* 2 (Fl 48) 80-90.
Sanchez, N. V. "Material for Fiction Writing in Early History of California." *Overland Mo* 88 (Ap 30) 109.
Sapir, Edward. "Realism in Prose Fiction." *Dial* 63 (22 N 17) 503-6.
Sartre, Jean-Paul. "American Novelists in French Eyes." *Atl* 178 (Ag 46) 114-8.
Schantz, B. T. "Sir Christopher Gardiner in Nineteenth-Century Fiction." *NEQ* 11 (D 38) 807-17.
Schönemann, Friedrich. "Die gegenwärtige amerikanische Romanliteratur." *Westermann's Monatshefte* 78 (Mr 34) 69-72.
Schorer, Mark. "Technique as Discovery." *Hudson R* 1 (Sp 48) 67-8.
Shepherd, Esther. "The Tall Tale in American Literature." *Pac R* 2 (D 21) 405-16.
Sherman, C. B. "A Brief for Fiction." *SAQ* 36 (Jl 37) 335-47.
——— "Farm Life Fiction." *SAQ* 27 (Jl 28) 310-24.
——— "Farm Life Fiction in the South." *SLM* 1 (Mr 39) 203-10.
Shurter, R. L. "The Utopian Novel in America, 1888-1900." *SAQ* 34 (Ap 35) 137-44.
Shuster, G. N. "The Retreat of the American Novel." *Cath World* 106 (N 17) 166-78.
Sillen, Samuel. "History and Fiction." *New Masses* 27 (14 Je 38) 22-3.
Smith, C. A. "The Novel in America." *SR* 12 (Ap 04) 158-66.
Smith, Harrison. "Sex and the Hysterical Novel." *Tomorrow* 1 (Mr 46) 65-8.
——— "Thirteen Adventurers: A Study of a Year of First Novelists, 1947." *SRL* 31 (14 F 48) 6-8, 30-1.

Smith, H. N. "Buffalo Bill, Hero of the Popular Imagination." *Sw R* 33 (Au 48) 378-84.

——— "The Dime Novel Heroine." *Sw R* 34 (Sp 49) 182-8.

——— "The Western Hero in the Dime Novel." *Sw R* 33 (Su 48) 276-84.

Smith, P. J. "From Harte to Saroyan." *SRL* 26 (30 O 43) 3.

Smith, R. W. "Catalogue of the Chief Novels and Short Stories by American Authors Dealing with the Civil War and Its Effects, 1865-1899." *Bul Bibl* 16 (1939) 193-4; 17 (1940) 10, 33, 53, 72.

——— "Portrait of an American: The National Character in Fiction." *Sw R* 21 (Ap 36) 245-60.

Snelling, Paula. "Southern Fiction and Chronic Suicide." *N Ga R* 3 (Su 38) 3-6, 25-8.

Spencer, B. T. "Wherefore This Southern Fiction?" *SR* 47 (O 39) 500-13.

Spotts, C. B. "The Development of Fiction on the Missouri Frontier (1930-1860)." *Mo Hist R* 28 (Ap, Jl 34) 195-205, 275-86; 29 (O 34, Ja 35) 27-34, 100-8.

Stafford, Jean. "The Psychological Novel." *KR* 10 (Sp 48) 214-27.

Stalnaker, J. M., & Eggan, Fred. "American Novelists Ranked: A Psychological Study." *EJ* (coll ed) 18 (Ap 29) 295-307.

Starke, Aubrey. "'No Names' and 'Round Robins.'" *AL* 6 (Ja 35) 400-12.

Steeves, H. R. "A Sober Word on the Detective Story." *Harper's* 182 (Ap 41) 485-92.

Stegner, Wallace. "Is the Novel Done For?" *Harper's* 186 (D 42) 76-83.

——— "New Climates for the Writer: A Novelist Turned Instructor Defends the University as a Place for Training." *N Y Times Book R* (7 Mr 48) 1, 20.

Steinhauer, H. "Eros and Psyche: A Nietzschean Motif in Anglo-American Literature." *MLN* 64 (Ap 49) 217-28.

Stern, P. D. "Books and Best-Sellers." *VQR* 18 (Wi 42) 45-55.

——— "The Case of the Corpse in the Blind Alley." *VQR* 17 (Sp 41) 227-36.

Stevens, George. "Lincoln's Doctor's Dog and Other Famous Best Sellers." *SRL* 17 (22 Ja 38) 3-4, 14-6, 18.

Stevens, H. R. "La Frontiera e la storiografia americana." *Il Ponte* 4 (Je 48) 552-9.

Stevenson, Lionel. "The Novelist as a Fortune-Hunter." *VQR* 13 (Su 37) 376-90.

Stewart, G. R. "The Novel Takes Over Poetry." *SRL* 23 (8 F 41) 3-4, 18-9.

Stratton, G. M. "Woman's Mastery of the Story." *Atl* 117 (My 16) 668-76.

Strauss, Harold. "Realism in the Proletarian Novel." *YR* 28 (D 38) 360-74.

Strong, L. A. G. "James Joyce and the New Fiction." *Am Merc* 35 (Ag 35) 433-7.

Swift, Benjamin. "The Decay of the Novel." *Critic* 42 (Ja 03) 59-61.

Swift, Lindsay. "Boston as Portrayed in Fiction." *Book Buyer* 23 (O 01) 197-204.

Tandy, J. S. "Pro-Slavery Propaganda in American Fiction of the Fifties." *SAQ* 21 (Ja, Ap 22) 41-50, 170-8.

Thompson, A. E. "Woman's Place in Early American Fiction." *Era* 12 (N 03) 472-4.

Thompson, A. R. "The Cult of Cruelty." *Bkm* 74 (Ja-F 32) 477-87.

——— "Farewell to Achilles." *Bkm* 70 (Ja 30) 465-71.

Tindall, W. Y. "Many-leveled Fiction: Virginia Woolf to Ross Lockridge." *EJ* 37 (N 48) 449-55; *CE* 10 (N 48) 65-71.

——— "The Sociological Best Seller." *CE* 9 (N 47) 52-66; *EJ* 36 (N 47) 447-54.

Tourtellot, A. B. "History and the Historical Novel." *SRL* 22 (24 Ag 40) 3-4, 16.

Trilling, Lionel. "Manners, Morals and the Novel." *KR* 10 (Wi 47) 11-27.

——— "New Yorker Fiction." *Nation* 154 (11 Ap 42) 425-6.

Turner, Arlin. "Fiction of the Bayou Country." *SRL* 18 (30 Ap 38) 3-4, 16.

——— "The Southern Novel." *Sw R* 25 (Ja 40) 205-12.

Uzzell, T. H. "Modern Innovations." *CE* 7 (N 45) 59-65.

Vagne, Jean. "Note sur le roman américain et le public français." *Renaissance* no 16 (S 45) 145-50.

Van Auken, Sheldon. "The Southern Historical Novel in the Early Twentieth Century." *J So Hist* 14 (My 48) 157-91.
Van Doren, Carl. "American Realism." *NRp* 34 (21 Mr 23) 107-9.
——— "Early American Realism." *Nation* 99 (12 N 14) 577-8.
——— "Notes on Some Early American Novelists." *Nation* 101 (23 D 15) 456-66.
Van Doren, Mark. "The Art of American Fiction." *Nation* 138 (25 Ap 34) 472-4.
Van Gelder, Robert. "The World of Books at War's End." *N Y Times Book R* (2 D 45) 1, 16.
Van Westrum, A. S. "The Christmas Books." *Lamp* 29 (D 04) 438-45.
Vincent, M. J. "Fiction Mirrors the War." *Sociol & Soc Res* 3 (N-D 45) 101-11.
Walcutt, C. C. "Fear Motifs in the Literature between Wars." *SAQ* 46 (Ap 47) 227-38.
——— "From Scientific Theory to Aesthetic Fact: The 'Naturalistic' Novel." *Quar R Lit* 3 (nd) 167-88.
——— "The Regional Novel and Its Future." *Ariz Q* 1 (Su 45) 17-27.
Waldman, Milton. "Tendencies of the Modern Novel: America." 140 *Fortnightly R* (D 33) 717-25.
Walker, Franklin. "Hollywood in Fiction." *PS* 2 (Sp 48) 127-33.
Wann, Louis. "The 'Revolt from the Village' in American Fiction." *Overland Mo* 83 (Ag 25) 299-301.
Watson, E. H. L. "The Censorship of Fiction." *Dial* 50 (16 Ap 11) 296-8.
West, H. L. "American Out-Door Literature." *Forum* 29 (Jl 00) 632-40.
West, R. B., Jr. "A Note on American Fiction: 1946 [1947]." *WR* 11 (Au 46) 45-8; 12 (Au 47) 58-62.
Wharton, Edith. "The Great American Novel." *YR* 16 (Jl 27) 646-56.
——— "Permanent Value in Fiction." *SRL* 10 (16 Ap 34) 603-4.
White, Mrs. T. E. "The New England Heroine in Contemporary Fiction." *N E Mag* ns 41 (F 10) 725-32.
Wilkinson, Hazel. "Social Thought in American Fiction, 1910-17." *Un Calif Stud Sociol* 3 (D 18).
Willcox, L. C. "The Content of the Modern Novel." *NAR* 182 (Je 06) 917-29.
——— "The South in Fiction: Virginia." *Bkm* 33 (Mr 11) 44-58.
William, Churchill. "Philadelphia in Fiction." *Bkm* 16 (D 02) 360-73.
Williams, S. T. "Aspects of the Modern Novel." *Texas R* 8 (Ap 23) 245-6.
Wilmer, R. H., Jr. "Collecting Civil War Novels." *Colophon* ns 3 (Au 38) 513-8.
Wilson, A. H. "Escape Southward." *NAR* 248 (Wi 39-40) 265-74.
Wilson, J. S. "The Changing Novel." *VQR* 10 (Ja 34) 42-52.
Wilson, J. W. "Delta Revival." *EJ* 38 (Mr 49) 117-24.
Winston, A. S. "America as a Field for Fiction." *Arena* 23 (Je 00) 654-60.
Winther, S. K. "The Sick American Novel." *PS* 1 (Wi 47) 105-12.
Wister, Owen. "Quack-Novels and Democracy." *Atl* 115 (Je 15) 721-34.
Woodbridge, Elisabeth. "The Novelist's Choice." *Atl* 110 (O 12) 481-91.
Woodruff, M. D. "Realism and Romance." *SAQ* 38 (Jl 39) 293-6.
Wright, L. H. "Propaganda in Early American Fiction." *PBSA* 33 (1939) 98-106.
——— "A Statistical Survey of American Fiction, 1774-1850." *HLQ* 2 (Ap 39) 309-18.
Wright, Luella. "Fiction in History." *Palimpsest* 28 (Ap 47) 97-111.
Wyatt, Edith. "The First American Novel." *Atl* 144 (O 29) 466-75.
Young, Vernon. "An American Dream and Its Parody." *Ariz Q* 6 (Su 50) 112-23.

FOREIGN INFLUENCES AND ESTIMATES. Anon. "American Culture Abroad." *CL News Letter* 4 (Mr 46) 41-5.
——— "Amerika und Sartre." *Prisma* 6 (Ap 47) 39-40.
——— "As Others See Us." *Living Age* 341 (N 31) 276-7.
——— "A British View of US in 1924." *N Y Times Mag* 81 (20 S 31) 15.
——— "Dickens in America." *TLS* (9 Ja 43) 20.
——— "Go Abroad, Carissimo!" *Freeman* 1 (1 S 20) 581-2.

——— "An Italian Estimate of American Authors." *Rev of Rev* 30 (O 04) 498.

——— "Liberty through Democracy: The Lesson of Tocqueville." *TLS* (9 Je 43) 261-7.

——— "Measuring Our Culture by Europe's." *Lit Dig* 101 (22 Je 29) 20-1.

Adamic, Louis. "The Yugoslav Speech in America." *Am Merc* 12 (N 27) 319-21.

Adams, C. F. "Milton's Impress on the Provincial Literature of New England." *PMHS* 42 (1909) 154-70.

Adams, C. M. "Macaulay on America, Once More." *BNYPL* 40 (My 36) 437-9.

Adams, J. T. "Americans Abroad." *N Y Times Mag* 80 (21 Je 31) 4-5.

Altick, R. D. "Dickens & America. Some Unpublished Letters." *PMHB* 73 (Jl 49) 326-36.

Anderson, Annette. "Ibsen in America." *SS* 14 (F, My 37) 65-109, 115-46.

Anikist, Alexander. "Soviet Finds Modernity in American Authors." *Lib J* 70 (Ja 45) 10-2, 26.

Apsluer, Alfred. "Writers from Across the Sea." *CE* 9 (O 47) 19-24.

Armstrong, E. K. "Chateaubriand's America." *PMLA* 22 (1907) 345.

Arndt, K. J. R. "American Utopias and Internationalism." *CL News Letter* 2 (My 45) 54-6.

Astre, G. A. "Less Origines de lettres américaines." *Critique* (Paris) 5 (Mr 49) 206-14.

Atherton, Gertrude. "The American Novel in England." *Bkm* 30 (F 10) 632-40.

Baldini, G. "Prespettive europea della letteratura d' oltre Atlantico." *Fiera Letteraria* 24 (12 Je 47).

——— "Tre secoli di poesia americana." *Nuova Antologia* (D 47).

Barnett, G. P. "First American Review of Charles Lamb." *PMLA* 61 (Je 46) 597-600.

Barthold, A. F. "French Journalists in the United States." *Franco-Am R* 1 (Wi 37) 215-30.

Barton, A. O. "Alexander Corstvet and Anthony M. Rud, Norwegian-American Novelists." *N Am Stud & Records* 6 (1931) 146-52.

Bataille, Georges. "La Souveraineté de la fête et le roman américain." *Critique* (Paris) 5 (Ag 49) 675-81.

Benson, A. B. "Cultural Relations between Sweden and America to 1830." *GR* 12 (Ap 38) 83-101.

Beyer, William. "The State of the Theatre: The Strindberg Heritage." *School & Soc* 71 (14 Ja 50) 23-8.

Biermann, Berthold. "Goethe im Urteil der Amerikaner." *Neue Schweizer Rundschau* 17 (S 49) 317-23.

Birss, J. H. "A Letter to Tobias Smollett." *N&Q* 164 (6 My 33) 315-6.

Blake, W. B. "Chateaubriand in America." *Atl* 101 (Ap 08) 559-65.

Blanc-Dufour, A. "A propos de romans américains." *Cahiers du Sud* 29 no 294 (1949) 291-8.

Blankenagel, J. C. "An Early American Review of *Die Wahlverwandtschaften*." *JEGP* 35 (Jl 36) 383-8.

Bogner, H. F. "Sir Walter Scott in New Orleans, 1818-1832." *La Hist Q* 21 (Ap 39) 420-517.

Bond, D. F., Carrière, J. M., & Seeber, E. D. "Anglo-French and Franco-American Studies: A Current Bibliography." *RR* 38 (Ap 47) 97-116.

Bourne, R. S. "Our Cultural Humility." *Atl* 114 (O 14) 503-7.

Boyd, Ernest. "Literary Internationalism." *VQR* 3 (Jl 27) 382-91.

Boys, R. C. "General Oglethorpe and the Muses." *Ga Hist Q* 31 (Mr 47) 19-29.

Bradsher, E. L. "The First American Edition of the Lyrical Ballads." *SAQ* 16 (Jl 17) 268-70.

Brée, Germaine. "The 'Interpenetration' of Literatures." *MLJ* 33 (D 49) 619-23.

Brewer, E. V. "The New England Interest in Jean Paul Friedrich Richter." *Un Calif Pub* 27 (1944) 1-26.

Brink, F. R. "Literary Travellers in Louisiana between 1803 and 1860." *La Hist Q* 21 (Ap 48) 394-424.
Brittain, Vera. "A Comment on Herbert Read in America." *Adelphi* 23 (Ja-Mr 47) 100-1.
Brogan, D. W., *et al.* "De l'Amérique et des Américains." *Renaissances* no 18 (F 46).
Brooks, J. G. "American Culture Abroad." *CL News Letter* 4 (Mr 46) 41-5.
Brown, R. E. "A French Interpreter of New England's Literature, 1846-1865." *NEQ* 13 (Je 40) 304-21.
Browne, C. A. "Joseph Priestley and the American 'Fathers.'" *Am Schol* 4 (Sp 35) 133-47.
Bryce, James. "Stray Thoughts in American Literature." *NAR* 201 (Mr 15) 357-62.
Cairns, W. B. "British Republication of American Writings, 1783-1833." *PMLA* 43 (Mr 28) 303-10.
Cardwell, G. A. "The Influence of Addison on Charleston Periodicals, 1795-1860." *SP* 35 (Jl 38) 456-70.
Carpenter, F. I. "The Vogue of Ossian in America." *AL* 2 (Ja 31) 405-17.
Carrière, J. M. "Unnoticed Translations of Balzac in American Periodicals." *MLN* 60 (Ap 45) 234-41.
Carus, Gustave. "Robert Burns and the American Revolution." *Open Court* 46 (F 32) 129-36.
Cestre, Charles. "Alexis de Tocqueville; témoin et juge de la civilisation américaine." *Revue des Cours et Conférences* (15 Ja 34) 275-88.
——— "American Literature through French Eyes." *YR* 10 (O 20) 85-98.
Chesterton, G. K. "Chesterton Sums Up." *N Y Times Mag* 80 (12 Jl 31) 4-5.
——— "Chesterton Views Our 'Puritan' Land." *N Y Times Mag* 80 (28 Ja 31) 7, 17.
——— "Why Chesterton Likes America." *N Y Times Mag* 80 (3 My 31) 1-2.
Chew, S. C. "Byron in America." *Am Merc* 1 (Mr 24) 335-44.
Childs, F. S. "French Opinion of Anglo-American Relations, 1795-1805." *FAR* 1 (Ja-Mr 48) 21-35.
Chinard, Gilbert. "Chateaubriand en Amérique." *MP* 9 (Jl 11) 129-49.
Clark, R. T. "The German Liberals in New Orleans (1840-1860)." *La Hist Q* 20 (Ja 37) 137-51.
Clemens, Cyril. "Housman in America." *Poet Lore* 49 (Au 43) 266-75.
Coatsworth, Elizabeth. "To Begin with the Hazlitts." *Chri Sci Mon* 40 (9 Ja 48) 8.
Colbron, G. I. "The American Novel in Germany." *Bkm* 39 (Mr 14) 45-9.
Connolly, Cyril. "On Englishmen Who Write American." *N Y Times Book R* (18 D 49) 1, 9.
Cook, Mercer. "The Literary Contribution of the French West Indian." *J Negro Hist* 25 (O 40) 520-31.
Cooper, Harold. "John Donne and Virginia in 1610." *MLN* 57 (D 42) 661-3.
Cowley, Malcolm. "American Books Overseas." *NRp* 115 (8 Jl 46) 16-20.
Curti, Merle. "The Great Mr. Locke: America's Philosopher 1783-1861." *Huntington Lib Bul* 11 (Ap 37) 107-51.
——— "The Reputation of America Overseas (1776-1860)." *Am Q* 1 (Sp 49) 58-82.
Cutler, B. D. "The Great Victorians Come to America." *Pub W* 122 (19 N, 17 D 32) 1927-30, 2255-7.
Damon, S. F. "Some American References to Blake before 1863." *MLN* 45 (Je 30) 365-8.
David, Jean. "Voltaire et les Indiens d'Amérique." *MLQ* 9 (Mr 48) 90-103.
Davis, R. B. "America in George Sandys's 'Ovid.'" *WMQ* 4: ser 3 (Jl 47) 297-304.
DeArmond, A. J. "Americans in England, 1835-1860." *Del Notes* 17 (1944) 37-90.
De Beauvoir, Simone. "An American Renaissance in France." *N Y Times Book R* (22 Je 47) 7, 29.

De Ritis, Beniamino. "L'America vista come paese della storia." *Nuova Antologia* 82 (S 47) 65-70.
Dinamov, Sergie. "American Literature in Russia." *Mod Q* 5 (Fl 29) 367-8.
Ditzion, Sidney. "The Anglo-American Literary Scene: A Contribution to the Social History of the Library Movement." *Lib Q* 16 (O 46) 281-301.
Doolaard, A. D. "A Study in Misunderstanding." *SRL* 32 (24 S 49) 6-7, 39-40.
Dudek, J. B. "The Czech Language in America." *Am Merc* 5 (Je 25) 202-7.
——— "Czech Surnames in America." *Am Merc* 6 (N 25) 333-6.
Duffy, Charles. "Thomas Campbell and America." *AL* 13 (Ja 42) 346-55.
Dummer, E. H. "Hermann Sudermann, a Contributor to American Culture." *AGR* 13 (F 47) 26-9.
Dunkel, W. D. "Ellen Kean's Appraisal of American Playgoers." *AL* 22 (My 50) 163-6.
Edgar, H. L., & Vail, R. W. G. "Early American Editions of the Works of Charles Dickens." *BNYPL* 33 (My 29) 302-19.
Edwards, Herbert. "Zola and American Critics." *AL* 4 (My 32) 114-29.
Elgstrom, A. L. "Vid den amerikanska diktens källor." *Samtid och Framtid* (Stockholm) 3 (Mr 45) 155-60.
Englekirk, J. E. "Obras Norteamericanas en Traducción Española." *Revista Iberoamericana* 9 (F 45) 125-66.
Evans, Oliver. "Letter from Rome." *Prairie Schooner* 23 (Fl 49) 299-301.
Everson, I. G. "Goethe's American Visitors." *AL* 9 (N 37) 356-7.
Falk, R. P. "Representative American Criticism of Shakespeare, 1830-1885." *Sum Doctoral Diss Un Wisc* 5 (1940) 248-60.
Falnes, O. J. "New England Interest in Scandinavian Culture and the Norsemen." *NEQ* 10 (Je 37) 211-42.
Falqui, E. "Sull' Americanismo." *Fiera Letteraria* 37 (19 D 46).
Fess, G. M. "The American Revolution in Creative French Literature (1775-1937)." *Un Mo Stud* 16 (1941) 1-119.
Fiore, Ilario. "L'America ha invaso l'Europa." *Fiera Letteratura* 15 (27 Mr 49).
Firebaugh, J. T. "Samuel Rogers and American Men of Letters." *Al* 13 (Ja 42) 331-45.
Fish, C. R. "The Pilgrim and the Melting Pot." *Miss Valley Hist R* 7 (D 20) 187-205.
Fisher, L. A. "The First American Reprint of Wordsworth." *MLN* 15 (F 00) 77-84.
Flanagan, J. T. "Captain Marryat at Old St. Peters." *Minn Hist* 18 (Je 37) 152-64.
Foerster, Norman. "Matthew Arnold and American Letters Today." *SR* 30 (Jl 22) 298-306.
——— "Wordsworth in America." *SP* 26 (Ja 29) 85-95.
Ford, W. C. "Some London Broadsides and Issues on Pennsylvania." *PMHB* 39 (1905) 65-9.
Francke, Kuno. "German Literature and the American Temper." *Atl* 114 (N 14) 655-64.
Frenz, Horst. "Georg Kaiser." *Poet Lore* 53 (Wi 46) 363-9.
——— "Karl Knortz, Interpreter of American Literature and Culture." *AGR* 13 (D 46) 27-30.
Frey, J. R. "America and Franz Werfel." *GQ* 19 (Mr 46) 120-31.
Frierson, W. C., & Edwards, Herbert. "Impact of French Naturalism on American Critical Opinion, 1877-1892." *PMLA* 63 (S 48) 1007-16.
Fucilla, J. G. "Dante Lands in America." *Ital* 27 (S 50) 208-10.
——— "Echoes of the American Revolution in an Italian Poet." *Ital* 11 (S 34) 85-7.
——— "The First Fragment of a Translation of the *Divine Comedy* Printed in America: A New Find." *Ital* 25 (Mr 48) 9-11.
Galantière, Lewis. "American Books in France." *Am Merc* 2 (My 24) 97-102.
Gassner, John. "Strindberg in America." *Theatre Arts* 33 (My 49) 49-52.

Gegenheimer, A. F. "They Might Have Been Americans." *SAQ* 46 (O 47) 511-23.
Gettman, R. A. "Turgenev in England and America." *Un Ill Stud Lang & Lit* 27 (1941) 51-63.
Gisolfi, A. M. "'The Beach of Heaven': Italy 1943-45 in American Fiction." *Ital* 27 (S 50) 199-207.
Goggio, Emilio. "Dante Interests in 19th Century America." *PQ* 1 (1922) 192-201.
——— "First Personal Contact between American and Italian Leaders of Thought." *RR* 27 (Ja-Mr 36) 1-8.
Gohdes, Clarence. "British Interest in American Literature during the Latter Part of the Nineteenth Century as Reflected by Mudie's Select Library." *AL* 13 (Ja 42) 356-62.
Green, M. L. "Stendhal in America." *Revue de Littérature Comparée* 10 (Ap-Je 30) 304-12.
Greenough, C. N. "Defoe in Boston." *PCSM* 28 (1935) 461-93.
——— "John Dunton Again." *PCSM* 21 (Ap 19) 232-51.
Griffin, R. A. "Mrs. Trollope and the Queen City." *Miss Valley Hist R* 37 (S 50) 289-302.
Grueningen, J. P. von. "Goethe in American Periodicals, 1860-1900." *PMLA* 50 (D 35) 1155-64.
Gulliver, H. S. "Thackeray in Georgia." *Ga R* 1 (Sp 47) 35-43.
Hainebach, Hans. "German Publications in the United States, 1933 to 1945." *BNYPL* 52 (S 48) 435-49.
Hamilton, Clayton. "European Dramatists on the American Stage." *Bkm* 31 (Je 10) 410-21.
——— "Strindberg in America." *Bkm* 35 (Je 12) 358-65.
Hand, A. C. "Ibsen's Reputation in America since His Death in 1906." *Un Colo Stud* 18 (O 30) 69-70.
Harrison, Katherine. "A French Forecast of American Literature." *SAQ* 25 (O 26) 350-60.
Hastings, G. E. "John Bull and His American Descendants." *AL* 1 (Mr 29) 40-68.
Hatfield, H. C., & Merrick, John. "Studies of German Literature in the United States, 1939-1946." *MLR* 43 (Jl 48) 353-92.
Hatfield, J. T. "Goethe and the Ku-Klux Klan." *PMLA* 37 (D 22) 735-9.
——— "*Götz von Berlichingen* in America." *GR* 24 (O 49) 177-83.
Haugen, E. I. "Ibsen in America: A Forgotten Performance and an Unpublished Letter." *JEGP* 33 (3Q 34) 396-420.
Hawkins, R. L. "Unpublished Letters of Alexis de Tocqueville." *RR* 20 (O-D 29) 351-6.
Hawley, C. A. "Gerald Massey and America." *Church Hist* 8 (D 39) 356-70.
Haxo, H. E. "America as Modern French Writers See It." *Quar J Un No Dak* 23 (1933) 211-51.
Healy, E. D. "Acadian Exiles in Virginia." *FR* 22 (Ja 49) 233-40.
Heiser, M. F. "Cervantes in the United States." *Hisp R* 15 (O 47) 409-35.
Helman, E. F. "Early Interest in Spanish in New England (1815-1835)." *Hispania* 29 (Ag 46) 339-51.
Hewitt, T. B. "German Hymns in American Hymnals." *GR* 21 (Ja 48) 37-50.
Hickey, R. L. "Donne and Virginia." *PQ* 26 (Ap 47) 181-92.
Hiden, P. H. "Education and the Classics in the Life of Colonial Virginia." *VMHB* 69 (Ja 41) 20-8.
Higginson, T. W. "English and American Cousins." *Atl* 93 (F 04) 184-92.
Hildreth, W. H. "Mrs. Trollope in Porkopolis." *Ohio State Arch & Hist Q* 58 (Ja 49) 35-51.
Hindus, Maurice. "What They Read of Ours in the U.S.S.R." *N Y Herald-Tribune Books* 22 (2 S 45) 1-2.
Hodge, Francis. "Charles Mathews Reports on America." *QJS* 36 (D 50) 429-99.
Holman, Harriet. "Matthew Arnold's Elocution Lessons." *NEQ* 18 (D 45) 479-88.

Hotson, C. P. "Swedenborg's Influence in America." *New-Church R* 37 (Ap 30) 188-207.

House, R. T. "Strong Meat in Hispanic-American Fiction." *Sw R* 29 (Wi 44) 245-51.

Houtchens, L. H. "Charles Dickens and International Copyright." *AL* 13 (Mr 41) 18-28.

Howard, Leon. "The Influence of Milton on Colonial American Poetry." *Huntington Lib Bul* 9 (Ap 36) 63-89.

——— "Wordsworth in America." *MLN* 48 (Je 33) 359-65.

Howe, M. A. DeW. "With Dickens in America; New Material from the Papers of Mrs. James T. Fields." *Harper's* 144 (My 22) 708-22.

Hubbell, J. B. "Thackeray and Virginia." *VQR* 3 (Ja 27) 76-86.

Jackson, S. L. "A Soviet View of Emerson." *NEQ* 19 (Je 46) 236-43.

Jantz, H. S. "German Thought and Literature in New England, 1620-1820." *JEGP* 41 (Ja 42) 1-45.

Johnson, E. G. "An Excited Swedish Novelist and the Civil War." *J Illinois State Hist Soc* 41 (Je 48) 1-13.

——— "Swedish Author's Only American Story." *J Illinois State Hist Soc* 41 (S 48) 285-304.

Johnson, L. H. "America in the Thought of Leading British Men of Letters, 1830-1890." *Sum Doctoral Diss Un Wisc* 8 (1944) 200-2.

——— "The Source of the Chapter on Slavery in Dickens's *American Notes*." *AL* 14 (Ja 43) 427-8.

Johnson, R. A. "Teaching of American History in Great Britain." *AHR* 50 (O 44) 73-81.

Johnson, Stanley. "John Donne and the Virginia Company." *ELH* 14 (Je 47) 127-38.

Jones, H. M. "American Comment on George Sand, 1837-1848." *AL* 3 (Ja 32) 389-407.

——— "American Literature and the Melting Pot." *Sw R* 26 (Ap 41) 329-46.

——— "Arnold, Aristocracy and America." *AHR* 49 (Ap 44) 393, 409.

——— "As Others See Us." *Books Abroad* 7 (O 33) 402-4.

——— "The Image of the New World." *Un Colo Stud* 2: ser B (O 45) 62-84.

——— "The Importation of French Books in Philadelphia, 1750-1800." *MP* 32 (N 34) 157-77.

——— "The Importation of French Literature in New York City, 1750-1800." *SP* 28 (O 31) 235-51.

——— "The Influence of European Ideas in Nineteenth-Century America." *AL* 7 (N 35) 241-73.

——— "Notes on the Knowledge of French in Eighteenth-Century America." *SP* 24 (Jl 27) 426-37.

———, & Aaron, Daniel. "Notes on the Napoleonic Legend in America." *Franco-Am R* 2 (Su 37) 10-26.

Jones, J. R. "Lord Byron in America." *Un Texas Stud Eng* 20 (1940) 121-36.

Jones, M. B. "'L'Attaque du Moulin' in American Translation." *MLN* 57 (Mr 42) 207-8.

——— "Henry Gréville et Émile Zola aux États-Unis (1870-1900)." *Revue de Littérature Comparée* 28 (O-D 48) 528-34.

——— "Two American Zola Forgeries." *FR* 16 (O 42) 24-8.

Kain, R. M. "The Literary Reputation of Turgenev in England and America." *Madison Q* 2 (Ja 42) 23.

Kalfavan, Armen. "United States in the Post-War Literature of France, 1919-31." *MLJ* 18 (Mr 34) 398-404.

Kelley, M. W. "Thomas Cooper and Pantisocracy." *MLN* 45 (Ap 30) 218-20.

King, H. S. "Echoes of the American Revolution in German Literature." *Un Calif Pub in Mod Phil* 14 (Jl 29) 1-193.

Klenze, Camillo von. "German Literature in the Boston *Transcript,* 1830-1880." *PQ* 11 (Ja 32) 1-25.
Kraus, Michael. "Eighteenth-Century Humanitarianism: Collaboration between Europe and America." *PMHB* 60 (Jl 36) 270-86.
——— "Literary Relations between England and America in the Eighteenth Century." *WMQ* 1 (Jl 44) 210-34.
Kummer, George. "Anonymity and Carlyle's Early Reputation in America." *AL* 8 (N 36) 297-9.
Lamb, C. F. "Some Anglo-American Literary Contacts." *Quar R* 285 (Ap 47) 247-58.
Landrum, G. W. "Sir Walter Scott and His Literary Rivals in the Old South." *AL* 2 (N 30) 256-76.
Lang, Cecil. "Swinburne and American Literature, with Six Hitherto Unpublished Letters." *AL* 19 (Ja 48) 336-50.
Lapp, J. C. "The New World in French Poetry of the Sixteenth Century." *SP* 45 (Ap 48) 151-64.
Larsen, S. A. "George Brandes' Views on American Literature." *SS* 22 (N 50) 161-5.
Larson, Harold, & Haugen, Einar. "Björnson and America—A Critical Review." *SS* 13 (F 34) 1-12.
Lawder, Donald. "W. L. George on American Literature." *Bkm* 52 (N 20) 193-7.
Lawton, W. C. "Classical Influences on American Literature." *Chautauquan* 30 (F 00) 466-70.
Leary, Lewis. "Leigh Hunt in Philadelphia: An American Literary Incident of 1803." *PMHB* 70 (Jl 46) 270-80.
——— "Ossian in America." *AL* 14 (N 42) 305-6.
——— "Thomas Day on American Poetry: 1786." *MLN* 61 (N 46) 464-6.
——— "Wordsworth in America." *MLN* 58 (My 43) 391-3.
Leavitt, S. E. "Latin American Literature in the United States." *Revue de Littérature Comparée* 11 (Ja-Mr 31) 126-48.
Lenormaud, H. P. "American Literature and France." *SRL* 11 (27 O 34) 244-5.
Levin, Harry. "Some European Views of Contemporary American Literature." *Am Q* 1 (Fl 49) 264-79.
Lewisohn, Ludwig. "German-American Poetry." *SR* 12 (Ap 04) 223-30.
Long, O. W. "Attitude of Eminent Englishmen and Americans toward *Werther.*" *MP* 14 (D 16) 454-66.
——— "English and American Imitations of Goethe's *Werther.*" *MP* 14 (Ag 16) 193-216, 455.
——— "Goethe's American Visitors." *AGR* 15 (Ag 49) 24-8.
Louchheim, K. S. "Ilya Ehrenburg on American Writers." *NRp* 114 (1 Jl 46) 931-2.
Ludeke, H. "American Literature in Germany: A Report of Recent Research and Criticism, 1931-1933." *AL* 6 (My 34) 168-75.
Lundkvist, Artur. "Amerikansk kritik." *Bonniers Litterära Magasin* 11 (Ap 42) 284-92.
——— "Amerikansk litteraturanalys." *Bonniers Litterära Magasin* 14 (N 45) 757-62.
——— "Böcker från Amerika." *Bonniers Litterära Magasin* 10 (Ja, F 41) 37-42, 127-34; 16 (My-Je, Jl-Ag 47) 412-7, 489-94.
——— "Böcker från Väster." *Bonniers Litterära Magasin* 9 (Ja 40) 28-36; 11 (Su 42) 448-57; 13 (Ap 44) 332-42; 14 (Ap 47) 304-11.
Lydenberg, H. M. "What Did Macaulay Say about America?" *BNYPL* 29 (Jl 25) 459-81.
Lynes, Carlos, Jr. "The 'Nouvelle Revue Française' and American Literature, 1909-1940." *FR* 19 (Ja 46) 159-67.
Mabbott, T. O. "*Arcturus* and Keats: An Early American Publication of Keats's 'La Belle Dame Sans Merci.'" *AL* 2 (Ja 31) 430-2.

——— "More American References to Blake Before 1863." *MLN* 47 (F 32) 87-8.
——— "More Early American Publications of Blake." *N&Q* 165 (21 O 33) 279.
——— "A Newly Found American Translation of Balzac." *MLN* 61 (Ap 46) 278-9.
MacClintock, Lander. "Sainte-Beuve and America." *PMLA* 60 (Mr 45) 427-36.
MacMinn, G. P. "English and American Appreciation of Rabelais." *Un Calif Pub in Mod Phil* 11 (1922) 139-51.
McCollum, J. D. "The Apostle of Culture Meets America." *NEQ* 2 (Jl 29) 357-81.
McCullers, Carson. "The Russian Realist and Southern Literature." *Decision* 2 (Jl 41) 15-8.
McDermott, J. F. "A Note on Mrs. Trollope." *Ohio Archaeological & Hist Q* 45 (O 36) 369-70.
——— "Voltaire and the Freethinkers in Early Saint-Louis." *Revue de Littérature Comparée* 16 (O-D 36) 720-31.
McDowell, Tremaine. "An American Robinson Crusoe." *AL* 1 (N 29) 307-9.
McFee, William. "The Cheer-Leader in Literature." *Harper's* 152 (Mr 26) 462-9.
Magidoff, Robert. "American Literature in Russia." *SRL* 29 (2 N 46) 9-11, 45-6.
Magyar, Francis. "American Literature in Hungary." *Books Abroad* 6 (Ap 32) 151-2.
Major, J. C. "American Writers' Home Town." *FAR* 3 (Ja-Mr 50) 63-9.
Marquardt, F. S. "Shakespere and American Slang." *AS* 4 (D 28) 118-22.
Marraro, H. R. "American Travellers in Rome, 1848-1850." *Cath Hist R* 29 (Ja 44) 470-509.
——— "Italian Culture in Eighteenth-Century Magazines." *Ital* 22 (Mr 45) 21-31.
——— "Italian Music and Actors in America during the Eighteenth Century." *Ital* 23 (Je 46) 103-17.
——— "Pioneer Italian Teachers of Italian in the United States." *MLJ* 28 (N 44) 555-82.
——— "The Teaching of Italian in America in the Eighteenth Century." *MLJ* 25 (N 41) 120-5.
Marshall, Margaret. "Notes by the Way." *Nation* 162 (2 F 46) 130-1.
Matthews, Albert. "Brother Jonathan Once More." *PCSM* 32 (1937) 374-86.
——— "Knowledge of Milton in Early New England." *Nation* 87 (1908) 624, 625, 650.
Matthews, Brander. "The Centenary of a Question." *Scribner's* 67 (Ja 20) 41-6.
Maurice. A. B. "American Invasion of Europe." *Bkm* 27 (My 08) 246-9.
Maurois, André. "L'Amérique vue par André Maurois." *Nouvelles Littéraires* (24 Je 39) 1-2.
Melz, C. F. "Goethe and America." *CE* 10 (My 49) 425-31; *EJ* 38 (My 49) 247-53.
Mendelson, M. "Amerikanskaya progressivnaya literatura poslednikh let." *Zvezda* (Leningrad) no 11 (N 49) 167-82.
Metzenthin-Raunick, Selma. "German Verse in Texas." *Sw R* 18 (O 32) 38-49.
——— "A Survey of German Literature in Texas." *Sw Hist Q* 33 (O 29) 134-59.
Miller, C. R. D. "Alfieri and America." *PQ* 11 (Ap 32) 163-6.
——— "American Notes in the Odes of Labindo." *RR* 21 (Jl-S 30) 204-8.
——— "Pasquale de Virgilii and L'Americano." *RR* 23 (Ja-Mr 32) 9-13.
Monaghan, Frank. "French Travellers in the United States, 1765-1931. A Bibliographical List." *BNYPL* 36 (Je, Jl, Ag, S, O 32) 427-38, 503-20, 587-96, 637-45, 690-702.
Moore, C. A. "Berkeley's Influence on Popular Literature." *SAQ* 14 (Jl 15) 263-78.
Moore, E. R. "Influence of the Modern Mexican Novel on the American Novel." *Revue de Littérature Comparée* 19 (Ja 39) 123-7.
Morgan, B. Q. "Sources of German Influences on American Letters." *AGR* 10 (F 44) 4-7, 35.
——— "Traces of German Influence in American Letters." *AGR* 10 (Ap 44) 15-8.
Morison, S. E. "Charles Bagot's Notes on Housekeeping and Entertaining at Washington, 1819." *PCSM* 26 (Ap 26) 438-46.

Morley, Malcolm. "American Theatrical Notes and Boz." *Dickensian* 44 (Au 48) 187-93.
——— "Early Dickens Drama in America." *Dickensian* 44 (Su 48) 153-7.
Mortensen, E. "American Songs by Danish Immigrants." *Common Ground* 5 (Sp 45) 84-6.
Mowbray, J. P. "Has America Outgrown Matthew Arnold?" *Critic* 40 (My 02) 409-13.
Muirhead, J. H. "How Hegel Came to America." *Philos R* 37 (My 28) 226-40.
Mumford, Lewis. "American Condescension and European Superiority." *Scribner's* ns 87 (My 30) 518-27.
Muray, Jean. "Regards sur les lettres Anglo-Américaines." *La Revue Française* no 19 (My 49) 63-4.
Myers, Elizabeth, & Gaimster, R. "Further Comment on America, de Tocqueville and Herbert Read." *Adelphi* 23 (Ap-Je 47) 166.
Myers, R. M. "The Old Dominion Looks to London: A Study of English Literary Influences upon *The Virginia Gazette,* 1736-1766." *VMHB* 54 (Jl 46) 195-217.
Nelson, J. H. "Some German Surveys of American Literature." *AL* 1 (My 29) 149-60.
Nenclaires, F. C. "El Viaje de Alejo de Tocqueville a America del Norte en 1830." *Revista de las Indias* 75 (Mr 45) 377-96.
Nolle, A. H. "The German Drama on the St. Louis Stage." *Ger Am Annal* ns 15 (1917) 29-65, 73-112.
O'Brien, Justin. "American Books and French Readers." *CE* 1 (Mr 40) 480-7.
O'Connor, W. V. "The Influence of the Metaphysicals on Modern Poetry." *CE* 9 (Ja 48) 180-7.
Orians, G. H. "Early American Travelers." *JEGP* 26 (4Q 27) 569-81.
——— "The Romance Ferment after *Waverley.*" *AL* 3 (Ja 32) 408-31.
Orrick, J. B. "Matthew Arnold and America." *London Merc* 20 (Ag 29) 389—97.
O'Sullivan, Vincent. "America and the English Literary Tradition." *Living Age* 303 (18 O 19) 170-6.
Parker, J. T. "Rudyard Kipling's Probable Introduction to American Literature." *AL* 14 (Ja 43) 426-7.
Pearce, R. H. "Sterne and Sensibility." *MLN* 59 (Je 44) 403-7.
Peckham, H. H. "Is American Literature Read and Respected in Europe?" *SAQ* 13 (O 14) 382-8.
Penrose, Boise. "The First Book about America Printed in England." *PMHB* 73 (Ja 49) 3-8.
Perry, Marvin, Jr. "Keats in Georgia." *Ga R* 1 (Wi 47) 460-9.
Peterson, R. M. "Echoes of the Italian Risorgimento in Contemporaneous American Writers." *PMLA* 47 (Mr 32) 220-40.
Pettit, Henry. "A Check-List of Young's 'Night Thoughts' in America." *PBSA* 42 (2Q 48) 150-6.
Peyre, Henri. "American Literature through French Eyes." *VQR* 23 (Su 47) 421-38.
Piccioni, L. "La Cultura in America no è di un solo colore." *Fiera Letteraria* no 24 (19 Je 47).
Pierson, G. W. "Alexis de Tocqueville in New Orleans, 1832." *Franco-Am R* 1 (Je 36) 25-42.
Pochmann, H. A. "Early German-American Journalistic Exchanges." *HLQ* 11 (F 48) 161-80.
Potter, C. F. "The Hindu Invasion of America." *Mod Thinker* 1 (Mr 32) 16-23.
Priestly, J. B. "Contemporary American Fiction: As an English Critic Sees It." *Harper's* 152 (Ja 26) 230-4.
Rabinovitz, A. L. "Criticism of French Novels in Boston Magazines, 1830-1860." *NEQ* 14 (S 41) 488-504.

Radine, Serge. "Ecrivains américains non-conformistes." *Suisse Contemporaine* (Lausanne) no 6 (Je 49) 287-95.
Randall, D. A. "Waverley in America." *Colophon* ns 1 (Su 35) 34-57.
Raunick, S. M. "A Survey of German Literature in Texas." *Sw Hist Q* 33 (O 29) 134-59.
Read, Herbert. "De Tocqueville on Art in America." *Adelphi* 23 (O-D 46) 9-12.
Reid, J. T. "As Other Americans See Our Literature." *SAQ* 40 (Jl 41) 211-9.
Remenyi, Joseph. "American Writers in Europe." *Ga R* 2 (Wi 48) 461-5.
Renstrom, A. G. "The Earliest Swedish Imprints in the United States." *PBSA* 39 (1945) 181-91.
Rice, H. C. "Seeing Ourselves as the French See Us." *FR* 21 (My 48) 432-41.
Riley, T. A. "New England Anarchism in Germany." *NEQ* 18 (Mr 45) 25-38.
Ritchie, H. S. "Thackeray's Letters from America." *Harper's* 148 (Mr 24) 536-44.
Robach, A. A. "Yiddish Writing in America." *Books Abroad* 8 (Ja 34) 15-7.
Roberts, C. "American Books in England." *World's Work* 8 (O 04) 5430-1.
Roberts, J. G. "The American Career of Quesnay de Beaurepaire." *FR* 20 (Mr 47) 463-70.
Roche, A. V. "Regis Michaud and American Literature." *Books Abroad* 13 (Su 39) 301-3.
Roll, Charles. "The Quaker in Anglo-American Cultural Relations." *Ind Mag Hist* 45 (Je 49) 135-46.
Roosebroeck, G. L. van. "Madame de Staël and the United States." *RR* 22 (Ap-Je 31) 154-6.
Roy, Claude. "Clefs pour l'Amérique et sa littérature." *Fontaine* 11 (O 47) 655-63.
Roz, Firmin. "L'Américain devient-il cosmopolite? *Revue des Deux Mondes* 40 (15 Jl 37) 340-61.
Russak, Ben. "Does Europe Want Our Books?" *Pub W* 153 (3 Ja 48) 32-6.
Russell, Phillips. "American Literature in France." *Freeman* 5 (16 Ag 22) 539-40.
Salls, H. H. "Joan of Arc in English and American Literature." *SAQ* 35 (Ap 36) 167-84.
Sanders, C. R. "William Strachey, the Virginia Colony and Shakespeare." *VMHB* 57 (Ap 49) 115-32.
Sartre, Jean-Paul. "American Novelists in French Eyes." *Atl* 178 (Ag 46) 114-8.
———, *et al.* "U. S. A." *Les Temps Modern* 1 nos 11-2 (Ag-S 46).
Schafer, Joseph. "Immigrant Letters." *Wisc Mag Hist* 16 (D 32) 211-5.
Schinz, Albert. "Le Livre français aux États-Unis." *Revue de Paris* (15 F 36) 893-906.
Schwartz, W. L. "L'Appel de l'Extrême-Orient dans la poésie des États-Unis." *Revue de Littérature Comparée* 8 (Ja 28) 113-26.
Sedgwick, H. D. "Literature and Cosmopolitanism." *Atl* 115 (F 15) 215-21.
Seeber, E. D. "Chief Logan's Speech in France." *MLN* 61 (My 46) 412-6.
Seitz, R. J. "Goethe in Chicago." *Open Court* 40 (Ag 32) 538-50.
Semmingsen, Ingrid. "Utvandringen, Amerikabrevene og norsk samfundsutvikling i det 19. aarhundre." *Samtiden* (Oslo) 52 (1941) 335-45.
Seznec, Jean. "Notes on Flaubert and the United States." *Am Soc Legion of Honor Mag* 17 (S 46) 391-8.
Sherrer, G. B. "French Culture as Presented to Middle-Class America in *Godey's Lady's Book*, 1830-1840." *AL* 3 (N 31) 277-86.
Sherzer, Jane. "American Editions of Shakespeare: 1753-1866." *PMLA* 29 (1907) 255.
Shorey, Paul. "Influence of the Classics on American Literature." *Chautauquan* 43 (Ap 06) 121-32.
Siegfried, André. "L'Europe devant la civilisation américaine." *Revue des Deux Mondes* 56 (15 Ap 30) 757-73.
Simon, Jean. "French Studies in American Literature and Civilization." *AL* 6 (My 34) 176-90.

Skard, Sigmund. "Studiet av amerikansk literatur." *Samtiden* (Oslo) 57 (1948) 225-42.
Smalley, G. W. "American Authors Abroad." *Munsey's* 26 (Mr 02) 774-7.
Smith, M. E. "Note on 'Shakespeare in America.'" *Shakespeare Assn Bul* 17 (Ja 42) 61-2.
Smith, O. D. "Joseph Tosso, the Arkansaw Traveler." *Ohio State Arch & Hist Soc Q* 56 (Ja 47) 16-45.
Spencer, Theodore. "Montaigne in America." *Atl* 177 (Mr 46) 91-7.
Spender, Stephen. "The Situation of the American Writer." *Horizon* 19 (Mr 49) 162-79.
Spiller, R. E. "Brother Jonathan to John Bull." *SAQ* 26 (O 27) 346-58.
——— "The English Literary Horizon: 1815-1835." *SP* 23 (Ja 26) 1-15.
——— "The Verdict of Sidney Smith." *AL* 1 (Mr 29) 1-16.
Sprengling, M. "Michael Naimy and the Syrian Americans in Modern Arabic Literature." *Open Court* 46 (Ag 32) 551-63.
Spurlin, P. M. "Rousseau in America, 1760-1809." *FAR* 1 (Ja-Mr 48) 8-16.
Stearns, Bertha-Monica. "Miss Sedgwick Observes Harriet Martineau." *NEQ* 7 (S 34) 533-41.
Stephen, A. M. "Dr. Samuel Johnson Views Our Poets." *Dalhousie R* 11 (Ja 32) 493-506.
Stevens, H. R. "La Frontiera e la storiografia americana." *Il Ponte* 4 (Je 48) 552-9.
Stevenson, Robert. "Watts in America." *Harvard Theol R* 41 (Jl 48) 205-10.
Stoke, H. W. "De Tocqueville's Appraisal of Democracy—Then and Now." *SAQ* 36 (Ja 37) 14-22.
Stolberg-Wernigerode, Otto zu. "Bismark and His American Friends." *VQR* 5 (Jl 29) 397-410.
Swan, M. W. S. "Gustavus Vasa Again." *SS* 18 (N 45) 307-16.
Syford, Ethel. "Ibsen in America." *N E Mag* 48 (S 12) 329-33.
Sypherd, W. O. "'Judith' in American Literature." *PMLA* 45 (Mr 30) 336-8.
Templeton, W. D. "A Note on Arnold's 'Civilization in the United States.'" *MLN* 59 (Mr 44) 173-4.
Thompson, Lawrence. "Fredrika Bremer as a Critic of American Literature." *Edda* (Oslo) 41 (Ap-Je 41) 166-76.
Thorndike, Ashley. "Shakespeare in America." *Proc British Acad* 13 (1927) 153-72.
Tinker, C. B. "Rasselas in the New World." *YR* ns 14 (O 24) 95-107.
Tower, R. A. "Attempts to Interest Germany in Early American Literature." *PQ* 7 (Ja 28) 89-91.
Vachot, Charles. "James Thomson et l'Amérique." *Revue de Littérature Comparée* 28 (O-D 48) 487-507.
Vagne, Jean. "Note sur le roman américain et le public français." *Renaissance* no 16 (S 45) 145-50.
Vaiciulaitis, A. "American Writers in Lithuania." *Books Abroad* 17 (Au 43) 334-7.
Vail, R. W. G. "The American Sketchbooks of a French Naturalist, 1816-1837." *PAAS* ns 48 (Ap 38) 49-155.
Vance, W. S. "Carlyle in America before *Sartor Resartus*." *AL* 7 (Ja 36) 363-75.
Van de Water, F. F. "Rudyard Kipling's Feud." *Harper's* 174 (My 47) 569-77.
Viatte, Auguste. "Les Franco-Américains de Nouvelle-Angleterre." *Renaissance* 2, 3 (1944-5) 322-35.
Virtanen, Reino. "Emile Montégut as a Critic of American Literature." *PMLA* 63 (D 48) 1265-76.
——— "Tocqueville on a Democratic Literature." *FR* 23 (Ja 50) 214-22.
Vittorini, Elio. "American Influences on Contemporary Italian Literature." *Am Q* 1 (Sp 49) 3-8.
Wadepuhl, Walter. "Goethe's Interest in America." *AGR* 15 (Ag 49) 29-32.
Wagner, L. E. "The Reserved Attitude of the Early German Romanticists toward America." *GQ* 16 (Ja 43) 8-12.

Wannamaker, W. H. "Some German Criticisms of America." *SAQ* 5 (Ap 06) 150-60.

Warner, Oliver. "How American Books Strike an English Reader." *Pub W* 123 (7 Ja 33) 31.

Warren, Dale. "American Books in Havana." *Pub W* 118 (2 Ag 30) 405-7.

Watson, Virginia. "Alfieri and America." *NAR* 196 (Ag 12) 244-53.

Wauchope, T. S. "What the French Think of Us." *Am Merc* 6 (D 25) 479-86.

Weber, C. J. "New England through French Eyes Fifty Years Ago." *NEQ* 20 (S 47) 385-96.

——— "Thomas Hardy and His New England Editors." *NEQ* 15 (D 42) 681-99.

Welleck, René. "The Minor Transcendentalists and German Philosophy." *NEQ* 15 (D 42) 652-80.

Werner, Alfred. "Goethe in America." *SAQ* 49 (Ap 49) 242-50.

West, Rebecca. "These American Men." *Harper's* 151 (S 25) 448-56.

——— "These American Women." *Harper's* 151 (N 25) 722-30.

Whicher, G. F. "Shakespeare for America." *Atl* 147 (Je 31) 759-68.

Whitford, R. C. "Mme. de Staël's Literary Reputation in America." *MLN* 33 (D 18) 476-80.

Whitridge, Arnold. "Brillat-Savarin in America." *Franco-Am R* 1 (Je 36) 1-12.

Wilkens, F. H. "Early Influences of German Literature in America." *Americana Germanica* 3 (1900) 110-36.

Willoughby, E. E. "The Reading of Shakespeare in Colonial America." *PBSA* 31 (1937) 45-6.

Wilson, A. H. "Expatriate French Literature in America during World War II." *Susquehanna Un Stud* 3 (1945) 19-34.

Wilt, Napier. "National Unity and Cultural Diversity." *AGR* 11 (F 45) 31-2, 36.

———, & Naeseth, H. C. K. "Two Early Norwegian Dramatic Societies in Chicago." *Norwegian Am Stud & Records* 11 (1938) 44-75.

Wimberly, L. C. "Oscar Wilde Meets Woodberry." *Prairie Schooner* 21 (Sp 47) 108-16.

Winship, G. P. "Remarks on the Second Part of Merry Drollery." *PCSM* 20 (D 17) 21-3.

Winters, Yvor. "The Symbolist Influence." *H&H* 4 (Jl-S 31) 607-18.

Withington, Robert. "Brother Jonathan." *CE* 6 (Ja 45) 200-6.

——— "A French Comment on the Battle of Bunker Hill." *NEQ* 22 (Je 49) 235-40.

Wittke, Carl. "The American Theme in Continental European Literature." *Miss Valley Hist R* 28 (Je 41) 3-26.

——— "The German Forty-Eighters in America: A Centennial Appraisal." *AHR* 53 (Jl 48) 711-25.

——— "Melting Pot Literature." *CE* 7 (Ja 46) 189-97.

Wood, G. A. "American Books and the American Dream." *Fortnightly D* ns 989 (My 49) 341-5.

Woolf, H. B. "Chaucer in Colonial America." *AN&Q* 2 (Ag 42) 71-2.

Yarmolinsky, Avraham. "The Russian View of American Literature." *Bkm* 44 (S 16) 44-8.

——— "Studies in Russian Americana." *BNYPL* 46 (Ap, My 42) 374-8, 451-75; 47 (Ja 43) 52-4.

Yutang, Lin. "When East Meets West." *Atl* 170 (D 42) 43-8.

Zandvoort, R. W. "American Studies." *Englische Studien* 12 (D 31) 209-18.

Zucker, A. E. "Southern Critics of 1903 on Ibsen's *Ghosts*." *PQ* 19 (O 40) 392-9.

Zylstra, Henry. "Mid-Nineteenth Century Dutch View of American Life and Letters." *PMLA* 57 (D 42) 1108-36.

FRONTIER. Babcock, C. M. "Vocabulary of Social Life on the American Frontier." *WF* 9 (Ap 50) 134-43.

Clark, T. D. "The American Backwoodsman in Popular Portraiture." *Ind Mag Hist* 42 (Mr 46) 1-28.
——— "Manners and Humors of the American Frontier." *Mo Hist R* 35 (O 40) 3-24.
Conant, C. A. "Literature of Expansion." *Int Q* 3 (Je 01) 719-27.
Dale, E. E. "Culture on the American Frontier." *Neb Hist* 26 (Ap-Je 45) 75-90.
Duncan, W. H. "Josiah Priest, Historian of the American Frontier." *PAAS* ns 44 (1934) 45-102.
Fox, D. R. "Civilization in Transit." *AHR* 32 (Jl 27) 753-68.
Hayes, C. J. H. "The American Frontier—Frontier of What?" *AHR* 51 (Ja 46) 199-216.
Howard, Leon. "Literature and the Frontier: The Case of Sally Hastings." *ELH* 7 (1940) 68-82.
Hubbell, J. B. "The Frontier in American Literature." *Sw R* 10 (Ja 25) 84-92.
Jones, H. M. "The Colonial Impulse: An Analysis of the 'Promotion' Literature of Colonization." *PAPS* 90 (1946) 131-61.
Macdonald, William. "Some Observations on the Spirit and Influence of the American Frontier." *PCSM* 26 (1927) 165-80.
Nixon, H. C. "Precursors of Turner in the Interpretation of the American Frontier." *SAQ* 28 (Ja 29) 83-9.
Paine, Gregory. "The Frontier in American Literature." *SR* 36 (Ap 28) 225-36.
Pierson, G. W. "American Historians and the Frontier Hypothesis in 1941." *Wisc Mag Hist* 26 (S, D 42) 35-60, 170-85.
——— "The Frontier and American Institutions." *NEQ* 15 (Je 42) 224-55.
Shipten, C. K. "The New England Frontier." *NEQ* 10 (Mr 37) 25-36.
Smith, H. N. "What Is the Frontier?" *Sw R* 21 (Au 35) 97-103.
Still, Bayrd. "Patterns of Mid-Nineteenth Century Urbanization in the Middle West." *Miss Valley Hist R* 28 (S 41) 187-206.
Wecter, Dixon. "Instruments of Culture on the Frontier." *YR* 36 (Wi 47) 242-56.
Wright, B. F., Jr. "American Democracy and the Frontier." *YR* 20 (Wi 30) 349-65.
Zaslow, Morris. "The Frontier Hypothesis in Recent Historiography." *Canadian Hist R* 29 (Je 48) 153-67.

HUMOR. Anon. "Humor and the 'Twenties.'" *SRL* 8 (28 N 31) 325-8.
——— "The Spirit of American Humor." *Living Age* 265 (11 Jl 10) 686-9.
Allen, G. W. "Humor in America." *SR* 40 (Ja-Mr 32) 111-3.
Bangs, J. K. "A Word Concerning American Humor." *Book Buyer* 20 (Ap 00) 205-8.
Benton, Joel. "American Humourists." *Bkm* 21 (Ag 05) 584-9.
Bergengren, Ralph. "The Humor of the Colored Supplement." *Atl* 98 (Ag 06) 269-73.
Blair, Walter. "Burlesques in Nineteenth-Century American Humor." *AL* 2 (N 30) 236-47.
——— "Laughter in Wartime America." *CE* 6 (Ap 45) 361-7; EJ 34 (Ap 45) 179-85.
——— "Our Literary Comedians." *Chicago Sun Book Week* 4 (7 My 47) 20.
——— "The Popularity of Nineteenth-Century American Humorists." *AL* 3 (My 31) 175-94.
Boatright, M. C. "The Art of Tall Lying." *Sw R* 34 (Au 49) 357-63.
——— "Frontier Humor: Depressing or Buoyant?" *Sw R* 27 (Sp 42) 320-34.
Boynton, H. W. "American Humor." *Atl* 90 (S 02) 414-20.
Bradley, Sculley. "Our Native Humor." *NAR* 242 (Wi 37) 351-62.
Bragin, Charles. "The Tousey Comics." *Coll J* 4 (Ja-F-Mr 34) 449.
Cazamian, Louis. "L'Humour de New York." *Revue Anglo-Américaine* 6 (Je 29) 393-405.

Charpentier, John. "Humeur Anglais et Humeur Américain." *Mercure de France* 264 (15 D 35) 475-501.
Chesterton, C. "The Salt of America." *Living Age* 295 (27 O 17) 243-6.
Chesterton, G. K. "American Humour and Bret Harte." *Critic* 41 (Ag 02) 170-4.
Chittick, V. L. O. "Ring-Tailed Roarers." *Frontier* 13 (My 33) 257-63.
Clark, J. A. "Ade's Fables in Slang: An Appreciation." *SAQ* 46 (O 47) 537-44.
Crane, F. "American Humor." *Reader* 9 (1906) 70.
Current-Garcia, Eugene. "Newspaper Humor in the Old South, 1835-1855." *Ala R* 2 (Ap 49) 102-21.
Davol, Ralph. "Contemporary New England Humorists." *N E Mag* ns 33 (F 06) 673-87.
Dickson, H. E. "A Note on Charles Mathews's Use of American Humor." *AL* 12 (Mr 40) 78-83.
Dorson, R. M. "America's Comic Demigods." *Am Schol* 10 (Au 41) 389-401.
Eastman, Max. "Humor and America." *Scribner's* 100 (Jl 36) 9-13.
——— "Wit and Nonsense: Freud's Mistake." *YR* 26 (S 36) 71-87.
Eaton, Clement. "The Humor of the Southern Yeoman." *SR* 49 (Ap-Je 41) 173-83.
Ferguson, J. DeL. "American Humor: Roots or Flowers?" *Am Schol* 4 (Su 35) 380-2.
——— "On Humor as One of the Fine Arts." *SAQ* 38 (Ap 39) 177-86.
——— "The Roots of American Humor." *Am Schol* 4 (Wi 35) 41-9.
Flanders, B. H. "Humor in Ante-Bellum Georgia: The Waynesboro *Gopher*." *Emory Un Q* 1 (O 45) 149-56.
Ford, F. L. "A Century of American Humor." *Munsey's* 25 (Jl 01) 482-90.
Gallacher, S. A. "The Ideal Hero of Antiquity and His Counterpart in the Comic Strip of Today." *SFQ* (Je 47) 141-8.
Hancock, E. L. "The Passing of the American Comic." *Bkm* 22 (S 05) 78-84.
Holliday, Carl. "Colonial Laughter." *EJ* 24 (F 36) 125-36.
Hooker, Brian. "The University and American Humor." *Bkm* 32 (Ja, F 11) 522-9, 580-8.
Howells, W. D. "Editor's Easy Chair." *Harper's* 133 (S 16) 626-9.
——— "Our National Humorists." *Harper's* 134 (F 17) 442-5.
Johnson, Burges. "The New Humor." *Critic* 40 (Ap, Je 02) 331-8, 526-32.
Johnston, Charles. "American Humor of the Vintage of Fifty-four." *Harper's W* 57 (18 Ja 13) 8.
——— "The Essence of American Humor." *Atl* 87 (F 01) 195-202.
——— "Old Funny Stories of the South and West." *Harper's Weekly* 57 (4 Ja 13) 21.
Jordan, P. D. "Humor of the Backwoods, 1820-1840." *Miss Valley Hist R* 25 (Je 38) 25-38.
Leacock, Stephen. "American Humor." *Nineteenth Century* 76 (Ag 14) 444-57; *Living Age* 283 (10 O 14) 92-102.
——— "Exporting Humor to England." *Harper's* 144 (Mr 22) 433-40.
Legman, G. "The First Comic Books in America: Revisions and Reflections." *AN&Q* 5 (Ja 46) 148-51.
Lippincott, H. M. "Quaker Humor." *Bul Friends Hist Assn* 35 (Sp 46) 10-6.
Lucas, E. V. "The Evolution of Whimsicality." *Harper's* 143 (Jl 21) 207-12.
McLuhan, H. M. "The New York Wits." *KR* 7 (Wi 45) 12-28.
McWilliams, Carey. "The Writers of California." *Bkm* 72 (D 30) 352-60.
Macy, J. A. "The Career of the Joke." *Atl* 96 (O 05) 498-510.
Masson, T. L. "Has America a Sense of Humor?" *NAR* 228 (Ag 29) 178-84.
——— "Humor and Comic Journals." *YR* ns 15 (O 25) 113-23.
Meine, F. J. "The Carpet-Bag." *Coll J* 4 (O-N-D 33) 411-3.
——— "Vanity Fair." *Coll J* 4 (Ja-F-Mr 34) 461-3.
Menard, Edith. "Jewish Humorists of the 20's." *Am Hebrew* 156 (4 Ap 48) 32, 72, 73.

Mendoza, Aaron. "Some 'Firsts' of American Humor, 1830-1875." *Pub W* 119 (21 Mr 31) 1603-5.
Mills, R. V. "Frontier Humor in Oregon and Its Characteristics." *Ore Hist Q* 43 (D 42) 339-56.
Mitchell, Langdon. "Comedy and the American Spirit." *Am Merc* 7 (Mr 26) 304-10.
Nesbit, W. D. "The Humor of To-day." *Independent* 54 (29 My 02) 1300-4.
Peters, Richard. "A Collection of Puns and Witticisms." *PMHB* 25 (1901) 366-9.
Quinn, A. H. "The Perennial Humor of the American Stage." *YR* ns 16 (Ap 27) 553-66.
Rayford, J. L. "Our Own Gods Are Always Comic." *Am Merc* 60 (Ap 45) 491-7.
Repplier, Agnes. "The American Laughs." *YR* 13 (Ap 24) 482-93.
——— "Cruelty and Humor." *YR* ns 6 (Ap 17) 537-47.
Robbins, L. H. "American Humorists." *N Y Times Mag* (8 S 35) 8-9.
Rourke, Constance. "Examining the Roots of American Humor." *Am Schol* 4 (Sp 35) 249-52.
——— "Our Comic Heritage." *SRL* 7 (21 Mr 31) 678-9.
Sanborn, K. A. "New England Women Humorists." *N E Mag* ns 35 (O 06) 155-9.
Stote, Amos. "Some Figures in the New Humor." *Bkm* 31 (My 10) 386-93.
Tietjens, Eunice. "Our Over-Developed Sense of Humor." *Arena* 41 (My 09) 320-1.
Trent, W. P. "A Retrospect on American Humor." *Century* 62 (N 01) 45-64.
Walker, Stanley. "What Is Humor?" *NAR* 243 (Sp 37) 176-84.
Weiss, H. B. "A Brief History of American Jest Books." *BNYPL* 47 (Ap 43) 273-89.
——— "Some Comic Histories of the United States." *BNYPL* 41 (Ap 38) 303-12.
Weitenkampf, Frank. "The Literary Hoax." *Am Merc* 59 (Jl 44) 112-3.
Wilkinson, C. W. "Backwoods Humor." *Sw R* 24 (Ja 39) 164-81.

INDIAN. Allen, Hervey, & Heyward, DuBose. "Poetry South." *Poetry* 20 (Ap 22) 35-48.
Austin, Mary. "American Indian Dance Drama." *YR* 19 (Je 30) 732-45.
Bass, Althea. "The Cherokee Press." *Colophon* 4 (Mr 33) Pt 13.
Beder, E. F. "Kingston to Newson to Balke; or, Bibliographical Adventures among the Indians." *BNYPL* 46 (Je 42) 525-30.
Carleton, P. D. "The Indian Captivity." *AL* 15 (My 43) 169-80.
Chamberlain, A. F. "The Contributions of the American Indian to Civilization." *PAAS* 16 (O 03) 91-126.
——— "Wisdom of the North American Indian in Speech and Legend." *PAAS* 23 (Ap 13) 63-96.
Densmore, Frances. "The Alabama Indians and their Music." *Pub Texas Folk-Lore Soc* 8 (1937) 270-93.
——— "The Songs of the Indians." *Am Merc* 7 (Ja 26) 65-8.
Dondore, Dorothy. "White Captives among the Indians." *N Y Hist* 13 (Jl 32) 292-300.
Fergusson, Harvey. "The Cult of the Indian." *Scribner's* 88 (Ag 30) 129-233.
Hale, E. E. "Aboriginal Languages of North America." *PAAS* 16 (O 04) 306-13.
Hartley, Alexander. "For an Indian Theatre." *Theatre Arts* 10 (Mr 26) 191-202.
Lyman, W. D. "Indian Myths of the Northwest." *PAAS* 25 (O 15) 375-95.
——— "Myths and Superstitions of the Oregon Indians." *PAAS* 16 (Ap 04) 221-51.
Munroe, J. A. "The Philadelawareans: A Study in the Relations between Philadelphia and the Delawares in the Late Eighteenth Century." *PMHB* 69 (Ap 45) 128-49.
Orians, G. H. "The Cult of the Vanishing American: A Century View, 1834-1934." *Un Toledo Stud* (D 34).
——— "The Indian Hater in Early American Fiction." *J Am Hist* 27 (1933) 34-44.
Pearce, R. H. "The Significances of the Captivity Narrative." *AL* 19 (Mr 47) 1-20.

Pearce, T. M. "American Traditions and Our Histories of Literature." *AL* 14 (My 42) 276-84.
Russell, J. A. "The Narratives of Indian Captivities." *Educ* 51 (O 30) 84-8.
Seeber, E. D. "Diderot and Chief Logan's Speech." *MLN* 60 (Mr 45) 176-8.
Walton, I. L. "Navaho Poetry: An Interpretation." *Texas R* 7 (Ap 22) 198-210.
Wroth, L. C. "The Indian Treaty as Literature." *YR* 17 (Jl 28) 749-66.

LIBRARIES AND READING. Anon. "Check List of Brooklyn and Long Island Papers in the New York Public Library." *BNYPL* 6 (Ja 02) 20-1.
——— "Dorothy Canfield Fisher Speaks on Book Clubs." *Pub W* 151 (17 My 47) 2494-6.
——— "Early Documents of the Library Company of Philadelphia, 1733-1744." *PMHB* 39 (1915) 450-4.
——— "Fiction in Our Public Libraries." *Atl* 94 (D 04) 859-60.
——— "Ideals for Americans at War Spread by Council on Books." *Pub W* 144 (25 D 43) 2300-13.
——— "Jam Session." *Scholastic* 53 (5 Ja 49) 24.
——— "The Library Company of Baltimore." *Md Hist Mag* 12 (D 14) 297-310.
——— "Proposals in a Public Library at Albany in 1758." *BNYPL* 12 (O 08) 575-6.
Adamic, Louis. "What the Proletariat Reads." *SRL* 11 (1 D 34) 321-2.
Aiken, Conrad. "The Great Audience Is Ready." *SRL* 30 (20 S 47) 7-8.
Barker, E. E. "What Crown Pointers Were Reading One Hundred Years Ago." *N Y Hist* 31 (Ja 50) 31-40.
Baym, M. E. "The 1858 Catalogue of Henry Adams's Library." *Colophon* ns 3 (Au 38) 483-9.
Bolton, C. K. "Circulating Libraries in Boston, 1765-1865." *PCSM* 11 (F 07) 196-208.
Borden, A. K. "Seventeenth-Century American Libraries." *Libr Q* 2 (Ap 32) 138-47.
Bowen, Dorothy. "Huntington and His Hobby." *SRL* 26 (30 O 43) 19-20.
Brayton, S. S. "The Library of an Eighteenth-Century Gentleman of Rhode Island." *NEQ* 8 (Je 35) 277-83.
Brett, G. P. "What the American People Are Reading." *Outlook* 75 (5 D 03) 778-81.
Brett, W. H. "American Libraries." *Dial* 28 (1 My 00) 346-9.
——— "Modern Library Enterprises." *Dial* 34 (1 F 03) 75-7.
Browne, R. J., & Zohn, Harry. "The Goethe Year in American Public Libraries." *GQ* 23 (Ja 50) 1-8.
Cadbury, H. J. "Harvard College Library and the Libraries of the Mathers." *PAAS* ns 50 (Ap 40) 20-48.
——— "John Harvard's Library." *PCSM* 34 (1943) 353-77.
Cahill, E. H. "The Life and Works of John Cotton Dana." *Americana* 24 (Ja 30) 69-84.
Canfield, J. H. "What Are College Students Reading?" *Outlook* 74 (16 My 03) 163-6.
Chamberlain, John. "Readers and Writers in War Time." *YR* 33 (S 43) 1-13.
Cleland, R. G. "The Research Facilities of the Huntington Library." *HLQ* 3 (O 39) 135-41.
Cole, G. W. "Early Library Development in New York State (1800-1900)." *BNYPL* 30 (N, D 26) 849-57, 917-25.
Conklin, Groff. "Pullman Reading." *Pub W* 128 (6 Jl 35) 11-2.
Cooley, L. C. "The Los Angeles Public Library." *Hist Soc So Calif Q* 23 (Mr 41) 5-23.
Crawford, N. A. "Literature in the Open Spaces." *Am Merc* 27 (O 32) 237-45.
Dana, J. C. "The Changing Character of Libraries." *Atl* 121 (Ap 18) 481-5.
——— "What the American People Are Reading." *Outlook* 75 (5 D 03) 775-8.

Davis, R. B. "Literary Tastes in Virginia before Poe." *WMQ* 19 (Ja 39) 55-68.
DeMille, G. E. "The Birth of the Brahmins." *SR* 37 (Ap 29) 172-88.
Deutsch, Babette. "The Public Library and the Public Need." *Dial* 64 (23 My 18) 475-7.
DeVoto, Bernard. "A Sagebrush Bookshelf." *Harper's* 175 (O 37) 488-96.
Dexter, F. B. "Early Private Libraries in New England." *PAAS* 18 (Ap 07) 135-47.
——— "The First Public Library in New Haven." *Papers New Haven Colony Hist Soc* 6 (1900) 301-13.
Eckert, R. P., Jr. "A Poet and His Library." *Colophon* 4 (O 33) Pt 15.
Edmunds, A. T. "The First Books Imported by America's First Great Library." *PMHB* 30 (1906) 300-8.
English, T. H. "One Hundred Famous Southern Books." *So Atlantic Bul* 13 (My 47) 1, 12-7.
Field, Ben. "What Kinds of Literature Do the People Want?" *Overland Mo* 91 (S 33) 123-4.
Fisher, D. C. "American Readers and Books." *Am Schol* 13 (Sp 44) 179-91.
——— "Book-Clubs." *BNYPL* 51 (My 47) 297-319.
Flanders, B. H. "Reading and Writing in Early Georgia." *Ga R* 1 (Su 47) 209-17.
Fleming, John. "One Hundred Influential American Books Printed before 1900." *Pub W* 151 (26 Ap 47) B353-4.
Fletcher, M. P. "Arkansas Pioneers: What They Were Reading a Century Ago." *Ark Hist Q* 8 (Au 49) 211-4.
Forman, H. B. "The Pleasures of a Book-man." *Atl* 105 (Je 10) 780-4.
Gold, W. J. "The Cause of Good Books in the South." *Pub W* 137 (10 F 40) 706-11.
Goodhue, A., Jr. "The Reading of Harvard Students, 1770-1781, as Shown by Records of the Speaking Club." *EIHC* 72 (Ap 37).
Gray, David. "A Modern Temple of Education." *Harper's* 122 (Mr 11) 562-76.
Greenberg, Herbert. "The Authenticity of the Library of John Winthrop, the Younger." *AL* 8 (Ja 37) 448-52.
Hall, H. J. "Two Book-Lists: 1668 and 1728." *PCSM* 24 (Ap 20) 64-71.
Hallenbeck, C. T. "A Colonial Reading List." *PMHB* 56 (O 32) 289-340.
Haraszti, Zoltán. "Harvard Tercentenary Exhibit." *More Books* 11 (S 36) 257-76.
Harris, D. G. "History of Friends' Meeting Libraries." *Bul Friends Hist Assn* 31 (Au 42) 52-62.
Hart, J. D. "A Puritan Bookshelf." *New Colophon* 1 (Ja 48) 13-26.
Henderson, Archibald. "An American Bookshelf." *SR* 22 (O 14) 483-93.
Herrick, C. A. "The Early New Englanders: What Did They Read?" *Library* 3: ser 9 (Ja 18) 1-17.
Hervey, J. L. "The Tribulations of an Amateur Book-Buyer." *Atl* 112 (S 13) 319-27.
Holmes, T. J. "The Mather Collection at Cleveland." *Colophon* 4 (Je 33) Pt 14.
Hutchins, J. K. "For Better or Worse, the Book Clubs." *N Y Times Book R* (31 Mr 46) 1, 24.
Irrman, R. H. "The Library of an Early Ohio Farmer." *Ohio State Arch & Hist Q* 57 (Ap 48) 185-93.
Jennings, J. M. "Notes on the Original Library of the College of William and Mary in Virginia, 1693-1705." *PBSA* 41 (3Q 47) 239-67.
Johnson, Clifton. "More Quaint Readers in the Old-Time School." *N E Mag* ns 29 (Ja 04) 626-37.
——— "The Readers Our Grandparents Used." *N E Mag* ns 29 (N 03) 376-85.
Kappel, J. W. "Book Clubs and the Evaluation of Books." *Public Opinion Q* 12 (Su 48) 243-52.
Kellogg, A. W. "The Boston Athenaeum." *N E Mag* ns 29 (O 03) 167-85.
Keyes, T. E. "The Colonial Library and the Development of Sectional Differences in the American Colonies." *Lib Q* 8 (Jl 38) 373-90.

Lamberton, E. V. "Colonial Libraries of Pennsylvania." *PMHB* 42 (Ja 18) 193-234.
Lancaster, E. R. "Books Read in Virginia in Early 19th Century, 1806-1823." *VMHB* 46 (Ja 38) 56-9.
Landis, C. I. "The Juliana Library Company in Lancaster." *PMHB* 43 (1919) 24-53, 163-81, 288-90.
Landrum, G. W. "Notes on the Reading of the Old South." *AL* 3 (Mr 31) 60-71.
Leonard, I. A. "A Frontier Library, 1799." *Hispanic Am Hist R* 23 (F 43) 21-51.
Lillard, R. D. "A Literate Woman in the Mines: The Diary of Rachel Haskel." *Miss Valley Hist R* 31 (Je 44) 81-9.
Linton, C. D. "The Tragic Comic." *Madison Q* 6 (Ja 46) 1-6.
Lydenberg, H. M. "A History of the New York Public Library." *BNYPL* 20 (Jl, Ag, S 16) 555-84, 623-60, 685-707; 21 (F, Ap 17) 71-80, 215-36; 24 (N, D 20) 587-616, 671-715; 25 (Ja, Mr. My, Jl, Ag, S 21) 3-38, 123-53, 307-20, 427-41, 495-530, 579-634.
McCutcheon, R. P. "Libraries in New Orleans, 1771-1833." *La Hist Q* 20 (Ja 37) 1-9.
McDermott, J. F. "Best Sellers in Early Saint Louis." *School & Soc* 47 (My 38) 673-5.
——— "Books in Eighteenth-Century Sainte Genevieve." *St Genevieve Fair Play* (17 Ag 35).
——— "Everybody Sold Books in Early St. Louis." *Pub W* 132 (Jl 37) 248-50.
——— "The Library of Barthelemi Tardiveau." *Illinois Hist Soc J* 29 (Ap 36) 89-91.
——— "The Library of Father Gibault." *Mid-America* 27 (O 35) 273-5.
——— "The Library of Henry Shaw." *Mo Botanical Garden Bul* 28 (Ap 40) 49-53.
——— "Public Libraries in St. Louis, 1811-1839." *Lib Q* 14 (Je 44) 9-27.
MacLeish, Archibald. "The Library of Congress Protects Its Collections." *Am Lib Assn Bul* 36 (F 42) 74-5.
Manning, J. W. "Literacy on the Oregon Trail: Books Across the Plains." *Ore Hist Q* 41 (Je 40) 189-94.
Martin, S. W. "Ebenezer Kellog's Visit to Charleston, 1817." *S C Hist & Gen Mag* 49 (Ja 48) 1-14.
Maura, Sister. "A Hundred Best Books." *Dalhousie R* 26 (O 46) 304-11.
Meadows, Paul. "Popular Culture in America." *Prairie Schooner* 22 (Su 48) 176-83.
Mershon, G. L. O. "The Kingston, New Jersey, Library of 1812." *Proc N J Hist Soc* 65 (Ap 47) 100-3.
Metcalf, J. C. "Virginia Libraries in Retrospect." *Madison Q* 6 (N 46) 154-62.
Miller, Merle. "The Book Club Controversy." *Harper's* 196 (Je 48) 518-24.
——— "The Book Clubs." *Harper's* 196 (My 48) 433-40.
Minot, J. C. "The Boston Athenaeum." *NAR* 225 (Mr 28) 331-3.
Moffat, L. G., & Carrière, J. M. "A Frenchman Visits Charleston, 1817." *S C Hist & Gen Mag* 49 (Jl 48) 131-54.
Mood, Fulmer. "The Continental Congress and the Plan for a Library of Congress in 1782-83: An Episode in American Cultural History." *PMHB* 72 (Ja 48) 3-24.
Morison, S. E. "The Library of George Alcock, Medical Student, 1676." *PCSM* 28 (F 33) 350-7.
Morris, E. P. "A Library of 1742." *Yale Un Lib Gaz* 9 (Jl 34) 1-11.
Mott, F. L. "The Banquet of the Boudoir." *SRL* 6 (23 N 29) 441.
Neuberger, R. L. "Reading in the Backwoods." *SRL* 30 (8 Mr 47) 10-1.
Newton, A. E. "The Amenities of Book-Collecting." *Atl* 115 (Mr, Ap 15) 336-47, 488-96.
——— "A Word in Memory: A Remembrance of Harry Elkins Widener." *Atl* 122 (S 18) 351-6.
Norton, A. O. "Harvard Textbooks and Reference Books of the Seventeenth Century." *PCSM* 27 (1935) 361-438.

O'Faoláin, Seán. "Getting at Which Public?" *VQR* 24 (Wi 48) 90-5.
Oliphant, J. O. "The Library of Archibald McKinley, Oregon Fur Trader." *Wash Hist Q* 25 (Ja 34) 23-6.
Palmer, H. R. "The Libraries of Rhode Island." *N E Mag* ns 22 (Je 00) 478-500.
Parma, V. V. "The Rare Book Collection of the Library of Congress." *Colophon* 2 (S 31) Pt 7.
Patrick, W. R. "A Circulating Library of Ante-Bellum Louisiana." *La Hist Q* 23 (Ja 40) 131-40.
———, & Taylor, C. G. "A Louisiana French Plantation Library, 1842." *FAR* 1 (Ja-Mr 48) 47-67.
Peery, William. "What Do You Read, My Lord?" *Am Schol* 6 (Su 37) 271-81.
Pennington, E. L. "The Beginnings of the Library in Charles Town, South Carolina." *PAAS* ns 44 (1934) 159-87.
Phillips, J. W. "The Sources of the Original Dickinson College Library." *Penn Hist* 14 (Ap 47) 108-17.
Potter, A. C. "Catalogue of John Harvard's Library." *PCSM* 21 (Mr 19) 190-230.
Powell, W. S. "Books in the Virginia Colony before 1624." *WMQ* 5 (Ap 48) 177-84.
Putnam, Herbert. "American Libraries in Relation to Study and Research." *Lib J* 54 (1 S 29) 693-8.
——— "The Library of Congress." *Pub W* 119 (24 Ja 31) 444-8.
Randall, D. A. "Books That Influenced America." *N Y Times Book R* (21 Ap 46) 11, 22.
Rice, H. C. "A Frontier Bibliophile." *Colophon* ns 1 (Au 35) 183-90.
Richardson, C. F. "The Sixth Reader." *YR* ns 5 (Jl 16) 832-40.
Robinson, C. F. & Robin. "Three Early Massachusetts Libraries." *PCSM* 28 (1935) 107-75.
Rodgers, J. T. "The Library of Congress." *NAR* 225 (Ap 28) 447-51.
Romberg, Annie. "A Texas Literary Society of Pioneer Days." *Sw Hist Q* 52 (Jl 48) 60-5.
Rosenbach, A. S. W. "The Libraries of Presidents of the United States." *PAAS* ns 44 (1934) 337-64.
Rothrock, M. U. "Nine States Look at Their Libraries." *So Packet* 4 (O 48) 1-3.
Rovere, R. H. "The Book of the Month Club: Librarian to the Nation." *Am Merc* 58 (Ap 44) 434-41.
Rugg, H. G. "Modern Authors in New England Libraries." *Col & Res Lib* 6 (D 44) 54-7.
Rush, O. N. "Maine's First Circulating Library." *Bul Maine Lib Assn* 3 (Ag 42) 13-4.
Schinz, Albert. "Ce qu'on lit aux Etats-Unis." *Mercure de France* 218 (15 F 30) 50-72.
Seybolt, R. F. "Student Libraries at Harvard, 1763-1764." *PCSM* 28 (1935) 449-61.
Shelley, F. "Manuscripts in the Library of Congress, 1800-1890." *Am Archivist* 11 (Ja 48) 3-19.
Silver, J. W. "Propaganda in the Confederacy." *J So Hist* 11 (N 45) 487-503.
Smart, G. K. "Private Libraries in Colonial Virginia." *Am Lib* 10 (Mr 38) 24-52.
Smith, Harrison. "Trends in American Literature." *SRL* 31 (24 Ja 48) 22.
Spectorsky, A. C. "The Future of Books in America." *CE* 6 (Mr 45) 303-10.
Spruill, J. C. "The Southern Lady's Library, 1770-1776." *SAQ* 34 (Ja 35) 23-41.
Starke, Aubrey. "Books in the Wilderness." *J Ill Hist Soc* 29 (Ja 36) 258-70.
Stern, P. Van D. "Books and Best Sellers." *VQR* 18 (D 41) 45-55.
Stokes, F. A. "The Case against the Book Clubs." *NAR* 228 (Jl 29) 47-56.
Thompson, C. S. "The Darby Library in 1743." *Un Penn Lib Chron* 11 (Ap 43) 15-22.
Thompson, Lawrance. "The St. Mary's City Press: A New Chronology of American Printing." *Colophon* ns 1 (Wi 36) 333-57.

Thorpe, James. "English and American Literature in the McCormick Collection." *PULC* 10 (N 48) 16-40.
Travous, R. L. "Pioneer Illinois Library." *J Ill Hist Soc* 42 (D 49) 446-53.
Tuttle, J. H. "Early Libraries in New England." *PCSM* 13 (Mr 11) 288-92.
——— "The Library of Dr. William Ames." *PCSM* 14 (1913) 63-6.
——— "The Libraries of the Mathers." *PAAS* 20 (Ap 10) 269-356.
Tweito, T. E. "Pioneer Mental Pabulum." *Palimpsest* 21 (Ja 40) 1-5.
Utley, G. B. "Newberry Library, 'Court of Last Resort.'" *Am Schol* 6 (Su 37) 372-6.
Wheeler, J. T. "Booksellers and Circulating Libraries in Colonial Maryland." *Md Hist Mag* 34 (Je 39) 1-137.
——— "The Layman's Libraries and the Provincial Library." *Md Hist Mag* 35 (Mr 40) 60-73.
——— "Reading and Other Recreations of Marylanders." *Md Hist Mag* 38 (Mr, Je 43) 37-55, 167-80.
——— "Reading Interests of Maryland Planters and Merchants, 1700-1776." *Md Hist Mag* 37 (Mr 42) 26-41.
——— "Reading Interests of the Professional Classes in Colonial Maryland, 1770-1776." *Md Hist Mag* 36 (Je 41) 184-201.
——— "Thomas Bray and the Maryland Parochial Libraries." *Md Hist Mag* 34 (1939) 246-65.
Whitford, R. C. "Horsethieves' Reading." *Am Bkm* 1 (Fl 44) 69-73.
Wood, A. L. S. "Keeping the Puritan Pure." *Am Merc* 6 (S 25) 74-8.
Wood, Eugene. "What the Public Wants to Read." *Atl* 88 (O 01) 566-71.
Wright, L. B. "The Classical Tradition in Colonial Virginia." *PBSA* 33 (S 39) 85-97.
——— "The 'Gentlemen's Library' in Early Virginia." *HLQ* 1 (O 37) 3-61.
——— "Pious Reading in Colonial Virginia." *J So Hist* 6 (Ag 40) 383-92.
——— "The Purposeful Reading of Our Colonial Ancestors." *ELH* 4 (Je 37) 85-111.
——— "Richard Lee II, a Belated Elizabethan in Virginia." *HLQ* 2 (O 38) 1-35.
Wright, L. M. "Iowa's Oldest Library." *Iowa J Hist & Pol* 38 (O 40) 408-28.
Wroth, L. C. "The St. Mary's City Press: A New Chronology of American Printing." *Colophon* ns 1 (Wi 36) 333-57.
——— "Toward a Rare Book Policy in the Library of Congress." *Lib Cong Quar J* 1 (Jl, S 43) 3-11.
Wyatt, E. A. "Schools and Libraries in Petersburg, Virginia, Prior to 1861." *Tyler's Quar Hist & Gen Mag* 19 (O 37) 65-86.
Yorke, Dane. "Three New England Libraries." *Am Merc* 9 (S 26) 83-7.
Yost, Genevieve. "The Reconstruction of the Library of Norborne Berkely, Baron de Botetourt, Governor of Virginia, 1768-1770." *PBSA* 36 (2Q 42) 97-123.

LITERARY CRITICISM. Anon. "The Author as Critic." *Atl* 121 (F 18) 282-4.
——— "The Embattled Humanists." *NRp* 61 (12 F 30) 315.
——— "Looking Back at the Critics." *SRL* 26 (30 O 43) 9.
——— "The Middle Distance." *TLS* 48 (27 My 49) 346.
——— "Mr. Mencken and the Prophets." *Freeman* 2 (13 O 20) 103-4.
——— "Our Critical Self-Consciousness." *Dial* 35 (1 O 03) 207-9.
——— "Professor Sherman's Tradition." *Freeman* 2 (27 O 20) 151-4.
Abel, Lione. "History, Snobbery, Criticism." *Nation* 138 (25 Ap 34) 474-6.
Adams, J. D. "Reviewing and Criticism." *Annals Am Acad Pol & Soc Sci* 219 (Ja 42) 145-50.
Aiken, Conrad. "American Writers Come of Age." *Atl* 169 (Ap 42) 476-81.
——— "The Mechanism of Poetic Inspiration." *NAR* 206 (D 17) 917-24.
Angoff, Charles. "The Intellectuals Discover America." *Am Merc* 69 (D 49) 748-54.
Babbitt, Irving. "The Critic and American Life." *Forum* 79 (F 28) 161-76.

——— "Humanists and Humanitarians." *Nation* 101 (2 S 15) 288-9.
——— "The Humanities." *Atl* 89 (Je 02) 770-9.
——— "On Being Original." *Atl* 101 (Mr 08) 388-96.
Bacon, Leonard. "The Ancient Well: Literature and the New Psychology." *Atl* 158 (Jl 36) 59-63.
Barrett, William. "A Present Tendency in American Criticism." *KR* 11 (Wi 49) 1-7.
Barzun, Jacques. "The American as Critic." *SRL* 23 (7 D 40) 30.
Beach, J. W. "American Letters between Wars." *CE* 3 (O 41) 1-12.
——— "The Holy Bottle." *VQR* 2 (Ap 26) 175-86.
Benson, A. C. "Vulgarity." *Atl* 98 (Ag 06) 229-32.
Benton, T. H. "Art and Reality: Reflections on the Meaning of Art in the Social Order." *UKCR* 16 (Sp 50) 198-216.
Bernbaum, Ernest. "The Practical Results of the Humanistic Theories." *EJ* (coll ed) 20 (F 31) 103-9.
Berryman, John, *et al.* "The State of American Writing, 1948." *PR* 15 (Ag 48) 855-94.
Bishop, J. P. "The Myth and Modern Literature." *SRL* 20 (22 Jl 39) 3-4, 14.
Blackmur, R. P. "A Burden for Critics." *Hudson R* 1 (Su 48) 170-86.
——— "For a Second Look." *KR* 11 (Wi 49) 7-10.
Bodenheim, Maxwell. "American Literary Critics." *Double Dealer* 3 (Ap 22) 206-10.
——— "Self-Glorification and Art." *Dial* 68 (Ja 20) 92-4.
Boyd, Ernest. "Literary Internationalism." *VQR* 3 (Jl 27) 382-91.
——— "Marxian Literary Critics." *Scribner's* ns 98 (D 35) 342-6.
Boyesen, Bayard. "Creative Criticism." *Dial* 63 (16 Ag 17) 95-8.
Boynton, P. H. "American Literature and the Tart Set." *Freeman* 1 (7 Ap 20) 88-9.
Bradford, Gamaliel. "The Mission of the Literary Critic." *Atl* 94 (O 04) 537-44.
Bromfield, Louis. "Calliope and the Critics." *SRL* 30 (27 D 47) 7-8, 26-7.
——— "A Case of Literary Sickness." *SRL* 30 (13 S 47) 7-8, 30.
Brooker, Bertram. "Idolators of Brevity." *SR* 39 (Jl 31) 263-8.
Brooks, Cleanth. "The New Criticism: A Brief for the Defense." *Am Schol* 13 (Su 44) 285-95.
———, & Warren, R. P. "The Reading of Modern Poetry." *Am R* 7 (F 37) 442-6.
Brooks, Obed. "The Literary Front." *Mod Mo* 7 (Mr, Ap 33) 115-7, 182-6.
Brown, E. K. "The National Idea in American Criticism." *Dalhousie R* 14 (Jl 34) 133-47.
Brown, Ivor. "Misrepresentative Drama." *Atl* 141 (My 28) 706-11.
Brownell, W. C. "Criticism." *Atl* 107 (Ap 11) 548-67.
Burgum, E. B. "Literary Form: Social Forces and Innovations." *SR* 49 (Jl-S 41) 325-38.
——— "Our Writers Are Winning Victories Too." *CE* 6 (Ja 45) 185-93.
Burke, Kenneth. "Acceptance and Rejection." *So R* 2 (Wi 37) 600-32.
Burman, B. L. "The 'Little Men' of Literature." *SRL* 31 (11 Ja 48) 5-6, 28.
Burroughs, John. "The Literary Treatment of Nature." *Atl* 94 (Jl 04) 38-43.
Bush, Douglas. "Pale-Eyed Priests and Happy Journalists." *Bkm* 75 (N 32) 699-702.
C., H. "Out of the Woods." *Poetry* 73 (D 48) 151-2.
Cabell, J. B. "Dizain of the Doomed." *N Y Herald-Tribune Books* 6 (27 Ap 30) 1, 6.
Calverton, V. F. "Pathology in Contemporary Literature." *Thinker* 4 (D 31) 7-16.
Canby, H. S. "Defining the Indefinable." *NAR* 215 (My 22) 633-40.
——— "The Expressionists." *Lit R* 3 (1922) 285-6.
——— "The New Humanists." *SRL* 6 (22 F 30) 749-51.
——— "The Reviewing of Books." *Atl* 180 (Ag 47) 115-8.
——— "What's Wrong with Criticism in America?" *SRL* 15 (13 Mr 37) 8.

Cargill, Oscar. "The Laggard Art of Criticism." *CE* 6 (F 45) 243-50.
Carten, Alfred. "Reproach for the Critics." *NMQR* 6 (Ag 36) 169-80.
Chamberlain, John. "Critic Finds New Authors Work Things Out in Their Own Ways." *Life* 22 (2 Je 47) 81-2.
Chase, Frederick. "The Intellectals' Black Beast." *SR* 50 (Jl-S 42) 349-56.
Chase, Richard. "New vs. Ordealist." *KR* 11 (Wi 49) 11-3.
Clark, H. H. "Literary Criticism in the *North American Review,* 1815-1835." *Trans Wisc Acad Sci, Arts & Letters* 32 (1940) 299-350.
Coindreau, Maurice-Edgar. "La Rapport Kinsey—une enquête américaine." *Revue de Paris* (Ja 49) 106-15.
Collins, Seward. "Criticism in America." *Bkm* 71 (Je, Jl 30) 241-56, 353-64, 400-15; 72 (O 30) 145-64.
Colum, M. M. "The American Mind in Literature." *Forum* 90 (D 33) 330-4.
——— "Self-Critical America." *Scribner's* 86 (F 30) 197-206.
Corbin, John. "Harking Back to the Humanities." *Atl* 101 (Ap 08) 482-90.
Corey, H. E. "Critics of Criticism." *Dial* 57 (16 N 14) 371-4.
Cowley, Malcolm. "Angry Professors." *NRp* 62 (9 Ap 30) 207-11.
——— "The Escape from America." *N Y Herald-Tribune Books* 6 (10 N 29) 1, 6.
——— "For Postwar Writers." *NRp* 113 (3 D 45) 751-2.
——— "Ivory Towers to Let." *NRp* 78 (18 Ap 34) 260-3.
——— "On Writing as a Profession." *NRp* 122 (24 Ap 50) 15-9.
——— "The War against Writers." *NRp* 110 (8 My 44) 631-2.
Cowley, W. H. "'All God's Chillun Got Wings.'" *School & Soc* 66 (30 Ag 47) 145-50.
Creek, H. L. "Creation or Criticism?" *SAQ* 17 (Jl 18) 207-16.
Crow, W. L. "The Devil in the Ink Bottle." *Dalhousie R* 18 (Jl 38) 138-42.
Cunningham, J. V. "The Ancient Quarrel between History and Poetry." *Poetry* 79 (S 49) 336-42.
Daiches, David. "The New Criticism: Some Qualifications." *EJ* 39 (F 50) 64-72; *CE* 11 (F 50) 242-50.
——— "The Scope of Sociological Criticism." *Epoch* 3 (Su 50) 57-64.
Davis, J. L. "A Survey of the Humanist Controversy." *Letters* 4 (N 30) 6-15.
Davis, R. G. "New Criticism and the Democratic Tradition." *Am Schol* 19 (Ja 50) 9-19.
DeMille, G. E. "American Criticism Today." *SR* 35 (Jl 27) 353-8.
——— "The Birth of the Brahmins." *SR* 37 (Ap 29) 172-88.
DeVoto, Bernard. "How Not to Write History." *Harper's* 168 (Ja 34) 199-208.
——— "The Rocking Chair in History and Criticism." *Forum* 89 (F 33) 104-7.
——— "A Sagebrush Bookshelf." *Harper's* 175 (O 37) 488-96.
——— "The Skeptical Biographer." *Harper's* 166 (Ja 33) 181-92.
Downes, W. H. "Training in Taste." *Atl* 93 (Je 04) 816-21.
Eastman, Max. "The Cult of Unintelligibility." *Harper's* 158 (Ap 29) 632-9.
———, & Farrell, J. T. "As to Value and Facts: An Exchange." *PR* 9 (My-Je 42) 203-12.
Eaton, W. P. "What Every Critic Knows." *Harper's* 141 (Je 20) 131-3.
Eliot, T. S. "Experience in Criticism." *Bkm* 70 (N 29) 225-32.
——— "Second Thoughts about Humanism." *H&H* 2 (1929) 339-50.
Elton, William. "A Glossary of the New Criticism." *Poetry* 73 (D 48, Ja 49) 153-62, 232-45.
Erskine, John. "The Characters Proper to Literature." *NAR* 217 (Mr 23) 393-408.
——— "The Cult of the Contemporary." *NAR* 217 (F 23) 247-62.
——— "The Cult of the Natural." *NAR* 217 (Ja 23) 68-83.
Fadiman, Clifton. "The Decline of Attention." *SRL* 32 (6 Ag 49) 20-4.
——— "The Reviewing Business." *Harper's* 183 (O 41) 472-9.
Farrar, J. T. "The Condition of American Writing." *EJ* 38 (O 49) 421-8.
Farrell, J. T. "Literature and Ideology." *CE* 3 (Ap 42) 611-23.

——— "A Note on Literary Criticism." *Nation* 142 (4, 11 Mr 36) 276-7, 314-5.
Feuillerat, Albert. "Scholarship and Literary Criticism." *YR* ns 14 (Ja 25) 309-24.
Field, L. M. "The Great Word War." *NAR* 230 (Jl 30) 101-6.
——— "What's Wrong with the Men?" *NAR* 231 (Mr 31) 234-40.
Firkins, O. W. "The Irresponsible Power of Realism." *NAR* 223 (Mr-Ap-My 26) 131-44.
Foerster, Norman. "Historian and Criticism of Letters: A Diagnosis." *H&H* 3 (O-D 29) 83-105.
——— "Humanism and Religion." *Forum* 82 (S 29) 146-50.
——— "Impressionists." *Bkm* 70 (D 29) 337-47.
——— "The Literary Prophets." *Bkm* 72 (S 30) 35-44.
——— "Literary Scholarship and Criticism." *EJ* 25 (Mr 36) 224-32.
——— "Matthew Arnold and American Letters Today." *SR* 30 (Jl 22) 298-306.
Fogle, R. H. "A Recent Attack on Romanticism." *CE* 9 (Ap 48) 356-61.
Follett, Wilson. "Confessions of a Literary Ex-Drunkard." *VQR* 11 (Ja 35) 16-33.
——— "Every Reader His Own Novelist." *Atl* 171 (Ap 43) 111-6.
——— "Literature and Bad Nerves." *Harper's* 143 (Je 21) 107-16.
——— "New England Aftermath." *Atl* 166 (S 40) 305-7.
Foster, Edward. "A Note on Standards." *SR* 49 (Jl-S 41) 305-12.
Frankenberg, Lloyd. "Some Intentions of Criticism." *N Y Herald Tribune Book R* (3 S 50) 3, 10.
Frohock, W. M. "What about Humanism?" *Sw R* 25 (Ap 40) 322-34.
Fuller, Edward. "Real Forces in Literature." *Atl* 91 (F 03) 270-4.
Gannett, Lewis. "A Quarter Century of a Weekly Book Review . . . and of the World." *N Y Herald Tribune Books* 26 (25 S 49) 4-5.
Gardner, Jerome. "Book Reviewing in the Deep South." *SRL* 25 (19 S 42) 15.
Garnett, Edward. "A Gossip on Criticism." *Atl* 117 (F 16) 174-85.
Gass, S. B. "Humanism as a Way of Life." *Forum* 81 (My 29) 282-7.
Gates, L. E. "Impressionism and Appreciation." *Atl* 86 (Jl 00) 73-84.
Geiger, Don. "Oral Interpretation and the 'New Criticism.'" *QJS* 36 (D 50) 508-13.
Gerould, K. F. "The Hard-Boiled Era." *Harper's* 158 (F 29) 265-74.
Gissen, Max. "Commercial Criticism and Punch-Drunk Reviewing." *AR* 2 (Su 42) 252-63.
Gleason, Arthur. "Distorted Standards." *Cath World* 140 (F 35) 577-82.
Glicksberg, C. I. "The Aberrations of Marxist Criticism." *QQ* 56 (Wi 49-50) 479-90.
——— "The Decline of Literary Marxism." *AR* 1 (Wi 41) 452-62.
——— "The Documentary in Action." *Ariz Q* 3 (Sp 47) 5-18.
——— "Marxism, Freudianism, and Modern Writing." *QQ* 54 (Au 47) 297-310.
——— "Two Decades of Literary Criticism." *Dalhousie R* 16 (Jl 36) 229-42.
Gohdes, Clarence. "The Theme-Song of American Criticism." *UTQ* 6 (O 36) 49-65.
Grattan, C. H. "Open Letters to Lewisohn, Krutch, and Mumford." *Mod Mo* 7 (Ap 33) 175-81.
——— "The Present Situation in American Literary Criticism." *SR* 40 (Ja-Mr 32) 11-23.
——— "What Is This Humanism?" *Scribner's* ns 87 (Ap 30) 423-32.
Hackett, Francis. "Literary Critics." *Am Merc* 60 (Mr 45) 367-74.
Hall, Dorothy. "The Function of Literature." *AR* 1 (S 41) 388-97.
Harrison, H. S. "Poor America." *Atl* 116 (D 15) 751-63.
Hart, Russell. "Authoritative Criticism of Poetry in America." *NAR* 198 (S 13) 413-5.
Hazlitt, Henry. "All Too Humanism." *Nation* 130 (12 F 30) 181-2.
——— "Standards (Loud Cheers)." *Nation* 131 (3 D 30) 613-4.
Healy, J. V. "Contemporary Poetry Criticism." *Poetry* 61 (Mr 43) 672-80.
Herron, I. H. "The Blight of Romanticism." *Sw R* 26 (Jl 41) 449-53.
Hessler, L. B. "On 'Bad Boy' Criticism." *NAR* 240 (S 35) 214-24.

Hibbard, Addison. "The Road of Modernism." *SRL* 19 (21 Ja 39) 3-4, 16.
Hicks, Granville. "The Crisis in American Criticism." *New Masses* 8 (F 33) 3-5.
——— "Literary Criticism and the Marxian Method." *Mod Q* 6 (Su 32) 44-7.
——— "Some Literary Fallacies." *CE* 6 (N 44) 69-75.
Hoffman, F. J. "Psychoanalysis and Literary Criticism." *Am Q* 2 (Su 50) 144-54.
Houghton, Norris. "Drama at the Crossroads." *Atl* 168 (N 41) 596-604.
Howe, M. A. DeW. "Back Bay Landfall." *Atl* 168 (Ag 41) 228-36.
Hyman, S. E. "Marxist Literary Criticism." *AR* 7 (D 47) 541-68.
——— "Psychoanalytic Criticism of Literature." *WR* 12 (Wi 48) 106-15.
Janes, G. M. "Literary Shibboleths: An Economist Looks at Literature." *SR* 41 (O-D 33) 385-95.
Jarrell, Randall. "Contemporary Poetry Criticism." *NRp* 105 (21 Jl 41) 88-90.
Jenkins, Iredell. "The Laissez-Faire Theory of Artistic Censorship." *JHI* 5 (Ja 44) 71-90.
Johnson, Burges. "The Alleged Depravity of Popular Taste." *Harper's* 142 (Ja 21) 209-15.
Johnson, Seneca. "In Defense of Ghost Writing." *Harper's* 179 (O 39) 536-43.
Jones, H. M. "The American Malady." *SRL* 32 (6 Ag 49) 24-7.
——— "Amidst the Encircling Gloom." *Scribner's* 87 (Ap 30) 405-11.
——— "Is There a Southern Renaissance?" *VQR* 6 (Ap 30) 184-97.
——— "Literary Scholarship and Contemporary Criticism." *EJ* 23 (N 34) 740-58.
——— "The New England Dilemma." *Atl* 165 (Ap 40) 456-67.
——— "Nobility Wanted." *Atl* 164 (N 39) 641-9.
Jones, R. E. "Romanticism Reconsidered: Humanism and Romantic Poetry." *SR* 41 (O-D 33) 396-418.
Kazin, Alfred. "American Fin-de-Siècle." *SRL* 21 (3 F 40) 3-4, 11-2.
——— "Criticism at the Poles." *NRp* 107 (19 O 42) 492-5.
——— "Nearer My Land to Thee." *NRp* 107 (12 O 42) 460-3.
Keith, L. J. "One Humanist to Another." *SR* 38 (O-D 30) 441-63.
Kirk, R. A. "Jefferson and the Faithless." *SAQ* 40 (Jl 41) 220-7.
Knickerbocker, W. S. "Humanism and Scholarship." *SR* 38 (Ja-Mr 30) 81-103.
Krieger, Murray. "Creative Criticism: A Broader View of Symbolism." *SR* 58 (Wi 50) 36-51.
Kronenberger, Louis. "Criticism in Transition." *PR* 3 (O 36) 5-7.
Krutch, J. W. "Half Truth of the Whole Truth." *Nation* 144 (2 Ja 37) 21-2.
——— "New, Newer, Newest." *Nation* 171 (15 Jl 50) 62-3.
——— "An Open Letter to Critics." *Nation* 155 (1 Ag 42) 95.
——— "What Is a Good Review?" *Nation* 144 (17 Ap 37) 438.
Levin, Harry. "America Discovers Bohemia." *Atl* 180 (S 47) 68-75.
——— "Literature and the Lively Sciences." *Atl* 155 (Mr 35) 303-11.
Lewisohn, Ludwig. "Blind Alley." *Harper's* 162 (D 30) 87-92.
Lind, R. L. "The Crisis in Literature." *SR* 47 (Ja-Mr, Ap-Je, Jl-S, O-D 39) 35-62, 184-203, 345-64, 524-51; 48 (Ja-Mr, Ap-Je 40) 66-85, 198-203.
Linebarger, P. M. A. "STASM: Psychological Warfare and Literary Criticism." *SAQ* 46 (Jl 47) 344-8.
Lüdeke, Henry. "Neuhumanismus und Demokratie im amerikanischen Geistesleben." *Germanisch-Romanische Monatschrift* 21 (My-Je 33) 220-33.
Lundkvist, Artur. "Amerikansk kritik." *Bonniers Litterära Magasin* (Stockholm) 11 (Ap 42) 284-92.
——— "Amerikansk litteraturanalys." *Bonniers Litterära Magasin* (Stockholm) 14 (N 45) 757-62.
Lutwack, Leonard. "A New Formula for Criticism." *Gifthorse 1949* (Ohio State) (44-7).
McClure, John. "The Domination of Literature." *Am Merc* 5 (Jl 25) 337-40.
McCole, C. J. "Our Literary Depressionists." *Cath World* 142 (Ja 36) 456-61.
McKelway, St. Clair. "Business Men, Get a Writer!" *Harper's* 181 (Ag 40) 270-8.

MacLeish, Archibald. "The Beginning of Things." *NAR* 219 (Mr 24) 367-71.
——— "The New Age and the New Writers." *YR* 12 (Ja 23) 314-21.
McWilliams, Carey. "Localism in American Criticism." *Sw R* 19 (Jl 34) 410-28.
Marshall, Margaret, & McCarthy, Mary. "Our Critics: Right or Wrong." *Nation* 141 (23 O, 6, 20 N, 4, 18 D 35) 468-72, 542-4, 595-8, 653-5, 717-9.
Martin, A. C. "Yggdrasill and the Gardener." *SR* 38 (Ap-Je 30) 129-32.
Masters, E. L. "The Artist Revolts." *Poetry* 22 (Jl 23) 206-9.
Matthiessen, F. O. "'The Great Tradition'—A Counter-Statement." *NEQ* 7 (Je 34) 223-34.
——— "The Responsibilities of the Critic." *Mich Alumnus Quar R* 55 (30 Jl 49) 283-92.
Mayer, F. P. "The Sad Story of Romance." *VQR* 2 (O 26) 577-93.
Mierow, C. C. "Through Seas of Blood." *SR* 41 (Ja 33) 1-22.
Mims, Edwin. "The Function of Criticism in the South." *SAQ* 31 (Ap 32) 133-49.
Mizener, Arthur. "Recent Criticism." *So R* 5 (Au 39) 376-400.
Monroe, Harriet. "Art and Propaganda." *Poetry* 44 (Jl 34) 210-5.
More, P. E. "A Revival of Humanism." *Bkm* 81 (Mr 30) 1-11.
Moses, M. J. "Should Dramatic Critics Be?" *NAR* 233 (Mr 32) 243-51.
Muller, H. J. "The Function of a Critical Review." *Ariz Q* 4 (Sp 48) 5-20.
——— "Literary Criticism: Cudgel or Scales?" *Am Schol* 8 (Su 39) 285-94.
——— "Pathways in Recent Criticism." *So R* 4 (Su 39) 187-208.
——— "The New Criticism in Poetry." *So R* 6 (Sp 41) 811-39.
Mumford, Lewis. "The New Tractarians." *NRp* 62 (26 Mr 30) 62.
——— "Origins of the American Mind." *Am Merc* 8 (Jl 26) 345-54.
——— "What Has 1932 Done for Literature?" *Atl* 150 (D 32) 761-7.
Munson, G. B. "American Criticism and the Fighting Hope." *YR* 20 (Mr 31) 568-82.
——— "Criticism for Black Sheep." *SR* 37 (O 29) 459-77.
——— "The Embattled Humanists." *Bkm* 68 (D 28) 404-11.
——— "Humanism and Modern Writers." *EJ* 20 (S 31) 531-9.
——— "The Young Critics of the Nineteen-twenties." *Bkm* 70 (D 29) 369-73.
Nathan, G. J. "Advice to a Young Critic." *Am Merc* 12 (O 27) 244-9.
Nock, A. J. "A Study in Literary Criticism." *Freeman* 3 (16 Mr 21) 10-2.
O'Connor, W. V. "The Aesthetic Emphasis before the Moderns." *NMQR* 17 (Sp 47) 5-16.
——— "A Short View of the New Criticism." *CE* 11 (N 49) 63-7; *EJ* 38 (N 49) 489-97.
Ong, W. J. "The Meaning of the 'New Criticism.'" *Mod Schoolman* 20 (1943) 192-209.
Osborn, M. E. "Too Much Incoherency." *SLM* 4 (Mr 42) 114-8.
P., B. "The New Literature." *Atl* 103 (Ja 09) 1-8.
Pacey, Desmond. "Literary Criticism in Canada." *UTQ* 19 (Ja 50) 113-9.
Parks, E. W. "Legaré and Grayson: Types of Classical Influence on Criticism in the Old South." *Sw R* 22 (Jl 37) 354-65.
Payne, W. M. "American Literary Criticism and the Doctrine of Evolution." *Int Q* 2 (Jl, Ag 00) 26-46, 127-53.
Peckham, H. H. "The Novelty Fallacy in Literature." *SAQ* 16 (Ap 17) 144-8.
Perry, Bliss. "The American Reviewer." *YR* ns 4 (O 14) 3-24.
——— "Literary Criticism in American Periodicals." *YR* ns 3 (Jl 14) 635-55.
Phillips, William. "Categories for Criticism." *Symposium* 4 (Ja 33) 31-47.
——— "The Intellectual's Tradition." *PR* 8 (N 41) 481-90.
———, & Rahv, Philip. "Some Aspects of Literary Criticism." *Sci & Soc* 2 (Je 37) 212-20.
Pritchard, J. P. "Aristotle's *Poetics* and Certain American Literary Critics." *Classical W* 27 (1934) 81-5, 89-93, 97-9.
Puffer, E. D. "Criticism and Aesthetics." *Atl* 87 (Je 01) 839-48.

Rahv, Philip. "The Cult of Experience in American Writing." *PR* 7 (N 40) 412-24.
——— "Paleface and Redskin." *KR* 1 (Su 39) 251-6.
———, & Phillips, William. "Criticism." *PR* 2 (Ap 35) 16-31.
Ransom, J. C. "The Basis of Criticism." *SR* 52 (Au 44) 556-71.
——— "Criticism, Inc." *VQR* 13 (Ag 37) 586-600.
Robertson, J. M. "On Criticism." *New Criterion* 4 (Ap 26) 244-61.
Roman, Jeannette. "How Do You Stand on Humanism?" *Pub W* 117 (8 Mr 30) 1327-9.
Salpeter, Harry. "Irving Babbitt: Calvinist." *Outlook & Independent* 155 (16 Jl 30) 421-3, 439.
Samson, Leon. "Chaos in Criticism." *Mod Thinker* 1 (Ap 32) 128-33.
Sedgwick, H. D. "The Mob Spirit in Literature." *Atl* 96 (Jl 05) 9-15.
Shafer, Robert. "The Definition of Humanism." *H&H* 3 (Jl-S 30) 533-56.
——— "Humanism and Impudence." *Bkm* 70 (Ja 30) 489-98.
——— "Our American Humanists." *Books Abroad* 3 (O 29) 330-1.
——— "In Wandering Mazes Lost." *Bkm* 71 (Mr 30) 37-9.
——— "What Is Humanism?" *VQR* 11 (Ap 30) 198-209.
Shapiro, Karl. "What Is Anti-Criticism?" *Poetry* 80 (Mr 50) 339-53.
Sherman, C. B. "The Vanishing Critique." *SAQ* 31 (Ja 32) 98-104.
Sherman, S. P. "A Conversation with Cornelia (Jan. 1924)." *Atl* 150 (N 32) 560-77.
Siegel, Eli. "Scientific Criticism: The Complete Criticism." *Mod Q* 1 (Mr 23) 37-50.
Skard, Sigmund. "The Use of Color in Literature: A Survey of Research." *PAAS* 90 (Jl 46) 163-249.
Smith, Bernard. "The Liberals Grow Old." *SRL* 10 (30 D 33) 377-8.
Spencer, Theodore. "The Critic's Function." *SR* 47 (O 39) 552-8.
——— "How to Criticize a Poem." *NRp* 109 (4 D 43) 816, 818.
Spingarn, J. E. "The Growth of a Literary Myth." *Freeman* 7 (2 My 23) 181-3.
Stauffer, D. A. "A Letter from the Critical Front." *KR* 4 (Wi 42) 133.
Steadman, R. W. "A Critique of Proletarian Literature." *NAR* 247 (Sp 39) 142-52.
Stewart, Randall. "The Social School of American Criticism." *SAQ* 43 (Ja 44) 22-6.
Streeter, R. E. "Association Psychology and Literary Nationalism in the *North American Review*." *AL* 17 (N 45) 243-54.
Sylvester, Harry. "A Note on Criticism." *Commonweal* 41 (23 Mr 45) 562-4.
Tate, Allen. "The American Caravan." *Bkm* 68 (N 28) 353-5.
——— "The Fallacy of Humanism." *Criterion* 8 (Jl 29) 661-81; *H&H* 3 (Ja-Mr 30) 234-58.
——— "The New Provincialism." *VQR* 21 (Sp 45) 262-72.
——— "Poetry and the Absolute." *SR* 35 (Ja 27) 41, 51.
——— "The Present Function of Criticism." *So R* 6 (Au 40) 236-46.
——— "R. P. Blackmur and Others." *So R* 3 (Su 37) 183-98.
——— "The Same Fallacy of Humanism." *Bkm* 71 (Mr 30) 31-6.
Taylor, H. W. "Some Nineteenth Century Critics of Realism." *Un Texas Stud Eng* 8 (1928) 110-28.
Taylor, W. F. "That Gilded Age: Plain Talk about Some Recent Criticism and the National Tradition." *SR* 45 (Ja-Mr 37) 41-54.
Thayer, W. R. "Pen Portraiture in Seventeenth Century Colonial Historians." *PAAS* ns 31 (Ap 21) 61-9.
Thompson, A. R. "Back from Nature." *Un Calif Chron* 32 (Ap 30) 211-25.
——— "Literature and Irresponsibility." *Am R* 7 (My 36) 192-202.
Thompson, C. M. "Honest Literary Criticism." *Atl* 102 (Ag 08) 179-90.
Thorpe, C. D., and Nelson, N. E. "Criticism in the Twentieth Century: A Bird's-Eye View." *EJ* 36 (Ap 47) 165-73.
Tomlinson, H. M. "Inappropriate to America." *N Y Herald-Tribune Books* (2 Mr 30) 12.

Trilling, Lionel. "Parrington, Mr. Smith and Reality." *PR* 7 (Ja 40) 24-40.
Trowbridge, Hoyt. "Aristotle and the 'New Criticism.'" *SR* 52 (Au 44) 551-2.
Urban, W. M. "The Crisis in Taste." *Atl* 110 (Jl 12) 53-9.
Van Doren, Mark. "Good Critics, Rare and Common." *Nation* 154 (24 Ja 41) 95-6.
Vann, W. H. "On the Liberal in Literature." *SW R* 24 (Jl 39) 472-4.
Wagenknecht, Edward. "Our Changing Literary Temper." *CE* 6 (My 45) 423-30.
Waggoner, H. H. "American Literature Re-Examined." *UKCR* 14 (Wi 47) 114-6.
Walcutt, C. C. "Critic's Taste or Artist's Intention." *UKCR* 12 (Su 46) 278-83.
Ward, Norman. "Novels and Social Science." *Dalhousie R* 26 (O 46) 297-303.
Webster, H. C. "Humanism as the Father Face." *Poetry* 70 (Je 47) 146-50.
West, R. B. "Truth, Beauty, and American Criticism." *UKCR* 14 (Wi 47) 136-48.
Williams, M. L. "The Scholar in Democracy." *Papers Mich Acad Sci, Arts & Letters* 25 (1940) 597-606.
Wilson, Edmund. "Literary Criticism and History." *Atl* 168 (N 41) 610-7.
——— "Notes on Babbitt and More." *NRp* 62 (19 Mr 30) 115-20.
——— "The Rag Bag of the Soul." *Lit R* 3 (1922) 237-8.
——— "Sophocles, Babbitt and Freud." *NRp* 65 (3 D 30) 68-70.
Winters, Yvor. "A Protest." *Am Schol* 19 (Sp 50) 227-30.
Wylie, I. A. R. "As One Writer to Another." *Harper's* 174 (F 37) 268-74.
Zabel, M. D. "The Condition of American Criticism." *EJ* (col ed) 18 (Je 39) 417-28.
Zinsser, Hans. "The Deadly Arts." *Atl* 154 (N 34) 530-43.

LITERARY HISTORY. Anon. "American New Writing." *TLS* no 2411 (17 Ap 48) 218.
——— Twenty-fifth Anniversary Issue. *SRL* 32 (6 Ag 49).
——— "Where We Stood in 1832." *Lit Dig* 114 (9 Jl 32) 17-8.
——— "Young U. S. Writers: A Refreshing Group of Newcomers on the Literary Scene Is Ready to Tackle Almost Anything." *Life* 22 (2 Je 47) 75-6, 78.
Abbott, E. H. "Being Little in Cambridge." *Ladies' Home J* 53 (Ja, F, Mr 36) 8-9, 43, 45; 14, 87-8, 90, 92; 54, 148-51.
Adair, Douglass. "The Authorship of the Disputed Federalist Papers." *WMQ* 1 (Ap, Je 44) 97-122, 235-64.
Adkins, N. F. "James Fenimore Cooper and the Bread and Cheese Club." *MLN* 47 (F 32) 71-9.
Alden, W. L. "Literary New York in the Sixties." *Putnam's* 3 (F 08) 554-8.
Aldridge, J. W. "The New Generation of Writers." *Harper's* 195 (N 47) 423-32.
Astre, G. A. "Les Origines de lettres américaines." *Critique* (Paris) 5 (Mr 49) 206-14.
Barzun, Jacques. "Twenty-five Years of American Sensuality." *Nation* 166 (27 Mr 48) 355-7.
Beers, H. A. "The Connecticut Wits." *YR* ns 2 (Ja 13) 242-56.
——— "Literature and the Civil War." *Atl* 88 (D 01) 749-60.
Bentley, E. "A Note on American Culture." *Am Schol* 18 (Sp 49) 173-84.
Betsky, Seymour. "Intellectual Life in the U. S. A.: Comment and Reply." *Scrutiny* 15 (D 48) 278-88.
Boas, George. "The Literature of Diversity." *NRp* 121 (17 O 49) 26-9.
Bodenheim, Maxwell. "On Literary Groups." *Am Merc* 3 (O 24) 206-8.
Boyd, E. A. "American Literature or Colonial?" *Freeman* 1 (17 Mr 20) 13-5.
Bragdon, Claude. "The Purple Cow Period." *Bkm* 69 (Jl 29) 475-8.
Brooks, Van Wyck. "Dr. Holmes's Boston." *Harper's* 181 (Jl 40) 138-46.
——— "On Creating a Usable Past." *Dial* 64 (11 Ap 18) 337-41.
——— "Toward an American Culture." *Seven Arts* 1 (Mr 17) 537-45.
Buffinton, A. H. "The Massachusetts Experiment of 1630." *PCSM* 32 (1937) 308-20.

Burch, E. E. "The Sources of New England Democracy, a Controversial Statement in Parrington's *Main Currents in American Thought.*" *AL* 1 (My 29) 115-30.
Campbell, Killis. "Recent Additions to American Literary History." *SP* 33 (Jl 36) 534-43.
Canby, H. S. "Anon Is Dead." *Am Merc* 8 (My 26) 79-84.
——— "Death of the Iron Virgin." *SRL* 30 (12 Ap 47) 11-3, 65.
——— "Footnotes to 1949." *SRL* 32 (6 Ag 49) 17-9, 175-6.
Carpenter, F. I. "The Genteel Tradition: A Re-Interpretation." *NEQ* 15 (S 42) 427-43.
Carter, Everett. "The Haymarket Affair in Literature." *Am Q* 2 (Fl 50) 280-8.
Cassady, E. E. "Muckraking in the Gilded Age." *AL* 13 (My 41) 134-41.
Chamberlain, John. "Critic Finds New Authors Work Things Out in Their Own Ways." *Life* 22 (2 Je 47) 81-2.
Clark, H. H. "Factors to Be Investigated in American Literary History from 1789-1800." *EJ* 23 (Je 34) 481-7.
——— "Suggestions Concerning a History of American Literature." *AL* 12 (N 40) 268-96.
Cowley, Malcolm. "Limousines on Grub Street." *NRp* 115 (4 N 46) 588-92.
——— "The Literary Atmosphere of Two Eras." *N Y Herald-Tribune Books* 26 (25 S 49) 6.
——— "'Not Men': A Natural History of American Naturalism." *KR* 9 (Sp 47) 414-35.
Craven, Thomas. "The Decline of Illustration." *Am Merc* 12 (O 27) 204-7.
Dangerfield, George. "The Insistent Past." *NAR* 143 (Sp 37) 137-52.
Davis, R. B. "The Early American Lawyer and the Profession of Letters." *HLQ* 12 (F 49) 191-206.
DeCasseres, Benjamin. "Five Portraits on Galvanized Iron." *Am Merc* 9 (D 26) 394-9.
Dell, Floyd. "Rents Were Low in Greenwich Village." *Am Merc* 65 (D 47) 662-8.
Dempsey, David. "Literature between Two Wars—and a Glance Ahead." *N Y Times Book R* (18 Ag 46) 7.
Deutsch, Babette. "The Plight of the Poet." *Am Merc* 8 (My 26) 66-8.
Dondore, Dorothy. "Points of Contact Between History and Literature in the Mississippi Valley." *Miss Valley Hist R* 11 (S 24) 227-36.
Drury, John. "Literary Landmarks of Chicago." *Chicago Schools J* 30 (N-D 48) 89-93.
Duffy, Richard. "When They Were Twenty-one." *Bkm* 37 (My 13) 296-304; 38 (Ja 14) 521-31.
Eaton, A. J. "The American Movement for International Copyright: 1837-1860." *Lib Q* 15 (Ap 45) 95-122.
Eisinger, C. T. "Land and Loyalty: Literary Expressions of Agrarian Nationalism in the Seventeenth and Eighteenth Centuries." *AL* 21 (My 49) 160-78.
Farrar, John. "The Condition of American Writing." *CE* 11 (O 49) 1-8.
Farrell, J. T. "The End of a Literary Decade." *Am Merc* 48 (D 39) 408-14.
Flesch, Rudolph. "What the War Did to Prose." *SRL* 32 (13 Ag 49) 6-7, 36-7.
Ford, F. M. "A Stage in American Literature." *Bkm* 74 (D 31) 375-6.
Freemantle, Anne. "World Literature at Mid-Century: I. The American Novel." *United Nations World* 4 (Ja 50) 60-2.
Friederich, W. P. "Die nordamerikanische Literatur zwischen zwei Kriegen." *N Y Staatszeitung und Herold (Sonntagsblatt)* (13 Ja, 10 F, 7 Ap 46).
——— "North American Literature between Two Wars." *N Y Staatszeitung und Herold* (5 My, 9 Je, 14 Jl, 18 Ag, 29 S, 10 N 46).
Friedman, L. M. "Jews in Early American Literature." *More Books* 17 (D 42) 455-74.
Gilman, Arthur. "Atlantic Dinners and Diners." *Atl* 100 (N 07) 646-57.

Glicksberg, C. I. "The Problem of Evil in Modern Literature." *Sw R* 32 (Au 47) 353-9.
Hale, E. E. "The Awakening." *Reader* 5 (Ja 05) 247-50.
——— "The Knickerbockers." *Reader* 5 (D 04) 121-9.
Harkness, R. E. E. "America's Heritage of Colonial Culture." *Crozer Q* 19 (O 42) 278-91.
Harrington, F. H. "Literary Aspects of American Anti-Imperialism, 1898-1902." *NEQ* 10 (D 37) 650-67.
Hatcher, Harlan. "The Second Lost Generation." *EJ* 25 (O 36) 621-31.
——— "The Torches of Violence." *EJ* 23 (F 34) 91-9.
Heilman, R. B. "Footnotes on Literary History." *So R* 6 (Sp 41) 759-70.
Henneman, J. B. "The Trend of Modern Literature." *SR* 11 (Ap 03) 161-8.
Herrick, Robert. "The War and American Literature." *Dial* 63 (3 Ja 18) 7-8.
Herzberg, M. J. "1946, Year of Doubt." *EJ* 36 (Mr 47) 109-15.
——— "Literary 1947 in Retrospect." *CE* 9 (Mr 48) 293-9; EJ 37 (Mr 48) 109-14.
Hicks, Granville. "The Fighting Decade." *SRL* 22 (6 Jl 40) 3-5, 16-7.
——— "The Twenties in American Literature." *Nation* 130 (2 F 30) 183-5.
Higginson, T. W. "Literature, 1857-1907." *Atl* 100 (N 07) 606-12.
——— "The Sunny Side of the Transcendental Period." *Atl* 93 (Ja 04) 6-14.
Hockett, H. C. "The Literary Motive in the Writing of History." *Miss Valley Hist R* 12 (Mr 26) 469-82.
Hodder, F. H. "Propaganda as a Source of American History." *Miss Valley Hist R* 9 (Je 22) 3-18.
Hoffman, F. J. "Philistine and Puritan in the 1920's." *Am Q* 1 (Fl 49) 247-63.
Hofstader, Richard. "Parrington and the Jeffersonian Tradition." *JHI* 2 (O 41) 391-400.
Holt, W. S. "The Idea of Scientific History in America." *JHI* 1 (Je 40) 352-62.
Howe, W. D. "Beginnings of American Literature." *Reader* 4 (O, N 04) 589-95, 715-20.
Hubach, R. R. "Nineteenth-Century Literary Visitors to the Hoosier State: A Chapter in American Cultural History." *Ind Mag Hist* 45 (Mr 49) 39-50.
Hubbell, J. B. "The Old South in Literary Histories." *SAQ* 48 (Jl 49) 452-67.
Hyman, S. E. "The Deflowering of New England." *Hudson R* 2 (Wi 50) 600-12.
Johnson, G. W. "American Writing, American Life." *N Y Times Book R* (1 My 49) 1, 17.
Jones, H. M. "The Colonial Impulse." *PAPS* 90 (1946) 131-61.
——— "Desiderata in Colonial Literary History." *PCSM* 32 (1937) 428-39.
——— "Literature and Orthodoxy in Boston after the Civil War." *Am Q* 1 (Su 49) 149-65.
——— "The Literature of Virginia in the Seventeenth Century." *Memoirs Am Acad Arts & Sci* (1946) 3-47.
Josephson, Matthew. "Historians and Myth-Makers." *VQR* 16 (Wi 40) 92-109.
Kane, H. F. "Notes on Early Pennsylvania Promotion Literature." *PMHB* 63 (Ap 39) 144-68.
Kimball, A. R. "The New Provincialism." *Atl* 88 (Ag 01) 258-62.
Knight, G. C. "The 'Pastry' Period in Literature." *SRL* 27 (16 D 44) 5-7, 22-3.
Knight, G. W. "On Eighteenth-Century Nationalism." *English* 3 (D 41) 243-6.
Kraus, Michael. "America and the Utopian Ideal in the Eighteen Century." *Miss Valley Hist R* 22 (Mr 36) 487-504.
Krishnamachari, V. "Transcendentalism in America." *Calcutta R* 116 (Je 50) 161-5.
Krutch, J. W. "The Usable Past." *Nation* 138 (14 F 34) 191-2.
Lawton, W. C. "Cosmopolitan Tendencies in American Literature." *SR* 14 (Ap 06) 149-60.
Levin, Harry. "America Discovers Bohemia." *Atl* 180 (S 47) 68-75.
Lillard, R. G. "A Year of Western Nonfiction." *PS* 2 (Au 48) 388-98.

Lipscomb, H. C. "Humanistic Culture in Early Virginia." *Classical* J 43 (Ja 48) 203-8.
MacLeish, Archibald. "The New Age and the New Writers." *YR* ns 12 (Ja 23) 314-21.
Marshall, R. P. "A Mythical Mayflower Competition: North Carolina Literature in the Half-Century Following the Revolution." *N C Hist R* 27 (Ap 50) 178-92.
Matthews, Brander. "The Centenary of a Question." *Scribner's* 67 (Ja 20) 41-6.
——— "Literature in the New Century." *NAR* 179 (O 04) 513-25.
Meeks, L. H. "The Lyceum in the Middle West." *Ind Mag Hist* 29 (Je 33) 87-95.
Millett, F. B. "American Literature (1940-5)." *English* 6 (Sp 47) 170-6.
Mims, Edwin. "The Renaissance in New England." *SAQ* 1 (Ap 02) 224-38; 2 (Ja 03) 10-22.
Monaghan, Jay. "Literary Opportunities in Pioneer Times." *J Ill State Hist Soc* 33 (D 43) 412-37.
Moore, C. L. "The Interregnum in American Literature." *Dial* 48 (1 My 10) 307-9.
——— "Tendencies of American Literature at the Close of the Century." *Dial* 29 (1 N 00) 295-7.
Muir, A. F. "Patents and Copyrights in the Republic of Texas." *J So Hist* 12 (My 46) 204-22.
Mumford, Lewis. "A Footnote to a Decade." *N Y Herald-Tribune Books* 140 (9 Ag 31) 1, 4.
Munson, G. B. "The Fledgling Years, 1916-24." *SR* 40 (Ja 32) 24-54.
Murray, M. R. "The 1870's in American Literature." *AS* 1 (Mr 26) 323-8.
Paine, Gregory. "American Literature a Hundred and Fifty Years Ago." *SP* 42 (Jl 45) 382-402.
Parr, Johnstone. "John Rastell's Geographical Knowledge of America." *PQ* 27 (Jl 48) 229-40.
Parrott, L. M., Jr. "The Literary Scene." *Theatre Arts* 33 (S 49) 48-9, 105-7.
Pattee, F. L. "Anthologies of American Literature before 1861." *Colophon* 4 (Mr 34) Pt 16.
——— "Call for a Literary Historian." *Am Merc* 2 (Je 24) 134-40.
——— "The Journalization of American Literature." *Unpopular R* 7 (Ja-Mr 17) 374-94.
Payne, W. M. "Three Centuries of American Literature." *Atl* 87 (Mr 01) 411-8.
Pearce, T. M. "American Traditions and Our Histories of Literature." *AL* 14 (N 42) 276-84.
Pelzer, Louis, *et al.* "Projects in American History and Culture." *Miss Valley Hist R* 31 (Mr 45) 499-522.
Putnam, Samuel. "Background to Flight." *Briarcliff Q* 3 (Jl 46) 100-17.
Quaife, M. M. "The Dictionary of American Biography." *Miss Valley Hist R* 17 (Je 30) 116-22.
Quinn, A. H. "American Literature and American Politics." *PAAS* 54 (1945) 59-112.
——— "The Passing of a Literary Era." *SRL* 1 (21 Mr 25) 1-2.
——— "Philadelphia: The Birthplace of the Arts in America." *Inquirer* (15 S 46) 1, 8.
——— "Pilgrim and Puritan in Literature." *Scribner's* 67 (My 20) 571-81.
——— "Some Phases of the Supernatural in American Literature." *PMLA* 25 (1910) 114.
——— "The Spirit of Independence as Revealed in the Letters of the Time." *Scribner's* 80 (Jl 26) 17-24.
Randall, J. G. "The Blundering Generation." *Miss Valley Hist R* 27 (Je 40) 3-28.
Richardson, L. N. "Men of Letters and the Hayes Administration." *NEQ* 15 (Mr 42) 110-41.
Rodabaugh, J. H. "A Decade of Reform." *SRL* 28 (6 Ja 45) 24-5.

Rose, L. A. "Shortcomings of 'Muckraking in the Gilded Age.'" *AL* 14 (My 42) 161-4.
Sachse, W. L. "The Migration of New Englanders to England, 1640-1660." *AHR* 53 (Ja 48) 251-78.
Sanborn, F. B. "A Concord Note-Book." *Critic* 47 (Je, Jl, Ag, S, N 05) 76-81, 121-8, 267-72, 349-56, 444-51; 48 (F, Mr, Ap, My 06) 154-60, 251-7, 338-50, 409-13; 49 (S 06) 273-81.
Schlesinger, A. M. "Social History in American Literature." *YR* 18 (S 28) 135-47.
Schlesinger, A. M., Jr. "Jackson and Literature." *NRp* 114 (27 My 46) 765-8.
Schneider, H. W. "A Century of Romantic Imagination in America." *Philos R* 56 (Jl 47) 351-6.
Sedgwick, Ellery. "Second Growth in New England." *SRL* 26 (22 My 43) 10-2.
Sellers, M. P. "New England in American Colonial Literature." *N E Mag* ns 28 (Mr 03) 100-7.
Shafer, B. C. "The American Heritage of Hope, 1865-1940." *Miss Valley Hist R* 37 (D 50) 427-50.
Smith, T. M. "Feminism in Philadelphia, 1790-1850." *PMHB* 68 (Jl 44) 243-68.
Spencer, B. T. "A National Literature, 1837-1855." *AL* 8 (My 36) 125-59.
——— "A National Literature: Post-Civil War Decade." *MLQ* 4 (Mr 43) 71-86.
Spender, Stephen. "Den amerikanske författarens situation." *Prisma* (Stockholm) 2 (1949) 3-15.
Spiller, R. E. "Critical Standards in the American Romantic Movement." *CE* 8 (Ap 47) 344-52.
——— "The Task of the Historian of American Literature." *SR* 43 (Mr 31) 70-9.
Stearns, B. M. "The Literary Treatment of Bacon's Rebellion in Virginia." *VMHB* 52 (Jl 44) 163-79.
Stegner, Wallace. "The Anxious Generation." *CE* 10 (Ja 49) 183-8.
Stewart, Randall. "American Literature between the Wars." *SAQ* 44 (O 45) 371-83.
——— "Puritan Literature and the Flowering of New England." *WMQ* 3 (Jl 46) 319-42.
Streeter, R. E. "Association Psychology and Literary Nationalism in the *North American Review*." *AL* 17 (N 45) 243-54.
Swift, Lindsay. "Our Literary Diplomats." *Book Buyer* 20 (My, Je, Jl 00) 284-91, 364-73, 440-9.
Taylor, W. F. "In Behalf of the Gilded Age." *CE* 6 (O 44) 13-7.
——— "That Gilded Age!" *SR* 45 (Ja-Mr 37) 41-54.
Trilling, Lionel. "Contemporary American Literature in Its Relation to Ideas." *Am Q* 1 (Fl 49) 195-208.
Van Doren, Carl. "The Flower of Puritanism." *Nation* 111 (8 D 20) 649-50.
——— "The Soil of the Puritans." *Century* 105 (F 23) 629-36.
Waggoner, H. H. "American Literature Re-Examined." *UKCR* 14 (Wi 47) 114-6.
Wells, B. W. "Nineteenth Century Literature—A Survey." *Book Buyer* 21 (O 00) 203-8.
Wood, Clement. "The Story of Greenwich Village." *Haldeman-Julius Q* 5 (O 26) 169-85.
Woodberry, G. E. "Beginnings of American Literature." *Harper's* 105 (Jl 02) 232-8.
——— "A Century of Achievement in American Literature." *Harper's W* 44 (17 N 00) 1079-80.
——— "Knickerbocker Era of American Letters." *Harper's* 105 (O 02) 677-83.
——— "The Literary Age of Boston." *Harper's* 106 (F 03) 424-30.
Wright, L. B. "The Classical Tradition in Colonial Virginia." *PBSA* 33 (1939) 85-97.
——— "Literature in the Colonial South." *HLQ* 10 (My 47) 297-316.
——— "Materials for the Study of the Civilization of Virginia." *PULC* 10 (N 48) 3-15.
Wyllie, J. C. "A West Virginia Broadside." *PBSA* 42 (4 Q 48) 322-3.

Yutang, Lin. "Do American Writers Shun Happiness?" *SRL* 33 (15 Jl 50) 7-8, 33.

NEGRO. Bennett, M. W. "Negro Poets." *Negro Hist Bul* 9 (My 46) 171-2, 191.

Billups, E. P. "Some Principles for the Representation of Negro Dialect in Fiction." *Texas R* 8 (Ja 23) 99-123.

Bland, Edward. "Racial Bias and Negro Poetry." *Poetry* 63 (Mr 44) 328-33.

——— "Social Forces Shaping the Negro Novel." *Negro Q* 1 (1945) 241-8.

Bonham, M. L., Jr. "A Rare Abolitionist Document." *Miss Valley Hist R* 8 (D 21) 266-73.

Bontemps, Arna. "The James Weldon Johnson Memorial Collection of Negro Arts and Letters." *Yale Un Lib Gaz* 18 (O 43) 19-26.

——— "Special Collections of Negroana." *Lib Q* 14 (Jl 44) 187-206.

Brawley, Benjamin. "The Negro in American Fiction." *Dial* 60 (11 My 16) 445-50.

——— "The Negro in American Literature." *Bkm* 56 (O 22) 137-41.

——— "The Promise of Negro Literature." *J Negro Hist* 29 (Ja 34) 53-9.

Brewer, J. M. "American Negro Folklore." *Phylon* 6 (4 Q 45) 354-61.

Brewster, Dorothy. "From Phillis Wheatly to Richard Wright." *Negro Q* 1 (1945) 80-3.

Brown, S. A. "The American Race Problem as Reflected in American Literature." *J Negro Educ* 8 (Jl 39) 275-90.

——— "Negro Character as Seen by White Authors." *J Negro Educ* 2 (Ap 33) 179-203.

Brown, Sterling. "The Negro Author and His Publishers." *Negro Q* 1 (1945) 7-20.

Bullock, Penelope. "The Mulatto in American Fiction." *Phylon* 6 (1 Q 45) 78-82.

Butcher, Philip. "In Print . . . Our Raceless Writers." *Opportunity* 26 (Su 48) 113-5.

Calverton, V. F. "The Negro and American Culture." *SRL* 22 (21 S 40) 3-4, 17-8.

Chamberlain, John. "The Negro as Writer." *Bkm* 70 (F 30) 603-11.

Chestnutt, C. W. "Post-Bellum—Pre-Harlem." *Colophon* 2 (F 31) Pt 5.

Cook, Mercer. "Edouard Lefebre de Laboulaye and the Negro." *J Negro Hist* 18 (Jl 33) 246-55.

Damon, S. F. "The Negro in Early American Songsters." *PBSA* 28 (1934) 132-63.

Dempsey, David. "Uncle Tom's Ghost and the Literary Abolitionists." *AR* 4 (Fl 46) 442-8.

DeRobertis, D. "Poesia negra americana." *La Fiera Letteraria* (Italy) no 30 (9 O 49) 2.

DuBois, W. E. B. "The Negro in American Literature and Art." *Annals Am Acad Pol & Soc Sci* 49 (S 13) 233-7.

Eaton, Clement. "Mob Violence in the Old South." *Miss Valley Hist R* 29 (D 42) 351-70.

Elgström, A. L. "Sångare i sorg." *Samtid och Framtid* (Stockholm) 2 (My 45) 294-301.

Ellison, Richard. "Recent Negro Fiction." *New Masses* 40 (5 Ag 41) 22-4.

Funkhouser, Myrtle. "Folklore of the American Negro." *Bul Bibl* 16 (Ja-Ap, My-Ag, S-D 37, My-Ag, S-D 38, Ja-Ap 39) 28-9, 49-51, 72-3, 108-10, 136-7, 159-60.

Gaines, F. P. "The Racial Bar Sinister in American Romance." *SAQ* 25 (O 26) 396-402.

Glicksberg, C. I. "The Furies in Negro Fiction." *WR* 13 (Wi 49) 107-14.

——— "The Negro Cult of the Primitive." *AR* 4 (Sp 44) 47-55.

——— "Negro Fiction in America." *SAQ* 45 (O 46) 477-88.

——— "Negro Poets and the American Tradition." *AR* 6 (Su 46) 243-53.

Gloster, H. G. "The Negro Writer and the Southern Scene." *So Packet* 4 (Ja 48) 1-3.

Gordon, Eugene. "The Negro Press." *Am Merc* 8 (Je 26) 207-15.

Gould, Jan. "The Negro in Show Business." *AR* 6 (Su 46) 254-64.

Grant, G. C. "The Negro in Dramatic Art." *J Negro Hist* 17 (Ja 32) 19-29.

Halper, Albert. "Whites Writing Up the Blacks." *Dial* 76 (Ja 29) 29-30.
Harrison, R. C. "The Negro as Interpretor of His Own Folk Songs." *Pub Texas Folk-Lore Soc* 5 (1926) 144-53.
Hill, M. C., & Foreman, P. B. "The Negro in the United States: A Bibliography." *Sw J* 2 (Su 46) 225-30.
Hubbell, J. B. "A Persimmon Beer Dance in Ante-bellum Virginia." *SLM* ns 5 (N-D 43) 461-6.
Huggins, Kathryn. "Aframerican Fiction." *SLM* 3 (Jl 41) 315-20.
Hughes, Langston. "Harlem Literati in the Twenties." *SRL* 22 (22 Je 40) 13-4.
Isaacs, J. R. "The Negro in the American Theatre." *Theatre Arts* 26 (Ag 42) 492-543.
Jefferson, M. M. "The Negro on Broadway, 1945-1946." *Phylon* 7 (2 Q 46) 185-96.
Johnson, J. W. "The Dilemma of the Negro Author." *Am Merc* 15 (D 28) 477-81.
——— "Race Prejudice and the Negro Artist." *Harper's* 157 (N 28) 769-76.
Jones, Joseph. "The 'Distress'd' Negro in English Magazine Verse." *Un Texas Stud Eng* 17 (1937) 88-106.
Kendall, J. S. "New Orleans Negro Ministrels." *La Hist Q* 30 (Ja 47) 128-48.
Koch, F. H. "A Gullah Negro Drama." *SLM* 2 (Ap 40) 236-7.
Krapp, G. P. "The English of the Negro." *Am Merc* 2 (Je 24) 190-5.
Lash, J. S. "The American Negro and American Literature: A Check List of Significant Commentaries." *Bul Bibl* 19 (S-D 46) 12-5.
——— "The American Negro and American Literature: A Check List of Significant Commentaries. Part II." *Bul Bibl* 19 (Ja 47) 33-6.
——— "On Negro Literature." *Phylon* 6 (3 Q 45) 240-7.
——— "The Study of Negro Literary Expression." *Negro Hist Bul* 9 (Je 46) 207-11.
——— "What Is Negro Literature?" *CE* 9 (O 47) 37-42.
Law, R. A. "Mrs. Peterkin's Negroes." *Sw R* 14 (Jl 29) 455-61.
Lawson, H. D. "The Negro in American Drama." *Bul Bibl* 16 (Ja, My 40) 7-8, 27-30.
Lewis, Theophilus. "The Frustration of Negro Art." *Cath World* 155 (Ap 42) 51-7.
Locke, Alain. "Broadway and the Negro Drama." *Theatre Arts* 25 (O 41) 745-50.
——— "Der Neger in der amerikanischen Kultur." *Prisma* 6 (Ap 47) 10-2.
——— "The Negro and the American Stage." *Theatre Arts* 10 (F 26) 112-20.
——— "The Negro Minority in American Literature." *EJ* 35 (Je 46) 315-9.
Lomax, Alan. "'Sinful' Songs of the Southern Negro: Experience in Collecting Secular Folk Music." *Sw R* 19 (Wi 34) 105-31.
McDowell, Tremaine. "The Negro in the Southern Novel prior to 1850." *JEGP* 25 (4 Q 26) 455-73.
Marley, H. P. "The Negro in Recent Southern Literature." *SAQ* 27 (Ja 28) 29-41.
Morse, G. C. "Broadway Re-Discovers the Negro." *Negro Hist Bul* 9 (My 46) 173-6, 189-91.
Nathan, Hans. "Charles Mathews, Comedian, and the American Negro." *SFQ* 10 (S 46) 191-7.
Oberstreet, H. A. "Images and the Negro." *SRL* 27 (26 Ag 44) 5-6.
——— "The Negro Writer as Spokesman." *SRL* 28 (2 S 44) 5-6, 26-7.
Pivano, E. "Letteratura negro americana." *La Rassegna d'Italia* (N 48).
Porter, Dorothy. "A Library on the Negro." *Am Schol* 7 (Wi 38) 115-7.
Pride, A. S. "Negro Newspaper Files and Their Microfilming." *JQ* 24 (Je 47) 131-4.
Redding, J. S. "American Negro Literature." *Am Schol* 18 (Sp 49) 137-48.
——— "The Negro Author: His Publisher, His Public and His Purse." *Pub W* 147 (24 Mr 45) 1284-8.
Rollins, H. E. "The Negro in the Southern Short Story." *SR* 24 (Ja 16) 42-60.
Simms, H. H. "A Critical Analysis of Abolition Literature 1830-1840." *J So Hist* 6 (Ag 40) 368-82.

Spingarn, A. B. "Books by Negro Authors in 1945." *Crisis* 53 (F 46) 46-7, 59-60.
Tandy, J. R. "Pro-Slavery Propaganda in American Fiction of the Fifties." *SAQ* 21 (Ja, Ap 22) 41-50, 170-8.
Tate, Allen. "Preface to *Libretto for the Republic of Liberia*." *Poetry* 76 (Jl 50) 216-28.
Turner, L. D. "Anti-Slavery Sentiment in American Literature Prior to 1865." *J Negro Hist* 14 (O 29) 371-492.
White, N. I. "American Negro Poetry." *SAQ* 20 (O 21) 304-22.
——— "Racial Feeling in Negro Poetry." *SAQ* 21 (Ja 22) 14-29.
Wilson, E. E. "The Joys of Being a Negro." *Atl* 97 (F 06) 245-50.
Wright, Richard. "Littérature noire américaine." *Les Temps Modernes* 3 (Ag 48) 193-221.

NEWSPAPERS AND PERIODICALS. Anon. "An Anniversary Retrospect." *Harper's* 121 (Je 10) 38-45.
——— "The Atlantic's Pleasant Days in Tremont Street." *Atl* 100 (N 07) 716-20.
——— "Check List of Newspapers Published in New York City Contained in the New York Public Library, December 31st, 1900." *BNYPL* 5 (Ja 01) 20-30.
——— "Is An Honest Newspaper Possible? By a New York Editor." *Atl* 102 (O 08) 441-7.
——— "The Limbo of the Magazines." *Freeman* 1 (28 Jl 20) 461-3.
——— "Lists of New England Magazines, 1743-1800." *PCSM* 13 (1911) 69-74.
——— "Little Magazines, What Now?" *NRp* 104 (31 Mr 41) 424.
——— "Magazine Activity." *Lit Dig* 120 (O 35) 28.
——— "Ninety Years On." *Living Age* 346 (My 34) 198-9.
——— "Our Little Magazines." *Pulse of the Nation* 1 (D 35) 13-5.
——— "Philadelphische Zeitung: The First German Newspaper Published in America." *PMHB* 24 (1902) 90-2.
——— "The Problem of the Associated Press, by an Observer." *Atl* 114 (Jl 14) 132-7.
——— "Sell the Papers! The Malady of American Jouralism." *Harper's* 151 (Je 25) 1-9.
——— "The Writer Celebrated Two Anniversaries." *Pub W* 151 (12 Ap 47) 2017-8.
Abrams, R. H. "The Copperhead Newspapers and the Negro." *J Negro Hist* 20 (Ap 35) 131-52.
Acheson, Sam. "Founding the News: Prelude to Journalistic History." *Sw R* 23 (Sp 38) 436-49.
Admari, Ralph. "Bonner and 'The Ledger.'" *Am Book Coll* 6 (My-Je 35) 176-93.
Aikman, Duncan. "The Springfield Republican." *Am Merc* 8 (My 26) 85-92.
Albjerg, M. H. "The New York *Herald* as a Factor in Reconstruction." *SAQ* 46 (Ap 47) 204-11.
——— "Times May Change But Does the *New York Times?*" *SAQ* 28 (Ap 29) 165-73.
Alden, H. M. "Magazine Writing and Literature." *NAR* 179 (S 04) 340-56.
Aldridge, A. O. "The Poet's Corner in Early Georgia Newspapers." *Ga R* 3 (Sp 49) 45-55.
Alger, G. W. "Sensational Journalism and the Law." *Atl* 91 (F 03) 145-51.
Allen, Charles. "The Advance Guard." *SR* 51 (S 43) 410-29.
——— "American Little Magazines." *Am Prefaces* 3 (N 37, Ja, Mr, Je 38) 28-32, 54-9, 94-6, 136-40; 4 (My 39) 115-8, 125-8.
——— "American Little Magazines, 1912-1944." *Ind Quar for Bkm* 1 (Ap 45) 43-54.
——— "The Dial." *Un R* 9 (Wi 43) 101-8.
——— "Director Munson's Secession." *Un R* 5 (Wi 38) 101-8.
——— "The Fugitive." *SAQ* 43 (O 44) 382-9.
——— "Glebe and Others." *CE* 5 (My 44) 418-23.
Allen, F. L. "The American Magazine Grows Up." *Atl* 180 (N 47) 76-82.

——— "One Hundred Years of Harper's." *Harper's* 201 (O 50) 23-6.
——— "Vocational Journalism." *Harper's* 147 (S 23) 559-61.
———, *et al.* "American Magazines, 1741-1941." *BNYPL* 45 (Je 41) 439-56.
Amacher, R. E. "New Jersey's First Magazine." *JRUL* 12 (D 48) 28-31.
Anderson, Sherwood. "The Country Weekly." *Forum* 85 (Ap 31) 208-13.
——— "New Orleans, *The Double Dealer* and the Modern Movement." *Double Dealer* 3 (Mr 22) 119-26.
Archer, William. "The American Cheap Magazine." *Fortlightly R* 93 (2 My 10) 921-32; *Living Age* 265 (4 Je 10) 579-87.
Arrowsmith, William. "*Partisan Review* and American Writing." *Hudson R* 1 (Wi 49) 526-37.
Asbury, Herbert. "Hearst Comes to Atlanta." *Am Merc* 7 (Ja 26) 87-95.
Auxier, G. W. "Middle Western Newspapers and the Spanish-American War, 1895-1898." *Miss Valley Hist R* 26 (Mr 40) 523-34.
Avary, M. L. "Success—And Dreiser.'" *Colophon* ns 3 (Au 38) 598-604.
Ayer, M. F. "Check-List of Boston Newspapers 1704-1780." *PCSM* 9 (1907).
Bacon, C. F. "College Literature and Journalism." *Critic* 37 (Jl 00) 21-30.
Baker, H. T. "Periodicals and Permanent Literature." *NAR* 212 (D 20) 777-87.
Baldwin, L. F. "Unbound Old Atlantics." *Atl* 100 (N 07) 679-84.
Barry, Iris. "The Ezra Pound Period." *Bkm* 74 (O 31) 159-71.
Beazell, W. P. "Tomorrow's Newspaper." *Atl* 146 (Jl 30) 24-30.
Benet, W. R. "Among the Slicks." *SRL* 11 (23 F 35) 501-2.
Benson, A. B. "The Essays on Frederika Bremer in the *North American Review.*" *PMLA* 41 (S 26) 747-55.
Bernstein, David. "The Little Magazines." *Scholastic* 25 (13 O 34) 10, 13.
Bigelow, D. N. "A Journal of 'Unquestionable' Loyalty." *N Y Hist* 27 (O 46) 444-57.
Billington, R. A. "Maria Monk and Her Influence." *Cath Hist R* 22 (O 36) 283-96.
Bishop, W. W. "Photostatic Productions of Early American Newspapers." *PBSA* 22 (1928) 45-51.
Bixler, Paul. "Little Magazine, What Now?" *AR* 8 (Sp 48) 63-77.
Bliven, Bruce. "Our Changing Journalism." *Atl* 132 (D 23) 743-50.
Blodgett, Marion. "A Little More about Little Magazines." *Lit Rec* 2 (Jl 37) 16-24.
Bolton, C. K. "Social Libraries in Boston." *PCSM* 12 (Ap 09) 332-8.
Botkin, B. A. "*Folk-Say* and *Space.*" *Sw R* 20 (Jl 35) 321-35.
——— "The Paradox of the Little Magazine." *Space* 1 (Ap 35) 113-5.
Boynton, H. W. "The Literary Aspect of Journalism." *Atl* 93 (Je 04) 845-51.
Bragdon, Claude. "The Purple Cow Period." *Bkm* 69 (Jl 29) 475-8.
Branch, E. D. "The Lily and the Bloomer." *Colophon* 3 (D 32) Pt 12.
Brayer, H. O. "Preliminary Guide to Indexed Newspapers in the United States, 1850-1900." *Miss Valley Hist R* 33 (S 46) 237-55.
Brigham, Clarence. "Bibliography of American Newspapers." *PAAS* 23-37 (1913-25) *passim.*
Bronowski, J. "Experiment." *Transition* no 19-20 (Je 30) 707-12.
Brown, Bob. "Them Asses." *Am Merc* 5 (D 33) 403-11.
Brown, H. R. "Elements of Sensibility in the *Massachusetts Magazine.*" *AL* 1 (N 29) 286-96.
——— "Richardson and Sterne in the *Massachusetts Magazine.*" *NEQ* 4 (Ja 32) 65-82.
Busch, N. F. "One Hundred Years of Town and Country." *Life* 21 (23 D 46) 83-90.
Bush, Douglas. "Pale-Eyed Pirates and Happy Journalists." *Bkm* 75 (N 32) 699-702.
Calverton, V. F. "The Decade of Convictions." *Bkm* 71 (Ag 30) 490-6.
Canby, H. S. "The Family Magazine." *NAR* 214 (O 21) 433-41.
Cantwell, Robert. "Little Magazines." *NRp* 79 (25 Jl 34) 295-7.

Cardwell, G. A. "The Influence of Addison and Steele on Charleston Periodicals, 1795-1860." *SP* 35 (Jl 38) 456-70.

——— "The *Quiver* and *Floral Wreath:* Two Rare Charleston Periodicals." *N C Hist R* 16 (O 39) 418-27.

——— "A Newly Discovered Charleston Literary Periodical." *AL* 14 (N 42) 306-8.

Catlin, G. P. "Adventures in Journalism: Detroit Newspapers since 1850." *Mich Hist Mag* 39 (S 45) 342-76.

Chambers, M. M. "Periodicals Covering Foreign Universities." *School & Soc* 68 (6 N 48) 321-3.

Churchill, Allen. "The Awful Disclosures of Maria Monk." *Am Merc* 37 (Ja 36) 94-8.

Clark, T. D. "The Country Newspaper: A Factor in Southern Opinion, 1865-1930." *J So Hist* 14 (F 48) 4-33.

Cleaton, Allen. "The Press in Petticoats." *VQR* 8 (O 32) 494-501.

Clement, E. H. "19th Century Boston Journalism." *N E Mag* ns 35 (N, D 06, Ja, F 07) 276-81, 415-21, 523-8, 707-13; 36 (Mr, My, Je, Jl, Ag 07) 41-9, 321-30, 462-7, 558-63, 729-35.

Cooney, J. P. "Among the Magazines." *Phoenix* 1 (Je-Ag 38) 134-50.

Coryell, Irving. "Josh of the 'Territorial Enterprise.'" *NAR* 243 (Su 37) 287-95.

Cowley, Malcolm. "The Little Magazines Growing Up." *N Y Times Book R* 52 (14 S 47) 5, 35.

——— "Magazine Business: 1910-46." *NRp* 115 (21 O 46) 521-3.

Cross, Wilbur. "The Yale Review Comes of Age." *YR* 21 (S 31) 1-9.

Crowell, C. T. "American Journalism Today." *Am Merc* 2 (Je 24) 197-204.

Cunningham, J. V. "Envoi." *H&H* 6 (O-D 32) 124-30.

——— "The Gyroscope Group." *Bkm* 75 (N 32) 703-8.

Current-Garcia, Eugene. "Newspaper Humor in the Old South, 1835-1855." *Ala R* 2 (Ap 49) 102-21.

Dargan, Marion. "Crime and the Virginia Gazette, 1736-1775." *Un N Mex Bul* 2 (1 My 34) 3-61.

Davidson, L. J. "Colorado's First Magazine." *Colo-Wyo J Letters* 1 (F 39) 47-52.

——— "O. J. Goldrick, Pioneer Journalist." *Colo Mag* 13 (Ja 36) 26-36.

——— "Out West, a Pioneer Weekly and Monthly." *Colo Mag* 14 (Jl 37) 135-42.

Derleth, A. W. "The Cult of Incoherence." *Mod Thinker* 11 (D 32) 612-8.

deRochemont, R. G. "The Tabloids." *Am Merc* 9 (O 26) 187-92.

De Roussy de Sales, Raoul. "Notes on American Newspapers." *Atl* 169 (Ja 37) 28-33.

Dillon, George. "The 'Little Magazine' Gimmick." *Poetry* 71 (O 47) 41-4.

Ditzion, Sidney. "The History of Periodical Literature in the United States." *Bul Bibl* 15 (Ja-Ap, My-Ag 35) 110, 129-33.

Dornbusch, C. E. "Stars and Stripes: Check List of the Several Editions." *BNYPL* 52 (Jl 48) 331-40; 53 (Jl 49) 335-8.

———, & Weeks, A. D. "Yank, the Army Weekly: A Check List." *BNYPL* 54 (Je 50) 272-9.

Drewry, J. E. "American Magazines Today." *SR* 35 (Jl 28) 342-56.

Duncan, J. G. "Literary Content of a Pioneer Michigan Newspaper." *Mich Hist* 33 (S 49) 195-209.

Dupre, Huntley. "The Kentucky Gazette Reports the French Revolution." *Miss Valley Hist R* 26 (S 39) 163-80.

Eastman, Max. "Bunk about Bohemia." *Mod Mo* 8 (My 34) 200-8.

——— "John Reed and the Old *Masses.*" *Mod Mo* 10 (O 36) 19-22, 31.

——— "New Masses for Old." *Mod Mo* 8 (Je 34) 292-300.

Eliot, T. S. "The Idea of a Literary Review." *Criterion* 4 (Ja 26) 1-6.

Elistratova, A. "New Masses." *Int Lit* 1 (1932) 107-14.

Ellison, R. C. "Newspaper Publishing in Frontier Alabama." *JQ* 23 (S 46) 289-301.

Ely-Estorik, Eric, & Fidell, O. H. "The Masses Tradition in Contemporary Literature." *Contempo* 3 (5 Ap 33) 1-3, 8.
Emmart, A. D. "The Limitations of American Magazines." *Mod Q* 1 (D 23) 17-26.
Evans, Oliver. "The Fugitives." *Commonweal* 40 (30 Je 44) 250-4.
Everett, Edward. "Jeffersonian Democracy and the *Tree of Liberty*, 1800-1803." *W Penn Hist Mag* 32 (Je 49) 11-44.
Fahrney, R. R. "Horace Greeley and the New York Tribune in the Civil War." *N Y Hist* 16 (O 35) 415-35.
Field, A. G. "The Press in Western Pennsylvania to 1812." *W Penn Hist Mag* 20 (D 37) 231-64.
Field, Ben. "Charles Fletcher Lummus." *Overland Mo* 87 (Jl 29) 197-203.
Fisher, Brooks. "The Newspaper Industry." *Atl* 89 (Je 02) 745-53.
Flanagan, J. T. "Early Literary Periodicals of Minnesota." *Minn Hist* 26 (D 45) 293-311.
Flanders, R. B. "Newspapers and Periodicals in the Washington Memorial Library." *N C Hist R* 7 (Ap 30) 220-3.
Fletcher, J. G. "Little Reviews: Yesterday and Today." *Space* 1 (D 34) 84-6.
Ford, E. H. "Colonial Pamphleteers." *JQ* 13 (Ja 36) 24-36.
——— "Southern Minnesota Pioneer Journalism." *Minn Hist* 27 (Mr 46) 1-20.
———, & Tyler, Parker. "Blues." *SR* 39 (Ja-Mr 31) 62-7.
Frese, J. R. "Some Notes on the 'United States Catholic Miscellany.'" *Rec Am Catholic Hist Soc Philadelphia* 55 (D 44) 389-400.
Friend, J. W. "Innocents Abroad." *Double Dealer* 4 (O 22) 201-4.
———, Moore, Marianne, Macleod, Norman, McAlmon, Robert, Frank, Waldo, & Munson, Graham. "Symposium on the Little Magazines." *Golden Goose* 3 (1951) 11-30.
Gale, Zona. "Editors of the Younger Generation." *Critic* 44 (1904) 318.
Gallacher, S. A. "Folklore in Periodical Literature." *JAF* 63 (Jl-S 50) 368-73.
Gannett, Lewis. "A Quarter Century of a Weekly Book Review . . . and of the World." *N Y Herald Tribune Books* 26 (25 S 49) 4-5.
Garrett, Kathryn. "The First Newspaper in Texas: *Gaceta de Texas*." *Sw Hist R* 40 (Ja 37) 200-15.
Garrett, O. H. P. "The Gods Confused." *Am Merc* 12 (N 27) 327-34.
Gavit, Joseph. "American Newspaper Reprints." *BNYPL* 35 (Ap 31) 212-23.
Gilmer, Gertrude. "A Critique of Certain Georgia Ante-Bellum Literary Magazines Arranged Chronologically, and a Checklist." *Ga Hist R* 18 (Je 34) 293-334.
——— "Maryland Magazines—Ante-Bellum, 1793-1861." *Md Hist Mag* 29 (Je 34) 120-31.
Gleason, E. G. "Newspapers of the Panhandle of Oklahoma." *Chron Okla* 19 (Je 41) 141-61.
Gohdes, Clarence. "*The Western Messenger* and *The Dial*." *SP* 26 (Ja 29) 67-84.
Graham, Walter. "Notes on Literary Periodicals in America before 1800." *W Reserve Un Bul* 20 (1927) 5-27.
——— "Poets of the American Ambulance." *SAQ* 19 (Ja 20) 18-23.
Grasty, C. H. "British and American Newspapers." *Atl* 124 (N 19) 577-91.
Gregory, Horace. "The Unheard of Adventure—Harriet Monroe and Poetry." *Am Schol* 6 (Sp 37) 195-200.
Griffin, M. L. "A Bibliography of New Orleans Magazines." *La Hist Q* 18 (Jl 35) 493-556.
Gross, Belia. "*Freedom's Journal* and *The Rights of All*." *J Negro Hist* 17 (Jl 32) 241-86.
Ham, E. B. "Journalism and the French Survival in New England." *NEQ* 11 (Mr 38) 89-107.
Hamilton, W. P. "The Case for the Newspapers." *Atl* 105 (My 10) 646-54.
Hanighan, F. C. "Vance Thompson and *M'lle New York*." *Bkm* 75 (S 32) 472-81.
Hanna, A. J. "A Confederate Newspaper in Mexico." *J So Hist* 12 (F 46) 67-83.

Hapgood, Hutchins, & Maurice, A. B. "Great Newspapers of the United States." *Bkm* 14 (F 02) 567-84.

Harding, G. L. "The Pacific News." *Colophon* 2 (Je 31) Pt 6.

Harger, C. M. "The Country Editor of Today." *Atl* 99 (Ja 07) 89-96.

——— "Journalism as a Career." *Atl* 107 (F 11) 218-24.

Harper, Allanah. "A Magazine and Some People in Paris." *PR* 9 (Jl-Ag 42) 311-20.

Harrison, J. G. "Nineteenth-Century American Novels on American Journalism." *JQ* 22 (S, D 45) 215-24, 335-45.

Hart, J. D. "Little Magazines and Their Battle." *Hesperian* (Sp 31).

Hartley, L. T. "The Midland." *Iowa J Hist* 47 (O 49) 325-44.

Haskell, D. C. "A Checklist of Newspapers and Official Gazettes in the New York Public Library." *BNYPL* 18 (Jl, Ag, S, O, N 14) 683-722, 793-826, 905-38, 1079-110, 1261-94; 19 (Jl 15) 553-69.

Hemens, R. D. "Magazines That Come Off the Presses." *SRL* 29 (8 Je 46) 11.

Heyl, Lawrence. "Little Magazines." *PULC* 2 (N 40) 21-6.

Higgins, Francis. "'Sniktau,' Pioneer Journalist." *Colo Mag* 5 (1928) 102-8.

Hochmuth, Marie. "In the Periodicals." *QJS* 33 (F 47) 105-13.

Hoeltje, H. H. "Iowa Literary Magazines." *Palimpsest* 11 (F 30) 87-94.

Hoffman, F. J. "The Little Magazines: Portrait of an Age." *SRL* 26 (25 D 43) 3-5.

——— "Research Value of the 'Little Magazine.'" *Col & Res Lib* 6 (S 45) 311-6.

Holden, W. C. "Frontier Journalism in West Texas." *Sw Hist Q* 32 (Ja 29) 206-21.

Hoole, W. S. "The Gilmans and *The Southern Rose*." *N C Hist R* 11 (Ap 34) 116-28.

Horwill, H. W. "The Training of the Journalist." *Atl* 107 (Ja 11) 107-10.

Howard, M. C. "*The Maryland Gazette*, an American Imitator of the *Tatler* and the *Spectator*." *Md Hist Mag* 29 (D 34) 295-8.

Howard, R. W. "Newspaper Mass Production." *NAR* 225 (Ap 28) 420-4.

Howe, M. A. deW. "Books and Nation." *Scribner's* ns 87 (Mr 30) 267-73.

——— "Personality in Journalism." *Atl* 100 (S 07) 419-24.

Howells, W. D. "Recollections of an Atlantic Editorship." *Atl* 100 (N 07) 594-606.

Hughes, R. M. "Inaccurate Numerations of *The Southern Literary Messenger*." *WMQ* 9 (Jl 29) 217.

Irwin, Wallace. "The American Newspaper: A Study of Journalism in Its Relation to the Public." *Collier's* 46 (18 F, 4 Mr 11) 14-7, 18-20.

Jackson, D. K. "An Estimate of the Influence of *The Southern Literary Messenger*, 1834-1864." *SLM* 1 (Ag 39) 508-14.

——— "Letter of Georgia Editors and a Correspondent." *Ga Hist R* 23 (Je 39) 170-6.

James, G. W. "The Founding of the Overland Monthly." *Overland Mo* ns 52 (Jl 08) 3-12.

James, Henry. "The Founding of *The Nation*." *Nation* 101 (8 Jl 15) 44-5.

Jennings, K. Q. "The New American Magazine." *JRUL* 13 (D 49) 29-31.

Jerome, J. K. "When I Was an Editor." *Harper's* 151 (Jl 25) 189-98.

Johnson, Burges. "The Newspaper's Lost Leadership." *NAR* 232 (Jl 31) 65-73.

Johnson, G. W. "Journalism below the Potomac." *Am Merc* 9 (S 26) 77-82.

——— "Newspapers on Guard." *Atl* 169 (F 42) 156-61.

——— "Southern Image-Breakers." *VQR* 4 (O 28) 508-19.

Jolas, Eugène. "Ten Years Transition." *Plastique* 3 (1938) 23-6.

——— "*Transition:* An Epilogue." *Am Merc* 23 (Je 31) 185-92.

Jones, Archer. "The Pulps—A Mirror to Yearning." *NAR* 246 (Au 38) 35-47.

Jordy, W. H. "The Magazines Are Loud." *Nation* 155 (29 S 42) 235-7.

——— "The Slicks Are Scared." *Common Sense* 11 (D 42) 408-10.

Keating, Isabelle. "Reporters Become of Age." *Harper's* 170 (Ap 35) 601-12.

Keidel, G. C. "Early Maryland Magazines." *Md Hist Mag* 28 (Je, S, D 33) 119-37, 244-57, 328-44; 29 (Mr, Je, S, D 34) 25-34, 132-44, 223-36, 310-22; 30 (Je 35) 149-56.
Kennedy, Fronde. "Russell's Magazine." *SAQ* 18 (Ap 19) 125-44.
——— "The Southern Rose-Bud and the Southern Rose." *SAQ* 23 (Ja 24) 10-9.
Kenny, R. W. "The Rhode Island Gazette for 1732." *R I Hist Soc Coll* 25 (O 32) 97-107.
Kimball, A. R. "The Invasion of Journalism." *Atl* 86 (Jl 00) 119-24.
——— "The Profession of a Publicist." *Atl* 92 (D 03) 804-10.
Kirk, Rudolf. "The Spirit of the Fair." *JRUL* 6 (D 42) 30-1.
Kirstein, Lincoln. "The Hound and Horn, 1927-1934." *Harvard Advocate* 121 (Christmas 34) 6-10, 92-4.
Knickerbocker, W. S. "Up from the South." *WR* 13 (Sp 49) 168-78.
Kobre, Sidney. "The First American Newspaper: A Product of Environment." *JQ* 17 (D 40) 335-45.
Konkle, B. A. "Enos Bronson, 1774-1823." *PMHB* 57 (O 33) 355-8.
Kramer, Dale. "The Revolt against the 'Little' Magazines." *Midwest* (Ag 36) 1, 8.
———, & Clark, G. R. "Harold Ross and the New Yorker; A Landscape with Figures." *Harper's* 186 (Ap 43) 510-21.
Lamont, T. W. "Journalism in the Nineties." *SRL* 29 (22 S 46) 13-5.
Larsen, Cedric. "The Rising Tide of Genealogical Publications." *Colophon* ns 3 (Wi 38) 100-2.
Laughlin, James. "The Little Mags: 1934." *Harkness Hoot* 4 (Ap 34) 41-8.
Law, R. A. *"The Texas Review,* 1915-1924." *Sw R* 10 (O 24) 83-90.
Lazarsfeld, P. F., & Wyant, Rowena. "Magazines in 90 Cities—Who Reads What?" *Public Opinion Q* 1 (O 37) 29-41.
Leacock, Stephen. "The British and American Press." *Harper's* 145 (Je 22) 1-9.
Leupp, F. E. "The Waning Power of the Press." *Atl* 105 (F 10) 145-56.
Lodge, H. C. "This 'Review': A Reminiscence." *NAR* 201 (My 15) 749-56.
Lundberg, Ferdinand. "News-Letters: A Revolution in Journalism." *Harper's* 180 (Ap 40) 463-73.
Luxon, N. N. "Niles' Weekly Register—Nineteenth Century News Magazine." *JQ* 18 (S 41) 273-91.
McCausland, Walter. "Some Early Texas Newspapers." *Sw Hist R* 49 (Ja 46) 384-9.
McCloskey, J. C. "The Campaign of Periodicals after the War of 1812 for National American Literature." *PMLA* 50 (Mr 35) 262-73.
——— "A Note on the *Portico.*" *AL* 8 (N 36) 300-4.
McDermott, J. F. "Best Sellers in Early Saint Louis." *School & Soc* 47 (My 38) 673-5.
——— "Everybody Sold Books in Early St. Louis." *Pub W* 132 (Jl 37) 248-50.
——— "The First Bookstore in Saint Louis." *Mid-America* 21 (Jl 39) 206-8.
——— "Louis Richard Cortambert and the First French Newspapers in Saint Louis, 1809-1854." *Bibl Soc of Am Papers* 34 (3Q 40) 221-53.
McDonald, G. P. "A Gift of *The New-York Gazette.*" *BNYPL* 40 (1936) 487-93.
——— "Unrecorded Numbers of *The New-York Gazette.*" *BNYPL* 46 (Jl 42) 685-8.
McKernon, Edward. "Fake News and the Public." *Harper's* 151 (O 25) 528-36.
MacMullen, Margaret. "Pulps and Confessions." *Harper's* 175 (Je 37) 94-102.
McMurtrie, D. C. "Eastern Records of Early Wyoming Newspapers." *Annals Wyo* 15 (Jl 43) 271-8.
——— "The First Texas Newspaper." *Sw Hist Q* 36 (Jl 32) 41-6.
——— "Washington Newspapers, 1852-1890." *Wash Hist Q* 26 (Ja 35) 34-64.
Maddox, N. S. "Literary Nationalism in *Putnam's Magazine,* 1853-1857." *AL* 14 (My 42) 117-25.
Maloney, Russell. "Tilley the Toiler: A Profile of the New Yorker Magazine." *SRL* 30 (30 Ag 47) 7-10, 29-32.

Marbut, F. B. "Early Washington Correspondents: Some Neglected Pioneers." *JQ* 25 (D 48) 369-74.

Markham, J. W. "Some Problems of Early Texas Newspapers." *N Mex Hist R* 22 (O 47) 342-50.

Marraro, H. R. "Rome and the Catholic Church in Eighteenth-Century American Magazines." *Cath Hist R* 32 (Jl 46) 157-89.

Marshall, H. E. "The Story of the Dial." *N Mex Q* 1 (My 31) 147-65.

Martin, Lawrence. "The Genesis of Godey's 'Lady's Book.'" *NEQ* 1 (1928) 41-7.

Matthews, Albert. "Bibliographical Notes to a Check-list of Boston Newspapers, 1704-1780." *PCSM* 9 (1907) 3-62.

——— "Lists of New England Magazines of the Eighteenth Century." *PCSM* 13 (Ja 10) 69-74.

——— "A Projected Harvard Magazine, 1814." *Harvard Grad Mag* 37 (Je 29) 445-7.

Maurice, A. B. "More 'Old Bookman' Days." *Bkm* 70 (S 29) 56-65.

Mayer, S. D. "The Poetry Magazines." *Scholastic* 26 (23 Mr 35) 6.

Meine, F. J. *"The Carpet-Bag." Coll J* 4 (O-N-D 33) 411-3.

——— *"Vanity Fair." Coll J* 4 (Ja-F-Mr 34) 461-3.

Mencken, H. L. "Newspaper Morals." *Atl* 113 (Mr 14) 289-97.

———, Pound, Louise, Malone, Kemp, & Kennedy, A. G. "'American Speech,' 1925-1945: The Founders Look Back." *AS* (D 45) 241-6.

Miller, E. E. "Das New Yorker Belletristische Journal, 1851-1911." *AGR* 8 (D 41) 24-7.

Millington, Y. O. "A List of Newspapers Published in the District of Columbia, 1820-1850." *PBSA* 19 (1925) 43-65.

Mills, George. "The Des Moines Register." *Palimpsest* 30 (S 49) 273-304.

Miltonson, T. "Brief Notes on Four Obscure New York Scandal Sheets." *AN&Q* 4 (N 44) 115-6.

Moore, Marianne. *"The Dial:* A Retrospect." *PR* 9 (Ja-F 42) 52-8.

Morrow, Marco. "Thoughts on Newspapers." *Atl* 157 (My 36) 572-5.

Moss, David. "A Bibliography of the Little Magazines Published in America since 1900." *Contact* 1 (F-O 32) 91-109, 111-24, 134-9.

Mott, F. L. "A Brief History of *Graham's Magazine.*" *SP* 25 (Jl 28) 362-74.

——— "The *Christian Disciple* and the *Christian Examiner.*" *NEQ* 1 (1928) 197-217.

——— "Facetious News Writing, 1833-1883." *Miss Valley Hist R* 29 (Je 42) 35-54.

——— "Fifty Years of 'Life': The Story of a Satirical Weekly." *JQ* 25 (S 48) 224-32.

——— "The Newspaper Coverage of Lexington and Concord." *NEQ* 17 (D 44) 489-505.

——— "One Hundred and Twenty Years." *NAR* 240 (Je 35) 163-5.

Mowery, W. B. "Convention of Themes in the Magazine Short Story." *Texas R* 8 (Jl 23) 369-83.

Muller, H. J. "The Function of a Critical Review." *Ariz Q* 4 (Sp 48) 5-20.

Munson, G. B. "The Fledgling Years, 1916-1924." *SR* 40 (Ja-Mr 32) 24-54.

——— "How to Run a Little Magazine." *SRL* 15 (27 Mr 37) 3-4, 14, 16.

——— "The Mechanics for a Literary 'Secession.'" *S 4 N* 4 (N 42).

——— "*The Others* Parade." *Guardian* 1 (Ap 25) 228-34.

——— "The *Sewanee Review* from 1892 to 1930." *SR* 40 (Ja-Mr 32) 1-4.

——— "The Skyscraper Primitives." *Guardian* 1 (Mr 25) 164-78.

Muntz, E. E. "The Newspaper as an Educational Agency." *SAQ* 35 (Ap 36) 137-49.

Murphy, L. W. "A Monopoly Daily of 1785 Looks at Its Obligations." *JQ* 26 (Je 49) 202-3.

Murray, M. R. "The 1870's in American Literature." *AS* 1 (Mr 26) 323-8.

Myers, R. M. "The Old Dominion Looks to London: A Study of English Literary Influences upon *The Virginia Gazette,* 1736-1766." *VMHB* 54 (Jl 46) 195-217.
Nelson, H. L. "American Periodicals." *Dial* 28 (My 00) 349-52.
Nichols, Nelson. "An Early Newspaper of Alexandria, Va." *BNYPL* 25 (O 21) 663-9.
Nixon, H. C. "DeBow's Review." *SR* 39 (Ja-Mr 31) 54-61.
North, Rachel. "The Limitations of American Magazines." *Mod Q* 1 (Mr, Jl, D 23) 2-12, 18-30, 17-26.
Norton, C. E. "The Launching of the Magazine." *Atl* 100 (N 07) 579-81.
O'Brien, E. J. "The Little Magazines." *Vanity Fair* 41 (O 33) 20-1, 58.
O'Brien, R. L. "The Last Half Century of *Transcript* History." *PMHS* 67 (1945) 500-14.
O'Connor, W. V. "The Direction of the Little Magazines." *Poetry* 71 (F 48) 281-4.
——— "Little Magazines in the Third Generation." *Poetry* 73 (Mr 49) 367-9.
——— "New Magazines, Here and Abroad." *Poetry* 71 (N 47) 104-7.
Ogden, Rollo. "Some Aspects of Journalism." *Atl* 98 (Jl 06) 10-20.
Ogg, F. A. "Newspaper Satire during the American Revolution." *N E Mag* ns 30 (My 04) 367-76.
Oppenheim, James. "The Story of *The Seven Arts.*" *Am Merc* 20 (Je 30) 156-64.
Owens, D. M. "The Associated Press." *Am Merc* 10 (Ap 27) 385-93.
P., M. J. "The Picture Gallery: A 'First' in American Magazines." *AN&Q* 3 (S 43) 83-5.
Paltsits, V. H. "New Light on *Publick Occurences:* America's First Newspaper." *PMHS* 59 (1949) 75-88.
Parker, C. M. "The New Poetry and the Conservative American Magazine." *Texas R* 6 (O 20) 44-66.
Parry, Albert. "Goodbye to the Immigrant Press." *Am Merc* 28 (Ja 33) 56-7.
Peffer, Nathaniel. "Editors and Essays." *Harper's* 172 (D 35) 78-84.
Pekor, C. F., Jr. "An Adventure in Georgia." *Am Merc* 8 (Ag 26) 408-13.
Penniman, T. D. "The Early History of the *Baltimore American.*" *Md Hist Mag* 28 (S 33) 272-8.
Pennypacker, I. R. "Philadelphia's Johnny Inkslingers." *Am Merc* 6 (N 25) 357-62.
Perkins, H. C. "The Defense of Slavery in the Northern Press on the Eve of the Civil War." *J So Hist* 9 (N 43) 501-31.
Perry, Bliss. "The Arlington Street Incarnation." *Atl* 150 (N 32) 515-8.
Perry, C. E. "The New Hampshire Press in the Election of 1828." *Granite State Mo* 61 (D 29) 454-8.
Peterson, E. T. "Journalists, Middlemen of Learning." *Am Schol* 2 (O 33) 479-86.
Peterson, W. J. "Beginings of Journalism in Iowa." *Iowa J Hist & Pol* 45 (Jl 47) 261-89.
Porterfield, Ruth. "Memoirs of a Wood Pulp Editor." *Am Merc* 33 (O 34) 180-4.
Pound, Ezra. "Small Magazines." *EJ* 19 (N 30) 689-704.
Powell, L. C. "'The Western American'—an Early California Newspaper." *PBSA* 34 (4 Q 40) 349-55.
Pride, A. S. "Negro Newspaper Files and Their Microfilming." *JQ* 24 (Je 47) 131-4.
Priestley, H. L. "History on File." *SRL* 26 (30 O 43) 18-9.
Pringle, H. F. "Politicians and the Press." *Harper's* 156 (Ap 28) 618-24.
Pulitzer, Ralph. "Newspaper Morals: A Reply." *Atl* 113 (Je 14) 773-8.
Ranck, M. A. "Some Remnants of Frontier Journalism." *Chron Okla* 8 (D 30) 378-88; 9 (Mr 31) 63-70.
Randall, J. G. "The Newspaper Problem in Its Bearing upon Military Secrecy during the Civil War." *AHR* 23 (Ja 18) 303-23.
Randall, R. G. "Authors of the *Port Folio* Revealed by the Hall Files." *AL* 11 (Ja 40) 379-416.

Ransom, J. C., Bixler, Paul, & Schwartz, Delmore. "The Misery and Necessity of the Quarterly." *Am Schol* 15 (Au 46) 550-4.
Raschen, J. F. L. "American German Journalism a Century Ago." *AGR* 12 (Je 46) 13-5.
Ratchford, Fanny. "The Rolling Stone: The Life History of an O. Henry Rarity." *Colophon* 5 (Je 34) Pt 17.
Rawlings, K. W. "Trial List of Titles of Kentucky Newspapers and Periodicals before 1860." *Proc N J Hist Soc* 56 (Jl 38) 263-87.
Repplier, Agnes. "American Magazines." *YR* 16 (Ja 27) 261-74.
Rhodes, J. F. "Newspapers as Historical Sources." *Atl* 103 (Ap 09) 650-7.
Robbins, J. A. "Fees Paid to Authors by Certain American Periodicals, 1840-1850." *SB* 2 (1949-50) 95-104.
Robin, Philip. "The Yiddish Press." *Am Merc* 10 (Mr 27) 344-53.
Robinson, E. B. "The Dynamics of American Journalism from 1787 to 1865." *PMHB* 61 (O 37) 435-45.
——— "The Public Leader: An Independent Newspaper." *PMHB* 64 (Ja 40) 43-55.
Rorty, James. "Life's Delicate Children." *Nation* 128 (17 Ap 29) 470-1.
Roscoe, Theodore. "A Quaker Journal." *Contemp R* no 985 (Ja 48) 62-3.
Rosenberg, Harold. "Literature without Money." *Direction* 1 (1938) 6-10.
Rovere, R. H. "American Magazines in Wartime." *NRp* 110 (6 Mr 44) 308-12.
Sales, R. deR. "Notes on American Newspapers." *Atl* 159 (Ja 37) 28-33.
Salisbury, William. "American Journalism." *Arena* 40 (D 08) 564-71.
Sanders, C. R. "South Atlantic Quarterly." *So Atl Bul* 8 (D 42) 1, 12-3.
Schappes, M. U. "New York's First Labor Paper." *New Masses* 48 (7 S 43) 15-7.
Schaub, E. L. "Harris and the Journal of Speculative Philosophy." *Monist* 46 (Ja 36) 80-98.
Schermerhorn, James. "A Quarter of a Century of Michigan Journalism, 1858-1884." *Mich Hist Mag* 19 (Sp-Su 35) 253-76.
Schlesinger, A. M. "The Colonial Newspapers and the Stamp Act." *NEQ* 8 (Mr 35) 63-83.
——— "The Khaki Journalists, 1917-1919." *Miss Valley Hist R* 6 (D 19) 350-9.
——— "Propaganda and the Boston Newspaper Press, 1767-1770." *PCSM* 32 (1937) 396-416.
Schultz, Esther. "James Hall in Vandalia." *Ill State Hist Soc J* 23 (Ap 30) 92-112.
Schwartz, Delmore. "*The Criterion,* 1922-1939." *Purpose* 11 (O-D 39) 225-37.
Scott, F. W. "Newspapers and Periodicals of Illinois." *Coll Ill State Hist Lib* 4 (1910).
Sedgwick, J. H. "Newspaper Cannibalism." *NAR* 225 (Ap 28) 415-9.
Shaaber, M. A. "Forerunners of the Newspaper in the United States." *JQ* 9 (1934) 339-47.
Shaw, Harry. "Pocket and Pictorial Journalism." *NAR* 243 (Su 37) 297-309.
Shearer, A. H. "French Newspapers in the United States before 1800." *PBSA* 14 (1920) 45-147.
Sheldon, C. M. "The Experiment of a Christian Daily." *Atl* 134 (D 24) 624-33.
Shelton, W. H. "The Comic Paper in America." *Critic* 39 (S 01) 227-34.
Shelton, W. L. "Checklist of New Mexico Publications." *N Mex Hist R* 24 (Ap, Jl, O 49) 130-55, 223-36, 300-31.
Sherrer, G. B. "French Culture as Presented to Middle-Class America by *Godey's Lady's Book,* 1830-1840." *AL* 3 (N 31) 277-86.
Shirer, W. L. "The Poison Pen." *Atl* 169 (My 42) 548-52.
Simpson, L. P. "*The Literary Miscellany* and *The General Repository:* Two Cambridge Periodicals of the Early Republic." *Lib Chron Un Tex* 3 (Sp 50) 177-90.
Singer, Herman. "The Modern Quarterly, 1923-1940." *Mod Q* 11 (Fl 40) 13-9.
Smart, G. K. "A Note on Periodicals of American Transcendentalism." *AL* 10 (Ja 39) 494-5.
Spargo, G. H. "Newspaper Paralysis." *NAR* 226 (Ag 28) 189-94.

Spaulding, E. W. "*The Connecticut Courant*, a Representative Newspaper in the Eighteenth Century." *NEQ* 3 (Jl 30) 443-63.
Spell, L. M. "The Anglo-Saxon Press in Mexico, 1846-1848." *AHR* 38 (O 32) 20-31.
Spiker, C. C. "*The North American Review* and French Morals." *West Va Un Bul* 4 (S 43) 3-14.
Spurlin, P. M. "The American and His Newspaper, 1760-1801." *Emory Un Q* 3 (Mr 47) 44-53.
Stearns, B. M. "Before *Godey's*." *AL* 2 (N 30) 248-55.
——— "Early New England Magazines for Ladies." *NEQ* 2 (Je 29) 420-57.
——— "Early Philadelphia Magazines for Ladies." *PMHB* 64 (O 40) 479-91.
——— "Early Western Magazines for Ladies." *Miss Valley Hist R* 18 (D 31) 319-30.
——— "New England Magazines for Ladies, 1830-1860." *NEQ* 3 (O 30) 627-56.
——— "Philadelphia Magazines for Ladies: 1830-1860." *PMHB* 69 (Jl 45) 207-19.
——— "Reform Periodicals and Female Reformers, 1830-1860." *AHR* 37 (Jl 32) 678-99.
——— "Southern Magazines for Ladies (1819-60)." *SAQ* 31 (Ja 32) 70-87.
Stearns, Harold. "The American Press since the Armistice." *Dial* 66 (8 F 19) 129-32.
Stephens, Ethel. "American Popular Magazines: A Bibliography." *Bul Bibl* 9 (1916) 7, 41, 69, 95.
Stern, Madeleine. "Mrs. Frank Leslie: New York's Last Bohemian." *N Y Hist* 29 (Ja 48) 21-50.
Stevens, W. B. "Joseph B. McCullough." *Mo Hist R* 27 (Ja, Ap 33) 151-6, 257-61.
Stimpson, M. S. "The Harvard Lampoon: Its Founders and Famous Contributors." *N E Mag* ns 35(F 07) 579-90.
Streeter, R. E. "Association Psychology and Literary Nationalism in the *North American Review*, 1815-1825." *AL* 17 (N 45) 243-54.
Strunsky, Simeon. "The Reporter Speaks for Publication." *Harper's* 146 (Mr 23) 474-80.
Swallow, Alan. "Postwar Little Magazines." *Prairie Schooner* 23 (Su 49) 152-7.
Tait, S. W., Jr. "The St. Louis *Post-Dispatch*." *Am Merc* 22 (Ap 31) 403-12.
Tassin, Algernon. "The Magazine in America." *Bkm* 40 (D 14) 669-73; 41 (Ap, My, Je, Ag 15) 138-51, 284-96, 369-80, 620-32; 42 (S, O 15) 58-72, 137-47.
Tate, Allen. "The Fugitive, 1922-1925." *PULC* 3 (Ap 42) 75-84.
——— "The Function of the Critical Quarterly." *So R* 1 (Wi 36) 551-9.
Taylor, Archer. "Biblical Conundrums in the *Golden Era*." *Calif Folklore Q* 5 (Jl 46) 273-6.
Thomas, J. W. "*The Western Messenger* and German Culture." *AGR* 11 (O 44) 17-8.
Thomases, Jerome. "Freeman Hunt's America." *Miss Valley Hist R* 30 (D 43) 395-407.
Thompson, Ralph. "The Maria Monk Affair." *Colophon* 5 (Je 34) Pt 17.
Todd, Ruthven. "The Little Review." *Twentieth Century Verse* 15-6 (F 39) 159-62.
Tompkins, R. S. "Princes of the Press." *Am Merc* 12 (O 27) 171-7.
Tourtellot, A. B. "In Defense of the Press." *Atl* 174 (Ag 44) 83-7.
Towne, C. H. "The One-Man Magazines." *Am Merc* 63 (Jl 46) 104-8.
Trowbridge, J. T. "An Early Contributor's Recollections." *Atl* 100 (N 07) 582-93.
Troy, William. "The Story of the Little Magazines." *Bkm* 70 (Ja, F 30) 476-81, 657-63.
Turner, A. L. "The *Sewanee Review*." *SR* 40 (A-Je, Jl-S 32) 129-38, 257-75.
Ulrich, C. F., & Patterson, Eugenia. "Little Magazines." *BNYPL* 51 (Ja 47) 3-25.
Vandiver, F. E. "The Authorship of Certain Contributions to *Russell's Magazine*." *Ga Hist Q* 31 (Je 47) 118-20.

Vaughan, C. C. "History of the Newspaper Business in Clinton County." *Mich Hist Mag* 19 (Sp-Su 35) 279-85.
Villard, O. G. "An Editor Balances the Account." *Atl* 163 (Mr 39) 452-60.
Wall, A. J. "Early Newspapers." *N Y Hist Soc Quar Bul* 15 (Jl 31) 39-67.
Walseley, R. E. "The Journalist as Autobiographer." *SAQ* 42 (Ja 43) 38-44.
Ward, J. H. "The *North American Review.*" *NAR* 201 (Ja 15) 123-34.
Warner, R. F. "Godey's Lady's Book." *Am Merc* 2 (Ag 24) 399-405.
Warren, Austin. "Some Periodicals of the American Intelligentsia." *New English W* 1 (6 O 32) 595-7.
Watkins, Ann. "Literature for Sale." *Atl* 168 (N 41) 557-66.
Watkins, E. W. "Amateur Periodicals of the New York Historical Society." *N Y Hist Soc Q* 31 (Ja 47) 21-4.
Watterson, Henry. "The Personal Equation in Journalism." *Atl* 106 (Jl 10) 40-7.
Wayland, J. W. "The Virginia Literary Museum." *Pub So Hist Assn* 5 (Ja 02) 1-14.
Wayne, J. L. "Some Little Magazines of the Past." *Hobbies* 45 (My 40) 106-7.
Weeks, Edward. "We Have Read with Interest." *Atl* 143 (Je 29) 735-44.
Wegelin, Oscar. "Etienne Derbec and the Destruction of His Press at San Francisco, April, 1865." *N Y Hist Soc Quar Bul* 17 (Ja 43) 10-7.
Weiss, H. B. "A Graphic Summary of the Growth of Newspapers in New York and Other States, 1704-1820." *BNYPL* 52 (Ap 48) 182-96.
Wells, Carolyn. "What a Lark!" *Colophon* 2 (D 31) Pt 8.
White, W. A. "The Country Newspaper." *Harper's* 132 (My 16) 887-91.
——— "Editors Live and Learn." *Atl* 170 (Ag 42) 56-60.
——— "Good Newspapers and Bad." *Atl* 153 (My 34) 581-6.
Wiley, B. I. "Camp Newspapers in the Confederacy." *N C Hist R* 20 (O 35) 327-35.
Wilson, T. C. "The Literary Avant-Garde." *Inland R* 1 (Ap 34) 10-4.
Winterich, J. T. "Through Fire and Flood with the Colophon." *Pub W* 152 (23 N 47) 2397-2402.
Wolf, Howard. "What about the Associated Press?" *Harper's* 186 (F 43) 258-66.
Woodruff, C. R. "Is Journalism Decadent?" *Dalhousie R* 5 (O 25) 304-10.
Wright, L. M. "Journalistic Literature." *Palimpsest* 19 (D 38) 503-14.
——— "The Midland Monthly." *Iowa J Hist & Pol* 45 (Ja 47) 3-61.
Yoder, D. H. "*Der Fröhliche Botschafter:* An Early American Universalist Magazine." *AGR* 10 (Je 44) 13-6.
Zabel, M. D. "The Way of Periodicals." *Poetry* 34 (S 29) 330-4.
Zucker, A. E. "*Die Abendschule,* 1853-1940: A Pioneer Weekly." *AGR* 8 (F 42) 14-7.

PHILOSOPHY AND PHILOSOPHICAL TRENDS. Anderson, P. R. "Hiram K. Jones and Philosophy in Jacksonville." *J Ill State Hist Soc* 33 (D 40) 478-520.
——— "Quincy, an Outpost of Philosophy." *J Ill State Hist Soc* 34 (Mr 41) 50-83.
Beers, H. A. "A Pilgrim in Concord." *YR* ns 3 (Jl 14) 673-88.
Bourne, Randolph. "Conscience and Intelligence in War." *Dial* 63 (13 S 17) 193-5.
Curti, Merle. "The Great Mr. Locke: America's Philosopher, 1783-1861." *Huntington Lib Bul* 11 (Ap 37) 107-55.
Faust, C. H. "The Background of the Unitarian Opposition to Transcendentalism." *MP* 35 (F 38) 297-324.
Fisch, M. H. "Evolution in American Philosophy." *Philos R* 56 (Jl 47) 357-73.
Forbes, Cleon. "The St. Louis School of Thought." *Mo Hist R* 25 (O 30, Ja, Ap, Jl 31) 83-101, 289-305, 461-73, 609-22; 26 (O 31) 68-77.
Gohdes, Clarence. "Aspects of Idealism in Early New England." *Philos R* 39 (N 30) 537-55.
Goudge, T. A. "Philosophical Trends in Nineteenth-Century America." *UTQ* 16 (Ja 47) 133-42.

Leonard, W. E. "Paul Carus." *Dial* 66 (3 My 19) 452-5.
Miller, Perry. "Jonathan Edwards to Emerson." *NEQ* 13 (D 40) 589-617.
Perry, C. M. "William Torrey Harris and the St. Louis Movement in Philosophy." *Monist* 46 (Ja 36) 59-79.
Pochmann, H. A. "The Hegelization of the West." *AGR* 9 (Je 43) 24-31.
——— "Plato and Hegel Contend for the West." *AGR* 9 (Ag 43) 8-13.
Riley, Woodbridge. "Two Types of Transcendentalism in America." *J Philos* 15 (23 My 18) 281-92.
Schneider, H. W. "A Century of Romantic Imagination in America." *Philos R* 56 (Jl 47) 351-6.
Shipton, C. K. "Puritanism and Modern Democracy." *New England Hist & Gen Reg* 101 (Jl 47) 181-98.
Smith, L. W. "The Drift toward Naturalism." *SAQ* 22 (O 23) 355-69.
Stevens, I. K. "Edmund Montgomery." *Sw R* 16 (Wi 31) 200-35.
Sweet, W. W. "Cultural Pluralism in the American Tradition." *Christendom* 11 (Su, Au 47) 316-26, 501-8.
Todd, E. W. "Philosophical Ideas in Harvard College, 1817-1837." *NEQ* 16 (Mr 43) 63-90.
Warren, Austin. "The Concord School of Philosophy." *NEQ* 2 (Ap 29) 199-233.
Wiener, P. P. "Peirce's Metaphysical Club and the Genesis of Pragmatism." *JHI* 7 (Ap 46) 218-33.

POETRY. Anon. "About Writing Poetry." *Harper's* 138 (Ja 19) 219-23.
——— "America's Golden Age in Poetry." *Century* 91 (Mr 16) 793-4.
——— "'Good Newes from Virginia, 1623.'" *WMQ* 5: ser 3 (Jl 48) 351-8.
——— "More about 'Yankee Doodle.'" *NAR* 189 (Ap 09) 638-9.
——— "Of Yankees and 'Yankee Doodle.'" *NAR* 187 (Ja 08) 150-6.
——— "The 1949 Awards." *Poetry* 75 (N 49) 93-7.
Adkins, N. R. "The Lyric Year." *Am Book Col* 3 (Mr 38) 148.
Aiken, Conrad. "Back to Poetry." *Atl* 166 (Ag 40) 217-23.
——— "Mortality of Magic." *Dial* 65 (19 S 18) 214-5.
——— "The Place of Imagism." *NRp* 3 (22 My 15) 75-6.
——— "Poetry in America." *Dial* 62 (8 Mr 17) 179-82.
——— "Return of Romanticism." *Dial* 65 (5 S 18) 165-7.
Alden, H. M. "Recent Poetry." *Dial* 61 (15 Jl 16) 59-65.
Aldridge, A. O. "The Poet's Corner in Early Georgia Newspapers." *Ga R* 3 (Sp (Sp 49) 45-55.
Allen, G. W. "Naval Songs and Ballads." *PAAS* ns 35 (Ap 25) 64-78.
Allison, Lelah. "Traditional Verse from Autograph Books." *Hoosier Folklore* 8 (D 49) 87-94.
Arnold, Adel. "Where Poets Are Reborn." *SRL* 26 (30 O 43) 7-8.
Arvin, Newton. "American Poetry since 1900." *Freeman* 8 (14 N 23) 236-7.
——— "Our Haughty Poets." *Cur Hist* 40 (Je 34) 308-14.
Atkins, Elizabeth. "Man and Animals in Recent Poetry." *PMLA* 51 (Mr 36) 263-83.
Austin, Mark. "Sources of Poetic Inspiration in the Southwest." *Poetry* 43 (D 33) 152-63.
Bacon, Leonard. "Americans and Poetry." *SRL* 20 (7 O 39) 3-4, 16-7.
Baker, H. T. "Poetry and the Practical Man." *Forum* 42 (S 09) 227-36.
Beach, J. W. "The Cancelling Out—A Note on Modern Poetry." *Accent* 7 (Su 47) 243-50.
Beatty, R. C. "The Heritage of Symbolism in Modern Poetry." *YR* 36 (Sp 47) 467-77.
Beck, Warren. "Poetry between Two Wars." *VQR* 18 (Su 42) 359-74.
Benét, W. R. "Poetry Today in America." *SRL* 22 (10 Ag 40) 3-4, 17.
——— "Poetry's Last Twenty Years." *SRL* 27 (5 Ag 44) 100, 102, 104.

——— "Remembering the Poets: A Reviewer's Vista." *SRL* 32 (6 Ag 49) 46, 48, 50, 52.
——— "Three Poets and a Few Opinions." *NAR* 243 (Sp 37) 195-201.
Bennett, M. W. "Negro Poets." *Negro Hist Bul* 9 (My 46) 171-2, 191.
Birss, J. H. "Parodies of American Poets." *N&Q* 162 (23 Ja 32) 62.
Bishop, J. P. "The Missing All." *VQR* 13 (Wi 37) 106-21.
——— "Reflections on Style." *Hudson R* 1 (Su 48) 207-20.
Blackmur, R. P. "Twelve Poets." *So R* 7 (Su 41) 187-213.
Blake, Howard. "Thoughts on Modern Poetry." *SR* 43 (Ap-Je 35) 187-96.
Blake, N. M. "A Dialogue between Arnold and Lord Cornwallis." *Archive* (Duke Un) 44 (D 30) 17-20.
Bland, Edward. "Racial Bias and Negro Poetry." *Poetry* 63 (Mr 44) 328-33.
Boas, Guy. "The Algebraic School of Modern Poetry." *Blackwood's* 245 (My 39) 632-9.
Bodenheim, Maxwell. "Modern Poetry." *Dial* 68 (Ja 20) 95-8.
——— "The Poetry Quibble." *NAR* 210 (N 19) 706-8.
——— "Tendencies in Modern Poetry and Prose." *NAR* 213 (Ap 21) 551-5.
Boie, Mildred. "A Wider Audience for Poetry." *NAR* 245 (Su 38) 408-14.
Bolwell, R. W. "*The Art of Pleading:* A 'Lost' Poem." *AL* 3 (N 31) 314-6.
Bonner, W. H. "The Ballad of Captain Kidd." *AL* 15 (Ja 44) 362-80.
Boynton, H. W. "Major and Minor Verse." *Atl* 89 (F 02) 275-82.
Boys, R. S. "The Beginnings of the American Poetical Miscellany, 1714-1800." *AL* 17 (My 45) 127-39.
——— "The English Poetical Miscellany in Colonial America." *SP* 42 (Ja 45) 114-30.
Bradley, W. A. "The New Freedom—in Verse." *Bkm* 41 (Ap 15) 131-2.
——— "Song-Ballets and Devil's Ditties." *Harper's* 130 (My 15) 901-14.
Bradshear, M. M. "Missouri Literature since the First World War. Part I—Verse." *Mo Hist R* 40 (O 45) 1-20.
Breit, Harvey. "The Case for the Modern Poet." *N Y Times Mag* (3 N 46) 58-61.
Bridges, Robert. "A Paper on Free Verse." *NAR* 216 (N 22) 647-58.
Brooks, Cleanth. "The Modern Southern Poet and Tradition." *VQR* 11 (Ap 35) 305-20.
——— "Three Revolutions in Poetry." *So R* 1 (Jl, Ag 35) 151-63, 328-38.
Brown, Leonard. "Our Contemporary Poetry." *SR* 41 (Ja-Mr 33) 43-62.
Brown, W. C. "'A Poem Should Not Mean But Be.'" *UKCR* 15 (Au 48) 57-63.
Bruncken, H. G. "The Poetry Trade." *NAR* 227 (Ap 29) 463-8.
Bryan. G. S. "American Renderings of the 'Aeneid.'" *SR* 15 (Ap 07) 208-14.
Burke, Kenneth. "The Problem of the Intrinsic." *Accent* 3 (Wi 43) 80-94.
——— "Recent Poetry." *So R* 1 (Su 35) 164-77.
Bushby, D. M. "Modern American Poetry: A Critique." *Overland Mo* 88 (Mr 30) 75-6.
——— "Poets of Our Southern Frontier." *Overland Mo* 89 (F 31) 41-52, 58.
Campbell, E. S. "Three Mississippi Poets of the Nineteenth Century." *J Miss Hist* 5 (Ja 43) 38-40.
Carruth, Hayden. "The Anti-Poet All Told." *Poetry* 74 (Ag 49) 274-85.
——— "The Bollingen Award: What Is It?" *Poetry* 74 (Je 49) 154-6.
Catel, Jean. "La Poésie moderne aux États-Unis." *Revue des Cours et Conferences* (15, 30 My 34) 247-59, 341-57.
Ciardi, John. "Letter from Harvard." *Poetry* 74 (My 49) 112-3.
——— "Poets and Prizes." *CE* 12 (D 50) 127-34; *EJ* 39 (D 50) 545-52.
Clark, E. M. "An Unpublished Bit of Jeffersonian Verse." *SAQ* 26 (Ja 27) 76-82.
Clark, J. A. "Why Poetry Languishes." *Mod Thinker* 4 (N 33) 44-9.
Coblentz, S. A. "The Poetic Puritans." *Texas R* 9 (Ja 24) 144-9.
——— "The Poetical War." *Texas R* 6 (Ap 21) 176-89.
——— "Poetry Brought Down to Earth." *Texas R* 8 (Jl 23) 323-8.

Cocke, Zitella. "The Future of American Poetry." *N E Mag* ns 45 (D 11) 375-81.
Coffin, R. P. T. "Poetry Today and Tomorrow." *J Aesth & Art Criticism* 3 (n.d.) 59-67.
Cohn, D. L. "Wanted: An All-American Bard." *Atl* 173 (Je 44) 101-4.
Collins, Churton. "The Poetry and Poets of America." *NAR* 178 (Ja, F, Mr 04) 86-102, 278-96, 439-53.
Collins, Joseph. "Lunatics of Literature." *NAR* 218 (S 23) 376-87.
Colum, Padriac. "Egoism in Poetry." *NRp* 5 (2 N 15) 6-7.
——— "The Imagists." *Dial* 62 (22 F 17) 125-7.
——— "Sapling Poets." *Bkm* 48 (O 18) 233-8.
Comer, C. A. P. "Poetry To-Day." *Atl* 117 (Ap 16) 493-8.
Conover, Robert. "Poets Who Can Speak for All of America." *Chicago Sun Book Week* 4 (4 My 47) 2.
Counsell, E. M. "Latin Verses Presented by Students of William and Mary College to the Governor of Virginia, 1771, 1772, 1773 and 1774." *WMQ* 10 (Jl 30) 269-74.
Cuff, R. P. "An Appraisal of the American Poets Laureate." *Peabody J Educ* 25 (Ja 48) 157-66.
Daskam, J. D. "The Distinction of Our Poetry." *Atl* 87 (My 01) 696-705.
Davidson, Donald. "The Southern Poet and His Tradition." *Poetry* 40 (My 32) 94-103.
Davidson, H. C. "The Sonnet in Seven Early American Magazines and Newspapers." *AL* 4 (My 32) 180-7.
Deats, R. Z. "Poetry for the Populace." *SR* 50 (Jl-S 42) 374-88.
DeRobertis, D. "Poesia negra americana." *La Fiera Letteraria* 30 (9 O 49) 2.
Deutsch, Babette. "The Poet and the War." *NRp* 107 (7 D 42) 741-3.
——— "Poetry at the Mid-Century." *VQR* 26 (Wi 50) 67-75.
——— "Religious Elements in Modern Poetry." *Menorah J* 29 (Ja-Mr 41) 21-48.
De Vis, Leo. "Is Modern Poetry Sense?" *Honolulu Merc* 1 (N 29) 51-5.
de Vries, Peter. "Poetry and War." *CE* 5 (D 43) 113-20.
Dobie, J. F. "Ballads and Songs of the Frontier Folk." *Pub Texas Folk-Lore Soc* 6 (1927) 121-76.
Dyboski, Roman. "Odrodzenie poezji Ameryce XX Wieku." *Twórczosc* 1 (S 45) 122-45.
Dykes, E. B. "The Poetry of the Civil War." *Negro Hist Bul* 7 (F 44) 105-6, 114-5.
Eagleton, D. F. "The Sonnet in Texas Literature." *Texas R* 2 (O 16) 150-66.
Earnest, Ernest. "Poets in Overalls." *VQR* 19 (Ag 42) 518-29.
Eastman, Max. "American Ideals of Poetry: I." *NRp* 16 (14, 21 S 18) 190-2, 222-5.
——— "Poetic Justice in the Art of Calling Names." *SRL* 25 (24 O 42) 9-10, 43-4.
——— "Poets Talking to Themselves." *Harper's* 163 (O 31) 563-74.
——— "The Poet's Mind." *NAR* 216 (Mr 08) 424.
——— "The Tendency toward Pure Poetry." *Harper's* 159 (Jl 29) 221-30.
Eaton, W. P. "The Influence of Free Verse on Prose." *Atl* 124 (O 19) 491-6.
Eaton, Wyatt. "Recollections of American Poets." *Century* 64 (O 02) 842-50.
Eberhart, Richard. "In Defense of Poetry." *Poetry* 77 (N 50) 89-97.
Elliott, G. R. "The New Poetry and New America." *Nation* 107 (30 N 18) 652-4.
Ellis, Milton. "Two Notes on the Early American Sonnet." *AL* 5 (N 33) 268-9.
Engle, Paul. "Five Years of Pulitzer Poets." *EJ* 38 (F 49) 59-66; *CE* 10 (F 49) 237-44.
Erskine, John. "The New Poetry." *YR* 6 (Ja 17) 379-95.
——— "When Will the Poets Speak?" *Am Schol* 10 (Wi 40) 59-66.
Fairclough, H. R. "The Classics and Our Twentieth Century Poets." *Stanford Un Pub Lang & Lit* 2 (1927) 1-50.
Fellows in American Letters of the Library of Congress, *et al.* "The Case Against the *Saturday Review of Literature*." *Poetry* special issue (O 49).
Ficke, A. D. "Modern Tendencies in Poetry." *NAR* 204 (S 16) 438-47.
——— "The Present State of Poetry." *NAR* 194 (S 11) 429-41.

Figueira, Gaston. "Poetas estadounidenses." *America* 10 (Ap-My 41) 38-43.
Firkins, O. W. "American Verse." *Nation* 103 (17 Ag 16) 488-9.
——— "Crickets on the Hearth." *Nation* 107 (27 Jl 18) 98-100.
——— "The New Movement in Poetry." *Nation* 101 (14 O 15) 458-60.
——— "Singers Old and New." *Nation* 102 (6 Ja 16) 12-4.
——— "Verse and Verse Criticism." *Nation* 106 (4 Ap 18) 399-400.
Fletcher, J. G. "The Modern Southern Poets." *Westminster Mag* 23 (Ja-Mr 35) 229-51.
——— "Poetry, 1937-1947." *Ga R* 1 (Su 47) 153-61.
——— "A Rational Explanation of Vers Libre." *Dial* 66 (11 Ja 19) 11-3.
——— "Some Contemporary American Poets." *Chapbook* 2 (My 20) 1-4.
Flint, F. C. "Five Poets." *So R* 1 (Wi 36) 650-74.
Ford, W. C. "The Isaiah Thomas Collection of Ballads." *PAAS* ns 33 (Ap 23) 34-112.
Frank, J. C. "Early American Poetry to 1820. A List of Works in the New York Public Library." *BNYPL* 21 (Ap 17) 517-78.
Frankenberg, Lloyd. "Meaning in Modern Poetry." *SRL* 29 (23 Mr 46) 5-6, 56-7.
Frantz, A. I. "The Poetry of the Airways." *SAQ* 42 (Ap 43) 172-8.
French, L. J. "The Younger Poets of New England." *N E Mag* 32 (D 05) 425-6.
Furst, Clyde. "American Poetic Theory." *SR* 19 (O 11) 450-61.
Garnett, Edward. "Critical Notes on American Poets." *Atl* 120 (S 17) 366-73.
Gierasch, Walter. "Reading Modern Poetry." *CE* 2 (O 40) 32-3.
Gilbert, Katharine. "Recent Poets on Man and His Place." *Philos R* 56 (S 47) 469-90.
——— "A Spatial Configuration in Five Recent Poets." *SAQ* 44 (O 45) 422-31.
Gillet, L. B. "Poets in the War." *NAR* 209 (Je 19) 822-36.
Glicksberg, C. I. "Documentary Poetry." *Ariz Q* 3 (Au 47) 213-24.
——— "The Malady of Modern Poetry." *Prairie Schooner* 21 (Sp 47) 9-15.
——— "Negro Poets and the American Tradition." *AR* 6 (Su 46) 243-53.
——— "Poetry and Democracy." *SAQ* 41 (Jl 42) 254-65.
——— "Poetry and the Freudian Aesthetic." *UTQ* 17 (Ja 48) 121-9.
——— "Poetry and the Second World War." *SAQ* 44 (Ja 45) 42-54.
Graham, Walter. "Poets of the American Ambulance." *SAQ* 19 (Ja 20) 18-23.
Gregory, Horace. "Prologue as Epilogue." *Poetry* 48 (My 36) 92-8.
——— "The Unheard of Adventure—Harriet Monroe and Poetry." *Am Schol* 6 (Sp 37) 195-200.
——— "Of Vitality, Regionalism and Satire in Recent American Poetry." *SR* 52 (O-D 44) 572-93.
Gummere, F. B. "The Old Case of Poetry in a New Court." *Atl* 89 (Je 02) 824-8.
Hagedorn, Hermann. "A Note on Contemporary Poetry." *NAR* 196 (D 12) 772-9.
Hart, Russell. "Authoritative Criticism of Poetry in America." *NAR* 198 (S 13) 413-5.
Hartsock, Ernest. "Roses in the Desert: A View of Contemporary Southern Verse." *SR* 37 (Jl 29) 328-35.
Hausserman, H. W. "Left-Wing Poetry." *Eng Stud* 21 (O 39) 203-13.
Haviland, T. I. "'King Tammany,' a Song." *N Y Folklore Q* 6 (Su 50) 97-8.
Hayakawa, S. I. "The Linguistic Approach to Poetry." *Poetry* 60 (My 42) 86-94.
——— "Poetry and Advertising." *Poetry* 67 (Ja 46) 204-12.
Hayes, Alfred. "The Relation of Music to Poetry." *Atl* 113 (Ja 14) 59-69.
Healy, J. V. "Contemporary Poetry Criticism." *Poetry* 61 (Mr 43) 672-80.
Heartman, C. F. "An Historical Ballad of the Proceedings at Philadelphia, May 24th and 27th, 1799." *Am Coll* 1 (O 25) 12-4.
Henderson, A. C. "American Verse and British Critics." *Poetry* 11 (Ja 18) 207-12.
——— "The Folk Poetry of These States." *Poetry* 16 (Ag 20) 264-73.
Heydrick, B. A. "[American] Poetry." *Chautauquan* 65 (Ja 12) 169-89.
Heyward, DuBose. "Contemporary Southern Poetry." *Bkm* 62 (Ja 26) 561-4.

Hibbard, Addison. "The Lyric South." *Lit R* 4 (1923) 1-2.
Hillyer, Robert. "Farrago." *Atl* 175 (Mr 45) 98-100.
——— "Modern Poetry vs. the Common Reader." *SRL* 28 (Mr 45) 5-7.
Holley, Horace. "The New Poetry." *Forum* 53 (My 15) 629-33.
Holliday, Carl. "The Philosophy of American Poetry." *SR* 13 (Ja 05) 86-101.
Hooker, Brian. "Present American Poetry." *Forum* 42 (Ag 09) 148-56.
Howells, W. D. "Editor's Easy Chair." *Harper's* 131 (S 15) 634-7; 134 (Ap 17) 746-9.
——— "A Hundred Years of American Verse." *NAR* 172 (Ja 01) 148-160.
Hubbell, J. B. "'On Liberty Tree': A Revolutionary Poem from South Carolina." *S C Hist & Gen Mag* 41 (Jl 40) 117-22.
Hudson, A. P. "Songs of the North Carolina Regulators." *WMQ* 4: ser 3 (O 47) 470-85.
Ingalls, Jerry. "The Classics and New Poetry." *Classical J* 40 (N 44) 77-91.
Ingianni, Ignacio. "In Defence of the New Poetic Movement." *Texas R* 7 (Ja 22) 84-94.
Jantz, H. S. "The First Century of New England Verse." *PAAS* ns 53 (O 43) 219-508.
——— "Unrecorded Verse Broadsides of Seventeenth-Century New England." *PBSA* 39 (1Q 45) 1-19.
Jarrell, Randall. "Contemporary Poetry Criticism." *NRp* 105 (21 Jl 41) 88-90.
Jillson, W. R. "The First English Poem on Kentucky." *Ky State Hist Soc Reg* 35 (Ap 37) 198-201.
Jones, Llewellyn. "Free Verse and Its Propaganda." *SR* 28 (Jl 20) 284-95.
Jones, R. F. "Nationalism and Imagism in Modern American Poetry." *Wash Un Stud* 11 (O 23) 97-130.
Jones, V. L. "Congress and Poetry." *Texas R* 6 (Ja 21) 108-18.
Kendall, Carlton. "California Pioneer Poetess." *Overland Mo* 87 (Ag 29) 229-30.
Pittredge, G. L. "Verses of Adam Winthrop." *Trans Col Soc Mass* 27 (1932) 187-94.
Knickerbocker, W. S. "The Fugitives of Nashville." *SR* 36 (Ap 28) 211-24.
Kreymborg, Alfred. "American Poetry after the War." *EJ* 25 (Mr, Ap 33) 175-84, 263-73.
Krutch, J. W. "On the Difficulty of Modern Poetry." *Nation* 142 (4 Mr 36) 283-4.
Larrabee, Ankey. "Three Studies in Modern Poetry." *Accent* 3 (Wi 43) 115-21.
Leonard, N. H. "Let's Look at Alabama Poets." *Ala School J* 66 (N 48) 16-8.
Lewisohn, Ludwig. "German-American Poetry." *SR* 12 (Ap 04) 223-30.
——— "The Problem of Modern Poetry." *Bkm* 48 (Ja 19) 550-7.
Lomax, J. A. "Half-Million Dollar Song: Origin of 'Home on the Range.'" *Sw R* 31 (Fl 45) 1-8.
——— "'Sinful' Songs of the Southern Negro: Experience in Collecting Secular Folk Music." *Sw R* 19 (Wi 34) 105-31.
Lowell, Amy. "The Case of Modern Poetry vs. Prof. Lewisohn." *Bkm* 48 (Ja 19) 558-66.
——— "A Consideration of Modern Poetry." *NAR* 205 (Ja 17) 103-17.
——— "In Defence of Vers Libre." *Dial* 61 (7 S 16) 133.
——— "Imagist." *NRp* 5 (18 D 15) 174.
——— "Is There a National Spirit in the New Poetry of America?" *Craftsman* 30 (Jl 16) 339-49.
——— "Modern Poetry: Its Differences, Its Aims, Its Achievements." *Mass Lib Club Bul* 9 (O 19) 8-10.
——— "Naturalism in Art." *Poetry* 5 (O 14) 33-8.
——— "The New Manner in Modern Poetry." *NRp* 6 (4 Mr 16) 124-5.
——— "Poems of Democracy." *Poetry R* 1 (Jl 16) 46-7.
——— "Poetry as a Spoken Art." *Dial* 62 (25 Ja 17) 46-9.
——— "Poetry, Imagination, and Education." *NAR* 206 (N 17) 762-77.

——— "The Rhythms of Free Verse." *Dial* 64 (17 Ja 18) 51-6.
——— "Some Musical Analogies in Modern Poetry." *Musical Q* 6 (Ja 20) 127-57.
——— "Two Generations in American Poetry." *NRp* 37 (5 D 23) 1-3.
——— "Vers Libre and Metrical Prose." *Poetry* 3 (Mr 14) 213-20.
——— "Walt Whitman and the New Poetry." *YR* ns 16 (Ap 27) 502-19.
Lynch, J. W. "Parnassus to Calvary." *Cath World* 139 (My 34) 178-81.
Mabie, H. W. "Later and Younger American Poets." *Ladies' Home J* 20 (F 03) 15.
——— "The Poetry of the South." *Int Mo* 5 (F 02) 200-23.
McClure, John. "The Substance of Poetry." *Am Merc* 2 (My 24) 103-8.
McCormick, V. T. "Is Poetry a Live Issue in the South?" *SR* 37 (O-D 29) 399-406.
McGill, Josephine. "Sing All a Green Willow." *NAR* 228 (Ag 29) 218-24.
Mackall, L. L. "The Most Familiar Lines in American Verse." *N Y Herald-Tribune Books* (26 My 35) 22.
MacLeish, Archibald. "Poetry and the Public World." *Atl* 163 (Je 39) 823-30.
Macy, John. "The New Age of American Poetry." *Cur Hist* 35 (Ja 32) 553-8.
Mann, D. L. "American Poetry." *Forum* 53 (F 15) 232-6.
Marks, Jeannette. "On Reading Poetry To-Day." *NAR* 215 (Je 22) 827-37.
Masters, E. L. "The Poetry Revival in 1914." *Am Merc* 26 (Jl 32) 272-80.
Matthews, Brander. "American Satires in Verse." *Harper's* 109 (Jl 04) 294-9.
Matthiessen, F. O. "American Poetry, 1920-1940." *SR* 55 (Ja-Mr 47), 24-55; "Amerikanische Poesie Zwischen 1920 und 1940." *Die Wandlung* 4 (Ap 49) 316-31.
Mayhall, Jane. "The Modern Poet and the Devils of Circumstance." *UKCR* 15 (Sp 49) 199-204.
Maynard, Theodore. "The Fallacy of Free Verse." *YR* 11 (Ja 22) 354-66.
Meland, B. E. "Kinsmen of the Wild: Religious Moods in Modern American Poetry." *SR* 41 (O-D 33) 443-53.
Meyer, G. P. "Poets and Dragonflies." *SRL* 28 (24 Mr 45) 10-1.
Miles, Josephine. "Pacific Coast Poetry, 1947." *PS* 2 (Sp 48) 134-50.
Miller, E. E. "Some American War Poetry." *SAQ* 16 (Ap 17) 133-43.
Miller, Joaquin, *et al.* "The Slump in Poetry." *Critic* 46 (Mr, Ap 05) 263-77, 347-50.
Miner, L. M. "The Affair of the 'Mercury' in Prose and Verse." *AL* 2 (Ja 31) 421-30.
Monroe, Harold. "The Imagistes." *Poetry & Drama* 1 (Je 13) 127.
Monroe, Harriet. "The Arrogance of Youth." *Poetry* 37 (Mr 31) 328-33.
——— "The Free-Verse Movement in America." *EJ* 13 (D 24) 691-705.
——— "In the Aboriginal Mode." *Poetry* 42 (S 33) 332-9.
——— "In the Defense of Poetry." *Dial* 54 (16 My 13) 409.
——— "Poetry and the Allied Arts." *Poetry* 19 (O 21) 31-7.
——— "Poetry of the Left." *Poetry* 48 (Jl 36) 212-21.
——— "*Poetry's* Old Letters." *Poetry* 47 (O 35) 30-9.
——— "Present-day Tendencies." *Poetry* 48 (Je 36) 152-7.
——— "Twenty Years." *Poetry* 41 (O 32) 30-40.
——— "Typographical Queries." *Poetry* 28 (Ap 26) 32-40.
——— "A Word about Prosody." *Poetry* 27 (D 25) 149-53.
Morrison, M. B. "Poetry of the Southern United States." *Westminster R* 176 (Jl 11) 61-72.
Morrison, Theodore. "'The Fault, Dear Brutus': Poetic Example and Poetic Doctrine Today." *PS* 1 (Su 47) 235-50.
Morse, J. H. "American Nature Poetry." *Independent* 72 (20 Je 12) 1357-61.
Mowbray, J. P. "The New Pagan Lilt." *Critic* 41 (O 02) 308-12.
Muller, H. J. "The New Criticism in Poetry." *So R* 6 (Sp 41) 811-39.
Murdock, K. B. Review of *The First Century of New England Verse,* by Harold S. Jantz. *JEGP* 46 (Jl 47) 319-22.
Neiman, Gilbert. "To Write Poetry Nowadays You Have to Have One Foot in the Grave." *Poetry* 74 (Ap 49) 30-6.

Nitchie, Elizabeth. "The Longer Narrative Poems of America: 1775-1875." *SR* 26 (Jl 18) 283-300.
O'Connor, W. V. "The Color of Modern Poetry." *Poetry* 69 (N 46) 88-93.
——— "The Influence of the Metaphysicals on Modern Poetry." *CE* 9 (Ja 48) 180-7.
——— "The Isolation of the Poet." *Poetry* 70 (Ap 47) 28-36.
——— "Nature and the Anti-Poetic in Modern Poetry." *J. Aesth & Art Crit* 5 (S 46) 35-44.
——— "The Poet as Esthetician." *Quar R Lit* 4 (1948) 311-8.
——— "The Pre-Moderns in American Poetry." *NMQR* 17 (Sp 47) 5-16.
Oppenheim, James. "The New Poetry." *Conservator* 21 (Mr 10) 9.
——— "The New Poetry." *Poet-Lore* 22 (1911) 155-9.
——— "Poetry—Our First National Art." *Dial* 68 (F 20) 238-42.
Osborn, M. E. "Two Much Incoherency." *SLM* 4 (Mr 42) 114-8.
Page, A. B. "An Early American Poem." *PCSM* 11 (D 07) 403-8.
Parker, C. M. "The New Poetry and the Conservative American Magazine." *Texas R* 6 (O 20) 44-66.
Pattee, F. L. "Anthologies of American Literature before 1861." *Colophon* 4 (Mr 34) Pt 16.
——— "Recent Poetry and the Ars Poetica." *Sw R* 10 (Ja 25) 16-32.
Patterson, W. M. "New Verse and New Prose." *NAR* 207 (F 18) 257-67.
Pearson, Norman. "The American Poet in Relation to Science." *Am Q* 1 (Su 49) 116-26.
Peckham, M. H. "Present Day American Poetry." *SAQ* 11 (Jl 12) 205-14.
Phelps, W. L. "The Advance of English Poetry in the Twentieth Century." *Bkm* 47 (Jl 18) 551-2.
Pierce, F. E. "New Poets in a New Age." *YR* 8 (Jl 19) 796-811.
Pirhalla, John. "America's Most Quoted Poets." *EJ* 21 (D 32) 838-41.
Pound, Ezra. "A Few Don'ts by an Imagiste." *Poetry* 1 (Mr 13) 200-6.
——— "Lucrum Tuum Damnum Publicum Est." *Poetry* 48 (Ag 36) 273-5.
——— "Manifesto." *Poetry* 41 (O 32) 40-3.
——— "Vorticism." *Forum* 102 (S 14) 461-71.
——— "The Wisdom of Poetry." *Forum* 47 (Ap 12) 497-501.
Pound, Louise. "The Future of Poetry." *CE* 5 (Ja 44) 180-6.
Pratt, J. W. "Creation and Comment: Some Recent Verse." *SAQ* 18 (Ap 19) 175-8.
——— "The Cumberland Mountains in Verse." *SAQ* 17 (Jl 18) 217-21.
——— "The New Poetry." *SAQ* 16 (Jl 17) 271-4.
——— "Recent Poetry by North Carolina Writers." *SAQ* 17 (Ja 18) 40-3.
——— "Tendencies in Modern American Poetry." *SAQ* 17 (Ap 18) 167-70.
Ransom, J. C. "Poetry: I. The Formal Analysis." *KR* 9 (Su 47) 436-56.
——— "Poets without Laurels." *YR* 24 (Sp 35) 503-18.
——— "The Psychologist Looks at Poetry." *VQR* 11 (O 35) 574-92.
Read, Herbert, *et al.* "The Present State of Poetry." *KR* 1 (Au 39) 359-98.
Reardon, M. S., III. "The Advantages of Clarity in Poetry." *Mark Twain Q* 8 (Wi 50) 11-2.
Reynolds, H. "Heart Throbs and Melodies." *Chri Sci Mon* 36 (22 Ja 44) 6.
Rittenhouse, J. B. "Contemporary Poetry." *Bkm* 46 (D 17, Ja 18) 438-44, 575-9.
——— "Love as a Dominant Theme in Poetry." *Forum* 56 (S 16) 341-9.
Rosenberg, Harold. "The Profession of Poetry." *PR* 9 (S-O 42) 392-413.
Sandburg, Carl. "Those Who Make Poetry." *Atl* 169 (Mr 42) 344-6.
Santayana, George. "Genteel American Poetry." *NRp* 3 (29 My 15) 94-5.
Sapir, Edward. "The Twilight of Rhyme." *Dial* 63 (16 Ag 17) 98-100.
Savage, D. S. "Form in Modern Poetry." *Poetry* 65 (O 44) 30-43.
Schauffler, R. H. "The Matter with the Poets." *NAR* 200 (O 14) 603-15.
Scott, Kenneth. "A Naval Ballad of the War of 1812." *Am Neptune* 7 (Ap 47) 167-9.

Scott, W. T. "Youth, Maturity, and American Poetry." *Poetry* 6 (Ja 47) 210-20.
Sergent, N. B. "High School Poets." *NAR* 230 (Jl 30) 113-20.
Sherman, C. B. "Our Rural Poetry." *SAQ* 37 (Ap 38) 200-14.
——— "Rural Poetry in the South." *SLM* 1 (Jl 39) 461-5.
Shuster, G. N. "Our Poets in the Streets." *Cath World* 105 (Jl 17) 433-45.
Simon, Jean. "Les Poètes Américains et leurs introductions français." *Les Langues Modernes* 42 (Ag-S-O 48) 441-5.
Smith, J. H. "Magazine Verse in Eighteenth-Century America." *SR* 33 (Ja 26) 89-90.
Smith, L. W. "The New Naïveté." *Atl* 117 (Ap 16) 487-92.
Spencer, Theodore. "How to Criticize a Poem." *NRp* 109 (4 D 43) 816, 818.
Spingarn, J. E. "Politics and the Poet." *Atl* 170 (N 42) 73-8.
Spitzer, Leo. "History of Ideas *vs.* the Reading of Poetry." *So R* 6 (Wi 41) 584-609.
Stanton, Theodore. "The Poet of the Stacks." *Freeman* 7 (13 S 22) 14.
Starke, A. H. "An Omnibus of Poets." *Colophon* 4 (Mr 34) Pt 16.
Stephen, A. M. "Dr. Samuel Johnson Views Our Poets." *Dalhousie R* 11 (Ja 32) 493-506.
Stevens, James. "The Northwest Takes to Poetry." *Am Merc* 16 (Ja 29) 64-70.
Stevenson, Lionel. "Mute Inglorious Miltons." *Un Calif Chron* 33 (Jl 31) 296-316.
Sutcliffe, E. G. "Whitman, Emerson and the New Poetry." *NRp* 19 (24 My 19) 114-6.
Swallow, Alan, *et al.* "Experimental Poetry." *NMQR* 16 (Wi 46) 417-44.
Swan, B. F. "Some Thoughts on the Bay Psalm Book of 1640, with a Census of Copies." *Yale Un Lib Gaz* 22 (Ja 48) 56-76.
Swett, Margery. "Free Verse Again." *Poetry* 25 (D 24) 153-9.
Tate, Allen. "American Poetry since 1920." *Bkm* 58 (Ja 29) 503-8.
——— "Confusion and Poetry." *SR* 38 (Ap-Je 30) 133-49.
——— "Poetry and the Absolute." *SR* 35 (Ja 27) 41, 51.
——— "Understanding Modern Poetry." *CE* 1 (Ap 40) 561-72.
Thompson, Lawrance. "Background for Modern Poetry." *AR* 2 (Sp 42) 90-102.
Tietjens, Eunice. "Apologia." *Poetry* 22 (Ag 23) 267-73.
Timrod, Henry. "A Theory of Poetry." *Atl* 96 (S 05) 313-26.
Tomlinson, Elizabeth. "The Metaphysical Tradition in the Modern Poets." *CE* 1 (D 39) 208, 222.
Trent, W. P. "The Poetry of the American Plantations." *SR* 8 (Ja 00) 73-88.
Triggs, O. L. "A Century of American Poetry." *Forum* 30 (Ja 01) 630-40.
Trimble, Neil. "The Decline of Light Verse." *Am Spect* 1 (Ag 33) 4.
Untermeyer, Louis. "Daughters of Niobe." *Am Spect* 1 (N 32) 4.
——— "New Meanings in Recent American Poetry." *VQR* 16 (Su 40) 399-412.
——— "Three Younger Poets." *EJ* 21 (D 32) 787-98.
Van Doren, Mark. "Poetry and Subject Matters." *SRL* 22 (10 Ag 40) 5-6.
——— "The Poetry of Our Day Expresses Our Doubt and the Time's Confusion." *N Y Herald-Tribune Books* 26 (25 S 49) 9.
Van Ghent, Dorothy. "When Poets Stood Alone." *New Masses* 26 (11 Ja 38) 41-6.
Viereck, Peter. "For a Third Force in Poetry Today." *N Y Herald-Tribune Books* (3 S 50) 3.
Walbridge, E. F. "Incense and Praise, and Whim, and Glory: Real People in Poetry." *Colophon* 4 (Mr 34) Pt 16.
Walton, I. L. "Navaho Poetry: An Interpretation." *Texas R* 7 (Ap 22) 198-210.
Warren, R. P. "A Note on Three Southern Poets." *Poetry* 40 (My 32) 103-13
——— "Pure and Impure Poetry." *KR* 5 (Sp 43) 237-40.
Weaver, W. "Poesia americana di guerra." *Aretusa* 1 (1944) 124-6.
Wells, H. W. "The Diction of Modern American Poetry." *Word Study* 24 (D 48) 1-3.
——— "The Predicament of Modern Poetry." *CE* 10 (Ap 49) 371-5.

——— "Recent Trends in American Verse: A Summary and Appraisal." *English* 7 (Au 48) 112-7.
White, M. E. D. "New England in Contemporary Verse." *N E Mag* ns 30 (Je 04) 408-18.
White, N. I. "American Negro Poetry." *SAQ* 20 (O 21) 304-22.
White, R. E. "Democracy and American Poetry." *N E Mag* ns 31 (Ja 05) 531-5.
Wilkinson, Mary. "Poets of the People." *Touchstone* 2 (F 18) 510-2.
Wilson, Edmund. "The Canons of Poetry." *Atl* 153 (Ap 34) 455-62.
Winters, Yvor. "The Poet and the University." *Poetry* 75 (D 49) 170-8.
——— "The Symbolist Influence." *H&H* 4 (Jl-S 31) 607-18.
Wolfert, Helen. "Wanted: An Audience for Our Poets." *N Y Times Book R* (30 D 45) 3, 10, 14.
Wood, Clement. "Charlie Chaplins of Poetry." *Independent* 93 (12 Ja 18) 64.
——— "Stocktaking: American Poetry, 1942." *SLM* 4 (Mr 42) 106-11.
Wood, G. A. "American Metaphysical Poetry." *Contemp R* 178 (O 50) 232-6.
Wood, R. C. "Life, Death and Poetry as Seen by the Pennsylvania Dutch." *Monatshefte für Deutschen Unterricht* 37 (N 45) 453-65.
Wright, L. M. "A Century of Verse." *Palimpsest* 27 (Jl 46) 217-24.
——— "Verse in the Newspapers." *Palimpsest* 19 (My 38) 173-84.
Wright, Richard. "Littérature noire américaine." *Les Temps Modernes* 3 (Ag 48) 193-221.
Wyatt, E. F. "The Adventures of a Poetry-Reader." *NAR* 209 (Mr 19) 404-15.
——— "Conversational Poetry." *YR* ns 9 (O 20) 157-67.
Zabel, M. D. "American Poetry: 1934." *NRp* 81 (12 D 34) 134-5.
——— "Two Years of Poetry." *So R* 5 (Wi 40) 568-608.
Zukofsky, Louis. "American Poetry 1920-1930." *Symposium* 2 (Ja 31) 60-84.
——— "Program: 'Objectivists' 1931." *Poetry* 37 (F 31) 268-72.

PRINTING. Anon. "The Best Sellers of 1946." *Pub W* 151 (25 Ja 47) 415, 418.
——— "The Best Sellers of 1947 According to Sales in Bookstores." *Pub W* 153 (24 Ja 48) 300-4.
——— "Book Production in the United States." *TLS* no 2506 (10 F 50) x.
——— "Confessions of a Best-Seller." *Atl* 104 (N 09) 577-85.
——— "Doubleday Plans Fiftieth Anniversary Celebration in 1947." *Pub W* 150 (21 D 46) 3284-94.
——— "Fifty Years of Textbook Publishing." *Pub W* 127 (13 Ap 35) 1508-11.
——— "The Finance of Authorship." *Manchester Guardian* 56 (2 Ja 47) 13.
——— "H. W. Wilson's 50 Years of Bibliographic Publishing." *Pub W* 153 (21 F 48) 1058-61.
——— "Literary Awards 1946." *Pub W* 151 (25 Ja 47) 410-4.
——— "Maeterlinck Sues Dodd, Mead as His Sales Decline." *Pub W* 152 (23 Ag 47) 731-2.
——— "The Old Corner Book-Store: The Famous Literary Landmark of Boston and the Men Who Met There." *N E Mag* ns 29 (N 03) 303-16.
——— "Oxford University Press, American Branch Celebrates 50th Anniversary." *Pub W* 150 (12 O 46) 2204-7.
——— "A Penny a Word." *Am Merc* 37 (Ja 31) 285-92.
——— "Points of View in Book Publishing: I—Book Censorship." *Pub W* 153 (24 Ja 48) 316-7.
——— "A Preface to *The Bay Psalm Book*." *More Books* 4 (Je 29) 223-9.
——— "Scribner—A Century of Publishing." *Pub W* 150 (7 S 46) 1184-95.
——— "Ten Thousand Books a Year." *Pub W* 119 (24 Ja 31) 411-2.
——— "Ten Years of Publishing at the Rutgers University Press." *Pub W* 150 (28 D 46) 3409-12.
Adams, R. G. "America's First Bibles." *Colophon* ns 1 (Su 35) 11-20.
——— "Notes and Queries." *Colophon* ns 2 (Wi 37) 283-4.

Alden, H. M. "Editor's Study." *Harper's* 133 (Jl 16) 310-2; 136 (D 17) 150-2.
Alden, John. "Scotch Type in Eighteenth-Century America." *SB* 3 (1950) 270-3.
Allen, Frederick. "Best Sellers: 1900-1935." *SRL* 13 (7 D 35) 3-4, 20, 24, 26.
Andrews, W. L. "Early American Bookbinding." *Bkm* 16 (S, O 02) 56-69, 164-75.
Arnold, W. H. "The Welfare of the Bookstore." *Atl* 124 (Ag 19) 192-9.
Ballou, R. O. "Goudy." *Am Merc* 7 (F 26) 230-4.
Banning, M. C. "The Problem of Popularity." *SRL* 14 (2 My 36) 3-4, 16-7.
Banta, R. E. "*The American Conchology:* A Venture in Backwoods Book Printing." *Colophon* ns 3 (Wi 38) 24-40.
Barrow, W. J. "Black Writing Ink of the Colonial Period." *Am Archivist* 11 (O 48) 291-307.
Batchelder, F. R. "Isaiah Thomas, the Patriot Printer." *N E Mag* ns 25 (N 02) 284-305.
Bates, A. C. "Some Notes on Early Connecticut Printing." *PBSA* 27 (1933) 1-11.
Baxter, W. T. "Daniel Henchman, a Colonial Bookseller." *EIHC* 70 (1934) 1-30.
Bevan, E. R. "Early Maryland Bookplates." *Md Hist Mag* 39 (D 44) 310-4.
Blanck, Jacob. "News from the Rare Book Sellers." *Pub W* 151 (15 Mr 47) B225-B226.
Bradsher, E. L. "The First American Edition of the Lyrical Ballads." *SAQ* 16 (Jl 17) 268-70.
Brand, R. F. "A General View of the Spanish Language Press in the United States." *MLJ* 33 (My 49) 363-70.
Breit, Harvey. "Best Sellers: How They Are Made." *N Y Times Book R* 53 (4 Ja 48) 25.
Brett, G. P. "Book-Publishing and Its Present Tendencies." *Atl* 3 (Ap 13) 454-62.
——— "How Books Achieve Circulation." *Outlook* 76 (27 F 04) 512-4.
Bridenbaugh, Carl. "The Press and the Book in Eighteenth Century Philadelphia." *PMHB* 65 (Ja 41) 1-30.
Brigham, C. S. "Bibliography of American Newspapers, 1690-1820." *PAAS* 23 (O 13) 247-403; 24 (O 14) 363-449; 25 (Ap, O 15) 128-293, 396-501; 26 (Ap, O 16) 80-184, 413-60; 27 (Ap, O 17) 177-274, 375-513; 28 (Ap, O 18) 63-133, 291-322; 29 (Ap 19) 129-80; 30 (Ap 20) 81-150.
——— "History of Book Auctions in America." *BNYPL* 39 (F 35) 55-89.
——— "James Franklin and the Beginnings of Printing in Rhode Island." *PMHS* 65 (Mr 36) 536-44.
Brown, H. G. & M. O. "A Directory of the Book-Art and Book Trade in Philadelphia to 1820, Including Printers and Engravers." *BNYPL* 53 (My, Je, Jl, Ag, S, O, N, D 49) 211-26, 290-8, 339-47, 447-58, 492-503; 54 (Ja, F, Mr 50) 25-37, 89-92, 123-45.
Burrus, E. J. "The First Literary Production of the New World." *Classical J* 43 (O 47) 31-3.
Cappon, L. J. "The Yankee Press in Virginia, 1805-1865." *WMQ* 15 (Ja 35) 81-8.
Carruth, Hayden, *et al.* "A Symposium: Poet, Publisher, and the Tribal Chant." *Poetry* 75 (O 49) 22-58.
Cerf, Bennet. "Publishers' Row Different in 1924-'25." *N Y Herald Tribune Books* 26 (25 S 49) 3, 75.
Chokla, Sarah. "Bookprinting in Texas." *Sw R* 21 (Ap 36) 319-29.
Clapesattle, Helen. "Out of the Mouths of Wise Men." *SRL* 30 (7 Je 47) 12-3.
Colwell, E. C. "The Publishing Needs of Scholarship." *Pub W* 151 (1 F 47) 516-9.
Compton, F. E. "Subscription Books." *BNYPL* 43 (D 39) 879-94.
Copeland, Fayette. "The New Orleans Press and the Reconstruction." *La Hist Q* 30 (Ja 47) 149-337.
Corbett, J. A. "The First Printing Press of the University of Notre Dame." *Ind Mag Hist* 41 (Mr 45) 50-6.
Couch, W. T. "Twenty Years of Southern Publishing." *VQR* 26 (Sp 50) 171-85.
Cowley, Malcolm. "The Literary Business in 1943." *NRp* 109 (27 S 43) 417-9.

——— "A Note on Publishing." *Nation* 116 (20 Ja 47) 3.
Crawford, N. A. "The Books of Dard Hunter." *Am Merc* 2 (Ag 24) 470-2.
Cutler, B. D. "The Great Victorians Come to America." *Pub W* 122 (19 N, 17 D 32) 1927-30, 2255-7.
Davis, D. T. "Bookmaking in the West." *Critic* 37 (S 00) 232-41.
Devoe, Alan. "A Literary Experiment." *Atl* 153 (Ap 34) 472-7.
Dingham, J. H. "American Bookselling and Booksellers." *Dial* 28 (1 My 00) 344-6.
Dittus, C. W. "Pioneering with a Press." *SRL* 29 (8 Je 46) 13.
Dreis, Hazel. "Lancaster, Pennsylvania, Bookbindings: An Historical Study." *PBSA* 42 (2Q 48) 119-28.
Eames, Wilberforce. "The First Year of Printing in New York." *BNYPL* 32 (Ja 28) 3-24.
Eaton, A. J. "The American Movement for International Copyright, 1837-1860." *Lib Q* 15 (Ap 45) 95-122.
Eaton, Clement. "The Freedom of the Press in the Upper South." *Miss Valley Hist R* 18 (Mr 32) 479-99.
Eddy, G. S. "A Work Book of the Printing House of Benjamin Franklin and David Hall, 1759-1766." *BNYPL* 34 (Ag 30) 575-89.
Edmonds, A. S. "The Henkels, Early Printers in New Market, Virginia." *WMQ* 18 (Ap 38) 174-95.
Edmunds, A. J. "A Spurious Philadelphia Bible of 1788." *N&Q* 165 (11 N 33) 332.
Ellison, R. C. "Early Baptist Printing in Alabama." *Ala R* 2 (Ja 49) 24-31.
Farrar, John. "Footnotes to a Publisher's Sunday." *Colophon* ns 3 (Wi 38) 67-91.
——— "Publisher's Eye View." *SRL* 30 (9 Ag 47) 11-2, 26.
Fedash, Mayteel. "State of the Catholic Press." *Cath World* 166 (F 48) 416-23.
Fletcher, Herbert. "Four Texas Publishers." *Sw Hist Q* 50 (Ja 47) 344-8.
Flynn, W. H. "A Bookseller Looks Back." *Pub W* 123 (22 Ap 33) 1329-31.
Ford, W. C. "Henry Knox and the London Book-Store in Boston, 1771-1774." *PMHS* 61 (Je 28) 227-303.
Freidel, Frank. "Lieber's Contribution to the International Copyright Movement." *HLQ* 8 (F 45) 200-6.
——— "The Loyal Publication Society: A Pro-Union Propaganda Agency." *Miss Valley Hist R* 26 (D 39) 359-76.
Gilbert, R. W. "Sower's Almanac as an Advertising Medium." *AGR* 15 (O 48) 9-11.
Gilkyson, Claude. "Henry Reed, 1825. Wordsworth's American Editor." *Gen Mag & Hist Chron* 38 (1936) 84-90, 163-72, 318-22, 355-71.
Goff, F. R. "The Rare Books Division of the Library of Congress." *Pub W* 150 (23 N 46) 2886-90.
Gomme, L. J. "The Little Book-Shop Around the Corner." *Colophon* ns 2 (Au 37) 573-93.
Goodspeed, G. T. "The Home Library." *PBSA* 42 (2Q 48) 110-8.
Green, S. A. "A Further List of Early American Imprints." *PMHS* 37 (Ja 03) 13-77.
Hacker, L. M., *et al.* "Unfinished Business for the Masses." *SRL* 29 (8 Je 46) 8-11.
Haines, H. E. "'Tis Fifty Years Since: *Publishers' Weekly* Office in an Earlier Day." *Pub W* 151 (18 Ja 47) 278-83.
Hall, J. N. "Too Many Books." *Atl* 150 (D 32) 458-60.
Hallenbeck, C. T. "Book-Trade Publicity before 1800." *PBSA* 32 (1938) 47-56.
Hamilton, J. G. DeR. "Three Centuries of Southern Records, 1607-1907." *J So Hist* 10 (F 44) 3-36.
Hamilton, Sinclair. "Early American Book Illustration." *PULC* 6 (Ap 45) 101-26.
Hansen, Harry. "The 1947 Literary Output, or The Biggest Book Marathon in Recent History." *Pub W* 152 (24 Ja 48) 292-4.
Harrison, H. S. "Adventures with the Editors: with a Reëxamination of an Ancient Inquiry: Why Are Manuscripts Rejected?" *Atl* 113 (Ap 14) 445-56.
Hart, Henry. "The Tragedy of Literary Waste." *New Masses* 24 (29 Je 37) 19-20.

Hart, I. H. "Best Sellers in Non-Fiction since 1920." *Pub W* 123 (4 F 33) 524-8.
Harwell, R. B. "Publishers Carry On." *SLM* 4 (Ja 42) 3-6.
Henry, E. A. "Cincinnati as a Literary and Publishing Center, 1793-1880." *Pub W* 132 (3, 10 Jl 37) 22-3, 24, 110-2.
Herrick, Robert. "The Mystery of the Best Seller." *EJ* 23 (O 34) 621-9.
Hockett, A. P. "Seventy-five Years of Booklisting." *Pub W* 151 (18 Ja 47) 335-6.
Holmes, T. J. "The Bookbindings of John Ratcliff and Edmund Ranger, Seventeenth Century Boston Bookbinders." *PAAS* ns 38 (Ap 28) 31-50.
Holt, Henry. "The Commercialization of Literature." *Atl* 96 (N 05) 577-600.
——— "Competition." *Atl* 102 (O 08) 516-26.
Howells, W. D. "Editor's Easy Chair." *Harper's* 135 (Je 17) 138-41.
Huebsch, B. W. "Footnotes to a Publisher's Life." *Colophon* ns 2 (Su 37) 406-26.
Jackson, Joseph. "First Catholic Bible Printed in America." *Rec Am Cath Hist Soc Phila* 56 (Mr 45) 18-25.
Kendall, J. S. "New Orleans Newspapermen of Yesterday." *La Hist Q* 29 (Jl 46) 771-90.
——— "Old-Time New Orleans Police Reporters and Reporting." *La Hist Q* 29 (Ja 46) 43-58.
King, M. I. "John Bradford and the Institution of Printing in Kentucky." *Letters* 4 (N 30) 26-9.
Knopf, A. A. "Effective Publishing of Scholarship in the Humanities and Social Sciences." *Pub W* 151 (1 F 47) 525-9.
Kobre, Sidney. "The Revolutionary Colonial Press." *JQ* 20 (1943) 193-204.
Kopman, H. L. "Modern American Printing." *Am Merc* 2 (My 24) 51-4.
Kup, Karl. "Books about Bookmaking." *Pub W* 154 (4 D 48) 2294-6.
Larremore, T. A. "An American Typographic Tragedy—The Imprints of Frederick Conrad Bursch. Part I. Through the Literary Collector." *Papers Am Bibl Soc* 43 (1Q 49) 1-38.
Legman, G. "The First Comic Books in America: Revisions and Reflections." *AN&Q* 5 (Ja 46) 148-51.
Lewis, Oscar. "The California School of Printing." *Colophon* (S 30) Pt 3.
——— "Mug Books." *Colophon* 5 (Je 34) Pt 17.
Long, Daniel. "Printing in the Southwest." *Sw R* 26 (Au 40) 37-49.
McCombs, C. F. "John Peter Zenger, Printer." *BNYPL* 37 (D 33) 1031-4.
McCulloch, William. "William McCulloch's Additions to Thomas's History of Printing." *PAAS* ns 31 (Ap 31) 89-247.
McCutcheon, R. P. "Books and Booksellers in New Orleans." *La Hist Q* 20 (Jl 37) 3-15.
McDermott, J. F. "Everybody Sold Books in Early St. Louis." *Pub W* 132 (24 Jl 37) 248-50.
——— "The Printing Press and Culture." *Am Book Coll* 6 (Ja 35) 13-5.
McDonald, Gerald. "Early Printing in the United States." *Pub W* 137 (6 Ja 40) 54-8.
MacDonald, H. L. "University of Minnesota Press Celebrates Twenty Years of Publishing." *Pub W* 151 (1 F 47) 544-50.
McKay, G. L. "American Book Auction Catalogues, 1713-1934. A Union List." *BNYPL* 39 (1935) 141-66, 389-410, 461-78, 490-521, 561-76, 638-63, 724-44, 815-28, 891-914, 955-80; 40 (1936) 56-78, 139-65, 375-90, 535-57, 671-703, 775-800, 859-77, 955-84, 1065-98; 50 (1946) 177-84; 52 (1948) 401-12.
——— "Early American Book Auctions." *Colophon* ns 1 (Je 39).
——— "A Register of Artists, Booksellers, Printers and Publishers in New York City." *BNYPL* 44 (Ap, My, Je 40) 351-7, 415-28, 475-87; 45 (Je 41) 483-99.
McMurtrie, D. C. "Additional Buffalo Imprints 1812-1849." *Grosvenor Lib Bul* 18 (Je 36) 69-91.
——— "Additional Geneva Imprints 1815-1849." *Grosvenor Lib Bul* 18 (Je 36) 93-9.

——— "The Beginnings of Printing in the District of Columbia." *Americana* 27 (Jl 33) 265-89.
——— "The Beginnings of Printing in New Hampshire." *Trans Bibl Soc Am* 15 (1934) 340-63.
——— "The Beginnings of Printing in Rhode Island." *Americana* 29 (O 35) 607-26.
——— "The Bibliography of American Imprints." *Pub W* 144 (19 N 43) 1939-44.
——— "A Bibliography of Books and Pamphlets Printed at Geneva, N. Y., 1800-1850." *Grosvenor Lib Bul* 17 (Je 35) 82-112.
——— "A Bibliography of Books and Pamphlets Printed in Ithaca, N. Y., 1820-1850." *Grosvenor Lib Bul* 19 (Je 37) 46-105.
——— "A Bibliography of Morristown Imprints, 1798-1820." *Proc N J Hist Soc* 54 (Ap 36) 129-55.
——— "A Bibliography of North Carolina Imprints, 1761-1800." *N C Hist R* 13 (Ja, Ap, Jl 36) 47-86, 143-66, 219-54.
——— "A Bibliography of South Carolina Imprints, 1731-1740." *S C Hist & Gen Mag* 34 (Jl 33) 117-37.
——— "Early Printing in Wyoming." *PBSA* 36 (4Q 42) 267-304.
——— "The First Printers of Illinois." *J. Ill State Hist Soc* 26 (O 33) 201-21.
——— "The First Twelve Years of Printing in North Carolina, 1749-1760." *N C Hist R* 10 (Jl 33) 214-34.
——— "The French Press of Louisiana." *La Hist Q* 18 (O 35) 947-65.
——— "The Green Family of Printers." *Americana* 26 (Jl 32) 364-75.
——— "Located Georgia Imprints of the Eighteenth Century." *Ga Hist Q* 18 (Mr 34) 27-65.
——— "Locating the Printed Source Material for United States History." *Miss Valley Hist R* 31 (D 44) 369-78.
——— "Our Medieval Typography." *Am Merc* 12 (S 27) 94-7.
——— "Pioneer Printing in Georgia." *Ga Hist R* 16 (Je 32) 77-113.
——— "Pioneer Printing in North Dakota." *No Dak Hist Q* 6 (Ap 32) 1-25.
——— "The Printing Press Moves Westward." *Minn Hist* 15 (Mr 34) 1-25.
——— "Some Supplementary New Mexican Imprints, 1850-1860." *N Mex Hist R* 7 (Ap 32) 165-75.
——— "Was There a Printing Press in Washington in 1844?" *Wash Hist Q* 24 (Jl 33) 193-4.
———, & Allen, A. M. "A Supplementary List of Kentucky Imprints, 1794-1820." *Ky State Hist Soc Reg* 42 (Ap 44) 99-119.
McPharlin, Paul. "The Spiral Press: Twenty Years." *Pub W* 150 (12 O 46) 2231-6.
Mann, D. L. "The First Bookseller's Convention in America." *Pub W* 118 (17 My 30) 2509-13.
Mansbridge, Ronald. "By the Scholars, for the People." *SRL* 30 (7 Je 47) 9-10.
Masson, T. L. "The Big Business of Books." *NAR* 227 (Ja 29) 42-8.
Merz, Charles. "The American Press, a Summary of the Changes in a Quarter-Century." *Century* 113 (N 26) 103-10.
Miers, E. S. "Richard Ellis, Printer." *JRUL* 5 (D 41) 39-59.
——— "The Sauce Thickens." *SRL* 30 (7 Je 47) 11-2.
Miller, G. J. "David A. Borrenstein: A Printer and Publisher at Princeton, N. J., 1824-1828." *PBSA* 30 (1936) 1-56.
Mills, Walter. "Hearst." *Atl* 148 (D 31) 696-710.
Moffit, Alexander. "A Checklist of Iowa Imprints, 1837-1860." *Iowa J Hist & Pol* 36 (Ja 38) 3-95.
——— "Iowa Imprints before 1861." *Iowa J Hist & Pol* 36 (Ap 38) 152-205.
Moore, I. H. "The Earliest Printing and the First Newspaper in Texas." *Sw Hist Q* 39 (O 35) 83-99.
Morehouse, C. P. "Origins of the Episcopal Church Press from Colonial Days to 1840." *Hist Mag Prot Episc Church* 11 (Jl 42) 201-318.
Moriarity, J. H. "Hoosiers Sell Best." *Ind Quar Bkm* 3 (Ja 47) 7-14.

Morton, J. B. "William Cobbett." *London Merc* 20 (Je 29) 176-85.
Mott, F. L. "The Beadles and Their Novels." *Palimpsest* 30 (Je 49) 173-89.
——— "Pioneer Iowa in Beadle Fiction." *Palimpsest* 30 (Je 49) 190-208.
Münsterberg, Hugo. "The Disorganization of the Book Trade." *Atl* 103 (Mr 09) 403-9.
Murphy, W. C., Jr. "The Catholic Press." *Am Merc* 9 (D 26) 400-8.
Nelson, William. "Some New Jersey Printers and Printing in the Eighteenth Century." *PAAS* 21 (Ap 11) 15-56.
Nichols, C. L. "The Boston Edition of the Basket Bible." *PAAS* ns 37 (Ap 27) 24-42.
——— "Is there a Mark Baskett Bible of 1752?" *PCSM* 21 (Ap 19) 285-92.
——— "Justus Fox: A German Printer of the Eighteenth Century." *PAAS* 25 (Ap 15) 55-69.
——— "Some Notes on Isaiah Thomas and His Worcester Imprints." *PAAS* 13 (Ap 00) 429-47.
Orcutt, W. D. "In Quest of the Perfect Book." *Atl* 136 (D 25) 800-9.
P., W. "The First Real University Press in the United States." *AN&Q* 6 (Ag 46) 67-71.
Paine, Nathaniel. "Remarks on the Early American Engravings and the Cambridge Press Imprints (1640-1692) in the Library of the American Antiquarian Society." *PAAS* 17 (Ap 06) 280-98.
Paltsits, V. L. "John Holt—Printer and Postmaster." *BNYPL* 24 (S 20) 483-99.
——— "John Holt, Public Printer of New York, to the President of the Senate." *BNYPL* 26 (O 22) 942-3.
Parry, Albert. "Goodby to the Immigrant Press." *Am Merc* 28 (Ja 33) 56-7.
Parsons, Wilfrid. "Early Catholic Publishers of Philadelphia." *Cath Hist Reg* 24 (Jl 38) 141-52.
Phillips, J. D. "Recollections of Houghton Mifflin Company Fifty Years Ago." *Pub W* 152 (1 N 47) 2165-7.
Philpott, A. J. "A Pioneer Publishing Romance." *Word Study* 7 (S 34) 5-10.
Powers, Alfred. "Chronicle of Western Books Published in 1941." *Ore Hist Chron* 43 (Mr 42) 63-81.
Reichman, Felix. "German Printing in Maryland: A Check List, 1768-1950." *Soc for the Hist of the Germans in Md* 27th Report (1950) 9-70.
Roach, G. W., *et al.* "Preliminary Check List of Batavia Imprints, 1819-1876." *N Y Hist* 24 (Jl, O 43) 423-32, 565-9; 25 (Ja, Ap, Jl 44) 67-79, 228-33, 381-7.
Robinson, H. M. "Mr. Beadle's Books." *Bkm* 69 (Mr 29) 18-24.
Robinson, R. V. "Confederate Copyright Entries." *WMQ* 16 (Ap 36) 248-66.
Rose, G. D. "Early Morristown Imprints." *Proc N J Hist Soc* 53 (Jl 35) 156-63.
Rosenburg, M. V. "One Book Traveler Looks at the South." *Pub W* 119 (3 Ja 31) 39-41.
Rugg, H. G. "Printing in Peacham, Vermont." *Proc Vt Hist Soc* 12 (Ap 44) 125-8.
Samuel, Ralph. "Four Centuries of Book Titles." *Colophon* 2 (D 31) Pt 8.
Schaper, Joseph. "A Question of First Again." *Wisc Mag Hist* 16 (S 32) 102-4.
Scheer, G. F. "First Printing in the Valley of Virginia." *Pub W* 150 (23 N 46) 2891-7.
——— "University of North Carolina Press Celebrates Its Silver Anniversary." *Pub W* 151 (1 F 47) 540-4.
Schinz, Albert. "Ce qu'on lit aux États-Unis: Expériences d'un éditeur américain." *Mercure de France* 218 (15 F 30) 50-72.
Schramm, J. R. "Publication as a Scientific Problem." *PAPS* 75 (1935) 527-36.
Shaw, C. B. "The University of Oklahoma Press." *SW R* 31 (Fl 45) 61-7.
Sherman, S. C. "Leman Thomas Rede's *Bibliotheca Americana*." *WMQ* 4: ser 3 (Jl 47) 332-49.
Silver, R. G. "The Boston Book Trade, 1800-1825." *BNYPL* 52 (O, N, D 48) 487-500, 557-73, 635-50.

——— "Printer's Lobby: Model 1802." *SB* 3 (1950) 207-28.

Skipper, O. C. "'De Bow's Review' after the Civil War." *La Hist Q* 29 (Ap 46) 355-93.

Smith, G. W. "Broadsides for Freedom: Civil War Propaganda in New England." *NEQ* 21 (S 48) 291-312.

Spargo, John. "Early Vermont Printers and Printing." *Proc Vt Hist Soc* 10 (D 42) 214-29.

Spell, L. M. "The Anglo-Saxon Press in Mexico, 1846-1848." *AHR* 38 (O 32) 20-3.

——— "Samuel Bangs: The First Printer in Texas." *Hispanic AHR* 11 (My 31) 248-58; *Sw Hist Q* 25 (Ap 32) 267-8.

Starker, L. G. "Benefactors of the Cambridge Press: A Reconsideration." *SB* 3 (1950) 267-9.

Stern, M. B. "Books in the Wilderness: Some Nineteenth-Century Upstate Publishers." *N Y Hist* 31 (Jl 50) 260-82.

——— "The First Half-Century of *Publishers' Weekly*." *Pub W* 151 (18 Ja 47) 286-306.

——— "The Fruits of Authorship." *AN&Q* 8 (O 48) 99-105.

——— "James D. Bemis: Country Printer." *N Y Hist* 29 (O 48) 404-27.

——— "Keen and Cooke: Prairie Publishers." *J Ill Hist Soc* 42 (D 49) 424-45.

——— "The Leslies of Publishers' Row." *Pub W* 152 (11 O 47) B233-7.

——— "Mrs. Frank Leslie: New York's Last Bohemian." *N Y Hist* 29 (Ja 48) 21-50.

——— "The Mystery of the Leon Brothers." *Pub W* 148 (17 N 45) 2228-32.

——— "Roberts Brothers, Boston." *More Books* 20 (D 45) 419-23.

Stevens, D. H. "Scholarly Publishing and the Foundations." *Pub W* 151 (1 F 47) 520-4.

Stoudt, J. J. "The German Press in Pennsylvania and the American Revolution." *PMHB* 59 (Ja 35) 74-90.

Sutton, Walter. "Cincinnati as a Publishing and Book Trade Centre, 1796-1830." *Ohio State Arch & Hist Q* 56 (Ap 47) 117-43.

Swan, B. F. "Some Thoughts on the Bay Psalm Book of 1640, with a Census of Copies." *Yale Un Lib Gaz* 22 (Ja 48) 56-76.

Swindler, W. F. "Press and Communications: An Annotated Bibliography of Journalism Subjects in American Magazines." *JQ* 26 (Mr 49) 100-11.

Sydnor, C. S. "The Beginning of Printing in Mississippi." *J So Hist* 1 (F 35) 49-55.

Tapley, H. S. "The Declaration of Independence." *EIHC* 85 (Ja 49) 1-8.

Tassin, Algernon. "The Story of Modern Book Advertising." *Bkm* 33 (Ap, My, Je 11) 182-90, 290-302, 405-14.

Taylor, C. H. "Some Notes on Early American Lithography." *PAAS* ns 32 (Ap 22) 68-80.

Taylor, L. G. "The Way of the Best Seller." *Colophon* 2 (Je 31) Pt 6.

Thomas, C. M. "Contrasts in 150 Years of Publishing in Ohio." *Ohio State Arch & Hist Q* 51 (Jl-S 42) 184-94.

Thwartes, R. G. "The Ohio Valley Press before the War of 1812-15." *PAAS* 19 (Ap 09) 309-68.

Tolman, J. J. "The Printing Presses of William Lyon Mackenzie, Prior to 1837." *Canadian Hist R* 18 (D 37) 414-8.

Tryon, W. S. "Book Distribution in Mid-Nineteenth Century America. Illustrated by the Publishing Records of Ticknor and Fields, Boston." *PBSA* 41 (3Q 47) 210-30.

——— "The Publications of Ticknor and Fields in the South, 1840-1865." *J So Hist* 14 (Ag 48) 305-30.

——— "Ticknor and Fields' Publications in the Old Northwest, 1840-1860." *Miss Valley Hist R* 34 (Mr 48) 589-610.

Twaddell, Elizabeth. "The American Tract Society, 1814-1860." *Church Hist* 15 (Je 46) 116-32.
Vail, R. W. O. "Seventeenth Century American Book Labels." *Am Book Coll* 4 (1933) 164-76.
Wagner, H. R. "Commercial Printers of San Francisco from 1851 to 1880." *PBSA* 33 (1939) 69-84.
——— "The First Book Printed in America." *Colophon* ns 1 (Wi 36) 453-4.
Waldman, Milton. "Subscription Sets." *Am Merc* 4 (F 25) 237-43.
Walsh, M. J. "Contemporary Broadside Editions of the Declaration of Independence." *HLB* 3 (Wi 49) 31-43.
Weeks, Edward. "The Best Sellers since 1875." *Pub W* 119 (21 F 34) 1503-5.
——— "A Modern Estimate of American Best Sellers, 1875-1933." *Pub W* 125 (21 Ap 34) 1506.
——— "What Makes a Book a Best Seller?" *N Y Times Book R* (20 D 36) 2, 15.
Wegelin, Oscar. "Six Early Western Imprints." *N Y Hist Soc Quar Bul* 25 (Ap 41) 73-6.
——— "Some Rare Americana from Eastern Presses Owned by the New York Historical Society." *N Y Hist Soc Quar Bul* 27 (O 43) 93-9.
Weiss, H. B. "The Printers and Publishers of Children's Books in New York City, 1698-1830." *BNYPL* 52 (Ag 48) 383-400.
——— "Samuel Wood & Sons, Early New York Publishers of Children's Books." *BNYPL* 46 (S 42) 755-71.
——— "Solomon King, Early New York Bookseller and Publisher of Children's Books and Chapbooks." *BNYPL* 51 (S 47) 531-44.
White, L. M., Jr. "The American Publishing Scene, 1831-1858." *Madison Q* 5 (N 45) 154-64.
White, W. A. "The Passing of the Free Editor." *Am Merc* 8 (My 26) 110-2.
Wiggins, R. H. "The Louisiana Press and the Lottery." *La Hist Q* 31 (Jl-48) 716-844.
Willey, M. M. "The Press in the University." *SRL* 29 (8 Je 46) 7.
Williams, Michel. "The Recent Growth of Catholic Publishing." *Pub W* 151 (22 F 47) 1239-41.
Wilson, T. J. "Without Profit-Motive." *SRL* 30 (7 Je 47) 13, 43.
Winkler, E. W. "Check List of Texas Imprints, 1846-1876." *Sw Hist Q* 46 (Ap 43) 336-57; 47 (Jl, O 43, Ja, Ap 44) 19-28, 143-59, 268-93, 371-87; 48 (Jl, O 44, Ja, Ap 45) 38-50, 219-37, 373-86, 484-98; 49 (Jl, O 45) 89-115, 245-66, 532-84; 51 (Ja 48) 230-51; 52 (O 48) 209-26.
——— "The First Book Printed in Texas." *Un Texas Lib Chron* 2 (Sp 47) 183-6.
Winshop, G. P. "Facts and Fancies and the Cambridge Press." *Colophon* ns 3 (Au 38) 531-57.
——— "Old Auction Catalogues." *Am Col* 4 (1927) 188-93.
——— "Recollections of a Private Printer." *Colophon* ns 3 (Sp 38) 210-24.
Winterich, J. T. "Early American Books and Printing." *Pub W* 120 (17 O, 21 N, 19 D 31) 1811-3, 2309-14, 2649-53; 121 (20 F 32) 856-68; 122 (16 Jl 32) 213-4; 123 (17 Je 33) 1972-4; 124 (15 Jl, 19 Ag, 16 S, 21 O, 18 N 33) 174-7, 510-1, 912-4, 1449-50, 1749-53.
——— "The Imprints of A. Edw. Newton & Co., 1887-1893." *Colophon* ns 1 (Sp 36) 510-22.
Wroth, L. C. "The First Press of Providence." *PAAS* 51 (15 O 41) 351-83.
——— "The St. Mary's City Press." *Colophon* ns 1 (Wi 36) 333-57; *Md Hist Mag* 31 (Je 36) 91-111.

PROSE. Anon. "American Prose." *SRL* 5 (12 D 31) 363, 366.
Clough, W. U. "The Rhythm of Prose." *Un Wyo Pub* 4 (Jl 39) 1-19.
Dobrée, Bonamy. "Modern Prose Style." *Criterion* 13 (Jl 34) 561-76.
Eaton, W. P. "More Thoughts on Modern Prose." *Freeman* 1 (9 Je 20) 296-7.

——— "On Burying the Essay." *VQR* 24 (Au 48) 574-83.
Heydrick, B. A. "The [American] Essay." *Chautauquan* 65 (F 12) 313-35.
Hornberger, Theodore. "A Note on Eighteenth-Century American Prose Style." *AL* 10 (Mr 38) 77-8.
Jones, H. M. "American Prose Style: 1700-1770." *HLQ* 6 (N 34) 115-51.
Josephson, Matthew. "Corporative Prose." *NRp* 85 (29 Je 38) 207-9.
Logan, J. D. "American Prose Style." *Atl* 87 (My 01) 689-96.
Lundkvist, Artur. "Amerikansk prosa." *Bonniers Litterära Magasin* 6 (Mr 37) 197-204.
Matthews, Brander. "American Epigrams." *Harper's* 107 (N 03) 862-5.
Repplier, Agnes. "The American Essay in War Time." *YR* ns 7 (Ja 18) 249-59.

REGIONALISM. Anon. "Articles on or Related to Alabama Appearing in Current Periodicals." *Ala R* 3 (O 50) 304-11.
——— "Minnesota Has a Writing Boom." *Life* 24 (8 Mr 48) 125-9, 131.
——— "Novels of Western Life." *Bkm* 32 (S 10) 20-1.
Abrahams, William. "The Disappearing Centre: Notes on Boston and Cambridge." *Horizon* 16 (O 47) 81-4.
Adams, Andy. "Western Interpreters." *Sw R* 10 (O 24) 70-4.
Adler, M. J. "The Chicago School." *Harper's* 183 (S 41) 377-88.
Adriance, G. N. "Literature of the Old West." *Overland Mo* 93 (Mr 35) 11.
Aikman, Duncan. "The Home-Town Mind." *Harper's* 151 (N 25) 663-9.
Allen, Charles. "Regionalism and the Little Magazines." *CE* 7 (O 45) 10-6.
Anderson, P. A. "The Intellectual Life of Pittsburgh, 1781-1836." *West Penn Hist Mag* 14 (Ja, Ap, Jl, O 31) 9-27, 92-114, 225-36, 288-309.
Anderson, Sherwood. "Why Must There Be a Midwestern Literature?" *Vanity Fair* 16 (Mr 21) 23-4.
Angoff, Charles. "Boston Twilight." *Am Merc* 6 (D 25) 439-44.
Atkeson, M. M. "A Study of the Local Literature of the Upper Ohio Valley, with Especial Reference to the Early Pioneer and Indian Tales, 1820-1840." *Ohio State Un Bul* 26 (S 21) 1-62.
Austin, Mary. "Regionalism in American Fiction." *EJ* 21 (F 32) 97-106.
———, *et al.* "Southwestern Culture: A Symposium." *Sw R* 14 (Jl 29) 474-94.
Bacheller, Irving. "American Backgrounds for Fiction: The North Country of New York." *Bkm* 38 (F 14) 624-8.
Bacon, E. M. "The Literary Associations of the Hudson." *Critic* 41 (S 02) 221-9.
Baker, J. E. "Four Arguments for Regionalism." *SRL* 15 (28 N 36) 3-4, 14.
——— "Provinciality." *CE* 1 (Mr 40) 488-94.
——— "Regionalism in the Middle West." *Am R* 4 (Mr 35) 603-14.
——— "Using Our Regional Past." *Am Prefaces* 7 (Su 42) 332-9.
——— "Western Man against Nature." *CE* 4 (O 42) 19-26.
Barr, Stringfellow. "The Uncultured South." *VQR* 5 (Ap 29) 192-200.
Bashford, Herbert. "The Literary Development of the Pacific Coast." *Atl* 92 (Jl 03) 1-9.
Baskervill, W. M. "Southern Literature." *PMLA* 7 (1892) 89-100.
Basso, Hamilton. "Letters in the South." *NRp* 83 (19 Je 35) 161-3.
Beath, P. R. "The Fallacies of Regionalism." *SRL* 15 (28 N 36) 3-4, 14, 16.
Berry, Edmund. "The Road to Concord." *Dalhousie R* 20 (Ja 41) 433-8.
Billington, Ray. "Writers in Revolt Against Society." *Chicago Sun Book Week* 4 (4 My 47) 8.
Bishop, J. P. "The South and Tradition." *VQR* 9 (Ap 33) 161-74.
Bland, H. H. "How Some of the Western Writers Work." *Overland Mo* ns 51 (Je 08) 511-3.
——— "Literary Monterey." *Overland Mo* ns 53 (Ja 09) 19-26.
——— "Literature of Oregon." *Overland Mo* ns 63 (Mr 14) 278-85.

Blythe, LeGette. "North Carolina's Books and Authors of the Year: A Review." *N C Hist R* 24 (Ap 47) 224-34
Boatright, M. C. "The Genius of Pecos Bill." *Sw R* 14 (Sp 29) 419-28.
——— "The Tall Tale in Texas." *SAQ* 30 (Jl 31) 271-9.
Bochstahler, O. L. "Contributions to American Literature by Hoosiers of German Ancestry." *Ind Mag Hist* 38 (S 42) 231-50.
Boie, Mildred. "The Myth about the Middle West." *Spectator* 145 (5 Jl 30) 9-10.
Bond, B. W., Jr. "American Civilization Comes to the Old Northwest." *Miss Valley Hist R* 19 (Je 32) 3-29.
Bonner, J. W., Jr. "Bibliography of Georgia Authors, 1949-1950." *Ga R* 4 (Wi 50) 253-67.
Botkin, B. A. " 'Folksay' and 'Space': Their Genesis and Exodus." *Sw R* 20 (Jl 35) 321-35.
——— "Regionalism: Cult or Culture?" *EJ* 25 (Mr 36) 181-4.
——— "We Talk about Regionalism." *Frontier* (My 33) 1-11.
Bowman, Heath. "Those Hoosiers." *SRL* 28 (6 Ja 45)6-7.
Bowyer, J. W. "Conflict in the South." *Sw R* 28 (Sp 43) 252-66.
Boyd, E. "The Literature of Santos." *Sw R* 35 (Sp 50) 128-40.
Boynton, H. W. "Literature by Piecemeal." *EJ* 23 (Mr 34) 179-88.
Bradley, W. A. "The Folk Culture of the Kentucky Cumberlands." *Dial* 64 (31 Ja 18) 95-8.
Brashear, M. M. "Missouri Literature since the First World War." *Mo Hist R* 40 (O 45) 1-20.
——— "The Missouri Short Story as It Has Grown Out of the Tall Tale of the Frontier." *Mo Hist R* 43 (Ap 49) 199-219
Brewton, W. W. "St. Elmo and St. Twelvemo." *SRL* 5 (22 Ja 29) 1123-4.
Brickell, Hershel. "The Literary Awakening in the South." *Bkm* 66 (O 27) 138-43.
Bright, Verne. "The Davy Crockett Legend and Tales in the Oregon Country." *Ore Hist Q* 51 (S 50) 207-15.
Brooks, Cleanth. "What the Deep South Needs." *SRL* 25 (19 S 42) 8-9.29.
———, & Warren, R. P. "Dixie Looks at Mrs. Gerould." *AR* 6 (Mr 36) 585-95.
Buck, E. H. "Early Literary Culture in Western Pennsylvania." *Pittsburgh Record* 9 (1935) 3-8.
Buley, R. C. "Glimpses of Pioneer Mid-West Social and Cultural History." *Miss Valley Hist R* 23 (Mr 37) 481-510.
Burford, William. "Big D." *Am Letters* 1 (D 48) 2-7.
Burkhart, J. A. "Texas, Texans, and Texanism." *AR* 9 (Fl 49) 316-31.
Burns, Aubrey. "Regional Culture in California." *Sw R* 18 (Su 32) 373-94.
Burpee, L. J. "Literature of the Western Fur Trade." *Dial* 42 (1 Ap 07) 212-4.
Bushby, D. M. "Poets of Our Southern Frontier." *Overland Mo* 89 (F 31) 41-2, 58.
Capers, Charlotte. "In the Mail: Letters from Dublin and Mississippi." *N Y Times Book R* (7 N 48) 45.
Cardwell, G. A. "On Scholarship and Southern Literature." *SAQ* 40 (Ja 41) 60-72.
Carroll, G. H. "New England Sees It Through." *SRL* 13 (9 N 35) 3-4, 14, 17.
Carruth, F. W. "Boston in Fiction." *Bkm* 14 (N, D 01, Ja, F 02) 236-54, 364-88, 507-21, 590-604.
Carson, W. G. B. "The Beginnings of the Theatre in St. Louis." *Mo Hist Soc Coll* 5 (1924) 129-65.
Cash, W. J. "Literature and the South." *SRL* 23 (28 D 40) 3-4, 18-9.
Cater, Catherine. "Four Voices Out of the South." *Mich Alumnus Q* (Wi 44) 166-73.
——— "Myth and the Contemporary Southern Novelist: A Note." *Midwest J* 2 (Wi 49) 1-8.
Caughey, J. W. "Shaping a Literary Tradition." *Pacific Hist R* 8 (Je 39) 201-15.
Chapman, A. "The New West and the Old Fiction." *Independent* 54 (Ja 02) 98-100.
Chapman, L. F. "Florida." *Am Merc* 6 (N 25) 337-42.

Chase, Daniel. "Local Color." *Chri Sci Mon* 34 (12 F 42) 8.
Chittick, V. L. O. "Ring-Tailed Roarers." *Frontier* 13 (My 33) 257-63.
Chokla, Sarah. "Bookprinting in Texas." *Sw R* 21 (Ap 36) 319-29.
Clark, J. A. "The Middle West—There It Lies." *So R* 2 (Wi 37) 462-72.
Clough, W. O. "Regionalism." *Rocky Mt R* 3 (Wi 38-9) 1-2.
Clugston, W. G. "The Collapse of Kentucky." *Am Merc* 6 (N 25) 265-71.
Cobb, L. M. "Drama in North Carolina." *SLM* 2 (Ap 00) 228-35.
Cole, A. C. "The Puritan and Fair Terpsichore." *Miss Valley Hist R* 29 (Je 42) 3-34.
Cole, W. I. "Maine in Literature." *N E Mag* ns 22 (Ag 00) 726-43.
Coleman, R. A. "Literature and the Region." *Pac Nw Q* 39 (O 48) 312-8.
Collins, C. E. "Nineteenth Century Fiction of the Southern Appalachians." *Bul Bibl* 17 (S-D 42, Ja-Ap 43) 186-90, 215-8.
Colomb, R. W. "Dufour's Local Sketches, 1847." *La Hist Q* 14 (Ap 31) 208-304.
Commager, Henry. "The Literature of the Pioneer West." *Minn Hist* 8 (D 27) 319-28.
Connor, L. R. "Southern Plays on the Gotham Stage." *SLM* 1 (Je 39) 407-11.
Conway, A. M. "Art for Art's Sake in Southern Literature." *SR* 24 (Ja 16) 81-7.
Cordell, R. A. "Limestone, Corn, and Literature." *SRL* 19 (17 D 38) 3-4, 14-5.
Couch, W. T. "Reflections on the Southern Tradition." *SAQ* 35 (Jl 36) 284-97.
Craven, Avery. "The Literature of the Old Northwest." *N Y Herald-Tribune Books* 14 (31 Jl 38) 1-2, 5.
——— "The 'Turner Theories' and the South." *J So Hist* 5 (Ag 39) 291-314.
Crowell, C. T. "Cowboys." *Am Merc* 9 (O 26) 162-9.
Curvin, J. W. "Regional Drama in One World." *QJS* 33 (D 47) 480-4.
Dabney, Virginius. "Virginia." *Am Merc* 9 (N 26) 349-56.
Dale, E. E. "The Cow Country in Transition." *Miss Valley Hist R* 24 (Je 37) 3-20.
Daniels, Jonathan. "F. O. B. Dixie." *SRL* 14 (29 Ag 36) 3-4.
Davenport, F. G. "Cultural Life in Nashville on the Eve of the Civil War." *J So Hist* 3 (Ag 37) 326-47.
——— "Culture versus Frontier in Tennessee 1825-1850." *J So Hist* 5 (F 39) 18-33.
Davis, Elmer. "The Indiana Faith." *SRL* 26 (4 D 41) 3-4.
Davidson, Donald. "A Meeting of Southern Writers." *Bkm* 74 (Ja-F 32) 494-6.
——— "Regionalism and Nationalism in American Literature." *Am R* 5 (Ap 35) 48-61.
——— "Regionalism as Social Science." *So R* 3 (Au 37) 209-24.
——— "Sectionalism in America." *H&H* 6 (Jl-S 33) 561-89.
——— "The Southern Poet and His Tradition." *Poetry* 40 (My 32) 94-103.
Daviess, M. T. "American Backgrounds for Fiction: Tennessee." *Bkm* 38 (D 13) 394-9.
DeCasseres, Benjamin. "The Broadway Mind." *Am Merc* 12 (O 27) 178-81.
Dell, Floyd. "Chicago in Fiction." *Bkm* 38 (N, D 13) 270-7, 374-9.
DeVoto, Bernard. "The Great Medicine Road." *Am Merc* 11 (My 27) 104-12.
——— "The Mountain Men." *Am Merc* 9 (D 26) 472-9.
——— "A Sagebrush Bookshelf." *Harper's* 175 (O 37) 488-96.
——— "Utah." *Am Merc* 7 (Mr 26) 317-23.
Dickason, D. H. "Clarence King's First Western Journey." *HLQ* 7 (N 43) 71-88.
Dickey, Dallas. "Southern Oratory: A Field for Research." *QJS* 33 (D 47) 458-63.
Dixon, Thomas. "American Backgrounds for Fiction: North Carolina." *Bkm* 38 (Ja 14) 511-21.
Dobie, C. C. "The First California Authors." *Bkm* 72 (F 31) 590-6.
Dobie, J. F. "The Writer and His Region." *SW R* 35 (Sp 50) 81-7.
Donald, David, & Palmer, F. A. "Toward a Western Literature." *Miss Valley Hist R* 35 (D 48) 413-28.
Dondore, Dorothy. "Points of Contact between History and Literature in the Mississippi Valley." *Miss Valley Hist R* 11 (S 24) 227-36.

Dorson, R. M. "Dialect Stories of the Upper Peninsula: A New Form of American Folklore." *JAF* 61 (Ap-Je 49) 113-50.
Dougherty, C. T. "Novels of the Middle Border: A Critical Bibliography for Historians." *Hist Bul* 25 (My 47) 77-8, 85-8.
Drew, H. L. "Literary Visitors to the Rock River Valley, 1832-1882." *Ill Lib* 18 (Ja 36) 42-52.
DuBois, A. E. "Among the Quarterlies: The Question of 'Regionalism.'" *SR* 45 (Ap-Je 37) 216-27.
Dykes, J. C. "Dime Novel Texas; or, the Sub Literature of the Lone Star State." *Sw Hist Q* 49 (Ja 46) 327-40.
Eagleton, D. F. "The Sonnet in Texas Literature." *Texas R* 2 (O 16) 150-66.
Eaton, W. P. "In Defense of the Puritan." *Am Merc* 1 (Ap 24) 424-8.
Emch, L. B. "Ohio in Short Stories, 1824-1839." *Ohio Arch & Hist Q* 53 (Jl-S 44) 209-50.
English, T. H. "One Hundred Famous Southern Books." *So Atl Bul* 13 (My 47) 1, 12-3.
Esarey, Logan. "The Literary Spirit among the Early Ohio Valley Settlers." *Miss Valley Hist R* 5 (S 18) 143-57.
Escoube, Lucienne. "Les Plantations et les États du Sud dans la littérature américaine." *Mercure de France* 303 (My 48) 64-77.
Evans, Medford. "Oxford, Mississippi." *So R* 15 (Au 29) 46-63.
Fairies, Elizabeth. "The Miami Country, 1750-1815, as Described in Journals and Letters." *Ohio State Arch & Hist Q* 57 (Ja 48) 48-65.
Ferril, T. H. "Writing in the Rockies." *SRL* 15 (2 Mr 37) 1-2, 13-4.
Field, L. M. "The South on Broadway." *SLM* 2 (Mr 40) 174-6.
Firkins, O. W. "Undepicted America." *YR* 20 (Au 30) 140-50.
Fitch, W. T. "Is There Literary and Artistic Culture in California?" *Overland Mo* 84 (D 26) 379, 408-12.
Fitzell, Lincoln. "Western Letter." *SR* 55 (Su 47) 530-5.
Flanagan, J. T. "Literary Protests in the Midwest." *Sw R* 34 (Sp 48) 148-57.
——— "Novels of the Midlands." *Chicago Sun Book Week* 4 (4 My 47) 4.
——— "Some Minnesota Novels, 1920-1950." *Minn Hist* 31 (S 50) 145-57.
——— "Texas Speaks Texan." *Sw R* 31 (Sp 46) 191-2.
Flanders, B. H. "Reading and Writing in Early Georgia." *Ga R* 1 (Su 47) 209-17.
Fleming, H. E. "Literary Interests of Chicago." *Am J Soc* 11 (N 05, Ja, My 06) 377-408, 499-531, 784-816; 12 (Jl 06) 68-118.
Fletcher, J. G. "American Regionalism." *Freeman* 7 (5 S 23) 621-2.
——— "Regionalism and Folk Art." *Sw R* 19 (Jl 34) 429-34.
Flower, B. O. "A Golden Day in Boston's History." *Arena* 32 (Ag 04) 151-66.
Foldes, Lili. "Charleston." *Common Sense* 14 (Ag 45) 28-9.
Frank, Waldo. "Mid-America Revisited." *Am Merc* 8 (Jl 26) 322-6.
Frazier, A. C. M. "The South Speaks Out." *SR* 35 (Jl 27) 313-24.
Frederick, J. T. "The Writer's Iowa." *Palimpsest* 11 (F 30) 57-60.
Fulks, Clay. "The Sacred Poesy of the South." *Am Merc* 12 (S 27) 75-80.
Gale, Zona. "The American Village Defended." *N Y Times Mag* 80 (19 Jl 31) 12-21.
Gardner, Jennie. "Book Reviewing in the Deep South." *SRL* 25 (19 S 42) 15.
Gathe, R. M. "Ketturah Belknap's Chronicle of the Bellfountain Settlement." *Ore Hist Q* 38 (S 37) 265-99.
Gerould, K. F. "The Aristocratic West." *Harper's* 151 (S 25) 466-77.
——— "A Yankee Looks at Dixie." *Am Merc* 37 (F 35) 217-20.
Glenn, Eunice. "Southern Writers Today." *Am Letters* 1 (Ja 49) 2-10.
Gloster, H. G. "The Negro Writer and the Southern Scene." *So Packet* 4 (Ja 48) 1-3.
Gray, James. "The Minnesota Muse." *SRL* 16 (12 Je 37) 3-4, 14.
Gulliver, H. S. "Thackeray in Georgia." *Ga R* 1 (Sp 47) 35-43.

H., H. "Chicago Develops Realistic Writers." *Holiday* 2 (My 47) 32-3.
Hale, E. E. "The Romantic Landscape of the Far West." *Union Col Bul* 23 (Ja 30) 5-17.
Hallgren, Mauritz. "Delaware." *Am Merc* 8 (Je 26) 173-9.
Harben, W. H. "American Backgrounds for Fiction: Georgia." *Bkm* 38 (O 13) 186-92.
Harris, L. H. "Southern Writers." *Critic* 47 (S 05) 260-3.
Harwood, W. S. "New Orleans in Fiction." *Critic* 47 (N 05) 426-35.
Hatcher, Harlan. "Connecticut Goes West." *SRL* 28 (6 Ja 45) 20-1.
Hawley, Edith. "Bibliography of Literary Geography." *Bul Bibl* 10 (Ap, Jl-S, O-D 18; Ja-Mr, Ap-Je 19) 34-8, 58-60, 76, 93-4, 104-5.
Hemstreet, Charles. "Literary Landmarks of New York." *Critic* 41 (Jl, Ag, S, O, N 02) 41-9, 158-65, 238-45, 333-40, 427-32; 42 (Ja, F, Mr, Je 03) 53-8, 143-8, 237-43, 517-23; 43 (Jl, Ag, S 03) 41-6, 153-8, 239-45.
Henderson, A. C. "The Folk Poetry of These States." *Poetry* 16 (Ag 20) 264-73.
Henneman, J. B. "The National Element in Southern Literature." *SR* 11 (Jl 03) 345-66.
Herbst, Josephine. "Iowa Takes to Literature." *Am Merc* 7 (Ap 26) 466-70.
Herron, I. H. "The Blight of Romanticism." *SW R* 26 (Su 41) 449-53.
——— "Charleston: Ante-bellum Magazine Center." *Sw R* 22 (O 36) 100-6.
——— "Texas Prose Anthologies." Dallas *Times Herald Book Sup* sec 2 (7 O 45) 5.
Hesseltine, W. B. "The Propaganda Literature of Confederate Prisons." *J So Hist* 1 (F 35) 56-66.
Hogan, W. R. "Amusements in the Republic of Texas." *J So Hist* 3 (N 37) 397-421.
Holliday, Carl. "One Phase of Literary Conditions in the South." *SR* 11 (O 03) 463-6.
Hornberger, Theodore. "Three Self-Conscious Wests." *Sw R* 26 (Jl 41) 428-48.
Howe, Irving. "The South and Current Literature." *Am Merc* 67 (O 48) 494-503.
Howe, M. A. DeW. "The Boston Religon." *Atl* 91 (Je 03) 729-38.
——— "The 'Literary Centre.'" *Atl* 92 (S 03) 346-55.
Howells, W. D. "Certain of the Chicago School of Fiction." *NAR* 176 (My 03) 734-46.
Hubach, R. R. "Illinois, Host to Well-Known Nineteenth-Century Authors." *J Ill State Hist Soc* 38 (D 45) 446-67.
——— "St. Louis: Host of Celebrated Nineteenth Century British and American Authors." *Mo Hist R* 38 (Jl 44) 375-87.
Hubbell, J. B. "The Decay of the Provinces." *SR* 35 (O 27) 473-87.
——— "The Frontier in American Literature." *Sw R* 10 (Ja 25) 84-92.
——— "The New Southwest." *Sw R* 10 (O 24) 91-9.
——— "The Old South in Literary Histories." *SAQ* 48 (Jl 49) 452-67.
——— "On 'Southern Literature.'" *Texas R* 8 (O 21) 8-16.
Jillson, W. R. "A Bibliography of Lexington, Kentucky." *Register Ky Hist Soc* 45 (Ja 47) 39-70.
Johnson, Clifton. "The Winter of the New England Poets." *N E Mag* ns 41 (D 09) 393-403.
Johnson, G. W. "The Horrible South." *VQR* 11 (Ap 35) 201-7.
——— "The South Takes the Offensive." *Am Merc* 2 (My 24) 70-8.
——— "Southern Image-Breakers." *VQR* 4 (O 28) 508-19.
Johnson, R. B. "The Tyranny of Local Color." *Critic* 48 (Mr 06) 266-8.
Johnston, Charles. "Old Funny Stories of the South and West." *Harper's W* 57 (4 Ja 13) 21.
Jones, H. M. "The Future of Southern Culture." *Sw R* 16 (Wi 31) 141-65.
——— "Is There a Southern Literary Renaissance?" *VQR* 6 (Ap 30) 184-97.

——— "Literature and Orthodoxy in Boston after the Civil War." *Am Q* 1 (Su 49) 149-65.
Jones, Idwal. "Letters on the Pacific Rim." *SRL* 15 (30 Ja 37) 3-4, 15.
Jones, Llewellyn. "Chicago, Our Literary Crater." *Bkm* 60 (Ja 25) 565-7.
Jordan, P. D. "Roots in the Valley." *SRL* 28 (6 Ja 45) 8-9.
Kendall, C. W. "Support of California Letters." *Overland Mo* 88 (N 30) 335.
Kendall, J. S. "New Orleans Negro Minstrels." *La Hist Q* 30 (Ja 47) 128-48.
Kendrick, B. B. "The Colonial Status of the South." *J So Hist* 8 (F 42) 3-22.
Keyserling, Hermann. "The South—America's Hope." *Atl* 144 (N 29) 605-8.
Klingberg, F. J. "The Value of Regional Literature." *Hist Mag Prot Episc Church* 10 (D 40) 399-401.
Knickerbocker, W. S. "Mr. Ransom and the Old South." *SR* 39 (Ap-Je 31) 222-38.
——— "Up from the South." *WR* 13 (Sp 49) 168-78.
Knight, G. C. "Bluegrass and Laurel: The Varieties of Kentucky Fiction." *SRL* 28 (6 Ja 45) 12-3.
Kroll, H. H. "Deep South—Never, Never Land." *SRL* 25 (19 S 42) 1-2.
Knowlton, Don. "Ohio." *Am Merc* 7 (F 26) 175-81.
LaFollette, Robert. "Interstate Migration and Indiana Culture." *Miss Valley Hist R* 16 (D 29) 347-58.
Leonard, N. H. "Let's Look at Alabama Poets." *Ala School J* 66 (N 48) 16-8.
Levy, B. M. "Mutations in New England Local Color." *NEQ* 19 (S 46) 338-58.
Lewis, C. L. "What Is a Southern Book?" *SLM* 3 (Ap 41) 194-6.
Lewis, N. B. "North Carolina." *Am Merc* 8 (My 26) 36-43.
Libby, O. G. "The New Northwest." *Miss Valley Hist R* 7 (Mr 21) 332-47.
Lomas, C. W. "Southern Orators in California before 1861." *So Speech J* 15 (S 49) 21-37.
Loomis, C. G. "'Four Shillings, Sir': Massachusetts vs. Missouri." *NEQ* 18 (D 45) 507-8.
Mabie, H. W. "The Poetry of the South." *Int Mo* 5 (F 02) 201-23.
——— "Provincialism in American Life." *Harper's* 134 (Mr 17) 579-84.
McCleod, Norman. "Regionalism: A Symposium." *SR* 39 (O-D 31) 456-83.
McDermott, J. F. "Books in Eighteenth Century Sainte Genevieve." *St Genevieve Fair Play* (17 Ag 35).
McDowell, Tremaine. "Regionalism in the United States." *Minn Hist* 20 (Je 39) 105-18.
McGill, Josephine. "Sing All a Green Willow." *NAR* 228 (Ag 29) 218-24.
McKee, Irving. "Notable Memorials to Mussell Slough." *Pac Hist R* 17 (F 48) 19-27.
McLeod, Norman, *et al.* "Regionalism: A Symposium." *SR* 39 (O-D 31) 456-83.
McLuhan, H. M. "The Southern Quality." *SR* 55 (Su 47) 357-83.
MacMinn, G. R. "The Gentleman from Pike in Early California." *AL* 8 (My 36) 160-9.
McMurtrie, D. C. "El Payode Nuevo-Mejico." *N Mex Hist R* 8 (Ap 33) 130-8.
McWilliams, Cary. "Localism in American Criticism." *Sw R* 19 (Jl 34) 410-28.
——— "Myths of the West." *NAR* 232 (N 31) 424-32.
——— "Swell Letters in California." *Am Merc* 21 (S 30) 42-7.
——— "The Writers of California." *Bkm* 72 (D 30) 352-60.
Macy, John. "The Passing of the Yankee." *Bkm* 73 (Ag 31) 616-21.
Maltby, J. E. "Exhibit of Western Writings." *Overland Mo* 89 (My 31) 154.
Marcosson, I. F. "The South in Fiction: Kentucky and Tennessee." *Bkm* 32 (D 10) 360-70.
Marshall, R. P. "A Mythical Mayflower Competition: North Carolina Literature in the Half-Century Following the Revolution." *N C Hist R* 27 (Ap 50) 178-92.
Martin, H. R. "American Backgrounds for Fiction: The Pennsylvania Dutch." *Bkm* 38 (N 13) 244-7.
Matchett, W. T. "Boston Is Afraid of Books." *SRL* 27 (15 Jl 44) 5-7, 21.

Maurice, A. B. "The New York of the Novelists." *Bkm* 42 (S, O 15) 20-39, 165-92.
Merriam, H. G. "Expression of Northwest Life." *N Mex Q* 6 (My 34) 127-32.
Merz, Charles. "Behind the Blocs: A New Explanation of Our Growing Sectionalism." *Harper's* 151 (Je 25) 76-81.
Miles, J. T. "Nineteenth Century Southern Literature and Its Five Great Poets." *SLM* 1 (S 39) 573-603.
Millard, Bailey. "San Francisco in Fiction." *Bkm* 31 (Ag 10) 585-97.
Miller, A. B. "Philadelphia." *Am Merc* 9 (O 26) 199-206.
Mills, R. V. "Emerson Bennett's Two Oregon Novels." *Ore Hist Q* 41 (D 40) 367-81.
Mims, Edwin. "The Function of Criticism in the South." *SAQ* 2 (O 03) 334-45; 31 (Ap 32) 133-49.
——— "A Semi-Centennial of North Carolina's Intellectual Progress." *N C Hist R* 24 (Ap 47) 235-56.
——— "The South's Intellectual Expression." *World's Work* 14 (Je 07) 8979-84.
Moody, A. D. "Dixie Debunked." *Am Merc* 43 (Ap 38) 392-403.
Moriarity, J. H. "Hoosiers Sell Best." *Ind Quar Bkm* 3 (Ja 47) 7-14.
Morley, S. G. "Cowboy and Gaucho Fiction." *NMQR* 16 (Au 46) 253-67.
Morris, R. L. "*Ozark* or *Masserue*." *Ark Hist Q* 3 (Mr 43) 39-43.
Morrison, M. B. "Poetry of the Southern United States." *Westminster R* 176 (Jl 11) 61-72.
Morrissette, Pat. "Notes on Mid-Western Oblivion." *Poetry* 34 (S 29) 346-55.
Morse, J. M. "Colonial Historians of New York." *N Y Hist* 23 (N 42) 395-409.
Moses, M. J. "Literary Life in the Tennessee Mountains." *Bkm* 36 (S 12) 47-52.
——— "The South in Fiction: The Trail of the Lower South." *Bkm* 33 (Ap 11) 161-72.
Mulder, Arnold. "Authors and Wolverines." *SRL* 19 (4 Mr 39) 3-4, 16.
Murray, A. M. "Early Literary Developments in Indiana." *Ind Mag Hist* 36 (D 40) 327-33.
Nadal, E. S. "Southern Literature." *Independent* 72 (8 F 12) 294-8.
Nathan, G. J. "New York versus America." *Am Merc* 59 (D 44) 692-6.
Neuberger, R. L. "Readers and Writers in Alaska." *N Y Times Book R* 52 (24 Ag 47) 28.
Nolle, A. H. "The German Drama on the St. Louis Stage." *Ger Am Annals* ns 15 (1917) 29-65, 73-112.
Oldham, J. N. "Anatomy of Provincialism." *SR* 44 (Ja-Mr, Ap-Je, Jl-S 36) 68-75, 144-52, 298-302.
Olson, J. C. "The Literary Tradition of Pioneer Nebraska." *Prairie Schooner* 24 (Su 50) 161-8.
Page, E. R. "I'm from Missouri." *SRL* 22 (27 Ap 40) 3-4, 19.
Parks, E. W. "Legaré and Grayson: Types of Classical Influence on Criticism in the Old South." *Sw R* 22 (Jl 37) 354-65.
Pattee, F. L. "The Soul of Florida." *SAQ* 43 (O 44) 338-48.
Peterkin, Julia. "One Southern View-point." *NAR* 244 (Wi 37-8) 389-98.
Piercey, J. K. "The 'Character' in the Literature of Early New England." *NEQ* 12 (S 39) 470-6.
Poley, I. C. "Quakers and Words: Some Stories about Friends." *Word Study* 24 (F 49) 1-3.
Pound, Louise. "Biographical Accuracy and 'H. H.'" *AL* 2 (Ja 31) 418-21.
Powell, J. B. "Missouri Authors and Journalists in the Orient." *Mo Hist R* 41 (O 46) 45-55.
Power, R. I. "The Hoosier as an American Folk-Type." *Ind Mag Hist* 38 (Je 42) 107-22.
Pratt, J. W. "The Cumberland Mountains in Verse." *SAQ* 17 (Jl 18) 217-21.
Pressly, T. J. "Agrarianism: An Autopsy." *SR* 49 (Ap-Je 41) 145-63.
Putnam, Samuel. "Chicago: An Obituary." *Am Merc* 8 (Ag 26) 417-25.

Ransom, J. C. "The Aesthetic of Regionalism." *Am R* 2 (Ja 34) 290-310.
——— "Modern with Southern Accent." *VQR* 11 (Ap 35) 184-200.
Rawlings, M. K. "Regional Literature of the South." *CE* 1 (F 40) 381-9.
Rascoe, Burton. "The Southern Accent." *Am Merc* 11 (My 27) 73-5.
Richardson, E. R. "The South Grows Up." *Bkm* 70 (Ja 30) 545-50.
Robinson, D. S. "Indiana's Cultural Heritage." *Ind Mag Hist* 34 (Je 38) 145-56.
Robinson, Ted. "Claims of the Buckeye." *SRL* 16 (7 Ag 37) 3-4, 13, 14.
Roe, V. E. "The Western Novel." *Overland Mo* 88 (Ja 30) 9.
Rogers, J. W. "A Round-Up of the Most Interesting Texas Books." *Times Herald* (Dallas) (7 O 45).
Romberg, Annie. "A Texas Literary Society of Pioneer Days." *Sw Hist Q* 52 (Jl 48) 60-5.
Rourke, Constance. "The Significance of Sections." *NRp* 26 (20 S 33) 148-51.
Salley, A. S. "A Bibliography of the Women Writers of South Carolina." *Pub So Hist Assn* 5 (Mr 02) 143-57.
Sampley, A. M. "Thin Harvest in Texas Literature." *Sw R* 31 (Fl 45) 92-4.
Sancton, Thomas. "The New York Myth." *NRp* 107 (27 Jl 42) 112-4.
Sandoz, Mari. "Some Tall Tales of Nebraska." *Neb Hist* 24 (Ja-Mr 43) 57-8.
Saunders, Lyle. "A Guide to the Literature of the Southwest." *NMQR* 16 (Su, Au, Wi 46) 240-6, 399-408, 523-7.
Sellers, M. P. "New England in American Colonial Literature." *N E Mag* ns 27 (Mr 03) 100-7.
Semmes, Raphael. "Vignettes of Maryland History from the Society's Collection of Broadsides." *Md Hist Mag* 39 (Je 44) 95-126.
Sergeant, E. S. "The Santa Fe Group." *SRL* 11 (8 D 34) 352-4.
Sherman, C. B. "Farm-Life Fiction in the South." *SLM* 1 (Mr 39) 203-10.
——— "Rural Literature Faces Peace." *SAQ* 42 (Ja 43) 59-71.
——— "Rural Poetry in the South." *SLM* 1 (Jl 39) 461-5.
Shipton, C. K. "Literary Leaven in Provincial New England." *NEQ* 9 (Je 36) 203-17.
Shyrock, R. H. "Cultural Factors in the History of the South." *J So Hist* 5 (Ag 39) 333-46.
Simkins, F. B. "The Everlasting South." *J So Hist* 13 (Ag 47) 307-22.
Smith, H. J. "The Midwest's Literary Background." *Midwest* 1 (S 34) 3.
Smith, H. N. "The Frontier Hypothesis and the Myth of the West." *Am Q* 2 (Sp 50) 3-11.
——— "Kit Carson in Books." *Sw R* 28 (Wi 43) 164-89.
——— "The Southwest: An Introduction." *SRL* 25 (16 My 42) 5-6,
——— "The Western Farmer in Imaginative Literature, 1818-1891." *Miss Valley Hist R* 36 (D 49) 479-90.
Smith, R. W. "The Southwest in Fiction." *SRL* 25 (16 My 42) 2-13, 37.
Snyder, H. N. "The Matter of Southern Literature." *SR* 15 (Ap 07) 218-26.
Spivey, H. E. "Southern Literary Culture: An Annotated Bibliography for 1946." *So Atl Bul.* Annually in May.
Spotts, G. B. "The Development of Fiction on the Missouri Frontier (1830-1860)." *Mo Hist R* 29 (O-Jl 35) 17-26, 100-8, 186-96.
Stace, F. "Michigan's Contribution to Literature." *Mich Hist Mag* 14 (Sp 30) 226-32.
Starke, Aubrey. "Books in the Wilderness." *J Ill State Hist Soc* 29 (Ja 36) 258-70.
Stearns, B. M. "Literary Rivalry and Local Books." *Americana* 30 (Ja 36) 7-19.
Stegner, Wallace. "The Trail of the Hawkeye." *SRL* 18 (30 Je 38) 3-4, 16-7.
Stewart, Randall. "Regional Characteristics in the Literature of New England." *CE* 3 (N 41) 129-43.
Stokes, F. M. "Fred Stocking and His Service to California Literature." *Overland Mo* ns 59 (F 12) 111-4.
Suckow, Ruth. "Iowa." *Am Merc* 9 (S 26) 39-45.

——— "Middle Western Literature." *EJ* 21 (Mr 32) 175-81.
Sutcliffe, Denham. "New Light on the Chicago Writers." *Newberry Lib Bul* 2: ser 5 (D 50) 146-57.
Swift, Lindsay. "Boston as Portrayed in Fiction." *Book Buyer* 23 (O 01).
Sydnor, C. S. "The Southern Experiment in Writing Social History." *J So Hist* 11 (N 45) 455-68.
Tait, S. W., Jr. "Indiana." *Am Merc* 7 (Ap 26) 440-7.
——— "Missouri." *Am Merc* 8 (Ag 26) 481-8.
Tate, Allen. "The New Provincialism." *VQR* 21 (Sp 45) 262-72.
——— "The Profession of Letters in the South." *VQR* 11 (Ap 35) 161-76.
Thompson, Maurice. "Hoosier Literature." *Independent* 52 (23 Ag 00) 2023-5.
Tinker, E. L. "Gombo: The Creole Dialect of Louisiana, with a Bibliography." *PAAS* ns 45 (Ap 35) 101-42.
Townsend, J. W. "A History of Kentucky Literature since 1913." *Filson Club Hist Q* 13 (Ja 39) 21-36.
Trent, W. P. "The Poetry of the American Plantations." *SR* 8 (Ja 00) 72-88.
——— "Southern Writers." *Reader* 6 (Jl 05) 236-8.
Trotter, Margaret. "Appalachia Speaking." *Mountain Life & Work* 13 (O 37) 25-7.
Turner, F. J. "The Children of the Pioneers." *YR* 15 (Jl 26) 645-70.
Tyler, L. G. "New England's Contribution to Virginia." *PAAS* 40 (Ap 30) 17-26.
Van Auken, Sheldon. "The Southern Historical Novel in the Early Twentieth Century." *J So Hist* 14 (My 48) 157-91.
Walcutt, C. C. "The Regional Novel and Its Future." *Ariz Q* 1 (Su 45) 17-27.
——— "Regionalism—Practical or Aesthetic?" *SR* 49 (Ap-Je 41) 165-72.
Warfel, H. R. "Contemporary Pennsylvania Literature." *Un Penn Lib Notes* 11 (1928) 71-80.
Waring, M. G. "The Gay Nineties in Savannah." *Ga Hist Q* 18 (D 34) 364-76.
Warren, Austin. "The Concord School of Philosophy." *NEQ* 2 (Ap 29) 199-233.
Warren, R. P. "Some Don'ts for Literary Regionalists." *Am R* 8 (D 36) 142-50.
Wasson, J. "The Southwest in 1880." *N Mex Hist R* 5 (Jl 30) 263-87.
Wauchope, G. A. "Literary South Carolina." *Bul Un S C* no 133 (D 23) 1-60.
Weaver, R. M. "Scholars or Gentlemen?" *CE* 7 (N 45) 72-7.
Webb, W. A. "Southern Poetry 1849-1881." *SAQ* 2 (Ja 03) 35-49.
Wecter, Dixon. "Literary Lodestone: 100 Years of California Writing." *SRL* 33 (16 S 50) 9-10, 37-41.
West, G. P. "The California Literati." *Am Merc* 8 (Jl 26) 281-6.
Westermeier, C. P. "The Cowboy—Sinner or Saint!" *N Mex Hist R* 25 (Ap 50) 89-108.
Wharton, A. H. "Philadelphia in Literature." *Critic* 47 (S-O 05) 324-31, 328-35.
Wheeler, E. J. "An Illinois Art Revivalist." *Cur Lit* 50 (30 Jl 32) 19.
White, M. E. D. "New England in Contemporary Verse." *N E Mag* ns 30 (Je 04) 408-18.
Willcox, L. C. "The South in Fiction: Virginia." *Bkm* 33 (Mr 11) 44-58.
William, Churchill. "Philadelphia in Fiction." *Bkm* 16 (D 02) 360-73.
Williams, Jack. "Georgians as Seen by Ante-Bellum English Travelers." *Ga Hist Q* 32 (S 48) 158-74.
Williams, M. L. "They Wrote Home About It." *Mich Alumnus Quar R* (Su 45) 337-51.
Wilson, A. H. "Escape Southward." *NAR* 248 (Wi 39-40) 265-74.
Wilson, C. M. "Elizabethan America." *Atl* 144 (Ag 29) 238-44.
Wilson, Edmund. "The Californians." *NRp* 25 (16 D 40) 839-40.
Wilson, J. S. "The South Goes Democratic." *SRL* 3 (28 My 27) 860.
Wilson, J. W. "Delta Revival." *EJ* 38 (Mr 49) 117-24.
Wish, Harvey. "Aristotle, Plato, and the Mason-Dixon Line." *JHI* 10 (Ap 49) 254-66.
Woodberry, G. E. "The Literary Age of Boston." *Harper's* 106 (F 03) 424-30.

——— "The South in American Letters." *Harper's* 106 (O 03) 735-41.
Wright, L. B. "Literature in the Colonial South." *HLQ* 10 (My 47) 297-316.
Wyllie, J. C. "Contemporary Virginia Literature." *Un Va News Letter* 14 (1 Ap 38) 3-4.
Wynn, Dudley. "The Southwestern Regional Straddle." *N Mex Quar* 5 (F 35) 7-14.
Yorke, Dane. "Shakespeare's New England." *Am Merc* 22 (Ja 31) 63-70.
Young, Vernon. "An American Dream and Its Parody." *Ariz Q* 6 (Su 50) 112-23.

RELIGION. Anon. "Gentility or Puritanism?" *SRL* 8 (26 Mr 32) 613, 615.
B., M. L. "The Pilgrim Ideal." *Chri Sci Mon* 26 (29 N 33) 7.
Barrett, E. B. "Modern Writers and Religion." *Thinker* 3 (My 31) 32-8.
Baskette, F. K. "Early Methodists and Their Literature." *Emory Un Q* 3 (D 47) 207-16.
Bates, Ernest. "The Puritan Mothers." *Am Merc* 46 (Ap 39) 400-2.
Beary, T. J. "Religion and the Modern Novel." *Cath World* 166 (D 47) 203-11.
Branch, E. D. "Jingle Bells: Notes on Christmas in American Literature." *SRL* 16 (4 D 37) 3-4, 20-4, 28.
Brown, R. W. "The Creative Spirit and the Church." *Harper's* 150 (D 24) 42-9.
Calverton, V. F. "The Puritan Myth." *Scribner's* 89 (Mr 31) 251-7.
Canby, H. S. "Quakers and Puritans." *SRL* 2 (2 Ja 26) 457-9.
Clapham, H. S. "The Influence of Puritanism on American Literature." *Living Age* 235 (4 O 02) 38-47.
Clark, F. E. "The Menace of the Sermon." *YR* 12 (O 22) 87-96.
Cooke, G. W. "Unitarianism in America." *N E Mag* ns 22 (My 00) 317-37.
Davin, Tom. "Our Not So Puritan Fathers." *Am Spect* 1 (S 33) 4.
East, R. A. "Puritanism and New Settlement." *NEQ* 17 (Je 44) 255-64.
Eddy, M. O. "Three Early Hymn Writers." *SFQ* 10 (S 46) 177-82.
Eisinger, C. E. "The Puritans' Justification for Taking the Land." *EIHC* 84 (Ap 48) 131-43.
Faust, C. H. "The Background of the Unitarian Opposition to Transcendentalism." *MP* 35 (F 38) 297-324.
Fedash, Mayteel. "State of the Catholic Press." *Cath World* 166 (F 48) 416-23.
Foster, H. D. "International Calvinism through Locke and the Revolution of 1688." *AHR* 32 (Ap 27) 475-99.
Francis, R. E. "The Religious Revival of 1858 in Philadelphia." *PMHB* 70 (Ja 46) 52-77.
Friedman, L. M. "Jews in Early American Literature." *More Books* 17 (D 42) 455-74.
Gabriel, Ralph. "Evangelical Religion and Popular Romanticism in Early Nineteenth Century America." *Church Hist* 19 (Mr 50) 34-47.
Gillis, J. M. "Problems of a Catholic Writer." *Cath World* 166 (Mr 48) 481-6.
Harding, F. A. J. "The Social Impact of the Evangelical Revival: A Brief Account of the Social Teachings of John Wesley and His Followers." *Hist Mag Prot Episc Church* 15 (D 46) 256-84.
Hawley, H. L. "Puritan Literature." *Hist Outlook* 21 (D 30) 369-72.
Hintz, H. W. "The Quaker Influence in American Literature." *Friends' Intelligencer* 96 (15 Jl, 5 Ag, 9 S 39) 455-7, 506-7, 523-4, 555-6, 585-6, 619-20.
Holmer, N. G. "John Campanius' Lutheran Catechism in the Delaware Language." *Essays and Studies in Am Lang & Lit* (Upsala) 3 (1946) 1-34.
Hudson, W. S. "Puritanism and the Spirit of Capitalism." *Church Hist* 18 (Mr 49) 3-17.
Johnson, G. W. "Saving Souls." *Am Merc* 2 (Jl 24) 364-8.
Jordan, P. C. "The Funeral Sermon." *Am Book Coll* 4 (S-O 33) 177-88.
Keller, A. F., Jr. "The Clergyman in Recent Fiction." *Lutheran Church Q* 20 (Ap 47) 193-8.

Kennedy, W. H. J. "Catholics in Massachusetts before 1750." *Cath Hist R* 17 (Ap 31) 10-28.
Klingberg, F. J. "Contribution of the S. P. G. to the American Way of Life." *Hist Mag Prot Episc Church* 12 (S 43) 215-24.
Lanier, J. J. "The South's Religious Thinkers." *SLM* 2 (Ja 40) 19-24.
Levitan, Tina. "Hebraic Mortar." *Am Hebrew* 157 (27 F 48) 2, 15.
Ludwig, Emil. "American Impressions." *Contemp R* no 987 (Mr 48) 141-6.
Macy, John. "A Glance at the Real Puritans." *Harper's* 154 (My 27) 742-50.
Margaret, Helen. "Religion and Literary Technique." *Cath World* 157 (Jl 43) 390-3.
Marraro, H. R. "Rome and the Catholic Church in Eighteenth-Century American Magazines." *Cath Hist R* 32 (Jl 46) 157-89.
Miller, Perry. "Declension in a Bible Commonwealth." *PAAS* 51 (Ap 42) 37-94.
——— "Jonathan Edwards to Emerson." *NEQ* 13 (D 40) 589-617.
——— "The Marrow of Puritan Divinity." *PCSM* 32 (1937) 247-300.
——— "Preparation for Salvation in Seventeenth-Century New England." *JHI* 4 (Je 43) 253-86.
——— "The Puritan Theory of the Sacraments in Seventeenth-Century New England." *Cath Hist R* 22 (Ja 37) 409-25.
——— "Religion and Society in the Early Literature: The Religious Impulse in the Founding of Virginia." *WMQ* 5: ser 3 (O 48) 492-522; 6 (Ja 49) 24-41.
Moats, F. I. "The Rise of Methodism in the Middle West." *Miss Valley Hist R* 15 (Je 28) 69-88.
Morais, H. M. "Deism in Revolutionary America (1763-1789)." *Int J Ethics* 42 (Jl 32) 434-53.
Morgan, D. L. "Mormon Story Tellers." *Rocky Mt R* 7 (F 42) 1, 3-4, 7.
Morgan, E. S. "Light on the Puritans from John Hall's Notebooks." *NEQ* 15 (Mr 42) 95-101.
——— "The Puritan Family and the Social Order." *More Books* 18 (Ja 43) 9-21.
——— "Puritan Tribalism." *More Books* 18 (My 43) 203-9.
——— "The Puritans and Sex." *NEQ* 15 (D 42) 591-607.
——— "The Puritan's Marriage with God." *SAQ* 48 (Ja 48) 107-12.
Murdock, K. B. "The Puritans and the New Testament." *PCSM* 25 (1924) 239-43.
Nichols, C. L. "The Holy Bible in Verse." *PAAS* ns 36 (Ap 26) 71-82.
O'Connor, T. F. "Catholic Archives of the United States." *Cath Hist R* 31 (Ja 46) 414-30.
Parkes, H. B. "The Puritan Heresy." *H&H* (Ja-Mr 32) 165-90.
Pew, W. A. "The Spirit of Puritanism." *EIHC* 67 (Ap 31) 137-44.
Poling, D. A. "Books with Religious Significance Reach an All-Time High." *Pub W* 151 (22 F 47) 1236-8.
Richardson, R. P. "The Rise and Fall of the Parliament of Religions at Greenacre." *Open Court* 6 (Mr 31) 129-66.
Roscoe, Theodore. "A Quaker Journal." *Contemp R* no 985 (Ja 48) 62-3.
Rowley, W. E. "The Puritan's Tragic Vision." *NEQ* 17 (S 44) 394-417.
Royer, Mary. "The Amish and Mennonite Theme in American Literature for Children." *Mennonite Quar R* 19 (O 45) 285-91.
Sampson, Ashley. "Religion in Modern Literature." *Contemp R* 147 (Ap 35) 462-70.
Schappes, M. U. "Anti-Semitism and Reaction, 1795-1800." *Pub Am Jewish Hist Soc* 38 (D 48) 109-37.
Schneider, H. W. "Evolution and Theology in America." *JHI* 6 (Ja 45) 3-18.
Seidman, A. B. "Church and State in the Early Years of the Massachusetts Bay Colony." *NEQ* 18 (Je 45) 211-33.
Sherwin, Oscar. "The Armory of God." *NEQ* 18 (Mr 45) 70-82.
Shipton, C. K. "The New England Clergy of the 'Glacial Age' (1680-1740)." *PCSM* 32 (1937) 34-54.
——— "A Plea for Puritanism." *AHR* 40 (Ap 35) 460-7.

——— "Puritanism and Modern Democracy." *New England Hist & Gen Reg* 101 (Jl 47) 181-98.

Stearns, R. P. "Assessing the New England Mind." *Church Hist* 10 (S 41) 246-62.

Stone, W. M. "The Holy Bible in Verse, 1698." *PAAS* ns 44 (Ap 34) 154-8.

Swan, B. F. "Some Thoughts on the Bay Psalm Book of 1640, with a Census of Copies." *Yale Un Lib Gaz* 22 (Ja 48) 56-76.

Sylvester, Harry. "Problems of the Catholic Writer." *Atl* 181 (Ja 48) 109-13.

Thomas, Norman. "Puritan Fathers." *Atlantic* 148 (N 31) 650-5.

Tolles, F. B. "Quietism *versus* Enthusiasm." *PMHB* 69 (Ja 45) 26-49.

Trinterud, L. J. "The New England Contribution to Colonial American Presbyterianism." *Church Hist* 17 (Mr 48) 32-43.

Vail, R. W. G. "A Check List of New England Election Sermons." *PAAS* 45 (O 35) 233-66.

Voigt, G. P. "The Spiritual Aspect of Recent American Literature." *Lutheran Church Q* 17 (Ja 44) 3-13.

Wach, Joachim. "The Rôle of Religion in the Social Philosophy of Alexis de Tocqueville." *JHI* 7 (Ja 46) 74-90.

Williams, Michael. "The Catholic Spirit in American Literature." *Forum* 80 (S 28) 441-9.

Winship, G. P. "Ballad from an Early Commonplace Book, Satirizing the Puritans." *PCSM* 26 (1927) 362-6.

SCIENCE. Baring-Gould, W. S. "Little Superman, What Now?" *Harper's* 193 (S 46) 283-8.

Bell, W. J. "The Scientific Environment of Philadelphia, 1775-1790." *PAPS* 92 (8 Mr 48) 6-14.

Clark, H. H. "The Influence of Science on American Ideas, from 1775 to 1809." *Trans Wisc Acad Sci, Arts & Letters* 35 (1943) 305-49.

Blicksberg, C. I. "Literature and Science: A Study in Conflict." *Sci Mo* 59 (D 44) 467-72.

Hornberger, Theodore. "The Date, the Source, and the Significance of Cotton Mather's Interest in Science." *AL* 6 (Ja 35) 413-20.

——— "The Effect of the New Science on the Thought of Jonathan Edwards." *AL* 9 (My 37) 196-207.

——— "Puritanism and Science." *NEQ* 10 (S 37) 503-15.

——— "Science and the New World." *Catalogue Huntington Lib* (1937) 3-18.

——— "The Science of Thomas Prince." *NEQ* 9 (Mr 36) 26-42.

Jones, A. E., Jr. "Darwinism and Its Relationship to Realism and Naturalism in American Fiction, 1860-1890." *Drew Un Bul* 38 (D 50) 1-21.

Jorgenson, C. E. "The New Science in the Almanacs of Ames and Franklin." *NEQ* 8 (D 35) 555-61.

Kincheloe, Isabel. "Nature and the New England Puritan." *Americana* 31 (1937) 569-88.

Kittredge, G. L. "Cotton Mather's Scientific Contributions to the Royal Society." *PAAS* ns 26 (1916) 18-57.

Loewenberg, B. J. "The Controversy over Evolution in New England, 1859-1873." *NEQ* 8 (Je 35) 232-57.

——— "Darwinism Comes to America, 1859-1900." *Miss Valley Hist R* 28 (D 41) 339-68.

——— "The Reaction of American Scientists to Darwinism." *AHR* 38 (Jl 33) 687-701.

McDermott, J. F. "Books on Natural History in Early St. Louis." *Mo Botanical Garden Bul* 23 (Mr 35) 55-62.

——— "Scientific Books in Early St. Louis." *School & Soc* 40 (D 34) 812-3.

Masterson, J. R. "Travelers' Tales of Colonial Natural History." *JAF* 59 (Ja-Mr, Ap-Je 46) 51-67, 174-88.

Payne, W. M. "American Literary Criticism and the Doctrine of Evolution." *Int Q* 2 (Jl, Ag 00) 26-46, 127-53.
Pearson, Norman. "The American Poet in Relation to Science." *Am Q* 1 (Su 49) 116-26.
Ratner, Sidney. "Evolution and the Rise of the Scientific Spirit in America." *Philos Sci* 3 (Ja 36) 104-22.
Stetson, S. P. "American Garden Books, Transplanted and Native, before 1807." *WMQ* 3 (Jl 46) 343-69.
Stimson, Dorothy. "Puritanism and the New Philosophy in Seventeenth Century New England." *Bul Inst Hist of Medicine* 3 (1935) 321-44.
Van Doren, Carl. "Beginnings of the American Philosophical Society." *PAPS* 81 (14 Jl 43) 277-89.
Wiener, P. P. "Chauncey Wright's Defense of Darwin and the Neutrality of Science." *JHI* 6 (Ja 45) 19-45.

SOCIAL ASPECTS. Anon. "American Writers Look Left." *TLS* (22 F 36) 145-6.
——— "Anthony Comstock in the Role of Literary Censor." *Cur Op* 55 (N 13) 353.
——— "The Censorship Forum." *Pub W* 117 (31 My 30) 2734-7.
——— "Points of View in Book Publishing: I—Book Censorship." *Pub W* 153 (24 Ja 48) 316-7.
——— "Socialism in Literature." *Bkm* 27 (Ap 08) 119-24.
Adams, R. M. "A Little Note on Literature and Sociology." *Epoch* 3 (Fl 50) 123-8.
Alger, G. W. "The Literature of Exposure." *Atl* 96 (Ag 05) 210-3.
Arvin, Newton. "Literature and Social Change." *Mod Q* 6 (Su 32) 20-5.
Barry, G. F. "The Commissar and the Free Lance Writer." *Cath World* 164 (Ja 47) 328-35.
Bestor, A. E., Jr. "Education and Reform at New Harmony: Correspondence of William Maclure and Marie Duclos Fretageot, 1820-1833." *Ind Hist Soc Pub* 15 (1948) 285-417.
Boyd, Ernest. "Adult or Infantile Censorship." *Dial* 70 (Ap 21) 381-5.
Braden, W. W. "The Lecture Movement, 1840-1860." *QJS* 34 (Ap 48) 206-12.
Brooks, Obed. "The Problem of the Social Novel." *Mod Q* 6 (Fl 32) 77-82.
Burgum, E. B. "Literary Form: Social Forces and Innovations." *SR* 49 (Jl-S 41) 325-38.
Cain, J. M., & Farrell, J. T. "Do Writers Need an 'AAA'?" *SRL* 29 (16 N 46) 9-10, 40-1, 44-5, 47.
Calverton, V. F. "Art and Social Change." *Mod Q* 6 (Wi 31) 16-27.
——— "Can We Have a Proletarian Literature?" *Mod Q* 6 (Fl 32) 39-52.
——— "Leftward Ho!" *Mod Q* 6 (Su 32) 26-32.
——— "Left-Wing Literature in America." *EJ* 20 (D 31) 789-98.
——— "Literature Goes Left." *Cur Hist* 41 (D 34) 316-20.
——— "Marxism and American Literature." *Books Abroad* 7 (Ap 33) 131-4.
——— "Pathology in Contemporary Literature." *Thinker* 4 (D 31) 7-21.
——— "Proletarianitis." *SRL* 15 (9 Ja 37) 3-4, 14-5.
Cardozo, B. W. "Law and Literature." *YR* ns 14 (Jl 25) 699-718.
Charvat, William. "American Romanticism and the Depression of 1937." *Sci & Soc* 2 (Wi 37) 67-82.
Clark, H. H. "Nationalism in Literature." *UTQ* 2 (Jl 33) 492-519.
Collins, J. H. "The American Grub Street." *Atl* 98 (N 06) 634-43.
Colum, M. M. "Marxism and Literature." *Forum* 91 (Mr 34) 145-9.
Daiches, David. "The Scope of Sociological Criticism." *Epoch* 3 (Su 50) 57-64.
Davidson, Carter. "The Immigrant Strain in American Literature." *EJ* 25 (D 36) 862-8.
Denison, J. H. "The Great Delusion of Our Time." *Atl* 93 (Je 04) 721-9.
DeVoto, Bernard. "Freud's Influence on Literature." *SRL* 20 (7 O 39) 10-11.

——— "Literary Censorship at Cambridge." *Harvard Grad Mag* 39 (S 30) 30-42.
Eaton, W. P. "Class-Consciousness and the 'Movies.'" *Atl* 115 (Ja 15) 48-56.
Eisinger, C. E. "The Freehold Concept in Eighteenth-Century American Letters." *WMQ* 4 (Ja 47) 42-59.
Eliot, T. S. "Poetry and Propaganda." *Bkm* 70 (F 30) 595-602.
Ely-Estorik, Eric, & Fidell, O. H. "The Masses Tradition in Contemporary Literature." *Contempo* 3 (5 Ap 33) 1-3, 8.
Farrell, J. T. "Notes for a New Literary Controversy." *NRp* 114 (29 Ap, 13 My 46) 616-8, 702-5.
——— "Social Themes in American Realism." *EJ* 35 (Je 46) 309-14.
Forbes, A. B. "The Literary Quest for Utopia, 1880-1900." *Social Forces* 6 (D 27) 179-89.
Glicksberg, C. I. "Literature and Freudianism." *Prairie Schooner* 23 (Wi 49) 359-72.
——— "Literature and the Marxist Aesthetic." *UTQ* 18 (O 48) 76-84.
——— "Marxism, Freudianism, and Modern Writing." *QQ* 54 (Au 47) 297-310.
Gohdes, C. H. "Three Letters by James Kay Dealing with Brook Farm." *PQ* 17 (O 38) 377-88.
Harrington, F. H. "Literary Aspects of American Anti-Imperialism, 1898-1902." *NEQ* 10 (D 37) 650-67.
Harris, L. I. "Brook Farm as It Is Today." *Lamp* 28 (F 04) 7-12.
Hazlitt, Henry. "Art and Social Change." *Mod Q* 6 (Wi 31) 10-5.
——— "Literature as Propaganda." *SRL* 20 (16 S 39) 13-5.
Hesseltine, W. B. "The Propaganda Literature of Confederate Prisons." *J So Hist* 1 (F 35) 56-66.
Hicks, Granville. "Literature and Revolution." *EJ* 24 (Mr 35) 219-39.
——— "Literary Criticism and the Marxian Method." *Mod Q* 6 (Su 32) 44-7.
Higginson, T. W. "The Cowardice of Culture." *Atl* 96 (O 05) 481-6.
Hunt, E. L. "The Social Interpretation of Literature." *EJ* 24 (Mr 35) 214-8.
Johnson, O. "The Monetary Control of Literature." *Mod Q* 5 (Wi 30-1) 517-23.
Jones, Joseph. "Utopia as Dirge." *Am Q* 2 (Fl 50) 214-26.
Jones, M. B. "Thomas Maule, the Salem Quaker, and Free Speech in Massachusetts." *EIHC* 72 (Ja 26) 1-42.
Kirk, C. M. "The Marxist Doctrine in Literature." *EJ* 24 (Mr 35) 209-13.
Kraus, Michael. "Slavery Reform in the Eighteenth Century." *PMHB* 60 (Ja 36) 53-6.
Krutch, J. W. "Literature and Propaganda." *EJ* 22 (D 33) 793-802.
Lewis, Wyndham. "The Propagandist in Fiction." *Cur Hist* 11 (Ag 34) 567-72.
Matthiessen, F. O. "'The Great Tradition'—A Counter-Statement." *NEQ* 7 (Je 34) 223-34.
Michaud, Regis. "Le Mouvement littéraire et social de gauche aux États-Unis." *Grande Revue* 149 (F 36) 575-93; 150 (My, Je 36) 461-82, 628-48.
Mitchell, A. M. "The Brook Farm Movement." *Cath World* 73 (Ap 01) 17-31.
Neill, T. P. "The Puritan Spirit in Eighteenth-Century Reform." *Hist Bul* 25 (Ja 47) 27-8, 37-9.
O'Faoláin, Seán. "Getting at Which Public?" *VQR* 24 (Wi 48) 90-5.
Preece, Harold. "Proletarian Writers." *Mod Thinker* 7 (D 35) 11-4.
Rahv, Philip. "Proletarian Literature: A Political Autopsy." *So R* 4 (Ja 39) 616-28.
Riddell, W. R. "Notes on Negro Slavery." *J Negro Hist* 16 (Jl 31) 322-7.
Samson, Leon. "A Proletarian Philosophy of Art." *Mod Q* 5 (Sp 29) 235-9.
Saunders, D. A. "Social Ideas in the McGuffey Readers." *Public Opinion Q* 5 (Wi 41) 579-89.
Schlesinger, A. M. "Learning How to Behave. A Study of American Etiquette Books." *More Books* 31 (Ja, F, Mr 46) 3-17, 53-9, 87-102.
——— "Social History in American Literature." *YR* 18 (S 28) 135-47.

Schneider, Isidor. "Freud and Literature." *New Masses* 55 (19 Je 45) 22-3.
Sedgwick, H. D., Jr. "Certain Aspects of America." *Atl* 90 (Jl 02) 5-12.
——— "A Girl of Sixteen at Brook Farm." *Atl* 85 (Mr 00) 394-404.
Shanks, C. L. "The Biblical Anti-Slavery Argument in the Decade 1830-1840." *J Negro Hist* 16 (Ap 31) 132-57.
Sherwin, Oscar. "The Armory of God." *NEQ* 18 (Mr 45) 70-82.
Slochower, Harry. "Freud and Mary in Contemporary Literature." *SR* 49 (Jl-S 41) 316-24.
Smart, G. K. "Fourierism in Northampton: Two Documents." *NEQ* 12 (Je 39) 370-4.
Smith, G. W. "Broadsides for Freedom: Civil War Propaganda in New England." *NEQ* 21 (S 48) 291-312.
Smith, H. N. "The Dilemma of Agrarianism." *Sw R* 19 (Ap 34) 215-32.
Smith, Winifred. "The Worker as Hero." *Am Bkm* 1 (Fl 44) 35-42.
Spiller, R. E. "What Became of the Literary Radicals?" *NRp* 115 (18 N 46) 664-6.
Steadman, R. W. "A Critique of Proletarian Literature." *NAR* 247 (Sp 39) 142-52.
Steele, Erskine. "Fiction and Social Ethics." *SAQ* 5 (Jl 06) 254-63.
Stephenson, G. M. "Nativism in the Forties and Fifties, with Special Reference to the Mississippi Valley." *Miss Valley Hist R* 9 (D 22) 185-202.
Stern, M. B. "Propaganda or Art?" *SR* 45 (O-D 37) 453-68.
Stovall, Floyd. "The Function of Literature in a Democracy." *CE* 6 (My 45) 440-4.
Strauss, Harold. "Realism in the Proletarian Novel." *YR* 28 (D 38) 360-74.
Sumner, J. S. "The Truth about 'Literary Lynching.'" *Dial* 71 (Jl 21) 63-8.
Swift, Lindsay. "Members, Scholars, and Visitors [at Brook Farm]." *Nation* 70 (22 F 00) 152.
——— "Organization and Life [at Brook Farm]." *Cur Lit* 28 (Ap 00) 70-3.
Tandy, J. S. "Pro-Slavery Propaganda in American Fiction of the Fifties." *SAQ* 21 (Ja, Ap 22) 41-50, 170-8.
Uzzle, T. H., *et al.* "A Symposium: The Status of Radical Writing." *A Year Mag* (D 33-Ap 34) 122-43.
Weaver, R. L. "The American Authors' Authority." *Canadian Forum* 27 (S 47) 133-4.
Wheeler, B. I. "A National Type of Culture." *Atl* 92 (Jl 03) 74-7.
Wilkinson, Hazel. "Social Thought in American Fiction, 1910-17." *Un Calif Stud Social* 3 (D 18).
Wilson, Edmund. "Literary Class War." *NRp* 70 (4 My 32) 319-23.
Wilson, Janet. "The Early Anti-Slavery Propaganda." *More Books* 19 (D 44) 393-405.
Wrage, E. J. "Public Address: A Study in Social and Intellectual History." *QJS* 33 (D 47) 451-7.
Wright, L. H. "Propaganda in Early American Fiction." *PBSA* 33 (1939) 98-106.

SOCIETIES. Anon. "History of the Virginia Historical Society." *VMHB* 39 (O 31) 292-362.
——— "The Tuesday Club of Annapolis." *Md Hist Mag* 1 (Mr 06) 59-65.
Andrews, F. E. "Foundations—A Modern Maecenas." *Pub W* 151 (8 Mr 47) 1464-6.
Arndt, K. J. "The Harmonists and the Hutterians." *AGR* 10 (Ag 44) 24-7.
——— "The Harmonists and the Mormons." *AGR* 10 (Je 44) 6-9.
Bestor, A. E., Jr. "Fourierism in Northampton." *NEQ* 13 (Mr 40) 110-22.
Dale, E. E. "The Frontier Literary Society." *Neb Hist* 31 (S 50) 167-82.
Faÿ, Bernard. "Learned Societies in Europe and America in the Eighteenth Century." *AHR* 37 (Ja 32) 255-66.
Fillmore, Parker. "Records of the MacDowell Club." *N Y Hist Soc Bul* 27 (Jl 43) 69-70.
Gohdes, Clarence. "A Brook Farm Labor Record." *AL* 1 (N 29) 297-303.
——— "Getting Ready for Brook Farm." *MLN* 49 (Ja 34) 36-9.

—— "Three Letters of James King Dealing with Brook Farm." *PQ* 17 (O 38) 377-88.
Greene, M. H. "Raritan Bay Union, Eagleswood, N. J." *Proc N J Hist Soc* 68 (Ja 50) 1-19.
Grosvenor, Gilbert. "The National Geographic Society." *PAAS* 52 (O 42) 235-62.
Haraszti, Zoltán. "Brook Farm Letters." *More Books* 12 (F, Mr 37) 49-69, 93-114.
Hellman, H. E. "The Influence of the Literary Society in the Making of American Authors." *QJS* 28 (F 42) 12-4.
Holbrook, S. H. "Brook Farm, Wild West Style." *Am Merc* 57 (Ag 43) 216-23.
Johnson, H. B. "The Carver County German Reading Society." *Minn Hist* 24 (S 43) 214-25.
Kraus, Michael. "America and the Utopian Ideal of the Eighteenth Century." *Miss Valley Hist R* 22 (Mr 36) 489-504.
Lind, L. R. "Early Literary Societies at Wabash College." *Ind Mag Hist* 42 (Je 46) 173-6.
Lyle, G. R. "College Literary Societies in the Fifties." *Lib Q* 9 (Jl 34) 487-94.
Pinckney, Josephine. "Charleston's Poetry Society." *SR* 38 (Ja-Mr 30) 50-6.
Prahl, A. J. "The Goethean Literary Society of Franklin and Marshall College; a Tribute." *AGR* 16 (O 49) 29-30.
Read, A. W. "The Membership in Proposed American Academies." *AL* 7 (My 35) 145-65.
—— "The Philological Society of New York, 1788." *AS* 9 (Ap 34) 131-6.
Scott, E. B. "Early Literary Clubs in New York City." *AL* 5 (Mr 33) 3-16.
Smart, G. K. "Fourierism in Northampton." *NEQ* 12 (Je 39) 370-6.
—— "A New England Experiment in Idealism." *Travel* 74 (N 39) 14-6.
Twaddell, Elizabeth. "The American Tract Society, 1814-1860." *Church Hist* 15 (Je 46) 116-32.
Uhler, J. E. "The Delphian Club: A Contribution to the Literary History of Baltimore in the Early Nineteenth Century." *Md Hist Mag* 20 (D 25) 305-46.
Vail, R. W. G. "Report of the Librarian." *PAAS* ns 43 (1933) 44-9.
Van Hoesen, H. B. "The Bibliographical Society of America—Its Leaders and Activities." *PBSA* 35 (3Q 41) 172-202.
Verlenden, Mrs. W. L. "The American Society Held at Philadelphia for Promoting Useful Knowledge." *PMHB* 24 (1900) 1-17.
Wesley, T. J. "The Conversational Club." *NEQ* 16 (Je 43) 296-8.
Wilson, Janet. "The Early Anti-Slavery Societies." *More Books* 20 (F 45) 51-67.
Wilson, J. B. "Antecedents of Brook Farm." *NEQ* 15 (Je 42) 320-31.

THEATER. Anon. "Album 1923." *Theatre Arts* 32 (Ag-S 48) 35-64.
—— "The Grand Old Days." *Theatre Arts* 15 (Je 31) 485-92.
—— "The National Theatre Approaches Reality." *Lit Dig* 120 (22 Je 35) 23.
—— "A Plea for the Unacted Drama." *Atl* 102 (O 08) 564-7.
—— "The Robinson Locke Dramatic Collection." *BNYPL* 29 (1925) 307-22; 33 (1929) 801.
—— "The 'Straw Hat' Theater." *AN&Q* 5 (Jl, Ag 45) 51-4, 67-9.
—— "Washington and the Theatre." *Rec Am Cath Hist Soc Phila* 60 (Mr 49) 57-8.
Allison, T. E. "The Theater in Early California." *Un Calif Chron* 30 (1928) 75-9.
Archer, William. "The Development of American Drama." *Harper's* 142 (D 20) 75-86.
—— "Puritanism and the Theater." *Critic* 37 (Jl 00) 57-60.
Atkinson, J. B. "Large Scale Drama Production." *NAR* 224 (D 27) 686-91.
Austin, Mark. "Spanish Drama in Colonial America." *Theatre Arts* 19 (S 35) 705.
Ayer, C. S. "Foreign Drama on the English and American Stage." *Un Colo Stud* (Je, D 09; N 13; N 14).

Bagley, R. E. "Theatrical Entertainment in Pensacola, Florida: 1882-1892." *So Speech J* 16 (S 50) 62-84.
Baker, G. P. "The Dramatist & His Public." *Lamp* 27 (N 03) 329-32.
Baker, L. C. "The German Drama in English on the New York Stage to 1830." *Ger-Am Annals* ns 13 (1915) 1-47, 98-130, 133-69; 14 (1916) 3-53.
Barnes, James. "American Theatricals." *Century* 81 (Mr 11) 670-9.
Barron, Samuel. "The Dying Theater." *Harper's* 172 (D 35) 108-17.
Beiswanger, George. "The Playwrights Company." *Theatre Arts* 27 (My 43) 299-306.
——— "Politicians in American Plays." *Theatre Arts* 24 (D 43) 741-50.
——— "Theatre Today, Symptoms and Summaries." *J Aesth & Art Crit* 3 (n.d.) 19-29.
Benchley, Robert. "The Return of the Actors." *YR* 23 (Mr 34) 504-13.
Benson, A. B. "Charles XII on the American Stage." *SS* 17 (N 43) 290-6.
Bentley, E. R. "The Drama at Ebb." *KR* 7 (Sp 45) 169-84.
——— "Drama Now." *PR* 12 (Sp 45) 244-51.
Berelson, Bernard, & Grant, H. F. "The Pioneer Theatre in Washington." *Pac Nw Q* 28 (Ap 37) 115-36.
Beyer, William. "The Return to Culture in the American Theatre." *School & Soc* 65 (25 Ja 47) 61-3.
——— "The State of the Theatre." *School & Soc* 66 (27 S, 25 O 47) 245, 325-8.
——— "The State of the Theatre: A New Season." *School & Soc* 68 (30 O 48) 301-4.
——— "The State of the Theatre: The Strindberg Heritage." *School & Soc* 71 (14 Ja 50) 23-8.
Blake, W. B. "Our Un-American Stage." *Independent* 72 (7 Mr 12) 503-8.
Blakely, P. R. "The Theatre and Music in Halifax." *Dalhousie R* 29 (Ap 49) 8-21.
Boas, F. S. "A Herod Play from America." *Contemp R* 144 (N 33) 575-80.
Boyd, Ernest. "The Role of the Little Theatre." *Freeman* 3 (22 Je 21) 352-3.
Boynton, Percy. "American Authors of Today: The Drama." *EJ* 12 (Je 23) 407-15.
Braverman, Barnet. "David Wark Griffith: Creater of Film Form." *Theatre Arts* 29 (Ap 45) 240-50.
Brede, C. F. "German Drama in English on the Philadelphia Stage to 1830." *Ger-Am Annals* ns 10 (1912) 3-64, 99-149, 226-48; 11 (1913) 64-99, 175-206; 13 (1915) 67-130, 170-94; 14 (1916) 69-110.
Briggs, H. E. & E. B. "The Early Theatre in Chicago." *J Ill State Hist Soc* 39 (Je 46) 165-78.
——— "The Early Theater on the Northern Plains." *Miss Valley Hist R* 37 (S 50) 231-64.
——— "The Early Theater on the Upper Mississippi." *Mid-America* 31 (Jl 49) 131-62.
Broch, H. I. "Sherlock Holmes Returns to the Stage." *N Y Times Mag* (10 N 29) 14, 20.
Brown, F. C. "The First Boston Theatre, on Federal Street, Charles Bullfinch, Architect." *Old-Time New England* 36 (Jl 45) 1-7.
Brown, H. R. "Sensibility in Eighteenth-Century American Drama." *AL* 4 (Mr 32) 47-61.
Bruce, P. A. "An Early Virginia Play." *Nation* 88 (11 F 09) 136.
Bueloch, J. M. "American Stage History." *N&Q* 167 (29 S 34) 219.
Burton, Katherine. "A Belated Falstaff." *AL* 4 (My 32) 187-91.
Cairns, W. B. "American Drama of the 18th Century." *Dial* 59 (15 Jl 15) 60-2.
Cameron, M. M. "Play-Acting in Canada during the French Regime." *Canadian Hist R* 11 (Mr 30) 9-19.
Campa, A. L. "Religious Spanish Folk-Drama in New Mexico." *N Mex Q* 2 (F 32) 3-13.

Campbell, C. L. "A National Theatre in America." *QJS* 34 (F 48) 59-64.
——— "Two Years towards a National Theatre." *QJS* 36 (F 50) 23-6.
Campbell, Marie. "Survivals of Old Folk Drama in the Kentucky Mountains." *JAF* 51 (Ja-Mr 38) 10-24.
Cantela, Giuseppe. "The Italian Theater in New York." *Am Merc* 12 (S 27) 106-12.
Carmer, Carl. "Adventures in Playmaking: Original Plays in Tributary Theatres." *Theatre Arts* 16 (Jl 32) 529-45.
Carruth, Hayden. "Malediction against Radio Announcers." *Poetry* 74 (S 49) 331-5.
Carson, W. G. B. "The Beginnings of the Theatre in St. Louis." *Mo Hist Soc Coll* 5 (1928) 129-65.
——— "Night Life in St. Louis a Century Ago." *Bul Mo Hist Soc* 1 (Ap 45) 3-9.
Chandler, Raymond. "Writers in Hollywood." *Atl* 176 (D 45) 50-4.
Cheney, Sheldon. "The American Playwright and the Drama of Sincerity." *Forum* 51 (Ap 14) 498-512.
——— "The New Movement in the Theatre." *Form* 52 (Ap 12) 749-63.
Clapp, H. A. "Reminiscences of a Dramatic Critic." *Atl* 88 (Ag, S, O, N 01) 155-65, 344-54, 490-501, 622-34.
Clark, B. H. "American Drama in Its Second Decade." *EJ* 21 (Ja 32) 1-11.
——— "Our Most American Drama." *EJ* (coll ed) 28 (My 39) 333-42.
Clarke, M. V. "Sauce for the Gander and Sawdust for the Goose." *Dial* 65 (14 D 18) 541-3.
Clarke, William. "An Unpublished Comedy." *PMHS* 57 (O 23) 72.
Cline, J. "Opera on America, 1735-1850." *Poet Lore* 41 (Su 30) 239-50.
Clurman, Harold. "Preface to the Younger Dramatists." *NRp* 121 (11 Jl 49) 14-6.
Coad, O. S. "The American Theatre in the Eighteenth Century." *SAQ* 17 (Jl 18) 190-7.
——— "The First Century of the New Brunswick Stage." *JRUL* 5 (D 41, Je 42) 15-36, 78-89; 6 (Je 43) 52-7.
——— "An Old American College Play." *MLN* 37 (Mr 22) 157-63.
——— "Stage and Players in Eighteenth-Century America." *JEGP* 19 (2Q 20) 201-23.
Cobb, L. M. "Drama in North Carolina." *SLM* 2 (Ap 40) 228-35.
Cocke, Zitella. "The Modern Stage Decadent." *N E Mag* ns 40 (Je, Jl 09) 399-409, 553-9.
Colby, Elbridge. "Early American Comedy." *BNYPL* 23 (Jl 19) 427-35.
Comstock, Sarah. "Early American Drama." *NAR* 225 (Ap 28) 469-75.
——— "What Makes a Play Succeed?" *Harper's* 157 (O 28) 628-36.
Connor, L. R. "Southern Plays on the Gotham Stage." *SLM* 1 (Je 39) 407-11.
Cook, Alistair. "A National Theatre on Trial." *Fortnightly R* ns 840 (D 36) 726-31.
Corbin, John. "The Dawn of the American Drama." *Atl* 99 (My 07) 632-44.
Craven, Thomas. "The Great American Art." *Dial* 81 (D 26) 483-92.
Crouse, Russel. "Whither Is the Theatre Bound?" *Stage* 15 (Mr 38) 12.
Curtis, John. "A Century of Grand Opera in Philadelphia." *PMHB* 44 (Ja 20) 122-58.
Curvin, Jonathan. "Realism in Early American Art and Theatre." *QJS* 30 (D 44) 450-5.
——— "Regional Drama in One World." *QJS* 33 (D 47) 480-4.
D'Amico, S. "Teatro americano en Italia." *Nuova Antologia* (Ja 45).
Damon, S. F. "Providence Theatricals in 1773." *R I Hist* 4 (Ap 45) 55-8.
Deland, L. F. "A Plea for the Theatrical Manager." *Atl* 102 (O 08) 492-500.
DeMille, W. C. "Our 'Commercial' Drama." *YR* ns 4 (Ja 15) 316-29.
Dickinson, T. H. "The Dawn of a New Dramatic Era." *VQR* 5 (Jl 29) 411-27.
Dodd, W. L. "The Well-Made Play." *YR* ns 2 (Jl 13) 746-62.
Dorson, R. M. "Jonathan Draws a Long Bow." *NEQ* 16 (Je 43) 244-79.
——— "Mose the Far-Famed and World-Renowned." *AL* 15 (N 43) 288-300.

——— "The Yankee on the Stage—a Folk Hero of American Drama." *NEQ* 13 (S 40) 467-93.
Douglas, W. A. S. "The Passing of Vaudeville." *Am Merc* 12 (O 27) 188-94.
Downer, A. S. "The New Theatrum Poetorum." *Poetry* 60 (Jl 42) 206-15.
Dye, W. S. "Pennsylvania versus the Theatre." *PMHB* 60 (O 31) 333-72.
Eastman, Fred. "A Challenge to the American Theater." *Harper's* 151 (Ag 25) 328-32.
Eaton, W. P. "A Back-Door to Beauty." *Freeman* 1 (14 Ap 20) 111-2.
——— "Broadway and National Life." *Freeman* 1 (17 Mr 20) 16-8.
——— "The Cambridge School of the Drama." *Harvard Grad Mag* 39 (O 31) 16-22.
——— "The Drama in 1933." *Am Schol* 3 (Wi 34) 96-101.
——— "The Failure of Our Younger Dramatists." *Collier's* 48 (21 O 11) 22.
——— "New Horizons." *Freeman* 1 (24 Mr 20) 44.
——— "Our Comedy of Bad Manners." *Am Mag* 71 (F 11) 534-44.
——— "Our Generation of Dramatists." *Am Mag* 71 (N 10) 120-9.
——— "The Plight of the Dramatist." *Harper's* 182 (Mr 41) 417-21.
——— "The Repertoire Theater in America." *Am Mag* 75 (Je 13) 58-63.
——— "The Theatre Mrs. Fiske Knew." *Theatre Arts* 16 (My 32) 371-6.
——— "Towards a New Theatre." *Freeman* 5 (12 Jl 22) 418-9.
——— "The Trail of the Serpent." *Freeman* 1 (21 Ap 20) 140.
——— "Why Do You Fear Me, Nellie? The Melodramas of Forty Years Ago." *Harper's* 183 (Jl 41) 164-70.
——— "A Year at the New Theater." *Atl* 105 (My 10) 689-96.
Eich, L. M. "The Stage Yankee." *QJS* 27 (F 41) 16-25.
Ellis, Milton. "Pioneers and the Drama." *AN&Q* 2 (Jl 42) 64.
Ernst, A. B. "Eugene's Theatres and 'Shows' in Horse and Buggy Days." *Ore Hist Q* 44 (Je, S 43) 127-9, 232-48.
——— "Thunderbird Dance: Native North American Theatre." *Theatre Arts* 29 (F 45) 118-25.
Eustis, Morton. "Writing as a Business." *Theatre Arts* 18 (Ap 34) 271-80.
Ferguson, C. B. "Rise of the Theatre at Halifax." *Dalhousie R* 29 (Ja 50) 419-28.
Ferguson, Francis. "Notes on the Theater." *So R* 5 (Wi 40) 559-67.
Field, L. M. "Cynics Leave the Theatre." *NAR* 232 (Jl 31) 49-55.
——— "The Drama Catches Up." *NAR* 234 (Ag 32) 170-6.
——— "Our Laggard Theatre." *NAR* 233 (Ja 32) 73-8.
——— "The South on Broadway." *SLM* 2 (Mr 40) 174-6.
Firkins, O. W. "Literature and the Stage; a Question of Tactics." *Atl* 109 (Ap 12) 477-83.
Fletcher, E. G. "The Beginnings of the Professional Theatre in Texas." *Un Texas Bul* (1 Je 36) 1-53.
Ford, W. C. "Prologue to Zara, 1776." *PMHS* 56 (F 23) 260-3.
Fox, D. R. "The Development of the American Theatre." *N Y Hist* 17 (Ja 36) 22-41.
Francke, N. "Iphigenie at Harvard." *Nation* 70 (29 Mr 00) 239-40.
Free, J. M. "The Ante-Bellum Theatre of the Old Nachez Region." *J Miss Hist* 5 (Ja 43) 14-27.
Freedley, George. "The American National Theatre." *Sw R* 31 (Au 46) 364-9.
——— "An Early Performance of 'Romeo and Juliet' in New York." *BNYPL* 40 (Je 36) 494-5.
Frenz, Horst. "American Drama and World Drama." *EJ* 6 (Mr 45) 319-25.
——— "Edwin Booth in Polyglot Performances." *GR* 18 (D 43) 280-5.
——— "The German Drama in the Middle West." *AGR* 8 (Je 42) 15-7, 37.
———, & Campbell, L. W. "William Gillette on the London Stage." *QQ* 52 (Wi 45-6) 443-57.
Friedland, L. S. "A Russian Dramatist and the American Stage." *Dial* 62 (31 My 17) 463-5.

Frohman, Daniel. "Tendencies of the American Stage." *Cosmopolitan* 38 (N 04) 15-22.
Gaffney, F. H. "Modern Dramatic Realism." *Arena* 29 (Ap 03) 390-6.
Gafford, Lucille. "The Boston Stage and the War of 1812." *NEQ* 7 (Je 34) 327-35.
——— "Transcendentalist Attitudes toward Drama and the Theatre." *NEQ* 13 (S 40) 442-66.
Gassner, John. "Aspects of the Broadway Theatre." *QJS* 35 (Ap, O 49) 190-8, 289-96.
——— "Strindberg in America." *Theatre Arts* 33 (My 49) 49-52.
Gates, W. B. "Performance of Shakespeare in Ante-Bellum Mississippi." *J Miss Hist* 5 (Ja 43) 28-37.
——— "The Theatre in Natchez." *J Miss Hist* 3 (Ap 41) 71-129.
Gay, F. L. "The First American Play." *Nation* 88 (11 F 09) 136.
Gilder, Rosamond. "A Picture Book of Play and Players: 1916-1941." *Theatre Arts* 25 (Ag 41) 562-609.
Gilman, Lawrence. "The Neo-Celtic Drama in America." *Lamp* 27 (O 03) 231-3.
Goodman, Edward. "American Dramatic Problem." *Forum* 43 (F 10) 182-91.
Gould, Jan. "The Negro in Show Business." *AR* 6 (Su 46) 254-64.
Gower, Herschel. "Nashville's Community Playhouse." *Holland's Mag* 67 (Mr 48) 10-1.
Graubel, G. E. "A Decade of American Drama." *Thought* 15 (S 40) 388-419.
Green, Paul. "Symphonic Drama." *CE* 10 (Ap 49) 359-65; *EJ* 38 (Ap 49) 177-83.
Greenlaw, Edwin. "Washington Irving's Comedy of Politics." *Texas R* 1 (Ap 16) 291-300.
Hale, L. C. "Historic Englishmen on the American Stage." *Bkm* 13 (Ag 01) 535-44.
Hale, Philip. "A Boston Dramatic Critic of a Century Ago." *PMHS* 59 (My 26) 312-24.
Halline, A. G. "American Dramatic Theory Comes of Age." *Bucknell Un Stud* 1 (Je 49) 1-11.
Hamar, C. E. "Scenery of the Early American Stage." *Theatre Annual* 7 (1948-9) 84-103.
Hamilton, Clayton. "European Dramatists on the American Stage." *Bkm* 31 (Je 10) 410-21.
——— "The New Realism in the Drama." *Bkm* 36 (F 13) 639-49.
——— "The One-Act Play in America." *Bkm* 37 (Ap 13) 184-90.
——— "The Younger American Playwrights." *Bkm* 32 (N 10) 249-57.
——— "What Is Wrong with the American Stage?" *Bkm* 39 (My 14) 314-9.
Hamilton, W. B. "The Theater of the Old Southwest." *AL* 12 (Ja 41) 471-85.
Harris, M. A. "The Renaissance of the Tragic Stage." *Atl* 87 (Ap 01) 533-9.
Harting, Frank. "The Little Theatre in Texas." *Bunker's Mo* 1 (Je 28) 870-81.
Hartley, Alexander. "For an Indian Theatre." *Theatre Arts* 10 (Mr 26) 191-202.
Hartley, Marsden. "John Barrymore's Ibbetson." *Dial* 64 (14 Mr 18) 227-9.
Hartt, R. L. "The Home of Burlesque." *Atl* 101 (Ja 08) 68-78.
Haskell, D. C. "List of American Dramas in the New York Public Library." *BNYPL* 19 (O 15) 739-86.
Haugen, E. I. "Ibsen in America." *JEGP* 33 (Jl 34) 396-420.
Hawkins, A. D. "The Poet in the Theatre." *Criterion* 14 (O 34) 29-39.
Haynes, William. "Romanticism and the Little Theatres." *Dial* 62 (19 Ap 17) 337-9.
Heffner, Hubert. "The Decline of the Professional American Theatre." *PS* 1 (Wi 47) 58-75.
——— "The Decline of the Professional Theatre in America." *QJS* 35 (Ap 49) 170-7.
Helburn, Theresa. "The Theater, Bloody but Unbowed." *NAR* 243 (Su 37) 231-42.
Held, M. W. "Special Lighting Effects on the Late Nineteenth-Century Stage." *Furman Stud* 33 (Sp 50) 61-77.

Henderson, Archibald. "America and the Drama: A Forecast." *Texas R* 1 (Jl 16) 210-9.
——— "The American Drama." *SR* 23 (Jl 15) 468-78.
——— "The American Drama: A Survey." *SR* 26 (Ap 18) 228-40.
——— "American Drama and the European War." *SAQ* 15 (O 16) 319-26.
——— "The Drama—After the War." *SAQ* 19 (Jl 20) 258-65.
——— "The Drama of the Future." *So R* 1 (Je 20) 16-9.
——— "Early Drama and Amateur Entertainment in North Carolina." *Reviewer* 5 (1925) 68-77.
——— "Early Drama and Professional Entertainment in North Carolina." *Reviewer* 5 (1925) 47-57.
Herbatschek, Heinrich. "Die Anfaenge des deutschen Theaters in Milwaukee." *AGR* 13 (F 47) 17-8.
Herbert, J. W. "Young Men on the American Stage." *Cosmopolitan* 28 (F 00) 419-24.
Herron, I. H. "Home Grown Plays." *Sw R* 34 (Sp 49) 202-15.
Heydrick, B. A. "The [American] Drama." *Chautauquan* 45 (D 11) 25-48.
Hilton, James. "Literature and Hollywood." *Atl* 178 (D 46) 130-6.
Hogan, W. R. "The Theatre in the Republic of Texas." *Sw R* 19 (Jl 34) 374-401.
Holbrook, Stewart. "Boston's Temple of Burlesque." *Am Merc* 58 (Ap 44) 411-6.
Hoole, W. S. "Charleston Theatres." *Sw R* 25 (Ja 40) 193-204.
——— "Charleston Theatricals during the Tragic Decade, 1860-1869." *J So Hist* 11 (N 45) 538-47.
——— "Two Famous Theatres of the Old South." *SAQ* 36 (Jl 37) 273-7.
Hopkins, Arthur. "New Theatre Freedoms." *Theatre Arts* 29 (F 45) 81-93.
Hornstein, L. H. "'Though This Be Madness': Insanity in the Theater." *CE* 7 (O 45) 7-9.
Howells, W. D. "Editor's Easy Chair." *Harper's* 133 (Je 16) 146-9.
Hutchens, J. K. "The Reviving Theatre." *Cur Hist* 44 (Ap 36) 44-8.
Issacs, Edith, & Gilder, Rosamund. "American Musical Comedy." *Theatre Arts* 29 (Ag 45) 452-93.
——— "Theatre with Father." *Theatre Arts* 27 (Ag 43) 459-503.
Jackson, Joseph. "The Shakespeare Tradition in Philadelphia." *PMHB* 40 (1916) 161-72.
Jefferson, M. M. "The Negro on Broadway, 1945-1946." *Phylon* 7 (2Q 46) 185-96.
Jerome, J. K. "Chronicles of a Playwright." *Harper's* 151 (Je 25) 67-75.
Johnston, Winifred. "Cow Country Theatre." *Sw R* 18 (O 32) 10-26.
——— "The Early Theatre in the Spanish Borderlands." *Mid-America* 13 (O 30) 121-31.
——— "Entertainments of the Spanish Explorers." *Chron Okla* 8 (Mr 30) 89-93.
Jones, H. A. "Literature and the Modern Drama." *Atl* 98 (D 06) 796-807.
Kendall, J. S. "'The American Siddons.'" *La Hist Q* 28 (Jl 45) 922-40.
——— "Joseph Jefferson in New Orleans." *La Hist Q* 26 (O 43) 1150-67.
——— "New Orleans Negro Minstrels." *La Hist Q* 30 (Ja 47) 128-48.
Kernodle, G. R. "Playwrights and Ancestors." *CE* 2 (Ja 41) 325-37.
——— "Time-frightened Playwrights." *Am Schol* 18 (Au 49) 446-56.
Kindersley, A. F. "Some Haunts of Clio in America." *Contemp R* 138 (N 30) 621-9.
King, Rolf. "Sketches of Early German Influence on Rochester's Theatrical and Musical Life." *AGR* 8 (D 41) 13-5.
Koch, F. H. "A Gullah Negro Drama." *SLM* 2 (Ap 40) 236-7.
Kronenberger, Louis. "The Decline of the Theatre." *Commentary* 1 (N 35) 47-51.
Krutch, J. W. "The Meaning of Modern Drama." *Nation* 141 (4, 11, 18, 25, S 35) 269-70, 291-3, 320-3, 351-3.
——— "Twenty Years of American Drama." *SRL* 27 (5 Ag 44) 36-7, 40-1.
Lancaster, A. E. "Historical American Plays." *Chautauquan* 31 (Jl 00) 359-64.
Land, R. H. "The First Williamsburg Theater." *WMQ* 5: ser 3 (Jl 48) 359-74.

Langner, Lawrence. "The Future of the Government in the Theatre." *YR* 27 (S 37) 64-76.
Laufe, A. L. "Not So New in the Theatre." *SAQ* 46 (Jl 47) 384-9.
Laurie, Joe. "The Theatre's All-Time Hit." *Am Merc* 61 (O 45) 469-72.
Law, R. A. "Early American Performances of Shakespeare." *Texas R* 1 (Ap 16) 358-9.
——— "A Diversion for Colonial Gentlemen." *Texas R* 2 (Jl 16) 79-88.
——— "Notes on Some Early American Dramas." *Un Texas Stud Eng* 5 (1925) 96-100.
Lawson, H. J. "The Negro in American Drama." *Bul Bibl* 17 (Ja-My 40) 7-8, 27-30.
Leary, Lewis. "First Theatrical Performance in North America." *AN&Q* 2 (S 42) 84.
Leete, William. "Theatre Collections." *Theatre Arts* 18 (Je 34) 459-63.
Leonard, Claire. "The American Negro Theatre." *Theatre Arts* 28 (Jl 44) 421-3.
Leonard, W. E. "Wanted: A Wagner for the Movies." *Dial* 65 (5 O 18) 257.
Liebert, Vera. "'Far from the Madding Crowd' on the American Stage." *Colophon* ns 3 (Su 38) 377-82.
Lippincott, H. M. "Amusements in the Nineties." *Gen Mag & Hist Chron* 52 (Su 50) 239-51.
Locke, Alain. "Broadway and the Negro Drama." *Theatre Arts* 25 (O 41) 745-50.
——— "The Negro and the American Stage." *Theatre Arts* 10 (F 26) 112-20.
Luhan, M. D. "A Bridge between Cultures." *Theatre Arts* 9 (My 25) 297-301.
Mabbott, T. O. "Richard Penn Smith's Tragedy of *Caius Marius*." *AL* 2 (My 30) 141-56.
Mabie, H. W. "American Plays Old and New." *Outlook* 102 (28 D 12) 945-55.
McAneny, Herbert. "Some Notes on Princeton Amusements, Civil War to 1887." *PULC* 4 (N 42) 10-29.
McCutcheon, R. P. "The First English Plays in New Orleans." *AL* 11 (My 39) 183-99.
McDavitt, E. E. "The Beginnings of Theatrical Activities in Detroit." *Mich Hist* 31 (Mr 47) 35-47.
Macgowan, Kenneth. "Antiquated Youth." *Dial* 64 (25 Ap 18) 390-2.
——— "Corrupted Dramatic Critics." *Dial* 64 (3 Ja 18) 13-5.
——— "Drama's New Domain—the High School." *Harper's* 159 (N 29) 774-9.
——— "A Gordon Craig from Broadway." *Dial* 64 (23 My 18) 478-9.
——— "A Happy Ending for the Little Theatre." *Dial* 64 (28 F 18) 187-8.
——— "Repertory from Judea." *Freeman* 1 (7 Jl 20) 402-3.
Mackay, F. F. "A National Art Theater in America." *Arena* 32 (Jl 04) 48-52.
Mackaye, Percy. "Self-Expression and the American Drama." *NAR* 188 (S 08) 404-14.
Macmillan, Ethel. "The Plays of Isaac Bickerstaff in America." *PQ* 5 (Ja 26) 58-69.
Magyar, Francis. "The History of the Early Milwaukee German Theatre." *Wisc Mag Hist* 13 (Je 30) 375-86.
Mammen, Edward. "The Old Stock Company." *More Books* 19 (Ja, F, Mr 44) 3-18, 49-63, 100-7.
Marraro, H. R. "Italian Music and Actors in America during the Eighteenth Century." *Ital* 23 (Je 46) 103-17.
Marshall, E. W. "The Weston Playhouse: Regional Drama Centre." *Vt Q* 15 (Ap 47) 121-4.
Mattefeld, Julius. "A Hundred Years of Grand Opera in New York, 1825-1925." *BNYPL* 29 (1925) 695-702, 778-814, 874-914.
Matthews, Albert. "Early Plays at Harvard." *Nation* 88 (10 Mr 09) 295.
Matthews, Brander. "Are the Movies a Menace to the Drama?" *NAR* 205 (Mr 17) 447-54.

——— "The Case of the Little Theaters." *NAR* 206 (N 17) 753-61.
——— "The Modern Novel and the Modern Play." *NAR* 180 (N 05) 699-711.
——— "The Playwright and the Playgoers." *Atl* 102 (S 08) 421-6.
——— "The Revival of the Poetic Drama." *Atl* 101 (F 08) 219-24.
Mersand, Joseph. "When Ladies Write Plays." *Players Mag* 14 (S 37) 7-8, 26, 28.
Metcalfe, J. S. "Dramatic Criticism in the American Press." *Atl* 121 (Ap 18) 495-9.
——— "Financing a National Theatre." *NAR* 180 (F 05) 198-209.
——— "Is the Theater Worth While?" *Atl* 96 (D 05) 727-34.
Meyer, A. N. "The Vanishing Actor: and After." *Atl* 113 (Ja 14) 87-96.
Mitchell, Langdon. "The Drama: Can It Be Taught?" *VQR* 4 (O 28) 561-80.
Moehlenbrock, A. H. "The German Drama on the New Orleans Stage." *La Hist Q* 26 (Ap 43) 361-427.
Moreland, James. "The Theatre in Portland in the Eighteenth Century." *NEQ* 11 (Je 38) 331-42.
Morgan, Frederick. "Notes on the Theatre." *Hudson R* 2 (Su 49) 269-77.
Morison, S. E. "Two 'Signers' on Salaries and the Stage, 1789." *PMHS* 62 (Ja 29) 55-63.
Morley, Malcolm. "Early Dickens Drama in America." *Dickensian* 44 (Su 48) 153-7.
Morse, G. C. "Broadway Re-Discovers the Negro." *Negro Hist Bul* 9 (My 46) 189-91.
Moses, M. J. "American Plays of Our Forefathers." *NAR* 215 (Je 22) 790-804.
——— "Cobwebs of Antiquity." *NAR* 231 (Ja 31) 81-8.
——— "A Hopeful Note on the Theatre." *NAR* 234 (D 32) 528-35.
——— "Our 'Come Seven, Come Eleven' Theatre." *NAR* 235 (Mr 33) 269-78.
——— "The Social Significance of Little Theatres." *NAR* 224 (Mr-Ap-My 27) 128-39.
——— "The Theatre in America." *NAR* 219 (Ja 24) 82-91.
Muir, A. F. "Diary of a Young Man in Houston, 1838." *Sw Hist Q* 53 (Ja 50) 276-307.
Munson, G. B. "Buoyant Experimenting." *Freeman* 1 (2 Je 20) 282-3.
Naeseth, Henriette. "Drama in Early Deadwood, 1869-1879." *AL* 10 (N 38) 289-312.
Nathan, G. J. "The Drama's Four Horsemen." *Am Merc* 65 (O 47) 455-60.
——— "Good News from Broadway." *Cur Hist* 40 (My 34) 185-90.
——— "Literature Returns to the Theatre." *SRL* 13 (14 Mr 34) 3-4.
Nathan, Hans. "Charles Mathews, Comedian, and the American Negro." *SFQ* 10 (S 46) 191-7.
Neidig, W. J. "The First Play in America." *Nation* 88 (28 Ja 09) 86.
Nettleton, G. H. "Sheridan's Introduction to the American Stage." *PMLA* 65 (Mr 50) 163-82.
Niles, William. "Nantucket Folk Theatre." *Theatre Arts* 26 (D 42) 793.
O'Brien, F. P. "Passing of the Old Montgomery Theatre." *Ala Hist Q* 3 (Sp 41) 8-14.
Oliver, Peter. "The Boston Theatre, 1800." *PCSM* 34 (1943) 554-70.
Page, E. R. "Rediscovering the American Drama." *Am Schol* 8 (Sp 39) 250-2.
Pattee, F. L. "The British Theatre in Philadelphia in 1778." *AL* 6 (Ja 35) 381-8.
Patterson, F. T. "The Author and Hollywood." *NAR* 244 (Au 37) 77-89.
Paul, H. N. "Shakespeare in Philadelphia." *PAPS* 76 (1936) 719-29.
Pearce, T. M. "'Los Moros y Los Cristianos': Early American Play." *N Mex Folklore Rec* 2 (Je 48) 58-65.
Peery, William. "American Folk Drama Comes of Age." *Am Schol* 11 (Sp 42) 149-57.
Peffer, Susan. "Dion Boucicault." *Letters* 2 (Ag 29) 7-18.
Pettit, P. B. "Showboat Theatre." *QJS* 31 (Ap 45) 167-74.
Phelps, W. L. "The Present Condition and Tendencies of the Drama." *YR* ns 1 (O 11) 81-98.
——— "Unmusical Non-Comedy." *NAR* 224 (S-O 27) 433-6.

Pollock, T. C. "Notes on Professor Pattee's 'The British Theatre in Philadelphia in 1778.'" *AL* 7 (N 35) 310-4.
Potter, Helen. "The Drama of the Twentieth Century." *Arena* 23 (F 00) 157-66.
Price, L. G. "American Undergraduate Dramatics." *Bkm* 18 (D 03) 373-8.
Quinn, A. H. "The Authorship of the First American College Masque." *Gen Mag & Hist Chron* 28 (1926) 313-6.
——— "Modern American Drama." *EJ* 12 (D 23) 653-62; 13 (Ja 24) 1-10.
——— "National Ideas in the Drama." *Scribner's* 74 (Jl 23) 63-71.
——— "New Notes and Old in the Drama." *Scribner's* 76 (Jl 24) 79-87.
——— "The Perennial Humor of the American Stage." *YR* ns 16 (Ap 27) 553-66.
——— "The Real Hope for the American Theatre." *Scribner's* 97 (Ja 35) 30-5.
——— "The Significance of Recent American Drama." *Scribner's* 72 (Jl 22) 97-108.
——— "The Study of American Drama." *Drama League Mo* 1 (Mr 17) 321-3.
Rahill, Frank. "Melodrama." *Theatre Arts* 16 (Ap 32) 285-94.
Rahv, Philip. "The Men Who Write Our Plays." *Am Merc* 50 (Ag 40) 463-9.
Ramos, J. A. "El Teatro Literario en Norte-América." *Revista Cubana* 9 (Ag 37) 162-93.
Rayford, J. L. "Paul Bunyan's Kin." *Theatre Arts* 29 (Mr 45) 161-5
Reed, P. I. "The Realistic Presentation of American Characters in Native Plays Prior to 1870." *Ohio State Un Bul* 22 (My 18).
Rhodes, H. G. "American Invasion of the London Stage." *Cosmopolitan* 33 (My 02) 25-32.
Rice, Elmer. "The First Decade." *Theatre Arts* 33 (My 49) 53-6.
Robinson, T. C. "Fascism and the Political Theatre." *SR* 44 (Ja-Mr 36) 53-67.
Roppolo, J. P. "Audiences in New Orleans Theatres, 1845-1861." *Tulane Stud Eng* 2 (1950) 121-36.
Rosenfield, John. "The Resident Arts: Villain Still Pursues Her." *Sw R* 34 (Au 49) 320-5, 395-8.
Rosenstock, Milton. "Reunion on Broadway." *SRL* 29 (26 Ja 46) 7-8, 48-9.
Ross, M. M. "The Theatre and Social Confusion." *UTQ* 5 (Ja 36) 197-215.
Rossman, K. R. "The Irish in American Drama in the Mid-Nineteenth Century." *N Y Hist* 21 (Ja 40) 39-53.
Rugg, H. G. "The Dartmouth Plays, 1779-1782." *Theatre Annual* (1942) 55-7.
Savage, Courtenay. "Catholic Theatre Looks Ahead." *America* 66 (21 F 42) 549-50.
Sayler, O. M. "The New Movement in the Theatre." *NAR* 213 (Je 21) 761-71.
Schem, L. C. "Two Latter-Day Hamlets." *Dial* 66 (8 Mr 19) 228-31.
Schick, J. S. "Early Showboats and Circuses in the Upper Valley." *Mid-America* 32 (O 50) 211-25.
——— "The Early Theater in Davenport." *Palimpsest* 31 (Ja 50) 1-44.
Seeber, E. D. "The French Theatre in Charleston in the Eighteenth Century." *S C Hist & Gen Mag* 42 (Ja 41) 1-7.
Seldes, Gilbert. "The Artist in the Theater." *Dial* 82 (F 27) 108-16.
Shockley, M. S. "American Plays in the Richmond Theatre, 1819-1838." *SP* 37 (Ja 40) 100-9.
——— "First American Performances of English Plays in Richmond before 1819." *J So Hist* 13 (F 47) 91-105.
——— "First American Performances of Some English Plays." *Un Colo Stud* 2: ser B (O 45) 302-6.
——— "The Proprietors of Richmond's New Theatre of 1819." *WMQ* 19 (Jl 39) 302-8.
——— "Shakespeare's Plays in the Richmond Theatre, 1819-1838." *Shakespeare Assn Bul* 15 (Ap 40) 88-94.
Shurter, R. L. "Shakespearean Performances in Pre-Revolutionary America." *SAQ* 36 (Ja 37) 53-8.
Simonson, Lee. "Prescription for an Ailing Theatre." *N Y Times Mag* (14 N 43) 16, 39.

——— "The Theatre: Gambler's Paradise." *NRp* 72 (7 S 32) 93-6.
Smith, A. M. "Transporting the Circus." *Hobbies* 54 (N 49) 34.
Smith, Cecil. "The Road to Musical Comedy." *Theatre Arts* 31 (N 47) 54-9.
Smith, H. J. "The Melodrama." *Atl* 99 (Mr 07) 320-8.
Smith, Winifred. "Mystics of the Theatre." *SR* 50 (Ja-Mr 42) 35-48.
Smither, Nellie. "A History of the English Theatre at New Orleans, 1800-1842." *La Hist Q* 28 (Ja, Ap 45) 85-276, 361-572.
Sothern, E. H. "Leg Shows and Billingsgate." *NAR* 227 (Mr 29) 308-14.
Sowers, W. L. "Pantomime in America." *Texas R* 2 (Ja 17) 235-47.
——— "Some American Experimental Theatres." *Texas R* 2 (Je 16) 26-40.
Spell, J. R. "Hispanic Contributions to the Early Theatre in Philadelphia." *Hisp R* 9 (Ja 41) 192-8.
Squire, Tom. "Church and Drama." *Theatre Arts* 23 (S 39) 653-60.
Stallings, Roy. "The Drama in Southern Illinois (1865-1900)." *J Ill State Hist Soc* 33 (Je 40) 190-202.
Straumann, von Heinrich. "Das moderne amerikanische Drama und seine gedanklichen Ursprünge." *Neue Schweizer Rundschau* 12 (Ap 45) 722-39.
Strunsky, Simeon. "The Show." *Atl* 113 (My 14) 622-9.
Sumner, J. S. "Thrill Addicts and the Theatre." *NAR* 224 (Je-Jl-Ag 27) 241-51.
Super, P. L. "Backgrounds of Naturalism in the Theatre." *QJS* 33 (F 47) 46-52.
Thomas, Ota. "Student Dramatic Activities at Yale College during the Eighteenth Century." *Theatre Annual* (1944) 47-59.
Turner, Vivian. "Our Colonial Theatre." *QJS* 27 (D 41) 559-73.
Vail, R. W. G. "Boston's First Play." *PAAS* ns 49 (O 39) 283-6.
——— "The Way to the Big Top!" *N Y Hist Soc Quar Bul* 29 (Jl 45) 137-59.
Walser, R. G. "Strolling Players in North Carolina, 1768-1788." *Carolina Play Book* 10 (D 37) 108-9.
Watts, Richard. "Postwar Broadway." *Am Schol* 15 (Au 46) 558-70.
Wegelin, Oscar. "An Early Iowa Playwright." *N Y Hist Soc Quar Bul* 28 (Ap 44) 42-4.
Westheimer, David. "Broadway in Houston." *Scene* 1 (Ap 47) 52.
White, Walter. "The Negro on the American Stage." *EJ* 24 (Mr 35) 179-88.
Whiting, F. M. "Theatrical Personalities of Old St. Paul." *Minn Hist* 23 (D 42) 305-15.
Wiley, Edwin. "A Glance at the American Stage and 'Semiramis and Other Plays.'" *SR* 13 (Jl 05) 292-304.
Wilson, Willard. "The Theatre in Hawaii before 1900." *QJS* 35 (O 49) 304-9.
Woodruff, John. "America's Oldest Living Theatre—the Howard Athenaeum." *Theatre Annual* 7 (1950) 71-81.
Wyatt, E. A. "Three Petersburg Theatres." *WMQ* 21 (Ap 41) 83-110.
Young, Stark. "The Apron String in our Theatre." *NAR* 216 (D 22) 833-42.
——— "Belasco." *NRp* 67 (17 Je 31) 123-4.
——— "The Garland of Dionysos: 1923-1924." *NAR* 219 (Je 24) 874-82.
——— "Mrs. Fiske." *NRp* 70 (2 Mr 32) 71-2.
——— "Theatre 1932, New York." *VQR* 9 (Ap 33) 262-76.
Young, V. A. "Theatre: A Middle-Class Failure." *Ariz Q* 3 (Au 47) 197-206.
Zucker, A. E. "The History of the German Theatre in Baltimore." *GR* 18 (Ap 43) 123-35.